THE OXFORD INDIA COMPANION
to Sociology and Social Anthropology

THE OXFORD INDIA COMPANION
to Sociology and Social Anthropology

WITHDRAWN

Edited by

VEENA DAS

OXFORD
UNIVERSITY PRESS

OXFORD
UNIVERSITY PRESS

YMCA Library Building, Jai Singh Road, New Delhi 110001

Oxford University Press is a department of the University of Oxford.
It furthers the University's objective of excellence in research, scholarship,
and education by publishing worldwide in

Oxford New York

Auckland Bangkok Buenos Aires Cape Town Chennai
Dar es Salaam Delhi Hong Kong Istanbul Karachi Kolkata
Kuala Lumpur Madrid Melbourne Mexico City Mumbai Nairobi
São Paulo Shanghai Taipei Tokyo Toronto

Oxford is a registered trade mark of Oxford University Press
in the UK and in certain other countries

Published in India
by Oxford University Press, New Delhi

© Oxford University Press 2003

ISBN 019 564582 0

Typeset in Sabon 11/14
by Eleven Arts, Keshav Puram, Delhi 110035
Printed by Thomson Press (I) Ltd.
Published by Manzar Khan, Oxford University Press
YMCA Library Building, Jai Singh Road, New Delhi 110001

Contents

Volume I

Acknowledgements		ix
Preface		xi
Contributors		xiii
Veena Das	Social Sciences and the Publics	1

1 THE OVERARCHING CONCEPTS AND CONTEXTS

	Introduction	32
André Béteille	Sociology and Social Anthropology	37
Satish Deshpande	Modernization	63
Richard Saumarez-Smith	The Historiography of Indian Society	99
J.P.S. Uberoi	Civil Society	114

2 THE ECOLOGICAL CONTEXT OF SOCIAL LIFE

	Introduction	136
Rita Brara	Ecology and Environment	141
Pravin and Leela Visaria	India's Population Its Growth and Key Characteristics	184
Aparna Rao and Michael J. Casimir	Movements of Peoples Nomads in India	219
Myron Weiner	Migration	262
Tetsuya Nakatani	Refugees	283

Paul Greenough	The Social and Cultural Framework of Health and Disease in India	303
James L. Wescoat Jr, Richa Nagar, and David Faust	Social and Cultural Geography	326

3 MORPHOLOGICAL CATEGORIES

	Introduction	368
Virginius Xaxa	Tribes in India	373
Brij Raj Chauhan	Village Community	409
Narayani Gupta	The Indian City	458
Christopher J. Fuller	Caste	477
Dipankar Gupta	Social Stratification Hierarchy, Difference, and Social Mobility	502
Satish Saberwal and N. Jayaram	Social Conflict	532

4 THE CULTURAL LANDSCAPE

	Introduction	564
Roma Chatterji	The Category of Folk	567
Heidrun Brückner and Elizabeth Schömbucher	Performances	598
Christopher Pinney	The Image in Indian Culture	625
Arjun Appadurai	Public Culture	654
Nita Kumar	Consumption and Lifestyle	675
Udaya Narayana Singh	Social Aspects of Language	695

5 RELIGIONS

	Introduction	770
T.N. Madan	Religions of India Plurality and Pluralism	775
Lawrence A. Babb	Sects and Indian Religions	802
Audrey Cantlie	Myth Text and Context	827
Masakazu Tanaka	Religion in Everyday Life	861
Rowena Robinson	Christianity in the Context of Indian Society and Culture	884
Gurpreet Mahajan	Secularism	908

Volume II

6 EDUCATION, KNOWLEDGE, AND HUMAN DEVELOPMENT

	Introduction	936
Olga Nieuwenhuys	The Paradox of Child Labour and Anthropology	939
Lawrence Cohen	Old Age and the Global Economy of Knowledge	956
Jean Drèze	Patterns of Literacy and Their Social Context	974
Sanjay Srivastava	Schooling, Culture, and Modernity	998
Suma Chitnis	Higher Education	1032

7 THE PERSONAL SPHERE AND ITS ARTICULATION

	Introduction	1058
Patricia Uberoi	The Family in India Beyond the Nuclear versus Joint Debate	1061
Thomas R. Trautmann	Patterns of Marriage	1104
Malavika Karlekar	Domestic Violence	1127
Margaret Trawick	The Person Beyond the Family	1158
Robert Desjarlais and James Wilce	The Cultural Construction of Emotion	1179

8 ECONOMIC ARRANGEMENTS

	Introduction	1206
Surinder Jodhka	Agrarian Structures and Their Transformations	1213
Narayan Sheth	Labour and Trade Unions	1243
Kuriakose Mamkoottam	Labour, Technology, and Industry	1266
Jan Breman	The Informal Sector	1287
Mario Rutten	The Study of Entrepreneurship in India In Need of a Comparative Perspective	1319
Denis Vidal	Markets	1342
Pranab Bardhan	Decentralization and the Poor	1361

9 POLITICAL INSTITUTIONS AND PROCESSES

	Introduction	1380
Robert Moog	The Significance of Lower Courts in the Judicial Process	1389
Thomas Pantham	The Indian Nation-State From Pre-colonial Beginnings to Post-colonial Reconstructions	1413
Sudipta Kaviraj	The Nature of Indian Democracy	1447
P. Radhakrishnan	Backward Castes/Classes as Legal and Political Entities	1474
Harold A. Gould	Local-level/Grassroots Political Studies	1494
Martin Fuchs and Antje Linkenbach	Social Movements	1524
Jonathan Spencer	Collective Violence	1564
Index		1581

6

Education, Knowledge, and Human Development

Several social science disciplines intersect in the field of education, knowledge, and human development—one common theme that unites them is the concern with social reproduction and social as well as individual transformation.[1] Education encompasses the contradictory aspects of reproduction and transformation—hence educational processes can be seen at the heart of familial, educational and work related contexts in a society. The broader discussion of these issues is dispersed over various chapters in the different sections. In this section the concern is more with questions of how education is intertwined in the different stages of the life-cycle, especially childhood. Simultaneously the way that these stages of the life-cycle become objects of disciplines within a global economy of knowledge is demonstrated with regard to both childhood and old age.

The chapter by Sanjay Srivastava on the school as an institution shows the intimate connections between the evolution of ideas of governance, the making of colonial subjects, nationalism, and the debates on education. The combined forces of neglect and actual hostility on the part of the British obliterated the indigenous network of educational institutions. If these institutions continued during the British rule, they acquired fossilized forms. The attempts of the Orientalists to preserve traditional knowledge gave impetus to those forms of knowledge that could be useful for governance (for example, in law courts for settlements of disputes between natives). There were also attempts to salvage traditional knowledge that were premised on the notions of its disappearance. The overall British concern however was to think of schools as places where the perceived lack in native personality could be remedied.

Srivastava makes creative use of Bakhtin's powerful idea of the chronotope to show how reformists such as Dayanand Saraswati or Sister Nivedita placed concerns arising out of the British critique of native personality at the heart of their reform programmes but projected these into some ancient past. Srivastava examines the reasons why Gandhi's idea of basic education, revolutionary in the way in which it placed learning through engagement with the material world at the heart of reform, did not find many supporters in independent India. The examples he gives of the way different ideologies were embodied in the structure of schools, ranging from Doon School to the various DAV schools, reposition debates about elite education and mass education into a more than binary opposition.

Jean Drèze looks at literacy and mass education from the perspective of a development economist. While literacy rates have shown substantial improvement in the country, the performance in relation to other countries, especially China, is disappointing. The lack of emphasis on mass education is particularly evident given that in the late 1940s China and India were in a comparable position with regard to literacy while today China has achieved near universal literacy leaving India far behind. Drèze's contribution shows the importance of cultural factors but it also breaks the myth of deep cultural resistance to literacy. Thus he finds that the achievements of Himachal Pradesh in the last decade are particularly remarkable because the state does not follow the Kerala model. Instead it is a combination of the resources put into primary education by the state coupled with relatively homogeneous village communities that led to substantial improvement in school attendance for both boys and girls in Himachal Pradesh.

Two conclusions drawn by Drèze will be of special interest to sociologists. First he shows that female literacy in India is largely a by-product of male literacy. It is the demand for educated brides among communities that have achieved certain educational levels for males that drives female education. This is consistent with research on literacy that suggests different kinds of uses for literacy among different social groups. Second, he argues that contrary to popular perceptions, it is not child labour that is an obstacle to sending children to school. As he says, productive work accounts for only a small share of the time utilization of children out of school. Instead it is the poor quality of schooling in terms of infrastructure, teacher accountability, and teaching methods that leads to school drop-outs. In other words, it is supply side failures that account for children dropping out of school rather than the demand for their labour at home.

The last point directly ties in with Olga Niewenhuys's chapter on the paradox of child labour. While the global discourse portrays childhood in terms of ideals of innocence, Niewenhuys argues that one could recast the current politics on child labour in terms of its inability to address the question of exclusion of children from remunerative employment. Age is used along with gender, she argues, to accord a low value to work performed by children. This paradoxically increases children's vulnerability to exploitation. Along with the findings of Drèze that most children engage in labour because they have already dropped out of school rather than the other way round, one must ask whether global visions of childhood obscure and even unintentionally collude in local practices that consistently exclude children in the production of value. This is obviously not to support child labour but to ask how we might rethink these issues in relation to the specificity of the research findings with regard to childhood in India.

The chapters by Suma Chitnis and Lawrence Cohen address, in different ways, the world of adulthood. In the context of her interest in higher education, Chitnis revisits the old Orientalist versus Anglicist debates—she argues that the British marginalized earlier forms of higher education as new institutions were created for new forms of knowledge. She suggests that there was a long tradition of institutions for the development and dissemination of knowledge in Indian society—this was by no means something new that the British introduced. In fact the stakes in higher education led to demands by various voluntary bodies for the establishment of universities in the colonial period. Thus, apart from the universities established by the British there were also institutions of higher learning established through voluntary effort. The list of such institutions is impressive—SNDT Women's University, Vishwa Bharati, Jamia Milia, and the Institute of Science at Bangalore. Chitnis's chapter shows the interplay between ideas of nationalism and higher education. Written from the perspective of an educational administrator, it shows the challenges faced by institutions of higher education in India both in the project of social development and in the new context of globalization.

Lawrence Cohen's chapter on aging has an important place in this section for he shows how narratives of aging are metaphors for the narratives of decline at the level of both anthropological positioning of this subject and in popular culture. The terms of this narrative assume that the history of old age only begins with the descent of Indian society into unhappy modernity. Like Nieuwenhuys, Cohen is most interested in the way in which knowledge and perceptions that circulate in the global public sphere interact with local modes of organizing the life cycle. He argues that a genealogy of these issues may be constructed at the intersection of images of old age in the international discipline of gerontology as well as in the specific images of the old body in colonial and independent India. The alarmist rhetoric of dependency ratios in the international arena intersects with the alarmist rhetoric of the decline of the joint family in India, constituting old age as a 'problem'. Instead of the normative comparisons in which anthropology of old age has been caught—is it better there or here?—Cohen argues that theorizing on old age mandates attention to processes of temporality, work, and rupture.

One wishes that it had been possible to look at adulthood and the engagement with forms and institutions of knowledge in India in a yet broader perspective. The essays here, I hope, are provocative enough to make one rethink many of the problems with regard to education, knowledge, and development as they become braided with questions of tradition and modernity in Indian history and sociology.

ENDNOTES

1. Unfortunately two important chapters relating to traditional systems of knowledge and the particular trajectory of science and technology in India could not be completed by the respective authors.

The Paradox of Child Labour and Anthropology*

 *Olga Nieuwenhuys*

In relating the child labour debate to the observed variety of children's work patterns, this chapter reveals the limits of current notions such as labour, gender, and exploitation in the analysis of this work. Particularly in the developing world, most work undertaken by children has for a long time been explained away as socialization, education, training, and play. Anthropology has helped disclose that age is used with gender as the justification for the value accorded to work. The low valuation of children's work translates not only into children's vulnerability in the labour market but, more importantly, in their exclusion from remunerated employment. I argue that current child labour policies, because they fail to address the exclusion of children from the production of value, paradoxically reinforce children's vulnerability to exploitation.

The Paradox of Child Labour

Irrespective of what children do and what they think of what they do, modern society sets children apart ideologically as a category of people excluded from the production of value. The dissociation of childhood from the performance of valued work is considered a yardstick of modernity, and a high incidence of child labour is considered a sign of underdevelopment. The problem with defining children's roles in this way, however, is that it denies their agency in the creation and negotiation of value. Illuminating the complexity of the work patterns of children in developing countries, recent anthropological research has begun to demonstrate the need to critically examine the relation between the condemnation of child labour on the one

*First published in *Annual Review of Anthropology*. 1996. 25:237–51. Permission for reprint is gratefully acknowledged.

hand and children's everyday work practice on the other. The emerging paradox is that the moral condemnation of child labour assumes that children's place in modern society must perforce be one of dependency and passivity. This denial of their capacity to legitimately act upon their environment by undertaking valuable work makes children altogether dependent upon entitlements guaranteed by the state. Yet we must question the state's role—as the evidence on growing child poverty caused by cuts in social spending has illuminated—in carrying out its mission.

This chapter is divided into three parts: (*a*) a discussion of the theoretical perspectives adopted by development theory as it has dealt with poverty and child labour, (*b*) an assessment of the contribution of anthropology to the child labour debate, and (*c*) a discussion of the need of future research based on the idea of work as one of the most critical domains in which poor children can contest and negotiate childhood. First, in the section on Approaches to Children's Work, I argue that from its inception the notion of child labour has been associated with factory work and hence was limited to western countries. The interest in children's work in the developing world can be traced back to theories of socialization, a preoccupation with population growth, and unfair economic competition. The section on Children's Work and Anthropology probes the paradox of the market impinging upon locally accepted forms of child work without transforming it into 'child labour'. Here, I discuss how anthropologists have criticized the simplistic views of child labour espoused by western development experts. Approaches to children's work undertaken from the anthropological perspective highlight the very complex interplay of gender and age in determining a child's work allocation. Third, in the section The Negotiation of Childhood, I propose to enlarge the notion of children's exploitation to include the more mundane aspects of work. Finally, I outline the direction future research should take to enable us to understand not only how children's work is negotiated and acquires its meaning but children's own agency therein.

Approaches to Childrens' Work

The recent concern with child labour draws on a shared understanding among development experts of how, from the mid-nineteenth century onward, western industrial society began to eliminate through legislation the exploitation of children. However, historians still debate more deep-seated reasons for the nineteenth-century outcry in Western Europe and the United States against child labour, which is probably as old as childhood itself. For instance, Nardinelli (1990) has questioned the assumption that this outcry was inspired, as some authors have argued (see Fyfe 1989; Thompson 1968; and Walvin 1982), by the brutal treatment of children working in factories. Besides humanitarian reasons, Nardinelli (1990) argued that there was a desire to protect initiatives to mechanize the textile industry from the uncontrolled competition of a labour force composed almost entirely of children. Another equally important reason was the fear of political instability created by a youthful working class not to be disciplined by the army, schools, or the church (Minge-Kalman 1978; Nardinelli 1990; Weiner 1991; Weissbach 1989). While some believe compulsory education was the single most important instrument leading to the elimination of child labour (Fyfe 1989; Weiner 1991), others have argued that changes in the perceived roles of children (Walvin 1982; Zelizer 1994) and the increase in family income (Nardinelli 1990), played a more decisive role.

Progressive state legislation has marked the major steps of child labour abolition in the West. However, while such legislation defined child labour as waged work undertaken by a child under a certain age, it also established the borderline between morally desirable and pedagogically sensible activities on the one hand, and the exploitation of children on the other. While condemning the relatively uncommon forms of waged labour as exploitation, it sanctioned a broad spectrum of other activities, including housekeeping, child minding, helping adults for no pay on family farms and in small shops, domestic service, street selling, running errands, delivering newspapers, seasonal work on farms, working as trainees in workshops, etc. In contrast with child labour, these activities were lauded for their socializing and training aspects (Davin 1982; Walvin 1982).

The distinction between harmful and suitable—if not desirable—work as defined by western legislation has become the main frame of reference of most contemporary governmental and bureaucratic approaches to children's work. Many countries in the world have now either ratified or adopted modified versions of child labour legislation prepared and propagated by the International Labour Organization (ILO) (ILO 1988, 1991). The implications are far-reaching. Legislation links child labour quite arbitrarily to work in the factory and excludes a wide range of non-factory work. It therefore sanctifies unpaid work in the home or under parental supervision, regardless of its implications for the child. In the words of an ILO report:

> We have no problem with the little girl who helps her mother with the housework or cooking, or the boy or girl who does unpaid work in a small family business. ... The same is true of those odd jobs that children may occasionally take on to earn a little pocket money to buy something they really want [see ILO 1993].

Many of the odd jobs mentioned here, as in the case of helping on the family farm or in shops and hotels, though strictly not prohibited, are felt by both children and the public at large to be exploitative. Legislation also selects chronological age as the universal measure of biological and psychological maturity, and it rejects cultural and social meanings attached to local systems of age ranking (La Fontaine 1978). More specifically, it denies the value of an early introduction to artisanal crafts or traditional occupations that may be crucial in a child's socialization (see section on The Negotiation of Childhood). Finally, legislation condemns any work undertaken by a child for his/her own upkeep—with the notable exception of work undertaken to obtain pocket money. The denial of gainful employment is the more paradoxical in that the family and the state often fail to provide children with what they need to lead a normal life (Zelizer 1994). These are some of the reasons why the industrial countries, despite much lip service to the contrary, have not succeeded in eliminating all forms of child work (Challis and Elliman 1979; Herpen 1990; Lavalette 1994; Lee-Wright 1990; Mendelievich 1979; Williams 1993).

Given the factory origins of the notion of child labour, it is hardly surprising that children's work in the erstwhile colonies caused no concern. Most colonial administrations passed factory acts excluding children under 14 from the premises soon after they had been passed at home. However, these laws carried only symbolic value. The colonies were merely seen as sources of cheap raw materials and semi-manufactured goods produced by rural villagers, while the factory system of production was energetically discouraged. The administration's main preoccupation was that the local rural population—men, women, and children—continue to find in the old forms of subsistence the means of surviving while delivering the agricultural goods necessary to maintain the colonial revenue (Nieuwenhuys 1993; White 1994).

This may explain why in the West social activists expressed outrage about child labour at home, while anthropologists romanticized the work of rural children in the colonies as a form of socialization well adapted to the economic and social level of pre-industrial society (Mead and Wolfenstein 1955; Whiting 1963; for a critique see Hull 1981). Engrossed with the intricacies of age ranking and passage rites, anthropologists seldom hinted at what this meant in terms of work and services required by elders from youngsters (Van Gennep [1908] 1960). The high premium put on the solidarity of the extended family as the corner-stone of pre-capitalist society overshadowed the possibility of exploitation occurring within the family or the village.

This perception changed with the identification in post-War development theory of population growth as the main obstacle to the eradication of poverty in the new nations of the Third World. Celebrated as an antidote to poverty during the colonial period, children's work contributions to the family economy came to be perceived as an indicator of poverty, if not its cause. In the 1960s and 1970s, a burgeoning literature on the 'population explosion' tried to show that the fast-growing numbers of poor children—non-workers with escalating expectations—were to be held responsible for consuming the developing world's scant resources (Dore 1982; Eisenstadt

1956). These allegations often masked the fear that the mounting frustrations of youngsters would 'fester into eruptions of violence and extremism' (McNamara 1968) and thereby threaten the stability of the post-War world order (Michaelson 1981; Schrijvers 1993). Large-scale foreign-funded research programmes were introduced in high-fertility countries to induce poor couples to control births. However, resistance to birth control was unexpectedly staunch. By the mid-1970s, research began to provide clues that the poor desired a large family because children represented an important source of free labour (Michaelson 1981). Mamdani's seminal work on the importance of children's work contribution for the reproduction of the peasant household in the Green Revolution areas of the Punjab cast an entirely new light on high fertility by suggesting that India's peasants needed many children to meet their labour demands (Mamdani 1972, 1974, 1981).

   Mamdani's research inspired a fresh approach to children's work in terms of its utility to the peasant household. During the 1970s, anthropologists carried out extensive and painstaking time-allocation and family-budget studies to show that even young children were contributing to their own sustenance by undertaking a whole range of activities in the subsistence sphere of the peasant economy (Hull 1981; Marcoux 1994; Mueller 1975; Nichols 1993; White 1975). The ensuing debate on the determinants of high fertility in peasant economies showed, however, that the claim that poor peasants' desire for children would be inspired by their value as workers was premature (Datta and Nugent 1984; Vlassoff 1979; 1982; Vlassoff and Vlassoff 1980; White 1982). Caldwell's (1976, 1981, 1982) work on Nigeria and India was particularly influential in mapping the wider setting of children's historical, social, and cultural roles (Caldwell 1976, 1981, 1982). Research on intra-household relations also questioned the concept of the household as an unproblematic unit, highlighting the outspoken inequality that exists not only between males and females but between seniors and juniors (Elson 1982; Folbre 1994; Jain and Banerjee 1985; Schildkrout 1980, 1981). Another criticism of the 'cost–benefit' analysis has been its exclusive focus on decision making at the level of the household; it ignores the larger context in which the actions of its members occur (Goddard and White 1982, Rodgers and Standing 1981; Wallerstein et al. 1982).

   In spite of such criticism, the neoclassical belief that child labour is essentially a problem of household economics has continued to be espoused in the studies of child labour published under the auspices of international agencies such as the United Nations International Children's Educational Fund (UNICEF), the World Health Organization (WHO), and the ILO following the International Year of the Child in 1979 (Bequele and Boyden 1988; Black 1995; Bouhdiba 1982; Challis and Elliman 1979; Fyfe 1989; Mendelievich 1979; Myers 1991; Rimbaud 1980). Similar views are expressed in the documents produced by international charities devoted to the welfare of children such as the International Catholic Bureau, Save the Children, Defence of Children International, Anti-Slavery International (for overviews, see Boyd 1994; Bureau of International Affairs, US Department of Labor 1994; Ennew 1994). Typical of these publications is a moral preoccupation with abolition through legislation and a zealous belief in the desirability of extending western childhood ideals to poor families worldwide. Their merit lies essentially in having staked out child labour as a new and legitimate field of global political and academic concern. As aptly stated by Morice and Schlemmer (1994), the continuous reference to (western) moral values, however, all too often not only supplants scientific analysis but may at times mask its very need. The emerging picture is one of conceptual confusion, in which ill-grasped notions from diverse analytical fields are indiscriminately used. The most glaring confusion is undoubtedly the one between the moral oppression and the economic exploitation of children (Morice 1981; Morice and Schlemmer 1994; Nieuwenhuys 1993). Reference to broad and ahistorical causes of the oppression of children such as poverty, illiteracy, backwardness, greed, and cruelty fail to go beyond the mere description of oppression and ignore the historical and social conditioning of exploitation (Sahoo 1995).

As a global solution to eliminate child labour, development experts are now proposing a standard based on the sanctity of the nuclear family on the one hand and the school on the other as the only legitimate spaces for growing up. If this becomes a universal standard, there is a danger of negating the worth of often precious mechanisms for survival, and penalizing or even criminalizing the ways the poor bring up their children (Boyden 1990; Cunningham 1991; Donzelot 1977). This criminalization is made more malevolent as modern economies increasingly display their unwillingness to protect poor children from the adverse effects of neoliberal trade policies (Amin 1994; Cornia et al. 1987; Fyfe 1989; Mundle 1984; Verlet 1994).

Children's Work and Anthropology

Children's lives have been a constant theme in anthropology. However, in-depth studies of their work remain few and have been inspired, as I have argued, by a critical concern with the neoclassical approach to the value of children. Two main areas of research have elicited anthropologists' interest: the family context of work and the relation between socialization, work, and schooling.

One of the leading themes of economic anthropology has been the conceptualization of work and its cultural meanings. The growing numbers of publications on child labour in the developing world have invoked renewed interest in the family context of work. Central to some of the most notable studies has been how children's work is constrained by hierarchies based on kinship, age, and gender, a constraint that results in its typically rural, flexible, and personalized character. Rather than a widespread form of exploitation, child employment is mostly limited by the free-labour requirement of families that is satisfied by giving children unremunerated and lowly valued tasks (Céspedes and Zarama 1994; Dube 1988; McEwen 1982; Melhuus 1984; Reynolds 1991; Wyers 1986).

Considering the low cost of children's labour, it is indeed surprising that employers do not avail themselves more fully of this phenomenal source of profit. Despite more than 100 million children in the age bracket 5 to 15 living in abject poverty in India, for example, a mere 16 million are employed, the vast majority of whom are teenagers who work in agriculture. About 10 per cent are employed by industries, largely producing substandard if not inferior products for the local market (Gulrajani 1994; Kothari 1983; Nieuwenhuys 1993).

There is more and more evidence that poor children who are not employed perform crucial work, often in the domestic arena, in subsistence agriculture, and in the urban informal sector (Campos et al. 1994; Gangrade and Gathia 1983; Marcoux 1994; Mies and Shiva 1993; Moerat 1989; Mutiso 1989; Nieuwenhuys 1994; Oloko 1991; Reynolds 1991; Salazar 1991). Theories explaining underdevelopment in terms of the persistence of precapitalist labour relations provide some clues about why these children are not employed (Martin and Beittel 1987; Meillassoux 1983; Southall 1988). The crucial aspect of underdevelopment in these theories is the unequal exchange realized in the market between goods produced in capitalist firms, where labour is valued according to its exchange value, and goods produced by the peasantry and the urban informal sector, where the use value of labour predominates. The latter group is paid only a fraction of its real cost because households are able to survive by pooling incomes from a variety of sources, undertaking subsistence activities and using the work of women and children to save on the costs of reproduction (Wallerstein et al. 1982). The unpaid work of children in the domestic arena, which turns them into 'inactives', is seen as crucial for the developing world's low labour cost rationality.

The reasons children are more likely than adults to be allotted unpaid work in agriculture or the household can be gauged by the work of feminist researchers that highlights how ideologies of gender and age interact to constrain, in particular, girls to perform unpaid domestic work (De Tray 1983; Dube 1988; Nieuwenhuys 1994; Oppong 1988; Reynolds 1991; Schildkrout 1980; 1981; Wyers 1986). The ideology of gender permits the persistence of an unequal system in which women are excluded from crucial economic and political activities and their positions of wives and mothers are associated with a lower status than men (Dube 1988; Folbre 1986; Jain and Chand 1979; Scheper-Hughes 1987). The valuation of girls' work is so low that it has been 'discovered' by feminist anthropologists making a conscious choice to include housework and child care in their definition of work (Folbre 1986; Jain and Banerjee 1985; Jeffrey et al. 1989; Schildkrout 1980; Sen and Sengupta 1985).

Girls are trained early to accept and internalize the feminine ideals of devotion to the family (Bellotti 1981; Kakar 1981). The role of caretaker of younger siblings has not only the practical advantage of freeing adult women for wage work, it also charges girls' work with emotional gratifications that can make up for the lack of monetary rewards (Leslie and Paolosso 1989; Myers 1992).

Elson (1982) has argued that seniority explains why children's work is largely valued as inferior: Inferiority is not only attached to the nature of the work but to the person who performs it as well. Poor children are not perceived as workers because what they do is submerged in the low status realm of the domestic. The effect of seniority is not limited to the control of children's work within the nuclear family. Anthropologists have also uncovered how children's work plays a cardinal role in the intricate and extensive kinship and pseudo-kinship patterns that are at the core of support systems in the developing world. While servicing the immediate household is young children's mandatory task, poor children coming of age may also be sent to work as domestics and apprentices for wealthier kin (Galdwell 1982; Kayongo-Male and Walji 1984; Morice 1982; Salazar 1991). For the parent-employer, this is a source of status and prestige (Caldwell 1982). The widespread African practice of fostering the children of poorer (pseudo-)relatives is just one example of the intricate way family loyalty and socialization practices combine to shape how poor children are put to work. Another example is the practice among the poor in some areas of India of pledging their children's work against a loan. Although the object of much negative publicity, the practice is seen by parents as a useful form of training, a source of security, and a way of cutting household expenditures (Gangrade and Gathia 1983; ILO 1992; Nieuwenhuys 1994). Old crafts such as carpet weaving, embroidery, silk reeling, artisanal fishing, and metal work lend themselves to protracted periods of apprenticeship in which a child is made to accept long hours of work and low pay in the hope of becoming master (Kambargi 1991; Morice 1981; Vijaygopalan 1983). While often exacting, children may experience apprenticeship or living in another household as valuable, particularly if it helps them learn a trade or visit a school. Children's valuation of the practice is nevertheless ambiguous, and they may prefer employment to servicing their kin (Fyfe 1989; Lee-Wright 1990; Nieuwenhuys 1994; Salazar 1991; Sinha 1991; White 1994).

There is a persistent belief, which finds its origins in the neoclassical approach, that schooling is the best antidote to child labour (Fyfe 1989; Weiner 1991). However, one consequence of the personalized character of children's work patterns is that this work is often combined with going to school. Reynolds' (1991) study of the Zambezi Valley describes how Tonga children need to work in subsistence agriculture while attending school simply to survive. Insecurity about the value of diplomas and marriage strategies is among the reasons girls in Lagos, Nigeria, spend much out-of-school time acquiring street-trading skills (Oloko 1991). In Kerala, India, where attending school is mandatory, children spend much time earning cash for books, clothes, and food (Nieuwenhuys 1993). Around the world children undertake all kinds of odd jobs, not only to help their families but to defray the fast-rising costs of schooling, be it for themselves or for a younger sibling (Bekombo 1981; Boyden 1991; Hallak 1990; La Fontaine 1978). However, children may also simply dislike school and prefer to work and earn cash instead (Kambargi 1991; White 1994).

Although to some extent schools and work can coexist as separate arenas of childhood, schooling is changing the world orientation of both children and parents. Among the most critical effects is the lowering of birth rates, which has been explained by the non-availability of girls for child care (Caldwell et al. 1985; Myers 1992). Another explanation, inspired by the neoclassical approach of balancing children's costs against the returns, is related to what Caldwell (1981) has called the 'intergenerational flow of wealth.' This notion suggests that schooling increases the costs of child rearing while reducing children's inclination to perform mandatory tasks for the circle of kin. The traditional flow of wealth from juniors to seniors is thus reversed. Perhaps of greater importance, schooling—despite the heavy sacrifices it may demand—provides children with a space in which they can identify with the parameters of modern childhood. It makes possible negotiations with elders for better clothes and food; time for school, homework, and recreation; and often payment for domestic work (Nieuwenhuys 1994). The proponents of compulsory education have also argued that literate youngsters are likely to be more productive later in life than uneducated ones, who may have damaged their health by early entrance into the labour market (Weiner 1991). For Purdy (1992), schooling reinforces the useful learning imparted by parents at home and may, for some children, be the only useful form of learning.

Schools are also said to have a negative impact. Illness, lack of support at home, or heavy work make poor children's performance often inadequate and repetition and dropping out common. Competition in the classroom helps breed a sense of inferiority and personal failure in poor children, turning their work assignments into a source of shame. The high costs of schooling, including the need to look respectable in dress and appearance, incites poor children to engage in remunerative work, which contradicts the belief that compulsory education would work as an antidote to child labour (Burra 1989; Fyfe 1989; McNamara 1968; Weiner 1991).

In the past few years, non-governmental organizations (NGOs) concerned with children have been encouraged to develop low-cost solutions to address the problem of child labour. The solutions are based on a combination of work and school and recognize the need of poor children to contribute to their own upkeep. The approach has gained support within the ILO, the organization that until recently was the most staunch defender of prohibition by legislation (Boyd 1994; Espinola et al. 1987; Fyfe 1994; Gunn and Oslas 1992; ILO/Government of Germany 1991). The poor quality of the education imparted, the heavy demands of studying after work, and above all the fact that they leave untouched the unjust social system that perpetrates children's exploitation are among the most problematic aspects of NGOs' interventions (Boyden and Myers 1995).

The articulation of gender, age, and kinship plays a cardinal role in the valuation of poor children's work and is instrumental in explaining why some work is condemned as unsuitable and some is lauded as salutary. Hierarchies based on gender, age, and kinship combine to define children's mandatory tasks as salutary work and condemn paid work. By legitimizing children's obligation to contribute to survival and denying them their right to seek personal gain, these hierarchies effectively constrain them to a position of inferiority within the family. It is then not so much their factory employment as their engagement in low-productivity and domestic tasks that defines the ubiquitous way poor children are exploited in today's developing world.

Anthropology has sought to explain the apparent inability of the market to avail itself more fully of the vast reservoir of cheap child labour by pointing out that the free-labour requirements of poor families are satisfied by giving children lowly valued tasks. This explanation questions child labour studies' conceptualization of the exploitation of poor children. Employment is clearly not the only nor the most important way children's work is exploited: child work contributions to the family are instrumental in its subsistence and in the production of goods that reach the market at prices far below their labour value. The moral assumption that poor children's socialization should occur through the performance of non-monetized work excludes this work from the same economic realm that includes child labour; it is as much a part of children's exploitation. This fact seriously questions the premises of modern childhood discussed in the next section.

The Negotiation of Childhood

Irrespective of what they do and what they think about what they do, the mere fact of their being children sets children ideologically apart as a category of people excluded from the production of value. The dissociation of childhood from the performance of valued work has been increasingly considered a yardstick of modernity. International agencies and highly industrialized countries now turn this yardstick into a tool to condemn as backward and undemocratic those countries with a high incidence of child labour (Bureau of International Affairs, US Department of Labor 1994). The problem with this way of defining the ideal of childhood, however, is that it denies children's agency in the creation and negotiation of value.

The view that childhood precludes an association with monetary gain is an ideal of modern industrial society (De Mause 1976; Zelizer 1994). Historians highlight the bourgeois origins of this ideal and question its avowed universal validity not only across cultures but across distinctions of gender, ethnicity, and class (Ariès 1973, 1980; Cunningham 1991; Donzelot 1977; Hoyles and Evans 1989). Some have argued that this ideal is threatened at the very core of capitalism and may be giving way to more diversified patterns of upbringing or even to the 'disappearance of childhood' (Evans 1994; Postman 1982). The current debate over children's rights is symptomatic of the discredit bourgeois notions of parental rights and childhood incompetence seem to have suffered (Archard 1993; Franklin 1986; Freeman 1983; Purdy 1992; Vittachi 1989). The exposure of child abuse in the western media during the 1980s and 1990s has, in this line, been explained as a display of excessive anxiety sparked by the growing fragility of personal relationships in late-modern society that cannot but also affect childhood. Late-modern experiences of childhood suggest that the basic source of trust in society lies in the child. Advances in children's rights or media campaigns against child labour or sex tourism would point to a growing sanctity of the child in late modernity (Jenks 1994). This sanctity, however, is essentially symbolic and is contradicted by actual social and financial policies, as borne out by the harshness with which structural adjustment programmes have hit poor children in developing countries and caused a marked increase in child mortality, morbidity, illiteracy, and labour (Amin 1994; Cornia et al. 1987; Folbre 1994; Fyfe 1989; Graham-Brown 1991; Mundle 1984). Under these conditions it is no wonder that, as noted by Jenks (1994), late-modern visions of childhood are now increasingly split between 'futurity' and 'nostalgia'.

As childhood becomes a contested domain, the legitimacy of directing children into economically useless activities is losing ground (Zelizer 1994). The need to direct children into these activities is linked to a system of parental authority and family discipline that was instrumental in preserving established bourgeois social order. The price of maintaining this order is high, because it requires, among other commitments, money to support the institutions at the basis of the childhood ideal, such as free education, cheap housing, free health care, sports and recreation facilities and family welfare and support services. Developing economies will unlikely be able to generate in the near future the social surplus that the maintenance of these institutions requires. As the neoliberal critique of the welfare state gains popularity, wealthy economies also become reluctant to continue shouldering childhood institutions. It is interesting to note that with the retreat of the state, the market itself has begun to address children as consumers more and more, explicitly linking their status to the possession of expensive goods, thereby inducing poor children to seek self-esteem through paid work (White 1994). Working children find themselves clashing with the childhood ideology that places a higher value on the performance of economically useless work. Although working for pay offers opportunities for self-respect, it also entails sacrificing childhood, which exposes children to the negative stereotyping attached to the loss of innocence this sacrifice is supposed to cause (Black 1995; Boyd 1994; Bureau of International Affairs, US Department of Labor 1994; Challis and Elliman 1979; Fyfe 1989; Myers 1991).

Rethinking the paradoxical relation between neoliberal and global childhood ideology is one of the most promising areas for research. Research should especially seek to uncover how the need of poor children to realize self-esteem through paid work impinges upon the moral condemnation of child labour as one of the fundamental principles of modernity. In stark contrast with what happened in the nineteenth-century West, the future may very well see employers, parents, children, and the state disputing the legitimacy of this moral condemnation. Women, in particular, as they expose the construction of gender roles as instrumental in their discrimination in the labour market, are likely to be girls' foremost allies in contesting modern childhood's ideal of economic uselessness (Folbre 1986, 1994). The ways children devise to create and negotiate the value of their work and how they invade structures of constraint based on seniority are other promising areas of future anthropological research. This type of research is even more relevant in that it may not only enrich our knowledge of children's agency but may prove seminal in understanding the process by which work acquires its meaning and is transformed into value.

REFERENCES

Amin, A.A. 1994. 'The Socioeconomic Impact of Child Labour in Cameroon'. *Labour Capital Society*. 27(2):234–49.

Archard, D. 1993. *Children, Rights and Childhood*. London: Routledge.

Ariès, P. 1973. *L 'Enfant et la Vie Familiale sous l'Ancien Régime*. Paris: Seuil.

———. 1980. 'Motivation for Declining Birth Rates in the West: The Rise and Fall of the Role of the Child'. *Population Development Review*. 6(4):645–50.

Bekombo, M. 1981. The Child in Africa: Socialisation, Education and Work.

Bellotti, E.G. 1981. *Dalla Parte delle Bambine, l'Influenza dei Condizionamenti Sociali nella Formazione del Ruolo Femminile nei Primi Anni di Vita*. Milano: Feltrinelli.

Bequele, A. and J. Boyden, eds. 1988. *Combating Child Labour*. Geneva: International Labour Organization.

Black, M. 1995. *In the Twilight Zone: Child Workers in the Hotel, Tourism and Catering Industry*. Geneva: International Labour Organization.

Bouhdiba, A. 1982. *Exploitation of Child Labour: Special Report of the Subcommittee on Prevention of Discrimination and Protection of Minorities*. New York: United Nations.

Boyd, J. 1994: 'Introduction: Child Labour Within the Globalizing Economy'. *Labour Capital Society*. 27(2):153–61.

Boyden, J. 1990. 'Childhood and the Policy Makers: A Comparative Perspective on the Globalization of Childhood'. In A. James and A Prout, eds, *Constructing and Reconstructing Childhood: Contemporary Issues in the Sociological Study of Childhood*. 184–215. London: Falmer.

Boyden, J. 1991. Working Children in Lima. In *Children of the Cities*; London, Zoo Books.

Boyden, J. and W.E. Myers. 1995. *Exploring Alternative Approaches to Combating Child Labour: Case Studies from Developing Countries*. Florence: UNICEF/Innocenti Occasional Paper 8.

Bureau of International Affairs, US Department of Labor. 1994. *By the Sweat and Toil of Children: The Use of Child Labor in American Imports*. Washington, D.C.: US Department of Labor.

Burra, N. 1989. *Child Labour and Education: Issues Emerging from the Experiences of Some Developing Countries of Asia*. Paris: UNESCO-UNICEF.

Caldwell, J.C. 1976. 'Towards a Restatement of Demographic Transition Theory'. *Population Development Review*. 2(4):321–59.

———. 1981. 'The Mechanisms of Demographic Change in Historical Perspective'. *Population Studies*. 35:5–27.

———. 1982. *Theory of Fertility Decline*. London: Academic.

Caldwell, J.C., P.H. Reddy and P. Caldwell. 1985. 'Educational Transition in Rural South India'. *Population Development Review*. 11(1):29–51.

Campos, R., M. Raffaelli and W. Ude. 1994. 'Social Networks and Daily Activities of Street Youth in Belo Horizonte'. *Child Development*. 65:319–30.

Céspedes, B.S. and M.I.V. Zarama. 1994. Le travail des enfants dans les mines de charbon en Colombie. *Travail Capital et Société* 27(2):250–69.

Challis, J. and D. Elliman. 1979. *Child Workers Today*. Middlesex: Quartermaine.

Cornia, G., R. Jolly, and F. Stewart, eds. 1987. *Adjustment with a Human Face*, vol. 1, *Protecting the Vulnerable and Promoting Growth*. Oxford: Clarendon.

Cunningham, H. 1991. *The Children of the Poor: Representations of Childhood since the Seventeenth Century*. Cambridge, MA: Blackwell.

Datta, S.K. and J.B. Nugent. 1984. 'Are Old-age Security and the Utility of Children in Rural India Really Unimportant?' *Population Studies*. 38:507–9.

Davin, A. 1982. 'Child Labour, The Working Class Family, and Domestic Ideology in 19th-Century Britain'. *Development Change*. 13(4):663–52.

De Mause, L., ed. 1976. *The History of Childhood*. London: Souvenir.

De Tray, D. 1983. 'Children's Work Activities in Malaysia'. *Population Development Review*. 9(3):437–55.

Donzelot, J. 1977. *La Police des Families*. Paris: Minuit.

Dore, R. 1982. *The Diploma Disease, Education, Qualification and Development*. London: Allen & Unwin.

Dube, L. 1981. 'The Economic Roles of Children in India: Methodological Issues'. pp. 179–213.

———. 1988. 'On the Construction of Gender in India, Hindu Girls in Patrilineal India'. *Economic and Political Weekly*. 30 April:WS11–24.

Eisenstadt, S.N. 1956. *From Generation to Generation, Age Groups and Social Structure*. New York: Free Press.

Elson, D. 1982. 'The Differentiation of Children's Labour in the Capitalist Labour Market'. *Development Change*. 13(4):479–97.

Ennew, J. 1994. *Street and Working Children: A Guide to Planning*. London: Save the Children.

Espinola, B., B. Glauser, R.M. Oriz and Cartzosa S. de Ortiz. 1987. *In the Streets: Working Street Children in Asunciòn: A Book for Action*. Bogotà: UNICEF.

Evans, D.T. 1994. 'Falling Angels? The Material Construction of Children as Sexual Citizens'. *International Journal of Children's Rights*. 2:1–33.

Folbre, N. 1986. 'Hearts and Spades: Paradigms of Household Economics'. *World Development*. 14(2):245–55.

———. 1994. *Who Pays for the Kids?* London/New York: Routledge.

Franklin, B., ed. 1986. *The Rights of Children*. Oxford: Blackwell.

Freeman, M.D.A. 1983. *Rights and Wrongs of Children*. London/Dover: Pinter.

Fyfe A. 1989. *Child Labour*. Cambridge: Polity Press.

———. 1994. 'Educational Strategies for Street and Working Children'. Presented at Conference on the Street Child. Psychoact. Subst.: Innov. Coop., World Health Organization, Geneva.

Gangrade, K.D., and J.A. Gathia, eds. 1983. *Women and Child Workers in the Unorganized Sector, Non Government Organization's Perspective*. Delhi: Concept.

Goddard, V.B. and White, eds. 1982. 'Child Workers Today'. *Development Change*. 13(4):465–78.

Graham-Brown, S. 1991. *Education in the Developing World, Conflict and Crisis*. London/New York: Longman.

Gulrajani, M. 1994. 'Child Labour and the Export Sector: A Case-study of the Indian Carpet Industry'. *Labour Capital Society*. 27(2):192–215.

Gunn, S.E., and Z. Ostas. 1992. 'Dilemmas in Tackling Child Labour: The Case of Scavenger Children in the Philippines'. *International Labour Review*. 131(6):629–46.

Hallak, J. 1990. 'Setting Educational Priorities in the Developing World'. In *Investing in the Future*. Paris: UNESCO/Internal Institute for Educaction Planning, Perganion Press: pp. 303.

Herpen, A. 1990. *Children and Youngsters in Europe: The New Proletariat? A Report on Child Labour in Europe*. Brussels: Centre for European Studies/European Trade Unions Commission.

Hoyles, M., and P. Evans. 1989. *The Politics of Childhood*. London: Journeyman.

Hull, T. 1975. *Each Child Brings Its Own Fortune: An Enquiry into the Value of Children in a Javanese Village*. Canberra: Australian National University.

———. 1981. 'Perspectives and Data Requirements for the Study of Children's Work'. pp. 47–80.

International Labor Organization (ILO). 1988. *Conditions of Work Digest: The Emerging Response to Child Labour*, vol. 7(1). Geneva: International Labor Organization.

———. Government of Germany. 1991. *International Programme of the Elimination of Child Labour (IPEC)*. Geneva: International Labor Organization.

———. 1991. *Conditions of Work Digest, Child Labour Law and Practice*, vol. 10(1). Geneva: International Labor Organization.

———. 1992. *Children in Bondage: A Call for Action*. Geneva: International Labor Organization.

———. 1993. *World of Work*. June 6–7. Geneva: International Labor Organization.

Jain, D. and N., Banerjee, eds. 1985. *Tyranny of the Household: Investigative Essays on Women's Work*. Delhi: Shakti.

Jain, D. and M. Chand. 1979. 'Rural Children at Work: Preliminary Results of a Pilot Study'. *Indian Journal of Social Work*. 40(3):311–22.

Jeffery, P., R. Jeffery and A. Lyo. 1989. *Labour Pains and Labour Power, Women and Childbearing in India*. Delhi: Manohar Publishers.

Jenks, C. 1994. Child Abuse in the Post-Modern Context: An Issue of Social Identity. In *Childhood Global Perspect* 2(3):111–21.

Kakar, S. 1981. *The Inner World, A Psycho-Analytic Study of Childhood and Society in India*. Delhi: Oxford University Press.

Kambargi, R. ed. 1991. *Child Labour in the Indian Subcontinent, Dimensions and Implications*. Delhi: Sage Publications.

Kayongo-Male, D. and P. Walji. 1984. *Children at Work in Kenya*. Nairobi: Oxford University Press.

Kothari, S. 1983. 'There's Blood on Those Matchsticks, Child Labour in Sivakasi'. *Economic and Political Weekly*. 13(27):1191–202.

La Fontaine, J.S. 1978. *Sex and Age as Principles of Social Differentiation*. London: Academic.

Lavalette M. 1994. *Child Employment in the Capitalist Labour Market*. Aldershot, UK: Avebury.

Lee-Wright, P. 1990. *Child Slaves*. London: Earthscan.

Leslie, J. and M. Paolosso. 1989. *Women, Work and Child Welfare in the Third World*. Boulder, CO: Westview.

Mamdani, M. 1978. *The Myth of Population Control, Family, Caste and Class in an Indian Village*. New York: Monthly Review.

———. 1974. 'The Ideology of Population Control'. *Concerned Demogr*. 4:13–22.

———. 1981. 'The Ideology of Population Control. pp. 39–49.

Marcoux, R. 1994. 'Des inactifs qui ne chô ment pas: une réflexion sur le travail des enfants en milieu urbain du Mail'. *Travail Capital et Société* 27(2):296–319.

Martin, W.G. and M. Beittel. 1987. 'The Hidden Abode of Reproduction: Conceptualizing Households in Southern Africa'. *Development Change*. 18:215–34.

McEwen, S.A. 1982. 'Changes in the Structure of Child Labour Under Conditions of Dualistic Economic Growth'. *Development Change*. 13(4):537–50.

McNamara, R. 1968. *The Essence of Security: Reflections in Office*. London: Hodder & Stoughton.

Mead, M. and M. Wolfenstein, eds. 1955. *Childhood in Contemporary Cultures*. Chicago: University, Chicago Press.

Meillassoux, C. 1983. 'The Economic Basis of Demographic Reproduction: From the Domestic Mode of Production to Wage Earning'. *J. Peasant Stud*. *11(1)*:50–61.

Melhuus, M. 1984. 'Cash Crop Production and Family Labour: Tobacco Growers in Corrientes, Argentina'. In *Family and Work in Rural Societies: Perspectives on Non-wage Labour*. London: Tavistock.

Mendelievich, E., ed. 1979. *Children at Work*. Geneva: International Labor Organization.

Michaelson, K.L., ed. 1981. *And the Poor Get Children: Radical Perspectives on Population Dynamics*. New York: Monthly Review.

Mies, M. and Vandana Shiva. 1993. 'The Impoverishment of the Environement: Women and Children Last'. In eds, *Ecofeminism*. M. Mies and Vandana Shiva, 70–91. London: ZED.

Minge-Kalman, W. 1978. 'The Industrial Revolution and the European Family: The Institutionalization of Childhood as a Market for Family Labour'. *Comparative Studies in Society and History*. 20:456–63.

Moerat. F. 1989. *A Study of Child Labour with Regard to Newspaper Vendors in the Cape Peninsula*. Cape Town: University of Cape Town.

Morice, A. 1981. The Exploitation of Children in the 'Informal Sector': Proposals for Research. 131–58.

_____. 1982: 'Underpaid Labour and Social Reproduction: Apprenticeship in Koalack, Senegal'. *Development Change.* 13(4):515–26.

Morice, A. and B. Schlemmer. 1994. La mise au travail des enfants: une problématique à investir. *Trav. Cap. Soc.* 27(2):286–94.

Mueller, E. 1975. The Economic Value of Children in Peasant Agriculture. Presented at Conf. Popul. Policy, Resour. Fut.

Mundle, S. 1984. 'Recent Trends in the Condition of Children in India: A Statistical Profile'. *World Development.* 12(3):297–308.

Mutiso, R. 1989. *Housemaids in Nairobi: A Review of Available Documents on the Subject of Female Domestic Workers in Nairobi*. Nairobi: Undugu.

Myers, R. 1992. *The Twelve Who Survive: Strengthening Programmes of Early Childhood Development in the Third World*. London/New York: Routledge.

Myers, W.E., ed. 1991. *Protecting Working Children*. London: ZED Books/UNICEF.

Nag, M., B. White and R.C. Peet. 1978. 'An Anthropological Approach to the Study of Economic Value of Children in Java and Nepal'. *Current Anthropology.* 19(2):293–306.

Nardinelli, C. 1990. *Child Labour and the Industrial Revolution*. Bloomington, IN: Indiana University Press.

Nichols, M. 1993. 'Third World Families at Work: Child Labor or Child Care?' *Harvard Business Review.* January/February: 12–23.

Nieuwenhuys, O. 1993: 'To Read and Not to Eat: South Indian Children between Secondary School and Work'. *Children Global Perspective.* 1(2):100–9.

_____. 1994. *Children's Life-worlds: Gender, Welfare and Labour in the Developing World*. London/New York: Routledge.

_____. 1995: 'The Domestic Economy and the Exploitation of Children's Work: The Case of Kerala'. *International Journal of Children's Rights.* 3:213–25.

Oloko, B.A. 1991. Children's Work in Urban Nigeria: A Case Study of Young Lagos Traders. 24–45.

Oppong, C. 1988. 'Les femmes Africaines: des épouses, des mères et des travailleuses'. In *Population et Sociétés en Afrique au Sud du Sahara*. Paris: Harmattan.

Postman, N. 1982. *The Disappearance of Childhood*. New York: Delacorte.

Purdy, L. 1992. *In Their Best Interests? The Case against Equal Rights for Children*. Ithaca/London: Cornell University Press.

Reynolds, P. 1991. *Dance Civet Cat: Child Labour in the Zambezi Valley*. London: ZED.

Rimbaud, C. 1980. *52 Millions d'Enfants au Travail*. Paris: Plon.

Rodgers, G. and G. Standing, eds. 1981. *Child Work, Poverty and Underdevelopment*. Geneva: International Labor Organization.

Sahoo, U.C. 1995. *Child Labour in Agrarian Society*. Jaipur/Delhi: Rawat.

Salazar, M.C. 1991. 'Young Workers in Latin America: Protection of Self-determination?' *Child Welfare.* 70(2):269–83.

Scheper-Hughes, N., ed. 1987. *Child Survival*. Dordrecht: Reidel.

Schildkrout, E. 1980. 'Children's Work Reconsidered'. *International Social Science Journal*. 32(3):479–90.

Schrijvers, J. 1993. *The Violence of Development*. Utrecht: International Books; Delhi: Kali for Women (Inaugural address).

Sen, A., and S. Sengupta. 1985. Malnutrition in Rural Children and the Sex Bias. 3–24.

Sinha, S.K. 1991. *Child Labour in Calcutta: A Sociological Sutdy*. Calcutta: Naya Prokash.

Southall, A. 1988. 'On Mode of Production Theory: The Foraging Mode of Production and the Kinship Mode of Production'. *Dialectical Anthropology*. 12:165–92.

Stadum, B. 1995. 'The Dilemma in Saving Children from Child Labor: Reform and Case-work at Odds with Families' Needs'. *Child Welfare*. 74(1):20–33.

Thompson, E.P. 1968. *The Making of the English Working Class*. Harmondsworth, UK: Penguin.

Van Gennep, A. [1908] 1960. *The Rites of Passage*. Chicago: University of Chicago Press.

Verlet, M. 1994. 'Grandir à Nima (Ghana): dérégulation domestique et mise au travail des enfants. *Travail Capital et Société*. 27(2):162–90.

Vijayagopalan, S. 1993. *Child Labour in the Carpet Industry: A Status Report*. Delhi: NCAER.

Vittachi, A. 1989. *Stolen Childhood: In Search of the Rights of the Child*. Cambridge: Polity Press.

Vlassoff, M. 1979. 'Labour Demand and Economic Utility of Children: A Case Study in Rural India'. *Population Studies*. 33(3).

_____. 1982. 'Economic Utility of Children and Fertility in Rural India'. *Population Studies*. 36:45–60.

Vlassoff, M. and C. Vlassoff. 1980. 'Old Age Security and the Utility of Children in Rural India'. *Population Studies*. 34(3):487–99.

Wallerstein, I., W.G. Martin and T. Dickinson. 1982. 'Household Structures and Production Processes: Preliminary Theses and Findings'. *Review*. 5(3):437–58.

Walvin, J. 1982. *A Child's World: A Social History of English Childhood 1800–1914*. Harmondsworth, UK: Penguin.

Weiner, M. 1991. *The Child and the State in India: Child Labour and Educational Policy in Comparative Perspective*. Princeton, NJ: Princeton University Press.

Weissbach, L.S. 1989. *Child Labour Reform in Nineteenth Century France: Assuring the Future Harvest*. London: Baton Rouge Louisiana University Press.

White, B. 1975. 'The Economic Importance of Children in a Javanese Village'. In M. Nag, ed., *Population and Social Organization*. 127–46. The Hague: Mouton.

_____. 1982. 'Child Labour and Population Growth in Rural Asia'. *Development Change*. 13(4):587–610.

_____. 1994. *Children, Work and 'Child Labour': Changing Responses to the Employment of Children*. The Hague: Inst. Soc. Study. (Inaugural address). Development and Change. 25:849–78.

Whiting, B.B., ed. 1963. *Six Cultures: Studies of Child Rearing*. New York: Wiley.

Williams, S. 1993. *Child Workers in Portugal*. London: Anti-Slavery Institute.

Wyers, J. 1986. 'Child Labour in Brazilian Agriculture'. *Critical Anthropology*. 6(2):63–80.

Zelizer, V. 1994. *Pricing the Priceless Child, The Changing Social Value of Children*. Princeton, NJ: Princeton University Press.

Old Age and the Global Economy of Knowledge

Lawrence Cohen

INTRODUCTION

Since the 1970s, gerontological writing in India has been dominated by a powerful and seldom challenged narrative of the decline of the Indian joint family and the consequent emergence of old age as a time of difficulty (Biswas 1987; Bose and Gangrade 1988; Desai 1982; Mishra 1989; Pati and Jena 1989; Sharma and Dak 1987; Sinha 1989; Soodan 1975). The narrative runs as follows: (1) Indian families once lived in multigenerational 'joint' households; (2) in such households, old people had all their needs taken care of, were listened to and respected, and had few complaints; (3) with the advent of westernization, industrialization, and urbanization—in a word, modernization—families began to break up and social support and respect for the elderly declined, along with their quality of life.

Despite its ubiquity, this version of the social history of old age is inaccurate. Evidence that most households were joint in the past is lacking (Shah 1996), as is evidence that most old people in the past had their economic or emotional needs met. Definitional criteria for 'old' tend to conflate chronological, biological, and social aging. The very terms of the narrative presume that the history of old age only begins with an axiomatic Fall into unhappy modernity; such terms render historical inquiry all but meaningless. Discussion of 'the old' as a uniform group diverts attention from those bodily and social assaults of old age which correlate with distinctions of class, community, and gender, particularly the assaults of undernutrition (De Souza 1981, De Souza and Fernandes 1982) and what we might term the 'respectful neglect' of family members.

The durability of this lapsarian version of aging in India, despite a lack of empirical justification, is rooted both in the dynamics of the international discipline of gerontology and in a specific genealogy of the old body in colonial and independent India. A discussion of international (predominantly American) gerontology and the subdiscipline of geroanthropology (Nydegger 1983) will be followed here by a discussion of Indian gerontology: in both cases, attention will be to the genealogy and sociology of gerontological knowledge. In the concluding section, some recent approaches to the critical sociology and anthropology of old age will briefly be addressed.

Making Old Age

The plight of the aged is continually rediscovered. Minois (1987) has attempted a history of old age 'from Antiquity to the Renaissance' in what he defines as the West; Tilak (1989) has offered a similarly broad survey of Indian engagements with old age from classical to contemporary literatures. Old age has always been good to think, to paraphrase (Lévi-Strauss) reflection on the old body and its voice, wisdom, danger, and decay has been central to the making of soteriologies, theodicies, and political philosophies across regions and across centuries. But claims of authoritative knowledge over this body, made to the state by scholars, emerge at discrete junctures and frequently in gendered terms. Thus the Renaissance critics of the *Malleus* and the rest of the apparatus of Inquisitorial witchcraft accusation, Reginold Scot and Weyer Jonathan, transform a generalized discussion of dotage as the mesocosm between the body and the social order into a new site of medical authority against the Church: *they are not witches,* the medical reformers claim, *they are doing old women* (Scot [1584] 1964; Weyer [1583] 1991).

From seventeenth-century European and colonial witchcraft panics to the nineteenth-century French physician Jean Martin Charcot's (1881) realization that the many indigent old women at the Salpetriere hospital offered the human material for a new medicine of old age, the old body becomes a site of scientific inquiry, particularly at moments when the curtailment of the rights of widows in land, livelihood, or access to family or community support produces an excess of visible old women. Charcot (1881) tells his students to *look around* the clinic and note how many old women are there. Leo Ignatz Nascher, the American who coined the term 'geriatrics' early in the twentieth century, describes the moment when he realized doctors were wrong to neglect the medical problems of the old as an epiphany: his preceptor refused to treat an old woman in a poorhouse they were visiting, but she persisted in following them on their rounds. In the old woman's refusal to disappear, young Nascher recalls suddenly realizing the prejudice behind the other man's inability to see old people as meriting serious medical attention (see Thewlis 1941).

This stubborn visibility of old women, drawing upon earlier gendered articulations of overly present elderly, the bawds and crones either ludically or uncannily troped folk and high narrative (Mignon 1947; Walker 1985), is taken up within the expanding regulative apparatus Michelle Foucault has described as biopower. In Foucault's (1978) enumeration, in the first volume of *The History of Sexuality*, of the bodies specified and iterated within the 'Victorian' will to discourse—the masturbating child, the hysterical woman, the responsible couple, the sexual pervert—old bodies do not figure prominently. One site where they matter, however, is in the biopolitics of empire. Stoler (1995) has added the racialized body of 'the native' to the domains central to nineteenth-century biopolitical elaboration, and one of the centrally iterated bodies within colonial tableaux is that of an old woman.

Ashis Nandy (1983) has noted the colonial splitting of the colonized other in age-specific terms in the case of British India: India as simultaneously childlike, not ready for autonomy or freedom, and senescent, a decrepit and corrupt Oriental culture. Critical work on British self-fashioning *in loco parentis* is by now commonplace, but colonial rhetoric also placed Britain *in loco filii*, in so doing drawing upon the importance of the old woman's body within a very different universe of discourse. Thus the Orientalist scholar and administrator William Jones (1792), in introducing his translation of the dramatist Kalidasa's work *Sakuntala*, cites a Bengali aphorism taught him by his Sanskrit teacher: poetry is a woman, birthed and raised by the Epic poets, married to Kalidasa, the beloved mother of later poets, but now an old woman with no family nor shelter, wandering from house to house. Jones (1792) offers Britain as the good son, arriving just in time to house and clothe the tottering crone . Throughout the subsequent century, old women are ubiquitous in colonial narrative, their bodies often metaphors for the Indian social body (Cohen 1998). As colonial difference is increasingly defined by the pathophysiology of the native body, old age becomes the secret lodged within the seductive surfaces of native *topoi*: from Henry Haggard's Ayesha in *She* (1886) to James Hilton's princess in *Lost Horizon* (1933) and beyond. Colonial medicine drew upon the gross pathology of old age and particularly the finding of cerebral softening in describing the *tropical softening* which differentially affected colonials and natives and which helped explain the native body's seeming tendency to ripen and rot prematurely.

Georges Canguilhem (1989) has examined the nineteenth-century emergence of the normal body in European biology and medicine (1989). From the outset of the troubled relationship between the normal and the pathological, old age has represented a limit to the coherence of norms. For Charcot (1881), this limit is definitional: the medicine of old age has to be grounded in the difficulty of articulating the boundary between sickness and health. But Nascher will see in this ambiguity the denial of clinical responsibility. In his book *Geriatrics* (1914), he strenuously attempts to effect a division between physiological and pathological aging, but despite his effort each side continually bleeds into the other. Thomas Cole (1992) roots the centrality of *normal aging* in the science of old age from Nascher onwards in an earlier Victorian moment of moral perfectionism, and indeed the nineteenth- and early twentieth-century concepts of *senile climacteric* and *senile involution*—both of which attempt to bridge the normal and the pathological—are shot through with the full armamentarium of moral therapy. Forms of sickness in old age—particularly mental impairment—are linked to questions of character and moral strength. These understandings inform and are informed by the old body of the native; senile involution becomes increasingly linked in the inter-War period to eugenic ideas of racial fitness (Warthin 1929). To survive and improve, the race and the species must avoid both the burden of too many elders and the inferior germ plasm of the old.

The comparative status of the elderly has been a benchmark of civilizational difference in social evolutionary thought, not only in the arguably parricidal modernist fantasy of eugenics but more significantly within anthropological understandings of kinship behaviour. Inuit practices of 'abandoning' the old, dehistoricized and decontextualized, become a marker of savagery and a subject for philosophical debate on moral relativism. More generally, age appears in late nineteenth-century anthropological thought in the linked figures of the victim of the totemic feast and of the dying king in Robertson Smith (1889) and James Frazer (1900). Here the old body threatens not only materially, as a drain on the limited resources of hunter-gatherers, but symbolically: the body of the father, chief, king, or god, with which the larger collective of the clan, tribe, populace, or cosmos is sympathetically identified, must remain free from the debilitating signs of old age, if necessary by its violent removal and replacement. Frazer's (1900) central theme—that cultural continuity was threatened by the visible signs of time upon the body of the cynosure—suggests the broad contours of an incipient symbolic anthropology of age not exhausted by a psychoanalytic reading. Though the explicit practitioners of magical thinking are primitives, peasants, and paupers, the Frazerian narrative of the dying and resurrected god-king is a fin-de-siécle critique of Christian myth and anticipates modernist demythologization.

But this narrative, which extrapolates from its vision of the savage Other to see violence at the heart of the signification of age, is displaced. Significantly, by the time of the second wave of anthropological modernization narrative—with the emergence of the Cold War, the neo-colonial operations of development, and the juggernaut of modernization theory—the fin-de-siècle and modernist manoeuvres by which the savage becomes the mirror of European society lose coherence in the face of a *pax americana* which collapses primitivism and the high decadence of India and China into a single category of the traditional. The relationship between modernity and care for the aged is reversed. Traditional societies are now seen to take care of the elderly and filial piety replaces the savage heart of darkness as the *sine qua non* of the classic order. Parricide becomes a property of the modern, and gerontophobia is the fly in the ointment of development initiative, the unfortunate but remediable consequence of modernization. Only fully developed, late modern societies can recuperate the lost values of the golden age through the new sciences of gerontology and geriatrics (see Achenbaum 1995; Katz 1996).

Though rooted in earlier industrial and ideological shifts, contemporary gerontology and geriatrics are primarily offspring of this Cold War moment, of the post-Second World War incarnation of social welfare as necessary societal regulation through a unified social science. Gerontology's close relation to the theoretical nexus of Parsons (1949) and his colleagues thus lies not only in the specific application of modernization theory to questions of old age—the subfield known as *aging and modernization theory*—but in the persistence of an epistemological and disciplinary style rooted in a social welfare rhetoric resistant to post-Parsonian transformations in the various social sciences. This resistance goes beyond the hermeneutic of suspicion towards theoretical jargon and faddism, arguably necessary for an effectively applied social science, for even where gerontology embraces more recent disciplinary shifts it remains a highly normative and dualistic practice, structured around the funding exigencies of American soft money.

Like other post-War social science, gerontology has been dominated by the American academy given the latter's size and relatively open access to state and foundation resources. Crudely, the American field may be framed as having progressed through three phases:

(1) *a modernization/disengagement phase*, in which the social obsolescence of the elderly is normalized both as a function of urban industrial society and as an embodied characteristic of a healthy and adaptive old age (Parsons 1949; Cumming and Henry 1961);

(2) *a critical/activity phase*, in which the norms of the first phase are challenged as *ageism* (Levin and Levin 1980), changes in the quality of life of the elderly are no longer reduced to the effect of industrial and demographic transitions (Fisher 1978), and the emergence of distinct retirement communities of old people (Hochschild 1973; FitzGerald 1986) is normalized through a rhetoric insisting on the *normality* of old age (Butler 1975);

(3) *a post-modern/triage* phase, in which the dramatic shift

between the first and second phases is recognized as representing a false opposition and yet is not only maintained but sharpened as an increasingly salient distinction between the *young old* and the *old old:* the latter increasingly defined through a medico-legal jargon of *frailty* and *futility* (Olson 1994; Schneiderman 1994; Tilson 1990): thus the new biopolitical genre of *memento mori* advocating more societal triage given the cost and futility of the intensive medicalization of the frail elderly (Callahan 1993; Nuland 1994).

One of the forms of second phase critique is a self-conscious *political economy of aging* (Minkler and Estes 1991; Olson 1982) that began to criticize the formation of professional gerontology as an apparatus which deflected attention from the relation between age, class, race, and gender by fetishizing 'age' as a sufficient category of analysis. Caroll Estes famously examines the ways in which gerontological institutions were part of an *aging enterprise* that profited off the dependency of the elderly even as it paradoxically demanded their 'independence' (Estes 1979, 1993). Central to gerontology as an aging enterprise is the almost missionary zeal by which its adherents argued that other scholars, who did not take aging seriously enough as a category of analysis, needed to be 'indoctrinated' or 'proselytized' (Cohen 1994, 1998).

Within the American anthropology of age, the dynamic is similar. Early writing stresses modernization theory paradigms (Cowgill and Holmes 1972). Subsequently, a burgeoning critical literature attacks the adequacy of aging and modernization approaches, troubling the contrast between a gerontophilic pre-colonial past and a gerontophobic neo-colonial or post-colonial present (Rhoads 1984). One turn away from aging and modernization theory involves the repatriation of anthropological critique (Myerhoff 1978); this turn reflects both the post-colonial challenge to first-world anthropology and the availability of research money for studies of the old age of Americans. With the growth of such funding and the more applied and positivist rather than critical or interpretive goals of founders, new methodological precision and expertise and therefore a new set of subdisciplines appear: grandparent studies, life history studies, caregiver studies, chronicity studies, and even critical gerontology as a subdiscipline with its own operationalizable methods and jargon. As a largely nativist subdiscipline, American geroanthropology utilizes 'culture' in two ways: in engaging the culture of the old or of particular cohorts and in examining ethnicity and race in terms of cultural difference. International cross-cultural difference is analysed similarly to national ethnic difference. The resulting analysis is more influenced by the impact of American identity politics and ideologies of multiculturalism upon bureaucratic liberalism than by the post-

Writing Culture collapse of the sufficiency of the culture concept (Clifford and Marcus 1986). Despite its growth and specialization, the subdiscipline remains organized around the same rhetoric of mission as gerontology overall: there are never enough anthropologists in gerontology, or gerontologists in anthropology.

'Aging in India'

At least two narratives of the career of old age in Indian social thought are possible; the first locates the persistence of the Decline of the Joint Family narrative within the incitements of international gerontology, and the second in contrast offers a genealogy of Indian modernity not reducible to colonial and post-colonial epistemes.

Post-Independence writing on old age in Indian social science locates itself explicitly as an extension of British and particularly American scholarship, even when the accomplishment of such writing is unique. Marulasiddaiah's, *Old People of Makunti* is an innovative ethnography of village elders in Karnataka which predates the routinization of gerontology into repetitions of alarmist demography (Katz 1996) and appeals to a Golden Age; the author, a social worker by training, grapples with the interpretive and practical issues involved in analysing intergenerational relations. Unlike contemporary work in which 'the old' were presented as a single homogenous group (see Wiser and Wiser [1930] 1971, where the old literally spoke with a single voice, representing the perspective of a past resistant to modern agricultural techniques and social practices), the Makunti study represents greater diversity in both the personal style and the material conditions of aging. Yet when I interviewed Marulasiddaiah in 1996, he argued that his methodology was based almost entirely on American gerontological social work.

With *Aging in India*, Soodan's (1975) study of Lucknow elderly, the gerontological monograph assumes a fixed form: appeals to demographic urgency and international legitimation are followed by enumerations of the needs of the elderly and relatively utopian visions of gerontological social welfare, and the Joint Family narrative is firmly in place. Even the title is routinized; book after book called *Aging in India* follow. As with the mainstream of American gerontology, the subdiscipline is fairly impervious to outside developments. For decades, sociologists, historians, and anthropologists have massively challenged the empirical and analytic sufficiency of the monolithic 'Joint Family' and the premises of its ahistoricity and decline: distinguishing kinship and household dimensions of 'family' (Gray and Mearns 1989; Madan [1965] 1989; Shah 1974); distinguishing household ideology from empirical structure (Dumont 1983; Madan 1987) and rethinking the basis of that ideology (Das [1977] 1982); making the political economy of aging central to the analysis of intergenerational relations (De Souza 1981; De Souza and Fernandes 1982); documenting extensive regional variation in family and household structure (Karve [1953] 1968, Kolenda 1987); documenting the divergent and varied transformations of rural (Epstein 1962, 1973) and urban (Ross 1961; Vatuk 1972) development on household size; challenging presumptions about how social security in old age relates either to 'tradition' or family structure (Agarwal 1994; Chen and Drèze 1992); and rethinking the relationship of family and household organization and ideology to the experience of pleasure or unhappiness in old age (Vatuk 1980, 1990). Despite these interventions, the dominant sociology of the family remains unyielding and unruffled, drawing on the ubiquitous proclamations of demographic apocalypse of international gerontology, the call to arms of international conferences like the 1982 World Assembly on Aging in Vienna, and the dire predictions of British and other European gerontological experts and of the non-governmental organizations (NGOs) they have helped found in India.

Demographic and health transitions *are* occurring in parts of India, but they are far from ubiquitous. They have not been accompanied by the parallel ideological shifts in the meaning of family and household presumed by the European and American literature. Neither have they occurred within a global economy resembling late-nineteenth- and early-twentieth-century Europe or North America. And they do not account for differences in the usefulness of dependency ratios (the ratio of persons too old or young to be in the labour pool to those who are in it) in contexts where the very old and very young are frequently employed. A social gerontology which does not presume consequences but analyses the specificity and impact of demographic change is slow in emerging, in India as elsewhere. Prior to useful quantification, extensive empirical ethnography in the tradition of Marulasiddaiah will be necessary.

Nor is the impact of demographic change upon the structures of knowledge production self-evident. In Kerala and Tamil Nadu, for example, a number of gerontological NGOs have emerged since the 1980s and geriatrics research programmes and clinics have developed in several cities. The often significantly different age distributions of south India may explain part of this institutional development, but several of these organizations and programmes (the gerontological research centres of Tirupati and Madurai) emerged early in the process of demographic transition and reflect the ideological commitments of their founders and backers as well as the subsequent and still limited social demand for these services.

Despite the appeals to international scholarship and the routinization of alarmist rhetoric, the recasting of European and American scholarly narratives often creates divergent possibilities. Ramamurthy's work (1979) on the psychology of old age and that of his students and other scholars (Mishra 1989) broadens an older western social adjustment literature to encompass most of geropsychology, and in so doing may reflect the salience of balance and adjustment metaphor in the intergenerational negotiations of many middle-class families (Cohen 1998). Venkoba Rao's extensive work (1989) on psychiatric morbidity in old age, based on his clinical and community studies in Madurai district, Tamil Nadu, draws upon the global epidemiology of geropsychiatric distress but resists the emerging global tendency to reduce the ontogeny of both suffering and behavioural change to dementia (see Lyman 1989).

The Age of Renunciation

The insistence of the decline of the joint family in much of the 'Aging in India' literature reflects more than the persistence of aging and modernization theory paradigms within a global economy of knowledge and expertise. The old body has been a central presence in Indian social thought, and the origins of its modern abjection predate Jones' (1792) claims *in loco filii* upon a tottering Mother India. The genealogy of such a body, despite Tilak's (1989) important work, has not yet been undertaken and any account must be speculative. Materials for an archive abound: abject old bodies have circulated for millennia, as *memento mori* and signs of the limits of medicine, comic and tragic figures, and both icons and indices of cosmic decay. The bodies of the renouncer and the widow in particular are critical for a genealogy of modernity, age, and abjection.

There are several approaches to the modernity of the old renouncer. J.P.S. Uberoi (1996) has argued, in his analysis of Sikhism as a paradigmatic Indian 'modernity', that the effect of the Sikh Gurus was to collapse a medieval Hindu and Muslim triad of esoteric religion, civil society, and the state into a community and symbolic order organized around exemplary practices of self-sacrifice. Uberoi is not suggesting that Sikhism is the necessary or sufficient ground for any genealogy of Indian modernity. But in decentring Europe and colonialism in the production of such geneologies, he, in effect, articulates an account of pre-colonial or at least para-colanial Indian modernity and suggests the importance of attending to shifts in ideologies and micropractices of renunciation in its constitution. One does not have to accept the details of Uberoi's particular historiography to recognize the enabling features of this manoeuvre.

One of the structural binaries that collapsed in the process of consolidation Uberoi details is that of the Hindu Epic, Puranic and later texts. This binary is often narrativized through the moral quandary of the aging body caught between the exemplary positions of the king and the renouncer: Yayati in the Mahabharata, Vinayashila in the Kathasaritsagara (Cohen 1998). If Uberoi's analysis of the structural collapse articulated through such a modernity is correct, then the narratively age-linked figure of the renouncer is encompassed by the worldly and vernacular ascetisicm of the Sikh Guru, a manoeuvre which relocates the axis of age as constitutive of the social imaginary.

Thus, criticizing the historiographic convention of framing the pacificist Guru Nanak against the martial Guru Gobind Singh, Uberoi rereads the deepening semiotic chain of the line of Gurus in terms of an emerging ethos of loving martyrdom. The distinction between the two Gurus is implicitly reworked: Nanak in his representation still bears the old and signifiably renunciate body of the *sanyasi*, whereas Gobind Singh's sacrifice is not marked through the axis of age but of generation: his martyred predecessor, his martyred sons. The effect of the incipient Indian modernity Uberoi articulates, independent of European ideology and its transformation, is to supplant the signifiably old body of the medieval renouncer, Dumont's (1980) free-floating individual located outside a social order marked by lineage, affinity, and difference, with a renunciate householder-king no longer abjected from the social order but bearing the mark of sacrifice upon the generational axes of lineal kinship partially constitutive of that order. Age, refigured as generation, is brought within the frame of the social and supplants both caste and kingship as its prime signifying axis. Time and decay no longer stand as the limit to the *dharma* of the householder and king, but are simultaneously incorporated as the martyrdom of the modern subject and displaced onto the bodies of generational others.

Whatever the status of Uberoi's historical narrative, it remains a rare effort to construct an ontogeny of modern Indian society not exhausted by the 'world system', Islamic conquest, British colonialism, or the contemporary nation-state and offers a challenge for any genealogy of the old body. Before a colonial gaze inserts itself *in loco filii*, the aging of the renunciate body has already emerged as a critical and new site of cultural work. By the time of Jones's Orientalism, the abject old Widow Poetry the administrator-poet takes *in loco filii* already has a history.

The frequent figure in several classical and medieval genres, the pathetic old man with his decaying body and contemptuous family standing for cosmic decay as *memento mori* (see Cohen 1994), is brought from the limits into the centre of the social as an abject parent and in the process is gendered: consider the abandoned old mother. In the nineteenth century, this mother is not only taken up by the colonizing imagination but more productively by the emergent colonized elite of the *bhadralok:* a paradigmatic image of apocalyptic modernity is the satiric *patua* cartoon Ghar Kali, showing the *babu* with his primping wife astride his shoulders, dragging his old mother by a leash of her *rudraksha* (rosary) (Cohen 1998). Apocalyptic old women abound in the colonial period, not only as abject signifiers of a pre-colonial modernity which illuminate the new cultural logics of British rule but also— through their inversion as figures of old madwomen—as signs of millenial transformation, as in the case of an 1861 movement among the eastern Uttar Pradesh community of fishermen (ibid.).

These linked figures of abject mothers and old madwomen extend into the twentieth century, in part through expanding forms of travel and religious patronage and the institutionalization of abject widowhood in Hindu *tirthas* like Brindavan and Kashi. In Premchand's *Garib ki Hay*, the widow Manga loses her savings to a corrupt *munshi*, and only in her growing madness does she have any recourse to his exploitation. But the abjection of the old mother is increasingly supplanted by a different figure, that of the old and usually paternal aunt: Premchand's *Burhi Kaki*, Bandopadhya's *Pather Panchali* and Satyajit Ray's film of the latter. The childless aunt, unlike the mother, does not point unambivalently to children whose modern callousness had caused her abjection. Rather, she embodies a world in which the ontogeny of suffering is less coherently signifiable through the chain of parents and children, through the order of generation alone. She signifies an old age located within the logic of family yet irreducible to it, and remains the anchor of a counter-narrative to the Decline of the Joint Family iteration of modern gerontology.

A Post-modern Life Course?

Despite the dominance of the professional 'Aging in India' literature and its resistance to scholarly inquiry, the early promise of Marulasiddaiah's work has been continued in a variety of fields. In anthropology, Vatuk in a series of articles develops a sophisticated analysis of the life course based primarily upon ethnography in Delhi: fleshing out the relevance of both renunciatory and familial ideals within the everyday practice of old women and men (1980), discussing dependence upon one's children as both a value and yet a source of tremendous anxiety (1990), insisting on the relevance of age to the emerging study of widowhood and rights in land (Agarwal 1994), and more recently turning to ethnohistorical studies of age and gender over the past two centuries within a Muslim *khandan* in Madras and Hyderabad. Lamb's (2000) study of a West Bengal village extends Vatuk's work in desire and dependency as themes in the life course, using the intersection of old age and gender to rethink the cross-cultural study of the self. Lamb documents the centrality of the 'loosening' in old age of the relational ties constituting rural personhood.

Vatuk (1980, 1990) and Lamb (2000) establish an interpretive anthropology thematizing the negotiation and experience of old age at the intersection of gender, generational, and cultural difference; Chatterji et al. (1998) and Cohen (1998) turn to the institutional and disciplinary matrices through which old age is officially and professionally fashioned, and locate the interpretive possibilities for hearing old voices within such contexts. Sangeeta Chattoo, in a dissertation on the negotiation of clinical reality in a government hospital in Kashmir, relates allopathic and specifically geriatric disciplinarity to the political economy of the old body between the Indian state and the household and to what is at stake in the Islamic body. Integrating Chattoo's work with Chatterji's study of the constitution of self and clinic in a Dutch old age home, Chatterji et al. (1998) note against an easy culturalism. They argue that in different ways both the Dutch and Kashmiri clinics demand the social death of the old patient and yet the structural limits preventing the totalization of Indian gerontology do not lead, as in Holland, to the disappearance of the old voice but queer's its pitch:

> The hospital in Srinagar provides a different perspective altogether precisely because aging has not been fabricated as a separate object of clinical discourse there. This does not mean that what we see in the hospital is some kind of idyllic scene for the treatment of the impaired elderly: instead the hospital appears as a kind of cross roads where elderly patients bring their disappointments with the family and with a callous society for an authentication of their experience with aging and with disability. Thus they appropriate the bio-medical discourse and its sites within their own life worlds [1998].

I similarly examine the old voice in the context of bodily and social weakness and their gendered and class specificity, with a focus on senility and dementia (see Cohen 1998). The core of my project is a study of how families, institutions, and the elderly across class in Varanasi confront and make knowledgeable claims about the radical transformation of the old voice, about the intersection of the rhetorics and practices constituting senility, weakness, imbalance and maladjustment, forgetfulness and remembering and anger, loneliness and despair. From this base I move out to evaluate the ways age and agelessness signify the limits to collectivity in nineteenth- and twentieth-century India and the United States, examining figures ranging from singer Lata Mangeshkar and former deputy prime minister Devi Lal to Ronald Reagan.

This turn to popular culture has characterized the new cultural studies of old age in Europe, North America, and Australia, an effort to supplement the Frankfurt School methodology of critical gerontology with the tools of rhetoric. Featherstone and Wernick's (1995) work on images of aging draws on Cole's (1992) discussion of a post-modern old age which moves beyond the Victorian legacy of moral perfectibility and allows for a cultural politics of late life encompassing both autonomy and dependency, 'normality' and its Other. The articles in the 1995 Featherstone and Hepworth edited collection extend Cole's analysis to recent market-driven images of 'positive aging'; analyse the American popularity of Indian physician and New Age guru Deepak Chopra as part of a 'postmodern life course' which 'engenders a simulated life-span, one that promises to enhance living by stretching middle age into ... timelessness' (Katz 1995); and suggest that the analysis of age must be central to the reflexive modernization of (Giddens) and (Beck), and vice versa. 'Aging intensifies the reflexivity which is forced upon us in a world in which we are all compelled to choose a lifestyle embodying tastes.'

But Deepak Chopra, bringing the agelessness of a Vedanta-Samkhya-Ayurveda pastiche to a West hungry for the consumption of forms of life marked as Indian, circulates within the same economy of cynosures that brought Mother Teresa to India, offering the agelessness of Christian charity and redemption to the dying of Calcutta slums. Those who lament the excision of an art of dying from the dominant representation of old age as contemporary market-driven positive aging intensifies Victorian regimes of perfectibility, often avert their attention from more global arenas of circulation which locate a far more persistent *ars moriendi* within the spaces of neocolonial and increasingly neoliberal triage. It is in the context of rising commodity prices and everyday generational triage in India that the relation between the ideology of filial piety and the social death of the elderly (at stake in both fictional narratives of old mothers and aunts and scholarly narratives of the decline of the family) is being reworked. It is this global dispersion of old bodies and dying spaces that Chatterji et al. (1998) call attention to in their effort to juxtapose the old age of the Dutch old age home with the Kashmiri government hospital. The anthropology and history of old age has been classically more interested in normative comparison—is old age better here or there, now or then—than in developing the tools to analyse the shifting ground of such dispersion.

Such tools may come in part from work in feminist and sexuality studies; Katz (1995) has pointed out the critical need for a convergence. Both Woodward and Das have discussed the gendering of how the Other across time—parent, child, grandparent, grandchild, age-different friend or lover, one's own past or future self, the suffering child or elder—is granted subjectivity; Woodward's rethinking of the psychoanalytic figure of the mirror offers a valuable interpretive device and suggests an approach to the global mirror work which produces undertheorized splittings of active/frail, autonomous/futile, agelessness/decay, Chopra/Teresa.

In theorizing age, we need remember that both the rhetoric and political economy of the body in time are grounded in a set of interpretive possibilities. Theorizing age mandates attention to process; to the work of anticipation, recollection, and amnesis; to difference; and to the confrontation with rupture. *Aging is process*, a point articulated by Moore, and its analysis requires the delineation and problematization of the multiple processual frames by which body and subject are temporally articulated: cellular and organic processes within nutritionally and environmentally contingent sites; political and institutional processes with their specificities of schedule, cohort size and morphology, entitlement, and triage; and ritual and secular processes and the increasingly performative practice by which their multiple temporalities are citationally deployed. *Aging is work*, an artifact fabricated through continual acts of projection, recollection, and forgetting, a point developed by psychoanalysis, and by more sociological efforts to address the collective work of aging. *Aging is difference*, a point developed both through French Marxist debates on the status of age as a form of class within the domestic mode of production (Meillassoux 1981) and American sociological discussions of age stratification. The relative elision of age in the grand theoretical elucidation of Derridean *différence* may have to do with its near identity with the narrative axis through which Derrida constitutes the notion of limit, the relation of signification to death. Binary gender, through both the radical potential of feminist thought but also the influence of psychoanalytic heteronormativism, has anchored social theory as the *Ur*-difference through which racial, colonial, and sexual difference can be theorized. Age, as the other grand axis along with gender constituting a rhetoric of the universalizably natural, begs consideration.

Finally, *age is rupture*, and here we come full circle to Frazer. The necessary illusion of synchrony in the constitution of the real is continually interrupted by the fact of time. Semiosis decays: it is this insight which attributes to Indian 'ethnosociology' as the idea of *unmatching*. From modern anthropology's origins in the conjunction of anxiety over Christ's body and the troubling violence constituting the wildness colonialism encounters and creates, the idea that a violent act was necessary for the maintenance of the totality of society and its governmentality has persisted: the figure of the sacrifice, offered by Kierkegaard as the quintessential modern totem and displaced through colonial productions like *The Golden Bough*, is continually recuperated through its reimagining. The anthropological question, in this 'postmodern' moment of compression, intensification, and the production of marginality and 'out of the way places', becomes a matter of examining the distributive economy of such semiotic decay, to theorize the still divergent ways the aging body comes to matter and to demand a voice.

REFERENCES

Achenbaum, W. Andrew. 1978. *Old Age in the New Land: The American Experience since 1790.* Baltimore: Johns Hopkins University Press.

———. 1983. *Shades of Gray: Old Age, American Values, and Federal Policies since 1920.* In Little, Brown, Series on Gerontology. Boston: Little, Brown.

———. 1995. *Crossing Frontiers: Gerontology Emerges as a Science.* Cambridge: Cambridge University Press.

Agarwal, Bina. 1994. *A Field of One's Own: Gender and Land Rights in South Asia.* Cambridge: Cambridge University Press.

Biswas, Suhas K., ed. 1987. *Aging in Contemporary India.* Calcutta: Indian Anthropological Society.

Bose, A.B. and K.D. Gangrade, eds. 1988. *The Aging in India: Problems and Potentialities.* New Delhi: Abhinav Publications.

Butler, Robert N. 1975. *Why Survive? Being Old in America.* New York: Harper & Row.

Callahan, Daniel. 1993. *The Troubled Dream of Life: Living with Mortality.* New York: Simon & Schuster.

Canguilhem, Georges. 1989. *The Normal and the Pathological.* Trans. Carolyn R. Fawcett. New York: Zone.

Charcot, Jean Martin. 1881. *Clinical Lectures on Senile and Chronic Diseases.* Trans. William S. Tuke. London: The New Sydenham Society.

Chaterji, Roma, Sangeeta Chattoo and Veena Das. 1998. 'The Death of the Clinic? Normality and Pathology in Recrafting Old Bodies'. In M. Shildrick and J. Price, eds., *Vital Signs: Feminist Reconfiguration Biological Body.* Edinburg: Edinburg University Press.

Chattoo, Sangeeta. 1992. *A Sociological Study of Certain Aspects of Diseases and Death: A Case Study of Muslims of Kashmir.* Unpublished Ph.D. dissertation of the University of Delhi.

Chen, Martha Alter and Jean Drèze. 1992. 'Widows and Health in Rural North India'. *Economic and Political Weekly.* (24–31 October): WS81–WS92.

Clifford, James and George E. Marcus, eds. 1986. *Writing Culture: The Poetics and Politics of Ethnography.* Berkeley: University of California Press.

Cohen, Lawrence. 1994. 'Old Age: Cultural and Critical Perspectives'. *Annual Review of Anthropology.* 23:137–58.

———. 1998. *No Aging in India: Alzheimer's, the Bad Family, and Other Modern Things.* Berkeley: University of California Press.

Cole, Thomas R. 1992. *The Journey of Life: A Cultural History of Aging in America.* Cambridge: Cambridge University Press.

Cowgill, Donald Olen and Lowell D. Holmes, eds. 1972. *Aging and Modernization.* New York: Appleton-Century-Crofts.

Cumming, Elaine and William E. Henry, eds. 1961. *Growing Old, the Process of Disengagement.* New York: Basic.

Das, Veena. [1977] 1982. *Structure and Cognition: Aspects of Hindu Caste and Ritual.* 2nd ed. Delhi: Oxford University Press.

Desai, K.G., ed. 1982. *Aging in India.* Bombay: Tata Institute of Social Sciences.

De Souza, Alfred. 1981. *The Social Organisation of Aging among the Urban Poor.* New Delhi: Indian Social Institute.

De Souza, Alfred and Walter Fernandes, eds. 1982. *Aging in South Asia: Theoretical Issues and Policy Implications.* New Delhi: Indian Social Institute.

Dumont, Louis. 1983. *Affinity as a Value: Marriage Alliance in South India, with Comparative Essays on Australia.* Chicago: University of Chicago Press.

Dumont, Louis. 1980. *Homo Hierarchicus: The System and its Implication.* Chicago: University of Chicago Press.

Epstein, Trude Scarlett. 1962. *Economic Development and Social Change in South India.* Manchester: Manchester University Press.

⸻. 1973. *South India: Yesterday, Today, and Tomorrow.* London: Macmillan.

Estes, Carroll L. 1979. *The Aging Enterprise.* San Francisco: Jossey-Bass.

⸻. 1993: 'The Aging Enterprise Revisited'. *Gerontologist.* 33(3):292–98.

Featherstone, Mike and Hepworth, eds. 1982. *Surviving Middle Age.* Oxford: Blackwell.

Featherstone, Mike and Wernick, eds. 1995. Images of Aging Cultural Representation of Later Life. New York: Routledge.

Fischer, David Hackett. 1978. *Growing Old in America.* 2nd ed. Oxford University Press.

FitzGerald, Frances. 1986. *Cities on a Hill: A Journey through Contemporary American Cultures.* New York: Simon and Schuster.

Foucault, Michel. 1978. *The History of Sexuality.* Vol. 1. Trans. Robert Hurley. New York: Pantheon Books.

Frazer, James George. 1900. *The Golden Bough: A Study in Magic and Religion.* 2nd ed. London: Macmillan.

Gray, John N. and David J. Mearns, eds. 1989. *Society from the Inside Out: Anthropological Perspectives on the South Asian Household.* New Delhi: Sage Publications.

Haggard, Henry. 1886. *She, A History of Adventure.* New York: McKinlay, Stone, and Mackenzie.

Hilton, James. 1933. *Lost Horizon.* New York: W. Morrow.

Hochschild, Arlie Russell. 1973. *The Unexpected Community.* Englewood Cliffs: Prentice-Hall.

Jones, William. 1792. 'Preface to his translation of Kalidasa'. *Sacontala, or The Fatal Ring: An Indian Drama.* London: Edwards.

Karve, Irawati Karmarkar. [1953] 1968. *Kinship Organization in India.* 3rd ed. New York: Asia.

Katz, Stephen. 1996. *Disciplining Old Age: The Formation of Gerontological Knowledge.* Charlottesville: University Press of Virginia.

⸻. 1995. *Fear and Trembling.* Trans. Alastair Hannaq. New York: Viking Penguin.

Kierkegaard, Sren. 1988. *Stages on Life's Way: Studies by Various Persons.* (Ed. and tran. by Howard V. Hong and Edna H. Hong). Princeton University Press.

Kolenda, Pauline. 1987. *Regional Differences in Family Structure in India.* Jaipur: Rawat Publications.

Kumar K.V., Y.S. Sivan, J.R. Reghu, R. Das and V.R. Kutty. 1994. 'Health of the Elderly in a Community in Transition: A Survey in Thiruvananthapuram City, Kerala, India'. *Health Policy and Planning.* 9(3):331–6.

Lamb, Sarah. 2000. White Sarees and Sweet Mangoes: Aging, Body, and Gender in North India. Berkeley: California University Press.

Levin, Jack and William C. Levin. 1980. *Ageism: Prejudice and Discrimination against the Elderly*. Belmont: Wadsworth.

Lyman, Karen A. 1989. 'Bringing the Social Back In: A Critique of the Biomedicalization of Dementia'. *Gerontologist*. 29(5):597–605.

Madan, T.N. [1965] 1989. *Family and Kinship: A Study of the Pandits of Rural Kashmir*. 2nd ed. Delhi: Oxford University Press.

———. 1987. *Non-renunciation: Themes and Interpretations of Hindu Culture*. Delhi: Oxford University Press.

Marulasiddaiah, H.M. 1969. *Old People of Makunti*. Dharwar: Karnataka University.

Meillasoure, Claude. 1981. *Maidens, Meals and Money: Capitalism and the Domestic Community*. New York: Cambridge University Press.

Mignon, Elisabeth. 1947. *Crabbed Age and Youth: The Old Men and Women in the Restoration Comedy of Manners*. Durham: Duke University Press.

Minkler, Meredith and Carroll L. Estes, eds. 1991. *Critical Perspectives on Aging: The Political and Moral Economy of Growing Old*. Amityville.

Minois, Georges. 1987. *Histoire de la Vieillesse en Occident: de l'antiquité à la renaissance*. Paris: Fayard.

Mishra, Saraswati. 1989. *Problems and Social Adjustment in Old Age: A Sociological Analysis*. New Delhi: Gian.

Myerhoff, Barbara G. 1978. *Number Our Days*. New York: Dutton.

Nandy, Ashis. 1983. *The Intimate Enemy: Loss and Recovery of Self under Colonialism*. Delhi: Oxford University Press.

Nascher, Ignatz Leo. 1914. *Geriatrics: The Diseases of Old Age and Their Treatment*. Philadelphia: P. Blakiston's.

Nydegger, Corinne. 1983. 'Introduction'. *Research on Aging*. 5(4):451–53.

Nuland, Sherwin B. 1994. *How We Die: Reflections on Life's Final Chapter*. New York: Knopf.

Olson, Laura Katz. 1982. *The Political Economy of Aging: The State, Private Power, and Social Welfare*. New York: Columbia University Press.

———. ed. 1994. *The Graying of the World: Who Will Care for the Frail Elderly?* New York: Haworth Press.

Parsons, Talcott. 1949. *Essays in Sociological Theory: Pure and Applied*. Glencoe: Free Press.

Pati, R.N. and B. Jena. 1989. *Aged in India: Socio-demographic Dimensions*. New Delhi: Ashish.

Ramamurthy, P.V. 1979. 'Psychological Research of the Aged in India: Problems and Perspectives'. In E.G. Parmeswaran and S. Bhogle, eds, *Developmental Psychology*. New Delhi: Light and Life.

Rhoads, Ellen C. 1984. 'Reevaluation of the Aging and Modernization Theory: The Samoan Evidence'. *Gerontologist*. 24(3):243–50.

Ross, Aileen D. 1961. *The Hindu Family in Its Urban Setting*. Toronto: University of Toronto Press.

Schneiderman, Lawrence J. 1994. 'Medical Futility and Aging: Ethical Implications'. *Generations*. 18(4):61–5.

Scot, Reginald. [1584] 1964. *The Discoverie of Witchcraft*. Arundel: Centaur.

Shah, A.M. 1974. *The Household Dimension of the Family in India*. Berkeley: University of California Press.

_____. 1996. 'Is the Joint Household Disintegrating?' *Economic and Political Weekly*. 31(9):537–42.

Shariff, Abusaleh. 1989. *Fertility Transition in Rural South India*. New Delhi: Gian.

Sharma, M.L. and T.M. Dak, eds. 1987. *Aging in India: Challenge for the Society*. Delhi: Ajanta.

Sinha, Jwala Nand Prasad. 1989. *Problems of Ageing*. New Delhi: Classical.

Smith, William Robertson. 1889. *Lectures on the Religion of the Semites*. Edinburgh: Adam and Charles Black.

Soodan, Kirpal Singh. 1975. *Aging in India*. Calcutta: Minerva.

Stoler, Ann Laura. 1995. *Race and the Education of Desire: Foucault's History of Sexuality and the Colonial Order of Things*. Durham: Duke University Press.

Taussig, Michael T. 1986. *Shamanism, Colonialism, and the Wild Man: A Study in Healing*. Chicagos: University of Chicago Press.

Thewlis, Malford Wilcox. 1941. *The Care of the Aged (Geriatrics)*. 3rd ed. St. Louis: C.V. Mosby.

Tilak, Shrinivas. 1989. *Religion and Aging in the Indian Tradition*. Albany: SUNY Press.

Tilson, David, ed. 1990. *Aging in Place: Supporting the Frail Elderly in Residential Environments*. Glenview: Scott, Foresman.

Uberoi, J.P.S. 1996. *Religion, Civil Society and the State*. Delhi: Oxford University Press.

Vatuk, Sylvia. 1972. *Kinship and Urbanization: White Collar Migrants in North India*. Berkeley: University of California Press.

_____. 1980. 'Withdrawal and Disengagement as a Cultural Response to Aging in India'. In Christine L. Fry, ed., *Aging in Culture and Society*. South Hadley: Bergin & Garvey.

_____. 1990. 'To Be a Burden on Others: Dependency Anxiety among the Elderly in India'. In Owen M. Lynch, ed., *Divine Passions: The Social Construction of Emotion in India*. Berkeley: University of California Press.

Venkoba Rao, A.K. 1989. *Psychiatry of Old Age in India*. Ahmedabad: Torrent Laboratories.

Walker, Barbara G. 1985. *The Crone: Woman of Age, Wisdom, and Power*. San Francisco: Harper & Row.

Warthin, Aldred Scott. 1929. *Old Age, the Major Involution: The Physiology and Pathology of the Aging*. New York: P.B. Hoeber.

Weyer, Johann [1583] 1991. *Witches, Devils, and Doctors in the Renaissance [De praestigiis daemonum]*. Ed., Georges Mora, Trans. John Shea. Binghamton: Medieval and Renaissance Texts and Studies.

Wiser, William H. and Charlotte Viall Wiser. 1971. *Behind Mud Walls, 1930–1960, with a Sequel: The Village in 1970*. Revised edition. Berkeley: University of California Press.

Patterns of Literacy and Their Social Context

Jean Drèze

INTRODUCTION

India's proverbial diversity applies in particular to literacy and education. At one end of the scale, remaining uneducated is almost unthinkable for the Tamil Brahmin, or the Bengali Kayasth, or the Goan Christian. At the other end, literacy rates in 1981 were as low as 2.2 per cent among the Musahars of Bihar and 2.5 per cent among the Kalbelias of Rajasthan (for women, the corresponding literacy rates were below one per cent).[1]

For those who are at the receiving end of these massive inequalities, educational deprivation is a many-sided burden. It affects their employment opportunities, reduces their health achievements, exposes them to corruption and harassment, and generally undermines their ability to participate successfully in the modern economy and society. Indeed, literacy is a basic tool of self-defence in a world where social interaction often involves the written media, and the same can be said of numeracy and other skills acquired in the process of basic education. As Anand Chakravarti notes in a recent study of agricultural labour in Bihar, 'lack of education is a factor of overwhelming significance in emasculating the capacity of labourers in general to cope with the conditions of existence imposed upon them'.[2]

This chapter was written before the 2001 census, and also before the publication of the 'Public Report on Basic Education in India' (PROBE Team, 1999). These and other recent studies have further enhanced our understanding of the literacy situation in India, and they also point to significant progress in this field in the 1990s. However, the basic issues discussed in this chapter retain their relevance.

Literacy and education are also essential for the practice of democracy. If democracy is interpreted in the narrow sense of electoral participation, then widespread education is not a pre-condition for it.[3] But if it means sustained, informed, and equitable participation in democratic institutions (electoral campaigns, public debates, village panchayats, the legal system, and so on), then universal elementary education is clearly central to the democratic project. The exclusion of a large majority of the population from effective political participation is a crippling limitation of Indian democracy.

To illustrate, consider the current debate on economic reforms. While this debate superficially appears to be lively and inclusive, it actually involves a tiny fraction of the population. As several recent surveys have shown, most Indians do not even know that economic reforms are taking place.[4] People can hardly be expected to have a view on this matter, let alone take active steps to oppose or support the reforms, if they have no awareness of what is going on. The recent public debate on India's achievements and failures after fifty years of independence has been no less elitist. The 'common man' (not to speak of the common woman) was nowhere to be seen, except in R.K. Laxman's refreshing cartoons.

This article focuses on the most elementary aspect of formal education, namely literacy. It begins, in the next section, with a brief recapitulation of the literacy situation in India today. We then proceed to examine various causes of educational deprivation among the disadvantaged sections of the population. Specific social disparities, relating in particular to caste and gender, are discussed in the penultimate section. This is also the occasion to note Himachal Pradesh's outstanding experience of educational advancement, which illustrates the mutually reinforcing effects of social equality and universal literacy. The last section presents some concluding remarks.

THE LITERACY SITUATION IN INDIA

At the time of the 1991 census, India's average literacy rate (defined as the proportion of literate persons in the age group of 7 and above) was 52 per cent. This is, of course, much higher than the corresponding figure of about 18 per cent at the time of independence, and vastly higher than India's literacy rate at the beginning of the twentieth century—around 5 per cent. Yet, the literacy situation in India remains unimpressive from several perspectives.

First, India has not done particularly well in comparative international terms. Here, a comparison with China is particularly relevant.[5] Careful examination of recent literacy rates in the older age groups suggests

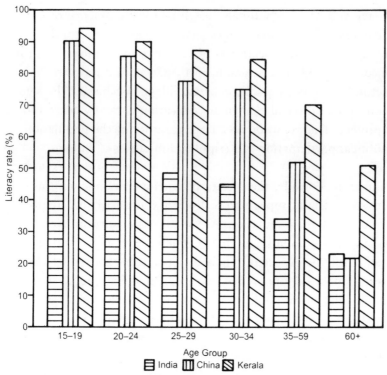

Fig. 1: *Source* : Government of India (1987) and State Statistical Bureau (1985).

Note: This graph shows 1981–82 literacy   rala. This
information can be used to assess age-specific literacy rates in *earlier* periods. For instance, the 20–24
literacy rate in 1981–82 can be considered as a good approximation to the 10–14 literacy rate in
1971–72 (since the two age groups correspond to the same cohort). This 'backward projection'
method is not entirely accurate, but it appears to be adequate for purposes of broad comparisons
between the three regions (see Drèze and Loh, 1995). By backward projection, this graph suggests
that, at the beginning of the 1950s, China and India had very similar literacy rates for the 30 plus age
group (roughly corresponding to the 60 plus age group in 1981–82), while Kerala was far ahead of
both countries. Thirty years later, China had caught up with Kerala, in terms of literacy rates in the
younger age groups, while India was left far behind.

that, in the late 1940s, India and China had similar levels of literacy (see
Figure 1). Today, however, China is far ahead of India, and even has literacy
rates comparable to those of Kerala in the younger age groups. Comparisons
with other east Asian countries, too, put India in a rather unfavourable light.
Even in sub-Saharan Africa, average literacy rates are higher than in India
(especially among women), according to World Bank data.[6]

Second, India still has a major problem of widespread illiteracy in
the younger age groups, which has been largely resolved in many other
developing countries. The issue is not just that a large number of Indian
adults are non-literate, because they did not get a chance to go to school
many years ago; even today, millions of children are deprived of that

opportunity. Nearly half of all adolescent girls, for instance, were unable to read and write in 1991.

Third, there are sharp disparities of literacy rates between different sections of the population. The gender gap is particularly striking (Table 1). Important differences in literacy achievements also exist between rural and urban areas as well as between different regions and communities.[7] When these contrasts are considered together, the chances of being literate vary enormously between different social groups, from close to 100 per cent for urban males in Kerala to less than 5 per cent for scheduled-caste women in rural Rajasthan.

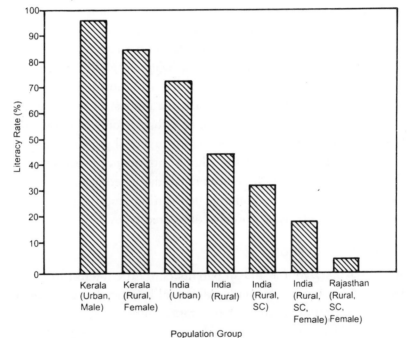

Fig. 2: *Source*: Census data presented in Tyagi (1993).

In assessing India's record in this field, it is useful to supplement literacy data with information on years of schooling. While 'total literacy' has become a focal point of public policy, it should be remembered that the Indian constitution directs all states to achieve much more: free and compulsory education for all children until the age of 14.[8] This roughly corresponds to eight years of schooling. In 1991, the proportion of adults who had actually completed eight years of schooling was as low as 30 per cent, with an even lower figure (16 per cent) for women.[9] Mean years of schooling were estimated at 2.4 years, compared with 5 years in China, 7 years in Sri Lanka, and 9 years in South Korea.[10]

In short, despite much improvement in the literacy situation since

Independence, a sharp contrast remains between constitutional goals and practical achievements. It is no wonder that, in a recent poll of Delhi residents, 88 per cent of the respondents agreed with the statement that 'our country's biggest failure has been in the field of education'.[11]

CAUSES OF EDUCATIONAL DEPRIVATION

In order to understand why so many Indian children do not go to school, the first thing to recognize is that sending a child to school on a regular basis requires a great deal of effort, especially in underprivileged families. There has to be money for books, slates, fees, clothes, and other expenses. The child has to be freed from full-time domestic chores or other work requirements. He or she needs attention and encouragement in the morning, at the time of preparing to go to school, and perhaps help with homework. The parents have to be convinced that what the child learns is worthwhile. The child may have to overcome the fear of a hostile reception from teachers or fellow pupils. Last but not least, the interest of the child in learning has to be sustained. This whole chain of efforts is only as strong as its weakest link. The fact that leaving school is, for practical purposes, an irreversible step adds to the fragility of the schools' attendance process.

Three specific obstacles have been much discussed in the literature: low parental motivation; economic deprivation; and the poor quality of schooling. Each of these is briefly considered below.[12]

Parental Motivation

It is often asserted that Indian parents have little interest in education. This view has been particularly influential in official circles, where it provides a convenient rationalisation of the state's failure to achieve universal elementary education in a reasonable time frame.[13] The myth of parental indifference, however, does not survive close scrutiny. Indeed, there is much evidence that an overwhelming majority of parents today, even among deprived sections of the population, attach great importance to the education of their children. To illustrate, one recent survey of the schooling situation in India's most educationally backward states found that the proportion of parents who considered it 'important' for a child to be educated was as high as 98 per cent for boy and 89 per cent for girls.[14] Further, educational aspirations were highly consistent with the constitutional goal of universal elementary education: only a small minority of respondents, for instance, aspired to fewer than 8 years of education for their sons or daughters. Only 3 per cent of parents were opposed to compulsory education at the primary level.

This is not to deny that lack of parental motivation may be an issue in specific contexts. Parental commitment to female education, in particular, is still rather inadequate in many areas (we shall return to the possible roots of this gender bias). And even parents who state that education is 'important' may not always translate that interest into practical efforts to send their children to school on a regular basis. Yet, it is important to take note of the generally positive disposition of most parents towards elementary education, and in particular, of the consistency between parental aspirations and the constitutional goal of eight years of education for all children.

It is also worth noting that parental attitudes towards education are far from immutable, and can be positively influenced through various means. For one thing, educational *aspirations* are not independent of the *opportunities* that people have (or perceive that they have). Attitudes towards education, especially female education, are also strongly influenced by cultural norms, role models, public discussions, and related factors. Indeed, educational aspirations and schooling decisions have a significant 'social' dimension. For instance, educational aspirations among parents and children of disadvantaged castes are bound to be influenced by *other* people's perceptions of the importance of education for the 'lower castes'. Ultimately, the task to be faced is not just to consolidate the motivation of individual parents, seen as isolated decision-makers, but to build a social consensus about the centrality of elementary education for every child's upbringing. The possibility of making rapid progress in that direction has been well illustrated in recent years in the context of the Total Literacy Campaign and related initiatives.[15]

Economic Deprivation

Poverty makes it harder to send a child to school in at least two ways. First, poor families sometimes depend on child labour for their survival. Second, poverty makes it harder to meet the direct costs of schooling.

Child labour is often seen as the main obstacle to universal schooling in India. In recent years, the movement against child labour has been particularly active in highlighting this problem. According to the Coalition Against Child Labour (1997), for instance, India has more than 60 million child labourers, working 12 hours a day on average. As one of the leading spokespersons of this movement recently put it, 'How can we make our country fully literate when 60 million of our children are engaged in full-time jobs as child labourers?'[16]

These figures may have some useful shock value, but their accuracy is another matter. In fact, studies of the time utilization of Indian children point to a very different assessment, namely that full-time workers account for a small proportion of out-of-school children.

To illustrate, Table 2 shows the distribution of children aged 5–14 by activity status according to the 1991 census. As the second column indicates, only 10 per cent of all out-of-school children in this age group were counted as 'workers' by the census enumerators.[17] Like all labour-force participation data, these figures have to be taken with a pinch of salt. It is quite likely, in particular, that domestic work is under-counted in these estimates. Recent research, however, has tended to corroborate the notion that productive work (*including* domestic work) accounts for only a small share of the overall time utilization of out-of-school children.[18] Bearing in mind that school hours are short and that schools are closed for about half of the days in the year in most Indian states, the proportion of children whose work activities are incompatible with that of the school is likely to be small.

It is also important to bear in mind that, when children work instead of going to school, the direction of causation need not run from child labour to non-attendance. In many cases, it is the other way round: drop out children take up productive work (of their own choice or through parental pressure) as a 'default occupation'. One recent case study of working children in Calcutta finds that two thirds of these children 'work as they have nothing else to do as the schools are not very attractive and teaching conditions are poor' (CINI-ASHA 1996). Similarly, Karin Kapadia (1997) observes that in rural Tamil Nadu 'it is very commonly the case that children are put to work by their parents to "keep them out of trouble" because they have dropped out of the hugely uninspiring (and underfunded) school system'.

In short, the role of child labour as an obstacle to universal schooling has often been over-emphasized. This is not to deny that India does have a serious problem of child labour, or to dismiss the vital role of the movement against child labour. The point is that it would be a mistake to regard child labour and educational deprivation as two sides of one coin, and even more of a mistake to see a simple causal link running from the former to the latter.[19]

Turning to direct costs, there is much evidence that elementary education in India is quite expensive, even in government schools. While the Constitution of India directs all states to provide 'free education', this term seems to have been interpreted by most state governments in the narrow sense that there should be no fees. A more pertinent interpretation is that elementary education should not involve any expenditure for the parents. In that broader sense, elementary education in India is far from free. According to one recent survey, sending a child to a government primary school in rural north India costs around Rs 360 a year on average, at 1996 prices.[20] This may look cheap, but poor parents are likely to differ. An agricultural labourer in

Bihar, for instance, would have to spend more than a month's earnings each year just to keep two children in such a school.

School Quality

As we noted earlier, sending a child to school on a regular basis demands a good deal of effort, especially in poor families. The willingness of parents to make that effort depends a great deal on what they perceive to be getting in return. If there is little activity in the classroom, or if the child does not make any progress, the game may not seem worth the candle. Similarly, the willingness of the child herself to make the effort of going to school often depends on whether the classroom activities stimulate her interest. Thus, the quality of schooling has an important influence on school attendance. Indian schools, however, leave much to be desired, particularly in rural areas.

The low quality of schooling has many aspects. To start with, the infrastructure is grossly inadequate. At the time of the sixth All-India Educational Survey (1993), 27 per cent of primary schools in India had only one classroom (if any), 21 per cent had a single teacher, and more than 60 per cent had at most two teachers.[21] It is hard to see how minimal teaching standards can possibly be achieved in schools where a single teacher handles children belonging to five different grades in a single classroom.

Second, low levels of teacher accountability have seriously undermined the effectiveness of the schooling system. Parents have no means of keeping the teachers on their toes, and the formal inspection system is a poor substitute for their vigilance. Since teachers have permanent posts, with salaries unrelated to performance, they have little incentives for exerting themselves. The accountability problem has been further enhanced by the collective political power of the teaching profession.[22]

Third, teaching methods in Indian schools are often stultifying. This is so even in urban middle class schools, as the recent report on the 'burden of learning' (Government of India 1994) clearly illustrates. In rural schools, the problem tends to take a different form (for example, lack of teaching activity, rather than over-exacting curriculum), but with a similar result, namely that the interest of the child is not sustained. Lack of class-room activity, non-comprehension of what is taught, fear of beating or humiliation, and social discrimination in the classroom are common causes of child discouragement.

In the light of these and other aspects of the low quality of schooling, it is not surprising that pupil achievements are abysmally low.[23] Nor is it difficult to understand why parents and children often lose patience with the schooling system.

Discussion

We have focused on three distinct reasons why children might be out of school: inadequate parental motivation, economic deprivation, and the low quality of schooling. It is difficult, of course, to arrive at a precise assessment of the relative importance of these factors. In many cases, when a child drops out of school, some combination of these influences is at work. Further research is required to go much beyond this general statement.

Meanwhile, a few basic conclusions can be drawn. First, single-focus explanations (highlighting one particular cause of educational deprivation and ignoring the others), which are common in public debates, do not survive close scrutiny. Second, as far as male education is concerned, parental motivation is very high in most social groups. The main problem here is not lack of motivation, but the fact that the abysmal quality of schooling discourages parents and children from making the effort required to achieve regular school attendance. Third, in the case of female education, there is, in some circumstances, an additional issue of low parental motivation (on which more below). Fourth, there is growing evidence that child labour is not a major general obstacle against regular school attendance, even though work burdens do have an adverse effect on schooling opportunities for specific categories of children.

In a sense, these findings are good news. If it were the case that parents are not interested in education, or that children from poor families are too busy to go to school, there might be good grounds for concern about the possibility of universalizing elementary education in a reasonable time frame. Contrary to this diagnosis, there is every reason to expect parents and children to respond positively to public initiatives aimed at facilitating their involvement in the schooling system. That expectation is amply confirmed by recent experience.

EDUCATIONAL DISPARITIES

As noted in the introduction, schooling opportunities in India are highly unequal. At one end of the scale, the offspring of the urban elite are likely to reach prestigious university colleges, with a good prospect of further studies abroad. At the other end, a girl born in a poor family in rural Rajasthan has a slim chance of entering (let alone completing) primary school. These educational disparities, which *contribute a* great deal to the persistence of massive inequalities in Indian society, also largely *derive* from more fundamental inequalities such as those of *class, caste* and *gender*. This section explores some of these connections.

Gender Bias

It is possible to link the neglect of female education in India (especially in the northern region) with specific social practices that create deep asymmetries between male and female education. Prominent among these social practices are the gender division of labour and the kinship system.

The gender division of labour confines many adult women to household work (and some family labour in agriculture). It is arguable that literacy and education are no less useful in these activities than in, say, white-collar employment. There is overwhelming evidence, for instance, that maternal education has a strong positive influence on child health.[24] The benefits of female education at home, however, are often less clearly perceived, and less strongly valued, than the economic returns to male education (for example, in terms of better employment and higher earnings). Hence the common statement, 'what is the point of educating our daughter, in any case after she grows up she will be cooking *rotis*?' (quoted in Senapaty 1997).

The kinship system, in many parts of India, involves the separation of an adult woman from her parents after her marriage, when she joins her husband's family. This implies that educating a daughter is of little benefit from the point of view of parental self-interest (with one qualification, discussed below). The situation is very different in the case of sons, since educated sons are expected to get better jobs and to look after their aged parents. This may seem like a cynical view of parental motivation for education, but there is much evidence that employment opportunities and old-age security do play a major role in schooling decisions.[25] The fact that educating a daughter does not bring any tangible benefits to her parents, and is no less costly than educating a son, may well be the most important cause of gender bias in schooling opportunities.

Aside from these basic problems, various other considerations discourage Indian parents from sending their daughters to school. For instance, parents are often reluctant to let their daughters wander outside the village. This prevents many girls from studying beyond the primary level, given that upper-primary schools are often unavailable within the village. Similarly, many parents rely on their elder daughters to look after young siblings (here again the gender division of labour is at work).

Against this background, the really interesting question is not so much why Indian parents show little interest in female education (that is relatively easy to understand), but rather why so many of them do send their daughters to school. One answer is that they do so out of concern for their daughters' well-being. This is certainly plausible, yet this explanation does not really help to understand variations in female school attendance between social groups and over time.

A complementary explanation is that, as the level of *male* education rises in a particular community, parents develop more positive attitudes towards female education. One specific reason for this arises from the relationship between female education and marriage prospects. Indian men often expect their spouse to be a little less educated than they are themselves, without the gap being too large. In a community with low levels of male education, a relatively well-educated daughter is often considered as a burden, because she may be difficult to marry.[26] In communities with high levels of male education, however, *uneducated* daughters may become a liability, for the same reason. In such communities, education is often considered (up to a point) to improve a daughter's marriage prospects.[27] Given that a daughter's marriage is often regarded as the overriding goal of her upbringing, these links between female education and marriage prospects are likely to have a significant influence on schooling decisions.

The notion that female literacy in India is largely a by-product of male literacy may seem depressing. However, we are talking here of historical patterns, not of what can be achieved today through public action. As far as the latter is concerned, there is much evidence that public campaigns can have a strong influence on social attitudes towards female education, and reduce the gender gap in school opportunities. The experience of the Total Literacy Campaign, in districts where it has received active support from the local administration and popular organisations, is quite encouraging in this regard.[28] Even in India as a whole, the gender gap in literacy has narrowed quite rapidly in recent years, and is likely to narrow further in the near future.

Caste and Tribe

The fact that literacy rates among disadvantaged castes (particularly the 'scheduled castes') are much lower than average is well-known. What is less clear is why this contrast happens to be so sharp and resilient, even when different castes share the same schooling facilities. Economic deprivation among the disadvantaged castes helps to explain this pattern, but there is much evidence of a strong caste bias in literacy rates even at a given level of income.[29]

This bias has several possible roots. First, the traditional upper-caste view that education is not appropriate for the 'lower' castes continues to have some social influence. This view is bound to reduce the educational aspirations of children from the disadvantaged castes, and the parental and social support they receive in pursuit of these aspirations.

Second, there may be objective differences in economic and other returns to education for different castes. For instance, an educated boy from an upper-caste family with good social connections often has better chances of finding a well-paid job than a low-caste boy with similar educational qualifications.[30]

Third, children from disadvantaged castes are still discriminated against within the schooling system. Blatant forms of caste-based discrimination (for example, denying school facilities to certain castes) have by and large disappeared, but more subtle forms of discrimination remain widespread. Some examples include discrimination against scheduled-caste settlements in the location of schools, teachers refusing to touch low-caste children, children from particular castes being special targets of verbal abuse and physical punishment by the teachers, and low-caste children being frequently beaten by higher-caste classmates.[31]

These causes of educational deprivation also apply, in many cases, to tribal communities. Tribal education, however, has also raised some further issues. One of these is the relevance of modern education, including literacy, to tribal children. On this, a common view is that tribal communities do not really 'need' modern education, or that they consider it as irrelevant. A variant of this theme is that tribal people have their own 'mode of knowledge', which modern education threatens to destroy. Another variant is that interest in education is inherently low among tribal communities.[32]

Little evidence, however, has been produced to substantiate the view that the educational needs and aspirations of tribal children are fundamentally different from those of other children. Of course, the school curriculum and teaching methods should be sensitive to the culture of tribal children—indeed of *all* children. But recognizing this basic pedagogical principle (and the fact that it is routinely overlooked in the schooling system today) is not the same as dismissing the relevance of modern education for tribal children. That dismissive view is far from widespread among tribal communities themselves, judging from the fact that tribal children have often taken to schooling like duck to water in areas where well-functioning educational facilities have been made available to them—notably in the north-eastern region, in the tribal districts of Himachal Pradesh, and in parts of southern Bihar and eastern Madhya Pradesh. The tremendous response of tribal communities in Madhya Pradesh to the 'education guarantee scheme' initiated in 1997 is another case in point.

These positive experiences suggest that the basic cause of educational deprivation among tribal communities is not so much a fundamental lack of interest in education on their part, as the dismal state of schooling facilities in most tribal areas. Until recently, for instance, single-teacher schools were the norm in these areas (when no schools existed at all). The general problem of official neglect of elementary education has tended to take an extreme form in tribal areas, partly due to the political marginalisation of tribal communities in most Indian states.

Some Regional Contrasts

Regional contrasts in literacy largely follow familiar patterns that also apply to many other indicators of 'social development' in India (see map): Kerala is far ahead; the southern states, with the notable exception of Andhra Pradesh, fare better than the northern region; and the large north Indian states (Bihar, Madhya Pradesh, Rajasthan and Uttar Pradesh) lag behind all others. Explaining these broad regional contrasts would call for historical enquiry of a kind that cannot be attempted in this short paper.[33] The weight of the historical legacy is evident from the fact that similar regional patterns already applied at the time of independence, and even much earlier.

Historical legacy is much less of an explanation for another (relatively little noticed) aspect of India's literacy map, namely the impressive achievements of the Himalayan region. Much of that region was considered as an underdeveloped backyard fifty years ago. Today, most Himalayan districts have literacy rates well above the all-India average, especially in the younger age groups.[34] Within the region, an outstanding case of successful expansion of literacy is Himachal Pradesh.

Starting with similar levels of literacy as, say, Bihar or Uttar Pradesh in the early fifties, Himachal Pradesh has virtually caught up with Kerala within forty years (see Figure 3). In 1991, literacy rates in the 10–14 age group in Himachal Pradesh were as high as 95 per cent for males and 86 per cent for females. And in 1992–3, 91 per cent of all children in the 6–14 age group were attending school (International Institute for Population Sciences 1995: 56).

In several respects, the experience of literacy expansion in Himachal Pradesh in recent decades is even more impressive than that of Kerala. First, the transition from mass illiteracy to near-universal primary education has taken place over a much shorter period of time in Himachal Pradesh. Second, educational expansion in Himachal Pradesh has been based almost entirely on government schools, with relatively little contribution from private schools, missionary organizations and related institutions. Third, Himachal Pradesh has an unfavourable topography; in particular, villages are scattered over large areas with poor connections (in sharp contrast with Kerala, where settlement patterns have been favourable to the expansion of public services in rural areas). Fourth, child labour used to play an important role in Himachal Pradesh's economy, partly due to the dependence of many households on environmental resources and also (in the case of girls) to the fact that a high proportion of adult women work outside the household.

The foundations of this success have not been fully explored, and this is not the place to do so. Let me just mention one contributing factor

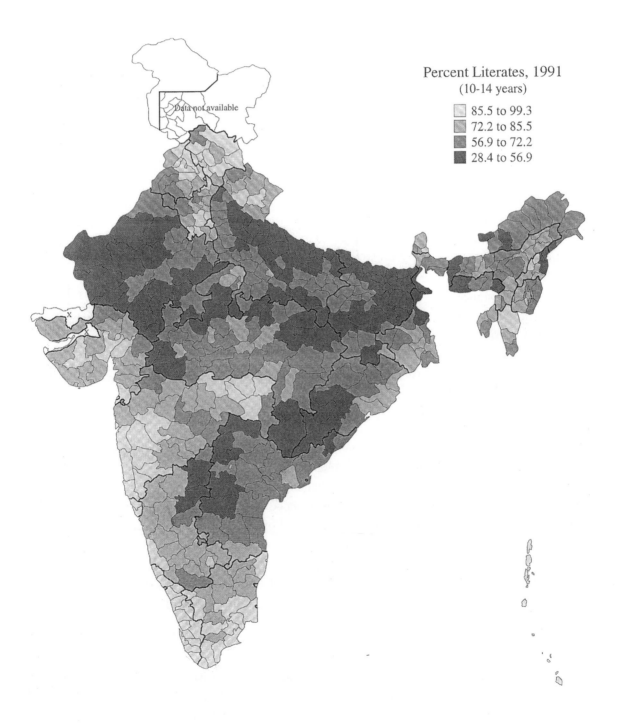

Percent Literates, 1991
(10-14 years)

85.5 to 99.3
72.2 to 85.5
56.9 to 72.2
28.4 to 56.9

Data not available

Map 1: Literacy in Indian Districts 1991
Source : Contributed by S.V. Subramanian (University of Portsmouth), based on 1991 census data.

which might be of interest to
sociologists and social
anthropologists: the relatively
equal social structure of
village communities in
Himachal Pradesh (or for that
matter in many other parts of
the Himalayan region). This
observation refers in
particular to the absence of
sharp inequalities of land
ownership (the incidence of
landlessness, for instance, is
very low in Himachal
Pradesh); to the relatively
narrow social distance
between different castes; and
to the high participation of
women in social life outside
the household.[35] This is not to
say that hill villages are
'egalitarian'. Nevertheless, the
divisions of class, caste and

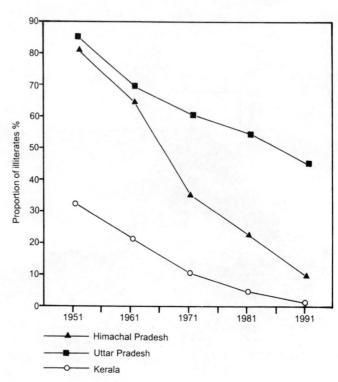

Fig. 3: Illiteracy Rate, Age 10–14
Source: Census of India, various years.

gender that have been so pernicious elsewhere in north India tend to be less
pronounced in this region. In particular, these social divisions do not preclude
a strong sense of collective interests at the village level.[36]

There are several reasons why the absence of sharp social
disparities might be expected to facilitate the spread of education. First, social
equality is conducive to the emergence of consensual social norms on
educational matters. Elsewhere in north India, it is perfectly possible for
children of one caste to go to school while children of another caste—in the
same village—are deprived of that opportunity. In fact, contrasts of this type
are necessary to sustain the inegalitarian social order. In Himachal Pradesh,
by contrast, the notion that schooling is an essential part of every child's
upbringing has acquired the character of a widely-shared social norm.

Second, social equality is likely to facilitate cooperative action for
the provision of local public services, including schooling facilities. To
illustrate, parents in Himachal Pradesh often cooperate to repair the village
school, a rare event in other north Indian states (Bhatty et al. 1997). Their
collective vigilance has also played an important role in preserving the
accountability of the schooling system.

Third, the absence of sharp social disparities can help to ensure that the demands made on the state by local communities and their representatives are oriented to basic social needs. In highly inegalitarian states such as Bihar and Uttar Pradesh, village leaders act as powerful intermediaries between the state and the people, and routinely use state resources as instruments of patronage and individual gain (Drèze and Gazdar 1997). In Himachal Pradesh, village leaders are more likely to clamour for collective facilities such as roads, electricity, drinking water and primary schools.[37]

These remarks are not intended to 'explain' Himachal Pradesh's success on their own. Other factors, such as rapid economic growth and a high level of central-government assistance, have also contributed. The preceding line of enquiry, however, does seem to be worth pursuing, especially because it helps to explain the rapid progress of education not only in Himachal Pradesh but also in other parts of the Himalayan region.

CONCLUDING REMARKS

From this account it should be clear that literacy achievements in India depend crucially on the social context: the gender division of labour, the kinship system, caste-related norms, economic entitlements, and so on. The statement is perhaps trivial, but it is worth noting that the overwhelming context-dependence of literacy achievements conflicts with the notion of elementary education as a basic right of all citizens.

As this book goes to press, the results of the 2001 census are putting the literacy situation in India in a fresh light. On the one hand, the basic patterns identified in this chapter (including the fundamental connection between educational deprivation and social inequality) continue to apply. On the other hand, there is evidence of accelerated progress towards universal elementary education in the 1990s. Literacy rates and school participation have substantially improved, the gender bias in educational achievements has narrowed, and some of the 'laggard' states (notably Rajasthan and Madhya Pradesh) are rapidly catching up.

Consolidating and extending these achievements calls for wider acknowledgement of elementary education as a fundamental right of all citizens. There has been some positive changes in this respect in recent years. The notion that every child has an inalienable right to learn is much more widely accepted today than it was (say) ten years ago, when the main focus of attention was on the pros and cons of 'compulsory education'. As things stand, the right to education is nowhere near being realised, but the 1990s have demonstrated the *possibility* of rapid progress in this field—a possibility that remains to be seized in full.

ENDNOTES

1. K.S. Singh (1993), pp. 658 and 966.

2. Anand Chakravarti (1997), p. 359.

3. Indeed, recent election studies conducted by the Centre for the Study of Developing Societies indicate that voter turnouts are, if anything, *lower* than average among relatively well-educated sections of the population (Yogendra Yadav, 2000).

4. See for example, Yogendra Yadav (1996) and The World Bank (1996). Those who claim some knowledge of the reforms often turn out, on further probing, to have something else in mind. Some respondents, for instance, believe that economic reforms are about the introduction of cooperative farming, or about the recent wave of corruption in high places (Yogendra Yadav, personal communication).

5. For a more detailed comparison, see Drèze and Loh (1995).

6. See for example, *World Development Report 1997*, pp. 226-7.

7. P.N. Tyagi (1993) provides useful data on regional and social disparities in literacy rates.

8. Indian Constitution, Directive Principles, Article 45. The target date for this goal (1960 according to the constitution) has been postponed again and again. The latest target date is 2005.

9. Calculated from unpublished 1991 census data.

10. *Human Development Report 1994*, p. 146.

11. *Sunday Times* (New Delhi), 21 September 1994, p. 24. In another recent poll of youth in major cities (reported in *The Times of India*, 15 August 1997), the respondents were asked to identify 'the most important thing in life'. 'Knowledge' was the most frequent answer (48 per cent of all responses), far ahead of 'love' (20 per cent), not to speak of 'money' (18 per cent).

12. For a more detailed examination of the evidence, see Kiran Bhatty (1998).

13. This tradition was already well established during the colonial period. Some observers went so far as to argue that active resistance to education was common: 'It may be stated generally that among the mass of people there is no desire for learning. The Jats as a body are not only illiterate but actually opposed to education, and in Jat villages thriving schools are very seldom to be found.' (Government of India 1922: 111). Interestingly, the same Jats now seem to have a passion for education, and are even deeply involved in the teaching profession (Craig Jeffrey, personal communication based on ongoing field work; see also Jeffery and Jeffery 1994).

14. See Bhatty *et al.* (1997).

15. See particularly Ghosh *et al.* (1994), who report that 'tremendous enhancement of demand for primary education and enrolment of children in primary schools have been noticed in many literacy campaign districts' (p. 23).

16. Kailash Satyarthi, quoted in *National Herald*, 2 January 1997.

17. For a detailed discussion of this pattern, see D.P. Chaudhri (1996).

18. See D.P. Chaudhri (1996), National Council of Applied Economic Research (1996, 1997), Preet Rustagi (1996), Rukmini Banerji (1997), Kiran Bhatty et al. (1997), Arup Maharatna (1997), R. Nagarajan (1997), National Sample Survey Organisation (1997), among others; also Manabi Majumdar (1998).

19. Such a causal link may however apply to specific categories of children, such as children of migrant labourers and eldest daughters in poor families.

20. See Bhatty *et al.* (1997). This figure is broadly consistent with independent estimates of the costs of schooling based on recent surveys by the National Council of Applied Economic Research and the National Sample Survey Organisation. On the latter, see also Tilak (1996), and the survey reports cited there.

21. Calculated from National Council of Educational Research and Training (1997). The schooling infrastructure has improved in recent years, but it remains completely out of line with the constitutional goal of universal education until the age of 14 (see for example, Kiran Bhatty et al. 1997).

22. Teachers, for their part, often complain about their difficult work environment, their low status in the administrative hierarchy, and the heavy burden of non-teaching duties. These complaints are frequently justified, and teachers do need better support. Enhanced accountability and improved support are best seen as complementary requirements of higher teaching standards.

23. In some schools, many pupils are still unable to read or write even after four or five years or schooling (Bhatty et al. 1997; Kapadia 1997). On pupil achievements, see also Govinda and Varghese (1993) and Sharma (1998), among others.

24. See Murthi et al. (1995), and the literature cited there.

25. See for example, Caldwell *et al.* (1985), Kashinath Bhoosnurmath (1991), Jeffery and Jeffery (1994), Bhatty et al. (1997), and the literature cited in Bhatty (1998).

26. Caldwell et al. (1985), for instance, note that in rural Karnataka some parents are worried that education 'would make daughters unmarriageable', because a woman 'must be married to a male with at least as much education'. For similar observations elsewhere, see also Committee on the Status of Women in India (1974:74), A. Almeida (1978:264), Seetharamu and Ushadevi (1985), van Bastelaer (1986:61), Khan (1993), among others.

27. See for example, Jeffery and Jeffery (1994), Jejeebhoy and Kulkarni (1989), Minturn and Kapoor (1993), Ursula Sharma (1980).

28. See particularly Ghosh et al. (1994).

29. See Drèze and Sharma (1998), Jayachandran (1997), Labenne (1995).

30. Caste-based reservation policies have probably reduced this advantage, without eliminating it. On the relationship between positive discrimination and investment in 'human capital', see Coate and Loury (1993); also Montgomery (1995) and the literature cited there.

31. For some illustrations, see Shami (1992:26), Varma (1992), Bashir et al. (1993:20-21), Lata (1995:32), Sinha and Sinha (1995), Drèze and Sharma (1998), Mehrotra (forthcoming).

32. Under the title 'why tribal children may not like school', for instance, the World Bank highlights the findings of a recent study of primary education in Andhra Pradesh, according to which 'a third of the children of school age did not attend school, preferring instead to spend their time moving freely around, swimming in ponds and streams, catching fish, climbing trees, hunting birds, collecting berries, riding on buffaloes, etc.' (World Bank 1997: 137). This rosy picture undoubtedly applies to some

children, but it is only a small part of the overall story of tribal exclusion from the schooling system.

33. For an early interpretation of these regional patterns, see Rudolph and Rudolph (1972); also David Sopher (1980).

34. It is also worth noting that, according to one recent World Bank survey, literacy rates in the younger age groups in Nepal are now considerably higher than in the large north Indian states. In other words, Nepal seems to fit in the general pattern of rapid educational progress in the Himalayan region (bearing in mind that literacy rates in Nepal used to be extremely low, even by South Asian standards).

35. On these aspects of village communities in Himachal Pradesh and the neighbouring Uttar Pradesh hills, see Berreman (1972), Parmar (1979), Guha (1989), Saraswat and Sikka (1990), Sax (1991), Sikka and Singh (1992), Moller (1993), Keith-Krelik (1995), and Bondroit (1998), among others. These studies are best read along with similar studies for other regions, since the point being made here is not that local social inequalities in Himachal Pradesh are unimportant, but rather that they are *less* significant than in many other parts of India.

36. The sense of village community, so weak elsewhere in India (Dumont 1980), appears to be quite strong in the hill region. Institutions and rituals such as village festivals, village deities and even village pilgrimages help to consolidate these bonds. See for example, Sax (1991), chapter 2.

37. Prof. N.S. Bisht (Department of Economics, Himachal Pradesh University), personal communication based on first-hand experience in Himachal Pradesh and Uttar Pradesh.

REFERENCES

Almeida, A. 1978. 'The Gift of a Bride: Sociological Implications of the Dowry System in Goa'. Université Catholique de Louvain, Louvain-la-Neuve, Belgium. Mimeo.

Baland, Jean-Marie and Platteau, Jean-Philippe. 1995. 'Does Heterogeneity Hinder Collective Action?' Discussion Paper No. 146, Centre de Recherche en Economie du Dévelopment, Université de Namur, Belgium.

————. 1997. 'Wealth Inequality and Efficiency of the Commons'. Discussion Paper No. 193, Centre de Recherche en Economie du Dévelopment, Université de Namur, Belgium.

Banerji, Rukmini. 1997. 'Why Don't Children Complete Primary School? A Case Study of a Low-Income Neighbourhood in Delhi'. *Economic and Political Weekly*. 32(32):9 August.

Bashir, Sajitha, et al. 1993. *Education for All: Baseline Survey of Three Districts of Uttar Pradesh, India*. Vol. 2. New Delhi: New Concept Consultancy Services.

Berreman, Gerald D. 1972. *Hindus of the Himalayas: Ethnography and Change*. 2nd ed. Delhi: Oxford University Press.

Bhatty, Kiran. 1998: 'Educational Deprivation in India: A Survey of Field Investigations'. *Economic and Political Weekly*, 33(27):1731–40.

Bhatty, K., A. De, J.P. Drèze, A.K. Shiva Kumar, A. Mahajan, C. Noronha, A. Rampal, Pushpendra and M. Samson. 1997. 'Class Struggle'. *India Today*. 13 October.

Bhoosnurmath, Kashinath. 1991. 'People's Perception of Importance of Education: A Field Experience in Dehradun District'. *The Administrator*. 36.

Bondroit, Marie-Eve. 1998. 'Les Aspects Economiques et Culturels Liés a l' Education des Filles en Inde'. M.A. dissertation, Faculté des Sciences Economiques, Université de Namur, Belgium.

Caldwell, J.C., P.H. Reddy and P. Caldwell. 1985. 'Educational Transition in Rural South India'. *Population and Development Review.* 11(1):29–51.

Chakravarti, Anand. 1997. 'Social Power and Everyday Class Relations: Agrarian Tansformation in North Bihar'. Delhi School of Economics. Mimeo. To be published as a monograph.

Chaudhri, D.P. 1996. *A Dynamic Profile of Child Labour in India, 1951–1991.* New Delhi: International Labour Organization.

CINI-ASHA. 1996. 'Our Present Day Understanding of Child Labour Issues'. *The Administrator.* 16:169–74.

Coalition Against Child Labour. 1997. 'Public Hearing on Child Labour: Reference Kit'. Document prepared for the 2nd National Convention of Child Labourers. 30–31 March 1997. New Delhi.

Coate, S. and G. Loury. 1993. 'Will Affirmative-Action Policies Eliminate Negative Stereotypes?' *American Economic Review.* 83:1220–40.

Committee on the Status of Women in India. 1974. *Towards Equality.* New Delhi: Ministry of Education and Social Welfare.

Drèze, Jean, and Amartya Sen. 1995. *India: Economic Development and Social Opportunity.* Delhi and Oxford: Oxford University Press.

――――. eds 1997. *Indian Development: Selected Regional Perspectives.* Delhi and Oxford: Oxford University Press.

Drèze, Jean and Haris Gazdar. 1997. 'Uttar Pradesh: The Burden of Inertia'. In Jean Drèze and Amartya Sen, eds, *Indian Development: Selected Regional Perspectives.* 33–128. Delhi and Oxford: Oxford University Press.

Drèze, Jean and Jackie Loh. 1995. 'Literacy in India and China'. *Economic and Political Weekly.* 11 November. 30(45) 2868–78.

Drèze, Jean and Naresh Sharma. 1998. 'Palanpur: Population, Society, Economy'. In P. Lanjouw and N. Stern, eds, *Economic Development in Palanpur Over Five Decades.* 3–113. Delhi and Oxford: Oxford University Press.

Dumont, Louis. 1980. *Homo Hierarchicus.* Revised ed. Chicago: University of Chicago Press.

Ghosh, A., U.R. Ananthamurthy, A. Béteille, S.M. Kansal, V. Mazumdar and A. Vanaik. 1994. 'Evaluation of Literacy Campaigns in India'. Report of an independent Expert Group appointed by the Ministry of Human Resource Development. New Delhi: Ministry of Human Resource Development.

Government of India. 1922. *District Gazetteer of the United Provinces of Agra and Oudh. Meerut.* Vol. 4. Comp. and ed. H.R. Nevill. Delhi.

Government of India. 1987. 'Social and Cultural Tables'. *Census of India 1981, ser. 1 (India), pt. IV-A.* New Delhi: Office of the Registrar General.

Government of India. 1994. *Learning Without Burden: Report of the National Advisory Committee appointed by the Ministry of Human Resource Development.* New Delhi: Ministry of Human Resource Development.

Govinda, R. and N.V. Varghese. 1993. 'Quality of Primary Schooling: An Empirical Study'. *Journal of Educational Planning and Administration.* 1.

Guha, Ramachandra. 1989. *The Unquiet Woods: Ecological Change and Peasant Resistance in the Himalaya*. Delhi: Oxford University Press.

International Institute for Population Sciences. 1995. *National Family Health Survey 1992–3*. Bombay: IIPS.

Jayachandran, Usha. 1997. 'The Determinants of Primary Education in India'. M. Phil. thesis, Department of Economics, Delhi School of Economics.

Jeffery, Patricia, and Roger Jeffery. 1994. 'Killing My Heart's Desire: Education and Female Autonomy in Rural North India'. In Nita Kumar, ed., *Women as Subjects: South Asian Histories*. 125–7. London: University Press of Virginia.

Jejeebhoy, S. and S. Kulkarni. 1989. 'Demand for Children and Reproductive Motivation: Empirical Observations from Rural Maharashtra'. In S.N. Singh, eds, *Population Transition in India*. 107–21. New Delhi: B.R. Publishing.

Kapadia, Karin. 1997. 'Emancipatory Processes in Rural Tamil Nadu Today: An Anthropological Study of Discourse and Practice Relating to Rights'. Research proposal, International Institute of Asian Studies, Amsterdam.

Keith-Krelik, Yasmin. 1995. 'Development, for Better or Worse: A Case Study on the Effects of Development on the Social and Cultural Environment of Spiti'. Unpublished dissertation, Department of Politics, University of Newcastle-upon-Tyne.

Khan, Sharukh R. 1993. 'South Asia'. In E. King, and A. Hill, eds, *Women's Education in Developing Countries: Barriers, Benefits and Policy*. Baltimore: Johns Hopkins University Press.

Labenne, Sophie. 1995. 'Analyse Econométrique du Travail des Enfants en Inde'. M.Sc. thesis, Department of Economics, Université de Namur, Belgium.

Lata, Divya. 1995. 'An Assessment of Early Child Care and Education Programmes Supported by SCF in India'. New Delhi: Save the Children Fund (UK). Mimeo.

Maharatna, Arup. 1997. 'Children's Work, Activities, Surplus Labour and Fertility: A Case Study of Six Villages in Birbhum'. *Economic and Political Weekly*. 32(7):363–69.

Majumdar, Manabi. 1998. 'Child Labor as a Human Security Problem: Evidence From India'. Harvard University: Harvard Center for Population and Development Studies. Mimeo.

Mehrotra, Nidhi. (Forthcoming), 'Primary Schooling in Rural India: Determinants of Demand'. Ph.D. thesis, University of Chicago.

Minturn, Leigh and Swaran Kapoor. 1993. *Sita's Daughters: Coming Out of Purdah, The Rajput Women of Khalapur Revisited*. New York: Oxford University Press.

Moller, Joanne. 1993. 'Inside and Outside: Conceptual Continuities from Household to Region in Kumaon, North India'. Ph.D. thesis. London School of Economics.

Montgomery. 1995. 'Affirmative Action and Reservations in the American and Indian Labor Markets: Are They Really That Bad?' University of Maryland, College Park. Mimeo.

Murthi, M., A.C. Guio and J.P. Drèze. 1995. 'Mortality, Fertility and Gender Bias in India: A District Level Analysis'. *Population and Development Review*. 21(4):745–82.

Nagarajan, R. 1997. 'Landholding, Child Labour and Schooling'. *Journal of Rural Development*. 16(2):193–217.

National Council of Applied Economic Research. 1996. *Human Development Profile of India. vol. II: Statistical Tables*. New Delhi: NCAER.

National Council of Applied Economic Research. 1997. 'Time Utilization of Children'. (provisional tables). MIMAP project. New Delhi: NCAER.

National Council of Educational Research and Training. 1997. *Sixth All-India Educational Survey*. New Delhi: NCERT.

National Sample Survey Organisation. 1997. 'Economic Activities and School Attendance by Children in India'. Revised Report No. 412 (based on the 50th round, 1993–4). New Delhi: NSSO.

Parmar, H.S. 1979. 'Subsistence Economy of Rural Himachal Pradesh: A Case Study of Three Small Villages'. *Economic Affairs*. 24(10–12):249–55.

PROBE Team. 1999. *Public Report on Basic Education in India*. New Delhi: Oxford University Press.

Rudolph. S.H., and L.I. Rudolph, eds. 1972. *Education and Politics in India: Studies in Organization, Society, and Policy*. Cambridge, MA: Harvard University Press.

Rustagi, Preet. 1996. 'The Structure and Dynamics of Indian Rural Labour Market'. Ph.D. thesis, Centre for Economic Studies and Planning, Jawaharlal Nehru University.

Saraswat, S.P., and B.K. Sikka. 1990. *Socio-economic Survey of an Affluent Village in Himachal Pradesh (A Study of Village Kiari in District Shimla)*. Shimla: Agro-Economic Research Centre, Himachal Pradesh University.

Sax, W. 1991. *Mountain Goddess: Gender and Politics in a Himalayan Pilgrimage*. New York: Oxford University Press.

Seetharamu, A.S., and M.D. Ushadevi. 1985. *Education in Rural Areas: Constraints and Prospects*. New Delhi: Ashish Publishing House.

Senapaty, Manju. 1997. 'Gender Implications of Economic Reforms in the Education Sector in India: Case of Haryana and Madhya Pradesh'. Ph.D. dissertation, University of Manchester.

Shami, N. 1992. 'Socio-Economic Survey of Village Patna Khurd'. Mussoorie: Lal Bahadur Shastri National Academy of Administration.

Sharma, Rashmi. 1998. 'Universal Elementary Education: The Question of "How"'. *Economic and Political Weekly*. 27 June. 33(26):160–47.

Sharma, Ursula. 1980. *Women, Work and Property in North-West India*. London: Tavistock.

Sikka, B.K. and D.V. Singh. 1992. 'Malana: An Oldest Democracy Sustainability Issues in Village Economy (Himachal Pradesh)'. Himachal Pradesh University, Simla: Agro-Economic Research Centre. Mimeo.

Singh, K.S. 1993. *The Scheduled Castes*. New Delhi: Oxford University Press.

Sinha, Amarjeet, and Ajay Sinha. 1995. 'Primary Schooling in Northern India: A Field Investigation'. Centre for Sustainable Development, Lal Bahadur Shastri National Academy of Administration, Mussoorie. Mimeo.

Sopher, David, ed. 1980. *An Exploration of India: Geographical Perspectives on Society and Culture*. Ithaca, NY: Cornell University Press.

State Statistical Bureau. 1985. *1982 Population Census of China*. Chinese edition. Beijing: Population Census Office.

Tilak, J.B.G. 1996. 'How Free is Free Primary Education in India?' *Economic and Political Weekly*. 31(5):275–82.

Tyagi, P.N. 1993. *Education for All: A Graphic Presentation*. 2nd ed. New Delhi: National Institute of Educational Planning and Administration.

UNICEF. 1997. *The State of the World's Children 1997.* Oxford and New York: Oxford University Press.

van Bastelaer, Thierry. 1986. 'Essai d'Analyse des Systèmes de Paiements de Mariage: Le Cas de l'Inde'. M.Sc. thesis, Facultés des Sciences Economiques et Sociales, Universite de Namur, Belgium.

Varma, Jyotsna. 1992. 'Lanka Kachuara: A Village Divide'. Lal Bahadur Shastri National Academy of Administration, Mussoorie. Mimeo.

Visaria, P., A. Gumber and L. Visaria. 1993. 'Literacy and Primary Education in India, 1980–81 to 1991: Differentials and Determinants'. *Journal of Educational Planning and Administration.* 7:13–62.

World Bank. 1996. Background papers on economic reforms and rural poverty. Prepared for the 1996 *Country Economic Memorandum.* Washington DC: World Bank.

World Bank. 1997. *Primary Education in India.* Washington, DC: World Bank.

Yadav, Yogendra. 1996. 'The Maturing of a Democracy'. *India Today.* 31 August.

_____. 2000. 'Understanding the Second Democratic Upsurge'. In F. Frankel, R.Z. Hasan, and R. Bhargava, eds., *Transforming India: Social and Political Dynamics of Democracy.* Oxford: Oxford University Press.

TABLES

Table 1: Educational Achievements in India, 1991

	Female	Male	Persons
Literacy rate (%)			
Age 7+	39	64	52
Age 15–19	55	75	66
Mean years of schooling (age 25+)	1.2	3.5	2.4
Median years of schooling[a] (age 6+)	0.0	4.8	2.5
Proportion of adults (age 20+) who have	16	44	30
Completed 8 years of education (%)			

[a] 1992–3.

Sources: Census of India 1991; International Institute for Population Sciences (1995), Table 3.9; *Human Development Report 1994*, p. 147. The literacy rates in the 15–19 age group have been calculated from unpublished 1991 census data, kindly supplied by the Office of the Registrar General; similarly with the proportion of adults who have completed eight years of education (strictly speaking, this refers to the completion of 'middle school and above').

Table 2: Child Work and School Attendance, 1991
(number of children aged 5–14 in different activity groups)

	Attending school (000s)	Not attending school (000s)	Total (000s)
Workers[a]	497 (0.5)	10,788 (10.2)	11,285 (5.4)
Non-workers	103,762 (99.5)	94,938 (89.8)	198,701 (94.6)
Total	104,259	105,726	209,986

[a] Both 'main' and 'marginal'.

Source: Census of India 1991, Social and Cultural Tables, Part IV, Table C-4. Figures in brackets are percentages of the column total.

Schooling, Culture, and Modernity

Sanjay Srivastava

The advent of the modern schooling system in India marks the consolidation of an educational regime which focuses on the 'native' personality and its shortcomings which are seen to be obstacles in the way of 'development' (in whatever form); further, this process is coterminous with the ascendance of the 'sciences' of psychiatry and psychology as important elements of the western knowledge regimes. Finally in this context, the consolidation of this schooling regime also inaugurates that elision so peculiar to standpoints aligned with nationalist discourses and projects: the marginalization of sociological and historical perspectives on society, and the exploration of *social* subjectivity. This, I think, is a crucial point: that modern schooling in India is firmly rooted in a 'science' of the native personality and the native body and ('modern') schools were to be the sites where 'lacks' and 'absences' could be analysed and rectified. Whilst this chapter is concerned with providing a broad outline of the main trends, opinions, and projects which have characterized the development of the primary and secondary educational system over the past 150 years or so, it will also concentrate on positioning these through the identification of specific discursive formations.

In the discussion which follows I will point to several contexts (or discursive formations) concerned with modern Indian educational thought and will characterize these as 'chronotopes' (Bakhtin 1990) in order to more fully express the idea that contexts/discourses can best be understood as expressions of temporal and spatial sensibilities. The literary theorist Mikhail Bakhtin suggested that the chronotope in its basic sense is 'a way of understanding experience; it is a specific form-shaping ideology for understanding the nature of events and actions' (Morson and Emerson 1990:

30). The name *chronotope,* Bakhtin says, is given 'to the intrinsic connectedness of temporal and spatial relationships that are artistically expressed in literature' (Bakhtin 1990: 84). Within each chronotope, 'spatial and temporal indicators are fused into one carefully thought-out, concrete whole. Time, as it were, thickens, takes on flesh, becomes artistically visible; likewise, space becomes charged and responsive to the movements of time, plot and history' (ibid.).

Rectifying Frivolity and Mischief: Natives and Education in the Nineteenth Century

The complicated history of elementary education in nineteenth-century India—the 'modern' period of Indian history—is made particularly prolix by the peculiarity of a society whose decentring tendencies have ensured that a wide variety of human endeavour has always lain outside the grids of bureaucracy and 'official' policy. Hence, through the greater part of the previous century, a wide variety of educational schemes and practices—influenced variously by a melange of sympathies and traditions—seemed to have found expression. What can be said with some confidence, however, is that as the century progressed there emerged a hegemonic discourse around the idea of—to quote the title of Charles Trevelyan's (1838) influential book—*Education and the People of India.* In another context, Connell has described 'hegemonic masculinity' as one 'constructed in relation to various subordinated masculinities' (Connell 1995: 183). We can say then that the hegemonic nineteenth-century educational discourse in India was one that defined itself through marginalizing a variety of other expressions and practices. This is not to say that forms of hegemony are always complete and look with satisfaction upon mute protests; they do, however, manage to dim other voices, suppressing their possibilities through processes of hierarchical classification.

Nurullah and Naik (1974) have noted that one of the greatest problems for a history of indigenous education at the beginning of the nineteenth century is the inadequacy of data, even for areas ruled by the British, notwithstanding the fact that surveys were commissioned to gather information on the extent and nature of the same. In the opening decades of the nineteenth century, surveys were carried out in the provinces of Madras, Bombay, and Bengal. In the Madras survey (1822), Thomas Munro estimated that there was 'one school to every 500 of the [male] population' (Nurullah and Naik 1974: 4). Munro also pointed out that to arrive at a more useful conclusion, one must also take account of the number of students given instruction in an informal setting, that is the home. This is an important point, one that may keep us from the historical reductionism that attributes learning to the existence of bureaucratic institutions. Indeed the prevalence of informal educational processes has also been a feature of our own time. In his autobiography ([1969] 1993) the poet Hariwanshrai Bacchhan, who was born in Allahabad in 1907, recalls that he received his first lesson in formal learning in the Urdu alphabet from his mother; and that for hours on end he would trace the letters of the alphabet she had written for him on a slate (Bacchhan [1969] 1993: 76). It is poignant that in a world where the figure of the mother was an important cultural icon as the transmitter of one's 'own' culture—a world where women were constructed as the custodians of 'tradition' (Chatterjee 1993a; Das 1996; Mani 1993)—Bacchhan's version of 'our (Indian) culture' un-self-consciously eschews any notion of allegiance to a single religion.

In the opening decades of the nineteenth century, the situation with regard to indigenous educational systems can be characterized without exaggeration (*or* romanticization) as approximating a limited system of mass education; limited in that in most accounts there is no mention of girl students being given any kind of formal schooling, and, in general, educational opportunities were also denied to members of the lower castes. However, as observers such as the missionary William Adam pointed out, there did appear to be an extensive system of elementary schooling encompassing both institutions specifically established and maintained for the purpose, as well as domestic education through privately employed tutors. And, further, that whilst there existed separate institutions for Hindus and Muslims offering different levels of education (the distinction between 'schools of learning' and 'elementary schools' made by Nurullah and Naik [1974], for example), there often existed a significant overlap between their respective clientele. So a mid-nineteenth-century report by a British official noted the presence of 'Persian schools' which 'were attended by a greater number of Hindus (Khatris) than Muslims' (Kumar 1991: 54). My reading of the situation does not purport to suggest a pre-colonial utopia of Hindu–Muslim relations, rather, only that we have yet to adequately capture the nature of intercommunal (and interpersonal across communities) relations that characterized pre-colonial and non-official contexts, but that this in itself is inadequate for *not* characterizing these situations as different (cf. van der Veer 1994).

The *formal* history—reports, surveys, acts, and schemes—of the establishment and consolidation of what I have referred to as the hegemonic educational discourse is, by now, of routine familiarity to most scholars of India. And whilst—for the sake of providing a context—I will go over this familiar territory, I should emphasize that my main purpose is to explore the nature of the discursive formation to which these elements belonged.

Missionary activity provided the earliest European contribution to schooling in India and the beginnings of the official system of education are generally attributed to the Charter Act of 1813 which expanded the inventory of duties of the Company to include responsibility for the establishment and maintenance of educational institutions. Between 1813 and 1854 debate raged over the object of educational policy, the medium of instruction, agency for its spread, and the method of its promulgation. The Wood's Education Despatch of 1854, formulated on the occasion of the renewal of the Charter of the East India Company, attempted to address some of these issues by declaring that official educational policy must concentrate on the promulgation of western knowledge and science among Indians.

The Despatch was wide-ranging in its review and recommendations with respect to Indian education. However, whilst it had the apparent effect of stimulating activity in various fields of educational policy, it is important also to remember its location within the colonial context; such contexts, no matter what their geographical occurrence, are hardly conducive to the unfettered welfare of the majority of the colonized population. It was thus in keeping with the imperatives of the colonized milieu—one where knowledge regimes which have the potential to compete with those of the colonizers are progressively marginalized—that in the period immediately following the issue of the Despatch, the vast and functional network of indigenous educational institutions was almost completely obliterated. And, in instances where such institutions continued to function, they became fossilized remnants of a discrete past, condemning their students to a marginalized existence in the realm of colonized (and, subsequently, post-colonial) existence.

The educational regime during the period following the 1854 Despatch was one marked by the neglect of indigenous educational institutions and traditions. Further, there appeared to be a consensus in both official and non-official circles that private Indian effort in the dissemination of education ought to be encouraged. Around this time there appear to have existed three schools of thought on educational matters: those followers of Hastings and Minto who believed in the encouragement of Sanskrit and Arabic studies; another group which wanted the progressive use of modern Indian languages as a vehicle for imparting 'western' knowledge; and those who took their cue from Charles Grant's thinking and 'advocated the spread of western knowledge through the medium of English' (Nurullah and Naik 1974: 61). It is important to remember, however, that most of these debates tended to be conducted among the British and 'Indian opinion' (or the class whose opinions passed as 'Indian') was largely absent from them. As has been copiously recorded by historians, these positions devolved into two broad oppositional stances, that of the Orientalists and that of those who decried the former stance as encouraging 'a great deal of what was frivolous, not a little of what was purely mischievous and a small remainder indeed in which utility was in any way concerned' (Despatch from the Court of Directors, 1824, quoted in Nurullah and Naik 1974: 65). The latter position was, of course, to be forcefully elaborated by Macaulay.

We should also remember that whilst official opinion in favour of disseminating western learning and the English language was gaining ground, there continued to exist a school of official opinion, which argued that 'every Native who possesses a good knowledge of his own mother-tongue, of Sanskrit and of English [possesses] the power of rendering incalculable benefit to his countrymen' (*Report of the Board of Education*, 1840–1: 35, quoted in Nurullah and Naik 1974: 83.) The nature of the debate differed across provinces. So while in Bengal the medium-of-instruction argument was carried out mainly in terms of the choice between classical languages and English, in Bombay it seems to have been well accepted that public instruction should primarily be imparted through the vernaculars. This position was only challenged during the 1840s. However, it is generally true that by the middle of the nineteenth century the opinions of those who argued for continued support to indigenous systems and methods of learning had been substantially marginalized. Along with this any possibility of a viable system of *mass* education was also undermined.

One of the strongest linkages between the marginalized condition of modern Indian languages within the educational system and the manoeuvres of a colonized polity can be traced to events in the late nineteenth century for this was the period during which the excoriation of the vernaculars was not effectively achieved through a combination of government policy and the perceptions of social advancement open to those with effective command of the English language. It is important to remember that whilst the general climate towards the use of the vernaculars as a medium of instruction may have been unfavourable, there nevertheless existed private efforts to the contrary. So in the Presidencies of Bombay and Bengal, a limited amount of medical education was sought to be provided in the vernacular. And whilst this education was chiefly designed for 'officers for the subordinate rank of the medical department' (ibid. 191), it resulted in an activity which carried the potential of radical reform in, and problematization of, existent educational philosophy regarding the 'suitability' of non-European languages for 'scientific' learning. Eminent doctors of Bombay's Grant Medical college 'wrote books in Marathi on all medical subjects' (ibid.) thus showing that vernacular languages were capable of communicating scientific thought.

The force of opinion against the use of vernaculars as a medium of instruction at all but the primary level of education was, however, during the second half of the nineteenth century, so strong, and the resources and rewards for committing energies towards this end so meagre, that these efforts met the terminal fate of all heroic efforts which do not—in a colonized society—have official sanction. So, whilst the Despatch of 1854 had recommended favourably on the encouragement of the vernaculars as a medium of instruction, by the closing decades of the century, the Indian Educational Commission (1882) came down in favour of English (Nurullah and Naik 1974: 190–9). By the turn of the twentieth century the idea of the use of vernaculars as a medium of teaching had been effectively effaced from the processes of policy formulation (ibid.). 'Progress' and 'civilization' required a cache of tools—the English language and western knowledge among these—that would enable all those were who wished to 'better' themselves to do so; those tools, to quote Foucault from a different context, which had ostensibly enabled historians to uncover the 'unmoving histories' concealed 'beneath the rapidly changing history of governments, wars, and famines' (Foucault 1982: 3).

We should keep in mind that the issue of the neglect of the vernaculars—by which I mean the creation of a two-tier post-colonial education system—can no longer simply be understood in terms of the internal dynamics of Indian society. We have to recognize that the fate of Indian vernaculars is quite similar to that of other languages that have no value in the global market-place of late capitalism. If colonialism is indispensable as an explanatory factor in their fate, their contemporary neglect is also linked to the economic and political (and hence cultural) power of languages such as English, French, and German. Quite clearly, no language has any intrinsic aesthetic or expressive quality that makes it a 'natural' and 'inevitable' choice as a language of global discourse. The popularity, or otherwise, of languages can only be understood in terms of historical and political factors, and both colonialism and the contemporary aspects of capitalism (the material affluence of western academia, for example) are part of this explanatory mosaic.

Recovering the Subject: The New Man of Post-coloniality

Though something akin to a nationalist sentiment had been gathering momentum in the closing decades of the nineteenth century, it was really during the first two decades of the twentieth century that what could be termed a nationalist educational agenda began to emerge. It is no coincidence that this period also witnessed the intensification of Gandhi's involvement in the national movement. It is not always clear that Gandhi's thought on education—as on many other matters—can be neatly categorized as part of a nationalist world-view. For on many points—such as the masculinity of the state and on the stubborn, though often implicit, questioning of the dichotomy between the 'manual' and the 'mental'—the complexity of his philosophy can be seen to problematize nationalist thought. This section is divided into two parts, and explores two different types of nationalist and modernist agendas. The first of these was formulated in the second half of the nineteenth century and found currency till the third decade of the twentieth, after which it was absorbed into a—second phase—modernist discourse that holds sway to the present. In addition to outlining current government initiatives, I will discuss the latter with reference to the establishment and functioning of the Doon School in Dehradun.

National histories in general seem to be informed by a millenarianism that foreshadows a new future through the means of an anthropomorphic promise. It is the promise of the 'coming man' (White 1992) whose character—ostensibly moulded at the intersection of 'rational' and 'modern' thinking—carries the key to a more 'progressive' thinking. In the Indian case, post-coloniality as a rupture upon the surface of an oppressive present unfolds through a dialogue of concurrence between colonial regimes of knowledge and their antagonists, the agitators for national Independence. The contemporary state of Indian education can, in turn, be linked to the nature of the latter group whose philosophical and material hegemony established very specific patterns of activity and development.

The history of Indian modernity and post-coloniality as a collaborative treatise—traces of which lie buried under the 'joyfulness' of its narrative of progress and 'national' good—can be found then in attempts to constitute modernist subjectivities.

One such attempt—the analysis of which provides some idea of the nature of the forces which constituted early Indian opinion on education—found considerable support among members of the Bengali academic community. In the foreword to a book on the 'origins' of the turn-of-the-century National Education Movement (NCE), Radha Kumud Mookerji speaks of a meeting to consider the implications of the student agitation against the planned partition of Bengal in 1905. The meeting, he cheerfully reports, was called by the Landholders' Association of Bengal and 'was a representative Conference of national leaders, of all men of light and learning in the country' (Mukherjee and Mukherjee 1957). The Conference resolved that open conflict with the government should be avoided and that 'the boycott of the Calcutta University Examinations be called off by the students concerned' (ibid.). However, it also resolved to plan for the education of the expelled students through the establishment of a National Council of Education (NCE). The National Education Movement, Mookerji continues, 'received a very good start by the donations announced on the spot by Brajendra Kishore Roy Chowdhury

(Zemindar of Gouripur) and Surya Kanta Acharya Chowdhury (Maharaja of Mymensingh)' (Mukherjee and Mukherjee 1957). It is in this light—the half-light of the consolidation of a 'national' consciousness in the 'coming man'—that we should appraise the banishment and disavowal of the 'feudal' from the *tableau vivant* of Indian modernity. In tracing the trajectory of Indian modernity, in other words, we should be mindful of not positing too sharp a break between its self-proclaimed milieu and that of its supposedly antithetical domains. Quite often we find that the two are, really, part of the same economy of praxis, expressions of shared commitments and contiguous emotions.

One of the most fruitful threads in contemporary theorizing on gender and sexuality can be summarized by the assertion that gender 'is a ... practical accomplishment—something accomplished by social practice' (Connell 1995: 76). Ironically, the colonial sphere appears to have provided particularly fertile grounds for the elaboration of this proposition. The 'social reformer' and associate of Swami Vivekanand, Margaret Noble, or Sister Nivedita as she came to be known, is a case in point. Though concerned with 'women's issues' Sister Nivedita spoke, above all, as an upper-caste male reformer of a fallen—'effeminized'—society (and hence the peculiarity of a recent study by Jayawardena [1995] which analyses Nivedita's work as part of a 'feminist gaze'). Sister Nivedita's thoughts on education drew upon an idealized and masculinized Hindu construction of a 'glorious' past that could be drawn upon as a resource for improving the present. The most important attribute of this ancient glory towards the rejuvenation of the Indian present lay in Nivedita's depiction of an undiluted antique essence whose traces could still be detected; further, it merely needed to be harnessed in the proper direction. This concerned the exceptional quality of the ancient Hindu mind, and the task of the present was to concentrate 'the Indian mind on the Indian problem' (Sister Nivedita 1923: 13). The slippages between 'Hindu' and 'Indian', male and female, and between Brahmanical and non-Brahmanical traditions were to become a regular part of the Indian nationalist discourse. Colonialism was marked by a convergence between ideas on the 'scientific temper', and the innate rationality of the 'industrial group'. 'Economic evolution', the economist Alfred Marshall was to assert, implied a movement towards the industrialized state. This was a movement away from 'savagery', a condition where humans exist 'under the dominion of custom and impulse; scarcely ever striking out new lines for themselves; never forecasting the distant future, ... governed by the fancy of the moment ...' (Marshall 1938: vii). This epistemological intersection was well represented in Sister Nivedita's thinking. A fundamental aspect of women's education in India, she said, must lie in making women more 'efficient' (Sister Nivedita 1923: 59). For, like 'Sita and Savitri', the modern Indian woman must acquire the skills of being 'at

once queen and housewife, saint and citizen, submissive wife and solitary nun
... daughters, sisters and disciples' (Sister Nivediter 1923: 57). Efficiency, then,
was Sister Nivedita's masculinist trope towards the reformation of Indian
womanhood. 'In order to achieve efficiency for the exigencies of the twentieth
century', she went on to say, 'a characteristic synthesis has to be acquired'
(Sister Nivediter 1923: 58). And as part of this 'efficiency drive' towards a new
society, the nation, women must be imparted a geographical sensibility for
geographical knowledge. The latter, she said, constitutes the fundamental building
block of the consciousness of national feeling (Sister Nivediter 1923: 59). This
might be achieved through resources already at 'our' disposal: 'the wandering
Bhagabatas or *Kathakas*, with the magic lantern, may popularise geography, by
showing slides illustrative of various pilgrimages' (Sister Nivedita 1923: 61):

> Picture, pictures, pictures, these are the first of instruments in trying to concretise
> ideas, pictures and the mother-tongue. If we would impart a love for the
> country [she said], we must give a country to love. How shall women be
> enthusiastic about something they can not imagine? [Sister Nivedita 1923: 61].

The education of Indian men, on the other hand, must ensure
obliteration of the dangers of effeminacy, and colonialism was a catastrophe
only in as much it has brought on modernity too suddenly (Sister Nivedita
1923: 66–7). The capacity to comprehend the changed situation brought about
by compressed modernity could, however, be developed through initiating
strategies for the restoration and reformation of Indian masculinity. Indeed
the 'uplift' of women was inextricably linked to the 'proper' education of men
and the ability to interest them in women's issues: 'Hundreds of young men
are necessary, to league themselves together for the deepening of education in
the best way amongst women' (Sister Nivedita 1923: 62); further, Indian history
provided ample evidence that men will work towards improving the educational
status of women: after all, Rammohun Roy provided the lead in the abolition
of *Sati*, and Ishwarchand Vidyasagar was instrumental in promoting
monogamy 'as the ideal of marriage' (Sister Nivedita 1923: 63). 'Let every
Indian woman', Sister Nivedita was to say, 'incarnate for us the whole spirit
of the Mother and the culture and protection of the Homeland, *Bhumyâ
Devi!* Goddess of the Homestead! *Bande Mataram!'* (Sister Nivedita 1923: 65).
The 'mind' as the object of educational reform is also the focus of
Aurobindo Ghose's recommendations in his *A System of National Education*
(1924). As is common in such perspectives, the social and political contexts of
educational projects come to be expressed in the conjunctional vocabulary of
biology and masculinity. Appropriately, then, the opening chapter is entitled
'The Human Mind' and opens with the words that 'the true basis of
Education is the study of the human mind'. Ghose then goes on to assert that

'the muscles of the mind must be trained by simple and easy means; then, and not till then, great feats of intellectual strength can be required of them' (Ghose 1924: 3). Perspectives which proceed from a philosophical commitment to the 'human mind' also carry within them (and are informed by) a deep commitment to individualism. In the Indian context this also becomes enmeshed with the broader context of the discourses of colonialism that justified imperialism through appeal to the *personal* qualities of the colonizing 'race' in comparison to the colonized. The response by Indians was usually in a similar currency, modified to insert the 'spiritual' integrity of the East where individualism was poured through the sieve of 'divine gift' to achieve perfection: 'Every one has in him something divine, something his own, a chance of perfection and strength in however small a sphere which God offers him to take or refuse' (Ghose 1924: 5).

Perhaps the most elaborate discourse on early education as foundational of the future national community can be found in the praxis of the nineteenth-century social reform movement known as the Arya Samaj. Founded in 1875 by Dayanand Saraswati (1824–83), the Samaj sought to reform a 'decaying' Hindu society and invigorate it through a return to the principles of the 'golden age' of a Vedic culture which through the centuries had been debased through practices such as idol worship and the caste system. As part of its 'reform' movement, the Samaj established a series of Dayanand Anglo-Vedic (DAV) colleges, the first of which was founded in Lahore in 1886. Several institutions for the education of girls were also established (the so-called Arya Kanya Gurukuls). The establishment of separate schools for boys and girls was in keeping with Dayanand's emphasis on celibacy of students, an attitude strongly redolent of British public school attitudes towards sexual and other 'degenerate' desires which stalked the young, though presented by the Samaj as a 'Vedic' principle. Female educational practice within the Arya Samaj, as others have pointed out (see Kishwar 1986), has followed the well-worn path of making strident demands for women's education in order to prepare wives who 'know how to manage home, rear children and at the same time participate in public social [sic], and even political life' (Pandit 1974: 197).

Primarily, the Samaj sought to revivify a 'fallen' society through the task of forming 'a sound, active and decisive character in students' (Pandit 1974: 193), a perceived 'drawback' of other nineteenth-century educational systems. The conjunctional site of the Arya Samaj discourses of a Hinduized past and present, of the centrality of the male citizen, of the male sexual regimen, and of national greatness through the development of 'personality' and 'character' was the Gurukul educational movement. The first of the Gurukuls was established in 1902 'in the Kangadi valley [Haridwar] on the banks of the river Ganges' (Pandit 1974: 211) and manifested a dissatisfaction within the Samaj with the direction of the DAV curricula which was seen to be taking on a 'foreign' character. This was sought to be stemmed through the propagation of the Gurukul movement—of 'ancient' and Vedic origin—within which 'the students were called *Brhamacharis* on the pattern of the Ancient Gurukulas' (Pandit 1974: 210).

Arya Samajis strongly emphasize that the founder of their creed held views which have since been validated by 'scientific' method, 'Swamiji [touched] upon what can be some of the vital aspects of and components of early childhood education which the modern child psychologists and educationists have priced highly' (Pandit 1974: 156). Thus, on the one hand, the Samaj was seen to be countering the 'degenerate' effects of westernization (and of missionary activity), while on the other hand the ultimate validation of its philosophy could only come from the knowledge regimes of the West. This is the well-known double bind of colonial cultural practice of 'wanting and not wanting a relation' (Metcalfe 1988: 197). The complex interweaving of temporal and spatial strategies in the educational philosophy of the Arya Samaj—the ancient and 'glorious' Hindu past, the space of the 'modern' present, the attempt to encompass the latter within the former, and, fundamentally, the resort to the encomia of 'scientific principles'—illustrates well the prolix chronotopicity of colonial and post-colonized situations; the terms of the struggle to retrieve an 'autonomous' self seem always to be borrowed from those of hegemonic knowledges which are sought to be resisted.

The mysticism that pervades much of Tagore's educational philosophy does, however, appear to seek to engage with an external reality which, though not fixed or objectively established, does have consequences for one's being in the world. Hence Tagore appeared to grant that the philosophy of 'inner transformation' may be inadequate strategy for societal transformation and that it may merely lead to the cul-de-sac of individualism. Hence he suggested that 'the twofold aim of education is first to help the individual consciousness to enter into and grow under the direct influence of the higher consciousness and secondly to externalise the inner change in life outside, in action; life and activities therefore are as important and indispensable as inner growth' (Sarkar 1961: 35).

We must also recognize Tagore's contribution to educational thought in his challenge to instrumental knowledge. His emphasis on the emotional and aesthetic dimensions of learning constituted a dissenting opinion on the Enlightenment rationality that had become such an integral aspect of the discourse of the 'modern' Indian intelligentsia. However, the chronoptope of 'ancient India' was never really far from Tagore's thoughts, and its 'Tapovana ideal and Upanashadic culture' (Sarkar 1961: 145) informed his notion of the post-colonized renaissance in which his educational experiments would play a part.

Of all the contributors to the debate on educational matters, it is perhaps only Gandhi who manages to question the authoritarian *guru-shishya* model which recommended itself to various thinkers primarily, it would seem, on the grounds of its supposed universality and antiquity. For the unquestioning deference to the *guru* as mode of transmission of learning and self-development, Gandhi substituted the dynamic of a physical relationship with materiality of the social world as the act of learning. The task of learning, Gandhi could be said to be suggesting, lies not in the phenomenological surrender to an (all-) knowing subject—the *guru*—but, rather, it must be constituted as an entirely decentred technology; here, there are no comforts of a 'truth' which is the 'reward' of sublimation in this philosophy, but only a complex learning and unlearning which mimic the warps and woofs of the products of the *charkha* (spinning wheel). In this way, his educational model also offered a way to engage with an Indian society which needed models of practice other than those drawn from a Hindu milieu.

However, in the wider context of the predominance of the Hindu viewpoint in public life, the liberal Bengali Muslim opinion seems to have been quite suspicious of the Wardha scheme of Basic Education.

> The main objection of the Bengali Muslims, it appears, was that the schools under the scheme would turn into *Ashram-schools* like *Vidya Mandir* and preach Hinduised Congress cult in the form of *Bharatmata, Bande Mataram,* non-violence and Gandhi cap. It was also feared that a reformed Hindustani would be forced upon the Muslims and this would drive out Urdu. ... not only the scheme but the bonafide of those who would be entrusted to implement the scheme was also in question [Acharya 1994: 174–5].

However, given Gandhi's own conception of Basic Education, it is not clear that these fears would have emanated *solely* from an engagement with the Gandhian educational philosophy. For example, with respect to religious training under his scheme, Gandhi noted that there would be 'no room for giving sectional religious training'. Instead he said that 'fundamental universal ethics will have full scope' (Gandhi 1951: 53). Further, though Gandhi was insistent that the unifying national language be Hindustani, he was just as clear that 'this common inter-provincial language can only be Hindustani written in Nagari or Urdu script. Therefore, pupils will have to master both the scripts' (Gandhi 1951: 53). It is, however, possible to understand Muslim fears in the context of non-Gandhian Hinduism that was, and continues to be, an important strain of Indian nationalism. Though

Gandhi was a deeply religious Hindu, he was careful not to equate India with Hinduism. In the wake of early-twentieth-century Indian nationalism, however, the cultural discourse which came to dominate was the one that emphasized an exclusive Indian identity, an identity shorn of the cultural complexity of life among contiguous and overlapping communities, in the flux of difference and commonality. The Wardha programme may not have had much in common with other contemporaneous schemes, but it could not escape the suspicions of those who were not Hindus. The exclusivist tendencies of other schemes were evident even in the 'enlightened' Tagore's *Santiniketan* experiment which made no attempt to investigate the possibilities of a more syncretic and inclusive educational philosophy.

In an age of disembodiment and alienation—industrial life, in other words—Gandhi's emphasis on bodily experience as learning had the frightening power to disorient. He was to assert,

> I hold that true education of the intellect can only come through a proper exercise and training of the bodily organs, e.g. hands, feet, eyes, ears, nose, etc. In other words an intelligent use of the bodily organs in a child provides the best and quickest way of developing his intellect. ... A proper and all-round development of the mind ... can take place only when it proceeds *pari passu* with the education of the physical and spiritual faculties of the child. They constitute an indivisible whole. According to this theory, therefore, it would be a gross fallacy to suppose that they can be developed piecemeal or independently of each other [Gandhi 1951; 10–11].

The Modern Regime

It is possible to argue that Gandhi's educational philosophy was part of a contradictory complex of ideas. Whilst it sought to disrupt the existing relations of power (his championing of the vernaculars as an educational medium is an example) he did not distance himself from rich and powerful in his public life (Sarkar 1983). Gandhi's scheme was really about the method of education rather than its substantive content, though it was through the latter that the former was formulated. However, the content through which 'education' could be achieved was not of an exclusionary kind and in this sense, his scheme was not about a concrete list of subjects. He argued, for example, that he was in no way opposed to 'literary' education. Rather, his concern was with the manner of its acquisition for he argued that literary education could not be separated from other kinds of learning, for to do so would be to resort to a disembodied sense of the self, one where the word and the world—sensuality and tactility—come to be seen as separable. Gandhi was to insist, that these were inextricably intertwined.

Despite the wide range of emotions aroused by Gandhi's thought, his educational scheme found few takers among the indigenous metropolitan post-colonial intelligentsia. One of the earliest pointers to the specificity of interests and ideologies which would come to dominate post-Independence educational thinking in India is contained in an incidental remark by Sir John Sargent, chief author of the Report of the Central Advisory Board of Education (CABE) on *Post-War Educational Development in India*, published in 1944. Writing in the 1960s of the process leading up to the publication of the so-called Sargent Report, he noted that 'when we had got all our financial and other statistics checked by experts, and gazed at the result, we felt rather like "stout Cortez and his men", only our peak was in Simla and we had a woman in our company' (Sargent 1968: xxii). The ideological topography of this observation—masculinist identity, proximity to centralized power, the civilizing mission—constitute also the landscape of the hegemonic schooling system of post-Independence India. In this section I will reflect upon these ideologies and discourses and conclude by pausing at a specific site, the Doon School, where these have been put into practice.

The legacy of colonialism, with its preoccupation with explaining differences between British and 'Oriental' societies grounded in a discourse of personality, gave way to a post-colonized educational philosophy similarly concerned with removing the perceived 'imperfections' of the native personality. The Zakir Hussain Committee Report (ZHC) of 1937 that evaluated Gandhi's Basic Education Scheme is a case in point. An indispensable aspect of Gandhi's scheme was its focus on the *social* process of the creation of privilege and the *historical* process of the creation of the mental/manual (or mind/body) dualism. Hence Gandhi considered it fundamental that all students undertake some kind of manual training as part of the schooling process. This *socio-historical* problematization of the very basis of knowledge formation—'instrumental rationalism' (Turner 1996: 10)—which held sway amongst the Indian intelligentsia offered a challenge that seemed just too frightening to engage with. The ZHC responded to Gandhi's disorientating ideas from within the fortified walls of a knowledge regime that fixed the shifting parameters of historical and social murk with a firm and classifying gaze, reducing structures and their historical dynamics to the vagaries of agency: it merely 'explained the principles and objectives of the scheme in terms of recognised doctrines of education and psychology' (ibid.).

The Sargent Report was also asked to evaluate the possibilities of educational development in India in the post-War period. In keeping with the, by then, deeply embedded world-view that explained 'success' and 'failure' in terms of the capacities of 'personality to the exclusion of social factors', the Board's report offered the following suggestion on school planning. Secondary education, it said, should be made selective and 'a pupil who does not happen to be selected shall not ordinarily be allowed to enter a High School' (Nurullah and Naik 1974: 395). For, it noted, 'The function of the High School is to cater for those children who are well above the average in ability' (ibid.). The social circumstance and specific histories of individuals—the sites of interaction between agency and structure, seem largely to have been submerged under the weight of a colonial epistemology. The report could be read to say that colonialism—the 'success' of one people over another—could itself be explained through the psychologized lexicon of innate ability and intrinsic traits. Of course, this aspect of the report also articulated an attitude implicit in much of post-colonized educational thinking that 'the duty of higher education [is] to produce an élite' (Sargent 1968: 87), and this was usually contextualized through stating that this elite was needed 'not for its own sake, but for that of the community' (ibid.).

The continuities between the classificatory regime of colonial rule, its naturalization of 'ability' through the psychologization of historically evolved positions of power, and post-colonized thinking are also starkly illustrated by some further recommendations of the Sargent Report. In a most remarkable discussion—chilling in its authoritarian ambitions—the report noted that special attention had to be paid towards training workers for the industrial life of the nation-to-be. With this in mind, it suggested a fourfold division of such workers, each category marked by special selection and training procedures. These categories were 'Chief Executives and Research Workers of the Future'; 'Minor Executives, Foremen, Charge Hands, etc.'; 'Skilled Craftsmen'; and 'Semi-skilled and Unskilled Labour' (Nurullah and Naik 1974: 398–9; Sargent 1968: 96–8).

These techno-bureaucratic gestures, born of a milieu where the imperatives of governmentality strained against the recalcitrance of diffuse practices of existence, also find constant play in our time; for in the post-colonized situation, 'instrumental-rationalism' has become a corner-stone of the 'nation-building' project, and, in its local recensions, has developed a most complex set of practices of policy. These, in the main, refer to themselves as touchstone and hence come to us as a pithy illustration of the Baudrillarian simulacra (Baudrillard 1994).

Situating Modernity[1]

As Lefebvre (1994) points out, ideologies need spaces to anchor their abstractions: to ground the fleeting figures of speech in an artefactual configuration that might, perhaps, be made to speak the self-referential language of proof and permanence. In the following section I wish to situate some of the issues raised in the preceding pages in a concrete context of practice, the Doon School. I will treat the Doon School as a historically significant site for the production and elaboration of a very specific discourse on Indian modernity and post-coloniality—including many of the ideas mentioned in the opening section of this chapter—and hence an important window to their analysis. My treatment of the Doon School[2] parallels Michel Foucault's (1979) use of the Panopticon as a model for investigating the relationship between people and institutions that may throw light on the Indian project of modernity and nationhood.

The relevance of the Doon School in the context of Indian modernity is manifold. The School's foundation (in 1935) coincides with what Pandey (1994) has called 'second-phase' nationalism marked by 'the dissociation of "nation" from any pre-existing communities and the construction of the purely national unambiguously, in terms of a new kind of community—the "India of our dreams"' (Pandy 1994: 239). Throughout its history the School has engaged actively with the wider discourses on modernity and citizenship in India. During this period it has also produced an intelligentsia (writers, academics, journalists, newspaper editors, social workers, corporate chiefs, etc.) whose influence on the public debate on nationalism and citizenship has been substantial. One could argue therefore that there exists a public space of debate and discourse on the nation, modernity, rationality, etc. which can be usefully examined through a historical, anthropological, and sociological study of the Doon School.

Fin de siècle debates on the future—post-colonial—Indian society seemed to have arrived at a consensus with respect to the 'attributes' required of the 'modern' personality of the citizen-to-be. Established by a coalition of interests which included members of the Indian Civil Service, the professional classes, and men of feudal background, the School's involvement in discourses of national identity had begun from its earliest days. Indeed, its founder S.R. Das, a barrister and cousin of the nationalist C.R. Das, was quite clear about the objectives of the 'Indian public school' he had decided to found ever since his return to India upon completing his education in England; in 1927, in a letter to one of his sons, Das despaired at what appeared to him a fractured sense of Indian identity and expressed his firm belief that 'his' school was 'going to be the real, though a very slow solution, of the problem of the nationality of Indians'. The School's educational and (one might say) philosophical agenda has also attracted wide support, some indication of which can be gained from the fact that the guest list for its opening-day ceremony in 1935 included representatives from the civil services, the defence forces, the landed classes, *as well as* a leading light in the cause of Hindu nationalism, Madan Mohan Malviya, and a member of the Muslim league, Chaudhri Zafarullah Khan (Srivastava 1998). Further, in 1952, the government appointed the Mudaliar Commission 'to survey the whole field of secondary education' (Sargent 1968: 85), and the Commission strongly supported the idea of private schools such as Doon (ibid.).

One of the moulds into which the School sought to cast the 'new' Indian personality was that of the rational, scientific subject. These were attributes specifically denied the 'natives' by the British who had commandeered the nineteenth century ontological space which conducted its business in vectors of 'objectivity', 'scientificity', and the critical 'this worldly' consciousness. The ability to lead a life of the mind was what set, so the argument went, the British apart from their subject races. The Doon School represented both an acceptance of this doctrine and an attempt to overcome it. The efforts of the School's founders were also informed by the philosophical deliberations of the age of capital and the ostensible requirements for participation in its enterprise. As the collective action of a class of men, the establishment of the School also represented the elevation of the individual as both a 'method' for understanding social predicament and a tool for the amelioration of the 'misfortunes' besetting a colonized society. An important context of the modernizing philosophy that marked the foundation of the School was that of the 'reformist' Brahmo Samaj. The School's founder S.R. Das (1872–1928) was an active member of the faith which advocated 'the substitution of a rational faith for the prevailing popular religions of the world, which, [the Samajis] thought, increasingly curtailed the freedom of human beings by enslaving them to mechanical rituals, irrational myths, meaningless superstitions and other worldly beliefs and values' (Kopf 1979: 1).

An important aspect of this dialogue in the colonial context was the manner in which social and economic stasis came to be represented as consequence of a 'lack' in the native body and mind. It was this 'lack'—one of which was the absence of the 'scientific temper'—that the Doon School set out to remedy. 'Personality' could now be seen as removed from the grasp of history: timeless, transcendent, and able at any time to be instantly transformed. It is only by situating the dialogue of Doon—the dialogue on 'nation building', the debates on the Doon man, the new Indian—within the universe of an ahistoricized present animated by the transubstantiative embrace of science and rationality, that we can fully understand its role as the propagator of a very specific kind of post-colonial world-view.

There were several ways in which the School sought to incorporate a 'scientific' world-view into its representational and educational practices. For a start, its founders decided upon the erstwhile campus of the Forest Research Institute (FRI; established 1906), one of the many colonial organizations concerned with 'scientific' mapping, classifying, and surveying, as the site for their institution. This decision sought to align the project of Indian modernity with that of the global Linnean enterprise (Pratt 1993) which was also a discourse of European identity, because organizations such as the FRI were also sites of self-representation by the British of their own subjectivity as ordered, rational, etc. It was entirely appropriate, then, that the search for a site for the birth and nurture of a new Indian identity should be a garden with flowers and laboratories—the garden of rational delights.

Several aspects of school life came to be viewed through the prism of 'rationality', and each of these constituted a procedure towards the construction of the scientific chronotope. In a 1947 edition of the *Doon School Weekly*, a popular forum for debates on 'national identity', Headmaster-designate John Martyn noted that 'Indian culture seems to me to be vast, unwieldy and diffuse', and that this 'diffuseness' was not suitable as ornamentation of a 'modern' nation. The 'problem' of Indian culture (its 'appropriateness' for the age of modernity), Martyn, an Englishman who had chosen to 'stay on', noted, 'concerns all those of us who are connected with education: It needs to be edited, clipped, trimmed, reduced to manageable proportions'. Ordinality—the fervour that reduces human endeavour to quantifiable units—was reflected in other areas as well. On 29 March 1943, the *Doon School Weekly* published results of 'Matrix' tests designed to measure the intelligence of the students divided into age, religious, caste, and regional categories. Percentiles were provided under the headings 'superior intellectual ability', 'above average', 'average', 'below average', and 'underdeveloped'. The students were further categorized according to whether they were 'Moslems', 'Brahmins', 'Kshatriyas', or 'other Hindu Castes', and according to the professional background of their fathers and their region of origin. The Matrix test was, of course, only one of the many ways through which the urge towards re-figuring the nation-state as an ordinal entity was made manifest. What is of greater interest is the institutionalization of these procedures in the wider processes of the nation-state, where well-being became a technocratic—the application of the 'right' procedures—rather than a complex social issue (see the discussion on the World Bank and mass education later).

We can say that the project of producing this new subjectivity took the form of a compact between men, since the young citizen in the making was now delivered from maternal care through the father's authority to the charge of other men, those in charge of the modern schooling system. This, in many ways, echoes the 'fraternal contract' (Pateman 1980) of the national project itself. However, it is important to understand that the post-colonized regime of modern educational thought is structured around a very specific notion of masculinity,[3] and that it came to be expressed in terms of the 'new' knowledges rather than through indices of corporeality; not for an ascendant Indian middle class the stereotypes of 'martial races' (Omissi 1991). Modern schooling in India is based, then, on a model of masculinity whose antecedents lie in the colonial experience. This model of education has also helped sustain a view of society where a certain ('modern') section of the population has come to represent itself as the harbinger of 'progressive' ideas, but has to constantly struggle against the atavistic recalcitrance of its 'primitive' populations. These national Others have come in the form of the 'unscientific' (and hence 'feminine'), the 'fundamentalists', the 'provincials', etc.

The system of schooling represented by the Doon School has recently received unprecedented homage from the nation-state via the establishment of Navodaya Vidyalyas (NVs) based on the Doon (boarding school) model. The NVs aim to make available 'good quality' school education to children 'irrespective of their capacity to pay for it'.[4] Children from rural backgrounds will particularly be encouraged to seek admission in the Vidyalayas, and the government will meet the educational costs of all students who qualify for study within a curriculum which borrows heavily from the Doon model of education (see also Scrase 1993).

Another important aspect of the modern schooling regime is connected with the issue of religion and how to deal with the multiplicity of religious voices that characterize Indian society. At Doon, it was most often manifested in the question of whether the curriculum should include religious instruction and whether it should arrange for (or encourage) religious worship. The search for the 'correct' religious attitude, and indeed the problematic of faith—interpreted primarily in terms of its perceived movement from the private to the public sphere—was (and continues to be) part of a wider, national, dialogue on the post-colonial 'modern' mind.

In English-speaking (and writing) circles in India, the realm of religion has increasingly come to be accompanied by a gloss on what is seen as its polar opposite, secularism. Secularism became an important part of the School's dialogue of self-representation and the various rituals of school life were, its proponents insisted, to be strictly organized around 'secular principles'. For many who were at the Doon School in the opening decades of its existence, and who were later to play important roles in the public life of the nation as part of the post-colonial intelligentsia—journalists, editors, novelists, social scientists, cultural functionaries of the state—secularism became a personal creed (Srivastava 1998). The School's policy on religion was expressed through a combination of textual practice and daily routine. So, while on the one hand, School magazines, newspapers, and other publications constantly reiterated—participating in the creation of the secular chronotope—its stand on religious matters, public rituals of the school such as the morning assembly were organized around the principle of religious syncretism. The latter procedure is particularly relevant to the creation of the School's secular chronotope, constituting as it does a graphic (ocular) demonstration of the organization of School space and time as the space and time of secularism; as a dramatization of the ethic of secularism, the assembly powerfully expressed and established the public face of the School.

It is possible to argue, however, that the Indian modernist dialogue on secularism is itself ensconced within a silent space of Hindu symbols and rituals. And that, in this manner, the Indian liberal-bourgeois discourse, of which the School is an important adjunct, speaks, unselfconsciously, through the vocabulary of majority opinion, with the gestures of that majority's cultural and religious universe. This is a situation that may be referred to as 'Hindu contextualism' and its form in the modern education system can be briefly outlined through reference to the Doon School. So, the representational space of the School—that occupied by the crest, the motto, special ceremonies, the field of visible impact, in other words—is, in fact, embedded within a very specific but *silent* configuration of signs. This is a configuration that belongs to the Hindu sacral caché of gestures, colours, and sounds. This silent space envelopes, so to say, the presence of the School, saturating the grounds of both its routine and non-routine existence. It also encompasses, and is encompassed by, the public voice of the School, the ethos of secularism. The School's crest is a long-stemmed oil lamp designated the 'lamp of learning'. The most immediate visible impact of the crest is to evoke the specific world of Hindu worship. The significance of oil lamps of various shapes and sizes in the Hindu ritual and cultural world—inaugurating a Kathakali performance, the *arati* ceremony during worship, and the symbolism of fire, *agni*, itself—need hardly be laboured (see, for example, Coomaraswamy 1964). I am not suggesting that those associated with the school consciously refer to the School's crest as an emblem drawn from the world of Hindu existence. On the contrary, one could speculate that such a consciousness is, in fact, absent. In this manner, one might say, what passes for a multi-religious or anti-religious environment is in fact lodged within a very specific universe, one evocative of the sights and sounds of the Hindu existence.

A similar argument can be mounted in the case of the *process* of selection of the School crest. Before the 'lamp of learning' was adopted in November 1937, several other designs had been submitted by students for consideration. All of the designs suggested by students incorporated motifs— or fragments—expressive of a Hindu aesthetic: the lamp, the sun, and the lotus (Singh 1985). These motifs, though removed from their original context, that is their specific role in Hindu life, nevertheless carry, to return to

Bakhtin, 'a certain chronotopic aura', a memory of their time and place: they 'remember' and resonate their past. It is not surprising, therefore, the political party with a public manifesto on Hindutva, the Bharatiya Janata Party, uses for its symbol the lotus flower (again, see Coomaraswamy 1964). Further, when, in 1953, Headmaster John Martyn put forward a selection of verses and aphorisms as possible options for a motto to accompany the crest, the entire selection was drawn from Sanskrit and Pali sources. The incorporation of the paraphernalia of the Hindu 'Great Tradition' (Singer 1972) at strategic intersections of visibility and permanence, is also apparent in other, more concrete ways: carvings and friezes depicting scenes from Hindu cosmology, and life-size statues of, among others, Mahavir, Buddha, Vivekananda, the torch-bearer of 'muscular-Hinduism', and the poet Tagore.

The point of the above discussion is not to censure efforts towards facilitating awareness of religious world-views. Rather, it is to problematize secularism as practice, for the modern system of education in India has played a considerable role in producing an intelligentsia which perceives Hindu contexts as synonymous with multi-religious ones.[5] Whilst there is a persistent tendency to ascribe 'fundamentalist' inclinations to those without access to 'modern secular historiography, still composed mainly in English' (Basu et al. 1993), 'we' have much to learn by turning 'our' attention to those processes and methods through which we have been produced as the avenging lights of secularism and the active subjects of modernity. It would appear to be of great importance to pay critical attention to the manner in which Aurobindo Ghose's (1924: 21) definition of the 'spirit of Hinduism' as the commitment to 'God ..., humanity ..., [and] country', and his observation that 'it is this spirit of Hinduism pervading our schools which ... should be the essence of Nationalism in our schools distinguishing them from all others', may indeed have come to fruition.

Official Policies and their Implementation

'The most unpardonable failure of our educational system', it has been suggested, 'is evidenced by the pathetic literacy rates'. And that, 'while the percentage of literates has increased at a snail's pace from 16.67 in 1951 to 36.23 in 1981, the number of illiterates has shot up from approximately 300 million to 437 million in the same period, and is expected to cross the 500 million mark by AD 2000' (Jayaram 1994: 210). As several studies have pointed out, parental reluctance is no longer an acceptable explanation—if it ever was—for this state of affairs (see Drèze this volume; Saldanha 1994).

Official figures for 'Recognised Educational Institutions' indicate that between 1950–1 and 1993–4, the number of primary schools grew from 209,671 to 572,923 (that is slightly less than threefold increase), whilst the number of universities ballooned from 27 to 213, amounting to an eightfold increase (*Annual Report of the Ministry of Education 1994* [ARE94]: 209). This phenomenal increase in the number of tertiary institutions did not, however, lead to (or was a reflection of) successes in the primary and tertiary sector whose graduates then created an overwhelming demand for higher study. On the contrary, data for the same period show sharp declines in stagewise enrolment, that is the numbers enrolling at primary, upper primary, and higher secondary levels (in any one year) follow a markedly downward trend (the phenomenon somewhat economistically referred to as 'wastage'). The corresponding declines for girls, and for students of Scheduled Caste and Scheduled Tribe backgrounds are greater at each stage. The most obvious conclusion to be drawn from this is that as students progress from grade to grade, schooling becomes a luxury for the vast majority of parents (or those in charge), and only those whose education does not impinge upon the family's ability to earn a subsistence are able to continue with it. In the Indian case, female children and those from Scheduled Caste and Scheduled Tribe backgrounds would seem to be the first affected by the strategies of survival. This is not, however, an assertion of a simplistic lack-of-demand hypothesis but points to the complexity of the nature of 'demand' for education. For example, the symptoms of Adivasi non-enrolment and drop out from educational institutions, cumulatively manifested in illiteracy, might be more meaningfully explained by reference to a wider context of deprivation where the choice between educating a child or putting him/her to work can present itself as a choice between bare subsistence or a calamitous effect upon that subsistence (Saldanha 1994: 90).

Census figures reported Indian literacy rate for 1991 ('for population aged seven years and above') at 52.21, that for males being 64.13 and for females 39.29 (ARE94: 203). Further disaggregation reveals that the proportion of literate to illiterate population is significantly higher in urban areas, and that the numbers for female literacy, both urban and rural, compare unfavourably with those for male literacy. It is also worth noting that certain states have shown stubbornly poor figures over the last forty years or so in all the categories of educational statistics mentioned above. These include, in descending order of literacy rate, Orissa, Madhya Pradesh, Andhra Pradesh, Uttar Pradesh, Rajasthan, and Bihar. The situation of female education and Scheduled Caste and Scheduled Tribe education is particularly sorrowful in these states. For 1991, Bihar recorded a female literacy rate of 22.89 per cent, that of Scheduled Castes at 19.49 and that of Scheduled Tribes at 26.78 per cent; the corresponding figures for Rajasthan were 20.44, 26.29, and 19.44 per cent respectively (ARE94: 205–8). There is ample evidence to show that this state of affairs cannot be attributed to any inherent resistance or obduracy towards educational acquisition on the part of the above groups. For example, it has been pointed out that in certain districts of Maharashtra, these very groups have made substantial contributions to literacy campaigns, and that as many as 68 per cent of learners belonged to the weaker section of society (Saldanha 1995: 1175).

The background to this situation is a slew of official policies and initiatives whose fulfilment (or, rather, lack of) becomes a variable of bureaucratic machinations and the casting of educational discourse in terms of the needs of the tertiary sector. The Operation Blackboard (OB) scheme of the National Policy on Education (NPE), 1986, was started in 1987–88 to bring all existing primary schools in the country to a minimum standard of physical facilities (ARE94: 35) which included buildings, teachers, as well as classroom equipment. Under the revised OB scheme launched in March 1994, girls' schools and 'SC/ST areas' are to be given high priority (ARE94: 35). Further, 'it has been made mandatory to the State Govts. that at least 50 per cent of the teachers appointed in future should be women' (ibid.). Historically, primary education, which ought to have been the most carefully planned and funded, has been a particularly neglected field. So, for example, Drèze and Loh point out that

> educational policy in China has given overwhelming priority to the expansion of primary education, and this contrasts with the elitist bias of India's educational system, which combines a resilient neglect of primary education with enormous public investments in higher education. Educational achievements are not only much lower in India than in China, they are also much less equitably distributed [Drèze and Loh 1995: 2870].

Reviews and Commissions at various times have emphasized that official energies should be particularly directed towards the effective dissemination of *primary education* at a mass level. Yet reality has usually been quite different. Historians and sociologists of education continue to record the sorry state of affairs in a sector that has the potential to benefit and empower the most marginalized groups in society. So, speaking of the OB project in Madhya Pradesh, Krishna Kumar points out that 'it could not proceed beyond the second phase when inquiries into charges of corruption in its handling resulted in stoppage of further utilisation of funds available under it' (Kumar 1995: 2720).

It is generally true to say, then, that the colonial tendency that favoured collegiate and secondary education (Viswanathan 1989) has tended to persist in the post-colonial period. And yet, just below the surface of a seemingly monolithic and intractable situation, there appear to have been gaps and fissures which, suitably exploited, may have led to quite a different scenario in terms of the development of a more effective system of mass education. So available evidence suggests that 'the adult literacy situation in [India and China] ... was very similar in the late 1940's. [And that] by 1981–82, there was virtually no difference between China and Kerala for the younger age group, while India was left far behind' (Drèze and Loh 1995: 2872). Drèze and Loh also point to the important role of the state in promoting educational activity in China and suggest that in regions of the country where such commitment has been lacking—such as Tibet—educational trends have been poor. The discussion in this chapter should make clear there is no dearth of official statements of intent in the sphere of mass education. However, it would appear that 'pious statements [regarding the need to promote a more equitable policy of basic education] are still to be matched with bold measures to ensure the universalization of primary education in the near future' (Drèze and Loh 1995: 2877). And yet it is important to remember that, quite often, local conditions play an important role in the unfolding of centrally developed plans, and that the impact of official policies need not be undifferentiated.

One such example is the case of Kerala. It has been suggested that Kerala has witnessed the growth of public politics and the fluctuation of women's roles over the past 150 years or so, which together produced the attributes of Kerala that produced the epithet model (Jeffrey 1992). During 1970s Kerala, a state poor in material terms, recorded the most remarkable achievements in terms of increased life expectancy of its inhabitants, decline in infant mortality, and improvements in literacy figures in general and in female literacy in particular. These have resulted, in a perceptible difference to the quality of life (United Nations Report, quoted in Jeffrey 1992: 6) of the people. Whilst there are no simple answers to the achievements summarized by the term 'the Kerala model', we can, nevertheless, say something 'about the extent to which a politically active population, in which women enjoy some autonomy, may force governments to carry out programs that ease people's lives' (Jeffrey 1992: 12). Some measure of the Kerala experience can be gauged by the fact that 'by the late 1950s, 87 per cent of primary-aged girls in Kerala were estimated to attend school' (Jeffrey 1992: 55). The official role in all this is most instructive and can be seen to offer hope for other models of governmental intervention in educational development. At the turn of the century, there already existed 'an extensive network of village schools' in the (present day) Kerala region (Jeffrey 1992: 56), and the Travancore Maharajas, a ruling class with an unusual sympathy for mass education, strongly supported these and laid particular emphasis on expanding facilities for education in the vernacular. Through a mixture of government policy and missionary influence, the initial dominance of the upper castes in these schools soon gave way to increasing numbers of students from lower-caste backgrounds. Jeffrey suggests that in part the later successes in the field of literacy can also be traced the place of women in matrilineal society [that] fostered widespread school-going habits (Jeffrey 1992: 58).

The combination of official initiatives and historical developments that fostered a climate of political assertiveness by the people led to achievements in the mass-literacy field which were unique, not only in the Indian context, but in the 'developing' world in general. An important aspect of the Kerala experience, another observer suggests, was the innovation in the design and use of literacy primers which incorporated the experiences and needs of learners (Chandran 1994). So for example, 'the lesson on food included discussions of its sources, availability, causes of hunger, malnutrition, dietary hygiene, etc.' (ibid.).[6] Kerala was declared fully literate in 1991, the first (and only, thus far) Indian state to achieve this distinction.[7] It is interesting to note that no other south Indian state has managed to replicate the 'Kerala experience', and that, in fact, one of these, Andhra Pradesh, is found in the company of the more 'backward' north Indian states in terms of statistics on literacy and education.

While it is true that no other Indian state has managed to replicate the 'Kerala experience', it need not imply a future characterized by absolute stasis in other regions. Drèze (this volume) reports that the last four decades in Himachal Pradesh have witnessed an astounding trend in educational achievements. Starting from the same levels of literacy as the most backward regions of the country, the literacy rate, for both males and females in Himachal, rivals that of Kerala. While the reason for this state of affairs may be complex, it does point to the possibility of change in even the most intractable of circumstances.

A considerable part of the problem may seem to lie in the fact that education planning and initiatives in India are often dissipated through their linkages to a plethora of non-educational bureaucracies and programmes. So,

> construction of school buildings is the major problem that State Govt. has been facing. This problem has, however, been sorted out with the Ministry of Rural Development, who have agreed not only to continue central funding for construction of school buildings under Jawahar Rozgar Yojna (JRY), but also make it a high priority item under newly introduced Employment Assurance scheme and the 120 backward districts identified under the intensive JRY [ARE94: 35–6].

In this way, the failures to achieve 'targets' can then be explained away in terms of the failures originating in the sectors with which educational plans have been crucially linked. This is the functioning of a bureaucratic simulacrum where it becomes impossible to say where responsibility for any failure lies, and explanations and refutations circulate in the form of cross-cutting concentric circles.

It is pointless, however, to view the career of the modernist schooling regime in isolation from the enmeshment of Indian society in a global configuration of knowledge whose worth is expressed through the index of 'usefulness', and through their 'inherent' propensity to 'normalize' human behaviour. An important aspect of this concerns the funding of mass-education schemes in India by international bodies such as the World Bank. This, as has recently been pointed out, has had the effect of establishing a clear nexus between the imperatives of global capital—the will to 'profitability'—and the conduct of educational practice in the Third World. This, in turn, carries within the possibility of submerging dissenting voices on educational practice in order to 'bring it in line with a homogeneous and globalised world propelled by the market' (Raina quoted in Kumar 1995: 2720). Such fears take on a concrete form as we learn more of the details of the strategy through which global capital seeks to 'normalize' backwardness, and quantify its efforts. The following excerpt comes from a World Bank office memorandum and needs little further gloss:

> Modern psychometric techniques will be applied to student learning achievement data and each country will produce a national report describing achievement levels and the distribution of school resources by geographical areas, and types of schools and students, provide an analysis of the determinants of student achievement, analyse the effects of any policy changes on learning achievement changes over time and draw overall conclusions [quoted in Kumar 1995].

What ought to be of concern is the manner in which such knowledge regimes find little contestation as they become institutionalized in official policy. So government documents are replete with information on 'microplanning' strategies for primary education, 'Centrally Sponsored Scheme of Restructuring and Reorganisation of Teacher Education', and on the Rajasthan Shiksha Karmi Project aimed at 'universalisation and qualitative improvement of primary education in remote and socio-economically backward villages in Rajasthan with primary attention given to girls' (ARE94: 35–9). Studies in the field seem to indicate that, more often than not, these pronouncements of policy are dissipated at various levels of bureaucracy, notwithstanding the fact of decentralization of administrative procedures at village level.[8]

In recent times, 'vocationalization of Higher Secondary education' has emerged as an important plank in contemporary educational policy. This aims to 'provide an alternative for those pursuing higher education without particular interest or purpose' (ARE94: 48). However, the NPE does not appear to be concerned with altering the fundamental character of an educational system that, in Indian society, plays a fundamental role in *legitimating* inequality. A more serious reform might have been to consider introducing *all* students to aspects of 'vocationalization' such that entrenched hierarchical differentiation between 'manual' (or bodily) labour and 'intellectual' (or non-corporeal) work might itself have been problematized. This was, of course, one of the great insights of Gandhi's educational philosophy.

Under the present circumstances, the most likely result of this compartmentalized 'vocationalization of Higher Secondary education' will be the continued institutionalization of a two-tier educational system which seems inerasably inscribed with the philosophies of both colonialism (or perhaps merely the Enlightenment) and capitalism; these legacies are reflected in the mind–body split inherent in the vocational–intellectual formulations, and in the educational Taylorism which continues to champion the 'conceivers and executants' (Preston and Symes 1992: 130) model of schooling. So, rather than arguing for problematizing the thinking–doing split, Indian educational planners merely proceed from the premise that there are indeed two different classes of human beings, those who must do the thinking and others who will act as the mechanical executors, 'a mere conduit for predetermined actions which have been timed and organised' (Preston and Symes 1992: 130). The *caveat* that vocational education 'is education which accommodates technocratic values and, insofar as it uncritically accepts society's hierarchies, it may perpetuate injustice, elitism and class and gender inequities' (Preston and Symes 1992: 135) would seem to be particularly germane in the Indian context.

The Future: Schooling 'Against the Grain'

One clear trend in the Indian educational milieu is the rapid proliferation of private schools to cater for the demand for public-school-type education by an emerging middle class. Many of these new schools are, in fact, boarding schools and use English as the medium; several of these have been established by corporate houses (the Goenkas, Living Media, the Shriram Group, and Magor and Macneill among them) as profitable business ventures in an era of the proliferation of global 'scapes' (Appadurai 1990), when the demand for the cultural capital they offer is particularly high. A recent report suggests that one of the entrants into the schooling-as-business sphere, the consumer-products giant Hindustan Lever (HL), hopes that its educational activities will, in fact, lead to greater demand for its products among previously 'resistant' market segments.[9] The rationale for opening a primary school in a rural area of Khamgaon district of Maharashtra (with others to follow) appears to be derived from the company's understanding of the link between education and the demand for consumer products as experienced in China. Hence a senior HL executive was quoted as saying that 'wherever the level of education is high, more people use products like soaps'. And, whilst the company does not intend to directly market its products through its schools, 'it is hoping the awareness brought by education [sic] would make people choose its products' both against those of its competitors and over traditional alternatives such as *sheekakai* (a plant variety used in powder form for washing clothes and hair) and coal powder. We may now truly be entering an era where certain forms of schooling may be directly implicated in producing 'ideal' consumers for late-twentieth-century capitalism.

In a time of continuing decline of the government-run schooling regime and the consolidation of a two-tier schooling system, perhaps the most innovative and cutting-edge education will originate from the non-government organization (NGO) sector. For there are indications that out of the struggle to come to grips with state hostility towards the marginalized, the institutionalization of statist, technocratic and authoritarian educational philosophies, and the proliferation of a corporatist ethos which whilst paying lip-service to progressive measures only serves to install a conservative agenda, an alternative educational agenda is emerging.

One of the most salient features of the private schooling system outlined above is the lack of commitment to mass education. With the exception of Gandhi's Basic Education Scheme, the various non-governmental philosophical debates and organizational efforts surrounding schooling were carried out—in addition to their Hindu and masculinist bias—within the quite explicit matrices of upper-caste and middle-class identities. This educational discourse maintained its contiguity with Indian nationalism in general through the shared hostility to non-upper-caste and non-middle-class milieux, representing conditions in the latter as a consequence of personality and character defects; among Hindus 'philosopher-statesman' Radhakrishnan (1975) was to note, there exist populations 'professing crude thoughts and submerged thoughts civilization has not had time to eradicate'. Whilst it is true that treatments of the past should avoid the twin pitfalls of glorification and condemnation, it is nevertheless reasonable to characterize recent NGO efforts in the educational field as a radical break from, and a problematization of, past positions.

Speaking of NGO efforts in Maharashtra, Saldanha (1994) notes that 'in contrast to the social welfarist approach to education, one sees the education efforts of the non-party political groups in the region focusing on

"social awareness" ' (1994: 105). He also points out that the approach of the
political activitsts 'offers a perspective for resolving some of [the] contradictions
which are confronted by the more institutionalised formal educational process
at the cultural and economic levels of *adivasi* existence by linking education to
the political act of social transformation along the lines of an alternate
development strategy' (ibid.). Further, the educational philosophy of
organizations such as the *Kahstkari Sangathana* and the *Shramik Mukti
Sangathan* (which works with *adivasi* children in Thane district) has provided
radical reinterpretations of the existent educational discourses through treating
'the generation of a critical social awareness' (Saldanha 1994: 96) as an
indispensable element of their activism. Indeed, whatever little change there has
been in official educational thought appears to have come about as a result of
NGO activism and pressure. An instance of this may be cited in the
formulation of the *Vigyan Shikshan Karyakram* (Vishika), 'embodying [an]
attempt to forge compatibility between intellectual creditability and utility'
(Rampal 1994), which was initiated in 1972 by a fortuitous collaboration
between voluntary activists, professional scientists and school teachers' (ibid.).
Though critics have pointed out that 'Vishika' also bases itself on models of
science education which have proved inadequate as modes of critical learning, it
is nevertheless an important marker towards the problematization of dominant
knowledge regimes. It can be said in this context that the most valuable
contribution of the NGO sector—one informed by the commitment to a critical
pedagogy which struggles against the statist and corporatist tendencies of the
'modern' schooling regime—has been to emphasize the constructed—rather
than 'objective' and immutable—nature of knowledge and 'truth'.[10]

In recent times, much has been made of the right of the private
education system to function in an unfettered manner since, as the most
common argument goes, it relies solely on 'private' resources and may expend
these as it deems appropriate. Post-colonized reality does not, however, bear
witness to the existence of such discrete realms of 'private' and 'public'
spheres and a detailed analysis would show that private schooling in India has
flourished through the munificence of the public purse. It is this silent
contract between the state and private—highly privileged—groups that ought
to be a continuing focus of critical scholarship on education. This contract
has a long history. A Congress spokesperson stated in 1940, 'Where do the
poor peasants of Bengal come in? The [private] schools are being run by the
fees of the students and by voluntary contributions from private sources and
not from any of the poor peasants of Bengal that do not receive their
education in them' (quoted in Acharya 1994: 183). In many ways this is the
biography of the nation-state itself. This is also a history of 'domesticated
difference': a situation where the modern education system has incorporated

within its fold a very wide range of opinions—the left, the right, the religious, the secular, the trade unionist and the corporate chief, the bureaucrat and the *laissez faire* proponent, etc.—all of whom are trained for an allegiance to a particular kind of modernity, and hence to an educational system which is seen as the font of that modernity.

Acknowledgements: I am grateful to Veena Das for various suggestions on the first draft of the chapter, and to Jean Drèze for making available a draft copy of his contribution to this collection.

ENDNOTES

1. This section of the chapter is adapted from Srivastava 1998.

2. Henceforth also referred to as the School.

3. Writing generally of gender issues in the context of schooling, Scrase (1993) notes that contemporary textbooks continue to reproduce sexist and stereotypic images of women, with the majority representing gender issues in a manner which derives from patriarchal ideologies of motherhood, the good wife, the pure and deferential sister, etc. And, as he points out, 'the textbook image of the happy and dutiful wife contests the notion that her position in that role results more from her exploitation as a woman than from any desire to be a good wife and mother—unemployed and confined to the home' (ibid.).

4. Navodaya Vidyalaya Samiti Annual Report, 1989: 63.

5. This conclusion derives from my fieldwork. Students' responses to the public symbols of school life almost exclusively identified them as 'Indian' and 'secular' rather than as Hindu or an allied religious content (see Srivastava 1998).

6. The concern with producing primers that pay attention to the specificity of local conditions has also been noted in another context. In the Dungarpur district of Rajasthan, an area with a large tribal population, two categories of primers were produced after consultation with the local people. The first of these utilized a local dialect and 'the second primer switches over to Hindi gradually' (Chandran 1994: 516).

7. The accuracy or otherwise of such a declaration is not as important as the fact that its claims have been modified rather than rejected by most independent scholars.

8. Drèze (this collection) provides an instructive—and depressing—account of the situation of female literacy in the post-Independence period (see also Karlekar 1994). For a discussion of government-backed initiatives which have succeeded, and of the conditions of possibility for such success, see Chandran (1994).

9. Lever to Open School; Pupils Potential Buyers', *The Indian Express*, 3 April 1998.

10. See Scrase (1993) for an interesting case study of an alternative schooling effort in a slum area on the outskirts of Calcutta.

REFERENCES

Acharya, P. 1994. 'Education and Communal Politics in Bengal: A Case Study'. In
   K. Kumar, ed., *Democracy and Education in India*. New Delhi and London: Sangam
   Books.

Adam W. 1941. *Reports on the State of Education in Bengal, 1835 and 1838*. Ed. A.N. Basu. Calcutta: University of Calcutta.

Ahmad, A. 1992. *In Theory: Classes, Nations, Literatures*. London: Verso.

Anderson, B.R. 1986. *Imagined Communities: Reflections on the Origin and Spread of Nationalism*. London: Verso.

Annual Report 1988–89. 1989. New Delhi: The Navodaya Vidyalaya Samiti.

Annual Report 1989–90. Part I. 1990. Department of Education, Government of India. New Delhi: Ministry of Human Resource Development.

Annual Report of the Ministry of Education 1994. 1994. New Delhi.

Appadurai, A. 1990. 'Disjunction and Difference in the Global Cultural Economy'. *Public Culture*. 2:1–24.

Bacchhan, H. [1969]. 1993. *Kya Bhooloon Kya Yaad Karoon* (in Hindi). Delhi: Rajpal and Sons.

Bakhtin, M.M. 1990. 'Forms of Time and of the Chronotope in the Novel: Notes towards a Historical Poetics'. In M. Holquist, ed., *The Dialogical Imagination. Four Essays by M.M. Bakhtin*. 84–258. Austin: University of Austin Press.

Basu, T., P. Datta, S. Sarkar, T. Sarkar, and S. Sen. 1993. *Khaki Shorts and Saffron Flags: A Critique of the Hindu Right*. New Delhi: Orient Longman.

Baudrillard, J. 1994. *Simulacra and Simulations*. Trans. Shiela Faria Glaser. Ann Arbor: The University of Michigan Press.

Bourdieu, P. 1986. 'The Forms of Capital'. In J.G. Richardosn, ed., *Handbook of Theory and Research in the Sociology of Education*. 241–58. New York: Greenwood Press.

Bourdieu, P. and J.C. Passeron. 1997. *Reproduction in Education, Society and Culture*. Trans. R. Nice. London: Sage Publications.

Chandran, K.N. 1994. 'Literacy in India and the Example of Kerala'. *Journal of Reading*. 37(6):514–17.

Chatterjee, P. 1986. *Nationalist Thought and the Colonial World. A Derivative Discourse?* Tokyo: Zed Books.

_____. 1993a. 'The Nationalist Resolution of the Women's Question'. In K. Sangari and S. Vaid, eds, *Recasting Women: Essays in Colonial History*. New Delhi: Kali for Women.

_____. 1993b. *The Nation and its Fragments: Colonial and Postcolonial Histories*. Princeton: Princeton University Press.

Connell, R.W. 1995a. *Gender and Power*. Oxford: Polity Press.

_____. 1995b. *O Masculinities*. St. Leonards: Allen and Unwin.

Connell, R.W., D.J. Ashenden, S. Kessler, and G.W. Dowsett. 1982. *Making the Difference: School, Families and Social Division*. Sydney: George Allen and Unwin.

Coomaraswamy, A.K. 1964. *The Arts and Crafts of India and Ceylon*. New York: Farrar, Strauss.

Das, V. 1996. *Critical Events. An Anthropological Perspective on Contemporary India*. Delhi: Oxford University Press.

de Souza, A. 1974. *Indian Public Schools. A Sociological Study*. New Delhi: Sterling Publishers.

Drèze, J. (Forthcoming). 'Patterns of Literacy and their Social Consequences'. In this collection.

Drèze, J. and J. Loh. 1995. 'Literacy in India and China'. *Economic and Political Weekly*. 30(45):2868–78.

Foucault, M. 1979. *Discipline and Punish. The Birth of the Prison*. New York: Vintage Books.

_____. 1982. *The Archaeology of Knowledge and the Discourse on Language*. New York: Pantheon Books.

Gandhi, M.K. 1927. 'Wanted Workers'. *Young India*, 10 March: 108–9.

_____. 1927. 'Three Speeches'. *Young India*. 2 September: 369–70.

_____. 1928. 'True and False Industrialisation'. *Young India*. 24 May: 756–7.

_____. 1951. *Basic Education*. Ahmedabad: Navjivan Publishing House.

_____. 1990. *An Autobiography: Or the Story of My Experiments with Truth*. Ahmedabad: Navjivan Publishing House.

Gathorne-Hardy, J. 1978. *The Old School Tie: The Phenomenon of the English Public School*. New York: Viking Press.

Ghose, A. 1924. *A System of National Education for India. Some Introductory Essays*. Calcutta: Arya Publishing House.

Hussain, Z. 1965. *The Dynamic University*. London: Asia Publishing House.

Iyer, R. 1987. *The Moral and Political Writings of Mahatma Gandhi*, vol. 3. New York: Oxford University Press.

Jayaram, N. 1994. 'Degeneration of Democracy and Education: Reflections on the Indian Scenario'. In K. Kumar, ed., *Democracy and Education in India*. New Delhi and London: Sangam Books.

Jayawardena, K. 1995. *The White Woman's Other Burden: Western Women and South Asia during British Colonial Rule*. London: Routledge.

Jeffery, R. 1992. *Politics, Women and Well-Being: How Kerala Became a Model*. London: Macmillan and Co.

Karlekar, M. 1994. 'The Slow Transition from Womanhood to Personhood: Can Education Help'. In K. Kumar, ed., *Democracy and Education in India*. New Delhi and London: Sangam Books.

Kishwar, M. 1986. 'The Daughters of Aryavarta'. *Indian Economic and Social History Review*. 23(2):151–8.

Kopf, D. 1969. *British Orientalism and the Bengal Renaissance: The Dynamics of Indian Modernization 1773–1835*. Berkeley: University of California Press.

_____. 1979. *The Brahmo Samaj and the Shaping of the Modern Indian Mind*. Princeton: Princeton University Press.

Kumar, K. 1989. 'Secularism: Its Politics and Pedagogy'. *Economic and Political Weekly*. 24(44–5):2473–6.

_____. 1991. *Political Agenda of Education*. New Delhi: Sage Publications.

_____, ed. 1994. *Democracy and Education in India*. New Delhi and London: Sangam Books.

_____. 1995. 'Learning and Money. Children as Pawns in the Dependency Game'. *Economic and Political Weekly*. 30(43):2719–20.

Kumar, R. 1985. 'All King's Men Dance to Doon's Tune'. *The Statesman*, 1 November.

Lefebvre, H. 1994. *The Production of Space*. Trans. D. Nicholson-Smith. Oxford: Blackwell.

Majumdar, R.C. 1960. *Glimpses of Bengal in the Nineteenth Century*. Calcutta: Firma K.L. Mukhopadhyaya.

Mani, L. 1993. 'Contentious Traditions: The Debate on Sati in Colonial India'. In K. Sangari and S. Vaid, eds, *Recasting Women: Essays in Colonial History*, New Delhi: Kali for Women.

Marshall, A. 1938. *Principles of Economics*. London: Macmillan and Co.

Metcalfe, A. 1988. *For Freedom and Dignity: Historical Agency and Class Structure in the Coalfields of New South Wales*. St. Leonards: Allen and Unwin.

Morson, G.S. and C. Emerson. 1990. *Mikhail Bakhtin: Creation of a Prosaics*. Stanford: Standord University Press.

Mukherjee, H. and U.U. Mukherjee. 1957. *The Origins of the National Education Movement (1905–1910)*. Calcutta: Jadavpur University Press.

Nurullah, S. and J.P. Naik. 1974. *A Students' History of Education in India (1800–1947)*. Delhi: Macmillan.

National Policy on Education 1986. New Delhi: Ministry of Human Resource Development, Government of India.

Nehru, J. 1960. *The Discovery of India*. New York: Anchor Books.

Omissi, D. 1991. 'Martial Race: Ethnicity, and Security in Colonial India, 1858–1939'. *War and Society*. 9(1):1–27.

Pandey, G. 1994. *The Construction of Communalism in Colonial North India*. Delhi: Oxford University Press.

Pandit, S.S. 1974. *A Critical Study of the Contribution of the Arya Samaj to Indian Education*. New Delhi. Sarvadeshik Arya Pratinidhi Sabha.

Pateman, C. 1980. *The Disorder of Women. Democracy, Feminism and Political Theory*. Cambridge: Polity Press.

Pratt, M.L. 1993. *Imperial Eyes: Travel Writing and Transculturation*. New York: Routledge.

Preston, N. and C. Symes. 1992. *Schools and Classrooms: A Cultural Studies Analysis of Education*. Melbourne: Longman Cheshire.

Radhakrishnan, S. 1975. *The Hindu View of Life*. New York: Macmillan Publishing Company.

Raina, V. 1995. 'Elementary Education: A Donor Driven Agenda'. In *The State of the Indian Economy 1994–95*. New Delhi: Public Interest Research Group.

Rampal, A. 1994. 'School Science in Search of a Democratic Order?' In K. Kumar, ed., *Democracy and Education in India*. 85–112. New Delhi and London: Sangam Books.

Report of the Education Commission 1964–66. Education and National Development. 1966. New Delhi, Ministry of Education, Government of India.

Saldanha, D. 1994. 'The "Socialisation" of Critical Thoght: Responses to Illiteracy amongst the Adivasis of Thane District'. In K. Kumar, ed., *Democracy and Education in India*. New Delhi and London: Sangam Books.

———. 1995. 'Literacy Campaigns in Maharashtra and Goa. Issues, Trends and Direction'. *Economic and Political Weekly*. 30(2):1172–95.

Sangari, K. and S. Vaid, eds. 1993. *Recasting Women. Essays in Colonial History*. New Delhi: Kali for Women.

Sargent, J. 1968. *Society, Schools and Progress in India*. Oxford: Pergammon Press.

Sarkar, S. 1983. *Modern India*. Delhi: Macmillan.

———. 1985. *A Critique of Colonial India*. Calcutta: Papyrus.

Sarkar, S.C. 1961. *Tagore's Educational Philosophy and Experiment*. Santiniketan: Visva-Bharati.

Scrase, T.J. 1993. *Image, Ideology, and Inequality: Cultural Domination, Hegemony, and Schooling in India*. New Delhi: Sage Publications.

Singer, M. 1972. *When a Great Tradition Modernizes: An Anthropological Approach to India*. New York: Praegar Publishers.

Singh, A. 1991. 'Ramamurthy Report on Education in Retrospect'. *Economic and Political Weekly*. 25(26):1605–13.

Singh, S. 1985. *Doon. The Story of a School*. Dehra Dun: Indian Public Schools Society.

Sister Nivedita. 1923. *Hints on National Education in India*. Calcutta: Ubodhan.

Srivastava, S. 1993: 'The Management of Water: Modernity, Technocracy and the Citizen of the Doon School'. *South Asia*. 16(2):57–88.

———. 1996. 'The Garden of Rational Delights: The Nation as Experiment, Science as Masculinity'. *Social Analysis*. 39:119–48.

———. 1998. *Constructing 'Post-Colonial' India: National Character and the Doon School*. London: Routledge.

Trevelyan, C.E. 1838. *On Education of the People of India*. London: Longmans, Orme, Brown, Green and Longmans.

Turner, B.S. 1996. *The Body and Society: Exploration in Social Theory*. London: Sage Publications.

van der Veer, P. 1994. *Religious Nationalism: Hindus and Muslims in India*. Berkeley: University of California Press.

Viswanathan, G. 1989. *Masks of Conquest: Literary Study and British Rule in India*. London: Faber and Faber.

Whilte, R. 1992. *Inventing Australia. Images and Identity 1688–1980*. St Leonards: Allen & Unwin.

Higher Education

Suma Chitnis

HIGHER EDUCATION AS A SOCIAL INSTITUTION
Definition

In 1962, forty-four nations participating in a UNESCO conference on higher education defined higher education as:

> all types of education (academic, professional, technological or teacher education) provided in institutions such as universities, liberal arts colleges, technological institutions and teacher colleges for which (a) the basic requirement is completion of secondary education, (b) the usual entrance age is about 18 years, and (c) in which the courses lead to the giving of a named award (degree, diploma or certificate of higher studies).

This definition, quoted in the reference on higher education in the fifteenth edition of the *Encyclopedia Britannica Macropedia* (1974), is perhaps the best one may use to cover most of the systems of university and other post-secondary school education in operation universally. These systems, according to the *Encyclopedia*, have evolved from the system that developed in medieval Europe and was firmly established there between the eleventh and the sixteenth centuries. Political and economic factors, together with other circumstances, produced modifications of the basic medieval pattern in different countries. The *Encyclopedia* states that the patterns that developed in France, Germany, England, the United States, and the Soviet Union are now recognized as the five basic models of this medieval system. Further, as each of these countries grafted or planted its systems of education in the countries it colonized, each generated its own variations (see *Encyclopedia Britannica Macropedia*). The system of higher education in operation in India today has evolved from the model, grafted on to India by the British in the course of their colonial rule.

Although the UNESCO definition satisfactorily covers most of the systems of higher education currently in operation in the world, it is somewhat inadequate in that it exclusively focuses on institutions that teach and give awards. Systems of higher education often include research institutions in which there is no teaching. Similarly, some institutions teach but do not offer degrees or diplomas. Thus one may use the UNESCO definition to denote higher education in most of the world today but one must accept that conceptually it is more appropriate to think of higher education in broader terms as an advanced phase in the exploration and transmission of knowledge in a *formal* system of education which is structured in phases. The emphasis on *formal* is important, because formal education as a social institution is what social scientists refer to and deal with when they analyse, reflect upon, or research into education. Education outside the formal system figures in this discourse only to the extent that it is relevant to the discussion of the formal system.

The Emergence of Formal Education

In simple societies, the conservation, advance, and transmission of knowledge proceeds informally within the family and the community. But as societies advance, knowledge expands and grows too large, complex, and specialized to be dealt with informally, and is thus organized into a formal system (Halsey et al. 1997).

The history of civilization reveals a fairly uniform pattern in the emergence of formal education as a social institution. Knowledge that addresses questions about life and death, about the power of the elements, about divinity and creation is the first to be formally organized. Esoteric in character, such knowledge generally originates with religious bodies or with the priesthood. Initially considered to be sacred and mystical, it gradually grows into a rich diversity of secular fields such as philosophy, mathematics, dialectics, grammar, and astronomy. Meanwhile the practices, procedures, rules, regulations, roles, relationships, and modes of behaviour involved in the conservation, advance, and transmission of this knowledge are shaped into a well-defined system and are firmly established as a social institution (Clark 1983).

While knowledge pertaining to some fields is thus formally organized, a vast body of knowledge, particularly pertaining to daily life continues to be informally conserved and nurtured in the crafts, trades and occupations that people practise, and by the values, beliefs, and customs that order their lives. This knowledge is transmitted informally in the family, at the workplace, and in the community. With the advance of civilization, this too grows in scale and complexity. When it can no longer be dealt with informally, occupational organizations, such as guilds, take on its responsibility. Thus a separate stream of organized knowledge administered by a well-established body is constituted, but is yet not recognized as formal education (Apple 1982).

In most societies, the advanced level of knowledge in this stream eventually merges with the advanced level in the formal stream to produce a more comprehensive system of higher education. The emergence of universities in medieval Europe is one of the best examples of this phenomenon (Clark 1983).

The Forces that Shape Systems of Education

The development of informal education into a formal system in a society and its subsequent growth and diversification are stimulated and shaped by demands and pressures from several quarters, (Bourdieu 1998) for instance by the demands of religious bodies; by the requirements of the state; by the exigencies of government; by the pressures exercised by the social and political elite; by the system of social stratification prevalent in a society; by the needs of the economy, and of trade and commerce; by political and social movements, philosophies, and ideologies; even by demographic changes in the composition of the population. The education system in turn affects and strongly influences many aspects of life in the society in which it functions. Its impact is strongest on the economy, the state, and the politics of governance, on social hierarchies and on the system of social stratification, on equations of power, and on the values and beliefs by which people live (Apple 1982).

The history of the growth and diversification of education in a society is essentially the history of the interaction between education and these other forces, whose predominance differs from society to society (Kemper and Williams 1996). Within the same society, they differ from one point of time to another and their impact may vary from one level of education to another. Above all, although the forces that shape education are the same in all societies, the nature and outcome of their interplay can be very different. In order to understand higher education as a social institution, it is necessary to understand this interplay, to identify the factors in the interplay, to locate the conflicts and contradictions in the pressures exercised by the different factors, to identify the choices or compromises made, and to trace how all this has influenced the objectives, organization and functioning of higher education (see Altbach 1991). The following overview of higher education in India over the period since the first formal system was in operation around 1000 BC attempts this task very briefly. The 3000-year period, during which higher education has functioned as a social institution in the country, has been divided into three periods namely the pre-colonial, colonial, and post-Independence periods, for convenience of discussion and presentation.

Higher Education in Pre-colonial India
Brahmanical Higher Education (Established in c. 1000 BC)

The Brahmanical system of higher education was the earliest system of higher education in India (Keay 1942). It is best understood in the context of the Hindu religious belief in the transmigration of souls and of knowledge as liberation. According to this belief, the soul is an immutable spark of the Divine, transmigrating through different forms of life, in a painful cycle of life and death. Spiritual salvation consists of *mukti* or liberation of the soul from this cycle and its union with the Divine Absolute. It is believed that mukti can be achieved by living strictly according to *dharma*, an ordering of life by which the individual's social, economic, and political obligations are prescribed in terms of a finely orchestrated system of ideals, practices, and conduct to be followed in the different spheres of daily life. Alternately, it can be achieved by acquiring *jnana* or knowledge of the whole truth, believed to be available in the four Vedas, mystically revealed to seers, and orally transmitted across generations.

Brahmanical higher education was structured around the study of the Vedas. Minimally, learning consisted of the memorization of the Vedas. But at a higher level, scholars searched for the meaning of these Vedas through reflection. Thus Brahmanical knowledge advanced. For instance, the quest for answers to questions regarding the universe and man's place in it led to the development of logic, philosophy, and astronomy just as ethics and law developed in the effort to define right and wrong. The attempt to understand the texts as well as the emphasis on grammar, philosophy, and etymology protected them from corruption in the process of oral transmission. Understanding and caring for the body as the abode of the soul led to the development of medicine, while mythology and legends evolved in connection with the explanation of ritual. The elaborate rules for the construction of altars for sacrifices, as specified in the Vedas, led to the development of geometry and algebra; and the desire to find propitious times for sacrifices gave rise to astrology and astronomy.

In the organization of Vedic learning, the basic unit was a teacher or *guru* and his students or *chelas,* residing in the *ashram* or home of the guru and his family. Here, under the close personal care of the guru, the shishyas not only studied the Vedas but also were firmly socialized into the values of society and its ways of life. They were not charged any fees but were expected to serve their guru and ashram in every way. Respect for the teacher, amounting to worship, was one of the cardinal principles of Brahmanical education. The shishya lived with his guru from the age of 8, for about twelve years. At the end of twelve years, most students entered the next stage of life as defined by dharma, that is *grihasthashram* or the stage of the householder. But some chose to study further, with the same teacher, or with another teacher, or at one of the universities.

Taxila (1000 BC), one of the most famous centres of Brahmanical higher education, is a good illustration of a Brahmanical university. It was a conglomeration of independent ashrams, offering different specializations. It generally took a student eight years to cover any one of the several specializations offered. While single ashrams, and conglomerations such as Taxila constituted the backbone of the Brahmanical system of higher education, there were other institutions such as *sabhas*, *sanghas*, and *parishads* that strengthened the system. The sabha was a conference of learned scholars, occasionally invited by the king as part of important celebrations. Invited scholars were expected to present their views, to debate the views of others, and to deliver discourses. Scholars from all parts of the country came to these sabhas. Some of the most critical advances in Vedic knowledge were made at these gatherings. The sanghas were assemblies where scholars themselves came together to share ideas and knowledge and to sharpen, discuss, and contest viewpoints. Parishads were settlements of learned Brahmins. They gave decisions on all issues connected with religion and learning (Keay 1942).

Initially, access to education in the Brahmanical system was available to all the four *varnas*—Brahmins, Kshatriyas, Vaishyas, and Shudras. Only the Chandalas—people conquered by the Aryans and considered to be outside the varna system—were excluded. Women were freely admitted. But by 500 BC, women were excluded and caste discrimination set in.

Buddhist Higher Education (Established in c. AD 400)

Like the Hindus, the Buddhists too believe in the doctrine of the reincarnation of the soul, and in the cycle of birth and death as bondage. But, whereas Hinduism prescribed *dharma* and *jnana-yoga* as avenues to the liberation of the soul, Buddha preached that those who seek liberation must, from the outset, renounce the world to live a life of meditation and philanthropic work as *bhikkus* and *bhikkunis* (mendicants). For this, he suggested that they live in monasteries or *viharas*. These viharas were responsible for the education of all Buddhists, religious as well as lay. Some viharas such as Nalanda (AD 425–1205), Vikramshila (AD 800–1203), and Valabhi (AD 600–1200) grew to be renowned centres of higher education (Keay 1942).

The structure of the Buddhist system of education was very similar to the Brahmanical systems. However, the range of disciplines offered in the former was far more diverse and the methods of teaching were more interactive. Admission was open to all, including women. Instruction was provided in several languages. In keeping with the Buddha's teaching, an effort was made to ensure that relationships within the vihara were democratic.

The major advances of the Buddhist system of higher education over the Brahmanical were its diversity, scale, reach, and highly sophisticated organization. For instance, it is mentioned that 10,000 monks resided at Nalanda. Of these, 1510 were teachers and 8500 were students. Students and monks came from as far off as Burma, Sri Lanka, Java, Sumatra, and China. Organizing for such large communities of scholars was a major task. So too was the provision of a diversity of disciplines, and the operationalization of equality. Organizational and administrative challenges also came from the fact that the viharas were enormously well endowed with splendid buildings, lands, orchards, and other forms of wealth (Keay 1942).

Mohammedan Higher Education (Established in c. AD 1174)

Mohammedan education arrived in India with Mohammeddan rule, from the centres of Islamic learning in Central Asia and the Middle East. It was provided through *maktabs* (schools) and *madrassahs* (institutions for higher education) generally attached to mosques. The courses taught at the madrassahs included Arabic, Persian, grammar, rhetoric, logic, theology, astronomy, metaphysics, philosophy, literature, jurisprudence, and science. The medium of instruction was Persian. But all students were required to study Arabic.

It is claimed that never in the history of India did art and literature, science and philosophy, and industry and commerce flourish quite as they did during the reign of the Mugals (AD 1526–1707). There is evidence to prove that technical knowledge and skills, in the production of textiles, jewellery, stone inlay, carving, woodwork, carpets, and other goods for which India was renowned, were highly advanced. So too were knowledge and skills in horticulture, architecture, and engineering. However, it is not known precisely how much of this was developed in the madrassahs and how much in the *karkhanas* or factories and guilds (Naik 1951).

Physically distanced from centres of Mohammedan learning in Central Asia and the Middle East, and affected by the fact that its patrons were continuously engaged in war, Mohammedan education in India remained weak. Meanwhile neglected, and often rejected by Mohammedan rulers,

Brahmanical and Buddhist education declined under Mohameddan rule. Thus, despite its proud history, indigenous higher learning was in a poor state when the British arrived in India at the dawn of the seventeenth century.

Higher Education in the Colonial Period
Establishment and Growth
Schools

The charter for trade with India was first granted to the East India Company in the year 1600, without the British government imposing any civic or religious responsibilities on the Company. But when the Company's charter was renewed in 1698, it carried a clause requiring the Company to maintain schools for the education of the children of its English and Anglo-Indian employees.

About the same time that the Company was charged with this responsibility, Christian mission schools were beginning to provide education for the children of Indians converted to Christianity. Firmly convinced that if Indians were taught the European language and introduced to English culture they would be drawn to Christianity, the missionaries also regarded these schools as instruments of conversion. The Hindu elite, initially reluctant to send their children to missionary schools, gave in as they realized that proficiency in the English language and acquaintance with European culture were vital to acquiring jobs in the British administration and to gain access to the social circles of the rulers. Later they launched parallel efforts and started their own schools (Dharampal 1983).

Colleges

Towards the end of the eighteenth century, the important Amending Act of 1781 forced the Company to take active initiative in the promotion of higher education. Prior to the passing of this Act, the Supreme Court in India had administered the English Civil Law, which often ran counter to the Hindu and Mohammedan religions. The Act attempted to remedy the situation with the requirement that 'inheritance and succession to lands, rents, and goods and all matter of contracts should be determined by Hindu and Mohammedan laws and usages' (Nurullah and Naik 1951: 66). To implement this Amendment, English judges needed assistants who could clarify and explain to them Hindu and Mohammedan law. In 1781, the Calcutta Madrassah was founded with the specific objective of providing Arabic and Persian education aimed at producing experts to clarify Mohammedan laws. In 1791, the Benares Sanskrit College was established with the objective of producing experts to clarify Hindu laws. As these two colleges flourished, they produced well-trained experts to advise British judges. Further, demonstrating that the Company was willing to provide higher education to equip Indians for important positions in the government (Dongerkery 1967), they also generated confidence in the Company's rule—an additional bonus.

Meanwhile, in response to the steadily mounting demand for European education at a higher level (Basu 1974), some of the schools run by missionaries as well as a few run by natives were developing into colleges. The Directors and the Officers of the Company could see that the European education provided by such institutions cultivated deep appreciation of the European culture and indirectly nurtured loyalty to British rule. Thus, when at the time of the renewal of the Company's Charter in 1813, the British government laid down the requirement that

> a sum of not less than one lakh of rupees each year shall be set apart and applied to the revival and improvement of the literature and the encouragement of the learned natives of India, and for the introduction and promotion of knowledge of science among the inhabitants of the British territories in India [Nurullah and Naik 1951: 66].

the Directors were more than willing to comply.

Controversies

Unfortunately there were four bitter controversies over how this directive was to be implemented.

Christian Missionaries

The first controversy was about whether Christian missionaries should be encouraged as educators or not. Initially the company had been appreciative of missionary activities in India and had supported missionaries. But, emboldened by the fact that Indians were reaching out to the education they offered, missionaries had become openly critical of the culture and the morals of the Hindus. After the Company acquired political power over India in 1765, some Directors of the Company in Britain and several of its officers in India were seriously worried that this would antagonize the Hindu elite and destroy their goodwill so essential to British commerce and political authority. They therefore advised the Company to withdraw its support to the missionaries and to adopt a policy of religious neutrality. However, other Directors and Officers firmly believed that reform through conversion to Christianity was urgently needed, and advocated support for the missionaries. Both points of view had strong lobbies in India and in Britain.

European Knowledge and Culture

The second major controversy, known as the controversy between the Anglicists and the Orientalists, centred on the value of indigenous learning vis-à-vis European learning. In 1792, in his *Observations on the State of Society among the Asiatic Subjects of Great Britain*, Charles Grant, who later, in 1805, became Chairman of the East India Company, remarked that Indians were ignorant and that their morals were in bad shape. He advised the communication of 'our European light and knowledge to them' to remedy this situation (Nurullah and Naik 1951: 60). Many others endorsed this view. For instance, Macaulay observed that 'a single shelf of a good European library was worth the whole native literature of India and Arabia' (quoted in Nurullah and Naik 1951: 105–7). On the whole Macaulay's minute conveys the impression that he wanted to create a class of people who would be 'Indians in blood and colour, but English in tastes, in opinions, morals and in intellect'. Some Directors of the Company did not accept this view. Several of its officers had genuine admiration for indigenous knowledge and culture. No less a person than Lord Minto, who was Governor General from 1806 to 1813, believed that Europe had a great deal to learn from India. Others like Munro in the province of Madras, Elphinstone in the province of Bombay, and Adam in the province of Bengal conducted surveys to validate and substantiate their opinion that although indigenous learning had visibly decayed and deteriorated, it had been of outstanding quality and deserved to be restored.

The Medium of Instruction

The third major controversy centred on the medium of instruction. Sanskrit, Arabic, and Persian, the three classical languages, together with the several vernacular languages spoken by the people, were used in indigenous schools (Dharampal 1983). In order to establish rapport with the people, the missionaries used the vernacular languages as the medium of instruction in their schools. A section of the Company's officials believed that this practice should continue. Another section believed that instruction should be through Sanskrit, Arabic, and Persian. But Englishmen like Grant, firmly committed to the propagation of European culture, insisted upon English (Kumar 1991).

Downward Filtration

The fourth major controversy concerned the quantum of education to be made available to Indians. Taking their cue from the situation at home in Britain, where education was being extensively promoted as an instrument for the alleviation of poverty, for the development of the economy, and for overall advance, officers like Adam advocated schooling for the Indian masses. But many officers feared that education provided so liberally would generate ideas of freedom and destabilize British rule. Others, who did not necessarily share this fear, subscribed to what has come to be known as the 'downward filtration theory' (Nurullah and Naik 1951: 181–5). They argued that there was no need to invest in the education of the masses because the benefits of education provided to the elite would trickle down to the masses anyway.

Resolution of the Controversies

These controversies, which had been brewing from the middle of the eighteenth century, were resolved only in 1854, when the Directors of the Company declared their decision on the four controversial issues in the context of their statement of the Company's policy on education in India. Their decision, communicated to the Company's officers in a document which has come to be known as the Wood's Despatch of 1854, may be summed up as follows:

1. Indigenous learning was not to be dismissed. On the contrary, its value and its continued relevance in some areas such as the administration of law was to be recognized. But the policy for British education in India would be to promote European learning.

2. Instruction was to be provided in English as well as in the vernacular languages. But the importance of the English language, both as an instrument for access to European knowledge as well as an instrument of administration, was to be emphasized.

3. Missionary schools were to continue to receive grants and Inspecting Officers were 'to take no notice' of the doctrines taught at these schools. But the schools owned and managed by the Company's government in India were to be strictly secular.

4. The idea of educating the masses was to be abandoned in favour of the downward filtration policy.

The Despatch contained policy recommendations on a variety of other issues. Among some of the most important of these were that women's education should be encouraged and that universities should be established for higher education in India (Nurullah and Naik 1951: 159–62; 170–7).

Growth of European Education and Decline of the Indigenous System

Despite the controversies, European education had grown steadily by the time of the Wood's Despatch in 1854. This growth was the result of a combination of at least six different factors. These were: a deep commitment on the part of the British government to do its duty by India; the active involvement of missionaries in education; the demand for European education by Indians who saw it as the means to their personal advance and prosperity; the keen interest taken by public-spirited Indians in providing facilities for education so as to enable Indians to advance; the Company's need to have educated Indians to assist with its administration; and the conviction on the part of the Company's managers that by promoting European culture through European education in India the Company could build loyalty to British rule. During the same period indigenous knowledge and education decayed and receded into insignificance. Indigenous schools were consciously replaced by schools that provided European learning. The Company did provide some support to Hindu and Muslim scholars, but not in the manner or on the scale required to maintain the quality and growth of indigenous scholarship. Indigenous knowledge and skills in fields such as engineering, architecture, textiles, or medicine which were highly advanced and which had flourished for centuries, withered as the British relied exclusively on European knowledge and skills (Dharampal 1983). Impressed by European science and technology, fascinated by European political and social philosophies, and conscious of its advantages for personal advance, Indians increasingly opted for European education in preference to the indigenous system. This was the climate when in 1857, following upon the recommendations in Wood's Despatch, the Company established the first three universities for European higher education in India at Bombay, Calcutta, and Madras.

British Universities in India

Structurally, these three British Universities were modelled after London University. As affiliating universities, they were exclusively examining and certifying bodies and did not carry any responsibility for teaching or for research. Teaching was conducted at colleges affiliated to the universities. The universities set down the conditions for admission to affiliated colleges, defined the courses to be taught, conducted examinations, evaluated students, and awarded diplomas and degrees.

These universities, however, did not offer the same range of disciplines or courses that were available at London University. They were only designed to offer some courses in European science and concentrated on Arts and the Humanities. In 1858, a year after the establishment of these universities, India passed from the Company to the Crown and the Company's government was replaced by the British government in India. Driven by its own needs, the British government did establish some facilities for higher education in medicine, engineering, teacher training, and law. A few technical institutions such as the School of Mining at Dhanbad were also established. But there was no effort to advance technical and technological education or to provide facilities for postgraduate education or research. Students, who aspired to an advanced education, were expected to go to Britain for further studies. Moreover, the governance of universities was not in the hands of scholars and academics. Rather, university authorities and governing bodies were constituted to ensure an adequate representation of members who could monitor and check the administration of the university on behalf of the British government.

No True Universities

These inadequacies did not remain unnoticed. For instance, in a carefully argued indictment that the Indian universities were not true universities, the report of the Calcutta University Commission (1902) pointed out that these universities did not carry responsibility for teaching or research, nor did they allow the colleges to perform these functions adequately. It complained that the closely defined syllabi and the manner in which examinations were structured left teachers very little space to be creative and did not allow students freedom to explore. The Commission also criticized the close control exercised over the universities by the government. But despite this criticism and constant pressure from the public to improve standards, very little was done to change the structure of universities. In fact the inadequacies pointed out by the Commission in 1902 remained till the end of British rule.

Voluntary Effort

Continuous public pressure on the government for the expansion of facilities for higher education as well as for improvement of existing facilities was among the most distinctive features of public life in British India. Although the Company neglected the demand for improvement of facilities, it did establish some new universities. By the time the British relinquished control over the country, there were twenty-five universities. However, the more notable achievement of public involvement in higher education was the establishment of voluntary effort and strong voluntary bodies dedicated to higher education—for instance the Bombay Native Society, the Servants of India Society, or the Deccan Education Society. Voluntary effort led to the establishment of several women's colleges including the S.N.D.T. Women's University, Benares Hindu University, Aligarh Muslim University, Vishwa Bharati, Jamia Millia, and institutions such as the Institute of Science at Bangalore and the Tata Institute of Social Sciences at Bombay. It is significant that the British government refused to 'recognize' some of these institutions.

Impact of Nationalism

As Indian nationalism burgeoned, nationalists resented the fact that the British government was holding back the growth of education in India (Naik 1981), particularly technical and technological education, essential for the country's industrial and economic advance. They acknowledged that British education was valuable and that it had brought western knowledge and science to India. They recognized that by introducing educated Indians to the social and political history and philosophies of western civilization, British education had laid the foundation for the nationalist movement for self-rule. But there was anger and unhappiness over the fact that it had destroyed indigenous learning, severed the links between formal education and the lives and occupations of the masses, neglected the vernacular languages, distanced educated Indians from their own culture, and thus struck Indian civilization at its roots.

Not unexpectedly, the establishment of a fully equipped system of higher education which would lead India on to industrialization and economic development to facilitate social and political development, have a symbiotic relationship with the country's culture, be responsive to its needs, and which would accept every deserving Indian who aspired to higher education was high on the nationalist agenda for the tasks to be taken up after Independence (Kumar 1991; Naik 1981).

Higher Education in Independent India
Basic Responsibilities

Planners for higher education in independent India organized the nationalist agenda into three basic responsibilities: first, to gear higher education to function effectively as an instrument of economic, social, and political development; second, to promote excellence, develop a world-class system of higher education, and liberate India from dependence on the developed countries for its higher education needs; third, to ensure full and equal opportunities for higher education (Association of Indian Universities 1995). The objectives of higher education in independent India have been redefined in terms of these responsibilities. The university system has been expanded massively and new institutions have been set up to ensure that the country is self-sufficient in higher education and fully equipped to meet the country's manpower development and training needs (Government of India 1986). Mechanisms have been set up to monitor excellence and quality and special policies and programmes have been instituted to ensure equality of educational opportunity. The government of independent India has invested heavily in all these efforts. Prior to Independence, the government's share of expenditure on higher education was roughly 58 per cent. Now, fifty-five years after Independence, it is estimated at more than 90 per cent.

New Objectives

As an instrument of development, higher education in independent India is expected to develop knowledge, skills, and the technically and technologically trained manpower required for the country's economic growth and for the advance and modernization of its services in different fields. As an instrument of social development, it is expected to promote rationality, to facilitate equality, and to inculcate secularism. As an instrument of political development (Hebsur 1997), it is expected to bring about national integration and contribute to the internalization of attitudes, values, and behaviour required to equip people to function as responsible citizens of an independent democratic nation. To meet the commitments to excellence and self-sufficiency, the system is expected to (a) bridge the knowledge and skill gap acquired from being confined to the needs of a colonial society, and (b) leap forward so as to be in the step with higher education in the developed countries. To promote equality of opportunities for education, it is expected to provide ample facilities and to ensure that access to these facilities is liberal and equal. It is significant that almost all these objectives are opposed to the objectives of higher education in British India (Chitnis and Altbach 1998).

Expansion and Upgradation Facilities

Affiliating universities, of the kind established by the British, continue to be the backbone of the system. But these have been enlarged in size, multiplied in number, and diversified to cover the full range of the academic universities. Thus an agricultural university has been set up in each state.

Further, in order to ensure that the country produces world-class manpower and becomes self-sufficient in higher education, a series of special national-level apex institutions have been set up in the fields of engineering, technology, management, medicine, and law. Many of these are 'deemed' to be universities. Small in size and well funded, some of these have been developed in consultation with experts from the developed countries and are in close and active collaboration with some of the best-known institutions in the same fields in these countries. Bodies such as the University Grants Commission, the All-India Council of Technical Education, and the Accreditation Council have been set up to monitor standards and to coordinate the growth of universities. Special advisory committees are regularly appointed as required.

Outside the university system there are a series of prestigious institutions for highly specialized research. These include the Council for Scientific and Industrial Research, the Indian Council for Agricultural Research, the Indian Council for Medical Research, the Indian Council for Social Science Research, and the Indian Council for Historical Research. More than a hundred research laboratories are run or supported by these bodies. They also support research projects and provide scholarships and fellowships to individual scholars. Apart from these Councils, these are several 'National Institutes' for a rich diversity of fields, ranging from

1046   THE OXFORD INDIA COMPANION TO SOCIOLOGY AND SOCIAL ANTHROPOLOGY

community development to immunology. Finally, there is a range of 'recognized' industrial and technical institutes and polytechnics that offer students certificate- and diploma-level courses on the completion of secondary school (10 years) or after higher secondary school (12 years).

Provisions for Equality of Educational Opportunity

Access to higher education has generally been facilitated by providing instruction in the vernacular languages, by keeping fees low and by setting up extensive facilities for distance education. There are scholarships for those who are economically disadvantaged. Special provisions have been made for the education of the Scheduled Castes (former untouchable castes), Scheduled Tribes, and women, the three categories identified as 'weaker sections' of society in the constitution of the country. The former have a quota of 'reserved' admissions in every institution of higher education in the country. They are also provided with special scholarships, hostel accommodation, and assistance for the purchase of books, etc. There are no reserved admissions for women, but the establishment of women's colleges and hostels for women students is firmly encouraged. Several states offer tuition waivers to women students. Departments of women's studies have been established at several universities.

Towards National Integration and Responsible Citizenship

Programmes such as the National Social Service, the Adult Education Programme, National Cadet Corps, and Extension Education have been established at universities with a view to involving students in social service and developing qualities essential for responsible citizenship. In order to promote national integration through higher education, universities are provided with funding to organize cultural festivals and sports meets which bring students from different universities in the country together. Prior to Independence, school and college education was organized differently in different parts of the country. In the interests of integration, it is now structured to run uniformly through a fifteen-year course consisting of ten years of schooling up to the completion of secondary school, two years for the completion of higher secondary school, and three years for the first degree.

Returns

The system of higher education in the country has yielded substantial returns, as it now produces all the manpower needed to serve industry and for services such as health care, communications, and transport. India is no longer dependent on higher education in the developed countries.

On the contrary, students from some of the other developing countries come to India for post-secondary school education. Products of Indian universities compete successfully for jobs in the international employment market. However, there are serious inadequacies. By way of illustration, some of the most disturbing are briefly described now.

Inadequacies

Inability to Satisfy the Demand for Admissions

When India acquired Independence in 1947, there were twenty-five universities, 700 colleges, and 105,000 students. The latest statistics available from the University Grants Commission (1996) show 225 universities/ university-level institutions, 8613 colleges, and 6,114,000 students. Today, India has the second largest system of higher education in the world. Despite this impressive growth of facilities it is not possible to accommodate all those who seek admission. This is because the demand for higher education has exploded exponentially.

While the system of higher education struggles to cope with this situation, the government is under pressure to reduce its funding for higher education in favour of primary education. This is because the task of the universalization of primary school education, meant to be accomplished by 1961, still remains incomplete. Those who press for further expansion of facilities for higher education point out that barely 6 per cent of the population in the relevant age group pursues higher education in India as against 25 per cent in Europe and roughly 75 per cent in North America. They demand education as their right and also point out that bodies such as the World Bank advise that further growth of higher education is critical to development.

Deterioration of Standards and the Operation of Vested Interests

Having stretched their facilities to accommodate this demand, universities and other institutions for post-secondary school education have become examination-driven diploma- and degree-vending machines. The knowledge and skills they provide have very little relevance to the country's development needs. With competing demands for its resources, the government is not in a position to provide the funds required to improve the quality of education and make it more relevant.

Privatization

Privatization in the sense of free enterprise in higher education is being seriously considered as an alternative (Tilak 1991). To a limited extent, privatization is in operation. But the government is unwilling to allow private enterprise to expand for fear that, left to market forces, the quality of education will deteriorate further, that it will become unaffordable, and that there will be sharp unevenness in facilities, rendering opportunities unequal. To an extent, these fears are valid. Already, 'education barons' run substandard colleges and use political leverage to get by (Kaul 1993). Yet private initiative and cooperative enterprise were primarily responsible for the advance of higher education in pre-Independence times. It is possible that there is something in the present functioning of the system that discourages honest, committed private enterprise and allows corrupt private bodies with vested interests to thrive. Meanwhile it is evident that the government itself has developed strong vested interests in higher education. And it is therefore also possible that the government is lukewarm towards the idea of privatization because it is unwilling to relinquish its own control over higher education (Singh 1991).

Inability to Function Fully as Instrument of Economic Growth

By far the greatest problem, however, is the unsatisfactory match between higher education and the needs of the economy (Shukla and Kaul 1998). University graduates are very well equipped to work in the urban, westernized, modern sector of the economy. They are able to compete successfully for employment in developed countries. But they are not similarly equipped to serve the traditional sector of the country's economy consisting of agriculture, farming, animal husbandry, fishing, forestry, the traditional trades, crafts, and services. This sector accounts for almost 70 per cent of the economy (Blaugh 1969).

This inadequacy can be traced to the British policy of isolating higher education from indigenous life. Thus isolated, institutions of higher education in India never developed the symbiotic relationship with the indigenous occupations required to respond to the needs of an economy (Singh and Sharma 1988, 1989). After Independence, when the decision to continue with and build upon the system of higher education inherited from the British was taken, the implications of this were not considered or addressed seriously. It was somewhat simplistically assumed that just as industries were to be set up with the help of transferred technology, advanced knowledge, technologies, and skills could be brought in from the developed countries and applied to help the traditional sector advance. But experience now indicates that technologies borrowed from countries that are highly advanced are often inappropriate for the level at which the traditional sectors stand. They have to be adapted or new appropriate technologies developed.

For this, or for that matter even to transfer technology, it is necessary to interact with people in this sector, to understand their skills and the technologies they use and the knowledge and beliefs by which they are guided and to find ways and means to link these with modern skills and knowledge. Over the course of the last two decades, some NGOs have succeeded in doing this. But, being inflexible in character and weighed down by the pressures of providing education to massive numbers, institutions for higher education are unable to respond to these challenges.

Other Problems

There are many other problems which include the bitter politicization of the policy of affirmative action on behalf of the Scheduled Castes and Scheduled Tribes (Chitnis 1984, 1986); the unionization of students, teachers, and administrative staff resulting in frequent strikes and protests that dislocate the system; bureaucracy, red tape, and the consequent inability to use existing resources optimally; political interference; corruption in the administration; the failure to develop indigenous course materials; the inability to conduct relevant research; and the tendency to depend upon the developed countries as leaders in knowledge. The most disturbing trend is that dissatisfied parents who are disillusioned with higher education in the country, send their children abroad for the first degree after completion of high school if they can afford to do so. This phenomenon is new. So too the fact that courses run by North American and European universities in India are in demand, despite being expensive. While this reflects the response of the users of higher education, a fair answer to the more basic question as to whether the system of higher education in post-Independence India has served the country satisfactorily, possibly is that the failures of the system are balanced by its successes.

The Colonial Heritage and Pressures of Development

Since the success and failure of higher education in independent India are generally measured against the performance of higher education in the developed countries of Europe and North America, it is important to understand how higher education has served these civilizations. It is also necessary to recognize how the context and the challenges for higher education in India are different from those in Europe or North America. The point may be illustrated with reference to higher education as an instrument of economic development and as an instrument of equality for women.

Higher Education and Economic Development

Prior to the Industrial Revolution, engineering and technology were not given much importance at European and North American universities. In fact these disciplines were often located outside universities, in polytechnics or technical institutes. However, as industrialization advanced and economic growth became increasingly dependent on a high level of knowledge and skills in engineering and technology, universities responded by developing these disciplines as well as other pertinent fields such as management studies. They took on the responsibility to generate the knowledge needed to sustain the advance of technology and management and to produce the specialized manpower required.

Since the dawn of the post-Second World War period, this process has acquired a new dimension. Education is now charged with responsibility for what is referred to as 'human capital formation' or 'human resource development'. This task is guided by the assumption that in every society there is a limited pool of individuals with a high level of intelligence, spread across all sectors of society. These talented individuals have to be selected and equipped with knowledge and skills, and promoted to run the engines of industrial growth. The others have to be suitably educated to serve as white-collar or blue-collar workers and supervisors. In the context of the doctrine of economic nationalism, it is believed that the prosperity of a nation depends on how well its system of education performs this task.

Now that economic nationalism is being replaced by globalization, fresh challenges have appeared (Gulati 1993; Mahanti et al. 1993). As technologies advance rapidly, the demand for highly specialized skills is steadily making way for more flexible capabilities that can adapt to rapid technological change. With the growth of powerful multinationals and the revolution in communications, the bureaucratic paradigm of organizational efficiency is being replaced by an entrepreneurial one. It is not enough that managers at the top are educated to be good administrators. They must be equipped to be innovators and leaders. Workers and supervisors must be equipped for teamwork. Education is expected to socialize all categories suitably.

From the beginning of the nineteenth century onwards, higher education in Europe and North America has thus steadily responded to and served the emerging knowledge and manpower needs of the economy. Its structural differentiation and internal functioning are so well tuned to economic growth that its relationship with the economy almost seems to be organic.

Faced with the difficult task of advancing the country's poor and backward economy to a level that would support an independent nation, planners for independent India decided to industrialize. They recognized that industrialization could only be achieved by borrowing technology as well as methods for the organization of production and for the management of business from the developed countries of Europe and North America. But they believed that after an initial period of development with help from these countries, India would be fully capable of advance on its own.

Education, particularly higher education, was charged with the responsibility of the provision of suitably trained manpower, and for the transfer as well as generation of knowledge required for the country to keep pace and compete with technological advances in the developed countries of the world. It was recognized that the university system inherited from the British was altogether inadequate for these responsibilities. It was strengthened with restructuring on the lines of courses offered at universities in the developed countries and with the establishment of special institutions for education in science and technology and for research, closely modelled after some of the best institutions of higher education in developed countries.

Thus equipped, higher education in independent India is expected to develop, within a few decades, knowledge and capabilities of a quality and level that the developed countries have reached through a process that has stretched over two centuries. This is difficult enough. But the task has become even more difficult because of the 'massification' of higher education, the burden of the policy of reservations, and the inadequacy of resources to maintain and upgrade facilities as needed. Above all, after more than a century of isolation from indigenous life and culture, it is proving to be extremely difficult for higher education to link with the economy in the manner required. The situation is further complicated by the fact that different sectors of the Indian economy are at different levels of growth, along a spectrum that stretches from simple food gathering and primitive agriculture to highly sophisticated industry and globalization. To satisfy the demands of development, higher education must simultaneously serve all these different levels of economic growth.

Educating Women for Equality

Experience obtained from the effort to use education as an instrument of equality for women illustrates another facet of the difficulties encountered, that is, the weight of tradition and the limitations to using policy and planned programmes as instruments of change (Blumberg 1980). In India the commitment to promote the education of women is not new. Over the course of the last two centuries, it has been inspired by several different concerns. However, the expectation that education must be used as an instrument to advance their equality is fairly recent (Chitnis 1989).

The history of education in India reveals that schooling for women was established in the nineteenth century. From the outset of the century, Christian missionaries had promoted the education of women with the idea of taking Christianity into Indian homes. From the 1830s onwards, women's education was firmly supported by social reformers who considered it to be the most effective instrument with which to fight practices such as *sati*, female infanticide, child marriage and the oppression of widows. The Wood's Despatch of 1854 recommended it for the same reason. By the later half of the century, the western-educated elite supported it, considering it prestigious to educate the women in their families, and as this also improved their marriage prospects. Finally it was encouraged because of an experienced need for women teachers and nurses. The country produced its first woman graduate towards the close of the nineteenth century.

The twentieth century is marked by an advance of higher education. In 1916 Maharishi Karve, a bold social reformer, established India's first university for women. His ambition was to educate women to be economically independent and self-reliant. Karve's university flourished, though his concept of education for economic independence and self-reliance has only recently made headway. Close upon the establishment of the women's university, Mahatma Gandhi gave the higher education of women a new meaning when he advised young women keen to join the nationalist movement to concentrate on their education, so as to be equipped to serve the country after Independence. From the Second World War onwards, the continuous increase in the cost of living and the growing aspirations for better standards of life combined to make it necessary for women to earn, and for this, to pursue higher education.

Thus, by the time the country acquired independence, the value of providing women with higher education was well established. Nevertheless the constraints to both their education and their utilization of education were so strong and so many that women's education did not progress very far. In 1947 women constituted only 12.28 per cent of the enrolment in higher education, and were largely confined to the faculties of arts and the humanities.

In independent India, the higher education of women has, from the outset, been accorded high priority in planned development (Government of India 1959, 1966). The constitution of the country identifies women, together with the Scheduled Castes and Scheduled Tribes, as a weaker section of society. It promises special provisions for the advance of this section. As part of these provisions the Scheduled Castes and Scheduled Tribes are provided with a quota of reserved admissions for students in all government-aided institutions for higher education as well as reserved faculty and administrative positions. They are also provided with a host of other facilities ranging from fee waivers to special coaching.

Although there are no reservations for women as for the other two categories, the government has supported extensive establishment of women's colleges and women's hostels. There were only 300 colleges for women in 1965–6. Today there are 1146. Several states provide tuition waivers for the higher education of women. The commitment of the government to women's education is consistently affirmed and reaffirmed in government documents and statements. During the international women's decade, the University Grants Commission sanctioned thirty-five departments of women's studies at as many universities. It also established an advisory committee for women's studies. So did the Indian Council of Social Science Research.

Despite all their efforts, neither official statements nor government policies and programmes for the higher education of women explicitly emphasized the promotion of equality for women until the 1980s. From this point of view, it is significant that in the 1959 report of the National Committee on the Education of Women, a long discussion on equal education for women concludes with the statement that women are basically mothers and home-makers and that therefore equal does not mean identical. The emphasis on education since the 1980s as an instrument of equality for women is therefore all the more significant. It has been underlined in the Seventh Five Year Plan, as well as in the document which spells out the programme of action for the National Policy of Education (1986). In the Ninth Five Year Plan, the concept of education for empowerment and equality of women is central to the planning of higher education. It is interesting to assess the present situation against this background.

The simplest course is to look at whether women have equal access to higher education. The facts are not particularly impressive. In 1998, at the end of almost five decades after the country's First Five Year plan was put in operation in 1951, women constituted only 34.4 per cent of the total enrolment in higher education. However they now have a significant presence in all disciplines. Moreover the growth in their enrolment has been consistently larger than the growth in the enrolment of men—by 149 per cent in the decade of the 1950s; 79 per cent in the decade of the 1960s; 42 per cent in the decade of the 1970s; and 43 per cent in the decade of the 1980s.

For a more rigorous assessment it is necessary to examine whether education has enabled women to achieve equality of social, political, and economic status. In the absence of suitable data and indicators, this is not possible. But a 1994 University Grants Commission study of the women's studies centres that were set up with a view to empower women, offers some valuable pointers. The study shows that very few of these centres are successful. Most have withered away or are stagnant. This is because of several factors, including the rigidity of the university structure, and a lack of the understanding and expertise required to translate an ideological concern into courses and syllabi. The few centres that have succeeded, happen to be administered by academics who are feminist activists or who otherwise have close links with the women's movement. These findings are significant in that they bring to the fore the limitations of initiating change or establishing new values through policy measures and planned interventions alone.

In Europe and North America, the emergence of new values and ideals is generally accompanied by processes and movements that make space for their operationalization in different spheres of life, including education. Following this pattern, the ideology of equality for women first found expression in the feminist movement. This movement criticized higher education for being gender-biased; argued that women's experiences, perceptions, and conceptions are very different from those presented in the courses taught at universities; complained that the courses offered at universities lean towards the occupational preferences of men; and pointed out that universities are reluctant to admit women to some of their most prestigious courses. In response to this criticism, institutions of higher education in Europe and North America have been making conscious efforts to take cognizance of gender differences in interpretations and viewpoints, and to establish special departments for women's studies and to promote the access of women to courses/departments in which they are poorly represented.

At Indian universities, departments for women's studies were not established in response to any such process or movement for change. Rather, they were set up in the hope that they would stimulate change. This is what planned development is. But experience from efforts to use higher education as an instrument of economic development as well as experience from the effort to use it as an instrument of equality for women illustrates how difficult it is to institute change without supportive public opinion or movements. From this point of view it is interesting to look at India's system of higher education as an offshoot of an institution that originated in Europe, was implanted into India, and was then shaped by the forces of colonialism and the pressures of development.

REFERENCES

Aikara, J. 1994. *Sociology of Education Research in Sociology and Anthropology: Third Survey Monograph*. Indian Council for Social Science Research, New Delhi.

Altbach, P.G. 1991. *International Higher Education: An Encyclopaedia*. New York and London: Garland Publishing.

Apple, M.W. 1982. *Education and Power*. Boston and London: Ark Paperbacks.

Association of Indian Universities. 1995a. *Policies of Higher Education*. Delhi: Association of Indian Universities.

Association of Indian Universities. 1995b. *Higher Education in India*. Delhi: Association of Indian Universities.

Basu, A. 1974. *The Growth of Education and Political Development in India*. Delhi: Oxford University Press.

Blaugh, M. 1969. *The Causes of Graduate Unemployment in India*. London: The Penguin Press.

Blumberg, R.L. 1980. *India's Educated Women—Options and Constraints*. New Delhi: Hindustan Publishing Corporation.

Bourdieu, P. 1998. *Homo Academicus*. Cambridge: Polity.

Chitnis, S. 1984. 'Positive Discrimination in India with Reference to Education'. In R. Goldmann and J. Wilson, eds, *From Independence to Statehood*. 31–44. London: Frances Printer.

_____. 1986. 'Positive Discrimination and the Educational Advancement of the Scheduled Castes in India'. In D. Rothermund and J. Simon, eds, *Education and Integration of Ethnic Minorities*. 108–29. London: Frances Printer.

_____. 1989. 'India'. In Gail P. Kelly, ed., *International Handbook Of Women's Education*. 135–62. New York: Greenwood Press.

Chitnis, S. 1992. *Sociology of Education in Survey of Research in Sociological and Social Anthropology*. Delhi: Indian Council of Social Science Research.

Chitnis, S. and P.G. Altbach. 1992. *Higher Education Reform in India*. Experiences and Perspectives. New Delhi: Sage Publications.

Clark, B.R. 1983. *The Higher Education System: Academic Organization in Cross National Perspective*. Berkeley and Los Angeles: University of California Press.

Cormack, M.L. 1961. *She Who Rides a Peacock*. Bombay: Asia Publishing.

Dharampal. 1983. *The Beautiful Tree: Indigenous Indian Education in the Eighteenth Century*. New Delhi: Biblia Impex Pvt. Ltd.

Dongerkery, S.R. 1967. *University Education in India*. Mumbai: P.C. Manaktala & Sons Pvt. Ltd.

Encyclopaedia Britannica Macropaedia. 1974. 15th ed. Chicago: Encyclopaedia Britannica Inc.

Government of India. 1959. *Report of the National Committee on Women's Education*. New Delhi: Ministry of Education.

Government of India. 1966. *Report of the Education Commission: Education and National Development*. New Delhi: Ministry of Education.

Government of India. 1986. *Programme of Action. National Policy on Education*. New Delhi: Ministry of Human Resources Development.

Green, A. 1996. *Education, Globalization and Nation State*. London: Macmillan.

Gulati, R.R. 1993: 'India's Brain Drain to the USA'. *Current Science*. 59(4).

Halsey, A.K., H. Lauder, P. Brown, and A.S. Wells. 1997. *Education, Culture, Economy and Society*. London: Oxford University Press.

Hassan, M. 1998. *Knowledge Power and Educational Institutions*. New Delhi: Lotus Collection Pub. Roll Books.

Hebsur, K.S. 1997. *Social Intervention for Justice*. Mumbai: Publications Unit; Tata Institute of Social Sciences.

Husen, T. and N. Postelwaite, eds. 1985. *International Encyclopaedia of Education*. Oxford: Pergammon Press.

Kaul, R. 1993. *Caste, Class and Education: Politics of the Capitation Fee Phenomenon in Karnataka*. New Delhi: Sage Publications.

Keay, F.E. 1942. *Indian Education in Ancient and Later Times: An Inquiry into its Origin, Development and Ideals*. London: Oxford University Press.

Kemper, K. and G. William. 1996. *The Social Role of Higher Education: Comparative Perspectives*. New York and London: Garland Publishing.

Khadria, B. 1998. 'Divides of the Development': Underdevelopment Relationship in Higher Education and Policy for Brain Drain. In S. Shukla & R. Kaul, eds, *Education, Development and Underdevelopment*. 175–98. New Delhi: Sage Publications.

Kumar, K. 1991. *Political Agenda of Education: A Study of Colonialist and Nationalist Ideas*. Delhi: Sage Publications.

Mahanti, S. et al. 1995. *Scientific Communities and Brain Drain*. New Delhi: Gyan Publishing House.

Naik, J.P. 1951. *A History of Education in India*. Bombay: Macmillan & Co.

Nurullah, S. and J.P. Naik. 1962. *A Student's History of Education in India*. London: Macmillan & Co.

Pai Panandiker, V.A. 1997. *The Politics of Backwardness in Reservation Policy in India*. Delhi: Konark Publications Pvt. Ltd.

Perkins, J.A. 1996. *The University in Transition*. New Jersey: Princeton University Press.

Reza, M. and N. Malhotra. 1991. *Higher Education in India: A Comprehensive Bibliography*. New Delhi: Concept. Publishing House.

Shukla, S. and R. Kaul. 1998. *Education, Development and Underdevelopment*. New Delhi: Sage Publications.

Singh, A. and G.D. Sharma. 1988. *Higher Education in India in the Social Context*. Delhi: Konark Publications Pvt. Ltd..

———. 1989. *Higher Education in India in the Institutional Context*. New Delhi: Konark Publications Pvt. Ltd.

Singh, R.P. 1991. *Private Initiative and Public Policy in Education*. New Delhi: Neeta Prakashan.

Tilak, J.B.G. 1991: 'Privatization of Higher Education'. *Prospects*. 21(2):227–39.

———. 1990. *The Political Economy of Education in India: Comparative Education Centre*. New York: SUNY Buffalo.

7

The Personal Sphere and
Its Articulation

The study of family and kinship has been central to the disciplines of sociology and social anthropology. The delineation of these areas as a specialized field of study in the nineteenth century was the invention of legal scholars. Hence the earliest concerns in kinship studies were about defining how biological relations were differentially coded in different societies to define rights and duties, privileges and obligations. Kinship was seen as an important marker of the type of society within the evolutionary paradigm of the nineteenth century. The earliest studies of kinship and marriage in India bore the mark of the political context of colonialism—translation of classical legal texts provided a framework for determining the 'personal laws' of the Hindus and the Muslims. At the same time recording of customary rules for determining such matters as systems of land tenure, rules of inheritance, and types of marriage, built an archive which came to be regarded by many as the foundation for the understanding of these institutions in India. The chapters in this section provide an understanding of the formal structure of kinship and marriage in India. But they also reconfigure the field of kinship by showing how the normativity of family (understood as heterosexual coupling closely tied to concerns of reproduction) may have obscured the critiques of family on the one hand, and different ways of defining the texture of relations that define personhood, on the other.

The subtitle of Patricia Uberoi's paper on the family (*Beyond the Nuclear versus Joint Debate*) gestures towards the way in which the study of family in India was tied for a long time to the discussion on the disappearance of the joint family. Seen as a marker of the Indian, and especially the Hindu, society in the colonial archive, the obsession with the significance of the so-called decline of the joint family haunts sociological and anthropological writings as well as debates in the public sphere even today. (on this point see also Lawrence Cohen in the previous section). Uberoi tries to show the ways in which the discourse on the family gets formulated and dispersed on different sites—such as that of politics and popular culture. The normativity of the family is further interrogated in Malavika Karlekar's paper on domestic violence which shows that the very norms through which heterosexual normative behaviour is regulated are also the ones which become the source of gendered violence as evidenced in practices such as immolation of widows or burning of brides. It is intriguing that while some influential scholars in the West, especially those interested in practices of gay kinship, have critiqued traditional kinship, studies for ignoring sexualities which are oriented not towards reproduction but towards annihilation of the self, the chapters by Uberoi and Karlekar show that gendered death has always been intricately woven into the fabric of kinship.

Margaret Trawick takes up the question of the way personhood is defined outside the sphere of family. The normativity of the heterosexual family is not critiqued in India through the formation of political identities around other sexualities (such as the gay movement in the United States). However, both traditional and modern articulations of the person have critiqued the ideology of family. Examples may be found in the ascetic or renunciatory models of personhood in the register of the traditional, as well as feminist critiques of the family, or the rejection of biological family in the search for a larger collective identity in the register of the modern. For instance, in many political movements (including militant movements) have recruited both men and women in defiance of kinship norms of honour and shame. Together these three chapters show that the notion that the normative is also the normal is particularly oppressive when women are placed in vulnerable positions as widows or single women. These chapters show both the strength of the family as a model of relatedness and the simultaneous rejection of its claims as the only way of imagining intimacy.

Thomas R. Trautman gives an overview of the patterns of marriage, showing not only the regional differences within systems of exchange but also the ideology which governs this exchange. His depiction of the relationship terminology and the patterns of exchange show that it is inadequate to think of a single distinction between the north and south in patterns of marriage as the subtle variations within these overarching models have much to teach us on the way in which local forms come to be articulated. The relation between the overall ideology of gift and exchange finds one particular expression in rules of marriage but has relevance for understanding other enduring institutions of Indian society. Thus the vast changes in that ideology of gift may lead to changes in many directions including that of commodification of the gift. Marriage patterns thus provide links between the different spheres of the legal, the political, and the personal—they explain the stability of structures even in the face of changes.

The chapter by Robert Desjarlais and James Wilce on emotions is included in this section because the construction of the person not only as a rational subject but as a bearer of affect is closely related to the intimate relations within which personhood as practice is forged. The authors review the various attempts made in the literature to capture the specificity of Indian society in the context of universal theories of emotion. Going far beyond the simple opposition of East and West, individualcentric and sociocentric theories of the person, they show the complex ways in which emotions are not only the products of socialization but might also break from given patterns of societal genres within which emotions are sought to be authorized and expressed.

The Family in India
Beyond the Nuclear versus Joint Debate

Patricia Uberoi

INTRODUCTION

A review of scholarly writings in the field of Indian family and
kinship studies suggests that the field is not, at least at present, a well-
integrated one. One of the problems is that the subject is partitioned between
several different social science disciplines whose protocols, problematics,
theoretical foci, and practical concerns are all rather different: Indology, law,
anthropology, sociology, psychology, psychiatry, economics, demography,
human geography, and social work. In particular, the 'metropolitan' division
of labour between the *anthropology of kinship* and the *sociology of the
family* in terms of theories, methods, and preoccupations has been faithfully
reproduced in the textbooks commonly used in Indian colleges and
universities, notwithstanding a widespread sentiment against differentiating
anthropology and sociology in the Indian context.[1]

Second, there has been an immense amount of empirical data
collected under the aegis of the Census of India and other socio-economic
survey instruments, but this vast material has only intermittently been brought
under sociological scrutiny. Indeed, much of it is deemed unsuitable for testing
sociologically meaningful hypotheses (see Shah 1999a). Third, the sociology
of Indian family and kinship has focused more on kinship *norms* than on
pathology, deviance, and breakdown. For this reason it has largely failed to
inform or to confront the practical challenges of social activism and public-
policy intervention.

This chapter does not deal directly with these issues of disciplinary
boundary maintenance, but approaches them indirectly, through a critical
reviewing of the single question that has dominated sociological discussion of

the Indian family as well as public discourse in India. This is the question of the future of the 'traditional' Indian joint family or, more precisely, the question of whether or not the joint family has been breaking down as a result of the processes of modernization. At one stage this issue seemed to have been satisfactorily resolved (or was it just wished away?) by the privileging of the supposedly more precise notion of 'household' over the more fuzzy-edged concept of 'family', but in retrospect it appears that gains in definitional precision have unduly restricted the range of questions that can be asked and the issues that can be addressed. I believe that there is a pressing need now to recover 'the family' as an integrated object of study and, by this means, to reclaim for the disciplines of sociology and anthropology themes that have been sidelined by the one-sided focus on questions of household type and composition. Ironically, in thus retracing the trajectory of an intellectual debate, this chapter has itself been shaped and constrained by the very preoccupation it sets out to critique. Some indications of the hiatuses in the present account and a number of suggestions towards a renewal of the field are made, however, by way of conclusion.

THE FAMILY IN INDIA

India occupies a special place in the comparative sociology of the family as a textbook case of the working of a 'joint family system' (see Goode 1963: Chapter 5; and 1964: 48–51). Nonetheless, few questions have been as confused, or as confusing, as that of the Indian joint family: its definition; its composition; its functions; its history; and, of course, its future trajectory. The ideal of the Indian joint family has long been an important ingredient in national self-imaging as the social institution that uniquely expresses and represents the valued aspects of Indian culture and tradition;[2] thus it has become rather difficult to separate fact from value, behaviour from norm and indeed, to talk dispassionately about the subject at all. This is more so since the joint family and its supporting value system (often termed 'familism', as distinguished from 'individualism') are widely believed to be under threat from alien values and an alien way of life.

Historically, the concept of the 'Indian joint family' was the product of the engagement of British colonial administration with indigenous systems of kinship and marriage, notably with respect to the determination of rights in property and responsibility for revenue payment. Seeking to understand the principles of Indian legal systems, the British turned to the Hindu sacred texts, the Dharmashastras (see Kane 1930–62), or parallely, for the Muslim population of the subcontinent, to the Shariat and the rulings of Muslim legalists (see Mulla 1972). This approach, retrospectively termed the

'Indological' approach to Indian family studies (see Shah 1973: 124–5), confirmed the 'joint family' as the typical and traditional form of family organization in India, located it within the discursive domain of the law, and defined its special features.

An important influence in putting the Indian family on the map of comparative family studies and in shaping the Indological approach to the Indian joint family was the pioneering work of Henry Sumner Maine (1822–88), Law Member of the Council of the Governor-General in India from 1862 to 1869. Relying on the classical textual sources of Hindu law, read along with contemporary ethnographic and administrative reports, Maine projected the Indian joint family as a living example of the earliest or 'ancient' form of the human family whose outlines could also be discerned in the legal system of ancient Rome as well as in Celtic and Slavic survivals of earlier forms of social organization (Maine [1861] 1972). Maine termed this type of family the 'patriarchal family' for the reason that it was constituted by a group of persons related in the male line and subject to the absolute power (*patria potestas*) of the seniormost male member. In Maine's understanding, the patriarchal family functioned as a sort of a 'corporation', existing in perpetuity, whose living members were coparceners in a joint estate. Family property was divided equally among sons before or after the death of the ascendant; alternatively, the undivided family might expand over several generations to become an organized and self-regulating 'brotherhood of relatives', the 'village community', that Maine believed to be a characteristic South Asian form of social organization. Maine proposed that this ancient form of social organization, based on the principle of 'status', would in due course evolve through several stages into one based on 'contract', with the patriarchal joint family being replaced by the monogamous conjugal family unit of the contemporary western type, associated with the individual ownership of property and linked to the power of testation (Maine [1861] 1972).

Many of the early generation of Indian sociologists identified the patriarchal joint family of the Sanskrit legal and sacerdotal texts as the 'traditional' form of the family in India. In a discursive environment shaped by the force of 'cultural nationalism', they regarded the joint family as a unifying civilizational ideal that had been 'very widely held by all Hindus—the rich as well as the poor, the learned as well as the lay, the city men as well as the village folk' (Prabhu [1940] 1955: 5). This viewpoint was vigorously propounded in the writings of the Sanskritist/sociologist G.S. Ghurye who, in his erudite *Family and Kin in Indo-European Culture* (1955), claimed an Indo-European pedigree for the Indian joint family. By implication, of course, he also excluded from this venerable heritage the structurally quite different subcontinental culture of Dravidian kinship, the kinship practices of non-Hindu communities, and a wide range of non-Brahmanic usages.

Reconciling the unitary Sanskritic heritage with the empirical variety of contemporary Indian family and kinship practices was a problem that several of Ghurye's students at the Sociology Department of Bombay University sought to address explicitly (see, esp., Kapadia 1955). For instance, following the general line of Lewis Henry Morgan (1871), Irawati Karve sought to link Indian kinship systems, through the structure of their vocabularies of kinship terms, to the major subcontinental language groups and sub-linguistic areas. By these criteria she identified four main types of kinship organization in India: (i) an Indo-European or Sanskritic type in the north, where kinship practices were essentially continuous with those described in classical Sanskrit sources; (ii) a Dravidian type in the south; (iii) a mixed 'central' zone between the two; and (iv) a geographically non-contiguous Austro-Asiatic type (of Mundari and Mon-Khmer linguistic affiliation) in the East (Karve 1953: Chapter 1). Counterbalancing this heterogeneity, Karve then proposed three *unifying* factors through the subcontinent: (i) the all-India institution of caste, notwithstanding its many regional variations (Karve 1953: 6–10); (ii) the patrilineal or matrilineal 'joint family' (which she defined as 'a group of people who generally live under the same roof, who eat food cooked at one hearth, ... hold property in common and ... participate in common family worship and [who] are related to each other as some particular type of kin' [Karve 1953: 10]); and (iii) the Sanskritic heritage, wherein one may find descriptions of almost all the kinship practices still found throughout the subcontinent (Karve 1953: 28). In Karve's formulation, then other words, the Hindu joint family had a positive role to play as a unifying force beneath the enormous variety of Indian kinship systems, as well as being an important instrument of social and economic security (Karve 1953: 301). It was another matter that, particularly in its northern variant (in continuity with the classical model), it was very hard on women: a price to be paid, perhaps, for the greater goal of civilizational continuity and unity.

THE MODERNIZATION THESIS

The conviction that the traditional Indian joint family system was in the process of breaking down gained currency following early British censuses which revealed that, empirically speaking, this type of family structure was by no means as prevalent as the strength and persistence of the ideal would have led one to expect (Shah 1973: 125–6). The Indological training of many of the first generation of Indian sociologists predisposed them to think likewise. However, the idea gained social scientific legitimacy in the post-World War II period when theorists of 'modernization' identified the Anglo-American nuclear family, focused on the conjugal couple, as the family type best adapted to the requirements of a modern, industrial society.

The most influential contribution to the sociology of the family in the post-War period was that of the eminent American sociologist and social theorist, Talcott Parsons, whose theory of family socialization and interaction was an important constituent in his structural-functional and comparative theory of society and social change (esp. Parsons [1949] 1959; Parsons and Bales 1955). Parsons was responding to the widespread post-War perception that the rising divorce rate, declining birth rate, and changes in sexual morality portended the imminent breakdown of the American family. To the contrary, he asserted that such changes were indicative of the stresses of a period of 'transition', and not signs of a trend to dysfunction and disorganization per se (Parsons and Bales 1955: 4). According to Parsons, American society was presently witnessing the culmination of a long-term process of the 'isolation', 'differentiation', and 'specialization' of the nuclear family as a bounded sub-system of society. This was the inevitable result of the logic of the modern occupational system with its emphasis on mobility and individual performance: 'As the occupational system develops and absorbs functions in society', Parsons wrote, 'it must be at the expense of the relative prominence of kinship organization as a structural component in one sense, and must also be at the expense of what previously have been functions of the kinship unit' (Parsons and Bales 1955: 12).

Complementing the isolation and loss of function of the nuclear family in modern societies, according to Parsons, was the enhanced emphasis on both the parental and the conjugal bonds (the latter, paradoxically resulting in increased strain on the institution of marriage). Now 'stripped down' to its elementary structural characteristics and 'root' functions, the contemporary American nuclear family afforded a unique empirical example of the 'minimal structural and functional essentials' of the human family as a special type of small social group (Parsons and Bales 1955: 354). That is, in its elementary structure, the family comprised four basic roles differentiated along the two axes of generation and of sex—father, mother, male child, female child—the differentiation of generation amounting to a differentiation in terms of power, and the differentiation of sex to a differentiation between 'instrumental' and 'expressive' functions.

There is something both candid and narcissistic about Parsons' formulation: candid in its recognition that the functional stability of the American nuclear family was dependent on a supposedly 'naturally' given generational hierarchy of authority and sexual division of labour, narcissistic in that the family pattern thus valorized within an evolutionary theory of societal development was both ideally and empirically typical of the white American, middle class family (father as breadwinner, mother as housekeeper), delegitimizing other family patterns (see Morgan 1975: 40–8). Writing in the 1950s, Parsons had clearly not envisioned that the 'transition' of the American family would be a continuing and open-ended process. A combination of demographic factors (declining birth and death rates), variations in sexual and conjugal arrangements (for example, gay and lesbian marriages, the legal recognition of live-in arrangements), as well as the impact of new reproductive technologies of motherhood and fatherhood, have since changed the face of the American family, even its white middle class variant. Moreover, with the introduction of programmes of economic liberalization, governments worldwide have begun to review the costs of their welfare programmes, seeking to restore to families the burden of care (of the young, of the aged, of the invalid, and the handicapped) that the modern state and its agencies had assumed during several decades of welfarism or socialist construction. The declaration of a UN International Year of the Family in 1994 was an indication of a growing and worldwide sense of crisis in the institution of the family, precipitated by the downsizing of welfare programmes, as are continuing appeals for the reinstitution of 'family values', marital fidelity, and premarital continence. In many countries this conservative backlash, targeted especially against the sexual emancipation of women, has also been associated with anti-western xenophobia and with the rise of religious fundamentalisms (see Hasan 1994; Jayawardena and de Alwis 1996).

Focusing on the typical family pattern of white, middle class Americans as the most 'advanced' type of kinship organization, functionally adapted to the requirements of modern industrial society, Parsons himself had little interest in *other* modes of family life except insofar as these served to validate his general theory (see Parsons and Bales 1955: Chapter 6). But his functionalist perspective on family organization, albeit slightly modified, was assimilated into the 'development' literature of the 1950s and 1960s, notably through the influential writings of William J. Goode (see 1963 and 1964).

Goode's *World Revolution and Family Patterns* (1963) is an ambitious comparative survey of modern changes in the family in five different areas of the world (the Arab world, Sub-Saharan Africa, India, China, and Japan), set against the background of the historical evolution of the family in the modern West. According to Goode, the process of industrialization is bound to bring critical pressures to bear on traditional family structures as increased physical and social mobility separates individuals from larger kin groups and as functions formerly performed by the kin group are taken over by other social agencies. Allowing that the actual patterns and directions of change would differ (depending on the characteristics of the traditional kinship and family systems concerned), Goode nonetheless concluded that *all* societies the world over were in the process of moving towards the same end, that is towards the institutionalization of what he termed the 'conjugal family' form:

> It is clear ... that at the present time a somewhat similar set of influences is affecting all world cultures. *All of them are moving toward industrialization, although at varying speeds and from different points. Their family systems are also approaching some variant of the conjugal system* [Goode 1963: 368, emphasis added].

In presenting the comparative evidence from the five different societies of his study, Goode had found the Indian case to be particularly problematic (Goode 1963: Chapter 5). First, as he candidly admitted, there was in fact no conclusive evidence that the majority of Indians had *ever* lived in extended families in the past (notwithstanding ideals to the contrary),[3] nor that Indian families were at present moving decisively towards a conjugal family pattern. Second, to the extent that there appeared to have been some changes in this direction (for instance increased emphasis on the husband–wife bond as against that of mother and son; a higher level of contact between a married woman and her natal family; a decline of patriarchal authority in the family; greater freedom of choice of marriage partner), these changes could not plausibly be attributed to the impact of industrialization per se, since they had in fact preceded any significant level of industrialization. Nevertheless, and remarkably in the face of the paucity of his evidence, Goode remained convinced of the historical inevitability of a global revolution in family patterns towards the conjugal pattern presently exemplified by the West. As he wrote in the conclusion to his monumental survey,

> In this investigation, we have, in a very deep sense, pointed to both the present and the future while attempting to make a sociological analysis of the past half-century: As an illustration, in suggesting that various of these family changes are now taking place in India and the Arab world, we are pointing in effect to data that *will* appear, behavioral patterns that *will* become more pronounced, attitudes that are emerging but *will* become dominant in the future. ... We are suggesting that processes are at work which will lead to the changes indicated [Goode 1963: 379, emphasis in original].

Needless to add here, perhaps Goode's conjugal family pattern was projected not merely as an 'ideal type' in the neutral Weberian sense of the term but, on balance, as a morally superior social and political ideal which (like capitalism as an economic system) institutionalized the individual's 'freedom' to 'choose', and offered people 'the potentialities of greater fulfilment, even if most do not seek it or achieve it' (Goode 1963: 380).

Two further aspects of Goode's reading of the Indian data on the modernization of the family might briefly be noted. First, Goode observed that in India, *ideological* change (expressed, for instance, in progressive legislation or in the opinions of the educated elite) was far ahead of *behavioural* change, which remained relatively slow. Second, reflecting on the resilience of traditional Indian family patterns, Goode suggested that these family patterns are not merely dependent variables, changing in response to the exogenous impact of industrialization, but that they 'embody or express most of the factors that have impeded India's social development' (Goode 1963: 203). This is a hypothesis that, in one form or another, has had a long history, notwithstanding the lack of sound empirical evidence to support it.[4]

Oft-cited as a refutation of Goode's thesis is Milton Singer's (1968) study of the family histories of nineteen Madras industrialists. While Singer had indeed found some inter-generational changes (in residence, household size and composition, occupation and educational levels) which he speculated might functionally be associated with urbanization and industrial entrepreneurship, he also noted an inter-generational persistence of joint family living in many cases, the constant interactions of both nuclear and joint families with their relatives in villages, the continued sense of joint-family obligations even on the part of those actually living in nuclear families, and the continuity of aspects of family occupation (for instance continuity in the professions of trade and business) despite new educational specializations (Singer 1968: 436–8). Singer interpreted his findings as indicating the potential of the Indian joint family for 'structural adaptation' to new circumstances (Singer 1968: 444). This type of joint family organization, he concluded, is not only compatible with the development of modern industry, but may even constructively *assist* the establishment of a modern industrial enterprise (Singer 1968: 445).

As a number of critics have pointed out, the value of Singer's study was compromised by his failure to define with precision the concepts of 'nuclear' and 'joint' family and his conflation of 'family'—a genealogical construct—and 'household'—a residential and/or commensal arrangement of persons who are mostly (if not invariably) kin. In retrospect, however, one can appreciate the importance of Singer's principle of 'structural adaptation' as a way of reconciling *both* persistence *and* change in the realm of Indian family and kinship.

HOUSEHOLD VERSUS FAMILY

The lack of uniform operational definitions of the concepts of 'joint' (or 'extended') and 'nuclear' ('conjugal' or 'elementary') family, and the conflation of 'family' and 'household' were not confusions peculiar to Milton

Singer's work. On the contrary, they were, and still remain, widely prevalent in studies on the Indian family in the discipline of sociology as well as in other social sciences. Under the circumstances, one wonders how the sociologist can be expected to answer the only question that anyone seems to want to ask of the Indian family: 'Is the joint family disintegrating?', and what general conclusions can be built on such shaky foundations.

Two sociologists in particular, A.M. Shah and Pauline Kolenda, working independently along rather similar lines, have contributed significantly to clarifying the conceptual issues involved in assessing trends in the composition of the Indian family. In a series of articles from 1964, now collected in *The Family in India* (1998), and in his earlier monograph on *The Household Dimension of the Family in India* (1973), A.M. Shah had sought to spell out the features of what he considered a properly 'sociological' approach to the Indian family (as distinct from the 'Indological' or 'legal' approach that had earlier prevailed). Shah's clarification had two distinct aspects. First, following M.N. Srinivas's emphasis on field-based, as against text-based, approaches to the study of Indian society, he stressed the importance of the empirical observation of kinship *behaviour* (in the 'field') as the proper basis of sociological generalization. He also cautioned against the methodologically dubious procedure whereby present ethnographic realities are posited against an ideal picture of family life derived from normative and prescriptive textual sources, and conclusions drawn therefrom on the nature and direction of social change (Nimkoff 1959).[5] Second, in line with current sociological usage, Shah recommended that the object of study should be what he called the *household* 'dimension' of the family, the household being defined as the strictly commensal and co-resident group. This focus discounts the features of 'coparcenership' and ritual corporateness that had defined the Hindu joint family in the Indologically oriented literature (Lardinois 1992).[6]

Substituting the commensal and co-resident 'household' group for the more imprecise and polysemous term 'family', the question, 'Is the joint *family* disintegrating?' is rephrased as, 'Is the joint *household* disintegrating?'. This question is supposedly more amenable to empirical verification—that is so long as comparable time-series data are available—but unfortunately, neither family nor household data have hitherto been elicited with uniform definitions in mind. However, Shah urged, meticulous attention to methodological questions, the judicious use of data sources, and a cautious approach to generalization can enable the sociologist to monitor longitudinal trends, at least in patchwork manner. Moreover, as time goes by there will be further opportunities for anthropologists and sociologists to restudy communities that they themselves or others had earlier studied, an exercise that is by now well under way (see Epstein 1973; Ghurye 1960; Kessinger 1974; Kolenda 1987: Chapter 3; Shah 1973: 86–93; 1998: Chapter 7; Wadley and Derr 1988).

Several household-classification schemes have been devised by sociologists to enable them to capture with greater precision the multiple forms of household composition and the dynamics of household change in India. Of these, the scheme that has had widest currency (in its original form, or somewhat modified) is the twelve-type classificatory scheme proposed by Pauline Kolenda in her pioneering 'Region, Caste and Family Structure: A Comparative Study of the Indian "Joint" Family', based on an analysis of twenty-six post-1949 ethnographic studies and household censuses (Kolenda 1968).[7] The scheme has proved pragmatically useful for highlighting aspects of household composition that tend to be obscured in the dichotomous classification of households into either joint/extended or nuclear/elementary types. For instance, by a dichotomous classification, the commonly encountered domestic group composed of a widowed mother or father along with a married son, his wife, and children, is classified by some analysts as a joint household (depleted), and by others as a nuclear household (supplemented): depending on the scheme adopted, the relative proportions of joint versus nuclear households in the population under study will be skewed accordingly (Kolenda 1968: 373ff; see also Vatuk 1972: 59–63). Again, a simple joint/ nuclear categorization obscures the phenomenon of single-person households, a household type which may be of both sociological and practical interest.[8]

It is no easy matter to sum up the burden of the empirical research that has been conducted on patterns of household composition and change in India. A number of observations may be hazarded, nonetheless, with the caution that they are more in the nature of the deconstruction of well-entrenched stereotypes than a positive input into remapping the field:

(1) The joint household is rarely the statistically predominant form of household; nuclear households are usually more numerous.[9] However, even with the majority of *households* being nuclear in composition, the majority of *persons* in a population might still reside in joint or supplemented nuclear families.[10]

(2) Overall, the proportion of joint over nuclear households does not appear to be *decreasing*. The average size of the household has actually been increasing over the last century and a half (see Shah 1998: 66; also Orenstein 1961) and, while there is no direct correlation between household size and household type, there is every likelihood that proportions of joint households have been increasing as well. Indeed, such an outcome would appear inevitable given population growth, increased longevity, greater pressure on land and housing, the usual norms of household formation, and

the preponderant rule of patri(viri)local residence, the absence of state-run social services, economic development and the accumulation of assets, and an overall encouragement in the wider political culture to the Sanskritization of custom. It is pertinent to note in this context that some longitudinal studies (in rural settings) have registered increase in *both* nuclear *and* joint household types over time, accompanied by a decline in households of other types (sub-nuclear or supplemented nuclear, for instance [see Kolenda 1987: Ch. 3; Shah 1973: 88–93; Wadley and Derr 1988]). The demographic fact of increased life expectancy may be the simple key to this latter type of change.

(3) Despite the predominance of nuclear households, many or most people would experience living in several different types of households. Households, like individuals, have a 'life-cycle' of development as individual life courses web in complex ways with trajectories of household expansion, fission and replacement, and with wider socio-economic forces. This is the phenomenon that anthropologists have termed 'the developmental cycle of the domestic group' (see Fortes 1962; Freed and Freed 1983; Gould 1968; Robertson 1991: esp. 11–16, 31–6; Vatuk 1972: 64–9; and from a demographer's angle, Raju 1998).

(4) A 'stem family' form (of parents residing with a married child), structurally if not developmentally similar to the classic pattern of Europe or Japan, may be an emerging pattern of family organization and an important social mechanism for care of the elderly. (Statistically, widowed or widower parents are frequent 'supplements' to the nuclear household [see Vatuk 1972: 64–72; also Shah 1999 (b)].

(5) Rural households tend on average to be larger than urban households (5.59 to 5.33 members respectively in 1991 [see Shah 1998: 66]); parallely, joint households are more numerous in rural than urban areas (Shah 1998: 74). However, it would be premature to accept these findings as supporting the proposition that urbanization *leads to* nuclearization, at least not without a very careful monitoring of longitudinal trends. Such composite figures may only conceal the complexity and heterogeneity of the processes involved. For instance, India has had a long history of urbanism, and probably a relatively high proportion of persons in the old cities live in joint households. On the other hand, while new migrants to the towns and cities may come initially as individual workers and then establish nuclear families, the passage of time combined with the governing principles of household formation and the pressures of urban living may well encourage the development of joint households in due course. Similarly, while the lifestyles and occupational mobility of the professional middle classes may discourage joint-household living, another section of the urban middle class (for instance those engaged in business enterprise) may prefer to maintain joint households

along with their joint business and property interests.[11] Such communities may also be the social reference groups in urban centres.

(6) There appear to be significant *regional* differences in the prevalence of joint households. Utilizing a combination of census data and anthropological field studies from the first decade after Independence, Pauline Kolenda had shown that the joint household is strongest through a contiguous belt across north India, and weakest in south India. This mapping coincides in its broad outlines with the distinctions that have been made between north and south Indian kinship systems, centring around marriage practices (Karve 1953; see also Bhat 1996; Dyson and Moore 1983).[12] In sum, Kolenda's work suggested that regional patterns may be more consistent than some of the other factors that have been hypothesized to correlate with preference for joint or nuclear households, for instance caste status or landownership (Kolenda 1968; also Basu 1992; Raju 1998; Vatuk 1972: 69).

(7) Notwithstanding nuclear-household *residence*, there is strong and generalized commitment to joint-family *values* and *norms* of kinship behaviour (see Desai 1964). While urban nuclear families may be relatively isolated from close kin, perhaps translating neighbourhood relations into a kinship idiom instead (see Sharma 1986; Vatuk 1972), in the village context individual households may well live under the same roof as close kin, or in adjacent houses (see Raju 1998). Property and ritual observances may be common, and codes of conduct (for instance a woman's veiling herself before senior affines) will apply as in the case of a regular joint household. Similarly, through much of India (especially north India) the norm of household formation follows the pattern whereby brides are initially recruited into the households of their husbands' patrilineal kin ('patri[viri]local residence'), although the young couple may move out of the joint household and set up separate residence in due course of time.[13]

While the work of Kolenda, Shah, and others has succeeded in nailing the myth of the ongoing 'disintegration' of the Indian joint household, an enormous amount of research still remains to be done to chart the dynamics of the household life cycle and the complex processes of family change in the South Asian region. Kolenda's data in the studies cited (1967, 1968, and 1989) is derived from ethnographic monographs and surveys of the first decade after Independence, and from the 1961 Census of India. Since the 1970s, some regions of the country have begun to register fertility decline, indicating significant changes in traditional family-building strategies. However, the task of monitoring these processes in all their heterogeneity— over regions, castes, classes and communities, and through individual life cycles—has barely begun.[14]

RECOVERING 'THE FAMILY'

Privileging the concept of 'household' over that of 'family' has no doubt introduced a welcome precision into scholarly discussion on the Indian family and has enabled more rigorous comparative studies of households across cultures and over time (Netting et al. 1984). At the same time, the exercise has also been self-limiting, if not actually self-defeating. Driven by the one-point agenda of pronouncing authoritatively (one way or another) on the fate of the Indian joint family in modern times, inquiry has been largely restricted to quantitative and morphological aspects of household form/ composition at the expense of the more ineffable dimensions of family life and relationships.[15] It has excluded address to the other reality of the family as a property-sharing or ritual unit *distinct from* the strictly co-resident or commensal group (Lardinois 1992), as well as investigation of the economics of the household as a unit of production, distribution, and consumption. Overemphasis on the household does not allow speculation on the role of the family in the organization of human reproduction, in the socialization of citizens, or in the provision of welfare—questions which are mostly left to other disciplines to address. The emphasis on household discounts as sociologically irrelevant the ubiquity of ideals of joint-family living that may be fervently ascribed to *even when* the individuals concerned actually live out some or the greater part of their life courses in nuclear households (see Desai 1964). Perhaps the time has now come to backtrack to the point from where sociologists of the Indian family had set out on their quest for greater precision, replicability, and general methodological rigour through the conceptual distinction of family and household, and to begin a more broad-based reconstruction of the field of Indian family and kinship studies.

Such an enterprise would include, but also go beyond, what has been described as a shift of focus in Indian family and kinship studies in the 1990s, from 'structure' to 'process' (see Wadley 1998: 119ff.). It might involve, for instance: (i) taking a new and critical look at revisions of the history of the family in Europe and North America (e.g. Goody 1990; Laslett 1972; Robertson 1991; Wall et al. 1983), and in other regions as well, themes so far taken up, if at all, mainly by social demographers (see Das Gupta 1995); (ii) a re-engagement with the now relatively disfavoured functionalist and structural-functional approaches to family and kinship in social anthropology and in Parsonian sociology, short of endorsing their status-quoist and sexist assumptions;[16] (iii) openness to insights from the 'cultural' approach to kinship studies as a means of understanding both the ideology of the joint family and, more generally, the nature of indigenous conceptions of relatedness (Schneider [1968] 1980); (iv) recognition of the structural implications of marriage alliance in determining the role of the family in the wider kinship system; (v) exploration of the political economy of the household—both the intrahousehold distribution of resources and the imbrication of the household economy within the wider national and global economies; (vi) consideration of the relations of contradiction and collusion between state, community, and household (see Agarwal 1988; Risseuw and Palriwala 1996); and (vii) a general openness to insights from other disciplines, taking back on board themes that have been largely marginalized in recent sociological research on the family in India.

This is a rather formidable agenda, and this chapter can only hope to indicate and comment on some general trends and hiatuses in the existing literature. As suggested earlier, some of these are the product of the informal division of labour between sociology and anthropology on the one hand, and between these disciplines and social work on the other. In many instances, as will be evident in the discussion that follows, one finds that the writings of feminist scholars have provided a bridge across these conventional disciplinary divides, and suggested new emphases and directions.

Kinship Ideology

Anthropologists studying primitive societies have had long-standing interest in indigenous theories of procreation—what are often called 'descent' or 'procreative ideologies' in anthropological parlance—linked, in particular, to the functioning of unilineal descent groups and justifying the rights and duties associated with membership in such groups. In the South Asian context, where kinship systems are largely (though by no means exclusively) based on patrilineal descent, such ideas are seen as the foundation of a pervasive 'patriarchal' ideology which rationalizes the differential access of men and women to the material and symbolic resources of society.

An influential input into this mode of thinking in the Indian context has been Leela Dube's paper (1986) on the ubiquitous South Asian procreative metaphor of 'seed and earth': man is the active principle, providing the 'seed' of the child's future identity, and woman merely the passive 'field' in which this seed is sown and nurtured (also Misri 1985). This theory of the unequal contribution of the sexes to the process of reproduction, Dube argues, 'provides the rationalization for a system in which woman stands alienated from productive resources, has no control over her labour power, and is denied rights over her offspring' (Dube 1986: 44; and 1997: esp. Chapter 3). By contrast, she observes, some of India's matrilineal communities have had quite different theories of procreation, along with their different understandings of women's entitlement (Dube 1986: 32–3, 51n.).

Other feminist writers have pursued this reasoning further, seeking correlations between the descent principle and a number of other features of the system of kinship, marriage, residence and succession, along with other indicators of women's status and 'bargaining power' (see Agarwal 1994; 1997), as has Dube herself in a recent comparative study of gender and kinship in South and South East Asia (Dube 1997). The connections thus made between the principle of patrilineal descent, its expression in a masculinist procreative ideology, and aspects of the 'secondary' status of women in south Asian society are both insightful and compelling, and of wide ramification through diverse domains of social life including public administration and law (see Agarwal 2000; Kapur and Cossman 1996: Chapter 2; Uberoi 1996a: Chapter 14). But this is clearly not the whole story. Dube's own paper shows that the status of the mother is *also* a significant component of the child's identity, since placement in the caste hierarchy is ultimately a function of the status of *both* parents, not of the father alone (see Das 1976; Hershman 1981: 129–33; Hsu 1963; Misri 1985; Tambiah 1975; Yalman 1963). The special status of motherhood in Hindu society is therefore not merely an extension of the mother's role as father's wife or ancestress, but derives from cultural understandings of the unique 'natural' bond that exists between mother and child in consequence of the mother's 'sacrifice' in bearing and nurturing the child with her blood and milk (see Das 1976; Madan 1983: 105). Also, as Louis Dumont and others have demonstrated (Dumont 1983b; Kane 1930–62: II, 1, 452ff.; Trautmann 1981: 246–71), the important concept of '*sapinda*' in Hindu kinship reckoning is not exclusively agnatic, but varies from an exclusively agnatic orientation in the context of oblations to ancestors, to a modified patrilineal emphasis in the context of birth and death pollution and inheritance rights, to a more even-handedly cognatic emphasis in the exogamous rules governing marriage.

In fact, the problem is not only with the rather uncomfortable fit between metropolitan kinship theory and ethnographic evidence from the non-western world but, it has been suggested, with the theory itself. In particular, the so-called 'descent' approach to kinship studies within the structural-functional tradition is problematic in several respects that have been highlighted in the anthropological literature, including from the perspective of the 'alliance' and 'cultural' approaches (see Uberoi 1995). It is to the latter— that is the 'cultural' approach—that I draw attention immediately, reserving for later some comments on the relevance of 'alliance' theory (see section entitled 'The Family in the "System" of families').

In his pathbreaking *American Kinship: A Cultural Account* (1980 [1968], David Schneider had set out to describe the 'meaning' of American kinship as a 'system of symbols' independent of the anthropologists' usual classificatory inventory of principles of descent, residence, inheritance, succession, etc.[17] Proceeding from analysis of the American kinship terminology, Schneider had characterized the cognitive universe of American kinship in terms of an opposition of relations by 'blood' (conceived as 'natural', permanent, and substantive), and different types of relations 'by marriage', that is, relations of a more contingent character, governed by an express 'code of conduct' and conceived as based in 'law' or 'culture' rather than in 'nature'.

In a patchy sort of way, different scholars have picked up and elaborated on different strands of Schneider's work in the Indian context. Inden and Nicholas, for instance, have looked at the principles of classification of relatives in the culture of Bengali kinship and the codes of conduct that these relations require, augmenting this analysis with consideration of the symbolic structure of Hindu rites of passage (*samskaras*) which work to ritually transform the person through successive stages of the individual life-cycle (Inden and Nicholas 1977). A number of chapters in Ostor, Fruzzetti, and Barnett's collection, *Concepts of Person* (1983), link the idiom of kinship in north and south India to constructions of personhood and, in particular, to caste identity. T.N. Madan (1983) has looked at the Kashmiri Pandits' ideology of householdership and its relation to their sense of community, while John Gray (1995: Chapter 2) has similarly argued that understanding the dynamics of the Nepali household as an institution must begin with an appreciation of the meaning of 'householdership' in the Nepali worldview. The Nepali household, he argues, is a 'structure of consciousness' before it is a group of persons or a set of shared functions.

In a rather different idiom, Margaret Trawick (1996) has elaborated on the meaning of 'love' in the culture of Tamil kinship—not merely the contrast of 'erotic', 'conjugal' love versus non-erotic 'consanguineal' love that Schneider (1968) proposes in the context of American culture, but love (Tamil, '*anpu*') construed as the multiple and contradictory attributes of 'containment', 'habit', 'harshness', 'dirtyness', 'humility', 'simplicity', 'servitude', the 'reversal' of normal social hierarchies, 'confusion' (Trawick 1996: Ch. 4)! Others see the culture of South Asian kinship as an instance of a more encompassing ontology that is reflected in many different domains: architecture, medicine, religion, law, land and labour relations, etc. (see Daniel 1984; Marriott 1990; Osella and Osella 1996).

From the viewpoint of the discussion here of the 'ideology' of the Indian joint family as a component of the wider kinship system, one of the most interesting inputs has been Veena Das's essay on Punjabi kinship (1976). Punjabis, she says, acknowledge the strong emotional bonds arising from the 'natural' sexual relation of husband and wife, and the 'natural' procreative relation of parent (especially mother) and child, but they insist that these emotions must be kept—socially speaking—'backstage', to be 'sacrificed' and transcended in the interests of the manifest solidarity of the patrilineal joint family (see also Trawick 1996: Chapter 4). In these terms, the joint family might be defined not so much as a specific type of household formation, but as an *ideology* and *code of conduct* whereby the relations of husband and wife and parent and child are expected to be subordinated to a larger collective identity. This ideology finds constant affirmation in the world of Indian popular cinema.

In fact, kinship 'ideologies' (ideas about how the family is constituted and how it functions) inform public discourse in many domains, including administration and the law, and are embedded in many provisions of public policy (see Agarwal 2000; Kapur and Cossman 1996: Chapter 2). Similarly, culturally embedded ideas of sexuality and procreation are seen to inflect judgements on points of Hindu personal law that are formally phrased in the quite different legal idiom of marriage as 'sacrament' versus marriage as 'contract' (see Uberoi 1996a: Chapter 14). Or judgements in rape cases disclose the pervasive cultural assumption that the violent 'sexualization' of a virgin girl devalues her currency as an object of exchange between men, and renders her effectively unmarriageable (see Das 1996).

With the studies just cited, one shifts from rural or village India to the 'modern' sector of Indian society, focusing on the urban middle and upper-middle classes whose self-image and concepts of person are projected on to the national canvas as *the* Indian culture of kinship. There remains, still, much scope for the continuation and refinement of the cultural approach, with reference to other ethnographic regions of the subcontinent as well as to the kinship ideology of the lower caste, tribal, and marginalized groups of Indian society of whose concepts of personhood one as yet knows very little (but see Khare 1984; Moffatt 1979).

The Social 'Functions' of the Family

Aside from the insights afforded by the cultural approach to family and kinship studies, it would be worthwhile to recall some features of the functionalist perspective on the family that are routinely rehearsed in most elementary texts on the family (see Goode 1964: Chapter 1; Murdock 1949: esp. Chapter 1).[18] In reviewing the current literature on these dimensions of Indian family life, it will be clear that sociologists/anthropologists have relinquished much ground to other disciplines. The suggestion is that this ground should now be reclaimed.

Biological Reproduction

Foremost among the family's social functions is its role as the usual and legitimate site of biological reproduction. Human fertility is both determined by and impacts upon family values and structures in the wider context of society and culture, but the complex mechanisms of this reciprocal action remain the subject of academic controversy. For instance, in an influential early article (1955), Kingsley Davis had speculated that the dysfunctional levels of fertility that presently characterize certain underdeveloped and agrarian societies, such as India, are linked to the prevailing type of family organization (that is unilinear descent groups and joint households). In such systems, Davis observed, the nuclear family of procreation is able to share the burden of child raising with a wider kin group. Consequently, the age of marriage tends to be quite young, and numerous offspring, especially male offspring, are viewed as a positive asset to the group, providing security to the parents in their old age when few other means are available (Davis 1955: 34–7).[19]

Considering their common focus on the reproductive functions of the family, one might have expected that anthropologists/sociologists and social demographers would be in constant dialogue. Regrettably, this has not usually been the case. In fact, sociologists have sometimes been quite dismissive of survey research methods applied to the sensitive area of human reproduction (a particular target has been the knowledge-acceptance-practice [KAP] focus of the early family planning surveys), and have insisted that reproductive behaviour can only be viewed in the wider context of culture and social structure (Srinivas and Ramaswamy 1977). For their part, demographers have been impatient with the ethnographic detail of micro-level fertility studies, and have questioned the generalizability of such studies to the wider canvas of regional or national population planning.

The position has changed somewhat since the 1980s, however, particularly with the more nuanced elaboration of a *regional* perspective on Indian demographic behaviour and family patterns (Raju et al. 1999; Singh 1993). A number of important studies (see Agarwal 1994; Basu 1992; Bhat 1996; Dyson and Moore 1983; Kolenda 1987: Chapter 2; Miller [1981] 1997, to cite just a few) have now demonstrated considerable consistency between demographic variables such as fertility rates, household size, sex ratios, sex-differentiated infant and child mortality, and women's age at marriage, and the regional patterns of kinship organization described by anthropologists, particularly the north/south contrast (Karve 1953; Trautmann 1981: esp. Chapter 3). These different patternings of kinship organization are seen to correlate with different degrees of 'female autonomy' (as measured by proxy variables such as the mean distance between natal and conjugal homes; freedom of divorce and remarriage; literacy rates; work participation rates; and women's inheritance rights), and with different degrees of 'son preference'. In general, the north Indian region (the states of Gujarat, Rajasthan, Uttar Pradesh, Madhya Pradesh, Punjab, and Haryana) is strongly masculinist on most measures; the south (the states of Kerala, Tamil Nadu,

Andhra Pradesh, Karnataka, and Maharashtra), much less so; while the eastern region (Bihar, West Bengal, and Orissa) lies in between, with mixed characteristics. These differentials also correspond, more or less, with the success or otherwise of state-sponsored measures of population control, though there are some notable exceptions to the pattern which merit close attention, and trends of change which promise to reverse long-established patterns (see Bhat 1996; Harriss-White 1999; *Public Report* 1999; Visaria 1999).

For their part, some sociologists have sought to test demographic hypotheses through intensive participant observation fieldwork at micro-level (a good recent example is Patel 1994), while others have used large-scale survey methods to confirm trends that are perhaps less obvious when viewed close up. Notable here is Monica Das Gupta's study (1987) of sex-differentiated child morbidity and mortality levels in a micro region of rural Punjab that had been intensively studied in the 1950s. Her work demonstrates the greatly impaired survival chances of higher birth order girls (as compared to their brothers and to first-born girls), despite the overall economic development of the region and significant declines in both fertility and mortality. She links this disparity with sex-differentiated access to food and clothing and, most crucially, medical attention. Revealingly, and disconcertingly, this disparity is shown to be inversely related to mothers' educational levels.

The collaboration of social demographers and anthropologists/sociologists has been stimulated by the urgent need for population control, but this narrow focus has produced some distortions and blind spots as well. First, notwithstanding recent changes in international population-control policies, the emphasis of research and intervention has been, until very recently, quite one-sidedly on *female* reproductive behaviour. (This emphasis appeared especially compelling following the politically disastrous promotion of male sterilization during the national Emergency in India [1975–7].) Second, focus on population magnitudes has tended to marginalize address to the social implications of the new reproductive technologies (NRTs) now patronized by the middle and upper-middle classes. The important exception here has been the linked practices of amniocentesis and sex-selective abortion, which have attracted much public attention (if not equally serious scholarly address) as pathological indicators of the strength of Indian son preference (Visaria 1999: 90–1). But there are several other dimensions to the NRTs which deserve greater sociological scrutiny for the light they throw on Indian kinship ideologies and family-building strategies, and for the connections they demonstrate between economic development, class formation and the exaggeration of some traditional features of Indian family organization. This may be another, and rather more malign, dimension of the 'adaptive' capacities of the Indian family that Milton Singer (1968) had alluded to. That is, traditional pathologies may be exaggerated, not eliminated, by processes of modernization and economic development.

Sexuality

Sexuality is one area where the disciplinary division of labour between sociology and anthropology is revealed most clearly. Considering the intimate connection between procreation and sexuality, it is remarkable that, after the pioneering work in this area of the redoubtable G.S. Ghurye (1973: Chapters 9 and 10), sociologists for the most part seem to have scrupulously avoided investigating Indian sexuality.[20] There is no Kinsey Report, no Hite Report, and no monitoring of changing sexual practices except from the very narrow perspective of conjugal procreative behaviour in the context of population control. Anthropologists, on the other hand, seem to have no such compunctions: in fact, exoticizing the sexual practices of object societies is a conspicuous sign of their 'othering' enterprise. Expectedly, then, the significant inputs into the study of sexuality have come from anthropologists, along with psychologists and psychoanalysts, social historians (particularly those influenced by the work of Michel Foucault), and social workers dealing with sexual pathologies, incest and domestic violence. Latterly, feminist researchers, too, have broken their self-imposed silence to address male and female sexuality as a major topic of both theoretical and practical concern (John and Nair 1998; Uberoi 1996a). Some of this work is referred to in the brief discussion that follows.

First, there, is the suggestive anthropological writing on 'procreative ideologies', already referred to, and the inputs of some psychologists and psychoanalysts who have sought to explore the oedipal tension of the mother–son relation in India, usually counterposed against the sexual dynamics of the conjugal relation (see Carstairs 1957; Kakar 1981: Chapter 3; and 1989; Nandy 1980). In addition to this, one may also note the continued reference to an 'Indological' or 'Sanskritic' model of conjugal sexual relations whereby sexuality is deemed legitimate only for the production of male offspring to continue the ritual offerings to ancestors: and not, primarily, for the production of pleasure. Otherwise, sexual activity for males is perceived as a source of sin, impurity, and danger which is likely to impair both physical well-being and spiritual development (see Allen 1982; Kapadia 1955: 159–60; Misri 1985; Prabhu [1940] 1995: 240–1).

A second exploration of sexuality may be found in the quite extensive anthropological literature on Hindu life-cycle rituals—particularly those of marriage, childbirth and, most conspicuously, female puberty (see Dube 1988; 1997; Good 1991). In many communities through south Asia, a girl's menarche is marked by a series of rituals which simultaneously celebrate her attainment of fecundity and marriageability while underlining her state of impurity and vulnerability and dramatizing the danger she now poses to her natal kin (see Bennett 1983: Chapter 6; Good 1991: Chapter 7; Kapadia 1995: Chapter 5; Yalman 1963). Once again, however, the richness of the ethnography of the 'traditional' sector of Indian society is in no way matched by comparable work on the urban and more 'modern' sector, and one is left to speculate on where and whether a girl's coming of age in the contemporary urban milieu is stigmatized or celebrated, ritually marked or unmarked, or transformed into some other idiom, secular or 'medicalized', through agencies such as the multinational pharmaceutical companies.

Yet another trend may be found in the recent critical literature, for the most part by 'Subaltern' historians and feminists, which has begun the process of reassessing the last century and a half of Indian social reform (see Nair 1996; papers in Hasan 1994; Kapur 1996; John and Nair 1998; and Uberoi 1996a). As is well known, Indian social reform efforts were largely concentrated on two issues: the removal of untouchability and the improvement of the social condition of women. A major emphasis of this latter project involved community and state interventions to regulate female sexuality inside and outside of marriage in line with upper-caste, Sanskritic norms and/or Victorian standards of propriety. Deconstruction of the discourse of social reform shows that both the nationalist and the reformist agendas, even on such questions as the abolition of *sati* and female infanticide or the raising of the Age of Consent, were more ambiguous and complex than superficial appearances and received opinion might suggest (Uberoi 1996a: Introduction). Particularly problematic was the process of the codification of customary and religious law, and interventions into the 'reform' of matrilineal systems of kinship and marriage (see Dube 1997; Nair 1996: Chapter 6; Saradamoni 1996), which often, in fact, placed new and untoward restrictions on women's freedom of action.

Finally, on the theme of sexuality, it is likely that the AIDS crisis will increasingly focus attention on aspects of Indian sexuality, beyond procreation, both inside and outside of marriage (see Bharat 1999). Indeed, the effect of this new and now donor-driven orientation, proceeding impatiently from research to policy recommendations, has already been felt, though to date more in social work than in anthropology/sociology proper.

Socialization

Following on from the family's role as the site of biological reproduction is its role as the first, the so-called 'primary', agency of socialization. After initial enthusiasm during the 1950s, when the study of child socialization practices was linked with the comparative study of personality types and political cultures (Minturn and Hitchcock 1963), sociologists/anthropologists appear to have almost abandoned the study of child socialization to the disciplines of psychology, psychoanalysis, and child development (see Kakar 1981). Indeed, with the exception of a paper by Urvashi Misri (1985) on the Kashmiri Pandit' understanding of the child and of childhood, sociologists have not reflected particularly on the cultural meaning of the concept of 'childhood' in the Indian context (Ariès 1962; Erikson 1950; Robertson 1991: Chapter 7).[21] The Pandits, according to Misri, see the child as both an individual with his or her own unique *karma,* and as a sharer in the inherited bodily substance of father and mother. Childhood is a process of separation of the child from divinity, with the child's loss of innate sacredness and purity being matched by the incremental attainment of adult community identity through successive rites of passage (*samskaras*).

Contrariwise, and in a more secular mode, Krishna Kumar points to the traditional continuity between the world of the child and the adult world (Kumar 1993; also Kakar 1981: esp. Chapter 4 and Appendix). Kumar suggests that contemporary social processes have brought about a new distantiation of the child and adult worlds in urban India as children's schooling on the one hand, and adult work schedules on the other, now structure childhood and adolescent experience. Obviously, too, the 'invention' of Indian childhood is being reinforced for the middle classes by the new post-liberalization consumerism, which has identified childhood and adolescence each as a distinctive life stage—and consumer market segment (for the latter, see Butcher 1999)!

Krishna Kumar's work has succeeded in bringing under examination the cultural practices of the Indian urban middle classes whose obsessive concern with their children's education, employment, and marriage instances the modern family's critical role in the reproduction of class status. Similarly, André Béteille has argued (1991) that in contemporary India it is the institution of the family (rather than the traditional caste group) that now ensures the social placement of the younger generation—through arranging school and college admissions, professional training, and employment opportunities.[22]

There is one aspect of the process of child socialization that *has* received considerable attention from sociologists/anthropologists. This is the process of socialization of the girl child and her internalization of feminine gender identity through a variety of social mechanisms (Das 1988; Dube 1988; Minturn 1993: esp. Chapter 12; Minturn and Hitchcock 1963). One of the important mechanisms of sex-role socialization is the sex-differentiated allocation of family resources (see later discussion). Another is the series of life-cycle rituals, particularly those of puberty (already mentioned) and of marriage

(Dube 1988 and 1997; Fruzzetti [1982] 1990; Good 1991; Hanchett 1988). In the north Indian patrilineal kinship system, in particular, a young girl is made aware early on that she will 'belong' after her marriage to another family, a family of strangers, and that, except in the greatest adversity, her rights, responsibilities and entitlements will pertain in that family.

As in all societies, the process of maturation involves the internalization of gendered codes of bodily deportment (see Das 1988) and of social space. Sex segregation is strongly, if unevenly, marked throughout much of South Asia where *purdah* (the veiling and seclusion of women) is practised to greater or lesser extent among Hindus as well as (albeit in different form) among Muslims (see Mandelbaum 1988; Minturn 1993: Chapter 3; Papanek 1982; Sharma 1978; Vatuk 1982). Women's relative seclusion and their inability to access the public domain on equal terms with men have been identified as important impediments to their economic independence and betterment (see Agarwal 1994: 268–70, 298–311, 458ff.; Sharma 1980: 3–7, 201–2).

Welfare

A major function of the family is that of care and nurturance—of the young, the handicapped, the sick, the unemployed, the aged. Indeed, in some 'biologistic' explanations, the care of the helpless infant and the protection of the pregnant and lactating mother are the very *raison d'être* of the human family as a social institution concerned with the reproduction of the species (see Fox 1967: esp. Chapter 1). As remarked earlier, in the upper income 'developed' societies, and especially in the erstwhile socialist states, many of these functions had been taken over by agencies of the state. However, the dismantling of socialist regimes and policies of liberalization have created a crisis of welfarism worldwide, stalling the aspiration for comprehensive social welfare in developing countries and restricting the state's commitment to areas of dire distress, or to sectoral investment in programmes which conspicuously further other developmental goals.[23] Perhaps this explains why the agency for initiating and prosecuting social-welfare schemes has been substantially relocated from the state to international organizations on the one hand, and to non-governmental organizations (NGOs) on the other (Risseeuw and Palriwala 1996; Uberoi 1996b).

In public discourse in India, problems in the delivery of welfare are often construed as evidence of a crisis in the *family*, rather than, for instance, a failure of state planning or a lack of political will. Thus it is widely believed that the Indian joint family is a type of family organization perfectly adapted to providing the maximum degree of security to its members (see Kapadia 1955: 248–51; Karve 1953: 301), but that this function has been seriously impaired by the expansion of an 'individualistic' ethos (Sharma

1989), and by new socio-economic trends such as occupational and spatial mobility, and the enhanced participation of women in some sectors of the workforce. This is all a matter of speculation. In fact sociologists tell us very little about how families cope with severe stress, about the ways in which familial care supplements or substitutes care provided by the community and the state and, in general, about the principles of the Indian moral economy in normal and abnormal times (but see Greenough 1982; Khare 1998). In consequence of the disciplinary division of labour between the theoretical and the applied sciences, such questions have not been a prominent focus of the sociology of the Indian family, and are largely left to social workers to address (Bharat and Desai 1991).

Feminist writers have been at the forefront of efforts to investigate the familial and extra-familial resources that households draw on to cope with adversity, whether these be the normal ups and downs of everyday life, or situations of extreme distress (Risseeuw and Palriwala 1996). At the same time, they have been wary of accepting at face value, the valorization of the family as an efficient instrument of care, perceiving here a convenient rationalization of the state's withdrawal from welfare responsibilities and its shifting of this burden to families (or rather, to *women*, who are the major care givers in the context of the family [Uberoi 1996b]). Similarly, they have critiqued the presumption that altruism is the governing principle of family relations, highlighting gender asymmetries in the allocation of family resources and bringing the issue of domestic violence prominently on to the public agenda (Karlekar 1998, and this volume).

The duality of the family as at once the site of oppression and violence and a 'haven in a heartless world' has been graphically illustrated in recent writing on the Indian Partition (Das 1995: Chapter 3). While male family members often took the lead in persuading their female kin to commit suicide for the sake of family honour, or themselves executed their own womenfolk, families also rallied to provide shelter and sustenance to victims and, wherever possible, to cover up the history of their women's abduction during those traumatic times. Similar stories could no doubt be told of the survival strategies of families in other situations of extreme distress and deprivation (Bharat and Desai 1991).

Production, Distribution, and Consumption

As noted, the distinction between 'family' and 'household and the definition of the household as the co-resident and commensal group were analytical refinements introduced to deal with two conceptual problems. The first is what one might term an 'enumerative' problem, arising from the fact that a house (as a material structure) might contain several distinctly demarcated social groups ('hearths') (see Madan [1965] 1989; Rao 1992; Shah 1998). The second is the confusion arising from the 'Indological' definition of the family as a property-sharing group. That is, as a result of the often uneven and staggered processes of family partition, the kinship group constituted by shared property interests might be smaller, or more likely larger, than the co-resident/commensal domestic unit. Ethnographers describe many cases where hearth-group units are separate, but where landed property continues to be jointly cultivated and the proceeds shared (see Madan [1965] 1989; Parry 1979; Raju 1998). That is why many sociologists had, *contra* the 'Indological' approach, discounted relations in property as defining features of 'household' membership. (Of course, the criterion of commensality in the definition of the household *does* imply a certain sharing of budgeting and consumption [Agarwal 1994].) Nonetheless, there has been a well-developed and continuing tradition in social anthropology which attends to the 'domestic group' as a unit of ownership, production, consumption, and distribution, as well as of reproduction (see Gray 1995; Madan [1965] 1989: Chapters 7 and 8; Mayer 1960), and this emphasis has now been strengthened by the important work of several feminist scholars (see Agarwal 1994; Sharma 1980).

Crucial to the familial organization of production is the sexual division of labour, both within the household itself and between the private realm of the household and the world outside. Feminist scholars, particularly those operating within a Marxist framework, have seen women's confinement to the domestic, reproductive sphere, their inability to access the public domain on equal terms with men, and the 'naturalization' of this arrangement at the ideological level ('woman's place is in the home') as the historical and contemporary source of women's subjection. They have particularly taken issue with those traditions in sociology/anthropology, and some earlier feminist writings (such as of Michelle Rosaldo 1974), that have placed the opposition of the private and the public realms at the centre of kinship theory (see Moore 1988: 21ff.; Yanagisako and Collier 1987). Following the suggestive lead of Jack Goody and S.J. Tambiah (Goody 1976; Goody and Tambiah 1973), feminist social scientists have recently sought to explore connections between the sexual division of labour in the household and the wider political economy, the structure of property rights, the nature of marriage payments (bride wealth or dowry), the frequency of divorce and remarriage, sexual permissiveness, restrictions on women's movement in public space (especially the institution of purdah), and modes of production in different ecological environments (see Agarwal 1994).

An outstanding example of the empirical investigation of the hypothesized connection between women's work (particularly their participation in agricultural labour) and their overall social status is Ursula

Sharma's comparative case study of women's economic roles in a village in Himachal Pradesh, where women participate actively in paid and unpaid agricultural work, and one in Punjab, where women have been increasingly withdrawn from the agricultural labour force (Sharma 1980). Though the Himachali women were publicly more visible, Sharma concluded that they did not *on this account* have conspicuously more domestic or extra-domestic 'social power' than their Punjabi counterparts.[24] She attributed this to a complex of social structural and cultural factors, but especially to women's effective exclusion from inheritance rights in land in both states (notwithstanding the formal provisions of the Hindu Succession Act of 1956), and their ultimate economic dependence on their male kin. Additionally, even where women did have title to property (in inherited land, in dowry goods, or in wages), Sharma stressed, this property was rarely—given cultural and social structural constraints—under their own control and management.

The measurement of women's socio-economic status in terms of the rate of their participation in the workforce is a somewhat problematic issue which one need not go into at this point, except to note that these measures fail to capture and account for the quantum and value of women's unpaid labour and their productive work in the domestic sphere, in home-based industry, and in reproducing class status through what Hanna Papanek has aptly termed 'family status production work' (see Papanek 1989). This latter aspect of women's work has also been addressed by Sharma in the course of a study of the economic roles of employed women and housewives in an urban centre of north India (Shimla, Himachal Pradesh) (1986). As in the rural study already mentioned (Sharma 1980), Sharma found that neither ownership of property nor monetary earnings *in themselves* could ensure women's economic independence, since their control over these resources was constrained by generational and sexual asymmetries of power within the household, and by social codes of feminine deportment. In any case, without reciprocal adjustments by their male kinsmen, women's participation in the labour force, for the most part, resulted in their shouldering the 'double burden' of unpaid housework and paid employment (see Kapur 1970; Karlekar 1982: Chapter 5).

The economic and political role of the household as an intermediary unit between the individual and the state is prominently acknowledged in public policy and administration, public goods and services being routinely allocated to the household as if it were a single unit of consumption. Similarly, the household is seen as a self-regulating administrative unit, whose individual members are identified in terms of their relations to the household 'head' (usually assumed to be the seniormost male member), who is their representative in the public domain and whose authority over other members is questioned only in the event of exceptional abuse of power.

These commonplace assumptions have been challenged recently—at the theoretical level within economics, as well as on pragmatic and ethical (equity) grounds. For instance, economist Amartya Sen (1983) has urged interrogation of commonplace assumptions on the nature of the household as an economic institution, arguing for its recognition as an arena of both cooperation and conflict, of the mutual 'bargaining' over resources, in which some members are structurally so placed that they are likely to get the worst end of the bargain. In the context of the Indian family, Sen points to gender as a major basis of disadvantage, affecting notions of entitlement and access to land, food, education and medical attention, and severely compromising the life chances of females vis-à-vis males, differentially through the life course (Das Gupta 1995; Kynch and Sen 1983; also Drèze 1990; Papanek 1990). This approach has been further elaborated by Bina Agarwal (1994: 53–71; and 1997) who, like Ursula Sharma (1980), has stressed that it is particularly their restricted access to *land* as the major productive resource in South Asia that has placed the greatest limits on women's bargaining position in the family.

Though the assumption of the 'unitary' household is not one that sociologists/anthropologists have been wont to make (as noted, Parsons had maintained that the modern nuclear family was a basic and functional unit of society *precisely because* of its generational hierarchy of authority and sexual division of labour), the economists' linking of the political economy of the household and the wider society with reference to the goal of distributive justice has been an important corrective to the status quoist assumptions of functionalist anthropology/sociology (see Morgan 1975: 95ff. and Chapter 5), as well as to the gender blindness of neoclassical economics.

Family Roles and Relationships

Though the analysis of family roles and relationships finds little place in discussions of change in household composition, descriptions of both normative expectations and behavioural patterns have been, and rightly continue to be, a mainstay of anthropological, sociological, and social psychological writing on the family (for excellent examples, see Bennett 1983; Das 1976; Ross 1961; Trawick 1990). Apart from interviews, surveys, and the participant observation of family-interaction patterns, sociologists and others have found in literature, the arts, the contemporary mass media and 'folklore' rich sources of data, albeit to be used with caution and sensitivity to the constraints of genre. In particular, folklore and women's genres have provided important insights into cultural norms, as well as evidence of vigorous critiques of these same norms from the viewpoint of the disadvantaged (see Chowdhry 1994; Raheja and Gold 1996: esp. Chapter 2; Srinivas 1942).

Among the issues that have dominated cross-cultural research especially on changes in family, the relative priority accorded to different dyadic relationships is of special interest. It has been proposed, for instance, that the family system of (patrilineal north) India is based on the father–son relationship, while that of North America is based on the conjugal relation (see Inden and Nicholas 1977). Others have argued that Indian kinship emphasizes the mother–son bond over that of husband and wife (Kakar 1981: Chapter 3; Nandy 1980) or of father and son (Hsu 1963). Still others argue that seen from the viewpoint of women, the overriding opposition is between a woman's role as daughter/sister (that is patrilineal kinswoman) and her role as wife (Bennett 1983; Karve 1953; Minturn 1993: Chapter 2); or that functions of sexuality and procreativity have been dichotomously projected on to the complementary social roles of the wife *versus* the 'other woman' as in the feminine role structure of Indian popular cinema [see Uberoi 1997]; and so on.

Certainly, most observers would agree that the introduction and valorization of the ideal of companionate and romantic marriage over the last century has simultaneously focused attention on the conjugal bond and given rise to cultural conflict over the 'meaning' of marriage and of wifehood. Feminist historians and historically minded sociologists have taken the lead in exploring this theme, using a variety of data sources, from public debates on legal reform to the arts and mass media (e.g. Sarkar 1993; papers in Uberoi 1996a).

As Talcott Parsons might have predicted, the new emphasis on the conjugal relationship and on values of romance and companionship within marriage has put the conjugal relationship under extra strain, directing the sociologist's attention to issues of domestic violence and marital discord and breakdown. Some of the most sensitive and suggestive ethnography of Indian marriage and family relations is to be found in studies by psychologists and psychoanalysts (e.g. Kakar 1989), and by social workers who seek to understand the cultural and social ambience in which 'violence is the form assumed by sexual love in a conjugal context', where antinomies of 'suspicion and sexual love', 'possession and desire', 'authority and affection' intersect in the husband's oftentimes brutal impress on his wife's body (Geetha 1998).

THE FAMILY IN THE SYSTEM OF FAMILIES

The academic and public focus on 'the family' as the prioritized object of study tends to obscure two important facts. The first is the empirical *variety* of family forms, of which, as noted, South Asia presents a great number.

From this perspective, to speak of *the* Indian family is to assign normative value to only one of these many types (that is the patrilineal joint family of the northern type). The second is the fact that 'the family' pertains only in the context of what one might term a *system* of families. It does not, indeed cannot, exist in itself. How such a system is to be interpreted, however, is the subject of much debate and the basis of theoretically opposed positions in the sociology/anthropology of family and kinship. For instance, in A.R. Radcliffe-Brown's structural-functional anthropology, 'the basic unit on which the kinship system is built' is the 'elementary family', consisting of a man, his wife and their children, and comprising the 'three basic relationships' of (i) parent and child, (ii) siblings, and (iii) husband and wife as parents of the same child or children (Radcliffe-Brown 1950: 51). Each member of the elementary family connects with a member of another elementary family in a second-order relationship (for example, mother's brother) and each again in a third-order relationship (for example, mother's brother's son), and so on: 'This interlocking of elementary families creates a network of ... genealogical relations, spreading out indefinitely' (Radcliffe-Brown: 52).

A not dissimilar perspective was proposed by Talcott Parsons who stressed that every individual is, uniquely, a member of *two* different conjugal families: that into which he was born, called the 'family of orientation', and the 'family of procreation' founded by his marriage (Parsons 1959: 242ff). These two conjugal families comprise 'the inner circle of the kinship structure', each member of which is a connecting link with another conjugal family (Parsons 1959: 245).

A very different orientation has been suggested, however, by the French anthropologist, Claude Lévi-Strauss. In his model, the basic unit of kinship is not the 'naturalized' elementary family but the 'family' of a brother-sister pair, the sister's husband and their child—or, more parsimoniously, the relationship of brothers-in-law. This elementary structure derives from the universal prohibition of incest. As Lévi-Strauss put it,

> *The prohibition of incest establishes a mutual dependency between families,* compelling them, in order to perpetuate themselves, to give rise to new families. ... For incest prohibitions simply state that families (however they should be defined) can only marry between each other and that they cannot marry inside themselves [Lévi-Strauss (1956) 1960: 277, emphasis added].

Supplementing the social function of the incest taboo, many societies also prescribe certain categories of kinsfolk as desirable marriage partners, setting up by this means intricate systems of marital 'exchange' (see Lévi-Strauss (1956) 1960: 279ff.; and [1949] 1969; Trautmann, this volume). Thus marriage is not (as it may appear from a commonsensical contemporary western perspective), primarily an arrangement between two *individuals*. It is an 'alliance' between two *families*, which is typically perpetuated into the next generation in the special relation of the mother's brother to his sister's children and perhaps, through further marital alliances, indefinitely.

As is well known, south Indian kinship is structurally distinct from north Indian kinship, having 'positive', not merely 'negative', rules of marriage. But in either case, as Louis Dumont in particular has argued (1966), it is the relationship of *affinity* (i.e. of marriage) that ultimately structures the kinship system. Expressed and consolidated in conventional patterns of gift giving and rules of kinship etiquette, Hindu marriage institutes a hierarchical relationship between 'wife-takers' (superior) and 'wife-givers' (inferior). In this way the kinship system of South Asian Hindus engages with the caste system, for each marriage not only links individuals and families, but also reproduces the hierarchy of Hindu caste society.

The 'alliance' perspective has been of singular importance in transforming the understanding of Indian family and kinship and its many varieties, and in rendering the institution of 'arranged marriage', so called, in a new, and rather less exoticized, light. That is, arranged marriage is not merely an expression of the authority of seniors over juniors in the family, but is essential to the reproduction of the family as a system of kinship *and* affinity embedded within the wider structure of caste. Needless to add, it also reproduces communitarian separateness.

CONCLUSION AND NEW DIRECTIONS

In reviewing the current state of Indian family and kinship studies, this chapter took as its starting point the single question that has dominated professional and popular discourse on the Indian family: namely the fate of the joint family in modern times. In particular, it has followed one trajectory of this debate in the sociological literature—the redefinition of the object of study as the co-resident/commensal household. This gesture, though it introduced new rigour into sociological studies of changes in family composition, has had little impact on the terms and direction of public discourse. This itself, perhaps, suggests a challenge: Is it not possible for the sociologist of the family to engage in a more constructive way with people's own understanding of their family life, rather than simply dismissing this understanding as the empirically unfounded product of cultural nostalgia? Second, the focus on household composition as the aspect of family that can be empirically *quantified* has been self-limiting. There is certainly a need for continued investigation of changing patterns of household formation, composition, and dispersion—over different regions, castes, communities, and classes in India. Apart from any other justification, this is intimately connected to public policy in several domains. But this should not become a pretext for ignoring the more ineffable aspects of family life and relationships and the wide range of functions that households/families typically perform.

This chapter has attempted to briefly survey the literature on these other dimensions of family life, underlining that these are areas where sociology and anthropology need to plumb their own disciplinary resources and histories as well as to engage actively with other social sciences. This does not imply acceptance of the idea that the family is functional, consensual, and homeostatic. On the contrary, sociologists need to confront (and not to abandon to psychology and social work) the dysfunctional and pathological aspects of family life, to recognize the family's capacity for adapting to changing circumstances, and indeed to acknowledge that questions of justice, human rights, distributional equity, directed social transformation, and policy formulation *are* the professional business of sociologists in general, and sociologists of the family in particular.

Third, in following the trajectory of the debate on the modern fate of the Hindu joint family, this chapter has, like the participants in that debate, colluded in the equation of *the* Indian family with the Hindu patrilineal joint family. It has thus marginalized consideration of the kinship patterns of non-Hindu and tribal communities, of communities following principles of matrilineal or bilateral descent, and of groups for whom the joint family is neither the cultural ideal nor an empirical preference (see Singh 1993). Some writers argue that *regional* patterns of kinship overwhelm communitarian differences (Agarwal 1994), but in general the perception of the Indian family that prevails, among sociologists and the wider public, is a generalized and hegemonic Indo-Aryan/north Indian one. This returns us to our earlier discussion of the mindset of the earlier generation of Indian sociologists, and our observations on the important role of the family as the trope for community and nation.

A broadening of the agenda for sociological studies of Indian family and kinship suggests going beyond head counting and genealogical reckoning to engaging in methodologically eclectic and unconventional ways with new sources of data—literature, the arts, popular culture and mass media (see Wadley 1998: 123), with the data sources of the public domain (law, politics, public administration [Agarwal 2000; Uberoi 1996a: Chapter 14]), and with historical records of various types. These are sources that sociologists have so far scarcely tapped.

The sociology of the Indian family, I have suggested here, seems to have been trapped in a debate which is no longer productive of new insights. It has also fallen victim to its own narcissistic preoccupations, in the sense that there is very little engagement with contemporary theoretical challenges in family and kinship studies, such as they are, nor much openness to insights from cross-cultural and historical research. This is ultimately impoverishing. South Asian ethnography in the past was simultaneously shaped by, and itself contributed to shaping, the evolutionist and diffusionist theories of the pioneers of family and kinship studies in anthropology and sociology—Henry Sumner Maine, Lewis Henry Morgan and W.H.R. Rivers (See Uberoi 1993: 7–20); it provided grounds for the exploration of the integrative social function of religious belief and ritual in relation to different levels of social organization (Radcliffe-Brown 1952); it afforded illustration of the structurating principles and inbuilt tensions of matrilineal kinship systems (Gough 1959; Radcliffe-Brown 1950: 72–82; Schneider and Gough 1961); it furthered the testing and elaboration of the alliance approach to kinship studies (Lévi-Strauss [1949] 1969; Dumont 1968 and 1983a; see Uberoi 1993: 20–31), as well as of the cultural approach in vogue during the 1970s (Inden and Nicholas 1977; Schneider [1968] 1980; Ostor et al. 1983); and it provided a well-documented instance of the impact of 'modernization' on the family in developing countries (Goode 1963: Ch. 5). Indian ethnography also substantiated the case for instituting a conceptual distinction between the 'family' as a genealogical construct and the 'household' as a residential-commensal unit in the context of historical and cross-cultural research on household dynamics (Wilk and Netting 1984; Carter 1984).

But that is all in the past: a legacy. For the present, I believe, there is urgent need for renewal.

ENDNOTES

1. I have possibly exaggerated here the opposition of the anthropology of kinship and the sociology of the family in the western academy to make this point. Certainly, pioneers of new or synoptic perspectives in the sociology of the family have often sought to bolster their claims to theoretical universality by reference to the data of comparative ethnography (see Goode 1964; Parsons and Bales 1955: Chapter 6; or latterly Robertson 1991). At the same time, anthropologists have intermittently sought to bring their distinctive perspectives and methodologies to bear on family, kinship, and marriage in advanced, industrial societies, or on ethnic communities within these societies (see Bott 1957; Firth et al. 1970; Schneider [1968] 1980). Nonetheless, the metropolitan distinction between the anthropology of kinship and marriage and the sociology of the family has been perpetuated in the syllabi of Indian universities, notwithstanding the overlapping disciplinary affiliations of many Indian anthropologists and sociologists.

2. The three social institutions commonly held to characterize 'traditional' Indian society are the caste system, the village community, and the joint-family (Kapadia 1955: 233; Karve 1953: Introduction). Of the three, it is the family which has been viewed most positively in both public and sociological discourse (see Béteille 1991). Attitudes to the caste system and village community have been more ambiguous, indeed, often hostile. On the latter, see Jodhka 1998.

3. In retrospect, it seems somewhat odd that the criterion for establishing an 'ideal type' of Indian family pattern should be seen to depend on the demonstration that *the majority* of persons, or of families, statistically conform to the pattern.

4. For a summary of views on this question, see Madan (1976).

5. This is not to say that such sources are irrelevant, for they indicate ideals of family life that continue to command prestige in Hindu society. Shah, in fact, finds a role for such ideals through M.N. Srinivas's concept of 'Sanskritization', that is the social process whereby lower-caste groups attempt to raise their status in the caste hierarchy by adopting the more 'Sanskritized' kinship (and ritual) practices of higher-caste groups such as a ban on widow remarriage.

6. Shah's definition of the household is more problematic than is apparent at first sight, combining as it does the three features of (i) kinship relationship, (ii) co-residence, and (iii) commensality. In practice anthropologists have often found it difficult to decide, for instance, whether a family member residing in the city but maintaining his village household and returning there frequently should or should not be counted as a member of the village household (perhaps even its 'head'). Census and National Sample Survey (NSS) definitions of the household have focused on features of residence and commensality, and have therefore included servants, sometimes even 'visitors', in their definition of the household. For a useful discussion of conceptual problems in different definitions of the household (the disciplines of anthropology/sociology, the Census, and the NSS), see Rao (1992).

7. The twelve types are as follows: (1) *nuclear family*, a couple with or without unmarried children; (2) *supplemented nuclear family*; (3) *sub-nuclear family*; (4) *single-person household*; (5) *supplemented sub-nuclear family*; (6) *collateral joint-family*; (7) *supplemented collateral joint-family*; (8) *lineal joint-family*; (9) *supplemented lineal joint-family*; (10) *lineal-collateral joint-family*; (11) *supplemented lineal-collateral joint-family*; and a residual category, (12) *other*. See Kolenda (1987: 11–13) and A.M. Shah's perceptive critique of this scheme (1973: 220–5).

8. For instance, a high or rising proportion of bachelor households may indicate a situation of migration or social upheaval, the bachelor household in one place being matched by a female-headed household in another; or it may indicate a situation provoked by imbalances in the sex ratios and consequent distortions in the marriage market. Or, should the single persons be widows, one may be confronting a category of extreme social and material deprivation that demands active intervention (e.g. Chen 1998; Drèze 1990). On the other hand, a marked increase in spinsterhood would indicate a major change in one of the most persistent features of Indian family life—the near universality of marriage for Indian women (see Raju et al. 1999: 80).

9. All-India figures for 1981 (using a dichotomous classification) indicate a slightly higher proportion of nuclear over joint families in both urban and rural areas (see Shah 1998: 74).

10. Kolenda calculates that with 30 per cent of more joint families in a population, over 50 per cent of persons would reside in such households (1968: 390).

11. In this connection, it is pertinent that M.S. Gore's study (1968) of families of the Aggarwal business community in and around Delhi was unable to demonstrate significant differences in family size and composition between the rural and urban sample

families, though he did report *attitudinal* differences on several counts, correlating with respondents' educational levels (cf. Vatuk 1972: esp. Chapters 3 and 7). See Abbi (1969) and Shah (1973: 204–7) for critiques of this well-known study.

12. To the usual distinction Kolenda has added some further points of difference: (i) differing cultural norms as to the appropriate timing of household partition (Kolenda 1967); (ii) differing degrees of what she calls women's 'bargaining power' in the family, as reflected in such features as women's relative freedom of divorce and remarriage, the institution of bridewealth versus that of dowry, and stronger ties with the wife's or the husband's kin (Kolenda 1967); (iii) for certain areas of rural Rajasthan which have registered unusually high proportions of joint households, traditions of young adolescent marriage related to region-specific customs such as sibling- and collateral-set marriages and multiple marriages (Kolenda 1989); and (iv) dependence on the joint family as a labour unit which is both a 'work team' and a 'well team' (Kolenda 1989). These and a number of other factors, including women's rights of inheritance to landed property, have been explored more consistently by Bina Agarwal in a major study of the geography of women's land rights through South Asia (1994). See also Raju et al. (1999) for a demographer's presentation of some of these factors.

13. The timing of this 'nuclearization', and the possible factors which facilitate or impede it, is the subject of a useful demographic study by K.N.M. Raju (1998). See also the detailed analyses of cases of household partition in Madan ([1965] 1989) and Parry (1979).

14. See, however, the important paper by P.N. Mari Bhat (Bhat 1996) on the regional distribution of joint families in the context of fertility limitation, based on data from the 1991 Census and the 1981 Census household tables; also S. Raju et al. (1999).

15. See Bharat (1996) for a social psychologist's self-critical discussion and assessment of the various 'measures' of aspects of family life that psychologists have devised or adapted for the Indian context.

16. For a critique of structural-functionalism in family studies, see Morgan (1975: Chapter 1, esp. 40–8).

17. This is, of course, a rather crude summary of a much more complex position, but it is not necessary to address these other aspects here.

18. This is not to disregard the heterogeneity of approaches classed as functionalist, nor to discount their several well-publicized limitations. D.H.J. Morgan (1975: Chapter 1) has summed up these limitations as emphasis: (i) on function more than dysfunction (whether for the individual or for society); (ii) consensus more than conflict; and (iii) stability rather than change.

19. There is probably much to commend Davis's formulation, which appears to be supported by macro-level data (see Bhat 1996), though its empirical corroboration at micro level has not actually been conclusive (see, for example, Patel 1994: 66). One reason for this, as Davis, himself had pointed out in the article referred to, is that nuclear households in India are often located in very close proximity to the larger kin group, so that fertility decisions are *still* likely to be influenced by the extended family, regardless of the formal type of family/household organization. See also Raju (1998).

20. An interesting exception here is Promilla Kapur's study of the life histories of Indian 'call-girls' (Kapur 1978).

21. Recent focus on the phenomenon of child labour and the 'rights of the child' has, however, drawn attention to the need for engagement between social scientists and policy makers on the concept of childhood. See Burra (1995); also Nieuwenhuys ([1994] 1999).

22. To these mechanisms for reproducing class identity, Béteille might have added the importance of strategies of matchmaking in recruiting influential affines. For an early reflection on the family's role in the social reproduction of class status, see Ross (1959).

23. For instance, providing old-age care or raising women's educational levels may be proposed as a means towards the achievement of population limitation, rather than as desirable social goals in themselves (see Uberoi 1996b).

24. More recent research has, however, confirmed a remarkable enhancement of women's 'capabilities' (education, literacy, health) in Himachal Pradesh, if not compared to neighbouring Punjab/Haryana, at least compared to other states of the 'northern' zone of kinship (See *Public Report* 1999).

REFERENCES

Abbi, Behari. 1969. 'Urban Family in India: A Review Article'. *Contributions to Indian Sociology* (n.s.). 3:116–27.

Agarwal, Bina. 1988. *Structures of Patriarchy: State, Community and Household in Modernizing Asia*. New Delhi: Kali for Women.

_____. 1994. *A Field of one's Own: Gender and Land Rights in South Asia*. Cambridge: Cambridge University Press.

_____. 1997. '"Bargaining" and Gender Relations: Within and Beyond the Household'. *Feminist Economics*. 3(1): 1–51.

_____. 2000. '"The Family" in Public Policy: Fallacious Assumptions and Gender Implications'. Ninth Lecture NCAER Golden Jubilee Seminar Series, National Council of Applied Economic Research, New Delhi.

Allen, Michael. 1982. 'Introduction: The Hindu View of Women'. In Michael Allen and S.N. Mukherjee, eds, *Women in India and Nepal*. 1–20. Canberra: Australian National University.

Ariès, Philippe. 1962. *Centuries of Childhood: A History of Family Life*. New York: Alfred Knopf.

Basu, Alaka. 1992. *Culture, the Status of Women and Demographic Behaviour: Illustrated with the Case of India*. Oxford: Clarendon Press.

Bennett, Lynn. 1983. *Dangerous Wives and Sacred Sisters: Social and Symbolic Roles of High-caste Women in Nepal*. New York: Columbia University Press.

Béteille, André. 1991. 'The Reproduction of Inequality: Occupation, Caste and Family'. *Contributions to Indian Sociology*. 25(1):3–28. (Reprinted in Patricia Uberoi, ed., 1993 *Family, Kinship and Marriage in India*. Delhi: Oxford University Press: 435–51).

Bharat, Shalini, ed. 1996. *Family Measurement in India*. New Delhi: Sage Publications.

_____. 1999. *HIV/AIDS Related Discrimination, Stigmatisation and Denial in India: A Study in Mumbai and Bangalore*. Mumbai: Unit for Family Studies, Tata Institute of Social Sciences.

Bharat, Shalini and Murli Desai, eds. 1991. *Research on Families with Problems in India: Issues and Implications*. 2 vols. Bombay: Tata Institute of Social Sciences.

Bhat, P.N. Mari. 1996. 'Contours of Fertility Decline in India: A District Level Study Based on the 1991 Census'. In K. Srinivasan, ed., *Population Policy and Reproductive Health*, 96–117. New Delhi: Hindustan Publishing Corporation and Population Foundation of India.

Bott, E. 1957. *Family and Social Network*. London: Tavistock.

Burra, Neera. 1995. *Born to Work: Child Labour in India*. Delhi: Oxford University Press.

Butcher, Melissa. 1999. 'Parallel Texts: The body and television in India'. In Christiane Brosius and Melissa Butcher, eds, *Image Journeys: Audio-visual Media and Cultural Change in India*, 165–96. New Delhi: Sage Publications.

Carstairs, G. Morris. 1957. *The Twice-born: A Study of a Community of High-caste Hindus.* London: Hogarth Press.

Carter, Anthony J. 1984. 'Household Histories'. In Robert McC. Netting Richard R. Wilk and Eric J. Arnould, eds, *Households: Comparative Studies of the Domestic Group*, 44–53. Berkeley: University of California Press.

Chen, Martha Alter, ed. 1998. *Widows in India: Social Neglect and Public Action*. New Delhi: Sage Publications.

Chowdhry, Prem. 1994. *The Veiled Women: Shifting Gender Equations in Rural Haryana, 1880–1990*. Delhi: Oxford University Press.

Daniel, E. Valentine. 1984. *Fluid Signs: Being a Person the Tamil Way*. Berkeley: University of California Press.

Das, Veena. 1976. 'Masks and Faces: An Essay on Punjabi Kinship'. *Contributions to Indian Sociology*. 10(1):1–30. (Reprinted in Patricia Uberoi, ed. 1993. *Family, Kinship and Marriage in India*. Delhi: Oxford University Press, 198–224).

———. 1988. 'Femininity and the Orientation to the Body'. In Karuna Chanana, ed., *Socialisation, Education and Women: Explorations in Gender Identity*, 193–207. New Delhi: Orient Longman.

———. 1995. *Critical Events: An Anthropological Perspective on Contemporary India*. Delhi: Oxford University Press.

———. 1996. 'Sexual Violence, Discursive Formations and the State'. *Economic and Political Weekly*. 31(35–7):2411–23.

Das Gupta, Monica. 1987. 'Selective Discrimination against Female Children in Rural Punjab, India'. *Population and Development Review*. 13(1):77–100.

———. 1995: 'Life Course Perspectives on Women's Autonomy and Health Outcomes'. *American Anthropologist*. 97(3):481–91.

Davis, Kingsley. 1955. 'Institutional Patterns Favouring High Fertility in Underdeveloped Areas'. *Eugenics Quarterly*. 2: 33–9.

Desai, I.P. 1964. *Some Aspects of Family in Mahuva*. Bombay: Asia Publishing House.

Drèze, Jean. 1990. *Widows in Rural India*. London School of Economics, Development Economics Research Programme Discussion Paper Series, no. 26.

Dube, Leela. 1986. 'Seed and Earth: The Symbolism of Biological Reproduction and the Sexual Relations of Production'. In Leela Dube, Eleanor Leacock, and Shirley Ardener, eds. *Visibility and Power: Essays on Women in Society and Development*, 22–53. Delhi: Oxford University Press.

———. 1988. 'On the Construction of Gender: Hindu Girls in Patrilineal India'. In Karuna Chanana, ed., *Socialisation, Education and Women: Explorations in Gender Identity,* 166–92. New Delhi: Orient Longman.

Dube, Leela. 1997. *Women and Kinship: Comparative Perspectives on Gender in South and South-East Asia*. New Delhi: Vistaar Publications.

Dumont, Louis. 1966. 'Marriage in India. The Present State of the Question, III. North India in Relation to South India'. *Contributions to Indian Sociology*. 9:90–114.

———. 1968. 'Marriage Alliance'. In D. Sills, ed., *International Encyclopaedia of the Social Sciences*. 10:19–23. New York: Macmillan and Free Press.

———. 1983a. *Affinity as a Value: Marriage Alliance in South India with Comparative Essays on Australia*. Chicago: University of Chicago Press.

———. 1983b. 'The Debt to Ancestors and the Category of *Sapinda*'. In Charles Malamoud, ed., *Debt and Debtors*, 1–20. Delhi: Vikas Publishing Hase.

Dyson, Tim and Mick Moore. 1983. 'On Kinship Structure, Female Autonomy and Demographic Behavior in India'. *Population and Development Review*. 9(1):35–60.

Erikson, E.H. 1950. *Childhood and Society*. New York: W.W. Norton.

Epstein. T.S. 1973. *South India: Yesterday, Today and Tomorrow*. London: Macmillan.

Firth, Raymond, James Hubert, and Anthony Forge. 1970. *Families and their Relatives: Kinship in a Middle-class Sector of London*. London: Routledge & Kegan Paul.

Fortes, Meyer. 1962. 'Introduction'. In Jack Goody, ed., *The Developmental Cycle in Domestic Groups*, 1–14. Cambridge: Cambridge University Press.

Fox, Robin. 1967. *Kinship and Marriage: An Anthropological Perspective*. Harmondsworth: Penguin Books.

Freed, Stanley A. and Ruth S. Freed. 1983. 'The Domestic Cycle in India: Natural History of a Will-o'-the-wisp'. *American Ethnologist*. 10(2):313–27.

Fruzzetti, Lina M. [1982] 1990. *The Gift of a Virgin: Women, Marriage and Ritual in a Bengali Society*. Delhi: Oxford University Press.

Geetha, V. 1998. 'On Bodily Love and Hurt'. In Mary E. John and Janaki Nair, eds, *A Question of Silence: The Sexual Economies of Modern India*, 304–31. New Delhi: Kali for Women.

Ghurye, G.S. 1955. *Family and Kin in Indo-European Culture*. Bombay: Oxford University Press.

———. 1960. *After a Century and a Quarter*. Bombay: Popular Prakashan.

———. 1973. *I and Other Explorations*. Bombay: Popular Prakashan.

Good, Anthony. 1991. *The Female Bridegroom: A Comparative Study of Life-crisis Rituals in South India and Sri Lanka*. Oxford: Clarendon.

Goode, William J. 1963. *World Revolution and Family Patterns*. London: Free Press of Glencoe.

———. 1964. *The Family*. Foundations of Modern Sociology Series. Englewood Cliffs, NJ: Prentice-Hall.

Goody, Jack. 1976. *Production and Reproduction: A Comparative Study of the Domestic Domain*. Cambridge: Cambridge University Press.

———. 1990. *The Oriental, the Ancient and the Primitive: Systems of Marriage and the Family in the Pre-industrial Societies of Eurasia*. Cambridge: Cambridge University Press.

Goody, Jack and S.J. Tambiah. 1973. *Bridewealth and Dowry*. Cambridge: Cambridge University Press.

Gore, M.S. 1968. *Urbanization and Family Change*. Bombay: Popular Prakashan.

Gough, E. Kathleen. 1959. 'The Nayars and the Definition of Marriage'. *Journal of the Royal Anthropological Institute.* 58(5):826–53.

Gould, H.A. 1968:. 'Time Dimension and Structural Change in an Indian Kinship System'. In Milton Singer and C. Bernard Cohn, eds, *Structure and Change in Indian Society,* 413–21. New York: Wenner-Gren Foundation.

Gray, John N. 1995. *The Householder's World: Purity, Power and Dominance in a Nepali Village.* Delhi: Oxford University Press.

Greenough, Paul R. 1982. *Prosperity and Misery in Modern Bengal: The Famine of 1943– 44.* New York: Oxford University Press.

Hanchett, Suzanne. 1988. *Coloured Rice: Symbolic Structure in Hindu Family Festivals.* Delhi: Hindustan Pubulishing.

Harriss-White, Barbara. 1999. 'Gender-cleansing: The Paradox of Development and Deteriorating Female-life-chances in Tamil Nadu'. In Rajeswari Sunder Rajan, eds, *Signposts: Gender Issues in Post-Independence India,* 124–53. New Delhi: Kali for Women.

Hasan, Zoya, ed. 1994. *Forging Identities: Gender, Communities and the State.* New Delhi: Kali for Women.

Hershman, Paul. 1981. *Punjabi Kinship and Marriage.* Delhi: Hindustan Publishing Corporation.

Hsu, Francis L.K. 1963. *Clan, Caste and Club.* Princeton, N.J.: D. Van Nostrand.

Inden, Ronald B. and Ralph W. Nicholas. 1977. *Kinship in Bengali Culture.* Chicago: Chicago University Press.

Jayawardena, Kumari and Malathi de Alwis, eds. 1996. *Embodied Violence: Communalising Female Sexuality in South Asia.* New York: St Martin's Press. *Contextualising Women's Sexuality in South Asia.* New Delhi: Kali for Women.

Jodhka, Surinder S. 1998. 'From "Book View" to "Field View": Social Anthropological Construction of the Indian Village'. *Oxford Development Studies.* 26(3):311–31.

John, Mary and Janaki Nair, eds. 1998. *A Question of Silence? The Sexual Economies of Modern India.* New Delhi: Kali for Women.

Kakar, Sudhir. 1981. *The Inner World: A Psychoanalytic Study of Childhood and Society in India.* Delhi: Oxford University Press.

———. 1989. *Intimate Relations: Exploring Indian Sexuality.* New York: Viking/Penguin.

Kane, P.V. 1930–62. *History of Dharmasastra,* 5 vols. Poona: Bhandarkar Oriental Research Institute.

Kapadia, K.M. 1955. *Marriage and Family in India.* London: Oxford University Press.

Kapadia, Karin. 1995. *Siva and Her Sisters: Gender, Caste and Class in Rural South Asia.* Boulder, CO: Westview Press.

Kapur, Promilla. 1970. *Marriage and the Working Woman in India.* Delhi: Vikas Publishing House.

———. 1978. *Life and World of Call-girls in India: A Socio-psychological Study of the Aristocratic Prostitute.* Delhi: Vikas Publishing House.

Kapur, Ratna. ed. 1996. *Feminist Terrains in Legal Domains: Interdisciplinary Essays on Women and Law in India.* New Delhi: Kali for Women.

Kapur, Ratna and Brenda Cossman. 1996. *Subversive Sites: Feminist Engagements with Law in India.* New Delhi: Kali for Women.

Karlekar, Malavika. 1982. *Poverty and Women's Work: A Study of Sweeper Women in Delhi*. Delhi: Vikas Publishing House.

———. 1998: 'Domestic Violence'. *Economic and Political Weekly*. 33(27):1741–51.

Karve, Irawati. 1953. *Kinship Organization in India*. Poona: Deccan College Monograph Series.

Kessinger, Tom G. 1974. *Vilyatpur, 1848–1968: Social and Economic Change in a North Indian Village*. Berkeley: University of California Press.

Khare, Ravindra S. 1984. *The Untouchable as Himself: Ideology, Identity and Pragmatism among Lucknow Chamars*. Cambridge: Cambridge University Press.

———. 1998. 'The Issue of "Right to Food" among the Hindus: Notes and Comments'. *Contributions to Indian Sociology*. 32(2):253–78.

Kolenda, Pauline. 1967. 'Regional Differences in Indian Family Structure'. In Robert I. Crane, ed., *Regions and Regionalism in South Asian Studies*, 147–228. Durham, South Carolina: Duke University Press. (Reprinted in Kolenda 1987: Chapter 2).

———. 1968. 'Region, Caste and Family Structure: A Comparative Study of the Indian "Joint" Family'. In Milton Singer and Bernard Cohn, eds, *Structure and Change in Indian Society*, 339–96. New York: Wenner-Gren Foundation. (Reprinted in Pauline Kolenda, *Regional Differences in Family Structure in India*, 1987. Jaipur: Rawat Publications, Chapter 1.)

———. 1987. *Regional Differences in Family Structure in India*. Jaipur: Rawat Publications.

———. 1989. 'The Joint Household in Rural Rajasthan: Ecological, Cultural and Demographic Conditions for its Occurrence'. In John N. Gray and David J. Mearns, eds, *Society from the Inside out: Anthropological Perspectives on the South Asian Household*, 55–106. New Delhi: Sage Publications.

Kumar, Krishna. 1993. 'Study of Childhood and Family'. In T.S. Saraswathi and Baljit Kaur, eds, *Human Development and Family Studies in India: An Agenda for Research and Policy*, 67–76. New Delhi: Sage Publications.

Kynch, Jocelyn and Amartya Sen. 1983. 'Indian Women: Well-being and Survival'. *Cambridge Journal of Economics*. 7:363–80.

Lardinois, Roland. 1992. 'Family and Household as Practical Groups: Preliminary Reflections on the Hindu Joint Family'. In K. Saradamoni, ed., *Finding the Household: Conceptual and Methodological Issues*, 31–47. New Delhi: Sage Publications.

Laslett, Peter. 1972. 'Introduction: The History of the Family'. In Peter Laslet and R. Wall, eds, *Household and Family in Past Time*, 1–89. Cambridge: The University Press.

Levi-Strauss, Claude. [1956] 1960. 'The Family'. In Harry L. Shapiro, ed., *Man, Culture and Society*, 261–85. 2nd ed. New York: Galaxy Books.

———. [1949] 1969. *The Elementary Structures of Kinship*. London: Eyre & Spottiswoode.

Madan, T.N. 1976. 'The Hindu Family and Development'. *Journal of Social and Economic Studies*. 4(2): 211–31. (Reprinted in Patricia Uberoi, ed., *Family, Kinship and Marriage*, 1993. Delhi: Oxford University Press: 416–34).

———. 1983. 'The Ideology of the Householder among the Kashmiri Pandits'. In Akos Ostor, Lina Fruzzetti and Steve Barnett, eds, *Concepts of Person*, 99–117. Delhi: Oxford University Press.

Madan, T.N. [1965] 1989. *Family and Kinship: A Study of the Pandits of Rural Kashmir*. 2nd ed. Delhi: Oxford University Press.

Maine, Henry Sumner. [1861] 1972. *Ancient Law*. London: Everyman edition.

Mandelbaum, David G. 1988. *Women's Seclusion and Men's Honor: Sex Roles in North India*. Tucson: University of Arizona Press.

Marriott, Mckim. 1998. 'The Female Family Core Explored Ethnosociologically'. *Contributions to Indian Sociology* (n.s.). 32(2):279–304.

———. 1990. *India through Hindu Categories*. New Delhi: Sage Publications.

Mayer, Adrian C. 1960. *Caste and Kinship in Central India: A Village and its Region*. London: Routledge & Kegan Paul.

Miller, Barbara. [1981] 1997. *The Endangered Sex: Neglect of Female Children in Rural North India*. Delhi: Oxford University Press.

Minturn, Leigh. 1993. *Sita's Daughters: Coming out of Purdah. The Rajpur Women of Khalapur Revisited*. New York: Oxford University Press.

Minturn, Leigh and John Hitchcock. 1963. 'The Rajputs of Khalapur, India'. In B. Whiting, ed., *Six Cultures: Studies in Child Rearing*. New York: Wiley.

Misri, Urvashi. 1985. 'Child and Childhood: A Conceptual Construction'. *Contributions to Indian Sociology*. 19(1):115–32.

Moffatt. Michael. 1979. *An Untouchable Community in South India: Structure and Consensus*. Princeton: Princeton University Press.

Moore, Henrietta. 1988. *Feminism and Anthropology*. Minneapolis: University of Minnesota Press.

Morgan, D.H.J. 1975. *Social Theory and the Family*. London: Routledge & Kegan Paul.

Mulla, D.F. 1972. *Principles of Mohamedan Law*. 20th ed. Bombay: N.M. Tripathi.

Murdock, George Peter. 1949. *Social Structure*. New York: Macmillan Company.

Nair, Janaki. 1996. *Women and Law in Colonial India: A Social History*. New Delhi: Kali for Women.

Nandy, Ashis. 1980. 'Woman *versus* Womanliness in India: An Essay in Cultural and Political Psychology'. In Ashis Nandy, ed., *At the Edge of Psychology: Essays in Politics and Culture*, 32–46. Delhi: Oxford University Press.

Netting, Robert McC., Richard R. Wilk, and Eric J. Arnould, eds. 1984. *Households: Comparative and Historical Studies of the Domestic Group*. Berkeley: University of California Press.

Nieuwenhuys, Olga. [1994] 1999. *Children's Lifeworlds: Gender, Welfare and Labour in the Developing World*. New Delhi: Social Science Press.

Nimkoff, M.F. 1959. 'The Family in India: Some Problems Concerning Research on the Changing Family in India'. *Sociological Bulletin*. 8: 32–8.

Orenstein, H. 1961. 'The Recent History of the Extended Family in India'. *Social Problems*. 8:341–50.

Osella, Filippo and Caroline Osella. 1996. 'Articulation of Physical and Social Bodies in Kerala'. *Contributions to Indian Sociology*. 30(1): 37–68.

Ostor, Akos, Lina Fruzzetti, and Steve Barnett, eds. 1983. *Concepts of Person: Kinship, Caste, and Marriage in India*. Delhi: Oxford University Press.

Papanek, Hanna. 1982. 'Purdah: Separate Worlds and Symbolic Shelter'. In H. Papanek and G. Minault, eds, *Separate Worlds: Studies of Purdah in South Asia*, 3–53. Delhi: Chanakya Publications.

_____. 1989. 'Family Status-production Work: Women's Contribution to Social Mobility and Class Differentiation'. In Maitreyi Krishnaraj and Karuna Chanana, eds, *Gender and the Household Domain: Social and Cultural Dimensions*, 97–116. New Delhi: Sage Publications.

_____. 1990. 'To Each Less than She Needs, from Each More than She Can Do: Allocations, Entitlements, and Value'. In Irene Tinker, ed., *Persistent Inequalities: Women and World Development*, 162–81. New York: Oxford University Press.

Parry, J.P. 1979. *Caste and Kinship in Kangra*. Delhi: Vikas Publishing House.

Parsons, Talcott. [1949] 1959. 'The Social Structure of the Family'. In Ruth Anshen, ed., *The Family: Its Function and Destiny*. Revised ed., 241–74. New York: Harper.

Parsons, Talcott and Robert F. Bales. 1955. *Family, Socialization and Interaction Process*. Glencoe, Ill: The Free Press.

Patel, Tulsi. 1994. *Fertility Behaviour: Population and Society in a Rajasthan Village*. Delhi: Oxford University Press.

Pillai, S. Devadas. 1997. *Indian Sociology through Ghurye: A Dictionary*. Mumbai: Popular Prakashan.

Prabhu, Pandharinath H. [1940] 1995. *Hindu Social Organization: A Study in Socio-psychological and Ideological Foundations*. 4th ed. Bombay: Popular Prakashan.

Public Report on Basic Education in India. 1999. Delhi: Oxford University Press.

Radcliffe-Brown, A.R. 1950. 'Introduction'. In A.R. Radcliffe-Brown & Daryll Forde, eds, *African Systems of Kinship and Marriage*, 1–85. London: Oxford University Press.

_____. 1952. 'Foreword'. In M.N. Srinivas, ed., *Religion and Society among the Coorgs of South India*, 5–9. Oxford: Clarendon Press.

Raheja, Gloria Goodwin and Ann Grodzins Gold. 1996. *Listen to the Heron's Words: Reimagining Gender and Kinship in North* India. Delhi: Oxford University Press.

Raju, K.N.M. 1998. *Family and Household Functions: A Demographic Study*. Bangalore: Sunrise Publications.

Raju, Saraswati, Peter J. Atkins, Naresh Kumar, and Janet G. Townsend. 1999. *Atlas of Women and Men in India*. New Delhi: Kali for Women.

Rao, N.J. Usha. 1992. 'Gaps in Definitions and Analysis. A Sociological Perspective'. In K. Saradamoni, ed., *Finding the Household: Conceptual and Methodological Issues*, 49–74. New Delhi: Sage Publications.

Risseeuw, Carla and Rajni Palriwala. 1996. 'Introduction: Shifting Circles of Support'. In Rajni Palriwala and Carla Risseeuw, eds, *Shifting Circles of Support: Contextualising Gender and Kinship in South Asia and Sub-Saharan Africa*, 15–47. New Delhi: Sage Publications.

Robertson, A.F. 1991. *Beyond the Family: The Social Organization of Human Reproduction*. Cambridge: Polity Press.

Rosaldo, Michelle Z. 1974. 'Woman, Culture and Society: A Theoretical Overview'. In Michelle Z. Rosaldo and Louise Lamphere, eds, *Woman, Culture and Society*. Stanford: Stanford University Press.

Ross, Aileen D. 1959. 'Education and Family Change'. *Sociological Bulletin*. 8:39–44.

Ross Aileen D. 1961. *The Hindu Family in its Urban Setting*. Bombay: Oxford University Press.

Saradamoni, S. 1996. 'Women's Rights and the Decline of Matriliny is Southern India'. In Rajni Palriwala and Carla Risseeuw, eds, *Shifting Circles of Support: Contextualising Gender and Kinship in South Asia and Sub-Saharan Africa*, 133–54. New Delhi: Sage Publications.

Sarkar, Tanika. 1993. 'Rhetoric against Age of Consent: Resisting Colonial Reason and Death of a Child Wife'. *Economic and Political Weekly*. 27(36):1869–78.

Schneider, David M. [1968] 1980. *American Kinship: A Cultural Account*. 2nd. ed. Englewood Cliffs, N.J.: Prentice-Hall.

Schneider, David M. and E. Kathleen Gough. 1961. *Matrilineal Kinship*. Berkeley: University of California Press.

Sen, Amartya. 1983. 'Economics and the Family'. *Asian Development Review*. 1(2):14–26.

Shah. A.M. 1973. *The Household Dimension of the Family in India*. Berkeley: University of California Press.

_____. 1998. *The Family in India: Critical Essays*. Delhi: Orient Longman.

_____. 1999a. 'The family in the Census of India'. *Sociological Bulletin*. 48(1–2):235–7.

_____. 1999b: 'Changes in the Family and the Elderly'. *Economic and Political Weekly*. 34(20):1179–82.

Sharma, Ursula. 1978. 'Women and Their Affines: The Veil as a Symbol of Separation'. *Man*. 13:18–33.

_____. 1980. *Women, Work and Property in North West India*. London: Tavistock.

_____. 1986. *Women's Work, Class and the Urban Household: A Study of Shimla, North India*. London: Tavistock.

_____. 1989. 'Studying the Household: Industrialisation and Values'. In John N. Gray and David J. Mearnsm, *Society From the Inside Out: Anthropological Perspectives on the South Asian Household*, 35–54. New Delhi: Sage Publications.

Singer, Milton. 1968. 'The Indian Joint Family in Modern Industry'. In Milton Singer and Bernard Cohn, eds, *Structure and Change in Indian Society*, 423–52. New York: Wenner-Gren Foundation.

Singh, K.S., ed. 1993. *An Anthropological Atlas* (Anthropological Survey, *People of India*, vol. 11). Delhi: Oxford University Press.

Srinivas, M.N. 1942. *Marriage and Family in Mysore*. Bombay: New Book Company.

_____. 1952. *Religion and Society among the Coorgs of South India*. Oxford: Clarendon Press.

Srinivas, M.N. and E.A. Ramaswamy. 1977. *Culture and Human Fertility*. Delhi: Oxford University Press.

Tambiah, S.J. 1975. 'From Varna to Caste through Mixed Unions'. In Jack Goody, ed. *The Character of Kinship*. Cambridge: Cambirdge University Press.

Trautmann, Thomas R. 1981. *Dravidian Kinship*. Cambridge: Cambridge University Press.

_____. 1987. *Lewis Henry Morgan and the Invention of Kinship*. Berkeley: University of California Press.

Trawick, Margaret. 1996. *Notes on Love in a Tamil Family*. Berkeley: University of California Press.

Uberoi, Patricia, ed. 1993. *Family, Kinship and Marriage in India*. Delhi: Oxford University Press.

Uberoi, Patricia. 1995. 'Problems With Patriarchy: Conceptual Issues in the Engagement of Anthropology and Feminism'. *Sociological Bulletin*. 44(2):15–221.

———. 1996a. *Social Reform, Sexuality and the State*. New Delhi: Sage Publications.

———. 1996b. 'The Family in Official Discourse'. In *Second Nature: Women and the Family. India International Centre Quarterly*. Winter: 134–55.

———. 1997. 'Dharma and Desire, Freedom and Destiny: Rescripting the Man-woman Relationship in Popular Hindi Cinema'. In Meenakshi Thapan, ed., *Embodiment: Essays on Gender and Identity*, 145–71. Delhi: Oxford University Press.

Vatuk, Sylvia. 1972. *Kinship and Urbanization: White Collar Migrants in North India*. Berkeley: University of California Press.

———. 1982. 'Purdah Revisited: A Comparison of Hindu and Muslim Interpretations of the Cultural Meaning of Purdah in South Asia'. In H. Papanek and G. Minault, eds, *Separate Worlds: Studies of Purdah in South Asia*, 54–78. Delhi: Chanakya Publications.

Visaria, Leela. 1999. 'Deficit of Women in India: Magnitude, Trends, Regional Variations and Determinants'. In Bharati Ray and Aparna Basu, eds, *From Independence towards Freedom: Indian Women since 1947*, 80–99. Delhi: Oxford University Press.

Wadley, Susans S. 1999. 'Anthropology'. In Joseph W. Elder, Edward C. Dimock, Jr., and Ainslie T. Embree, eds, *India's Worlds and US Scholars*. 111–37. Delhi: Manohar/American Institute of Indian Studies.

Wadley, Susan and Bruce W. Derr. 1988. 'Karimpur Families Over Sixty Years'. *South Asian Anthropologist*. 9(2):119–32. (Reprinted in Patricia Uberoi, *Family, Kinship and Marriage in India*, 1993. Delhi: Oxford University Press, 393–415)

Wall, Richard, Jean Robin, and Peter Laslett, eds. 1983. *Family Forms in Historic Europe*. Cambridge: Cambridge University Press.

Wilk, Richard R. and Robert McC. Netting. 1984. 'Households: Changing Forms and Functions'. In Robert McC. Netting, Richard R. Wilk and Eric J. Arnould, eds, *Households: Comparative Historical Studies of the Domestic Group*, 1–28. Berkeley: University of California Press.

Yalman, Nur. 1963. 'On the Purity and Sexuality of Women in the Castes of Ceylon and Malabar'. *Journal of the Royal Anthropological Institute*. 93(1):25–58.

Yanagisako, Sylvia Junko and Jane Fishburne Collier. 1987. 'Toward a Unified Analysis of Gender and Kinship'. In Jane Fishburne Collier and Sylvia Junko Yanagisako, eds, *Gender and Kinship: Essays toward a Unified Analysis*, 14–50. Stanford: Stanford University Press.

Patterns of Marriage

Thomas R. Trautmann

Marriage is of central importance in all societies and has been so in each of the civilizations, but the configuration of marriage relations and the weight they are given vary enormously. In Indian civilization the emphasis on the married state has risen to a very high pitch over the long duration of its history. Thus the age at which marriage and its preliminaries take place has become ever younger. Until the last century the married state, so to say, had colonized a greater part of the life cycle of the individual. Correspondingly the condition of unmarried adults was marginalized, except for those who become monks or nuns, and that of widows and widowers was diminished. With an increasingly lower age at marriage, the renunciation of marriage for religious reasons has also had to occur at an ever earlier age than was the case in ancient times, as for example the *bala-pravrajika* (renunciation while still a child) of the Madhva monks of Udipi (Rao 1997) which occurs before puberty, or following the death of a partner.

In keeping with this centrality, marriage in India has acquired an extensive written record, especially in the Sanskrit texts on *dharma* (the Dharmashastra), through which these long-term tendencies can be traced and by which they were propagated and became Indiawide in their influence. The authority of the Dharmashastra for marriage was perpetuated until recent times by the colonial regime under the name of Hindu law (together with the Muslim law deriving from the Shariah) and was not displaced until after Independence with the enactment by Parliament of laws for Hindu marriage. There is thus a rich body of legal literature on marriage in the colonial period as well, that takes the Dharmashastra as its point of reference and source of authority. This literature has come to have a decided value for sociological and social-anthropological study, of which, indeed, it forms a beginning (a relevant example of this literature would be Gharpure [1943] on the concept of *sapindya*). Because of the existence of this written record and long history, the study of marriage in India by sociologists and social anthropologists has often combined the study of Dharmashastra and other ancient texts with field or studies of marriage in the present. This was especially true of Bombay sociologists G.S. Ghurye (1962, 1972), K.M. Kapadia (1947) and Irawati Karve (1965, among many other writings), and of French sociologist Louis Dumont (for example 1953, 1957, 1961–6). All studies of marriage in India, to a certain degree, take cognizance of this civilizational aspect of marriage.

Although marriage is powerfully shaped by norms thought to be eternal and propagated by the Dharmashastra, which make for a unitary Hindu culture of marriage that is Indiawide in scope, deviations from those norms by different castes and regions is not only tolerated but officially recognized. This is under the notions of *jati* dharma (customary laws of caste) and *desha* dharma (customary laws of regions) specific to and valid for certain castes or regions, though incapable of forming universal norms. So the norms of the Dharmashastra have always coexisted with an abundance of variations and contradictions of its tenets, with its express sanction. The unitary character of the Hindu culture of marriage has always been a loose synthesis presiding over a pluralism of particular cultures that cannot be deduced from the texts although they point to it. In particular there are specific patterns of marriage that have proved extremely durable, associated with the three large families of languages, Dravidian, Munda, and Indo-Aryan out of whose conjuncture Indian civilization emerged. Further, these regional patterns subtending Hindu marriage are also found among many others including among most of Muslim castes, so that while the Hindu/Muslim difference has governed the legal aspect of marriage since colonial times, the regional patterns are far more salient sociologically and historically, quite independent of the great religious traditions. Thus any discussion of marriage patterns in India has to attend both to the regional patterns and the legal cultures of marriage associated with the great religious traditions.

Marriage is itself central to sociology and social anthropology as the point of articulation of gender relations and the centrepiece of family structure, making it a privileged site for two of the major topics of investigation in the social sciences. It points beyond the family, being the means by which relations of alliance are formed *between* families, forming patterns that get their shape from the rule of marriage and the associated terminology of kinship. These patterns will be the object of examination here. It has been this extra-familial, 'alliance' dimension of marriage and its association with kinship terminology that has been the special discovery of social anthropology. Study of Indian marriage patterns has played a signal part in the first formation of social anthropology and sociology as well. In the work of L.H. Morgan (*Systems of Consanguinity and Affinity of the Human Family* 1871), for example, India was central to a comparison of kinship terminologies of Asia, Europe and the Indians of North America, and in *The Ancient City* (1864) some of the English literature on Hindu law generated by the colonial regime (principally translations of Manu and the *Mitakshara*) entered into Fustel de Coulanges's reconstruction of early Indo-European family law and ancestor worship.

DRAVIDIAN MARRIAGE PATTERNS

The outstanding example of a distinctive regional pattern of marriage is the south-Indian rule of cross-cousin marriage among speakers of the Dravidian languages. Its great antiquity is proved by the fact that it is discussed in the earliest period of the Dharmashastra literature, that of the *sutras*, where it is a question of the desha dharma of the Dravidas or southerners. The beauty and clarity of the Dravidian system, in which the semantic pattern of the terminology for kinship relations and the rule of marriage entail each other in a simple and transparent way, has made it a classic location for the study of marriage, and makes it a good starting point for a survey of marriage patterns in India.

We may say that cross cousins are the children of a brother and sister or, from the point of view of the children themselves, my cross cousin is my mother's brother's child or my father's sister's child. Cross cousins of opposite sex not only may, but should, marry. Conversely the children of a pair of brothers, or of a pair of sisters, are parallel cousins and must not marry, being like brothers and sisters to one another. Indeed they are called by the brother and sister words in the Dravidian languages (usually divided into elder and younger brother and sister). All the more remote cousins are also sorted out into the two groups of 'siblings' and cross cousins by the logic of cross-cousin marriage, the 'siblings' being unmarriageable and the cross cousins marriageable, so that the rule of marriage concerns a fairly large category of kin, not just first cousins. In a sense, we need to speak a Dravidian language to state more exactly what is meant by cross and parallel cousins in the Dravidian marriage rule, for all cousins are put in these two categories.

Moreover, the distinction between cross and parallel relatives is made not only in Ego's generation, but in those of the parents and the children, so that the three medial generations are bisected by the distinction between cross and parallel. In the parents' generation, the parents' same-sex siblings are assimilated to the parents; thus the father's brother is called father ('big' or 'little' father depending on his age in relation to the father: FB = F:), the mother's sister is a big or little sister (MZ = M). Because of these equations the children of such 'parents' are also my brothers and sisters, and are unmarriageable (FBCh = MZCh = Sb). But the parents' opposite-sex siblings (father's sister, mother's brother) are 'aunt' and 'uncle' or cross kin to me, and their children are my cross cousins. Conversely, the generation below me is divided into parallel kin consisting of my children and those assimilated to them (for a man, the brother's child, for a woman, the sister's child), and my cross kin (a man's sister's child or a woman's brother's child), who are 'nephews' and 'nieces' and who are marriageable to my children. The classification follows the logic of the marriage rule: 'children' or parallel kin

		♂				♀	
	X		II				X
G^2		*pāṭṭa* FF, MF				*pāṭṭi* FM, MM	
periya G^1 cinna		*māman* MB, FZH SpF	*periya-* FeB, MeZH *ciṇṇa-* FyB MyZh	*appā* F	*ammā* M	periya- MeZ, FeBW ciṇṇa- MyZ, FyBW	*attai* FZ, MBW SpM
G^0	e	*attāṇ* e(MBS), e(FZS)	*aṇṇaṇ* eB, e(FBS), e(MZS)		*akkā* eZ, e(FBD), e(MZD)		*mayni* e(MBD), e(FZD)
				ego			
	y	*maccinaṇ* y(MBS), y(FZS)	*tampi* yB, y(FBS), y(MZS)		*taṇkacci* yZ, y(FBD), y(MZD)		*koḷunti* y(MBD), y(FZD)
G^{-1}		*marumakaṇ* ♂ZS, ♀ BS	*makaṇ* S, ♂BS, ♀ ZS		*makaḷ* D, ♂BD, ♀ ZD		*marumakaḷ* ♂ZD, ♀ BD
G^{-2}		*pēraṇ* SS, DS				*pētti* SD, DD	

Fig. 1: Box diagram of a Dravidian kinship terminology (Nanjilanttu Vellalar)
Source: Trautmann (1981: 40).

are my own children and those of my same-sex sibling, who is assimilated to me, plus those of my opposite-sex cross cousin (whom the logic of the terminology assumes I have married); and my 'nephews' and 'nieces' or cross kin are the opposite, namely children of my same-sex cousins and opposite-sex siblings. In short, the three medial generations of the kinship terminology are completely

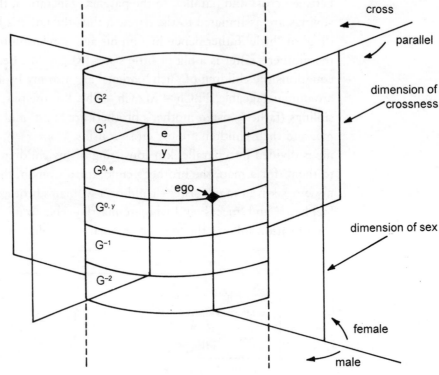

Fig. 2: Diagram of a Dravidian kinship terminology inscribed on a cylinder *Source:* Trautmann 1981: 41.

bifurcated by the distinction of crossness—that is the cross/parallel distinction—which applies in a checkerboard fashion to alternating bands of more distant kin. One could picture the universe of one's kin as being inscribed on a sheet of paper that is rolled up into a cylinder and divided into two sets based on two degrees of nearness and marriageability: parallel kin, at a distance of 0 and therefore not to be married, and cross kin at a distance of 1 and to be married, as shown in Figures 1 and 2.

A further feature of Dravidian terminologies is that the words for relationships created by marriage, such as 'mother-in-law' and 'father-in-law', tend to be merged with relations of descent, in these cases with the father's sister and mother's brother, again under the assumption of a rule of cross-cousin marriage.

This is outline is the structure of Dravidian kinship but, as shall be seen, it is subject to a great deal of variation on the ground. Before considering variant structures of particular Dravidian systems (as systems of rules and categories), however, it is worth saying that the actual marriages of individuals may in fact show a great deal of deviation from the model. Further, the system is less an account of behaviour than a representation of an ideology, in the sense that it represents the outcomes of marriage choices as if they conformed to the rule of cross-cousin marriage even if they do not do so. It continually reinterprets the actuality of marriage matches in the light of the normative pattern. For example, my 'father-in-law' becomes my 'uncle' (mother's brother) after my marriage, whether or not he was my mother's brother before the event. Thus non-conformity to the marriage rule is turned into conformity to the rule by the terminology. The system influences behaviour, but changing patterns of marriage behaviour do not seem to change the system readily; to the contrary, the system has shown an ability to remain recognizably the same for the last two thousand years and more. There is, of course, a great deal of play in each actual marriage choice, and the strategic deployment of interest leads often to contested versions of what the rules actually are, or how the categories are to be applied (or manipulated) in any given circumstance. This individual level of variability in kinship behaviour, which the praxis theorists have insisted upon (see Bourdieu 1977), is undoubtedly important. But approaches to marriage which focus upon the strategic pursuit of interest would not uncover and cannot account for the immense longevity of the Dravidian system.

Structural variation within the Dravidian system is very great but not boundless. There is good reason to think that the original, proto-Dravidian kinship system had the rule that one marry the *bilateral* cross cousin, that is the mother's brother's child or father's sister's child and their equivalents, which are generally indistinguishable in the terminology. But in several particular systems within the Dravidian region we find that a rule or preference stipulates the *matrilateral* cross cousin (so-named for the mother's brother's daughter; she, of course, marries the reciprocal relative, her father's sister's son) in some castes, and (more rarely) others stipulate the *patrilateral* cross cousin (father's sister's daughter marries her mother's brother's son).

These three variants of the rule of cross-cousin marriage have structural properties that have been much discussed by anthropologists, notably by Leach (1951) and Lévi-Strauss (1969). Thus the bilateral rule permits a continuous exchange of marriage partners between two lineages; the matrilateral rule permits a directional exchange between lineages, A giving partners to B, B to C and, perhaps, C to A, requiring a minimum of three lineages to complete the cycle of exchange; and the patrilateral rule produces a pattern of alternate exchange over time between two lineages, A to B in one generation, reciprocated in the next generation by an exchange going from B to A. All these patterns are found in the Dravidian region. (In Figure 3 patrilineal descent, which is dominant in India, is assumed but the effects are the same for matrilineal descent.)

The matrilateral rule (MBD)

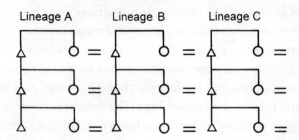

The patrilateral rule (FZD)

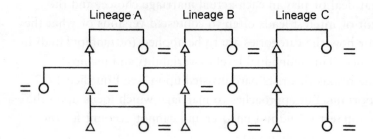

The bilateral rule (MBD, FZD)

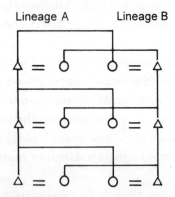

Fig. 3: Structural implications of three rules of cross-cousin marriage
Source: Trautmann 1981: 202.

Other variant patterns as well are found in the Dravidian region, that deform the pattern based on bilateral cross-cousin marriage still further. Three of them deserve mention. The first variant is the marriage of the elder sister's daughter with her mother's younger brother, a pattern widely found among upper-caste groups in Tamil Nadu and Karnataka with some cases in Andhra Pradesh and Maharashtra (see Good 1980; 1981). This pattern of marriage distorts the terminology of kinship in a characteristic and systematic way, because it merges kin of adjacent generations which the original pattern keeps strictly separate. The scholarly consensus is that this is a further development of the patrilateral pattern (FZD marries MBS), of which it is a kind of anticipation; that is a man marries his elder sister's daughter who would otherwise be married by his son (see Figure 4).

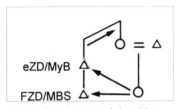

Fig. 4: The marriage of the elder sister's daughter with the mother's younger brother, and the marriage of patrilateral cross cousins
Source: Trautmann 1981: 207.

A second variant permits marriage of cross kin of alternate generations but not adjacent ones; this is found in central India among Gonds, but is generally prohibited elsewhere in the Dravidian region. Naturally the marriage of persons of alternate generations—those of oneself and of one's grandparents, for example—must be rare on account of disparity of age, but in societies where kinship categories extend to distant collateral kin there may be some of alternate generations who are near in age. What is striking about such systems is not the practice but the structural possibility of such marriages. They are accompanied by an extension of the distinction of crossness to the grandparents' generation, which is not found in most parts of the Dravidian region. This central-Indian variant of the Dravidian pattern is incompatible with the previous pattern, of marriage with the elder sister's daughter, and it has some resemblance to Munda patterns (see section on Munda patterns ahead). It is impossible to tell whether the proto-Dravidian kinship pattern had the features of this variant, or of the more widespread one in which the distinction of cross and parallel is lost in the generations of the grandparents and the grandchildren.

A third variant, that obtained among the Nayars of Kerala in recent historic times, distorts the basic pattern to the point that it is only barely recognizable. The matrilineal and matrilocal Nayar extended families (*tarawad*) retained little of the characteristic Dravidian pattern in their terminology, and had a very attenuated form of marriage relation in which women and men entered into and ended marriages at will but resided in the (different) tarawads of their mothers; husbands visited their wives in their own tarawads. A remnant of the general Dravidian structure remains, however, in the ritual marriages that are performed at puberty, in which the boys of one tarawad become, briefly, the ritual husbands of the girls of another tarawad (see Figure 5), as an initiation into adulthood and with it the capacity to form marriages of the kind previously described. These tarawad-to-tarawad relations of ritual marriage are hereditary, so that the ritual marriages of each passing generation recapitulate the form of the previous ones. Succeeding generations are related to one another as structural equivalents of cross cousins:

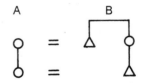

Fig. 5: Ritual marriages between two Nayar tarawads
Source: Trautmann 1981: 212.

The pattern of alliance is the equivalent of matrilateral cross-cousin marriage or, if the boys of both tarawads marry girls of the other in a direct exchange, it is the equivalent of the ancestral pattern of bilateral cross-cousin marriage. The intriguing complexities of the Nayar pattern, which have made it a classic case for social anthropological study, cannot be fully examined here (see Gough 1959; 1961). But it is worth noting that the pattern accommodates the fact that married people live separately in the families of their mothers and not together, as a couple. The accommodation includes a splitting of marriage into two species, one of them a ritual marriage that has heavy family-to-family alliance functions but does not form lasting couples, and another, more lasting but non-ritualized kind of marriage which forms loving couples but lacks the density of family-to-family relations formed by arranged marriage (see Trautmann 1981; pp. 208–14).

The Dravidian pattern of marriage and terminology of kinship is exceedingly durable and not subject to rapid or dramatic change from the play of strategic marriage choices of individual families or statistical and demographic ebbs and flows. Like language itself, patterns of marriage and terminology contain within them traces of a deep past that remain legible in spite of the changes that inevitably come with the passage of time. Perhaps the most striking example of such durability is the way in which the Dravidian pattern remains imprinted upon the terminology of groups lying beyond the region of the Dravidian languages, such as the Mer of Saurashtra, who speak Gujarati, an Indo-Aryan language (see Trivedi 1954; Trautmann 1981: 124–33). In such cases we see clearly that the pattern is not one of vocabulary but of the semantics of kinship, shaped by the rule of cross-cousin marriage. Traces of the Dravidian pattern in Gujarat and Maharashtra, and in the Ganges valley (the Maler), tend to confirm the view of the linguists, that Dravidian languages were once spoken throughout India (Trautmann 1981).

Thus language and patterns of marriage, in part, point to the deep past and identify the cultural constituents out of whose conjuncture India's civilization was formed, namely, the Dravidian, the Indo-Aryan and the Munda language families, and the patterns of marriage and kinship terminology associated with the societies speaking these languages. Having considered the Dravidian pattern, let us take up the others in turn.

MUNDA MARRIAGE PATTERNS

Munda-speakers make up a thin scattering of groups in the east-central and eastern parts of the subcontinent, with their linguistic congeners in the larger Austroasiatic family of which they are the westernmost branch being found mostly in the Indo-China peninsula (the most prominent being

Khmer, the language of the Cambodians). Many of the Munda-speaking groups are 'tribal' (the term is increasingly awkward, but a better one has not yet been found) and though some are large of scale, in the aggregate they make up less than 1 per cent of the population of India. They are, nevertheless, one of the three pieces making up the puzzle of Indian civilization, and the problem of their contribution to its construction remains very much an open one.

We can generalize confidently about the Munda pattern of marriage because it has been the subject of a comprehensive comparative study by Parkin (1992; see also Parkin 1991). It resembles the Dravidian pattern, in that it distinguishes cross and parallel kin in part of the terminology and promotes the repetition of marriage alliance between groups. And yet it differs from the Dravidian in very definite ways. We can take stock of its features by listing the ways in which the Munda pattern differs from the Dravidian pattern of bilateral cross-cousin marriage and terminology. First, cross and parallel cousins are merged with one another and with siblings; that is in Ego's generation everyone is called by the 'brother' and 'sister' terms, much as in Hindi (as we shall shortly see), and quite unlike the Dravidian pattern. To put it another way, the distinction of cross and parallel is absent in Ego's generation, though it divides kin of the parents' and the childrens' generations, as in the Dravidian pattern. Second, since siblings are unmarriageable, and since cousins of all kinds are called brother and sister, it follows that the marriage of cross cousins is *not* allowed (there are some exceptions). Third, kin of adjacent generations may not marry (few exceptions), as happens in the Dravidian region where we find the pattern of a man marrying his elder sister's daughter. Fourth, there is a separate vocabulary for affines or relatives by marriage, where in Dravidian terminologies they tend to be merged with terms for consanguines.

One may well ask then whom may one marry in the Munda pattern if everyone of one's own generation is a kind of sibling and hence unmarriageable, and if those of the adjacent two generations are forbidden? The fundamental Munda pattern of marriage thus is that a marriage alliance formed between two sets of people cannot be repeated in the next generation (that is, by the marriage of first cousins), but it should be repeated in one or three generations, that is, with more distant (second or fourth) cousins, so that the alliances a group forms by marriage are opened out somewhat to form a more far-flung network. These more distant cousins are generally categorized not as siblings, which would construct them as unmarriageable consanguines, but through the affinal terminology, which is to say through the initial marriage which they recapitulate. Thus calling the cousins siblings in the Munda terminology acts to push out the marriage of close kin and to widen the marriage network accordingly, but the existence of a rich affinal terminology gives a path by which those networks close up again at a distance from the closer kin.

The odd number of generations and the 'rules of delay' to which they attach are the heart of the Munda marriage pattern in Parkins's interpretation. The pattern rests on two fundamental Munda principles. One is the 'alternation of generations', according to which kin of alternate generations, such as Ego's generation and that of the grandparents and grandchildren, tend to be merged in the terminology and otherwise identified with one another culturally and socially; the same tendency unites the parents' with the childrens' generations. Persons categorized in alternate generations who are close in age, as might happen in societies where kinship categories extend to practically everyone, may marry, but those categorized in adjacent generations may not. (As we have seen, some Dravidian patterns of central India show this tendency, and it is not settled whether it was part of the ancestral pattern; the coincidence with the Munda pattern may be significant.)

The other fundamental principle is the rule of repeated bilateral marriage alliance, bilateral in the sense that alliances may be directly reciprocated rather than being systematically oriented in one direction only, by means of a radical distinction of wife-giving from wife-taking affinal relatives (as shall be seen later, in Hindi).

The Munda pattern of alliance shows a general structural similarity to the ancestral Dravidian pattern of bilateral cross-cousin marriage, excepting only the rules that delay the repetition of a marriage alliance for one or more generations, and the similarity grows when we compare it to the Gond and other central-Indian groups speaking Dravidian languages showing alternation of generations—exactly the territory where Dravidian and Munda come together. What this may mean historically is uncertain, since the two language families are not known to be related. In other ways the Munda pattern seems to show the influence of the Indo-Aryan pattern, especially in subsuming all cousins under the brother and sister terms, and in having a separate affinal terminology.

INDO-ARYAN MARRIAGE PATTERNS

The speakers of languages of the Indo-Aryan family in north India form the largest segment of the Indian population. But for the associated pattern of marriage and kinship terminology we do not have the benefit of a comprehensive comparative study more recent and detailed than Karve's overview of Indian kinship and social organization (1965). Nevertheless we can get a sense of the broad features by examining a case from the Hindi-speaking area, from Vatuk (1969), in contrast with the Dravidian system.

The terminology of kinship in Hindi lacks the distinction of cross and parallel kin that we find in the three medial generations of Dravidian terminologies, and the associated rule of marriage in north India is, in a word, to marry a non-relative. Since the marriage of relatives is prohibited, we do not find the kinds of equations of relatives that make the Dravidian terminological pattern so recursive and the vocabulary so comparatively brief. We can list the differences as follows. First, in the parents' generation, the parents' siblings and their spouses are distinguished by separate words; the parents' same-sex siblings are not merged with the parents as in the Dravidian system (in which FB = F; MZ = M). Second, correlatively, my children, my sister's children, and my brother's children are all distinguished, whereas in Dravidian terminologies my same-sex sibling's children are merged with my own children (♂BCh = ♂Ch; ♀ZCh = ♀Ch). Third, in Ego's generation, all cousins are classed as brother and sister, with no distinction of cross and parallel cousins. Fourth, there is a separate terminology for affines, whereas in Dravidian systems the affines tend to be merged with consanguines.

The contrast is marked when we track the Hindi word *māmā* (mother's brother) and its cognates, which are found in almost all families of languages in India. In Tamil, a Dravidian language, the cognate word *māman* means mother's brother; father's sister's husband, on the assumption that mother's brother and father's sister, being cross cousins to one another, have married; and the spouse's father, since the child of the mother's brother is a cross cousin, and to be married. Thus we may say that Tamil makes the equations MB = FZH = SpF. Hindi breaks these equations open and has quite separate words for the three relationships: *māmā* (MB), *phūphā* (FZH), and *sasur* (SpF); moreover, the semantic association of *māmā* is not with the father's sister, as in Dravidian, but with his own wife, *māmī* (MBW) (Figure 6).

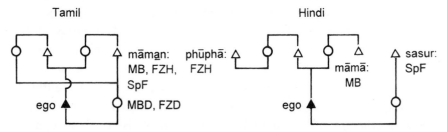

Fig. 6: Tamil and Hindi terms for mother's brother, father's sister's husband, and spouse's father
Source: Trautmann 1981: 24.

Thus, by comparison with the Dravidian pattern of kinship terminology, Hindi and Indo-Aryan terminologies generally make fewer equations or (which is the same thing), make more discriminations among kinds of relatives, and have a separate terminology for affines. The Munda pattern is somewhat between the two, and has certainly been influenced to some degree by the Indo-Aryan pattern.

Rules of marriage in the Indo-Aryan speaking region of India generally require the marriage of a non-relative, and this non-relative in most cases is to be found within one's own caste. The rules generally forbid direct exchange of siblings, that is where two men marry each other's sisters. But since the brother and sister words tend to be extended without limit within the caste, which would make it impossible to find a marriage partner within the caste, the rules are generally framed in terms of prohibited degrees of relationship beyond which one may marry. Where exogamous patrilineal clans (gotra, got) exist they may bear the burden of accomplishing this. For example, among Jats and Rajputs there is often found a rule forbidding marriage to persons whose gotra is the same as one's own, one's mothers, one's father's mothers, and one's mother's mothers (differently said, the gotras of the four grandparents). This has the effect of ruling out marriage with all agnates (all persons of one's own patrilineal clan), and cognates within the second-cousin range, but permitting some beyond that range.

The non-marriageability of close kin is visible in the semantic organization of the terminology in Ego's generation. As stated earlier said, the terminology has brother and sister terms for all consanguineous relations, and a separate set of terms for affines. On closer inspection the affinal terms are separable into two sets, those that are wife-giving relatives (such as wife's brother and sister) and those that are wife-taking relatives (such as husband's brother and sister) which are distinguished from one another. Thus we have three sets in all, consanguines (C), wife-givers (G), and wife-takers (T). Second-order relatives (a relative's relative) are classified by a logic in which the combination of opposite kinds of affines turns such relatives into consanguines. That is, a wife-giver's wife-taker, or a wife-taker's wife-giver, is a consanguine. Examples would be a wife's sister's husband's siblings (called brother and sister) (GT→C) or a husband's brother's wife's siblings (also called brother and sister) (TG→C). In these and other cases the spouses and siblings of a pair of sisters or a pair of brothers are related to one another as siblings, by a logic that rules out the direct exchange of marriage partners. Thus persons who are in the same relation to a pair of sisters (as wife-takers of their family) or brothers (as wife-givers to their family) must be siblings to one another.

HINDU MARRIAGE PATTERNS

In addition to the features we have discussed, which fall into three distinguishable patterns of marriage associated with the three language families that have come together in the formation of Indian civilization, there are other aspects of marriage-forming patterns that are Indiawide in scope. They are the patterns of Hindu marriage, and their classic formulation is in the science of dharma, the Dharmashastra.

The Dharmashastra treatment of marriage presupposes the Hindu ritual of marriage which, although it varies from caste to caste and region to region by the addition of many purely local elements, is in its central structure a Vedic sacrifice, involving Brahmin priest, *mantras*, fire, and offerings. Indeed, at a time when ancient Vedic sacrifices are rarely performed, the Hindu wedding ceremony remains a living representative, and a very robust one at that, of the Vedic ritual complex.

The structure of the wedding ritual has a three-part movement: the processional of the groom's family to the bride's home; the wedding proper, centring upon the sacred fire and the ritual acts performed before it, including the gift of the bride by her father to the groom *(kanyādāna)*, the clasping of hands *(panigrahana)*, taking of seven steps with the ends of the bride's and groom's garments knotted together *(saptapadi)*, and putting *sindhūr* (vermillion) in the parting of the bride's hair *(sindhuradāna);* and the recessional of the bridal couple to the groom's home. The ritual has the threefold character of *gift*, of *initiation*, and of *sacrament*. The *gift* elements have to do with the incorporation of the bride into the family of the groom and its ancestors. Marriage is said to be the *initiation* for girls, comparable to the thread ceremony for boys, marking the transition to spiritual adulthood. And, because of the use of fire and Vedic mantra, it is a *sacrament,* creating a bond between the couple that is indissoluble and that makes them a single unit capable of performing rituals. Divorce is an impossibility and the marriage bond is, in a sense, prolonged into the next life, in which deceased male ancestors and their wives are ritually fed by the married householders who are their living descendants. The model of the family underlying this structure is of a set of males related to one another by patrilineal descent, their in-marrying wives *(kula-vadhu)* and their daughters who are given in marriage *(pratta)* to other families, a highly gendered structure in which the destinies of boys is to remain in their family of birth as shareholders of its property, and that of girls is to grow up in the family of birth but leave it to marry into another, taking with them their claim upon the family wealth in the form of a dowry.

Polygamy has been legal for Hindus till recent times, in the form of polygyny (multiple wives) but not polyandry (multiple husbands), except in the legendary and exceptional case of Draupadi and the Five Pandavas of the *Mahabharata*. The fully sacramental character of Hindu marriage as just described, is typically reserved for the principal marriage, and various forms of secondary marriage do exist. Even in sacramental Hindu marriage it is important to be clear that the prohibition of jural separation (divorce) does not extend to conjugal separation; if anything, the absence of a legal remedy for failed marriage entails social remedies of separate living while staying married under law. Secondary marriages may be unmade without legal hindrance and with relatively little formality.

Two aspects of the treatment of marriage in the Dharmashastra require a closer look, because they reveal the complex relations which Hindu marriage patterns hold to the Indo-Aryan and Dravidian regional patterns: the rules of marriage, and the conception of marriage as the gift of a maiden from one family to another.

The rules of marriage in the Dharmashastra are essentially two: a man is to marry a woman who is not of the same gotra (*a-sa-gotra*) or patrilineal clan, and who is not a relative through a common *pinda* or funeral offering to the ancestors (*a-sa-pinda*). The first rule refers only to Brahmins, and their exogamous, patrilineal clans whose members are notionally the descendants of the ancient sages (*rshis*) to whom the Vedas were revealed; though other castes may have clans called gotras the Dharmashastra takes little cognizance of them, and leaves such matters to be governed by the customary law of castes. In the marriages of Brahmins, the bride abandons the gotra of her father and acquires that of her husband upon marriage (*gotrantara*). The second rule, which applies to all castes, is a law of prohibited degrees, specifying (in one influential formulation) that marriage is forbidden with relatives who fall within five or seven degrees (generations) on the mother's and the father's side—very wide bounds indeed, which have the intent of prohibiting marriage more or less wherever a relationship is traceable.

There can be no doubt that both rules essentially express the north Indian or Indo-Aryan pattern of prohibiting marriage of the same patrilineage and among close cognatic relatives; they make no provision as such for the Dravidian pattern of cross-cousin marriage. Nevertheless it has not escaped the ingenuity of southern pandits (specifically, Devannabhatta in his *Smritichandrika* and Madhava in his commentary on the *Parashara Smriti*) to argue that, if the bride changes gotra upon marriage, it can be said that a brother and sister are no longer related after her marriage, so that their children (who are cross cousins) might by that reasoning, marry. This is the gist of a classic argument supporting the practice of cross-cousin marriage in the south.

Thus there is a division of learned opinion within the Dharmashastra tradition on this issue, and Brahmins of the north and of the south have for a very long time married differently, according to the Indo-Aryan and Dravidian patterns respectively.

The matter of marriage as gift of a maiden (kanyādāna) has a quite different bearing. In the Dharmasastra, kanyadana is by no means universal; it is recognized as only one form of the marriage transaction among others, which include purchase, the elopement of lovers, and forcible abduction. Although the forms of marriage that depart from kanyādāna are disparaged, they are nevertheless valid under certain circumstances (for example for non-Brahmins) and have as great a claim to antiquity as it has, as has the self-choice of a princess (svayamvara) which seems to be found in many early Indo-European cultures, not just in India. The payment of bride wealth in particular has been widespread in India till recently, and seems to have been part of Vedic culture; it is quite opposed to the kanyadana pattern with its accompaniment of dowry. It is evident that it is the jurists themselves who have propagated kanyādāna through the Dharmashastra as a universal ideal by disparaging and limiting the scope of the alternatives.

The conception of marriage as gift is a highly theorized one, in which marriage is but a special case of a more general theory of gift. This theory comes out of the reinterpretation of the Veda in the light of the reincarnation doctrine, in response to the challenge of the anti-Vedic religions of Buddhism and Jainism. It is the project of the school of interpretation called the Mimamsa, on which the Dharmashastra draws. According to this theory, reciprocated gifts bear a 'seen' (dṛishta) recompense and are worldly; but dharmic gifts are those scripturally enjoined gifts which, because they are not reciprocated, bear an 'unseen' (a-dṛishta), karmic recompense in the next life (see Trautmann 1981: 239–40). This point of view reinterprets marriage as a non-reciprocal transaction, in which all gifts beginning with the bride herself flow from her family to the groom's but not vice-versa, since reciprocal gifts cancel the dharmic character of the principal gift, the bride. And it textures the asymmetrical relation such that it puts the groom's family in a superior role, as the object of unrequited gifts yielding 'unseen' future benefits. The asymmetrical relation between bride's and groom's families and the doctrine of non-reciprocity serves to promote the radical distinction of wife-givers and wife-takers in the Hindi terminology and in north Indian practice generally. In the south, the Dravidian pattern can be accommodated to this asymmetry by limiting marriage to the matrilateral form (MBD marries FZS), which has the result that there is no reciprocal exchange of children in marriage between families.

Overall, it is apparent that the kanyadana ideal, which has become ever more pervasive in the course of India's history, is, in relation to the three regional patterns, a new creation forming a pattern claiming universality, and as such builds an all-India culture of marriage.

A further aspect of the Dharmashastra norms informing the Hindu marriage pattern is the way in which marriage is connected with caste. The Dharmashastra envisions three possibilities, that marriage will be with a person of the same caste *(sa-varna)*, or that the bride will marry a groom of higher caste *(anuloma,* 'with the hair'), or a groom of lower caste *(pratiloma,* 'against the hair'), giving them names lovelier than the scientific Greek the anthropologists use: isogamy, hypergamy, hypogamy. The first is best and the last worst; but the texts, though they do not fully approve of inter-caste marriage, nevertheless give qualified recognition to the hypergamous direction of marriage, the direction that is most consistent with the kanyadana idea.

The hypergamous direction of marriage is very visible at certain places in the ethnographic record, especially in north India, where among Rajputs, for example, there has been an overall hypergamous flow of brides from lower- to higher-status clans and not in the opposite direction (see Shah and Desai 1988). The ideal of intra-caste marriage, which is the dominant one, provides that family-to-family relations of alliance will be implemented through marriage, but that caste-to-caste relations will exclude marriage. This ideal coexists in tension with that of hypergamy, through which the marriage pattern tends to overspill the bounds of caste and to organize relations between castes.

THE ISLAMIC PATTERN AND SOUTH ASIAN MUSLIMS

The marriage patterns of Indian Muslims often resemble those of their Hindu neighbours, especially among the non-Ashraf groups. Among the Ashraf groups (those upper-status lineages claiming an ancestral origin that is Arab, Persian, or Central Asian), the Islamic pattern formalized in the Shariah and perpetuated through the colonial period in the Anglo-Muhammedan law to the present, adds a further complication to the picture of marriage patterns in India.

This pattern derives from Arabia. It is essentially the Arab pattern associated with segmentary lineages of classic type based on patrilineal descent, with a propensity to form alliances with other lineages and lineage segments based on a calculus of segmentary nearness. Associated with this pattern is a kinship terminology that is 'descriptive' in the sense that it makes few of the equations we find, for example, in Dravidian terminologies, distinguishing the different kinds of aunts, uncles, and cousins.

What is distinctive of the Arab pattern is the strongly endogamous tendency of the lineage, or, put another way, the reluctance to form alliances through marriage with distant or non-related lineages, against whom one's own lineage and other close lineages might very well be called upon to take up arms. These tendencies crystallize in a canonical preference for the *bint 'amm*, the father's brother's daughter, who of course is of the same patrilineal group, while the other first cousins are not forbidden in marriage. It is unfortunate that anthropological discussion of this pattern sometimes refers to it as a preference for the patrilateral parallel cousin, since of course there is no distinction of cross and parallel in the Arabic terminology of kinship (see Murphey and Kasdan 1959); the logic of the distinction is not supplied by considerations of crossness, which is absent, but by the segmentary patrilineage and its characteristic ways of forming alliances against enemies. This pattern, then, is quite different from the Dravidian pattern, and it leans in the opposite direction from the Indo-Aryan one, preferring to find marriage partners close to home within the structure of patrilineages, rather than (as in the latter) strictly forbidding marriage within patrilineal lineages or clans and encouraging the formation of dispersed alliances.

Two other concomitants of the Arabic pattern that Islam brings to South Asia are the payment of a bride price *(mahr),* and the conception of marriage as a contract made by persons who can dissolve it at will. Both features differ from those associated with the idea of kanyadana and the sacramental character of the principal marriage among Hindus.

The various groups of Indian Muslims follow Dravidian, Indo-Aryan, and Arab patterns or variants of them. Because of the different logics of the patterns (repetition of alliances, dispersed alliance, endogamous alliance) the difference among Muslim groups taken together is considerable.

Change in Recent Times

These general patterns of marriage had cohabited in India for a long time before the colonial period. The Orientalist policy of Warren Hastings, promulgated in 1772, provided for the administration of Hindu and Muslim law in courts of British India, in matters of marriage, inheritance, and caste, based on Dharmashastra and Shariah law and the judicial decisions of the courts themselves, much as in Europe matters pertaining to marriage often came under the jurisdiction of church law. The colonial rulers, hoping to gain the affection or at least avoid the unnecessary disaffection of their subjects, did not wish to interfere with these most intimate and sensitive of practices which, being neither Hindu nor Muslim themselves, they had no moral standing to alter. This position proved decisive for the colonial period. The decision to recognize distinct Hindu and Muslim realms of personal law affecting marriage among other things continued until Independence, and created the post-colonial predicament for India which still persists.

There were several more immediate consequences. In the first place, although the courts came to recognize and uphold the regional and local peculiarities of marriage patterns (such as the cross-cousin marriage of the south) the formation of Hindu and Muslim personal laws had the effect of separating the two more emphatically than they may have been in practice, leaving thereby a difficult legacy of communal strife, and in other ways promoting the authority of the Dharmashastra and the Shariah over that of custom than had previously been the case.

In the second place, the reluctance of the British to interfere with Hindu and Muslim marriage made them unable to undertake legislation for the reform of marriage laws. The main legislative initiatives concerning marriage in the colonial period had to do with providing for what the Hindu and Muslim law did not, principally the Special Marriage Act of 1872 making civil marriage available to persons marrying outside their castes. It is symptomatic of the British unwillingness to interfere with the religious law that it was necessary for the parties to declare that they did not profess the Hindu, Buddhist, Sikh, Jain, Muslim, Jewish, Parsi, or Christian faith in order to avail themselves of the opportunity of civil marriage, a provision which the Parliament of independent India soon did away with, by the Special Marriage Act of 1954. The one reformatory measure of the colonial regime was the Hindu Widows' Remarriage Act (1856) which gave legal recognition to the remarriage of Hindu widows, which of course was a permissive measure requiring no massive change of behaviour or opinion (Smith 1963). At the same time, marriage was under intense debate among Indian reformers, missionary critics, and others. The colonial situation had the effect of fuelling debate and stultifying change at the same time. Similarly, the nationalist effort to end colonial rule had the general tendency to put reform of marriage on the back burner as a divisive issue when solidarity was needed for the freedom struggle.

Independence broke the logjam in a certain sense, and in 1955 the Hindu Marriage Act was approved by Parliament together with other bills covering inheritance, guardianship, and adoption, though only after strong criticism from opposing directions. The voices of Hindu traditionalism were particularly loud over provisions for divorce in the bill which, it was argued, was destructive of the sacramental character of Hindu marriage. In general the new Act and its companions had the effect of displacing the Dharmashastra from the law courts, and replacing its authority with that of the legislative power of the people through its representatives, which was certainly a major change, and rendered marriage patterns subject to rearrangement whenever the Parliamentary majority chose. Other critics of the Act pulled in the opposite direction, calling for a secular and progressive marriage law that applied to everyone irrespective of religion, and argued that creating a Hindu Marriage Act would promote communalism. The framers of the Indian Constitution provided for a uniform civil code as one of the items among the Directive Principles of State Policy. The backers of the Hindu Marriage Act construed it not as a settled resolution of the reform issue, but as a way station towards a future uniform code.

Thus contradiction between emerging reformist views of marriage and the relatively unchanging and unchangeable state of the law at the end of the colonial period was rectified shortly after Independence in respect of Hindus (and also for Jains and Sikhs who were included in its provisions) by this and other laws recognizing widow remarriage, ending polygamy, making provision for separation and divorce, and giving daughters inheritance rights in land. But the obstacles continue, in respect of Muslim law. Muslim religious leadership in India has tended to oppose interfering with the Shariah-based Anglo-Muhammedan law, contending that the legitimacy of the (non-Muslim) government of India for Muslims depends upon its countenance. Parliament, inevitably having a non-Muslim majority, finds itself in a predicament not unlike that of its colonial predecessors, having the power but lacking the moral authority to reform the law of marriage for Muslims. The impasse continues, and is central to the post-colonial quandary. The legal framework of marriage patterns in India, then, is one of a reformed regime of marriage for Hindus and others, and a continuing, unreformed and unreformable regime of the Anglo-Muhammedan law for Indian Muslims. The huge controversy over the Shah Bano affair is a symptom of this impasse.

Against the background of that framework of law, marriage patterns have been subject to a variety of pushes and pulls in recent times that have changed them in many ways, though in ways not easy to capture in a country so pluralistic as India. We may mention four of them: the increasing scope and intensity of kanyādāna marriage and dowry; the decline of cross-cousin marriage; the emergence of a norm of post-puberty marriage; and the strengthening of the ideals of intimacy and companionship between the man and woman forming a married couple.

The idea of marriage as the gift of a maiden was promoted by the writers of the Dharmashastra against other accepted conceptions of the marriage transaction, as part of an overall philosophy of the gift that bears 'unseen' fruit in another life. It is a paradox that modern conditions, which have promoted the critical examination of marriage in India, have also promoted the further spread of this conception, and of the practice of dowry, at the expense of the use of bride price which was customary in many localities until recently—a clear case of modern conditions fostering what Srinivas calls Sanskritization (Srinivas 1955). The dowry itself, in an emerging economy of consumerism, grows without limit in the imagination and has become a highly visible social pathology in the epidemic of dowry deaths over the last several decades.

Another pattern, the Dravidian rule of cross-cousin marriage, has been in retreat in the twentieth century, and although it remains imprinted upon the terminology the incidence of its practice declines. One very evident factor at work here is the belief that the marriage of close relatives leads to physical defects in the children. This belief has been under discussion in the West for over a century, leading to legislation against the marriage of close cousins, and it is notable that it began well before modern genetics proposed a scientific basis for it in the idea of recessive genes and their often deleterious character. These ideas have been taken up in India and form part of a kind of modern common sense that frowns upon the Dravidian custom, although the long survival of the Dravidian rule argues against it having been so very deleterious in practice. The forces that promote individual choice in marriage partners tend in the same direction, towards lower incidences of the marriage of cross-cousins. One effect which might congeal into a settled pattern is the tendency to ban the marriage of first cousins, but to find second or more distant cousins in the cross-cousin category, which is similar to the Munda pattern, and is more compatible with north Indian norms (see Rajadhyaksha 1995).

A third point concerns the rising age at marriage. After many centuries over which the marriage of children before puberty had become more prominent, it is on the wane in this century and individual choice or voice is greater than ever before. Marriage no longer colonizes so great a part of one's early life. Effects of the receding age of marriage upon girls have been studied by Rajadhyaksha (1995). Menstruation is a complex symbol in Hinduism, combining ideas of temporary impurity, which requires temporary segregation from contact with others in the family, with those of fertility, which is to be celebrated but needs to be secured by the family of a husband. Under the old regime of child marriages, the onset of menstruation followed marriage and was welcomed and ritually marked, and monthly periods were known to all by the observance of certain rules of temporary withdrawal. Modern ideas have reversed the secular trend towards securing fertility by ever earlier marriage, and as the age at marriage has increased, the menstruating girl who is not yet married has emerged as a new phenomenon. Her menstruation is a cause of anxiety both to her—who must bear the burden of it without celebration and indeed in silence—and a worry to her parents, who know their daughter is capable of becoming sexually active, a dangerous period of life until she is safely married. The new dispensation may be better, but it is more isolating and some of the collective and ritual burden lifting is no longer available (Rajadhyaksha 1995).

The final area of change to be addressed here is the development of ideals of intimacy and companionship in marriage. The desire for intimacy and companionship is no doubt always a part of marriage, but it must be balanced with other social objectives, and in India while the married state and the married couple as normative are highly stressed, public expression of intimacy by the couple is generally suppressed out of deference to elders and the occasions for experiencing intimacy may be quite limited. Divorce is the obverse of the coin of intimacy, and the demand for a legal remedy for marriages that have gone bad on the part of those who led newly independent India was a part of the rethinking on marriage that had been going on during the previous century. What has tended to decline with the greater demand for intimacy between the married couple is the competing demand for familial solidarity and the alliance aspect of marriage, so strongly developed in India's history, now receding, unevenly and variously (Jain 1996; Kakkar 1996). More than ever before, marriages that are 'out of pattern' and that are governed less by considerations like the family-to-family relations that are made by marriage, and more by the desire for intimacy by the couple forming the marriage, are a possibility for a larger numbers of Indians.

REFERENCES

Bourdieu, Pierre. 1977. *Outline of a Theory of Practice*. Cambridge Studies in Social Anthropology. Cambridge: Cambridge University Press.

Dumont, Louis. 1953. 'The Dravidian Kinship Terminology as an Expression of Marriage'. *Man*. 34–9.

_____. 1957. *Hierarchy and Marriage Alliance in South Indian Kinship*. Occasional papers of the Royal Anthropological Institute of Great Britain and Ireland, no. 12. London: Royal Anthropological Institute of Great Britain and Ireland.

_____. 1961–6. 'Marriage in India: The Present State of the Question'. 'I. Marriage Alliance in South-East India and Ceylon'. *Contributions to Indian Sociology*. 5:75–98. Postscript to Part I and II. 'Marriage and Status; Nayar and Newar'. *Contributions to Indian Sociology*. 7: 78–98. II. 'North India in Relation to South India'. *Contributions to Indian Sociology*. 9:90–114.

Fustel de Coulanges, Numa Denis. 1864. *La cité Antique*. Paris: Durand.

Gharpure, J.R. 1943. *Sapindya or the Law of Sapinda Relationship*. Collection of Hindu Law Texts, vol. 27. Bombay: V.J. Gharpure.

Ghurye, G.S. 1962. *Family and Kin in Indo-European Culture*. 2nd ed. Bombay: Popular Book Depot.

_____. 1972. *Two Brahmanical Institutions: Gotra and Charana*. Bombay: Popular Prakashan.

Good, Anthony. 1980. 'Elder Sister's Daughter's Marriage in South Asia'. *Journal of Anthropological Research*. 36:474–500.

_____. 1981. 'Prescription, Preference, and Practice: Marriage Patterns among the Kondaiyankottai Maravar of South India'. *Man* (n.s.). 16:109–29.

Gough, Kathleen E. 1959. 'The Nayars and the Definition of Marriage'. *Journal of the Royal Anthropological Institute of Great Britain and Ireland*. 89:23–34.

————. 1961. 'Nayar: Central Kerala'. In David M. Schneider and Kathleen Gough, eds, *Matrilineal Kinship*. Berkeley/Los Angeles: University of California Press.

Jain, Madhu. 1996. 'A Search for Intimacy'. *India Today*. December 11:98–105.

Kakkar, Sudhir. 1996. 'Emergence of the "Jodi"'. *India Today*. 11 December:105–6.

Kapadia, K.M. 1947. *Hindu Kinship: An Important Chapter in Hindu Social History*. Bombay: Popular Book Depot.

Karve, Irawati. 1965. *Kinship Organization in India*. 2nd ed. Bombay: Asia Publishing House.

Leach, E.R. 1951. 'The Structural Implications of Matrilateral Cross-cousin Marriage'. *Journal of the Royal Anthropological Institute of Great Britain and Ireland*. 81:23–55.

Lévi-Strauss, Claude. 1969. *The Elementary Structures of Kinship (Les structures élémentaires de la parenté, 1949)*. Rev. ed. and trans. James Harle Bell and John Richard von Sturmer, and ed. Rodney Needham. London: Eyre & Spottiswoode.

Morgan, Lewis Henry. 1871. *Systems of Consanguinity and Affinity of the Human Family*. Washington, D.C: Smithsonian Institution.

Murphey, Robert F., and Leonard Kasdan. 1959. 'The Structure of Parallel Cousin Marriage'. *American Anthropologist*. 61:17–29.

Parkin, Robert. 1991. *A Guide to Austroasiatic-speakers and Their Languages*. Honolulu: University of Hawaii Press.

————. 1992. *The Munda of Central India: An Account of Their Social Organization*. Delhi: Oxford University Press.

Rajadhyaksha, Tarini. 1995. 'Symbolism of the Female Life-cycle with Special Reference to the Female Body in Everyday Life: A Case Study from Maharashtra'. Unpublished Ph.D. thesis, Department of Sociology, University of Delhi.

Rao, Vasudeva. 1997. 'A Sociological Study of the Madhva Monastery in Udipi'. Unpublished. Ph.D. thesis, Department of Sociology, University of Delhi.

Shah, A.M. and I.P. Desai. 1988. *Division and Hierarchy: An Overview of Caste In Gujarat*. Delhi: Hindustan Publishing Corporation.

Smith, Donald Eugene. 1963. *India as a Secular State*. Princeton: Princeton University Press.

Srinivas, M.N. 1955 'Sanskritization and Westernization'. *Far Eastern Quarterly*. 14:481–96.

Trautmann, Thomas R. 1981. *Dravidian Kinship*. Cambridge: Cambridge University Press. (Reprinted in 1985 by Vistaar Publications, New Delhi.)

Trivedi, Harshad. 1954. 'Some Aspects of Kinship Terminology among the Mers of Saurashtra'. *Journal of the Maharaja Sayajirao University of Baroda*. 3:157–68.

Vatuk, Sylvia. 1969. 'A Structural Analysis of the Hindi Kinship Terminology'. *Contributions to Indian Sociology* (n.s.). 3:94–115.

Domestic Violence

Malavika Karlekar

INTRODUCTION: DEFINITION OF VIOLENCE[1]

This section focuses on violence against women and girl children in the home with an emphasis on physical acts of abuse and neglect. Though domestic violence is the specific context, the growing ubiquity of gender-specific violence in public spaces is evident from statistics and the discourse on rape and sexual harassment at the workplace (Das 1996; Agnes 1993; Krishna Raj 1991; Pati 1991; PUDR 1991; Samuel 1992; S. Sarkar 1994; T. Sarkar 1991; Sunder Rajan 1993). The sexual violation of women in times of political, communal, and ethnic strife has led to innovative analyses based on archival research, life stories, and narrative techniques (Bhasin and Menon 1994; Butalia 1993, 1998; Das 1990; Das and Nandy 1986; Menon and Bhasin 1998; Sarkar and Butalia 1995), encouraging an interrogation of established representations of major events such as Partition and, more recently, religious strife. There is also some discussion of sex workers and of aberrant events such as *sati* (widow immolation), witch-hunts, stripping and shaming of women—particularly those from the lower castes, often as punishment for their community's transgressions (see Vyas et al. 1996 for a comprehensive guide to material available).

The present chapter, however, does not go into a discussion of such forms of violence and while it is well established that psychological (Carstairs 1983; Ghadially 1987; Kakar 1983) and indeed symbolic (Bondurant 1965; Bourdieu 1977) manifestations of violence are as widespread, these are by and large, beyond the scope of this chapter. Though the discussion on entitlements does touch upon attitudes and stereotypes which result in denial and neglect, in the Indian context there is urgent need to spend far more time and resources on the mental-health aspect of violence. This has so far been an area largely neglected by government and police agencies, voluntary organizations, and researchers. In part the neglect can be explained by the overall social attitude of suppressing—if not ignoring—factors which reflect on the inner life of individuals and families and cannot easily be classified as an 'illness'. An alarming finding of the latest World Development Report (1993) was that, globally, rape and domestic violence account for about 5 per cent of the total disease burden among women in the age group of 15–44. Disease is defined as both, physical as well as non-physical ailments. It need hardly be pointed out that these figures possibly represent only a fraction of actual violence-induced psychological and somatic disorders. As the focus is on the household, the term domestic violence is preferred to family violence: the former helps focus on the physical unit of the home rather than the more amorphous context of the family, even though the underlying world-view may be that of the larger familial and kin group.

      An overview of studies in a communication paper circulated by Anveshi, Research Centre in Women's Studies in Hyderabad (1995), shows that while there is no gender difference in severe mental disorders such as schizophrenia and manic depression, twice as many women than men are afflicted with common mental disorders such as anxieties, phobias, and obsessive-compulsive behaviour. The paper concluded that when mental illness has a biological basis, the prevalence was the same across genders; however 'where mental illness has a psycho-social basis, women are far more frequently ill than men' (Anveshi 1995: 2). In other words, there is a strong correlation between women's life situations and their mental and physical health (see Davar 1995).

      There is also limited recognition of the fact that a physical act, catastrophic event, or violent abuse can result in a range of symptoms known generically as post-traumatic stress disorders (PTSD). Evidence proves that the impact of these disorders can often be far greater and last much longer than the act or event itself. A report on global mental health (Desjarlais et al. 1995) point out that PTSD is a 'persistent response', and one that can impede the functioning of some of those exposed to a particular trauma. As an instance, it may be worth pointing out that in India, the 'possession' of women by malevolent spirits is socially and culturally accepted; elaborate procedures for exorcism—which are often violent in nature—bring into focus the woman or girl, who as a victim of this particular affliction, is expected to behave in ways which violate conventional norms of appropriate conduct. (see Kakar 1983 for a discussion of feminine possession). This state of possession, often caused by severe familial, social, and sexual abuse and trauma, may be classified as part of the PTSD syndrome.

Quite apart from the silence around the non-physical acts of aggression, such as verbal abuse and denial of food, education, and care, there is surprisingly little material available in the form of books or academic essays or papers on the entire issue of violence against women in India; despite the fact that a battery of statistics and reports made available by official sources and the media reinforce the view that this form of gendered violence is fast becoming a feature of daily living in contemporary India, it has yet to become a priority area of research. Further, of what is available, about half relates to violence within the family (Vyas et al. 1996). In Patricia Uberoi's ([1994] 1995) opinion, this silence is explicable by a certain hesitance in subjecting the family and its intimate relationships to scrutiny; at the same time, if there is any data base on the nature and kind of violence that goes on behind locked doors, it has become available largely due to the activities of NGOs, those in the women's movement and the police.[2]

Uberoi feels that though the 'family is also a site of exploitation and violence ... sociologists appear to eschew issues of social pathology, at least in regard to the family' ([1994] 1995: 36). This is because the family is 'a cultural ideal and a focus of identity', its inviolability as an institution being reaffirmed by an environment which limits interaction and discourse between the professional academic and the activist. The situation is compounded by the fact that familial concern with propriety, honour (*izzat*), and reputation makes it difficult for those researchers interested in investigating violence within the home to gain access to those perceived as victims. Thus it is hardly coincidental that a large percentage of available data on violence against women locates the family as a major cause of oppression and subsequent ill health and loss of identity. The Anveshi paper noted that 'all our analyses point to the fact that marriage and the family are necessary stressors in the cause of mental illness among Indian women' (Anveshi 1995: 3–4). It thus becomes necessary to 'pay attention to the violence of everyday life' (Das 1997).

Put simply, violence is an act of aggression, usually in interpersonal interaction or relations. It may also be aggression of an individual woman against herself, such as suicide, self-mutilation, negligence of ailments, sex determination tests, food denial, and so on. Basically, then, violence brings into question the concept of boundary maintenance (Nedelsky 1991) and a sense of self as well as a perception of another's autonomy and identity. It implies that when the body—and indeed the self—is vulnerable to violation, individuals have a very different notion of 'what is one's body and what is done to one's body' (Litke 1992: 174). Indian scholars in the field of women's studies have emphasized the dynamics of power and powerlessness involved in a violent act. It is a coercive mechanism 'to assert one's will over another, to prove or to feel a sense of power' (Litke 1992: 174).

Given that violence is not limited to any single group, 'it can be perpetuated by those in power against the powerless or by the powerless in retaliation against coercion by others to deny their powerlessness' (Poonacha 1999). Further, Govind Kelkar (1991) situates violence against women 'in the socio-economic and political context of power relations'. She feels that the view that violence is 'an act of illegal criminal use of force', is inadequate and should include 'exploitation, discrimination, upholding of unequal economic and social structures, the creation of an atmosphere of terror, threat or reprisal and forms of religio-cultural and political violence' (Kelkar 1991: 1).

This wide definition of violence finds resonance in a hierarchical society based on exploitative gender relations. Violence often becomes a tool to socialize family members according to prescribed norms of behaviour within an overall perspective of male dominance and control. The family and its operational unit, the household, are the sites where oppression and deprivation of individual psyches and physical selves are part of the structures of acquiescence: often enough, those being 'moulded' into an acceptance of submission and denial are in-marrying women and children. Physical violence, as well as less explicit forms of aggression, are used as methods to ensure their obedience. At every stage in the life cycle, the female body is both the object of desire and of control (Thapan 1997b; Karlekar forthcoming).

The Indian family, its forms, structure, and functions have been important areas of study. Debates on definitions and concepts which continue, are by no means free of contradictions (Desai 1980). Relevant areas of concern relate to whether the basic family unit is joint or nuclear in structure (Desai 1980; Desai 1964; Gore 1968; Shah 1964, 1973, 1988), and how to distinguish between the family and the household. These have direct bearing on the status of women, not only in terms of the number and quality of relationships to which they have to adapt and the distribution of functions and roles, but also with regard to the allocation of resources. All these aspects can be, and indeed are, areas for differences of opinion. Clearly a joint or extended family imposes certain emotional and physical burdens on the daughter-in-law, at the same time it provides much-needed support in child rearing and care (Gore 1968; Karlekar 1982; Kasturi 1990).

The fact that in most parts of India, women enter as strangers into an already structured world of consanguineally related men generates its own tensions and conflicts in loyalties and commitments. The exceptions are castes such as the Tamil–Brahmins which practice cross-cousin and maternal uncle-niece marriages. In fact, according to M.S. Gore, the two main causes of strain in the joint family are the evolution of a strong conjugal relationship and 'the difficulty of socialising the women members into developing a community outlook and a sense of identity with the family groups' (Gore

1968: 25). In the present context, conflicting identities are particularly significant for an understanding of the external dynamics of a group united on the basis of blood, and living together with those from other families. They raise, for instance, the question of whether, for any analysis on women's status, the household is more relevant or the family.

There is no simple answer to this question, particularly as 'the very attempt to distinguish between family and household in India, if not elsewhere too, goes hand in hand with establishing a relationship between the two' (Shah 1983: 34). By and large, households 'are task-oriented residence units' while families are 'kinship groupings that need not be localised' (Netting et al. 1984: xx). To put it somewhat simplistically, the household implies a physical structure, goods and services held in common, and a core membership. On the other hand, the family is more amorphous, spread over time and space, characterized by a 'developmental process' (Shah 1983:4) in roles and relationships. A household is the operational unit which functions broadly within the parameters of a family and kinship ideology; this would include rules of marriage, residence, property ownership, roles and functions determined according to age and gender. As Rajni Palriwala writes, 'While the household forms the grid for a major part of women's activities and interpersonal relations, various facets of kinship provide necessary cultural and social structural contexts' (Palriwala 1990: 17). In other words, these contexts provide the ground, so to speak, for a working out of family ideologies around specific roles and expectations.

There are, as Veena Das (1976) has commented in the context of Punjabi kinship, certain moral rules which influence the trajectory of individual lives. It can be argued that these moral rules operate to maintain a certain gender-biased order internal to families and kinship systems. In arguing that the family more than the caste system is responsible for reproducing inequalities within society, André Béteille feels that entire families work towards 'transmitting its cultural and social capital to its younger members, despite psychological failures of many kinds' (Béteille 1998: 440). Clearly, moral rules of a family do operate with an eye to a shoring up on, as well as acquisition of, Bourdieuan capital; however, what Béteille overlooks is that embedded in this very process is a gender-based inequality. In looking at the role of the family in socialization, Béteille has glossed over the inequality that is often institutionalized between the 'older' and 'younger members'. This inequality is embedded in oppressive structures of a family ideology committed to an age and gender hierarchy which is worked out within a household. Who shall have access to which scarce resource of capital is thus determined by the gender as well as age of the family member. As will be clear soon, the girl child is often the victim of such discrimination as families devise coping mechanisms on resource sharing. However, there is a tendency to perceive domestic violence only in terms of inter-spousal violence: in a study among professionals—paediatricians, general physicians, and psychiatrists—dealing with victims of domestic violence, as well as a sample of the victims themselves, researchers from the Delhi-based Multiple Action Research Group (MARG) found that 'by the large, there appeared to be no clear understanding of "domestic violence". Each case is treated symptomatically even if it traced to violence in the family' (MARG 1996: 25). Thus violence against children and the aged was hardly perceived as instance of domestic violence. Studies that speak of discrimination against the girl child or the old grandparents in terms of the food and nutrition they receive, would view this as the physical impact of deprivation; rarely would it be regarded as an act of violence. If there are meagre data on violence against the elderly, there are even less on abused single women and men in families. Using the life cycle approach, the following section argues that at every stage, there is discrimination and violence, particularly against girl children and later women within the household, either natal or conjugal. With age, problems are compounded as increased dependency, illness, and fatigue arise. Finally, it also suggests that despite the ubiquity of violence, micro-studies may well point to the emergence of alternate discourses which question a dominant familial ideology in many ways.

VIOLENCE IN THE NATAL HOME
Female Foeticide and Infanticide

A major gain from the women's movement has been the emergence of a rich storehouse of information and data on women at every stage of the life cycle-exposure of the prevalence of the acts of foeticide and infanticide being a case in point. While both these methods of dealing with unwanted daughters go back in history, is the misuse of medical tests for female foeticide and increasing incidence of infanticide in parts of the country where it was once unknown are of recent origin. Apart from the medical issues involved, there are important ethical questions being raised: if abortions are legal, why are different standards applied to sex-determination tests which may or may not be used to influence sex-selective abortions? How can one combat the logic of those who argue that it is better to avoid the suffering imposed on unwanted girl babies by not allowing them to be born (Padmanabhan 1993)? In a democratic society, why should the state interfere in the right of couples to decide whether they want girls or not?

This is particularly so in India where abortion (medical termination of pregnancy or MTP) is a form of birth control actively encouraged by the medical establishment. In a well-argued article where she places the Indian debates around abortion and female foeticide in the wider context of the rights discourse, Nivedita Menon points out that

> there is a profound philosophical incoherence involved in arguing for abortion in terms of the right of women to control their bodies and at the same time demanding that women be restricted by law from choosing specifically to abort female foetuses. It is essential that feminists should avoid being forced to counterpose the rights of (future) women to be born against the rights of (present) women to have control over their bodies [Menon 1996: 374].

In other words, feminists and concerned citizens have to acknowledge that in asking for women to have the right to control their bodies, they have to accept for caveat that women may themselves work against future generations of their gender. However, those who want to make a distinction between a gender-neutral abortion and abortion induced following sex-selective tests, argue that the latter actively works against equality and the right to life for girls.

Keeping these arguments in mind, a discussion of the violence of female foeticide and infanticide follows, arguing that how women control their bodies is often the manifestation of a dominant ideology which valorizes the male child. While some studies have seen the discrimination against female children to be validated by economic functions (see Miller 1981 for an analysis of region-wise differences on son and daughter preferences in the context of their productive roles in the family), other studies point to a far more deep-seated yearning for the male child, who, among other things, facilitates the passage of a Hindu to the next world. (Prabhu [1940] 1995)

Female foeticide has become popular with the spread of amniocentesis, a medical technique evolved to discover birth defects. A part of the test involves establishing the sex of the foetus. Introduced in 1974 at a leading government-run hospital in New Delhi, the new technology was quickly appropriated by medical entrepreneurs. A spate of sex-selective abortions followed. Though a series of government circulars from 1977 onwards conveyed the ban on the tests, 'the privatization and commercialization of the technology' was well under way within a few years of its introduction (Mazumdar 1992).

A case study from a hospital in a city in western India conducted from June 1976 to June 1977 revealed that of the 700 women who sought prenatal sex determination, 250 were found to have male foetuses and 450 females. While all the foetuses were kept to term, 430 of the 450 female foetuses were aborted (Ramanamma and Bambawale 1980). According to Kuntal Agarwal, 'amniocentesis tests and female foeticide have been prevalent since 1977, but have become popular (only) since 1982 and thereafter small towns and cities are also experiencing their effect' (Agarwal 1988). A field study conducted by Dr Sanjeev Kulkarni of the Foundation for Research in Community Health (1986) brought to light the fact that in the 1980s, five thousand amniocentesis tests were carried out annually in Bombay for determining foetal sex. Eighty-four per cent of the gynaecologists contacted by him admitted to having performed the amniocentesis tests for sex determination. Of these, seventy-four per cent had started performing the tests since 1982 and only a few cases of genetic defects were detected. The overwhelming majority of 'patients', most of whom were of middle or upper class status, came merely to obtain information about the sex of the foetus. Many women who came for the tests already had at least two daughters. Several clinics were run under the guise of maternity homes, clinical laboratories and family health centres, and costs ranged from Rs 70 to Rs 600. Thirty per cent of the doctors believed that their patients came to them under some kind of pressure. At the same time, there is also evidence that women often took the decision on their own (Juneja 1993). It is a moot point whether mothers-to-be genuinely believed that girls were burdensome or whether they were socialized into such a world-view.

Today there are clinics throughout the country and 'Gujarat topped the list with SD clinics spreading even in small towns' (Ravindra 1993). Despite the efforts of women's organizations, voluntary groups, and the media to the contrary, sex-determination (SD) tests are becoming increasingly common.

A far more pernicious manifestation of an ideology which devalues girl children is the recent resurgence of female infanticide. In 1870, the British government in India outlawed infanticide (see Kasturi 1994; Pakrasi 1970 and Panigrahi 1972, for discussions of the practice), but over a century later, there are alarming reports of baby girls being murdered in areas where the custom did not previously exist. In a study in the 1970s, based on a study of historical records, Barbara Miller had noted that 'female infanticide in nineteenth century India was practiced primarily in the higher social groups of the North, though this point is debatable' (Miller 1981: 55). The author relate this practice to the control and distribution of property and variations in the tradition of dowry. Further, fieldwork and analysis of census data, led her to conclude that there was a distinct son preference in the north, related to inheritance patterns as well as to sex-related work roles. Today, the growing number of incidents of female infanticide from the south fly in the face of well-argued research results of social scientists who have been concerned over these issues. What has happened in the years between?

The obvious answer readily proffered is the all-pervading menace of dowry and the concomitant negative attitudes towards girl children. What is particularly disquieting is the spread of dowry among communities which practised bride price or bride wealth, and where, historically, women had a high status, such as, for instance, among the Mizos and the Kallars of Tamil Nadu. The obsessive hold of Sanskritization is evident among the prosperous sections of the Kallar community which is seen to 'claim comparability with upper caste culture' (Devi 1991; Mazumdar 1992). Social sanction and legitimization of infanticide are surely important in communities where the poor fear dowry, and the rich, a fragmentation of property.

In a study of twelve villages of K.V. Kuppan Block, North Arcot, Ambedkar district of Tamil Nadu state, which began in September 1986 and continued for four years, it was found that of a population

> of 13,000 there were a total of 773 births recorded, involving 759 live births of which 378 were male and 381 female. Further, among the cohort of live born infants, 56 died in the period of two and a half years and of these there were 23 males and 33 females. ... Of these deaths, 19 were confirmed infanticides (which were all female infanticides).

The research further indicated that the villages in which 'female infanticide occurred are less "developed" in terms of urban linkages, services and education than the non-infanticide villages' (George, et al. 1992: 1153).

A recent study done by the Community Service Guild of Madras in collaboration with Adithi, a Patna-based organization for the development of rural women with a branch in Chennai, shows that in Salem district of Tamil Nadu, female infanticide is rampant (Venkatachalam and Srinivasan 1993). Though the study covered Christians, Hindus, and Muslims, the practice of female infanticide was found only among Hindus. Of the 1250 families in the sample—most of whom were Goudas with a few Naickers, Vanniars and Chettiars—covered by the study, 606 had only one girl child and 111 admitted that they had done away with the unwanted girl child. Equally alarming was the fact that 476 respondents said that 'they would have to commit female infanticide when more than one female child was born to them' (Venkatachalam and Srinivasan 1993: 26). Most women said that they had killed their babies under pressure from their husbands: 'Women said that sometimes the men would beat them up insisting on the murder of new born daughters' (Venkatachalam and Srinivasan 1993: 53).

A detailed study of juvenile sex ratios and data from Primary Health Centres (PHC) in Tamil Nadu (Chunkath and Athreya 1997) established two additional facts: analysis of juvenile sex ratios may lead to surprising conclusions as well as provide the data for a longitudinal assessment of the prevalence of female infanticide. For instance, for the 1991

Census, the three districts of Dharmapuri, Salem, and Madurai accounted for forty-one out of the forty-six blocks in Tamil Nadu, with a juvenile female sex ratio of less than 900 to a 1000. Further, as is evident from a study of earlier census reports, this sharp decline is of fairly recent origin. The authors concluded that 'this would be true of female infanticide as well' (Chunkath and Athreya 1997: WS-22). Analysis of PHC data also corroborated this observation.

Poverty, alcoholism among men, ignorance of family planning, and cost of dowry are the possible causes of this practice of infanticide, and there is scattered evidence to suggest that it is more prevalent in other parts of India than is readily acknowledged. At the same time, while instances of infanticide are indicative of negative attitudes towards girls, a certain caution needs to be exercised before extrapolating on the likely spread of this social malaise; it is also useful to keep in mind Chunkath and Athreya's observation that birth order also determines the fate of a girl child; analysis of household data where female infanticides had occurred in 1995 showed that 'the first female infant is, in a majority of cases not a victim of female infanticide (Chunkath and Athreya 1997: WS-28), the second girl child would often escape, and it was the third girl who was invariably the victim.

The Abused Child

An area in which there is little available research is that of child abuse within the home. This includes sexual aggression, beating, as well as extracting hours of labour from children who should be in school or at play. Nonetheless, nearly all available studies have shown that children are victims of substantial abuse of a physical, psychological, and emotional nature (MARG 1996). In part, this abuse is caused by the life situation of families, where, for instance, children become part of the labour force due to poverty. Recent studies have shown that, in absolute terms, child labour is on the increase, particularly for those who work as marginal workers. For girls the expansion has been dramatic in both rural as well urban areas (Chaudhuri 1996). Neera Burra (1995) has divided child labour into four categories—those who work in factories, workshops, and mines; those who are bonded; street children; and children who form part of the familial labour force. Working in inhuman conditions often for a pittance, children are abused at work and within homes where their earnings become the property of their parents. Not unexpectedly, then, child labour has become an emotive issue resulting in a sense of moral outrage in the international community and the concomitant boycott of products using this form of labour; however, banning child labour is a simplistic response to a much deeper problem, which lies embedded in structures of power, availability of alternatives and schooling, as well as the overall immiseration of at least a third of the population (see Raman forthcoming, for a discussion of the issue). For those children who do not work for a wage but contribute to the family workforce, leisure, education, and anything remotely regarded as the rights of the child need to be defined keeping in mind the cultural specificities of notions of childhood, play, learning, and consequently exploitation and abuse.

Apart from the physical burden of working before the body is ready for it, children are often enough subjected to beatings and lashings in a range of situations. Amarjit Mahajan and Madhurima (1995) have argued that punishment per se does not constitute violence; however, when an act of punishment involves substantial injury, it is no longer legitimate punishment but violence against a defenceless child. In a study carried out in a village in Haryana, 200 children in the age group 7–14 years were interviewed. The majority came from landless families, and 97 per cent of fathers in this category said that they punished their children as against 83 per cent of the landowners; interestingly, both sets of fathers preferred physical punishment. However, the reasons for punishment were different: 72 per cent of the landowners punished the children for non-compliance with family norms and standards of discipline; for the landless, the major concern was with unwillingness to work—for 'when the child shirked work, he was given severe punishment' (Mahajan and Madhurima 1995: 86). It was also this category of children who were injured more often in the course of punishment. Most parents, irrespective of their background, felt that there were positive consequences associated with beating. On the other hand, the study found that routinely abused children started hating their parents, became more obstinate, and a few even ran away from home.

In a 1982 study of a 1000 victims of child abuse, Dave et al. (1982) found that 81 per cent could be classified as victims of physical abuse, 7 per cent of what the authors call physical neglect, 9.3 per cent of sexual abuse, and 2.7 per cent of emotional abuse. None of these categories can be treated as exclusive and it is important to note that studies of this kind are extremely difficult to undertake, particularly so in the area of sexual relations where the overall attitude of secrecy and suppression that governs any discussion or reference to sex, makes it difficult to come to definite conclusions on the extent of sexual abuse of children. Yet, of the available figures, of almost 10,000 reported rapes in 1990, an alarming 25 per cent are of girl children below the age of 16, and about a fifth are of those under ten. A recent analysis done by the Crimes Against Women Cell, Delhi Police, points out that of the 381 rape cases registered between January and August 1997, 270 or almost 75 per cent of the victims were in the age range 7–18 years. Only 57 of the rapists were unknown to the victims. Most were immediate neighbours; ten girls were raped by their fathers; and three by step fathers (*The Pioneer*, 29 September 1997).

Such alarming figures are indicative not only of the sexual vulnerability of the girl child in and around her home, but also of a social climate which encourages her violation. In an interesting presentation at a seminar on child rape organized by the National Commission for Women (NCW) in New Delhi, in October 1992, Sobha Srinath from NIMHANS, Bangalore pointed to an important, though perhaps little thought about, fact: a young child below the age of ten need not always be aware that her sexual violation is in fact qualitatively different from thrashing and abuse: it is only with the onset of puberty that she becomes aware of her sexuality. In fact, in an environment where physical contact, both affectionate and abusive, by relatives of both sexes is not uncommon, child rape needs to be viewed a little differently from the rape of a post-pubertal girl.

Not unexpectedly, families rarely talk about the rape of their young daughter; when the rapist is a father or a brother, the chances of reporting are even lower. Members of voluntary organizations said that a mother would often suppress and wish away the event, not only because of a sense of shame and outrage, but also out of fear of reprisals from her husband, son, or other relatives (NCW Seminar, October 1992, personal observations). Interestingly, in 1992–3, there were eight cases of rape and molestation reported by mothers to the Crime against Women Cell in Delhi; officials at the Cell pointed out that this was a significant development as hardly any such instances were reported earlier. At the same time, wives expected the police to merely caution their husbands, filing a case against them would be unheard of (Wadhwa 1993). If there is a silence around the sexual violation of the girl child in the family, this is equally true of cases of sodomy and abuse of the male child.

Inequality in the Household

The prevalence of a dominant ideology which confines girls and women to definite roles and obligations leads to their devaluation and discrimination in a range of areas. The basic assumption is that girls are inferior, physically and mentally weak, and above all sexually vulnerable. In a society which lays so much stress on purity and pollution, various oppressive structures—including early marriage—are encouraged so as to confine the physical mobility of girls and women. A declining sex ratio (929 women to 1000 men according to the Census of 1991) would suggest endemic female mortality and morbidity (Agnihotri 1997; Deshpande 1991; Irudaya Rajan et al. 1991, Mazumdar 1992, Reddy 1991) caused by consistent neglect and sustained discrimination, both manifestations of violence and oppression.

In this context, the notions of expectations and entitlements are particularly important. An entitlement (Papanek 1990; Sen 1983, 1987) represents the right to a share of resources such as health care, nutrition, education and material assets, as well as to parental attention and interest. The distribution of these resources is usually in keeping with a family ideology and can be seen in intra-household allocation of resources. Evidence indicates that girls and women are usually far less privileged than boys in access to material resources (Basu 1989; Batliwala 1983; Gopalan and Chatterjee 1985; Gulati 1978; Kumari 1989; Minocha 1984; Sen and Sen Gupta 1985). However, these often vary according to the birth order of the girls, and, as mentioned already, it is often the case that excess female child morality is more common in families which already have a daughter (Das Gupta 1987; Das Gupta and Chen 1995).

Rural health surveys in north India show that women and girls are ill more often than boys and men. At the same time a study of records at medical institutions (Batliwala 1983) reported that there was only one woman user to every three men who use hospital facilities. Hospital records (Kynch and Sen 1983) indicate a similar pattern of crises-related admissions. A recent study of 1853 persons who came to a general health facility found that 193 (10.4 per cent) had psychological problems. Most were women in the age group 16 to 45 years, who had come to the facility from a far greater distance than those with physical disorders. For a majority of this group, 'the cause of stress lay in personal and family life' and specifically, for 10 per cent, marital and sexual reasons were the cause of distress (Srinivasa Murthy, 1992). It would be fairly safe to hypothesize, then, that while a sizeable percentage of women's health problems lie rooted in familial dynamics and tension-ridden relationships, more often than not women tend to get treated for physical disorders.

The fact that forms of discrimination in food exist in upper caste, middle class homes as well, indicates that factors other than scarcity are crucial. Further, the ailments of boys and men are more likely to get treated, or if women do get attention, much less is spent on their ailments (Dandekar 1975). In an analysis of state- and district-level data, Sunita Kishor found that 'a critical manifestation' of discrimination against girl children 'is the under-allocation of medicine and food' (Kishor 1995: 48). Making a distinction between survival rates and discrimination, she points out that while the former seems to rise with the socio-economic status of the household, there is not enough evidence to suggest that discrimination declines with higher status: observations from the field show that upper caste, upper-middle-class families, discriminate against girls with respect to the access they have to higher education, as well as in matters such as protein intake, games and extra- and co-curricular activities (Karlekar 1987).

Other data (Das Gupta 1987; Kumari et al. 1990) indicate a definite bias in feeding boys milk and milk products and eggs, while both boys and girls have equal access to cereal and vegetables. Taboos associated with giving girls meat, fish, and eggs which are regarded as hot food, are fairly widespread (Dube 1988, Kumari et al. 1990). In Rajasthan and Uttar Pradesh, it was usual for girls and women to eat less, and usually after the men and boys had eaten (Kumari et al. 1990). Greater mobility outside the home provided boys with the opportunity to eat sweets and fruit from saved-up pocket money or from money given to buy articles for food consumption (Khan et al. 1986). In case of illness, it is usually boys who are given preference for receiving health care (Chanana 1990; Das Gupta 1987; Desai and Krishna Raj 1987; Kanhere 1987; Mankekar 1985). In fact, a study in rural Punjab established that there were wider sex differentials in access to medical care than in food allocation: more was spent on clothing for boys than for girls, which had an effect on morbidity (Das Gupta 1987). Thus familial views on what should be a girl's expectations take precedence over the right to greater individual entitlement and, on the whole, reinforce her growing sense of marginalization, powerlessness, as well as vulnerability. Here again ethnographic studies would be useful in furthering an understanding of the dynamics of feminine socialization, availability of resources, and patterns of oppression. For instance, apart from the usual indicators of caste, class, religion, and so on, observations from the field on availability of resources, and infrastructure such as PHCs, schools, and hospitals would show whether their existence appreciably influences girls' access to a better quality of life. Also, size of family, differences of attitudes towards children on the basis of birth order, spacing between siblings and, age of the mother, may also influence attitudes towards allocations not only between boys and girls but among female siblings as well.

Violence in the Conjugal Home

Marriage continues to be universally regarded as essential for a girl, in India, irrespective of class, caste, religion, and ethnicity, as control of her sexuality and its safe transference into the hands of the husband is given prime importance. Concern over the conduct of the sexually vulnerable girl is important cause of early marriage. According to the Census of 1991, about 30 per cent of women in the ages group 15–19 were married; as the official age for marriage is 18 for girls, it is possible that a large percentage of these marriages were of under-age girls. Though the age of marriage is rising gradually, it is important to note that girls are barely out of their teens when they leave their natal homes for another unknown residence. The exception is the familiarity characterizing cross-cousin marriages. Subsequent expectations and relationships impose a considerable load on those who are as yet girls, ill-equipped to adjust to a totally new environment, and a set of unfamiliar relationships. For, in India, marriage establishes a network of interacting individuals: it is rarely only a highly personal relationship between a man and a woman (see Das 1976 for a discussion of *biradari*).

The persistence of a dominant family ideology which enjoins a strict sexual division of labour and age and gender hierarchy means that young wives have to invest a considerable amount of time and energy in forging new relationships, not all of which are caring or accommodative. These take precedence over all other relationships in the natal home. Nothing describes the transient nature of a girl's brief life in her parent's home or her inherent worth better than the north-Indian saying that a girl is *paraya dhan* or another's wealth. It not only establishes the very notion of belonging but also that, a girl is wealth (dhan) which belongs ultimately elsewhere (paraya).

Is wealth the same as property? What does the concept of women as wealth mean? It can be argued that both property and wealth involve ownership, control, and right of disposal. They also imply the capacity to generate more assets, if properly utilized. Clearly, such an understanding is more comprehensible in the context of physical goods and immoveable assets. In the case of human resources, it would include intangibles such as skills, education, reputation, and physical attributes as well. In the traditions of marriage for most of India, 'the bride is a vehicle for the passage of valuables from her own kin to that of her husband' (Hirschon 1984: 11). The unequal nature of the marital relationship sanctified by significant gift exchanges, rituals, and expectations establishes the parameters of subsequent intra-familial behaviour patterns.

Based on her field data from Papua New Guinea, anthropologist Marilyn Strathern has argued, 'If women are passed between groups of men, equated with the wealth that flows between them, then they must be treated as objects themselves. As objects they must be a form of property' (Strathern 1988: 163). But, she asks, what about their personhood and their capacity to assert their identities? She points out that 'the definition of personhood is not tied up with the manipulation of things' (Strathern 1988: 144). Strathern's position is worth taking note of in the context not only of dowry but the present-day ramifications of the system, namely the violence and even physical annihilation associated with this form of gift giving. The very notions of personhood and identity are under threat from familial power structures where the in-marrying woman's sense of self is constantly assailed. Of course, with age and gain in status within the family as the mother of sons and, ultimately, a mother-in-law, a distinct identity emerges. In fact, it is an identity which, in the popular imagination, is often linked to oppression of new female entrants to the family. Bollywood has had an important role to play in the stereotyping of the evil mother-in-law and the oppressed, submissive daughter-in-law.

Within this framework of matrimony and affinal relationships, many women attempt to negotiate space for themselves, to assert their personhood. The capacity to do so is dependent on a range of factors such as age, maternal status, and position in the hierarchy of senior or junior daughters-in-law. It is also often enough the case that intra-couple discord (which may later escalate into a dowry-related demand and expectation syndrome) is over roles, their performance or otherwise, and a woman's quest for her identity. It is this which distinguishes inanimate wealth/property from an animate being who may be the reason or vehicle for transactions, but nonetheless resists being treated in the same manner as a disposable commodity. That, often enough, a woman loses out is a symbol of the unequal power play within the home.

An important part of the power relationship between spouses and indeed their families, relates to dowry and its ramifications. In the Indian context, the preference for structural asymmetry between the two families and the consequent burden of gift giving on the bride's family strengthens inequality. Anthropological studies, particularly of north-Indian marriage and kinship patterns, indicate that hypergamous unions establish a permanent asymmetry in gift giving and prestations. Here the notion of property in marriage acquires another meaning: not only is the in-marrying girl viewed as the property of her husband if not of the conjugal family, but also, the event marks the unequal flow of goods and even property between the two kin groups (Dumont 1975; Goody and Tambiah 1973; Madan [1965] 1989; Sharma 1984; Stri Kriti Samiti 1984; Patnaik and Sadual 1988; Ranjana Kumari 1989; Uberoi [1994] 1995; Vatuk 1975; Verghese 1997). Based on her fieldwork in north-India, Ursula Sharma has argued persuasively that dowry, or what the bride's family gives to the groom's family at the time of hypergamous marriages, is 'a concrete form of property in which members of the household, both men and women, have different kinds of interest and over which they have different kinds of control' (Sharma 1984: 62). Important for later analysis is the communal aspect of dowry, nor is it a one time transaction: ritual occasions, festivals, and indeed any minor pretext result in more demands being made on the daughter-in-law's family.

In India, there is a tendency to club most marital violence under the overall heads of 'dowry', 'dowry deaths', and 'dowry violence'. This categorization glosses over the other causes of violence which pervade the familial context. However, to argue that dowry is not always the cause behind marital discord is not to ignore the fact that it is one of the major factors responsible for domestic violence. While keeping this fact in mind it is necessary to work towards a fuller understanding of the institution of dowry and its impact on inter-family relationships. Madhu Kishwar (1986) feels that oppression of wives for bringing inadequate dowry is one more excuse for using violence against them: in other words—and in fact evidence from other countries has indicated as much—even without the additional 'attraction' of dowry, interspousal violence is endemic. She has also pointed out that dowry payments in themselves do not transform girls into burdens but rather 'dowry makes daughters "burden-some" only because daughters are unwanted to begin with' (Kishwar 1986). For instance, middle class parents who save to pay lakhs as capitation fees for sons in medical or engineering colleges do not view them as burdensome; but similar sums set aside for daughters' marriages are regarded differently.

Though it is difficult to be categorical on the background of those either harassed or killed for dowry, it is clearly a phenomenon on the increase among all social categories. In a study of dowry victims in Delhi, Ranjana Kumari (1989) commented that 'dowry has become inseparably interlinked with the general status of women in our society'. Her study shows that in a sample of 150 dowry victims, one-fourth were murdered or driven to commit suicide, and more than half, i.e. 61.3 per cent, were thrown out of their husband's house after a long-drawn-period of harassment and torture. Dowry-related killings followed two patterns. First the young brides were either murdered or forced to commit suicide (18.4 per cent) when their parents refused to concede to continuing demands for dowry. Second, the murders were committed also on the pretext of 'complex family relations'. Extramarital relationships were alleged in 52.6 per cent cases of death. It was also discovered that the conflicts intensified because of the refusal by young brides to yield to overtures made by father-in-law, uncle-in-law or brother-in-law. There were also cases where wives alleged that the husband was impotent.

In 69.3 per cent cases, parents sent their daughters back to the husbands while being fully aware of the torment they were undergoing. Of these, 77.9 per cent returned only to be deserted and 11.5 per cent to be murdered. In 72 per cent of cases, parents were more willing to put thousands of rupees in the hands of a man who tortured their daughter than to spend even a fraction (10 per cent) of the dowry to train the girl to survive independently, because they did not consider independent survival of women as respectable. Ranjana Kumari also found dowry giving and taking to be universal across caste, religion, and income groups. However, she observed that 'while desertion and harassment cases are more among higher income groups, middle income groups show higher dowry death rates'. She also found that only 5 per cent of marriages were love marriages while 11 per cent were inter-caste. The rest had married according to the prevailing social norms of 'arranged' matches (see Ranjana Kumari 1989: 88–91 for this discussion; see also Mahajan and Madhurima 1995; Sinha 1989).

There is no satisfactory explanation for why the system of dowry is growing and indeed spreading to communities where it earlier did not exist. Nonetheless, its role in perpetuating violence within the home is substantial. Of particular relevance is the fact that dissatisfaction over dowry payments and subsequent prestations result in abuse of the wife not only by her husband but by other affines as well. This, however, is not the only reason for ill-treatment of married women. Apart from ill-health and stress, a violent home environment can led to a total psychological remoulding such as the internalization of deception, manipulative techniques, and feigning. It can also lead to anticipation and provocation, a macabre expectation of the inevitable (see Agnes 1988; and Kakar 1990, for perceptive interpretations of inter-spousal violence).

Thus wife abuse, a practice shared with many other cultures, acquires a different connotation in Indian society due to the institution of dowry. Here, the term 'abuse' includes physical as well as non-physical acts. There is enough evidence to suggest that such abuse often receives wider familial sanction. It is institutionalized in various forms that range from inhumanly long hours of labour, often within and outside the home, food denial, neglect of ailments, and verbal abuse by affines to physical violence by the husband and sometimes other family members. In this context, it is important to note the growing number of cases being registered under section 498A of the Indian Penal Code (IPC, 1983) which indicts a husband or relative of the husband for cruelty against a wife. For instance, all-India police data under this head that are available from 1989 onwards record a steady increase: from 11,803 cases registered in 1989 cases went up to 15,949, or by 37.5 per cent in 1992. As entire families and indeed the state become involved in the ramifications of inter-spousal disputes, the incidence of these events continues to spiral upwards, occasionally with macabre outcomes: personal communications with police officials indicated that the unnatural deaths of wives were on the increase each year.

Abuse of wives and wife beating—or in more extreme cases wife battering—is the most common form of abuse worldwide irrespective of class, religion, community, and in the case of India, caste background (Bogard 1988; Chen 1922a; Cheung and Law 1990; Dong Xing 1995; Finkelhor et al. 1983; Gelles 1980; Gelles and Loseke 1993; Hoff 1990; Jahan 1994; KWDI 1993; Strauss 1980; Walker 1983). In India, studies have correlated childhood abuse, alcoholism, unemployment, and poverty with the growth of this malaise (Ahuja 1987; Kaushik 1990; Mahajan and Madhurima 1995; Sinha 1989; Sood

1990). It has also been argued that it is not a woman's dependence which makes her particularly vulnerable: a wife in a high-status job may be beaten more than her unemployed neighbour (Pawar 1988). Battered women are also seen as lacking self-esteem and self-confidence and being apathetic and nervous (Kaushik 1990).

In an interesting study of the impact of wife beating on the women themselves as well as on other members of the family, Vijayendra Rao (1995) found that in three multi-caste villages in the southern state of Karnataka, only 22 per cent women claimed to have been abused by their husbands. In fact, during fieldwork, two women were hit by their husbands; but, in response to a question, the very same women did not say that they had been abused. The researcher concluded that it was only if the beatings were very severe that women perceived of themselves as being abused: the odd slap or blow was regarded as routine husband-like behaviour. There was wide societal tolerance for wife abuse, which was even considered justifiable under certain circumstances: 'Disputes over dowries, a wife's sexual infidelities, her neglect of household duties, and her disobedience of her husband's dictates are all considered legitimate cause for wife-beating' (Rao 1995: 11). Observations during fieldwork for a project on domestic violence also confirmed a high degree of acceptance of male violence: it was only when the torture became unbearable or death appeared imminent that most women appeared willing to speak out (Karlekar et al. 1995).

In a detailed discussion of wife abuse, Flavia Agnes (1988) has convincingly rebutted the popular myths which surround the phenomenon of wife beating in India, such as middle class women do not get beaten; the victim of violence is a small, fragile, helpless woman belonging to the working class; and the wife beater is a man who is frustrated in his job, an alcoholic, or a paranoid person, aggressive in his relationships. Nor is it true that so-called loving husbands do not beat their wives or that women provoke men to beat them. Yet many of these myths seem to pervade the analysis of wife beating and feminine expectations in Indian society.

For instance, based on an analysis of cases which had come to the Delhi-based women's organization Saheli, it was evident that wife beating was common among all social classes as it 'is a reflection of the power relationship between a husband and wife', which mirrors a woman's secondary social status (Saheli 1988:1) However, the pattern of violence differs from one class to another, with the whole neighbourhood being witness when a slum-dweller beats his wife while a middle class professional's physical oppression of his spouse is extremely private in nature.

Like child rape within the family, another area about which little is known and which is hardly discussed is that of marital rape: in India. Despite some thinking along these lines by feminists and legal experts, there has as yet been no amendment in law to include sexual violence as rape within marriage. The only exception is if the wife is below 16 years of age. Though figures on marital rape as well as other sexually demeaning and violent acts are difficult to obtain, discussions[3] with counsellors working with abused women indicated that a very large percentage of their clients were tortured with forced sexual intercourse.

Feminine socialization which stresses docility, compliance, and shame predisposes a wife to accept a range of physical behaviour from her spouse, where, without doubt, her sexual satisfaction is of little consequence. On the basis of her fieldwork among upper-middle-class and middle-class women in Delhi, all of whom had contracted 'so-called "love" marriages', Meenakshi Thapan (1997) concludes that women had internalized notions of the perfect female body and of femininity; consequently, they were often complicit in the mechanisms of oppression, particularly those aspects which dealt with physical and sexual attractiveness. However, that such psychological and physical oppression can equally develop into a site for resistance—a point not addressed by Thapan—is discussed later. It would not be too extreme to hypothesize that much male physical violence in marriage is related to sexual activity: detailed interviews and discussions at the women's shelter for battered women[4] quite often led to admission of sexual excesses; when a woman resisted, she was beaten; or if she did not satisfy her husband's demands (which could quite often be perverse in nature), the outcome was physical abuse. It is indeed ironical that for long, the family, viewed as an individual's ballast against the world, becomes the arena for legitimate physical and mental oppression of women. While the legal and police systems have, after 1975, become more receptive to certain excesses, much remains unstated, invisible and repressed.

The Aging Person within the Home

With a decline in rates of mortalities there are a growing number of aging people in families and households. In a recent demographic study of the aged, Kumudini Dandekar (1996) has concluded that in a rural population of about 640 million, about 45 million or 7 per cent are above 60; half of this population is poor and at least 10 per cent of those above 60 are helpless and in the category of requiring financial support. While there is little information on attitudes and behaviour of younger family members towards the elderly, a few studies have established that a situation of dependency on the younger generation results in neglect and in some cases, ill-treatment and different forms of violence against older people, in particular, women. For instance, neglect of ailments by family members which is quite common, is extremely demoralizing for the aged (Shankardas 1997).

Researchers in the West have tried to make a distinction between active and passive neglect while others have viewed neglect and abuse differently (see Mahajan and Madhurima 1995). Reluctance to speak of their trauma and a concern with the family's reputation or *izzat* coupled with a dependence on others has meant that 'elder abuse becomes known to the authorities through a third party' (Mahajan and Madhurima 1995: 106).

While in India, institutionalization of the elderly is virtually unknown, there is evidence that households are increasingly disinclined to invest scarce resources on those whom they feel will have little to contribute to a family's success and mobility (personal observations during fieldwork for various projects on the position of women in India). A report brought out by the women's organization Karmika (quoted in MARG 1996: 18–19), characterized the habitual scolding, nagging, non-communication, as well as feigned ignorance about their needs and ailments as informal violence; this form of violence, argued the report could be 'sometimes worse than physical injury' (MARG 1996: 18).

In a study of 749 elderly working-class persons in the districts of Haryana of whom 369 were men above 60 years of age and 380 women above 55, Mahajan and Madhurima found that over 30 per cent of all respondents 'admitted that quite often or sometimes they were abused by family members' (Mahajan and Madhurima 1995: 120). Further enquiries indicated that inability to work, lack of finances, and failing health accounted for ill-treatment. Interestingly, the level of satisfaction among women was higher than among men. Aging siblings, some of whom may or may not have married, old couples who have to rely on one another, and destitutes are other categories of the elderly about whom very little is known.

The position of the aged in rural areas and situations of in chronic poverty is a much neglected area of study. During a recent field trip to households suffering from severe food shortages in Madhya Pradesh, Veena Das encountered two very old women who existed on the margins of society: as widows and destitutes, they did not figure in the welfare measures instituted by the local-level bureaucrats, and were paid scant attention by the villagers. She concludes that the preponderant emphasis on the married woman in the reproductive cycle has led almost to an effacement of other categories such as the elderly, the never married, and the disabled (Das 1997). In fact, before the declaration of the Year of the Girl Child a few years ago, not much was known about female children either.

Irrespective of their geographic location, little is known about the treatment and neglect of the elderly who have lost their spouses. A recent study of widows established that 'of the poor in India, widowed women are in all likelihood the most disadvantaged, both socially and economically' (HIID-WIDER Workshop 1992: 1). Not only do widows and their lot slip through the net in discussions on poverty, but also little is known about their treatment within families. In a study of north-Indian widows, Martha Chen and Jean Drèze observed that marginalization, social as well as physical, was usual and the widow 'remains highly vulnerable to neglect' resulting in poor health and high mortality rates (Chen and Drèze 1995: 283). Importantly, the widow who headed her own household which included an adult son had the lowest mortality risk. Extrapolating from these data, we can conclude that food discrimination, inadequate health care, lack of living space, and excessive expectations as far as domestic work is concerned make the widow's situation extremely tenuous. When these are combined with lack of access to property and assets, it is not difficult to envisage the overall situation of denial and deprivation they face.

Increase in domestic workload, loss of self-respect, as well as tendency to neurosis was observed in a study of 350 widows in Haryana which also found that most felt that survival and accommodation were major problems (Sandhya 1994). In a study which probed the entire question of violence against widows, Mukesh Ahuja (1996) found that of the 190 widows interviewed in Jaipur city, the most common complaint was that of verbal abuse from their in-laws; such behaviour ranged from sarcastic comments to scolding, shouting, and humiliating remarks in the presence of others. A large percentage said that they had been denied access to their husbands' assets. While 12.5 percentage said that they had been physically beaten by their in-laws, another 15 percentage said that their children too were beaten and ill-treated (Ahuja 1996: 88). Of the twenty-nine women who had grown-up children, fourteen reported abusive behaviour by their sons and daughters-in-law.

Sexual vulnerability of the widow is a prevalent though little-discussed and-acknowledged fact of their existence. Twenty-six of Ahuja's respondents said that they had been victims of sexual attacks; well over 60 per cent said that the assailants had been affines while the rest had been molested by neighbours, employers, or friends' brothers (Ahuja 1996: 93). A woman's physical and sexual vulnerability is accentuated in times of social and political stress, communal disturbances being a case in point. Recounting their experiences at a centre at Tilak Vihar in west Delhi, activists spoke poignantly of the sixty young Sikh widows they were trying to rehabilitate after the holocaust of November 1984, following the assassination of Prime Minister Indira Gandhi. The typical familial response of 'settling' the widow was to marry her to a brother-in-law, in itself an old practice. The results were often disastrous as 'very few have been able to resist the onslaught of these cruel societal norms' (Srivastava 1989: 65). Those who had the courage to resist faced social and familial ostracism as well as 'drunken beating and exploitation or worse at the hands of their men' (Srivastava 1989: 65). Prostitution was encouraged by affines even as the women were trying to piece together their lives. Thus, despite the will to survive, 'the stringent codes of conduct of Indian society crushes them again into keeping the family's interest and name and fame above their own and their children's hope for a better life' (Srivastava 1989: 64). Clearly then, widowhood exposes a woman to new forms and networks of exploitation and violence.

Conclusion

The ever-present fact of violence, both overt and covert, physical and non-physical has overwhelming influence on feminine identity formation. A child's sense of self is greatly dependent on how others think, feel, and behave towards her. This fundamental difference in identity formation between the sexes has deep roots in the socialization processes, resource allocation within families, the impact of external influences such as mass media, pornography, and the educational system. While identity, notions of self, roles, and obligations are worked out fairly early in a woman's life, no stage of her life-cycle is without change and questioning of received norms. Thus feminine identity and a woman's position within the family continue to be open to modification, depending on her situation in the life-cycle. What is important in this context is that these modifications are often determined by the collectivity: individual self-expression is repressed and subjugated and the anger at being violated is internalized.

There is clearly much more that needs to be understood about the Indian family and its internal dynamics. For instance, to pin all violence against the girl child on the fear of dowry appears a convenient rationalization, shrouding a range of motivations. Is it to be assumed that dowry giving is such a widespread and prevalent practice as to influence every parent who goes in for female foeticide, abortion, or infanticide? While, in the absence of adequate data, it is difficult to be categorical, there is clearly a need to further investigate the family's strategies for survival and mobility as well as how dependency of the young, the housewives, and the elderly conditions responses to these conditions. It is clear that far from being a refuge from the outside world, the family is complicit in processes and mechanisms of socialization, many of which are oppressive if not extreme in nature.

The validity of field studies in filling the gaps in knowledge has been stressed more than once in this chapter. These would not only enhance the data base on various phases in the female life cycle, but would also help in gauging the voices of resistance. Whether it is the covert activities of Bangladeshi housewives who find innovative ways of hiding a part of their earnings; the systematic putting away of a measure of grain by village women in the Bankura district of West Bengal; or the uninhibited account of a battered wife narrated to a police official, women are finding ways of challenging the established familial hierarchy, based on male domination and control (personal observations).

Despite the ubiquity of violence against women, both within the home and in public spaces, the celebration of individual experiences has led to the emergence of alternate discourses where the 'truth' and validity of established structures, norms, and roles are called into question. In order to appreciate how individual experience may become the ground for alternative discourses to emerge it is necessary to see the family and its individual members in an emerging context with many players in the field: an interface between them, the state, the law, and the women's movement becomes increasingly relevant (see Agnes 1995; Gandhi and Shah 1992; Kapur and Cossman 1996; Kumar 1993; Nair 1996). As retelling and reinterpretation become the sites for differing realities, it is clear that contemporary understandings of domestic violence will need to interrogate a familial ideology based on unity and patriarchal dominance in a manner that does not valorize victimhood alone but takes note of agency and resistance as well.

ENDNOTES

1. Much of the work on this section is based on the introductory chapter in 'Violence against Women—Domestic Violence', unpublished report of a study by Malavika Karlekar with Anuja Agarwal, Maithili Ganju, and Meena Mukherjee, Centre for Women's Development Studies, New Delhi, undertaken for the Government of India, 1995. However, I have added more material and my later perceptions owe a lot to discussions with Veena Das. I am grateful to her for useful suggestions as well as for help in locating additional references.

2. It is a global fact official police data, in particular statistics, deal with crime rather than with the much more pervasive phenomenon of violence. One reason for this variance is that the police data on crime are based on complaints and cases registered, which in turn depend on willingness to report and police receptivity to acts as crimes against women as well as the inclination to investigate these. It would not be an exaggeration to state that crime figures are merely the proverbial tip of the iceberg.

3. Some cases have been discussed in 'Violence against Women—Domestic Violence'. On the basis of the study a workshop was held in 1995 and its report entitled 'No Safe Spaces—Report of a Workshop on Violence against Women' by Malavika Karlekar et al. (1995), was circulated.

4. See Karlekar et al. (1995: Chapter 3).

REFERENCES

Abraham, Margaret. 1995. 'Ethnicity, Gender and Marital Violence: South Asian Women's Organization in the United States'. *Gender and Society*. 9(4):550–68.

Agarwal, Kuntal. 1998. 'Survival of Females in India'. Paper presented at International Conference of Women, Development and Health, Michigan State University, Michigan.

Agnes, Flavia. 1988. 'Violence in the Family: Wife Beating'. In Rehana Ghadially, ed., *Women and Indian Society: A Reader*, 151–66. New Delhi: Sage Publications.

_____. 1993. 'The Anti-Rape Campaign: The Struggle and the Setback'. In Chaya Datar, ed., *The Struggle against Violence*, 99–150. Calcutta: Stree Publications.

_____. 1995. *The State, Gender and the Rhetoric of Law Reform*. Bombay: RCWS, SNDT Women's University.

Agnihotri, Satish Balram. 1997. 'Unpacking Juvenile Sex Ratios in India'. Paper presented at a UNICEF-UNIFEM-UNDP-SDC Conference on Ending Violence against Women and Girls in South Asia. Kathmandu, 21–4 October.

Ahuja, Mukesh. 1996. *Widows: Role Adjustment and Violence*. New Delhi: Vishwa Prakashan.

Ahuja, R. 1987. *Crimes against Women*. Jaipur: Rawat Publication.

Anveshi. 1995. 'Women in India and Their Mental Health'. Communication paper.

Basu, A.M. 1989. 'Culture and the Status of Women in North and South India'. In Singh et al. eds, *Population Transition in India*. Delhi: B.R. Publishing Corporation.

Batliwala, S. 1983. 'Women in Poverty: The Energy, Health and Nutrition Syndrome'. Unpublished paper.

Béteille, André. 1998. 'The Reproduction of Inequality: Occupation Caste and Family'. In Patricia Uberoi, ed., *Family, Kinship and Marriage in India*, 435–51. Delhi: Oxford University Press.

Bhasin, Kamala and Ritu Menon, eds. 1994. *Against all Odds: Essays on Women, Religion and Development in India and Pakistan*. New Delhi: Kali for Women.

Bograd, M. 1988. 'Feminist Perspective on Wife Abuse: An introduction'. In K. Yllö and Bograd, eds, *Feminist Perspective on Wife Abuse*, 11–25. Newbury: Sage Publications.

Bondurant, Joan. 1965. *Conquest of Violence: The Gandhian Philosophy of Conflict*. Berkeley and Los Angeles: University of California Press.

Bourdieu, Pierre. 1977. *Outline of a Theory of Practice*. Cambridge: Cambridge University Press.

Burra, Neera. 1995. *Born to Work: Child Labour in India*. Delhi: Oxford University Press.

Butalia, Urvashi. 1993. 'Community, State and Gender: On Women's Agency during Partition'. *Economic and Political Weekly*. 28(17):12–24.

_____. 1998. *The Other Side of Silence: Voices from the Partition of India*. New Delhi: Viking.

Carstairs, M. 1983. *Death of a Witch: A Village in North India 1950–1981*. London: Hutchison.

Chanana, Karuna. 1990. 'Structures and Ideologies: Socialisation and Education of the Girl Child in South Asia'. *Indian Journal of Social Science*. 3:53–71.

Chaudhuri, D.P. 1996. *A Dynamic Profile of Child Labour in India 1951–1991*. New Delhi: ILO.

Chen, Martha A. and Jean Drèze. 1995. 'Widowhood and Well-being in North India'. In Monica Das Gupta et al., eds, *Women's Health in India: Risk and Vulnerability*, 245–88. Delhi: Oxford University Press.

Chen, R. 1992. 'Marital Violence in Taiwan: Characteristics and Risk Factors'. *Journal of Sociology*. 21:123–60.

Cheung, F.M. and J.S. Law. 1990. 'Victims of Sexual Assault: A Summary of the Crime Victimization Surveys of 1978, 1981 and 1986'. In F.M. Cheung, R.G. Audry, and R.C. Tam, eds, *Relevance on Rape and Sexual Crime in Hong Kong*, 1–18. Hongkong: The Hong Kong Institute of Asia Pacific Studies. CUHK.

Chunkath, Sheela Rani and V.B. Athreya. 1997. 'Female Infanticide in Tamil Nadu: Some Evidence'. *Economic and Political Weekly*. 32(17) (26 April): Review of Women's Studies, WS 22–9.

Dandekar, K. 1975. 'Has the Proportion of Women in India's Population been declining?' *Economic and Political Weekly*. 10(42):1663–7.

———. 1996. *The Elderly in India*. New Delhi: Sage Publications.

Das, Veena. 1976. 'Masks & Faces: An Essay on Punjabi Kinship'. *Contributions to Indian Sociology* (n.s.). 10(1):1–30.

———, ed. 1990. *Mirrors of Violence: Communities, Riots and Survivors in South Asia*. Delhi: Oxford University Press.

———. 1996. 'Sexual Violence, Discursive Practices and the State'. Paper presented at the International Conference on Gender Perspectives in Population, Health and Development in India. 12–14 January.

———. 1997. 'Gender Sensitivity: Research and Action'. Presentation made at the National Assembly of Voluntary Organizations, Indian Social Institute, New Delhi. 2–4 October.

Das, Veena and Ashis Nandy. 1986. 'Violence, Victimhood and the Language of Silence'. In Veena Das, ed., *The World and the World*. New Delhi: Sage Publications.

Das Gupta, Monica. 1987. 'Selective Discrimination against Female Children in Rural Punjab, India'. *Population and Development Review*. 13(1):77–100.

Das Gupta, Monica and Lincoln Chen. 1995. 'Overview'. In Monica Das Gupta, L. Chen and T.N. Krishnan, eds, *Women's Health in India—Risk and Vulnerability*, 1–18. Bombay: Oxford University Press.

Datar, C. 1993. *The Struggle against Violence*. Calcutta: Stree Publications.

Davar, Bhargavi. 1995. 'Mental Illness among Indian Women'. *Economic and Political Weekly*. 30(45):2879–86.

Dave, A.B., et al. 1982. 'Child Abuse and Neglect (CAN), Practices in Drug Abuse in a District of Madhya Pradesh'. *Indian Pediatrics*. 19:905–12.

Desai, A.R. 1980. *Urban Family and Family Planning in India*. Bombay: Popular Prakashan.

Desai, I.P. 1964. *Some Aspects of Family in Mahuva*. New Delhi: Asia Publishing House.

Desai, Neera and Maithreyi Krishna Raj. 1987. *Women and Society in India*. New Delhi: Ajanta Books.

Desjarlais, Robert, Leon Eisenberg, Bryon Good, and Arthur Kleinman. 1995. *World Mental Health: Problem and Priorities in Low-Income Countries*. New York: Oxford University Press.

Desphande, A. 1991. 'Census Underlines Anti-women Bias'. *The Telegraph*, 24 March.

Dong, Xing. 1995. 'Study of Domestic Violence'. *Sociology and Research* (third issue).

Dube, Leela. 1974. *Sociology of Kinship: An Analytical Survey Literature*. Bombay: Popular Prakashan.

Dube, Leela. 1986. 'Seed and Earth: The Symbolism of Biological Reproduction and Sexual Relations of Production'. In Leela Dube, Eleanor Leacock, and Shirley Ardner, eds, *Visibility and Power: Essays on Women in Society and Development*, 22–53. Delhi: Oxford University Press.

_____. 1988. 'Socialisation of Hindu Girls in Patrilineal India'. In K. Chanana, ed., *Socialisation, Education and Women*, 168–92. New Delhi: Orient Longman.

Dumont, L. 1975. 'Terminology and Prestations Re-visited'. *Contributions to Indian Sociology* (n.s.). 9(2):197–215.

Finkelhor, David, Richard Gelles, Gerald T. Hotaling, and Murray A. Strauss, eds. 1983. *Dark Side of Families: Current Family Violence Research*. Beverly Hills: Sage Publications.

Gandhi, Nandita and Nandita Shah. 1992. *The Issues at Stake*. New Delhi: Kali for Women.

Gelles, Richard. 1980. 'Violence in the Family: A Review of Research in the Seventies'. *Journal of Marriage and Family*. 42(4).

Gelles, K. and D.R. Loseke. 1993. *Feminist Controversies in Family Violence*. New Delhi: Sage Publications.

George, Sabir, Abel Rajaratnam, and B.D. Miller. 1992. 'Female Infanticide in Rural South India'. *Economic and Political Weekly*. 27(22):1154–6.

Ghadially, Rehana, ed. 1987. *Women in Indian Society*. New Delhi: Sage Publications.

Goody, Jack and Stanley J. Tambiah. 1973. *Bridewealth and Dowry*. Cambridge: Cambridge University Press.

Gopalan, C. and Meera Chatterjee. 1985. 'Gender Bias in Health and Nutrition Care'. *NFI Bulletin*. 8(4).

Gore, M.S. 1968. *Urbanization and Family Change*. Bombay: Popular Prakashan.

Gulati, Leela. 1978. *Profiles in Female Poverty*. New Delhi: Hindustan Publishing House.

HIID-WIDER. 1992. Proceedings of the Workshop on 'Widows in Rural India'. 2–5 March, New Delhi.

Hirschon, Renee. 1984. *Women and Property—Women as Property*. London: Croom Helm.

Hoff, Lee Ann. 1990. *Battered Women as Survivors*. London: Routledge.

Jahan, Roushan. 1994. *Hidden Danger: Women and Family Violence in Bangladesh*. Dhaka: Women for Women.

Juneja, R. 1993. 'Women should also be Punished for Foeticide'. *Pioneer*. 11 August.

Kakar, Sudhir. 1983. *Mystics, Shamans and Doctors*. Delhi: Oxford University Press.

_____. 1990 *Intimate Relations: Exploring Indian Sexuality*. Delhi: Oxford University Press.

Kanhere, Usha. 1987. *Women and Socialisation: A Study of Their Status and Role in Lower Castes of Ahmedabad*. Delhi: Mittal.

Kapur, Ratna and Brenda Cossman. 1996. *Subversive Sites: Feminist Engagements with Law in India*. New Delhi: Sage Publications.

Karlekar, Malavika. 1982. *Poverty and Women's Work*. New Delhi: Vikas.

_____. 1987. 'Education'. In Desai and Krishnaraj, eds, *Women in India*, Delhi: Ajanta Press..

_____. 1998a. Review of Henrietta Moorea. 1995. *A Passion for Difference: Essays in Anthropology and Gender*. Cambridge: Polity Press; and Review of Meenakshi Thapan, ed. 1997. *Embodiment: Essays on Gender and Identity*. Delhi: Oxford

University Press (for the Nehru Memorial Museum and Library). *The Book Review*. 22(1–2):10–3.

———. 1998b. *Breaking the Silence and Choosing to Hear: Perceptions of Violence against Women*. New Delhi: Sage Publications.

Karlekar, Malavika, Anuja Agarwal, and Maithali Ganjoo. 1995. 'No Safe Spaces'. Report on a Workshop on Violence against Women. New Delhi: Centre for Women's Development Studies.

Kasturi, Leela. 1990. 'Poverty, Migration and Women's Status'. In Veena Mazumdar, ed., *Women Workers in India*, 3–169. New Delhi: Chanakya.

Kasturi, Malavika. 1994. 'Law and Crime in India: British Policy and the Female Infanticide Act of 1870'. *Indian Journal of Gender Studies*. 1(2): 169–93.

Kaushik, Sunanda. 1990. 'Social and Treatment Issues in Wife Battering: A Reconsideration'. In S. Sood, ed., *Violence against Women*, 23–34. Jaipur: Arihant Publications.

Kelkar, Govind. 1991. *Violence against Women in India: Perspectives and Strategies*. Bangkok: Asian Institute of Technology.

Khan, et al. 1986. *Health Practices in India*. Bombay: Operations Research Group.

Kishor, Sunita. 1995. 'Gender Differentials in Child Mortality—A Review of Evidence'. In M. Das Gupta et al. eds, *Womens Health in India: Risk and Vulnerability*, 19–54. Bombay: Oxford University Press.

Kishwar, Madhu. 1986. 'Dowry to Ensure her Happiness or to Disinherit her?' *Manushi*. 34:2–13.

Krishnaraj, Maitheryi. 1991. *Women and Violence: A Country Report. A Study sponsored by UNESCO*. Bombay: RCWS, SNDT Women's University.

Kulkarni, Sanjeev. 1986. *Pre-natal Sex Determination Tests and Female Foeticide in Bombay City*. Bombay: The Foundation for Research in Community Health.

Kumar, Radha. 1993. *The History of Doing*. New Delhi: Kali for Women.

KWDI. 1993. *A Study on the Prevention and Future Directions of Domestic Violence*. Seoul: Korean Women's Development Institute.

Kynch, J. and A. Sen. 1983. 'Indian Women: Well-being and Survival'. *Cambridge Journal of Economics*. 7(3–4).

Litke, Robert. 1992. 'Violence and Power'. *International Social Science Journal*.

Madan, Triloki N. [1965] 1989. *Family and Kinship: A Study of Pandits of Rural Kashmir*. Bombay: Asia Publishing House.

Mahajan Amarjit and Madhurima. 1995. *Family Violence and Abuse in India*. New Delhi: Deep & Deep Publications.

Mankekar, Purnima. 1985. *The Girl Child in India: Data Sheet on Health*. New Delhi: UNICEF.

Mazumdar, Veena. 1992. 'Aminocentesis and Sex Selection'. Paper Presented at WIDER, Helsinki.

Menon, Nivedita. 1996. 'The Impossibility of "Justice": Female Foeticide and Feminist Discourse on Abortion'. In Patricia Uberoi, ed., *Social Reform, Sexuality and the State*, 369–92. New Delhi: Sage Publications.

Menon, Ritu and Kamala Bhasin. 1998. *Borders and Boundaries: Women in India's Partition*. New Delhi: Kali for Women.

Miller, Barbara. 1981. *The Endangered Sex*. Ithaca: Cornell University Press.

Minocha, Aneeta. 1984. 'Mother's Position in Child Feeding and Nutrition: Some Sociological Consideration'. *Economic and Political Weekly*. 12(48):2045–8.

Mitchell, Juilet. 1963, *Women's Estate*. New York: Random House.

————. 1974. *Psychoanalysis and Feminism*. New York: Penguin.

Multiple Action Research Group (MARG). 1996. *Within Four Walls—A Profile of Domestic Violence*. New Delhi: MARG.

Nair, Janaki. 1996. *Women and Law in Colonial India: A Social History*. New Delhi: Kali for Women.

Nedelsky, Jennifer. 1991. 'Law, Boundaries and the Bounded Self'. *Representations*. Spring.

Netting R. McC., R.A. Wilk and E.J. Arnould et al. eds. 1984. *Households: Comparative and Historical Studies of the Domestic Group*. Berkeley: University of California Press.

Padmanabhan, M. 1993. 'Outlawing Sex-determination, No Solution'. *Pioneer*. 22 September.

Pakrasi, Kanti B. 1970. *Female Infanticide in India*. Calcutta: Temple Press.

Palriwala, Rajni. 1990. 'Introduction'. In Leela Dube and Rajni Palriwala, eds, *Structures and Strategies: Women, Work and Family*, 15–55. New Delhi: Sage Publications.

Panigrahi, Lalita. 1972. *British Social Policy and Female Infanticide*.

Papanek, Hannah. 1990. 'Socialization for Inequality: Issues for Research and Action'. *Samya Shakti*. 4–5:1–10.

Pati, Biswamony. 1991. 'Women, Rape and the Left'. *Economic and Political Weekly*. 21(5):219–20.

Patnaik M.M. and M.K. Sadual. 1988. 'The Problem of Dowry, Domestic Violence and Legal Literacy in India'. Paper Presented at the Fifth National Conference on Women's Studies on Religion, Culture and Politics.

Pawar, M.S. 1988. 'Women and Family Violence: Policies and Programmes'. *Social Change*. 8(3):26–40.

People's Union of Democratic Rights. 1991. *Custodial Rape*. New Delhi: The Union.

Poonacha, Veena, ed. 1999. *Women and Violence*. Bombay: SNDT University.

Prabhu, P.H. [1940]. 1995. *Hindu Social Organization: A Study in Socio-Psychological and Ideological Foundations*. Bombay: Popular Prakashan.

Rajan, Irudaya et al. 1991. 'Decline in Sex Ratio: An Alternative Explanation?' *Economic and Political Weekly*. 26(51):2963–4.

Raman, Vasanthi. Forthcoming. 'A Question of Child Rights'. *Indian Journal of Gender Studies*. 5(1).

Ramanamma, A. and U. Bambawale. 1980. 'The Mania for Sons: An Analysis of Social Values in South Asia'. *Social Science and Medicine*. 14B:107–10.

Ranjana Kumari. 1989. *Brides are not for Burning: Dowry Victims in India*, New Delhi: Radiant.

Ranjana Kumari, et al. 1990. *Growing up in Rural India: Problems and Needs of Adolescent Girls*. New Delhi: Radiant Publishers.

Rao, Vijayendra. 1995. 'Wife-beating in a Rural South Indian Community'. Research Memorandum no. 143. Center for Development Economics, Williams College, Mass, USA.

Ravindra, R.P. 1993. 'The Campaign against Sex Determination Tests'. In Chhaya Datar, ed., *The Struggle against Violence*. 51–98. Calcutta: Stree Publications.

Reddy, P.H. 1991. 'Perpetual Gulf in Male–Female Ratio'. *Deccan Herald*. 4 May.

Saheli. 1988. 'Wife Battering: Creating Choices for Individual Women, the Role of Government and Issues Facing the Women's Movement'. Paper Presented at the National Workshop on Family Violence against Females. 15–18 Feb. New Delhi.

Samuel, Hazel. 1992. 'Report of the Seminar on Harassment of Women in the Workplace'. *Vikasini*, 7(1).

Sandhya. 1994. *Widowhood—A Socio-Psychiatric Study*. New Delhi: Mohit Publications.

Sarkar, Lotika. 1994. 'Rape: A Human Rights versus a Patriarchal Interpretation'. *Indian Journal of Gender Studies*. 1(1):69–92.

Sarkar, Tanika. 1991. 'Reflections on Birati Rape Cases—Gender Ideology in Bengal'. *Economic and Political Weekly*. 21(5):215–8.

Sarkar, Tanika and Urvashi Butalia. 1995. *Women and the Hindu Right*. New Delhi: Kali for Women.

Sen, A. 1983. 'Economics of the Family'. *Asian Development Review*. 1(2).

———. 1987. 'Gender and Cooperative Conflicts'. Harvard Institute of Economic Research. Discussion Paper No. 1342.

Sen, A. and S. Sengupta. 1985. 'Malnutrition of Rural Children and Sex Bias'. In Devaki Jain and N. Banerjee, eds, *Tyranny of the Household*, 3–24. New Delhi: Shakti Books.

Shah, A.M. 1964. 'Basic Terms and Concepts in the Study of Family in India'. *Indian Economic and Social History Review*. 1(3):1–36.

———. 1973. *The Household Dimension of the Family in India*. Delhi: Orient Longman.

———. 1983. 'Issues in Family Studies: Some Notes'.

———. 1988. 'The Phase of Dispersal in the Indian Family Process'. *Sociological Bulletin*. 37(1–2).

Shankardas, Mala Kapur. 1997. 'The Plight of Older Women: Victims of Domestic Violence'. In Kalyan Baghi ed., *Elderly Females in India: their Status and Suffering*, 79–88. New Delhi: Society for Gerontological Research and Help Age, India.

Sharma, Ursula. 1984. 'Dowry in North India: Its Consequences for Women'. In R. Hirschon, ed., *Woman and Property: Women as Property*, 62–74. London: Croom Helm.

Sinha, Niroj. 1989. *Women and Violence*. New Delhi: Vikas Publishing House.

Sood, Sushma. 1990. *Violence against Women*. Jaipur: Arihant Publishers.

Srinivasa Murthy, R. 1992. 'Mental Health'. In *State of India's Health*. New Delhi: VHAI.

Srivastava, Jaya. 1989. 'The Widows of November 1984'. In Pramila Dandevate et al., eds, *Widows Abandoned and Destitute Women in India*, 63–7. New Delhi: Radiant Publishers.

Strathern, Marilyn. 1988. 'Out of Context: The Persuasive Fictions of Anthropology'. *Current Anthropology*. 28(3).

Straus, M.A. 1980. 'Sexual Inequality and Wife Beating'. In Straus and Hotaling, eds, *The Social Crisis of Husband-Wife Violence*. Minneapolis. University of Minnesota Press.

Stri Kriti Samiti. 1984. 'On the Dowry Question'. Unpublished paper presented at the Second National Conference on Women's Studies. 9–12 April, Trivandrum.

Sunder Rajan, Rajeshwari. 1993. 'Life after Rape'. In Rajeshwari Sunder Rajan, ed., *Real and Imagined World: Gender, Culture and Postcolonialism*, 63–82. London: Routledge.

Thapan, Meenakshi ed. 1997a. *Embodiment: Essays on Gender and Identity*. Delhi: Oxford University Press.

———. 1997b. 'Femininity and its Discontents: Woman's Body in Intimate Relationships'. In Meenakshi Thapan, ed., *Embodiment: Essays on Gender and Identity*, 172–93. Delhi: Oxford University Press.

The Pioneer. 29 September 1997.

Uberoi, Patricia [1994]. 1995. 'Introduction'. In Patricia Uberoi, ed., *Family, Marriage and Kinship in India*, 1–44. Delhi: Oxford University Press.

Vasanthi Devi. 1991. *Socio-Economic Context of Female Infanticide. A Study of Usilanpatti, Taluk in Tamil Nadu*. Madras: Madras Institute of Development Studies.

Vatuk, S. 1975. 'Gifts and Affines in North India'. *Contributions to Indian Sociology* (n.s.). 9:155–96.

Venkatachalam, R. and Viji Srinivasan. 1993. *Female Infanticide*. New Delhi; Har-Anand Publications.

Verghese, J. 1997. *Her Gold and Her Body*. 2nd ed. Ghaziabad: Vikas Publishing House.

Vyas, Anju, Naheed Mohsini, and Madhushree. 1996. *Voices of Resistance, Silences of Pain: A Resource Guide on Violence against Women*. New Delhi: Centre for Women's Development Studies.

Wadhwa, S. 1993. 'Incest Cases Pose Challenge for Authorities'. *The Pioneer*. 16 August.

Walker, L.E. 1979. *The Battered Woman*. New York: Harper and Row.

———. 1983 'The Battered Women Syndrome Study'. In D. Finkelhor et al., ed., *Dark Side of Families: Current Family Violence Research*, 31–48. Beverly Hills: Sage Publications.

World Development Report. 1993. *Investing in Health*. New York: Oxford University Press.

The Person Beyond the Family

Margaret Trawick

The Family Dilemma

No person can come into being without some kind of family. A human child needs caretakers, s/he needs other people from whom to learn language and culture, and from whom to acquire a sense of her or his own value as a person. In childhood as well as in later life, a person needs emotional and material support, and some sense of enduring connectedness. The family provides all of these things but it also constrains the actions of its members. This chapter examines some of the ways in which Indian people act to overcome the constraints of family ties, to resist and transcend family-based determination of their meaning and value as persons. There is a continuum from prescribed ways to forbidden ways of overcoming family constraints. Some of the prescribed ways are radical and rarely resorted to. Some of the forbidden ways are, in practice, fairly widespread.

That Indian people are more family oriented than, say, Americans is by now a truism (Roland 1988). Marriage and childbearing are for most Indian people absolute necessities. Few can imagine why anyone would choose not to marry, and many, especially women, consider the bearing and raising of children to be their sole purpose in life. Children are valued not only as future providers for their parents, but also in and of themselves, for what they are as children—beautiful, affectionate, mischievous sources of joy and constant surprise. Many Hindu gods and saints are adored as children or for their childlike attributes. South Asian Christians and Muslims also regard children as central necessities of life (Mishri 1985; Das 1991).

From the time they can talk, if not before, Indian children learn that they are part of a multiplex family network. People, whether kin or not, are more often addressed by kin terms than by name, and a babbling two-year-old can be heard reciting these terms and the possessive pronouns that properly accompany them. In Tamil, a major Indian language, there are over a dozen central kin terms (mother, father, mother's older sister, mother's younger sister, father's older brother, father's younger brother, older brother, younger brother, older sister, younger sister, grandfather, grandmother, mother's brother, father's sister, male cross-cousin, female cross-cousin, grandson, granddaughter). When one meets a person, one chooses what kin term to call them by, and with each kin term goes a complex set of ways to behave, so that as soon as you have decided what kin term to call a person by, you also know how to behave toward them, and what you can expect from them (Das 1976).

Ideally, each person should have, during their lifetime, one or more kinsfolk in each category. To be missing a key kinsperson, such as a brother or sister, is to be deprived of something precious. A fortunate child grows up among a wide range of kin and an equally wide set of personal satisfactions: a person to joke with, a person to turn to for comfort, a person from whom to seek protection, a person to protect, and so forth (Trawick 1990).

In many sections of South Asian society, a person is defined first and foremost by who s/he is kin to. The behaviour of each individual in a kin network reflects upon each of the others, in roughly direct proportion to how close the given kinspeople are. No matter what you do, unless you run away from your family entirely, you can never escape the shine or the shadow of your brothers and sisters, your aunts and uncles.

Additionally, a South Asian person grows up having their family within them, perhaps to a greater extent than is true of people elsewhere. While any child anywhere will incorporate personality traits of her caregivers, a normal and healthy South Asian person may be so close to some of her kin that she may continue in conversation with them in dreams even after they are dead. For the dreamer, such dream conversations are not mere fantasies, they are as real as waking speech with the living. Close kin ties may also be expressed as a psychic connection during life, such that if something happens to one member of such a closely bonded kin-dyad, the other member will immediately know it. Brother–sister bonds are undeniably sacred (Petersen 1986).

Clearly, such kinship embeddedness has both positive and negative consequences for the individual. On the positive side, one is never really alone; there are many people to whom one can turn for help if one needs it. The emotional richness of South Asian lives is unmatched in the West, such that the horror of personal isolation is the first thing that hits many South Asians who emigrate to western countries.

On the negative side, the burdens of family life, especially on women but also on men, can be severe. Family honour takes precedence over individual welfare in many instances. For the sake of preserving family honour, a rape victim is expected to carefully conceal what happened to her, or, alternatively, marry her rapist. Some regard suicide, or murder of the victim by her kin, as the most appropriate response to rape. Beyond even this, many consider kin ties, and marital ties established by sexual intercourse, as bonds that cannot be broken even by death. Kin and marital ties and bonds are just that, crippling as ropes and chains. 'The husband shackles the feet and the children shackle the hands', is a Tamil women's adage.

Responsible people must meet their obligations toward their kinsfolk, even if the kinsfolk do not reciprocate adequately. Quarrels between close kinsfolk over issues to do with who has given how much and who owes what to whom seem almost unavoidable. Marital ties determine the fortunes of whole extended families. The dowry system, though it has been denounced by reformers of all sorts for many decades, continues to spread throughout South Asia, causing serious intra-familial tensions, even murders, where it is practised (see Karlekar, this volume). Divorce is stigmatizing, and while men (often in defiance of disapproving talk) may take mistresses or second wives, women are rarely allowed such options (Dumont 1986; Dhagamwar 1993). Responsible adult men may be burdened with large numbers of people to feed, clothe, house, educate, and marry—not only their own offspring but orphaned or widowed or abandoned kinsfolk who have nowhere else to turn for support. The embeddedness, in India, of family systems within caste systems restricts marriage options and for both women and men with high personal aspirations, the necessity of devoting one's life to mundane concerns such as money making (for men) and housekeeping (for women) can be stifling. Lifelong bondedness to people one cannot get along with can be immiserating (see Ramanujan 1971). Finally, the dynamics and clamour of a large household can drive peace-loving individuals to distraction, even if the family is fundamentally happy.

Religious Responses
Renunciation

The nature of what I am calling the family dilemma has been widely attested in Indian literature and folklore. For men in Indian society of many places and in many ages, the dilemma is stated in fairly clear terms: should one be a family man ('householder') with all the rewards and punishments that such a role entails, or should one renounce family life and enjoy the spiritual freedom of an ascetic? In mythology, the god Siva is represented as oscillating between the two extremes, epitomizing both

(O'Flaherty 1973). Because Siva is a deity, he can get away with impossibly contradictory behaviour, and have the best of all worlds, but human beings are not so lucky and must make hard choices (Gold 1992). The Dharmashastras (Sanskrit texts of around the first century BC, prescribing codes for human conduct) contain long passages discussing the relative merits of householdership versus renunciation (Manu 2: 97, 3: 77–9, 6: 73–97). The householder is the upholder of the human world, but his involvement in the world necessarily entails that he accrue sin. The ascetic can keep his hands clean, as it were, but he contributes little if anything to the world or human society.

Sannyasis are people, usually men, who renounce all worldly ties and choose a life of mendicancy and undistracted devotion to their chosen deity. As there are many homeless in India, it is sometimes difficult to distinguish between a 'real' religious mendicant and a homeless man who has donned religious garb in hope of collecting more alms. Few Indian parents would want their sons to become wandering mendicants, regardless of how lofty the son's motivations might be. For these and other reasons, sannyasis are ambiguous figures in the Indian imagination. They are, at best, people who have deserted their families so that they can seek the divine. They may be holy men or they may be tricksters and scoundrels. Folklore about them describes them as all three (Narayan 1972). Female renouncers also exist in Indian legend, but whereas male sannyasis may be found wandering Indian streets, female renouncers are less visible and perhaps more rare (Narayan 1989; McDaniel 1989).

Many people live in a state of what might be called partial renunciation of family. These are people who have family obligations and attachments that they cannot simply walk away from, but who in various ways seek a state of temporary isolation of self from family and world. Some engage in repeated, prolonged periods of meditation. Some undergo fasts, during which time their physical interactions with their families are reduced as many of these interactions revolve around food and feeding; some people leave their households and stay in temples for the duration of long fasts. Some people temporarily remove themselves from their families by going on pilgrimages alone or in the company of other pilgrims to distant holy places (Daniel 1984; Gold 1988). The pilgrimage may last as long as a month, and it may entail a prior period of celibacy and fasting.

Therefore, while states of aloneness and famililessness are generally dreaded, there is in Indian society a counter-current of longing for separation from family and isolation of self that is expressed in many ways. In Patanjali's Yogasutras AD 200, the liberation of soul from body is called *kaivalya* which means precisely isolation, aloneness. This notion of liberation as absolute aloneness contrasts markedly with visions of heaven-after-death in which the person is surrounded by hosts of congenial beings, including the spirits of earthly family members. It also contrasts with the view that ultimate reward is union with a loving God. Even people who hold this latter view may express a sense of overt tension or contradiction between devotion to family and devotion to deity. Even in the midst of family life, they may go through the motions of being good wives and mothers (or husbands and fathers), but in their hearts and in their dreams they are with their god, and their families are nowhere about. The classic model for women in this mode is Mirabai (see Obeyesekere 1990).

Old age may be a time when, after childhood, a person needs his or her family most; it is also a time when, in many families, the person is perceived as burdensome and no longer needed. In *varnasharamadharma* of the Dharmashastras, only the second stage of life, householdership or *grihastha,* of the four stages *(ashramas),* entails involvement in the family. Childhood is skipped over in this schema, and the first stage of life (for a man) is life as a student celibate; the third is life as a forest-dweller; and the fourth is life as a wandering mendicant (see Malamoud 1997). When he sees the face of his first grandson, a man is called by this plan to leave his home and children and go live a life of asceticism in the forest, taking his wife with him if he chooses. In the last stage of life, he should leave everything behind and live as a mendicant. Some men actually do this, although most do not. In one case known to me (as an example) an old man chose to live as a wandering mendicant after his three sons were killed in war.

Alternative Families

Spirit mediumship and possession cults both offer escape from oppressive family situations, and tend to duplicate certain aspects of family life (Claus 1975). Spirit possession in South Asia has been interpreted by modern psychologists as a dissociative response to childhood sexual trauma (Castillo 1994). Given that a large number of the spirit possessed in South Asia are young brides, the psychological argument has plausibility and further drives home the point that at least certain forms of religiosity in South Asia are direct consequences of familial oppression. Identification with the possessing deity, and/or experiencing that deity as an idealized family member (for instance as mother or spouse), seems to help make the afflicted person well again (Trawick 1983).

In Chennai male worshippers of Krishna may assume the role of *gopis* (Krishna's cowgirl lovers) during collective worship ceremonies; during this time as gopis, they are not men, they are women, and they might be said to constitute Krishna's family of clandestine co-wives. Although this identity contrasts with and appears to a western observer to contradict the worshippers' identities as businessmen with wives and children, to the men themselves who raise their families in one context and become gopis in another, there is no contradiction (Singer 1972).

However, in other cases where an individual is a member both of an earthly family and of a divine one, the contradiction may be acutely felt. Like men who are torn between the householder and ascetic ideals, women who act as mediums for the mother goddess—which means that they both identify with her and interact with her intimately as though she were a real mother—can feel torn between their love of their families and their devotion to the Mother (Srinivas 1976; Trawick 1983). Some suffer from this perceived contradiction even as their earthly families subsist on their earnings as mediators with the divine.

Monastic life is another traditional alternative to family life. In colonial and pre-colonial India, some monastic orders exercised substantial political power, interlaced with the powers of families, castes, and kingdoms. Boys who entered such monasteries were not necessarily exercising the kind of personal choice to renounce or suspend family life that characterizes the religious decisions outlined in the preceding paragraphs (Pinch 1996). Buddhist monks in modern Sri Lanka retain the secular power and militancy that faded from Indian Hindu orders with the rise of Congress secularism (Tambiah 1992). In India of this century, monastic life has become an option for Indian men and occasional non-Indians who wish to seek God and who for personal reasons do not wish to have families (Masson 1980; Agehananda Bharati 1980).

Lesbian and homosexual activities and transsexuality in South Asia have only recently begun to receive serious scholarly attention. Gay and lesbian lovemaking are graphically portrayed in ancient Indian poetry and plastic arts (Kumar 1996; see also Trawick 1990: 33–5). It is rather amazing that so little has been said about these portrayals, and what they may mean about actual gender and sexual relations among the people who created them. Ayurvedic texts of two millenia ago state matter-of-factly that human beings come in three sexes. Easy androgyny among modern South Asians has been noted with distaste, or more recently with approval, by psychologists, social scientists, and others writing about South Asian cultures and societies (Agarwal 1997). Whether lesbianism can be called an extra-familial activity in South Asia is a matter of question, as it does not necessarily stand in opposition to, or as a substitute for, regular cross-gender marriage and familial relations. The long-standing community *of religiously motivated male-to-female transsexuals*, called *hijras*, does consist of renunciation of 'regular' family life and the formation of alternative families consisting entirely of hijras. The hijras have a role in the domestic religion of places where they live, bringing fertility by dancing for gifts at births and weddings (Nanda 1990). Hijras' participation is prominent and necessary in at least one major temple festival, both for the sake of the festival, and for the affirmation of the hijras' complicated identity (Hiltebeitl 1995). Though they may have become an icon of Indian social tolerance, in fact the life of hijras is not easy, entailing all the danger and humiliation of male prostitution, plus some. The fact of being castrated is required proof that the hijra is the person s/he claims to be (Cohen 1995).

Finally, female prostitution must be named as a traditional Indian outside-family occupation, and communities of prostitutes as sometime substitutes for families. The condition of prostitutes in India, as in other large nations, ranges from relatively privileged to severely oppressed. Long-standing, well-structured, and self-protective communities of sexually active women outside of traditional families include wives of Jagannath (*devadasis*) in Orissa, and the courtesans of Lucknow (Marglin 1985; Oldenburg 1990). The wives of Jagannath are a religious community; the courtesans of Lucknow are not defined in religious terms. But the two communities have several features in common. They perceive themselves to be in many respects more fortunate than ordinary family women. They are able to reject constructions of themselves as 'polluted' and to define themselves as incapable of sexual defilement; they control their own reproductive capacities to suit their interests; and they are financially independent.

Non-religious Responses
Feminism

Perhaps the most serious challenge to the construction of personhood in South Asia as family-bound is the range of feminist movements and ideologies that have grown up on the subcontinent (Gandhi and Shah 1991; Kumar 1993; Mohanty and Martin 1986, Calman 1992). This is so just because throughout South Asia women have been kept more tightly bound to family and household than men. Most forms of feminism seek to loosen the bondage of women to family. If personhood stated simply is the terms in which a person is defined by self and others, and if a South Asian woman is defined, more than a South Asian man, as the parent of x, the spouse of y, and the child of z, then feminism encourages her to be defined also as the author of a, the director of b, the creator of c. Feminism allows her to be a complete person even if she has no connections with z, and x and y do not exist.

If one is to judge by the quantity of publications, social action organizations, people in key positions, and their assorted successes, it appears that feminism in South Asia is stronger than it is in western Europe, the UK, or the US (to say nothing of Australia, New Zealand, China, Japan, and Africa!).

Just as over-strong family orientation may be a cause of the abundance of renunciatory movements and devices in South Asia, so one (not the only) contributing factor to the vitality of feminism there may be the very magnitude of the problems with which South Asian women, over many generations, have had to contend. Many of these problems spring from women's status within their families.

Here, space allows only a brief enumeration of some of the forms of feminism existing in India and neighbouring countries, and some of the ways they enable women to establish personhood outside of their respective families.

Women's non-government organizations (NGOs) are numerous throughout South Asia. Many of them concentrate on assisting women to establish independent incomes by giving them low-interest loans to start up small businesses. Others address problems of domestic violence by bringing women who are victims of such violence together and helping them organize to act collectively against serial rapists and wife beaters. Through such organizations, women learn that domestic abuse is a social problem and not merely a private one. In general, for a person to break the rule of keeping family problems within the family is a difficult but important step towards establishing a sense of self, independent of family (Desai 1996; Gandhi and Shah 1991).

Eco-feminism in India likewise has the effect of breaching the boundaries between private/familial and public/social by calling women who depend on a balanced ecological environment for subsistence to mobilize against projects that threaten that environment. One dramatic example of eco-feminism in India has been the mobilization of women who gather firewood from forest floors to bodily obstruct forest-clearing projects in areas where they live (Agarwal 1986). A woman who acts together with women to protect the environment, like a woman who joins other women to combat spousal abuse, becomes part of a horizontally solidary group that may complement or, in some cases, subvert the hierarchical solidarity of the woman's individual family. If eco-feminists identify themselves with the earth mother, they may in some respects be affirming the traditional (trodden on) status of women, but in action they challenge this role by stepping beyond concern for their particular families and acting to protect something greater (Shiva 1989).

Academic feminism in India starts at the level of all those who support education for girls and women and work to improve it—the parents who pay to send their girls to college and the people who set up and run those colleges, as well as the girls and women who choose to become educated. One consequence of feminism at this level has been the relatively large percentage of women in professions such as medicine and engineering (Jakobsen and Wadley 1992).

At another level, academic feminism in India consists of feminist research and writing. It is far beyond the scope of this chapter to survey the work of Indian feminist academics, but some of the more famous writing with respect to women and family may be mentioned. Perhaps because their role is more social criticism than social back patting, Indian academics have tended to be pessimistic about the chances of Indian women to escape oppressive family structures, pointing to the paternalism of caste, religion, and state (Das 1995), and pointing to the fact that women's voices as women are continually suppressed or erased in the masculine discourses that shape colonial and post-colonial ideologies (Spivak 1987; 1988). In the former view, if a woman by choice or force moves beyond the family, she then encounters large structures that duplicate familial hierarchies. In the latter view, likewise, a woman's choices are between colonialist paternalism and anti-colonialist paternalism. It has even been suggested that modern *satis* (women who self-immolate on their husbands' funeral pyres) may be deliberately choosing to perform an act that defies colonialist values and norms and affirms indigenous ones (Mazumdar 1978).

Media feminism—consisting of the expression of feminist concepts and values in cinema and television shows—is a growing concern in India. Media-feminist expressions may be relatively conservative and not at all challenging to the overall notion of a woman as an essentially familial being, showing heroically assertive women acting in defence of family, such as a wife who saves the life of her endangered husband, rather than vice versa (the popular Tamil-Hindi film 'Roja'). Another portrayal of woman as free agent is the Tamil television serial drama 'Taayumaanavar', about a family in which the wife works outside the home in a professional career, while the husband stays home, does the housework, and raises the children. The husband is a handsome, muscular union leader with high ideals, and it is interesting to note that he is not mocked, as men with strong wives so often are on American TV shows. Public acceptance of men in traditionally female roles may be facilitated by the fact that men in India more easily assume such roles than men elsewhere (cf. the Krishna cults mentioned earlier, and the case of Gandhi mentioned in the later discussion). A step further in media encouragement of women becoming individuated from family is the Tamil film 'Vidhi', depicting a rape victim who takes legal public action against her rapist, wins the paternity suit, and then chooses to raise her child alone. Finally, the English-language film 'Fire' by Deepa Mehta has helped bring Indian lesbianism out of the closet.

Print feminism in India is best exemplified by the famous periodical *Manushi* edited by Madhu Kishwar. This periodical has achieved long-term international success despite the fact that it accepts no advertisements and subsists by subscriptions and voluntary donations alone. It publishes a wide variety of articles about women in South Asia, written from many different perspectives. Women writers are abundant in South Asia and many achieve international success, the most currently celebrated being Arundhati Roy, author of the Booker Award-winning *God of Small Things*. Taslima Nasrin, a quiet Bangladeshi woman who challenged some anti-feminist Islamic tenets in writing and provoked great controversy plus a *fatwah* on her head, is another well-known example (Weaver 1994). By the very fact of their spending time as writers, South Asian women who do so, step outside of family and become, through their work, persons in themselves, so long as their work receives a public audience. Additionally, many such authors question the value of traditional family structures, and implicitly or explicitly advocate women's moving beyond such structures. Roy, for instance, provoked wrath from some quarters by writing sympathetically of a cross-caste, extramarital love affair.

Folk feminism consists of acts by women (or men) alone or in groups that may be deemed both traditional and feminist at the same time. In Rajasthani women's folk songs, for instance, small subversions of paternalism and androcentrism often take place, forbidden language may be used, marriage may be lamented, and adultery celebrated (Gold and Raheja 1994). Certain enactments of the concept of *shakti*—power as a feminine principle—may be deemed folk feminism almost by definition; some of these enactments entail reversal of male–female hierarchies and transcendence of family ties. In Tamil Nadu, a village street-theatre performance I saw of the folk tale *Adiparasakti* was ardently feminist, mocking the pretences of male gods and demons, celebrating the power of female solidarity, and paying homage to the goddess in the form of a tall, green, ugly woman. The wives defeated the husbands completely, the goddess killed the demon who wanted to marry her, and the message, stated in just these words, was, 'Women are better than men.' In accordance with street-theatre tradition, all the roles, both male and female, were played by men.

Female militancy, in which women renounce familial subordination, acquire combat training, and go for active combat duty, has received surprising support in conservative Sri Lankan Tamil society (Trawick 1997; Somasundaram 1998). A pre-existing, unreflective confidence in the strength of women, many of whom engage in hard agricultural labour and also head large families, may have facilitated this acceptance. Both males and females step out of family when they join the LTTE.

Finally, there exist in some parts of South Asia well-established kinship patterns that partly free women from bondage to family and enable them to do other things. Joint and extended families, in which women share childcare and housework, are effectively set up to free some women to some extent. In other words, family structure itself may sometimes facilitate liberation from family—for some, if not for all. How valid is the application of the word feminist to such families is a matter of one's definition of feminism, as well as of the particular characteristics of the family in question.

Work and Education

Work for money has been mentioned earlier as a domain in which a person may exist and/or be defined in partial independence of family. The kind and degree of independence achieved is a matter of the kind of work that is done. Most people bring their earnings back to their families. Some use a portion for themselves. When wages are small, any habitual selfish use of money earned can cause problems for the family. Hence smoking and drinking in South Asia are specifically anti-familial acts, and although these habits are widespread, they are frowned upon in most communities.

Work, as the source of financial support for the family, is part of the familial world. However, it is also a basis for valuation of the individual that is separate from family. In any part of South Asia, a person will be respected more if s/he bears the title 'doctor'. The more a person has studied, and the more degrees s/he has, the higher s/he will be ranked on the evaluative scale that pertains to work. The higher one ranks on that scale, the higher the pay one is likely to get—if one gets work commensurate with one's education. Both social and material rewards are closely tied, therefore, to education. This is why education is so important in South Asia, and this is why blood has been shed and lives have been lost over such issues as reservations and quotas in universities (Béteille 1991). The kind of work that can be gotten through education is the only viable means for individual persons to overcome low familial and caste status and a legacy of poverty; it is also one of the means by which privileged families maintain their privilege generation after generation.

At a more fundamental psychological level, the work world constitutes a large portion of an adult's total experienced world and hence contributes its own structure of concepts to the person's total world-view and, finally, self-image.

One notable example of the moulding influence of work on perceptions of the person is the difference in bodily form between physical labourers and people who do not engage in such labour. Physical labourers if they are healthy, maintain well-formed bodies into old age and have darker skin because of being in the sun all the time. Non-physical labourers are more likely to grow fat and may have lighter skin from avoiding the sun. In general, hard physical work is held to be damaging to health, and such work is lowly esteemed, especially by those who do not do it. Prevalent aesthetic evaluations of male and female bodies in South Asia still favour the fat and light skinned (Osella and Osella 1996). However, there is a current of masculinism which favours the 'wrestler's body' (akin to the labourer's body) while disregarding attractions of the feminine physique (Alter 1994).

Aficionados of the wrestler's body are young male cinema goers who are not necessarily wealthy and may work as physical labourers themselves. At least one moderately successful female cinema star specializes in fighter roles. She plays an attractive unmarried policewoman who skilfully battles and beats bad guys. She does her own stunts, her body is curvy-athletic, and she is not fat. It would be interesting to learn who her fans are.

In general, muscularity and fighting ability (that is fitness for violence) are closely associated; likewise non-muscularity and non-violence go together. Gandhi commented on this in his autobiography. In Ayurvedic thought, building a muscular body entails eating muscle, that is meat. The flesh of carnivores is concentrated strength-building food (Zimmerman 1987). A fleshless diet yields a more *sattvika* body—sweet, peaceful, and knowing.

There seems to be a still unexplored sharp divide between people who are proud of their ability to do hard physical work and those who find such work demeaning. As with the two kinds of body, so with the two kinds of knowledge held by the two kinds of people. An educated boy from a farming background may proudly proclaim that he does not know how to farm. But, especially in rice-growing regions, knowledge of how to raise a crop is complex and demanding. The nature of this knowledge is reflected in the agricultural vocabulary of workers, which pervades oral discourse in other domains of life as well, and contributes to an image of the human body that is overtly plant-like. Girls at first menstruation are said to 'blossom', moustaches on young men are said to 'sprout', side sprouts on rice stalks are referred to as 'children', a nubile girl is a 'vine', and so also is a matriline, with its members being flowers and fruits on the vine (Egnor 1978; Trawick 1986 and 1988). The poetry of modern Sri Lankan Tamils is filled with imagery of vegetative propagation—sprouts grow from severed limbs, it is said that where one fighter falls two more will spring up in her place, the bodies of fallen fighters are buried like 'seeds' in the ground, and the blood of the murdered blossoms in the red flowers of spring. Such examples could be multiplied indefinitely. I should add that most of the fighters among Sri Lankan Tamils come from poor families in rice-growing regions of the east.

While family of origin may determine which category a person falls into—labouring or non-labouring—bodily experience is a formative factor in self-definition which has little to do with family per se. Likewise with the quality of knowledge a person has that is gained in the extra-familial work world, whether that world be the field or the school or some combination of the two.

The knowledge acquired through formal education likewise has a powerful influence on a person's self-perception, his/her perception of the world, and the world's perception of him or her. Education and physical labour such as farming have in common a kind of levelling property which is independent of family or caste background—either one passes an exam or one fails it; either one can carry a burden or one cannot; either one ploughs at the right time or the wrong time; either one makes a correct diagnosis or one makes an incorrect one. Such things are matters of personal skill and knowledge, not matters of who is one's brother or father.

The passage of universal childhood education laws in India has had the effect of making a person's fate somewhat less dependent on his or her family. Children of many castes are put into one village classroom, and they learn the same lessons as well as learning from each other about each other. There are still vast inequalities in educational opportunities, however.

Knowledge acquired through formal education that affects personhood in fundamental ways includes the ability to read and write and the ability to do more than basic arithmetic (and hence run a business). Beyond this, formal education may—for good or evil—instil or strengthen a person's sense of ethnicity, making him or her feel kin to all the other people who speak the same language, have read the same books, and participate in the same mytho-history. Through education and reading, the imagined family supercedes to some degree the real one (Anderson 1991). One comes to think of one's identity generally in terms of something broader than a certain kin or caste group. The effect of literature and literacy on ethnic group consolidation in South Asia may be seen in language-based ethnic affiliations, as well as in the cleft between Hindutva and Islam, both of which are dependent on literacy and the written word, though in different ways. Islamic identity is based upon belief in a book, the Quran. Affiliation to Islam as a distinct ethnic identity has resulted in the rise of numerous Islamic schools throughout South Asia, where boys and girls learn to memorize this book, and are also taught Islamic rules and values. Hindu identity is based on orientalist literature that created out of numerous local praxes and texts an essential thing called Hinduism. One may know the story of the Ramayana, and identify oneself as 'Hindu' without being able to read (just as many Muslims cannot read the Quran) but the basic identity is still dependent on certain trans-regional texts, and the presence in the community of specialists who know them.

Identity through education and the employment gained thereby has rendered obsolete caste-based occupational identities such as potter and oil-presser. These old occupational statuses were all inherited through family. The ones that count today are not.

Social Activism

Individual South Asian people may become involved in social-action projects that take precedence over their involvement in family. Alternatively, the family may be pulled willy-nilly into the project. The paradigmatic example is Mahatma Gandhi, who was a great transformer of Indian society, but whose family suffered as a result of his refusal to compromise his ideals, and his inattention to their needs.

Reform movements often focus on family reform: issues such as the right of widows to remarry, the right of girls not to be married in childhood, limitation of family size, opposition of widow self-immolation and general maltreatment of widows, and opposition to the dowry system. Because of the high embeddedness of persons in families, some of these problems have proved seriously intractable.

People who oppose the dowry system, and are reformers in that sense, face the difficult task of finding acceptable young men who do not demand a dowry together with the daughter's hand in marriage. The family may have to search far and wide, and go beyond their usual network of connections in order to find such a young man, while even in conventional marriages, finding suitable husbands for daughters is generally hard enough. Ironically, a daughter given away without dowry may suffer precisely because her parents opposed the dowry system because it results in suffering of young married women such as their daughter. Families who have both sons and daughters may demand dowries from their daughters-in-law so that they can make up what they lose when they give their daughters away. Or they may want the dowry to help pay for the education of their children, as education of daughters and sons and the marriage of daughters are the two greatest expenses an Indian family generally faces. A dowry is seen as a deposit on the future material security of the daughter: it should buy her a home and a secure place within a secure new network of kin. All too often, however, the dowry is taken but the daughter-in-law who brought it is abused and neglected by her affines. If she is forced to leave, they keep the wealth she brought them. A marriage under this system is always a serious gamble. But bucking the system is also a gamble. If a family opposes the system in practice, and the marriage fails, the family who opposed the system will be blamed, and the life chances for younger family members will be jeopardized. This is not to say that dowriless marriages, necessarily end in failure. If a boy and girl from two reformist families decide to marry each other without dowry, or if a reformist father of a daughter is fortunate enough to find a reformist father of a son, and the boy and girl are suited to each other, then the marriage can be happy. Many such marriages take place among well-educated cosmopolitan families where valuation of a person on the basis of personal accomplishments (as opposed to family background) is already strong.

'Love marriages' may be undertaken in a reformist spirit, for instance in the case of cross-caste marriages and marriages between Hindus and Muslims. People who enter into such marriages assert the priority of the individual's right to happiness over maintenance of the integrity of the whole—including caste, community, and family. Thus their formation of a new family is a kind of anti-family act, insofar as 'family' means family as traditionally conceived. They must live without many of the supportive structures in which traditional families are embedded. By acting to assert the rights of individuals to happiness, they may thereby renounce some of the happiness, such as personal security, that devolves from a successful traditional marriage.

People who risk their lives for a social cause, for instance a nationalist movement, may face a similar contradiction—they may die for the sake of people (their own family and the imagined community beyond it) who need them to live.

Total renunciation of family—that is refusal to marry at all—for non-religious reasons, is rare but not unheard of. Some women may choose not to marry because they wish to devote full-time attention to their professions, such as medicine or scholarship. Such a choice entails a lifetime of celibacy in a family-based society and is more than a personal decision; it is a clear social statement. To decide against marriage, however, a person whether male or female must have substantial non-family-based means of support, as few natal families would accept such a decision on the part of a child. The family renouncer risks extreme social isolation. In extraordinary cases though, if their behaviour is saintly, they may be revered.

Effects of Diaspora upon South Asian Personhood with Respect to Family

For hundreds of years there have been South Asian diasporas—communities of people living in scattered places outside the subcontinent who expect never to return except for brief visits. They nevertheless retain a respect for their ancestral roots in the subcontinent and seek also to continue in its new context the culture that makes them think of themselves, despite expatriation, as still 'Bangladeshi' or 'Punjabi' or 'Sri Lankan' or 'Indian' or 'Tamil' or 'Brahman' or some intersection or subset of such broad categories. In some respects, South Asian cultures are pre-adapted to migration and mixing with others (Ghosh 1989) and this facility is reflected in the success of people in the diaspora.

One feature of their home culture that people in a South Asian diaspora may seek to maintain is their own set of customs regarding family relations and marriage. Adaptations of old customs may be maintained over generations, with international intra-community marriages becoming the norm in some cases—as with New Zealand Gujaratis. However, migration overseas has the effect of loosening ties between person and family through an assortment of processes (Ballard 1996). Geographical separation from the extended kinship network in which the family itself was originally embedded reduces the number and kind of family- and kin-based activities that people can engage in, and therefore diminishes the significance of family itself in the life of the person.

The pervasive influence of the majority society in which South Asian immigrants settle is only fractionally offset by the protection of South Asian ethnic enclaves, where they exist. Children go to school with members of the majority-society and are strongly influenced by the habits, actions, and plans of majority-society children. In everyday life outside the home (or even on TV) they are 'bombarded' with 'messages' telling them to be one way and not another. Parent–child rifts in first-generation immigrant families are difficult to avoid.

Expatriate South Asian families are likely already to have been multilingual and cosmopolitan even before they left South Asia. It takes money and influence, after all, to be allowed entry into a new country. Some members of the diaspora may well feel that they should not be incarcerated in a geographically circumscribed fixed culture (Appadurai 1992) in which family is one of the fixtures. The choice to migrate may after all be a positive choice, entailing the belief that there are definitely better places than home (Rushdie 1991; 1992). For young people, especially, leaving home means leaving family, and a sense of freedom can accompany that move. But feelings will be mixed. Together with freedom, loneliness in the new country may heighten feelings of autonomy, feelings that one must find within oneself the resources one needs to survive and become a person of worth (Lessinger and Swerdlow 1983; Gajjala 1994; 1997; Mukherjee 1988).

Experiences and activities of the diaspora reflect back into India through communications and visits between kin and friends at home and abroad. Since the West is still perceived by many in South Asia as a kind of Mecca, on the whole a better place than home to live, activities that would not be condoned by most people in South Asia—such as hamburger eating and short skirt wearing—are tolerated by family members (such as children of brothers and sisters) who live in Toronto or Sydney. Young people in South

Asia may compare themselves with their cousins abroad and contemplate acting like them. Special challenges to the integrity of South Asian families are presented by such situations. Conversely, when South Asians in the diaspora become more independent of family and assert autonomous self-worth, western-style, they may find themselves suspended between two identities, unable to reconcile one to the other.

Is There Such a Thing as South Asian Personhood and is Family Essential to It?

In South Asia, the magnet of the West and the longing for individuation sometimes seem to pull in the same direction. But the longing for individuation has been in evidence in South Asia since Upaniṣadic times, long before the West, as presently construed, came into being.

I have suggested in the preceding discussion that longing for autonomy and freedom from family is caused by the very strength of South Asian family bonds, and, further, that some aspects of what is perceived as quintessentially South Asian religiosity derive from family experience. Hindu gods are conspicuously family people and so also was the Prophet Mohammed. Jesus, by contrast, was single and demanded of his followers that they renounce their families (pace modern Christian 'family-values' advocates). These two values of 'Indianness'—familism and religiosity—are therefore closely linked. They are linked also among non-Indian South Asians.

Whatever has accounted for the apparent lastingness of South Asian social and cultural structures, the endurance of South Asian family structures is surely a contributing factor. South Asian families depend upon the embeddedness of persons within them—that is they depend for their strength on people's dependence on them. Traditional alternatives to dependence on family seem to have been, for the most part, radical (involving much risk and sacrifice) and religious (oriented toward deities and/or ultimate personal salvation). The path of the renouncer is the best-known South Asian alternative to familism.

Modern alternatives often (not always) involve less sacrifice, are more overtly economic in character, and show more obvious influence of models from the far West. These models are now more easily available because of great changes in communication technology over the past century. If there is any truth to the claim that the West, in particular America, values individualism more than South Asia does, then emanations from the West into South Asia may be expected to change South Asian culture in the direction of individualism. I know such claims are both simplistic and fraught with controversy. But in a chapter under this title, those claims have at least to be acknowledged.

Will the power of the West eventually erode Indian society as it is presently constructed? Will 'family' be reduced to its minimal limit? If we imagine such processes as evolving quickly within the span of one lifetime, what effects might they have on actual individual? Can one be raised with a strong kinship orientation and live happily as an adult with one's orientation toward extra-familial matters? Can a person be both non-religious and independent of family and still be 'Indian'?

Such questions might be turned around and one might ask in Dumontian fashion, can a society endure in which the needs of the individual take precedence over the needs of the whole (the whole in this case being the family)? Is the family-embedded 'Indian' person somehow more natural than the individualistic 'American' person? Or is high valuation of the individual person, as Marcel Mauss argued, the mark of advanced socio-cultural (and moral and religious) evolution?

I am not a believer in unilinear socio-cultural evolution, nor in the premise that there is always only one best way of doing things. Deep embeddedness of persons in family may be appropriate to some contexts and inappropriate to others. It is no longer possible to think of timeless structures, it is possible only to think of change. It is not even possible to think of long-term change, but only of short-term. Eventually there will come a time when there is no such thing as 'India' and no such thing as an 'Indian person' (nor 'America' nor an 'American person') and all the questions posed above will be moot.

To think in terms of short-term change then: as economic conditions tilt to favour and disfavour different categories of people, as media and communications systems reach still more of those people both favoured and disfavoured, as options for individuals grow and shrink, the experienced worlds of South Asian people will be different. No matter how adaptable established family structures are, conditions will arise with which they cannot cope in any of their present manifestations. Transformations and rebellions as yet unimagined—forced by persons within the family as well as by powers outside it—are likely to take place.

REFERENCE

Agarwal, Bina. 1986. *Cold Hearths and Barren Slopes: The Woodfuel Crisis in the Third World*. Delhi: Institute of Economic Growth.

Agehananda Bharati, Swami. 1980. *The Ochre Robe: An Autobiography*. Santa Barbara, CA: Ross-Erikson Publishers.

Agarwal, Anuja. 1997. 'Gendered Bodies: The Case of the "third gender" in India'. *Contributions to Indian Sociology* (n.s.). 31(2):273–92.

Alter, Joseph S. 1994. 'Celibacy, Sexuality, and the Transformation of Gender into Nationalism in North India'. *The Journal of Asian Studies*. 53(1):45–66.

Anderson, Benedict. 1991. *Imagined Communities: Reflections on the Origin and Spread of Nationalism*. London and New York: Verso.

Appadurai, Arjun.1992. 'Putting Hierarchy in Its Place'. In George E. Marcus, ed., *Rereading Cultural Anthropology*, 34–47. Durham and London: Duke University Press.

Ballard, Roger. 1996. *Desh Pardesh: The South Asian Presence in Britain*. Delhi: South Asia Books.

Béteille, André. 1991. 'The Reproduction of Inequality: Occupation, Caste and Family'. *Contributions to Indian Sociology* (n.s.). 25(1):3–28.

Calman, Leslie J., ed. 1992. *Women and Movement Politics in India*. Boulder: Westview.

Castillo, Richard J. 1994. 'Spirit Possession in South Asia, Dissociation or Hysteria? Part II: Case Histories'. *Culture, Medicine, and Psychiatry*. 18(2):141–62.

Claus, Peter. 1975. 'The Siri Myth and Ritual: A Mass Possession Cult of South India'. *Ethnology*. 14(1):47–58.

Cohen, Lawrence. 1995. 'The Pleasures of Castration: The Postoperative Status of Hijras, Jankhas, and Academics'. In P.R. Abramson and S.D. Pinkerton, eds, *Sexual Nature and Sexual Culture*, 276–304. Chicago: University of Chicago Press.

Daniel, E.V. 1984. *Fluid Signs: Being a Person the Tamil Way*. Berkeley: University of California Press.

Das, Veena. 1976. 'Masks and Faces: An Essay on Punjabi Kinship'. *Contributions to Indian Sociology* (n.s.). 10(1):1–30.

———. 1991. Voices of Children. Dac: *Journal of the American Academy of Arts and Sciences*. 91–108.

———. 1995. *Critical Events: An Anthropological Perspective on Contemporary India*. Delhi: Oxford University Press.

Desai, Manisha. 1996. 'Informal Organizations as Agents of Change. Notes from the Contemporary Women's Movement in India'. *Mobilization*. 1(2):159–74.

Dhagamwar, Vasudha. 1993. *Law, Power, and Justice: The Protection of Personal Rights in the Indian Penal Code*. Delhi: Sage Publications.

Dumont, Louis. 1986. *A South Indian Subcaste: Social Organization and Religion of the Pramalai Kallar*. Translated from the French by M Moffatt and L. and A. Morton. Revised by the author and A. Stern. Delhi: Oxford University Press.

Egnor, Margaret Trawick. 1978. 'The Sacred Spell and Other Conceptions of Life in Tamil Culture'. Unpublished Ph.D. Dissertation. University of Chicago, Department of Anthropology.

Gajjala, Radhika. 1994. 'Couch Notes'. *Committee on South Asian Women Bulletin*. 9 (1–4).

———. 1997. 'Some More Couch Notes'. In *Jabberwocky*. Electronic text. http:/ernie.bgsu. edu/radhika/jabberwocky. html#The Couch

Gandhi, Nandita and Nandita Shah. 1991. *The Issues at Stake: Theory and Practice in the Contemporary Women's Movement in India*. New Delhi: Kali for Women.

Ghosh, Amitav. 1989. 'The Diaspora in Indian Culture'. *Public Culture*. 2(1):73–8.

Gold, Ann Grodzins. 1988. *Fruitful Journeys: The Ways of Rajasthani Pilgrims*. Berkeley: University of California Press.

———. 1992. *A Carnival of Parting: The Tales of King Bhartrhari and King Gopi Chand as Sung and Told by Madhu Natisar Nath of Ghatiyali, Rajasthan*. Berkeley: University of California Press.

Gold, Ann Grodzins and Gloria Goodwin-Raheja. 1994. *Listen to the Heron's Words*. Berkeley, CA: University of California Press.

Hiltebeitl, Alf. 1995. 'Dying before the Mahabharata War: Martial and Transsexual Body-building for Aravan'. *Journal of Asian Studies*. 54(2):447–73.

Jakobsen, Doranne and Susan Wadley. 1992. *Women in India: Two Perspectives*. Delhi: South Asia Books.

Kumar, Mina. 1996. 'Some Indian Lesbian Images'. *Trikone Magazine*. 11(3):12–4.

Kumar, Radha. 1993. *The History of Doing: An Illustrated Account of Movements for Women's Rights and Feminism in India*. New Delhi: Kali for Women.

Lessinger, Hanna and Amy Swerdlow, eds. 1983. *Class, Race and Sex: The Dynamics of Control*. Boston: K.G. Hall.

Malamoud, Charles. 1997. *Cooking the World: Ritual and Thought in Ancient India*. French Studies in South Asian Culture and Society. Trans. David White. Delhi: Oxford University Press.

Manu. 1991. *The Laws of Manu*. Trans. Wendy K. Doniger and Brain Smith. London: Penguin Books.

Marglin, Frederique. 1985. *Wives of the God-king: The Rituals of Devadasis in Puri*. Oxford: Oxford University Press.

Masson, Jeffrey Moussaieff. 1980. *The Oceanic Feeling: The Origins of Religious Sentiment in Ancient India*. Boston: D. Reidel.

Mauss, Marcel. 1938. 'Une categorie de l'esprit humain: la notionne de personne, celle de "moi"'. *Journal of the Royal Anthropological Institute*. 68.

Mazumdar, Veena. 1978. 'Comment on Suttee'. *Signs*. 4(21):269.

McDaniel. June. 1989. *The Madness of the Saints: Ecstatic Religion in Bengal*. Chicago: University of Chicago Press.

Mishri, Urvashi. 1985. 'Child and Childhood: A Conceptual Construction'. *Contributions to Indian Sociology* (n.s.). 19(1):115–32.

Mohanty, Chandra Talpade and Biddy Martin. 1986. 'Feminist Politics: What's Home Got to Do With It?' In Teresa de Laurentis, ed., *Feminist Studies/Critical Studies*, 191–212. Bloomington: Indiana University Press.

Mukherjee, Bharati. 1988. 'The Management of Grief'. In Bharati Mukherjee, *The Middleman and Other Stories*. New York: Grove Press.

Nanda, Serena. 1990. *Neither Man Nor Woman: The Hijras of India*. (Wadsworth Modern Anthropology Library). Boston: Wadsworth Publishing Company.

Narayan, R.K. 1972. 'God and the Cobbler'. In R.K. Narayan, *Malgudi Days*. New York: Viking Press.

Narayan, Kirin. 1989. *Storytellers, Saints, and Scoundrels: Folk Narrative in Hindu Religious Teaching*. Philadelphia: University of Pennsylvania Press.

Obeyesekere, Gananath. 1990. *The Work of Culture: Symbolic Transformation in Psychoanalysis and Anthropology*. Chicago: University of Chicago Press.

O'Flaherty, Wendy Doniger. 1973. *Eroticism and Asceticism in the Mythology of Siva*. Delhi: Oxford University Press.

Oldenberg, Veena. 1990. 'Lifestyle as Resistance: The Case of the Courtesans of Lucknow, India'. *Feminist Studies*. 16(2):259–87.

Osella, Filippo and Caroline Osella. 1996. 'Articulation of Physical and Social Bodies in Kerala'. *Contributions to Indian Sociology* (n.s.). 30(1):37–68.

Patanjali. 1996. *Yoga: discipline of freedom: the Yoga Sutra attributed to Patanjali.* Trans. with commentary, introduction, and glossary of keywords by Barbara Stoller Miller. Berkeley: University of California Press.

Petersen, Indira V. 1986. 'The Tie That Binds: Brothers and Sisters in North and South India'. Paper presented at the Conference on Religion in South India, Craigsville, Massachusetts.

Pinch, William. 1996. *Peasants and Monks in Ancient India.* Berkeley: University of California Press.

Ramanujan, A.K. 1971. *Relations: Poems.* Chicago: University of Chicago Press.

Roland, Alan. 1988. *In Search of Self in India and Japan: Toward a Cross-Cultural Psychiatry.* Princeton: Princeton University Press.

Rushdie, Salman. 1991. *Imaginary Homelands: Essays and Criticism 1981–1991.* London: Granta.

———. 1992. *The Wizard of Oz.* London: BCI Publishing.

Singer, Milton. 1972. *When a Great Tradition Modernizes: An Anthropological Approach to Indian Civilization.* New York: Praeger.

Shiva, Vandana. 1989. *Staying Alive: Women, Ecology and Development.* London: Zed Books.

Somasundaram, Daya. 1998. *Scarred Minds: The Psychological Impact of War on Sri Lankan Tamils.* New Delhi: Sage Publications.

Spivak, Gayatri Chakravorty. 1987. *In Other Worlds: Essays in Cultural Politics.* New York and London: Methuen.

———. 1988. 'Can the Subaltern Speak?' In Gary Nelson and Lawrence Grossberg, eds, *Marxism and the Interpretation of Culture,* 271–313. Urbana: University of Illionis Press.

Srinivas, M.N. 1976. *The Remembered Village.* Berkeley: University of California Press.

Tambiah, Stanley J. 1992. *Buddhism Betrayed?: Religion, Politics and Violence in Sri Lanka.* Chicago: University of Chicago Press.

Trawick, Margaret. 1983. 'The Changed Mother, or What the Smallpox Goddess Did When There Was No More Smallpox'. *Contributions to Asian Studies.* 18:24–45.

———. 1986. 'Internal Iconicity in Paraiyar Crying Songs'. In Stuart Blackburn and A.K. Ramanujan, eds, *Another Harmony: New Essays on the Folklore of India,* 294–344. Berkeley: University of California Press.

———. 1988. 'Spirits and Voices in Tamil Songs'. *American Ethnologist.* 15(2):193–215.

———. 1990. *Notes on Love in a Tamil Family.* Berkeley: University of California Press.

———. 1997. 'Reasons for Violence: a Preliminary Ethnographic Account of the LTTE'. *South Asia.* 20:153–80.

Weaver, Mary Ann. 1994. 'A Fugitive from Injustice'. *The New Yorker.* 12 September. 49–60.

Zimmerman, Francis. 1987. *The Jungle and the Aroma of Meats: An Ecological Theme in Hindu Medicine.* Berkeley: University of California Press.

The Cultural Construction of Emotion

Robert Desjarlais • James Wilce

From the bonds of love evident in Hindu families to dysphoric bouts of 'soul loss' suffered by ethnically Tibetan peoples in Nepal, emotions play an important role in the lives of South Asians. These emotions are culturally constructed in several interconnected ways. Cultural dynamics pattern the way in which emotions are felt, named, understood, spoken of, and managed in everyday life. They also shape how people communicate, acknowledge, and interpret feelings and emotions through various verbal and non-verbal means. Although most of our ethnographic examples concern Hindu communities, other examples come from ethnographies of Muslim and Buddhist communities. The social relations and psychological formations common to certain societies can help to establish certain emotional bonds and sensibilities among family members or members of a community. They can also contribute to particular forms of illness and affliction. In turn, religious and ritual practices, such as pilgrimages, exorcisms, and healing performances, as well as different art forms, such as theatre, literature, dance, song, and film, can work to heighten, lessen, articulate, inculcate, or transform different emotions and affective sensibilities among the participants and audiences of such performances. We might call this an 'environmental' take on the phrase 'the cultural construction of emotion' in the sense that we become environments for one another and that social environment can influence affect, and even physiology, directly (as Mauss envisioned). Without mediation by the more cognitive dimensions of culture (Mauss [1953] 1973). Finally, perspectives on emotion are often integral to ideologies of personhood, caste, and gender, and help to reinforce or legitimate political relations and systems of domination and inequality. Considerations of these perspectives pertain to what we might call the 'discursive' or 'ideological' approach to the cultural construction of emotion.

All researchers investigating the nature of emotions in South Asia have faced the perennial problem of anthropological translation. Is there a Hindu, Buddhist, or South Asian concept of emotion? Or, is the anthropology of 'emotion' another example of a category error in which a western category like 'depression' is used to translate local ideas that might entail something quite different (Shweder 1985; Obeyesekere 1985)? This question is evident in scholarly musings on *bhava*, which is a key concept for many in South Asia (McDaniel 1990). While bhava means 'emotion, sentiment' in its secular sense, religious devotees describe states of bhava with metaphors of 'drowning' or 'absorption' into a greater self, other spiritual entities, or higher spiritual states. Its interpersonal, otherly connotations lead Sullivan (1996, forthcoming), to translate bhava (glossed as 'emotion' by others) as 'relationships'. He therefore renders the desirable *dasya* bhava towards Krishna not as 'servant feeling' but as 'servant relationship'. One of the most significant implications of such reflections is that a dominant Indic analogue of the English concept of 'emotion' is fundamentally relational, not individualistic.

Given the apparent sociocentric underpinnings of selfhood and emotions in South Asia, emotions are often understood to have a strong moral dimension to them. In a study of the moral and psychological sensibilities of the Newars of Bhaktapur, Nepal, for instance, Steven Parish describes a common emotion among the Newars known as *lajya*, which 'combines feeling and evaluation; it is an emotion and a moral state' (1994: 199) variably involving sentiments of shame, embarrassment, shyness, or modesty, especially in regard to one's hierarchical superiors in the family and caste system. As with lajya, other emotions in South Asia similarly carry important moral connotations because they index or underscore the morally attuned social relations between people living in a community.

Thus emotions in South Asia do not strictly entail divides between feeling and thinking, or between mind and body, as many in Europe and North America assume to be the case. The Yolmo Sherpa of north-central Nepal, for example, understand that processes of thinking, feeling, imagining, and moral evaluation occur in the *sem* or 'heartmind', located in the centre of the chest; many emotional processes have a strong cognitive and moral quality to them, and many thoughts are imbued with affective resonances (Desjarlais 1992). Owen Lynch reports that the Hindi *man* is similarly understood to be 'the seat of thought and of feeling' (1990: 102), while Stephen Tyler notes that the Dravidian languages 'do not so fastidiously separate "knowing" and "feeling" in the way SAE [standard average European] terms do (1984: 36). The Yolmo also tend not to distinguish sharply between what people in

English-speaking cultures would call 'emotions' and 'sensations', with the result that moments of grief or sadness are not simply psychological events but are felt in deeply embodied ways. Yolmo folk songs thus allude to such sentiments through images of 'weary bodies' and 'the sorrow of little feet hurting' as well as speak of the need to 'cut' the pain of grief and heartache from the bodies of those feeling pain (Desjarlais 1992). Despite the fact that many emotions have a strong bodily basis, however, decades of cross-cultural research make it clear that these and other emotions are not natural biological constants for which a culture merely provides a label.

People in different cultures feel differently, and yet they do feel. As Richard Shweder puts it, 'Three-year-olds, Ifaluk islanders, and psychoanalysts (in other words, almost everyone, except perhaps the staunchest of positivists) recognize that emotions are feelings' (1985: 183). It therefore makes sense to stick with the English word 'emotion' in discussing the lives and concerns of people in South Asia. Yet it also makes sense to conclude that, given the variation in emotional functioning in different societies, extreme care must be taken in mapping out the semantic and phenomenal contours of any emotional processes. Researchers following this creed have consistently found that emotions in South Asia are often heartfelt, embodied, semiotically mediated, and morally and ideologically charged sentiments that relate as much, if not more, to interpersonal concerns as to the psychological functioning of an individual.

Psychoanalytic Approaches

In trying to understand the psychodynamic constitutions of various peoples in South Asia, psychiatrists, clinicians, and anthropologists have traced certain patterns of emotional experience and social relationships among Hindu adults to the nature of emotional bonds between children and their parents. Like Freud, these researchers assume that a child is the father of man. In accord with the tenets of the 'culture and personality' school of psychological anthropology, however, they also acknowledge that the lives of children in different societies produce different social and psychological concerns in the adults of those societies. In one of the first and most influential accounts, G. Morris Carstairs (1958) connects social relationships and other aspects of 'Hindu personality' to patterns of child rearing. According to him, there is a great deal of physical and emotional closeness between the Hindu mother and her child, with mothers indulging their children in various ways. Since children do not become accustomed to frustration prior to weaning, that transition is difficult and tempestuous, provoking many days of crying and anger, and is experienced as an abrupt rejection by the mother. Fathers, remaining cool and distant authority figures, never become warm enough to undo the damage. One consequence of such an upbringing is that an 'underlying mistrust' clouds many adult personal relationships (Carstairs 1958: 158). The serenity that prevails in a well-adjusted Hindu family, in turn, 'is perhaps a precarious calm, based on the suppressing rather than on the resolving of underlying tensions, but still it reflects a gracious and civilized way of life' (Carstairs 1958: 168–9). In hindsight, Carstairs's comparison between western and Indian processes and outcomes of childrearing seems starkly invidious, as is his evaluation of the tenuousness of his subjects' hold on civility and decency, who to him are decent only when bound by formalism.

Alan Roland (1988), who practised psychoanalysis in India and Japan, finds a particular pattern to the restraint described by Carstairs: culturally proscribed emotions such as personal ambition or anger find indirect expression through the cultivation of an inner private self as well as through passive–aggressive behaviour and 'somatization' (which, incidentally, was the most frequent sort of 'psychiatric' symptom reported in Carstairs and Kapur's 1976 study of psychiatric morbidity in an Indian village). Roland does find a form of narcissism to be prevalent, but this 'self-love' involves what he calls the 'we-self' more than an 'I-self'. This Indian form of selfhood underlies the tendency to avoid open-faced threats and to engage in reciprocal, role-based nurturing. Culturally valorized sentiments like interdependence, we can deduce, must be cultivated through such practices as having adults and children sharing sleeping spaces within a household. These practices manifest a capacity for emotional empathy built within Indian households, which Carstairs, however, found lacking. Agreeing with Carstairs and others that Indian fathers tend to be emotionally aloof towards their sons, Roland argues that such distance forces sons to be even more emphatically sensitive, enhancing a 'radar-like' ability that contrasts with the emotional 'gyroscope' of the self-contained western individual. Like Carstairs, however, Roland does find the repressive extreme of indirection with regards to the expression of anger and sexuality (that is, the variety of 'defence mechanisms' used by Indian persons to parry the thrusts of passion) to generate psychopathology in the Indian context as, he notes, it would elsewhere.

In his wide-ranging psychoanalytic study of India, Sudhir Kakar (1978) builds on the work of Carstairs to trace themes in social organization to the structures of personality formed in early childhood. Whereas Kakar finds that the core of emotional life in India 'is anxiety and suffering', Indian social organization is 'therapeutic', oriented to meeting dependency needs (Kakar 1978: 124–5). Like Carstairs, Kakar explains pervasive male sexual anxiety largely in terms of identification with the 'bad' side of a split

Mother image, but he goes further to find echoes of this throughout Indian religious imagery and popular culture. Kali thus represents a projection of infantile rage at this 'bad' mother from whom a male child is, at times, perforce separated. Kakar agrees with Carstairs that Oedipal conflict must be experienced by Indian boys, but then transcends Carstairs's account of it, to find explanations in the ways mothers pin such great emotional hopes on sons—not only because sons represent a promise of increased status for their mothers, but also because women's desires for intimacy with their husbands are frustrated by their in-laws. The predominant, problematic resolution of this Oedipal conflict leads to the 'narcissistic vulnerability' of the male ego by way of a passive homo-eroticism (Kakar 1978: 132). Consequently, for Kakar, 'the emotional self-absorption of the masculine psyche in India' arises from the combination of the prolongation of a symbiotic mother–son bond and its rupture, followed by a disappointing relationship with the father (Kakar 1978: 133). This infantile experience, Kakar argues, is the emotional ontogeny of what Dumont calls 'Homo hierarchicus'—the subjection of the individual (male) to the (male-dominated) group. The emotion most indicative of this particularly Indian form of selfhood is the fear of separation-in-autonomy, a fear which arises when death approaches (Kakar 1978: 36) but which also finds expression in many popular genres, where 'pathos [particularly that which is evoked by separation from love] is everything' (Kakar 1978: 33). Finally, Kakar's unique contribution is to show that the child is not only the father of man, but of the nation as well. Kakar anticipating his own 1996 arguments with regard to male vulnerability in the face of fiery communalist rhetoric, argues in *The Inner World* that the Indian-male resolution of the Oedipal conflict potentiates a 'communal conscience' in place of an individual one, and the emotional significance invested in individual leaders in India (Kakar 1978: 135–7).

With the exception of Ewing's (1990; 1991) work in Pakistan, the psychoanalytic literature on South Asia has followed Carstairs in focusing on Hindus. Ewing (1990) exemplifies more recent work inspired both by Freud and those, such as Lacan, who interpret Freud as a semiotician. Thus she takes 'the experience of wholeness' among Pakistani women as largely resulting from mechanisms Freud described—condensation, displacement, transference, and identification—which are reinterpreted as semiotic processes. That is, such mechanisms are seen as ways in which the self becomes a sign to itself. Such semiosis of the self is a (meta) emotional process as well, Ewing argues. 'Shifts of mood' correspond with shifts in 'self-image' (Ewing 1990: 270). The present authors see what Ewing notes as the need to maintain 'the illusion of [the self's] wholeness' as a transcultural manifestation of a primal desire or longing (Lacan 1977).

Illness and Psychopathology

More than a few illnesses in South Asia involve forms of malaise that are largely sensorial-emotional in nature. Bruce Kapferer (1979; 1983), for instance, notes that Sinhalese Buddhists suffering demonic illness are understood to be in a state of physical and psychological 'aloneness'. Such illnesses usually occur when a person is alone and suddenly frightened or startled and a demon or ghost takes a firm emotional and physical grip on that person. The demons and ghosts, who are consistently associated with such desires, passions, and emotions as lust, pride, greed, cruelty, anger, and sorrow, then immerse the afflicted person in a state of general mental and emotional disquiet. Those caught in a demon's 'gaze' are consumed by thoughts, which concentrate on the frightening aspect of demons and express such extreme emotional states as fear, anger, or acute sexual longing; adopt a dominant serious mood and an inability to laugh; and often withdraw into themselves and reject normal sociable intercourse.

The Yolmo Sherpa suffering from 'spirit loss' encounter a comparable range of symptoms (Desjarlais 1992: 135–56). As with many peoples in the world who understand that one can lose one's life forces, the Yolmo assume that a person typically loses his or her *bla* or 'spirit' when he or she is alone and startled by some unforeseen event, like birds rustling in a dark forest. When a healthy bla is intact, it enables a person to be energetic, vital, wilful, attentive, and altogether 'spirited' in life. When it is lost, a person can fall into a lethargic, absent-minded slumber, wanting neither to eat, work, sleep, or talk with others. Desjarlais (1992) finds that such 'spirit loss' is one of the most prevalent forms of illness in the Yolmo communities where he conducted ethnographic research. He attributes the prevalence of spirit loss to several interrelated factors. An aesthetics of everyday life leads the Yolmo to value themes of balance, personal and interpersonal harmony, bodily and social integration, and mindful presence; while health is characterized by the presence of these themes in a person's life, illness is often defined by their absence. People are, therefore, primed to experience illness in terms of fragmentation, dispersal, and absence. At the same time, residence and kinship patterns, in which daughters and sons often leave their natal villages and families, are constantly threatened with fissions when brothers set up their own households this promotes a lingering ethos of loss and sadness in the community. This ethos can come to the fore when people fall ill, fall on hard times, or suffer losses in their own lives. Finally, the predicaments of young women, who must leave their natal villages and marry into a new and sometimes inhospitable family miles away, can sometimes spawn a general, dysphoric state of spiritlessness (whereas in Bangladesh women faced with similar problems suffer from spirit possession (see Blanchet 1984).

The affinities between European and American ideas of 'depression', demonic possession among the Sinhalese, and spirit loss among the Yolmo raise the question of whether the latter two states are really depression after all. Psychiatrists working in South Asia such as Rao (1984) and Mullick et al. (1994) find that depression is a universal disease and that many South Asians in fact suffer from it. In a psychiatric study of Havik Brahmin women in a south-Indian village, for instance, Helen Ulrich (1987) found that twenty-five of forty-five women she interviewed had a history of depression. Ulrich attributes such a high rate of depression to the fact what women in Havik Brahmin society are culturally devalued and thus often become dependent on their husbands and families. This dependence, in turn, places women at risk to life events which, along with the lack of close relationships and a poor marital relationship, can predispose them to depression. This is particularly true for elderly women; (eleven of thirteen women over 50 interviewed had a history of depression). As Ulrich notes, 'Old age for women in this society often meant powerlessness and shame. A widow who does not appear clinically depressed is rare' (Ulrich 1987: 284). Similarly, A. Venkoba Rao (1984) finds depression as common in India as elsewhere in the world. In fact, Rao finds descriptions of depression-like constellations of symptoms in the Ramayana and Mahabharata. In contemporary India, not only is suicide carried out but suicidal ideation is observed clinically (see Rao 1984: 308; and Mullick et al. 1994). Rao and others agree that a dysphoric mood is rarely expressed, particularly as a presenting problem, while somatization (the expression of distress in somatic terms) is a common presenting idiom. Yet, for Rao, the problem is waiting to be expressed, requiring only an insightful clinical listener to elicit it (Rao 1994: 304).

Anthropologists, however, caution that there are problems in applying a psychiatric category devised and accepted in western settings to peoples who live in different cultural worlds. Gananath Obeyesekere (1985), for example, argues that sentiments of sorrow and revulsion towards one's body in South Asia are irrevocably rooted in Buddhist cultural traditions, and are in fact highly valued by some Buddhists who meditate on these sentiments in order to seek a more enlightened understanding of the world. Anything that might be labelled as depression in the West, therefore, assumes a radically different set of meanings among Buddhists in South Asia. Shweder (1985), in turn, inverts the typical psychiatric line, which would find that soul loss is, at heart, depression, and suggests that depression is founded in the basic, universally shared feeling of soul loss, in which one feels dispirited, empty, and unwilful. In sifting through such findings and perspectives, it appears that people in South Asian cultures commonly suffer from various dysphoric states. Yet, given the designated differences between categories like depression and soul loss (Yolmo spiritlessness, for instance, never involves ideas of guilt, self-worthlessness, or suicidal intent, ideas which are basic to psychiatric definitions of depression and which are salient according to many psychiatrists in South Asia), it is best to conclude in the spirit of Wittgenstein (1953) that there is a 'family resemblance' between the two categories, with both involving feelings of dysphoria but also with cultural dynamics shaping each in characteristic and sometimes culturally specific ways.

Other factors to consider are the culturally constituted 'idioms of distress' (Nichter 1981) that pattern how people signal and embody distress. Roland (1988), for instance, interprets somatization in Indian women, in particular, in relation to constraints on their communication of distress. Nichter (1981), also presuming limits on the ability of south-Indian women to 'ventilate' or verbalize distress within or outside of the home, finds a somewhat broader range of alternative idioms of distress in addition to 'illness idioms': eating disturbances, obsession with purity, reports of evil eye, spirit possession, and involvement in *bhakti* cults. Similarly, Gananath Obeyesekere (1974) interprets Sinhalese women's *dola-dukha* ('sorrows' or cravings that coincide with pregnancy) as a culturally constituted idiom. For these women, pregnancy is a time when the expression of symbolically charged desires is permitted to them (Blanchet 1984 offers a similar interpretation of desires expressed by possessed women in Bangladesh). In other studies that combine psychoanalytic and anthropological theory, Obeyesekere (1981; 1990) documents the ways in which unconscious sentiments of desire and guilt motivate the lives of Sri Lankans and sometimes lead to situations of distress, illness, or frail cures as manifested in demonic attacks, divine possession, and ritual practices.

Families, Child Rearing, and Emotion

Several anthropologists working along the lines of the 'culture and personality' school of psychological anthropology have generated findings that both complement and enable rethinking on the psychoanalytic and ethnographic insights noted earlier. Leigh Minturn and John Hitchcock (1963), who conducted ethnographic research among the Rajputs of Khalapur, India, in the early 1960s for the collaborative 'Six Cultures' study of child rearing, concluded that, in comparison to parents in other societies studied, Khalapur parents were not openly warm or overly affectionate with their children. Further, Khalapur mothers, although generally attentive to their children's needs, did not lavish individual attention on them, insisting that 'all children are alike' (Minturn and Hitchcock 1963: 111). As Minturn and Hitchcock put it, 'The child is always a secure member of a group, but he is never an important individual. His needs are cared for, his reasonable demands met, but he never monopolizes his mother's time' (1963: 112). In general, they found that parents' sanctions against their children were best thought of as 'status oriented' rather than 'love oriented' because they capitalized on fear of lost status and consequent abandonment by the social group rather than fear of loss of love from a particular person. Quantitative analyses that compared these and other observations to those conducted in other cultures found that Khalapur mothers, who scored below all others on a maternal-warmth factor, were 'unusual in their lack of warmth in interaction with their children' (Minturn and Lambert 1964:238) and that Indian children ranked high on an authoritarian-aggressive dimension and low on a sociable-intimate dimension (Whiting and Whiting 1975).

In a similar vein, Ronald Rohner and Manjusri Chaki-Sircar (1988), comparing the level of maternal warmth perceived by both children and mothers themselves in both high- and low-caste Hindu households in Bengal, find higher levels of affection in low-caste households. Along with Minturn and Lambert (1964) they attribute this to the fact that high-caste households are more likely to consist of extended families than are low-caste households. Susan Seymour (1975) reported similar results in her study of child rearing among Hindu families in Bhubaneswar, but interpreted them differently. According to her, 'The care of children in Bhubaneswar was strikingly casual and impersonal. Children were taken for granted and their basic needs attended to, but they received little other special attention or stimulation' (Seymour 1975: 47). At the same time, in low-status joint households, family members besides mothers, offered children a great deal of spontaneous positive affect (Seymour 1983). While agreeing that the extended family household dilutes the intensity of affection which mothers provide their own offspring, she follows the hypothesis of Margaret Mead (1928) in Melanesia that affective bonds and caretaking roles in larger households are diffused across a greater number of relationships. Seymour also points out the need to consider interpersonal touching and physical contact when studying the nature of affective behaviour and emotions in India (1983: 276).

Stanley Kurtz (1992) draws from these and other studies in arguing that the psychoanalytic studies of Carstairs and Kakar overemphasize both the intimacy between mother and infant before weaning and the emotional fallout that arises when the child separates from the mother and enters the world of adult males. Shying away from psychoanalytic models that give priority to relations between individuals, such as a mother and child, Kurtz finds that neither the mother nor other family members are engaged in an intimate exchange or reflection of emotions with the child. The mother's behaviour and attitudes towards her child, where she attends to that child's needs but simultaneously suggests that complete self-indulgence is neither acceptable nor admirable behaviour, work towards gently pushing the child away from a direct and exclusive link with the natural mother and towards a sense of immersion in, or unity with, the family group (Kurtz 1992: 59) This gradual and negotiated movement from the orbit of the mother's care towards the loving protection of a larger group generates the Hindu emphasis on detachment from emotional bonds as well as a sense of unindividuated belonging to a larger group. Rather than finding in this the roots of pathology, Kurtz argues that the diffusion of affective bonds leads to a healthy but uniquely Indian and rather sociocentric resolution of the conflict that western societies experience as 'Oedipal'. In fact, he interprets teasing, unfulfilled threats, and the avoidance of overt praise along with unique maternal attention to each child (interpreted by Kakar as a failure to provide what self psychologists call 'empathic mirroring') as highly functional in a matrix designed to produce hierarchically oriented, sociocentric adults (Kurtz 1992: 57–9).

Other anthropological studies make further contributions to our understanding of the role of emotions in South Asian family life. In her 1990 ethnography, *Notes on Love in a Tamil Family*, Trawick details the attributes of the Tamil concept of *anpu* or 'love', as gathered from her informant's views of it in their everyday lives. Anpu is a ruling principle for the Tamils that Trawick came to know during her fieldwork. Among other things, anpu is understood to be a dangerous, habit-forming force that must be 'contained' and 'hidden' lest it overflow its boundaries and harm both the recipients and the givers of love. A mother, for instance, should never gaze lovingly into her child's face because that gaze could harm the child; spouses were expected to keep loving affection and sexual feelings for one another hidden; and family members would hide love by openly downgrading a loved one. Trawick also finds that Tamils understood that love is 'cruel and forceful' as much as it is tender and slow. The bonds of affection are cruel in part because, when the bonds are broken, those affected suffer pain. Love is also cruel and harsh in the sense that, out of love for their children, Tamil parents often beat them or force them to act in certain ways just as they try to train their children to be tough and learn how to share. As Trawick notes, these sentiments are necessary in a world of scarcity and hardship. As a result, in the family Trawick became close to, she found that 'mothers deliberately spurned or mistreated their own children, forcing their own and their children's affection away from the closest blood bond' (1990: 103). These assessments could, as Kurtz suggests, reflect the pain that parents might feel in turning the child from exclusive intimacy with them toward wider bonds with 'other mothers' and fathers of the extended family. These themes also recall the self-control and emotional detachment that Carstairs and others observe, although this valorization and love-based account of restraint undercuts their descriptions of 'cold' and emotionally distant Hindu families. Trawick's account also points to the limitations of research based on observations of behaviour alone, for such research can fail to capture the webs of meanings, ideologies, and sentiments that motivate such behaviour.

Although Trawick's model leaves room for conflicting viewpoints, she does not provide the sort of examples needed to disturb her readers' assumption that the ideology of love projected by her host family is Tamil truth. The notion that love, especially maternal love, must be hidden, for example, is an ideology reflecting the interests of some parties more than others. This ideology is actually challenged, as Vatuk's (1982) study of kin terms demonstrates. Vatuk's north-Indian experience shows the way kin terms used in address modulate emotional bonds, but not always as senior lineage members would hope. In order to insert the cultural principle of cross-generational hierarchy into what is regarded as the 'natural' bond between mothers and their own children, north-Indian grandmothers train their children to call them 'mother'. The aim is to transfer the affectionate power of the term to the grandmother.

> It is somewhat ironic that when the mother term is preempted by the grandmother—either on her own initiative or at the instigation of the young mother herself—in order to reinforce her bond with her son's child and to reaffirm his [sic] belonging to the wider family group—the term adopted for addressing the natural mother usually comes to connote in turn the specialness and uniqueness of the mother child relationship' [Vatuk 1982: 96]. In the end, therefore, we see patterns of address between mothers and their own children, and the emotional connotations acquired in that use, subverting a cultural definition of the mother's love for her child as selfish and disruptive of patrilineal solidarity.

Trawick (1990) explicitly argues that it is precisely tensions between conflicting desires (culturally constituted sentiments, not biological essentials) that sustain the system of kinship ideals and, in fact, the broad Tamil social order. Those ideal-objects of desire centre on four relationships, each of them conflicted: mother–daughter, father–son, husband–wife, and brother–sister. The two vertical relationships are characterized by an asymmetry of desire: fathers and daughters desire continuity across the generations (with sons and mothers, respectively); while mothers and sons long for more independence as they have less to lose and more to gain therein. The marital bond is conflictual but hard to sever, while the sibling bond is strong and idealized but 'must be denied'. Overall, the kinship system is a linguistically projected ideal that becomes an object of aesthetic pleasure in itself, while the bonds (particularly the four just mentioned) inscribed within that linguistic system hold forth the promise of pleasure for at least one party.

Trawick's Lacanian interpretation of kinship finds that family members are often involved in a tragic combination of agonism and desire, the very sort of dynamic, says Trawick, which is necessary to sustain such an ideal over time. Such emotion, she implies, is more than socially constructed for it sustains the social order itself (Trawick 1990: 117–86).

In a Foucault-inspired exploration of the colonial production of discourse and 'disciplines' in Hindu India, Pradip Kumar Bose (1995) considers the role of a child-rearing manual, *Santāner Caritra Gaṭhan,* an exemplar of an extremely popular genre of expert manuals produced in colonial Calcutta. Bose argues that these manuals co-opted 'family' and some older cultural values for use in a new discourse that placed discipline at the pinnacle of a reformulated hierarchy of values. In this framework, the family is redefined as a private and intimate sphere in which warm but restrained private affective experience produces character for the sake of a disciplined nation. Even semen loss is somewhat re-symbolized in economic terms as 'waste'. Guilt becomes a tool and a goal along the way to producing a nation both self-reliant and, in recognition of India's poverty, appropriately ascetic. The ascetic strain in disciplined love is thus a manifestation of the post-colonial internalization of the image of the impoverished nation. While it is difficult to determine the impact of such discourses on everyday child-rearing practices in Hindi communities, Bose's work points to the need to consider the broader cultural and ideological parameters of conceptions of childhood, family care, and emotions.

Several studies lend support to the sociocentric focus of personhood and emotions in South Asia while also noting the often troublesome presence of individual desires and sentiments in adult lives. One thing that becomes clear through these studies is that, while there is a strong focus on collective identity among South Asians, there are also important concerns for individual autonomy and personal needs and desires (McHugh 1989). In a psychoanalytically inclined study of the psychological concerns of Pakistani women, for instance, Ewing (1991) takes the cultural demand for sociocentric allegiance to the family group as a given, but also finds evidence that these women have either achieved or else experienced a painful lack of intra-psychic autonomy. Some Pakistani women leave their natal families with an 'ability to maintain enduring mental representations of sources of self-esteem' (Ewing 1991: 132), an internalized sense of their parents' warm regard towards them, undergirding their own self-esteem. The lives of others, however, are marked by adjustment difficulties as evident in bouts of spirit possession, depression, and hostility. Ewing contends that these emotional dynamics can be 'passed on' from one generation to another, but she also notes that any pathology entailed in these dynamics accords not to any universal psychoanalytic norm, but to what is possible, healthy, and normal in the Pakistani world.

Steve Derné (1995a), who conducted extensive interviews with Hindu men living in joint households in the city of Benāras, found that these men are driven by a collectivist model of action which leads them to see 'social fear/respect' *(samaj ka dar)* as an exemplary emotion. Because these men focus on how action is rightly guided by social pressures, group opinion, and the threat of moral censure, they understand that fear, prompted by loving respect for authority, is one of the main motivating forces that leads people to act in socially proper ways. Hindu men find that individual desires can threaten the solidarity of joint households, just as love that becomes too focused on one individual or aspect of life is a dangerously wild, powerful, and unpredictable emotion that can blind a person to family obligations, such as the care of one's parents. They, therefore, often try to limit love that pulls them towards their wives and instead value a less threatening kind of love that is based on duty and extends towards many in a family. Despite this dominant emotional paradigm, however, many men also recognize the benefits of unconstrained love and the costs of social fear. Thus a 'second language' that emphasizes individual desires, complements the focus on being guided by social pressures.

Aesthetics, Religious Practices, and Ritual Performances

Derné (1995a, 1995b) finds that Hindi films, which are especially popular among young Hindu men, both court and commercialize this second language in presenting individuals who struggle alone against injustice and family pressures and learn to give priority to romantic love over social fear. After the parents of two young lovers withdraw their support in one popular film, for instance, the hero sings, 'We are lovers. We are not fearful of the world' (Derne 1995b: 177). In conveying such messages the films apparently have the potential to do several things at once. They can provide a liminal forum through which men can momentarily escape from the authority of home and work; they can indulge men's fantasies; allow them to live vicariously the love that they often believe they cannot achieve in their daily lives; help them recognize their own desires along with family duties; and emphasize the joys of exclusive love for a uniquely special person. But in simultaneously reminding viewers of the costs of abandoning one's parents for love, these films also express the dominant view of love as a madness that should not be allowed to jeopardize family honour. The cultural force inherent in these cautionary tales is suggested by the fact that the male film-goers interviewed by Derné continue to insist that love marriages never succeed and that parental support is essential to a couple's success. Despite the fantastic, desirable worlds pictured in the films, men's fears of social censure and the loss of parental support in real life continue to shape how they think, feel, and act.

Other artistic media in South Asia work in other ways to pattern how and what people feel. Of great importance to many of these media is the classical aesthetic theory of *rasa,* a word which literally means 'taste' or 'flavour' but usually entails the idea of a generalized mood that can be intuitively perceived and understood by other persons in similar states (see, among others, Hiriyanna 1954; Dimock et al., 1974; Bhat 1984). In poetic or dramatic contexts, the eight bhavas or quotidian feelings that all persons experience in their lives—love, mirth, grief, energy, terror, disgust, anger, and wonder—can be transformed into a corresponding rasa or mood that is general and common to all men who are receptive, but also so transcendent and fleeting that is requires special dramatic techniques to establish it among the audience of a play. Unlike the dramatic techniques common to western theatre, which, as Aristotle noted, largely involve ideas of dramatic plots, emotional catharsis, and unique and changeable characters, these techniques do not focus on individual awareness, accidental or private experience, or transformations of character in either the audience or the characters portrayed. Rather, they work to promote an immediate but depersonalized and generalized awareness of and participation in the dominant rasa that the play at hand entails. This is, therefore, an emotion-centred, rather than plot-, action-, or character-centred, kind of drama. A dramatic performance determines and promotes the dominant emotional tone of a play through two major means: by establishing the conditions of character and setting through the use of language, formulaic gestures, and dramatic events; and by artfully setting the fledgling sentiment against various transitory emotional states as well as against other, potentially dominant emotions. By prompting a certain emotional tone through words and gestures and then maintaining and enlivening that tone through contrast with other emotional states, a play can, if successful, enable its participants to apprehend a generalized aspect of mind and experience that usually remains hidden and implicit.

The orientations to drama and emotion inherent in the theory of rasa are evident in a range of other art forms and dramatic and religious performances. Edwin Gerow (1974b) shows that the aesthetic means of several Bengali novels work along the lines of the theory of rasa. Bibhutibhushan Banerji's novel, *Pather Panchali* (1968), for instance, sets up characters, events, and particular moods in order to advance a dominant emotional mood: namely that of the innocent, untainted wonder of a child's view of the world. As Gerow (1974b) puts it,

The effect, the rasa, can be nothing else than the sympathetic translation of the everyman in us back to that state that preceded involvement, wherein all things were understood for what they were and not for what they could profit us. Banerji's *defi* has been first to amalgamate the esthetic standpoint of pure rasa with the social proposition that such a standpoint is naturally manifest in a child's outlook [Gerow 1974b: 237].

Arjun Appadurai (1990) convincingly argues, meanwhile, that acts of 'praising' in Hindu India are unconsciously anchored 'in the living logic of worship' and rooted in rasa-like forms of emotional expression. Beggars, for instance, try like actors on the classical stage to create certain emotional bonds and communal understandings through formulaic gestures and utterances:

> As in *rasa* theory, what beggars do, by drawing on a publicly negotiable set of expressions, is to draw the audience (and their potential benefactor, who is sometimes the sole member of the audience) into a 'community of sentiment' whose pragmatic consequence (if the performance is skillful) is that the benefactor bestows some favor on the beggar [Appadurai 1990: 108].

Like-minded efforts to create a certain emotional climate are found in Donna Wulff's (1995) account of *Līlākīrtan* in West Bengal and Brindavan. Through these celebrations of *līlā*, which in this context refers to the divine play of Krishna with his beloved Radha and their close associates, each performance represents a single *pala* or episode in the life of Krishna or of Caitanya. The affinities with models of rasa is evident in Wulff's observation that all of the episodes performed

> centre not on actions but on emotions, often a single emotion or complex of emotions of Radha or Kṛṣṇa or both. Insofar as the *pālās* have plots, the elements of those plots are largely means of making manifest Radha's or Kṛṣṇa's emotional states and the devotion of their close friends and associates toward them. In the persons of these secondary characters, the devotees present at a *kīrtan* performance find proper models for emulation. The performance itself thus provides guidance and practice in the ideal emotions of Vaiṣṇava devotion [Wulff 1995: 106].

As Wulff notes, the techniques of the performance also work along the lines of classical theatre. The performers try to evoke, direct, and intensify the emotion being conveyed by a particular episode, through a powerful combination of music, song, dance, and dramatic gesture. Sentiments of grief as well as bliss are thus promoted.

> 'Yet, in the classical theory of *rasa,* the experience is not that of the raw human emotion but of a transmutation of that emotion brought about by aesthetic means. ... By becoming absorbed in the emotions of Radha and

Kṛṣṇa and their intimate friends and associates, devotees at a *kīrtan* performance are privileged not only to witness but also to participate in the divine *līlā*, which in the Bengali Vaiṣṇava worldview is nothing less than ultimate reality [Wulf 1995: 109].

The close links between dramatic performance, emotional experience, and divine sentiments in these and other performance, illustrate what scholars have often noted: that there is no strict divide, as there reputedly is in the modern West, between aesthetic and religious practices. As Gerow notes, 'Art is Religion' for many in South Asia (1974a: 143). Accordingly, emotions are often understood to be a valid and exemplary means of salvation or transcendence. This is especially true of bhakti or devotional religious activities that are common to many Hindu peoples of south and north India, such as the followers of the Krishna sects. Bhakti religions, which are based on the rasa-influenced premise that those who develop a loving, devotional relationship with a deity can easily free the human spirit and attain a blissful state of divine grace, swept across northern India and into Bengal from the fourteenth through the seventeenth centuries. Given that the primary characteristics of the bhakti movements are—along with devotion to the deity—an emphasis on transcendence, a relatively liberal attitude towards caste, the use of regional languages instead of Sanskrit for religious expression, and anti-Brahmanism (Naim 1974:181–4), there is often a democratizing aspect to such movements (Wulff 1995:99). Indeed, in discussing the cults associated with Krishna, with their stress on uninhibited responses to the playful god, Kakar (1978) finds that 'the psycho-social meaning of *bhakti* is that it provides for, and actually uses, 'democratic' fantasies in which the inner and outer repressions exacted by life in a rigidly structured and highly stratified social order are lifted' (Kakar 1978:141). Other research alludes to the affinities between such devotional practices and the ethos of Hindu family life, especially the love and devotion cultivated between mother and child (Kakar 1978; Trawick 1990; Kurtz 1992).

Ecstatic love is an emotion nurtured in the traditions of Bengali mysticism; the particular form it takes is entwined with Indian forms of religiosity, especially Shakta and Vaishnava and the syncretic form practised in Bengal by the Bauls (McDaniel 1990). For Bauls and members of other sects, as for the Tamil families studied by Trawick, love involves a mingling of persons and genders, and religious enlightenment involves the realization that union entails a return to an original state. In Baul discourse, the divine splits itself into two, male and female, so that the Self could experience rasa as aesthetic pleasure: 'Because he wished to do this, he divided himself in half, into a female form. She was created for pleasure and sexuality. Because of her existence, the Self could taste the best and sweetest of the emotions (*śṛṅgāra rasa)*. Such emotion is both the joy of love and the foundation of creation' (McDaniel 1990: 180).

While the theory of rasa promotes understandings of meaning and action markedly different from the ideas of emotional catharsis invested in Aristotle's theory of poetics (and, accordingly, in Freud's understanding of the symbolic expression of unconscious drives), it is not necessarily the case that cathartic acts do not occur in South Asian religious practices. An exemplary account of the potentially cathartic function of ritual is presented in Obeyesekere's 1984 study, *The Cult of the Goddess Pattini*. Obeyesekere observes that the *ankeliya* or 'horn-game' rituals associated with the Pattini cult in Sri Lanka constitute a 'cathartic enactment' that helps the participants of these rites to act out the psychic problems that are common to Sinhala men (Obeyesekere 1984: 381–508) The rituals, which present humorously ribald scenes of playfully sexual and violent engagements, enable the men who participate (women are prohibited from attending) to express three major emotional problems to which Sinhala culture predisposes them: impotence anxiety, castration anxiety, and a deep-seated wish for anal intercourse. By participating either directly in the dreamlike, primary-process material presented through the rituals or indirectly through vicarious participation, individuals who usually must act with restraint 'have the opportunity to "let themselves go" and give expression to deep psychological states, feelings, or needs that simply cannot be expressed, or even consciously recognized, in normal everyday life' (Obeyesekere 1984: 484). Obeyesekere also notes that, while the *ankeliya* as a ritual is out of vogue in Sinhala society, one of its main models of action—'public vilification and abuse'—dominates in everyday social life (1984: 508).

Other religious observances in South Asia work to transform the emotional and spiritual constitution of religious adepts. Bruce Long's (1972) account of *Shivaratri*, the most auspicious religious observance among Hindu saivas of Madras, details how its participants try to secure the goals desired in this life—union or communion with Lord Shiva in his heavenly realm on *Mount Kailasha* and, thereby, final emancipation after death—by fasting during an entire lunar day, keeping a wakeful vigilance throughout the night, and performing with a pure heart continuous worship of Shiva during the day through the repetition of his divine names. Long concludes that the rites enable the devotee to experience 'a renewal of life and faith':

> A regeneration of his very life-forces *(élan-vital)* enables him to continue living with a renewed sense of purpose. What had become weak with the passage of time, has now been made strong. What had become lifeless, has been revitalized. What had become tasteless and filled with drudgery, has been enriched [Long 1972: 37].

Of particular interest is the fact that these goals are achieved in part through a ritualized reformation of the senses. The act of fasting, for instance,

> is merely a means of promoting control of the senses and of restraining them from wandering in search of deluded objects. The withdrawal of food from the physical body is conducive to the starvation of lust, greed and envy, so that the mind and heart may be pure abodes for Divinity [Long 1972: 38].

A comparable reworking of the senses is evident in a Hindu pilgrimage to visit Lord Ayyappan, who resides on a mountain known as Sabari Malai in central Kerala. As chronicled by E. Valentine Daniel (1984), an anthropologist who participated in one of the annual pilgrimages, the pilgrimage, symbolically a progressive movement from a state of physical, mental, and spiritual lethargy to one of equipoise, salvation, and perfect knowledge, involves and demands the overcoming of the five corporeal senses and eight *ragas* or negative emotions (which might be glossed as 'lust', 'jealousy', 'avarice', 'presumptuousness', 'arrogance', 'persistence', and 'showiness' (Daniel 1984: 270). One way that these hindering senses and emotions are overcome is through the arduous physical and mental exertions required of the pilgrim: elaborate preparations, including vows of austerity prior to beginning the journey; ritual defecation and urination in the company of other pilgrims; and a painful climb up the mountain all to the transformation of the pilgrim's emotional and spiritual sensibilities. As one pilgrim recounted to Daniel, 'At one moment everything is pain. But at the next moment everything is love *(anpu)*. Everything is love for the Lord' (Daniel 1984: 269). As is the case elsewhere, the significance of the often formalized 'list' of seven or eight ragas, which one may hear from Sufis in Bangladesh as often as Vaishnavite Hindus in Tamil Nadu, is its construction of key emotional aspects of human nature as objects to be transformed by religious discipline.

Many healing rites in South Asia work directly to alter the emotional make-up of people understood to be ill. In Sri Lanka, Sinhalese Buddhists rely on a set of ritual exorcisms to sever the relationship between a patient and demons and ghosts who have caught that person in their 'gaze' (Kapferer 1979; 1983). Exorcists themselves point out that their cures derive not only from their ability to magically sever the link between patients and demons and bring the demons under control with the aid of various deities, but also from their ability to 'change the emotional and mental condition of the patient' (Kapferer 1979: 156). They achieve such a change by inducing an atmosphere of emotional quiet through ritual and symbolic means and by weakening the hold of the demonic through dramatic, musical, and comic performances that first present demons in their frightening, terrifying aspect but then show their absurd, comic, and foolish characteristics. In all, 'a shift in mood' is established that enables the patient to laugh once again, to redefine reality in accord with the conceptions of healthy others at the rite, and to escape the disquieting, frightening wrath of the demonic.

Among the Yolmo Sherpa of north-central Nepal, shamanic healers try to alleviate bouts of 'soul loss' and other maladies through a range of ritual practices. In a typical night-long healing performance shamans will try, among other things, to divine the causes of a patient's illness, 'cut' pain and disease from a patient's body, and recover lost life forces. Several of these acts tie directly into the patient's emotional world. Oracular divinations, for instance, often 'show' the hidden emotional turmoil of patients and other family members; one shaman's divination revealed that a young woman was suffering from illness-spawning 'confusion' and 'anxiety' at the hands of her in-laws' family (Desjarlais 1992: 169–84). 'Soul-calling' rites, in turn, work ostensibly to retrieve lost life forces that are wandering the landscape. Yet, by creating a powerfully charged world of music, taste, sight, touch, and kinesthesia, in which the patient's mind, body, and senses are 'awakened', the rites also help to change how the patient feels, negating a sensibility bound by dysphoric spiritlessness and creating a new one of vitality, mindful presence, and emotional well-being (Desjarlais 1992: 198–222; 1996). Significantly, many of those susceptible to 'soul loss' and other spiritual afflictions end up summoning a shaman several times a year. The need for repeated cures suggests that Yolmo shamans are more adept all alleviating the symptoms of distress by reforming the emotional and sensory worlds of their clients than they are at addressing the social, psychological, and biological roots of such distress.

Another important medium for the articulation and potential transformation of emotions among Yolmo are the *tsher glu* or 'songs of pain' that villagers sing and dance to at funerals or during other religious or communal events (Desjarlais 1992: 90–134). These songs, which often speak of sentiments of tsher *ka* or 'heartache', can work simultaneously to express a person's or community's feelings of distress and sadness, outline the semantic and moral connotations of such feelings, and teach children and youth how to both feel and 'hide' one's feelings in culturally appropriate ways. The poetics of some songs also have the potential to move singers and listeners from a state of grief or despair to one of contentment and well-being.

Several other anthropologists find that South Asian laments are sites for the social construction of emotion, gender, and power (Zbavitel 1961; Wadley 1983; Vaudeville 1986; and Wilce 1998b). In ritualized weeping (and, to some extent, in rarefied literary reflections, such as *bilap, baramasya,* and *zarigan*) affect as sentiment can be displayed via culturally recognized and shared aesthetic traditions. Far from being idiosyncratic, lament performances at times of death or separation embody convention, representing the linguistic code as well as 'symbols of excess' (Das 1986: 197f). For example, brides are expected not only to performatively demonstrate their grief in leaving their natal families but also follow traditional forms of expression in doing so. Laments ritually express not only sadness but romantic or sexual desire (Vaudeville 1986) as well as rage and resistance to power (Wilce 1998a, 1998b). They can thus serve as social protests that might otherwise be inexpressible by women and other subalterns. Although associated by South Asians (and others around the world) with women, ethnographic observations of men's and women's emotion performances and accompanying discursive evaluations reveal an ideological dimension to that gendering.

Das reports from the Punjab that 'it is not that women feel more grief than men. It is rather that the culture allows and even enjoins upon them the obligation to display symbols of excess. Whatever the personal grief that a man may feel, immobility and silence are the only languages available to men' (1986: 198). Going somewhat further, we would argue that when men do weep—as Das also notes they do—or even verbalize laments (Wilce 1998b) they may not only be 'admonished' but their behaviour is also soon forgotten in the semiotic reduction of complexity that 'gender' entails.

Gender, The Colonial Legacy, and Ideologies of Emotion

Ideologies, in fact, constrain the experience and discursive projection of gender and emotion in such broad ways that we must conclude by noting the positioning of all discourse regarding emotion in formerly colonized nations, especially the emotions attributed to subaltern groups in South Asia. Emotion is, in fact, a construction not only in the 'environmental' sense but also in the 'ideological' sense that discourses about the emotionality of others can be invidious and often reflect the West's dichotomization of thought and feeling, its valorization of rationality, and its relegation of emotion to the subjugated feminine.

Whatever their origin, such ideologies of emotion are influential in South Asia; the construction of affectivity *per se* has reflected dominant cultural forces in India. Emotionalism is pervasively associated with lower-status groups by both Muslims and Hindus. According to Patricia Jeffery (1979), Pirzada women, wives of the caretakers of an important Sufi shrine in Old Delhi, were 'derisive' when told how a non-Pirzada woman visiting the shrine went into a trance, swinging her loosened hair until it whipped those nearby. 'Only ignorant women who don't know any better go into ecstacy' (Jeffrey 1979: 95). The definition of self of these Pirzada women requires 'reserve and diffidence' and careful attention to avoidance rituals, even between the generations of women. These 'requirements' are reminiscent of Carstairs's image of high-caste Hindus; comparing a high-caste Hindu village with a Bhil village not far from it, Carstairs concludes that the Bhils are as 'spontaneous [and] violent[ly] ebullien[t]' as high-caste Hindus are 'controlled [and] inhibited' (1958: 136).

Similarly, among the Hindus of Bengal, certain forms of ecstatic religion, including healing and possession *(bhar)*, are so closely associated with women and the lower castes, that high-caste ecstatics attempt to place semantic distance between their experience and practice, which is understood to involve divine emotion or bhava, and that of disdained groups, which is understood to involve bhar or possession (McDaniel 1990). Emotionality is contrasted with the ideal of self-control to which persons in prestige categories seem to strive. This has strong parallels in other parts of the world, such as Senegal, West Africa, where affectivity in speech styles is strongly associated with a stance of submissiveness by association of that expressive style with low-status 'griots' whose hereditary occupation included praising members of the noble caste. (Irvine 1990). As Allen and Mukherjee (1982) see it, women's options can be constrained by this negative cultural construction of emotionalism, since they can choose to reject the value system (restraint, self-control, ritual purity, etc.) that renders women polluted, but to do so links them with others (including ecstatics) who have rejected caste but have not achieved status in the society at large.

The intersection in Bangladesh of forces including urbanization, 'tradition', 'modernity', global-media penetration, and Islamization has produced new discourses on emotion and new lifestyles that threaten the vitality of once valued genres of emotional expression. The lament genres mentioned earlier are now associated not only with women but with the less-educated rural classes, and are performed in Dhaka only by recent rural immigrants. Along with wept 'song', ludic songs once sung during that part of weddings knows as *gaye halud*–richly emotional, seditiously celebratory songs which provided a venue for women to challenge structures of gender and sexuality (see Raheja and Gold 1994)—are also vanishing. So are the evocative genres of tale telling which were, like ballads, once performed tunefully. An oft-heard ideological critique of funerary laments draws on Islamic prohibitions of 'loud' wailing over the passing of one of God's people as well as to fears that the passage of the departed soul will be disturbed by such wailing. In general, artistic and resistant expressions and celebrations of emotion are yielding to demystified rationality; silent weeping at death in Dhaka represents the new order of affective control and interiority. At the same time, discourses of selflessness, a normative standard to which Bangladeshi women in particular are often held, ideologically render emotional self-assertion 'mad' and define 'madness' as emotionalistic self-indulgence. This reminds us of the situatedness of ideological assertions about relationality versus individuality as characteristic of this or that group.

Links between a history of colonial domination and emotions (particularly 'violent emotion') are complex enough to invite syntheses of psychoanalytic interpretation with critical sociology. Nandy (1983) and

Kakar (1996) combine the perspectives of clinical-psychoanalytic practice and historiography in their explorations of two, seemingly unrelated themes: the construction of identity among colonizers and the colonized, and the roots of communalism and communal rioting. These exemplify, respectively, what we are calling 'ideological' and 'environmental' takes on the construction of emotion in India. Paralleling Nandy's approach, Sanjay Joshi (1995) argues that a strong (middle) class base for communalist voices fills those voices with contradiction, trapping the discourse of communalism within another, of liberalism and reason, while projecting violent passions onto the Other. Joshi and Nandy stress how colonialist representations of power, which identified Europeans with masculinity and placed masculinity above femininity and androgyny in a hierarchy of gendered selfhood, potentiated angry assertions of virility through nationalism and communalism. Kakar (1996), in turn, finds that the roots of communal violence lie in a social identity that is, for him, no less primal and unconscious than individual identity. Like Carstairs (1958) before him, Kakar traces the production of hostility to intra-psychic 'splitting' of good and bad selves and the projection of the bad self onto other objects, persons, and groups. Capitalizing on the unconscious formation of personal and social identity, religious demagogues are thus able to rekindle primal identification with one's own group and paranoid hatred of the Other.

In general, analyses such as these help explain defensive masculinity, the arousal of violent passions, and 'emotionalism'—or at least its pejoration and projection onto lower-status groups by higher ones—as reactions to domination by Others. Entwistle (1987), Hein (1982; 1986), and O'Connell (1976) attribute the rise of emotionalism in Indian religion (bhakti) to the frustration of Hindu political fortunes under Muslim domination, while Nandy and Joshi treat Hindu expressions of 'virile' rage as a response to western constructions of gender and power. It is important, however, to work towards a model that would encompass the indigenous and exogenous roots not only of particular sentiments and passions but also of class- and caste-based stances towards emotion and emotionalism. The model to strive for would also 'gender Orientalism' (Lewis 1996) or our understandings of shifting historical productions of emotion in India. Such attempts have recently been made by Menon (1993), who describes how the sufferings of women who were raped and abducted by the Other at the time of the Partition became key symbols to be rhetorically manipulated for political gain (a theme that had been exploited in Indo-English literature since the Raj), (Paxton 1992; see also Das 1996). The model whose pieces are on the table but whose whole is projected here, is one that questions essentializations of emotion while also rethinking such ideas as 'emotion in India is relational'.

REFERENCES

Allen, Michael and S.N. Mukherjee. 1982. *Women in India and Nepal*. Canberra: Australian National University.

Appadurai, Arjun. 1990. 'Topographies of the Self: Praise and Emotion in Hindu India'. In L. Abu-Lughod and C. Lutz, ed., *Language and the Politics of Emotion*, 92–112. Cambridge: Cambridge University Press.

Banerji, Bibhutibhushan. 1968. *Pather Panchali*. Trans. T.W. Clark and Tarapada Mukherji. Bloomington: Indiana University Press.

Bhat, G.K. 1984. *Rasa Theory and Allied Problems*. Baroda: The M.S. University of Baroda.

Blanchet, Thérèse. 1984. *Women, Pollution and Marginality: Meanings and Rituals of Birth in Rural Bangladesh*. Dhaka: The University Press.

Bose, Pradip Kumar. 1995. 'Sons of the Nation: Child Rearing in the New Family'. In Partha Chatterjee, ed., *Texts of Power: Emerging Disciplines in Colonial Bengal*, 118–43. Minneapolis: University of Minnesota Press.

Carstairs, G. Morris. 1958. *The Twice-born: A Study of a Community of High-caste Hindus*. London: Hogarth Press.

Carstairs, G. Morris and R.L. Kapur. 1976. *The Great Universe of Kota: Stress, Change and Mental Disorder in an Indian Village*. Berkeley: University of California Press.

Daniel, Valentine, E. 1984. *Fluid Signs: Being a Person the Tamil Way*. Berkeley: University of California Press.

Das, Veena. 1986. 'The Work of Mourning: Death in a Punjabi Family'. In Merry I. White and Susan Pottack, eds, *The Cultural Transition: Humen Experience and Social Transformation in the Third World and Japan*, 179–210. Boston: Routledge Kegan Paul.

———. 1996. 'Language and the Body: Transactions in the Construction of Pain'. *Daedalus*. 125:67–92.

Derné, Steve. 1995a. *Culture in Action: Family Life, Emotion, and Male Dominance in Banaras, India*. Albany: State University of New York Press.

———. 1995b. 'Popular Culture and Emotional Experiences: Rituals of Filmgoing and the Reception of Emotion Culture'. In C. Ellis and M. Flaherty, eds, *Social Perspectives on Emotion*, vol. 3, 171–97. Greenwich, CT: JAI Press.

Desjarlais, Robert. 1992. *Body and Emotion: The Aesthetics of Illness and Healing in the Nepal Himalayas*. Philadelphia: University of Pennsylvania Press.

———. 1996. 'Presence'. In C. Laderman and M. Roseman, eds, *The Performance of Healing*, 143–64. New York: Routledge Press.

Dimock, Edward, Edwin Gerow, C.M. Naim, A.K. Ramanujan, Gordon Roadarmel, and J.A.B. van Buitenen. 1974. *The Literatures of India: An Introduction*. Chicago: University of Chicago Press.

Dumont Louis. 1970. *Homo Hierarchicus*. Chicago: University of Chicago Press.

Entwistle, A.W. 1987. *Braj: Centre of Krishna Pilgrimage*. Groningent: Egbert Forsten.

Ewing, Katherine P. 1990: 'The Illusion of Wholeness: Culture, Self and the Experience of Inconsistency'. *Ethos*. 18(3):251–78.

———. 1991. 'Can Psychoanalytic Theories Explain the Pakistani Woman? Intrapsychic Autonomy and Interpersonal Engagement in the Extended Family'. *Ethos*. 19:131–60.

Gerow, Edwin 1974a. 'The Dhvani School of Criticism'. In Edward Dimock et al., eds, *The Literatures of India: An Introduction*, 136–43. Chicago: University of Chicago Press.

———. 1974b. 'The Persistence of Classical Esthetic Categories in Contemporary Indian Literature: Three Bengali Novels'. In Edward Dimock et al., eds, *The Literatures of India: An Introduction*, 212–38. Chicago: University of Chicago Press.

Hein, Norvin. 1982. 'Comments: Rādhā and Erotic Community'. In J. Stratton Hawley and D.M. Wulff, eds, *The Divine Consort: Rādhā and the Goddesses of India*, 116–24. Berkeley: Berkeley Religious Studies Series.

———. 1986. 'A Revolution in Kṛṣṇaism: The Cult of Gopāla. *History of Religions*. 25:296–317.

Hiriyanna, M. 1954. 'Art Experience-2'. *Art Experience*, 29–42. Mysore: Kavyalaya Publishers.

Irvine, Judith. 1990. 'Registering Affect: Heteroglossia in the Linguistic Expression of Emotion'. In Catherine Lutz and Lila Abu-Lughod, eds, *Language and the Politics of Emotion*, 126–61. Cambridge: Cambridge University Press.

Jeffery, Patricia. 1979. *Frogs in a Well: Indian Women in Purdah*. London: Zed Press.

Joshi, Sanjay. 1995. Empowerment and Identity: Middle Class and Hindu Communalism in Colonial Lucknow, 1880–1930'. Unpublished Dissertation, University of Pennsylvania.

Kakar, Sudhir. 1978. *The Inner World: A Psychoanalytic Study of Childhood and Society in India*. Delhi: Oxford University Press.

———. 1996. *The Colors of Violence: Cultural Identities, Religion, and Conflict*. Chicago: University of Chicago Press.

Kapferer, Bruce. 1979. 'Emotion and Feeling in Sinhalese Healing Rites'. *Social Analysis*. 1:3–19.

———. 1983. *A Celebration of Demons: Exorcism and the Aesthetics of Healing in Sri Lanka*. Oxford, Washington, D.C.: Berg/Smithsonian Institution.

Kurtz, Stanley N. 1992. *All the Mothers Are One: Hindu India and the Cultural Reshaping of Psychoanalysis*. New York: Columbia University Press.

Lacan, Jacques. 1977. *Écrit: A Selection*. Trans. A. Sheridan. New York: W.W. Norton.

Lewis, Reina. 1996. *Gendering Orientalism: Race, Femininity and Representation*. London: Routledge.

Long, J. Bruce. 1972. 'Festival of Repentance: A Study of Mahāśivarātri'. *Journal of the Oriental Institute*. 22:15–38.

Lynch, Owen M. 1990. 'The Social Construction of Emotion in India'. In O. Lynch, ed., *Divine Passions: The Social Construction of Emotion in India*, 3–34. Berkeley: University of California.

Mauss, Marcel. [1935] 1973. 'Techniques of the Body'. Trans. Ben Brewster. *Economy and Society*. 2(1):70–88. (Originally published in *Journal de psychologie normal et pathologigue*. Paris: Année. 32:271–930).

McDaniel, June. 1990. *The Madness of the Saints: Ecstatic Religion in Bengal*. Chicago: University of Chicago Press.

McHugh, Ernestine. 1989. 'Concepts of the Person among the Gurungs of Nepal'. *American Ethnologist*. 16:75–86.

Mead, Margaret. 1928. *Coming of Age in Samoa*. New York: Mentor.

Menon, Ritu. 1993. 'Her Body and Her Being: The Dispute over the Abducted Woman in Post-Partition in India'. Paper presented at the Association for Asian Studies, Annual Meeting, Los Angeles.

Minturn, Leigh and John Hitchcock. 1963. 'The Rājpūts of Khalapur, India'. In B. Whiting, ed., *Six Cultures: Studies of Child Rearing*, 203–361. New York: John Wiley and Sons.

Minturn, Leigh and William Lambert. 1964. *Mothers of Six Cultures: Antecedents of Child Rearing*. New York: John Wiley and Sons.

Mullick, M.S.I., M.E. Karim, and M. Khanam. 1994. 'Depression in Self-Harm Patients'. *Bangladesh Medical Research Council Bulletin*. 20(3):123–8.

Naim, C.M. 1974. 'Ghazal and Taghazzul'. In E. Dimock et al., eds, *The Literatures of India: An Introduction*, 181–97. Chicago: University of Chicago Press.

Nandy, Ashis. 1983. *The Intimate Enemy: Loss and Recovery of Self under Colonialism*. Delhi: Oxford University Press.

Nichter, Mark. 1981. 'Idioms of Distress: Alternatives in the Expression of Psychosocial Distress: A Case Study from South India'. *Culture, Medicine, and Psychiatry*. 5:379–408.

Obeyesekere, Gananath. 1974. 'Pregnancy Cravings (Dola-duka) in Relation to Social Structure and Personality in a Sinhalese village'. In R. Levine, ed., *Culture and Personality*, 202–21. Chicago: Aldine.

_____. 1981. *Medusa's Hair: An Essay on Personal Symbols and Religious Experience*. Chicago: University of Chicago Press.

_____. 1984. *The Cult of the Goddess Pattini*. Chicago: University of Chicago Press.

_____. 1985. 'Depression, Buddhism, and the Work of Culture in Sri Lanka'. In A. Kleinman and B. Good, eds, *Culture and Depression*, 134–52. Berkeley: University of California Press.

_____. 1990. *The Work of Culture: Symbolic Transformation in Psychoanalysis and Anthropology*. Chicago: University of Chicago Press.

O'Connell, Joseph T. 1976. 'Caitanya's followers and the Bhagavad Gita'. In Bardwell E. Smith, ed., *Hinduism: New Essays in the History of Religion*, 33–52. Leiden: E.J. Brill.

Parish, Stephen. 1994. *Moral Knowing in a Hindu Sacred City: An Exploration of Mind, Emotion, and Self*. New York: Columbia University Press.

Paxton, Nancy. 1992. 'Mobilizing Chivalry: Rape in British Novels about the Indian Uprising of 1857'. *Victorian Studies*. 36:5–30.

Raheja, Gloria Goodwin and Ann Grodzins Gold. 1994. *Listen to the Heron's Words: Reimagining Gender and Kinship in North India*. Berkeley: University of California Press.

Rao, A. Venkoba. 1984. 'Depressive Illness in India'. *Indian Journal of Psychiatry*. 26:301–11.

Rohner, Ronald and Manjusri Chaki-Sircar. 1988. *Women and Children in a Bengali Village*. Hanover and London: University Press of New England.

Roland, Alan. 1988. *In Search of Self in India and Japan: Toward a Cross-Cultural Psychology*. Princeton: Princeton University Press.

Seymour, Susan. 1975. 'Child Rearing in India: A Case Study in Change and
    Modernization'. In T.R. Williams, ed., *Socialization and Communication in Primary
    Groups*, 1–58. The Hague: Mouton.
_____. 1983. 'Household Structure and Status and Expressions of Affect in India'. *Ethos.*
    11:263–77.
Shweder, Richard A. 1985. 'Menstrual Pollution, Soul Loss, and the Comparative Study of
    Emotions'. In A. Kleinman and B. Good, eds, *Culture and Depression*, 182–215.
    Berkeley: University of California Press.
Sullivan, Bruce M. 1996. 'Paradise Polluted: Religious Dimensions of the Vrindavana
    Ecology Movement'. In R. Gottlieb, ed., *This Sacred Earth: Religion, Nature,
    Environment*, 565–71. London: Routledge.
_____. Forthcoming. 'Theology and Ecology at the Birthplace of Kṛṣṇa'. In L. Nelson,
    ed., *Ecological Concern in South Asian Religion*. Albany, NY: State University of
    New York Press.
Trawick, Margaret. 1988. 'Spirits and Voices in Tamil Songs'. *American Ethnologist.*
    15:193–215.
_____. 1990. *Notes on Love in a Tamil Family*. Berkeley: University of California.
Tyler, Stephen. 1984. 'The Vision Quest in the West, or What the Mind's Eye Sees'.
    Journal of Anthropological Research. 40:23–40.
Ulrich, Helen. 1987. 'A Study of Change and Depression among Havik Brahmin Women in
    a South Indian Village'. *Culture, Medicine, and Psychiatry*. 11:261–87.
Vatuk, Sylvia. 1982. 'Forms of Address in the North Indian Family: An Exploration of the
    Cultural Meaning of Kin Terms'. In Á Östör, L. Fruzzetti, and S. Barnett, eds,
    Concepts of Person: Kinship, Caste and Marriage in India, 118–42. Cambridge, MA:
    Harvard University Press.
Vaudeville, Charlotte. 1986. *Bārahmāsā in Indian Literatures: Songs of the Twelve Months
    in Indo-Aryan Literatures*. Delhi: Motilal Banarsidass.
Wadley, Susan. 1983. 'The Rains of Estrangement: Understanding the Hindu Yearly Cycle'.
    Contributions to Indian Sociology. 17:51–85.
Whiting, Beatrice and John Whiting. 1975. *Children of Six Cultures: A Psycho-Cultural
    Analysis*. Cambridge: Harvard University Press.
Wilce, James M. 1997. 'Discourse, Power, and the Diagnosis of Weakness: Encountering
    Practitioners in Bangladesh'. *Medical Anthropology Quarterly*. 11(3):352–74.
_____. 1998a: 'The Pragmatics of "Madness.": Performance Analysis of a Bangladeshi
    Woman's "Aberrant" Lament'. *Culture, Medicine, and Psychiatry*. 22(1):1–54.
_____. 1998b. *Eloquence in Trouble: The Poetics and Politics of Complaint in Rural
    Bangladesh*. Oxford Studies in Anthropological Linguistic. Wm. Bright, ed. New
    York: Oxford University Press.
Wittgenstein, Ludwig. 1953. *Philosophical Investigations*. Trans. G.E.M. Anscombe. New
    York: Macmillan.
Wulff, Donna. 1995. 'The Play of Emotion: *Līlākīrtan* in Bengal'. In W. Sax, ed., *The
    Gods at Play: Līlā in South Asia*, 99–114. Oxford: Oxford University Press.
Zbavitel, Dusan. 1961. 'The Development of the Baromasi in the Bengali Literature'.
    Archiv Orientalni. 29:583–619.

8

Economic Arrangements

This section on economic arrangements opens with a chapter by Surinder Jodhka on agrarian structures. Debates on the peasantry in eastern and central Europe were concerned with the place of the peasantry within class analysis and the importance of the peasant household as a unit of both production and consumption in agriculture. Such debates influenced the Marxist approaches to peasantry in India. In contrast, the peasantry as a class was not the focus in American sociology. There, studies in agricultural innovation and rural social structure were located in the sub-discipline of rural sociology which was developed in polytechnics and agricultural extension schools in North America and was then incorporated in the curricula of sociology in Indian universities and agricultural extension schools as well. Village studies in India had a somewhat different focus, concerned as these were with questions of caste hierarchy and the relation between great and little traditions. While disciplinary influences are important, it is also essential to keep in mind that the empirical impetus for gathering detailed data on patterns of landholding, cropping, agricultural labour, and rural indebtedness in the colonial period came from the needs of revenue collection and governance. The wide range of topics covered under official commissions of inquiry, ranging from reasons for peasant indebtedness to the description of irrigation practices, provides rich documentation on many of these issues.

The complex pattern of knowledge/power relations came to the fore in the formation of landholding patterns in different regions in India. Jodhka shows how British decisions on land settlement were influenced both by the nature of debates on ownership and control in the metropolitan centres and by the experience with revenue extraction in the colonies. Questions of rural unrest, peasant indebtedness, and the interest in surplus extraction engaged the British, but the governmental techniques of dealing with these issues were subject to continuous experimentation—they were not put in place once and for all. Thus the experience with the permanent settlement in Bengal and the problems with governance it created led to the adoption of a different system of land tenure (the *ryotwari* system) in parts of southern and western India. This was followed by the *malguzari* tenure system in parts of Punjab and the Central Provinces. Under this system, the village was treated as a collectivity for revenue purposes.

Modes of agricultural organization are tied to issues of food security and famines in India, as Jodhka shows. The pressure on land, the cash needs of households especially in areas where cash revenue payments were enforced by the British, and the development of markets severely affected traditional arrangements of food security. Jodhka provides an excellent overview of the changing political and intellectual context of debates on modes of production in agriculture. The emergence of categories such as semi-feudal modes of production dominated discussion in the seventies. The impact of the green revolution on capitalization of agriculture engaged scholars in this period but its long term impact on class relations in rural areas and on environmental degradation developed only as changes in agriculture became more entwined with new regional and social inequalities. Jodhka's overview of these issues also shows us the complex relation between the categories of caste and class; the interweaving of ritual and economic practices, and the complex regional patterns of differential developments in the postcolonial period in India. The green revolution is an important site for examining the importance of global practices and transnational policies and programs for changes in Indian agriculture. With some exceptions, though, there has been less attention paid to this in the analysis of the green revolution.

Against the notion of the unchanging village, Jodhka's paper argues for a closer understanding of peasant resistance and peasant movements. While studies of peasantry have taken the relation between state and village as a central problematic, the specific historical context of peasant mobilization as part of the nationalist movement shows the role of the peasantry in anti-colonial movements. Read along with the papers on the village, social ecology, and social movements respectively, this paper provides an important overview of the peasantry in relation to economic and political life in India.

The twin processes of industrialization and urbanization have been classically placed at the moment of the origin of modernity in social science literature. Narayan Sheth gives us a chronology of the important moments in the process of industrialization. Despite a rich history of crafts and markets for trade much before the advent of the East India Company, the technological and organizational changes consequent on the introduction of coal mining, introduction of railways and setting up of textile mills in the first half of the nineteenth century, constituted the beginning of industrial production and its associated social processes. These marked an important rupture in economic and social arrangements. Sheth argues that changes in the landholding patterns and decline of food security in peasant households led to pauperized peasants seeking work in the new industrial centers. Yet we know that rural to urban migration was not simply a process of unanchored pauperized rural labour drifting into urban centers. Sheth shows the complex ways in which labour recruitment practices came to be linked to village institutions. For instance, rural–urban networks of caste and kinship were important for the *pattern* of movements between rural and urban areas. In addition, recruitment practices of industrial labour in which middlemen played a crucial role depended upon activation of such networks between town and village. Since the industrial labour force in India was never completely severed from its rural moorings, many of the so-called 'problems' of industrialization such as absence of labour commitment were traced to the continuing hold of the village on urban migrants. Sheth's acute analysis shows that such problems as that of labour absenteeism were not only highly exaggerated but were generated as much by employer policies of recruitment and retention as by continued links with the village. In any case, concerns with the creation of a disciplined labour force led to the appointment of several official commissions on industrial labour, sponsored by the colonial state. These constitute an important archive for documenting the processes of industrialization. As an archive, these texts reveal the underlying processes of state formation and also tell us about the conditions of industrial labour.

The industrial proletariat is the motor of history in Marxist teleology—it comes to represent *correctly* the course of history through its position in the processes of production. It is therefore interesting to see the effect that the experimentation with alternatives (such as the Gandhian ideology of trust) had on the trade-union movement in India—especially with respect to anti-colonial struggles and national politics. Over the years, however, Sheth feels that trade unions have lost their pivotal role in aligning the worker movements with broader social movements despite their formal alignment with party politics. He argues that managerial and state practices, on the one hand, and bitter union rivalries, on the other, led to a steady decline in the role played by worker movements in the representation of worker interests in national politics. The emergence of labour movements in the unorganized sector marks an important shift in our understanding of worker movements. Far from being seen simply as the lumpen proletariat, various categories of workers in the informal economic sector such as hawkers, self-employed women, and children employed in small-scale industry have entered into contests over rights and entitlements within the democratic framework of politics in India. Since the organized labour force constitutes only two per cent of the total labour force, it is the struggles for worker rights within the unorganized or informal sector and its alliance with non-governmental organizations that seem most important for securing worker rights. This is particularly important in view of the fact that the labour of women and children was socially devalued, resulting in a lack of voice within trade unions.

As in the case of the green revolution in the agricultural sector, the emergence of new technology (especially information technology) in industry is also an important site for examining the way that global changes are affecting economic arrangements in India. Kuriakose Mamkoottam explores the changes brought about by information technology in managerial practices, the shop floor, and the nature of temporality at the workplace. Flexibility is considered to be the hallmark of this technology. This is reflected in changes in processes of task allocation, workforce composition, and flexible financial networks, all of which have jointly changed the relations between management and labour. The strict division between home and work and the rigid working day have given place to a variety of managerial and labour arrangements. However, there is tremendous variation in the way that this technology has influenced the different sectors of the economy. Trade union responses have also varied—ranging from active resistance to the new technologies to new demands for flexible training to develop worker expertise. Unfortunately sociological work on new technologies in the workplace is still rudimentary. It seems while flexibility is introduced in some spheres, in others there is enhanced surveillance through new technologies, such as the extensive use of e-mail to monitor worker time. How notions of work and the construction of subject positions change in relation to information technology is an inviting area of research.

The importance of the informal sector in the Indian economy has been alluded to earlier. Jan Breman points out in his chapter that one cannot talk about strict demarcation between the formal and informal structures of the economy. Instead, he proposes that the capitalist transformation of the urban milieu has created a variety of economic activities and economic arrangements that have created a workforce of irregularly working people who are at the bottom of the economic hierarchy. The size and composition of this sector are hard to calculate, both because of lack of terminological clarity and because these economic actors are not part of a stable economic regime. Yet those engaged in work in the informal sector are not only the self-employed. They may also be part of the industrial workforce, receiving wages on piecemeal basis. Or they may work in the expanding service sector, employed both in the private and public sectors, but on an irregular basis. Various employment practices in the formal sector keep them as temporary workers, thus depriving them of any legal entitlements. Most Indians working in urban areas are familiar with the practice of various institutions (including governmental ones) of employing casual labour for long periods of time. The legal rights and entitlements of such groups have been the subject of some important judicial interventions. For instance, the right of hawkers to particular parts of pavements in order to carry on their trade has been recognized by the Supreme Court—this has, however, not stopped sporadic governmental actions to 'clean' up the city, leading to displacement of hawkers. The relation established between the economic actors in this sector and the state is manifested at several levels, but is especially visibility in interactions with the street-level bureaucracies such as the police or food inspectors who become recipients of rent in the form of bribes. Thus it may be inappropriate to classify the range of activities and varieties of relations to the state under these economic arrangements as part of the informal sector, especially if it leads to the perception that this sector is outside the formal sector. Breman shows us both the precariousness of the lives of those who survive through work in this sector and also the economic opportunities it presents to the marginal urban populations. Once we move to questions of policy for improving the position of the rural and urban poor, and consider what kind of alternatives are available for ameliorating the hardships of poverty, it becomes imperative to engage with questions of organization. In his thought-provoking contribution, Pranab Bardhan asks whether the move to greater decentralization advocated by many critics of development paradigms would deliver the results that are expected. By a careful comparison with other countries, Bardhan concludes that decentralization in itself is not sufficient for the empowerment of the poor for if local communities are divided according to the existing fault lines of caste, class and gender differentiation. Indeed, as an economist Bardhan is interested in general models of development and decentralization but he is also one of the few economists who takes the question of local power structures into account in showing the limits of arguments that do not take the difficulties of implementation of particular policies into account.

The linkages between rural and urban networks and also the movement through trade and commerce depend on the central role of the market in the economic and social arrangements in the country. Monetary transactions are not only important but are dispersed over several kinds of sites ranging from large economic and commercial institutions to the peasant household. Yet as Denis Vidal writes in his chapter on the markets, these processes have been neglected because of the belief that markets are a recent imposition on traditional forms of sociality. In critiquing this view, Vidal points to the widespread practices in which money has been incorporated within ritual and caste practices so that monetary transactions, though having a strong economic component, are not seen as strictly economic activities between anonymous actors. Simmel's influence on social theory had led many to believe that there is suspicion of money in all traditional cultures, for as a symbol of modernity that reduces difference to a single measure, it has the potential to dissolve the close ties forged traditionally through exchanges in other mediums. Drawing from the literature on gift exchange in India, Vidal shows that gift exchange differs from money exchange in that the former is marked by a series of highly ambivalent implications of self and other. Thus one cannot presume a clear a priori equivalence between tradition, habit, and gift exchange on the one hand, and novelty, modernity and monetary exchange, on the other. Vidal argues for the importance of empirically studying the different circuits of exchange in order to see what kinds of sociality they embody. Because food was traditionally been seen as the principle example of an object of consumption that is destroyed once it reaches the hands of the final consumer, we have few studies that examine the relation between production and consumption as contiguous and on-going activities as is the case for other objects of consumption. In the case of objects other than food, consumption is not an act in which the object is destroyed—rather it becomes a point in which new social trajectories are entered and elaborated through socially informed practices of consuming and even reproducing the object in a new mode. This is true not only for such cultural objects as cinema or poetry but also for material objects such as clothes.

Vidal draws attention to social and cultural specificity by showing that in the Indian case brokerage plays a central role in the constitution of the market itself. Thus, behind the final act of the exchange between the seller and the buyer in the market there are vast chains of linkage through practices of brokerage that traverse networks along social trajectories. Vidal's argument is important because it shows that we cannot think of production as the central moment in the economic processes and consumption as secondary. Rather, production and consumption are mutually implicated at every moment of the economic and social process.

Mario Rutten in his chapter argues that studies of entrepreneurship in India have been thwarted by undue emphasis on the Weberian question—namely whether capitalist development was impeded by Indian religions. The famous (or infamous) thesis proposed by Max Weber, that Indian religions were not conducive to the development of the ever-watchful and prudent self that was engaged in worldly activities, led many to study the trader castes or groups such as the Jains or Marwaris to see whether the traditions of caste and joint family shackled them in the pursuit of rational economic activities. There were other studies in which emphasis was placed on the ways in which the colonial experience obstructed the development of indigenous industrial capital or threw up aberrant types of entrepreneurship in India. However, Rutten argues that there is paucity of empirical studies on entrepreneurship. The experience of South East Asia, that is both its recent success and its trauma, should encourage studies of the various ways in which economic reasoning operates in different social and cultural milieus. It is obvious that forms of economic reasoning are strongly enmeshed in different forms of sociality but these need to be demonstrated empirically.

Together, these chapters would lead us to examine the forms of economic reasoning deployed by social actors both in terms of cultural and social factors in a dynamic social context. Rather than assuming that culture gives scripts to social actors that determine behaviour, one has to see how social actors placed within changing political and economic scenarios are able to improvise and act. From the survival strategies of the poor to the economic innovations of the old and new entrepreneurial classes, this is a rich area in which new problems are emerging and need to be addressed.

Agrarian Structures and Their Transformations

Surinder Jodhka

All economic activity is carried out in a framework of social relationships. Production is organized socially, markets function as social institutions, and consumption patterns are shaped by social norms and cultural values. Agriculture is no exception. The institutional framework of agricultural production determines how and by whom land is cultivated, what kinds of crops can be produced and for what purpose, how food and agricultural incomes can be distributed, and in what way or on what terms the agrarian sector is linked to rest of the economy/society.

However, agrarian structures and their transformations have not been the major concern of sociologists and social anthropologists. Western sociology, since the days of its classical traditions, has remained preoccupied with the study of social life in urban-industrial societies. As Shanin rightly points out, in its most fundamental self-image, the western capitalist world defined itself as a 'world without peasants'. The division of societies into 'modern' and 'backward' in the evolutionist schema of early social theory also meant that conceptually the agrarian populations, or the peasants, were reduced to an unspecified part of the mixed bag of 'remainders of the past' (Shanin 1987: 468).

In their search for 'pure' and 'primitive' cultures, early practitioners of social anthropology—the discipline that was supposed to study 'pre-modern' societies—invariably chose the pre-agrarian 'tribal/folk communities' for their field studies. Even when they began to look at the 'village', they viewed it as a closed, unchanging community of 'ascriptive groupings' organized around a normative belief system that essentialized it into an 'oppositional other' of the western type of modern urban societies (Inden 1990).

It was outside the mainstream western tradition of social sciences, in peripheral eastern and central Europe, that the 'agrarian question' became important on the political and intellectual agenda. The famous debate between the populist thinkers led by the Russian economist Chayanov (1987) on the one side, and the Marxist class analyses of the Russian countryside by Lenin (1899; 1908) along with Kautsky's work on the 'agrarian question' (Banaji 1976) on the other, laid the foundation of what later came to be known as 'agrarian studies'.

Though the 'Russian debate' during the early twentieth century made substantial contributions to the field, 'agrarian studies' could really take off only after the Second World War. The emergence of the 'new states' following decolonization during the post-War period played an important role in changing the research agenda of the social sciences. The most characteristic feature of the newly emerged 'Third World' countries was the dependence of large proportions of their populations on a 'stagnant' agrarian sector. The struggle for freedom from colonial rule had also developed new aspirations among the 'masses' and the 'elites' of these societies. In some of these struggles, the peasantry had played a crucial role. Thus the primary agenda for the new political regimes was the transformation of their 'backward' and stagnant economies. Though the strategies and priorities differed, 'modernization' and 'development' became common programmes in most Third World countries. It was in this historical context that 'development studies' emerged as one of the most important areas of interest in the global academy.

Since a large majority of the populations in Third World societies were directly dependent on agriculture, understanding the prevailing structures of agrarian relations and working out ways and means of transforming them emerged as important priorities within 'development studies'. Western political interest in the rural inhabitants of the Third World and the growing influence of modernization and development theories also brought with them a good deal of funding for the study of peasant economies and societies (Silverman 1987: 11). It was at this time that the concept of 'peasantry' found currency in the discipline of social anthropology. At a time when primitive tribes were either in the process of disappearing or had already disappeared, the 'discovery' of the peasantry provided a vast new field of investigation to the discipline of social anthropology (Béteille 1974b: 40).

As distinct from the isolated 'primitive communities' of tribal society, peasant communities were defined as 'part societies with part cultures' (Krober 1948). Redfield (1965) argued that peasant societies had similarities all over the world. He particularly emphasized their attachment to land and the pursuit of agriculture as a way life. Peasant societies, unlike tribal communities, also produced a surplus that was generally transferred to a dominant group of rulers in the city (Wolf 1966:4). Thus peasant society could not be seen as self-sufficient and isolated, for it was the surplus produced by peasants that partially supported the activities of rulers.

Corresponding to the idea of the peasantry having something generic about it, Shanin offered an 'ideal type' of peasant society with the following features. First, the peasant family was the basic unit of production and consumption in a multidimensional social organization. Second, land husbandry was the major means of livelihood. Third, there was a distinct traditional culture linked to the way of life of peasant communities. Fourth, an elite living outside the community dominated the peasantry (Shanin 1987: 3–5).

Whereas peasants were by definition pre-modern and hence were primarily seen as 'subject matter' for social anthropologists, or later for those in 'development studies', 'rural sociology' had come into existence in the United States much before peasant studies became popular. The civil war in the late nineteenth century and the ensuing 'farm crisis' saw the emergence of farmers' organizations demanding federal aid to solve the problems of rural areas afflicted by severe depression. Rural sociology, as an applied discipline, came into existence essentially in response to this crisis (Newby 1980: 10).

The main concern of 'rural sociology' came to be the understanding and diagnosing of the social and economic problems of farmers. More emphasis was placed on issues such as the internal structures of 'community life' and the changing composition of rural populations (Schwarzweller 1984: xi) than on their relationships with land or the social aspects of agricultural production. Theoretically, rural sociology remained caught up in bipolar notions of social change, where 'rural' often got defined as the opposite of 'urban'. 'Rurality' was conceptualized as an autonomous sociological reality (Bonnano 1989). The identification of 'rural sociology' with 'rural society' has also raised questions about its relevance in the western context where no rural areas were left anymore and almost the entire population had become urbanized (Friedland 1982: 590).

In response to these critiques of rural sociology, a new sub-discipline of sociology emerged that operated largely within the functionalist paradigm and was preoccupied with the study of the community life of rural people. This sub-discipline, known as sociology of agriculture, focused its attention on understanding and analyzing the social framework of agricultural production and the structures of relations centered around land (Friedland 1989). It raised questions about how and on what terms the agrarian sector was being integrated into the system of commodity production and about the unequal distribution of agricultural incomes and food among the different social categories of people (Friedland 1989; 1984). The sociology of agriculture also distinguished itself from 'peasant studies' on the grounds that its focus was on capitalist farming, where the production was primarily for the market, not on peasants producing for their own consumption by using family labour. Thus, it claimed more kinship with the tradition of the 'political economy' of agriculture or 'agrarian studies'. At the methodological level, historical inquiries became as relevant as ethnographic/empirical studies. This conceptual shift during the early 1970s also helped in bringing sociologists working on agrarian issues in the western countries closer to those concerned with agrarian transformations in the Third World.

This chapter is an attempt to look at the Indian agrarian context broadly from the perspective of the 'sociology of agriculture'. Though the focus is on the contemporary agrarian scene, I approach it from a historical perspective.

THE INDIAN CONTEXT

The Indian agrarian context occupies special status, both in the social scientific literature on India and in the literature on agrarian societies in general. However, unlike studies on caste, kinship, village community, or, more recently, gender, study of agrarian relations did not occupy a central position in Indian sociology. Though some sociologists, particularly those working on developmental issues, were writing on agrarian issues, it was with the publication of André Béteille's *Studies in Agrarian Social Structure* in 1974 that 'agrarian sociology' gained professional respectability within the two disciplines.

'Peasant studies', in a way, arrived in India with 'village studies'. The vastly influential collection of essays, *Village India*, edited by Marriot (1955) with its emphasis on 'little communities' and 'great communities' was brought out under the direct supervision of Robert Redfield. It is therefore interesting to see Béteille's (1974b) critique of the assumption that the village in India could conceptually be equated to peasant communities in Europe. Béteille pointed out that the Indian village was characterized by a baffling variety of land relations and a complex hierarchy of ownership rights over land. By defining 'little communities' not in relation to land but through other social institutions, such as kinship, religion, and the social organization of caste, there was a shift away from looking at the rural population in relation to agriculture and land (there were some notable exceptions to this broad trend such as Bailey 1958; Gough 1955; Mukherjee 1971). Caste hierarchy came to be defined in terms of ritual or social interaction over institutions of commensality and marriage. Nearly universal acceptance of functionalism among the social anthropologists of the 1950s made them overemphasize the need to understand what produced social order. Even when they found evidence to show that neither the village nor the caste system was an unchanging reality, it was not reflected in the overall picture of the village that they presented (Jodhka 1998). There was a perceived dualism in thinking on caste and class. Studies of land and agriculture came to be associated with the domain of economics while the sociologist/social anthropologist specialized in caste (Béteille 1974a: 7–34).

Much before village studies were initiated by professional anthropologists during the early 1950s, social life in the Indian village and its agrarian structures were extensively documented by colonial ethnographers, though, as with many other practices of colonial historiography, the accounts were written in a manner that justified colonial subjugation of India (Cohn 1987: 212). Along with the earlier writings of James Mill, Charles Metcalfe's notion of the 'Indian village community' set the tone for much of the later writing on rural India. Metcalfe, in a celebrated remark, stated that:

> the village communities are little Republics, having nearly everything they want within themselves, and almost independent of foreign relations. They seem to last where nothing else lasts. Dynasty after dynasty tumbles down; revolution succeeds revolution; Hindu, Pathan, Mughal, Mahratta, Sikh, English are masters in turn; but the village communities remain the same [quoted in Cohn 1987: 213].

This construction emphasized the fact that these communities were harmonious, relatively isolated, and, above all, unchanging, thus blocking from view the impoverishment caused by colonial policies. Perhaps the most critical element of this construct was the assumption about the absence of private ownership of land; land was thought to be owned by the village community collectively. Since there had been no private rights over land, the British believed that there would have been no significant economic differentiation in the Indian village.

Later historical research in different regions of pre-colonial India has convincingly shown that this was at best a superficial understanding of the Indian village. Since land was in abundant supply, there was no sale or purchase of land in most parts of the Indian countryside. However, not everyone had equal rights of cultivation or claims over land produce: these were instead based upon custom or upon grants made by the king (Neale 1962: 21). Irfan Habib, writing on the Mughal period, points out that these rights could even be purchased and sold (Habib 1963: 154). 'The village did not hold its land in common. Common were its officials and servants' (Neale 1962: 21).

Historians have also gathered enough evidence to show that claims that the Indian village was internally undifferentiated, self-sufficient, and stable were incorrect. According to Irfan Habib, during the Mughal period of Indian history

> economic differentiation had progressed considerably among the peasantry. There were large cultivators, using hired labour, and raising crops for the market, and there were small peasants, who could barely produce food grains for their own subsistence. Beyond this differentiation among the peasantry, there was still sharper division between the caste peasantry and the 'menial' population (Habib 1982: 247).

Dharma Kumar also argues that there was a sizeable population of those who primarily worked as agricultural labourers in pre-colonial south India and generally belonged to some specific caste group (Kumar: 1992).

The village was linked to the central authority through the revenue bureaucracy. Land revenue worked as the dominant mode of surplus appropriation during 'medieval' times. Mughal authorities discriminated between the classes of landowners while fixing the revenue demands. The larger landholders, such as *zamindars*, headmen or a favoured community, were required to pay less per unit (Kumar 1992: 239–40).

Pre-colonial agrarian relations were also not free of conflicts and tensions. Whenever the revenue demands became unbearable, the typical response of the peasantry was to flee en masse to other territories where conditions were more conducive to land cultivation (Habib 1963; Moore 1966: 332). There were also instances of the peasantry revolting against local rulers. Most of these revolts, however, were unorganized, inspired by some religious ideology or a millenarian dream (Dhanagare 1983: 29).

The notion of the '*jajmani* system' was also popularized by the colonial enthography. It tended to conceptualize agrarian social structure in the framework of exchange relations. In its classical construct, different caste groups specialized in specific occupations and exchanged their services through an elaborate system of division of labour. Though asymmetry in position of various caste groups was recognized, what it emphasized was not inequality in rights over land but the spirit of community. For instance, Wiser argued, 'Each served the other. Each in turn was master. Each in turn was servant. This system of inter relatedness in service within Hindu community was called the Hindu Jajmani system' (Wiser 1969: xxi). Central to such a construction of exchange is the idea of 'reciprocity' (Gouldner 1973: 173–220) with the implicit or explicit assumption that it was a non-exploitative system where mutual gratification was supposed to be the outcome of the reciprocal exchange (Bhattacharya 1985: 114–15).

How far is this construct correct? Later research has questioned the assumption that jajmani relations were non-exploitative. On the contrary, it has been argued that the dominant landlords used the system of hereditary obligations and occupational duties to perpetuate and legitimize the local variety of pre-capitalist/feudalistic relations (Beidelman 1959:6; Djurfeldt and Lindberg 1976:42). Moreover, what was projected as a pan-Indian reality that had been in practice since antiquity was only a local system confined to northern parts of India with a rather short history (Mayer 1993).

AGRARIAN CHANGES DURING COLONIAL RULE

Apart from theories on the Indian village produced by the colonial empire, British rule also had far-reaching material effects on the Indian countryside. It may however be relevant to stress that although British colonial rule had a significant impact on the village economy, the initial representation of the village as having been unchanging and static in earlier periods does not stand up to historical scrutiny.

After having established its political supremacy, the colonial regime initiated the task of reorganizing local society in a framework that would make governance easy and manageable. This process began with the introduction of new property rights in land. The first, and historically the most controversial, was the Permanent Settlement introduced in Bengal in 1793. Under this the intermediary zamindars (the tax-collecting officials in the earlier regime) were granted ownership rights over lands from which they previously only had the rights to collect revenues. Moore argues that apart from simplifying things, the colonial rulers saw in the local zamindars a counterpart of the 'enterprising English landlord', who, they believed, had the capacity to 'establish prosperous cultivation' if provided with secure and permanent ownership rights over land (Moore 1966: 345). Others have argued that the Permanent Settlement also had politico-strategic implications, for in the landlord the British rulers saw a possible support base in local society (Desai 1976: 39).

At least during the initial years, for the peasantry the new system just meant an increase in revenue demands. The additional economic burden also weakened the 'traditional' structure of patron–client relations between the zamindars and the local tenants, leading to a disintegration of what Scott calls 'the moral economy of the peasantry' (Scott 1976). Contrary to the expectations of the colonial rulers, Permanent Settlement accelerated and intensified the trend towards 'parasitic landlordism' (Moore 1966: 346). By the middle of the nineteenth century the entire area under Permanent Settlement was in a state of crisis.

Learning from the Bengal experience, the colonial regime tried a new arrangement in the regions of Madras, Bombay, and Berar. This came to be known as the *ryotwari* system. Under this, the actual landholders (*ryots*) were given formal proprietary rights. The ryot in theory was a tenant of the state, responsible for paying revenue directly to the state treasury, and could not be evicted as long as he paid his revenue (Baden-Powell 1892: 126). Stokes argues that the growing influence of Utilitarian philosophy in England during the time also produced distaste for landlordism and led to the introduction of new systems of revenue assessments (Stokes 1978).

Another variety of land settlement known as *mahalwari* or *malguzari* was introduced in the United Provinces, Punjab, and the Central Provinces. Under this, the village was identified as the unit of assessment. As such the mahalwari system was not very different from the ryotwari. Effective ownership of the cultivated land was vested in the cultivator here as well, but the revenue was collectively paid by the village. A villager of 'good social standing' was generally given the responsibility of collecting the revenue from individual cultivators and paying the assessment on behalf of the village.

Despite differences in arrangement, the patterns of change experienced in land relations were more or less similar in most parts of the empire. Though the new settlements changed the formal structures of authority, the colonial policies also reinforced and revitalized older, 'quasi-feudal' structures which for the peasant meant 'not less but in many cases more intensive and systematic exploitation' (Guha 1983: 7). The new land revenue systems also forced the peasants to become increasingly involved with the market, even when they did not have the capacity to produce surplus.

Commercialization of Agriculture

The expression 'commercialization of agriculture' is used to describe two related processes: first, a shift in the agrarian economy from production for consumption to production for the market; and second, a process where land starts acquiring the features of a commodity and begins to be sold and purchased in the market, like other commodities.

Though it grew both quantitatively as well as qualitatively during British rule, production for the market was not an entirely new phenomenon for Indian agriculture. As Habib points out, the big peasants during the Mughal period produced cash crops such as cotton, tobacco, and sugar cane (Habib 1982). However, these markets were generally local in nature and the demand for such things was limited. Establishment of colonial rule changed the entire scenario. The laying of the railways and the opening of the Suez canal made the Indian village a part of the global market.

The Industrial Revolution in England around the same time

generated fresh demands for some specific agricultural products required as raw material in the new industries. The manifold increase in the land revenue at the same time compelled the peasantry to shift to crops that had better market value, which effectively meant switching over from food crops to cash crops. According to one estimate, in Rayalseema region of southern India, the area devoted to food crops declined from 78.2 per cent in 1901–4, to 58.2 per cent in 1937–49, while at the other end it increased from 17.0 per cent to 30.1 per cent for cash crops during the same period (Satyanarayana 1991: 57). Similarly, from the state of Punjab a large proportion of food and non-food crops began to be exported. While there was a rapid increase in the agricultural production of the region from 1921 onwards, the per capita output of food crops experienced a decline. According to the estimates made by G. Blyn for the entire country, exportable commercial crops grew more than ten times faster at 1.31 per cent annually, compared to only 0.11 per cent increase per annum for foodgrains from 1894 to 1947. He also estimated that per head availability of foodgrains declined by 25 per cent during the inter-War period. This decline was highest in Bengal, Bihar, and Orissa at 38 per cent, while the relatively prosperous state of Punjab also saw a decline of 18 per cent (Blyn 1966).

One obvious consequence of this shift in cropping patterns and a growing involvement of the peasantry in the market was a significant increase in the vulnerability of local populations to famines. Forced commercialization of agriculture disintegrated the traditional systems of food security. India experienced a number of serious famines, particularly during the second half of the nineteenth century and the first half of the twentieth century. According to an estimate, 3.5 to 4 million people (one-tenth to one-eighth of the total population of the region) perished during the 1876–8 famine in parts of southern India (Kumar 1982: 231).

Similarly Bengal was transformed from a prosperous region to a region with frequent famines. In one of its worst famines during 1943–4, nearly 3.5 million people died. Though the official reports and 'inquiries' by colonial rulers attributed these famines to scarcity of food due to crop failures, the per capita availability of food in Bengal in the year 1943 was not substantially different from the previous year and there were no widespread crop failures in 1942 (Sen 1976; Greenough 1982).

According to Sen (1976) it was not the scarcity of food but the changes in the 'exchange entitlements' that caused the 1943 Bengal famine. The year 1942–3 saw unprecedented inflation, mainly resulting from War expenditure, and the absolute level of prices moved rapidly upward. But the prices of different commodities did not move in the same way. While food prices went up, wage rates, particularly of rural unskilled labour, remained low. This was reinforced in certain regions of Bengal by a direct decline in employment arising from loss of agricultural activity due to cyclonic destruction, making the exchange entitlements worse for certain groups. While some classes benefited from the incomes newly created by the war economy, others faced higher prices of food without a corresponding rise in their monetary incomes and therefore starved (Sen: 1976; 1977). Greenough adds that there were also some cultural patterns specific to Bengal which explain the selective starvation and death during the famines. There was cultural acceptance in Bengali society of 'abandoning' those dependents who were deemed inessential for the reconstitution of family and society in the post-crisis period and of protecting those whose survival was held essential for the future (Greenough 1982: 265).

Commodification of Land

While the new land settlements conferred formal and transferable/ alienable rights over land, the growing revenue demands and the increasing market orientation of agricultural production created conditions under which land began to acquire the features of a commodity. The new administrative and judicial system also introduced laws against defaults of legal dues that included default of rent, revenue, and debts. The moneylender, who until then lent keeping a peasant's crops in mind, began to see his land as a mortgageable asset against which he could lend money. Further, an increase in population during the nineteenth century made good-quality cultivable land scarce.

Apart from an absolute increase in population, colonial rule also led to what has been called the 'de-industrialization' of the Indian economy. Displacement of the native rulers after the conquest of India by the East India Company resulted in a sudden and almost complete collapse of old urban handicrafts in the absence of patronage. The influx of cheap machine-made goods from England after the Industrial Revolution hastened this process. Economic ruination of urban and village artisans increased the pressure on land considerably (Gadgil 1933). The net result was an ever-growing burden of debt for a majority of peasants.

Indebtedness as such was not an entirely new thing for the Indian peasant. Moneylenders as a distinct social category had always been a part of village social life. In most regions, they existed as a separate caste group. Whenever the peasant's stocks finished, he could go to the *sahukar* (moneylender) for a loan of grain. The local sahukar was also the customary source for peasants who generally needed an occasional loan. He was more of a functional category, a 'crude balance wheel to even out periods of scarcity and prosperity' (Moore 1966: 358). He evaluated the creditworthiness of a particular peasant on the basis of his ability to pay back, and decided on how much could be advanced to a particular peasant. The prevailing system of credit was perhaps close to what Weber conceptualized as 'neighborhood help' (Weber 1978: 361).

As land became both scarce and transferable, and the economic environment began to change, the moneylender started advancing much more than before, provided the peasant was willing to offer his land as guarantee against a possible default. At this stage rich landowners also entered the credit market, more with the intention of usurping the lands of smaller peasants than to earn interest. Thus began the process of 'land alienation'.

Land alienation was a pan-Indian development irrespective of the system of revenue settlement: zamindari, ryotwari, or mahalwari (Dhanagare 1983). This impoverished the small and, often also, the middle peasant, and strengthened the position of big landowners and moneylenders in rural society. The professional moneylender generally did not evict the peasant from his land. If the peasant could not pay back his loan, the moneylender asked for the transfer of ownership rights over land while the peasant continued cultivating land, but as a tenant of the moneylender. Where moneylenders were also landlords, the indebted peasant could end up being a landless labourer. Thus tenancy as well as landlessness grew significantly in most parts of the British empire. According to one estimate, out of the total population of male agricultural labourers in the state of Punjab, the proportion of those coming from peasant and landowning castes went up from 0.8 per cent in 1911 to as much as 29.7 per cent in 1931 (Bhattacharya 1985: 136). Similarly, in the case of Orissa, Bailey argues that once a market in land developed, peasants began to sell their lands whenever they were faced with a 'contingent need' (Bailey 1958).

Peasant indebtedness and land alienation acquired such gigantic proportions that even the colonial administrators began to see this as 'a problem' (Darling 1947; Thorburn 1983). Reports on growing discontent among the peasantry from different parts of the empire added to their worries. The Deccan riots of 1875 only confirmed these apprehensions. Colonial rulers responded to the growing unrest in the countryside by passing legislations such as the Deccan Relief Act of 1879 and the Punjab Alienation of Land Act of 1901. The main thrust of these legislative measures was to stop the transfers of agricultural land to members of non-agricultural castes. However, in the absence of any significant change in the revenue structure or in the overall politico-ideological framework of colonial rule, these legislative measures hardly brought any relief to the peasantry. For the poor peasants the only difference these measures made was that they now had to depend more on the credit of the richer landowners from the cultivating castes. The discontent among the peasantry continued to grow and expressed itself in a series of revolts and protest movements, particularly during the first half of the twentieth century.

The study of these movements became quite popular in the 1970s and 1980s. While scholars such as Desai (1979), Gough (1979), and Dhanagare (1983) explored these mobilizations from the conventional perspectives of social movements and Marxist class analysis, the famous 'Subaltern Studies' pioneered by Guha (1982) raised the issue of the relationship between peasant mobilizations and the nationalist movement. These studies questioned the dominant historiographies of the colonial period, which tended to subsume the politics of the peasantry within the broader framework of the nationalist struggle led by middle-class elite, thereby erasing the question of the agency of the subaltern classes. Guha argued for a perspective that gave autonomy to peasant consciousness and looked at the 'politics of the people' independently of the domain of elite politics.

The question, 'What did the agrarian policies of the colonial rulers do to the Indian village?' has most frequently been raised by Marxist scholars. Marx himself had almost celebrated the colonial conquest of India, which he thought would break the earlier stagnant system and help private property relations, and hence contradictions, to grow in Indian society. Though guided by its own 'vilest' self-interest, Marx argued that British rule was responsible for 'causing a social revolution in Hindustan' (Marx 1959: 18). Some later Marxists have also argued that high indebtedness of the peasantry, forced commercialization of agricultural produce, land alienation, and increasing domination of rich landowners and moneylenders over tenants and peasants was a specific form of 'the primitive accumulation of capital' which, in the ultimate analysis, led to 'a formal subsumption of labour under capital' (Alavi 1990; Fox 1987).

More popular has been the thesis of 'conservation-dissolution', which is that while colonial rule destroyed some of the local pre-capitalist structures, it also preserved many. As Patnaik argues, colonial rule 'broke down' the earlier structures without 'reconstituting' them, and 'bourgeois property relations' developed without a corresponding 'development of capitalist relations of production' in Indian agriculture (Patnaik 1990: 41). In certain cases, colonial rule in fact introduced semi-feudal relations to perpetuate itself. 'Unlike its parent mode of production in the West, distinguished historically by its continuous expansion of the productive forces, the mode of production installed in the colonies reduced the entire process of production to an immense super exploitation of the variable capital' (Banaji 1990: 126). The colonial West reinforced 'backward relations of exploitation' and transmitted to its colonies the pressures of the accumulation process in the metropolis without unleashing any corresponding expansion in the forces of production (Banaji 1990: 126). Alavi also argued that colonial or 'peripheral capitalism' was not the same as 'metropolitan capitalism'. While it was an integrated process of development in the West, 'peripheral capitalism brought about a disarticulated form of generalized commodity production' because the surplus generated in agriculture was reinvested not in the local economy but in the metropolitan centres (Alavi 1990: 170). Though with a different emphasis, Guha too argued that the fusing of landlordism and usury by colonial rule made a possible development of capitalism difficult both in agriculture and in industry. However, unlike Alavi, Guha emphasizes that the composite apparatus of dominance over peasantry and their subjection to the triumvirate—*sarkari* (of the state), *sahukari* (of the moneylender), and *zamindari* (of the landlord)—was primarily a political fact (Guha 1983: 8).

AGRARIAN CHANGES AFTER INDEPENDENCE

In many ways, independence from colonial rule in 1947 marked the beginning of a new phase in the history of Indian agriculture. Having evolved out of a long struggle against colonial rule with the participation of the people from various social categories, the Indian state also took over the task of supervising the transformation of its stagnant and backward economy to make sure that the benefits of economic growth were not monopolized entirely by a particular section of society. It is with this background that 'development' emerged as a strategy of economic change and an ideology of the new regime.

However, even though the political system had changed in a very fundamental sense, at a micro level the structures that evolved during colonial rule still continued to exist. The local interests that had emerged over a long period of time continued to be powerful in the Indian countryside even after the political climate had changed. Speaking at the Delhi School of Economics in 1955 after his extensive trips to different parts of independent India, Daniel Thorner was among the first to conceptualize this fact. He argued that the earlier structure of land relations and debt dependencies, where a small section consisting of a few landlords and moneylenders (who usually belonged to the local upper castes) were dominant, continued to prevail in the Indian countryside. The nature of property relations, the local values that related social prestige negatively to physical labour, and the absence of any surplus with the actual cultivator for investment on land ultimately perpetuated stagnation. 'This complex of legal, economic, and social relations uniquely typical of the Indian countryside served to produce an effect' that Thorner described as 'a built-in depressor' (Thorner 1956: 12). Thorner's formulation was, in a sense, symptomatic of the way in which agrarian issues began to be framed in the context of development studies and modernization of agriculture debates.

Land Reforms

The 'agrarian question' had also been an important topic of discussion for leaders of the Indian freedom movement, starting with Ranade and Dutt, who extensively wrote and debated on how Indian society and economy ought to be reorganized after independence from colonial rule (see Joshi 1987). The 'land question' had become one of the most hotly debated topics during the final years of the struggle for Independence.

Land reforms also became a question of considerable academic interest and debate in the discourse about planning and development. They were viewed as necessary for initiating modernization in agriculture. While there was a general agreement that the prevailing agrarian structures, marked by absentee landlordism and semi-feudal relations of production, needed to be reorganized, two extreme positions were taken on the following crucial questions: 'What kind of agrarian reforms are required and which would work the best?' and 'Is there an economic logic behind land reforms?' The competing answers to the latter question came to be known as the 'farm size-productivity' debate.

The first view was that of the 'institutionalists', who argued that the way out for Indian agriculture lay in a radical reorganization of land-ownership patterns that would not only democratize the village and revive the independent 'peasant economy', but also increase the productivity of land. Thus the slogan, 'land to the tiller' (Thorner 1956; Herring 1983). They also argued that smaller-sized holdings gave higher productivity (see Herring 1983: 239–67). The second viewpoint argued against the redistribution of land on the grounds that it was both unviable, as not enough land was available for everyone, and that it worked against the logic of 'economics'. The modernization of agriculture, it was argued, required landlords' reorientation. They needed to be motivated to cultivate their own land with wage labour and using modern technology. The land reforms, according to them, would only divide the land into 'unviable holdings', rendering them unfeasible for the use of modern technology (Bauer and Yamey 1957; Lewis 1963). Speaking from a very different position, some Marxist scholars also argued against the 'institutionalists' who reminded them of the neo-populist Narodanics of Russia. They thought that the argument in favour of small farms emanated from the Chayanovian logic of the peasant economy, which was in their view historically untenable (Patnaik 1972).

However, the process of agrarian reforms is inherently a political question (Ghose 1984:6) and not a purely technical or economic one. The choices made by the Indian state and the actual implementation of land reforms were determined by the 'politics' of the new regime rather than by the theoretical superiority of a particular position. The Indian state chose to reorganize agrarian relations through redistribution of land, but not in a comprehensive and radical manner. Joshi described it as 'sectorial or sectional reforms' (Joshi 1987: 56). The Government of India directed its states to abolish intermediary tenures, regulate rent and tenancy rights, confer ownership rights on tenants, impose ceilings on holdings, distribute the surplus land among the rural poor, and facilitate consolidation of holdings. A large number of legislations were passed by the state governments over a short period of time. The number of these legislations was so large that, according to Thorner, they could be 'the largest body of agrarian legislations to have been passed in so brief a span of years in any country whose history has been recorded' (Thorner 1956: 14).

The actual implementation of these legislations and their impact on the agrarian structure is, however, an entirely different story. Most of the legislations had intentionally provided loopholes that allowed the dominant landowners to tamper with land records by redistributing land among relatives—at least on papers—evicting their tenants, and using other means to escape the legislations. In the absence of a concerted 'political will' (Joshi 1976), land reforms could succeed only in regions where the peasantry was politically mobilized and could exert pressure from below (Radhakrishanan 1989).

Despite overall failure, land reforms succeeded in weakening the hold of absentee landlords over rural society and assisted in the emergence of a 'class of substantial peasants and petty landlords as the dominant political and economic group' (Bell 1974: 196). In a village of Rajasthan, for example, though the 'abolition of *jagirs*' (intermediary rights) was far from satisfactory, it made considerable difference to the overall landownership patterns and to the local and regional power structures. The Rajputs, the erstwhile landlords, possessed much less land after the land reforms than they did before. Most of the village land had moved into the hands of those who could be called small and medium landowners. In qualitative terms, most of the land began to be self-cultivated and the incidence of tenancy declined considerably (Chakravarti 1975: 97–8). The fear of losing land induced many potential losers to sell or rearrange their lands in a manner that escaped legislations (Byres 1974).

However, it was only in rare cases that the landless labourers living in the countryside, most of whom belonged to the ex-'untouchable' castes, received land. The beneficiaries, by and large, belonged to middle-level caste groups who traditionally cultivated land as a part of the calling of their castes. Otherwise also the holding structure continued to be fairly iniquitous though the proportion of smaller and medium-size landowners has been expanding (see Table 1).

Provision of Institutional Credit

While land reforms were supposed to deal with the problem of landlordism, the hold of moneylenders over the peasantry was to be weakened by providing credit through institutional sources, initially by credit societies and later by the nationalized commercial banks.

According to the findings of an official survey carried out immediately after Independence from colonial rule, up to approximately 91 per cent of the credit needs of cultivators were being met by informal sources of credit (RBI 1969: 15). Much of this came from usurious moneylenders (69.7 per cent). It was in recognition of this fact that the Indian state planned to expand the network of cooperative credit societies. With the imposition of 'social control' and later their nationalization, commercial banks were also asked to lend to the agricultural sector on priority basis. Over the years, the dependence of rural households on informal sources has come down significantly. While in 1961, an average of only 18.4 per cent of the total credit needs were being fulfilled by institutional sources of credit, in 1981 the corresponding figure had risen to 62.6 per cent (Gadgil 1986: 296).

However, this is not the entire story. The assessment studies on the cooperative credit societies showed that much of their credit went to the relatively better off sections of rural society, and the poor continued to depend on the more expensive informal sources (Thorner 1964; Oommen 1984). This was explained as a consequence of the prevailing structure of land tenures (Herring 1977). The state response was to bureaucratize the cooperative societies. Though in some regions this helped in releasing credit societies from the hold of big landowners, bureaucratization also led to rampant corruption and increasing apathy among those whom they were supposed to serve (Jodhka 1995a). Although banks were never controlled directly by the rural rich, the benefit of their credit has largely gone to those who had substantial holdings (Jodhka 1995b). Yet, despite this inherent bias of institutional credit against the rural poor, its availability played an important role in making the green revolution a success, and it definitely helped to marginalize the professional moneylender in the rural power structure.

Community Development Programme (CDP)

As a strategy of development, the CDP was conceptually very different from both land reforms and the idea of making cheap institutional credit available to cultivators. While the earlier programmes reflected an 'institutionalist' perspective, the CDP had emanated from the 'productionist' approach to rural development. It had been inspired by the agricultural extension service in the United States (Dube 1958: 8) and was based on a notion of the harmonious village community without any significant internal differences and conflict of interests (Dhanagare 1984). There was hardly any mention of the unequal power relations in the village. Its objective was to provide a substantial increase in agricultural production and improvement in basic services, which would ultimately lead to a transformation in the social and economic life of the village (Dube 1958). Its basic assumption was that 'the Indian peasant would of his own free will, and because of his "felt needs", immediately adopt technical improvements the moment he was shown them' (Moore 1966: 401).

The Programme was launched on 2 October 1952 in a few selected 'blocks' and it was soon extended to the entire country. However, the enthusiasm with which the Programme was started could not be sustained. A non-political approach to agrarian transformation resulted in helping only those who were already powerful in the village. Most of the benefits were cornered by a small section of the rural elite.

THE GREEN REVOLUTION AND AFTER

Of all the developmental programmes introduced during the post-Independence period, the green revolution is considered to have been the most successful. It was celebrated the world over and has been studied and debated quite extensively in academia. The green revolution led to a substantial increase in agricultural output, to the extent that it almost solved India's food problem. It also produced significant social and political changes in the Indian village and, in a sense, did bring about an 'agricultural revolution'. In purely economic terms, the agricultural sector experienced growth at the rate of 3 to 5 per cent per annum (Byres 1972), which was many times more than what the rate of growth had been during the colonial period (less than 1 per cent).

The green revolution conceptualized agrarian change in purely technological terms and was based on the 'trickle down' theory of economic growth. The expression 'green revolution' was deliberately coined to contrast it with the phrase 'red revolution'. It carried the conviction that 'agriculture was being peacefully transformed through the quiet working of science and technology, reaping the economic gains of modernization while avoiding the social costs of mass upheaval and disorder usually associated with rapid change' (Frankel 1971: V). The United States played an active role in its conception and implementation. Many have argued that this was because of the strategic, geopolitical interests that the US had at the time in the changing social and economic conditions in the countries of the Third World (Harriss 1987).

The term 'green revolution' had been first used during the late

1960s to refer to the effects of the introduction of higher yielding variety (HYV) seeds of wheat and rice in developing countries. However, the green revolution was not just about the use of HYV seed. It was a package. The new varieties of seeds required fertility-enhancing inputs, i.e. chemical fertilizers, controlled irrigation conditions, and plant-protecting chemicals (pesticides). The other components of the package consisted of providing cheap institutional credit, price incentives, and marketing facilities. In order to back up the application of new technology on local farms, a large number of agricultural universities were also opened in the regions selected for the new programme. It was under the direct supervision of the Ford Foundation that the Intensive Agricultural Development Programme (IADP) was started in 1961. Initially the IADP operated in 14 districts on an experimental basis; it was later extended to 114 districts (out of a total of 325) under the name of the Intensive Agriculture Areas Programme (IAAP) in 1965.

Its advocates argued that the new technology was 'scale neutral' and could be used with as much benefit by small as well as big landowners. However, in the actual implementation, small holdings were not found to be viable units for technological change. Joan Mencher observed that the concerned agriculture officers were far from neutral. 'What they thought was needed to further the green revolution was to forget about small farmers ... because they could not really contribute to increased production. To these officials, progressive farmers are those who have viable farms and who are fairly well-off' (Mencher 1978: 239–40). Interestingly, though, a study from Punjab showed that not only were the smaller landowners as eager to adopt the new technology but that their per acre income from land was slightly higher than that of the bigger farmers (Bhalla and Chadha 1983: 78).

But, participating in the green revolution did not mean the same thing to smaller farmers as it did to bigger farmers. While bigger farmers had enough surplus of their own to invest in the new capital-intensive farming, for smaller landowners it meant additional dependence on borrowing, generally from informal sources. My study of three villages in a green revolution district of Haryana showed that their average outstanding debt from informal sources was the highest even in absolute terms when compared with other categories of farmers (Jodhka 1995c: A124). Although theoretically the new technology was 'scale neutral', it was certainly not 'resource neutral' (Harriss 1987: 231). The new technology also compelled widespread involvement with the market. Unlike traditional agriculture, cultivators in post-green revolution agriculture had to buy all farm inputs from the market for which they often had to take credit from traders or institutional sources. In order to clear the debts, they had no choice but to sell the farm yield in the market even when they needed to keep it for their own consumption. They sold their farm yield immediately after harvesting when prices were relatively low, and bought later in the year for consumption when prices were higher. Thus although the small farmers took to the new technologies, the fact that their resources were limited meant that these technologies ushered in a new set of dependencies. On the other hand, it has definitely strengthened the economic and political position of rich farmers.

One of the manifestations of the growing market orientation of agrarian production was the emergence of a totally new kind of mobilization of surplus-producing farmers who demanded a better deal for the agricultural sector. Interestingly, these 'new' farmers' movements emerged almost simultaneously in virtually all the green revolution regions. Though initiated in the late 1970s, these movements gained momentum during the decade of the 1980s. Using the language of neo-populism (Dhanagare 1991; Brass 1994) and in some cases also invoking traditional social networks and identities of the landowning dominant castes (Gupta 1997), its leaders argued that India was experiencing a growing division between the city and the village. And the village, i.e. the agrarian sector, was being exploited by the city or the industrial sector through the mechanism of 'unequal exchange'.

Those who led these movements were mostly substantial landowners who had benefited most from the developmental programmes and belonged to the numerically large middle-level caste groups, whom Srinivas had called the 'dominant castes' (Srinivas 1994). The members of this new 'social class' not only emerged as a dominant group at village level but they also came to dominate regional/state-level politics in most parts of India. They had an accumulated surplus that they sought to invest in ever more profitable enterprises. Some of them diversified into other economic activities (Rutten 1991) or migrated to urban areas (Upadhya 1988) or entered agricultural trade (Harriss-White 1996). Culturally also, this new class differed significantly from both the classical peasants and the old landlords. As an observer comments:

> A typical family of this class has a landholding in its native village,
> cultivated by hired labour, *bataidar*, tenant or farm servants and supervised
> by the father or one son; business of various descriptions in town managed
> by other sons; and perhaps a young and bright child who is a doctor or
> engineer or a professor. It is this class that is most vocal about injustice done
> to the village (Balagopal 1987: 1545).

The changes produced by the green revolution also generated an interesting debate among Marxist scholars on the question of defining the prevailing 'mode of production' in Indian agriculture. Though the debate raised a large number of questions, the most contentious revolved around whether capitalism had become dominant in Indian agriculture or was still characterized by the semi-feudal mode of production. A good number of scholars, with some variation in their formulations, argued that the capitalist tendency had started in India with the disintegration of the old system during colonial rule, and that after Independence the process of accumulation had gathered momentum (Patnaik 1990; Thorner 1982). Another set of scholars, on the basis of their own empirical studies mostly from eastern India, asserted that Indian agriculture was still dominated by a semi-feudal mode of production. This position was best articulated by Bhaduri (1984). He argued that landlords-cum-moneylenders continued to dominate the process of agricultural production. Peasants and labourers were tied to them through the mechanism of debt that led to 'forced commercialization' of labour and agricultural yield. This produced a self-perpetuating stagnant and exploitative agrarian structure that could be at best described as 'semi-feudal'. The internal logic of this system worked against any possibility of agricultural growth or the development of capitalism in Indian agriculture (Bhaduri 1984).

However, towards the end of the debate there seems to have emerged a consensus that though it may have its local specificities and considerable regional variations, the capitalist mode of production indeed was on its way to dominating the agrarian economy of India and most certainly that of the regions which had experienced the green revolution (Thorner 1982).

Agrarian Changes and Agricultural Labour

Did the benefits of the green revolution 'trickle down' to agricultural labourers? How did it affect them relationally? These have been among the most debated questions in the literature on agrarian change in India.

In a study comparing wage rates of a pre-green revolution year with those of a year after the new technology had been adopted, Bardhan (1970) showed that while cash wages of agricultural labourers had gone up after the introduction of the new technology, their purchasing power had in fact come down due to overall increase in prices. Though not everyone would agree with Bardhan, few would dispute that though the green revolution brought an overall prosperity to the countryside, it also multiplied income inequalities both within the village and among different regions of the country (Bagchi 1982; Dhanagare 1988). In a way, it was in recognition of the failures of the 'trickle-down' thesis that 'target-group' oriented programmes for poverty alleviation were started during the second half of the 1970s.

During the decade of the 1970s, the proportion of agricultural labour to total population dependent on land also experienced a significant increase. According to one estimate it went up from 16.7 per cent in 1961 to 26.3 per cent in 1971 (Prasad 1994: 15). However, micro-level studies have shown that the increase was not an effect of land sales by marginal landholders. A substantial proportion of the new labourers were tenants evicted from land after the land reforms or they were those who did not own land but were previously self-employed in traditional occupations (Bhalla 1976). The green revolution made many of the traditional occupations redundant and the 'jajmani relations' disintegrated rapidly (Aggarwal 1971; Karanth 1987).

It is generally believed that the process of agricultural modernization is accompanied by a change in the social relations of production, leading to freeing of agricultural labour from relations of patronage and institutionalized dependencies. Some scholars did report in their studies that such a process was under way in the Indian countryside, particularly in the regions where the green revolution had been a success. Breman (1974), for example, observed a process of 'depatronization' being experienced in the farmer–labourer relationship in the villages of south Gujarat. In a later study, he again argued that the inter-generational bondage characterized by extra-economic coercion no longer existed in south Gujarat and that the existing system of attached labour was no longer an unfree relation (Breman 1985). In his study of a Tanjore village in Tamil Nadu, Béteille (1971) had also observed a process of formalization in the relation of landowning castes with village artisans and landless labourers. They had 'acquired a more or less contractual character' (Béteille 1971). On the basis of her study in the same region, Gough too reported that the old type of attached labour that was mainly paid in kind was being replaced by casual day labour, paid largely in cash (Gough 1989:142). Similarly, despite the elements of continuity that she observed, Bhalla reported that in the Haryana countryside relations between farmers and attached labourers were also changing into formalized contractual arrangements (Bhalla 1976).

Highlighting the elements of continuity reported by Bhalla in her study, Bhaduri (1984) argued that the presence of attached labourers and their high indebtedness meant that the relations of production even in the green revolution belt of Haryana were 'semi-feudal'. However, Bardhan (1984) and Rudra (1990) strongly contested the argument that the prevalence of attached labour necessarily meant 'semi-feudal' relations. Bardhan argued that the post-green revolution voluntaristic attached labour was very different from the feudal institution of bonded labour marked by hereditary and long-term indebtedness, entailing continuous and exclusive work for the creditor-employer. On the basis of his own work, he contended that the modernization of agricultural technology had in fact increased the demand for attached labourers, as they were seen to be useful in overseeing the work of casual labourers. Similarly, Rudra argued that the attached labour in the post-green revolution agrarian setting was more like permanent employment in the organized sector than an unfree relationship.

Arguing in a very different mode, Brass (1990) questioned the claims that offered a positive conceptualization of attached labour. Contesting the assumption that the voluntarity of attached labour meant freedom, Brass argued that 'while the recruitment may itself be voluntary, in the sense that labourer willingly offers himself for work, it does not follow that the production relation will be correspondingly free in terms of the worker's capacity to re-enter the labour market' (Brass 1990: 55). Brass argued that in post-green revolution Haryana, where he did a field study, farmers used the mechanism of debt and attachment to 'discipline' labour and 'decompose/recompose' the labour market, which led to 'deproletarianization' of labour. He asserted that the indebted labourers of the Haryana countryside were in fact 'bonded slaves'.

On the basis of my study (Jodhka 1994) in the same region, I have argued that while the attached labourers in Haryana were certainly not like permanent employees in the organized sector, as suggested by Rudra, and that elements of lack of freedom were obvious in their relationship with farmers, they could not be viewed as bonded slaves because of the overall change in the social framework of agricultural production in contemporary Haryana. I have suggested that attached labour in the post-green revolution agriculture should be seen more as 'a system of labour mortgage' where labourers, despite an acute dislike for the relationship, were compelled to accept attachment for interest-free credit. However, their loss of freedom being temporary in nature, they could not be characterized as bonded slaves. There were many cases where the labourers after having worked as attached labourers for some time, could leave the relationship. The growing integration of the village in the broader market and the increasing availability of alternative sources of employment outside agriculture, along with the changing political and ideological environment, had been leading to a process that weakened the hold of landowners over labourers. In some cases developmental schemes such as the Integrated Rural Development Programme (IRDP) being run by the central government also helped.

More recently, scholars have been exploring new questions relating to the process of development and agrarian transition. Some of these could have far-reaching implications for the classical theories of agrarian change. Such studies allow us to inquire into the specific effects of new agrarian

technology on the changing position of women in the household and on the
farm. Apart from pointing to the 'gender blindness' of much of the
development theory and the empirical surveys on issues such as poverty and
land rights of women in the region (Dube 1986; Agarwal 1988; 1994),
students of gender and agrarian change have also shown how the new
technology had a clear bias against women. It marginalized female
agricultural wage labour both in terms of work as well as earnings
(Chowdhry 1994). Similarly, the questions of ecology and displacement (Guha
1989; Das 1996; Kothari 1996) and the new social movements (Baviskar 1995)
against the construction of big dams, once considered 'the temples of modern
India', have raised serious critiques of the present models of development.

CONCLUSION

After his extensive tours of the Indian countryside during the
early 1950s, Daniel Thorner (1956) suggested that one conceptualize the
Indian agrarian structure on the basis of the form of income derived from the
soil, the type of right in the soil, and the form of actual field work that is
done. Conceptualized in this way, the Indian agrarian structure can be
thought to constitute three main social categories: *maliks* (the landlords or
proprietors), kisan (the working peasants), and mazdoors (the labourers).
Although speaking from a different perspective, around this time Srinivas
(1955) conceptualized the structure of social relations in the Mysore village in
a framework of patron–client relationships and vertical ties between landlord
and tenant, between master and servant, and between creditor and debtor. He
also mentioned that these relations did not always correspond with the
structure of caste hierarchies.

Another set of formulations of the prevailing agrarian structure
in India before it embarked upon the path of 'development' came from
different groups of Marxist scholars. As mentioned earlier, Bhaduri (1984)
saw agrarian relations in eastern India as a classical case of a 'semi-feudal'
mode of production where the landlord virtually controlled everything
through his monopoly over land and credit. Similarly, Bhardwaj (1974)
argued that agrarian relations in the Indian countryside were structured
around a network of unequal exchange relations between those who
possessed land, labour and credit. However, these exchange relations were
not among individuals with free will but were 'interlocked' with each other
in such a manner that the prevailing structure worked in favour of the
'strong' and against the 'weak'.

Common to all these formulations was a stress on the fact that a
small section of big landowners dominated a large section of agricultural
producers through control over resources and ideologies. They were the

people who rarely did any physical labour themselves. As Béteille (1980) points out, there was, in fact, an inverse relationship between the extent of manual work performed and the degree of control over land.

Despite a considerable degree of continuity and significant regional variations, these relations have definitely experienced many changes over approximately the last fifty years. Independence from colonial rule and the launching of development programmes started a new phase in the history of Indian agriculture. At a purely quantitative level, the limited institutional changes—i.e. partial implementations of land reforms, adoption of new technology, and state support to the cultivators—have led to considerable expansion in the area under cultivation and the total volume of production.

A substantial volume of the literature shows that the agrarian structure has transformed the direction of a capitalist mode of organization at least in areas that experienced the green revolution, which have extended from traditional crops such as wheat and paddy to new crops such as oil seeds and soya bean. The Indian farmer has increasingly become outward looking, orienting his needs to demands of the market rather than local conventions and earlier traditions, yet the impact of the change on the different categories defined by caste and gender has been a differential one. This is why the changes in agriculture have not secured a better quality of life for all social categories in the agrarian structure of village communities.

REFERENCES

Agarwal, B. 1988. *Structures of Patriarchy: State, Community and Household in Modernising Asia*. New Delhi: Kali for Women.

———. 1994. *A Field of One's Own: Gender and Land Rights in South Asia*. New Delhi: Foundation Books.

Aggarwal, P.C. 1971. 'Impact of Green Revolution on Landless Labourers: A Note'. *Economic and Political Weekly*. 6(47):2363–5.

Alavi, H. 1990. 'Structure of Colonial Formations'. In Utsa Patnaik, ed., *Agrarian Relations and Accumulation: The 'Mode of Production Debate in India'*, 165–82. Delhi: Oxford University Press.

Baden-Powell, B.H. 1892. *Land Systems of British India*. 3 vols. London: Oxford University Press.

Bagchi, A.K. 1982. *The Political Economy of Underdevelopment*. Cambridge: Cambridge University Press.

Bailey, F.G. 1958. *Caste and the Economic Frontier: A Village in Highland Orissa*. Bombay: Oxford University Press.

Balagopal, K. 1987. 'An Ideology of the Provincial Propertied Class'. *Economic and Political Weekly*. 21(36–7):2177–8.

Banaji, J. 1976. 'A Summary of Kautsky's *The Agrarian Question*'. *Economy and Society*. 5(1):2–49.

———. 1990. 'For a Theory of Colonial Modes of Production'. In Utsa Patnaik, ed.,

Agrarian Relations and Accumulation: The 'Mode of Production Debate in India',
119–31. Delhi: Oxford University Press.

Bardhan, P. 1970. 'Green Revolution and Agricultural Labour'. *Economic and Political Weekly.* 5(29–31):1239–46.

_____. 1984. *Land, Labour and Rural Poverty: Essays in Development Economics*. Delhi: Oxford University Press.

Bauer, P.T. and B.S. Yamey. 1957. *The Economy of Underdeveloped Countries*. Cambridge: Cambridge University Press.

Baviskar, A. 1995. *In the Belly of the River: Tribal Conflict over Development in the Narmada Valley*. Delhi: Oxford University Press.

Bell, C. 1974. 'Ideology and Economic Interests in Indian Land Reform'. In D. Lehmann, ed., *Agrarian Reform and Agrarian Reformism: Studies of Peru, Chile, China, and India*, 190–220. London: Faber and Faber.

Beidelman, T.O. 1959. *A Comparative Analysis of the Jajmani System*. New York: Association for Asian Studies.

Béteille, A. 1971. *Caste, Class and Power: Changing Patterns of Stratification in a Tanjore Village*. Berkeley: University of California Press.

_____. 1974a. *Studies in Agrarian Social Structure*. Delhi: Oxford University Press.

_____. 1974b. *Six Essays in Comparative Sociology*. Delhi: Oxford University Press.

_____. 1980. 'The Indian Village: Past and Present'. In E.J. Hobsbaum et al., eds, *Peasants in History: Essays in Honour of Daniel Thorner*, 107–20. Delhi: Oxford University Press.

Bhaduri, A. 1984. *The Economic Structure of Backward Agriculture*. Delhi: Macmillan.

Bhalla, G.S. and G.K. Chadha. 1983. *Green Revolution and Small Peasants: A Study of Income Distribution among Punjab Cultivators*. New Delhi: Concept Publishing House.

Bhalla, S. 1976. 'New Relations of Production in Haryana Agriculture'. *Economic and Political Weekly*. 11(13):A23–30.

Bhattacharya, N. 1985. 'Agricultural Labour and Production: Central and South-East Punjab'. In K.N. Raj, ed., *Essays on the Commercialization of Indian Agriculture*, 105–62. Delhi: Oxford University Press.

Blyn, G. 1966. *Agricultural Trends in India 1891–1947*. Philadelphia: University of Philadelphia Press.

Bonnano, A. 1989. *Sociology of Agriculture*. New Delhi: Concept Publishing House.

Brass, T. 1990. 'Class Struggle and Deproletarianization of Agricultural Labour in Haryana (India)'. *The Journal of Peasant Studies*. 18(1):36–67.

_____. 1994. 'Introduction: The New Farmers' Movements in India'. *The Journal of Peasant Studies*. 21(3–4):50–77.

Breman, J. 1974. *Patronage and Exploitation: Changing Agrarian Relations in South Gujarat India*. Berkley: University of California Press.

_____. 1985. *Of Peasants, Migrants and Paupers: Rural Labour Circulation and Capitalist Production in West India*. Delhi: Oxford University Press.

Byres, T.J. 1972. 'The Dialectics of India's Green Revolution'. *South Asian Review*. 5(2):99–106.

_____. 1974. 'Land Reforms, Industrialization and Marketed Surplus in India: An Essay on the Power of Rural Bais'. In D. Lehmann, ed., *Agrarian Reform and Agrarian Reformism: Studies of Peru, Chile, China, and India*, 221–61. London: Faber and Faber.

Chakravarti, A. 1975. *Contradiction and Change: Emerging Patterns of Authority in a Rajasthan Village*. Delhi: Oxford University Press.

Chayanov, A.V. 1987. *The Theory of Peasant Economy*. Ed. Daniel Thorner. Delhi: Oxford University Press.

Chowdhry, P. 1994. *The Veiled Women: Shifting Gender Equations in Rural Haryana 1880–1990*. Delhi: Oxford University Press.

Cohn, B.S. 1987. *An Anthropologist among the Historians and Other Essays*. Delhi: Oxford University Press.

Darling, M. 1947. *Punjab Peasantry in Prosperity and Debt*. Bombay: Oxford University Press.

Das, V. 1996: 'Dislocation and Rehabilitation: Defining a Field'. *Economic and Political Weekly*. 31(24): 1509–14.

Desai, A.R. 1976. *Social Background to Indian Nationalism*. Bombay: Popular Prakashan.

———, ed. 1979. *Peasant Struggles in India*. Bombay: Oxford University Press.

Dhanagare, D.N. 1983. *Peasant Movements in India: 1920–1950*. Delhi: Oxford University Press.

———. 1984. 'Agrarian Reforms and Rural Development in India: Some Observations'. *Research in Social Movements, Conflict and Change*. 7(1):178–93.

———. 1988. 'The Green Revolution and Social Inequalities in Rural India'. *Bulletin of Concerned Asian Scholars*. 20(2):2–13.

———. 1991. 'An Apoliticist Populism: A Case Study of BKU'. In K.L. Sharma and Dipankar Gupta, eds, *Country–Town Nexus: Study in Social Transformation in Contemporary India*, 104–22. Jaipur: Rawat Publications.

Djurfeldt, G. and S. Lindberg. 1976. *Behind Poverty: The Social Formation of a Tamil Village*. New Delhi: Oxford and IBH.

Dube, L. 1986. *Visibility and Power: Essays on Women in Society and Development*. Delhi: Oxford University Press.

Dube S.C. 1958. *India's Changing Villages: Human Factors in Community Development*. New Delhi: Allied Publishers.

Fox, R. 1987. *Lions of the Punjab: Culture in the Making*. New Delhi: Archives Publishers.

Friedland, W.H. 1982. 'The End of Rural Society and the Future of Rural Sociology'. *Rural Sociology*. 47(4):589–608.

———. 1984. 'Commodity Systems Analysis: An Approach to the Sociology of Agriculture'. In H.K. Schwarzweller, ed., *Research in Rural Sociology and Development*, vol. 1:221–35. Greenwich: Jai Press.

Frankel, F.R. 1971. *India's Green Revolution: Economic Gains and Political Costs*. Bombay: Oxford University Press.

Gadgil, D.R. 1933. *Industrial Evolution of India in Recent Times*. London: Oxford University Press.

Gadgil, M.V. 1986. 'Agricultural Credit in India: A Review of Performances and Policies'. *Indian Journal of Agricultural Economics*. 14(3):282–309.

Geertz, C., ed. 1963. *Old Societies and New States: The Quest for Modernity in Asia and Africa*. New York: The Free Press.

Ghose A.K., ed. 1984. *Agrarian Reforms in Contemporary Developing Countries*. New Delhi: Select Books.

Gough, K. 1955. 'The Social Structure of a Tanjore Village'. In M.N. Srinivas, ed., *India's Village*, 90–102. Bombay: Asia Publishers.

_____. 1979. 'Peasant Resistance and Revolt in South India'. In A.R. Desai, ed., *Peasant Struggles in India*, 719–42. Bombay: Oxford University Press.

Gouldner, A.W. 1973. *For Sociology: Renewal and Critique in Sociology Today*. Harmondsworth: Penguin.

Greenough P.R. 1982. *Prosperity and Misery in Modern Bengal: The Famine of 1943–1944*. Oxford: Oxford University Press.

Guha, R. 1982. *Subaltern Studies-I: Writings on South Asian History and Society*. Delhi: Oxford University Press.

_____. 1983. *Elementary Aspects of Peasant Insurgency in Colonial India*. Delhi: Oxford University Press.

Guha, Ramchandra. 1989. *The Unquiet Woods: Ecological Change and Peasant Resistance in the Himalaya*. Delhi: Oxford University Press.

Gupta, D. 1997. *Rivalry and Brotherhood: Politics in the Life of Farmers in Northern India*. Delhi: Oxford University Press.

Habib, I. 1963. *Agrarian Systems of Mughal India*. Bombay: Asia Publishers.

_____. 1982. 'Agrarian Relations and Land Revenue: North India'. In, T. Raychaudhury and Irfan Habib, eds, *The Cambridge Economic History of India*, vol.1:235–48. Delhi: Orient Longman.

Harriss, J. 1987. 'Capitalism and Peasant Production: The Green Revolution in India'. In T. Shanin, ed., *Peasants and Peasant Societies*, 227–45. London: Blackwell.

Harriss-White, B. 1996. *A Political Economy of Agriculture Markets in South India: Masters of the Countryside*. New Delhi: Sage.

Herring, R.J. 1977. 'Land Tenure and Credit-Capital Tenure in Contemporary India'. In R.E. Frynkenberg, ed., *Land Tenure and Peasants in South Asia*, 120–58. New Delhi: Manohar.

_____. 1983. *Land to the Tiller: The Political Economy of Agrarian Reforms in South Asia*. Delhi: Oxford University Press.

Inden, R. 1990. *Imagining India*. Oxford: Basil Blackwell.

Jodhka, S.S. 1994. 'Agrarian Changes and Attached Labour: Emerging Patterns in Haryana Agriculture'. *Economic and Political Weekly*. 29(39):A102–6.

_____. 1995a. 'Bureacratisation, Corruption and Depoliticisation: Changing Profile of Credit Co-operatives in Rural Haryana'. *Economic and Political Weekly*. 30(1):53–6.

_____. 1995b. *Debt, Dependence and Agrarian Change*. Jaipur: Rawat Publications.

_____. 1995c. 'Who Borrows? Who Lends?: Changing Structure of Informal Credit in Rural Haryana'. *Economic and Political Weekly*. 30(39):A123–31.

_____. 1998. 'From "Book View" to "Field View": Social Anthropological Constructions of the Indian Village'. *Oxford Development Studies*. 26(3):311–31.

Joshi, P.C. 1976. *Land Reforms in India: Trends and Perspectives*. New Delhi: Allied Publishers.

―――. 1987. *Institutional Aspects of Agricultural Development: India from Asian Perspective*. New Delhi: Allied Publishers.

Karanth, G.K. 1987. 'New Technology and Traditional Rural Institutions: The Case of Jajmani Relations'. *Economic and Political Weekly*. 22(51):2217–24.

Kothari, S. 1996. 'Whose Nation? Displaced as Victims of Development'. *Economic and Political Weekly*. 31(24):1476–85.

Krober, A.L. 1948. *Anthropology*. New York: Harcourt, Brace and Co.

Kumar, D. 1982. 'South India'. In Dharma Kumar and Meghnad Desai, eds, *The Cambridge Economic History of India*, vol. II:207–41. Delhi: Orient Longman.

―――. 1992. *Land and Caste in South India*. New Delhi: Manohar.

Lenin, V.I. [1899] 1960. *The Development of Capitalism in Russia*. In *Collected Works*, vol. 3. Moscow: Foreign Languages Publishing House.

―――. [1908] 1962. *The Agrarian Programme of Social-Democracy in the First Russian Revolution 1905–1907*. In *Collected Works*, vol.13. Moscow: Foreign Languages Publishing House.

Lewis, W.A. 1963. *The Theory of Economic Growth*. London: George Allen and Unwin.

Marx, K. 1959. *The First Indian War Of Independence: 1857–1859*. Moscow: Progress Publishers.

Marriot, M., ed. 1955. *Village India: Studies in Little Community*. Chicago: Chicago University Press.

Mayer, P. 1993. 'Inventing Village Tradition: The Late 19th Century Origins of the North Indian Jajmani System'. *Modern Asian Studies*. 27(2):357–95.

Mencher, J.P. 1978. *Agriculture and Social Structure in Tamil Nadu: Past Origins, Present Transformations and Future Prospects*. New Delhi: Allied Publishers.

Moore, B.Jr. 1966. *Social Origins of Dictatorship and Democracy*. Middlesex: Penguin.

Mukherjee, M. 1985. 'Commercialization and Agrarian Change in Pre-Independence Punjab, 1870–1940'. In K.N. Raj, ed., *Essays on the Commercialization of Indian Agriculture*, 51–104. Delhi: Oxford University Press.

Mukherjee, R. 1971. *Six Villages of Bengal*. Bombay: Popular Prakashan.

Neale, W. 1962. *Economic Change in Rural India: Land Tenure and Reform in Uttar Pradesh, 1800–1955*. New Haven: Yale University Press.

Newby, H. 1980: 'Trend Report: Rural Sociology'. *Current Sociology*. 28 (Spring): 1–41.

Oommen, T.K. 1984. *Social Transformation in Rural India*. New Delhi: Vikas Publishing House.

Patnaik, U. 1972. 'Economics of Farm Size and Farm Scale'. *Economic and Political Weekly*. 7(31–3):1613–24.

―――. 1996. 'Export Oriented Agriculture and Food Security in Developing Countries and India'. *Economic and Political Weekly*. 31(35–7):2429–50.

―――, ed. 1990. *Agrarian Relations and Accumulation: The 'Mode of Production Debate in India'*. Delhi: Oxford University Press.

Prasad, K.N. 1994. *Four Decades of Indian Agriculture*. Delhi: Manas.

Radhakrishanan, P. 1989. *Peasant Struggles, Land Reforms and Social Change: Malabar 1836–1982*. New Delhi: Sage Publications.

Redfield, R. 1965. *Peasant Society and Culture*. Chicago: University of Chicago Press.

Reserve Bank of India. 1969. *Report of the All India Rural Credit Review Committee*. Bombay:RBI.

Rudra, A. 1990. 'Class Relations in Indian Agriculture'. In Utsa Patnaik, ed., *Agrarian Relations and Accumulation: The 'Mode of Production Debate in India'*, 251–67. Delhi: Oxford University Press.

Rutten, M. 1991. *Capitalist Entrepreneurs and Economic Diversification: Social Profile of Large Farmers and Rural Industrialist in Central Gujarat, India*. Rotterdam: Academisch Proefschrift.

Satyanarayana, A. 1991. 'Commercialization, Money Capital and the Peasantry in Colonial Andhra, 1900–1940'. In S. Bhattacharya et al., eds, *The South Indian Economy: Agrarian Change, Industrial Structure and State Policy 1914–1947*, 51–77. Delhi: Oxford University Press.

Schwarzweller, H.K., ed. 1984. *Research in Rural Sociology and Development*, vol. 1. Greenwich: Jai Press.

Scott, J. 1976. *The Moral Economy of the Peasantry: Rebellion and Subsistence in Southeast Asia*. New Haven: Yale University Press.

Sen A. 1976. 'Famines as Failures of Exchange Entitlements'. *Economic and Political Weekly*. 11(31–3):1273–80.

———. 1977. 'Starvation and Exchange Entitlements: A General Approach and its Application to the Great Bengal Famine'. *Cambridge Journal of Economics*. 1(1):33-59.

Shanin, T., ed. 1987. *Peasants and Peasant Societies*. London: Blackwell.

Silverman, S. 1987. 'The Concept of Peasant and the Concept of Culture'. In J. Mencher, ed., *Social Anthropology of Peasantry*, 7–31. Bombay: Somaiya Publications.

Srinivas, M.N. 1955. 'The Social Structure of a Mysore Village'. In M. Marriot, ed., *Village India*, 1–35. Chicago: University of Chicago Press.

———. 1994. *The Dominant Caste and Other Essays*. Delhi: Oxford University Press.

Stokes, E. 1978. *The Peasant and the Raj*. New Delhi: Vikas Publishing House.

Thorburn, S.S. 1983. *Musalmans and Moneylenders in Punjab*, Delhi: Mittal Publications.

Thorner, A. 1982. 'Semi-Feudalism or Capitalism? Contemporary Debate on Classes and Modes of Production in India'. *Economic and Political Weekly*. 17(49–51):993–99; 2061–86.

Thorner, D. 1956. *The Agrarian Prospects of India*. Delhi: Oxford University Press.

———. 1964. *Agricultural Co-operatives in India*. Bombay: Asia Publishers.

Upadhya, C.B. 1988. 'The Farmer-Capitalists of Coastal Andhra Pradesh'. *Economic and Political Weekly*. 23(27–8):1376–82.

Weber, M. 1978. *Economy and Society: An Outline of Interpretative Sociology*, vol.1. Eds, G. Roth and C. Wittich. Berkeley: University of California Press.

Wiser, W.H. 1969. *The Hindu Jajmani System*. Lucknow: Lucknow Publishing House.

Wolf, E. 1966. *Peasants*. New Jersey: Prentice-Hall, Inc.

TABLE

Table 1: Changing Structures of Landholdings during the Post-Independence Period

Size	1960–1		1976–7		1990–1	
	Number of holdings (%)	Area operated (%)	Number of holdings (%)	Area operated (%)	Number of holdings (%)	Area operated (%)
Marginal	40.70	6.70	54.60	10.70	59.00	14.90
Small	22.30	12.20	18.00	12.80	19.00	17.30
Semi-medium	18.90	20.00	14.30	19.90	13.20	23.20
Medium	13.40	30.40	10.10	30.40	7.20	27.20
Large	4.70	30.70	3.00	26.20	1.60	17.40
Total	100.00	100.00	100.00	100.00	100.00	100.00

Source : Indian Agriculture Sector-A, Compendium of Statistics. September 1995.

Labour and Trade Unions

Narayan Sheth

Labour, in a broad sociological sense, refers to human effort in the production of some form of goods or services for the satisfaction of needs of people in society. The process and product of labour in a social situation reflect institutionalized relations involving rights and obligations between workers and those who control the use of their labour resource and its products (employers, government, and consumers). When performers of labour in a given social context become aware of their common interest and pursue it through formal organization and collective action, a labour organization or trade union develops and seeks legitimacy and recognition as an interest group within the larger society. In a typical democracy, a trade union is an integral part of its social, economic, and political organization.

Labour and Society

Economists characteristically define labour with reference to economically active population in society. This includes those who work within the framework of the principle of division of labour and whose output adds value to the existing base of capital in society. This view of labour excludes some areas of work which have considerable significance for the sociologist. For instance, the work of a housewife in the domestic sphere and work performed under institutionalized compulsions such as slavery or serfdom, do not constitute work in the economist's reckoning, although they have much value in determining the nature and character of a society. Economists seem to have produced an artefact in their definition of labour for convenience of measurement and avoidance of controversial phenomena. Kalpagam (1994) documents an interesting ideological debate in Britain on women's work in the household. The debate ended in a clear recognition of those who provided labour within the family as dependents, as against workers who supported the family. This dichotomy reinforces the idea of male dominance and makes it difficult to predict whether and how the dependent status of women in the domestic domain will find incorporation in the definition of the workforce in the wake of the growing demand for gender equality across the world.

Labour in Pre-industrial Days

There are two sets of views among social scientists on the existence of labour in the modern sense in ancient India (see Vyas and Shivamaggi 1975). Some scholars believe that a distinct category of workers could not have existed in self-sufficient village communities containing occupationally divided and economically interdependent castes in which peasants and artisans pursued their respective callings in their entirety. The other view is based on the presence of large holdings of land and craft enterprise. This implies the need for consistent supply of labour outside family units. Saran (1957) argues that the required workforce was supplied by the lowest categories in the *varna* hierarchy and by non-Aryan communities recruited as slaves. Women were employed in crafts such as dyeing and embroidery and also in the fine arts of dancing, singing, and prostitution. Saran, in fact, documents from scriptural texts the existence of economic bonds between peasants and workers as well as rudimentary norms regarding conditions of work, fair wages, wage bargaining, settlement of disputes, labour guilds, and social security.

It is now well known that Indian society before the advent of British rule was far more complex than the much-romanticized image of self-sufficient villages would have us believe. It contained a good measure of social mobility and urban centres with services and crafts well beyond those characterizing village communities. India through its early and medieval history was dotted with a variety of political and economic upheavals involving entries and exits of rulers, looters, traders, builders, craftsmen, travellers, scholars, and reformers. All such enterprises could not have been undertaken and maintained without the availability of labouring masses with some degree of specialization. Social historians seem to have shown little interest in labour in medieval India, barring brief references in studies like Habib (1963) and Kumar (1965). The rural economy in pre-British times was based essentially on caste-linked occupational division and interdependence with patron–client bonds involving structured barter of goods and services (*jajmani*). Elements of monetization entered the urban economy in stages and led to mixed compensation involving cash and kind. Traders and artisan-entrepreneurs in urban communities formed guilds (*mahajan*). These functioned mainly as philanthropic agencies and business cartels, but occasionally indulged in regulation of wages and welfare of labour.

Emergence of Labour Market

The emergence of labour as a distinct socio-economic phenomenon in India is usually ascribed to the impact of the Industrial Revolution and British rule. Modern technology implied mass production and complex organization in the factory, with increasing specialization of jobs and a structured division of labour. Accordingly, the Indian economy began to graduate from status to contract. Employer–employee relations in the urban-industrial sector were governed by three principal factors: the contract of employment, cash nexus, and the superordinate role of the state as the custodian of the interests of all citizens. Labour assumed the form of a marketable commodity and became a factor of production.

In agriculture, ownership and labour continued to remain indistinguishable for the most part, as the production process involved owners, tenants, their families, and neighbours in a complex set of socio-economic mutuality that would elude the identification of labour as a discrete force. Those who worked exclusively as farm labourers were also governed by traditional ties of patronage and bondage. Wage labour in agriculture emerged slowly and painfully in the wake of land reforms introduced by the British rulers before Independence and subsequently by successive governments in regional contexts. Consequently, agricultural labour in India has conventionally been recognized as a distinct category for socio-economic analysis and intervention. However, a large proportion of farm workers own some land and thus fall in the categories of small or marginal farmers, although many of them live close to or well below subsistence level. With constantly growing population pressures on rural resources, large masses of farm workers live with seasonal employment and continually move along the spectrum of employment, partial employment, and unemployment. At the end of the spectrum there are landless labourers who live totally on wages offered by employers or on government aid and subsidies. All this makes it difficult to unequivocally designate a section of population as agricultural labour. The conditions and problems of farm labour can be dealt with in the context of local situations and traditions.

The labour employed by craftsmen and artisans was bound by relations of socio-economic mutuality. Subsistence, minimum insurance (for old age, crisis etc.), and perpetual bondage characterized labour relations. Exceptional cases of kindness and affection would have led to occasional episodes of mobility of workers into the role and status of craftsmen. Generally, however, there were distinct communities of employers and workers.

Modern Enterprise and Unions

The emergence of modern trade unions in India in the wake of the impact of machine technology and the factory system is well documented by Punekar (1948), Sharma (1962), Subramanian (1967), and others. Industrialization began with coal mining in eastern India in the 1820s and assumed significance with railways and textile mills in the 1850s. At the same time, the pressure of growing population on land and other sources of livelihood had begun to force the poor low-caste people in rural areas to look for work in urban centres. The labour force needed for industrial enterprises therefore mainly consisted of pauperized migrants from rural areas who were recruited through the agency of labour contractors. These middlemen were also responsible for ensuring availability and discipline of labour, absolving the employer of direct accountability for workers' security and welfare. Their workloads and schedules depended entirely on the need and convenience of employers. Migrant workers lived in cheap, crowded, unclean settlements in the neighbourhoods of their workplaces. Their families were, as a rule, left behind in villages. They therefore needed to frequently visit their village homes to fulfil numerous socio-economic obligations. Industry employed women and children for relatively less arduous jobs, paid them lower wages, and exploited them in many ways. These conditions led to the emergence of an urban-industrial proletariat living in extreme poverty and helplessness (Mukhtar 1930; Sharma 1962).

The pauperization of industrial labour soon attracted the attention of liberal-minded social observers and reformers in India and Britain. They cajoled the government to inquire into the prevailing labour conditions. An official commission visited industrial centres in 1875 and reported on the conditions of workers with regard to safety, welfare, child labour, etc. Thus began the process of formal documentation of the social reality of Indian industrial labour. Consequently, the government imposed legal obligations on employers to ensure minimum safety at the workplace and protection for female and child labour. The government thus assumed the role of monitor and regulator of labour relations. The process of official inquiry into conditions of industrial labour was repeated in 1884, 1907, and 1931. In each case, the inquiry was followed by new regulatory legislation to control exploitation of workers and to improve their lot (Royal Commission on Labour in India 1931).

The exercise of documentation of labour conditions by inquiry commissions led to the emergence of exigent combinations among workers to represent their common experiences. A collective consciousness of the industrial proletariat thus began to emerge among the Indian labour scene. This was reinforced by the attempts of social reformers to ameliorate workers' destitution and ignorance. Similar welfare organizations were formed among railway workers in 1897 and printing workers in 1905. A trade union in the modern sense was launched by Gandhi and his colleagues in Ahmedabad in 1917 (Patel 1987) and by Wadia in Madras in 1918. Gandhi's concept and programmes of trade unionism were predominantly informed by the philosophy of harmony, trusteeship, and resolution of disputes by mutual understanding or arbitration.

The All-India Trade Union Congress was formed in 1920 in response to the need to represent Indian labour at a tripartite international meeting sponsored by the International Labour Organization. Until 1926, however, trade unions did not enjoy legal recognition. Attempts to organize workers or raise demands on their behalf were treated by employers and government as breach of civil contract between employer and worker. Union leaders and workers engaged in union activity were often punished or persecuted for forming illegal combinations. The Indian Trade Unions Act, (1926) conferred on unions legal immunity for legitimate union action. The law also permitted up to half of a union executive body to be drawn from non-workers. The role of the outsider in trade unionism was thus approved in law. It has since been the subject of much controversy in discussions on trade-union democracy and effectiveness (Punekar 1948; Sharma 1962).

The growth of trade unionism nearly coincided with the development of the Indian nationalist consciousness and movement. In the train of their concurrent progress, trade union objectives and leadership became subservient to nationalist goals and political leadership. This historical connection between Indian unions and politics has become the hallmark of the progress of unionism in the country and its influence on the effectiveness of unions to achieve their principal objectives of articulating, protecting, and promoting workers' collective interests. From their inception until the early years of Independence, trade unions passed through episodes of unity and dissension, combination and division, directly as a consequence of such episodes among political parties. However, union leaders were all influenced by a combination of nationalist and socialist ideologies. These ideologies and the leaders' participation in the freedom movement endowed them with the missionary spirit of selfless service (Sharma 1962; Subramanian 1967).

Governance and Research

Trade unions gradually secured for workers benefits in wages, perquisites, welfare, stability, and security. The growth of the public sector was accompanied by a reinforcement of government's role as model employer, apart from its responsibility as arbiter and moderator of employer–employee relations. A tripartite forum called the Indian Labour Conference was set up in 1942 for periodical reviews and action plans regarding the resolution of disputes and the promotion of mutual understanding and cooperation among employers, unions, and government.

This process of maturation in labour relations anticipated the availability of information on various aspects of labour and employment. The periodical inquiry commissions during the British regime, as mentioned earlier, had paved the way for the compilation of socio-economic data on workers in industry. The government appointed an expert committee in 1946 to assess the socio-economic conditions of industrial labour. The findings of this committee provided the basis for the prescription of minimum wages on the principles of basic needs of workers and social justice. These developments raised interest in labour among economists, sociologists, and other social scientists. The economists' special interest in labour culminated in the birth of the Indian Society for Labour Economics during 1957–8. They began the convention of an annual conference of labour economists and launched the *Indian Journal of Labour Economics (IJLE)*. Interestingly, this fraternity co-opted sociological and psychological research on labour within their fold. From the beginning, the research work reported in *IJLE* covered a wide spectrum of issues in labour and industrial relations, including female and child labour, personnel management, technological change, labour welfare, humanism, and industrial democracy. A glance through the contributions made to *IJLE* over the years shows that the scholars and researchers in labour were predominantly driven by the democratic-socialist ideology emphasizing social equality and justice, dignity of labour, and workers' control over their own fate.

At the level of government, the strategy and programmes of planned development required detailed information on labour in all sectors. The central and state governments gradually undertook the documentation of labour conditions through their own research establishments or through academic researchers. Inquiries were conducted from time to time to study the conditions of labour in various sectors, including agriculture and women. The central government also began in 1957 to compile periodical digests and bibliographies on labour research. A specialized unit called the Labour Bureau was promoted to collect statistical data on all aspects of labour and to disseminate the information for use by government and other parties through an official periodical called the *Indian Labour Journal*. The Planning Commission also encouraged and supported research on labour, as did some employers' organizations and trade unions. Various social science departments in universities and autonomous research institutions, some set up primarily for research on labour, also undertook research on labour and labour relations.

These include the National Labour Institute, Shri Ram Centre for Industrial Relations, and Gandhi Labour Institute. The Indian Council of Social Science Research undertook in 1969–70 a survey of literature on the entire range of research areas including labour and trade unions. The National Commission on Labour during 1967–9 surveyed various aspects of labour and trade unions in different industries and regions, apart from a thematic report on the sociology of labour–management relations (National Commission on Labour 1969). In subsequent years, the government appointed national commissions for other sectors of the economy, including agriculture, rural labour, and self-employed workers. The efforts of all these agencies have contributed much information and sociologically relevant insights. Punekar and Varickayil (1989) have brought out a compilation of various official reports and petitions made by people on matters of labour and labour relations.

Labour and Sociology

As mentioned above, official inquiries into the conditions of labour during the early decades of industrialization led to the documentation of socio-economic conditions of workers. Sociologically significant information was also occasionally compiled by sensitive observers and reformers. Subramanian (1967) describes the publication of a British journalist's account of the oppression of workers by employers in Bombay in 1905. Sharma (1962) likewise has stated how a section of the elite Brahmin youth in Bengal was disturbed by the slave-like conditions of plantation workers. Sharma's account includes the adventure of a young man who disguised himself and worked as a coolie and then published his experiences of the condition of labour.

However, significant sociological interest in labour emanated from a different source. By the turn of the century, eminent western social analysts like Marx and Weber had drawn a depressing picture of the prospects of industrialization in tradition-bound societies such as India. Weber regarded the Indian caste system, the joint family, Hindu beliefs and rituals, and the rural-agricultural nexus of Indian society as antithetical to the growth of a rational urban-industrial culture. Such gloomy prognoses induced some early western scholars and administrators in the British regime to study the Indian labour scene. Their conclusions, represented by Broughton (1924) and the Royal Commission on Labour in India (1931), predicted a bleak future for industrialization in the country. They noticed that workers came largely from rural areas, lower castes, and agricultural occupations. There was evidence of high rates of absenteeism and labour turnover accompanied by low productivity. Such data led the observers to the diagnosis that Indian workers lacked commitment to industrial work. Lack of commitment was looked upon as a symbol of the cultural impediments to the growth of industrialization. As the Second World War and Indian colonialism drew to an end, western social scientists began to examine the process of industrialization in developed and developing societies in a comparative framework. This search led to the construction of a logic of industrialism, which was perceived as embodied in the rational, liberal-individualist culture of the West labelled as modern, as against the traditional cultures of the developing societies. Consequently, an incompatibility was postulated between modern technology and traditional cultures. The perceived lack of commitment among workers then became a 'problem of labour commitment' and invited the attention of students of labour and industry (see Myers 1958; Niehoff 1959; Patel 1963; and Mehta 1960).

Concrete studies of industrial workers began to reveal that by using an inadequate database, earlier observers had misconstrued the problem of labour commitment. It was pointed out (Morris 1960; Thorner 1957) that indices of poor commitment like high absenteeism and turnover and low productivity, were a function of employers' aversion to committed labour rather than a simple manifestation of workers' primordial loyalties and aversion to urban-industrial culture. These findings lent a new perspective to the sociological studies of industrial labour that followed. Some scholars studied labour commitment in terms of statistical measures of employees' conformity to workplace discipline and employees' attitudes to work and employer (Lambert 1963; Sharma 1974). Others laid greater stress on the participant-observation approach (Sheth 1968; Holmstrom 1976). These studies marked the beginning of comprehensive sociological research on industrial workers in India. They revealed that industrial workers were more open to an industrial way of life and less enslaved by primordial ties than postulated by earlier observers. The demands on workers from industry (work technology, discipline, etc.) and those from their traditional socio-cultural loyalties were not always contradictory. Institutional obligations and commitment to work could coexist and allow workers to compartmentalize their behaviour in order to resolve emergent contradictions. Traditional and modern institutions not only coexisted but also offered choices to workers in specific situational contexts. Holmstrom (1976), Sheth (1979), and Uma Ramaswamy (1983) provide valuable examples of the multiplicity of social, economic, and political forces influencing behavioural choices of industrial workers. At the same time, socio-economic studies of labour have continued to be made at universities and research institutions for doctoral, post-doctoral, and other projects, although many of these seem to remain unpublished (see Kher 1984 and Chaturvedi 1987).

The Wider Perspective

Meanwhile, progressive trade-union action on behalf of labour and government's active role in labour relations resulted in a wide variety of monetary and social benefits. In this background, sociological interest in labour shifted from the commitment discourse to the reality of labour conditions. This reality was to be seen as a part of the dynamics of labour relations involving workers, employers, trade unions, government, and the social forces governing the behaviour patterns of each of these categories of stake holders. The structural approach adopted by sociologists like Lambert and Sharma to study workers' behaviour and attitudes was subsequently used by others to research managerially significant aspects of performance and behaviour. Thus began an era of sociological interest in organizational and socio-cultural factors influencing behavioural factors such as productivity, motivation, attitude to work, and labour–management cooperation. It was gradually realized that the conventional definition of a worker needed to be expanded to cover all sections of employees including white-collar and managerial cadres governed by the contract of employment (see Punekar and Savur 1969; Sharma 1987 and 1991). The growing impact of modern information technology and computers has begun to change the socio-economic profile of labour which is likely to have far-reaching implications for the behaviour, performance, and role of workers in industry and society. Considerable information on this trend is published in popular and serious periodicals. Ramaswamy's recent publications (1994b and 1997) contain precious sociological clues in this regard.

On the other hand, the managerial perspective of labour studies and the motivation–alientaion view of labour productivity gave rise to a composite socio-technical view of people's behaviour and output in the workplace. This view engineered a variety of productivity-oriented experiments in redesigning work groups to create scope for more collaborative, adaptive, and dignified relationships among workers and supervisors. Some of these experiments have been documented and offer valuable sociological insights into workplace behaviour (see De 1977). Unfortunately, as far as I am aware, all such experiments failed to survive the economic, political, and social realities of the enterprises in which they were launched.

Trade union Studies

The planned process of industrialization in the post-Independence era facilitated the emergence of trade unionism as an effective force not only in the context of employment relations but also in its direct and indirect effect on the economy at all levels. This encouraged scholars and practitioners to examine the socio-economic conditions of trade unions. The early attempts in this direction were limited to the compilation of factual information about unions—history, organization, membership, ideology, leadership, major achievements, and such other descriptions. The more scholarly attempts among these studies dealt with issues such as political connections of unions, the dominance of outside leadership, problems of organizational strength and bargaining power within their complex legal-political framework, and lack of interest among the ranks of members (see Punekar 1948; Karnik 1966). Studies conducted by sociologists were principally guided by questions of the effects of socio-cultural factors (caste, religion, urban–rural origin, education, etc.) on interest and involvement of leaders and workers in their unions (Punekar and Madhuri 1967; Sheth and Jain 1968; Reindorp 1971). They emphasized the dominating role in unions played by outsiders with political preoccupation and oligarchic tendencies. Leaders and workers were unequal in terms of social, economic, and educational status, which distanced them from each other in their expectations and perceptions regarding trade-union goals and activities. Workers among themselves were socially and culturally heterogeneous and fragmented into regional, religious, and caste divisions that blocked their identity as workers and hence their involvement in unions.

These early attempts in unfolding the Indian trade-union reality were based more on quick general observations than on adequate information and understanding of workers and unions. Munson's overview of Indian unions (1970) enabled him to distinguish three types of union orientation. Apart from the stereotypical political unions controlled by political parties, he identified a category of unions which were dependent on employers or government for their sustenance or growth. A third type of unions was called member centred because such unions were predominantly guided by workers' needs and interests. Against this background, Ramaswamy's (1977) study of trade unions in Coimbatore was a pioneering effort in an intensive sociological analysis of trade unionism. Ramaswamy discovered considerable political consciousness among workers and a network of social, economic, and political interconnections among workers and leaders. Leaders depended on workers' acceptance of their leadership and were therefore forced to be democratic in their management of union organization as well as workers' needs and grievances. These findings effectively challenged the prevailing view of trade unions as being led by an oligarchy of leadership and weakened by a heterogeneous and fragmented membership. The kind of trade union reality brought by Ramaswamy was unlikely to be widely prevalent. In fact, one of the unions covered by Ramaswamy in the same study showed clear signs of oligarchy and subordination of workers' interests to leaders' political ideology and expediency.

A similar study of trade unionism in Jamshedpur (Mamkoottam 1982) brought out a carefully nurtured collusion between union leaders and management across their respective hierarchies. The result was gross disregard for workers' problems and needs, although the union was ostensibly democratic and free from political control. These studies, apart from their substantive contribution, underscored the need for sociological research in trade unions to be based on examination of the interconnection of all socio-cultural forces influencing the behaviour of workers and leaders. However, micro studies were not undertaken on a large scale. Information and insights into the conditions of labour and trade unions seem to come more from journalistic accounts than from detailed sociological studies.

Ramaswamy's subsequent study (1984) revealed the dynamics of power among trade unions, employers, and government. He showed that the treatment received by a union from employers and government depended on equations of political power in given situations. The political and bureaucratic wings of government were commonly used to promote the interests of protege unions and to exploit or victimize those who posed any threat to the ruling clique. This resulted in union militancy, violence, constant rivalries, and loss of production.

In large industrial centres, union leadership has fallen into the hands of professional careerists and opportunists who have lumpenized the power of unions. These leaders use personal charisma, physical prowess, and mafia tactics to plunder the membership of established unions and then force employers and workers to obey their commands regardless of their consequences (see Sherlock 1996). Today, it is not uncommon for employers and unions to create and settle conflicts in employment relations with the help of mafia elements. The famous strike in the Bombay textile industry in the early 1980s was as much a consequence of bitter and brutal union rivalries as of management practices and government policy (Wersch 1992).

The general picture of the reality of trade unions does not apply to all unions in the country. There are unions which represent their members and conduct their affairs in tune with the fundamental rationale of trade unionism in a democratic society. Such 'normal' unions are less likely to attract public or academic attention. In rare cases, unions have done exemplary work by taking over and managing sick units on behalf of workers. Such experiences have given rise to hopes regarding promotion of a workers' sector in industrial entrepreneurship (Bhowmik 1991).

Trade unions today cover less than a fifth of workers in the organized sector and barely 2 per cent of the total workforce in India. Some sections of labour in the organized sector enjoy satisfaction and security in spite of their remaining non-unionized due to legal protection and entitlements or due to humanist employers. However, a large portion in this category, especially the poor and weak among them, remain out of bounds for union support.

On the other hand, trade unionism has grown with special force among white-collar and managerial workers. These sections found themselves neglected or exploited in the wake of the rising power of blue-collar unions during the post-Independence period. With the growth of educated, urban, upper-caste sections in the worker population, the social barriers between blue and white collar began to collapse. The only way in which the white collar could gain benefits and security was by unionizing. For some time, it was hoped that white- and blue-collar unions would combine to form a formidable working class. But the interests and orientations of the two were divergent (see Kanhere 1987; Sreenivasan 1989). Hence white-collar unions became a independent force and gradually acquired power. Gradually, collective action yielded benefits and attracted elite categories of professional workers like lawyers, teachers, and doctors to unionism. They indulged in militancy too. Today, they often wield more power than blue-collar workers.

The profile of the unionized blue-collar workers has changed in recent years. The relatively young, educated, and socially mobile worker is increasingly influenced by the consumerist culture. On the other hand, the growing competitiveness in industry in the wake of globalization and liberalization has pushed employers into desperate moves to rationalize labour resources by retrenchment, voluntary retirement schemes, and redefined workloads. Trade unions have been unable to help workers facing actual and potential unemployment or increased work pressures. In fact, union leaders have often supported employers in bargaining for greater benefits for a smaller workforce at the cost of retrenched or retired employees. This has created a sense of alienation among workers in relation to union leadership. Consequently, trade unions have been losing membership as well as the strength to truly represent the workers' interests (Ramaswamy 1988).

This trend of progressive weakening of trade unions seems to be a global phenomenon. The new market-driven global village probably has less tolerance for conventional trade unions than yesterday's capitalist and socialist fraternities. Some observers regard trade unions as irrelevant to the emerging global economy and society (Sheth 1993; Davala 1994). Some advocate a new role for tomorrow's unions in the form of community welfare and social reform. Others predict growing socio-economic alienation among workers as a result of rising affluence and consumerism and anticipate a new role for trade unions in managing new forms of discontent among workers (Sadri et al. 1994). Meanwhile, employers have begun to employ the new concepts and methods of human resource development (HRD) and participative management in the hope of co-opting workers and trade unions into a collaborationist view of labour–management relations (Venkata Ratnam 1994, Jomon 1997). It remains to be seen whether this new approach can catalyse the ground-level realities of labour, capital, and management into an arena of mutual trust and understanding.

Some entrepreneurs and social workers influenced by Gandhian ideology have, since Independence, tried to practise the trusteeship concept by involving workers in ownership and management of enterprise. Some economists have occasionally favoured financial stake of workers in enterprise by holding a part of equity. In a few cases, as mentioned earlier, workers took over total management of industrial units after they became unviable due to management failure. However, these attempts have so far met with extremely modest success. Whenever an innovative measure implying major participation of workers or unions in enterprise appears on the horizon, trade unions and scholars tend to become euphoric and build hopes and expectations about the growth of a workers' sector. These hopes and expectations are related to the democratic aspirations of reduction of poverty and inequality and of raising the dignity of labour and empowerment of the weaker segments in society. However, plans and efforts in this direction have not moved beyond stray experiments which have mostly proved short-lived. Entrenched interests do not easily yield to euphoric bouts of ideology.

The Informal Sector

The informal sector of labour and employment covers a wide variety of labour conditions and employer–employee relations. In urban areas, it includes small industrial units which are either not governed by any labour law or where employers violate legal obligations with the connivance of government or by clever manipulation of law and authority. It also includes vast masses of workers employed in the commercial sector, wayside enterprises, domestic services, self-employed artisans, and vendors etc. In rural areas, the vast majority of labour in agriculture (Chopra 1994; Singh 1997) and cottage industry, as also self-employed craftsmen and artisans, fall within the informal sector. Apart from these segments of labour, those who are unemployed or underemployed deserve recognition as part of a society's labour force. The National Commission on Rural Labour has documented and analysed the various dimensions of socio-economic conditions of rural labour and employment (Government of India 1991). Women and children have lately been given special attention in studies of labour in view of the growing awareness of discrimination and exploitation suffered by them both in social conduct and policy in the sphere of government as well as in civil society. I have therefore discussed female labour and child labour briefly in separate sections in the following pages.

It is known that the informal and formal sectors of employment do not exist as exclusive worlds for labour (Holmstrom 1984; Breman 1994). Not all workers in the formal sector are highly paid or enjoy job protection and socio-economic welfare benefits. On the other hand, some segments of workers in the informal sector are well paid and protected, either due to the generous outlook of employers or organized action led by trade unions or non-government organizations. There is also socio-economic interdependence between the two sectors as members of a family or larger kin group are often divided between them and provide mutual support and security, especially in times of crisis such as unemployment or loss of jobs. The growing incidence of industrial sickness has often pushed industrial workers back to casual labour or self-employment.

Glimpses into the socio-economic conditions of rural labour are available in studies like Patel (1952), Daniel and Alice Thorner (1962), and Kumar (1965). A pioneering study of agricultural and rural labour was made by Breman, who has documented elements and degrees of bondage of farm workers in Gujarat and the farmers' control over their existence and exploitation (Breman 1974). The workers were aware of their low status but lacked political power in spite of numerical strength. Breman showed how this weakness was compounded by fragmentation among workers and exploited by employers. Breman's continuing interest in rural and agricultural labour has yielded valuable insights into various facets of labour relations (Breman 1985; 1993; 1994; and 1996) and the effects of migration of rural workers to urban centres. His studies show that the entry of rural migrants into channels of recruitment to jobs in industry creates a link between the formal and informal sectors in a continuum. Primordial loyalties such as caste and religion are important in recruitment. Scarcity of jobs gradually erodes the significance of education and leads to downward social mobility among workers. Such forces create disunity and fragmentation among workers, preventing them from fighting for their rights or common interests.

As trade unionism took root in the industrial sector, the socio-economic conditions of labour in agriculture and the unorganized industry made union leaders aware of the need for the unionization of workers in these sectors. Employers were all-powerful. Workers were socially and economically heterogeneous and perennially under patronage and indebtedness in relation to employers. In such an environment, it was hardly feasible for the largely urban-oriented trade unions to penetrate labour relations in rural areas. Some unions such as the Textile Labour Association in Ahmedabad and those with socialist ideologies in the eastern and southern regions made efforts in this direction, but did not succeed beyond a few modest projects. One suggestion made by some scholars was to set up workers' cooperatives to provide union-type protection and support (Aziz 1978). However, such ideas could not be converted into concrete experience. As an alternative measure, some organizations like the National Labour Institute undertook action research in rural labour. This enabled scholars to study the reality of rural labour even as they were engaged in rural service in the form of raising awareness among rural workers about their conditions, rights, and opportunities within the contemporary legal and socio-political framework (Ghatak 1977, Maharaj et al. 1977). Along with such attempts, the formation of a band of social workers and reformers in rural communities sought to look after the welfare and development of the people, especially those suffering from social disability, disadvantage, and exploitation. The liberal-socialist elements in political parties also began to advocate and struggle for a better deal for workers in the rural and unorganized sectors. Consequently, minimum wages for rural labour were prescribed by law in various states and enforcement agencies were set up to ensure compliance and resolve disputes.

Such measures have contributed to improvement in the conditions of rural workers. However, it is widely known that employers violate the norms of minimum wages and can easily persuade government invigilators to collude with them. Exploitation of labour, especially women and children, continues. Political dominance or influence enjoyed by employers usually gives them greater leverage to exploit labour. Since labour as a rule is from lower socio-economic sections than employers, its exploitation is often coloured by disputes or conflicts between castes or caste combinations. Such conflicts, especially in some northern states, worsen the plight of workers, as they involve violence and destruction of life and property.

Female Labour

Increasing attention has been paid over the last two decades to the social reality and problems of female labour. According to the 1981 census, only a fifth of women in India were in the labour force, of whom a third were marginal workers (Gulati 1985). The 1991 census recorded 89.7 million female workers (about 28.5 per cent) in a total workforce of 314.1 million. Of these, 28.1 per cent of the female workers were marginal workers, as against 1.2 per cent of male workers (Datt 1997).

A good deal of information on patterns of female participation in the Indian labour force (Visaria 1991) and the implications of the changing economic scenario for women (Bannerji 1991) is available to researchers and other observers. The trend of growth in the proportion of women at all levels of work and employment is likely to continue in the wake of some well-known forces of socio-economic change such as rise in female literacy, changing mores about the role and status of woman in family and society, escalating need for family earnings to meet consumerist ideas of prestige and comfort, and employers' preference for women in some segments of employment. As more and more women join the labour force, they are likely to enhance the pace of liberalization in terms of gender equity and individual rights. At the same time, female employment seems to generate intricate problems of harassment and exploitation at work. Women workers fight on two fronts, against male domination at home and against oppressive and exploitative employers. They suffer from helplessness and indebtedness and are often relegated to a position of slavery (Shobha 1987). The National Commission of Self-Employed Women has reported on the conditions of self-employed women in various sectors such as home-based producers, providers of services, petty vendors, processing workers, and manual workers (SEWA 1989). They found that a vast majority of these women were landless. They were perceived not as workers but just as women by themselves and by others, despite the fact that they contributed substantially to family incomes.

The labour market in the informal sector is thus biased against women. The lowest paid occupations employ a disproportionately high number of women. Modernization and technological change have adversely affected female labour participation. Traditional avenues of work and employment are closing down. Women from Scheduled Castes and Tribes as well as minority communities are at a special disadvantage in the labour market (Jumani 1991). Women end up looking for consistent but inferior work with lower wages in relation to men. Mies et al. (1987) also emphasize the oppression of and discrimination against women workers in the patriarchal culture of India. Skills are usually withheld from women. Women mostly work in marginal sectors of employment with low wages and insecure jobs. This often gives the impression that their incomes are subordinate to men's incomes, whereas they may actually carry the main burden of sustaining the family. The dominant role of men reinforces this impression. Issues of the conditions of women at work and inequity in working conditions and incomes are examined by scholars such as Cherian and Prasad (1995) and Everett and Savara (1994). The National Commission on Self-Employed Women pleaded for a new perspective on women's role in the workforce. It suggested that women's bargaining power should be raised through action for women's cooperatives. Bajpai (1997) has discussed some aspects of the rights of women at the workplace. An overview of the problems of empowerment of women in work and life is contained in studies like Carr et al. (1996) and Rao et al. (1996).

Child Labour

Child labour as a major social problem of developing societies has been examined and debated with growing concern in recent years. It is well known that employment of children in the informal sector is rampant as a strategy to reduce labour cost and contain labour protest against injustice. Child labour predominantly implies denial of individual freedom and opportunity to children and often unspeakable exploitation and abuse by employers, parents, and others.

Salient aspects of the dynamics and growth of child labour in India are discussed by scholars like Jain (1996) and Chaudhri (1996). From 1951 to 1991 child labour has increased more in urban areas than in rural and more among girls than boys. Total full-time child labour has decreased by 12 per cent in absolute terms, but urban child labour has increased by 59 per cent. On the other hand, marginal child labour has increased by 338 per cent between 1981 and 1991. This increase includes figures of 588 per cent among urban boys, 733 per cent among urban girls, 103 per cent among rural boys, and 405 per cent among rural girls. There has thus been an alarming increase in child labour among girls and among urban children of both sexes.

There is considerable awareness of the evil effects of child labour in India as well as at global level (Hirway 1987; Sharma and Mittal 1990; Burra 1989; Mishra and Pande 1996). Legislation for the abolition of child labour and the awareness and protest programmes conducted by dedicated activists and organizations do not seem to have had much effect on child labour. It is recognized that the problem runs into a vicious spiral in a situation of low economic growth. Absence of a demographic transition, effective public policies, static economy, and inferior technology reinforce each other to restrain effective measures against child labour. It is hoped that increase in real incomes will lead to higher literacy and greater female participation in the workforce and will help create a positive climate against child labour.

The Tailenders

The social reality of labour in seasonal and irregular avenues of employment is examined purposively at national and regional levels by official agencies and research institutions. They bring out the ephemeral nature of employment, poor compensation (often below subsistence level), lack of protection by law or organized action, and bleak prospects of improvement. In some regions such as Maharashtra, the government has launched schemes for providing minimum economic protection to those who are either totally unemployed or marginally employed in an irregular manner. The Employment Guarantee Scheme takes care of unorganized labour in dire need. Employment is also available to unemployed and underemployed people under other government schemes such as the Jawahar Rozgar Yojana (JRY) and the Integrated Rural Development Programme (IRDP). But all these efforts contribute only marginally to the problem of unemployment and underemployment (Hirway and Terhal 1990).

Empowering the Poor

The need for organizing unorganized workers has been felt over the years. In fact, the new climate of economic liberalization has strengthened the awareness of this need, as it has resulted in an increasing casualization of labour. Datt's compilation on the subject (1997) has catalogued the recent attempts at worker organization in various parts of India. About two million workers have been organized through trade unions or non-government organizations (NGOs). An umbrella organization called the National Confederation of Labour, involving trade unions and NGOs concerned with organizing the unorganized, was recently established (Bidwai 1995). The various studies included in Datt (1997) highlight ways in which the unorganized sectors can be unionized. Some advocate NGOs forming or joining trade unions and participating in the regular trade-union movement. Others would like trade unions to assist poor workers in setting up production systems with adequate financial support, implying an entrepreneurial role for unions. Still others would like the government to play a leading role in promoting viable enterprises for unorganized workers with the help of trade unions and NGOs. Workers' cooperatives are suggested as one way of helping poor workers. These efforts towards the amelioration of the poverty, deprivation, and social injustice suffered perennially by the unorganized masses of labour are still in a nascent stage. The power of the powerless is still in the realm of hope and dream. Jhabvala (1995) presents an interesting account of the growing global concern about the plight of poor unorganized workers and the efforts to recognize their problems and give them their due.

Further Literature

As mentioned in the main text, sociologists have shown relatively modest interest in labour and trade unions. It would be quite educative to study the socio-political contexts of some normal, copy-book trade unions with a history of stable collective bargaining and peaceful bilateral resolution of disputes. Such unions may provide useful clues to the future of trade unionism in the years to come. Some scholars continue to pursue the paradigm of labour as a social class and explore its contemporary organizational and social factors (Dev Nathan 1987; Patel 1994 and 1997; Wilson 1996; Sadri et al. 1995). The institution of trade unionism is based on the premise of class consciousness and confrontation. We need to learn how this institution is moulded or modified to cope with the rising importance of the computer and information technology, along with the growing threat to human capital. The growth of consumerism, the knowledge worker, and the multinational corporation will increasingly divide and marginalize the working masses. At the same time, every section or fragment of the labour force will need to indulge in countervailing power to further their respective interests (Sheth 1996). Thus, while trade unions as organizations may go through a process of decline, trade unionism as a social force may grow in a criss-cross pattern. Will this phenomenon create greater disharmony and conflict in society? Will society evolve new structures or forces to contain this seemingly dysfunctional trend? Are there viable forms and systems of participative management available to replace conventional collective bargaining? (see Ramaswamy 1994a; Custers 1995).

Meanwhile, more attention needs to be paid to the social situation of workers in the informal sector (Srinivasulu 1997; Mishra et al. 1996; and Singh 1991). Ironically, the more we idealize human dignity and human resource development, the farther we push the poorer sections of workers into marginalization and casualization. What options in social, economic, and political action are available to these people to acquire minimum standards of human dignity and social security? Our ability to design situationally meaningful answers to this question will indeed determine how far we can view and treat Indian labour as a coherent socio-economic category rather than as a disjointed collectivity of consuming producers.

REFERENCES

Aziz, Abdul. 1978. 'Unionizing Agricultural Labourers in India: A Strategy'. *Indian Journal Of Industrial Relations*. 13(3): 307–20.

Bajpai, Asha. 1997. 'Women's Rights at the Workplace: Emerging Challenges and Legal Interventions'. *Indian Journal of Social Work*. 58(1):111–25.

Bannerji, Nirmala, ed. 1991. *Indian Women in a Changing Industrial Scenario*. Delhi: Sage Publications.

Bhowmik, Sharit K. 1991. 'Is a Workers' Sector Viable?' *Economic and Political Weekly*. 14 December: 2854–6.

———. 1991. 'State Intervention and the Working Class Movement'. *Economic and Political Weekly*. 28 December: L39–44.

Bidwai, Praful. 1995. 'Mutiny of 290 Million: Informal Workers get Organized'. *The Times of India*. Ahmedabad. (3 June): 6.

Breman, Jan. 1974. *Patronage and Exploitation*. Berkeley: University of California Press.

———. 1985. *Of Peasants, Migrants and Paupers: Rural Labour Circulation and Capitalist Production in Western India*. Oxford: Oxford University Press.

———. 1993. *Beyond Patronage and Exploitation: Changing Agrarian Relations in South Gujarat*. Delhi: Oxford University Press.

———. 1994. *Wage Hunters and Gatherers: Search for Work in the Urban and Rural Economy of South Gujarat*. Delhi: Oxford University Press.

———. 1996. *Footloose Labour: Working in India's Informal Economy*. Cambridge: Cambridge University Press.

Broughton, G.M. 1924. *Labour in Indian Industries*. Milford.

Burra, Neera. 1989. *Child Labour in the Brassware Industry of Moradabad. Uttar Pradesh, India*. New Delhi: ILO-ARTEP.

Carr, M., M. Chen, and R. Jhabvala, eds. 1996. *Speaking Out: Women's Economic Empowerment in South Asia*. New Delhi: Vistaar Publications.

Chaudhri, D.P. 1996. *A Dynamic Profile of Child Labour in India 1951–91*. New Delhi: Child Labour Action and Support Project.

Chaturvedi, Abha. 1987. *Workers' World: Socio-economic Profile of Pune Workers*. Pune: Times Research Foundation.

Cherian, J. and K.V.E. Prasad. 1995. *Women, Work and Inequity: The Reality of Gender*. Ghaziabad: National Labour Institute.

Chopra, Radhika. 1994. 'Voices from the Earth: Work and Food Production in a Punjabi Village'. *Sociological Bulletin*. 43(1):79–91.

Custers, Peter. 1995. 'The Race Between Ford and Toyota: Struggle for World Dominance'. *Economic and Political Weekly*. 25 November: M151–8.

Datt, Ruddar, ed. 1997. *Organizing the Unorganized Workers*. New Delhi: Vikas Publishing House.

Davala, Sarath. 1994. 'New Economic Policy and Trade Union Response'. *Economic and Political Weekly*. 19 February:406–8.

——. 1994. *Unprotected Labour in India*. New Delhi: Friedrich Ebert Stiftung.

De, Nitish R. 1977. 'Participative Redesign of Work System and Enrichment of Quality of Work Life'. *National Labour Institute Bulletin*. 3(5):184–200; and 3(6):237–53.

Dev Nathan. 1987. 'Structure of Working Class in India. *Economic and Political Weekly*. 2 May:799–809.

Everett, Jana and M. Savara. 1994. *Women and Organizations in the Informal Sector*. Delhi: Himalaya Publishing House.

Ghatak, Maitreya. 1977. 'The Agricultural Labour: A Case Study from West Bengal'. *National Labour Institute Bulletin* 3(5):201–20.

Government of India, Ministry of Labour. 1991. *Report of the National Commission on Rural Labour*. Delhi: Government of India.

Gulati, Leela. 1985. 'Women in the Unorganized Sector with Special Reference to Kerala'. Working Paper 172. Trivandrum: Centre for Development Studies.

Habib, Irfan. 1963. *The Agrarian System of Mughal India (1556–1707)*. Bombay: Asia Publishing House.

Hirway, Indira, ed. 1987. *Child Labour*. Bombay: Oxford and IBH.

Hirway, I. and P. Terhal. 1990. *Towards Right to Work in India: Indian and International Experiences in Rural Works Programmes*. New Delhi and The Hague: ICSSR-IMWOO.

Holmstrom, Mark. 1976. *South Indian Factory Workers*. Cambridge: Cambridge University Press.

——. 1984. *Industry and Inequality: The Social Anthropology of Indian Labour*. Cambridge: Cambridge University Press.

Jain, Mahaveer. 1996. 'Child Labour: A Growing Phenomenon in India'. *Social Engineer*. 5(1):50–9.

Jhabvala, Renana. 1995. 'Invisible Workers Reach International Heights'. *Economic and Political Weekly*. 9 December:3133–6.

Jomon, M.G. 1997. 'The New HRD Manager'. *Manas* 1(1):16–22.

Jumani, Usha. 1991. *Dealing with Poverty: Self-Employment for Poor Rural Women*. Delhi: Sage Publications.

Kalpagam, U. 1994. *Labour and Gender: Survival in Urban India*. Delhi: Sage Publications.

Kanhere, Usha. 1987. *Managerial Trade Unionism*. Delhi: Mittal Publications.

Karnik, V.B. 1966. *Indian Trade Unions: A Survey*. Bombay: Manaktalas.

Kher, Manik. 1984. *Profile of Industrial Workers: A Study of Pune Industrial Belt*. Pune: Times Research Foundation.

Kumar Dharma. 1965. *Land and Caste in South India: Agricultural Labour in the Madras Presidency during Nineteenth Century*. Cambridge: Cambridge University Press.

Lambert, R.D. 1963. *Workers, Factories and Social Change in India*. Princeton, N.J.: Princeton University Press.

Maharaj, R.N. et al. 1977. 'Bilaspur Visited'. *National Labour Institute Bulletin*. 3(3):100–12.

Mamkoottam, K. 1982. *Trade Unionism: Myth and Reality*. Delhi: Oxford University Press.

Mehta, A.B. 1960. *The Domestic Servant Class*. Bombay: Popular.

Mies, Maria et al. 1987. *Indian Women in Subsistence and Agricultural Labour*. Geneva: International Labour Organization.

Mishra, G.P. and D.M. Diwakar. 1996. 'Child Labour in Glass Industry: Some Field Notes'. *Indian Journal of Labour Economics*. 39(1):163–70.

Mishra, G.P. and P.N. Pande. 1996. *Child Labour in the Carpet Industry*. New Delhi: APH Publishing Corporation.

Morris, M.D. 1960. 'The Labour Market in India'. In W.E. Moore and A.S. Feldman, eds, *Labour Commitment and Social Change in Developing Areas*, 173–200. New York: Social Sciences Research Council.

Mukhtar, A. 1930. *Factory Labour in India*. Annamalainagar: Annamalai University.

Munson, Fred C. 1970. *Indian Trade Unions: Structure and Function*. Ann Arbor: University of Michigan.

Myers, C.A. 1958. *Labour Problems in the Industrialization of India*. Cambridge: Harvard University Press.

National Commission on Labour. 1969. *Report*. New Delhi: Ministry of Labour.

Niehoff, A. 1959. *Factory Workers in India*. Milwaukee: Milwaukee Public Museum.

Patel, Kunj. 1963. *Rural Labour in Industrial Bombay*. Bombay: Popular.

Patel, Pravin J. 1994. 'Trade Union Participation and Development of Class Consciousness'. *Economic and Political Weekly*. 3 September:2368–77.

———. 1997. 'Trade Unions and Class Mobilization of Workers'. *Economic and Political Weekly*. 30 August:L23–36.

Patel, S.J. 1952. *Agricultural Labourers in Modern India and Pakistan*. Bombay: Current Book House.

Patel, Sujata. 1987. *The Making of Industrial Relations: The Ahmedabad Textile Industry 1918–1939*. Delhi: Oxford University Press.

Punekar, S.D. 1948. *Trade Unionism in India*. Bombay: New Book Company.

Punekar, S.D. and S. Madhuri. 1967. *Trade Union Leadership in India*. Bombay : Lalvani.

Punekar, S.D. and M.G. Savur. 1969. *Management White-Collar Relations*. Bombay: Popular.

Punekar, S.D. and R. Varickayil, eds. 1989. *Labour Movement in India*, vols I and II. Delhi: Indian Council for Historical Research.

Ramaswamy, E.A. 1977. *The Worker and His Union: A Study in South India*. Delhi: Allied Publishers.

——. 1984. *Power and Justice*. Delhi: Oxford University Press.

——. 1988. *Worker Consciousness and Trade Union Response*. Delhi: Oxford University Press.

——. 1994a. *Countdown: Essays for Trade Unionists*. New Delhi: Friedrich Ebert Stiftung.

——. 1994b. *Rayon Spinners: The Strategic Management of Industrial Relations*. Delhi: Oxford University Press.

——. 1997. *Question of Balance: Labour, Management and Society*. Delhi: Oxford University Press.

Ramaswamy, Uma. 1983. *Work, Union and Community*. Delhi: Oxford University Press.

Rao, Nitya, L. Rurup, and R. Sudarshan, eds. 1996. *Sites of Change: The Structural Context for Empowering Women in India*. Delhi: UNDP-Friedrich Ebert Foundation.

Reindorp, Julian. 1971. *Leaders and Leadership in the Trade Unions in Bangalore*. Madras: The Christian Literature Society.

Royal Commission on Labour in India. 1931. *Report*. Calcutta: Royal Commission on Labour in India.

Sadri, S. et al. 1994. 'Labour within the Economy and the Polity in India'. *The Indian Journal of Labour Economics*. 37(4):73–80.

——. 1995. 'A Study of the Employee Collectivity and Working Class Consciousness among Senior Civil Servants in India'. *Indian Journal of Industrial Relations*. 30(3):241–55.

Saran, K.M. 1957. *Labour in Ancient India*. Bombay: Vora & Company.

SEWA. 1989. *A Summary of the Report of the National Commission on Self-Employed Women and Women in the Informal Sector*. Ahmedabad: Self-Employed Women's Association.

Sharma, B.K. and Vishwa Mittal, eds. 1990. *Child Labour and Urban Informal Sector*. New Delhi: Deep and Deep.

Sharma, Baldev R. 1974. *The Indian Industrial Worker*. Delhi: Vikas Publishing House.

——. 1987. *Not by Bread Alone*. New Delhi: Shri Ram Centre for Industrial Relations and Human Resources.

——. 1991. *Organizational Commitment among Managers*. New Delhi: Wiley Eastern.

——. 1993. *Managerial Unionism: Issues in Perspective*. Delhi: Shri Ram Centre for Industrial Relations and Human Resources.

Sharma, G.K. 1962. *Labour Movement in India: Its Past and Present (1885–1990)*. Jaipur: University of Rajasthan.

Sherlock, Stephen. 1996. 'Class Reformation in Mumbai: Has Organized Labour Risen to the Challenge?' *Economic and Political Weekly*. 28 December:L34–8.

Sheth, N.R. 1968. *The Social Framework of an Indian Factory*. Bombay: Oxford University Press.

——. 1979. 'Industrial Man of India: Some Observations and Reflections'. *Economic and Political Weekly*. 24 November:102–14.

Sheth, N.R. 1993. 'Our Trade Unions: An Overview'. *Economic and Political Weekly*. 6 February:231–6.

———, 1996. 'We, The Trade Unions'. *Indian Journal of Industrial Relations*. 32(1):1–20.

Sheth, N.R. and S.P. Jain. 1968. 'Workers, Leaders and Politics: A Case Study'. *Indian Journal of Industrial Relations*. 3(3):268–300.

Shobha, V. 1987. *Rural Women and Development*. Delhi: Mittal Publications.

Singh, Manjit. 1991. *Labour Process in the Unorganized Industry*. New Delhi: Manohar.

———. 1997. 'Bonded Migrant Labour in Punjab Agriculture'. *Economic and Political Weekly*. 15 March:518–19.

Sreenivasan, N. 1989. 'Growth of Professional Managerial Unionism: The Indian Experience'. *Economic and Political Weekly*, 25 November:M169–77.

Srinivasulu, K. 1997. 'Impact of Liberalization on Beedi-Workers'. *Economic and Political Weekly*, 15 March:515–17.

Subramanian, K.N. 1967. *Labour-Management Relations in India*. Bombay: Asia Publishing House.

Thorner, Daniel. 1957. 'Casual Employment of a Factory Labour Force. The Case of India: 1850–1939'. *The Economic Weekly* (Annual Number). January.

Thorner, Daniel and Alice Thorner. 1962. *Land and Labour in India*. Bombay: Asia Publishing House.

Venkata Ratnam, C.S. 1994. 'Changing Role of Trade Unions in a Period of Transition'. Background paper for a conference on the Role of Trade Unions in a Period of Transition held in New Delhi during 10–12 May.

Visaria, Pravin. 1991. 'Women in the Indian Working Force: Trends and Differentials'. *Artha Vijnana*. 39(1):1–136.

Vyas, V.S. and B. Shivamaggi. 1975. 'Research on Genesis and Growth of Agricultural Labour'. In *A Survey of Research in Economics,* vol. IV *Agriculture,* Part II, 172–273. New Delhi: ICSSR.

Wersch, H. van. 1992. *Bombay Textile Strike 1982–83*. Delhi: Oxford University Press.

Wilson, Kalpana. 1996. 'Cooptation or Confrontation? New Challenges for Indian Trade Unions'. *Economic and Political Weekly*. 6 January:16–8.

Labour, Technology, and Industry

Kuriakose Mamkoottam

INTRODUCTION

The intimate relation that exists between technology, market dynamics, and other social institutions is a well-accepted fact; but the nature and direction of their linkages have been subject to debate. It is not difficult to identify the areas and extent of technology diffusion/application, and noticeable changes in the trends of production/services, on the one hand, and the pattern of employment, quality of human resources, organizational changes, and other labour-market variables, on the other. But neither is it easy to establish how far these shifts and changes are directly attributable to technological changes/innovations. The emergence of new technologies based on microelectronics since the 1970s, has given new impetus to this debate.

Although the technology–labour interface has been attracting the attention of scholars, Braverman's (1974) theory that degradation of work and polarization of skills resulted from the implementation of new technology gave a new direction to the ongoing technology debate. A major focus of discussion in recent years among sociologists has been the consequences of process applications of microelectronics. Unprecedented changes in the form of automated guided vehicle systems (AGVS), automated storage/retrieval systems (AS/RS), computer numerical control (CNC) machines, computer-aided design and manufacturing (CAD/CAM), industrial robots, computer-aided process planning (CAPP), manufacturing automation protocol (MAP), and similar innovations have transformed the traditional assembly-line production process to flexible manufacturing systems (FMS) based on the principles of just-in-time (JIT), continuous improvement, and zero defect.

Sociologists have used the Durkhemian concept of the division of labour (Durkheim 1933) to explain the interaction between technological change on the one hand, and the organization of work and generation and distribution of skills, on the other. Since Durkheim, different views have emerged in industrial sociology on the technology and labour relationship. The first view which is called the decline and rise of skills, as proposed by Woodward (1965), suggested that after the degradation of work roles, their evolution was in the direction of upgrading and enrichment. This reversal of the trend was seen as an evolutionary process and attributed to technology and the increasing prevalence of continuous-process production.

The second view, which is known as the degradation of work or polarization of skills approach, as exemplified by Braverman (1974) was that in capitalist production, complex work roles are continuously broken up and divided in two ways: on the one hand, into lower-grade, more routine, simple, and monotonous roles within a more segmented organization of work flow; and, on the other, into more demanding, responsible, and varied roles founded on more elaborated education and training.

Both these views are based on a deterministic view of technological change and work. A third approach which stresses the importance of socio-technical choice, founded on research at the Tavistock Institute, suggests that the evolution of work was in no way determined by the course of technological change but by the strategic choices adopted by key decision makers in the organization. This view suggests that the development of the technical, the social, and the sentient systems of an organization are founded on a strategy of enriching skills and achieving an overlapping, rather than divisive, organization of tasks. Subsequent research on the applications of microelectronics (Sorge and Streeck 1988; Kern and Schumann 1987; Hyman and Streeck 1988, and others) has followed this view.

New Technology and Modern Management

Postmodern industrial society has been distinguished by the predominance of information technology (IT) one the one hand, and the prevalent application of management methods and principles, on the other. The enormous attention paid by scholars and practitioners alike to the field of management has contributed to the development of new ways of manufacturing and marketing of products/services and of managing people, finances, and organizations in recent years. Among other things, information technology, in particular, has had the most serious impact on management philosophy and systems. Unprecedented competitiveness of the modern (globalized) market has put in place an all-important focus on concepts of quality, design, and flexibility. These developments have, at the same time, influenced and been influenced by the occupational structure and skill composition, organizational structure and communication, trade-union density, and quality of working life.

Firms would have to innovate in order to secure the most productive use of investments—manpower, raw materials, and energy—while at the same time offering improved service and quality to the ever-discerning customer. The global market today poses the biggest challenge by demanding simultaneous objectives of high productivity and wide flexibility from the firm. Faced with the emerging challenge of the global market, manufacturers have increasingly been turning to new technology. The application of new technology has not only improved communication and control activities across a broad range of manufacturing, but has also brought about the all-important task of integration. It has brought together previously discrete items of equipment into more powerful, multifunction systems. Today's integrated manufacturing systems offer high levels of computer integration while retaining their flexibility.

Computer-integrated manufacturing (CIM) technologies have brought about immense improvements in factors of effectiveness including lead times, inventory, and quality standards. James Womack et al. (1990) in the much-acclaimed book *The Machine That Changed the World,* state that just as mass production swept away craft production, so a new way of making things, called lean production, is now rapidly making mass production obsolete. Lean production welds the activities of everyone from top management to line workers and suppliers into a tightly integrated whole that can respond almost instantly to marketing demands from customers. It can also double production and quality, while keeping costs down. Its adoption, as it inevitably spreads beyond the auto industry, will change almost every industry and consequently how we work, how we live, and the fate of companies and nations as they respond to its impact.

New technology is almost always equated with IT and its applications. In fact, a very major part of activities in modern organizations, whether manufacturing or service, is based on convergence and application of computers and communication technologies. The potential for using a technology which offers dramatic improvements in the way in which we manage information activities is very significant. Unlike earlier technologies which are specific to a particular process or area in manufacturing, IT is seen as a pervasive and integrative technology which offers significant improvements across a broad front in quality, flexibility, and productivity. New technology is a powerful strategic weapon and, if used effectively, can help to pursue the long-term strategic goals of organizations.

Flexibility is key characteristic of modern business and industry. It is an all-pervasive concept covering product design and manufacturing, production process, and labour. Labour flexibility refers to a variety of decisions affecting geographical and occupational change of workers, recruitment, deployment, and working hours. Flexibility enables a course of action to be modified in accordance with an encountered situation which may surprisingly deviate from prior anticipation. Central to the notion of flexibility is the capability of a system to generate a variety so that options are available to do things differently or do something else if the need arises. Flexibility, thus, provides agility, versatility, and resilience—qualities which a modern industry must possess. Flexibility is also required to cope with fluctuations in market demand which may vary wildly in response to changing tastes, seasonal demands, advertising, and many other variables. Inability to meet market demand and customer needs can damage business viability.

Customers also want reliable products, easy availability, and rapid response, in terms of sales and after sales service. An increasing degree of flexibility is also required in the routing and scheduling of materials and production processes within the factory itself. More efficient use of capital invested in plant and equipment would also demand a more flexible use of these for producing a number of different products. Firms are moving towards greater flexibility by producing smaller volumes with a high degree of specialization and customization.

As reported by Bessant (1990), Atkinson (1984) identified three different aspects of a flexible firm: first, functional flexibility—the ease with which tasks performed by workers can be adjusted to meet changes in technology, markets, or other contingencies. This is possible because of the multi-skilling of the workers; second, numerical flexibility—the ease with which the number of workers can be adjusted to meet fluctuations in demand or other contingencies. There is also a trend to operate with a core plus peripheral workforce, the core remaining the main and permanent force, while the peripheral is retained and recalled for shorter periods on part-time and contractual bases; and third financial flexibility—the extent to which the structure of pay encourages and supports numerical and functional flexibility. The attempt is to find less rigid payment systems which can motivate individual performance and reward accordingly. The need for greater flexibility questions some of the basic principles of traditional (production) work organization based on rigid systems and elaborate division of labour.

Occupational Structure and Skills

The relationship between technological change, occupational structure, and skills is a complex one. While it may be seen that skills act as a constraint on new technology, the latter may facilitate the development of the skills. As Campbell and Warner (1992: 54–5) observe, high levels of technological change will be increasingly associated with hybrid (or mixed) skills where workers and managers will have less specialized training and broader ranges of taught capabilities to cope with the evolving technological challenges. Low levels of technological change may be found with low skill levels.

By far the most serious concern is for suitable skills and expertise to support the application of new technology. In general, IT poses a number of challenges for new and broader skills both to support it directly and to supervise and manage systems based around it. Skills in systems analysis and programming to develop new applications; skills in maintaining and testing microelectronics; and skills in managing the increased flow of information made available to organizations are some examples of the emerging requirements of skills.

The new trend in skill composition is a shift from operating skills to those of design, programming and analysis, maintenance, diagnosis and supervision. This pattern has been reducing the number (of employees) and increasing skill levels in industry. In some countries, this trend has created serious problems as there may not be enough skilled people available to support a microelectronics-based system. Countries like Japan and the Republic of Korea have invested heavily in developing appropriate skills and therefore do not face such problems. The range of skills is also expanding, with a major requirement for core skills, as also an increasing convergence of skills. It is also important to stress that higher levels of skill are required not just at operator and maintenance levels but also at managerial level. Absence of such professional skills at managerial level could limit the ability to exploit new technology to its full advantage, as cases from developing countries, in particular, indicate.

As products are customized using flexible technology, the ways in which the machines are used affect the occupational profile at the workplace (Campbell and Warner 1992). Better-skilled operatives backed up by highly trained technicians and engineers are becoming more predominant at the workplace. According to Schumann (1990), a holistic approach with reduced division of labour is being found to be more efficient than traditional 'Tayloristic rationalisation' patterns. Studies of British engineering industry have shown how technological changes have altered the occupational structure in favour of higher-skilled upper strata. Fewer people will be employed in manufacturing and these will be the white-coat labour force (Henderson 1989; Senker and Beesley 1986). A mushroom-shaped organization profile in which a small number of managers direct a much larger number of engineers supported by a much smaller number of technicians and a diminishing number of other ranks seem to be replacing the traditional pyramidal structure. Microelectronics has gradually been displacing labour-intensive operations with miniaturization and automation.

Campbell and Warner (1992) suggested that changes in skills mix are likely to occur at the workplace in two ways: first, there will be employees with distinctly new skills represented at the workplace, and second, because many workers will have several new skills mixed with their existing ones, there will be a hybridization of skills. While a higher degree of specialization of functions was associated with industrialization and technological change in the past, a reversal of the trend seems to be occurring with the application of microelectronics. The single disciplined craftsman has no foreseeable future, with the shift to multiskilled professional work.

Workers would have to cooperate across occupational boundaries, with theoretical knowledge in a range of fields matched by practical experience and diagnostic skills. Such a 'skills mix' and cooperation at the workplace enable workers to cope with a greater variety of tasks across different related functions such as production and maintenance. Increasingly, mixtures of operator and maintenance skills are required to function effectively with new technologies. Reports from fieldwork in a large firm making IT equipment in the electronic industry show that employees may learn a wider range of less narrow skills and/or more or fewer more specialized ones (Campbell and Warner 1992). Maintenance craftsmen may need to have a wider mix of engineering and electrical skills as well as new electronic technician skills. Similar developments were also observed in the automobile and textile companies in Spain (Mamkoottam and Herbolzeimer 1990).

New technologies, in other words, affect the structure of employment and the skill requirement at work. Differentiating skills into three categories of cognitive, interactive, and motor skills, Howell and Wolf (1991) noticed a decline in the growth of cognitive skills and a slight decline in the rate of growth of interactive skills from the 1960s to 1970s for professional, technical, and managerial staff. They also observed that cognitive skill levels of job grew faster for non-supervisory workers than for supervisory workers, and interactive skills grew substantially faster in the supervisory category. The shift in skill levels has been attributed to the introduction of new technologies which resulted in a reduced need for jobs with low cognitive skill requirements in the manufacturing sector. The same reason lead to relatively rapid growth in the average cognitive skill level for non-supervisory occupations, as team work, inter-functional coordination, and integration were required in the new work environment.

The New Worker

The integrating nature of the new technology requires increasing competence across a range of traditional and new disciplines. Maintenance of industrial robots, for example, requires skills in microelectronics, in electrical and mechanical engineering, in hydraulics, pneumatics, as well as in diagnostic and systems analysis. Evidence from other sectors such as process industries, banking and finance, food processing, electronics, engineering, and services shows similar trends towards greater integration of tasks and a need for 'cross-trading' and demand for multiskilling. The new technology calls for a new worker, who possesses not only greater technical knowledge but greater adaptability to new situations, an ability to respond quickly to technical problems as well as a capacity for team work, rather than physical strength and individual work ability.

The new technology calls for a polyvalent and professional worker, who understands not only the basic process of production but also the basic functioning and operation of the machines. As the new machines are flexible and versatile, so should the new employee be so as to operate them efficiently. It is also important that the employee should be competent both conceptually and in technical matters, she should be open-minded and willing to learn and cooperate with others to work effectively in teams. The new employee, in a way, is expected to be superhuman and will function in a versatile, flexible and multifunctional position.

Such workers perform a larger number of tasks. They occupy positions embodying broader job descriptions within a reduced hierarchy of division of labour. In general, this is reflected in the overall reduction in the number of employees required to perform a given set of operations. Such a reduction would be more prominent in the unskilled and semi-skilled categories as these are easily mechanized and replaced by machines. The traditional three-tier categories of unskilled, semi-skilled, and skilled are being replaced by the less skilled and highly skilled categories. The unskilled category would be gradually reduced and eliminated and merged with the less skilled group, while the skilled category would increase in size and importance. The change in the structure of the organization would become much more accentuated as there would be an increase in the number of skilled workers in the organization.

Evidence suggests that there is an increase in the requirement for professional engineers, technicians, and managers. This is also reflected in the changes in educational aspirations of individuals who are more conscious of the need for higher educational aspirations of individuals who are more conscious of the need for higher levels of qualification and a desire for greater personal growth and development. There is greater emphasis on flexibility and creative problem solving and the need to understand and appreciate the whole system, rather than a small part. Cross-trading and continuous education and training to update skills and fight the ever-faster rate of obsolescence are also evident from various studies. While traditional models involved narrowly defined, predictable, and predetermined tasks, the emerging trend is one which demands a flexible and professional response. The important skills required are agility, open-mindedness, and adaptability to switch quickly across different skills.

As a consequence, greater importance is given to training and development. The emerging pattern is one in which skills often have a short life cycle and where the ability to acquire new skills and to update old ones becomes critical for one's own survival. This, in turn, shifts the focus from task-related training to personal development. Tacit knowledge and ability to acquire and dispose skills in a flexible fashion become increasingly important factors in getting new technology to perform effectively, and many firms are now beginning to recognize the advantages offered by becoming a 'learning organization' (Bessant 1990).

Major changes are also taking place in the composition of the workforce in terms of gender, age, and education. An increasing number of women are entering the workforce, especially in developing countries, where relatively few women have been absorbed so far. William Johnston (1991) has observed that the trend towards women leaving home-based employment and entering the paid workforce is an often overlooked demographic reality of industrialization. As cooking and cleaning technologies ease the burden at home, agricultural jobs diminish, and other jobs, especially in the service sector, proliferate, women would be absorbed increasingly into the industrial sector. More than half of all women between the ages of 15 and 64 are now estimated to work outside the home; and women comprise nearly one-third of the world's workforce.

However, developed nations have absorbed many more women into the labour force than developing nations. According to a recent survey (*Financial Times*, 14 July 1996), more than 50 per cent of all jobs are held by women in the Scandinavian countries.

A larger presence of women workforce at the workplace will have implications on working conditions and terms of employment. Demand for services such as fast food, day care for children, home cleaners, and nursing homes is expected to go up as more and more women join the labour force. As women have more demands on them at home than men do, they are likely to be away from work more often than men, and the workplace may have to restructure the time schedule, giving way to flexi-time and other innovative methods of deployment.

Technology and Organization Structure

Studies have shown that the full benefits of new technologies can come only if simultaneous changes are brought about in physical layout, organization structure, manpower skills, and work culture (Rush et al.1990). As it was found in the case of Spanish automobiles and textiles, the absence of such a simultaneous approach can delay, if not totally stop, the introduction of new technologies (Mamkoottam and Herbolzeihmer 1990; 1991). In order to avail of the advantage of what Fleck (1987) has termed as 'configurational technologies', it is essential that firms should adopt an approach based on 'synchronous innovation' as suggested by Ettlie (1988).

Organizational Change

It is generally accepted that technological change requires some degree of innovation and organizational change. As Peter Drucker (1985) explains, innovation is the specific function of entrepreneurship. It is the means by which the entrepreneur either creates new wealth-producing resources or endows existing ones with enhanced potential for creating wealth. There are innovations that spring from a flash of genius. However, most innovations, especially the successful ones, result from a conscious, purposeful search for innovation opportunities which are found only in a few situations. Innovation theory also suggests that compatibility, that is the degree to which an innovation fits into the context in which it is being placed, is an important determinant of adoption success. In the case of a changeover to new technology, this is particularly true and many commentators have talked about the need for 'a new way of thinking'. The adaptation of new technologies would require a 'paradigm shift' integrating the production and process innovations along with new patterns of organization designs (Bessant 1993).

Technological change demands significant adaptation by going beyond the normal organization learning curve and finding new and radically extended answers to the new challenges being posed. These changes, moreover, are multidimensional, in the sense that they impact the entire organization in its every aspect. Such a process often requires an element of 'un-learning' and 'creative destruction'. However, change does not happen automatically with the introduction of new technology, but has to be initiated deliberately and implemented effectively. Such changes have to be introduced at individual level, group level, inter-functional level, and at the level of the organization. The traditional model of 'Fordism', which was based on assembly-line, mass production, is giving way to the new model of 'Toyotism', which is based on lean and mean methods, using techniques such as JIT, zero inventory, and zero defect. Such a shift also brings about major changes in the areas of skills, work organization, functional integration, control, interorganizational relationships, and organizational culture. In the absence of one 'best choice' in any of these areas, organizations would be expected to make their own strategic choices from a variety of options and contingencies. As Child (1977) suggested, strategic choices have to be made in the context of given environmental contingencies, technologies, and structure of the organization. Such choices in an increasingly uncertain world demand a highly flexible organization to deal with these contingencies.

Work Organization

Technology may be seen essentially as a system involving both tools and the organization around using those tools. Unless technology is seen and managed as a total system with appropriate attention to the organizational dimensions, it would not deliver the full benefits. As manufacturing/service systems become more complex and interdependent and the environments become more unpredictable, the need for flexibility further increases. The new technology requires a greater degree of cooperation among the employees who should also possess a larger amount of skills for information processing and decision making in the uncertain environment. In order to be able to respond quickly, a work organization which encourages local autonomy and decentralized decision making allowing sufficient degree of functional flexibility is considered to be more suitable. In such an organization, workers would be given a broad task specification within which they are expected to organize themselves by allocating roles and scheduling tasks, etc.

According to Bessant (1993), 'a factory within the factory' is created by functional flexibility and a greater degree of functional integration, bringing many specialist functional roles within the same organization. The increasing technological integration forces functional groups to work more closely together. CAD/CAM, for example, requires a much closer relationship between design and manufacturing. Similarly, to maintain quality standards, a very close relationship would be required between production, maintenance, and quality control.

Similar changes would take place in the traditional process of control and monitoring, from direct supervision to local autonomy and decentralized decision making. Highly interdependent systems designed to deal with high levels of uncertainty and local diversity would require decentralization of control to the operating point at local levels. It is argued that flexible response can be offered through a combination of flexible technology and flexible organization.

Culture

Technological change has often been seen as a 'paradigm shift', and all paradigm shift would involve values and norms. Organizational changes always involve a shift in organizational culture, which would be necessary to introduce technological innovations. Technological change implies also a shift in the prevailing system of beliefs and priorities; all technologies may be seen to be couched in a 'way of thinking' as well. It is the *organic* type of organization as against the *mechanistic* organization, as characterized by Burns and Stalker (1961), which is considered to be suitable to accept technological changes. Organic organizations encourage innovation, lateral rather than vertical communication, and higher degree of decentralization, flexibility and integration. Drawing from Child (1977) and Handy (1979), Bessant (1993) suggests that organizational change is possible only if values and goals are shared by all members within the organization. Such commitment would be characterized by a sense of ownership and participation/involvement of the workers as against the traditional model of organizations where the worker is marginalized.

However, it is also observed that the kind of options available in work-organization design are dependent on the available skills in the organization. Wherever levels of skills are high and there has been training to support multifunctionality, options would be open. It has been observed that experiments in team working and in the use of multiskilled workers are more prevalent in Scandinavia and Japan than in the UK, the USA, or other parts of the world where relative skill levels are much lower and distributed more narrowly across the workforce (Senker and Senker 1990; Rush and Bessant 1989).

Quality of Work Life

The physical and socio-psychological implications of new technology are not without ambiguities and contradictions. While the new worker would be better skilled and would be performing a larger job with more responsibilities compared to her/his earlier counterpart, his wages may not always be correspondingly enhanced. This is more so as often the worker may not necessarily be given a promotion to a higher level within the organization with acquisition of new or higher skills. In fact, trade unions argue that introduction of new technology often leads to a fall in real wages of the employees. Although the new worker performs a job with more functions and greater responsibilities and may be subjected to greater job stress, her/his job classification may remain just the same as before. The results of a study based on a number of new technology agreements in the UK during 1979–80 showed that though unions have often secured agreements with a guarantee for no reduction in earnings and no downgrading for those offered redeployment, they have seldom secured an increase in earnings for those operating new technology (Manwaring 1981; Mamkoottam and Herbolzeimer 1990).

Human skills are increasingly incorporated into machines which can automatically perform many simultaneous and sophisticated functions with the help of microprocessors and electronic data-processing applications. In this process, the worker would increasingly become subservient to the machine mainly assisting and maintaining it to perform the major operations. Robotization and incorporation of microelectronics in the manufacturing and service functions provide evidence of how the machines control the worker by setting the process and pace of work. This not only increases the monotony of the work, but also his isolation, because often a single worker manages a whole unit of automated processes.

In the context of new technology, while the worker receives less direct supervision and thus enjoys greater autonomy in the traditional sense, greater control is imposed on him by the machines, which immediately reduces the area of his freedom. Moreover, as the rate of technological change becomes faster, workers in general, and those in the older age groups in particular, find it extremely difficult to retain themselves in the face of a faster rate of (technological) obsolescence. While new technology creates a cleaner work environment by reducing the level of dust, dirt, noise, and physical strain, it seems to increase mental and psychological stress of the worker. Although team work, job rotation, group tasks, and employee-involvement schemes are meant to reduce these negative elements, they are as yet to become a popular practice in most cases.

Employment

Recent trends in unemployment are particularly disturbing. Despite steady improvement in the world economy, open unemployment has grown in many countries. The new phenomenon characterizing the 1990s and beyond has been termed as jobless growth. Employment growth has lagged behind both output growth and growth of labour force. Similarly, a widening gap is projected in terms of growth in labour force and growth in employment.

More specifically in the Indian context, there is a wide gap between growth in population and growth rate of employment. While the number of workers in the total population increased by 26.80 per cent between 1981 and 1991, the growth in employment between 1977–8 and 1987–8 has been only 1.95 per cent, registering an all India unemployment rate of 3.77 (Government of India 1994–5).

Papola (1989) observes that labour-saving technological changes have taken place in practically all branches of Indian industry. In industries and units where technological changes have been rapid and significant, employment potential has declined. However, employment is declining also in the older industries where technological change has been delayed or slow, due to stagnation in output. In other words, the interesting observation is that introduction as well as non-introduction of technological change is found to produce an overall adverse effect on employment generation.

While it is true that new technology incorporates human skills and manual labour into machines and thereby reduces and replaces human labour, it may also be observed that more of the new jobs available in the services and manufacturing sectors are in the area of new technology. In other words, there are also new employment opportunities that may be filled either by those de-skilled and displaced from traditional activities or by newer entrants. So the question of whether or not microelectronics poses a skills problem depends on choices made about training. The general trends in skill change related to microelectronics are towards higher levels, wider breadth, and greater flexibility.

Subcontracting

In response to technological changes, organizations have been developing a two-tier segmented labour force. The workforce often consists of a group of flexible and multiskilled workers clustered around a stable core as the permanent force and others who are hired on contractual and temporary basis exist at the periphery. As the market expands, the periphery grows to take up the slack; as growth slows down, the periphery contracts. Those at the periphery are the subcontracted part-time workers, the self-employed, and several others in the category of casual home-based temporary employment. These are comparatively low paid, on shorter-term contracts, and are not protected by trade unions or other benefits of permanent employment. Though subcontracting has always existed, it appears to increase with the introduction of new technology. The indication is that the trend in subcontracting will continue and perhaps increase. Although trade unions have been trying to restrain management from subcontracting jobs, the new tendency of what is commonly referred to as neo-liberal flexibilization and their legitimization by state legislation will make subcontracting more popular and easier. This increasing tendency towards subcontracting, in turn, leads to a higher level of labour segmentation. More and more jobs will be removed from the core sector to the peripheral sector, which will become less secure and more isolated from the external labour market and wider trade union protection.

Papola (1989) observes that growth of employment in India has been widely divergent and the real explanation for this lies in the practice of subcontracting. Favourable conditions have emerged for large-scale sub-contracting. A large number of small units have come up during the recent years, particularly in the manufacturing sector, which are not in a position to compete with the large units with brand names and market share. In fact, these small units produce for the use of larger units, and the latter find it economical to use the capacity of the smaller units. The wage costs are usually much lower in the smaller units, and the parent firm avoids the problems associated with the management of a large workforce, including industrial relations and post-retirement and other benefits. The wage rates in the small units are usually about two-thirds of those paid by large units and social security and other benefits are not provided in the subcontracted units. Subcontracting is widespread in almost all sectors. According to an estimate, not more than 40 per cent of production is undertaken in the parent unit.

Worker and Union Response to New Technology

Global experiences have shown that workers' response and trade-union strategies towards technological changes vary depending on the labour legislation operating in that environment. Based on three large-scale surveys of around 2000 British workplaces undertaken in 1980, 1984, and 1990 Daniel and Milward (1993) observe widespread support for technical changes including advanced technical changes, among both manual and non-manual workers, and even stronger support among their trade-union representatives. However, the same study pointed out that organizational changes provoked much more mixed reactions. Organizational change was resisted more often than it was supported among manual workers. Reactions to organizational change among office workers were fairly evenly balanced between favourable and unfavourable, but they were much less supportive than towards technical change.

According to Daniel and Millward, new technology represented progress and advance; the benefits of new machines were concrete and demonstrable, and represented competitive advantage. Investment in new technology represented confidence in the future and improved long-term job prospects and security. Workers were familiar with many features of new technology and valued their benefits. Overall, the introduction of new technology tended to be associated with success. Organizational change that was introduced independent of new equipment, on the contrary, tended to be more frequently associated with failure. It was often seen as an admission of unproductive organization in the past. It was more often viewed with suspicion as the benefits derived from different forms of organization were often seen as a matter of judgement and not self-evident. Moreover, the idea of change is not often effectively communicated to lower levels in the organization before it can be implemented.

Muneto Ozaki (1992) suggested in an ILO study that workers have had limited influence on the process and pattern of technological change in most countries except in Sweden where they have played a direct role in the planning of technological change. According to the study, unions and workers had little or no influence on planning of technological change in Japan or in the machine-tool industry in the US. In Sweden, semi-autonomous work groups, which are funded by public policy, play a direct role in the introduction of technological change and in the creation of new work roles. As Willman (1986) suggested, trade-union behaviour in the face of technical change will depend upon changes in the political and economic climate, the incidence and impact of innovations, changes to union structure, and collective bargaining. Studies on technological change in the UK,

Italy (Treu 1984), Australia (Deery 1986), and Spain (Fina and Hawksworth 1984; Mamkoottam and Herbolzeimer 1991) show that technological changes were mostly introduced unilaterally by management and faced little resistance from trade unions.

The Indian Scenario

Technological changes have been strongly resisted by trade unions in India during the recent past. A key feature of Indian industrial relations has been the dominant role played by the state, affecting almost every possible dimension, which has considerably reduced and restricted labour flexibility is and slowed down the introduction of new technologies. The fifteenth session of the Indian Labour Conference held in 1957, in principle, limited the possibilities of introducing technological change by adopting the 'Model Agreement' which approved a 'no-retrenchment' clause on account of technological change. Employers were required to provide workers with suitable alternative jobs in the same establishment or under the same employer. All along, the Indian government has been following a cautious path to effect changes in labour laws relating to retrenchment of workers. Although the government had promised to announce an exit policy in 1991, in the face of strong opposition from trade unions of the organized sector, including officers' associations of the various public sector companies, gradually the focus has shifted to what is called a 'structural reforms with a human face' approach, by which changes in labour laws would be introduced in phases.

Trade unions find it difficult to accept technological changes as there is fear in the minds of employees and unions that the envisaged changes, if implemented, will adversely affect the labour and employment situation in different ways. Major technological changes with the accompanying structural and organizational changes could affect the existing occupational structure, manpower skills, employment patterns, and other related areas. Moreover, new technology has important implications for the structure and strategy of trade unions. The evolution of technological changes has shaped and reshaped the labour movement. As Gill (1987) suggested, perhaps it is in the history of the labour movement that the discontinuous nature of technological change can be seen most clearly.

Ranabir Samaddar (1995), based on a case study of the newspaper industry, has taken a position that new technology is weapon in the hands of management to eliminate trade unions. On the other hand, Mamata Roy (1995) concludes from her study on the banking industry that the worker may become an eager supporter of technological change.

K.B. Akhilesh and M. Mathew, (1989) have suggested that mostly management have taken workers for granted while introducing technological change. In general, the management tend to believe that workers' (and unions') resistance can be overcome by monetary rewards by way of exgratia benefits. These studies have noted that such efforts to introduce technological change for improving productivity and quality could not succeed unless accompanied by efforts in creating awareness about new technologies among the workers.

In fact, it is worth noting that workers (and unions) are not concerned about introduction of technological change per se; what concerns them is the shop-floor reorganization resulting from such changes in terms of job loss, internal redeployment, change in work methods, etc. As noted by Manik Kher (1997), although workers and unions have been resisting shop-floor changes directly and technological changes indirectly, companies in the private sector have been able to bring about major changes on the shop floor while introducing technological changes by incorporating counter demands in wage settlements. In a recent ILO study by me on 'Productivity Linked Wages in South Asia' (Mamkoottam 1998), it has been found that the management has not only preserved the rights to introduce technological changes and redeploy workers to enhance productivity, but have also often made wage increases conditional on such changes in the negotiated agreements signed between the management and union(s).

In a study of technological change in the steel, textile, and engineering sectors in India, Manik Kher (1997) has observed variations which may be explained by the nature of the production process, educational qualifications of workers, industrial-relations environment, and the overall economic development of the region. Although modernization processes in steel, engineering, and textile were intended to improve quality and reduce costs, the implementation of the modernization programme varied in each case across the pubic sector and the private sector. Public-sector management with the remarkable exception of the Greenfield plant, were found complacent, non-committed, with a lower level of morale. Such work atmosphere affected the quality of decisions in terms of timeliness and reliability. In the private sector, on the other hand, decision making was quicker. The competitive spirit drove them towards greater commitment and concerted efforts (Kher 1997: 70).

Although unions have been coping with technological changes and shifting their focus of bargaining, the recent changes appear to be so swift and radical that they have nearly threatened the very foundation of trade unions. Major aspects of new technology annul the very foundation of traditional trade unions. Flexibility, for example, questions the fixed rules and norms of work determination. Job demarcations and occupational identities are increasingly being blurred and gradually disappearing. Decentralization disperses production/service centres and reduces collective strength. Unskilled and semi-skilled workers have been the backbone of traditional trade-union centres, and their gradual reduction and elimination and the simultaneous trend in subcontracting are threatening the future of trade unions. More and more organizations are becoming smaller in size and flatter in structure with fewer unskilled and semi-skilled workers. Above all, the new worker is better educated, well informed, and professionally oriented. Her/His aspirations, needs, and problems are different from those of the traditional worker.

In order to be relevant and meaningful in the new context, the unions may need to shift their almost exclusive focus from traditional wage bargaining, which is characterized by quantitative post facto conflictual bargaining, to an ante facto (proactive) bargaining and enlarge the union expertise into technological and organizational matters. A new cooperative bargaining model based on a continuous problem-solving approach rather than the conflict model may be required in the context of the new technology. As in the case of Scandinavian countries, much of the union activity in several parts of the world is already concerned with developing expertise within the union to understand technological developments and their implications on health, environment, employee, skills and their education and retraining.

REFERENCES

Akhilesh K.B. and M. Mathew. 1989. 'Technological Change: Management Initiatives and Trade Union Response'. Unpublished draft.

Albeda, W. 1983. 'Reflections on the Future of Full Employment'. *Labour and Society*. 8(2):57–71.

Altshuler, A. et al. 1986. *The Future of Automobiles*. Massachusetts, MIT Press.

Amberg, S. 1993. 'Institutional Framework and Production Systems: The Contribution of Skilled Workers to the Flexibility of American Automobile Industry'. *International Contributions to Labour Studies*. 3:51–66.

Atkinson, H. 1984. *The Flexible Firm*. Sussex University: Institute of Manpower Studies.

Batstone, E. et al. 1987. *New Technology and the Process of Labour Regulation*. Oxford: Clarendon Press.

Bessant, J. 1990. 'Fifth Wave Manufacturing: The Management Implications of New Manufacturing Technology'. Mimeo. Brighton Business School.

———. 1993. 'Towards Factory 2000: Design Organizations for Computer Integrated Technologies'. In J. Clark, ed., *Human Resource Management and Technological Change*, 192–211. London: Sage Publications.

Blauner, R. 1964. *Alienation and Freedom: The Factory Worker and His Industry*. Chicago: Rand-Mcnally.

Braverman, H. 1974. *Labour and Monopoly Capital*. New York: Monthly Review Press.

Burns, T. and G.M. Stalker. 1961. *The Management of Innovation*. London: Tavistock.

Campbell, A. and M. Warner. 1992. *New Technology, Skills and Management*. London: Routledge.

Child, J. 1977. *Organization: A Guide to Problems and Practices*. London: Harper and Row.

Clark, J., ed. 1993. *Human Resource Management and Technological Change*. London: Sage Publications.

Daniel, W.W. 1997. *Workplace Industrial Relations and Technological Change*. UK: Frances Printer.

Daniel, W.W. and N. Millward. 1993. 'Findings from the Workplace Industrial Relations Surveys'. In J. Clark, ed., *Human Resource Management and Technological Change*, 45–77. London: Sage Publications.

Deery, S. 1986. 'New Technology, Union Rights and Management Prerogatives: The Australian Experience'. *Labour and Society*. 9(2):67–81.

Drucker, Peter. 1985. 'The Discipline of Innovation'. *Harvard Business Review*. May–June: 67–72.

Durkheim, Emile. 1933. *The Division of Labour in Society*. London: The Macmillan Company.

Edgren, G., ed. 1989. *Restructuring, Employment, and Industrial Relations*. Asian Regional Team for Employment Promotion. ILO.

Ettlie, J. 1988. *Taking Charge of Manufacturing*. San Francisco: Jossey-Bass.

Fina, L. and R. Hawksworth. 1984. 'Trade Unions and Collective Bargaining in post-Franco Spain'. *Labour and Society*. 9(1).

Fleck, J. 1987. 'Innofusion or diffusation'. *Working Paper*. University of Edinburg.

Freedman, D.H. 1983. 'Seeking a Broader Approach to Employment and Work Life in Industrialized Market-economy Countries'. *Labour and Society*. 8(4):107–21.

Freeman, C. 1988. 'The Factory of the Future: The Productivity Paradox, Japanese, Just-in-time and Information Technology'. Policy Research Paper No. 3. Science Policy Research Unit, University of Sussex.

Gill, C. 1987. 'New Technology and Industrial Relations'. In B. Tuner, ed., *Industrial Relations Practice*. London: Kegan Paul Ltd.

Government of India, 1994–5. *World of Work*. Ministry of Labour. Annual Report. New Delhi.

Handy, C.B. 1979. *Gods of Management*. London: Pan.

Hart, A.G. 1973. 'Anticipation, Business Planning and the Cycle'. *Qaurterly Journal of Economics*. February.

Henderson, J. 1989. *The Globalisation of High Technology of Production*. London: Routledge.

Howell, D. and E. Wolf. 1991. 'Trends in the Growth and Distribution of Skills in the US Workplace 1960–1985'. *Industrial and Labour Relations Review*. 44(3):486–502.

Hyman R. and W. Streeck, 1988. *New Technology and Industrial Relations*. New York: Basil Blackwell.

Johnston, W. 1991. 'Global Workforce 2000: The New World Labour Market'. *Harvard Business Review*. March–April:115–27.

Kern, H. and M. Schumann. 1987. 'Limits of the Division of Labour'. *Economic and Industrial Democracy*. 8(2):151–70.

Kher, Manik. 1997. *Coping with Technological Change*. New Delhi: Response Books.

MacInnes, J. 1988. 'Gender, Class and Work'. In R. Hyman and W. Streeck, eds, *New Technology and Industrial Relations*. New York: Basil Blackwell.

Mamkoottam, K. 1994. 'Globalisation and the Emerging Labour Management Relations'. In C.S. Venkata Ratnam et al., eds, *Labour and Unions in a Period of Transition*, 167–88. New Delhi: Frederich Ebert Stiftung.

_____. 1998. *Productivity Linked Wages in South Asia*. New Delhi: ILO-SAAT.

Mamkoottam K. and E. Herbolzeimer. 1990. 'Interface of New Technology and Human Resource Management: A Case of Automobiles and Textiles in Spain'. EFMD, Brussels. Mimeo.

_____. 1991. 'Human Resource Implications of New Technology: A Case of Automobiles in Spain'. *Indian Journal of Industrial Relations*. 26(3):205–26.

Manwaring, T. 1981. 'The Trade Union Response to New Technology'. *Industrial Relations Journal*. 12(4):7–26.

Noguchi, T. 1983. 'High Technology and Industrial Strategies in Japan'. *Labour and Society*. 8(4):383–92.

Nuki, T. 1983. 'The Effect of Microelectronics on the Japanese Style of Management'. *Labour and Society*. 8(4):393–400.

Ozaki, Muneto, ed. 1992. *Technological Change and Labour Relations*. Geneva: ILO.

Papola, T.S. 1989. 'Restructuring in Indian Industry: Implications for Employment and Industrial Relations'. In G. Edgren, ed., *Restructuring, Employment and Industrial Relations*, 29–80. ILO: Asian Regional Team for Employment Promotion.

Roy, Mamata. 1995. 'Indian Banks, Information Technology and Bargaining'. In A.K. Bagchi, ed., *New Technology and the Worker's Response*, 123–44. New Delhi: Sage Publications.

Rush, H. and J. Bessant. 1989. 'Revolution in Three Quarters Time: Lessons from the Diffusion of Advanced Manufacturing Technology'. Centre for Business Research. Brighton Business School, Mimeo.

Samaddar, Ranabir. 1995. 'New Technology at the Shopfloor Level: The Story of Deunionisation in Some Indian Newspapers'. In A.K. Bagchi, ed., *New Technology and the Workers' Response,* Supra.

Schumann, M. 1990. 'Changing Concepts of Work and Qualifications'. In M. Warner et al., eds, *New Technology and Manufacturing Management*. London: Wiley.

Senker, J. and P. Senker. 1990. 'Technical Change in the 1990s: Implications for Skills, Training and Development'. Working Paper. University of Sussex.

Senker P. and M. Beesley. 1986. 'The Need for Skills in the Factory of the Future'. *New Technology, Work and Employment*. 1(1):9–17.

Sorge A. and W. Streeck. 1988. 'Industrial Relations and Technical Change'. In R. Hyman and W. Streeck, eds, *New Technology and Industrial Relations*, 19–47. New York: Basil Blackwell.

Treu, T. 1984. 'The Impact of Technologies on Employment, Working Conditions and Industrial Relations'. *Labour and Society*. 9(2).

Willman, P. 1986. *Technological Change, Collective Bargaining and Industrial Efficiency*. Oxford: Clarendon Press.

Womack, J.P. et al. 1990. *The Machine That Changed the World*. New York: Maxwell Macmillan.

Woodward, J. 1965. *Industrial Organisation: Theory and Practice*. Oxford: Oxford University Press.

World Bank. 1995. *The World Development Report 1995*. New York: The World Bank.

The Informal Sector

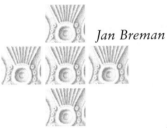

Jan Breman

INTRODUCTION

The term, 'informal sector' dates from the early 1970s when it was coined by Hart in a study on Ghana to describe urban employment outside the organized labour market. This category includes a great diversity of occupations characterized by self-employment (Hart 1971). His chapter, which was based on anthropological fieldwork, brought attention to the enormous variety of economic activities carried out by a large part of the population of Accra in order to survive. These activities were not registered anywhere and were often clandestine in nature or at any rate outside the framework of official regulations. The improvised and inadequate manner whereby this took place demonstrated that the people engaging in them lived mostly in poverty and were to be found at the bottom of the urban landscape.

The concept quickly became popular when the International Labour Organization (ILO), as part of its World Employment Programme, sent out missions to examine the employment situation outside the modern, organized, large-scale, and capital-intensive sectors of the economy. The first of these country reports investigated Kenya and the Philippines (ILO 1972 and 1974). These studies were followed by reports that examined the particular features of the 'informal sector' in a number of Third World cities such as Calcutta, Jakarta, Dakar, Abidjan, and Sao Paulo.[1] To supplement these case studies, the ILO commissioned a number of more analytical essays such as those authored by Sethuraman (1976) and Kanappan (1977), and the World Bank published a paper by Mazumdar (1975).

As a result of the way the concept had been framed and the attention it subsequently drew from development economists and policy makers in particular, the informal sector became, to a significant extent, associated with the economy of the large cities of Africa, Asia, and Latin America. Most of these cases concern societies with a predominantly rural-cum-agrarian identity in which the process of urbanization began relatively recently. The dynamics of this spatial shift in settlement patterns include the declining importance of agriculture as the principal source of economic production and the expulsion from village habitats particularly the growing proportion of the land-poor peasantry. However, this transition has not been marked by a concomitant expansion in the metropoles of 'technologically advanced' and 'modernly organized' industries, aimed at enabling the accommodation of this newly mobile section of the population from the rural hinterland. Only a small part of the labour that reaches the urban areas manages to penetrate the 'secure' zones of regular, more-skilled and hence better-paid work. The majority of migrants must be satisfied with casual labour which is unskilled or pseudo-skilled, has no fixed working hours, provides a low income which, moreover, fluctuates significantly and, finally, is only available seasonally.

The description of the informal sector is characterized by analytical vagueness. In order to indicate the wide repertoire of occupations, commentators often confine themselves to an arbitrary enumeration of activities which one comes across walking through the streets of the Third World metropoles. Included in this parade are market-stall holders, lottery-ticket sellers, parking attendants, vendors of food and drink, housemaids and market women, messengers and porters, ambulant artisans and repairmen, construction and road-building workers, transporters of people and cargo, and shoe polishers and newspaper boys. Numerous occupations on the seamy side of society such as pimps and prostitutes, rag pickers and scavengers, quacks, conjurers and confidence tricksters, bootleggers and drug pedlars, beggars, pickpockets, and other petty thieves are not omitted. It is a colourful arrangement of irregularly working people that scratches around for a living close to or at the bottom of urban society and which, in the overwhelming majority of cases, both lives and works in extremely precarious circumstances.

Origins

The division of the urban economy into two sectors can be seen as a variant of the dualism theories that had gained currency at an earlier time. Basing himself on colonial Indonesia, the Dutch economist Boeke voiced the idea at the beginning of this century that native producers had not internalized in their behaviour the basic principles of the homo economicus. Unlimited needs and their deferred gratification in accordance with a rational assessment of costs and benefits did not stand at the forefront of the peasant way of life in the Orient. What marked the orient was the immediate and impulsive indulgence of limited wants. This colonial doctrine of what Boeke referred to as homo socialis would return in later development studies as the image of the working masses in underdeveloped countries obstinately refusing to respond to the primacy of economic stimuli.[2]

The rejection of the axiom that there is a real difference in rationality and optimalization behaviour between western and eastern civilizations ended in the construction of a new contradistinction in post-colonial development economics, namely that between the countryside and the city. This spatial contrast corresponded more or less with a sectoral division between agriculture and industry. Western mankind was superseded by the city-industrial complex as the dynamic factor, against which village and agriculture were seen as static and diametrically opposed. The new dualism theory, like its precursor, was associated with the rise of capitalism as the organizing principle of economic life. While the bulk of the peasants in the villages were attributed an outlook restricted to subsistence, modern industry was expected to concentrate outside the agrarian sector and in the urban milieu. According to this line of thinking, the contradiction between both sectors was indeed not of a fundamental nature but merely reflected different stages of social development which corresponded with the traditional–modern dichotomy. The dualism concept in this sense was used first by Lewis (1954) and subsequently by Fei and Ranis (1964) with the aim of examining the outflow of superfluous labour from the rural subsistence economy and to trace the arrival of this labour in urban growth poles as part of the gradual expansion of non-agrarian production. The evolution of social transformation in developing countries is, in this scheme of interpretation, similar to the capitalist process of change that took place in the Atlantic part of the world in an earlier phase.

It is against this background that the latest version of the dualism model, now under discussion, should be understood. Urban agglomerations are not growing exclusively or even predominantly as centres of technologically advanced industrial production along capitalist lines. In addition to the presence of an economic circuit that does fit this description, there is also a sector consisting of a plethora of activities of a completely different nature. Key terms such as 'modern management' and 'capitalist organization' appear to be scarcely relevant for this sector. The combination of a slow pace of factorized industrialization, the presence of excess labour due to increased demographic growth and the expulsion from the agricultural economy, are given as the principal causes leading to a dualist system in cities of the Third World. The lower echelons in this bipolar order consist of the mass of the working poor who have a much lower rate of productivity than those in the technologically advanced section of the economy. To the latter, this rapidly increasing segment of urban population, as yet and perhaps forever, cannot obtain access.

Can the wide range of activities which informal-sector workers have to depend on for their survival be seen as 'traditional'? This is the stereotypical notion of those modes of production in which emphasis is laid on their old-fashioned and outmoded character. They depend on fairly simple occupational skills and employ very meagre as well as inadequate tools. The sparse availability of means of production based on superior technology results in a return on labour that is almost always quite low. A consequence is that, in order to scrape together a minimum income, the working day is extremely long while the work is also so physically demanding that poor health is a common occurrence. An argument against the tendency to portray the informal sector as traditional and 'pre-capitalist' is the fact that among the enormous variety of activities that fall under this category, very many in fact were created by the capitalist transformation of the urban milieu. It would be misleading to suggest that the observed urban dualism is shaped, on the one hand, by a dynamic growth pole marked by advanced technology and innovative organizational management and, on the other, by a more or less static circuit of long-established, miscellaneous, and stubbornly surviving but outdated pre-capitalist activities. Instead of speaking of a gradually disappearing contradiction between 'modern' and 'traditional', or capitalist versus non-capitalist, in my opinion what should be emphasized is the drastic restructuring of the entire economic system whereby the interdependence between different sectors needs to be identified as the most important element. This conclusion is in part derived from an appraisal of the transformation which took place in the western world over a period of more than a century and for which the dual processes of urbanization and industrialization were of major importance. Without wanting to suggest that societies that until recently were rural/agrarian are currently experiencing a similar process of change, I would nevertheless like to draw attention to the fact that what is now referred to as the informal sector, characterized by many different forms of self-employment and petty commodity production, has for a long time remained a marked feature in the urban economies of the northern hemisphere as well (see Stedman Jones 1971). Research on the various forms of the informal sector in developing countries, as it has been conducted since the 1970s, is handicapped by the virtual lack of comparison with the very profound changes in the organization of work and labour which went together with the emergence of metropolitan economies elsewhere in the world in the last two centuries. This lack of historical perspective coincides with the disciplinary background of the majority of researchers, mainly development economists and policy makers, who have little affinity with the need to understand the problem stated in a time span; they see little need for highlighting instead of obfuscating the continuing effects of the past on the present.

Clarification and Definition of Concepts

One of the first ILO reports on this subject discussed the informal sector by focusing on a set of characteristics: 'easy entry for the new enterprises, reliance on indigenous resources, family ownership, small scale operations, unregulated and competitive markets, labour intensive technology, and informally acquired skills of workers' (ILO 1972). The assumption behind this description is that the opposite of all these features applies to the formal sector of the economy. In this definition, which is built on an implicit contrast, it is not the type of economic activity but the way it is practised that is used as the differentiating criterion. In slightly different formulations, and supplemented with new suggestions, the above list of characteristics is found in a myriad of later studies. It is certainly possible to question the inclusion of some of these traits. For example, highly trained formal-sector professionals such as lawyers or accountants often run their businesses in a manner which does not satisfy the criterion of large-scale operation. And again, it is just as misleading to presume that at the bottom echelons of the urban economy newcomers can establish themselves without any trouble as vendors, shoe polishers, or beggars. Furthermore, features that were initially accorded great importance—such as the foreign origin of capital or technology, the use of mainly waged labour, the large and impersonal distance between the supply of and demand for commodities and services—appear, on closer examination, not to constitute the watershed between formal and informal. The easy answer to this criticism is that urban dualism must be understood not by assuming the validity of each and every separate characteristic but rather by looking at the total fabric in an ideal-type construction. Informal would then be the whole gamut of economic activities characterized by small scale, low capital-intensity, inferior technology, low productivity, predominantly family labour and property, no training or only that obtained 'on the job', easy entry, and finally a small and usually poor clientele. In this formulation, the emphasis lies on the subdivision of the urban economy into two independent circuits, each with its own logic, structural consistency, and dynamics.

Another form of the concept of economic dualism derives from the contrast made between an activity which is officially registered and sanctioned by official legislation and that which is not. The term informal, in this case, refers to operations which are kept out of the sight and control of the government and in this sense are also denoted as the 'parallel', 'underground', or 'shadow' economy. The legal recognition on which the formal sector can rely is not only expressed in the levying of taxes but also in the promulgation of various protective regulations. The much easier access to the state apparatus enjoyed by the owners or managers of formal-sector enterprises leads to disproportionate advantages in the granting of various facilities, such as credit and licences, as well as the selective use of government ordinances as to what is permitted and what is not. The privileged treatment claimed by formal-sector interests creates disadvantages or even renders criminal informal-sector activities when, for instance, these are seen as a hindrance to traffic on the street or as threatening 'public order'. Unregulated activities may also clash with the prevailing state ideology. In the former socialist regimes of central and eastern Europe, producers supplemented their income with transactions on the black market both outside and during official working hours. The conversion of the party leaders in post-Maoist China to free-market thinking went together with the legalization of various economic activities of an informal nature which, until then, had not been allowed or to which a blind eye had been turned.

When first using the concept, Hart did not omit to draw attention to the criminally inclined nature of some of the activities he enumerated. The association of informal with subversiveness or illegality is partly a result of an unwillingness to recognize the economic value of these goods and services. It should also be realized that excluding this great army of the deprived from access to space, water, and electricity, only encourages them to make clandestine use of these services and to contravene public health instructions. Yet the authorities are not slow to conduct large-scale campaigns against such violations of the law. In any case, it is clear that the government is not absent in this milieu but, on the contrary, actively concerns itself with disciplining the sector.

Furthermore, the dividing line in the two-sector model has to be drawn very differently when it comes to the observance of legislation and official regulations. There is a tendency to conceive of the informal economy as an unregistered, unregulated, and hence untaxed circuit. This, however, ignores the ease with which power holders, particularly the personnel in government agencies responsible for implementing formal regulations and laws, see this industry as their private hunting ground once it has been made invisible. Moreover, it would be a great distortion of reality to dissociate phenomena such as fraud, corruption, demands for the payment of speed, protection money, and bribes and, more generally, the conversion of public resources into private profits, from operations in the formal-sector economy where they primarily occur. This goes a long way in explaining why not only the legal incomes of politicians and policy makers, who are part of the elite, but also the basic salaries of many low-ranking health-care workers, police constables, and teachers lag far behind their incomes of an 'informal' nature.

The third and last variant of the formal- informal-sector dichotomy is related to the existence of bifurcated labour markets. A first feature to be discussed is the degree of division of labour. Formal-sector labour is usually performed in a complex work organization that consists of a set of specific tasks which are interrelated but are hierarchically and differently valued and which, to differing degrees, require previous training. The small scale, in combination with the low capital intensity, of informal-sector employment implies very little or no task differentiation and requires skills and knowledge which are picked up in daily practise.

Due to a lack of accurate and ongoing or periodical data collection, there is little known about the size, origin, and composition of the working population in the informal sector. The labour statistics which are maintained are mainly restricted to the supply and demand of permanent workers, who are recruited and dismissed on the basis of objectified criteria in the higher echelons of the urban economy. This registration is a result of, as well as condition for, greater control of the economy by official regulations. It is, therefore, not very surprising that studies of employment and labour relations have primarily focused on the upper segment of the urban order.

Given the above-mentioned characteristics, the alternative name for the informal sector as the zone of unorganized or unregistered labour is understandable, and just as clear as a third synonym, the unprotected sector. There are simply no legal rules concerning either entry into this sector or the conditions and circumstances under which informal-sector labour is put to work. If some elementary standards have been introduced—such as the fixing of a minimum wage, the ban on labour which is deleterious for health and the environment, and the prohibition of child labour or practices of bondage—a machinery for their enforcement is lacking. The organized, registered, and protected character of formal-sector labour is in diametrical opposition to this situation. In terms of organization, there is another advantage enjoyed by formal-sector workers, namely the possibility of setting up their own organizations in order to defend their common interests when dealing with employers or the government. This form of collective action increases the efficacy of the existing protection and is, at the same time, a means of extending this protection. In the informal-sector landscape, trade unions are only rarely encountered. This absence contributes further to the maintenance of low wages and to the social vulnerability and miserable conditions of employment in this sector.

The introduction of the concept 'informal sector' has irrefutably drawn attention to the jumbled mass of activities—unregulated, fragmented, and infinitely diverse—whereby a large part of the working population manages to survive, usually with a great deal of difficulty. Research on urban

employment in the past was almost always restricted to labour in factories
and other modern enterprises. Its recurring themes were the rural origin of
the new working population, its adjustment to an industrial lifestyle, and the
labour relations in these large-scale enterprises. With the shift in focus from
the formal to the informal sector, the long-fostered idea that the large mass of
workers who have not been incorporated in the labour process in a regular
and standardized manner should, in fact, be seen as unemployed has been
done away with.

On the other hand, the discussion on the informal sector has
begged more questions than it has answered. This is the result of a lack of
precision in the definition, where everything that is not regarded as belonging
to the formal sector is categorized as 'informal'. This assumption, made very
early on, gives a distinctly tautological slant to the difference made between
the two sectors.[3] The dualism that has been discussed above relates sometimes
to the labour market, sometimes to the economic circuits with different modes
of production, and, in other cases, to permissible versus clandestine or plainly
criminal economic activities. There is often a combination of all these
variants with the implicit or explicit suggestion that the different criteria of
the dual division run parallel to each other.[4] I fundamentally disagree with
this idea. One of the definitional problems arises precisely from the discord
between the different dimensions of the dualism concept. For example, it is
simply not true that informal-sector workers produce goods and perform
services only or even principally for clients in their own milieu, just as it is
true that innumerable formal-sector commodities find their way to informal-
sector consumers. Furthermore, formal-sector regulations are often avoided by
transferring some or even all business activities and industrial production to
the informal sector. These are only some arbitrarily chosen examples,
amongst many, of the interdependence of the two sectors.

It is significant that authors who base their work on empirical
research are often the most critical of this dual conceptualization. From my
own long experience of studying rural and urban labour relations in western
India, I conclude that the concept is useful in an 'ideal' sense only.[5] I believe
that the informal sector cannot be demarcated as a separate economic circuit
and/or a segment of the labour force. Attempts to persist with this strict
demarcation create innumerable inconsistencies and problems which are
discussed later. Instead of a two-sector model, there is a much more complex
differentiation of the urban economy which should be the point of departure
for structural analysis. The reduction to two sectors, the one capitalist and the
other non- or early capitalist, does not reflect the reality of the much greater
complexity of work and production. A final objection of perhaps greater
importance is that, in assuming such a dualist system, the interrelationships

between the various components of the economy threaten to be lost from sight. Instead of splitting up the urban system into two sectors, I want to emphasize the fragmented character of the total labour market and the need to see these fragments not as mutually exclusive, but as connected. This argument is central to my analysis (Breman 1994; 1996).

Size and Dynamics

Estimates of the size of the informal sector are not very precise and the figures which have been reported for various countries or cities differ greatly. This is a variation which does not, however, necessarily signal real differences in economic structure or developments over time. The most frequently cited estimates fluctuate between 30 and 70 per cent of the urban workforce. This very broad range is indicative of the serious lack of terminological clarity. Since the first use of the concept, a trend of upward correction has become apparent—both of the total number of workers and the proportion accounted for by the informal sector. Virtually all recent studies on this subject assume that at least half of the population in large Third World metropoles can be categorized as belonging to the informal sector, while this proportion is even higher for the smaller-sized cities and towns. The changing criteria used—including the nature of the work (industry, trade, transport, or services); the scale of operation (more or fewer than ten workers for each enterprise); use of other production factors than labour (energy and technology)—virtually exclude a systematic comparison of the estimates for different places and years. Based on official statistics, derived from the requirement to register the formal-sector labour, Visaria and Jacob estimated that, in 1972–3, 18.8 million of the total of 236.7 million working people in India belonged to the formal sector. In 1991 their number had increased to 26.7 million out of a total of 343.5 million. Hence, in both the first and last year, formal-sector employment came to less than 8 per cent of the total workforce (1995: 14). I may add here that I have little confidence in the completeness and reliability of the figures on which these estimates are based. Moreover, it should be realized that the data banks on employment and labour relations collected by international organizations such as the ILO and the World Bank are not much better.[6]

A serious methodological problem is that on both sides of the dividing line the working population is constituted very differently. Even the use of the term 'economically active' is of problematic significance for the informal sector. Women, the elderly, minors, and even the less able often participate in the work process, although their labour power is neither always nor fully used. This also applies to the labour power of able-bodied male adults at the peak of their physical strength. The ratio of earners to non-earners in homogeneous, informal-sector households is higher than that in pure formal-sector households. On the other hand, the working members of formal-sector households are more permanently employed. But to estimate that, of the working members of informal-sector households only one in eight is a woman—as Papola calculated on the basis of research in Ahmedabad—indicates significant under-registration in terms of gender (1981: 122). Similarly, until recently there has been systematic underestimation of the extent of child labour. The information to be found in the same source, that children constitute only 8 per cent of the workers in non-registered hotels and restaurants, is highly unlikely. The actual proportion of these young 'helpers' between 5 and 14 years must be at least double this figure.

The length of the working day in the informal sector is considerably greater than that in the formal sector and work often continues into the night. There are also no weekly off days, while annual festivals are celebrated much less or not at all. On the other hand, there are far greater seasonal fluctuations in the annual work cycle. The net effect of all these factors for the size and intensity of the labour power in the formal and informal sectors is difficult to ascertain. In order to obtain an insight into the living conditions of the poor masses, empirical research at the level of the household deserves priority. It is possible to understand the relative elasticity with which unemployment, greatly fluctuating incomes and other adversity are countered only by assuming that many, if not all members of households at the bottom of the urban heap—regardless of age, sex, or degree of physical ability—are, or want to be, partially or completely incorporated in the labour process.[7]

The specific nature of work arrangements in the informal sector seems to suggest a gradual continuum from employment to non-employment rather than a sharp break. The consequence of this peculiarity is that permanence and security are not marked features of informal work performance and that irregularity and vulnerability dominate instead. This particular trait of the informal sector makes an analysis of the labour market an extremely arbitrary and even disputable matter. The attempts to subject non-standardized and irregular work to quantitative analysis in terms of exact measures and clear counts might stem from a research methodology which is based on formal-sector notions. The recurrent complaints from researchers about the chaotic appearance and lack of transparency of the informal sector should be seen in this light. This explains why sociological and economic analyses of the labour market are so strongly distorted in favour of data collection on formal-sector enterprises. Of course, the small size of this sector does not at all justify this bias.

The contrast between the top and bottom of the urban economy is easy to describe. In the broad social spectrum between these polar ends, however, where informal and formal labour merge into each other, there is no clear dividing line. Consequently, I conclude that the image of a dichotomy is much too simple and can better be replaced by the idea of a continuum.

The first studies of the informal-sector concept created the impression that this segment of the urban economy functioned as a waiting room for a rapidly increasing stream of migrants pushed out from the rural economy. It was merely meant to be their first 'stay' in the new environment. The work that they performed provided them with craftsmanship and stimulated them to develop their talents as micro-entrepreneurs. Those who completed this apprenticeship successfully would in the end cross the gap which separated them from the formal sector. The promise of social mobility expressed by this optimistic scenario, however, appears in practice to be fulfilled for only a tiny minority. Time and again the results of numerous investigations show that a very considerable proportion of informal-sector workers are born and raised in the city and, at the end of their working lives, have not come much further than where they started.

A completely different dynamic, in an institutional and not an individual sense, arises from the idea that the informal sector is nothing more than a transitory phenomenon caused by the massive expulsion from the agrarian-rural economy. Given that the growth of formal-sector employment is slower than would be necessary to accommodate fully and immediately the size of this exodus, there is a temporary excess of people in the lower layers of the urban system. As economic growth accelerates, the need for and significance of employment in the informal sector declines and eventually little or nothing of this 'buffer zone' will remain. In my conclusion, I shall show that this representation is nothing more than hopeful expectation.

An Urban Phenomenon?

One of the shortcomings in the debate on the informal sector is the unflagging preoccupation with the urban economy. It is difficult to maintain that there is dualism in the urban order and that the countryside is in contrast characterized by homogeneity. To be sure, the peasant economy *in toto* demonstrates a number of features which are very similar to informal-sector activity. This is true for the way production takes place and it is also reflected in the pattern of employment. On the other hand, it is not so far-fetched to classify plantations, mines, or agro-industries in the rural areas as formal-sector enterprises, as they possess most of the dominant characteristics of this category. Why is attention in the majority of studies on this subject then focused on the urban economy? This preoccupation appears to originate in two misplaced suppositions: first, that the countryside is almost exclusively the domain of agriculture and, second, that agricultural labour is performed by a virtually homogenous peasant population. We are concerned here with a monolithic image which does not allow a sectoral division in terms of formal and informal. Moreover, this three-compartment (one rural and two urban) model seems to indicate the direction of social dynamics: peasants migrate to the city where they find work and an income in the informal sector before making the jump to the formal sector of the economy. Against this line of reasoning inspired by wishful thinking, I maintain that regardless of the reservations that one may have about the validity of the informal-sector concept, it is both theoretically and in practice impossible to declare that this concept is exclusively applicable to the urban domain. There are some other researchers who share this view and focus attention on dualist features manifest in the organization of agrarian production (Jaganathan 1987).

Analyses based on the comprehensive totality of economic activities, irrespective of whether they are located in urban or rural areas, emphasize the small volume of formal-sector employment in India. As mentioned earlier, for example, Visaria and Jacob (1995) arrived at a figure of not more than 8 per cent. According to them this extremely skewed division is primarily caused by the dominant position of the agrarian working population, consisting almost exclusively of informal-sector workers. The ratio of 92:8 is so highly uneven that it cannot be considered as a sound basis for sectoral analysis. This leads me to exclude agriculture, both in terms of production and labour, and to employ the formal–informal dichotomy as a framework of analysis for all other branches of the economy together (in other words, without dividing them according to city or countryside). It is a point of departure which takes care of my objection that there is a tendency to see the informal sector only as an urban phenomenon and helps to highlight the magnitude of informal non-agrarian employment in the rural economy. Skilled crafts of all sorts, trade and transport, as well as services in differing degrees of specialization have always been important occupations in the past as well as at present. The size and importance of this non-agrarian work, performed either as the worker's main or subsidiary activity, has increased significantly in many parts of India in recent decades. Table 1 illustrates the shift in the composition of the workforce in the last twenty years—the declining importance of employment in agriculture in the face of the growth, particularly in informal-sector activity in other economic sectors.

Even if all possible criticism of the accuracy of the figures, in Table 1, which are derived from government statistics, is taken into account, the data are still sufficiently robust to provide an insight into the trend of economic transformation in the long term. First, agricultural employment declined from 74 per cent in 1972–3 to 65 per cent fifteen years later. During the same period, non-agricultural labour rose from 26 to 35 per cent. The number of people employed in agriculture increased from 61.8 million in the first year to 113.6 million in 1987–8. According to another study, non-agricultural work was the main source of income for one out of four men and one out of six women in all rural households in India at the end of the 1980s (Chadha 1993). The growth indicated by these figures is principally propelled by activities which fall under the informal sector. The annual rate of increase in this sector is 4.9 per cent, more than double that of the formal sector.

It is important to observe that an acceleration in the diversification of the rural economy does not correspond to an increasing formalization of employment. One example concerns the emergence of a major agro-industry in the south of the state of Gujarat: every year huge armies of migrant labourers are mobilized from nearby Maharashtra and other catchment areas for the large-scale harvesting and processing of sugarcane; at the end of the campaign, they return (Breman 1994:133–287). I will discuss in the conclusion, this stagnation of formal-sector employment is a more general phenomenon which goes far beyond the city–country contrast; hence, it must be understood in a broader context.

Employment Modality

Self-employment is described in a large part of the literature as the backbone of the informal sector (see Sanyal 1991; Portes et al. 1989). When introducing the concept, Hart mentioned this as the most significant feature. 'The distinction between formal and informal income opportunities is based essentially on that between wage earning and self-employment' (1973: 86). Subsequently, many authors expressed themselves in a similar vein. A quite arbitrary example is Sanyal who, in an analysis of informal-sector policy states, without any reservation or empirical evidence, that the majority of the urban informal-sector population lives from the income gained from self-employment (Sanyal 1991: 41). This is, of course, the well-known image of the army of odd-jobbers and jacks-of-all-trades that travel around in the open air or survive from put-out work performed at home, but always do this on their own account and at their own risk. In such descriptions, emphasis is laid firmly on the ingenuity, the stamina, and the alert reaction to new opportunities demonstrated by these small-scale self-employed workers and last, but certainly not least, on the pride they show in being their own bosses. Some authors speak of these workers as mini-entrepreneurs and tend to describe the informal sector as a breeding ground for more sophisticated entrepreneurship which, as it is larger-scale and capitalist, can only be developed in the formal sector. Under this unrestrained apology for the free market, not only are informal workers trained and hardened in the struggle for daily existence—one can recognize here the profile of self-made men who started small—but once mature, they are able to develop into true captains of industry.

Another and more critical school of thought is represented by authors who describe and analyse the informal sector in terms of petty commodity production (see Smith 1985). In these writings the emphasis lies on the limited room for manoeuvre in which the self-employed have to operate. These works also discuss the dependence of the self-employed upon suppliers who overburden them with poor quality or overpriced products, moneylenders who charge extortionate rates of interest for short-term loans, street vendors who are easy prey for the police, sex workers who are in the hands of their pimps, slumlords who demand protection money, home-workers who can offer no resistance in the face of the practices of contractors or agents who commission their work, etc.

What is portrayed as own-account work carried out at the risk of the producer is in fact a more or less camouflaged form of wage labour. There is a wide diversity of arrangements which actually show great similarity with tenancy or sharecropping relationships in agriculture, where the principle of self-employment is so undermined in practice that the dependency on the landowner is scarcely different from that of a contract labourer. This is true for many actors operating in the informal sector such as the 'hirers' of a bicycle or motor taxi who must hand over a considerable proportion of their daily earnings to the owner of the vehicle, or for the street vendors who are provided their wares early in the morning on credit or commission from a supplier and then in the evening, after returning the unsold remainder, learn if and what they have retained from their transactions.

The façade of self-employment is further reinforced by modes of payment which are often associated with informal sector practices. For example the sub-contracting of production to home-workers is a common occurrence. Piece-rate and job work suggest a degree of independence which differs from the relationship between regular wage workers and employers. In the latter case, the time worked is the unit of calculation of the wage, while the wage is also paid regularly—per day, week, or month. The actual payment of this regular wage confirms the status of the worker as a permanent employee. Putting-out and one-off jobs, on the other hand, are in this aspect much closer to self-employment. And last but not least, there is no valid reason to describe wage labour as a phenomenon that is inextricably bound with the formal sector. The informal sector landscape is covered with small-scale enterprises that not only make use of unpaid labour, requisitioned from the household or family circle, but even more of personnel hired for a special purpose. This does not, however, always take the shape of an unequivocal and direct employer–employee relationship. There are different intermediaries—those who provide raw materials and then collect semi-finished or finished products from home workers, or jobbers who recruit and supervise gangs of unregistered workers— who function as agents for the ultimate patron. In all these cases, it would be incorrect to construct a sharp contrast between self-employment and wage labour corresponding to the informal–formal divide.

Such a division would also conflict with the occupational multiplicity that is characteristic of casualized labour. The bulk of these workers are continually in search of sources of income and perform a wide range of odd jobs within a relatively short time period—a week, a day, or even a few hours. These activities sometimes appear to be characterized by self-employment, sometimes by wage labour, and sometimes by a combination of both. For those involved, the nature of and the manner in which they perform these jobs is not of importance, but what they will pay is. The necessity not to specialize in one occupation but to show interest in a multitude of diverse activities arises from the seasonal fluctuations which are inherent to informal-sector economy. The alteration between the dry and the wet season, or between summer and winter, corresponds with the uneven annual rhythm of a great deal of these open-air occupations. During unsuitable seasons much less use, and sometimes no use at all, is made of the services of building and road-construction workers, quarrymen, brick makers, street vendors, itinerant artisans, and other street workers. But significant fluctuations throughout the year also occur in the demand for labour for numerous activities which take place in roof-covered and enclosed spaces. In their case, it is not the climatic conditions but the changing demand in the annual cycle of certain commodities and services that is the main factor. The months preceding the wedding season are a period of peak production for the manufacture of embroidered *saris,* while religious festivals also give a large but temporary incentive to associated industries. The same applies for the great variety of workers in the tourist industry. Cessation of production, or perhaps a sudden spurt, can be determined by stagnation in the supply of raw materials, cuts in the electricity supply or availability of transport, and price rises or falls. It is a characteristic of informal-sector employment that the use of labour, in size and intensity, is seen as derived from all these market imperfections of a structural or conjunctural nature. In other words, the business risk is passed on to the workers. They must remain available for as long as there is need of their labour, not only in the daytime but also in the evening and at night. Periods of overemployment are then followed by shorter or longer periods of enforced idleness. However, they can derive no rights from this pattern of irregular or suddenly changing working hours in the form of wage supplements or continued payment of wages for hours, days, or seasons during which work was stopped or declined in intensity. The excessive subjection of labour to the highly variable demands made by the production process arises from the presence of an almost inexhaustible labour supply, if not actually then at least potentially. This reserve army consists of men and women, both young and old, who differ from each other more in the degree of previous experience and suitability than in the preparedness to make the required effort for the lowest possible price. To speak of superexploitation of wage workers by employers in the informal sector, but then to regard the self-employed as responsible for their own degree of exploitation, gives, in my opinion, an exaggerated picture of the differences between both categories and ignores their similarities.

The standardization of the conditions of employment in the formal sector of the economy—in terms of wage scales, length of the working day, security, and social benefits—equally applies to obtaining access to the sector. This observation implies that recruitment and promotion are subject to fixed rules related to training, seniority, and other objectively determined qualities of the workforce concerned. Conversely, access to industry in the informal sector is characterized by much greater coincidence and arbitrariness. This difference is, of course, consistent with the more permanent employment in the formal sector and the much more casual and shorter-lasting jobs which dominate in the lower zones of the labour hierarchy. Without wanting to contest that access to employment in both sectors can be differentiated on the basis of these criteria, I would like to add that these differences become blurred when increasing pressure is put on the formal-sector labour market. When supply also exceeds demand in this sector, the standardized rules make way for more subjective considerations in the selection policy. Formalized labour arrangements then appear to be anything but free of arbitrary personal preferences and prejudices which are more often used to describe practices of recruitment and dismissal in the informal sector.

The conclusion that I draw from the above is that the diverse modalities of employment do not confirm the image of a dualist but rather of a fragmented labour market. The distinction made between the two sectors is further complicated by the manner whereby the occupants of formal and informal labour positions try to build fences or barriers in order to guarantee access to the conquered niche of employment for candidates hailing from their own circle, with maximal exclusion of 'outsiders'. The latter are those who do not belong to the category of close family members, neighbours and friends, nor are they members of the same caste, religious group, tribe, linguistic group, regional or ethnic group. Of vital importance for the organization of the labour market is a pronounced state of fragmentation, that is expressed in the innumerable compartments of employment, of which some assume a fluid form while others are demarcated by fairly hard partitions in both the higher and lower levels of the economy.

Social Identity

The very broad spectrum of activities grouped together under the concept of the informal sector are performed by heterogeneously composed categories of working people. Despite the diversity, there are still a number of common features in the social profile of these masses. In the first place, these workers have little or no formal training and the majority are often totally illiterate.

Second, they have no source of income besides the earnings from their own labour. Even the acquisition of the most simple tools—a shovel and basket or bowl for carrying earth in the case of road workers; a barrow, oil lamp, and scales for a street vendor; a little wooden box with polish and brushes for shoe polishers—represents an investment which beginners cannot afford out of their own savings and for which they have to take a loan. The moneylenders operating in this sector charge a high interest rate even for the small amounts and short-term repayments which they grant.

The acute lack of creditworthiness of informal-sector workers is closely connected to a third feature: the extremely low wages which they receive for their strenuous efforts. It is precisely these paltry returns that force informal-sector workers to make use of all hands, big ones as well as nimble fingers, which are available in their household. In the case of migrants, this leads them to leave behind 'dependent' family members who are no longer (or not yet) able to work to an extent that would at least compensate for the extra costs needed for their maintenance. In this weighing up of pros and cons, a role is also played by how much of the income should be spent on housing. In order to keep this expenditure as minimal as possible, seasonal migrants in particular make do with a very primitive roof over their heads, improvised from waste material that happens to be available, or they even set up a bivouac under the open sky. Migrants who establish themselves for longer periods far from home may sometimes hire living space together, in the case of single men, or attempt, if accompanied by wife and children, to find their own accommodation preferably with water and sanitary facilities, however primitive, in the immediate vicinity.

A fourth feature is the much higher participation of both women and children in the informal sector of the economy. The vulnerability of this labour force has also to be understood in gender and age tems. Even more exploited and subordinated than men are children and women. A wide variety of studies has documented the magnitude, identity, and conditions of work of both these categories (see Mies 1982; Karlekar 1982; Banerjee 1985; Tom 1989; Banerjee 1991; Kapadia 1995; Banerjee 1979; Rodgers and Standing 1981; Jugal et al. 1985; Punalekar 1993 and Sahoo 1995).

Finally, informal work has a low status. This is partly the sum of the features mentioned in the preceding paragraphs in combination with the substitutability and irregularity of the work, and partly the result of the socially inferior origin of this workforce: in India the large majority of them are members of backward or Untouchable castes. Although the word 'coolie' is no longer fashionable, the derogatory connotation implied by its use in the past covers quite well the lack of respect that is associated with this sort of work. The strenuous physical effort that is often demanded, goes with sweat, filth, and other such bodily features which bear the odium of inferiority and subordination. Besides being tainted with the stigma of pollution, these characteristics also undermine the health of the workers in a way which leads to their being prematurely worn out. In addition to all these hazards, the women and children are often exposed to sexual harassment. Female and child domestic servants are at risk from their employers, and such members of workgangs from the foremen. Lack of dignity results from their inability to cope with misfortune, such as illness, or to save for the considerable expense involved in important life-cycle rituals which have to be observed. By taking an advance on these occasions they try to meet their social obligations even though it leads to a form of labour attachment to their employer or an intermediary, which restricts even further their already limited room for manoeuvre.

Does it follow from the above that informal-sector workers have a style of living and working in common with each other which could categorize them as belonging to one homogeneous social class? In comparison with the labour aristocracy employed at the top of the formal-sector economy—permanently employed, well educated, with a daily rhythm in which work and free time are sharply marked, reasonably well paid and hence creditworthy, living in reasonable comfort and consequently aware of their social dignity and respect—the many-times-greater army of workers without all these prerogatives form one uniform mass. But closer examination reveals that there is no simple division into only two classes. At the very broad bottom of the economic order there are striking differences between, for example, migrants forced to wander around various sites of employment in the open air and labourers who operate power looms or other simple machines in small workshops. It is true that the textile workers go every day to work for the same boss, at least for the time being, but they cannot derive from their regular employment at the same site any claim to decent treatment or even the right to a minimum form of security.

In an earlier work (Breman 1994) I classified informal-sector workers into three classes:

First, a petty bourgeoisie who, besides the owners of mini-workshops, self-employed artisans, small traders and shopkeepers, also include those who earn their keep as economic brokers or agents, such as moneylenders, labour contractors, intermediaries who collect and deliver piece-work and home work, and rent collectors. Compared with the lower ranks of formal-sector labour, the income of this category is not infrequently on a much higher level. In reports which tend to value the informal sector as a breeding ground for entrepreneurs, the emphasis lies on the right type of behaviour. Those who belong to this social category set great store by their relative autonomy—they exhibit a need to avoid subordination to others in general and an aversion to wage dependence in particular—and show, by good bourgeois attributes such as thrift and hard work, that they are striving to improve their individual positions within the social hierarchy.

Second, the subproletariat, who subsume the largest segment of informal-sector workers, consists of a colourful collection of casual and unskilled workers who circulate relatively quickly from one location of temporary employment to another. It includes both labourers in the service of small workshops and the reserve army of labour who are recruited and dismissed by large-scale enterprises according to the need of the moment. The subproletariat also include, itinerant semi-artisans who offer their services and (paltry) tools for hire at morning markets, day labourers, home workers, vendors, and the long parade of occupations practised in the open air, including the shoe polisher and messenger. They differ from the residual category by having, if not a permanent, at least a demonstrable form of accommodation, and by keeping a regular household even if all the members are not always able to live together as a family. This is achieved by a labour strategy that is based on a rational choice of options which are time and place bound and by attempts to invest in education, health, and social security, even though the irregularity of their existence and the inability to accumulate consistently, excludes any firm plans for the future. Although their misery (from which many often escape into drunkenness) is great, these workers are still distinguished from the category of the last resort, which I am inclined to describe as 'paupers'. These are the lumpen, the dregs of society with criminal features, whose presence nobody values. They are the 'declassed' who have often broken contact with their family or village of origin, who have no fixed accommodation, and who maintain no regular contacts with other people in their immediate environment. These people not only lack all means of production but also do not have the labour power and stamina needed to be able to meet their daily minimal requirements in full. Thus alienated even from the means of consumption, they easily fall into a state of pauperization and form a ragbag of crushed, broken-spirited rejects—single men, widows or divorced women with children, children without parents, the mentally or physically handicapped, and the superfluous elderly.

It is important to note that this classification does not mean that an unambiguous, clearly hierarchical formation of three discrete social strata has crystallized. A household can consist of members who have been absorbed in the labour process in various ways; it is not always the case that all members of one household work in either the formal or informal sector. A consequent lack of consistency in terms of class position and associated lifestyle is, however, rectified by part of the household sometimes breaking away or being pushed off to form a new household.

The fluidity in the transition between the different social classes, as well as shifts in the proportional distribution among them that occur over time, under influence of contraction or expansion of the economy, mitigate against a division which is either unduly rigid or too static. It is hence empirically not easy to delimit the largest segment of the working population, the subproletariat, from the other collectivities. Upward and downward mobility are both possible, in theory, and occur in practice at all levels to some degree, although it is very exceptional for this mobility to apply for one individual all the way from the bottom to the top or vice versa. In most cases, mobility is limited to much shorter movements.

Organization and Protection

One of the most common criteria for the operationalization of the formal–informal-sector dichotomy is whether or not labour has managed to get organized. The protection enjoyed by workers in large-scale and capital-intensive enterprises is the result of action taken by them for the collective promotion of their interests, including wage levels, rules for recruitment, promotion, and dismissal, hours of work, and secondary terms of employment. Not all those who have found a niche in the formal sector are in fact members of such trade unions. On the other hand, it is even less common for workers in the informal sector to join together in an effort to improve their position. Still, this has actually occurred in a limited number of cases and it is interesting to observe that these initiatives arise from or focus on very vulnerable groups. This applies, for example, to the Self-Employed Women's Association (SEWA) which is based in Ahmedabad. In Kerala, both within and outside agriculture, different trade-union-like organizations have been established with the explicit objective of reinforcing the rights of informal-sector workers (Kannan 1988; Pillai 1996). Becoming acquainted with the occasional successful experience is relevant for answering the question of how the emergence of trade unions can be facilitated in the lower echelons of the economy. There is hardly any difference of opinion concerning the urgent need for such a course of action. Why then, with a few exceptions, are they absent in the informal-sector landscape?

The explanation must be sought firstly in the subaltern identity of these working masses and the manner in which they are absorbed in the labour process. The workers concerned are mostly young men and women who belong to the lowest levels of the social hierarchy, who can often neither read nor write, and who have arrived in an alien environment as migrants. They manage to survive with casual and irregular work which often gives them the appearance of being self-employed. The work performed is not connected with a fixed location but is subject to constant change. Besides having to move from place to place looking for employment they also need to engage themselves in a variety of different activities at intervals of a year, season, week, or even day.

This profile of occupational multiplicity demonstrates how difficult it is to bring together in an organization these casual, unskilled, itinerant, fragmented, and poverty-stricken masses on the basis of their common interests. Furthermore, any attempts at unionization made in the separate branches of informal-sector industry, come up against barriers erected by employers and their agents, such as intermediaries and labour contractors. This resistance is sometimes expressed in the form of intimidation or instant dismissal of workers who not only try to press for their own interests but also for those of others. Even worse, it can come to actual violence or the terrorizing of labour activists by gangs of thugs or hired killers whom the employers don't hesitate to use.

Are the existing trade unions established by and for formal-sector labour who have permanent jobs, are better trained, and usually higher paid, aware of the miserable state of the masses who populate the lower zones of the economy? And more important still, can they be persuaded to see these irregular workers, with low social visibility and fragmented into unconnected, fluid segments, as potential members of their organization? The answer seems to be 'no', or at least 'hardly at all'. This disinclination arises partly from all sorts of practical problems such as, for instance, the difficulty involved in mobilizing an amorphous and floating multitude on the basis of shared interests. The task set is further complicated by the necessity encouraging these differing and diverse interests to have bargaining dialogue with a very great number of micro-employers. This effort requires large overhead costs which would be impossible for members who belong to the economically most-vulnerable categories to finance. Furthermore, experience shows that the needs and problems of informal-sector workers are quite different from labour arrangements in the formal sector of the economy. These differences in needs demand a type of organization and promotion of interests of which conventional trade unions have little experience, many of them not at all. Even more important, the union leadership is not prepared, in the light of these much wider aims, to reformulate its mission and to operationalize the new agenda into a concrete plan of action. In the final analysis, the trade unions close ranks to restrict access. The miserable lot of informal-sector workers is not seen as a challenge but as a threat to the much better deal—the outcome of a long-lasting struggle for a reasonable degree of security, prosperity, and dignity—enjoyed by labour in the formal sector. The strategy of fending off the mass of excluded workers explains why, conversely, the latter feel little affinity with the recognized trade-union movement. Both the union leadership and members do not appear to unduly worry themselves over the question of how they could contribute to improving the lot of the informal workers and instead tend to see them as scabs. They regard the reserve labour army with scorn, as it supplies the strike-breakers who unscrupulously accept the jobs, temporarily made available by formal-sector workers who have gone on strike, in the hope of being able to occupy them permanently. Only in recent years, and under the pressure of stagnating or even declining levels of employment in the formal sector, have the established labour organizations dropped their indifferent or even hostile attitude. At the initiative of the International Congress of Free Trade Unions (ICFTU), a conference was held in 1988 on the transformation of the international economic order and the concomitant trend of informalization of employment modalities. It had become clear to insiders as well as outsiders that the trade-union movement was threatened with marginalization by its exclusive concentration upon a relatively small elite engaged under formal terms of employment. The leadership finally realized that a large part of the working masses did not recognize the trade-union movement as an ally in the struggle against deteriorating working conditions. The unions that were members of this international federation were urged to make the informal-sector issue a high priority one. A report that appeared only a year later described as a first aim the formalization of the gigantic army of unprotected and unorganized workers (ICFTU 1989). They should enjoy the same legal protection as employees in the formal sector. It will be clear that this demand was characterized by a woefully inadequate sense of reality. Moreover, it demonstrated a very poor understanding of the dynamics of the informal sector. The formula to achieve this new goal was confined to the suggestion about accelerating what, according to conventional wisdom, would be the predictable result of the process of economic development. It was a naive supposition, and after this recommendation very little has happened in the routine practice of trade-union activities.

The lack of support from the established trade-union movement does not mean that informal-sector workers passively accept the labour regime forced upon them. Many make efforts, often repeatedly so, to combat the insecurity and miserable conditions of employment by trying to negotiate a somewhat better deal with their particular employers. They do this by emphasizing their subordination and loyalty to their patrons in exchange for which they appeal to the patrons' discretionary power to grant favours. Given the abundant supply and limited demand for labour, employers are bent upon reducing even further the already small space in which the massive army in search of work must operate. Thus they use all sorts of arrangements which lead to a curtailment of their employees' room for manoeuvre. Mechanisms to tie the worker further to the employer, such as providing an advance on salary or paying in arrears show similarities with forms of unfree labour which occurred in the past (Breman 1993), but differ from them by a more articulated contractual and capitalist slant. Against this background, it is understandable why much labour resistance assumes the shape of sabotage, obstruction, avoidance, and other deeds of covert protest, summarized by the term, 'weapons of the weak' (Scott 1985, 1990).

Despite the severe sanctions which are brought to bear on attempts to form a common front and openly express latent feelings of solidarity, collective signals of resistance are the order of the day in the informal sector. Reasons discussed in the preceding paragraphs explain why, for example, strikes 'suddenly' break out, rarely spread to the whole branch of the industry, and also die out relatively quickly. The weak capacity to resist makes it understandable why these actions are usually spontaneous, local, and short in duration. But there is also in part an under-reporting of some forms of resistance, as they occur infrequently, or not at all, in employment under formal conditions. The registration of labour resistance has been unduly focused on the nature and course of the social struggle in the formal sector. Proto-trade unions, such as those that existed in Europe's pre-industrial past, could be an interesting point of departure for comparison with the manifestation of labour unrest and industrial action in the informal sector of the economy of today.[8]

The protection enjoyed by formal-sector workers arises from a gradual shift in the balance of power between capital and labour over a period of roughly one hundred years. The introduction and implementation of separate legislation for protecting labour (in the same way, although not to the same extent, that the rights of capital were safeguarded) would be inconceivable without the intermediary role of the state. What has been the role of national and local government in regulating the informal sector of the economy? For one thing, the impression often created that there is absolutely no official interference is incorrect. Where there is universal suffrage, which is actually exercised with reasonable freedom in India since Independence, the political system cannot afford to ignore completely the working masses which make up the majority of the electorate. This consideration is of relevance for explaining why minimum wages have been fixed for landless labourers, why the practices of illegal labour contractors are restricted, why various ordinances regulate the movement of migrants, and why violations of the prohibition of bonded labour are punishable by law, to mention just a few examples. In many states of India, there are detailed rules regulating employment for many occupations, even for casual labour that is limited to particular seasons of the year (Breman 1996). What is lacking, however, is an effective machinery to implement these regulations, as well as the appointment of an adequate number of officials responsible for their enforcement. Moreover, civil servants who are allocated inspection responsibilities in practice make use of their mandate to obtain extra income; it is an example of the abuse of public authority for private advantage that occurs at all levels of bureaucracy.

Policy and Globalization of the Labour System

After the 'discovery' of the informal sector, amazement was expressed in many publications that such a large part of the population survived or even thrived on it. The reaction of the authorities was evidence of the need felt for regulation. At the same time, the way in which regulation took place made it clear that this involvement was not motivated so much by the desire to improve the lives of these workers but arose largely from irritation over their escape from government control. In this negatively coloured assessment, the informal sector was seen as a conglomerate of activities which were inconvenient and caused trouble. The parasitic or openly criminal features attributed to these workers reinforced the tendency of the government to protect the public and the economy from these 'useless, unhealthy, or downright dangerous' elements. Bicycle taxis and peripatetic vendors were driven from the streets, while 'unfavourably' located slums, if they were not razed to the ground, were removed from public view by enclosures. City beautification was the slogan which in many countries was used to justify this persecution and banishment (Breman 1983).

The plea for a more positive attitude, first made by the ILO in particular, was the beginning of a new direction that at least promised to end the open hunt on informal-sector workers and their trades. The argument in support of this policy was that the returns from these activities not only provided a living for those involved but also that they were of genuine use from a more general economic perspective. In order to increase the efficiency and effectiveness of this sector, an extensive package of supportive measures was recommended, varying from better training, more (and more accessible) credit, expansion of the markets for informal commodities as well as services, to, finally, greater tolerance in issuing government permits. Whether these proposals should be understood as reflecting a policy of formalization remains unanswered, as most of them were never implemented. A scenario with which policy makers felt more at ease was to not involve themselves with the informal sector at all, in either a positive or negative sense. The persecution and unbridled mania for regulation by bureaucrats at all levels was discontinued but without switching over to active protection. A well-known and influential advocate of this formula, with a very strong neo-liberal leaning, is De Soto, who has created great enthusiasm for it among leading politicians and international agencies (De Soto 1986). This is understandable, as the policy of non-state intervention he advocated tends to leave the existing relations of deep-seated inequalities in the distribution of property and power untouched and goes on to legitimize a situation which guarantees the domination of formal-sector interests, both capital and labour.

I have already indicated in the preceding discussion that in populist-inspired interpretations of the informal-sector phenomenon, attention has been focused, to a significant extent, on self-employment as an important element in the definition of the sector. To suggest that these workers operate on their own account and at their own risk leads to an analysis focusing on micro-entrepreneurship with all its positive features: ingenuity, versatility, boldness, industriousness, and flexibility. This is also an image that pleases these neo-liberal politicians and policy makers because, in their perception, success or failure is purely an affair of the actors themselves as individuals. They feel no need to look for the causes of this success or failure in the structure of society, of which informal-sector workers form such a major segment, nor in the unequal opportunities which are inherent to it.

The continuous formalization of employment in the urban and rural economy did not eventually materialize. In most cases, including India, there has even been a reversal of the trend: a chipping away of the formal conditions of employment which are being replaced by casual and short-term labour arrangements as part of an overall change in the organization of industrial production. An example is the closure of textile factories in Bombay and Ahmedabad. In these locations, power looms for the manufacture of rayon were transferred to thousands of small-scale workshops in new urban growth poles such as Surat (Breman 1996). The new international economic order demands the addition of more capital to the industrial process, but this takes place in a manner that guarantees the availability of abundant labour and the payment of very low wages, and provides employment only when needed. The pattern of employment still runs along informal-sector lines, to the extent of becoming, in recent decades, an ideological maxim, a credo. What is heralded as the 'flexibilization of production' is actually contracting-out of work, replacing time-wage with piece-rate and permanent with casual workers. This trend implies not only a deterioration in the working conditions of formal-sector workers, but also undermines the role of the trade unions which have promoted the interests of this privileged section.

The further implementation of the recent policy calls for the dismantling of the existing labour legislation. In addition to a considerable drop in wages, the inevitable result is a cutting back of the social-security benefits that have been built up over many years and, in the end, a reappraisal of perceptions of dignity and self-esteem. The decline in the quality of workers' lives has been exacerbated in many developing countries by the simultaneous introduction of structural adjustment programmes. These schemes, imposed by the World Bank and the International Monetary Fund (IMF), have included a drastic reduction in subsidies which kept food and transport prices low, and of expenditure meant to facilitate public access to education, health, and housing.

Labour in an Integrating World is the title of the 1995 World Bank Annual Report. According to this document, the dualism that determines the organization of the labour market arises from the unjustified preferential treatment of formal-sector workers. In this view, the labour arrangements in the informal sector are not perceived as a problem, or as modalities of employment which contribute to the perpetuation of poverty. Rather, they are recommended as a solution to the situation of immense deprivation suffered by such a large part of humanity. The argument made for the withdrawal of state involvement in the labour system, for the repeal of existing protective legislation, and for the abolition of more effective enforcement of minimum-wage regulations, is part of a political-economic doctrine founded upon the unfettered freedom of the market as the guiding principle. The organization of economic production, in a period of growth characterized not by a lack of labour but of capital, benefits the latter at the cost of the former. The providers of work, under these conditions, pay the lowest possible price after the rejection of social-security rights which, directly or indirectly, require wage supplements.

The crumbling away of the welfare state where it had previously existed, as well as its halting development where it had only just begun to come into sight, can be seen as confirmation of a trend in which the slowly advancing emancipation of labour in recent decades appears as if it were being reversed into subordination and insecurity. The progressive polarization of social classes accompanying these dynamics has given rise in Europe to a debate which concentrates on the inclusion-exclusion contrast, which seems to mark the return of the old dualism concept in yet another form.

ENDNOTES

1. For Calcutta, see Lubell (1974) and Bose (1974); for Dakar, see Gerry (1974); for Jakarta, see Sethuraman (1976); for Abidjan, see Joshi et al. (1976); and for Sao Paulo, see Schaefer (1976).

2. Examples are 'the law of inverse wage elasticity' formulated by Boeke (1953) and the idea of the 'target worker' which enjoyed such great popularity in the early literature on the essence of the development process (Nurkse 1953).

3. 'The informal sector, as its name suggests, is not formal in its character', according to Sethuraman (1977: 196); see also Gerry (1974: 1).

4. One author who subscribed to this idea was Oteiza, who predicted that 'the end of the century will see, to an even more pronounced degree, the existence of two labour markets with two different occupational structures and levels of income, corresponding to two clearly distinctive sectors of the economy—the modern and the traditional sector' (1971: 196). Without using the terms 'modern' and 'traditional', Sethuraman (1976: 10–12) suggests the same distinction.

5. In the sense understood by Weber, namely the almost exaggerated emphasis on the principal characteristics in a way which seldom occurs in social reality.

6. For critical comments raised on the lack of adequate quantitative evidence in the documents published by both organizations, see Mazumdar (1995: 19).

7. See also Bienefeld (1975: 20). A complicating factor is that not all members of a household are necessarily employed in the same sector. This fact argues in favour of a choice to be made between income levels and type of economic activity when elaborating the formal/informal opposition. A combination of both leads to contradictions or discrepancies in the operationalization of the dichotomy.

8. See various contributions in the volume edited by Lis et al. (1994).

REFERENCES

Aziz, A. 1984. *Urban Poor and Urban Informal Sector.* New Delhi: Ashish Publishing House.

Banerjee, B. 1985. *Women in the Unorganised Sector.* Delhi: Sangam Books.

_____. 1986. *Rural and Urban Migration and the Labour Market.* Bombay: Himalaya Publishing House.

_____. 1991. *Indian Women in a Changing Scenario.* Indo-Dutch Studies on Development Alternatives. 5. New Delhi: Sage Publications.

Banerjee, N. 1978. *Unorganised Women Workers: The Calcutta Experience.* CSSSC Occasional Paper. Calcutta: Centre for Studies in Social Sciences.

Banerjee, S. 1979. *Child Labour in India: A General Review with Case Studies of the Brick making and Zari-embroidery Industries.* London: Antislavery Society.

Bhalla, A. and F. Lapeyre. 1997. 'Social Exclusion: Towards an Analytical and Operational Framework'. *Development and Change.* 28(3):413–34.

Bienefeld, M. 1975. 'The Informal Sector and Peripheral Capitalism: The Case of Tanzania'. *Institute of Development Studies Bulletin.* 6:53–73.

Bose, A.N. 1974. *The Informal Sector in the Calcutta Metropolitan Economy.* Geneva: ILO.

Boeke, J.H. 1953. *Economics and Economic Policy of Dual Societies as Exemplified by Indonesia.* Haarlem: H.D. Tjeenk and Zoon.

Breman, Jan. 1983. 'The Bottom of the Urban Order in Asia; Impressions of Calcutta'. *Development and Change.* 14:153–83.

———. 1985. *Of Peasants, Migrants and Paupers: Rural Labour Circulation and Capitalist Production in West India.* Oxford: Clarendon Press.

———. 1993. *Beyond Patronage and Exploitation: Changing Agrarian Relations in South Gujarat.* Delhi: Oxford University Press.

———. 1994. *Wage Hunters and Gatherers: Search for Work in the Urban and Rural Economy of South Gujarat.* Delhi: Oxford University Press.

———. 1995. 'Labour, Get Lost; A Late-Capitalist Manifesto'. *Economic and Political Weekly.* 30:2294–300.

———. 1996. *Footloose Labour: Working in India's Informal Economy.* Cambridge: Cambridge University Press.

Bromley, R. and G. Gerry, eds. 1979. *Casual Work and Poverty in Third World Cities.* New York: John Wiley & Sons.

Brown, P. and R. Crompton, eds. 1994. *Economic Restructuring and Social Exclusion.* London: UCL Press.

Chadha, G.K. 1993. 'Non-farm Employment for Rural Households in India: Evidence and Prognosis'. *The Indian Journal of Labour Economics.* 36:296–327.

De Soto, H. 1986 [1997]. *El Otro Sendero.* Lima: Editorial E L Barranco. In English translation: *The Other Path; The Invisible Revolution in the Third World.* New York: Harper & Row.

Fei, J.C. and G. Ranis. 1964. *Development of the Labour Surplus Economy; Theory and Policy.* Illinois: Homewood.

Gerry, C. 1974. *Petty Producers and the Urban Economy: A Case Study of Dakar.* World Employment Programme, Working Paper 8. Geneva: ILO.

Gerry, C. and C Birkbeck. 1981. 'The Petty Commodity Producer in Third World Cities: Petit Bourgeois or "Disguised" or Proletarians'. In Beckhoffer and Euiot, ed., *The Petite Bourgeoisie: Comparative Studies of the Uneasy Stratum,* 121–53. London: Mcmillan.

Gore, C., G. Rodgers, and J. Figueiredo. 1995. *Social Exclusion: Rhetoric, Reality, Response.* Geneva: International Institute for Labour Studies.

Government of India. Report of the Committee on Child Labour. 1979. Ministry of Labour.

Gulati, L. 1982. *Profiles in Female Poverty: A Study of Five Poor Working Women in Kerala.* Delhi: Hindustan Publishing Corporation.

Hart, K. 1973. 'Informal Income Opportunities and Urban Employment in Ghana'. In R. Jolly, ed., *Third World Employment* 66–70. Harmondsworth: Penguin.

Holmstrom, M. 1984. *Industry and Equality: The Social Anthropology of Indian Labour.* Cambridge: Cambridge University Press.

ICFTU. 1989. *On Organising Workers in the Informal Sector.*

ILO. 1972. *Employment, Incomes and Equality: A Strategy for Increasing Productive Employment in Kenya.* Geneva: ILO.

———. 1974. *Sharing in Development: A Programme of Employment, Equity and Growth for the Philippines.* Geneva: ILO.

———. 1976. *World Employment Programme: Research in Retrospect and Prospect.* Geneva: ILO.

Jaganathan, N.V. 1987. *Informal Markets in Developing Countries.* Delhi: Oxford University Press.

Jolly, R., E. de kadt, H. Singer, and F. Wilson, eds. 1973. *Thrid World Employment* Harmondsworth: Penguin.

Joshi, H. and V. Joshi. 1976. *Surplus Labour and the City: A Study of Bombay.* Delhi: Oxford University Press.

Joshi, H., H. Lubell, and J. Mouly. 1976. *Abidjan: Urban Development and Employment in Ivory Coast.* World Employment Programme. Geneva: ILO.

Jones, Stedman G. 1971. *Outcast London.* London/Oxford: Clarendon Press.

Jugal, B.N. et al. 1985. *Child Labour: The Twice Exploited.* Varanasi: Gandhian Institute of Studies.

Kanappan, A., ed. 1977. *Studies of Urban Labour Market Behaviour in Developing Countries.* Geneva: ILO.

Kannan, K.P. 1988. *Of Rural Proletarian Struggles: Mobilization and Organization of Rural Workers in South-West India.* Delhi: Oxford University Press.

———. 1992. 'Labour Institutions and the Development Process in India'. In T.S. Papola and G. Rodgers, eds, *Labour Institutions and Economic Development in India,* 49–85. IILS, Research Series no. 97, Geneva.

Karlekar, M. 1982. *Poverty and Womens' Work: A Study of Sweeper Women in Delhi.* Delhi: Shakti Books.

Kapadia, K. 1995. *Siva and Her Sister: Gender, Caste and Class in Rural South India.* Boulder/Oxford: Westview Press.

Lewis, W.A. 1954. 'Economic Development with Unlimited Supplies of Labour'. *The Manchester School of Economic and Social Studies.* 22:139–91.

Lis, C., J. Lucassen, and H. Soly, eds. 1994. *Before the Unions: Wage Earners and Collective Action in Europe, 1300–1850.* International Review of Social History, Supplement 2. Cambridge: Cambridge University Press.

Lubell, H. 1974. *Calcutta: Its Urban Development and Employment Prospects.* Geneva: ILO.

Mathew, P.M. ed. 1995. *Informal Sector in India; Critical Perspectives.* New Delhi: Khama Publishers.

Mazumdar, D. 1975. *The Urban Informal Sector.* World Bank Staff Working Paper. Washington: World Bank.

———. 1995. 'Labor Issues in the World Development Report: A Critical Assessment'. Unpublished paper, Centre for International Studies, University of Toronto.

Mies, M. 1982. *The Lace Makers of Narsapur.* London: Zed Books.

Nieuwenhuys, O. 1994. *Children's Life Worlds: Gender, Welfare and Labour in the Developing World. An Anthropological Study of Children and Their Work in a Kerala (Indian) Village.* London: Routledge.

Noronha, E. 1996. 'Liberalisation and Industrial Relations'. *Economic and Political Weekly* (Review of Labour). 31:L14–L20.

Nurkse, R. 1953. *Problems of Capitals Formation in Underdeveloped Countries*. New York: Oxford University Press.

Oteiza, E. 1971. 'The Allocation Function of the Labour Market in Latin America'. *International Institute for Labour Studies Bulletin*. 8:190–205.

Papola, T.S. 1981. *Urban Informal Sector in a Developing Economy*. New Delhi: Vikas Publishing House.

Papola, T.S. and G. Rodgers, eds. 1992. *Labour Institutions and Economic Development in India*. International Institute for Labour Studies, Research Series no. 97. Geneva: IILS.

Pillai, S.M. 1996. 'Social Security for Workers in Unorganised Sector. Experience of Kerala'. *Economic and Political Weekly*. 31:2098–107.

Punalekar, S.P. 1993. *Seeds of Marginalization and Instability: A Study of Children in Gujarat Cities*. Surat: Centre for Social Studies.

Portes, A. M. Castells, and L.A. Benton. 1989. *The Informal Economy: Studies in Advanced and Lesser Advanced Countries*. Baltimore: Johns Hopkins University Press.

Rodgers, G. and G. Standing, eds. 1981. *Child Work, Poverty and Underdevelopment*. Geneva: ILO.

Safa, Helen, ed. 1982. *Towards a Political Economy of Urbanization in Third World Countries*. Delhi: Oxford University Press.

Sahoo, U.C. 1995. *Child Labour in Agrarian Society*. Jaipur/Delhi: Rawat Publications.

Sanyal, B. 1991. 'Organizing the Self-Employed'. *International Labour Review*. 130:39–56.

Schaefer, K.1976. *Sao Paulo: Urban Development and Employment*. World Employment Programme. Research Working Papers. Geneva: ILO.

Scott, J.C. 1985. *Weapons of the Weak: Everyday Forms of Peasant Resistance*. New Haven: Yale University Press.

———. 1990. *Domination and the Arts of Resistance: Hidden Transcripts*. New Haven: Yale University Press.

Sethuraman, S.V. 1975. 'Urbanisation and Employment: A Case Study of Djakarta'. *International Labour Review*. 112:191–205.

———. 1976. *The Urban Informal Sector: Concept, Measurement and Policy*. World Employment Programme Research (Working Papers). Geneva: ILO.

———. 1977. 'The Informal Sector in Developing Countries: Some Policy Implications'. *Social Action*. July–September.

Singh, M. 1990. *The Political Economy of Unorganised Labour: A Study of the Labour Process*. New Delhi: Sage Publications.

Smith, G. 1985. 'Reflections on the Social Relations of Simple Commodity Production'. *The Journal of Peasant Studies*. 13(1):99–108.

Tom, I. 1989. *Women in Unorganised Sector: Technology, Work Organisation and Change in the Silk Industry, South India*. Delhi: Usha Publication.

Van Der Loop, Th. 1992. *Industrial Dynamics and Fragmented Labour Markets: Construction Firms and Labourers in India*. Netherlands Geographical Studies, 139. Utrecht/Amsterdam: Netherlands Geographical Studies.

Visaria, Pravin and P. Jacob. 1995. *The Informal Sector in India: Estimates of its Size, and Needs, and Problems of Data Collection*. Gujarat Institute of Development Studies, Working Paper Series no. 70. Ahmedabad: Gujarat Institute of Development Studies.

Wertheim, W.F. and G.H. van der Kolff, eds. 1966. *Indonesian Economics; The Concept of Dualism in Theory and Policy*. The Hague: W. van Hoeve Publishers.

World Bank. 1995. *Workers in an Integrating World. World Development Report 1995*. New York: Oxford University Press.

TABLE

Table 1: Agricultural and Non-agricultural Workers (in millions) Classified According to Formal/Informal Sector 1972–3 to 1987–8

Branch of Industry	1972–3			1977–8			1983			1987–8		
	Formal	Informal	Total	Formal	Informal	Total	Formal	Informal	Total	Formal	Informal	Total
Agriculture	1.1	173.8	174.9	1.2	189.7	190.9	1.3	206.3	207.6	1.4	209.7	211.1
Non-agriculture*	17.7	44.1	61.8	20.0	57.9	77.9	22.7	72.5	95.2	24.3	89.3	113.6
Total	18.8	217.9	236.7	21.2	247.6	268.8	24.0	278.8	302.8	25.7	299.0	324.7

* : This category includes mining and quarrying, manufacturing, construction, electricity, gas and water, trade, hotels and restaurants, transport, storage and communication services.

Source : National Sample Survey (NSS) as cited in Visaria and Jacob (1995: 17–18),

The Study of Entrepreneurship in India
In Need of a Comparative Perspective

Mario Rutten

Asia's recent economic success has led to renewed interest in the study of entrepreneurship in Asia. Most studies on this topic focus on the specificity of the business strategies employed by entrepreneurs in East and Southeast Asia. In particular, these studies focus on the nature of Japanese management practices and Chinese business networks to explain the rapid economic developments in this part of the world. Studies on the business strategies of entrepreneurs in South Asia, above all India, do not seem to play any role in the present-day discussion on the nature of Asian entrepreneurship. Taking into account India's long, established tradition in entrepreneurship studies and the prominent role research on Indian businessmen has played in earlier debates on the nature of entrepreneurship, this absence seems quite remarkable.

The purpose of this chapter is to present a brief, selective overview of the study of entrepreneurship in India over the past few decades and to indicate the need for a comparative perspective. This overview is not intended to be a comprehensive review of the literature only, it highlights some of the central issues that have dominated this field. Studies of Indian entrepreneurship over the past few decades have employed a variety of theoretical perspectives, but they can be divided into two major categories which, for the purpose of this discussion, I have rudimentarily labelled the 'cultural perspective' and the 'structural perspective'. In the first section, of this chapter I discuss the main characteristics of the cultural perspective, which was the dominant approach to the study of Indian entrepreneurship in the 1950s and 1960s. This approach was inspired by Max Weber's (1976) Protestant ethic thesis and explored the compatibility or incompatibility of Hindu religious values and other cultural factors with industrial entrepreneurship in India.

Taking over the field from this cultural perspective, structural analysis became the dominant approach to the study of Indian entrepreneurship in the 1970s and 1980s. In the second section of this chapter, I discuss the main characteristics of this structural perspective, which was mostly based on Marxist theories of capitalist transformation. These studies emphasized macroeconomic or political factors to explain the development of Indian entrepreneurship, or lack of it.

Following this brief, selective overview of the study of entrepreneurship in India over the past few decades, in the third and final section of the chapter I argue that structural perspective in research on Indian entrepreneurs has indisputably produced a very substantial and significant body of knowledge. But the downside is that it has contributed to the increasing isolation of the study of entrepreneurship in India from the discussions taking place in other parts of the world. Entrepreneurship studies in the 1970s and 1980s regarded comparisons of the behaviour of Indian entrepreneurs with general models about the rise of the class of industrialists in Europe as a Eurocentric brand of historical determinism and therefore unconditionally rejected such attempts. This, however, did not prevent comparisons with European developments from taking place, but it did 'force' these comparisons to burrow below the surface, thereby becoming unverifiable. Even more disappointingly, the almost exclusively structural focus of entrepreneurship studies in India in the 1970s and 1980s isolated these studies from similar discussions on entrepreneurship in East and South East Asia—where the cultural perspective remained dominant throughout the 1970s and 1980s—and thereby contributed to the segmentation of debates on entrepreneurship in different regions of Asia. In order to solve these problems of the compartmentalization of knowledge—which is equally true of studies on entrepreneurs in Europe, and in East and South East Asia—in this chapter I argue for a comparative perspective in the study of Indian entrepreneurship, stressing particularly the need to combine the findings on entrepreneurship in India with similar discussions on entrepreneurs in East and South East Asia, and with discussions on early and present-day industrialists in Europe.

THE CULTURAL PERSPECTIVE

Discussions on the nature and manifestations of entrepreneurship in India in the 1950s and early 1960s were directly linked to investigations of the basic causes of India's economic backwardness. The dominant approach at that time was the modernization theory, which originated in the assumption that Indian cultural and religious values were incompatible with the spontaneous development of industrial capitalism. This 'cultural perspective' was inspired by Max Weber's Protestant-ethic thesis (1976, 1978), which emphasized the cultural embeddedness of capitalist development and the ideological motivation for rational profit-seeking among early European capitalists. This approach was represented in studies that explored the compatibility, or lack thereof, of Hindu religious values with industrial entrepreneurship. A number of early studies carried out in India tested Weber's thesis by looking for an equivalent of the Protestant ethic, or some kind of 'this-worldly asceticism', in Hindu religion that could have contributed to the development of capitalist entrepreneurship. Cases in which this association was claimed included the Jains and the Parsis.[1]

A more influential approach within this modernization framework came from scholars who turned their attention to elements in Hinduism that were generally considered hindrances to entrepreneurial development. Following Weber's analysis of Hindu society (1958), these scholars argued that the spirit of enterprise was inhibited among the indigenous populations of India by the religious philosophy of resignation embodied in the doctrine of karma and by the rigid social organization of the caste system and the joint family.[2] According to this cultural perspective, these negative elements were viewed as important factors in explaining India's retarded economic growth. A nice formulation of the prevailing view is given by Dwijendra Tripathi in his critique of this Weberian brand of scholarship. Tripathi writes 'The result was that the Indian personality, by and large, remained unentrepreneurial, if not anti-entrepreneurial,' a view reported—not shared—by Dwijendra Tripathi (1992: 77).

This alleged incompatibility of Indian ideology and values with economic enterprise was held responsible for India's failure to make a successful transition to industrial development along the lines followed in western Europe at the beginning of industrialization. In his study on the European transition from 'feudalism to capitalism', Maurice Dobb [1947] (1976) traced two possible ways in which industrial capitalism usually emerges. Under the first route, small producers develop from craftsmen into industrial entrepreneurs. The second route is the one employed by merchants who become involved in the production process by controlling the producers through the buying and delivering of raw materials and the selling of finished products. Dobb claims that it was the first of these two roads to industrial capitalism which was critically important in the early industrial development of western Europe. By combining productive and commercial functions, small artisan producers started to manufacture on a larger scale, for which they made use of wage labour that had been freed from the handicraft restrictions of the guilds. The activities of the European merchants, on the other hand, remained limited to the mechanics of buying and selling without any real involvement in the internal organization of production and production techniques.[3]

Development in India is assumed to have taken the opposite path.

Because of their 'resistance to change' and the restrictions of the caste system, Indian artisans did not form an important source of entrepreneurial talent in modern industrial development. This was pointed out by Weber (1958) who emphasized the traditionalism of Indian artisans which, he thought, was reinforced by the fact that the caste structure was an obstacle to occupational mobility and socio-economic change.[4] Those authors who studied industrial development in India in the 1950s and 1960s within the overall modernization framework had a similarly low opinion of artisans, stressing that their contribution to India's industrial development had been negligible. One of the best-known views in this respect is that of Davi McClelland (1961) who was inspired by Weber's notion that religion, norms and values, behaviour, and economic—that is to say capitalist—developments are all interconnected. McClelland argued that the presence of a specific motivational structure, the desire to achieve purely for the sake of achievement—i.e. the 'achievement motivation'—is of critical importance to successful entrepreneurship. In 1957, he had already said that Indian artisans lacked entrepreneurial values and motives, a conclusion he based on his experience with handloom weavers in Orissa. The way McClelland saw it, these Indian weavers lacked 'the importance of maintaining quality of workmanship, concern for a long run relationship with consumers, and the assumption of personal responsibility for the product of one's own work'.[5] Staley and Morse wrote that only a very small proportion of artisans in India commanded the talent and motivation to become successful entrepreneurs owing to the fact that they were bound by traditional norms, values, and obligations (1965: 71). This negative judgement of the entrepreneurial behaviour of Indian artisans was further confirmed in an account of an experiment testing McClelland's theory carried out in Kakinada, south India (McClelland and Winter 1969).

Along with this view that, in contrast to western Europe, small artisan producers did not play a critical role in the development of industrial capitalism in India, there was a strong focus on the category of merchants as the prime movers behind the transition to industrial capitalism. To a large extent, this position is consistent with the historiography of Indian industrial development (Berna 1960: 8).[6] Following Weber, however, there have long been doubts about the suitability of Indian traders to becoming industrial entrepreneurs. Weber argued that the most important reason why Indian traders would not be able to make the transition from 'pariah capitalism' to 'rational capitalism' was to be found in their rituals and in the caste structure. In their ritual seclusion Indian traders remained 'in the shackles of the typical oriental merchant class, which by itself has never created a modern capitalist organization of labour' (1958: 112).

In line with Weber's analysis, studies conducted on Indian

entrepreneurs emphasized the specific commercial style and poor reputation attributed to Indian traders, which were said to stand in their way to establishing modern businesses. These studies argued that Indian moneylenders and traders, given their stark profit motivation, could not be considered a significant reservoir of industrial entrepreneurial recruits. They consider the production process to be something fixed and static and are not prepared to invest more than the absolute minimum amount of capital in installations and machines. This commitment towards rapid and not necessarily honest profits closely parallels the traditional Vaishya ethic, according to which, in this view, such activities can find religious sanction. For Indian traders, wealth is to be amassed and then, at intervals, consumed in magnificient marriages, religious services, and funerals that enhance the status of the family (Elder 1959: 17). The upshot is that Indian businessmen ultimately remain committed to trade and quick turnover as the most important sources of profit, and place a high premium on the flexibility of capital. In this view, Indian entrepreneurs with a trading background are contrasted to those industrial entrepreneurs who are production oriented, work within a long-term framework, are patient, tend to reinvest profits into industry, promote technological improvements, and are prepared to take risks.[7]

This notion of the unsuitability of Indian traders to industrial entrepreneurship was dwelt on in studies conducted on Indian businessmen in the 1950s and 1960s (see McCrory 1956; Berna 1960; Hazelhurst 1966; and Fox 1969).[8] In this view, the cultural disposition and subsequent commercial orientation of Indian businessmen with a trading background was supposed to have turned the highly developed profit motivation of Indian entrepreneurs not towards productive investments of significant scope but towards consumption and less risky and more immediately profitable fields of economic activity.[9] Partly basing himself on McCrory (1956), who carried out a study in the 1950s among owners of small industrial firms in a north-Indian city, James Berna, for example, argued that Indian entrepreneurs with a background in trade are 'opportunistic businessmen with very short time horizons, interested only in fast turnover and quick profits, completely unconcerned with technology, unwilling to invest more than the bare minimum in fixed capital, and still preoccupied far more with trade than with industry' (Berna 1960: 217). This was also expressed by Leighton Hazlehurst who concluded, on the basis of research among Banias in a Punjab town, that rural traders invested their capital in productive enterprises only very reluctantly (1966: 145). Richard Fox, who studied Banias in another small north-Indian town, also argued that these businessmen were more willing to accept smaller profits as long as they covered essential expenses, rather than to invest in more profitable long-term enterprises in which they risked losing their investments (Fox 1969: 143).

The cultural perspective that dominated research on entrepreneurship in India in the 1950s and 1960s was not an isolated case, but was part of a wider attempt to apply Weber's Protestant-ethic hypothesis to material drawn from various parts of Asia. The most well-known examples of such analyses outside India are the study by Robert Bellah on Jodo Buddhism and the Hotoku and Shingaku movements in Japan (Bellah 1957), and the study by Clifford Geertz on the Santri Muslims of Java, Indonesia (Geertz 1968). In some instances, attempts were made to discuss these separate analyses of entrepreneurial groups in various regions of Asia within a comparative perspective (see Bellah [1963], 1968; and Eisenstadt 1968). In these attempts towards achieving a comparative analysis of Asian entrepreneurship, early studies on Indian businessmen seem to have played a prominent role. David McClelland's 'achievement motivation', for example, was based largely on examples from India (McClelland 1961), while the discussion that followed Milton Singer's analysis (1956) of several Indian examples was not confined to India but became part of a wider debate on the Protestant-ethic analogy in Asia (see Bellah 1968, Eisenstadt 1968, and Singer 1966).[10]

As Bellah (1968) points out, this early focus on the motivational factor in Asia gave way later to a broader 'institutional' perspective based on a less narrow reading of Weber, in which capitalist development is thought to depend on a basic transformation in social structure rather than only on ideological predisposition. This shift in Weberian studies on Asia was most clearly present in the studies on entrepreneurship in India. Milton Singer (1972), for example, challenged Weber's thesis by arguing that Hindu industrialists in Madras compartmentalize their religious lives and their business activities. He also argued, in opposition to most scholars, that joint-family organization plays a positive role in industrial entrepreneurship.[11]

In spite of these early attempts to include social and institutional aspects in the cultural perspective, the focus of most of the early approaches to Indian entrepreneurship in the 1950s and 1960s was unifactoral, accentuating cultural factors to explain the alleged bottleneck in the supply of entrepreneurship as one of the main reasons for India's retarded economic growth. Moreover, in their anxiety to justify the assumption that the social and religious values of a community are bound to influence economic behaviour, these early studies were essentially deductive in character and Eurocentric in orientation. By applying Weber's analysis to Asia, these early studies on Indian entrepreneurship made use of a model that was explicitly shaped by the European experience of the rise of industrial capitalism. Absorbed in their own model, they hardly paid attention in their analysis to the actual experiences of Indian businessmen and the way they adapted their entrepreneurial strategies to changes in the material environment. Their focus was on studying Hindu religion and norms of social organization in order to gain insight into their compatibility with economic development. Having an all-India perspective, these early works often viewed India as a discrete cohesive system, ignoring the fact that various regions of India might manifest different kinds of entrepreneurial behaviour.[12]

THE STRUCTURAL PERSPECTIVE

In the 1970s and 1980s, this cultural approach to the study of Indian entrepreneurship was attacked and superseded by what I have called a structural perspective. Such studies, based mostly on theoretical views of a Marxist persuasion, criticized the cultural approach, and the modernization theory underlying it, for its lack of understanding of the exploitative relations between developing countries and the economically advanced countries, both at present and in a historical perspective. Contrary to these cultural analyses, the structural perspective related variations in entrepreneurial development in India to the broader politico-economic and historical context, particularly to the experience of colonialism and neo-colonialism. In these studies, the emphasis was no longer on the values and social prerequisites of industrialization. Instead, they tended to shift to socio-economic structures and the relations of exploitation embodied in these structures. The overall notion was that these structural factors had impeded the creation of indigenous industrial capital or had thrown up aberrant types of entrepreneurship in India.[13]

The first point these various scholars challenged was the previously held view on the relative contribution of caste- or religion-based groups to India's industrial development. These authors emphasized the prominence of several hereditary business communities in the formation of the modern business class in India. Studies of specific communities and castes illustrated aspects of the investment behaviour of the various Indian communities involved in business and industry. The rise of business corporations and corporate management in India indicated that Indian businessmen were capable of perceiving new opportunities and developing a distinctive style of management consistent with their needs and social structures. The tight organization as a commercial community that characterized such groups as the Marwaris and Parsis, for example, certainly helped the members of those communities to compete on more than equal terms with the rest of the population. However, these studies argued strongly against the prevailing cultural notions in which these communities were viewed as inherently more dynamic by virtue of race, superior social customs, or some sort of Protestant religious-cultural ethos (Kennedy 1965; Timberg 1978). Seeking a reason for the success of these communities, it was pointed out that the decisive factor was not so much their cultural disposition or religious mentality, but their social networks and the strategic positions they had carved out for themselves early on by virtue of acting as the collaborators of the Europeans in the Asian trade (Ray 1992: 1–69; Dobbin 1996: 77–155).

The question of the relative contribution of artisans and merchants to India's industrialization, a question which was central to the cultural perspective in the 1950s and 1960s, also played a prominent role in the structural approach to Indian entrepreneurship in the 1970s and 1980s. This time the outcome was very different. In the structural approach of the 1970s and 1980s, the earlier cultural notions of Indian entrepreneurship were challenged in various ways. The alleged failure of Indian artisans to engage in industrial enterprise was not explained by reference to their 'traditional' orientation, but by reference to the colonial policy and the process of de-industrialization. Authors writing from a structural perspective argued that, in essence, Indian artisans did have at their disposal the very values and motivations which McClelland and others contended they lacked. In their analysis, they placed the emphasis on the economic factors inhibiting industrial development rather than seeking an explanation in cultural compulsions. They harped upon the fact that the artisanal motivations and standards in India suffered enormously under British rule. Imperialism by its very nature was exploitative and the heavy yoke of British domination, with its mercantilist strategy of import tarrifs on textiles from India, was too much for the Indian economy to bear, and beyond their capability to try to circumvent. Consequently, Indian business developments were inevitably bound to be retarded and the entrepreneurial ability of Indian artisans could not find its full expression. This process has been described as 'de-industrialization' or 'peasantization'. Whatever name we attach to it, the process was one in which British rule led to a decline in urban and village handicraft production and to a displacement of traditional manufacturers as suppliers of consumption goods to the internal Indian market.[14]

Other scholars working within the structural perspective stressed that the previously held cultural notions about the contribution of artisans should be corrected on the grounds that, in many instances, artisans in India did in fact become industrial entrepreneurs. Mark Holmström, for example, has pointed out that 'in some cases artisan castes adapted their traditional crafts to new products: some handloom weavers bought powerlooms; the Karkhanedars or Muslim armourers of Delhi became blacksmiths under the British, and later went into light engineering products like ball bearings and motor parts' (Holmström 1985: 85–6). This transition from artisan to industrialist occurred in other parts of India as well. Satish Saberwal (1976) described in detail how, after 1930, carpenters and blacksmiths in a Punjabi city worked their way up to become industrial entrepreneurs. To a large extent this is true for the state of Punjab as a whole, as is shown in a study by G.K. Chadha (1986), who described how artisans—blacksmiths, masons, and carpenters—turned into good engineers who played a vital role in the regeneration of the agro-industry in Punjab, setting up small industrial workshops, many of which grew in due course into full-fledged industrial enterprises.[15] In his study on small-scale industrialists in two small Gujarat towns, Hein Streefkerk also showed that artisan-caste members, namely carpenters and blacksmiths, were the first to become actively involved in the transition to industrial production. Based on his own findings, combined with a review of studies in other places of India that showed how members of the artisan castes were involved in the process of industrial development, Streefkerk concludes that a 'correction ... must be made to the dominant version of native industrial development, namely rejection of the claim that members of artisan castes were, and are, unable for cultural and socio-psychological reasons to make a contribution to industrial development' (1985: 124).

With regard to the prevailing notion about the contribution of merchants to industrial development in India, the structural perspective in the 1970s and 1980s no longer tended to accentuate the alleged lack of entrepreneurship, but turned attention to the quality of the entrepreneurial behaviour of industrialists in India. Within these studies, the volume of entrepreneurship was no longer considered a major bottleneck, but economic and political factors were used to explain the specific 'commercial' orientation of Indian entrepreneurs. These studies indicated that considerations of caste, family, and kinship were still very important for entry into the business of manufacturing and for the style of management. Furthermore, these studies viewed the commercial orientation of Indian industrialists as the typical Indian style of entrepreneurship. According to these studies, Indian industrialists expended considerable effort on the purchasing and marketing aspects of their firms but paid very little attention to the actual production process. Rather than applying their energies to reducing the costs of production through the utilization of full capacity, appropriate technology, labour productivity, and so on, industrialists in India were inclined to concentrate on the reduction of purchasing costs and the enhancement of sales receipts. On top of this, they tended to have interests in a number of activities simultaneously, and to engage in a large variety of activities over time. Instead of reinvesting their profits in the industrial enterprise in order to advance technology and increase the scale of industrial operation, industrialists in India were said to be notoriously quick to shift investments into new fields in search of quick profits. These frequent shifts deterred the attainment of proficiency in any single line of production, and militated against the improvement of quality and technological advance. These authors claimed that this aspect of commercialism—that is the inclination to involve oneself in a wide range of disparate commercial and industrial activities, whether successively or simultaneously—was the most typical distinguishing characteristic of Indian industrialists.[16]

Studies on Indian entrepreneurship in the 1970s and 1980s emphasized that the typical pattern found in India—the concentration of business activity in trading rather than industry, and the prevalence of certain forms of organization such as family-controlled firms and business networks based on 'primordial ties'—were a response to structural factors such as imperfect markets or lack of an adequate institutional framework. Structural features in the economy or the interference of the state were thought to encourage non-productive forms of entrepreneurial activity in India, including the spreading of risks, through diversification of investment and a preference for high-profit speculative activities rather than long-term commitment.

In the structural approach to entrepreneurship studies in the 1970s and 1980s, the focus was therefore placed on the economic and political factors as a means of explaining this commercial orientation of Indian industrialists. These authors argued that if the commercial climate is made favourable—that is if there is availability of market incentives, governmental support, and sufficient banking and transport facilities—industrial entrepreneurship will be bound to develop. In this approach the development of entrepreneurship—that is the employment of capital and other productive means for industrial production—was placed in a broader political and economic frame. Commercialism was considered not to be the characteristic of a specific social group but inherent in the Indian socio-economic structure. Van der Veen (1976), for example, tried to understand the inconsistency and the dispersion of activities of Gujarat entrepreneurs largely in terms of economic factors. He accounted for the commercialism he found primarily in terms of, and as a rational response to, economic factors, being the direct result of state intervention, above all of the import-substitution strategy. Official efforts to ration inputs had created opportunities for entrepreneurs to earn windfall profits. It was the availability of these windfall profits that 'reinforce[d] the "natural" tendency of small-scale industrial entrepreneurs to adopt a commercial orientation' (van der Veen 1976: M-93). On similar lines, Hein Streefkerk (1985) stressed that the most important explanation for the commercial behaviour of industrialists in India must be sought in two sources: the economic structure and the social setting, both of which encouraged rather than prevented diverse investments and the spreading of risks. 'Risk-spreading and inconsistency are obvious choices; commercialism is more rewarded than punished. Such an orientation will clearly be manifest by those with access to raw materials and sales markets and who exercise influence over politico-administrative matters' (Streefkerk 1985: 170).

On the basis of these characteristics, most industrialists in India were viewed as 'routine entrepreneurs' (Leibenstein 1978), 'imitative entrepreneurs'/'meta-innovators' (Broehl 1978), 'financier-industrialist' (Holmström 1985), or 'commercialists' (Streefkerk 1985). They financed industrial production as a commercial undertaking and started industries to fill a known gap in the production chain or to manufacture a specific known component. In contrast to true 'innovators' (Schumpeter 1934) and 'technician-industrialists' (Holmström 1985), who learned new skills and production techniques by trial and error and improvisation, and who built up their businesses gradually by reinvesting profits, most industrialists in India were thought to have no interest in developing either the production process or the production capacity, but were credited with a strong tendency to get involved in a number of different commercial activities, either successively or simultaneously.

With this emphasis on the quality of industrial entrepreneurship in India rather than on its volume, the structural perspective of the 1970s and 1980s created further doubts about the validity of the emphasis on the lack of Indian entrepreneurship that characterized the cultural approach in the 1950s and 1960s. In comparison to the earlier studies of culture, entrepreneurship studies published in the 1970s and 1980s often placed strong emphasis on empirical research. In this, they displayed a welcome shift away from the purely deductive approach of the 1950s and 1960s by incorporating entrepreneurial-managerial experiences in their analyses, usually based on in-depth surveys and intensive fieldwork. Pertinently, structural studies conducted in the 1970s and 1980s had a regional focus rather than an all-India perspective and often combined socio-cultural and structural factors in their analysis to explain the specificity of business strategies of Indian entrepreneurs.

A COMPARATIVE PERSPECTIVE

When we look at the history of the emphasis on structural aspects within the 'mode of production' style of analysis initiated [or 'practiced'] by Karl Marx and on cultural aspects within the 'spirit of capitalism' style of analysis initiated [or 'practiced'] by Max Weber we will find that both analyses were originally closely related, sharing a common concern with the origins and likely course of evolution of industrial capitalism in western Europe. More specifically, Weber saw the economic conditions that Marx believed determined the development and future transformation of capitalism as embedded within a unique cultural totality (Giddens 1972). Therefore, the cultural and the structural approaches have common roots in nineteenth-century European social thought and share certain assumptions about the nature of capitalist development. But there was a significant difference. A characteristic feature of the structural analysis of the 1970s and 1980s was that studies on entrepreneurship in India implicitly, indeed sometimes even explicitly, turned away from general theoretical models in an attempt to avoid the trap of Eurocentric historical determinism which characterized the earlier cultural approach to entrepreneurship. It was generally assumed that the emergence of the entrepreneurial class in India was a historically unique phenomenon and that the factors leading to it were so specific that they could not be compared with the rise of the early industrialists in Europe. Accordingly, the emergence of entrepreneurial classes in India was usually regarded as a historically unique phenomenon which could not be compared with similar processes in European history, and research during the last two decades has focused almost exclusively on the study of India in its own right. Any comparison of industrialization in India with the European path of industrial transition has often been regarded as historical determinism and therefore rejected outright.[17]

To a large extent, this is of course correct. History does not repeat itself mechanically. A nineteenth-century pattern of development could hardly be repeated in detail today. All processes of change have their own prerequisites, which will differ from country to country and from one period to another. That the emergence of an entrepreneurial class in India would be an exact duplicate of the rise of the class of industrial capitalists in eighteenth- and nineteenth-century Europe is of course ridiculous and should indeed be rejected out of hand.

While this turning away from Eurocentric paradigms has of course been beneficial, there is some danger in rejecting completely any kind of comparison between capitalist development in India today and that of Europe in the past. The terminology employed to describe Indian entrepreneurs shows that comparisons with the European experience are in fact still being made, but not explicitly. Characterizations of Indian industrialists as 'commercialists' or 'financier-industrialists' are often based on a particular conception of industrial capitalism which in turn is derived from what early European capitalism, and the trajectory of its development, is thought to have been like. This conception is derived from a particular reading of the industrialization experience in Western Europe, particularly in Britain. Whether the focus is on the economic and technological preconditions for industrialization, or on the socio-cultural or ideological bases of entrepreneurship, the model is shaped by Europe. In this model, industrialization is a unilinear process which leads to the development of large-scale factory production, wage labour, and private investment by thrifty, innovative, and individualistic entrepreneurs. Forms of productive organization, labour relations, investment strategies, or entrepreneurial behaviour which do not conform to the model are counted as deviant. Indian entrepreneurs are often portrayed negatively in the literature because of their diversification of economic activities, preference for quick and high profit-yeilding trading activities, speculative practices, and expenditure on luxury consumer goods. They are said to lack the qualities that 'true' or 'genuine' industrialists possess, a stereotype that is usually derived from an ideal-typical (not necessarily realistic) notion of what the early European industrialists were like.[18]

In an earlier chapter (Rutten 1994), I gave a brief overview of economic historical studies on the early industrialists in Europe. On the basis of that discussion, I concluded that the characterizations of the entrepreneurial class in Asia are partly based on assumptions about the origin and nature of the first industrialists in Europe that are often highly questionable.[19] Here I would like to take this line of reasoning one step further and argue that in the transfer of the debate on the development of capitalism in Europe to Asia, the two approaches to entrepreneurship that were in essence closely linked to each other became disconnected. After an emphasis on the cultural perspective in India in the 1950s and 1960s, studies on Indian entrepreneurs pursued a more Marxist analysis and focused almost exclusively on the structural aspects of entrepreneurial behaviour. In doing so, the structural perspective in the study of entrepreneurship in India in the 1970s and 1980s produced a very substantial and significant body of knowledge, but it also resulted in increasing isolation from similar discussions on entrepreneurship in East and South East Asia remained inspired by the analysis of Max Weber and focused almost exclusively on the cultural aspects of entrepreneurial behaviour.

Following Max Weber's original analysis of the cultural set-up that stimulated the rise of capitalism in western Europe in the eighteenth and nineteenth centuries (and his subsequent studies on other world religions), studies on East and South East Asia concentrated analysis on the specificity of the cultural set-up of Confucianism, Buddhism, Islam that supported or hindered a similar kind of development in Asia. The types of entrepreneurship found in the region were attributed to the value systems or religious backgrounds of businessmen. The 'dependent' nature of entrepreneurs was associated with a specific mentality or business culture in which public and private interests mixed effortlessly. According to this view, Muslim and Chinese businessmen in South East Asia, for example, display a strong inclination to make use of politically secured economic priviliges to accumulate capital, and are characterized by an underlying inclination to take a slice of someone else's wealth rather than creating it for themselves (see Clad 1989; Abdullah 1994; and Muhaimin 1990).[20] A more recent version of the cultural approach is the 'Confucian-culture' argument (see Redding 1990; Silin 1976; and Wong 1989). While cultural factors were first used to explain why Chinese businessmen were unable to develop corporate businesses and thereby to become successful entrepreneurs, the same argument was later turned around to explain the recent rapid development of East and South East Asian countries by emphasizing the contribution of traditional Chinese 'values' and modes of social organization to entrepreneurial behaviour.[21] Although there have therefore been some shifts in perception and ideology among the scholars working within this perspective, the culturally oriented approach has always been the dominant perspective in the study of entrepreneurship in East and South East Asia.[22]

In this light, variations in forms of business entrepreneurship in India in the 1970s and 1980s have usually been explained in terms of structural or political-economic imperatives, while studies on variations in forms of business entrepreneurship in East and South East Asia continued to be inspired by the analysis of Weberian style cultural explanation. The empirical finding of studies of entrepreneurs indicate that there are many similarities in both economic behaviour and life-style between the entrepreneurial class of India and their counterparts in other areas of Asia.[23] Despite this foundation, practically no attempt has been made to look at the business classes across Asia within a broad comparative perspective. Another obstacle is that the research for such studies is usually designed—and the finding analysed—in relation to debates that are specific to their own regions rather than to a wider theoretical problematic. This has clearly contributed to the segmentation of debates on entrepreneurship in different regions of Asia. The difference in analytical emphasis in the entrepreneurship literature in India as compared to East and South East Asia tends to mask the similarities on the grounds—economic, social, and political—that seem to unite the business classes of various countries.

It is important to point out that the cultural and structural approaches to Indian entrepreneurship described above are not mutually exclusive and that various scholars, especially recently, have tried to include both perspectives in their studies. Even so, most entrepreneurship studies are unsatisfactory because they tend to privilege one type of explanation over the other rather than integrating them. Here I am not advocating either a structural or a culture-centred analysis, but argue instead for the development of a fresh approach that combines both by looking at how political, economic, and cultural processes interact within the historical process of capitalist development.[24] Such an approach should facilitate in-depth research on the question of the extent to which a capitalist style of entrepreneurship produces similar cultural features across the globe. In contradistinction to the earlier universalistic theories of industrial development, recent research suggests that industrial capitalism may be highly adaptable to various social and economic forms. Significant variations are found around the world in the organization of business enterprises and transactions, mode of labour exploitation, and entrepreneurial behaviour and ethos.[25]

While earlier studies on entrepreneurs in India and other parts of Asia tended to stress variability in the forms of business organization, recent studies point to the view that there are striking resemblances in entrepreneurial behaviour across the globe.[26] This observation suggests that there may be certain imperatives inherent in capitalist entrepreneurship that are manifested in various ways in different cultural contexts. Just as the division between labour and capital is a central feature of production under industrial capitalism, the requirements of investment, risk taking, and the organization of production and marketing appear to structure the behaviour of entrepreneurs in particular ways. For example, there is a strong element of rational pursuit of profit and decision making based on instrumental rationality, as specified in Weber's model. But this is qualified by the fact that entrepreneurs are not driven solely by the profit motive; goals such as desire for prestige, and constraints such as obligations towards kin, also determine their actions. Another common feature is that the economic transactions of entrepreneurs are often also social transactions, in the sense that they are usually embedded in social relations and not just determined by impersonal market forces. What is needed therefore is to reconnect the cultural and structural approaches and to come up with an overall theoretical framework that will help us in understanding and explaining the present-day economic, social, cultural, and political mobility of the entrepreneurial class in India and other parts of Asia. Such a framework has to be built up within a comparative perspective and should also include the findings on the entrepreneurial class in Europe, both at present and in the past.

This brings me back to the question of drawing comparisons between European and Asian development. The rejection of general theoretical models for comparative study after the 1970s led to a concentration of research on Asia in its own right. The post-modernization trend has been to emphasize the cultural uniqueness of business organization in different contexts, as seen, for example, in the literatures on Indian business communities, Japanese companies, or Chinese business networks.[27] However, a critique of Eurocentric models need not end up in cultural essentialism. Now that a significant body of knowledge about economic development in India and other Asian countries has been produced, the time has come to look again at European history and contemporary developments, employing insights gained from the Asian experience. It is also time for experts on Europe to look at the Asian examples. Such a comparative analysis needs to take into account the wide diversity in forms of business organization and entrepreneurship within and between Asia and Europe, and it should look for the conditions that promote or inhibit the growth of industrial entrepreneurship and investment without relying on Eurocentric stereotypes of entrepreneurial behaviour. If processes such as those described in the preceding paragraphs are understood within the overall framework of the expansion of world capitalism—which while exerting certain pressures towards uniformity also interacts with local structures and cultures, producing many variations—we will be able to account for both similarities and differences in entrepreneurial behaviour at various times and places. Therefore, one aim of comparative analysis should be to describe and account for various forms of entrepreneurship without resorting to stereotypes of what constitutes 'correct' capitalist behaviour or capitalism proper. A first step towards such an analysis is to acquire more in-depth knowledge about entrepreneurs in different parts of Asia and Europe, at present and in the past. With this chapter, I hope to have aroused the curiosity needed to lay the groundwork for such a comparative perspective.

ENDNOTES

1. See, for example, David McClelland who discussed the Jains and the Parsis (1961: 368–9), and Milton Singer who discussed several Indian examples in his 'Cultural Values in India's Economic Development' (1956: 81–91). The article by Milton Singer received comments from various scholars (Goheen et al. 1958).

2. For examples of such studies, see Elder (1959) and Kapp (1963).

3. Dobb's study on the issue of the transition from 'feudalism to capitalism' has provoked varied reactions, many of which have been collected in a volume by Hilton (1976).

4. Although from a different perspective, in 1934 Buchanan also explained the phenomenon that relatively few Indian craftsmen had successfully converted their businesses into factories by the fact that Indian artisans lacked ambition and were unwilling to change (Buchanan 1934: 11).

5. Cited in Singer (1960: 263).

6. See also Streefkerk (1985: 30–1) who emphasizes that the native industrialization which took place after 1850, and which was mainly based in cities such as Bombay, Ahmedabad, and Calcutta, was realized principally by traders such as Vaishnava Banias, Jain Banias, and Parsis.

7. See Berna (1960) who draws a distinction between industrial

entrepreneurs with short-term and long-term approaches. The former are said to be particularly typical of industrialists with a background in trade.

8. In the 1930s, Buchanan had already stated that the commercial activities of the Banias included those peculiarities which prevented them from starting modern factories, since they did not know how workers should be organized (Buchanan 1934).

9. For an overview of these ideas, see Streefkerk's discussion of commercialism versus production orientation (1985: 162–4).

10. Studies on Indian craftsmen also played an important role in the argument that artisans in Asia, or, for that matter in developing countries in general, were unsuitable material for the formation of industrial entrepreneurs. The conclusion by Staley and Morse that only a very small proportion of artisans in developing countries command the talent and motivation to become successful entrepreneurs was mainly based on references to artisans in India who, according to these authors, were bound by traditional norms, values, and obligations (1965: 71). In his *Asian Drama* Gunnar Myrdal had little confidence in the entrepreneurial ability of artisans in Asia, a conclusion which he based on a single study dealing with carpet making in north India (1968: 1100). Hein Streefkerk's remark in a footnote also drew my attention to this aspect (Streefkerk 1985: 125, fn. 2).

11. For examples of other studies, see Kennedy (1965) and the excellent collection of articles in Singer (1973). See also Fox (1973) for a critique of much of the Weberian literature. Contrary to his earlier work, in this paper, Fox rejected the notion of the unsuitability of Indian traders for industrial entrepreneurship and argued that Banias were certainly capable of organizing modern industrial undertakings (1973: 22–31).

12. See also Tripathi (1992: 76–81) for a critical evaluation of these earlier studies on entrepreneurship in India.

13. Such structural analyses have been inspired in part by Marxist mode-of-production theories which focus on class formation and the economic conditions of capitalist development. For an overview of the literature, see for example Tripathi (1992), Streefkerk (1985), and Rutten (1995).

14. The question of the growth of industrial capitalism, or lack thereof, has been central to Indian economic history, and structural explanations of India's economic backwardness have usually centred on the role of British capital and the colonial state (Bagchi 1972, 1988). For an overview of this perspective, see Streefkerk (1985: 27–36) and Tripathi (1992: 77). From the discussions on the economic effects of British imperialism, it is clear that a good deal of variation must be accounted for. Urban handicrafts were affected earlier than village ones and the different types of village crafts were harmed in varying degrees. Furthermore, there were regional differences. See for example Bagchi (1976); Desai (1966); Dutt (1940); Gadgil ([1924] 1971); Matsui (1968); Morris (1968); and Mukherjee (1958). Recently, revisionist historians have challenged the prevailing notion that industrial entrepreneurship in colonial India was solely in the hands of the British (Goswami 1989; Mahadevan 1992).

15. See Chadha (1986: 33), who also refers here to a study by Devendra Gupta (1982) on rural industry in Punjab.

16. For an extensive discussion of the aspect of commercialism among industrialists in India, see Streefkerk (1985: 162–71). More recently, Gorter (1996) and Streefkerk (1997) discussed this aspect of commercialism in connection with the change from a cultural to a structural perspective in the study of Indian entrepreneurship.

17. Christer Gunnarson (1985) suggests that the outright rejection of the European experience as an object of comparison for developments in Third World countries can be partly explained by the Marxist and Rostovian connotation such a comparison involves. At a general level, both the Rostovian and the Marxist theories on economic development argued that what the newly industrializing countries are doing is to follow the road shown by the western, developed countries. It was Karl Marx who stated that 'the industrially more developed countries present to the less developed countries a picture of the latters' future' (Marx 1978: Preface). W. Rostow (1971) followed a similar type of generalization in his 'Non-Communist Manifesto' in which he presented his take-off model of industrialization and economic progress in different stages by making a generalization from one example, England, to claim validity for all forms of development in the past, at present, and in the future. By postulating that there is only one type of industrialization, that is the European type of industrialization, of which the Third World type is a mere repetition, the Marxian and Rostovian models represented a serious type of misinterpretation and thereby gave comparative history a bad reputation (Gunnarsson 1985: 189).

18. Of course, this Eurocentric model of development has been challenged on many sides, such as by dependency and world-systems theories, but it still tends to linger on in much of the literature on entrepreneurship and economic history of Asian countries. For example, Chandavarkar (1985) has shown how 'teleological' conceptions of industrialization based on the British experience have pervaded and shaped the writing of Indian economic history.

19. This notion of early European capitalists seems to be based more on the eighteenth-century *ideology* of capitalism in Europe than on *actual* European experience. That ideology has also informed neoclassical economics, which takes the ahistorical and asocial individual actor as the basis of its model. Because economic theory cannot account for Asian business networks, it sees these economies as 'distorted' or 'imperfect' (Biggart 1991: 212–13).

20. The original studies along these lines were by Geertz (1963; 1968).

21. See McVey (1992) for a discussion of this turnaround in the cultural argument in the Chinese case.

22. I do not suggest that there are no studies on East or South East Asia that relate the state-dependent mode of capitalist development to the specific political-economic formations of these countries, particularly the pre-eminence of Chinese capital and the efforts of these states to subvert this dominance. For such arguments with regard to Malaysia, see Jomo (1988); for Indonesia, see Robison (1986).

23. For a comparison of case studies on small-scale entrepreneurs in South, South East, and East Asia, see Rutten and Upadhya (1997).

24. The argument that follows was developed together with Carol Upadhya and was recently published in our introduction to the volume on *Small Business Entrepreneurs in Asia and Europe: Towards a Comparative Perspective* (see Rutten and

Upadhya 1997). However, I alone am responsible for presenting it in its present form and for any possible mistakes.

25. Recently a number of anthropologists have turned to these issues and are investigating how the advance of global capitalism is being worked out in culturally disparate ways in various localities. See Blim (1996) for a review of this literature. A major point of debate in this literature is whether such diverse local forms of economic organization should be regarded as hybrids produced by the impact of the world capitalist system on pre-existing 'cultures', or as an integral part of the history of capitalism (understood as economic *and* cultural system to which 'local capitalisms' contribute). In the latter view, European capitalism can be understood as just one form of capitalism (even though it originally gave rise to industrialism), which existed alongside later forms that were produced through the articulation of local socio-economic systems with expanding capitalist markets. An intermediate position would hold that the world economy has its own logic but is historically contingent on encounters with local formations, pre-capitalist and capitalist.

26. For case studies on contemporary entrepreneurs in different parts of Asia and Europe, see the collection by Berger (1991) and Rutten and Upadhya (1997). For a historical comparison of entrepreneurs in different parts of Asia, see Dobbin (1996).

27. For examples of such arguments with regard to Indian business communities, see Tripathi (1984); for Japanese companies see Dore (1973, 1987), Fruin (1978), Abegglen and Stalk (1985); for Chinese business networks see Redding (1990), Hamilton (1991), Wang (1994), and Brown (1995).

REFERENCES

Abdullah, Irwan. 1994. 'The Muslim Businessmen of Jatinom: Religious Reform and Economic Modernisation in a Central Javanese Town'. Ph.D. thesis, University of Amsterdam.

Abegglen, James C., and George Stalk. 1985. *Kaisha: The Japanese Corporation.* New York: Basic Books.

Bagchi, Amiya K. 1972. *Private Investment in India, 1900–1939.* Cambridge: Cambridge University Press.

_____. 1976. 'De-Industrialization in India in the Nineteenth Century: Some Theoretical Implications'. *The Journal of Development Studies.* 12(2):135–64.

_____. 1988. 'Colonialism and the Nature of Capitalist Enterprise in India'. *Economic and Political Weekly.* 23 (30 July); PE-38–50.

Bayly, C. 1992. 'The Origins of Swadeshi (home industry): Cloth and Indian Society'. In A. Appadurai, ed., *The Social Life of Things: Commodities in Cultural Perspective,* 285–321. Cambridge: Cambridge University Press.

Bellah, Robert N. 1957. *Tokugawa Religion.* New Yor: Free Press.

_____ [1963]. 1968. 'Reflections on the Protestant Ethic Analogy in Asia'. In S.N. Eisenstadt, ed., *The Protestant Ethic and Modernisation; A Comparative View,* 243–51. New York: Basic Books. (Originally published in *Journal of Social Issues* 19:52–60.)

Berger, Brigitte, ed. 1991. *The Culture of Entrepreneurship.* New Delhi: Tata Mcgraw-Hill.

Berna, James G. 1960. *Industrial Entrepreneurship in Madras State*. Bombay: Asia Publishing House.

Biggart, Nicole W. 1991. 'Explaining Asian Economic Organization: Toward a Weberian Perspective'. *Theory and Society*. 20(2):199–232.

Blim, Michael. 1996. 'Cultures and the Problems of Capitalisms'. *Critique of Anthropology*. 16(1):79–93.

Broehl, W.G. 1978. *The Village Entrepreneur: Change Agents in India's Rural Development*. Cambridge: Cambridge University Press.

Brown, Raj A., ed. 1995. *Chinese Business Enterprise in Asia*. London and New York: Routledge.

Buchanan, D.H. 1934. *The Development of Capitalist Enterprise in India*. New York: Macmillan.

Chadha, G.K. 1986. *The State and Rural Economic Transformation: The Case of Punjab, 1950–85*. Delhi: Sage Publications.

Chandavarkar, Rajnarayan. 1985. 'Industrialization in India before 1947: Conventional Approaches and Alternative Perspectives'. *Modern Asian Studies*. 19(3):623–68.

Carrithers, M. and C. Humphreys, eds. 1991. *The Assembly of Listeners: Jains in Society*. Cambridge: Cambridge University Press.

Clad, James. 1989. *Behind the Myth: Business, Money and Power in Southeast Asia*. London: Unwin Hyman.

Desai, A.R. 1966. *Social Background of Indian Nationalism*. Bombay: Popular Prakashan.

Dobb, Maurice. [1947] 1976. *Studies in the Development of Capitalism*. Reprint. New York: International Publishers.

Dobbin, Christine. 1996. *Asian Entrepreneurial Minorities: Conjoint Communities in the Making of the World-Economy 1570–1940*. London: Curzon Press.

Dore, Ronald P. 1973. *British Factory, Japanese Factory*. Berkeley: University of California Press.

———. 1987. *Taking Japan Seriously: A Confucian Perspective on Leading Economic Issues*. Stanford: Stanford University Press.

Douglas, M. and B. Isherwood. 1978. *The World of Goods*. Harmondsworth: Penguin.

Dutt, R.P. 1940. *India Today*. London: Victor Gollanoz.

Eisenstadt, S.N., ed. 1968. *The Protestant Ethic and Modernisation: A Comparative View*. New York: Free Press.

Elder, Joseph W. 1959. 'Industrialism in Hindu Society: A Case Study in Social Change'. Ph.D thesis Harvard University. Cambridge: Mass.

Fanselow, F.S. 1990. 'The Bazar Economy or How Bizarre is the Bazar Really?'. *Man* (n.s.). 25:250–65.

Fox, Richard G. 1969. *From Zamindar to Ballot Box: Community Change in a North Indian Market Town*. Ithaca: Cornell University Press.

———. 1973. 'Pariah Capitalism and Traditional Indian Merchants, Past and Present'. In Milton Singer, ed., *Entrepreneurship and Modernisation of Occupational Cultures in South Asia,* 16–36. Durham: Duke University Press.

Fruin, Mark W. 1978. 'The Japanese Company Controversy'. *Journal of Japanese Studies*. 4(2):267–300.

Gadgil, D.R. [1924] 1971. *The Industrial Evolution of India in Recent Times, 1860–1939*. Reprint. Bombay: Oxford University Press.

Geertz, Clifford. 1963. *Peddlers and Princes: Social Development and Economic Change in Two Indonesian Towns*. Chicago: University of Chicago Press.

_____. 1968. 'Religious Belief and Economic Behaviour in a Central Javanese Town'. In S.N. Eisenstadt, ed., *The Protestant Ethic and Modernisation; A Comparative View*, 309–42. New York: Free Press.

Giddens, Anthony. 1972. *Politics and Sociology in the Thought of Max Weber*. London: MacMillan

Goheen, John, M.N. Srinivas, D.G. Karve, and Milton Singer, 1958. 'India's Cultural Values and Economic Development; A Discussion'. *Economic Development and Cultural Change*. 7(1):1–12.

Gorter, Pieter. 1996. 'Small Capitalists or "Agents of Underdevelopment"? A Case Study of a Large Industrial Estate in South Gujarat'. *The Journal of Entrepreneurship* 5(1):41–64.

Goswami, Omkar. 1989. 'Sahibs, Babus, and Banias: Changes in Industrial Control in Eastern India, 1918–50'. *Journal of Asian Studies*. 48(2):289–309.

Gunnarson, Christer. 1985. 'Development Theory and Third World Industrialisation'. *Journal of Contemporary Asia*. 15(2):183–206.

Gupta, Devendra. 1982. *Rural Industry in India: The Experience of the Punjab Region*. Delhi: Institute of Economic Growth.

Hamilton, Gary, ed. 1991. *Business Networks and Economic Development in East and South Asia*. Hong Kong: Centre of Asian Studies, University of Hong Kong.

Hazlehurst, Leighton W. 1966. *Entrepreneurship and the Merchant Castes in a Punjabi City*. Duke University Programme in Comparative Studies on Southern Asia, Monograph 1.

Hilton, Rodney, ed. 1976. *The Transition from Feudalism to Capitalism*. London: NLB, Foundations of History Library.

Holmström, Mark. 1985. *Industry and Inequality: The Social Anthropology of Indian Labour*. Cambridge: Cambridge University Press.

Howard, M. and J. Jones. 1991. 'Jain Shopkeepers and Moneylenders'. In M. Carrithers and C. Humphreys eds, *The Assembly of Listeners: Jains in Society*, 109–38. Cambridge: Cambridge University Press.

Jomo, Kwame S. 1988. *A Question of Class: Capital, the State, and Uneven Development in Malaya*. New York: Monthly Review Press.

Kapp, William H. 1963. *Hindu Culture, Economic Development, and Economic Planning in India*. New York: Oxford University Press.

Kennedy Robert E. 1965. 'The Protestant Ethic and the Parsis'. In Neil J. Smelser, ed., *Readings in Economic Sociology*, 16–26. NY: Englewood Cliff.

Leibenstein, H. 1978. *General X-Efficency Theory and Economic Development*. London: Oxford University Press.

Mahadevan, Raman. 1992. 'The Pattern of Industrial Control in Colonial Madras: Some Critical Observations on the Relative Position of Indian and Foreign Capital, 1930–50'. In Arun Ghosh et al., eds, *Indian Industrialisation, Structure and Policy Issues*, 333–64. Delhi: Oxford University Press.

Marx, Karl. 1978. *Capital: A Critiue of Political Economy*. London: Penguin.

Matsui, Toru. 1968. 'On the Nineteenth-century Indian Economic History: A Review of "a Reinterpretation"'. *The Indian Economic and Social History Review*, 5(1):17–33.

Mayer, P. 1993. 'Inventing Village Tradition: The Late Nineteenth-century Origins of the North Indian "Jajmani System". *Modern Asian Studies*. 27:357–95.

McClelland, David C. 1961. *The Achieving Society*. Princeton: Princeton University Press.

McClelland, David C. and D.G. Winter. 1969. *Motivating Economic Achievement*. New York: Free Press.

McCrory, J.T. 1956. *Small Industry in a North Indian Town: Case Studies in Latent Industrial Potential*. Delhi: Government of India, Ministry of Commerce and Industry.

McVey, Ruth. 1992. 'The Materialisation of the Southeast Asian Entrepreneur'. In Ruth McVey, ed., *Southeast Asian Capitalists*, 7–33. Cornell University Studies on Southeast Asia. Ithaca, NY.

Miller, ed., 1995. *Acknowledging Consumption*. London: Routledge.

Morris, M.D. 1968. 'Towards a Reinterpretation of Nineteenth Century Indian Economic History'. *The Indian Economic and Social History Review*. 5(1):1–15.

Muhaimin, Yahya. 1990. 'Muslim Traders: The Stillborn Bourgeoisie'. *Prisma*. 49:83–90.

Mukherjee, R. 1958. *The Rise and Fall of the East India Company: A Sociological Appraisal*. Berlin: VEB Deutscher Verlag der Wissenschaften.

Myrdal, Gunnar. 1968. *Asian Drama: An Inquiry into the Poverty of Nations*. New York: Twentieth Century Fund and Pantheon Books.

Plattner, S. ed., 1985. *Markets and Marketing*. Lanham: University Press of America.

Ray, Rajat K., ed. 1992. *Entrepreneurship and Industry in India, 1800–1947*. Delhi: Oxford University Press.

Redding, Gordon. 1990. *The Spirit of Chinese Capitalism*. Berlin: Walter de Gruyter.

Robison, Richard. 1986. *Indonesia: The Rise of Capital*. Asian Studies Association of Australia, Southeast Asia Publication Series, no. 13. Sydney: Allen & Unwin.

Rostow, W. 1971. *The Stages of Economic Growth: A Non-Communist Manifesto*. 2nd edition. Cambridge: Cambridge University Press.

Rutten, Mario. 1994. *Asian Capitalist in the European Mirror*. Comparative Asian Studies, no. 14. Amsterdam: Free University Press.

———. 1995. *Farms and Factories: Social Profile of Large Farmers and Rural Industrialists in West India*. Delhi: Oxford University Press.

Rutten, Mario and Carol Upadhya, eds. 1997. *Small Business Entrepreneurs in Asia and Europe; Towards a Comparative Perspective*. Delhi: Sage Publications.

Saberwal, Satish. 1976. *Mobile Men: Limits to Social Change in Urban Punjab*. Delhi: Vikas.

Sahlins M. 1976. *Culture and Practical Reason*. Chicago: Chicago University Press.

Schumpeter, J.A. 1934. *The Theory of Economic Development*. Cambridge: Massachusetts.

Silin, Robert H. 1976. *Leadership and Values: The Organization of Large-Scale Taiwanese Enterprises*. Cambridge: East Asian Research Center, Harvard University.

Singer, Milton. 1956. 'Cultural Values in India's Economic Development'. *The Annals of The American Academy of Political and Social Science*. May: 81–91.

Singer, Milton. 1960. 'Changing Craft Tradition in India'. In Wilbert, E. Moore and Arnold S. Feldman, eds, *Labour Commitment and Social Change in Developing Areas*. New York: Social Science Research Council.

———. 1966. 'Religion and Social Change in India: The Max Weber Thesis Phase Three'. *Economic Development and Cultural Change*. 14(4):497–505.

———. 1972. 'Industrial Leadership, the Hindu ethic and the Spirit of Socialism.' In Milton Singer, ed., *When a Great Tradition Modernizes: An Anthropological Approach to Indian Civilization*, 272–380. New York: Praeger.

———. ed. 1973. *Entrepreneurship and Modernisation of Occupational Cultures in South Asia*. Durham: Duke University Press.

Staley, E. and M. Morse. 1965. *Modern Small Industry for Developing Countries*. New York: McGraw Hill.

Streefkerk, Hein. 1985. *Industrial Transition in Rural India: Artisans, Traders and Tribals in South Gujarat*. Bombay: Sangam Books.

———. 1997. 'Gujarati Entrepreneurship; Historical Continuity against Changing Perspectives'. *Economic and Political Weekly*. 32(8):M-2-M-10.

Timberg, Thomas A. 1978. *The Marwaris; From Traders to Industrialists*. New Delhi: Vikas

Tripathi, Dwijendra, ed. 1984. *Business Communities of India: A Historical Perspective*. Delhi: Manohar Publications.

———. 1992. 'Indian Business Houses and Entrepreneurship: A Note on Research Trends'. *Journal of Entrepreneurship*. 1(1):75–97.

Upadhya, Carol and Mario Rutten. 1997. 'In Search of a Comparative Framework; Small-scale Entrepreneurs in Asia and Europe'. In Mario Rutten, and Carol Upadhya, eds, *Small Business Entrepreneurs in Asia and Europe; Towards a Comparative Perspective*, 13–43. Delhi: Sage Publications.

Veen, J.H. van der. 1976. 'Commercial Orientation of Industrial Entrepreneurs in India'. *Economic and Political Weekly*. 11(35):M91-M94.

Wang, Yeu-Farn. 1994. *Chinese Entrepreneurs in Southeast Asia: Historical Roots and Modern Significance*. Working Paper 34. Stockholm: Center for Pacific Asia Studies at Stockholm University.

Weber, Max. 1958. *The Religion of India*. Ed. and trans H.H. Gerth, and D. Martindale. Glencoe: Free Press.

———. 1976. *The Protestant Ethic and the Spirit of Capitalism*. London: George Allen & Unwin. (Originally published in Gesammelte Aufsätze zur Religionssoziologie, Töbingen, 1920-1. First published as a two-part article in 1904-05, in the Archive för Sozialwissenschaft und Sozialpolitik.)

———. 1978. 'The Origins of Industrial Capitalism in Europe'. In W.G. Runciman, ed., *Max Weber, Selections in Translation*, 331–40. (Originally published in Gesammelte Aufsätze zur Religionssoziologie, Töbingen, 1920-1.)

Wong, Siu-lun. 1989. 'The Applicability of Asian Family Values'. In Peter Berger and Michael, Hasiao, eds, In *Search of an East Asian Development Model*. New Brunswick: N.J., Transaction Books.

Markets

Denis Vidal

Markets and trade have always played an important role in Indian history. Whilst there is evidence of the significance of markets and monetary transactions in medieval India (Subrahmanyam 1994), it is concerning the eighteenth century that we find an abundance of information about the intricate networks of markets which characterized the Indian economy of that period. Such networks linked the periodical market (*hat*) of the countryside with the local urban markets (*mandi, ganj, qasbah*) of small towns, the great bazaars of important commercial cities, and the outposts for long-distance trade outside India (Chaudhuri 1994; Habib and Raychaudury 1982; Bayly 1983). Historians have also demonstrated that monetary transactions were not only limited to the domains of trade or to the collection of state revenue but also entered into other aspects of social life in pre-colonial India. For example, Dirk Kolff has shown the importance of a military labour market both for state formation and for the maintenance of the village economy (Kolff 1990). This richness of historical material makes it surprising that the study of markets and monetary transactions has played such a minor role in the development of the social and cultural anthropology of India. Ironically the main reason for this neglect is that the market has often been perceived as a relatively recent phenomenon and an alien imposition on Indian society and culture.

This neglect does not only concern India. It begs more general questions about the way markets have been studied within the framework of the social sciences and of economic anthropology in particular. It is probably true to say that the progressive hegemony of neoclassic theory in economic literature does not blend well with sociological approaches to the market in spite of recent efforts at reconciliation made by the so-called 'new institutional economics' school.[1] But it is not enough for anthropologists and sociologists to blame economists for monopolizing the field with their limited model of the market; the former are also partially responsible for the development of the situation.

On the one hand, sociologists criticize the neoclassic approach for its failure to consider the social and cultural factors which influence economic behaviour. On the other hand, the same critics will insist that social relationships and cultural values are obliterated by the market. In the first instance, they question the relevance and interpretative value of economic theory from a sociological point of view; but in the second, they find themselves implicitly validating the economist's model of the market, even if they intend to do the opposite. If anthropologists and sociologists are to escape from this double bind, they need not only to question the applicability of the economist's model, but to go one stage further to develop an alternative approach.

Paradoxically, it is amongst anthropologists working in non-western cultures, often perceived as not having market economies, that the tendency to endorse the standard economic interpretation of the market has been most apparent. Placing the emphasis on the social and the cultural specificities of the societies they study, these scholars inevitably recognize the discrepancy between the economic practices they observe and the economic model thought to characterize western societies. However, rather than using their observations to contest the model developed in the West, they tend to assume its relevance only for the West and that its limitation is simply that it cannot be applied cross-culturally.

The intensification of this debate in the anthropological literature of the 1960s and 1970s can be traced back to the influential role played by the work of Karl Polanyi (1886–1964). Polanyi attempted to show that the market economy characterized a specific and very particular moment of western society. It was therefore inappropriate to apply a model which had been built out of these specific circumstances to other societies. He also questioned the notion that the market economy was more 'rational' or more efficient than other forms of economic organization based on different principles. Like many other intellectuals of his time, Polanyi believed that the period of western history which had been marked by economic liberalism was coming to an end.

The ambition of Polanyi and his followers, who became known as the 'substantivists', was to draw up a typology of different kinds of economic organization found throughout the world at different periods in history. In effect, he identified three main economic principles: reciprocity, redistribution, and exchange: 'Reciprocity denotes movements between correlative points of symmetrical groupings; redistribution designates appropriational movements toward a centre and out of it again; exchange refers here to vice-versa movements taking place as between 'hands' under a market movement' (Polanyi 1992: 35). He was also anxious to avoid any form of evolutionism and did not want to give undue privilege to the sort of economic organization which characterized modern western societies. The social scientists who opposed this view, and who were collectively known as the 'formalists,' argued to the contrary that, in spite of the obvious differences in the economic organization of societies, the main task at hand was to delineate a few fundamental principles which could be applied to all.

According to the substantivists, the main characteristic of the domination of economic liberalism in the West lay in the separation of the economic domain from social and cultural values and constraints. By contrast, in more 'traditional' societies, economic relationships were 'embedded' within the social fabric and were subordinate to non-economic considerations. Such a conception corresponds well to that developed by Louis Dumont in the Indian context, and it is no coincidence that it was this author who wrote the preface of the French translation of Polanyi's major work, *The Great Transformation* (1957). Basing his argument both on ancient Hindu texts and contemporary ethnography, Dumont argued that one of the fundamental characteristics of Hindu society was that the economic and political domain (*artha*) was subordinate to the moral exigencies of a higher order (*dharma*). This hierarchy of principles was thought to inform the ideology of Indian society as a whole (Dumont 1970).

Most sociologists and anthropologists working in India have, at some level, proved 'substantivist' in their approach. They have tended to place emphasis on the logic of redistribution rather than monetary transactions, as if the latter could be dismissed as an alien imposition on Indian culture and society. Once market exchanges were perceived purely as a modern development, it became possible by contrast to define the ideological features which were supposed to characterize the 'traditional' economic system in India.

However, from the 1980s onwards this simplistic divide between so-called 'traditional' and 'modern' economic systems has been more and more contested. On the one hand, the use of the notion of 'tradition' has been questioned in the works of historians, cultural theorists, and anthropologists (Hobsbawm and Ranger 1983; Breckenridge and Van der Veer 1994). On the other hand, new approaches to economic sociology have emerged. As a result of these developments we find two new tendencies in Indian economic sociology. The first is to recognize and take a fresh look at the importance of markets in Indian culture, the second is to begin to question the dominant model of the market from an Indian perspective. It is on these two tendencies that I wish to focus.

Rediscovering the Importance of the Market in Indian Sociology

Sociologists and anthropologists have tended to draw a clear distinction between monetary transactions and other forms of exchange such as gift giving. The latter has generally been perceived as positive in value as opposed to the former which is thought to dehumanize social relationships. According to this view, it was usually taken for granted that exchanges of gifts not only expressed the values of a society but also reinforced social relationships within it; whilst money transactions implied the erosion of social solidarity and cultural values (Bloch and Parry 1989).

There is no doubt that gifts have positive connotations in western culture; and it is equally true that market transactions are often looked at with suspicion, particularly in certain spheres of life where commercialization may seem sacrilegious from a moral point of view. A good illustration of this is Viviana Zelizer's interesting discussion of the history of life-insurance companies in the United States (Zelizer 1992). She analyses the development of this specific market in terms of a complicated negotiation between mercantile values and particularly sacred human values which seem to contradict each other. She goes on to show that Americans were not only resistant to the idea that life could be evaluated in monetary terms but also to the idea that payment was appropriate as compensation for someone's death. The question raised by such an example is whether monetary transactions and market relationships are always evaluated in the same way in different societies. If economists have tended to universalize western economic logic, anthropologists have tended to universalize anti-market rhetoric. Joel Kahn put it neatly in his critique of Taussig's well-known monograph, '*The Devil and Commodity Fetishism in South America* (1980), when he argues that Taussig's approach 'places a Young Hegelian critique of commodities and markets into the mouth of Latin American peasants' (Kahn 1997: 75).

It is precisely this question which has been addressed by Jonathan Parry in his analysis of different types of economic transaction in Varanasi (Parry 1989). Parry argues that one cannot make a clear-cut distinction between gifts and commercial transactions in terms of the morality attached to them. Moreover, in India, it is gift relations, not monetary ones, which are perceived as a potential threat to social relations. Parry also demonstrates that commercial and monetary transactions are treated in a much more neutral perspective in India than in the West and in many other societies.

It is possible to question the generality of Parry's study, located as it was amongst the priests of Varanasi. There are, of course, many varied traditions and streams of thought in Indian culture, some of which do not fit his argument. Sanjay Subrahmanyam, for example, has shown that many currents of medieval poetry and literature in India express a range of ambivalent attitudes to money and trade (Subrahmanyam 1994) However, one should not undermine the importance of Parry's findings. There is, in fact, a large body of evidence in anthropological and historical literature to support his thesis. For example, we find often in India a more lenient and morally neutral attitude to debt and credit than that found generally in the West. In spite of the exploitation of debtors by creditors and of sporadic resistance, there is not as much moral condemnation of the former as one might expect (Vidal 1997; Hardiman 1987, 1996).

Parry's argument is not limited to India. In fact, he goes on to suggest that the condemnation of market relationships seems everywhere to be linked to the valorization of self-sufficiency in the economic domain— whether in the West or in Melanesia. So, reverting the conventional perspective on Indian society, Parry argues that it may be precisely because economic autarky has never been considered an ideal in Indian society that monetary transactions have not posed a serious threat to cultural values or social relationships. Such insights echo the mounting criticism of the idea that local economic relations can be understood purely in terms of what is known as the *jajmani* system.

The Jajmani System

The jajmani system is a term commonly used by sociologists and anthropologists to summarize economic relationships between members of different castes in the Indian village context. Jajmani relationships were thought to be based on a system of redistribution in kind where the monetarization and commercialization of goods and services hardly existed. This made economic interactions largely independent of market forces. Rather, they were deeply embedded in the social and ritual structures of the caste system.

W.H. Wiser is generally acknowledged to be the first author to have emphasized the importance of the jajmani system in village relations (Wiser 1958). But most village studies from the 1950s onwards make use of the concept even if some of them offer a much more nuanced picture of the rural economy than others, thereby pointing out some of the limitations of the jajmani model (Harper 1959; Pocock 1969). But in spite of these criticisms, the jajmani system came to be identified as some sort of normative principle at the very root of economic relations in village India, making it easy to contrast it with the logic of the market as defined by the West. The jajmani system was a good example of what Polanyi termed a 'redistributive' system, and its study allied Indian sociologists with the substantivist school.

It is for this reason that when C.J. Fuller (1989) and Peter Mayer (1993) systematically exposed the methodological weakness of the arguments which overstressed the importance of the jajmani system in the rural economy a turning point in the economic anthropology of India was reached. In particular, Fuller demonstrated the huge discrepancy which had always existed between the theorization of jajmani relations and the empirical evidence about them. In fact, he showed, beyond any possible doubt, that there was no general economic principle which corresponded to the variety of economic formations found in different parts of India. Neither could it be said that highly localized economic structures could be understood purely in terms of jajmani relations. Monetary transactions often existed alongside transactions in kind and were often an accompaniment to jajmani relations.

Once it is recognized that monetary exchanges are not incompatible with Indian social and cultural values, it becomes possible to re-evaluate the place of the market and trade within the sociological study of India.

Actors in the Market

In Indian markets, the social identity of local traders is often highly specific. Even in major cities like Delhi with a complex history of migration and rapid economic change, the vast majority of traders belong to specific socio-religious groups. Often a particular market is dominated by a particular community. For example, in the principal grain market of Delhi we find that most of the traders belong to the business communities of Haryana. Though the economic context of this market has changed considerably since Independence, there is evidence to suggest that it was these same communities which dominated it back in the first half of the nineteenth century (Bayly 1983: 332). Similarly, in local towns throughout south India grain markets tend to be dominated by traders belonging to specific communities (Harris-White 1996). While such a pattern is no doubt common in many places throughout India, and constitutes an important element of the sociology of the market, it is important to avoid the types of misinterpretations which are often made about its significance.

The first misinterpretation is about how such clusters reproduce themselves. If a trader's son becomes a trader, it is not because he is compelled to continue the tradition of his caste in any simplistic way. Rather, he is likely to explain his choice in terms of the fact that by following the family profession, he will have the best opportunity in terms of immediate access to business know-how, social and trading networks, and material facilities. However, one finds members of the same caste in a variety of different professions.

More generally, gender, caste, regional origin, and economic power are all significant factors of the identity of traders but their particular relevance varies according to specific markets, localities, and professions. It is possible to find a group of traders all of the same caste, even when this caste is not conventionally associated with trading activities. For example, in the street market for Gujarati embroidery in Ahmedabad, all the traders are from the same caste and most are linked by close kinship ties, yet their ancestors had no links with this trade (Tarlo 1997). What matters is not caste identity as such, but the types of networks that a person's identity enables him or her to tap into, both in terms of business opportunities and social connections. This is true not only for traders but for all types of participants in the market. For example, in the grain market of Delhi, it is not only the traders who have a specific identity, but also accountants, peons, and coolies. In each case it is different criterion that is emphasized. In the case of coolies in the grain market of Delhi, for example, it is regional origin, rather than caste identity, which forms the most important basis on which networks are established.

The example of the coolies in Old Delhi also highlights another common stumbling block in the sociological interpretation of markets. It is often assumed that markets can be distinguished according to whether they are organized along corporate or individual lines. However, in old Delhi we find that some coolies are operating purely on an individual basis whilst others, by contrast, pool all their earnings and work together in teams.

Finally, it is a mistake to consider that networks based on different aspects of social identity (caste, religion, locality, kinship, etc.) are necessarily obstacles to the smooth functioning of the market, as economists from Adam Smith onwards have tended to assume. Not only can one demonstrate that it is often by the mobilization of such networks that Indian markets are constituted (Tarlo 1997) and maintained (Lachaier 1997), but also that social networks play an equally crucial role in markets in the West which are generally supposed to be the purest incarnation of neoclassic economics (Carrier 1997).

Once we recognize that the perspective of the conventional economist is undersocialized whilst that of the conventional social anthropologist is generally oversocialized, it becomes clear that the study of socio-economic networks is essential to any empirical understanding of the market. And once such networks are placed at the centre of the analysis, the distinction usually drawn between economic transactions in western and non-western societies rapidly dissolves. Not only do economic transactions in non-western countries appear much less embedded than previously assumed, but also economic transactions in western societies appear much more embedded than economists have supposed (Granovetter 1992).

By rediscovering the importance of markets in India, anthropologists can now make use of the advances made in other social sciences. On the one hand, they can take advantage of research on markets in other parts of the world for studying markets in India, without either sacrificing or exaggerating Indian specificities. On the other hand, they can take advantage of the studies done in India which may have a real sociological content but were conducted under the umbrella of other disciplines such as economic geography, economic history, and political economy. The question which then emerges is how can one make use of these different works, not only in order to get a more satisfying picture of the history, geography, and sociology of markets in India, but also to reconsider the concept of the market itself in a broader context.

Redefining Markets

Analysing the economic writings of Indian nationalist thinkers (from Justice Ranade and his classic address on the Indian Political Economy, delivered at Pune in 1892 to the works of K.T. Telang, Dadhabhai, Bipen Chandra Pal, or G. Subramanya Iyer and others), Bipan Chandra has shown their awareness of the Eurocentric bias of economic theory. This, they felt, limited both its significance and its applicability to India (Chandra 1966). This tradition of defiance helps explain why economists who have worked either in or about India have kept a distance from neoclassic theory, many pointing out its limitations and recognizing the legitimacy of historical and sociological approaches. But although many have criticized the neoclassic theory of the market from the perspective of the political economy, this exercise has often proved little more than an intellectual routine (Basu 1994: 111–18).

Goods, Money, or Commodities?

Markets have been criticized both for dissolving social bonds and for reducing goods to commodities. This point of view has been perpetuated as much by economists as anthropologists. The latter have generally maintained a clear-cut distinction between the status of things which circulate as gifts and those which circulate as commodities (Mauss 1970). In the former case objects are thought to retain something of the quality of the giver whereas in the latter case they become neutralized through the market.

However, as Appadurai and others have shown, such a distinction only makes sense if one ignores the trajectories which objects follow before and after they enter the market context (Appadurai 1986).

In his anthropological study of the Muria Gonds, Alfred Gell points out that consumption is generally identified with the destruction of goods and that this may well be because our notion of consumption is conceptualized on the basis of eatables. He goes on to argue that 'consumption as a general phenomenon really has nothing to do with the destruction of goods and wealth, but with their reincorporation into the social system that produced them in some other guise' (Gell 1986: 112). One only has to consider the land market to recognize the inappropriateness of the metaphor of destruction. Such observations highlight the deficiencies of the economic categories so often accepted as uncontested truths.

To take another example, let us consider the market for jewellery which plays a very important role in Indian social and economic life. Much of a woman's jewellery is given to her at the time of marriage. This means that shortly after being purchased in the market place, jewellery will apparently lose its status as 'commodity' and acquire the new status of 'gift.' In fact, jewellery serves several functions at once. Not only is it both a beautifier and symbol of status and wealth but also it is considered a form of quasi-money which can be exchanged for other commodities or used in pawnbroking as a guarantee for loans. Viewed in this context, jewellery plays a very significant role in the monetization of the Indian economy.

What is true for jewellery is also true for other things. In a fascinating historical study, Christopher Bayly has demonstrated the diverse range of roles played by cloth in socio-economic life in India during the eighteenth and nineteenth centuries. He demonstrates how the Moghuls used textiles in a complex circuit of tribute and redistribution in such a way that 'at no point did cloth become "merely" a commodity whose production and distribution was solely determined by market forces'. Bayly also argues that even when cloth is acquired through the market place, it nevertheless retains the qualities associated with the conditions of its production and sale. So, even from this point of view, the distinction usually made between gift relationships and market relationships loses much of its relevance. As with the jewellery example it is not only the distinction between 'gifts' and 'commodities' that is called into question but also that between 'money' and 'commodities'.

The Market and the State

In India, as elsewhere, most of the public debates surrounding the market in the last two decades have focused on the issues of economic liberalization and deregulation. In its crudest and most ideological version, which is also its most common form, the whole debate is reduced to a simplistic dichotomy between the influence of the state, thought to impede the optimal functioning of the economy, and the influence of market institutions, thought to encourage it.

A more refined version of the same argument—largely developed nowadays in economic literature—consists in arguing that non-markert institutions cannot simply be regarded as negative and arbitrary influences on economic life which can be removed at will. State intervention can in fact be motivated by the 'failure' of markets. In such cases 'non-market' institutions are considered a 'rational' answer to the functioning of the economy. This is the line of argument first used by economists like R.H. Coase then Oliver E. Williamson in their explanations of the existence of firms, and on which the theoretical advances put forward by the 'new institutional economics' school are built (Williamson and Winter 1993).

A more socially sensitive form of the same argument is found in the work of Amartya Sen and Jean Drèze, though they would not necessarily identify with this school (Drèze and Sen 1995). In order to widen the debate from its narrow concentration on issues of liberalization, they insist on the importance of distinguishing between different domains: those where state intervention may be considered an impediment to the efficiency of the market and those where state intervention should be considered not only necessary but also desirable. For example, in areas like primary education or public health, they argue that it does not make sense to consider that there is (or could be) any real competition between the market and the state in a country like India. As a matter of fact, state intervention needs to be increased. So whilst it makes sense to debate the relative efficiency of the state and the market in domains where they are 'excluding' each other, one must also recognize that there are many domains where they should rather be complementary (Drèze and Sen 1995: 9–27).

From a sociological and anthropological point of view, the dichotomy between market and state is more than just a question of economic policy. First, in these disciplines, it is generally taken for granted that state and market are largely interdependent institutions. But the interaction between market and state is also much more complicated than is generally assumed. For example, every time individuals are confronted with one or another form of corruption, they are obliged to settle the debate about the 'deregulation' of government activities on their own terms and for their own use. So, an immediate consequence of corruption in ordinary life is to 'privatize' a debate which is more often analysed as a public one. More fundamentally, the accumulative result of this is to blur precisely the sort of distinctions that Drèze and Sen attempt to establish between 'market-complementary' governmental activities and 'market-excluding' ones. For example, access to public social amenities and services in the fields of health and education are often more 'privatized' than they appear. Moreover, while simple acts of corruption displace rather than abolish the distinction between monetary transactions and public services, such a distinction rapidly becomes irrelevant in the case of more insidious forms of corruption based on social networks and patronage. Such considerations are interestingly taken into account by an economist like Kaushik Basu, when he argues that 'the problem with the Indian economy is not that its market is less or more free but that its freedom is in the wrong domains' (Basu 1994: 154).

Buying and Selling

It is not only corruption but also a certain laxity in the enforcement of social and legal norms which must be taken into account for analysing the functioning of the market in India. Such, for example, is the case with the real-estate market. In all Indian cities, but particularly in major ones, a large amount of land is bought, built on, or sold without legal authorization. As a consequence of this, property rights cannot be taken for granted. And even when property rights are not questioned as such, broken contracts are very common and the legal apparatus for dealing with them is slow and inefficient. More generally, in the context of Indian markets, transactions are often made without formal contracts to fall back on. Such occurences are well known and scholars as different as Kaushik Basu and Amiya Kumar Bagchi have noted the importance of taking them into consideration when studying markets in India (Basu 1989: 51–5). This is also why both insist on the importance of trust in market transactions where there is always 'a time lag, however brief, between each agent performing his side of the exchange' (Basu 1989: 53). But even if it is worth noticing that 'where contract-adherence norms are weak, markets function poorly and may not even exist' (Basu 1989: 53), one should also point out the possibility of the opposite phenomenon. In some contexts it is precisely because the level of trust that exists between all sorts of actors that the time lag between transactions may, in fact, be extended as different categories of intermediaries become involved, and the market thereby expands.

The Key Role of Intermediaries

At first sight markets in large Indian cities look as if they might conform to the neoclassic paradigm: the choice of goods is plentiful, as is the competition; customers are free to purchase goods where they wish, to enquire about their quality and to negotiate prices to their advantage. And as long as they are willing to pay cash, the anonymity of buyers and sellers does not impede negotiations. However, only a very small proportion of commercial transactions actually conform to such a description. More usually, customers know exactly where they want to buy. This may be because they are regular clients of a particular shop or because a particular shop has been recommended to them. This is not to say that price and quality do not enter the equation, but rather that commercial transactions are usally enmeshed in a series of other factors where the identities of sellers and buyers are taken into account. These interactions are not dissimilar from what Clifford Geertz describes in his study of Moroccan bazaars (Geertz 1992). The merit of Geertz' analysis is his avoidance of the trap of assuming that one should give a central role to social and cultural factors in explaining bazaar transactions on the one hand, and discarding them automatically while describing market principles on the other. He bases his distinction between markets and bazaars on the way in which knowledge and information are acquired in each.In bazaars, the search for information is primarily intensive because knowledge has to be acquired by asking a large number of diagnostic questions to a few people, rather than a handful of index questions to a large number of people. The former approach, exploring nuances rather than canvassing populations, is what characterizes the bazaar economy in Geertz's view.

However, when one tries to apply Geertz's model of the bazaar to the Indian context, one finds that his analysis applies only to retail transactions. Only here can one draw an effective contrast between 'extensive' and 'intensive' forms of search for economic information; or that one can oppose anonymous styles of market interactions with more personalized ones between buyers and sellers. But when one analyses the sort of commercial transactions which take place between buyers and sellers at the wholesale level, not only the style but also the whole process and inner logic of the transactions totally changes. Not only can one no longer contrast different sorts of economic transactions on the basis of the knowledge that buyers and sellers individually possess, but, more fundamentally, one can no longer consider the confrontation between buyers and sellers as a the central element of the market institution. Rather, it is the presence of intermediaries and the different functions they assume that defines the characteristics of the market.[2]

At first sight, the activity of brokerage might seem a simple act of mediation between supply and demand, and the percentage taken on negotiations made via a broker might simply be considered as one of the many 'transaction costs' known to characterize any market. However, it needs to be recognized that the very existence of brokerage does, in fact, radically change the characteristics of the market. What it does is allow buyers to know what is available in a market well beyond their individual capacities for acquiring information. It also allows traders to know about the demand in the market place well beyond their capacities to accumulate information directly through their networks of clients; third, the mediation of brokers introduces a degree of trust between market partners who would not otherwise know each other sufficiently for entering into commercial relations. This is a particularly crucial point because all significant transactions involve financial credit which presupposes both trust and knowledge about the credibility of the partners involved.

In other words, brokerage cannot be dismissed as marginal to the functioning of the maket; on the contrary, it is the most decisive element in the constitution of the market itself. It is through the broker that supply and demand are defined and that the evaluation of customer and trader is made. The same trader may be presnted as a simple shopkeeper to some and as a commercial intermediary or potential business partner to others. Similarly, a customer who might not be taken seriously if unknown to a trader might be considered an important client if introduced in the right manner by the right broker. In other words, both the market actors and the supply and demand undergo a constant process of redefinition with the result that the same market will appear in a very differnet light according to the identity of different actors.

The role of brokerage in Indian markets is one example which shows why it is necessary to reconsider most of the hypothesis which lies at the foundation of the standard interpretation of markets. What characterizes the institution of brokerage is precisely the fact that it blurs the sorts of distinctions which are usually made between markets and bazaars but, more generally, between 'neoclassic markets' and supposedly less 'rational' economic institutions. Basically, in any market where brokerage prevails, all transactions are concretely made on a very personalized basis between people and intermediaries. And yet, at the same time, the buyers and sellers often remain anonymous to each other.

All over the world, markets are intricate institutional or quasi-institutional spaces in which different sorts of actors, often with different sets of values, interact, and which cannot be understood purely in terms of a confrontation between buyers and sellers. This is certainly the case with India. Barbara Harris-White's work on the grain market (1996) confirms the impossibility of reducing the function of trade to a simple intermediary stage between production and consumption. In the entire sample of merchant firms that she studied, none limited its activities to buying and selling. All of them were involved to varying degrees in other activities which ran all along the economic chain from agricultural production until the delivery of products to the final selling point. The pattern of their involvement was so diverse that she considered it impossible to classify according to function and had to devise new ways of analysing them in a pluri-functional perspective. Her example demonstrates the impossibility of reducing the market to a simple encounter between buyers and sellers or, at a more abstract level, between demand and supply.

Demand and Supply

Until quite recently, two sorts of theoretical perspectives have dominated the debate in economic literature. On the one hand there are those who insisted on the crucial importance of production in the economic process; on the other are those who focused on exchange. It was also taken for granted by many sociologists that to analyse society from an economic perspective, it was necessary to focus on the domain of production which was considered the driving force behind social and cultural identities. In most of these approaches, the role of consumption was largely ignored. The works of scholars like Werner Sombart or Thorstein Veblen were unusual in according a significant role to the consumption process. However, from the 1970s onwards, an increasing number of social scientists began to insist on the declining importance of the sphere of production in post-industrial societies. Follwoing thinkers like Jean Baudrillard and Roland Barthes, renewed importance was given to the symbolism of consumption and, more particularly, its importance for defining identities (Douglas and Isherwood 1978).

It is no coincidence that this new trend should find an echo in social and cultural anthropology. Most anthropologists, with the exception of Marxists, have always privileged the process of exchange above the process of production. Nevertheless, as I have already suggested, the one form of exchange which anthropologists rarely considered worthy of study was monetary transactions in 'ordinary' markets. So, in spite of the obvious importance of market culture in India, there were very few studies by sociologists and anthropologists which delineated the sorts of cultural practices displayed in Indian markets. Until recently, Ostor's study of bazaars in Bengal could be considered an exception (Ostor 1984). Nevertheless, new research has now been undertaken in this domain (cf., for example, Carrithers and Humphreys 1991; Cadene and Vidal 1997). The other dominant tendency in economic anthropology was to consider consumption and the use of objects largely in terms of their symbolic meaning rather than their utilitarian use. It is only recently that the importance of consumption in the making of social identities has been highlighted in different case studies (Appadurai 1986; Breckenridge 1993). For example, Emma Tarlo's study of the clothing choices made by different groups in India highlights the symbolic importance of consumption practices (Tarlo 1996).

Such works undoubtedly give new insights into a previously neglected domain; but it is also interesting to reflect on the reasons for this sudden interest in consumption in the social sciences.[3] A historical comparison may be helpful here. William Reddy has shown, for example, that until the second half of the eighteenth century, market people in France possessed considerable expertise concerning the goods in which they dealt but had very little interest in how these goods were produced (Reddy 1986). Nevertheless, in the few decades which preceded the French Revolution, new attitudes developed and market people started taking a strong interest in the details of production they had happily ignored until then. Reddy argues that this apparently small change was part of a larger cultural shift which was to completely transform the existing perceptions of the economic process; and this cultural shift took place before any technological transformation had occurred. The question is, might the sort of demonstration that Reddy makes for eighteenth-century France be helpful for understanding contemporary trends? Is it not the case that another cultural shift of similar importance is taking place today in the economic field? But while, in eighteenth-century Europe, the consequence was to affirm the link between the market and production, today it is to reinforce the link between the market and consumption.

Conclusion: Towards an Anthropological Study of Markets

To summarize, the study of markets in the social sciences has long been dominated by two perspectives: the dominant tendency, especially among economists, to analyse the functioning of the market in a formalist manner, leaving little space for sociological or historical considerations, and a counter-tendency, especially among sociologists and anthropologists, to dismiss the abstract model of the market because of its ideological content and to focus on the destructive characteristic of the market economy. However, in the case of India, what was fundamentally lacking was the attempt to reformulate the analysis of markets on the basis of Indian material. As far as economists and economic historians were concerned, the question was rather to know which of the existing frames of analysis Indian markets could better illustrate. Whilst attempts to impose a neoclassic frame were few,[4] there was much discussion concerning the exact nature of the Indian economy at different stages of its history, especially from a Marxist point of view.[5] Whilst most sociologists shared the same debates and sometimes the same perspective as economists (Breman 1985) the majority of anthropologists simply ignored the existence of the market altogether because it did not fit their idea of India.

There has, nevertheless, been an important renewal of interest in the anthropology of markets in the last two decades. This interest has taken two directions. On the one hand, the study of networks came to play a central role in the study of markets both in non-western and in western contexts. On the other hand, diverse notions and interpretations of the market—including academic ones—have ceased to be perceived either as pure ideologies in the Marxist sense or as more or less adequate representations of the 'real world'. Finally, a few sociologists and anthropologists attempted to contextualize interpretations of 'the market' and to study how people were using such interpretations (Carrier 1997). It was, in a way, only to be expected. This is, after all, what they have done for most institutions they have studied in different cultures.

One of the main strengths of the new sociological perspective on markets is that it should help definitively to dissolve the false dichotomy which has survived for so long between the study of markets in the West and non-West. On the one hand, it enables us to recognize the discontinuities in the progress of market culture in the West. On the other hand, it helps us also to recognize the exaggerated nature of the civilization gap assumed by the distinction between market economy and all other forms of economic organization. As a result, recent advances in economic sociology of the market are no more confined to western economies as the two collective volumes edited by Stuart Plattner and by Roy Dilley show (Dilley 1992). The study of Indian markets is playing an increasing role in this wider process. Kaushik Basu points out:

> A developing country provides a fascinating range of institutions. A lot of these remains unexplored because these phenomena are not of primary interest to economists in developed countries and economists in developing nations have a tendency to choose their research agenda from ongoing themes published in the major journals of developed countries [Basu 1994: 115].

In economic sociology and economic anthropology, this trend is slowly being reverted.

ENDNOTES

1. For an anthropological evaluation of this school, cf. Harris et al. 1995.
2. For another interpretation of bazaar transactions in India, cf. Panselow 1990.
3. For one critical interpretation of this trend, see Carrier and Heyman 1997.
4. For an exception, see M.D. Morris 1967.
5. For a critical assessment of these debates, see Subrahmanyam 1994 and 1996.

REFERENCES

Aggarwal, B.L., ed. 1989. *Alternative Economic Structures*. Delhi: Allied Publishers.

Appadurai, A., ed. 1986. *The Social Life of Things: Commodities in Cultural Perspective*. Cambridge: Cambridge University Press.

Basu, K. 1989. 'Limitations of the Free Market: Conjectures, Customs and Norms'. In B.L. Agarwal, ed., *Alternative Economic Structures, 51–5*. Delhi: IAS and Allied Publishers.

———. 1994. *Of People, of Places: Sketches from an Economist's Notebook*. Delhi: Oxford University Press.

Bates, R.H. 1995. 'Social Dilemmas and Rational Individuals: An Assessment of the New Institutionalism'. In J. Harris, J. Hunter and M. Lewis, eds, *The New Institutional Economics and Third World Development, 27–48*. London: Routledge.

Bayly, C.A. 1983. *Rulers, Townsmen and Bazaars: North Indian Society in the Age of British Expansion, 1770–1870*. Cambridge: Cambridge University Press.

Bloch M. and Parry, J. ed. 1989. *Money and the Morality of Exchange*. Cambridge: Cambridge University Press.

Breckenridge, C.A. ed. 1993. *Consuming Modernity: Public culture in contemporary India*. Delhi: Oxford University Press.

Breckenridge, C.A. P. and Van der Veer, eds 1994. *Orientalism and the Postcolonial Predicament*. Delhi: Oxford University Press.

Breman, J. 1985. *Of Peasants, Migrants and Paupers: Rural Labour Circulation and Capitalist Production in West India*. Delhi: Oxford University Press.

Cadène, P. and D. Vidal, eds. 1997. *Webs of Trade*. Delhi: Manohar Publishers.

Carrier, J.G. ed., 1997. *Meanings of the Market: The Free Market in Western Culture*. Oxford: Berg

Carrier, J.G. and J.M.C. Heyman. 1997. 'Consumption and Political Economy'. *Journal of the Royal Anthropological Institute* (n.s.). 3:355–73.

Carrithers, M. and C. Humphreys, eds. 1991. *The Assembly of Listeners: Jains in Society*. Cambridge: Cambridge University Press.

Chakravarty, S. 1993. 'Prologue: Economics as Seen by a Dissenting Economist'. In *Selected Economic Writings*. Delhi: Oxford University Press.

Chandra, B. 1966. *The Rise and Growth of Economic Nationalism in India*. Delhi: People's Publishing House.

Chaudhuri, K.N. 1994. 'Markets and Traders in India during the Seventeenth and Eighteenth Century'. In S. Subrahmanyam, ed., *Money and the Market in India 1100–1700,* Delhi: Oxford University Press.

Dilley, R., ed. 1992. *Contesting Markets; Analyses of Ideology, Discourse and Practice*. Edinburg; Edinburg University Press.

Douglas, M.and B. Isherwood. 1978. *The World of Goods*. Harmondsworth: Penguin.

Drèze, J. and Amartya Sen. 1995. *India: Economic Development and Social Opportunity*. Delhi: Oxford University Press.

Dumont, L. 1970. *Homo Hierarchicus: The Caste System and Its Implications*. London: Weidenfeld and Nicholson.

Fuller, C.J. 1989. 'Misconceiving the Grain Heap: A Critique of the Concept of the Indian Jajmani System'. In M. Bloch, and J. Parry, eds, *Money and the Morality of Exchange, 33–63*. Cambridge: Cambridge University Press.

Geertz, C. 1992. 'The Bazzar Economy: Information and Search in Peasant Marketing'. In M. Granovetter and R. Swedberg, eds, *The Sociology of Economic Life*, 225–32. Boulder: Westview Press

Gell, A. 1986. 'Newcomers to the World of Goods: Consumption among the Muria Gonds'. In A. Appadurai, ed., *The Social Life of Things: Commodities in Cultural Perspective*, 110–38. Cambridge: Cambridge University Press.

Granovetter, M. 1992. 'Economic Action and Social Structure: The Problem of Embeddedness'. In M. Granovetter and R. Swedberg, eds, *The Sociology of Economic Life*, 53–81. Boulder: Westview Press.

Granovetter, M. and R. Swedberg, ed. 1992. *The Sociology of Economic Life*. Boulder: Westview Press.

Habib, I. and T. Raychaudhury, eds. 1982. *The Cambridge Economic History of India*, vol. 1 (c.1200–c1750). Delhi: Orient Longman.

Hardiman, D. 1987. *The Coming of the Devi: Adivasi Assertion in Western India*. Delhi: Oxford University Press.

———. 1996. *Feeding the Baniya: Peasants and Usurers in Western India*. Delhi: Oxford University Press.

Harper, E.B. 1959. 'Two Systems of Economic Exchange in Village India'. *American Anthropologist*. 61:760–78.

Harris, J., J. Hunter and M. Lewis, eds. 1995. *The New Institutional Economics and Third World Development*. London: Routledge.

Harriss-White, B. 1995. 'Maps and Landscapes of Grain Markets in South Asia'. In J. Harris, J. Hunter and M. Lewis, eds, *The New Institutional Economics and Third World Development*, 87–108. London: Routledge.

———. 1996. *A Political Economy of Agricultural Markets in South India*. New Delhi: Sage Publications.

Hobsbawm, E. and T. Ranger, eds. 1983. *The Invention of Traditions*. Cambridge: Cambridge University Press.

Kahn, J.S. 1997. 'Demons, Commodities and the History of Anthropology'. In J.G. Carrier, ed., *Meanings of the Market*, 69–99. Oxford: Berg.

Kolff, D.H.A. 1990. *Naukar, Rajput & Sepoy: The Ethnohistory of the Military Labour Market in Hindustan, 1450–1850*. Cambridge: Cambridge University Press.

Lachaier, P. 1977. 'The Merchant Lineage Firm and the Non-Invisible Hand: Pune, Maharashtra'. In P. Cadène and D. Vidal, eds, *Webs of Trade*, 23–52. Delhi: Manohar Publishers.

Mauss, M. 1970. *The Gift*. London: Cohen and West.

Morris, M.D. 1967. 'Values as an Obstacle to Economic Growth in South Asia: An Historical Survey'. *Journal of Economic History*. 27(4).

Ostor, A. 1984. *Culture and Power: Legend, Ritual, Bazaar and Rebellion in a Bengali Society*. New Delhi: Sage Publications.

Parry, J. 1989. 'On the Moral Perils of Exchange'. In M. Bloch and J. Parry, eds, *Money and the Morality of Exchange*, 64–93. Cambridge: Cambridge University Press.

Pocock, D.F. 1969. 'Notes on *jajmani* relationships'. *Contributions to Indian Sociology*, 6:78–95.

Polanyi, K.1957. *The Great Transformation: The Political and Economic Origins of Our Time*. Boston: Beacon Press.

Polanyi, K. 1992. 'The Economy as Instituted Process'. In M. Granovetter and R. Swedberg, eds, *The Sociology of Economic Life,* 29–52. Boulder: Westview Press.

Polanyi, K., C.M. Arensberg, and H.W. Pearson, eds. 1957. *Trade and Market in the Early Empires.* Glencoe: The Free Press.

Reddy, W.M. 1986. 'The Structure of a Cultural Crisis: Thinking about Cloth in France before and after the Revolution'. In A. Appadurai, ed., *The Social Life of Things: Commodities in Cultural Perspective,* 261–84. Cambridge: Cambridge University Press.

Stein, B. and S. Subrahmanyam, eds. 1996. *Institutions and Economic Change in South Asia.* Delhi: Oxford University Press.

Sombart, W. 1967. *Luxury and Capitalism:* Ann Arbor: University of Michigan Press.

Subrahmanyam S. ed. 1994. *Money and the Market in India 1100–1700.* Delhi: Oxford University Press.

Subrahmanyam S. 1996. 'Institutions, Agency and Economic Change in South Asia: A Survey and Some Suggestions'. In B. Stein and S. Subrahmanyam, eds, *Institutions and Economic Change in South Asia,* 14–47. Delhi: Oxford University Press.

Tarlo, E. 1996. *Clothing Matters: Dress and Identity in India.* Delhi: Viking.

———. 1997. 'The Genesis and Growth of a Business community: A Case Study of Vaghri Street Traders in Ahmedabad'. In P. Cadène & D. Vidal, eds, *Webs of Trade,* 53–84. Delhi: Manohar Publishers.

Taussig, M. 1980. *The Devil and Commodity Fetishism in South America.* Chapel Hill: The University of North Carolina Press.

Veblen, T. 1967. *The Theory of the Leisure Class.* New York: Penguin.

Vidal, D. 1997. 'Rural Credit and the Fabric of Society in Colonial India: Sirohi District, Rajasthan'. In P. Cadène and D. Vidal, eds, *Webs of Trade,* 85–107. Delhi: Manohar Publishers.

Williamson, O.E. and S.G. Winter, eds. 1993. *The Nature of the Firm; Origins, Evolution and Development.* New York: Oxford University Press.

Wiser, W.H. 1958. *The Hindu Jajamani System.* Lucknow: Lucknow Publishing House.

Zelizer, V.A. 1992. 'Human Values and the Market: The Case of Life Insurance and Death in 19th-Century America'. In M. Grandovetter, and R. Swedberg, eds, *The Sociology of Economic Life,* 285–304. Boulder: Westview Press.

Decentralization and the Poor

Pranab Bardhan

After fifty years of Independence it is a matter of national shame that India is the largest single-country contributor to the number of extremely poor and illiterate people in the world. As we approach a billion in our total numbers, more than one-third of the population live at a consumption level below even the crude minimum poverty line of government statistics. Nearly half of the adults are illiterate. One in nine babies born alive dies before its fifth birthday; half the children under age 5 are underweight.

While not denying that there has been significant progress over the last five decades, economists try to explain this miserable performance in various ways. One way is to suggest that until recently the overall growth rate of the economy has been rather low, due largely to a policy regime of controls, regulations, and an overextended state that stifled individual initiative and hampered productive efficiency. This meant that there were very few resources to trickle down to the poor. Others suggest that the state did not do enough for the poor in terms of direct poverty-alleviation programmes, aid in employment, credit, food security, health, education, etc. Yet a very large part of the over-extension of the state in the economy has been explicitly in the name of the poor, and even direct anti-poverty programmes (like the Integrated Rural Development Programme, Jawahar Rozgar Yojana, the Public Distribution System for food, expenditures for primary and secondary education, and public health and sanitation) absorb a substantial part of government budget both at central and state levels each year. Why did the poor not derive commensurate benefits? The answer to this question may have much to do with our governance structure at local level, and that is why the issue of decentralization is so important.

For a long time, development planners, often in isolation from the masses for whom and on whose behalf they plan, have devised elaborate schemes for the centralized state to uplift people from poverty. State-designed and directed technocratic development projects, which do not involve people but simply treat them as recipient objects of the development process, have not always been successful. In spite of the best intentions of the designers and the directors, such projects have often ended up primarily as conduits of largesse for elite groups—middlemen, contractors, officials, politicians, and favoured special interest groups—with little reaching the intended beneficiaries. Even when a significant amount did reach these people the benefits were sometimes of the wrong kind. These benefits were technologically and environmentally inappropriate, unsustainable, were corrosive of local institutions of community bonding and self-help. Thus development planners usually left untapped, the large reservoir of local potential, initiative, and information.

On account of its many such failures the centralized state has lost a great deal of legitimacy in recent years. Liberal economists, i.e. those who point to the inefficiencies and injustices of the regulatory and intrusive state, highlight the importance of the market as a coordinating mechanism in a decentralized system of numerous individual economic decisions. But an increasing and diverse body of social thinkers (including many social anthropologists, post-modernist cultural critics, Gandhian anarchists, small-is-beautiful populists, grassroots environmental activists, and supporters of the cause of indigenous peoples and technologies)—in the absence of a better unifying name, I shall call them anarcho-communitarians—take a position that is both anti-market and anti-(centralized) state: their common cause is to defend the small producers and local communities against the onslaught of both large-scale capitalism and the modernizing, bureaucratic nation-state. The emphasis on decentralization in the sense of devolution of central decision-making power and an instantiation of local self-government provides a meaningful way out of the bipolar state-versus-market debates that often dominate studies of political economy. On the other hand, the anarcho-communitarians sometimes tend to romanticize the value of decentralized development and overlook many problems the poor may face in a self-governing local community. In this chapter I discuss some of the strengths and weaknesses of decentralization, keeping the poor in the local community as the focus of my analytical enquiry.

II

I begin by enumerating the advantages of decentralization in the sense of devolution. In a closely interactive local community such devolution places decision-making in the hands of those who have information that outsiders lack, an incentive advantage qualitatively similar to that enjoyed by the market mechanism over the state. Local information can often identify cheaper and more appropriate ways of providing public services, apart from getting a better fit for locally diverse preferences (or getting rid of uniformity constraints in service delivery that a centralized supplier is sometimes compelled to adopt). In remote regions of poor countries, decentralization also provides a more effective channel of transmitting (and acting upon) early warnings about problems which might develop into disasters (droughts, epidemics, etc.).

While sharing with the market mechanism the same advantage in mobilizing localized information, a self-governing local community can sometimes be superior to the market in coordination and enforcement. Markets may fail as a coordination mechanism when private information renders individual market contracts incomplete or unenforceable. One example of this is the situation of what are called moral hazard and adverse selection in credit and insurance markets, when without adequate collateral against loan-default risks or the ability to convincingly signal their true risk status, the poor are often left out of such market. In such cases a local community, if it has a stable membership and well-developed structures of transmission of private information and norms among the members, and if it has the power of social sanctions (or political sanctions of the local government), has the potential of providing a more efficient coordination device. Examples are provided by the widely cited success stories of the Grameen Bank in Bangladesh (where small groups of poor women take joint responsibility for repayment of loans and thus assuage the information and monitoring problems that the lenders facing default risks worry about) and SEWA in Gujarat (where the local women's organization provides peer monitoring in enforcing loan repayment and also insures the poor self-employed borrower against health-related income risks that impair such repayment).

It may, of course, be asked why a central government cannot procure for itself the informational advantage of proximity by hiring local agents. In some countries the central government uses such representatives at local level (like the 'préfets' in France and Italy or the 'intendentes' in Chile) for this purpose. It may even be argued that the central government can have economies of scope in the collection of information. But the main reason why in practice the local government still retains the informational advantage has to do with political accountability. In democratic countries, the local politicians may have more incentive to use local information than would national or provincial politicians, since the former are answerable to the local electorate while the latter have wider constituencies (where the local issues may get diluted).

If, in an otherwise democratic country, the institutions of local democracy and local accountability are weak—as in large parts of north India—problems such as absenteeism of salaried teachers in village public schools and of doctors in rural public health clinics are commonly observed. The villagers are usually aware of the problem but do not have the institutional means of correcting it because under the insufficiently decentralized system state-funded teachers and doctors are not answerable to the villages. On the other hand, in non-democratic China, the local Communist Party officials have sometimes been quite responsive to local needs (at least as long they are not conflicting with the Party's programme), as the comparative study of two villages in China and India by Drèze and Saran (1993) shows in the context of China's far better performance in the provision of primary education at local level. (Similar accounts are available of more effective public pressure in rural basic education and health services in Cuba compared to some of the more democratic regimes in Latin America.) There are, of course, many authoritarian countries where local accountability is completely absent and the situation is much worse than in north India.

In parts of India (like Karnataka), a relatively effective decentralization has significantly improved the attendance of schoolteachers in recent years and, in general, so has the speed and quality of official response to popular pressure and appeals areas as well. This is discussed by Crook and Manor (1994) in their comparative study of the performance of decentralized governments in Karnataka, Bangladesh, Cote d'Ivoire, and Ghana. Of these four cases they find the responsiveness to be the best in Karnataka. They explain this not so much in terms of popular participation levels (in their Bangladesh case the participation levels were slightly better), but in terms of effective systems of democratic accountability, a good administrative and financial resource situation, and a well-established party system and free press—one or more of which was lacking in the other three cases.

Accountability usually brings responsibility in decision making and in implementation, which helps in improving quality and cost-efficiency. There is some scattered evidence of such quality improvement and cost savings (see *World Development Report 1994* on Infrastructure). In Mexico under the municipal fund project introduced in 1990, community committees (Comites de Solidaridad) manage rural investment in simple infrastructures such as small water supply systems, rural roads and bridges, and school buildings. Studies have found that these projects often cost one-half to two-thirds as much as similar projects managed by state or federal agencies. A review of World Bank data for forty-two developing countries found that where road maintenance was decentralized backlogs were lower and the condition of roads better. Data for a group of developing countries reveal that per capita costs of water in World Bank-funded water projects are four times higher in centralized than in fully decentralized systems. A study of 121 completed rural water-supply projects, financed by various agencies, showed that projects with high participation in project selection and design were much more likely to have the water supply maintained in good condition than would be the case with more centralized decision making.

In most of the examples discussed in the preceding paragraphs, decentralization with local accountability improves service in publicly supplied facilities. But such decentralization may also help in resolving collective action problems in the management of common-property resources and in avoiding the so-called tragedy of the commons. The daily livelihood of the poor, particularly in rural areas, depends vitally on local environmental resources like forestry, grazing, irrigation, and fisheries. The local commons also provide an elementary insurance function for poor peasants, for example as a fallback food and fodder source in bad crop years. With the erosion of the local commons—decimation of forests and grazing lands, silting and increasing toxicity of rivers and tanks, depletion of aquifers, and soil erosion and desertification—the life of the rural poor in many parts of the world has become in some ways more insecure and impoverished. Many of these countries have actually had a long history of balanced resource management under highly informal local-community arrangements. The erosion of the local commons set in only with the major demographic and institutional changes of recent years; they were often accelerated by private commercialization or bureaucratic appropriation of the traditional historical rights of local communities over these resources.

It is commonly suggested in economics that these problems of overuse and degradation of environmental resources primarily reflect the lack of well-defined private-property rights in these local common-pool resources. Private-property rights can certainly go a long way in reducing uncertainty in interaction among agents and in inducing them to conserve resources and internalize externalities. But privatization of these common resources often implies disenfranchisement of the poor: from the enclosure movement in English history to the current appropriations of forests and grazing lands in developing countries by timber merchants and cattle ranchers, it has been the same sad story.

Although privatization has its problems, nationalization of the local commons and their management by a distant bureaucracy is rarely any better, and in some cases it is actually much worse. It leads to insufficient utilization of local information and initiative. As ineffective or corrupt government supervision replaces traditional control structures, a common property resource can become a hunting ground for overexploitation and malfeasance by influential interest groups, and an object of predation by even formerly responsible, now dispossessed, local users. The widespread depletion and degradation of the commons in many poor countries where they were taken over by the colonial and post-colonial governments bear testimony to the ravages of this system.

Contrary to the popular belief of many economists of the property-rights school and that of many bureaucrats eager to protect tribals and other illiterate villagers from their own irresponsibilities, there are several documented examples of successful and autonomous local-community-level cooperation in management of common-property resources (see Ostrom 1990). There are, of course, more numerous cases of the failure of such cooperation in poor countries, leading to an anarchical regime in the scramble for common resources. In recent years there have been a number of studies (see Bardhan 1984: chapter 16, 1993; Wade 1987; Ostrom 1990; and Baland and Platteau 1995) trying to understand the conditions working for and against sustainability of local cooperation on the commons. It is generally agreed that cooperation works better in small groups with similar needs and clear boundaries, and shared norms and patterns of reciprocity. In such communities monitoring is easier, the 'common-knowledge' assumption of strategic cooperation (in models of repeated games) is likely to be more valid, and sanctions are easier to implement through reputation mechanisms and social multiplex relationships of face-to-face communities. It is clear that decentralization in the sense of devolution of power to such local communities may succeed in regulating, conserving, and maintaining these common resources in areas where centralized bureaucratic systems have clearly failed.

Even limited decentralization in the sense of delegation of implementation tasks to local-level agencies can make a difference. Wade (forthcoming) points to interesting contrasts between the modes of operation of the Korean irrigation bureaucracy (under an authoritarian regime in the recent past) and the Indian, and the clearly more effective performance of the former. The Indian canal systems are large, centralized hierarchies in charge of all functions (operations and maintenance as well as design and construction). Their ways of operation (including promotion and transfer rules for officials, rules designed to minimize identification between the irrigation patrollers and local farmers, and the frequent use of low-trust management and supervision methods) and source of finance (most of the irrigation department's budget comes in the form of a grant from the state treasury) are totally insensitive to the need for developing and drawing upon what Putnam (1993) and others have called local 'social capital'.

In Korea there are functionally separate organizations in the canal systems. The implementation and routine maintenance tasks (as opposed to policy making and technical design work) are delegated to the Farmland Improvement Associations, one per catchment area, which are staffed by local part-time farmers (selected by the village chiefs), who are knowledgeable about changing local conditions, largely dependent for their salary and operational budget on the user fees paid by the farmers, and continually drawing upon local trust relationships. Korea at this time did not have a democratic political regime or a free press, but farmers were better informed about and had better access to the local irrigation organization. This is one more example that there is no one-to-one relationship between the strength of democracy at national political level and that of institutions of accountability at local level.

III

Some of the common arguments in favour of decentralization have been discussed in the previous section. But there are many reasons why it often fails, making some form of central control necessary, even in the case of goods or services whose spatial characteristics do not encompass the whole country (like national defence or money supply). The major trade-off is, on the one hand, between the need for policy coordination at some central level when there are economies of scale and of scope and interjurisdictional externalities, and, on the other, for local information and accountability. The importance of the two sides in this trade-off varies from case to case, and it is difficult to pass generic judgement on the appropriate extent of decentralization without looking into the empirical details of each case.

There are very few studies of scale economies in the supply of local public services. For many local public goods it is unlikely that the optimum scale in production exceeds a reasonably sized local jurisdiction, and so one may not require a national or provincial administration to utilize the scale economies. On the other hand, a proliferation of agencies in multiple jurisdictions sometimes unnecessarily increases overhead and administrative costs. A decentralized administration of education, for example, may make it difficult to reap scale economies in curriculum development, textbook production, examinations, teacher training, etc. A related point is that some degree of centralization is necessarily involved in setting national standards and defining minimum requirements in areas like education and health. Local consumers should definitely have some say, but they are not always the best judges of quality, particularly when merit goods are involved, and local public providers of these goods may have an incentive to hide their low standards. There are large fixed costs in setting up organizations that serve as quality watchdogs, which often only the central government can afford. Centrally supported but locally controlled projects should, therefore, have built-in provisions for periodic renewals contingent on independent evaluation of performance quality.

Similarly, there are agglomeration economies in attracting qualified people in bureaucracies. In most countries central bureaucracies attract better talent (sometimes with better reward structure, career paths, and diversity of tasks), and a pool of talent draws others through the usual self-reinforcing mechanisms of human capital externalities emphasized in recent growth theory. In many developing countries the quality of staff in local bureaucracies (including accounting and record keeping) is very low, hampering their technical and institutional capacities; even more professional and technical people suffer from the disadvantages of isolation, poor training, and low interaction with other professionals. As Bird (1995) puts it simply information asymmetry thus works both ways: the central government may not know *what* to do; the local government may not know *how* to do it.

Of course, this problem is of differential importance in different services. Providing for street cleaning or garbage collection may not require sophisticated expertise, but power production and transmission, bulk supply of clean water, and public sanitation do. Decentralization will often work better in the former kind of services than in the latter. It has also been pointed out that sometimes centralized systems use unnecessarily expensive services of specialized technicians. For some of the basic needs for poor people, local youths with minimum training as primary health workers or primary-school teachers can be adequate. In other, more technical, projects, there is a lot of scope for improving access to engineering, project design, and administrative skills.

Supra-local coordination may also be necessary in the case of interjurisdiction externalities, which the local authorities may be unable and sometimes even unwilling to cope with. In cases of positive externalities across localities there may, for example, be underinvestment in infrastructural facilities (say, in road building or labour training), the benefits of which spill over to other communities. In cases of negative externalities local control mechanisms may be inadequate as, for example, upstream deforestation causes flooding and soil erosion in downstream communities.

Supra-local intervention and involvement are also necessary for credit and insurance. In an agricultural community, for example, risks are often covariate, requiring a pooling of risks with other geographically distinct communities for insurance purposes. Covariate risks coupled with seasonal synchronicity in demand for credit make the development of locally based rural deposit banking or credit cooperatives difficult. Without territorial diversification and supra-local coordination in credit and insurance functions, local community organizations can remain desperately vulnerable. Traditional community risk-coping strategies (like kinship networks, gift exchange, seasonal migration, and private remittances) are highly imperfect substitutes, and requisite adjustments can be costly for efficiency and innovations.

It has often been observed that in developing countries the problem of corruption afflicts local governments more than national governments. We know from the recent literature on corruption (see, for example, Shleifer and Vishny 1993) that decentralized corruption can be more costly in terms of efficiency than centralized corruption, as the former system fails to internalize the (negative) externalities of one bribe transaction on another. The concept of decentralization used in this literature is somewhat wider in terms of economic agency than that used in the literature on political and administrative decentralization, but the logic can be applied to this context. Applying the same logic to the general case of rent seeking, one can say that decentralization may lead to larger subsidies for the economy as a whole, as the lobby for subsidy in each locality does not take into account the effects of the lobbies of other localities—this is an example of what in the theoretical literature in political economy is called a common agency problem. It is likely, for instance, that the massive government subsidy in the form of electricity or water underpricing in India would have been somewhat less if it were centrally rather than regionally determined.

A major reason for higher local corruption may be the fact that arm's-length relationships among the various parties involved (officials, politicians, contractors, and interest groups) are much more scarce at local level. One of the central results of the literature on collective action is that small group size and proximity help collective action. Collusions are thus easier to organize and enforce in proximate groups, risks of being caught and reported are easier to manage, and the multiplex interlocking social and economic relationships among the local influential people act as formidable barriers to entry into these cosy rental havens. In rent seeking at national level there is more competition; 'capture' of central-government institutions is more difficult as the local mafia of different regions neutralize one another to some extent. On account of more competition at the central level there are also more institutional mechanisms for checks and balances in place. These include not only the various constitutional forms of separation of powers and adjudicatory systems in some countries, but also more regular auditing of public accounts, which is often absent or highly ineffective at local level.

There is clearly some tension here between local accountability and the increased possibility of local-level collusion in corruption. This is why in the Indian administrative system, even with the recent attempts at decentralization (following upon the 73rd and 74th Constitutional Amendments), there is much more concern for accountability upwards (that is to the higher-up funding authority) than downwards to the local people, and the financial autonomy of the local bodies is severely restricted. It is, however, arguable that when institutions of local democracy are firmly in place (they are not in many parts of India), along with a vigorous opposition party and free press, the political process is more transparent and the theft of funds and the sale of influence become more visible compared to the system of centralized corruption. This, as Crook and Manor (1994) point out on the basis of indirect but strong evidence in the case of Karnataka in south India, may reduce the overall amount of money and resources siphoned off through corruption. Even though there are more hands in the till, it is difficult for people to steal very much (in big central-government projects, on the other hand, a single transaction can yield very large bribes). But, ironically, on account of the increased openness and visibility of the system compared to the earlier centralized system, local people believed, often wrongly, that corruption has increased.

In many parts of India the recent attempts at devolution of power have been partly neutralized by state-government officials and politicians trying to retain their authority in the local bodies (for fear that they will lose their command over the local patronage network). This has also resulted in a great deal of dual authority structure and overlapping administrative jurisdictions at local level, observed in Gaiha's study (1996) of the *panchayats* in Uttar Pradesh, Maharashtra, and Karnataka. It seems that large-scale theft and corruption may be more effectively resisted if regular local elections to select representatives in the local bodies are supplemented by an institutionalized system of public hearings on items of major public expenditure. Some people have attributed the relative success of the decentralization experiments in parts of rural West Bengal to these public hearings in villages and small towns (apart from the influence of a relatively disciplined ruling party in restraining decentralized malfeasance). It is heartening to note that even in backward districts of Rajasthan a movement is growing (under the leadership of the Mazdoor Kisan Shakti Sangathan) for villagers to demand information in public hearings (*jan sunwayis*) about bills, vouchers, and muster rolls on development works. There is also some demand for repealing the Official Secrets Act of 1923 which officials usually cite as an excuse for not making information public.

The 'capture' problem discussed in the preceding paragraphs is more severe in cases of marked social and economic inequalities. It is possible to think of situations in which decentralization may leave the poor grievously exposed to the mercies of the local overlords and their malfeasance. There are certain fixed costs of organizing resistance groups or lobbies. As a result the poor may sometimes be more unorganized at local level than at the national level, where they can pool their organizing capacities. In these situations they may even occasionally be able to play a pivotal role in national coalitions and obtain the redistributive transfers that are in their favour under centralized systems. (In the history of the United States, for example, movements in favour of 'state rights', which diminish the power of the federal government, have often been interpreted as regressive, working against poor minorities.) Decentralization without adequate redistributive transfers also exacerbates inter-regional inequality, as localities with better endowments and infrastructure tend to do better (generating the usual centripetal forces of the growth process, analysed in the economic geography literature).

Finally, there are administrative imperatives for going beyond the usual centralization–decentralization dichotomy, as Prud'homme (1995) suggests. For many economic activities and services two or three levels of government have to be involved simultaneously, as each level of government will have different, but equally legitimate, interests and comparative advantages. Prud'homme gives the example of primary education: the local government can provide accountability to its specific needs; the regional government can have the economies of scale in designing curricula and correct for the inequities of local financing of schools; the central government can provide minimum quality standards and auditing and evaluation of local performance. The important task is to design mechanisms of cooperation among these three levels of government and to avoid unnecessary treading on one another's toes in overlapping jurisdictions and perverse incentives (like free-riding opportunities, leading to negligence of essential functions). To take an example from a different area, there have been some successful cases in India of joint management of forest resources between the central forest service and local community organizations. Another successful example of cooperation between central and local agencies is the Malawi Self-Help Water Project, which is one of the outstanding rural water projects in Africa.

Sometimes it may also be useful to have special single-purpose quasi-political government agencies (such as water districts or school boards) to which some functions of the local government may be delegated. At any level, if the government has too many tasks, while this may bring the benefit of internalizing the spillover of information across tasks, political accountability gets diluted, as the electorate has to judge a government in terms of its overall performance. On the other hand, special-purpose bodies may compete for the same resources and weaken a local government.

IV

The last two decades in China have shown some striking ways in which decentralization has unleashed the forces of rapid economic growth at local level, leading to unprecedented reductions in poverty, particularly in the coastal provinces. In particular, the dramatic success story of the township and village enterprises (TVE) in rural industry has important lessons for the economic theory of decentralization.

There is already a large and growing literature on the TVEs, and analysts differ considerably on the explanations of their success. I shall concentrate here on the incentive structures they face and their impact on economic performance. There are many variations among TVEs, but in general the control rights in these enterprises are vested in local government (see Wang and Chang 1994, and Che and Qian 1994). Even though they are thus in some sense public enterprises (and not entirely free from rent appropriation by bureaucrats and politicians), the crucial difference from the usual state-owned enterprises lies in the incentive structures they face. The three aspects of the institutional mechanism of the TVE that make a big difference are: (a) vigorous competition among the enterprises of different localities for the market (the local governments do not have the administrative authority and capacity to protect the enterprises by erecting barriers to keep out competition); (b) a hard budget constraint implemented by the higher-tier fiscal and credit authorities—unlike the state-owned enterprises the TVEs may go bankrupt and lay off workers, without any bail-out from above; and (c) residual claimancy status by which the enterprises and the local government keep much of the profits they make. Not all these aspects apply with equal force in the case of TVEs in different parts of China, but in the successful coastal provinces, the combination of these three aspects provides a decentralized incentive structure that compels local governments to be self-reliant and fiscally prudent and at the same time encourages them to 'get rich gloriously' (to cite Deng's famous maxim). Qian and Weingast (1994) call this system 'market-preserving federalism', which is rather unique among developing countries in its institutional mechanism of effective economic decentralization.

In many parts of the world, including India, while there have been isolated cases of somewhat effective decentralization, more often than not the mobilization of local resources has been difficult. Take the case of rural West Bengal in India, where under the leadership of a leftist government over the last eighteen years some institutions of genuine local democracy have struck roots, as noted earlier. But the main success so far has been with respect to the fact that sections of the rural poor have been mobilized to demand and acquire some of the benefits and subsidies flowing from the top, subsidies which in other Indian states are often misappropriated by the rich. The institutions of local democracy in West Bengal have so far not succeeded in mobilizing any significant amount of their own resources or in launching self-reliant cooperative projects of rural development.[1] The case of Chinese TVEs suggests that under appropriate incentive structures decentralized public authorities at local level can initiate projects of rural industrialization and raise resources for funding rural infrastructure from the resultant profits.

The market competition under which TVEs operate plays an important role here. Decentralized decision makers have an inherent bias (see Sah and Stiglitz 1986) for a general discussion of the architecture of economic systems) towards accepting too many bad projects (what is known as Type II error)—just as centralized hierarchies tend to reject too many good projects (Type I error)—and the market process directly help, in disciplining against Type II errors. (In India it is not uncommon to find the protagonists of decentralized development, who are otherwise opposed to state interventions, quite vocal in demanding centralized state protection of inefficient small-scale enterprises when they are threatened by market competition from the large units). But the most difficult part is for a decentralized democracy to credibly precommit to maintaining a hard budget constraint; when a publicly sponsored local enterprise is in danger of folding with hundreds or thousands of livelihoods at stake the pressure on democratic politicians for a bail-out is likely to be inexorable.

This is not to deny that there is considerable scope for mobilizing contributions from the intended beneficiaries of small, locally specific infrastructural projects when their consensus and involvement are sought early in the process of the formulation of the projects and when there is initial financial pump-priming on the part of the government. The usual problems of free ridership and the strategic (mis)revelation of preferences that are emphasized in the public economics texts are (or can be) limited in the case of most such local public goods in small communities. Even the poor who may not be able to contribute in cash are often willing to contribute labour and local materials for construction and maintenance. As Klugman (1994) shows a detailed survey of development resources and constraints in one of the better-administered sub-districts in Bangladesh, reveals that among those people who indicated their readiness to contribute to local developmental activities (about half the respondents), the poorer groups were more willing to do so that the better-off, provided that they did not have to carry a disproportionate share of the burden. The *World Development Report 1994*, cites examples from successful self-help initiatives in constructing suspension bridges in the Banglung district in Nepal, in constructing roads in Gurage villages in Ethiopia, and in supplying power in the village of Purang in Nepal's Mustang district. Similar examples from poor urban areas are provided by the Orangi project in a Karachi slum in Pakistan which mobilized self-help activities to co-finance and construct water, sanitation and other facilities, and in poor districts of Lima, Peru, by informal local community associations financing projects such as roads and sewerage by systems of informal taxation. People are often unwilling (even hostile) to contribute in the form of taxes or user fees if the services are poor, enforcement is weak, the funds are wasted or misappropriated, or the central government reneges on its promised contribution.

V

For far too long in developing countries large-scale technocratic development projects have been directed from above, administered by a distant, uncoordinated, and occasionally corrupt bureaucracy, insensitive to local community needs and concerns. These projects have not involved the local people and have instead simply treated them as objects of the development process. Vast sums of money have been spent in the name of the poor, but very little has actually reached them. Even when it does reach them it often perpetuates a cycle of dependency and an attitude of malfeasance and opportunism among the poor with an eye to milking the state cow for its uncertain bounties.

Many development practitioners are now coming around to the view that participation by the intended beneficiaries improves project performance considerably, although the case studies usually cited in favour of this view are not always econometrically convincing. The econometric objections to the claimed association between project participation and performance relate to the subjectivity in much of the data, investigator bias (as some of the investigators start with the prior belief that participation is good, it creates a 'halo effect' in their observations), and a simultaneity problem (better project performance may cause increased beneficiary participation rather than vice versa). In a rare and careful attempt to deal with these objections Isham, Narayan, and Pritchett (1995) show (on the basis of the 121 diverse rural water projects referred to in Section I), that the strong causal relation between participation and project performance still survives relatively unscathed. More such exercises for projects in other sectors are useful.

As mentioned at the beginning of the chapter, one should resist the temptation to romanticize the value of decentralized participatory development. We have already seen that such development, for all its undoubted advantages, cannot resolve some major equity and efficiency problems. In particular, in situations of elite domination in local governance structures, the percolation benefits to the weaker sections of the population will be slow and uncertain. This is so, for example, even in the case studies of decentralization (especially in

Karnataka) of Crook and Manor (1994). One can, of course, cite the cases of Indonesia and Taiwan where substantial decentralization of expenditures on social and economic infrastructure in recent years has contributed to a sharp decline in poverty, but such examples are more difficult to find from countries that are growing at a much slower rate.

If decentralization in the context of pre-existing inequality is of limited benefit to the poor, it may also be asked if inequality helps or hinders the cause of decentralization. In general, the complex relationship between socio-economic inequality and successful collective action in building self-governing institutions at local level is still an under-researched area in economics. On the one hand, there is the well-known suggestion of Olson (1965) that in a heterogenous group a dominant member enjoying a large part of the benefits of a collective good is likely to see to its provision even if he has to pay all of the cost himself (with the small players free-riding on the contribution of the large player). On the other hand, there are cases where the net benefits of coordination for each individual may be structured in such a way that in situations of marked inequality some individuals (particularly those with better exit options) may not participate. In this case, the resulting outcome may be more inefficient than in the case with greater equality.[2] Besides, the transaction and enforcement costs for some cooperative arrangements may go up with inequality.

Empirically, there is some fragmentary evidence[3] that community-level institutions work better in enforcing common agreements and cooperative norms when the underlying property regime is not too skewed and the benefits generated are more equitably shared. Putnam's (1993) study of the regional variations in Italy also suggests that 'horizontal' social networks (that is those involving people of similar status and power) are more effective in generating trust and norms of reciprocity than 'vertical' ones. One beneficial by-product of land reform, underemphasized in the usual economic analysis, is that such reform, by changing the local political structure in the village, gives more 'voice' to the poor and induces them to get involved in local self-governing institutions and management of local public goods. It is also arguable that the market discipline and the hard budget constraint that have contributed to the success of decentralized development in China (led by the TVEs) were rendered politically tolerable by the secure social safety net made possible by the highly egalitarian redistribution of private access to land that the post-1978 decollectivization has effectively implied for the rural population.

In this chapter the various advantages and disadvantages of decentralization and also the conditions that predispose toward success or failure in beneficial decentralized development have been discussed. In particular, I have focused on the argument that in governance structures control rights should be assigned to people who have the requisite information and incentives and at the same time will bear responsibility for the (political and economic) consequences of their decisions. In many situations this calls for more devolution of power to local authorities and communities (including the local citizens' right to information and public hearings on major projects of public expenditure). I have also attempted a balanced assessment of the efficiency and equity effects of such assignments of control rights and of how they operate differentially under different initial conditions. One should add that the analysis in this chapter suggests that a more nuanced theory of the state than is usually available from the age-old state-versus-market debate is needed. On the one hand, we should, of course, recognize the limitations of the state as an economic governance structure arising from its lack of access to local information and local accountability and its vulnerability to wasteful rent-seeking processes. On the other hand, the state is not to withdraw into its minimalist role of classical liberalism. Instead, it is to play an activist role in enabling (if only as a 'catalyst') mobilization of people in local participatory development, providing supra-local support in the form of pump-priming local finance and underwriting risks (but at the same time avoiding the moral hazard of encouraging dependency), supplying technical and professional services towards building local capacity, acting as a watchdog for service quality standards, evaluation and auditing, investing in larger infrastructure, and providing some coordination in the face of externalities across localities. This is a delicate but complex task for any state, underappreciated by the usual enthusiasts for decentralization.

ENDNOTES

1. In the last few years the West Bengal government has started an interesting experiment in local mobilization of resources in minor irrigation. There are now hundreds of small tubewell groups, where the beneficiaries (usually small and marginal farmers) have taken over the responsibility of financing the operations and maintenance of their public tubewells.

2. For a theoretical analysis on these lines, see Dayton-Johnson and Bardhan (1996).

3. See Bardhan (1993) for examples from local irrigation communities.

REFERENCES

Baland, J.M. and J.P. Platteau. 1995. *Halting Degradation of Natural Resources: Is There a Role for Rural Communities.* Oxford: Oxford University Press.

Bardhan, P. 1984. *Land, Labour and Rural Poverty: Essays in Development Economics.* New York: Columbia University.

———. 1993. 'Analytics of the Institutions of Informal Cooperation in Rural Development'. *World Development Report.* September. Delhi: Oxford University Press, World Bank.

Bird, R.M. 1995. 'Decentralising Infrastructure: For Good or For Ill?' In A. Estache, ed., *Decentralising Infrastructure: Advantages and Limitations.* World Bank Discussion Papers 290. Washinton D.C.: World Bank.

Che, J. and Y. Qian. 1994. 'Boundaries of the Firm and Governance: Understanding China's Township and Village Enterprises'. Unpublished paper. Stanford University.

Crook, R. and J. Manor. 1994. *Enhancing Participation and Institutional Performance: Democratic Decentralisation in South Asia and West Africa.* Report to Overseas Development Administration, UK

Drèze, J. and M. Saran. 1993. 'Primary Education and Economic Development in China and India: Overview and Two Case Studies'. Unpublished paper. London School of Economics.

Dayton-Johnson, J. and P. Bardhan. 1996. 'Inequality and Conservation on the Local Commons: A Theoretical Exercise'. *Department of Economics Working Paper.* Berkeley: University of California.

Estache, A., ed. 1995. *Decentralising Infrastructure: Advantages and Limitations.* World Bank Discussion Papers 290. Washington DC: World Bank.

Gaiha, R. 1996. 'Participation or Empowerment of the Rural Poor: The Case of the Panchayats in India'. Unpublished paper: Delhi.

Isham, J., D. Narayan, and L. Pritchett. 1995. 'Does Participation Improve Performance? Establishing Causality with Subjective Data'. *World Bank Economic Review.* May. 9(2):175–200.

Klugman, J. 1994. 'Decentralisation: A Survey of Literature from a Human Development Perspective'. *Human Development Report Office Occasional Papers* 13. New York: UNDP.

Olson, M. 1965. *The Logic of Collective Action.* Cambridge, Mass: Harvard University Press.

Ostrom, E. 1990. *Governing the Commons: The Evolution of Institutions for Collective Action.* New York: Cambridge University Press.

Prud'homme, R. 1995. 'The Dangers of Decentralisation'. *World Bank Research Observer.* August.

Putnam, R.D. 1993. *Making Democracy Work: Civic Traditions in Modern Italy.* Princeton: Princeton University Press.

Qian, Y. and B.R. Weingast. 1994. 'Beyond Decentralisation: Market-Preserving Federalism with Chinese Characteristics'. Unpublished paper. Stanford University.

Sah, R.K. and J.E. Stiglitz, 1986. 'The Architecture of Economic Systems: Hierarchies and Polyarchies'. *American Economic Review.*

Wade, R. 1987. *Village Republics: Economic Conditions for Collective Action in South India.* Cambridge: Cambridge University Press.

———. Forthcoming. 'How Infrastructure Agencies Motivate Staff: Canal Irrigation in India and the Republic of Korea'. In A. Mody, ed., *Infrastructure Strategies in East Asia.* EDI. World Bank, Washington D.C.

Wang, Y., and C. Chang. 1994. 'Towards a Model of the Organisations in China as a Partially Reformed Development Economy'. Unpublished paper. University of Minnesota.

World Development Report. 1994. Infrastructure for Development. September. Delhi: Oxford University Press, World Bank.

9

Political Institutions
and Processes

The chapters in this section provide an overview of political life in contemporary India. The authors have described the historical contexts in which political institutions developed, thus providing temporal depth to the understanding of important transformations taking place in this field. While many take it for granted today that the nation-state is the most 'natural' expression of collective political life, it is important to guard against a historical teleology of the kind favoured by nineteenth-century social science that placed the nation-state as the institutional expression of an enlightened rationality. It is also necessary to keep in mind that forms of sociality in contemporary India have a significant impact upon the way that the nation-state functions. Furthermore, while the power that the state exercises makes it imperative for other forms of collective and social life to come to terms with its form of rationality (and irrationality), we should not reduce all forms of politics to the politics of the nation-state.

The issue of location of political institutions is directly addressed in the chapter by Thomas Pantham who argues that the modernity of the nation-state in India was located not in a complete break from tradition but in its reconfiguration. The nationalist movement saw the post-colonial state as realizable only within a pluralistic, civic-communitarian nationalism rather than a Hindu nationalism. Pantham gives a historical account of the idea of kingship as contained in the texts on the *Shanti Parva* in the *Mahabharata* and the *Arthashastra* but it is clear that despite some attempts here and there, a systematic genealogy of how such notions may have impacted upon the notions of sovereignty of the modern state in India has not been achieved. Scholars of medieval India have attempted to show the transformation in the ideas of nation and state—especially in relation to the segmented state in the southern kingdoms and the emergence of patrimonial bureaucracy in Mughal India. Clearly these transformations did have an impact on political institutions and some of the arrangements may still be discernible in patterns of local governance, but it is not easy to show this in a systematic way because of the dominance of colonial archives in the historical research on India. In this sense, not only did the colonial state bring about significant ruptures in the forms of governance but also determined the trajectories of social science and historical research on these issues. It would appear that a rethinking on the relation between notions of sovereign power and disciplinary power as it worked out in the colonial and post-colonial scenarios in India is both, empirically and theoretically, one of the most challenging task before us. While the social sciences have responded to the threat of a majoritarian Hindu nationalism through important public-spirited debates on such issues as pluralism and secularism, a rethinking on how notions of sovereignty and discipline are deployed *together* in the shaping of the state invites serious philosophical, legal, and social science reflection. Pantham alludes to the importance of the Partition and the Emergency on the political culture of the country, but the impact of these important moments, constituted as 'breaks' on the everyday conduct of politics, has only now begun to be addressed.

Sudipta Kaviraj's chapter on democracy in India is very relevant in relation to this set of questions for he locates the working of democracy in India within the problematic of translation. He argues that democracy was not a simple western import and that while being receptive to western ideas about equality and justice, political thought in India combined this with a critique of individualism as the only value on which ideas of choice and consent could be based. Thus democratic ideals were infused with a sense of a community-oriented democratic set-up with questions about rights of communities becoming part of this discourse. Further, intellectuals in India were very much aware of the fact that the ideals of equality and justice, or for that matter of due process in law, were severely compromised in the colonies. However, this intellectual critique in itself would not have been sufficient to mount a serious challenge to the colonial regime. It was Gandhi's political strategy of combining the intellectual critique with mass mobilizatiion that gave the nationalist movement its power. Like Pantham, Kaviraj also emphasizes the importance of the idea of the cultural unity of India as made up of a pluralistic, layered form of nationalism. The legacy of the Congress Party, then, was not only the allegiance to a constitutional form of democracy but also the political style of compromise between antagonistic conceptions and interests.

Kaviraj's chapter gives a remarkable account of the complex patterns of change in the democratic institutions. The fourth general elections in 1967 saw the emergence of new political parties and the decline of the Congress. New and powerful lobbies such as the farmer lobby began to function through new political parties rather than as factions within the Congress—thus expanding the range of interests that found institutional expression in the political arena. Simultaneously, there was an abrogation of internal democracy within the Congress and subsequently within other parties. Kaviraj traces the rise of insurgency movements and a politics of confrontation to both institutional decline and the perpetual confrontationist attitude of the Congress under Indira Gandhi. The Emergency is seen as a watershed—it not only crystallized the way in which democratic processes and procedural rules could be abandoned in the political arena including in the functioning of bureaucracy; but also though it lasted only a brief period, the processes it brought out into the open, including the issue of political corruption, continue to haunt politics in India.

Pantham and Kaviraj both see the 1980s as a period of the rise of identity politics. Political parties came to be based more on ethnic, religious, or caste identity and less on associational ties. At one level, this has allowed political expression to groups that were hitherto suppressed and that could not find a voice in the earlier political structures. At another level, it gave an impetus to groups espousing a Hindu majoritarian state (in substance if not in form) and its counterpart—the rise of movements demanding separate territorial units as a part of self-determination that fed into fears of political fragmentation. Kaviraj's acute analysis, however, does not pose a simple dichotomy between politics of redistribution versus politics of recognition. In fact, the entire debate around reservations that followed the acceptance of the Mandal Commission Report by the V.P. Singh government was framed around caste politics that was being rhetorically fought on the issue of social justice. And while the question of caste is important in considering political formations, it is equally striking that in the demands for social justice no political party seems to have moved beyond reservations to mobilization for mass education or health. The politically blunt instrument of the mandate, as Kaviraj points out, is not sufficient for any electorate to get the policy decisions to its liking—yet if democracy fails to provide mechanisms to fulfil the specific expectations for redistribution, if it leaves a large populace out of the wealth that is created—then it fails to sustain the consent of the governed. Thus while democracy may have been successful in bringing conflicts out into the open, its legitimacy depends upon being able to generate consent that goes beyond the electoral mandate. To that extent the affinity between democratic institutions and institutions of the market has to go beyond formal mechanisms of choice to a more substantial engagement with questions of the meaning of belonging to a political collectivity for those whose economic survival is at stake.

While the first two chapters provide an important perspective on the nation-state and democracy from a macro perspective, Harold A. Gould's analysis of local-level/grassroots politics gives us an understanding of the complex entanglement of local-level intuitions with the processes of political mobilization and state building. The emergence of village studies in the 1960s generated impressive research on political formations at village level, identified as village-level factions that often cut across caste formations. These structures of local power interacted with formal institutions of village governance in complex ways. So, on the one hand, local-level concerns could get articulated through the penetration of new forms of politics into the village and, on the other hand, the political parties themselves were shaped by their need to align with such structures of local-level politics.

Electoral politics and mobilization at the level of the region led to the development of caste associations for articulation of demands in the political arena that resulted in the crystallization of *mega castes*. While on the surface it may appear that this was simply a continuation of traditional caste-based loyalties finding expression in the political arena, Gould argues that there was a subtle mixture of ascriptive traits of caste and sect with the traits usually associated with class. The historical analysis presented in his chapter demonstrates how legislative changes instituted by the colonial regime, beginning with the Morley-Minto reforms of 1909, led to communal differentiation. But Gould is careful to show that separate Muslim constituencies came into being equally in response to grassroots demands for redressing local disparities as the national-level rhetoric of that period. The enormous expansion of the electorate following introduction of universal franchise in independent India led to the politicization of every level of the political structure. The articulation between these different levels shows an enormous investment in democratic politics and provides support to the claims of Pantham and Kaviraj that democratic forms of governance are not simply imports from the West but are a result of the involvement of large sections of the population in shaping the politics of the country.

The articulation between different levels of politics is important for generating an understanding of the politics of reservation that has a long history in south India but gained salience in the public discourse at the national level only since the adoption of the Mandal Commission Report in the early 1990s. In his chapter on this issue, P. Radhakrishnan gives us an analysis of the changes in the size and composition of backward classes for these are not static categories. Although the various categories of caste formations defined as 'Scheduled Castes' and 'Backward Castes' were basically administrative categories defined for purposes of educational concessions and employment in the government, it is clear that different kinds of social actors came to have stakes in the politics of these categories. Thus one cannot assume a one to one correspondence between backward classes as legal, administrative, political, and social entities. Instead, discourse and practice in each sphere has impacted upon the formations in other spheres. Radhakrishnan gives an account of the evolution of policy with regard to reservations during the colonial period and also the experimentation with categories through processes of inclusion and exclusion in the vigorous legal pronouncements that have been part of the struggle of these groups for greater resources. Instead of the assumption that 'backwardness' is easily defined, courts have wrestled with the legal and constitutional issues with regard to who is to be included in this category and how claims of individual rights are to be balanced against claims for redressal of historical harms.

The legal battles around reservation have to be seen in the light of the political processes that led to the emergence of backward classes as a powerful political category. It is commonplace now that not all castes included under the rubric of backward castes or classes could be counted as backward if we took into account the local power structures in rural India. The increasing use of the political rhetoric of social justice and empowerment and the importance of vote banks account for the fact that no political party has been able to oppose reservations or to suggest limiting the beneficiaries of these provisions. The increasing use of global categories assimilates reservations to affirmative action despite significant differences. A comparative account of how reservations operate in different social settings has not been seriously attempted in India. For instance, the serious conflicts that have arisen between different sections of the Backward Castes in Bihar and the Scheduled Castes in Andhra Pradesh leading to court cases, or the political conflicts between Backward Castes and Dalits in regional politics, points to the complexity of the politics of representation. Yet the categories of forward/backward are deployed in political discourse as if these were self-evident categories. Finally, it is important to recognize that the politics of the dispossessed as evidenced in various social movements (including the Dalit movement) cannot be confined to the politics of reservation alone.

The study of social movements provides an important window into the everyday life of political communities. As Martin Fuchs and Antje Linkenbach suggest, social movements are increasingly seen as a regular part of social life rather than as cataclysmic events. They define social movements as rooted in an experience of difference from political society. Social groups that experience such difference come to be reflexively engaged in an active interpretation of their present with a view to re-imagining and shaping a different future. The authors demonstrate their theoretical points by concrete examples taken from four types of social movements—peasant movements, tribal movements, the Dalit movement—and the women's movement, in India. In each case there are common questions of similarity and difference, inclusion and exclusion, as well as issues pertaining to the specificity of the struggles that have engaged the participants of these movements.

As is well known, 'new social movements' have addressed issues ranging from the environment to domestic violence, thus expanding the scope of what is considered to be political action. Fuchs and Linkenbach show an acute sensitivity to the historical context of these movements in India—they draw attention to transformation of these movements rather than only to their 'newness'. Analysis of peasant movements has been haunted by the question of whether the conditions of agricultural production lead to the development of a unified peasant consciousness. The idea of the family farm as representative of the peasant mode of production has drawn sharp criticism in

India. Many historians have argued that the peasant movements in India are better analysed as lying on the intersection of other kinds of movements rather than as representing a consciousness that was formed primarily through engagement with conditions of agrarian production and surplus extraction. The role of Gandhi in mobilizing the peasantry as an essential strategy of the nationalist movement led to the formation of peasant organizations such as the *Kisan Sabhas*. It is interesting to see how the specific demands of the peasantry, such as the demand for reduction of taxes, were folded into protests against 'outsiders' such as the colonial state as well as against 'internal' oppressors such as corrupt moneylenders or local zamindars. In recent years the work of Subaltern historians has done much to make us aware that knowledge interests that assimilate all peasant politics in the colonial era to the nationalist movement are suspect. These historians have argued for an understanding of peasant politics (including peasant movements), not as adjuncts to other movements but as expressive of the role of the peasantry in both local and national politics. The attempt is to recover their consciousness, their voice in history.

Tribal movements in India have been cast in recent years in terms of 'clash of cultures'—many scholars have read millennial movements among tribal groups as attempts to articulate a tribal identity as distinct from the surrounding Hindu identity. Questions of similarity and difference haunt these movements too—for the social geography of tribal groups shows distinct differences between the tribal groups of the north-eastern region and those in central India or in the hill regions of the north. Added to this is a further caveat—experiences of tribal groups in south India have received less scholarly attention, so we do not know how questions of identity inform their politics. Finally, groups that were once identified as tribes such as the Jats in north India have slowly come to consider themselves as castes. Clearly there are divergent strategies and meanings of self-determination as far as different tribal groups are concerned. The emergence of the discourse of the rights of indigenous peoples in the global institutions has led to a further recasting of identity in cultural terms or in terms of an opposition between original inhabitants and later settlers—a distinction that is not easy to maintain in the Indian context. In contrast to the uses of the past to establish an authentic tribal identity, there are important concerns about the present among tribal populations that relate to developmental policies and projects such as the building of roads and large dams. These have often led to displacement of tribal groups so that there is a complex interweaving of demands for economic and social justice with demands for cultural rights. The ways in which the political arenas are defined also influences the language deployed—for instance the demand for a separate state in the Jharkand region was articulated and processed within the democratic structure of the country while movements for territorial autonomy by the Nagas or the Mizos whose tribal allegiances cut across the newly created post-colonial states of Burma (now Myanmar) and India were articulated in terms that involved actors across states. The maturity of the democratic institutions, as Kaviraj suggested in his chapter, would be reflected in their capacity to balance these different conceptions and interests. The record of the state in India has been mixed on these counts—demands for self-determination, instead of being treated as counters in the opening of a political conversation, have often been treated as signs of dissidence that require the use of force, leading to violation of human rights. This in turn gets entangled both with geopolitical interests that can use these movements for their own ends and with global institutions that monitor human rights and thus provide important resources for countering the power of the state. The social geography of these movements also shows that creation of borders is not a one-time process—rather border-making practices are ongoing and are deeply implicated in the making of modern states and citizenship.

The final two movements discussed in this chapter—the Dalit movement and the women's movement—have focused much more on issues of violence and the redefining of a sociality in which victims have to suffer humiliation in everyday life. Both these movements have relied on the evidence of experience and the presentation of life histories and narratives as a way of converting individual biographies into socially meaningful texts. Questions of representation have been central to these concerns. Rather than looking for political actors who would act on their behalf, both Dalits and women have taken positions of leadership in articulating their own demands and negotiating questions of similarity and difference within the movements. Another distinctive feature of these movements has been the focus on reform of everyday life. Thus the Dalit literature is not simply about political demands but about the cruelty of the everyday practices of caste. Similarly the women's movement aims to question the very basis of patriarchy to allow for different possibilities of defining gender, body, and sexuality. Yet similarity of aims in these general terms does not mean that these movements are allies in the political arena for discriminatory gender practices and domestic violence do not stop at the boundaries of the higher castes.

As the literature on social movements shows, society is always in a relation of non-identity to itself. Obviously if conflict is normal to society then the legal institutions in which claims and counterclaims can be settled are very important for the health of a democracy. Yet rule of law is not simply a question of an abstract allegiance of the *idea of rule of law*—it is also a question of how legal institutions function. Robert Moog's chapter examines law not as enshrined in the Constitution or in the body of opinions given by legal luminaries but in the way that it is encountered in everyday life in the practices of lower courts. He argues that scholars have paid relatively little attention to the functioning of lower courts—yet the delays, poor judgments, and pending cases at this level not only clog the system at the level of the upper courts but may also lead to disillusionment with the rule of law itself.

Although delays in settlement of legal disputes in India are fantastically notorious—there is a famous case on inheritance that lasted 745 years—in fact the number of people who use courts for the resolution of their problems is not large. Moog writes that the most extensive use of courts is by the government itself, which initiates a large percentage of cases. Even in other cases the courts are seen more as an arena in which one can harass political opponents or buy time, rather than as a means of conflict resolution. The judgements in lower courts often leave the door open for appeals and writs, thus overburdening the higher courts. In terms of a social audit it would be interesting to see how the functioning of the law folds into local-level conflicts. While Moog draws attention to some village-level studies, there is a tremendous gap in the literature on how courts are actually used in ongoing patterns of conflict within communities and institutions. Moog's plea is that the judiciary should be seen as an integral system and that studies of lower level courts are imperative for generating an understanding of the law in India. One hopes for closer attention to these processes in the coming years.

The final chapter in this section is on collective violence and contests the usual view that looks at violence as an aberrant phenomenon. Jonathan Spencer argues that violence occupies a curious position in social theory that has sanitized the violence of the trenches in the First World War, the Nazi concentration camps, and the bombing of Hiroshima and Nagasaki by treating it as *atypical* and hence outside the purview of normal politics. Social theory has relied upon a particular conceptualization of human nature that treats violence as an aberrant phenomenon. This is what accounts for the trope of horror with which violence makes its appearance in social theory and description.

In Spencer's formulation, the anthropology of violence is part of the new anthropology of the body—it shows how other people's ideas about violence, gender, and personhood can seriously undermine powerful western assumptions about human nature. Further, what is named as violence and what is not named as violence is itself evidence of the alignment of social theory with dominant western notions of governance and order. Spencer makes the innovative argument that violence and non-violence are coeval and interdependent and that the boundaries between violence and power, state and society, or official and private violence are fuzzy. Recent work on collective violence in south Asia demonstrates that what is at stake is not the moment of horror but the normal functioning of the state in which lines between legality and illegality are continuously blurred and violence is an ever-present possibility for resolution of conflict or for infliction of order. Thus instead of the residual place given to collective violence—that which belongs neither to the state nor to the domestic—Spencer's review urges us to look at the interconnections between these forms of violence. His essay is a salutary reminder that social theory is deeply implicated in the way in which we come to recognize what we call 'facts'.

I hope the nuanced reading of the political processes in India offered by the authors here shows how social theory has not been simply applied to Indian experience—it has been moulded and enriched by it.

The Significance of Lower Courts in the Judicial Process

Robert Moog

INTRODUCTION

In the pursuit of their personal research agendas, scholars have tended to divide India's judiciary into its component parts (Supreme Court, High Courts, and lower or subordinate courts), and to isolate one from the others. While this concentration on one or another of the three tiers of the court system provides valuable insights and analyses into the workings of each of the levels, such an approach cannot possibly grasp the significance of the interactions among the various courts. As a unified judiciary (there is no bifurcation between separate national and state court systems), the formal and informal influences that pass among these three tiers take on enormous significance. These influences not only flow downwards from the Supreme Court to the High Courts and then the lower courts, but from the bottom upwards as well. The suggestion presented here is that although the horizontal linkages to other actors or institutions at a given level, whether it be district, state, or national, remain important in explaining the functioning of India's courts,[1] vertical linkages within the judiciary itself have for too long been largely ignored.

The three levels of courts within the Indian judiciary are bound together not only by the formal appeals processes open to litigants, but also by supervisory and disciplinary links. In addition, credibility or legitimacy is a fluid attribute which cannot be compartmentalized within each of the three levels. While it is almost certain that the different courts have varying degrees of acceptability, or legitimacy with the public, it is also true that one level's acceptability or lack of it, is likely to influence that of the other courts as cases flow up and down through the judicial system. Without considering these interactions and their ramifications for the system as a whole, any policy decisions regarding reform of any one level of the courts may be misguided or even counter-productive.

This chapter provides only a beginning of what a more systemic view of the Indian courts might produce. While it is primarily concerned with the problems confronting lower-level courts, it attempts to draw attention to their links with the High Courts, using the courts in Kerala and Uttar Pradesh (UP) as examples.[2] In doing so, it must be emphasized that the flow of influence moves both up and down within the court hierarchy and district courts, as the foundation upon which the Indian judiciary rests, can be either the source of either tremendous problems or solutions to other courts.

LOWER COURTS
Significance

India's lower courts are districtwide organizations, subdivided into three levels—district judge, civil judge, and *munsif*.[3] The district judge's jurisdiction is primarily appellate, the civil judge's both appellate and original, and the munsif's almost exclusively original. The head judicial officer, charged with the administrative responsibilities of the district courts, is the district judge. (Others at that level are referred to as additional district judges.) The courts tend to be located in the larger 'district towns', although in some cases there has been an attempt at decentralization to facilitate access by opening branch courts outside of larger towns.[4]

These district courts have generally been ignored by academics. The exception has been primarily in sociological and anthropological studies at district level. However, these studies have focused either on the lower courts as institutions, nor as part of a judicial hierarchy. Rather, they have tended to concentrate on actors outside the courts, considering the courts primarily as tangential factors affecting the lives of these people, or they have studied the functioning of particular groups located within the lower courts, but not the courts as a whole.[5]

There are a number of reasons for the general dearth of interest in subordinate courts beyond sociological and anthropological studies. Certainly Jerome Frank's (1935: xiv) 'appellate courtitis' plays a part. It refers to a fascination with appellate court decision making, particularly that of courts of ultimate appeal, which appears to be universal. This is the case whether the issue pertains to school desegregation (*Brown v. Board of Education*, 347 US 483 [1954]) or abortion rights (*Roe v. Wade*, 410 US 113 [1973]) in the United States, or Parliament's power to amend the constitution (*Kesavananda Bharati v. State of India*, AIR 1973 SC 1461) or the rights of bonded labourers (*Bandhua Mukti Morcha v. Union of India*, AIR 1984 SC 802) in India. These are the courts that make policy for a nation and have the final say in interpreting the constitution. Scholars are attracted to them because of the broad scope of their authority and the potential impact of their decisions.

Other factors, peculiar to India, make working on the upper courts more attractive to many academics. High Court and Supreme Court proceedings are conducted in English, not in the regional language as is the case with district-level courts. In addition, their decisions are reported. Both of these make it easier not only for scholars from overseas to work on these courts, but also for Indian scholars to do research outside of their home region. Besides, record keeping at district level is often quite poor, and reliable data may be hard to find. In UP, for example, the High Court stopped publishing its annual reports on the administration of justice in 1976. Whatever districtwide data are sought for the state must ordinarily be collected at district level, and what is available varies from district to district.[6] However, not all states are in the same situation. The Kerala High Court has continued to publish its annual reports on the district-level judiciary at least through 1992–3.[7] These types of disparities make interstate and often intra-state comparisons very difficult. An additional factor that certainly makes research at district-level unattractive for some is the lack of amenities available in many of the district towns compared with those in New Delhi or the larger cities where the High Courts are located.

This lack of academic interest in the lower courts is also reflected in a general lack of concern of policy makers regarding the well-being and reform of these institutions. Despite the occasional comment about the plight of the lower courts, little has been done by those in government to alleviate their problems. In 1992, the Supreme Court expressed its frustration over this matter in a fit of judicial activism. In *All India Judges' Association v. Union of India* (AIR 1992 SC 165), the then Chief Justice, Ranganath Mishra, issued an order requiring the government to take a series of steps to rehabilitate the lower courts. In 1995, when the Supreme Court was concerned about the seeming lack of progress in policy implementation, returned to the issue demanding more information from the government on what steps had been taken towards fulfilment of certain aspects of the earlier order (*All India Judges' Association v. Union of India* [1995 (2) SCALE 374]).

The danger in the plight of the lower courts needs to be understood in light of its effects on the judiciary as a whole. It is easy to compartmentalize the effects of the problems plaguing these courts and confine them to the district level. However, whether it be the delays, pending cases, worthless decisions,[8] or lack of credibility engendered by these courts, they can affect the upper courts in at least two ways. The first is the problem of an increased flow of cases to High Courts and the Supreme Court in the form of appeals, revisions, reviews, or the use of the upper courts' writ jurisdiction to avoid the district courts entirely. A second, and more insidious problem in the long run, is the extent to which public disillusionment or cynicism about the lower courts spreads upwards. There is the danger that the higher courts may be perceived as extensions of an often misused process, rather than bodies to remedy mistakes from below.

The district courts are the ones to which most Indians are exposed. Even when a villager has not been personally involved in a court case, he/she is likely to know someone who has been, and to have formed some opinion about these bodies. Many of the previously cited anthropological and sociological studies are valuable in this regard, providing insights into villagers' perceptions of the local courts. For most Indians, it is district-level courts that are most readily accessible, geographically, financially, as well as jurisdictionally, and, therefore, it is these courts that can be expected to influence the public's opinion of the judiciary as a whole.

Problems

The problems confronting India's lower courts have attained near legendary proportions with stories of litigation lasting 745 years (Clad 1990: 18).[9] While such anecdotal evidence unquestionably sensationalizes the plight of the lower courts, it makes their problems no less real. On occasion, the Supreme Court has expressed its frustration with delays and pending cases in these courts, noting in one case, 'It is common knowledge that currently in our country criminal courts excel in slow-motion.'[10] While individual dramatic instances and criticisms from well-placed sources attract some media and public attention, the reaction, if any, has been short-lived, and the lower courts proceed with little serious reform attempted. What scattered evidence there is, however, suggests that delays, pending cases, and worthless decisions do plague many of the district courts in India (see Moog 1997: Chapter 3; Law Commission of India 1978).[11]

While no one appears to know the precise number of pending cases in India's courts, one estimate from 1991 placed the figure at roughly twenty million, with slightly over two million of these at High Court and Supreme Court levels.[12] Any attempt at providing an average length for these cases would be largely meaningless because of the wide diversity of variables that can affect any particular case, from local legal culture to caseload to the delaying tactics of litigants and advocates. However, to suggest that such numbers do not represent a serious ongoing problem for India's courts is to ignore the historical record. The subordinate courts, at least from the time of the East India Company, have been subject to charges of inefficiency and inordinate delays, among other things.[13]

The delays, pending cases, worthless decisions, and allegations of corruption that periodically surface regarding these courts all serve to damage their credibility and discourage their use as forums of dispute resolution.[14] This also increases the search for alternatives, which range from versions of the more traditional *panchayats* (village or caste), such state-run forums as *lok adalats* (people's courts) or the widening variety of tribunals, to 'lumping it' or resorting to 'self-help'.

Despite the delays and pending cases, when comparing figures on filings per 100,000 population in India with those from other nations, it is clear that Indians do not resort to the lower courts in unusually large numbers. In fact, in some states they appear to be doing so in surprisingly small numbers. Figures for 1992–3 from Kerala show that civil cases were filed in district-level courts at a rate of 187 per 100,000 population.[15] However, Kerala is an unusual state for a number of reasons, not the least of which is its extremely high literacy rate—93.62 per cent male and 86.17 per cent female. By comparison, the all-India figures are 64.13 per cent and 39.29 per cent respectively (*Census of India* 1991). However, when similar data are collected for UP, the results indicate a restraint in the use of the lower courts uncommon in many other nations. In UP, the most recent figures available are from 1976. They show a rate of 88 civil filings per 100,000, which compares favourably with Kerala and is far below the figures published from other nations.[16] For example, the data from Kerala and UP are quite low when compared with recent figures from state courts in the United States.[17]

The figures cited in the preceding paragraph indicate that the Indian public, at least in Uttar Pradesh and Kerala, does not resort to the lower courts in comparatively large numbers. However, due to the large number of cases involving various governmental agencies, even those figures may be misleadingly high when discussing the propensity of Indians to institute suits in the lower courts. The central government alone is involved in a considerable number of the cases that are filed in court. The Indian Law Commission has complained about court dockets 'clogged' with government and public-sector litigation, and it has stated that the government's resort to the courts is 'prodigious'. Former Supreme Court Chief Justice A.M. Ahmadi is among those who have pleaded with the government to reduce its use of the courts (*Times of India*, 28 June 1995). Figures provided by the Law Commission in its 126th report show that for the five years prior to its publication in 1988, 787,450 cases had been filed by or against the Government of India alone. Unfortunately, the filings are not broken down into those instituted by and against the government, but comments such as those in the report and by the Chief Justice suggest that the government is responsible for a significant amount of the litigation.[18]

Despite the evidence presented in the preceding pararaphs, and the conclusion that Indians do not resort to the district courts in relatively large numbers, the fact remains that there is a clientele for these courts. Cases are instituted and revisions, reviews, and appeals are filed in order to create the delays and backlogs of cases found in many parts of the country. A series of studies completed during the 1960s and 1970s provide some insight into the explanations for many of these filings. Bernard Cohn summarized these as follows, 'Cases are brought to court to harass one's opponents, as a punishment, as a form of land speculation and profit making, to satisfy insulted pride, and to maintain local political dominance over one's followers' (Cohn 1965: 105). Others have described similar findings elsewhere (see Kidder 1973: 109; Morrison 1974–5: 52; and Sharma 1979: 3 & 54). Kidder's study of the courts in Bangalore, citing repeated use of the courts by 'court birds' or 'career litigants', suggests the possibility of an entertainment value to litigation as well (1974–5: 32). More recent research in eastern UP confirms these findings (Moog 1997: 100–2).[19]

It is difficult to determine what percentage of the total cases filed in any one district stem from these motivations, but they certainly have a damaging effect on the lower courts' credibility as dispute-resolution forums. In many of these cases a quick, final, and just resolution of the matter is not desired and/or expected. Writing of a village in Jaunpur district in eastern Uttar Pradesh, Cohn observed that 'the villagers do not expect a settlement that will end the dispute to eventuate from recourse to the state courts' (1965: 105). In Bangalore, Kidder (1974–5) noted that most cases ended in compromise, but a key to the process was ensuring delay in the courts. An attorney who was interviewed admitted that he was hired to delay matters, and added, 'It is not a question of winning the cases' (Kidder 1974–5: 31). Such openly held expectations and attitudes can have a damaging effect on the credibility of these courts in their role of resolving disputes. A significant number of people simply do not expect efficient or effective dispute resolution to result from them, nor do they expect justice. Kidder argued that only the 'novice' litigants expected justice to result from going to court (1973: 134). When allegations of corruption are added to the mix, notions of just resolutions recede farther into the background. Erin Moore, in her study of a village in Rajasthan, concluded, 'the courts are seen as an arena of and for the powerful' ... '(A)ll the actors—

witnesses, lawyers, judges, and police—are vulnerable to bribes'
(1993: 531).

Certainly the argument can be made that the use of district-level
courts discussed in these studies results in damage to the legitimacy of
these institutions as dispute-resolution forums. However, this does not
imply that they serve no other useful purpose. Providing an arena for the
defence of *izzat* (honour) or for the non-violent expression of local
political battles may fulfil a valuable social control function, albeit in a
relatively expensive fashion. However, playing such a role may simply
exacerbate a court's difficulties in adequately serving the public in its
conventional role of resolving disputes efficiently and effectively. For
example, in matters of honour, settling may be seen as 'selling out'. Under
such circumstances it is likely that cases will be approached from an
emotional standpoint, rather than a rational one which would be more
conducive to an early settlement. In cases of harassment or speculation,
delay becomes a key element to financially break or thoroughly embarrass
the other party.[20]

For those interested in efficient resolution of conflict, this
translates into avoidance of the district courts entirely, where it is feasible. If
that is impossible, there is the realization that the case will wind its way
through the lower courts with the possibility of its moving back and forth to
the upper courts from a final and/or interlocutory order below. This lack of
finality accorded to lower court decisions by advocates and litigants, partially
stems from a function which is of use to the lower courts for purposes other
than dispute resolution, and partially the lack of legitimacy of these courts
when dispute resolution is the goal. This has two effects on the upper
courts—an increased case flow moving among all three levels and what one
may call 'guilt by association'. The upper courts can be perceived as more a
part of the problem than as a solution to it. Through procedural devices open
to advocates they become an extension of the delaying process, leading to a
greater number of pending cases and worthless decisions. In this course of
events, the problems of the lower courts can envelop the judiciary as a whole
and become problems for the upper levels as well.

HIGH COURTS—KERALA CASE STUDY
Caseload 1990–1994

For those seeking expeditious, authoritative dispute resolution,
and an escape from lower courts, the High Courts may seem to offer some
solace. However, using the Kerala High Court as an example, one can see that
escape to the next level may provide little comfort.

Using Kerala's categorization of cases for reporting purposes, the jurisdiction of the High Courts can be broken down into the three main categories—civil matters, criminal matters, and miscellaneous petitions. Civil matters were subdivided into twenty-six sub-categories, criminal five, and miscellaneous petitions nine. It is miscellaneous petitions which are most numerous, but they are generally handled in an administrative manner and are therefore listed separately.[21]

Table 1 provides annual figures for filings, disposals, and pending cases in the Kerala High Court at Ernakulam from 1990 to 1994. The overwhelming majority of these cases are on the civil side.[22] As is indicated, filings have increased significantly during the five-year period covered (45 per cent overall) but disposals have not kept pace, resulting in a 91 per cent increase in pending cases.[23]

Table 2 takes the same data used in Table 1 but divides it by original and appellate sides. While the work is not evenly divided, there are a significant number of filings from each side. Original filings range from 60 per cent of the total in 1990 to a high of 67 per cent in 1993. Regarding disposals, the pattern is similar, although the span is somewhat larger. It varies from a low of 56 per cent of disposals from the original side in 1990 to 70 per cent in 1992. While the Table clearly shows that the court continues to have substantial amounts of work on both the original and appellate sides, it also indicates a general trend toward greater use of its original jurisdiction.

There is one category of cases that stands out in the data provided. Table 3 gives statistics for the sub-category of original petitions only. When the figures in Table 3 are placed in the context of those in Table 1, one can see that original petitions accounted for over one-half of all filings for each of the years under study, over one-half of the disposals in each year except 1990 (when they were 46 per cent), and between 42 per cent (1990) and 46 per cent (1993) of all pending cases.

Many of these original petitions may represent a convenient short cut to the High Court. Article 226(1) of the Indian Constitution provides High Courts with the jurisdiction to issue writs for the enforcement of fundamental rights (those found in Part III of the Constitution) and for any other purpose. That is, High Courts may intervene when a breach of any legal right is alleged (Bakshi 1995: 130). This latter clause presents a possible opening for those with the resources and desire to use the High Courts as an alternative to district courts. What the data from Kerala do not indicate is how many of the total of 79,688 original petitions filed during the five years under study were writ petitions based on issues which were suitable for disposal in the lower courts.[24] However, it has been suggested by an ex-Chief Justice of Kerala High Court that the use of writ petitions in such cases is not unusual, and is a major contributor to the backlog in the Court.[25] Writ petitions have become the major source of the court's filings, and have thereby transformed the court into a forum with over one-half of its caseload on the original side.

Another way to highlight the significance of the High Court's original jurisdiction is to compare the number of civil filings with the total civil filings in the state for the lower courts.[26] In 1990 the High Court received 23 per cent as many original civil filings as all the subordinate courts in the state; in 1991 the percentage increased to 24 per cent; and in 1993 to 34 per cent. In all likelihood, the High Court has become the single most active trial court in the state of Kerala.

On the appellate side the High Court's jurisdiction is quite diverse.[27] The most significant areas, based on the number of filings for 1994, are the following: civil revisions (2804); writ appeals (1698); miscellaneous first appeals (1302); criminal revisions (1209); land acquisition appeals (1052); second appeals (946); and criminal appeals (883).[28]

In 1978, it was claimed by a respected student of the Indian courts that the frequency of appeals in India is greater than in any other country (Derrett 1978: 1949). There is little indication that Derrett's observation has become less applicable over time. The Ministry of Law, Justice, and Company Affairs, recognizing the problem that a liberal appeals policy can cause, recommended in its 1993–4 Report that more appeals be handled at district level by raising the fee amount necessary to take one to the High Court. In order to discourage those appeals deemed frivolous, the Report also urged strict enforcement of Order 41, Rules 11 and 11A of the Code of Civil Procedure regarding dismissal of appeals (Ministry of Law, Justice, and Company Affairs 1994: 38).

The frequency of appeals is not merely a function of questionable decision making at trial level. More importantly, it is partly a function of the lack of credibility accorded to lower courts, and, as a result, the lack of finality attached to their decisions. It is also partially the result of the goals some litigant's have in mind when resorting to the courts. For Cohn's villagers referred to in earlier pages, and others who are interested in harassment, speculation, or defence of honour, appeals can be key element of their strategy.

One other set of figures will help to highlight the caseload burden under which the Kerala High Court operates. That is the number of justices sitting in Ernakulam at any given time. Of the figures provided here, the first represent the number of positions (permanent and additional) that had been sanctioned for the Court, and the second the number actually filled: 1990–1—

26/23; 1991–2—24/20; 1992–3—24/20.[29] When only pending cases (exclusive of miscellaneous petitions) are considered, this means that in 1990–1 there were 1739 cases pending for each justice. In 1991–2 the number increased to 1818, and in 1992–3 to 2331.[30]

Supervisory/Disciplinary Authority

In addition to their role as an appellate and trial courts (largely through their writ jurisdiction), High Courts are also linked in other ways to the subordinate judiciary. They control the budgets of the lower courts in their states, and while any given district judge is responsible for the day-to-day running of his/her court compound, the High Courts establish guidelines for the administration of those compounds.[31]

Constitutionally, the High Courts are granted supervisory and disciplinary authority over subordinate courts. Articles 233–6 of the Indian Constitution pertain to the role of the High Courts in the appointment, posting, promotion, transfer, as well as disciplining of subordinate court officers.

The intent of these articles is to protect the independence of the subordinate judiciary by limiting the influence the executive and legislative political branches can exercise over it (see Basu 1991: 256–61; Pandey 1995: 420–4). Through a series of decisions, the Supreme Court, has proved to be quite supportive of this goal.[32] Most would agree that such independence is essential to the functioning of a system of checks and balances, and therefore of a democratic polity. However, depending upon how the High Courts exercise their disciplinary and supervisory authority can be a double-edged sword. On the one hand, it does partially insulate the subordinate courts from the possible political influence of the other branches. But such a judicial system depending upon how the High Courts choose to exercise their control, can still have a chilling effect[33] on the actions of judges. In other words, the value of this organization upon how fair the High Court in question appears in scrutinizing the work of lower court judges as well as any complaints filed against them.

The Supreme Court warned of the dangers inherent in such a situation in *Ishwar Chand Jain v. High Court of Punjab and Haryana* ([1988] 3 SCJ 38). Responding to a resolution from a local bar association, the High Court of Punjab and Haryana conducted an inquiry into the work and conduct of an additional district and sessions judge, ultimately recommending his termination from the service. The recommendation was challenged by the judge in question through a writ petition to the High Court which was dismissed. The state government then terminated his employment. In reviewing the matter, the Supreme Court held that the bar association's resolution was unjustified and the officer's dismissal from the service should be set aside. The Court noted that the High Courts have a 'constitutional obligation to guide and protect judicial officers' (*Ishwar Chand Jain v. High Court of Punjab and Haryana* [1988] 3 SCJ 38:48). Justice K.N. Singh then concluded with a warning:

> An honest strict judicial officer is likely to have adversaries in the *mofussil* courts. If complaints are entertained on trifling matters relating to judicial orders which may have been upheld by the High Court on the judicial side no judicial officer would feel protected and it would be difficult for him to discharge his duties in an honest and independent manner. ... If judicial officers are under constant threat of complaint and enquiry on trifling matters and if [the] High Court encourages anonymous complaints to hold the field the subordinate judiciary will not be able to administer justice in an independent and honest manner. It is therefore imperative that the High Court should take steps to protect its honest officers by ignoring ill-conceived or motivated complaints made by unscrupulous lawyers or litigants [*Ishwar Chand Jain v. High Court of Punjab and Haryana* ([1988] 3 SCJ 38:48)].

There is evidence, at least from UP, that complaints filed with the High Court are a serious concern of lower court officers (Moog 1997: 81–2, 119–21). These complaints (anonymous or otherwise) can come from advocates, courthouse staff, or even litigants. The danger inherent in such a situation is the possible deterioration of confidence and trust between levels of the judiciary, resulting in passive lower court judges. If the High Court is perceived to be unsupportive of or indifferent to their plight,[34] they are likely to become more concerned with 'not making waves' than exercising their independence in decision making. This can translate into a hesitancy to confront or challenge advocates in the courtroom, for example over delaying tactics, or even the ministerial staff working under them.

India's Judiciary: An Integrated Whole

The material provided up to this point reinforces the images fostered in government documents and scholarly research of India's lower courts mired in a bog of delays, pending cases, and worthless decisions, and its High Courts overburdened with filings on both the original and appellate sides. However, what has also been suggested is that these problems are integrally related and that policy makers when searching for solutions, and researchers, when studying them, should treat them as such.

Those who concentrate on the High Courts, or even the Supreme Court, need to recognize that with the deterioration of the legitimacy of the subordinate courts as dispute-resolution forums, the caseload burdens on the High Courts and Supreme Court increases and a perpetuation and perhaps even further expansion of their roles as trial/service courts also occurs.[35] As the upper courts remain caught up in this more mundane dispute-resolution process, it cannot help but detract from the time and resources they spend on cases involving broader policy issues.

The problems thus created become evident not only in the High Courts, as indicated by the figures from Kerala, but at Supreme Court level as well. It has been estimated that the justices spend 50 per cent of their time on admissions matters alone (Dhavan 1986: 74 and 85). For the three years from 1989 to 1991 the Court averaged 44,215 new filings and 65,854 disposals annually (Ministry of Law, Justice, and Company Affairs 1992; 1993). As of 30 June 1993, 62,925 admission matters and 34,245 regular hearing matters were pending with the Court.[36] Taking into consideration the fact that the justices do not employ clerks for research purposes, as is done in the United States, and that the computerization process is in its infancy, the magnitude of the problem confronting the Court becomes even more daunting.

Part of the cause of this tremendous caseload burden can be categorized as structural and traced to the comparatively broad jurisdiction of the upper courts in India.[37] But part of it is also a function of a desire to see that justice is done in both a substantive and procedural sense. It is a well-intentioned attempt to enable as many litigants as possible, and who so desire, to proceed to a higher authority, even if the case is ultimately dismissed at the admission stage. However, this version of judicial populism creates a 'Catch-22' situation for the judiciary. At this point, facilitating access to the High Courts and Supreme Court on the premise of ensuring justice further undermines the public's perception of the quality of justice they receive from the subordinate courts. These very liberal appeals and writ policies encourage the impression that justice ultimately flows from the High Courts and/or the Supreme Court. They also feed the image that what the lower courts produce is a lower quality of justice, compounding the credibility problems these courts already have. These courts therefore become hurdles or barriers to get over, or avoid altogether (for example, through the writ jurisdiction), rather than forums from which final resolution of disputes is expected, But the problems such policies produce go beyond the subordinate courts. Leaving the door so loosely ajar for appeals and writs overburdens the upper courts. If time spent on cases has any relation to the quality of decision making, then this desire to see justice done ironically results in the deterioration of justice at the Supreme Court and High Court levels.

Just as facilitating access to the upper courts may have unintended negative consequences for the subordinate courts, so may the supervisory and disciplinary roles of the High Courts. Designed to ensure that a certain quality of justice is provided in the lower-level courts, when not tempered by deserved support for judges at district level, this oversight can result in undermining the security of these officers and produce a 'chilling effect'. Officers in the subordinate courts may begin to perceive threats from various sources which without a sympathetic High Court they believe they are relatively helpless to combat. That can translate into passive officers, more concerned with not offending advocates and staff for fear of triggering a review procedure, than with pursuing an effective and efficient justice process.[38]

The ease of access to the upper levels and the lack of finality that therefore attaches to decisions at district level, combined with the perception of unsupportive High Courts, can undermine the authority of the subordinate judiciary. This leaves it marginalized in terms of its status, not only within the judicial hierarchy, but in the larger Indian polity as well. In their traditional role of dispute-resolution forums, these lower courts, in many cases, remain as much an obstruction as part of the solution. Therefore, for many of those who desire efficient and effective resolution of conflict, it would seem these courts are to be avoided at all costs.

There are other factors that can add to the marginalization process. Symbolically, the failure to create an All-India judicial service for the district judges in these courts, despite the urgings of the Supreme Court (*All India Judges' Association v. Union of India* AIR 1992 SC 165), has left the perception that they remain a notch below those in the Indian Administrative Service who also work at district level. Also, the fascination with creating alternatives to these courts, ostensibly to reduce the burden on them, may simply be removing certain classes of cases from their purview and thereby limiting the issues with which they deal.[39] This may, or may not, produce a more efficient and effective dispute-resolution process for the cases removed, depending on the functioning of any particular alternative forum. However, it fails to address the root causes of the problems that plague the lower courts.[40] The use of alternatives may make reform of these lower courts less urgent by removing from the process many of those with the influence and resources to most effectively voice their complaints.

There is a tragic irony that attaches to the Indian judiciary and its attempts to facilitate and expedite access to justice. Much of what has been attempted arguably further erodes the creditability of the system's foundation, the district-level courts, by facilitating avoidance of them or undermining their authority. And that, in turn, may be damaging the quality of justice delivered by the upper levels, and ultimately their credibility as well. What is needed is not merely the material support Chief Justice Mishra spoke of in the *All India*

Judges' Association case (*All India Judges' Association v. Union of India* AIR 1992 SC 165). That is certainly helpful, but more important is encouragement and support from the upper levels, to increase the respect and finality accorded to lower court decisions. And, where it does not exist, a relationship of trust must be developed between subordinate judges and their superiors in the High Courts. However, the High Courts are in a difficult position. Their dual roles of policing the lower courts and at the same time supervising them can clash. But, as the Supreme Court observed, the authority of the High Courts is not just to discipline. As cited earlier, they also have a 'constitutional obligation to guide and protect judicial officers' (*Ishwar Chand Jain v. High Court of Punjab and Haryana* [1988] 3 SCJ 38:48). There needs to be a balance struck between these two.

The research presented here is simply a preliminary attempt to try better understand the interactions that take place between the various levels of the Indian judiciary. From the data available the system appears top heavy, with the upper levels handling a disproportionate share of the litigation load. But before specific remedies can be suggested, much more needs to be explained regarding the information that we have. Far too much of what scholars and policy makers claim to know about the lower courts, in particular, is based on conclusions drawn from old or incomplete data, anecdotal evidence, or extrapolations from related research. Certainly, more complete figures regarding the movement of cases between levels of courts and information on the percentage of cases that result in a lower court order (interlocutory or final) being overturned, would help in understanding the advantages, real and perceived, of taking cases to the upper courts. A closer look at writ petitions, including a breakdown of the types of cases in which they have been used, would provide a valuable insight as to their ability to do justice in the subordinate courts and the motives for what may amount to over half the filings in the High Courts. This would begin to address the avoidance factor discussed earlier. Why is so relatively little use, in terms of original filings, made of the far more numerous lower courts than the upper courts? Who is using, and not using, the various levels of courts and why? The sociological and anthropological studies cited earlier provide a beginning, but those works need to be integrated with research on the relationships among the various levels of courts themselves in order to more fully understand what is happening in the courts and why. Without it, even the most well-intentioned reformers will find it difficult to take a comprehensive approach in formulating policy which conceives of the judiciary as an integrated system.

ENDNOTES

1. At district level these relations can include those between the courts and the district collector, the police, and litigants (both repeat players and one-shotters). At Supreme Court level, the most significant relationship may be with the executive/legislative branch.

2. These two states are used because they are the two in which the author has conducted research.

3. These are the titles used in UP. While the labels may differ somewhat from state to state, the three-tier structure remains the same.

4. This has been the case in some of the districts in UP.

5. Typical of the former are: M.N. Srinivas's study of the Rampura village and the social pressures exerted on villagers not to use the courts (1955); Bernard Cohn's articles on why villagers resort to the courts (1959–60; 1965); R.S. Khare's piece on indigenous culture and lawyer's law (1972); and Erin Moore's monograph of dispute resolution in a Rajasthani village (1985) as well as her later article on the same topic (1993). Dominating the latter group are a range of studies of the district level bar (Galanter 1968–9; Rowe 1968–9; Morrison 1972a; Kidder 1974–5; Desai 1981; Sathe et al. 1982–3; 1983; Menon et al. 1983; and Oommen 1983). Added to these are others relating to *munshis* (Morrison 1974–5), advocates' relations with munshis (Morrison 1972b), and their relations with touts (Gandhi 1982). In addition to these sociological and anthropological works, an attempt has been made to explain the seeming weakness of district-level judges in UP by focusing on structural factors and judge–advocate relations (Moog 1992). See also Upendra Baxi's book, *Towards a Sociology of Indian Law*, for a review of much of this literature pertaining to advocates (1986: 113–7).

6. While working in two districts (Varanasi and Deoria) in north-eastern UP in 1987, I found it impossible to collect comparable data on case filings and pending cases covering the post-1976 period. This was despite the cooperation of the district judges from both districts.

7. To the best of my knowledge the High Court in Kerala continues to publish its annual reports, but is very likely the only one or one of the few to do so. But merely publishing the reports does not solve the researcher's problems. These reports are not widely circulated, and even the High Court library in Ernakulam did not have a complete set.

8. In its annual reports on the administration of justice in the state, the High Court in UP had been reporting data on wholly satisfied, partially satisfied, and worthless decisions. In each of the twenty-seven years from 1948 to 1976 for which figures were available, over one-half of the judgments turned out to be valueless after an application for execution had been filed (see Moog 1997: 47).

9. During research conducted in eastern UP in 1987, local advocates told me of a case which lasted 110 years, and had just been resolved the year before I arrived.

10. This was in response to a special leave petition filed with the Supreme Court to reinstate a defamation case which had been quashed in Karnataka High Court (quoted in the *Indian Express*, 21 April 1995).

11. There are two major problems in collecting evidence to support these contentions nationwide. The initial one remains the lack of reliable data on these courts. The second problem, also noted earlier, is the lack of researchers interested in compensating for the scarcity of state-generated information by working with these courts and generating their own.

12. By 1994, according to India's Law Minister, the number of cases pending in India's High Courts and Supreme Court had risen to slightly over 2,851,000 (cited in *Indian Express*, 27 March 1995). One unofficial estimate has placed the total figure at nearly 40 million (*India Abroad*, 4 February 1994).

13. The history of such problems in the districts courts is a long and well-documented one. Three of the more significant publications during the course of the twentieth century are: *Civil Justice Committee Report 1924–25* (1925); *Law Commission of India 14th Report* (1956); and *Law Commission of India 77th Report* (1978). For a more personal account, by a district and sessions judge in the Punjab, of delays and other problems infecting the lower courts in the early twentieth century, see Roe's treatise on the administration of justice (1927). However, the issue of inefficient handling of cases predates the twentieth century. In a report on the administration of justice in British India, Sir James Fitzjames, the law member of the Governor General's Executive Council in the 1870s, categorized the district bench in both Bengal and the North West Province as 'shamefully inefficient' (1870: 39).

14. It is difficult to gauge the credibility of judges among the public, but in 1995 the *Times of India* published the results of a public opinion poll in which 66 per cent of the respondents answered 'yes' when asked if they believed judges are corrupt (14 January 1995). The survey was limited to large urban centres, and it failed to distinguish among judges in the subordinate courts, High Courts, and Supreme Court. Despite these weaknesses, the results indicate a serious credibility problem for the judiciary.

15. This is based upon the most recent figure available on civil filings in the state at the time the research was conducted (*Administrative Report for the Civil Justice in Kerala for the Year 1992–93*, 1994: 22). The population for Kerala (29,098,518), is from the *Census of India, 1991* 157).

16. The UP figure is from the *Report on the Administration of Justice in the State of Uttar Pradesh, 1976*, 1982: Central Statement, no. 2), and is based on the population figure from the 1971 census. In a 1983 article, Marc Galanter provided figures from fifteen other countries and the data from India compare favourably with all of them. Spain was the closest to Kerala and UP with a rate of 345 per 100,000 (Galanter 1983: 53). Any international comparison of caseload statistics must be read with caution. Variations in court jurisdiction, record-keeping practices, legal culture, accessibility, and availability of alternatives are among the problems confronted. With these limitations in mind, the comparisons are still offered in order to provide some context in which the Indian data can be placed.

17. Among the thirty-four jurisdictions for which there were state totals given, the trial court civil caseloads in the United States for 1993 ranged from a low of 3301 filings per 100,000 population in Puerto Rico to 20,897 per 100,000 in Virginia (Court Statistics and Information Management Project 1995: 147–54).

18. Whether or not the government actually initiated the suit by filing in court is not necessarily an accurate indication of which side is responsible for the litigation. An unyielding or unreasonable position by a government official may leave an individual with little alternative but to file a lawsuit. Then Chief Justice Ahmadi noted this when he suggested that 'governments should pull up officers who failed to discharge their duties, leading to litigation' (*Times of India*, 28 June 1995).

19. It is interesting to note that these types of uses of the lower courts are not peculiar to independent India. Comments regarding such 'misuse' of the judicial process can be traced back to the colonial period (see, eg., Roe 1927).

20. For a more thorough discussion of the causes of delays in these courts, see Moog (1992).

21. While the High Court itself does not ordinarily include miscellaneous petitions in its total of pending cases, the Ministry of Law, Justice, and Company Affairs, in its national report, did so in 1995. This resulted in a significant inflation in the number of pending cases notionwide. For example, in Kerala, as of the week of 17 March 1995, there were 64, 394 civil and criminal matters listed as pending, but 114,317 miscellaneous petitions pending (data provided by the High Court of Kerala).

22. For example, the 1994 data showed 4107 criminal filings, 3387 disposals, and 5048 pending cases. The figures in Tables 1, 2, and 3 do not include miscellaneous petitions, since the High Court itself did not include them in its totals in the annual figures supplied.

23. The problem of overburdened upper courts has been discussed extensively by a number of committees and commissions. The *Report of the Arrears Committee, 1989–90* (also known as the Malimath Committee Report) gave a listing of sixteen other reports, beginning with the Rankin Committee Report in 1924, which dealt in part or in whole with this issue (1990: viii). The Malimath report listed the total number of pending cases in all High Courts as 1,421,589 as on 1 January 1990 (1990: 165).

24. Kerala is not unique with regard to the high number of petitions filed on the original side. An earlier study of Allahabad High Court indicated that the original side there had essentially become the writ jurisdiction (Dhavan 1986: 126–8).

25. Interview, Ernakulum, 1 April 1995. The Chief Justice noted that many of the cases to which he was referring involved property issues that advocates framed in such a way as to fit within the writ jurisdiction of the High Court.

26. The following are the numbers for all levels of lower courts for the corresponding years: 1990–1—54,801; 1991–2—59,411; 1992–3—54,430 (*Administrative Report for the Civil Justice in Kerala for the Year 1990–91; 1991–92; 1992–93.* 1993; 1994). In the High Court the numbers of original filings on the civil side were: 1990—12,436; 1991—14,221; 1992—18,686 (Kerala High Court records). While the years do not match because fiscal years were used for the lower courts and calendar years for the Higher Court, the members still clearly indicate the significance of the High Court's original side. The categories of cases included in the civil, original side are: original suits; original petitions; contempt-of-court cases; election cases; banking company petitions; banking company claims; company petitions; miscellaneous company applications; civil miscellaneous cases; *devaswom* board cases; and *devaswom* board petitions.

27. For the purposes of this chapter, revisions, reviews, and references are all considered part of the appellate side of the court's jurisdiction.

28. All of the data in this section were supplied by the High Court of Kerala.

29. These figures were collected from the *Administrative Report for the Civil Justice in Kerala* for the years 1990–1; 1991–2; and 1992–3. These reports are issued on a fiscal-year basis. The data provided in Tables 1, 2, and 3 were collected directly from the High Court, and are for calendar years.

30. The number of pending cases used were for the years 1990, 1991, and 1992 as found in Table 1.

31. For example, in UP the *General Rules (Civil)* (1987), a compendium of rules for the operation of the lower courts, was issued by the High Court and approved by the state government.

32. For example, concerning a governor's obligation to have 'meaningful' consultations with the High Court prior to appointment of district court judges, see *Chandramouleshwar v. Patna High Court*, AIR 1970 SC 375 and *Chandramohan v. State of Uttar Pradesh*, AIR 1966 SC 1987. Other examples of the Supreme Court's activity in this area include the High Courts' control over the transfer of lower court judges (*State of Assam v. Ranga Mohammad*, AIR 1967 SC 903), and the authority of the High Courts to discipline lower court judges other than in matters of dismissal which resides with the Governors (*State of West Bengal v. Nripendra Nath*, AIR 1966 SC 447). Even in the latter case, the Supreme Court has stated that the High Court's opinion is to be given great consideration. When a High Court is of the opinion that an officer should not continue in service, the Governor 'will act in harmony with the recommendation of the High Court as otherwise the consequences will be unfortunate' (*Tejpal Singh v. State of Uttar Pradesh*, 1986 3 SCJ 353: 361). These last three decisions were based on Article 235 and the 'control over district courts and courts subordinate thereto' which it grants to High Courts.

33. 'Chilling effect', as used here, refers to the disciplinary process and its potential effect of unreasonably constraining judges' freedom to act in a manner they feel is most appropriate in any given situation. In the same vein, Philip Kurland referred to some of the methods adopted for policing of judges in the United States as 'little more than polite blackmail' (Kurland 1969: 667–8).

34. In *Samsher Singh v. State of Punjab* (AIR 1974 SC 2192), the Supreme Court confronted a situation in which the High Court involved appeared indifferent to its obligations. Scolding the High Court for transferring an enquiry of a subordinate officer to the state government, the Court observed that the lower judiciary is not only under the control of the High Court, but is 'also under its care and custody.' High Courts are looked to 'not only for discipline but also for dignity' (*Samsher Singh v. State of Punjab* AIR 1974 SC 2192:2207).

35. The concept of a service court was used by Rajeev Dhavan to describe the plight of the Supreme Court. 'A service court is one which services dispute settlement at trivial levels not linked to policy issues.' His concern was that the Supreme Court had been converted into a predominantly service court (Dhavan 1986: 94).

36. Ministry of Law, Justice and Company Affairs (1994: 27). The total of 97,170 cases pending did not include miscellaneous matters which had been included in many of the Ministry's previous reports.

37. This becomes obvious when comparing the Supreme Courts in the United States and India. In the latter case, the writ jurisdiction under Article 32 of the Indian Constitution, combined with very liberal standing requirements, has provided the Indian public with far greater direct access to its Supreme Court (see *S.P. Gupta v. Union of India* AIR 1982 SC 149: 185–96).

38. For further analysis of the issue of passive subordinate officers as it relates to UP, see Moog (1992).

39. Any discussion of the alternative forums presently in use or under consideration is beyond the scope of this chapter. However, with the spread of less formal institutions such as lok adalats (people's courts) and the more formal 'tribunalization' process, more work needs to be done on any effects these may have on the lower courts. Whether they are reducing the burden on the lower courts and thereby expediting the process, or rather, simply allowing certain groups to escape the lower courts thereby reducing pressure that might otherwise build to reform them, remains an open question. If the latter is the case, then these forums would just be adding to the marginalization process without any corresponding benefit to the subordinate courts. For information concerning the working of lok adalats, see Baxi (1976); Legal Aid Unit (NSS) Campus Law Center (1985); Saxena (1986); Gupteswar (1988); Kassebaum (1989); Kumar (1990); Moog (1991); and Whitson (1992).

40. By 'root causes' 'I am referring' in particular, to litigant and advocate abuse of the process, as well as to structural factors that inhibit judges from asserting control over the process.

REFERENCES

Administrative Report of the Civil Justice in Kerala for the Year 1990–91; 1991–92; 1992–93. 1992; 1993; 1994. Ernakulam: Government Press.

Bakshi, P.M. 1995. *The Constitution of India*, 2nd ed. Delhi: Universal Book Traders.

Basu, Durga Das. 1991. *Constitutional Law of India.* 6th ed. New Delhi: Prentice-Hall of India.

Baxi, Upendra. 1976. 'From *Takrar* to *Karar*: The *Lok Adalat* at Rangpur—A Preliminary Study'. *Journal of Constitutional and Parliamentary Studies.* 10:52–116.

———. 1986. *Towards a Sociology of Indian Law.* New Delhi: Satvahan Publications.

Census of India 1971. General Report. Uttar Pradesh, Part 1-A.

Census of India 1991. Primary Census Abstract, Part II-B(i), General Population, vol. 1, Series 1.

Civil Justice Committee. 1925. *Civil Justice Committee Report, 1924–25.* Calcutta.

Clad, James. 1990. 'Grave Judgments'. *Far Eastern Economic Review.* 12 July:18.

Cohn, Bernard. 1959–60. 'Some Notes on Law and Change in North India'. *Economic Development and Cultural Change.* 8:79–83.

———. 1965. 'Anthropological Notes on Disputes and Law in India'. *American Anthropologist.* 67(6, Part II):82–122.

Court Statistics and Information Management Project. 1995. *State Court Caseload Statistics: Annual Report 1993*. Williamsburg, Va.: National Center for State Courts.

Derrett, J. 1978. 'The Concept of Duty in Ancient Indian Jurisprudence: The Problem of Ascertainment'. In Wendy Doniger, O'Flaherty and J. Duncan M. Derrett, eds, *The Concept of Duty in South Asia*, 18–65. New Delhi: Vikas Publishing House.

Desai, D.A. 1981. 'Role and Structure of the Legal Profession'. *Journal of the Bar Council of India*. 8:112.

Dhavan, Rajeev. 1986. *Litigation Explosion in India*. Bombay: N.M. Tripathi.

Frank Jerome. 1935. *Law and the Modern Mind*. New York: Tudor Publishing Co.

Galanter, Marc. 1968–9. 'The Study of the Indian Legal Profession'. *Law & Society Review*. 3:201–17.

———. 1983. (second printing). 'Reading the Landscape of Disputes: What We Know and Don't Know (and Think We Know) about Our Allegedly Contentious and Litigious Society'. *U.C.L.A. Law Review*. 31:4.

Gandhi, J.S. 1982. *Lawyers and Touts*. Delhi: Hindustan Publishing Corporation.

General Rules Civil. 1987. 2nd ed. Allahabad: Alia Law Agency,.

Gupteswar, K. 1988. 'The Statutory *Lok Adalat*: Its Structure and Role'. *Journal of the Indian Law Institute*. 30:174.

Hayden, Robert. 1984. 'A Note on Caste *Panchayats* and Government Courts in India: Different Kinds of Stages for Different Kinds of Performances'. *Journal of Legal Pluralism*. 23:43.

Kassebaum, Gene. 1989. 'ADR in India: The *Lok Adalat* as an Alternative to Court Litigation of Personal Injury and Criminal Cases in South India'. Working Paper Series, Program on Conflict Resolution, University of Hawaii at Manoa.

Khare, R.S. 1972. 'Indigenous Culture and Lawyers Law in India'. *Comparative Studies in Society and History*. 14 (January). 71–96.

Kidder, Robert. 1973. 'Courts and Conflict in an Indian City: A Study in Legal Impact'. *Journal of Commonwealth Political Studies*. 11:121–39.

———. 1974–5. 'Formal Litigation and Professional Insecurity: Legal Entrepreneurship in South India'. *Law & Society Review*. 9:11–37.

Kumar, Ashok. 1990. 'Lok Adalat in Allahabad'. *Supreme Court Journal*. 50.

Kurland, Phillip B. 1969. 'Constitution and the Tenure of Federal Judges: Some Notes from History'. *University of Chicago Law Review*. 36:665.

———. 1978. *Law Commission of India. 77th Report*. New Delhi: Ministry of Law.

———. 1988. *Law Commission of India. 126th Report*. New Delhi: Ministry of Law and Justice.

Law Commission of India. 1956. *Law Commission of India. 14th Report*. New Delhi: Ministry of Law.

Legal Aid Unit (NSS) Campus Law Centre. 1985. 'Lok Adalat in Delhi: A Report From a Legal Education Perspective'. *Indian Bar Review*. 12:415.

Menon, N.R. Madhava, S. Rama Rao, and V. Sudarsen. 1983. 'Legal Profession in Tamil Nadu: A Sociological Study'. *Indian Bar Review*. 10:553–83.

Ministry of Law, Justice, and Company Affairs. 1992, 1993, 1994. *Annual Report 1991–92; 1992–93; 1993–94*. New Delhi.

Moog, Robert. 1991. 'Conflict and Compromise: The Politics of *Lok Adalats* in Varanasi District'. *Law & Society Review*. 25(3):545.

_____. 1992. 'Delays in Indian Courts: Why Judges Don't Take Control'. *The Justice System Journal*. 16(1):19.

_____. 1997. *Whose Interests Are Supreme? Organizational Politics in the Civil Courts in India*. Ann Arbor: Association for Asian Studies.

Moore, Erin. P. 1985. *Conflict and Compromise: Justice in an Indian Village*. Berkeley: Center for South and Southeast Asia Studies, University of California.

_____. 1993. 'Gender, Power, and Legal Pluralism: Rajasthan, India'. *American Ethnologist*. 20(3):522–42.

Morrison, Charles. 1972a. 'Kinship in Professional Relations: A Study of North Indian District Lawyers'. *Comparative Studies in Society and History*. 14:100–25.

_____. 1972b. '*Munshis* and Their Masters: The Organization of an Occupational Relationship in the Indian Legal System'. *Journal of Asian Studies*. 31:309–28.

_____. 1974–5. 'Clerks and Clients: Paraprofessional Roles and Identities in Indian Litigations'. *Law & Society Review*. 9:39–61.

Oommen, T.K. 1983. 'The Legal Profession in India: Some Sociological Perspectives'. *Indian Bar Review*. 10:1–46.

Pandey, J.N. 1995. *Constitutional Law of India*. 28th ed. Allahabad: Central Law Agency.

Report of the Arrears Committee, 1989–1990. 1990. New Delhi: Supreme Court of India.

Report on the Administration of Justice in the State of Uttar Pradesh, 1976. 1982. Allahabad: Superintendent, Printing and Stationary.

Roe, B.O. 1927. *A Short Treatise on the Administration of Justice in the Punjab and India*. Lahore: The Civil Military Gazette.

Rowe, Peter. 1968–9. 'Indian Lawyers and Political Modernization'. *Law & Society Review*. 3:219–50.

Sathe, S.P., Shaila Kunchur, and Smita Kashikar. 1982–3. 'Legal Profession—Its Contribution to Social Change: A Survey of the Pune City Bar'. *Banaras Law Journal*. 18 and 19:40.

_____. 1983. 'Pune Bar: A Study in Sociology of the Profession'. *Indian Bar Review*. 10:47–81.

Saxena, Manohar Raj. 1986. 'Legal Aid Advice Scheme and Lok Adalat'. *All India Reporter*. 73:103.

Sharma, Miriam. 1979. *The Politics of Inequality: Competition and Control in an Indian Village*. Delhi: Hindustan Publishing Corporation.

Srinivas, M.N. 1955. 'The Social System of a Mysore Village'. In McKim Marriot, ed., *Village India*, 1–35. Chicago: University of Chicago Press.

Stephen, James Fitzjames. 1870. 'Minute by the Hon'ble Mr. Stephen on the Administration of Justice in British India'.

Whitson, Sarah Leah. 1992. '"Neither Fish nor Flesh nor Good Red Herring" *Lok Adalats*: An Experiment in Informal Dispute Resolution in India'. *Hastings International and Comparative Law Review*. 15 (Spring):391.

Cases—India

All India Judges' Association v. Union of India, AIR 1992 SC 165.
All India Judges' Association v. Union of India, 1995(2) SCALE 374.
Bandhua Mukti Morcha v. Union of India, AIR 1985 SC 802.
Chandramohan v. State of Uttar Pradesh, AIR 1966 SC 1987.
Chandramouleshwar v. Patna High Court, AIR 1970 SC 375.
Ishwar Chand Jain v. High Court of Punjab and Haryana (1988) 3 SCJ 38.
Kesavananda Bharati v. State of Kerala, AIR 1973 SC 1461.
S.P. Gupta v. Union of India, AIR 1982 SC 149.
Samsher Singh v. State of Punjab, AIR 1974 SC 2192.
State of Assam v. Ranga Mohammad, AIR 1967 SC 903.
State of West Bengal v. Nripendra Nath, AIR 1966 SC 447.
Tejpal Singh v. State of Uttar Pradesh, 1986 3 SCJ 353.

Cases—United States

Brown v. Board of Education, 347 US 483 (1954)
Roe v. Wade, 410 US 113 (1973).

TABLES

Table 1: Filings, Disposals, and Pending Cases in Kerala High Court 1990–1994

	Filings	Disposals	Pending cases
1990	23,021	24,359	32,992
1991	26,068	22,703	36,357
1992	32,394	22,139	46,612
1993	32,584	24,126	55,070
1994	33,402	25,448	63,024

Source : Kerala High Court records.

Table 2: Filings, Disposals, and Pending Cases on the Original and Appellate Sides 1990–1994

	Filings	Disposals	Pending cases
1990			
Original	13,863	13,531	14,820
Appellate	9158	10,828	18,172
1991			
Original	15,827	13,550	17,097
Appellate	10,241	9153	19,263
1992			
Original	20,367	15,391	22,073
Appellate	12,321	6748	24,539
1993			
Original	21,671	16,681	27,063
Appellate	10,913	7445	28,027
1994			
Original	21,364	17,508	30,919
Appellate	12,038	7940	32,105

Source : Kerala High Court records.

Table 3: Original Petitions Filed, Disposed, and
Pending 1990–1994

	Filings	Disposals	Pending
1990	12,109	11,158	13,765
1991	13,822	11,544	16,043
1992	17,355	13,188	20,151
1993	17,993	13,613	24,531
1994	18,409	14,446	28,494

Source : Kerala High Court records.

The Indian Nation-State
From Pre-colonial Beginnings to Post-colonial Reconstructions

Thomas Pantham

The Indian nation-state, imagined and struggled for during the anti-colonial movement, was formally inaugurated in 1947 and given constitutional sanction in 1950. Of its two components, viz. state and nation,[1] the former was largely an adapted continuation of the modern apparatus of the colonial state, whereas the latter was the anti-colonial creation of the Indian national movement, especially of its Gandhi-Nehru phase. In the processes leading to, and culminating in, the transfer of power from the British rulers to the leadership of the Indian nationalist movement and the attendant process of constitution making, the state apparatus of colonial modernity became transformed by, and anchored in, the moral-political concerns of Indian nationalism. Appropriately stressing the newness of the independent nation-state, Jawaharlal Nehru, India's first Prime Minister, announced its birth, at midnight of 14–15 August 1947, as 'a moment, which comes but rarely in history, when we step out of the old to the new, when an age ends, and when the soul of a nation, long suppressed, finds utterance' (Nehru 1949: 3).

How was this 'nation' suppressed by colonialism and how has it found its new expression in the post-colonial state? What has been its post-Independence career?

In their different ways, the British colonial state in India and the anti-colonial nationalist movement which it gave rise to, marked major departures from the structure of political authority and the culture of political identities as they had existed in pre-colonial/pre-modern Indian society. Those departures or discontinuities constitute the birthmarks of the distinctive identity of the contemporary Indian nation-state. This state, however, even while resolutely pursuing modernity, does claim a certain moral-cultural or cultural-political continuity with tradition or, to repeat Nehru's words, with the long-suppressed 'soul' of the Indian nation. This continuity is formally expressed, often for symbolic purposes, in several different places and ways, some of which include: (i) Article 1 of the Constitution, which identifies India as '*Bharat*', reminiscent of *Bharatvarsha* (the land of the progeny of Bharat, celebrated in the great epic, Mahabharata); (ii) the use of an adaptation from the Sarnath lion capital of Mauryan emperor, Ashoka, as the state emblem of India; (iii) the incorporation, into that emblem, of the inscription, *satyameva jayate* (Truth Alone Triumphs), which is taken from the *Mundaka Upanishad;* (iv) the incorporation of Ashoka's *dharmachakra* (Wheel of Law) on the national flag of India; and (v) the constitutionally directed (Article 40) efforts of the state to promote *panchayati raj*, the form of village republics in ancient India.

What then were the characteristics of state formations and their patterns of legitimization in India in pre-colonial times?

The Subcontinental State Under the Mauryan and Gupta Dynasties

In India's long pre-colonial history, a centralized pan-Indian state was the exception rather than the rule. The prevailing pattern was one of resilient power structures at the level of the village community and several regional kingdoms of varying power with changing interrelationships with one another. True, many of these regional states did often pursue ambitions for subcontinental hegemony, but only on very few occasions were they successful. In fact, prior to British colonial rule, there have been only three brief periods 'when the parochial loyalties of family, caste, and region have been transcended by a larger pan-Indian vision of what a united India might be' (Larson 1997: 140–1). These three 'pan-Indian visions' were those of the Mauryan empire under Ashoka (third century BC), whose legitimacy rested partly on Kautilya's *Arthashastra* (science of wealth) and partly on the Buddhist *dhamma*; the Gupta empire under Chandra Gupta II (fourth and early fifth centuries AD), with its legitimation by a composite Hindu religious culture which absorbed several ideas from Buddhism and Jainism; and the Mughal empire under Akbar (sixteenth century) with its largely Indo-Islamic legitimation.

The infrequency of the formation of centralized or strong subcontinental states and their early mortality in India's long history are generally interpreted as having to do partly with the frequency of foreign invasions and partly with the fact that structures of political authority remained rooted 'in lineage and kinship networks and primordial loyalties rather than in associational structures and impersonal norms'

(Kumar 1997: 398). The power of the dominant clans, lineages, and castes of a given local society was legitimized by the Brahmanical religion (Frankel 1989: 2). In ancient India, the transition from nomadic and semi-nomadic tribal communities to agricultural settlements took the form of caste society, which has proved to be a change-inhibiting system of social stratification (Kulke and Rothermund [1986] 1998: 39–41). In caste society, the political agency of the people was either circumscribed (in the case of the Brahmins and the Kshatriyas) or altogether precluded (in the case of the other, lower castes, namely the Vaishyas and Shudras, as well as the untouchables, the Aspriyas). Moreover, there was a peculiar embedding or reinforcing relationship between the ritual hierarchy based on religious notions of purity and pollution and the hierarchies of wealth and power—peculiar in the sense that the lowest levels of all these hierarchies tended to coincide, whereas their highest levels were differentiated from each other. In this ingenious system of social stratification, it was extremely difficult for the ordinary people to pinpoint any locus of compounded privileges or the social/human causation of, or political responsibility for, the compounded deprivations of those who found themselves at the bottom of the hierarchies of status, wealth, and power. This had a change-inhibiting impact, especially at the level of the local village community. Its social order, which was indeed one of inequality, was interpreted by the Brahmins as 'natural' or 'pre-given' (in/by the immutable, sacred *shruti* [revealed] texts), and not politically constructed by historically situated human agents. In a society which is thought to be made up of such 'pre-ordered' or 'pre-governed' village communities, the state or the political sphere had only a very limited or marginal role to play. It had no sovereignty in any political sense; it did not have to engage in any legislative or judicial activities for creating or transforming the social order, be it the order of gender relations or of production relations. Thus, as Francine Frankel writes, 'the failure of centralized states to emerge in the subcontinent was directly linked to the strength of Brahmanical ideology in providing sacral legitimation for localized dominance relations. These religious beliefs made the state unnecessary for the preservation of social harmony [1989: 1–2]'.

This is not to deny the limited space which the Brahmanically legitimized social order assigned to the state or the political-administrative sphere (of the Kshatriyas). Under Brahmanical edict, the state had to uphold or maintain, without any change, the pre-given social order of *varnashramdharma* and punish those who infringed it. The state of course also had to perform the basic function of providing protection to the community from its external enemies. Accordingly, the caste system provided for a very limited functional autonomy to its 'political' segment, the Kshatriyas, to raise and administer the required revenues and to manage its bureaucracy, police, and army. A part of the state's revenues had to be used to construct and maintain temples, whose priests crowned the kings and advised them on their *rajadharm* (king's duty) of upholding the varnashramdharma.

Given the limited or constrained nature of their differentiation or autonomy from the Brahmanically legitimized 'pre-given' or 'natural' social order, the institutions of the state could not develop as political institutions. Hence the formation of the first centralized pan-Indian state, namely the Mauryan empire, could come about only through radical departures from the old religiously legitimized social order—departures which established a clear differentiation or autonomy of the political sphere from the socio-religious sphere.[2] Such departures were made since the sixth century BC, first, by heretical movements within religion, namely, Buddhism and Jainism,[3] and, second, by the radically new, secular-pragmatic theory of the state and government contained in the *Arthashastra*, attributed to Kautilya, the mentor and minister of Chandragupta Maurya (c. 321–298 BC), the founder of the Mauryan empire.

As noted by Romila Thapar, some of the ways in which the 'reforms' or 'heresies' of Buddhism and Jainism contributed to changing the socio-economic system, were: the support of the investment of economic surplus in commercial activities rather than its consumption in ritual functions,[4] the formation of the Buddhist *sangha*, with the monastery, which was supported by the lay followers; as its main institution; and the participation of the emperors, qua *chakravartins* (universal rulers with not only administrative functions but also legislative and judicial sovereignty), in the Buddhist Councils held at Rajagrha and Pataliputra. The most important departure of Buddhism and Jainism from Brahmanism was their advocacy of a universalistic ethics for 'the entire range of castes in an effort to equate people not socially but at least at the level of ethical action' (Thapar 1984: 109–11; Prasad 1974: 209–11).

Buddhism and Jainism, however, were primarily heretical movements within the religious sphere and, with the exception of the later phase of Ashoka's rule, did not exert much direct influence on the state.[5] According to Louis Dumont, the Jain and Buddhist reaction against Brahminic supremacy 'has been effected through renunciation, and not within the social order itself; in other words it occurred on a level transcending society' (Dumont 1970: 74). I would, however, maintain that the affirmation of human agency by the individual in her/his religious life did have a revolutionary impact on political life in the sense that the political agency of the individual could no longer be de-legitimized by Brahmanical ideology. In fact, since its beginning, Buddhism has been associated with a republican view of political life and a contractarian view of the state. Moreover, during the time of Ashoka, Buddhism 'was not merely a religious belief; it was in addition a social and intellectual movement at many levels, influencing many aspects of society' (Thapar [1966] 1997: 85).

Yet it cannot be denied that the earlier strand of Buddhism, with its emphasis on renunciation and monastic life, could not have been the answer to the need for political unity and centralization in the wake of the incursions into India by Alexander of Macedon. That need was met by the theory of state which was provided by Kautilya's *Arthashastra*. According to it, the answer to the dangers of anarchy was to be found neither in renunciation nor in excessive individualism, but in a strong, centralized state under a sovereign king. What was required, in other words, was a clear or secular differentiation or autonomy of the political from the socio-religious. The *Arthashastra* provided for such a clear autonomy. As V.R. Mehta writes: 'While the earlier literature [e.g. the *Dharmasutras*] had subordinated the king to brahmanical authority, and the *Shantiparva* gave the king some discretion, when we come to Kautilya, we find that the king is given the last say in all matters' (Mehta 1992: 86). The autonomy of the political sphere from the socio-religious sphere was stretched to the extent of giving to the former its own moral standard, namely the principle of the end justifying the means. With the acquisition of such a sovereignty by the state, religion became a private affair of the citizens. Moreover, according to Kautilya, the king is no more a mere protector or upholder of a pre-given socio-religious order; he has sovereign legislative, judicial, and executive powers. 'In the Arthashastra,' writes Dumont, 'the king exerts a complete hold on everything, and in the first place on the soil' (1970: 83).

It was this radically new theory of state that guided and informed the formation and consolidation of the first centralized imperial Indian state under the Mauryan dynasty of Chandragupta, Bindusara, and Ashoka. Its formation through conquests and consolidation through a centralized bureaucracy rested on the fiscal security provided by an economy of expanding agriculture, craft guilds, and trade. The intervention of the state for such expansion, however, was by and large confined to the metropolitan or core region of the empire, whereas in the peripheral regions the presence of the imperial state, through its centralized administration, was usually confined to the collection of taxes, tributes and, during campaigns or conquests, plunder. The taxes and tributes thus collected were used to pay the large army and bureaucracy and the spies, who worked in the guise of ascetics, mendicant women, prostitutes, merchants, and students.

Romila Thapar has used the symbolism of the wheel and the *mandala* theory of state to describe the relationship between the core region of the Mauryan empire, which served as a firm and secure 'hub of power', and its peripheral areas. Just as a wheel is marked by a differential distribution of power, so in the Mauryan empire there was 'a differentiation between power at the centre of the circle and at the rim' (Thapar 1984: 161). Or, as the mandala theory stipulates, the core region and its peripheral areas stood in a kaleidoscopic; relationship marked by a constant vacillation between friendship-and-hostility, between the central king and his circle (mandala) of friendly, hostile, and neutral kings (cf. Ghoshal 1959: 93–4).

Towards the close of Ashoka's rule, the Mauryan state experienced some severe socio-economic and religious conflicts, namely conflicts between the Brahmins and the heterodox sects (Buddhists and Jains) and the disaffection of the rising mercantile communities whose interests clashed with the revenue requirements of the bureaucratic-militaristic state. Taxes were in fact collected 'from every conceivable human activity with which the state could be associated' (Thapar 1984: 160). Heavy taxation and bureaucratic controls did not contribute to the expansion of economic activity. The harassment of traders blocked economic progress and led to a fiscal crisis of the state (Kosambi 1970: 165 and 1975: 216).

Confronted by these problems, Ashoka felt that the *Arthashastra* framework of double or separate standards for the state and for the people had to be replaced by, or at least brought under the purview of, a new common or universal ethics that would not only unite the state and its citizens but also bring about toleration among the religious sects. Accordingly, he expounded and propagated a new, universal dhamma (the Prakrit word used in Buddhist literature for the Sanskrit word, dharma). Dhamma, for Ashoka, meant neither piety nor the rules of caste society, but a spirit of righteous conduct and social responsibility. Its main principles were non-violence, public works or people's welfare, and, most importantly, toleration, especially of opposing religious sects. In one of his rock edicts, he propagated the principle of toleration in the following way:

> The Beloved of the Gods [i.e. Ashoka] does not consider gifts of honour to be as important as the essential advancement of all sects. Its basis is the control of one's speech, so as not to extol one's own sect or disparage that of another on unsuitable occasions. ... On each occasion one should honour another man's sect, for by doing so one increases the influence of one's own sect and benefits that of the other man, while, by doing otherwise, one diminishes the influence of one's own sect and harms the other man's ... therefore concord is to be commended so that men may hear one another's principles [(Thapar (1966) 1977: 87)].

Although Ashoka's actual policy of dhamma made only a very small contribution to bringing about social unity and political stability, his role in emphasizing the need for moral legitimacy of the actions of the state has remained a lasting legacy in India. 'It can even be said,' to quote Kosambi, 'that the Indian national character received the stamp of *dhamma* from the time of Asoka. The word soon came to mean something else than "equity", namely religion—and by no means the sort of religion Asoka himself professed' (1970: 165).

The Brahmanic reaction to the Buddhist dhamma was one of the factors contributing to the decline of the Mauryan empire. The former led eventually to a great religious-cultural resurgence and creativity, culminating in what is referred to as the 'classical Hindu' period of Indian history under the imperial rule of the Gupta dynasty (AD 320–500). However, the Hindu religion from which the legitimacy of the imperial rule of the Gupta emperors was derived was a remarkably pluralist religion, containing within it three major sects/cults (of Shiva, Vishnu/Krishna, and Durga/Kali). The Gupta rulers were also tolerant towards and supportive of other religions, notably Buddhism and Jainism. There was also a Christian community in South India. According to many historians, the Gupta emperors pursued a composite pan-Indian moral-cultural vision that accommodated religious and regional differences. The *Lawbook of Yajnavalkya*, which served as a guide to the Gupta rulers, not only drew a clear distinction between secular and religious law but also removed some of the legal discriminations against the Shudras and some of the legal privileges which the Brahmins had earlier enjoyed. Yet it must be remembered that the primary interest of the Gupta rulers was to rule and not to bring about social revolution. Their rule sustained and was sustained by the 'Aryan patriarchal society', which, among other things, practised pre-puberty marriages and *sati* (Thapar [1966] 1977: 152 and 166; Dandekar [1958] 1988: 236–40). Under the rule of the Gupta dynasty, there was a revival of some aspects of the old Brahmanical ideology (for example caste hierarchy, Vedic rituals, and the horse sacrifice). The Gupta period was also associated with some new additions to, or redactions of, the *smriti* literature, especially the *Dharmashastra* and the *Bhagwad Gita*, which, among other things, presented the moral philosophy of *nishkama karma* (the duty of disinterested action).

The religious pluralism and toleration of the imperial state of the Guptas was associated with the flourishing of trade and commerce both across the regions within the empire and across the oceans, especially with Southeast Asia, where both Buddhists and Hindus visited and settled. There was also an association between the religious pluralism of the imperial state and the considerable degree of political and administrative autonomy which the provinces or regions had.

The degree of centralization of rule which was achieved under the Mauryan or the Gupta dynasties was not continued or repeated until the coming of the Mughals in the sixteenth century. In the intervening period, the Indian polity was loosely integrated under a succession of what has come to be alternatively designated as 'pyramidally segmented states' (Stein 1980) or 'imperial formations' (Inden 1990). In their separate ways, theoretical constructs such as these are meant to differentiate the medieval Indian polity from the unitary, centralized, territorial state of European modernity.

Pyramidally Segmented States or Imperial Formations?

According to Burton Stein (1980), a pyramidally segmented type of state was formed in medieval south India, especially during the Pallava, Chola, and Vijayanagara periods, by the interlinking of 'relatively self-sufficient, enduring, and often quite ancient localized societies'.

> Such a state is not an amalgamation or absorption of localised units into an organic greater unit such as implied in the unitary state, but is an arrangement in which the local units—segments—retain their essential being as segmental parts of a whole. One reason why each of the segmental units remains autonomous is that each is pyramidal, that is, each consists of balanced and opposed internal groupings which zealously cling to their independent identities, privileges, and internal governance, and demand that these units be protected by their local rulers [Stein 1980: 275].

In this polity, sovereignty was dual in the sense that while the king exercised an essentially ritual sovereignty in all the zones (*nadus*) of the state, he wielded actual political sovereignty or control only in the core or central zone of the state system, leaving the intermediate and peripheral zones to the political sovereignty or control of the 'little kings' and chiefs. However, because all the segmentary units recognized the king as the single, incorporative, ritual authority, they together constituted a state system of the segmentary type. It was segmentary rather than unitary or centralized in the sense that it had a vertical discontinuity of actual power relations, with the 'little kings' and chiefs of the peripheral zones retaining their own armies and administrators. Inter-segmentary cooperation was brought about in acts of defence or aggression against others and was cemented by their common recognition of the ritually incorporative sovereignty of the king of kings. This came about in Tamil Nadu during the Pallava period, when the Aryan/Brahmanical conception of 'ritually incorporative kingship' or sovereignty was introduced. To quote Stein again: 'The pre-Pallavan, or Classical, period was one in which three kingships and a great number of chieftainships existed among Tamils; from the Pallava period, the Tamils could have but one great king, one who, by means of ritual, incorporated all lesser rulers' (1980: 276).

Because its political unity was based only or essentially on the sacral or ritual rulership of the king over the segmentary units, which were in complementary opposition to one another, the pre-modern, pyramidally segmented state, in contrast to the modern, unitary, centralized state, constituted a fluid and indeterminate political structure with vague boundaries and shifting capitals. The fixed or stable elements of the state existed only at local levels, which were under the control of dominant cultivating or merchant groups and of the 'little kings'. As protectors of the locality, these 'little kings' could obtain resources by force. But since their rulership had a ritual or sacral character as well, they had to redistribute some of their amassed resources through the '*dharmic* activities' of giving *dana*s (gifts) to temples and Brahmins. The hundreds of nadus which comprised south Indian society under the Pallavas or the Cholas were unified not through any technical or bureaucratic mechanisms but through the 'idiom of a *dharmic* universe realized through the sacral kingship' of the ruling dynasty (Stein 1980: 365).[6]

The segmentary model of the state in 'medieval' south India has been criticized for its overemphasis on the segmentariness of the polity and the essentially ritual nature of the sovereignty of its king. Alam and Subrahmanyam (1998: 34) feel that the regular fiscal flows which were maintained between the localities and the core region of the Vijayanagar kingdom made it more than a mere segmentary state based essentially on ritual sovereignty. According to Ronald Inden (1990), the Indian polity during the so-called medieval period had a greater and, indeed, different type of unity than what is granted to it by Stein's notions of pyramidal segmentation and ritual sovereignty. Rejecting Stein's dichotomy between the higher ritual sovereignty of the Great King and the lower political sovereignties of the 'little kings', Inden seems to suggest that the so-called ritual or dharmic activities were also political activities and vice versa.

Instead of Stein's dichotomy between the ritual/sacral sovereignty of the Great King and the political sovereignty of the 'little kings', Inden speaks of the chakravartin's 'compound activity' whereby he seeks both *dig-vijaya* (conquest of the quarters, whereby other kings are brought into 'the circle of kings' or the imperial formation) and dharma-vijaya (cosmomoral victory). Inden writes

> All of the major [Indian] religious orders incorporated into their soteriologies the idea of a universal monarch or paramount king of India, a 'great man' (*mahapurusha*) who, endowed with special powers, was able to complete a 'conquest of quarters' of India in the name of a still greater agent, the one taken as overlord of the cosmos. The names given to this compound activity, the 'conquest of quarters' (*dig-vijaya*) and 'conquest in accord with cosmomoral order' (*dharma-vijaya*), referred to a royal progress

that was supposed to display the performer of it as the overlord of each of the four directional regions, together with a middle region, taken to comprise the whole of the earth [Inden 1990: 229–30].

Inden does concur with Stein in denying to the medieval-Indian state the centralized political control and administration that characterize the modern nation-state. He also sees in medieval India a succession, not of mere ritually integrated kingdoms, but of real 'imperial formations' which approximate the *Arthashastra* model of the 'circle of kings' (mandala, *rajamandala*) under the paramount control or domination of a chakravartin (universal monarch).[7] Each one of these imperial formations consisted of 'one (or more) empires and a number of other kingdoms'. Through 'dialectical and eristical relations with one another', they together formed 'a scale of polities, or rulerships that overlapped one another'. Among them, there was frequent competition for the position of the 'highest polity in the scale' (Inden 1990: 267).

According to Inden, the Indian polity functioned as an imperial formation under the Chalukyas, the Rashtrakutas, the Cholas, and the Vijayanagara rulers. Under their rule, the core or middle region of Indian polity was displaced from the Ganga-Yamuna region on to their own imperial domains. He also claims that Indian polity under the rule of the Rashtrakuta dynasty (AD 753–975) was one of a total of only four imperial formations which made up the whole of Eurasia and North Africa in that period, the others being the Arab, Chinese, and Greek imperial formations.

Patrimonial-Bureaucratic States

The Mughal empire, especially under Akbar's rule (1556–1605), has been viewed as 'the culmination of pre-modern state administration in India' (Kulke 1995: 32). It had a centralized administrative machinery, called the *mansabdari* system, in which there was a fusion of military and civil services into a single, hierarchic bureaucracy under the emperor. Each administrative-military officer had a definite number rank (*mansab*), generally determined by the number of cavalry (*sawars*, horsemen), he had to raise and maintain out of his emoluments and which, when needed, were available to the emperor. The payments were either in cash or by an assignment of the land-revenue of a specified area (*jagir*), under the control of the mansabdar and his subordinate revenue collectors, including the *zamindars*.

The empire was divided into *subahs* (provinces), *sarkars* (subdivisions), and *mohallas* (revenue circles). More or less the same administrative structure was developed in each subah. Yet, as pointed out by Alam and Subrahmanyam, there was noticeable variation in land-revenue administration from region to region, rather than an 'unremitting centralization based on an elaborate and uniform bureaucracy which has "penetrated" the countryside (1998: 15). The zamindars in the countryside as well as bankers and traders retained a certain degree of autonomy. Moreover, as many new regions were conquered and incorporated into the empire, regional and local variations had to be recognized so that the state eventually resembled a "patchwork quilt" rather than a "wall-to-wall carpet"' (Alam and Subrahmanyam: 33). Notwithstanding the absence of any 'unremitting centralization' in the administrative set-up of the Mughal empire, it needs to be noted that the Mughal state was seen 'in all of the subcontinent as the only true source of sovereignty' (Alam and Subrahmanyam 1998: 57).

The rise and consolidation of this great patrimonial-bureaucratic state in India coincided with, and was, in its later phase, helped by, the dawn of modern technology in Europe. Especially significant was the role of artillery, 'the most brilliant and dreadful representative of modern technology' in those times, when there also arose absolute monarchies in Europe (Ali 1995: 264). As pointed out by M. Athar Ali (1995: 274–5), even though the Mughal army was mainly a cavalry force, artillery did play a significant role in it. Its infantrymen included 'match-lock men, gunners, cannoneers[,] and rocketeers' and thus they had a decisive advantage against the traditional chiefs, including the Rajputs.

Another product of early European modernity was the influx of silver into the international market, resulting from the Spanish 'discovery' of South America. This made it possible for the Mughal emperors, especially Akbar, to replace the existing debased coinage (largely of copper content) that had a new currency system, with the highly valued silver-based rupee as the basic unit. This contributed to the expansion of commerce and credit, and also to the centralization of the state.

Some of the subjects of the Mughal state became aware of early modern European scientific knowledge and questioned the finality of traditional knowledge. For instance, Abul Fazl, Akbar's ideologue, propagandist, and adviser, questioned those who were opposing sciences that were not based upon the Quran (Ali 1995: 275). There were also 'revisionist' movements, like the Mahdavi movement, which challenged earlier interpretations of Islamic doctrines. 'All these,' writes M. Athar Ali, 'were symptoms of a cleft in the hitherto solid structure of faith in the traditional cultural heritage of Islam' (1995: 276). Partly in response to this new situation and partly for other reasons (like the majority status of the Hindus in the population and Akbar's marriage to a Hindu princess), Akbar pursued a policy of religious tolerance and promoted regular, inter-religious discussions. More importantly, he devised a new, eclectic set of beliefs called Divine Faith (*Din-el-Ilahi*), which contained elements from Islam, Hinduism, and Zoroastrianism. Din-e-Ilahi, however, was not made a state religion. Moreover, in the administration of justice, Akbar assumed the role of an interpreter of the Islamic law, which he occasionally supplemented by imperial edicts (*qanun-e-shahi*).

Despite these advances in military-fiscal organization and moral-political legitimation, the Mughal state basically remained a patrimonial-bureaucratic state, in which the empire was identified with the person of the emperor and personal loyalty to the emperor was equated with loyalty to the state. This is well expressed by J.F. Richards:

> From an external perspective, the bureaucratic structure of the empire[,] with its specialized offices, systematic procedures, and hierarchies of technically proficient officials, was the most impressive aspect of the empire. However, the core of the imperial system embedded within the outer structure was formed by the complex matrix of ties of loyalty and interest between the *amirs* and the emperor [1998: 129].

Some of the patrimonial-bureaucratic features of the Mughal state are brought out by Stephen Blake in his reading of Abul Fazl's *Ain-i Akbari* (Institutes of Akbar), as follows:

> In its depiction of the emperor as a divinely aided patriarch, the household[,] as the central element in government, members of the army as dependent on the emperor, the administration as a loosely structured group of men controlled by the Imperial household and travel as a significant part of the emperor's activities, the Ain-i Akbari supports the suggestion that Akbar's state was a patrimonial-bureaucratic empire [1995: 302].

A variant of the Mughal patrimonial-bureaucratic state was the patrimonial-*sultanist* state of Tipu Sultan (1783–99), which functioned as a semi-independent state under the carapace of the sovereignty of the Mughal state. Under this sultanism, the army was the first institution of the state and its ruler was above all a war commander, demanding the personal loyalty of the subordinates. Sultanism essentially meant the elimination of the tribute-paying intermediaries and the instantiation of a centralized machinery of fiscal control.[8]

Given its essential character as an extended patrimonial-bureaucratic system, the Mughal state cannot be said to have been constituted according to the distinctly modern values and principles of the formation and legitimation of the state. In effect, the subcontinent of India, to quote M. Athar Ali once more, 'had a centralized quasi-modern state without any developing sense of nationhood' (1995: 277) among the mass of the imperial subjects. In fact, one of the contributing factors to the decline of the Mughal imperial authority was the resistance movements not only of the peasants and other regional and local groups but also of the zamindars, who capitalized on the peasants' grievances against the state and mobilized them for their own political ends (Alam 1998: 472; Bhadra 1998).

The patrimonial-bureaucratic structures of the Mughal state were initially relied upon by the colonial regime, which, as we shall see below, eventually replaced it by the fully bureaucratized, modern, unitary state based on European principles (Stein 1985: 412–13). Another point of continuity and change between the Mughal and colonial states pertained to the use of what Foucault calls the modern technologies of power (Foucault 1979: part 3, ch. 3). The Mughal state did use some rudimentary, early modern versions of modern technologies of power and surplus extraction such as surveys, measurements, accounts, and audits. Also, panopticons-style prisons (designed to enable the warder to directly observe prisoners without being seen by them) were built at Poona and Ratnagiri. Through these new technologies of power exercise, the Mughal state eliminated some of the intermediary structures and acquired direct control over its subjects. These early modern technologies of power/knowledge, however, were more fully developed and used by the colonial state and used for substantively new purposes (Perlin 1985: 263, 475, 477).

The Colonial State

The British colonial state in India marked a substantial break with the previous state forms. This had to do with its European origins and orientations or purposes, which were inextricably linked with the career of capitalist modernity on a world scale.

The English East India Company, founded in London in 1600 under the Charter rights given by the British government, began its trading activities in India by securing privileges from Mughal emperor Jahangir, in 1619 for setting up and fortifying 'factories' or trading centres. Operating from those trading centres, the functionaries of the Company eventually resorted to political conspiracies, military conquests, and the instantiation of Company raj. These actions constituted the proto-state of colonial modernity, to be replaced, after the 1857 Great Revolt, by the fully designed and formally proclaimed colonial modern state.

The Company's securing of *Diwani* (the high office entitling its incumbent to collect all revenues) in Bengal in 1765 from the Mughal emperor constituted the 'inaugural moment of the *raj*' (Guha 1997: 156). Diwani enabled the Company to legitimize its military conquest of Bengal (in the battles of Plassey and Buxar) and to launch its new career as the incipient proto-state of British colonialism in India. As *Diwan*, the Company claimed legality for its new function of administering civil justice and collecting and administering land revenues, which were used to finance further trade and military conquests, and to pay an annuity of 400,000 pounds sterling as tribute to the British exchequer. By the Pitt's India Act of 1784, the British government brought the Company raj under its indirect rule. After the suppression of the Great Indian Revolt of 1857, the indirect rule of Great Britain over India was converted into direct imperial rule. This was effected through an Act passed by British parliament and proclaimed in India by Queen Victoria in November 1858. By this Act and Proclamation, the British Indian colonial state was formally created, with its sovereignty appropriated by the British Crown. This colonial state came to exercise direct rule over two-thirds of the territory and four-fifths of the population of the country, while the rest of the territory and population were left to the rule of the native princes, subject to the 'paramount' overseeing of resident agents of the Viceroy.

The Company raj received initial support from Indian financial and merchant capitalists, who saw themselves as standing to benefit more from the larger trade networks of the East India Company than from the military fiscalism of the Mughal *nawabs* or from the sultanist or warrior states of Mysore, the Marathas, or the Sikhs. For instance, Robert Clive's victory in the Battle of Plassey was crucially dependent on the support he received from the merchant bankers Jagat Seth and Omichand. As the Company raj became consolidated, Indian commercial and trading groups were reduced to very inferior status, although some of them found avenues for business in some of the British colonies in Africa, West Asia, and Southeast Asia.

Being both colonial and modern at the same time, the state of the British Indian empire marked a substantial departure from India's pre-modern/pre-colonial state structures as well as from its modern mother state in England. The most obvious way in which the colonial state differed from the pre-colonial states lay in the greatness and pervasiveness of its activities. Commenting on some of those 'great' activities of the new state on the eve of its reorganization according to the Government of India Act of 1935, Edward Thompson and G.T. Garratt wrote:

> On the merely material side the new Federal Government will take over the largest irrigation system in the world ... some 60,000 miles of metalled roads; over 42,000 miles of railway ...; 230,000 scholastic institutions ...; a great

number of buildings. The vast area of India has been completely surveyed, most of its lands assessed, and a regular census taken of its population and its productivity. ... The postal department handles nearly 1500 million articles yearly, the Forestry Department not only prevents the denudation of immense areas, but makes a net profit of between two and three crores. These great State activities are managed by a trained bureaucracy, which is today almost entirely Indian [Thompson and Garratt (1934) 1962: 654].

These 'great State activities', which, as noted by Thompson and Garratt ([1934] 1962) were to leave a 'permanent mark upon Indian life', had to do with the colonial state's superiority in military technology, financial resources, administrative or bureaucratic rationality, and, above all, its colonizing purpose, namely the incorporation of India, as a colony, into the imperialist capitalist system. The central task of the colonial state was the internal disarticulation of the colonial economy and the external articulation of its segments with the requirements of the metropolitan or core country of the then emerging imperialist system of capitalist production and exchange. Some of the requirements of that core country, namely Britain, were the import of raw materials, especially agricultural and mineral products, and the export of its own manufactured goods. Accordingly, the colonial state, departing from the military fiscalism of the Mughal state and its subordinate/ successor sultanist kingdoms in the region, developed modern, centralized, sovereign state institutions for transforming and restructuring the economy, culture, laws, etc. of the colony. Thus, besides promoting or supporting colonial plantations, forced cultivation of indigo or opium, irrigation, mining, trade, transport, communications, and selected industries, the new state introduced institutions of modern western education and bourgeois legal and judicial systems (Kaviraj 1994: 36 and 38).

For carrying out these unprecedented, mammoth tasks, the colonial state replaced the erstwhile, patrimonial-sultanist, civil-cum-military bureaucracy with a modern, specialized military and civil bureaucracy, based on a colonial version of the rational, impersonal, non-arbitrary, competitive principles of merit, efficiency, neutrality, etc. The colonial state constituted a curious mixture of modernity and tradition. It tried to accommodate its own modern, unitary sovereignty with the sovereignties of the traditional rulers, the *rajas* and *maharajas*. Even its own modern, paramount, unitary sovereignty was initially presented, for the purpose of legitimation, as a continuation and improvement of the institutional and symbolic order of the pre-colonial state, for example the institution of the Mughal *durbar* (Cohn 1983; Kaviraj 1994). By doing so, the colonial state secured legitimacy for its rule from the forces of tradition, which, in turn, received a fresh lease of life under the paramountcy of the modern-colonial state. For the sake of social stability and state legitimacy, the colonial state also followed the personal laws of the Islamic *sharia* and an order of precedence according to caste hierarchy.

As mentioned in earlier paragraphs, the colonial state marked a radical departure not only from its pre-colonial predecessor states but also from its mother state in Britain, to which it was in fact held responsible. Colonialism was based on the justificatory assumption that the colony and its people were different from, inferior to, and therefore colonizable by the 'enlightened' or 'rational' masters of the modern, industrialized metropolis. The colonial state therefore sought to 'prove' the truth of that assumption in two interrelated ways. First, it subjected the land and people of India to the specifically modern regime of power and knowledge, which, following Michael Foucault (1979), we may refer to as the power of cognitive regimes or disciplining categories of knowledge and rules of logic. Thus, under colonial rule,

> not only was the law codified and the bureaucracy rationalized, but a whole apparatus of specialized technical services was instituted in order to scientifically survey, classify, and enumerate the geographical, geological, botanical, and meteorological properties of the natural environment and the archaeological, historical, anthropological, linguistic, economic, demographic, epidemiological characteristics of the people [Chatterjee 1993: 19–20].

These new or modern technologies of disciplining knowledge/ power/rule, namely surveys, enumerations, classifications, accounting and auditing, and the associated conceptual baggage and binary logic of rational exclusion or marginalization, were put into operation by the colonial state in order to bring about an unprecedented centralization of rule, especially of the monetary system. As noted earlier, the revenues extracted from the traditional society by the modern, specialist cadres went into supporting the military operations or the international trading activities of the Company raj. This led to 'money famines', demonetization of the countryside, and the decline both of indigenous banking and manufacturing industries (Perlin 1985: 477–8). After the replacement of the Company raj by direct Crown rule through the Secretary of State and the Viceroy, the Indian economy had to pay what were called 'home charges', which included the cost of the Secretary of State's office (in London), costs of wars fought to expand or defend the empire, pensions for the military and civilian personnel, and a guaranteed annual interest on the investment in Indian railways. There was also a substantial de-valuation of the silver-based Indian rupee when it was plugged onto the gold-based exchange standard (Bose and Jalal 1998: 99–100).

The second way in which the colonial state attempted to 'prove' the justificatory assumption of colonialism (namely that the colonial subjects were a racially inferior people) was by 'demonstrating' that the legitimizing principles of the modern, liberal-democratic state, for example the principles of liberal equality, rule of law, and responsiveness to public opinion, were not universalizable until after the fulfilment of the so-called 'civilizing mission' of colonial rule. Even though the colonial state did set up institutions of modern western education in India and even though some of the constitutional reforms of the colonial rulers did provide for restricted Indian representation in provincial and central legislative assemblies as well as in municipal and other local boards, the colonial government did not give Indian judicial officers the same rights as their British counterparts to try cases in which European British subjects were involved.[9] Similarly, the principle of the freedom of opinion and expression was denied to the colonized subjects by the colonial government, whenever that opinion and expression clashed with those of the European community.[10]

The colonial state was formed by, and for, an alien bourgeois class. While the rule of that class was hegemonic in its home country as there was, in its civil society, widespread acceptance of the bourgeois-liberal conceptions of the individual, society, state, and democracy, its state in the colony lacked any such hegemony.[11] No doubt, the colonial state was responsible to the parliamentary-democratic government and public opinion of Britain. Those, however, were, for the historical period in question, avowedly imperialistic. The colonial state maintained its rule or power partly through coercion, partly through the continuation of some of the old discourses and practices of legitimation, and partly by forming a new middle class of English-educated Indians, who, it was hoped, would appreciate and advocate the benefits of the modern state that was imported from Britain. As it turned out, it was this middle class, whose acquisition of modern education made them see the utter illegitimacy or 'untruthful' nature of the colonial state and who provided the moral-intellectual and organizational leadership of the successful anti-imperialist nationalist movement.

In the course of the Indian nationalist movement, many of its leaders emphasized the fact that while in the entire tradition of Indian political thought and practice, the state had to seek its legitimacy in terms of moral-political principles, such as the principles of dhamma, dharma, or Din-e-Ilahi, the colonial state made itself the source of the law which created and sustained the colonial mode of the drain of wealth from India to the imperialist circuit of modern capitalism. This colonial-modern conception of the role of the state and of the rule of law was in fact inscribed over the seat of imperial power at the Central Secretariat in New Delhi. It read: 'Honour the State, the Root of Law and Wealth' (Sudarshan 1995: 59).

The Indian Nation-State—Democratic, Secular, and Developmental

It was in resistance to that state and its laws that the anti-colonial nationalist movement took shape in India and eventually succeeded in securing the transfer of power from the colonial rulers to its own leadership. The nationalist movement was spearheaded by the western-educated middle-class intelligentsia and the emergent indigenous bourgeoisie. Under the leadership of Mahatma Gandhi, the movement acquired a mass base among the peasantry, who had been the worst sufferers of the colonial system and who had previously risen in uncoordinated, violent rebellions (Chatterjee 1986 and 1993). The Gandhian era also saw a major reorganization of the Indian National Congress, whereby its provincial units were made to correspond to the linguistic regions rather than to the administrative provinces of the colonial state. The structure and functioning of the party were also made democratic. These democratic and linguistic-federal practices of the Indian National Congress, which were in clear opposition to the arbitrary and despotic practices of the colonial state, were thought to prefigure the future, independent nation-state. In fact, the central objective of the nationalist movement, in its mature phase, was the replacement of the colonial state by a democratic, sovereign nation-state, which, unlike the colonial and pre-colonial states, was to play a central, directing role in economic development and social justice.

The future, independent state was 'imagined' by the nationalist movement, especially in its final, Gandhi-Nehru phase, to be one which would sustain, and be sustained by, a complex conception of pluralist, civic-communitarian nationalism, rather than by any simple ethnic, religious, or linguistic nationalism. The former, unlike the latter, entailed a state-centred (rather than, say, caste- or religion-oriented) 'imagining' or 'construction' of a composite or pluralist national political community marked by the equal citizenship of all the peoples of India, irrespective of their religious, caste, linguistic, regional, or gender differences. 'In effect,' writes Rajni Kothari (1995a), 'it was stateness that gave to the new entity, at once, an encompassing, representative, and transcendent quality.' The state, moreover, was to respect the principle of the equality of all religions. The relationship of the new nation-state to the diverse pre-existing social, regional, linguistic, religious, or cultural identities was imagined 'in part to be one of transcendence, though it was far more to be one of encompassing them and in some ways even representing them in a composite manner' (Kothari 1995b). In the Indian nation-state, as imagined by the nationalist movement,

there was no way ... for any person to be *only* Indian and nothing else;
indeed, one could not be an Indian without being some other things at the
same time. Being a Bengali or Tamil or Punjabi, or Hindu, or Muslim or
agnostic, was not contradictory to being an Indian. Indianness was a
complex and multilayered identity which encompassed other such identities
without cancelling them [Kaviraj 1995c: 119].

The Indian nation-state, as pointed out by Bhikhu Parekh is both
an association of individuals and a community of communities, recognizing
both individuals and communities as bearers of rights. The criminal law
recognizes only individuals whereas the civil law recognizes most minority
communities as distinct legal subjects (1992: 171).

Only a democratic, federal, 'secular' state could sustain and be
sustained by such a rich or great 'composite' nation.

Actually, however, the end of the career of the British colonial state
in India in 1947 came about through the formation of *two* sovereign nation-
states, India and Pakistan.[12] Why the country was partitioned and how the
colonial state [or, how the end of the colonial state] contributed to defining the
state–religion relationship within, and interstate relations between, them are
some of the most important questions to be addressed in any study of the post-
colonial states of the Indian subcontinent. Such an exercise falls outside the
purview of the present work. I will, however, briefly consider the implications
of partition for the 'secular' and centralized nature of the Indian nation-state.

The demand of the Muslim League for a separate state for Indian
Muslims was based on the claim that they constituted a distinct 'nation', and
not just a 'minority'. Those, like the leaders of the Indian National Congress,
who opposed that demand did so on the counter-assertion that the Muslims
and the other religious communities together constituted the 'composite' or
'pluralist' Indian nation. Eventually, the creation of Pakistan as a separate
nation-state was not done through any homologous translation of the
religious identity of the Indian Muslims into a national-political identity.
Actually, partition was the result of a modern, political-ideological use of
religion, which Jinnah and the Muslim League pursued and which was agreed
to, quite readily, by the colonial rulers (who had earlier introduced the system
of separate electorates for minorities) and, more reluctantly, by the Indian
National Congress. Pakistan was created not as an Islamic state of all the
Indian Muslims, but as a separate state made up of the territory of only the
Muslim-majority provinces and Muslim-majority districts of Punjab and
Bengal.[13] After Partition, Pakistan had a Muslim population of about 60
million, while about 40 million Muslims continued to live in various parts of
India. Hence the idea of India as a 'composite', 'pluralist', or 'secular' nation-
state did not become less salient after Partition.

In fact, the Indian Constitution contains explicit provisions that guarantee to all persons equal freedom of conscience and religion and that prohibit the state from discrimination against any citizen on grounds of religion (Smith 1963; Pantham 1997; Bhargava 1998). In 1973, a full bench of the Supreme Court ruled that secularism is a constitutive feature of the basic structure of the Constitution. In 1976, the Constitution was amended to add the word 'secular' to the Preamble and to make the preservation of 'the rich heritage of our composite culture' a fundamental duty of all citizens.

Since the 1980s, however, there has been a shift in the legitimizing ideology of the Indian nation-state from secular nationalism to a religious-majoritarian nationalism. Associated with this, there has also been a shift in the state's developmental ideology from socialism or 'growth with justice' to the idea of the liberalizing state. These shifting trends are briefly sketched below.

It is pertinent to recall here that the partition of the country had a centralizing effect on state building in India (as well as in Pakistan). This is well brought out by Partha Chatterjee who writes that partition

> provided the state-builders in India with the opportunity to consolidate the powers of the state under a centralized political leadership which had a reasonably clear consensus on the objectives of state policy and which faced relatively little organized political opposition. The presence of a strong Muslim League opposition with potential support from large landed interests and the princes would have definitely made the task far more difficult [1998: 7].

Chatterjee goes on to maintain that Partition facilitated the formation of a new, relatively more cohesive ruling-class coalition, which was led by the industrial bourgeoisie and the urban middle-class intelligentsia and which also included, for reasons of electoral mobilization of the masses, locally dominant rural propertied classes.

A strong, centralized state, rather than a Gandhi-inspired decentralized system of government, was chosen by the state builders of independent India, led by Nehru and Sardar Vallabhbhai Patel, for coping with certain immediate problems of governance, such as Partition-related riots between Hindus and Muslims, the incursion of tribesmen from Pakistan's North West Frontier Province into Kashmir, a peasant uprising in Telengana, and problems connected with the integration of the hundreds of princely states, in one of which (Hyderabad) the Indian army had to intervene.[14] A strong, centralized state was also seen to be necessary for pursuing one of the major goals of the nationalist movement, namely-planned economic development, especially industrialization.[15] Hence it seemed sensible to the leadership of the independent nation-state to continue with the centralized structure of the colonial state apparatus. Not only the structure but also the Indian personnel of the civil bureaucracy, the police, and the army were retained and expanded in a big way. Also retained was the judicial system along with the system of civil and criminal laws. In fact, about two-thirds of the Constitution of independent India was drawn from the (colonial) Government of India Act of 1935.

The major institutional departures from the colonial state were: (i) the institutions of sovereign statehood (the indirectly elected President as Head of State) and parliamentary democracy based on universal adult franchise; (ii) a set of constitutionally guaranteed fundamental rights to all citizens, a set of principles to guide state policies; (iii) a centrally tilted federal system with a constitutional distribution of powers between the States; and the Union of India, and an independent judiciary vested with certain powers of judicial review.

The overriding objectives of the new independent nation-state were the preservation of its national sovereignty and unity and the fostering of economic development and social justice. These objectives had been the guiding motives of the Indian nationalist movement. Its opposition to the colonial state was based on the grounds that it was an alien institution serving to exploit and underdevelop India for the benefit of the people of the imperialist country. The independent Indian nation-state was imagined to be the historically necessary and legitimate means to end imperialist exploitation and to usher in a process of national economic development *with* social justice.[16]

> Concerning the state's role in economic development, Partha Chatterjee writes: A developmental ideology ... was a constituent part of the self-definition of the postcolonial state. The state was connected to the people-nation not simply through the procedural forms of representative government, it also acquired its representativeness by directing a programme of economic development on behalf of the nation. The former connected, as in any liberal form of government, the legal-political sovereignty of the state with the sovereignty of the people. The latter connected the sovereign powers of the state directly with the economic well-being of the people (1997: 86–7).

Whatever strategy of economic development was to be chosen by the state, it had to be in conformity with the newly acquired national Independence and the newly established democratic framework. No doubt, state power was controlled by a ruling-class coalition of the indigenous bourgeoisie, the rich farmers, and the professional-bureaucratic class. The interests of these classes had to be accommodated in the developmental strategy.

The actual strategy of economic development chosen by the state under Nehru's leadership was a state-planned or 'mixed' path of capitalist industrialization. According to it, the state or 'public' sector undertook the responsibility for the development of heavy industries and social overheads, with the medium and consumer industries as well as the agriculture being left to the private sector. The state sector of heavy industries was intended to bring about a pattern of import-substituting industrialization leading to a self-reliant economy.

Obviously, this state-planned and state-dependent capitalist industrialization required both capital accumulation and democratic legitimation; this was a historically unprecedented pair of requirements. In the pioneer capitalist countries (England and France), the democratization of the franchise took place only after the primary or 'primitive' accumulation required for the launch of capitalist industrialization had been obtained through a variety of non-democratic, coercive methods of appropriating the means of production from the peasants. And when it did eventually take place, those capitalist countries were able to secure the democratic legitimation of the state not merely through the institutions of liberal-representative democracy but also through social-democratic or welfare-state measures.

In India, the capital required for setting up the state-controlled heavy industries was obtained through taxation, loans, and foreign assistance, especially from the USSR. The requirement of democratic legitimation of the state and its 'mixed' capitalist strategy of economic development was attended to in two ways. First, the planning of economic development was entrusted to a body of technical experts and bureaucrats who were not directly tied to the requirement of electoral legitimation. Second, the state leadership gave up the claims to socialism proprie dicta or to welfare-state democracy, which some of them had been propagating earlier. Instead, a vaguely defined ideology of a 'socialistic pattern of society' was used to secure electoral legitimation for the state, with the 'public-sector' heavy industries being presented as the necessary means to take India along an independent or self-reliant 'middle' path between free-enterprise capitalism and state-dominated communism.

Nehru genuinely believed that he was leading the construction of a post-colonial, secular-democratic nation-state and launching a 'socialistic', 'third way' of self-reliant development.[17] There can be no denying that the Nehruvian phase of the Indian nation-state does have a very impressive record of achievements in many areas. The preservation of the unity and sovereignty of the Indian nation-state and its democratic and secular character is indeed a most significant achievement. Thanks to it reconstruction under the Gandhi–Nehru leadership, the Indian nation-state has been able to produce 'the most noteworthy spell of democratic governance for about a fifth of mankind for close to a half century' (Kaviraj 1995a: 128). Another praiseworthy achievement of the Nehruvian state is its preservation of India's political sovereignty through an ingenious and impressive foreign policy of non-alignment. Also notable is a certain degree of self-reliance achieved in the heavy industries sector as well as a fairly good infrastructure for further industrialization. 'Almost alone among non-Communist states,' writes Sunil Khilnani, 'it [India's developmental state] managed to prolong until the 1980s a quite exceptional insulation from the vagaries of the global economy' (1992: 204). Other accomplishments include the elimination, through land reforms, of some of the most glaring anomalies of feudal landlordism and the establishment of free primary schools and health centres.

Along with these praiseworthy achievements, there have also been some glaring distortions and decelerations in the process of economic change. The five-year plans, the series of periodically revised industrial policies, and the system of tax reliefs and state financial aid to the private sector, combined with a system of licensing and controls, resulted in the formation of 'a centralized powerful state, combining its monopoly of the means of repression with a substantial ownership of the means of production, propelling as well as regulating the economy' (Bardhan 1984: 36). The actual course of economic change, despite the aforementioned achievements, led to a retarded pattern of industrial development and an associated fiscal crisis of the state. This had to do with the growth-inhibiting 'rationalities' which were pursued by each of the three major partners of the dominant/ruling-class coalition.

Of them, industrial capitalists pursued their interest in securing inputs from the public sector at below-market prices, export subsidies, etc., while rich farmers managed to obtain subsidized fertilizers and seeds, higher procurement prices, etc. The latter also stalled land reforms[18] and derived benefits from the state in the name of the Green Revolution (Kaviraj 1995b: 120, 123; Frankel 1978). The third partner of the coalition, the political-bureaucratic class, reaped 'ruler's rents' and other benefits through state controls and regulations. The newly set-up public sector undertakings also served to increase their power and patronage enormously. By exercising its licensing, regulative, and controlling role in a selective manner, this class has been able to prevent any class-based challenge from industrialists and traders. In this way, as pointed out by Bardhan, the autonomy of the Indian state is reflected more often in its regulatory (and hence patronage-dispensing) than developmental role (Bardhan 1984: 39).

It must nevertheless be acknowledged that the Nehruvian state did set up a regime of curbs on monopoly houses and of some transfers 'not only to the landed rich, but also to broad sections of the peasantry, the working class, and to a miniscule extent, even to the rural poor' (Patnaik 1995: 204). Even though the monopoly houses did *actually* gain from the operations of the Nehruvian state, the latter did not officially identify the 'national interests' with the interests of any particular social class. Specifically; the relative autonomy of the Indian economy from metropolitan capital was maintained. This was obviously beneficial to Indian economy in general and to the domestic bourgeois and proto-bourgeois groups in particular in the 1950s and 1960s. However, in the 1970s, when the world economy went through a pronounced transnationalization of production, the opportunities it provided were not seized by India's state-bureaucratically managed strategy of import-substituting industrialization (Kaviraj 1995a: 123).

Re-imagining the Nation-State: Majoritarian Democracy and Economic Liberalization

Since the late 1980 and early 1990s, both domestic regulation of private capital and the protection of the Indian economy from penetration by foreign capital have been supplanted by a regime of economic liberalization, which provides for, among other things, domestic deregulation of private-sector enterprises, import liberalization, export facilitation, privatization or 'disinvestment' of profitable public-sector units, and the opening up of the domestic economy to foreign private capital.

Underlying this change is a shift in the legitimizing ideology of the state from one of a 'socialistic pattern of society' to that of a market-friendly, liberalized, open-door economy. Associated with this, there is also a shift in the ideology of the electoral legitimation of the state. The state has moved from the secular/pluralist notions of nationalism and democracy to religious-majoritarian redefinitions of these terms. These post-1980 shifts were the political responses of state leaders to a series of crises affecting the legitimacy, governability, and fiscal viability of the nation-state—crises in the making of which some of their own earlier actions and some of the actions of their predecessors had played a role.

In the latter part of the 1960s, there was an intense power struggle within the Congress party between Indira Gandhi and a powerful group of (regional) state-level bosses who had initially backed her rise to leadership. The former proved victorious through some clever left-leaning, populist moves, which undercut the power of the state-level bosses of the party and undermined the norms and procedures of inner-party democracy. In the name of a left-leaning populism, Gandhi's government nationalized the large banks and abolished the privy purses of the former rulers of the princely states.

These steps were put to good use by Indira Gandhi in the 1971 parliamentary elections, when, bypassing the regular party organization and its regional 'vote-banks', she made direct appeals to the electorate in the name of a populist-socialist programme of *garibi hatao* (poverty removal). The huge electoral success of this strategy contributed to overcentralization of power in her hands. This had adverse effects on both the democratic functioning of the Congress party and on the federal framework of the relationship between centre and states. At the same time, the masses, who had given electoral support to garibi hatao, started popular movements (especially in Bihar and Gujarat) demanding radical reforms from the government. Those protest movements had the backing of the urban middle class as well as the rural 'vote banks', whom Indira Gandhi had defeated in the elections. Neither the ruling Congress party nor the governmental bureaucracy was prepared to translate populist radicalism into any programme for the structural transformation of society in favour of the poor. In the wake of the ensuing 'steep decline in the legitimacy of the government in an unusually short time', the government under Indira Gandhi imposed Emergency (1975-7) and exhorted people to suspend their political rights to enable the government to bring about socio-economic change (Kaviraj 1995c: 113). Freed from democratic pressures, the government undertook or supported, among other things, such measures as the eviction of beggars from the big cities and forced sterilization of the poor in some urban locales. Some ideas were also floated in favour of a Brazilian-type liberalization of the economy (Kaviraj 1995a and 1995b).

Indira Gandhi's party was voted out of power in the 1977 elections. The victorious but heterogeneous Janata coalition fell apart after just three years of running the government. In 1980, Indira Gandhi and her party were returned to power. This time, the challenge to the power of the central government headed by her came from regionalist movements in the Punjab, Telugu Desham, Assam, and, indeed, Kashmir. These were vertically, and *not* horizontally mobilized movements, which combined the numerical strength of the poor and the financial resources of the well-to-do. The conflicts between these vertically mobilized united regions/states and the centre led Indira Gandhi to make a shift in her own mobilizational strategy from a horizontal to a vertical approach, which included a religious-majoritarian approach. This was obviously a shift away from secularism. There was also a simultaneous shift away from the socialistic, 'poverty removal' role (or promises) of the state towards a new role, namely the liberalization of the economy. The government successfully negotiated 'for the largest loan ever granted by the IMF' and took steps to liberalize imports, 'automatically' license some twenty important industries, and decontrol the pricing of certain industrial products (Kohli 1989: 308).

In the final phase of Indira Gandhi's rule, then, there was a certain shift in the ideology of the Indian nation-state away from secular-socialist democracy and nationalism towards a religious-majoritarian conception of nationalism and democracy and a vaguely conceived idea of a liberalized economy. An insight into the nature of the association between economic liberalization and the religious-majoritarian redefinition of the democratic nation-state may be gained from the following observation by Atul Kohli:

> Those who wanted to argue for business interests faced a dilemma: in a poor democracy like India, how do you mobilize the support of the majority, who are after all very poor? One solution to this puzzle was to cut the majority-minority pie at a different angle. If the poor were majority by the criterion of wealth, Hindus were the religious majority. Appeals to the majority religious community against minority communities, then, can be an alternative strategy for seeking electoral majorities by downplaying class issues [1989: 309].

The religious-majoritarian approach to electoral democracy and nation building is professed and practised in an unambiguous way by the Bharatiya Janata Party, which is leading the ruling coalition of parties at the present. That approach is a distortion of secular, pluralist democracy in the sense that it upholds one of the basic principles of the latter, namely that of majority rule, by dissociating it from what in fact is its twin, inseparable principle, namely that of the inviolability of the fundamental rights of the minority, be it a present minority or some future minority—of conscience, opinion, belief, religion, or even disbelief in any religion.[19]

The policy of economic liberalization has also been continued and progressively stepped up under all the succeeding governments since the late 1980s. The proximate reason for the change of track by the post-colonial, developmental nation-state on to a path of economic liberalization, entailing a closer integration into the global market economy, was the escalation of the government's fiscal deficit, which culminated in a very severe balance-of-payments crisis in 1991. In that year, India did not have enough foreign-exchange reserves to pay for its imports for even two weeks. The loans which the Indian government successfully negotiated with the International Monetary Fund and the World Bank to meet the crisis were tied to the conditionaliities requiring India to follow a programme of short-term macro-economic stabilization measures and long-term 'structural adjustment and reform', whereby the state is rolled back from the arena of production and regulation and the economy is left to be shaped by private initiative and the private sector rather than by state intervention or the public sector. This programme includes, besides the devaluation of the rupee, steps to curb inflation and to reduce the government's fiscal deficit (by reducing its subsidies and capital expenditures and by disinvestment of the shares of profitable public-sector units) and liberalize or free private capital from the regime of regulations, quotas, licences, controls, import-restrictions, etc. Another important feature of the new policy is the opening up of the Indian economy to foreign private capital, be it productive capital or finance capital.

An assessment of the pros and cons of this liberalizing 'structural adjustment programme', which the Indian nation-state has been pursuing since its fiscal and foreign-debt crisis of the late 1980s and early 1990s, is beyond the scope of the present chapter.[20] It is, however, pertinent to mention some of the ways in which these liberalizing reforms may be seen to be intimating a fundamental change in the nature and role of the nation-state. First, the state is withdrawing from long-term developmental activity and is now yielding space to the private sector. For instance, the capital expenditure of the central government showed a steady decline from 5.9 per cent of the GDP in 1990–1 to 3.6 per cent in 1994–5. Second, the state is changing from a market-controlling to a market-friendly institution.[21] Liberalization, to state the obvious, frees market forces from the erstwhile regime of state controls. Finally and most importantly, the nation-state is losing, to a considerable extent, the 'post-colonial' relative autonomy which it has hitherto had vis-à-vis metropolitan capital. For instance, as acknowledged by the World Bank in its 1995 Economic Memorandum on India, the '[c]onditions on portfolio investment by foreign institutional investors ... are much more liberal in India than in Korea ... Taiwan and China' (Kurien 1996: 90).[22] Yet it needs to be asserted that a not-too-insignificant measure of effective political autonomy is still available to the nation-state of India as it is to developing countries—a measure of autonomy that, alas, does not find appropriate reflection in the current liberalizing regime of structural adjustments and reforms!

Acknowledgements

The research for this paper was undertaken while I was a C.R. Parekh Visiting Fellow in the Department of Politics, University of Hull. The helpful discussions I have had with Bhikhu Parekh are gratefully acknowledged.

ENDNOTES

1. The modern 'nation-state' is the product of a process of 'state building', which, according to Charles Tilly (1975: 27), entails 'territorial consolidation,

centralization, differentiation of instruments of government from other sorts of organization, and monopolization (plus concentration) of the means of coercion'. In Europe, this process of state building passed through three stages of political unification and consolidation: (i) the formation of composite states under the leadership of a single dynasty, without any administrative unification; (ii) the institutionalization of absolute sovereign monarchies or military-fiscal states; and (iii) the transformation of the former into absolute, popular, 'national' sovereignty or, in other words, the modern representative republic (cf. Hont 1994: 179). As Hont points out,

> The difference between a modern 'absolutist' state, striving to unite the country and homogenize its institutions, and a 'nation-state' is thus no more than a higher stage of the very same 'state-building' process, a 'nation-state' is merely an 'absolutist' state whose subjects or citizens identify themselves with it, and regard it as a collective expression of themselves as a 'nation'. The pairing of the notions of 'nation' and 'state' makes sense when in people's imagination their nationality and their territorial political unit, which has emerged from a history of 'conquest and coalescence', becomes [sic.] fused [1994: 182].

On the meaning of the modern concept of the 'state', see Skinner (1989) and Parekh (1996). A stimulating discussion of 'the changing idea and/or mythology of the Indian state' may be found in Nandy (1989, 1992).

2. An impetus for political consolidation was provided by the invasion of north India by Alexander of Macedonia in 327–25 BC.

3. Interestingly, the founders of Jainism and Buddhism came from the Kshatriya castes of tribal republics.

4. According to A.L. Basham (1988 [1958]: 116), some of the Buddhist texts encouraged 'a solid bourgeois morality'. Similarly, Jainism, with its stress on frugality, facilitated commercial activity. Its emphasis on non-violence made it favour trade and urban life over agriculture which involved the killing of insects and pests (Thapar [1966] 1977: 65).

5. Towards the close of his reign, Chandragupta Maurya is believed to have patronized Jainism and eventually become a Jain monk, while the most illustrious of Mauryan emperors, Ashoka, embraced and promoted Buddhism after his victory in the Kalinga war.

6. Stein's 'segmentary state' has some similarity with Stanley Tambiah's 'galactic polity' (1976), in which, to use S.H. Rudolph's words, the leading king, the *rajadhiraj*, and the lesser rulers are 'unified by a field of force characterized by both repulsion and attraction' (1987: 739).

7. Inden (1990: 238, n. 22) too feels that Tambiah's 'galactic polity' (1976) comes close to his own conception of the 'imperial formation'.

8. It is interesting to note that sultanism attracted Max Weber's attention, as he saw in it a stage fairly close to the rationalized bureaucracy of the modern state. See Weber (1978: vol. I, 231–2).

9. In this connection, see the analysis of the so-called Ilbert Bill Affair in Partha Chatterjee (1993: 20–1).

10. In this context too Partha Chatterjee (1993: 22–4) makes a relevant examination of what has come to be known as the Nil Durpan Affair.

11. For a very insightful study of colonial rule as 'dominance without hegemony', see Guha (1997). See also Kaviraj (1994).

12. Pakistan went through a subsequent split in 1971, when Bangladesh seceded and became a new sovereign state. These two states, together with the Indian state, have been interpreted by L.I. Rudolph and S.H. Rudolph as representing 'two latter-day representatives of the regional kingdom and one of the subcontinental imperial state' (1987: 66).

13. As invented by Chaudhri Rahmat Ali, a Cambridge University student, in 1933, the name 'PAKISTAN' stands for Punjab ('P'), the Afghan Province ('A'), Kashmir ('K'), Sind ('S'), and Baluchistan ('tan').

14. The army also intervened to liberate Goa from Portuguese control in 1960.

15. L.I. Rudolph and S.H. Rudolph refer to this as 'high stateness' and associate it with India's 'imperial legacies and the contemporary requirements of an interventionist, managerial state pursuing welfare and socialist objectives' (1987: 73).

16. Articles 38 and 39 of the Indian Constitution direct the state 'to promote the welfare of the people by securing and protecting as effectively as it may a social order in which justice—social, economic, and political—shall inform all the institutions of the national life' and to ensure that 'the operation of the economic system does not result in the concentration of wealth to the common detriment'.

17. Partha Chatterjee and Sudipta Kaviraj have shown that the Nehruvian strategy of economic development was actually a strategy of 'passive' capitalist revolution, in which the bourgeoisie, because of its underdevelopment by imperialism, is required to make compromises with the old or pre-capitalist dominant classes (Chatterjee 1997; Kaviraj 1988. See also Pantham 1980, 1995: Ch. 3).

18. The reasons for, and consequences of, the absence of thoroughgoing land reforms in India's strategy of capitalist development are analysed in Patnaik (1998: 39–48).

19. As pointed out by Sudipta Kaviraj, the main problem with the religious-majoritarian conception of democracy is that by demanding 'unequal rights of permanent dominance on grounds of a purported majority', it imposes 'permanent disabilities on other groups' (1995c: 118).

20. Several aspects of the policy of economic liberalization in India are critically examined in Byres (1997); Bhaduri and Nayyar (1996); and Nayar (1992); Sridharan (1993); Kohli (1989); Kurien (1996); and Patnaik (1995 and 1996).

21. It must indeed be admitted that economic liberalization makes a belated recognition of the market as a positive institution of the economy. The market, however, cannot be a substitute for the state just as the state cannot be a substitute for the market. Hence the role of the state under economic liberalization has to be examined not so much in terms of the extent of state intervention as in terms of the nature and purpose of such intervention. In fact, the liberalizing programme of 'structural adjustment and reform' represents a transformed, rather than a reduced, form of state intervention. That transformation tends to go in the direction of a more centralized and authoritarian state. This, to a great extent, has to do with the 'conditionalities' of the international financiers and the so-called 'discipline' of the 'market forces'. see Ghosh (1997); Patnaik (1995 and 1996); and Bhaduri and Nayyar (1996).

22. Kurien (1996: 89) shows that the international capital that has come to India since liberalization has been more of finance capital than productive capital. He maintains that under liberalization, India has opened up its economy to foreign capital 'way beyond what was necessary and prudent'.

REFERENCES

Alam, M. 1998. 'Aspects of Agrarian Uprisings in North India in the Early Eighteenth Century' in M. Alam and S. Subrahmanyam, eds, *The Mughal State. 1526–1750.* Delhi: Oxford University Press.

Alam, M. and S. Subrahmanyam, eds. 1998. *The Mughal State, 1526–1750.* Delhi: Oxford University Press.

Alavi, H. 1973. 'The State in Postcolonial Societies: Pakistan and Bangladesh'. In K. Gough and H.P. Sharma, eds, *Imperialism and Revolution in South Asia.* 145–73. London: Monthly Review Press.

Ali, M.A. 1995. 'Towards an Interpretation of the Mughal Empire'. In H. Kulke. ed. *The State in India*, 1000–1700, 267–77. Delhi: Oxford University Press.

Austin, G. 1996. *The Indian Constitution: Cornerstone of a Nation.* Oxford: Clarendon Press.

Bayly, C. 1990. *Indian Society and the Making of the British Empire.* Cambridge: Cambridge University Press.

Bardhan, P. 1984. *Political Economy of Development in India.* Delhi: Oxford University Press.

———. 1997. 'The State against Society: The Great Divide in Indian Social Science Discourse'. In S. Bose and A. Jalal, eds, *Nationalism, Democracy and Development: State and Politics in India,* 184–95. Delhi: Oxford University Press.

Basham, A.L. [1958] 1988. 'Jainism and Buddhism'. In Wm. T.de Bary et al., comps, *Sources of Indian Tradition.* Reprint. Delhi: Motilal Banarsidass.

Bhadra, G. 1998. 'Two Frontier Uprisings in Mughal India'. In M. Alam and Subrahmanyam, eds, *The Mughal State. 1526–1750.* Delhi: Oxford University Press.

Bhaduri, A. and D. Nayyar. 1996. *The Intelligent Person's Guide to Liberalization.* New Delhi: Penguin Books.

Bhargava R. ed. 1998. *Secularism and Its Critics.* Delhi: Oxford University Press.

Blake, S.P. 1995. 'The Patrimonial-Bureaucratic Empire of the Mughals'. In H. Kulke, ed., *The State in India 1000–1700.* Delhi: Oxford University Press.

Bose, S., and A. Jalal, eds. 1997. *Nationalism, Democracy and Development: State and Politics in India.* Delhi: Oxford University Press.

———. 1998. *Modern South Asia: History, Culture, Political Economy.* Delhi: Oxford University Press.

Bose, Sumantra. 1997. '"Hindu Nationalism" and the Crisis of the Indian State'. In S. Bose and A. Jalal, eds, *Nationalism, Democracy and Development: State and Politics in India.* 104–64. Delhi: Oxford University Press.

Byres, T.J. 1988. 'A Chicago View of the Indian State'. *Journal of Commonwealth and Comparative Politics.* November: 246–69.

———. ed. 1997. *The State, Development Planning and Liberalization in India.* Delhi: Oxford University Press.

Chandra, B. 1980. 'Colonialism, Stages of Colonialism and the Colonial State'. *Journal of Contemporary Asia.* 10(3):272–85.

Chatterjee, P. 1986. *Nationalist Thought and the Colonial World.* Delhi: Oxford University Press.

_____. 1993. *The Nation and Its Fragments: Colonial and Postcolonial Histories.* Delhi: Oxford University Press.

_____. 1997. 'Development Planning and the Indian State'. In P. Chatterjee, ed., *State and Politics in India.* 271–97. Delhi: Oxford University Press.

_____. ed. 1998. *The Wages of Freedom: Fifty Years of the Indian Nation-State.* Delhi: Oxford University Press.

Cohn, B.S. 1983. 'Representing Authority in Victorian India'. In E. Hobsbawm and T. Ranger., eds, *The Invention of Tradition,* 165–209. Cambridge: Cambridge University Press.

Dandekar, R.N. [1958] 1988. '*Artha,* the Second End of Man'. In Wm.T.de Bary et al., comps, *Sources of Indian Tradition,* 236–57. Reprint. Delhi: Motilal Banarsidass.

Dirks, N. 1987. *The Hollow Crown: Ethnohistory of an Indian Kingdom.* Cambridge: Cambridge University Press.

Doornbos, M. and S. Kaviraj. eds. 1997. *Dynamics of State Formation: India and Europe Compared.* New Delhi: Sage Publications.

Dumont, L. 1970. *Religion, Politics and History in India.* Paris: Mouton Publishers.

Dunn, J. ed. 1992. *Democracy, the Unfinished Journey.* Delhi: Oxford University Press.

_____, ed. 1995. *Contemporary Crisis of the Nation-State.* Oxford: Basil Blackwell.

Eisenstadt, S.N. and H. Hartman, eds. 1997. 'Historical Experience, Cultural Traditions, State Formation and Political Dynamics in India and Europe'. In M. Doornbos and S. Kaviraj, eds, *Dynamics of State Formation: India and Europe Compared.* 35–53. New Delhi: Sage Publications.

Embree, A.T. 1977. 'Frontiers into Boundaries: From the Traditional to the Modern State'. In R.G. Fox, ed., *Realm and Region in Traditional India,* 255–80. New Delhi: Vikas.

Foucault, M. 1979. *Discipline and Punish: The Birth of the Prison.* Harmondsworth: Penguin.

Frankel, F.R. 1978. *India's Political Economy 1947–1977.* Princeton: Princeton University Press.

_____. 1989. 'Introduction'. In F.R. Frankel and M.S.A. Rao, eds, *Democracy and State Power in Modern India,* vol. I. Delhi: Oxford University Press.

_____. 1990. 'Conclusion: Decline of a Social Order'. F.R. Frankel and M.S.A. Rao, eds, *Democracy and State Power in Modern India.* 482–517. Delhi: Oxford University Press.

Ghosh, J. 1997. 'Development Strategy in India: A Political Economy Perspective'. In S. Bose and A. Jalal, eds, *Nationalism, Democracy and Development*; State and Politics in India. 165–83. Delhi: Oxford University Press.

Ghoshal. 1959. UN. *A History of Indian Political Ideas.* Bombay: Oxford University Press.

Guha, R. 1997. *Dominance without Hegemony: History and Power in Colonial India.* Cambridge, Mass: Harvard University Press.

Hont, I. 1994. 'The Permanent Crisis of a Divided Mankind: "Contemporary Crisis of the Nation-State" in Historical Perspective'. *Political Studies.* 42:166–231.

Inden, R. 1990. *Imagining India*. Oxford: Basil Blackwell.

Kaviraj, S. 1988. 'A Critique of the Passive Revolution'. *Economic and Political Weekly*. November (Special Number):2429–44.

_____. 1991. 'On State, Society and Discourse in India'. In J. Manor, ed., *Rethinking Third World Politics*. 72–99. London: Longman.

_____. 1994. 'On the Construction of Colonial Power: Structure, Discourse, Hegemony'. In S. Engels and S. Marks, eds, *Contesting Colonial Hegemony: State and Society in Africa and India*. 19–54. London: British Academic Press.

_____. 1995a. 'Crisis of the Nation-State in India'. In J. Dunn, ed., 115–129. *Contemporary Crisis of the Nation-State*. Oxford: Basil Blakwell.

_____. 1995b. 'Dilemmas of Democratic Development in India'. In A. Leftwich, ed., *Democracy and Development*, 114–138. Cambridge: Polity Press.

_____. 1995c. 'Democracy and Development in India'. In A.K. Bagchi, ed., *Democracy and Development*. 92–130. Delhi: Macmillan.

_____. 1997. 'The Modern State in India'. In M. Doornbos and S. Kaviraj, eds, *Dynamics of State Formation: India and Europe Compared*. New Delhi: Sage Publications.

Khilnani, S. 1992. 'India's Democratic Career'. In J. Dunn, ed., *Democracy, the Unfinished Journey*. Delhi: Oxford University Press.

_____. 1997. *The Idea of India*. London: Hamish Hamilton.

Kohli, A. ed. 1988. *India's Democracy: An Analysis of Changing State-Society Relations*. Princeton: Princeton University Press.

_____. 1989. 'Politics of Economic Liberalization in India'. *World Development*. 17(3):305–28.

_____. 1990. *Democracy and Discontent: India's Growing Crisis of Governability*. Cambridge: Cambridge University Press.

Kosambi, D.D. 1970. *The Culture and Civilization of Ancient India in Historical Outline*. Delhi: Vikas.

_____. 1975. *An Introduction to the Study of Indian History*. Bombay: Popular Prakashan.

Kothari, R. 1988. *The State against Democracy: In Search of Humane Governance*. New Delhi: Ajanta Publications.

_____. 1995a. 'Globalisation and Revival of Tradition: Dual Attack on Model of Democratic Nation-Building'. *Economic and Political Weekly*. 25 March.

_____. 1995b. 'Under Globalisation: Will Nation-State Hold?' *Economic and Political Weekly*. 1 July.

Kulke, H., ed. 1995. *The State in India, 1000–1700*. Delhi: Oxford University Press.

Kulke, H. and D. Rothermund. [1986] 1998. *A History of India*. London: Routledge.

Kumar R. 1997. 'State Formation in India: Retrospect and Prospect'. In M. Doornbos and S. Kaviraj, eds, *Dynamics of State Formation: India and Europe Compared*. New Delhi: Sage Publications.

Kurien, C.T. 1996. 'Economic Reforms–7: What Next?' *Frontline*. 23 February: 88–91. This seven-part series of articles have appeared in book-form, *Economic Reforms and the People*. Delhi: Madhyam Books.

Larson, G.J. 1997. *India's Agony over Religion*. Delhi: Oxford University Press.

Mehta, V.R. 1992. *Foundations of Indian Political Thought*. Delhi: Manohar Publishers.

Mitra, S. 1990. 'Between Transaction and Transcendence: The State and the Institutionalization of Power in India'. In S. Mitra, ed., *The Postcolonial State in Asia*. 73–99. Hermel Hempstead: Wheatsheaf.

_____. 1991. 'Desecularising the State: Religion and Politics in India after Independence'. *Comparative Studies in Society and History*. 755–77.

Moore, B. 1966. *Social Origins of Dictatorship and Democracy*. Boston: Beacon Press.

Nandy A. 1989. 'The Political Culture of the Indian State'. *Daedalus*. 118:1–26.

_____. 1992. 'State'. In W. Sachs, ed., *The Development Dictionary*, 264–74. London: Zed Books.

Nayar, B.R. 1989. *India's Mixed Economy*. Bombay: Popular Prakashan. 264–74.

_____. 1992. 'The Politics of Economic Restructuring in India: The Paradox of State Strength and Policy Weakness'. *Journal of Commonwealth and Comparative Politics*. 30(2):145–71.

Nehru, J. 1949. 'A Tryst with Destiny' (speech in the Constituent Assembly of India at the midnight of 14–15 August 1947). In J.L. Nehru. *Independence and After*, New Delhi: Government of India, Publications Division.

Pantham, T. 1980. 'Elites, Classes and The Distortions of Economic Transition in India'. In Sachchidananda and A.K. Lal, eds, *Elite and Development*. 71–96. New Delhi: Concept Publishing House.

_____. 1995. *Political Theories and Social Reconstruction: A Critical Survey of the Literature on India*. New Delhi: Sage Publications.

_____. 1997. 'Indian Secularism and its Critics'. *Review of Politics*. 59(3):523–40.

Parekh, B.C. 1992. 'The Cultural Particularity of Liberal Democracy'. *Political Studies*. (Special Issue). 40:160–75.

_____. 1995. 'Jawaharlal Nehru and the Crisis of Modernization'. In U. Baxi and B.C. Parekh, eds, *Crisis and Change in Contemporary India*. 21–56. New Delhi: Sage Publications.

_____. 1996. 'The Nature of the Modern State'. In D.L. Sheth and A. Nandy, eds, *The Multiverse of Democracy*. 27–49. New Delhi: Sage Publications.

Patnaik, P. 1995. 'Nation-State in the Era of Globalization'. *Economic and Political Weekly*. 19 August: 2049–54.

_____. 1996. 'A Note on the Political Economy of the Retreat of the State'. In P. Patnaik, *Whatever Happened to Imperialism and Other Essays*. 194–210. New Delhi: Tulika.

_____. 1998. 'Political Strategies of Economic Development'. In P. Chatterjee, ed., *The Wages of Freedom: Fifty Years of the Indian Nation-State*. 37–60. Delhi: Oxford University Press.

Perlin, F. 1985. 'State Formation Reconsidered'. *Modern Asian Studies*. 19(3):415–80.

Prasad, B. 1974. *Theory of Government in Ancient India*. Allahabad: Central Book Depot.

Richards, J.F. 1998. 'The Formation of Imperial Authority under Akbar and Jahangir'. In M. Alam and S. Subrahmanyam, eds, *The Mughal State*. 1526–1750. Delhi: Oxford University Press.

Rudolph, L.I. and S.H. Rudolph. 1985. 'The Subcontinental Empire and the Regional Kingdom in Indian State Formation'. In P. Wallace, ed., *Region and Nation in India*. 40–59. New Delhi: Oxford and IBH.

_____. 1987. *In Pursuit of Lakshmi: The Political Economy of the Indian State*. 731–46. Hyderabad: Orient Longman.

Rudolph, S.H. 1987. 'Presidential Address: State Formation in Asia—Prolegomenon to a Comparative Study'. *Journal of Asian Studies.* 46(4).

Sathyamurthy, T.V. 1996. 'State and Society in a Changing Political Perspective'. In T.V. Sathyamurthy, ed., *Social Change and Political Discourse in India,* vol. 4. *Class Formation and Political Transformation in Post-Colonial India.* 437–75. Delhi: Oxford University Press.

Sen, A. 1982. *The State, Industrialization, and Class Formations in India.* London: Routledge and Kegan Paul.

Skinner, Q. 1989. 'The State'. In T. Ball et al. eds, *Political Innovation and Conceptual Change.* 90–131. Cambridge: Cambridge University Press.

Smith, A. 1991. 'The Nation: Invented, Imagined, Reconstructed?' *Millennium: Journal of International Studies.* 20(2):353–68.

Smith, D.E. 1963. *India as a Secular State.* New Delhi: Oxford University Press.

Sridharan, E. 1993. 'Economic Liberalization and India's Political Economy: Towards a Paradigm Synthesis'. *Journal of Commonwealth and Comparative Politics.* 31(3): 1–29.

Stein, B. 1980. *Peasant State and Society in Medieval South India.* Delhi: Oxford University Press.

———. 1985: 'State Formation and Economy Reconsidered'. *Modern Asian Studies.* 19(3):387–413.

Stokes, E. 1959. *The English Utilitarians and India.* Delhi: Oxford University Press.

Sudarshan, R. 1995. 'The Political Consequences of Constitutional Discourse'. In T.V. Sathyamurthy, ed., *Social Change and Political Discourse in India,* vol. I: *State and Nation in the Context of Social Change.* Delhi: Oxford University Press.

Tambiah, S.J. 1976. *World Conqueror and World Renouncer: A Study of Buddhism and Polity in Thailand against a Historical Background.* Cambridge: Cambridge University Press.

Thapar, R. [1966] 1977. *A History of India.* vol. 1. Reprint. Harmondsworth: Penguin Books.

———. 1980. 'State Formation in Early India'. *International Social Science Journal.* 4:655–60.

———. 1984. *From Lineage to State: Social Formations in the Mid-First Millennium BC in the Ganga Valley.* Delhi: Oxford University Press.

Thompson, E. and G.T. Garrat. [1934] 1962. *Rise and Fulfilment of British Rule in India, 1600–1935.* Reprint. Allahabad: Central Book Depot.

Tilly, C. 1975. 'Reflections on the History of European State-Making'. In C. Tilly, ed., *The Formation of National States in Western Europe.* Princeton: Princeton University Press.

Wallerstein, I. 1986. 'Incorporation of the Indian Subcontinent into Capitalist World Economy'. *Economic and Political Weekly.* 21(4).

Washbrook, D. 1981. 'Law, State and Agrarian Society in Colonial India'. *Modern Asian Studies.* 15:649–721.

———. 1990. 'South Asia, the World System and World Capitalism'. *Journal of Asian Studies.* 49(3):479–508.

Weber, M. 1978. *Economy and Society.* Ed G. Roth and C. Wittich, vol. I. Los Angeles: University of California Press.

Yadav, Y. 1990. 'Theories of the Indian State'. *Seminar.* 367. (March): 1–5.

The Nature of Indian Democracy

Sudipta Kaviraj

THE PROBLEM OF INDIAN DEMOCRACY

It is often assumed, without enough clarification, that the continued success of democracy in India is in some senses a surprise, that the continuance of democracy itself is some kind of a problem to be explained. There are several possible grounds for such scepticism. The most common view sees the obstacle to democracy as economic. Without some economic development, it is argued, political democracy is not possible. The reason for this is that sharing in a general atmosphere of economic prosperity reduces the desperation and sharpness of social conflicts. The second argument is based on social structure or, alternatively, culture. The most familiar form that this argument takes is as follows. Indian society has traditionally been based on caste and other strong community identities. Caste is explicitly based on principles of hierarchy, and goes against political equality. Attachment to traditional communities or sects is resistant to the principles of abstract equal citizenship under a common state. The successful operation of democracy requires that individual electors should vote on the basis of their considered individual judgement, and on the basis of their perception of their self-interest. Caste and community attachments, it is argued, would defeat a succesful operation of democracy. The historical record of Indian democracy, however, shows that such objections are indecisive. Despite continued poverty, and the undeniable influence of caste and communities on political choice, the democratic system in India has functioned with vitality.[1] However, the social and cultural conditions in which democratic institutions have functioned have made Indian democracy operate in ways which are quite locally specific.

The Nature of Indian Democracy

John Stuart Mill began his treatise on representative government by noting two different ways of thinking about governments. The first theory treated governmental institutions like machinery that is deliberately conceived and constructed by human contrivance, without much regard for the form or kind of society in which this machinery is supposed to work. The second, Mill thought, regarded governmental forms as institutions which grow out of the fundamental tendencies of the social structure. Interestingly, in the literature on Indian democracy we can find traces of these two unreconstructed views of either extreme constructivism or sociological determinism. Broadly, the early academic works on Indian democracy accepted an uncritical legal constructivism, and spent its intellectual resources in perfecting legal institutions when faced with political challenges.[2] Since the 1970s, the academic study of Indian democracy has tended to move away from institutional formalism towards political sociology. Now the central questions about the 'nature' of Indian democracy involve an analysis of what has happened to the recognizable forms of institutional democracy adopted by the Indian state after Independence, what the structure of society has done to these state forms, and what the state form, in its turn, has done to the structures of social life. Democracy can be viewed in two rather different ways and is said to contain two contradictory types of possibilities. The idea of democratic government was evidently regarded as historically transformative by the political elite which established the state after Independence. It believed that operating under the principles of democratic government ordinary people would learn new rules of political and social equality. But historical comparisons of democratic experience show that democratic government also has a tendency to bring social cleavages into overt, public expression through the openness of its political process. And evidently, in certain circumstances there can be a tension between these two sides of the historical consequences of democratic government.

The Origins of Indian Democracy

Although the political elite after Independence behaved as if the choice of democracy as a form of government was a foregone conclusion, that belief itself is an interesting fact to explain. Neither traditional Indian social rules, nor the rules according to which British authorities governed India for about two hundred years, could be called democratic: that is based on a recognition of political or social equality.[3] Why did the successful national movement think of democracy as the only appropriate form of government? The historical sources of Indian democratic thought were several, and it was also a history of considerable complexity. First, the intellectual following of democratic ideas was historically uneven. Indian writers and political groups were quick to discern the internal differentiations and complexities of the democratic idea in the West. They noticed the difference particularly between a liberal, individualist, legalistic strand which embraced both individualism and emphasis on legal procedures and a radical, populist strand intolerant of procedural obstacles to social justice. Internal discussions on democracy would usually form a conversation between three different positions, to simplify the considerable variations of emphasis and inflexion. Some writers opposed the idea of any implantation of institutions from the West on the grounds that these were inappropriate for Indian culture. But, increasingly, two other strands were to emerge to make powerful arguments for adoption of western practices. One was a strand of liberal, individualistic thought which used rationalistic arguments to undermine justifications of the caste system and reject religious superstitions.[4] And a second, community-oriented, political strand interpreted democracy in a more radical, and at the same time less individualistic, fashion. The weight of political opinion and actual political support fluctuated between these three types of thinking. After the early influence of liberal and individualistic ideas, in the second half of the nineteenth century in Bengal one sees a clear emergence of a critique of western forms of ideology and a distinct preference for what was regarded, sometime quite erroneously, as more indigenist social forms and principles.[5] However, there was a second kind of complexity always accompanying this explicit debate. Even the strands which supported western ideological trends had to introduce startling translations and improvisations, especially when [or, 'mainly because'] they wrote in the vernacular—translations which would be difficult to characterize in terms of standard western categories.[6]

Administrative and cultural practices of colonialism contributed to the growth of democratic ideas in some ways. Colonial rule had immense impact on the systems of property holding in Indian society; much of colonial law insisted on private property. The meticulous institutionalization of private property in various spheres, like landholdings, introduced crucial ideas about individual ownership and assisted individuation with regard to economic practices in elite Indian culture. Perhaps more significantly, the colonial government in the nineteenth century introduced ideas of procedural as opposed to arbitrary government. Conceptions of fair procedure and just government existed in traditional society, but these were different from the modern ideas about impersonality of power and associated notions of legal impartiality. This familiarized Indians with ideas of a rule of law, though it was common practice to suspend it in case of European offenders. But the fact that some of the most powerful individuals associated with early colonialism, individuals who often acted like medieval despots, when away from the restrictions of the British Parliament, were formally tried and indicted, reinforced the idea that modern governance was a rule of law. Under the new dispensation, political activity did not consist in turning the arbitrary will of the rulers in one's favour, but to act in a public sphere to pressurize them into enacting more equitable laws. The introduction of western education was driven by a complex combination of motivations on the part of colonial rulers, and showed the extreme diversity of opinion among them. In part, it was driven by the condescending altruism of giving to Indians the knowledge on which modern civilization was based; in part, it was meant to produce a class of reliable bureaucratic under-labourers. But the most strikingly paradoxical effects of modern education were political. The more British education sought to convince Indians about the wonderful narrative of western enlightenment and freedom, the more it undermined the ideological grounds of colonial rule.[7] Familiarity with the history and the institutions of the West enabled Indians to desire more perfect forms of such institutions and helped them criticize British authority on the basis of principles which the British could not morally reject. But, obviously, the processes by which Indians could acquire a strong preference for democratic government in the strict sense were severely restricted in colonial India. Such preferences were found mainly in elite groups which have access to English education or among those who have serious contacts with the institutions of colonial legality; it was only in those groups that could either understand, value, feel attracted towards, or reflect critically on the western democratic ideals.

Democratic ideas emerged more powerfully and circulated more widely after the rise of the nationalist movement, particularly after it assumed mass character with the coming of Gandhi in the 1920s. Gandhi's tactics bridged the crucial gap between two broad strands of anti-colonial politics that had existed before him but never managed to converge. Middle class dissatisfaction with British rule assumed the form of constitutionalist-liberal agitation against the colonial government, which constantly emphasized the procedural and legalistic elements of modern politics and tried to embarass the British authorities by quoting their own principles, thereby proving the 'un-British' character of governance in India. The colonial adminsitrative discourse operated inside the British political ideology of the times, which generally advocated democracy as the best form of government, but argued that Indians were unprepared for self-government on cultural grounds. Liberal-constitutional agitation, however, sought to prove the Indian middle class was capable of governing. But since this agitation was confined primarily to the new colonial middle classes, it had little support outside the colonial cities. By contrast, peasant uprisings represented the most radical form of protest against colonial rule, but these were usually restricted to particular regions, and often showed utter incomprehension of the system of legal rules that the colonial administration had put in place (see Guha 1981). Understandably, peasant militants showed less regard for the intricacies of colonial legality as compared to the lawyers who mostly formed the leadership of the Indian National Congress in its early stages.

As long as the two strands of opposition to colonialism remained separate, British authorities in India could retain their power without much difficulty. The constitutionalist agitation of the middle classes rarely broke out of the strict limits of political mendicancy, and the anger of the peasantry, though much more troublesome and destructive, could always be surrounded and eventually crushed by the use of military power. Gandhi's emergence as the prime leader of Indian nationalism brought these two social forces into a powerful combination for the first time, immediately posing far more difficult problems for British colonial power.

The legacy of the Congress for Indian constitutional democracy was far more direct and positive, although not entirely free of paradoxes. Nehru claimed in the *Discovery of India* that Congress was the most democratic organization he knew, defending it against the British colonial charge that it was an organization dominated by a small elite and manipulated by its major leaders. But the practice of political procedure inside the Congress is interesting because it shows some trends which would persist in post-Independence Indian politics. The formal organizational structure of the Congress was certainly democratic, with members choosing Pradesh Congress Committees which sent their delegates through a democratic representative process to the annual sessions of the AICC, the major forum for the declaration of policies, if not their actual formulation. The Congress maintained an astonishing adherence to formal rules of procedure. Even large-scale agitations, which were to convulse India for long periods, were ceremonially launched at Congress sessions by the procedurally fastidious passing of resolutions, like the famous Quit India resolution of August 1942.

Political practice in the Congress thus showed a shrewd awareness that democracy required a balance between the participatory and procedural sides of the democratic idea: unlike many other popular movements, the Congress never claimed that large mobilizations of people were their own justifications.[8] Under the conditions of stress and enthusiasm in which successful national movements function, this was an amazing characteristic and not a mean achievement. However, Gandhi was always particular about his rather idiosyncratic notion of discipline, which he contrasted to the anarchy and disorder associated in his mind with violence. His construal of what discipline meant in particular circumstances could be extremely odd. But his ability to impose a certain kind of political discipline and orderliness on the potentially anarchic forces of Indian nationalism was quite evident from the success with which he could bring to instant suspension huge mass movements in the middle of their disorderly career. The manner in which the civil disobedience movements of the 1920s and 1930s were brought to a sudden but orderly end were miracles of control, though it is quite natural that his critics interpreted these acts very differently.

Communists and socialists like Nehru evidently associated more value with the participatory, mobilizational, activist side of the idea of democratic movements, and deplored Gandhi's sudden withdrawals as arbitrary and authoritarian, in the sense that what appeared the right course of action to Gandhi was allowed to trump what the thousands of activists in the movement actually thought. So while these were enormous acts of will for Gandhi mythicized his political role, it implied a totally illegitimate assumption of their capacity of decision by him, and evidently had a strongly negative impact on democratic politics. They correctly detected the small seed of authoritarianism at the heart of even the most benign form of charismatic politics. At other times, when the Congress was not engaged in leading mass movements but occupied in more mundane politics of the everyday, Gandhi's attitude towards procedural forms could be deeply puzzling. When Subhas Chandra Bose defeated Pattabhi Sitaramayya, the candidate he had favoured, Gandhi declared this as his own defeat, forcing a reluctant Bose to step down, eventually splitting the Congress. From another angle, however, Gandhi was usually willing to compromise with political opponents—his critics inside the Congress, Jinnah and the Muslim League, and, most significantly, the British. His actions, however, often had an air of moral generosity which was suited to his ethical style but they were really somewhat removed from the rejection of extremism required by political liberalism.

Despite these complexities, the Congress legacy was mainly positive in its contribution to a democratic form of government in independent India in two ways: first, its internal functioning was often startlingly attentive to procedures and legal niceties; and second, from the early part of the century, and especially after 1937, it took part in representative government at the provincial level. Until the very end, the institutions were based on only limited representation, never involving more than about 16 per cent of the entire population. The eve of constitution making was marked by several interesting contradictions. The Congress, which had campaigned for the introduction of adult suffrage which it considered essential for a possible Constituent Assembly, eventually accepted the unrepresentative assembly that the departing British administration offered.

At the same time, it is remarkable that most sections of political opinion about the form of government to be adopted after Independence chose some form of parliamentary democracy. The constitution, which introduced universal suffrage, was adopted by an Assembly which was not, to crown the irony, itself based on adult franchise. But this shows several peculiar features of the institutional form of Indian democracy. It was not a form of government that emerged out of irresistible popular demand, but rather a paternalistic elite construction driven by two rather different impulses. The educational and political culture of the Indian elite made it likely that they would regard parliamentary democratic government as the most appropriate to India after Independence. But it was also somewhat tragic luck which gave it its actual form.

The historical circumstances of Partition fatally weakened those forces which might have been less than enthusiastic about liberal democratic procedural forms—both the Muslim League with its fear of Hindu majoritarian rule and the assorted opposition to liberal-democratic ideas found from Hindu chauvinists to communists. There was a window of opportunity for the more democratic section of the Indian elite to construct the constitution relatively unhindered. The property restrictions in voting which chose members of the Constituent Assembly also appear to have favoured this institutional construction. Communists, for instance, had only one member in the Assembly, while in the first general elections, they formed the largest opposition group. The moment of constitution making therefore marked a strange and tragic elite consensus.[9] The politics of colonial India, despite the largely democratic ideals of the Congress, failed to produce any consensual or even compromise result, and failed to tackle the most serious conflict about religious nationalism. But after that serious opposition hived off from India, the business of finding relatively consensual settlements among the Indian elite became much easier.

The Constitutional Structure of Democracy

The preamble to the constitution declared with suitable solemnity that the people of India had resolved 'to give to themselves' the classical principles of freedom, equality, fraternity, and justice. A minor irony of this gesture was that it was made in English, a language understood by a small segment of the population, and some of its more indigenist members regretted weakly at the end of its deliberations that it would have been more appropriate if these principles had been given to the people in a language of their own.[10] Yet, given the complexity of the situation, even that was not an uncontested or simple issue. In the Constituent Assembly, there was little contestation about the adoption of democratic government. Because of the elite consensus in India's politics at that moment, no one doubted that parliamentary democracy was the most appropriate form of government for India. Most of the discussions in the Assembly concerned more detailed matters of institutional architecture: of combining elements from the American with the basic structure of the Westminster model. The eventual constitutional arrangement adopted a Westminster-style parliamentary government with a cabinet and the principle of collective responsibility to the central legislature.

It adopted a constitutional president as head of state, but sought to demarcate the difference in executive authority by making his election indirect. However, a troublesome flaw in the constitution was leaving the jurisdiction of the President, in times of confusion or absence of a clear-cut majority in parliament, strangely, to be governed by the conventions of British parliament. This assumed that future generations of legislators would be as conversant with the technicalities of British law and Erskine May as the one who wrote the constitution. It is hardly surprising that as legal training of legislators has declined in later years, such matters, in the absence of clear constitutional directives, have become increasingly contentious.

Independent India also slowly developed a very different culture of legality, with much less emphasis on legal technicality and the pertinacious accumulation of precedents. Consequently, after the decline of the comfortable majorities of the Congress in the 1980s, governmental changes have become increasingly uneasy; they are heavily dependent on the judicious use of discretionary powers by the President. If his decisions are politically awkward, morally questionable, and contested by major parties, this could become a source of serious problems for the smooth procedural functioning of Indian democratic institutions. In ordinary times, however, there has been little controversy about the powers of the cabinet and the President. The major institutional innovations of Indian democracy lay in the manner in which its draftsmen combined elements of more consensual forms with the majority rule of the Westminster model. The second chamber, the Rajya Sabha, was based on democratic but not numerically equal representation of the states, and several important types of legislation were made dependent on special majorities.[11] The Constitution accepted the principle of representation of constiuent states along with that of popular representation, which was expressed in a federal structure. In accordance with federal principles, the constitution distributed powers between the central and state governments, but the experience of the Partition changed legal thinking on federalism fundamentally.

Before Partition became a certainty, it was generally acknowledged that after Independence India would have a very loose federal structure; after

Partition, the understandable anxiety about territorial integrity favoured a far more centralized federalism. The central government not merely received a much larger number of subjects, but also the most insignificant ones, including the undefined residual powers.[12] Besides, the Constitution gave the central government power to dislodge state administrations in circumstances in which the former thought constitutional government had become impossible. In the aftermath of Partition, this highly centralized federal design drew little protest from regionally based political groups. But after 1967, in situations where the centre and the states were controlled by different parties, this emergency power has been used with alarming frequency and often with questionable justification. Political evolution after the 1960s saw increasingly strident demands for greater regional autonomy from parties which recognized that their influence was unlikely to expand beyond specific regions.

However, in several areas the constitutional structure improvised to produce legal rules to suit Indian conditions, and came out with remarkably interesting features. Because of the specific historical conjuncture, and the unrestricted influence of reformist leaders in the Constituent Assembly, the institutional structure paid serious attention to the eradication of caste discrimination, which it expected, along with affiliation to religious communities, to be the primary obstacle to the working of formal democracy. The first innovation was in the definition of the underlying form of nationalism which supported the institutions of the constitution. Historically, Indian nationalism had been an internally variegated ideology, with often strongly contradictory trends coexisting within its capacious spread. Apart from the question of how to deal with the two-nation theory which asserted that the two main religious communities constituted natural nations, there was the further problem of how the two levels of nationalist-patriotic sentiments could be reconciled. Historically, nationalism, rode on the back of intense cultural self-assertions of regional language cultures and the rise of modern vernacular literatures. The constitutional system had to find a way in which the nationalism of the linguistic regions and of the entire country could properly be reconciled.

The institutional solution to the problem of regional and administrative diversity was of course federalism. But underlying the entire idea of Indian federalism was the question of how far the ideal of the cultural unity of the new nation should be taken, and what its form should be. In the Constituent Assembly, there was an opinion which followed the precedent of western nation-states and demanded a single indigenous language to form the basis of a single national culture. In the aftermath of the Partition, it was particularly plausible to argue that without the unifying structure of a single culture based on a single language the new state would fall apart, or simply lack cultural substance as a nation.[13] It was also likely that this line of argument would increasingly slide towards a Hindu self-definition of the Indian nation. Despite strong representations of this strand within the Constituent Assembly, the drafting committee defended its idea of a pluralistic, two-tier nationalism. It recognized the legitimate demands of linguistic cultures and did not consider them hindrances to a feeling of an all-India nationalism. Federalism therefore was not just an administrative-territorial arrangement, it reflected the pluralistic and layered form of the nationalism that was officially accepted by the state.

Adoption of this idea was necessarily incomplete in the first stage of institution making. The Constitution initially established a Byzantine and complicated system of different types of states, but the reorganization of the states in linguistic terms after 1956 brought legal structures in line with this pluralistic conception of Indian nationalism.[14] The Nehruvian state remained concerned about the long-term effects of this concession to linguistic nationalism of the regions.[15] In its early stage, Nehru's government energetically, pursued a policy of propagation of Hindi which brought hostile reaction and political discontent in south India and West Bengal, leading to Nehru's retreat in the face of dissatisfaction. This, however, had rather contradictory consequences over the longer term. The imposition of Hindi on reluctant regions immediately after Independence, may have created difficult political problems similar to ones that the neighbouring state of Pakistan faced because of an unwisely homogenizing linguistic policy. But leaving things without reform meant unrestrained continuance of the cultural and professional privilege of English and the classes who controlled it—a policy unlikely to ever contribute to a democratic eradication of cultural access to social privilege. Fortunately, however, the Indian state has not faced direct trouble over the question of language and its distribution of life chances.

Another important innovation of the constitutional structure of democracy was the set of provisions for reverse discrimination in favour of groups which were considered historically backward. The Constitution not only formally abolished untouchability, but enacted provisions against discrimination on the basis of caste, the most common principle of conventional Hindu social life. The adoption of measures directed against caste practices was not a direct inheritance of a nationalist consensus. At least two strands of Indian nationalism were seriously opposed to the abolition of caste-based conduct. Hindu nationalists were, for obvious reasons, opposed to the abolition of castes, so central to the practice of common Hinduism, though it must be noted that modern Hindu nationalism always contained a serious reformist tradition as well, which, while using Hinduism as the basis of the Indian nation, wished internal hierarchies on the basis of caste to be abolished.[16] Yet the caste question could produce paradoxically complex issues. Gandhi, for instance, was intensely opposed to the practice of untouchability, but not to everyday conduct based on caste.[17] The radical approach to everyday conduct on caste therefore received its support mainly from the reformist, socialist elements in Congress around Nehru and the crusading zeal of B.R. Ambedkar who came to play a crucial role in the drafting of the Constitution. Thus the Constitution established a number of crucial provisions for reverse discrimination in favour of the former untouchable castes. About a fourth of government jobs and educational places were to be reserved for these Scheduled Castes and Tribes. This expressed a foundational belief in the connection between constitutional democracy and social change in the direction of greater equality. Government moves towards extending the scope of reservations for the lower castes(with the Mandal Commission recommendations, for instance) have often been bitterly disputed by parties drawing their support from the higher caste groups, but interestingly, no organized section in Indian politics has asked for an abolition of the existing reservations.

THE HISTORICAL TRAJECTORY OF INDIAN DEMOCRACY

Democratic politics in India during the Nehru years (1946–64) seemed to follow the rules and conventions associated with western democracy. First of all, the procedural rules of democratic government were in general punctiliously observed, though sections of political opinion were at times unhappy about individual cases. Elections were held punctually, and generally there were no strident complaints about vote rigging or violent exclusion of particular groups. Former untouchable groups, however, have later claimed that they simply did not vote in the early general elections in ceratin parts of the country.[18] Formal rules of cabinet government were also carefully observed. Some important incidents showed, however, that in case of disputes of an extremely serious nature, such procedural observances could be fragile. The most celebrated case of this kind was when the Communist government in Kerala, elected by a thin but eventually firm majority, was dismissed by the Nehru government on the wholly unconvincing excuse that constitutional government was becoming impossible. In fact, the government had undertaken radical measures which affected the Catholic church's control over the state's educational structure. This showed that if radical attacks were planned through perfectly constitutional means by a duly elected government, even a normally procedurally correct government under Nehru could construe these as constitutional anarchy and dismiss it. Similarly unsavoury incidents took place with far greater frequency after the Congress experienced its first major loss in elections in 1967.

Indira Gandhi and Institutional Decline

The fourth general elections of 1967 marked a watershed in the history of Indian democracy in several ways. At the level of party politics, they obviously marked the end of a period in which the Congress could simply assume electoral victory and concentrate on developmental policies entirely free of immediate electoral pressures. This introduced a new kind of politics in which government policies were to have a much more direct and visible connection with electoral commitments. Sometimes, such commitments were so general and radical as to be entirely unrealizable, and certainly the making of such commitments eventually harmed the parties that made them, although Congress under Indira Gandhi (1966–84)[19] initially gained an immense advantage through the slogan of *garibi hatao* (remove poverty). The 1967 elections also showed a more interesting sociological trend. Congress policies for heavy industrialization placed obvious emphasis on industrial groups and looked after their interests through protectionism, low pricing of raw materials, etc. Although the agricultural sector also gained by the absence of an agricultural income tax, powerful farmers' lobbies, formed by the mid-1960s complained against an urban-industrial bias and clamoured for greater attention to agricultural interests. There was a slow but steady alienation of farmers' groups from the Congress in the northern states from the late 1950s. By the fourth general elections, these disgruntled elements left the Congress and formed their own political parties, usually siding with the opposition. Thus for the first time in the history of elections, the opposition votes were unified, to the great disadvantage of the Congress. Apart from asserting the new power of the farmers' interests in national politics, this also started the process of the splintering of the Congress party. Eventually, the absence of a single ruling party and the unending squabbles among opposition groups introduced an utterly chaotic period of constant defections. This showed how the institutional structure, essentially drawn from some major western models, could face serious crisis with a change in the social composition of the party elites. If party leaders, unlike the Nehru period, were ignorant or defiant of known legal conventions, the institutional system might prove extremely fragile. In fact, the following decade of Indira Gandhi's regime offered a misleading picture of apparent orderliness that was actually created by the irresistibility of Mrs Gandhi's power rather than by a restoration of institutional discipline.

Historically, Indira Gandhi's rule reversed some of the fundamental principles by which Nehru's regime had ruled India and conducted the business of Indian democracy. First, she re-established the control of the Congress over the Indian political system by entirely abrogating the internal democratic functioning of her party. As the Congress in the 1970s still occupied so much of India's political space, this raised the question of how the democratic functioning of parties related to the democratic operation of the formal system. It was hardly surprising that as Indira Gandhi got away with disregard of procedural rules inside her party, she would try to extend this behaviour to state institutions as well. She began to ignore institutional conventions in appointment of Supreme Court judges and conduct of cabinet affairs, but as opposition to her government intensified and slowly turned into an unprecedented nationwide movement which she was unable to control, she eventually took resort to a quasi-legal authoritarianism. The Emergency (May 1975–December 1979) had a very thin legality. It was adopted by a legislature elected by a large but clearly outdated, over which Indira Gandhi exercised undisputed control; it put to mendacious use provisions put into the Constitution to avert threats to the entire institutional system or the territorial integrity of the country. Emergency provisions were meant to avert threats to the state, not to individual politicians. Although it was technically within its formal provisions, the Emergency violated the spirit of the Constitution, and mainly sought to deflect the effect of a ruling by Allahabad High Court questioning the method of Indira Gandhi's election in the previous general elections. The politics of populism leading to the Emergency, again, showed some interesting features of democratic evolution in India. It was dramatic evidence of a dissonance between participation and procedure. The fact that Indira Gandhi faced a rebellion in much of the country only three years after she had won an unprecedented majority showed a disconnection between the elective procedure and popular opinion. By her populist rhetoric and partly because of the success in the war with Pakistan, Indira Gandhi won an immensely impressive mandate. But this actually deflected attention from the record of her previous government so popular discontent spilled onto the streets soon after her resounding victory. The declaration of the Emergency passed off without much popular protest, with major political groups watching with caution a situation which was entirely without precedent. But when they were allowed some minimal freedom to organize, the other political groups reasserted themselves and set up a single party to oppose the Congress in 1977.

The episode of the Emergency showed, paradoxically, both the fragility of democratic institutions and their underlying legitimacy, if not strength. Their fragility was demonstrated by the weary and unenthusiastic manner in which advent of the first authoritarian regime in India was treated, and by the fact that for about two years it faced little resistance except of unorganized local people driven to desperation. Yet its end showed in some ways the opposite: a failure of nerves on Indira Gandhi's part to rule indefinitely without electoral sanction, though she was so immensely misinformed by a sycophantic bureaucracy that she probably expected to get a reduced mandate. This was in any case a reluctant acknowledgement of the principle that the exercise of political power required elective sanction. When the electorate was given a chance, they showed their determination for the continuance of democratic government by voting her out comprehensively. Indira Gandhi's period in uncontested authority also marked a departure from the liberal rules of democracy that Nehru followed. One of the major features of Nehru's government, as of the structure of the Congress party itself, was a commitment to compromise—between various ideological positions, regional interests, and social classes. Majority rule, therefore, never polarized opinions or interests to an extent where some political groups would become irretrievably alienated from the political process and the state itself.[20]

Indira Gandhi's tendency to use her electoral majority to destroy and alienate opposition, and to deny her adversaries even the general protection democratic procedures provide, led to a kind of political hostility that although it was initially expressed through democratic processes was new. Parties began to dredge more deeply for slogans and often began to mobilize along caste and religious community based ties. Indira Gandhi's years in Indian politics worked an astonishing transformation in the language and issues of politics. During the Nehru years, the main lines of party demarcation and political conflict were broadly ideological. The Communists and the Swatantra Party represented ideologically leftist and right-wing opposition to the Congress's resolute centrism. From the point of view of understanding democracy, this contrast can be seen not only as a conflict between ideological positions, but also as a conflict between political extremism and a politics of compromise. One of the major departures of Indira Gandhi from Nehru's political style was a conversion of Congress politics into one of perpetual confrontation. Excessive centralization ironically resulted in major outbreaks of regional discontent, sliding, because of her abrasive handling, into immediate militancy and, eventually, insurgency. By the time Indira Gandhi was assassinated, she had left behind seriously impaired institutions and a string of regional insurgencies which have proved intransigent to all subsequent governments.

Non-dominant Coalitions

After Indira Gandhi's death, Indian democracy clearly entered a new historical phase. The aspects of this phase were the decline of the Congress, which had previously occupied centre stage in Indian politics, and the rise of Hindu nationalism in various forms, primarily the growing influence of the Bharatiya Janata Party (BJP). After Independence, the nationalism of the state was represented by the Congress, and despite its many internal complexities and undoubted untidiness, the party held its ideology and political practice within some generally recognized parameters. It rarely succeeded in realizing the shining ideals of complete secularism, an unequivocal commitment to egalitarianism, or the perfect observance of procedures. Judged against such high standards, the Congress always came out seriously tarnished and sordid. Despite that, in retrospect, it achieved success of a kind. This success was to be measured, paradoxically, in negative terms: despite furtive use of religious feelings, it did not use overt communalism; its members did not always observe rules but could be shamed into retreating when serious procedural flaws could be revealed; it did little directly for social equality but admitted a general commitment of the state in that direction—at least had a bad conscience.

The historic achievement of the Congress lay not in what it achieved but in what it averted. Consequently, the Congress's slow fragmentation and apparently irreversible decline inevitably left a huge ideological vacuum in Indian politics. Two very different forces have tried to fill it in recent years. There is still considerable support in India for a strong, territorially integrated, powerful nation-state. The groups who promulgate such a position are naturally disappointed by the collapse of the Congress version of nationalist ideology which animated this nation-state. The strongest alternative to this nationalist vision is now the one offered by the BJP with a Hindu nationalist conception of India. This ideology shares with the Congress ideal the territorial integrity of the nation-state. What it does not share with the Congress ideal is the principle of secularism and pluralism as fundamental, inalienable aspects of the definition of nationalism (Jaffrelot 1996: Ch. 11)—it is not merely a Hindu majoritarian vision, but also necessarily hostile to the implicit pluralism of Indian culture. Thus it is opposed to two central principles of Indian society, one traditional, the other modern. It is opposed to the pluralist and politically egalitarian conceptions of modern secular democracy,[21] but, ironically, it is equally opposed to the traditional pluralism of Hindu religion. The success of the Hindu nationalists would preserve the territorial integrity of India, but turn its internal political culture into something utterly different. If experience with BJP regional governments is any guide, it might not offer a remarkably superior administration, but would certainly destroy the confidence of India's large religious minorities in the neutrality of the nation-state.

The second type of political force which might offer an alternative to the Congress is a congeries of regional groups which have no national perspective or vision and simply bargain with other regions and whichever party is at the centre for maximum regional advantage. Although it is customary for nationalists to deride these groups for their parochialism, in the long run this null nationalism might be an excellent foil to the BJP's tendency towards homogenization. The fact that these groups do not have a strong, determinate idea of what the nation should be like, or what should be its cultural form, ideological content, etc. tends to indicate that they would accept a pluralistic nationalism and, collaterally, a procedural conception of democracy. These parties are likely to be satisfied by a decision arrived at by a particular procedure (consultation, compromise, some form of weighted voting, etc.) rather than a strong association with a particular content of nationalism. For similar reasons, they are also less likely to impose a particular cultural, linguistic, ideological, or religious character on the whole nation, simply because they implicitly recognize their inability to speak for the nation as a whole. Given the strength of their respective support and social bases, it is unlikely that in the short term any of the main contenders in democratic politics in India would completely overwhelm the other. The BJP's support is unlikely to fade away or collapse suddenly. Although the Congress might fragment and decline even further, the counterweight to the BJP in the form of a coalition of groups which oppose it on secular or caste grounds is not likely to have an imminent collapse. Indian politics looks bound in the foreseeable future to muddle through on the basis of perishable coalitions. This might strengthen the procedural aspects of democracy by bringing into relief how important institutional forms are in case of indecisive electoral results. Since all parties suffer from insecurity in electoral terms, they might all equally value the impartiality of titular and supervisory agencies like the Election Commission or the President and state Governors. In a strange fashion, this might also gladden the hearts of economic liberalizers by shifting effective powers from the state to the market and by immobilizing the state agencies for long periods. But this consequence would go against the long-term tendency of Indian democracy to allow the state to extend its control over steadily larger areas of economic life, and marginal groups have tried to acquire some control over state resources by means of electoral power. Reduction of the effective control of the state's realm of decisions would mean a restriction of the scope of social life which was amenable to democratic power.

Major Features of Indian Democracy
The Problem of Representation

Indian democracy in its early years was marked by a paradox: its formal principles were democratic, based on formal equality of citizens, but the actual social structure through which it functioned was still highly aristocratic. Thus the political elite, who represented different social and political groups in the highly verbal arena of democratic politics were usually members of the educated middle class, predominantly urban elite. Democratic politics gives greater importance to certain types of assets: by nature, it values cultural capital. It is thus not surprising that in the first two decades of the operation of democratic government the legislators and politicians, irrespective of their political opinions, came from a narrow, recognizably homogenous urban upper-class elite. Political activities of all kinds in the narrower sense—in state institutions, the file-maintaining work of the bureaucracy, the verbal disputations inside the legislatures, and the legally technical proceedings of judicial process—were all carried out in impeccable English. This, of course, restricted access to the relevant democratic forms for ordinary people who did not have the right education or cultural capital. Political representatives of untouchable castes were figures like Ambedkar or Jagjivan Ram who shared the culture of the elite and could speak their 'language'. Similarly, Communist legislators were mostly from educated cultural and social backgrounds, despite their political sympathies. Representation, one of the most fundamental processes, was thus of a specific kind—representatives who could represent interests of marginal or less dominant groups like the former untouchables or the workers and peasants through the trade-union movements and Communist parties, were socially and culturally unlike the groups they spoke for.

Slowly, over the late 1950s and early 1960s, some inevitable consequences of democratic politics were discernible. Land reforms in the countryside, particularly in areas where formerly the *zamindari* system was in place, created a space for the emergence of a new class of richer farmers who acquired wealth and political influence locally, but did not immediately aspire to the culture of the urban elites. Their representatives slowly broke into the state legislatures initially altering their internal patterns of functioning, use of language and styles, and, finally, the entire internal culture of legislative and electoral politics. Democratic politics also slowly mobilized underprivileged groups like the lower castes and the poorer peasantry. Gradually, this led to a fundamental restructuring of the representational system of the parties. In the 1950s most parties were ideological, and claimed to represent mixed constituencies, mobilized on the basis of distributive principles of various sorts. Congress, Swatantra, the Communists, and the Socialists were all 'national' parties in a certain sense, and felt unwilling to be associated with the interests of any particular primordial group. The Communists claimed particular title to represent the working class. This was not based on primordial identity, but rather on an economic interest defined in terms of class.

By the 1970s, the early signs of a fundamental redefinition of this format of representation were clearly observable. Two processes occurred simultaneously to alter the meaning of representation in the party system.

First, there was a subtle but undeniable change in the nature of some parties. The Socialists from the 1960s slowly lost all other support and became a northern regional party except in name. The Communists, after their splits in 1964 and 1968,[22] slowly lost influence in other regions and became entrenched in West Bengal, Kerala, and Tripura and started behaving much like a regional party. The Congress did the same, only in a way that was less discernible because it continued to retain some influence in most regions. Under Indira Gandhi, the Congress began using appeals to religious identities, especially clearly in Punjab and Jammu and Kashmir, wooing the Hindu minorities in these states and alienating the Sikh and Muslim majorities. But what was more permanently damaging to democratic institutions was the enticement to religious groups to think of themselves as political communities. This undermined the randomness of outcomes and the indeterminacy of the constitution of majorities, slowly forcing the politics of these states in the direction of irresoluble conflict between religious communities.

But the more obvious shift in the field of political parties has been the development of straightforward identity-based parties which have equated the idea of identity with that of interest. Since the 1980s, two types of parties have emerged as the most powerful players in the political field. First, there are parties based on religious identities like the Akali Dal in Punjab, the BJP in most of north and western India and some of the political groups in Kashmir which drifted from an initially regionalist to a clearly religious self-indentification, and caste-based parties of various types, galvanized by the suggestions and opposition to the recommendations made by the Mandal Commission.[23] Between these two types of new political parties, political parties based on other types of affiliations, especially associational ones, have constantly been on the retreat. One accompanying feature of such homogeneous identity-based parties, unsurprisingly, has been a different form of representation. To represent a backward-caste group, it is now seen as necessary to have the outward manifestations of behaviour that both its members and others associate with these groups. The idea that any other individual who does not have the necessary identity features can represent them or their interest politically has been fatally undermined.

Politics of this kind acknowledges only representation by likeness. Often this logic of representation has been carried even further by implicating the bureaucracy into this politics. For instance leaders of successive governments in Uttar Pradesh have openly declared that only Scheduled-caste officers can advance the interests of Scheduled-caste groups, and therefore have promoted officers from these groups quite openly. This brings the logic of segmentation on which the caste order is based into the operation of democratic government with potentially unpredictable results. Although a departure from the previous idea of representation, which was at the bottom was aristocratic, democratizes politics in a certain sense. There are certainly precedents of this type from the history of western democracy, particularly from the history of labour parties, which often based the idea of representation on this kind of social resemblance. At the same time, it complicates the question of trust which must underlie modern institutions, including democratic political forms. It might introduce something like a non-territorial social partition between different identity groups. The effect of this has been that the discourse of rights has assumed increasingly complex form. While most groups speak in terms of a language of rights, the bearers of these rights are increasingly seen to be communities and primordial groups rather than individuals and their associational interests. The obvious consequence of this will be, if this trend is taken to its logical end, that democratic decisions will become frozen into segmented groups aligned in relations of unalterable, permanent majorities and minorities—a condition under which democratic decisions would become increasingly misleading and meaningless.

The politics of representation has another aspect as well. Democracy is often justified as a government based on the choice of the people. Obviously, this is an idea that has to be further refined. If choice means taking actual decisions about policies or outcomes, it is misleading to say that the electorate chooses. It seems necessary to think of the process of choice as stretching from a wide and general end where the electorate participates through elections to a narrow, specific end at which the government or its relevant bodies take actual decisions about individual policies. This does not deny the reality of an exercise of choice by the electorate, it locates choice in the relations between political parties and their personnel, with some very broad, occasionally ambiguous declarations of policies. This should properly be seen as a mandate, to be distinguished, in a strict sense, from a choice. Further down the line, there can be other forms of choice like assent or acquiescence to general directions or policy objectives, which are eventually further focused by the real act of policy decisions. One of the major questions in a democracy is how the electorate can use the necessarily blunt instrument of a mandate to get policy decisions of its liking. The change in the nature of political formations in India is closely associated with a change in the nature of the mandates that parties have put forward to the electorates. There is a broad trend of parties which is far away from large ideological postures like socialism or laissez faire, which were too broad to affect people's livelihoods or incomes, to far more specific expectations of redistribution of government resources for particular groups. The lack of interest in large public investments like infrastructure, observed by economists, might be linked to this political fact. The fragmentation of the party system has made the adoption of economic policies benefiting sectional interests more likely than government investment in general welfare or common interests.

It has been widely noted that the success of democracy has led to results that appear paradoxical in terms of conventional modernization theories. Those theories assumed that with the rise of industries and the entrenchment of modern democratic politics, social individuation would be greatly advanced and ordinary people would feel less attached to their primordial communities. But the actual consequence of democratic processes has confounded such expectations. As democracy applied pressure on groups to combine and use the pressure of large numbers, voters have been mobilized often on the basis of their community self-understandings. Through this caste identities have been politically reinforced. Instead of caste affiliations slowly fading and disappearing from political life, these identities have become incresingly assertive and important in the making of party political moves, baffling observers.[24] At the same time, it is difficult to regard these parties as manifestations of traditional caste identities. Conventional caste practices were concerned with social activities like marriage, commensality, and enjoyment of property. New caste forces are concerned primarily with the acquisition and maintenance of political power. Since political power in a democratic regime depends on large numerical groups, the trend in caste politics has gone in the direction of forming new kinds of alliances across the traditional segmentation of caste groups. This has led to the formation of entirely new kinds of caste affiliations like Scheduled Castes(created by Constitutional contrivance) or 'intermediate castes' created by the drive for large coalitions for electoral purposes. The consequence of this has been equally puzzling: instead of the principle of equality reducing caste identification, there is increasingly a tendency to assert caste identities while claiming equality *among* them. The imbrication of particularist, identity-based-claims and universalist, equality-based-claims was entirely unforeseen by the earlier theory or by constitutional designs or indeed by the traditional principles of the caste order. Thus democracy has certainly affected the structure of social inequality in India in terms of caste. It has surely reduced the practice of caste inequality both by the first wave of constitutional reforms in the 1950s and the second wave of electoral politics of the 1980s and 1990s. While the first set of moves intended to work towards greater individual equality, the second set have mobilized opinion against hierarchical caste practice by mobilizing and reinforcing caste identities themselves, not by trying to abolish them.

Democracy and Regional Interests

Sceptical views about Indian democracy often regard regional pluralism as a threat to democratic government. In the institutional arrangements of politics, regional diversity is supposed to be addressed by devices of federalism rather than of democratic government. But if democracy is interpreted as government by consent, where political solutions would not be imposed on people who do not like them, a strong connection between principles of federalism and democracy can be seen: federalism is a representative arrangement for India's various regions. Representation for regions has worked in two different ways. Initially, it functioned through the internal federalism of the Congress party itself, not through regional parties. In the Nehru period, the Congress maintained its earlier consensual principles of functioning by making sure representatives of various regions enjoyed office, which was also reflected in cabinet making. Although from a formal point of view, the first three decades Indian politics might appear to have been totally dominated by a single 'national' party, with very little power to regional groups, regional representation has in fact worked quite well through the Congress. However, centralizing tendencies in the Congress during Indira Gandhi's time led to more intense regional resentment against her regime, with regional parties successfully capturing state governments. Irresponsible and partisan use of the Constitutional clause for dismissing state governments exacerbated this relation, and the 1970s and 1980s were marked by increasingly insistent demands for redistribution of financial powers between the states and the centre. Regional parties have been primarily of two types, representing quite different types of opposition to the centre. Some groups were simply confined to regions in terms of support, such as the Socialists in the Hindi areas in the 1960s, or the Communists in West Bengal and Kerala since the mid-1960s. Since the 1960s, however, regional parties appeared which had merely regional political demands, and therefore could not aspire to any national influence. The Akali Dal, the DMK, the AGP, etc., owed their political existence to regional issues. In some cases, when outplayed by the Congress or a nationalist coalition, some of these regional groups have tended to move in the direction of secessionism. The relation between democracy and regional disaffection presents a complex and mixed picture in Indian politics. In at least three cases—Punjab, Kashmir, and Assam—attempts to resolve conflict through democratic elections have not succeeded, because, some claim, democratic procedures were not punctiliously observed for a long time in earlier phases. If regional demands are not reconciled early, they have tended to move uncontrollably towards confrontation and have eventually led to the disruption of the state itself. The movements for regional autonomy in these regions claimed not a better deal within the Indian Union but the right to break away from the Indian state itself. There have been other cases, by contrast, where serious concessions by the central government successfully defused conflict and brought intense regional secessionism back into the folds of electoral politics. The DMK in Tamil Nadu, the nativist agitation in Andhra, the Mizo separatist movement, and even the National Conference in Kashmir under Farukh Abdullah were enticed back into parliamentary politics after serious conflict. In the 1990s, with the decline of 'national' parties the relation between regional politics and Indian democracy is falling into a different pattern. Since neither the Congress nor the BJP appears likely to command a stable and unassisted majority in parliamentary elections, national governments would have to depend on coalitional support of regional parties. Suddenly, the relation between regional and national parties might become strangely altered. Since major parties would depend on their support for forming governments, they would have to concede substantial governmental power and influence to regional groups. Instead of thinking of themselves as players confined to regional politics, and having a predominantly negative relation with dominant national groups, regional parties would now have to play an increasingly significant role at central level. Ironically, this might induce them to look at the central government in a different light, and alter the rules by which the centre–states game has been played for the last fifty years.

Democracy and Economic Policy/Development Policy

Theorists of democracy with a predominant interest in political economy were wont to argue once that democracy is probably detrimental to economic growth. The primary reasons given for this were two: first, democratic politics led to instability of government policies regarding economic matters. Business groups found it difficult to adjust to potentially conflicting economic strategies followed by ideologically divergent political parties who might succeed each other in office. Authoritarian governments, by contrast, were able to follow stable economic strategies over long periods, making it easier for business to make long-term calculations. Second, democratic politics, it was often suggested, made for too close a connection between electoral politics and government distribution of economic resources. Since winning elections depends quite often on making short-term economic promises to particular sectional interests, democratic regimes are chronically incapable of making detached, long-term policies about deveopment of the whole economy, because such policies does not manage the requisite 'insulation' of economic policy making from electoral pressures. Democracy in India shows a rather paradoxical picture in this respect. First, on long-term continuity of economic or development strategy, government change rarely affected fundamental strategy. On the contrary, at times, the continuity was quite startling. For example, in 1977 when the Janata Party succeeded Indira Gandhi's Congress, it was logical to expect serious change, since it was a combination of political groups which had opposed Congress policies of state-led development on various grounds. Yet the government did little to alter the basic package of policy orientations on economic matters. Curiously, the most significant shifts in economic strategy marked by liberalization since the early 1990s were introduced by a minority Congress government, but no party seriously opposed them at the time. After a coliation of leftist and regional parties replaced the Congress government, they deliberately continued with the policies of liberalization instead of scrapping them. Short-term concessions of economic policy before elections have also been rare at central level, though in state elections such quick distribution of state resources has been fairly common. However, since the state governments' resources are generally quite meagre, the effect of such behaviour has not been significant.

Indian democratic politics, however, shows the impact of democracy on economic policies in a different way. Democratic politics was surely responsible for the continuous increase of the sphere of the state's interference in the economy. Though originally introduced by standard Fabian Socialist arguments, taken from Britain, about capturing the 'commanding heights' of the economy, it slowly degenerated into a different kind of politico-economic practice. The state's control over enormous economic resources meant that these could be used for political purposes by political elites. The only means of acquiring control over these resources was through winning elections. Despite important differences about economic policy, nearly all groups of politicians benefited from this access. This meant, by implication, that electoral politics determined, to some extent, how this reservoir of resources was to be spent.

Paradoxically, the tendency towards economic liberalization, though justified by liberal arguments about the harmony between democracy and markets as systems of choice, is likely to reduce this indirect popular control over state resources. If the state is slimmed down, and this fund of resources wrenched away from its grasp, the impact of political democracy in the structural operations of the Indian economy is bound to be significantly reduced. This tends to show that not under all circumstances are the logics of democracy and capitalism fully congruent; in the Indian case, at least, liberalization would tend to make them diverge dramatically..

Democracy and Social Inequality

At the time of the adoption of the Constitution, one of the major arguments in favour of adult suffrage was that it would eventually reduce social inequality. But social inequality in India existed in two forms. The first is status inequality based on caste, which is still, despite socio-economic changes during the colonial period, deeply entrenched in Indian society. The Constitution abolished status inequality on the basis of caste, at least in public matters, by the radically simple device of the legal declaration of the right to equality. But legal declarations, while powerful statements about a society's principles, do not always necessarily change social behaviour. Advantage based on caste could not be simply abolished by legal delcaration because social inequality also meant unequal economic conditions and life chances. Curiously, the rights in the Constitution bestowed status equality on its citizens and helped maintain economic inequality at the same time, since some essential aspects of social inequality—especially in property and incomes—were part of the liberal regime of rights. It was believed at the time of Constitution making that democracy would support social equality in two different but complementary ways. First, the Constitution gave the state the right to use reverse discrimination in favour of backward castes, reserving academic places for them and, more directly, reserving government jobs. To the extent, lower-caste individuals got these jobs or places, they acquired either equality of condition or a chance to secure it. State employment, however, offered opportunities for a relatively small number of people, and the importance of reservations of posts in government service was often of symbolic rather than of great statistical significance. Reservations in education and other measures were expected to work as a larger process of bringing in social equality, and the Constitution envisaged a phasing out of these reservation rules after opportunities had become more generally equal. It is in the second kind of measures that the effect of democracy has been disappointing. Democratic pressure on legislatures has constantly extended the reservation rules of the state, both in terms of time and in terms of their coverage, most notably through the recommendations of the Mandal Commission. But democratic politics has failed to bring pressure on the state to provide greater equality in the provision of education, health, and skills through which economic inequality can be addressed in the long term. In recent decades, the shift in political conflict to questions of identity, like caste and religion, has tended to overshadow this apsect of social equality. It must be noted, however, that the demands for advance of the lowest castes, although made on the grounds of identity, do have an effect on economic equality in an indirect fashion.

In India, historical experience appears to show that democratic politics tends to bring social conflicts out into the open. It makes them more public, occasionally magnifies them and, only at times makes them easier to settle because of this publicity. If the outer parameters of the state are accepted, it does tend eventually to assist in the resolution of conflicts. In democratic contexts, due to immediate expression of popular or sectional grievances, both the government and the ruling elites as well as other parties with opposed interests get to know about these disaffections quite quickly. Democratic openness thus works as a kind of early warning system, and allows other groups to adjust to such demands. But once demands have gained currency, democratic government has encouraged two rather contradictory tendencies: it allows radical groups to exacerbate differences of opinion and conflicts of interests. But at the same time, since demands of either social groups like castes or classes or regional forces have to argue their case against other views, it tends to create a climate in which accommodation is eventually possible. This can lead to the trend towards the composition of differences and de-radicalization that liberal theorists have usually found in democratic politics. After fifty years of Independence, the historical strength of Indian democracy is undeniable, and this is shown in the fact that no major party ever offers arguments against democracy. But the subtler threat to democracy might come from forces which wish to use the power of democracy in a way which keeps some sections of society permanently excluded, which would mean a violation of the spirit of democracy through the use of its electoral forms.

ENDNOTES

1. Rajni Kothari argued ingeniously that traditional Indian culture was based on religious pluralism, and could thus form a cultural base for the functioning of democracy. (Kothari 1970).

2. For an example of the constitutionalist approach to the problems of Indian democracy, see (Pylee). Besides these, however, there was an immensely detailed and erudite literature on technical constitutional law, of which one of the best known works.

3. For an account of the evolution of colonial government in India.

4. This strand was represented in Bengal, where some of these early intellectual moves were played out by the movement called Young Bengal.

5. For a detailed analysis of three writers who represent this tendency—Bankimchandra Chattopadhyay, Bhudev Mukhopadhyay and Vivekananda—see Raychaudhuri 199?

6. To take a well known example—again from late-nineteenth-century Bengal, there was a great deal of discussion about the exact semantic connotations of *Dharma* and religion, and Haraprasad Shastri the famous socio-linguist wrote about these translation problems.

7. The best example of this kind of argument is to be found in Dadabhai Naoroji's *Poverty and the Un-British Rule in India*, first published in Britain in 1899.

8. Thus the arguments, taken from Hannah Arendt's analysis of totalitarian politics, widely used in the conventional political science literature of the 1950s and 1960s against popular nationalist mobilizations could not be used against the Congress.

9. For detailed analyses of the workings of the Constituent Assembly, see Austin (1964); Chaube and; Dattagupta (1978).

10. Rajendra Prasad, the president of the Constituent Assembly expressed his regret in the valedictory session, speaking in Hindi.

11. The most important of these provisions is, of course, the amendment of the Constitution itself.

12. The division of powers between the central and state governments is set down in the ninth schedule of the Indian Constitution, with the centre awarded 97 separate heads, the states 64, treated as concurrent subjects on which the centre's laws would override the states', with the residuary powers given to the centre.

13. For discussions on the Constituent Assembly, see Austin (1964: Ch. 12).

14. For an account of the evolution of Indian federal institutions in this period, see Chandra (1965: Ch. 2).

15. Nehru's reservations about conceding linguitsic states are recorded in Gopal (1989: vol. II, Ch.).

16. Christophe Jaffrelot (1996) provides a detailed historical analysis of the various trends in Hindu nationalist thinking. See esp. Ch. 1.

17. Because of his odd belief that caste practices could be non-discriminatory, that is a registration of difference rather than inequality.

18. These complaints have been made mainly to academic researchers or journalists covering elections in rural constituencies.

19. But this phase of renewed Congress dominance could be stretched to 1990, the death of Rajiv Gandhi and the coming of the first Congress minority regime under P.V. Narasimha Rao.

20. Some critics of the argument that asserts the difference in political styles between Nehru and Indira Gandhi point to Nehru's attitude towards Naga rebels and the general troubles in India's north-eastern region. But those were cases of areas which were never properly integrated into the Indian state, rather than of areas pushed into militant opposition by government policy.

21. The BJP claims that its politics represents true secularism, and those of other parties 'pesudo-secularism' that concedes illegitimate concessions to the minorities. But the claim that religious minorities must conform to certain ideas, laid down eventually by the Hindu majority, goes against the fundamental principle of equal treatment of religious groups.

22. The Communist Party of India first split in 1964. Subsequently, the larger fragment, the CPI(M), split again in 1968, with the radical wing, popularly known as the Naxalites, forming a militant anti-electoral movement committed to winning power by violent revolution. While the CPI(M) has thrived electorally in specific regions, while slowly becoming de-radicalized, the Naxalite movement was crushed by the state's use of force, and later splintered into a number of warring groups.

23. The Mandal commission was appointed by the central government to look into the operation of reverse discrimination policies over the long term, and to make further suggestions. The Commission suggested a substantial increase in the scope of reservations, at times increasing it well beyond 50 per cent. This has polarized Indian political opinion as nothing else had for the last several decades. Its views have drawn

primarily three types of response. First, some groups have enthusiastically supported them as a means of realizing social justice. Second, other parties, based understandably on upper caste support, have condemned them as denial of rights to equality of opportunity and treatment. Some other groups, while not openly contesting the recommendations, have supported drastic reduction of state control over employment and resources, since these principles are more difficult to apply to the private sector.

24. The earliest, and in some ways the best, analysis of this trend remains Kothari's (1970) analysis.

REFERENCES

Austin, Granville. 1964. *The Indian Constitution: Constitution of a Nation.* Oxford: Clarendon Press.

Brown, Judith. *Modern India: The Origins of an Asian Democracy.* Oxford University Press.

Chandra, Asok. 1965. *Federalism in India.* London: George Allen and Unwin.

Dattagupta, S. 1978. *Justice and Political Order in India.* Calcutta: K.P. Bagchi.

Gopal, S., ed. 1989. *Jawaharlal Nehru,* vol. II. London: Frank Cass.

Guha, Ranajit. 1981. *Elementary Aspects of Peasant Insurgency in Colonial India.* Delhi: Oxford University Press.

Jaffrelot, Christophe. 1996. *The Hindu Nationalist Movement and Indian Politics.* London: Hurst.

Kothari, Rajani. 1970. *Politics in India.* Delhi: Orient Longman.

———. 1970. *Caste in Indian Politics.* Delhi: Orient Longman.

Naoroji, Dadabhai. [1889]. *Poverty and the Un-British Rule in India.*

Raychaudhuri, Tapan. 199. *Europe Reconsidered.* Oxford University Press.

Backward Castes/Classes as Legal and Political Entities

P. Radhakrishnan

The term 'Backward Castes' is used here for those caste groups which constitute the overwhelming majority of the population entitled to the compensatory benefits provided by the Indian Constitution. Also, the term 'Backward Classes' is used as a generic one for these intended beneficiaries, and for the corresponding social groups from other religious communities such as Muslims and Christians. To minimize confusion, following Galanter (1984: 3), 'backward classes' will be used without capitalization in a broad and inclusive sense for the Scheduled Castes, Scheduled Tribes, and the Other Backward Classes, and with capitalization in a narrow sense, exclusively for the Other Backward Classes.

If Srinivas in 1957 said that 'in Independent India, the provision of constitutional safeguards to the backward sections of the population, especially the Scheduled Castes and Tribes, has given a new lease of life to caste' (1962: 15), the same is being said today with greater vehemence because of the increasing importance of the compensatory principle.

As backward classes are reformulations of colonial categories, their emergence, as legal and political entities should be understood in the context of the processes at work since the late nineteenth century in the interactions between society, economy, and polity. It is possible to discern at least six of these processes:

(1) The expansion of the economic frontier, the emergence of new professions that were not ascriptive or prescribed by caste; through a series of 'social closures', the latter helped backward castes gain access to the opportunity structure of society from which they were excluded. Urban growth led to new forms of caste solidarity, and accelerated the

transition of caste from an 'organic' system to a 'segmentary' one—that is, from a structure to a juxtaposition of substances.

(2) The spread of social movements, some of which, such as the ones led by Jotirao Phule and B.R. Ambedkar in Maharashtra, Narayana Guru in Kerala, and E.V. Ramasamy Naicker in Tamil Nadu, gave a certain militancy to their anti-caste thrust, while others, such as the movements of the non-Brahmin, backward-classes and the depressed-classes in peninsular India, sought to nestle under the caste system by efforts to move up its hierarchy. These latter movements also weakened caste, at least in so far as they affected the Brahmins, by sapping their prestige and depriving them of their dominance in administration.

(3) The conflicting public postures on caste by Ambedkar and Mahatma Gandhi. Ambedkar, who campaigned for the emancipation of the Untouchables and for the annihilation of caste, condemned *chaturvarnya* (the fourfold classification of Hindu society) as a degrading social organization that deadens, paralyses, and cripples the people. Though Gandhi campaigned for the abolition of untouchability, he did not attack caste. Instead, he extolled *chaturvarnya*, and appealed to caste Hindus to elevate Untouchables to the status of Sudras in the *varna* system, and for making their unclean work honourable.

(4) The broad-basing of the nationalist movement, which provided the much-needed socio-political basis for the articulation of the rights of the backward castes, though importantly enough was also 'subversive' of the caste system.

(5) The British responses to the new stirrings in Indian society, stirrings which threatened its very stability through, among other things, its patronage politics, which created in the disprivileged sections increasing awareness of the close nexus between English education and government employment.

(6) India's adoption in 1950 of a Constitution committed to adult franchise, formal equality for all, and special dispensation for the historically disadvantaged sections of society, which made castes in general and backward castes in particular important political categories in the newly introduced number game of electoral/vote-bank politics, and helped the backward castes improve their life chances.

It is not possible to elaborate on all these processes within the limited space of this chapter. All the same, in understanding the backward castes in perspective it is important to note that it is these processes which loosened the caste structure, created the much needed social and political space for the backward castes to take on the system which has oppressed and exploited them, and brought about partial reordering of the social order and power structure.

Castes as Social Entities

Caste, the most complex and ubiquitous of India's social institutions, the structural basis of Hindu society and the classic expression of institutionalized inequality, has also traditionally been the principal category of social ordering and control. Conventionally, it has had two distinct meanings: *varna* and *jati*, both of which distinctly express the principle of hierarchical inequality.

Varna/Jati Dichotomy

Describing the features of the caste system *implicit* in the varna scheme, and how they differ from, or conflict with, the system as it actually functions, Srinivas wrote:

> According to the *varna* scheme there are only four castes excluding the Untouchables, and the number is the same in every part of India. But even during the Vedic times there were occupational groups which were not subsumed by *varna* even though it is not known whether such groups were castes in the sense sociologists understand the term. Today, in any linguistic area there are to be found a number of castes. According to Prof. Ghurye, in each linguistic region, there are about 200 caste groups which are further sub-divided into about 3000 smaller units each of which is endogamous and constitutes the area of effective social life for the individual. The *varna*-scheme refers at best only to the broad categories of the society and not to its real and effective units [1962: 65].

These real and effective units are the jatis or local caste groups. Srinivas also drew a distinction between two types of caste hierarchy: the traditional (articulated in religious terms) and the emergent (1962: 95–6).

While both meanings of caste are still recognized, caste is now understood more as jati than as varna, consistent with the shift in emphasis from the traditional to the emergent, and from religion to politics in matters relating to caste. Despite this shift, as shown by Galanter, the varna theory is still relevant:

> The power of the *varna* theory is shown by the common tendency to describe the caste system as made up of four 'castes' of which the endogamous caste groups are merely sub-divisions. (Hence the usage 'sub-caste'.) Groups seeking to better their position in the local hierarchy often phrase their claims in terms of a more prestigious *varna* identification by adopting names and practices associated with one of the three higher *varnas* [1984: 10].

Galanter has also drawn attention to the fact that the second Backward Classes Commission (Mandal Commission) which proposed, a major extension of preferential treatment to a vastly enlarged group of beneficiaries, revived the varna classifications dismissed by its predecessor a quarter century earlier (Galanter 1984: 20). The acrimonious debates on the Mandal report and the references in related judicial pronouncements also had the effect of reviving these classifications.

Backward Castes: Past and Present

Though varnas are taxonomic categories rather than functional groups, they are still reference groups to a number of castes. These categories offer a twofold forward–backward dichotomy in both the traditional (colonial) and contemporary contexts. In one Brahmins are forward, and non-Brahmins (the Kshatriya-Vaisya-Sudra combine) are backward. In the other, all but Sudras are forward. Of these, the second dichotomy is relevant mainly for north India (the Aryan heartland) and not for the rest of the country, especially east and peninsular India, where Kshatriya and Vaisya only refers to the local Sudra castes who have claimed to be belonging to these categories by virtue of their martial and occupational traditions.

In both these dichotomies Sudras, the overwhelming majority of the population subsumed by the four varnas, are clearly accounted as inferior to the three 'twice-born' varnas. They are, however, very heterogeneous:

> The category of Shudra subsumes in fact the vast majority of non-Brahminical castes which have little in common. It may at one end include a rich, powerful and highly Sanskritized group while at the other end may be tribes whose assimilation into the Hindu fold is only marginal. ... One of the most striking features of the caste system as it actually exists is the lack of clarity in the hierarchy, especially in the middle regions [Srinivas 1962: 65–6].

As the Sudra category subsumes all the backward castes (excluding Untouchables), who form the majority of the Sudras, its heterogeneity is shared by these castes as well, and consists of a multitude of hierarchized and strongly differentiated social aggregates. Hence, although backward castes are pan-Indian categories, there are no pan-Indian patterns of their backwardness or criteria to determine them.

As the compensatory provisions are primarily for the advancement in education and employment of the backward sections of society, backward castes should be seen from the Constitutional perspective of restitution or reparation to offset the entrenched and cumulative nature of group inequalities and deprivations suffered by the historically disadvantaged sections. Seen in this way, only those sections of Hindu society which are overwhelmingly backward in education and employment ought to be treated as backward castes.

Backward Castes/Classes as Colonial Categories

The term 'Backward Classes' has been in use in different parts of the country since the late nineteenth century. It began to gain currency in Madras presidency since 1872, in the princely state of Mysore since 1918, and in Bombay presidency since 1925.

Beginning in the 1920s, a number of organizations united around the issue of caste, sprang up in different parts of the country. The rise of these organizations was in response to several developments in the greater political culture, the most important of which are: the new benefits doled out by the government, the emerging bargaining culture and the growing awareness that caste played a vital political role in the formation of larger collectives. These included the United Provinces Hindu Backward Classes League, All-India Backward Classes League, Madras Provincial Backward Classes League, Bihar State Backward Classes Federation, and the All-India Backward Classes Federation. Galanter has noted that Majumdar (1955: 474–5) in 1954 counted 88 organizations working for the Backward Classes in 15 states, of which 74 represented individual communities and 14 Backward Classes in general, on a local or state basis (Galanter 1984: 162). Considering the great importance of the compensatory principle for the Backward Classes, and the great importance of Backward Classes in India's vote-bank politics, it is only to be expected that the number of such organizations has increased manifold in the subsequent years, with some of them either merging with or transforming themselves into political parties.

The major decisions taken and policies laid down by the colonial administration were from an all-India perspective, and Madras Presidency was far ahead of other provinces in evolving backward castes and classes as colonial categories and offering concessions and preferences to them in education and employment. Notwithstanding regional variations, an overview of the developments in Madras presidency should provide a broad idea of the developments in the rest of the country as well.

Popular Instruction

In his controversial Minute of 2 February 1835, drawn up at the instance of Governor General William Bentinck, Thomas Babington Macaulay, President of the General Committee of Public Instruction, asserted that 'we must, at present, do our best to form a class who may be interpreters between us and the millions whom we govern, a class of persons Indian in blood and colour, but English in taste, in opinions, in morals and intellect.' However, by the early 1850s the British administration realized that shaping men of the high castes in this 'Macaulay mould' was no longer the only necessary and desirable motivation of its educational policy in India. The emergence of backward classes as educational categories was an outcome of this realization.

Implicit in this realization was a belated concern for broad based colonial paternalism. That explains the consideration of the Court of Directors (the governing body of the East India Company) which speaks in its Despatch of 19 July 1854 (the Charles Wood despatch), of 'how useful and practical knowledge suited to every station in life might be best conveyed to the great mass of people, who are utterly incapable of obtaining any education worthy of the name by their own unaided efforts'—a consideration which by the Court's own admission had been neglected until then. But more pressing than this concern was the abiding concern for Imperial interests. The acrimonious debates on Indian education in both England and India in the wake of and immediately after the 'mutinies' of 1857; the Government of India resolution of 7 August 1871 on Muslim education which regretted that so large and important a class should stand aloof from active cooperation with its educational system; the Government of Madras follow-up resolution of 29 July 1872 stressing that the gradual disappearance of Muslims from the public service was injurious to the most vital interests of the Empire; and the special treatment of Muslims with regard to education and employment in the subsequent years—were all expressions of this paternalistic concern.

In fact, Muslims were the first to be treated as a backward class in Madras presidency. That was in 1872, following the two previously mentioned resolutions. At that time they were not labelled as a backward class. But the idea was to treat them so, by holding out, as reported in the Government of India resolution of 15 July 1885 (in response to a memorial of February 1882 by the National Muhammadan Association), 'special inducements to a backward class' for promoting their education and employing those qualified among them in the public service.

Just about a decade after this began the saga of backward classes categories. That was in the context of the education of the lower strata of society, or what the public instruction department then termed popular instruction, by both governmental and private efforts, especially Christian missionaries.

Soon after the public instruction department was organized during 1855–6 following the Despatch of 1854, it acknowledged the utter neglect of such instruction. By its own admission it produced little or no effect upon the mass of the population and its action was almost entirely confined to those that hoped to secure employment in the public service. It regretted that while the university examinations, with the honours they held out, and the uncovenanted service examinations, which presented direct pecuniary advantages as well as a share of credit, afforded a powerful leverage for the improvement of superior and middle class education, no such machinery afforded itself for the spread of primary instruction. By 1880 the department became more candid about this neglect, or what it soon characterized as the reproach that the educational efforts of the government had hardly touched the lowest castes.

Education Commission

Meanwhile, the government's failure to build up a system of mass education through grants-in-aid (as envisaged by the Despatch of 1854), and their failure to foster secondary and higher education—a failure which marked the neglect of the pressure from Christian missionaries for a review of educational developments since 1855—led to the appointment of an Education Commission of twenty members in 1882 by Governor-General Ripon, with W.W. Hunter, a member of his Executive Council, as chairman.

In its report of 1883, this Commission dwelt at length on the classes requiring special treatment. These were the chiefs and nobles at one extreme and, at the other, the 'aborigines', defined loosely and indefinitely as those races which had not been Hinduized and which preferred the freedom of forest or mountain and the pursuit of game to the monotony of school; the 'low castes', a euphemism for the Untouchables, a large population found in every Hindu village community, usually living on the outskirts of the village settlement; 'Musalmans' as certain sections of the Muslim community, which had sunk into a deplorable state of ignorance; and the 'poorer classes' as the poor families irrespective of caste. Of these, only the chiefs and nobles do not figure in the backward classes categories.

The Commission noted that there was a gradual shading off between the aborigines, who were partially Hinduized, and the Hindus themselves which rendered it difficult to determine the dividing line between the two. It also noted that though instances of great poverty were not confined to the lowest classes of society but existed in every caste, including Brahmins, such instances increased as the caste descended in the social scale.

These descriptions of various policies in conjunction with an attempt to trace the genealogy of backward classes as socio-historical categories should bring out the close nexus between the categories of tribe and caste that I have described thus far and those envisaged by the Indian Constitution: the bulk of the non-Hinduized aborigines are the Scheduled Tribes and the Untouchable low castes are the Scheduled Castes. As borderline cases, some of the partially Hinduized aborigines are Scheduled Tribes and some Scheduled Castes. While the poorer classes are spread over the entire society, only those comprising the lower strata just above the Scheduled Castes are the Backward Classes. For, as the Commission itself contended, instances of great poverty are more among these than among the upper strata; and poverty of the poor among the lower strata is not only economic but also social and cultural, whereas that of the poor among the upper strata is primarily economic.

Classificatory Schemes

Though the Commission broadly indicated the classes requiring special treatment, and though the public instruction reports actually followed the Commission's recommendations, the problem was that each of these classes was of an unwieldy and amorphous character comprising several groups of disparate size and socio-cultural background. Therefore, political considerations notwithstanding, governmental efforts to impart education among these heterogeneous ensembles entailed their classification. Each of the categories so classified differed from the rest for certain educational concessions and overlapped with them for certain others depending upon the official perception of it and of its educational needs. This process of classification was well on its way even before the appointment of the Education Commission. The annual and quinquennial public instruction reports classifying the population under instruction into different categories served as a useful tool for the Commission. Until 1890 the general classification was into Europeans/Eurasians, Native Christians, Hindus, Muhammadans, and Others. In 1891 the new category of Aborigines was introduced. The sub-classification of Hindus was into Brahmins, Vysyas, Sudras, and Other Hindus from 1883 to 1890; and Brahmins, Non-Brahmin Hindus (Vysyas and Sudras), and Paraiyas and kindred classes since 1891. Thus, within only the five years between 1880 and 1884 there appeared the categories of poor pupils, backward races, backward or indigent races or castes, indigent or backward classes, and backward classes proper. By this time, the Director of Public Instruction in Bombay also allowed (in 1878) fee concessions in primary schools to some of the castes which fell under various disabilities, and later instituted scholarships in secondary schools and colleges for boys from some of these castes (Ghurye [1932] 1979: 276).

Backward Classes

To begin with, the term backward classes was used for aborigines and low castes in the remarks of the Madras government in Chapter 9 of the Education Commission Report on the education of classes requiring special treatment sent to the Government of India. It was used in 1885 for Muslims, in 1886 in the School-Free Notification as a synonym for backward or indigent classes, and often thence by the public instruction department, before it crystallized in the second decade of the twentieth century as categories comprising the numerous historically disadvantaged bottom groups.

In 1892 the government permitted children of the backward or indigent classes specified in the Grant-in-aid Code (along with girls, and also Muslims and Oriyas permitted during 1872–3) to pay only half the standard rate of fees in institutions under public management. This half-fee concession was extended to Muslims in all professional colleges in 1896, and to the backward or indigent classes in 1908. The introduction of these concessions since 1892 led to a scramble for backward-class status (a scramble which still continues), and to the rapid lengthening of the backward-classes list.

Basis for Inclusion

Inclusions in the list were mostly on the basis of petitions by caste members or caste associations, or recommendation of the Director of Public Instruction, either of his own accord or based on the reports of the inspecting officers or collectors, or both.

The principal criterion for inclusion was educational backwardness, which in many cases coincided with low socio-economic status. But this criterion was seldom used with rigour and consistency. In 1913 the education department itself admitted that the list was not drawn scientifically; castes admitted according to this criteria were of every degree of literacy, ranging from one per mile to over 300. Some entries were caste titles, names of sub-castes, etc., some were not found in the recognized list of castes in Edger Thurston's work and the census reports. Besides, some were duplications, with the same caste shown under more than one name. The department, however, felt that not much good would come of going into the limitations, while omission of names already in it would be certain to evoke protests from missionaries who had schools full of the 'backward'.

Growth and Diversification

Though the fee concession was made general only in 1892, the list began to lengthen even a decade earlier. Its first major expansion was in 1884, following the extensive revision of the Grant-in-aid Code that took into consideration the recommendations of the Education Commission. Its second expansion was in 1913, following the Government of India resolution of 21 February 1913 to extend primary education and assist local governments with large grants from Imperial revenues by adding considerably to the backward-classes list on the basis of the 1911 Census. An important characteristic of the list was that names were often added to it but seldom deleted from it.

Closely related to the rapid growth of the list was its diversification, from as early as 1884. That year the Paraiyas and kindred classes (alias Panchamas, alias Adi-Dravidas, and Adi-Andhras, as these classes were renamed subsequently), were added to it. Panchamas, literally the fifth class, was brought into use by 1892 not only for brevity but also for replacing the terms Paraiyas, outcastes, etc., all of which had some embedded ideas of social degradation associated with it. Though these classes were then only a part of the list, they were singled out for special treatment by the public instruction department, and treated as a separate category in its reports since 1891. This indicated the increasing concern for their social ameliotion and their emerging identity as a separate category within the backward-classes list.

Besides the backward castes, backward classes also include the constitutional categories of Scheduled Castes (Untouchables) and Scheduled Tribes. As the present chapter is concerned with the backward castes, these other categories are not discussed here. What is, however, more relevant to note here is the growth and diversification of the backward-classes lists in Madras presidency, from just 11 names in 1883 to 39 in 1893, 46 in 1903, 122 in 1913, 131 in 1923, 182 in 1933, 238 in 1943, 270 in 1953, 302 in 1963, and well over 323 in 1997. Clearly this shows that far from being a creation of the Indian Constitution these categories were created by the British administration and supported and sustained by missionary educationists and the numerous bottom groups craving for social advancement. These lists, with minor modifications, have been used to fill the backward-class categories envisaged by the Constitution.

When the Constitution of India came into force in 1950, all the entries in the list of Scheduled Castes—comprising all the supposedly polluting castes of the then existing list of Depressed Classes as well as groups that were added to this list from the pre-existing category of 'Castes other than the Depressed'—filled the Constitutional category of Scheduled Castes. All groups with 'tribal characteristics' from the second list (renamed along with the introduction of the list of Scheduled Castes as renamed 'Castes other than the Scheduled Castes') filled the new list of Scheduled Tribes. The remaining groups in the second list filled the new list of Backward Classes, ('Socially and Educationally Backward Classes, as used by the judiciary).

Backward Castes/Classes as Legal Entities

If until the 1950s the backward classes were mere administrative categories, the introduction of compensatory provisions added a new dimension, enabling them over the years to emerge as an important legal entity. Understanding the related processes requires a recapitulation of the rationale behind the compensatory principle, the nature of the compensatory provisions, the categories entitled to them, and their identities as envisaged by the Constitution.

Merit versus Need

In a society where everyone (with the exception of a minuscule elite) is socially and ritually underprivileged, and the privileged are also overwhelmingly successful in every kind of competition, adoption of meritocracy alone would only have sharpened existing inequalities (Béteille 1992: 16; Srinivas 1992: 36–7). This situation explains the stress in the Constitution on both the meritarian and compensatory principles through which India's goal of an egalitarian society is sought.

The meritarian principle perceives merit as an individual attribute irrespective of caste/community. The compensatory principle limits the claims of merit by those who need in order to the victims of past discrimination to catch up with those who are ahead of them. While the perception of merit as an individual attributes itself is a radical departure from previous communist (or at least non-secular) views of the person, the idea of compensation is even more radical: it articulates a principle of social justice from the point of some of the most historically disabled communities in Indian history; it aims to give a centralized voice to groups of people who have almost always existed on the margins of social and economic life. (Béteille 1992: 10–18). The following observations by G.B. Pant made during a speech that moved the constitution of the Advisory Committee on fundamental rights, minorities, etc. clearly echoed this view:

> We have to take particular care of the Depressed Classes, the Scheduled Castes and the Backward Classes. ... We must do all we can to bring them up to the general level. ... The strength of the chain is measured by the weakest link of it and so until every link is fully revitalised, we will not have a healthy body politic [Rao 1968: 2, 63].

Backward Classes in the Constitution

Backward classes, as mentioned earlier, are Scheduled Castes, Scheduled Tribes, and Backward Classes. The core compensatory provisions for them are the following:

(1) Reservation of seats, in proportion to their numbers, for Scheduled Castes and Scheduled Tribes, in the Lok Sabha (House of people or the Lower House of parliament) (Article 330), and legislative assembly of every state (Article 332).

(2) Consideration of the claims of the members of Scheduled Castes and Scheduled Tribes, consistent with the maintenance of efficiency of administration, in the making of appointments to services and posts in connection with the affairs of the union or of a state (Article 335).

(3) Making any special provision for the advancement of any socially and educationally backward classes of citizens or the Scheduled Castes and Scheduled Tribes (Article 15 [4]).

(4) Making reservation of appointments or posts in favour of any backward class of citizens which, in the opinion of the state, is not adequately represented in the services of the state (Article 16 [4]).

As Scheduled Castes and Scheduled Tribes are the most backward, the principal compensatory measures for them are mandatory. But since the Backward Classes are a residual category, the measures for them are state based. This category is, however, the most controversial. Among the reasons for this are its extraordinary heterogeneity, large size, and ambiguity of identity; the conflict of interests and confrontation between castes declared as backward and those not; and the increasing animosity between castes competing for compensatory benefits. It is also crucial to India's vote-bank politics.

Judiciary and Backward Classes

When the traditional hierarchy of power and privilege is confronted by democracy and equalitarianism, and laws are used for reshaping recalcitrant social patterns, the results can be unsavoury: Some examples of this are the political moves and counter moves that have characterized events on the ground, mostly centring around the Backward Classes, and governmental superimposition of administrative categories as beneficiaries in the complex struggle for group and personal identity, with far-reaching implications for shaping and reshaping backward castes/classes as legal and political entities. So also the proliferation of jurisprudential views, classificatory schemes, and reservation formulae since the 1950s as a concomitant to and corollary of the politics of backwardness, which has been both chaotic and formidable. The Supreme Court's rulings of 16 November 1992 by a nine-judge Bench, were expected to put an end to this pernicious trend and settle the question of Backward Classes and reservations finally and authoritatively. Though the rulings were in the context of Article 16 (4), they have been extended by the judiciary to regulate the implementation of Article 15 (4) as well. A summary of these rulings follows:

(1) Article 16 (4) speaks only of any 'backward class of citizens' and does not contain the qualifying phrase 'socially and educationally'. Hence the expression 'backward classes' in Article 16 (4) is wider than the expression 'socially and educationally backward classes' in Article 15 (4). Though this is a major departure from the earlier rulings which treated both the expressions as synonyms, the judiciary has not followed this up with separate classificatory schemes.

(2) If the Backward Classes are similarly situated in their backwardness as the Scheduled Castes and Scheduled Tribes, they would, by Presidential order, find a place in these categories and no longer belong to the Backward Classes. Hence the earlier rulings that the backwardness of the Backward Classes should be comparable to that of Scheduled Castes and Tribes are invalid.

(3) The accent in the use of the term 'backward' is for purposes of Article 16 (4) upon *social backwardness*. Hence, the caste–class nexus is central to the understanding of what this expression signifies and how the classes within its ambit should be identified.

(4) The use of class for purposes of Article 16 (4) is as a *social class*, denoting a number of persons having certain common traits which distinguish them from the other, and not as understood in Marxist 'jargon'. (The usage is as in the judgements.) Such a class is often a caste inasmuch as a caste has all the attributes of a class, is also a class of citizens, is nothing but a social class, and is a socially and occupationally homogeneous class. Hence the nexus between class and caste is very close.

(5) The classification is not on the basis of caste itself but on the ground that the caste is found to be a Backward Class not adequately represented in the services of the state. In order to constitute a Backward Class the caste concerned must be socially backward and its educational and economic backwardness must be on account of its social backwardness. A caste that does not satisfy the agreed formulae, the primary test of social as well as economic and educational backwardness, generally cannot fall within the definition of a backward class of citizens under Article 16 (4).

(6) As economic backwardness is the bane of a majority of the people, if poverty by itself were the test of backwardness most people would be in a position to claim reservation, and reservation for all is reservation for none. Reservation is meant to remedy and undo the handicap of those historical injustices and discriminations that impeded the access of classes of people to public administration, and so social backwardness cannot be determined without regard to evidence of the persisting evil effects of such discrimination. Economic or educational backwardness which is not the result of social backwardness cannot be the criterion of backwardness under Article 16 (4). The determination of backwardness only and exclusively with reference to economic criteria is invalid, though economic criteria may be a consideration along with and in addition to social backwardness.

(7) Despite the recognition of the caste-occupation-poverty cycle as an ever-present reality strikingly apparent in rural India, with lowly occupation resulting not only in low social position but also in poverty—a vicious nexus and a vicious circle—actual identification of the Backward Classes is still not a settled issue. There is no set or recognized method, no law or other statutory instrument prescribing the methodology, and no such thing as a standard or model approach and procedure for such identification. Since the objective is to locate and identify social backwardness, a concerted effort should be made to consider all the available groups, sections, and classes of society. The following procedure should be undertaken: begin with

castes since these represent identifiable social classes and/or groups or spread over an overwhelming majority of the country's population; apply to them the criteria of backwardness involved; and either after or while performing an exhaustive coverage of caste groups, take up for consideration other occupational groups, communities, and classes.

(8) In a Backward Class as defined under Article 16(4), if the connecting link is social backwardness, it should broadly be the same across a given class. If some of the members are far too advanced socially (which in the context necessarily means economically and may also mean educationally) the connecting thread between them and the remaining class snaps. As they would be misfits in the class, only if they are excluded would the class be a compact class. Such exclusion benefits the truly backward. Hence it is imperative to exclude the advanced sections from the Backward Classes, which is a major departure from the earlier practice of treating the entire group as eligible for reservation benefits.

BACKWARD CASTES/CLASSES AS POLITICAL ENTITIES

The emergence of backward castes/classes as political entities has occurred both in the colonial and post-colonial contexts.

The colonial policy of distributing patronage on the basis of caste compelled caste members, by the sheer logic of the politics of numbers, to stay within their caste for social and political identity in institutional life. It also influenced similarly placed caste groups to unite themselves and to form what has been termed a 'horizontal stretch'. Caste thus began to lose its ritual content and became more and more secularized for political mobilization.

The great attention paid to caste in the decennial census since 1872, especially since 1901, also played a major role in the politicization of caste. Among other things, the census prompted caste groups to claim higher status in the caste hierarchy. The result was an extraordinary revival of the 'caste spirit', and the emergence of numerous caste *sabhas* (associations) to assert the dignity of the social groups which they claimed to represent.

The strengthening of caste as a political entity greatly accelerated since Independence because of adult franchise and the compensatory principle. In 1957 Srinivas argued for the following link between the strengthening of caste and the context of modern politics: 'the power and activity of caste has increased in proportion as political power passed ... to the people from the rulers' (1962: 23).

The failure of the Government of India (henceforth called the centre) to implement the provisions of Articles 15(4) and 16(4) for the

Backward Classes from 1950 to 1990, and its attempts to implement them partially since 1990, further strengthened the backward castes as political entities.

Backward Classes and Central Commissions
The Kaka Kalelkar Commission

The failure mentioned in the previous paragraph was mainly the result of the centre's rejection in 1956 of the report of the first Backward Classes Commission appointed in 1953. In its report of 1955, this Commission listed 2399 communities as Backward Classes (with 837 of them as Most Backward) and recommended reservation of at least 25 per cent jobs in class 1; 33.3 per cent in class 2; 40 per cent in classes 3 and 4; and 70 per cent seats in all technical and professional institutions for them.

The report was placed before parliament in 1956 along with a memorandum from Home Minister G.B. Pant. The memorandum criticized the Commission's criteria and conclusions. It saw the caste system as the greatest hindrance to India's progress to an egalitarian society and observed that recognition of certain specified castes as backward may serve to maintain and even perpetuate the existing distinctions based on caste.

The report was not discussed by parliament, and no alternative criteria were evolved. However, in 1961 the centre wrote to the states that while each of them had the discretion to choose its own criteria for defining backwardness, in its view it would be better to apply economic tests than to go by caste.

If the centre's rejection of this report was due to the caste factor, the disarray caused by its withdrawal only reinforced this factor. Without going into specific details it may be said that there have been wide variations between the states in the zeal with which they protect the interests of Backward Classes, in the extent of reservation provided, and in the criteria adopted to determine backwardness.

In most 'non-southern' states which are latecomers to reservation for the Backward Classes, governments have generally been indifferent and upper castes have been hostile to reservations, as revealed by the anti-reservation agitations of Bihar in 1978 and Gujarat in 1980–1 and 1985. By contrast, in the southern states which have had reservations from at least the 1920s, governments have been generally responsive to the demands for reservations and upper castes have been acquiescent, albeit reluctantly, to such responses. In fact, by enhancing reservations and expanding the Backward Classes lists these states have converted potential anti-reservation agitations into pro-reservation agitations.

The Mandal Commission

The victory of the Janata Party in the 1977 elections brought the Backward Classes onto the national political agenda. And, pursuant of its electoral promise, Morarji Desai, India's first non-Congress Prime Minister, appointed another Commission in 1979, with B.P. Mandal, a former Chief Minister of Bihar, as chairman along with five other members. This Commission listed 3743 communities among the Hindus alone as Backward Classes. It estimated 52 per cent of the Indian population as Backward Classes and recommended 27 per cent educational and employment reservations for them by the centre and the states. When it submitted its report in 1980 the Congress (I) was in power. Though in 1982 parliament adopted the report, Prime Minister Indira Gandhi was unwilling to act on it. When Rajiv Gandhi became Prime Minister in 1984, he too avoided 'having a ball with Mandal', apparently as a stand against casteism, a stand for the far-fetched Constitutional perception of 'a classless and casteless society'.

The revival of this report by the V.P. Singh-led National Front (with Janata Dal, a rehash of the Janata Party, as its main constituent) government, through its decision of 7 August 1990, and the related notification of 13 August 1990 to introduce 27 per cent job reservations at the centre was ostensibly to honour a poll promise. It was, however, widely seen as a political ploy, in particular to shore up the National Front's support base among the Backward Classes and seek a realignment of political forces along caste lines. It also came in a context of increasing Hindu revivalism and continuing opposition to the report by the Bharatiya Janata Party and the Congress (I). The result was an unprecedented violent backlash, especially in north India and by educated urban youth.

Important among the subsequent events are the Supreme Court's Order of 1 October 1990 staying the notification of 13 August 1990; before fall of the V.P. Singh ministry barely eleven months after its induction; and before rejection of the National Front in the 1991 mid-term polls despite efforts to project Singh as the 'Mandal Messiah', and his efforts to make reservation a matter of 'national social justice'.

The Supreme Court's directive to the minority Congress (I) government which the elections brought to power to make its stand clear on the Mandal report, again brought the reservation issue to the fore in the political arena. With by-elections round the corner and political survival as its overriding concern, the government changed its attitude to the report from opposition to support, and issued on 25 September 1991 a modified notification. Besides the 27 per cent notified by Singh, it set apart 10 per cent for the economically backward among the forward communities. The Supreme

Court's rulings of 16 November 1992 were mainly in the context of these two notifications.

CONCLUSION

Stating that the unanimous and enthusiastic endorsement by parliament on 11 August 1982 of the Mandal report constitutes an important landmark in the history of contemporary India, Béteille wrote a few days later:

> If Parliament has acted in full awareness of the likely consequences of its action, we are perhaps entering a new phase in the reconstitution of Indian society. This reconstitution may be no less far-reaching in its scope than the one attempted by the new Constitution which Indians fashioned for themselves on achieving independence [1992: 60].

Though Béteille did not elaborate on the nature of this reconstitution, the Mandal report and the Supreme Court rulings have certainly pushed Indian society in to a new phase. The widely varying reactions to the Supreme Court rulings, the increasing use of social justice and empowerment in political discourse and populist rhetoric, and the emergence of Backward Classes as a powerful political category are indications of this push.

The reactions to this new era of Indian politics and the Supreme Court rulings are marked by adherence, evasion, defiance, and subversion. Adherence is evinced by the introduction of reservation for the Backward Classes for the first time in over four decades, and its introduction in a number of states such as Orissa, Rajasthan, Uttar Pradesh, and West Bengal. It can also be seen in the increase in the quota for the Backward Classes in some states such as Gujurat and Punjab. This is all in addition to the statutory reservation for the Scheduled Castes and Scheduled Tribes. Evasion is marked by the circumvention of the Supreme Court ruling on the creamy layer as in Bihar, Kerala, and Uttar Pradesh. One sees a tone of defiance in the continuing existence of reservation far in excess of the judiciary's ceiling and in vehement opposition to the creamy layer exclusion, as in Tamil Nadu. It is also seen in the arbitrary stretching of reservation to an even higher level, as in Karnataka, and in inclusion of various groups previously deemed ineligible in the Backward Classes list prima facie advanced.

Subversion is enacted by the Congress (I), which was in power at the centre from 1991 to 1996, by giving assent to the Bills passed by the Tamil Nadu and Karnataka Assemblies to circumvent the ceiling of 50 per cent as the overall reservation for the Scheduled Castes, Scheduled Tribes, and the Backward Classes combine. Congress also enacts its subversive role by fixing the judiciary and by including the Tamil Nadu Act in the Ninth Schedule, thereby exempting it from judicial review.

The overriding consideration in all these reactions is political. That is, what is crucial recognition of the fact that introduction and expansion of the quota and lengthening of the Backward Classes lists will provide an easily manipulatable instrument to capture vote banks, whereas the creamy-layer exclusion will alienate the ruling party from the influential sections among Backward Classes. While the effects of these reactions are expected to result in a further increase in caste activity in politics and public life, intrinsic to and implicit in the use of this instrument is the enormous mass appeal of reservation, which itself is symbolic of certain fundamental changes in society: questioning the very basis of caste as an ascriptive category and converting it as a secular entity for political mobilization. The traditional criteria are irrelevant now, and caste distinctions have much less weight. What matters is not caste as such, but for what purpose it is used, that is the content of caste actions. This conceptual shift explains the scramble for Backward Class status, demands for an increased quantum of reservation for the Backward Classes by various castes and communities in different parts of the country, and the ongoing controversies about classification of Dalit Christians (Untouchable converts to Christianity) in the Scheduled Castes list, and sub-classification of the Scheduled Castes (as in Andhra Pradesh).

With his announcement of 7 August 1990, V.P. Singh at one stroke brought the question of the Backward Classes onto the national agenda. He also ensured that it would stay there for decades to come and provided a basis for a politically stable governing alliance of the Scheduled Castes, Backward Classes, and religious minorities. Finally, he made Mandal not only an employment scheme but, more importantly, an *empowerment* scheme. When Singh took up the Mandal Commission recommendations, there was tremendous opposition to them not only from vested interests but also from the press, especially the English press, and the academic community. Sociologists G.S. Ghurye, A.R. Desai, and K.M. Kapadia all had condemned employment and educational reservations for categories other than the Scheduled Castes on the grounds that they promoting caste spirit, though in default of this corrective measure all civil service posts would be in the hands of high castes. This refrain (of promoting caste spirit) was forcefully and even aggressively used against the V.P. Singh ministry's notification as well, especially by Singh's political opponents. But, as it turned out, Mandal does not need political parties now; political parties have become part of it.

As a result, the *Dalits* and other socially backward castes have emerged as the most important social class whom the political parties can ignore only at their own peril. The most conspicuous of this development is taking place in Uttar Pradesh, where the Bahujan Samaj Party (BSP) has assumed a great deal of significance particularly after the 1993 Assembly elections—in a state where till recently political leadership was a preserve of upper castes.

The backward castes/classes as they exist now, manifest themselves as four broad types of entities: social, administrative, legal, and political. Of these, the first is larger than the second and third, as it is from the first that the other two are picked and chosen. The fourth is, however, the largest. Its largeness does not mean that all the groups under its rubric are really backward. All that it means is reservation is now a rallying point for political mobilization and vote-bank politics.

REFERENCES

Bandyopadhyay, Sekhar. 1990. *Caste, Politics and the Raj: Bengal 1872–1937*. Calcutta: K.P. Bagchi and Co.

Béteille, André. 1992. *The Backward Classes in Contemporary India*. Delhi: Oxford University Press.

Burman, Roy B.K. 1997. 'Criteria for Identification of the Backward Classes'. In A.M. Shah, B.S. Baviskar, and E.A. Ramaswamy, eds, *Social Structure and Change*, vol. 4, (*Development and Ethnicity*) 163–89. New Delhi: Sage Publications.

Desai, I.P. et al. 1985. *Caste, Caste Conflict and Reservations*. Delhi: Ajanta Publications.

Dumont, Louis. [1966]. 1980. *Homo Hierarchicus: The Caste System and Its Implications*. Chicago: The University of Chicago Press.

Frankel, Francine R. and M.S.A. Rao, eds. 1989–90. *Dominance and State Power in Modern India: Decline of a Social Order*. 2 vols. Delhi: Oxford University Press.

Fuller, C.J., ed. 1996. *Caste Today*. New Delhi: Oxford University Press.

Galanter, Marc. 1984. *Competing Equalities: Law and the Backward Classes in India*. Delhi: Oxford University Press.

Ghurye, G.S. [1932] 1979. *Caste and Race in India*. Bombay: Popular Prakashan.

Government of India. 1883. *Education Commission Report*. Calcutta: Government Printing.

———. 1995. *Report of the Backward Classes Commission*. Delhi: Government of India Press.

———. 1956. *Memorandum on the Report of the Backward Classes Commission*. Delhi: Government of India Press.

———. 1980. *Report of the Backward Classes Commission*. Delhi: Government of India Press.

Government of Maharashtra. [1979] 1989. *Dr Babasaheb Ambedkar: Writings and Speeches*. vol. 1. Bombay: Education Department.

Irschick, Eugene. F. 1986. *Tamil Revivalism in the 1930s*. Madras: Cre–A.

Karlekar, Hiranmay. 1992. *In the Mirror of Mandal: Social Justice, Caste, Class, and the Individual*. Delhi: Ajanta Publications.

Kothari, Rajni. 1994. 'Rise of the Dalits and the Renewed Debate on Caste'. *Economic and Political Weekly*. 29(26):1589–94.

Majumdar, Nabendu Dutta. 1995. 'The Backward Classes Commission and Its Work'. In

Social Welfare in India (Issued on behalf of the Planning Commission). New Delhi: Government of India.

O'hanlon, Rosalind. 1985. *Caste, Conflict, and Ideology: Mahatma Joti Rao Pule and Low Caste Protest in Nineteenth Century Western India.* Hyderabad: Orient Longman Ltd.

Omvedt, Gail. 1976. *Cultural Revolt in a Colonial Society: The Non-Brahmin Movement in Western India, 1873–1880.* Bombay: Scientific Socialist Education Trust.

_____. 1991. 'The Anti-Caste Movement and the Discourse of Power'. *Race and Class.* 33(2):15–27.

Panandiker, Pai, V.A., ed. 1997. *The Politics of Backwardness: Reservation Policy in India.* New Delhi: Konark Publishers P. Ltd.

Radhakrishnan, P. 1989. 'Tamil Nadu Backward Classes'. *MIDS Bulletin.* 19(10):500–12.

_____. 1990. 'Backward Classes in Tamil Nadu: 1872–1988'. *Economic and Political Weekly.* 25(10):509–20.

_____. 1992. 'Communal Representation in Tamil Nadu, 1850–1916: The Pre-non-Brahmin Movement Phase'. *Economic and Political Weekly.* 28(31):1585–97.

_____. 1996a. 'Mandal Commission: A Sociological Critique'. In M.N. Srinivas, ed., *Caste, Its Twentieth Century Avatar,* 203–20. Delhi: Penguin Books India (P) Ltd.

_____. 1996b. 'Backward Class Movements in Tamil Nadu'. In M.N. Srinivas, ed., *Caste, Its Twentieth Century Avatar,* 110–34. Delhi: Penguin Books India (P) Ltd.

Rao M.S.A. 1979. *Social Movements and Social Transformation: A Study of Two Backward Classes Movements in India.* Madras: The Macmillan Co. of India Ltd.

Rao, Shiva, B., ed. 1967. *The Framing of India's Constitution: Select Documents.* New Delhi: The Indian Institute of Public Administration.

Singh, Parmanand. 1982. *Equality, Reservation and Discrimination in India: A Constitutional Study of Scheduled Castes, Scheduled Tribes and Other Backward Classes.* Delhi: Deep and Deep Publications.

Srinivas, M.N. 1962. *Caste in Modern India and Other Essays.* Bombay: Asia Publishing House.

_____. 1992. *On Living in a Revolution and Other Essays.* Delhi: Oxford University Press.

_____. ed. 1996. *Caste, Its Twentieth Century Avatar.* Delhi: Penguin Books India P. Ltd.

Supreme Court of India. 1992. *Judgements on Indra Sawhney and Others Vs Union of India and Others.* Delhi: LIPS Publications P. Ltd.

Thimmaiah, G. 1993. *Power Politics and Social Justice: Backward Castes in Karnataka.* Delhi: Sage Publications.

Zelliot, Eleanor. 1992. *From Untouchable to Dalit: Essays on Ambedkar Movement.* New Delhi: Manohar Publications.

Local-level/Grassroots Political Studies

Harold A. Gould

The roots of the scientific study of local-level politics in India lie in the village studies undertaken by the first generation of post-Independence social scientists. Their interest in these communities grew out of projects initiated from the 1950s both by the Government of India and external agencies such as the Ford and Rockefeller foundations. These projects were undertaken as aspects of the planning process that had become a central preoccupation of newly independent India. The purpose, of course, was to promote and evaluate the country's social and economic progress. This type of research inevitably necessitated establishing links with scholarly communities in India and the West from where various forms of relevant expertise could be drawn. In this manner, a nexus emerged within the ambit from which the data and conceptualization needed for the pursuit of developmental goals were generated. These projects also became a basis for expanding existing academic programmes and creating new ones in India and abroad (especially in the United States, Great Britain, and western Europe) whose purpose was to broaden the horizons of research on developing societies. Inevitably they also led to a burgeoning of careers in administration, politics, and scholarship which had ramifications far beyond the immediate scope of development research and project implementation.

The quest for a detailed understanding of how planned change was impacted ordinary persons in their day-to-day life generated not only empirical data on the subject but also a growing body of conceptualization that enriched the social sciences but as well as other disciplines. It can be said that the field of South Asian area studies grew out of these beginnings.

Especially affected in the early stages were anthropology and sociology because of the heavy emphasis that was placed on village communities as a means of attaining micro-level insight into the impact of social policies. Scores of postgraduate students and senior research scholars from these two disciplines were initiated into South Asian studies as members of the research teams that were assembled during this period.

While village studies sought to comprehend all aspects of culture and social organization (kinship, caste, class, religion, agrarian structure, and economic interaction) that could be used to create baseline data for evaluating the planning process, it was inevitable, as the pace of economic and political development accelerated, that these investigations would move beyond individual peasant communities and focus on ways in which such communities were part of larger wholes. It meant, as Atal (1968) puts it, treating the village 'as an *isolable unit* rather than an isolate', thereby recognizing both its 'unity and extensions' (Atal 1972: p. 24; see also Gould 1959). Local communities came to be viewed in the context of administrative units (such as districts), development blocks, cooperatives, political constituencies, and ultimately even cultural regions and fragments of nation. This, in turn, meant focusing on systems of power (the domain of the political scientist), particularly on the interface between the various forms of dominance which prevailed at the grassroots throughout India's pre-Independence history and the emerging forms of dominance associated with the transition to a modern social order with autonomous political institutions. This rapidly became a crucial consideration because India had opted for a so-called 'open society'— that is for a society with a democratic polity which, on the one hand, encouraged maximal popular participation in processes of social change and social reform while, on the other, simultaneously endeavoured, as much as possible, to preserve traditional values and institutions which purportedly gave texture and meaning to the enormous variety of cultures—rooted in race, nationality, religion, and ethnicity—which India, a land of European proportions, encompassed.

One of the earliest attempts at conceptually differentiating the political aspects of village social life was the study undertaken by a research team headed by Professor Oscar Lewis, at the time a Consulting Anthropologist for the Ford Foundation.[1] Published in 1954 by the Programme Evaluation Organization of the Planning Commission, under the title *Group Dynamics in a North Indian Village: A Study of Factions*,[2] this research systematically identified several political formations in the Jat village of Rampur, termed 'factions', among whom power was subdivided and between whom power was competed for. Although the stated purpose of this research was to identify the most suitable channels through which village-level workers could most effectively achieve entry into village social networks for purposes of community development, the process of identifying these networks revealed the lineaments of intra-village sub-groups that would become crucial aspects of processes of politicization at grassroots level as India's post-Independence political system continued to develop. In the researchers' words, 'Our data underline the well known dangers of working only or primarily through the official headmen of the village'. Doing so, 'one would find it difficult to reach all the villagers, and even worse, might offend or estrange a large portion' of them(Lewis with Dhillon 1954: 30).

More intensive concentration on the specifically political dimensions of individual rural communities quickly followed. These were soon augmented by studies which expanded the scope of grassroots political research to include the interplay between the most elemental, traditionally rooted structures of local power in agrarian society, the new formally structured units of popular participation in local self-government (that is *panchayati raj*), and the administratively driven, party-structured provincial and national levels of political integration. These latter systematically entered the picture shortly after the adoption of the 1950 Constitution of India which guaranteed human rights and mandated universal franchise elections. The First General Election in 1952 brought this latter dimension of political research in India to fruition. From this point onwards, especially with regard to the study of grassroots politics, the disciplines of anthropology, sociology, social history, and political science converged both methodologically and conceptually.

The transition to this broadened nexus of political research was well documented in a small study authored by Retzlaff (1962) entitled *Village Government in India*. Promulgated under the auspices of the Cornell University Field Research Project, another of the collaborative 'programme evaluation' undertakings of the 1950s and 1960s, this study undertook a detailed examination of two successive panchayat elections held in the village of Khalapur in the Saharanpur district north of Delhi. It noted the village's caste diversity and the differential demographic weights of the castes (for example 82 per cent of the village's population were concentrated in ten of thirty-six castes), and that candidates for *gaon* panchayat offices (for example president or *pradhan*) and for seats on this body formed inter-caste coalitions in their quest for votes. From the outset, open politics was more pragmatically than ideologically oriented even with regard to local offices. 'The motivation to support a candidate on the part of each of these groups was to insure its own position would be protected and a reasonable degree of personal aspiration would be aided and abetted by the 'new administration' (Retzlaff 1962: 113).

Here was the link to the larger political system. Peasants perceived and voted their interests not only in intra-village terms, but in terms of the encompassing emerging political order as well. In the first and second general elections (1952 and 1957), they cast their votes for and against candidates within their encompassing assembly and parliamentary constituencies according to their perception of what they believed their MLA and MP had done or could do for them at the higher levels of the political system where control over resources ultimately lay. Retzlaff's data showed that in this single village, as a measure of increasing internal socio-political differentiation, electoral support for the Congress MLA representing them in Lucknow declined from 'a near 100 per cent in 1951–52 to less than 66 per cent in 1957' (Retzlaff 1962: 117). It was the need to describe and interpret this increasing socio-political differentiation that gave impetus to methodologies and conceptualizations which carried the social science disciplines far beyond the original tendency to concentrate on individual villages, even as 'isolable' units of analysis. While village communities were not henceforth ignored, they were viewed as aggregate aspects, along with cities and towns, of social domains (what Bailey [1969] ultimately labelled 'arenas') where politics interacted with many facets of the Indian social order.

One of the most important of these 'facets' was caste. This defining social structure had long been the object of almost limitless examination of its history, religious meaning, and cultural details. But the coming of the modern social order, which stressed merit-oriented status differentiation and mobility, created conditions which increasingly emphasized the class and ethnic implications of this ancient system of social stratification at the cost of its socio-religious and ritual aspects (see Marriott 1960; Dumont and Pockok 1957–66; Gould 1987, 1988). The introduction of open politics strongly accelerated this transformational process.

Even prior to Independence, the class and ethnic aspects of caste had become the basis for certain kinds of political mobilization. Most noteworthy in this regard, of course, were caste associations which started to spring up as early as the nineteenth century once British census taking began to provide empirical basis for socially identifying and assigning demographic weight to these uniquely Indian hereditary status groups. The statistical objectification of caste made it possible for advocates of social reform to focus on its class attributes in their demands for entitlement to modern education, access to modern occupations, insistence on social justice, and eligibility for public office. By the early 1930s, G.S. Ghurye, a pioneer Indian sociologist, could declare, 'The community-aspect of caste has thus been made more comprehensive, extensive and permanent' (Ghurye 1957: 214). Although, like all nationalists of his day, he deplored this 'intensification' of caste feeling, Ghurye was nevertheless documenting the transition of caste from a predominantly socio-religious structure to an ethnically structured social formation which, as democratic politics spread, was factored into the calculations of politicians in search of popular support and into the formulations of social scientists engaged in grassroots political analysis.

One of the first to recognize the importance of this transition was M.N. Srinivas. In a milestone essay, Srinivas undertook 'to demonstrate that the power and activity of caste has increased in proportion as political power passed increasingly to the people from their rulers' (Srinivas 1957: 23). Many studies followed in quick succession which sharpened a scientific understanding of the manner in which selective aspects of caste stratification (that is those with class implications) were being successfully, indeed decisively, integrated into the contemporary political culture. These documented the initial stages of a process which eventually came to be known as the 'ethnicization' of caste. Srinivas's own research in Mysore, as well as Patterson's in Maharashtra, Harrison's in Andhra, and Hardgraves's in Tamil Nadu, revealed how profoundly electoral politics in India was being influenced by the crystallization in each state of megacastes whose social characteristics resembled in some ways ethnic groups in the West (Patterson 1954; Harrison 1959; Hardgrave 1969). Basing their cohesion on a putative hereditary identity (Barth 1969) derived from their status and roles in the traditional caste hierarchy, and their power to influence the political process through their formidable demographic weight, these social formations made themselves forces to be reckoned with and essentially set the tone of politics at grassroots level everywhere in India. Kothari saw that emerging modernity meant for India not the abandonment or suppression of traditional social and cultural institutions like caste (as has been the case with comparable ascriptive social formations in many other parts of the world) but to an important degree their adaptive transformation. As he aptly puts it, the 'Indian approach' led to a 'quickening of traditional identity, [to] its reinterpretation and rejuvenation, and [to] its consolidation in the framework of new institutions and ideas' (Kothari 1972).

Work published both by Indian and western scholars from the 1960s onward provided growing insight into the complex patterns of interactions which India's democratically structured political system was generating as the process of democratization itself penetrated even deeper into the fabric of Indian society. Gould spoke of the 'adaptive functions' of caste, declaring that 'caste is not disappearing in India because the solidarities inherent in it perform important functions in the contemporary non-traditional society' (Gould 1963: 156). Lloyd and Susanne Rudolph provided the terminological by-word for what was taking place by entitling their book, *The Modernity of Tradition* (1967). The value of their work was to confirm and provide theoretical reinforcement for the observations emanating from numerous prior sources that the class and ethnic dimensions of traditional institutions like caste, sect, and regional culture were finding a viable place in the domains of contemporary political and economic life. Béteille's *Caste, Class and Power* (1965) yielded a classic statement concerning the changes wrought by modernity: 'In traditional society', Béteille wrote, 'there was much greater consistency between the class system and the caste structure'. There is less congruence today because, 'new bases of power have emerged which are, to some extent, independent of both caste and class' (Beteille 1965: 199).

Mariott (1968) recognized that in the contemporary 'metropolitan' socio-political order, the 'felt locus of each caste' depended upon which of 'the several possibly relevant hierarchies and audiences' proved to be of most instrumental value to its members in the pursuit of power and mobility. These included, in 'zonal' terms, local, regional, or national reference models as well as 'only partially enclosing hierarchies of categories, such as those based on religious affiliation' or on 'sectarian values in diet and in other ritual conduct' (Marriott 1968: 110–11). Cohn (1955) provided one of the earliest case studies of how the application of the class aspects of caste to political mobilization was destined to affect local-level politics. In 1952–3, a panchayat election in the village of Madhopur in Azamgarh district (UP) resulted in the complete overthrow of a typical Thakur-dominated oligarchy when Chamars and other lower castes formed a coalition which they called the Praja (tenant) party. Although it did not endure for long, this emergence of a 'microparty' composed of castes possessing distinct ethnic characteristics but manifesting comparable relationships to the means of production (and, thus, common class interests), proved capable of challenging the long-sacrosanct traditional power system, and presaged the forms which political behaviour would increasingly display as open politics found its way into the country's grassroots. The presence of multiple reference models made possible by a democratic constitutional structure had become a resource through which mobilizing social groups could select the individual and collective identities which seemed to offer the best opportunities for material advancement and enhanced status.

F.G. Bailey's (1958) research, initially in the Orissa village of Bisipara, and ultimately the entire state, showed how the new economy and political order were creating opportunities for heretofore downtrodden castes to dramatically alter their relationships to the system of power. The reason, as Bailey saw it, was changes in the economic frontier. That is, the penetration of 'world commerce' and 'the administrative frontier' into the village community, brought about a radical change because land not only ceased to be the sole form of wealth but itself became commoditized—just another good to be bought and sold (Bailey 1958: 65). Once that happened, land could be 'bought by persons who have a source of income other than cultivation alone'. This meant opportunities for 'the small man to make money' and rendered vulnerable 'even the largest estate in the village' because land could be acquired by anyone with enough money (Bailey 1958: 48). One major result was the loosening up of the traditional social order (Bailey 1958; 1963).

A most striking manifestation of the consequences of this loosening-up process was the impact on the Boad Distillers in Bisipara who were able to profit from the liquor trade and, then employ their newly acquired monetary wealth to force changes in their hierarchical status and correspondingly, 'to a heightening of their political aspirations'. The 'class transformation' of this caste was prototypical of what the new political economy was giving rise to throughout grassroots India. The countryside was being transformed into a mosaic of local structures of power sorted and defined by the class attributes each was able to put into play in the political arena. It was for the allegiance of these formations that organized political groups increasingly competed. When viewed at state level, Bailey depicted Orissa politics as a vast panoply of competition between formally and informally structured parties. These functioned as machines preoccupied with crafting strategies and tailoring ideologies that appealed to the material appetites and mobility aspirations of ethnically differentiated status groups whose primordial identities were rooted in caste, religion, language, and nationality. This pattern and these attributes everywhere formed the essence of the emergent political system.

The Impact of National Elections

With the advent of electoral politics on a national scale, the methodological and conceptual skills of the political scientist and the anthropologist inevitably converged as the search intensified for detailed understanding of the relationship between the social and demographic characteristics of electorates, the distribution of power at the grassroots, the choices people made at election time, and the conduct of government.

One of the earliest attempts to gather data from this perspective was that made by Weiner and Kothari in the context of the Third General Elections in 1962. The constituency, instead of the individual community, was to be the unit of investigation, and within each constituency analysis was to be focused on the polling station. This locale was thought to yield detailed data on how ordinary Indians, in their indigenous socio-cultural milieux, interacted with state, region, and party. 'I suggested', declared Weiner, 'that each contributor conduct field research in one constituency—either for the legislative assembly or the national parliament—and report, not so much on the techniques of the candidates or the mechanics of the elections, but rather on the factors which affected the way in which Indians cast their ballots'. This meant above all providing 'detailed statistical data on how various social or economic groups in the constituency, or selected portions of the constituency, voted' (Weiner and Kothari 1965, emphasis added). These studies covered eleven constituencies—urban and rural, assembly and parliamentary—and were the first sociologically grounded portraits of grassroots voter behaviour garnered from different parts of India.[3] A most critical aspect of this approach, as noted, was the use of polling-station results which allowed the investigator to ascertain, with considerable precision, the manner in which caste and other personalistically structured social formations were interfacing with party-structured political formations.

Kothari and Sheth (1965), in their study of the Baroda East assembly constituency, illustrated the importance of micro-level data for identifying the manner in which caste and community were influencing voter behaviour, but their work also pointed to the the limits of demographic differentiation as an explanatory variable. Their data revealed a clear relationship between caste concentrations in certain clusters of urban polling stations and voter preferences. For example, in fifteen polling booths where 76 per cent of the population were upper caste and predominantly Bania, a Swatantra Party candidate, himself a Bania, won almost 53 per cent of the vote. In fifteen booths where over 70 per cent of the population consisted of Backwards, Harijans, and Muslims (who alone numbered 48.5 per cent), the Congress candidate (a Muslim) got almost 74 per cent of the vote. Yet demographic distribution might be said to have been a necessary but not sufficient factor to account for the election's outcome. Ethnicity established certain parameters within which voter behaviour was predictable to the extent that these parameters reflected the broad class orientations of the relevant hereditary status groups. But, as the authors observed, 'secular factors such as ideology and organization cut across and modify communal identities' (Kothari and Sheth 1965: 21). The capacity of parties to mobilize voters, command resources, promulgate their ideology, and penetrate local structures of power had as much to do with political success or failure as did caste or community per se. Caste was seen as one resource among several, albeit an extremely crucial one. Other contributors to this project found similar patterns regardless of the level or context of political behaviour they investigated.

Their findings, however, opened the floodgates for similar studies in all subsequent Indian elections. In 1972, Kothari edited a series of studies in which several western and Indian scholars specifically addressed the role of caste ethnicity in the political process in several of the major Indian states— Maharashtra, Gujarat, Tamil Nadu, Andhra Pradesh, Rajasthan, Bihar—plus two cities, Agra and Poona.[4] These studies demonstrated how pervasively in post-Independence open society caste was functioning as a traditionally legitimized mechanism through which Indians were asserting their claims for access to the modern system. Why were caste and other particularistic forms of group mobilization proving this pervasive? Because, in Kothari's words, 'Politics is a competitive enterprise, its purpose is the acquisition of power for the realization of certain goals, and the process is one of identifying and manipulating existing and emerging allegiances in order to mobilize and consolidate positions' (Kothari 1972b: 4). A democratic polity it is a process dominated by pragmatism and in such polities the spoils go to those groups that make their votes count at election time. Elliott summed it up well in her contribution on caste politics in Andhra: 'Caste is important less as a symbol of cohesion', she declared, 'and more as a network of groups which the party's or party's faction representatives try to activate by contacting village caste groups and awarding benefits to prominent members' (Elliott 1972: 162).

Qualitative and quantitative research on Indian politics revealed the existence of an electorate so highly pluralized that no single class or ethnic community had enough demographic clout to win an election on its own. This compelled political parties to assemble coalitions composed of several ethnically structured groups with shared class and/or other interests if they were to succeed. Béteille, in his chapter on Tamil Nadu saw this clearly and refers to a passage from Lipset (1963: 21) which relates the Indian case to modern polities in general: 'All major political parties include supporters from many segments of the population' (quoted in Béteille 1972: 293). However, this pragmatically driven need to diversify the party's support base had, in the Indian case, a major impact on the viability of the traditional caste system because it inevitably undermined the principle of ritual hierarchy. The cost of intensifying the ethnic and class aspects of caste (what Marriott calls their attributional properties) for bondable political purposes was the progressive erosion of its corporate aspects (see Marriott 1968) upon which the system of ritually determined ranks depended.

Studies of State-level Political Behaviour

Another type of research growing out of fieldwork at grassroots level was the intensive study of party politics in the various states. It stemmed from the realization that in India's federal system, state politics determined who represented the people and to what ends in New Delhi. Like European countries, the Indian states encompassed nationalities with separate linguistic, cultural, and historical identities; they possessed distinctive economic characteristics, manifested their own admixture of tribes, castes, and religious groups; and had experienced, as a consequence, distinctive patterns of political development. Each state was, in its turn, subdivided into districts, each one of which had its own mix of castes and other ethnic communities reflecting its social history, demographic structure, and economic characteristics. Therefore, to an important extent, the study of Indian politics required determining how Congress and competing political parties arose and functioned in the separate states, and the manner in which they found themselves able to translate power in the states into power at the centre.

The first systematic study of party politics at state level based on comprehensive fieldwork in situ was undertaken by Brass in the early 1960s (Brass 1965). Its focus was the Congress Party in India's most populous state, Uttar Pradesh. He chose a single state for his venue because he realized that from its inception, and particularly after Independence, the Congress is in essence a 'coalition of state parties' which 'are themselves coalitions of semi-independent district party organizations', and that it is within the districts 'that the Congress organizations interact with the traditional societies' (Brass 1965: 2–3).

Since at the time when Brass's research commenced, Congress was overwhelmingly dominant both at the centre and in most of the states, he understandably concluded that the principal bases for the pursuit of power were intra-party political formations, or factions. Competitors for control of the UP Congress, and by extension the Congress or any other party in any province where the 1950 Constitution was in full effect, formed coalitions by reaching into every district of the state in search of alliances with local groups whose interests might conceivably coincide with their own. Factions were seen almost as thermostatic mechanisms which determined the party's political viability in any district and, therefore, the capacity of its local leadership to be significant players at higher levels of party integration. Thus, Brass wrote 'The factional character of internal politics in the state also tends to produce a patternless politics. Districts which have been consistently strongly pro-Congress may suddenly become very weak Congress districts when the local organizations become divided by intense factional strife' (Brass 1965: 21).

Behind these conclusions, of course, lay a fundamental judgement regarding the nature of party politics in the context of India's post-Independence political culture: In the pursuit of power through the electoral process, Congress stressed instrumentalism over ideological rigour. In the local political environments where votes are cast and counted, existing interest groups were taken as givens to be bargained with and accommodated. Such groups were not to be transformed or eliminated if their values or demands ran contrary to the party's publically proclaimed social doctrines and political goals. In Brass's words: 'The Congress has chosen to make adjustments and accommodations rather than transform the traditional order' (1965: 2). Through highly detailed case studies of five UP districts (Gonda, Aligarh,

Deoria, Meerut, and Kanpur), he showed that in an Indian province there were as many Congress parties as there were districts because every district had its own political subculture with which Congressmen had to work. As a result, Congress at state level was a loosely synthesized amalgam of its district branches. By implication, therefore, Congress at national level was also a loosely synthesized amalgam of its provincial branches. The decision to perpetuate a post-Independence version of the old British dictum to 'honour native custom'—that is, accommodate the traditional social order—lay behind this state of affairs. Honouring native custom in this case meant accepting the traditional social formations (caste, religion, the landed elite, etc.) that dotted the countryside as 'givens' with and through which the party was committed to work in its pursuit of electoral success.

Brass subsequently applied his conceptual orientation to, as it were, the next level of abstraction and examined ethnicized political competition *between* states—which are called 'national movements' (Brass 1972), although in the Indian context they might be more appropriately called 'sub-national movements'. This approach revealed that the processes of competition and conflict observed in the intra-state political arena are different in scale but not in kind from those that operate between states. As political mobilization in districts revolves around the demands of local groups for differential access to symbolic and material resources commanded by the state government, so regional demands emanate from the country's nationalities for differential access to the symbolic and material resources controlled by the central government. Out of this latter process, says Brass, four rules evolved defining the parameters of acceptable political representation of regional demands: 'All demands short of secession [were] allowed full expression'; 'regional demands based on language and culture [were] accommodated' as long as they were not 'explicitly based on religious differences'; 'regional demands [were not] conceded capriciously', which means concessions were to be made only after political mobilization reached a level where demands had to be taken seriously by the centre; and 'demands for the division of multi-lingual states [had to] have some support from different linguistic groups' (Brass 1972: 17–18).

Through this type of analysis Brass was able to show how the interplay between 'a set of written and unwritten rules' and the social composition of the Indian electorate, at both state and national levels, resulted in a 'strategy of accommodation' which facilitated the relative stability of the Indian political system. The strategy reduced 'conflicts directed against the central government', encouraged '[regionalized] politics', and led to 'increased political participation' including 'increased political organization in several states' (Brass 1972: 19).

In two works which reflected the results of research initiated coterminously with Brass's pioneering study, Weiner provided a broader comparative focus for the analysis of grassroots political behaviour. The first was an edited volume in which a number of scholars contributed chapters on several Indian provinces (Weiner 1968a).[5] The purpose was to take advantage of a unique scientific opportunity presented by the continental proportions of the post-Independence Indian state. Because 'the Indian states function within a common political system and operate within the same constitutional structure and national constraints, we have a rare opportunity to observe developmental changes in a system controlled for governmental structures' (Weiner 1968b: 17). Thus, if differences exist between the states 'as to the type of party systems', or 'in the way state governments respond to new efforts at mass participation', or 'in the effectiveness of chief ministers in controlling their legislatures', (Weiner 1968b: 17) then we know it can only be due to variations in the socio-cultural characteristics of the state societies themselves.

In his second work, Weiner looked at this issue from a slightly different but conceptually comparable angle. He undertook case studies of party-building processes in three districts and two cities located in five Indian states (Weiner 1967). These were Kaira district in Gujarat, Guntur district in Andhra, Belgaum district in Karnataka, Madurai city in Tamil Nadu, and the city of Calcutta in Bengal. In this instance, he showed how each *pradesh* party organization throughout the country had evolved idiomatic configurations of political traits emanating from the regional milieu which had spawned it. These differing traits strongly influenced the nature and magnitude of the roles party leaders played in intra-party affairs in their state organizations and ultimately, of course, for those who moved onwards, in their national organization as well.

As Brass learned in UP, party building in each district and province followed certain common patterns because everywhere the Congress system had been the principal force behind the structuring of politics during the formative years. If in the districts, the mix of castes, classes, communities, and demographics varied, between the provinces, the linguistic, cultural, and regional identities varied. But the manner in which the party mobilized and manipulated these ethnic assets was the same everywhere. What Weiner (1967) said of the Belgaum district in Karnataka applied equally to the other four units upon which he concentrated, or indeed to any district in the country regardless of its provincial venue. 'With few exceptions', he declared, 'men do not build their political careers merely by working within the party organization.' On the contrary, at the most elemental level, party careers are conditioned by previously established political identities. A person's pathway to party membership and leadership lies through acquiring 'influence within his village', controlling the local cooperative, moving into 'the taluks development board and the District Local Board,' and getting 'elected to the board of the District Cooperative Bank' (Weiner 1967: 274). At some point in this climb through the local socio-political hierarchy, he caps his rise by induction into the Congress party and by becoming an office-bearer in it. Or this, at least, is the way it was during Congress's political heyday. What has changed today is the availability of more than one party organization through which this mobility process can take place.

Inevitably, many more studies followed which employed similar methodologies and produced results which reinforced the findings of those who initially factored grassroots perspectives into their analytical procedures. In 1972, Sisson published a case study of what he called political institutionalization in Rajasthan showing how Congress had achieved political ascendancy there by 'providing a dominant integrative structure in a highly segmented and pluralistic society' (Sisson 1972: 125). More than a decade later, Fadia (1984) would follow with a two-volume work on state-level party building in which the first volume was entirely devoted to analyses of the institutional and sociological aspects of political integration at state level, while the second, very much in the Weiner/Brass tradition, presented empirical studies of several states (Andhra, Bihar, Haryana, Kerala, Orissa, Punjab, Rajasthan, Tamil Nadu, Uttar Pradesh, and West Bengal) designed to provide an array of concrete illustrations of how these factors consistently manifested themselves on the ground, throughout the Indian Union.

During this same period, Weiner and Field also produced a four-volume assemblage of empirical studies which concentrated on the manner in which electoral politics in the Indian states was affecting specific aspects or domains of Indian society, such as the Communist parties of West Bengal (1974), three so-called 'disadvantaged sectors' of Indian society (namely the ex-princely states, tribal societies, and women, 1975), modernization (1977), and party systems and cleavages (1975).

Together, this body of research by both Indian and western scholars created not only large reservoirs of data on the workings of democracy at the grassroots in one of the world's largest and most ethnically complex new nations, but also conceptual tools that could be employed to understand the meaning of such data anywhere in the world where comparably complex nation-states were to be found. An important effect of this type of research in the Indian context was to move political studies away from an elitist perspective, perpetuated by two centuries of colonial rule and the dominance of high-caste Indians in the colonial administrative structure, which viewed political processes and development almost exclusively from the top down.

Social Historical Perspectives

Despite analytical biases engendered by pre-Independence oligarchy, an objective social history eventually did develop which showed that the behavioural foundations of grassroots politics in India grew out of a somewhat independent line of development, which would later converge with the developing nationalist movement. These grew out of the political interaction that occurred, particularly over the last century of colonial rule, between the British *Raj* and indigenous Indian society in the districts and the towns. What this scholarship has revealed is that the economic, social, and political impact of ramifying modernity created a 'dialogue' between the colonial regime and the Indian people, resulting in the progressive introduction of increasingly comprehensive self-governing institutions. A crucial milestone in this progression was the establishment of an electoral process for local bodies under the provisions of the Resolution on Local Self-Government originated by Lord Ripon in 1882, two years after his arrival in India as an appointee of Gladstone's Liberal party.[6]

The decision to facilitate a limited measure of representative government was a response to a number of factors growing out of the colonial experience. Most important, of course, were increasing demands for a say in their own governance by a growing Indian middle class which the economic and social changes wrought by British rule had made possible. Increasingly attuned to western political thought and aware of the disparity between democratic political practices in Britain and the oligarchic political institutions through which Britain ruled her premier colony, Indians with modern educational and professional credentials turned increasingly to political means to express their social grievances, including demands for greater access to the system of power. This had led to the Ripon initiative. Three years later it resulted in the establishment of the Indian National Congress, India's first modern political party. By the end of the first two decades of the twentieth century, as is well known, a full-blown, mass-based nationalist movement had arisen.

Another factor, noted by Robinson (1974), grew out of the quest of India's rulers to make their colony cost-effective. With the rise of the increasingly articulate middle class's resistance to imperial taxation policies, the British were encountering the same problem which had plagued the American colonies prior to their eighteenth-century rebellion: objections to 'taxation without representation'. To cope with fiscal demands, notes Robinson, 'Government placed greater reliance on the development of local responsibility in province, district and town'. This meant that from 1872, 'certain heads of expenditure were assigned to local government charge'. There was, in other words, a downward devolution of control over expenditures from centre to province which inevitably posed a dilemma for the latter. If local government wished to spend more on public services, it was told that it must raise taxes in order to do so. 'But this could be done only with the development of local self-government: more taxation meant more representation' (Robinson 1974: 135). As I stated in an earlier study, 'Ripon's role as Viceroy, therefore, seems to have been very much a matter of providing a framework within which political idealism and imperialist venality could converge and be leavened by a policy of limited political reforms' (Gould 1994: 33).

However, these limited political reforms, tenuous and tinged with fiscal practicality as they may have been, set in motion processes which led ineluctably to the evolution of an open political system in India.

The immediate effect of the Ripon reforms was to transform the municipal boards of numerous towns throughout India into political arenas where secret-ballot elections were mandated for at least some (and usually a majority of) seats. The franchise was severely restricted, in most cases to no more than 1 or 2 per cent of the adult population who possessed what were deemed appropriate educational, professional, and property qualifications. Nevertheless, by 1885, there were 725 municipal boards operating in India of which 472 (65.1 per cent) had partly or wholly elected members (Tinker 1967). What was important about these bodies was not their number, the proportion of elective seats available on them, the meagre size of their electorates per se, nor the limitations placed on their decision-making powers, but the opening which the modification of these bodies produced for genuine grassroots political processes to commence in India. Subsequent political reform, responding to the rising voice of nationalism which demanded increased participation in representative government, progressively widened the scope of these processes.

Competitive politics literally sprang into existence following the introduction of secret-ballot elections. Caste and communal (that is ethnically structured) identities instantly became the principal bases upon which political mobilization took place and through which coalitions were assembled in pursuit of the seat majorities needed to select board chairmen and conduct municipal affairs in accordance with one's class predilections. This was not the result which the colonial government envisioned when for the first time it established limited-franchise elective arenas at municipality level. It was actually done this way because the authorities contended that Indians must only imbibe the arts of democratic government in small doses. Those designated to acquire such experiences should be members of a socially homogeneous class of educated or otherwise qualified middle class citizens who theoretically would be inclined to eschew casteism and communalism and place statesmanship above parochialism in their pursuit and exercise of public office. The problem was that realistically speaking it was impossible to identify any stratum of Indian society that was free of the presence of hereditary social groups. And in an open polity, such differences would inevitably be inclined to assert themselves. The more localized the political environment, in fact, the greater the probability that ethnicity in its narrowest and most parochial manifestations would come into play. In politics, mighty oaks from tiny acorns do not necessarily grow!

In Faizabad-cum-Ayodhya municipality this was evident as soon as the municipality became fully functional as an 'open' arena shortly before the turn of the century. For a generation, two coalitions rooted in ethnic differentiation perennially opposed each other in municipal politics. One called itself the Kayastha party, and the other called itself the Khattri party; each had a multicaste composition. Although each was led by a pleader from these respective castes, the supporters explicitly identified with particular castes and with select segments of the Muslim community. Their distribution in one or the other microparty reflected patterns of traditional rivalry between the caste communities: thus Khattris and Kayasthas had a long history of mutual antagonism revolving around access to modern professions and government service; Vaishyas (UP trading castes) and Khattris (a trading and landholding caste originating in the Punjab) harboured historic enmities arising from mercantile competition; Thakurs (or Rajputs) distrusted Kayasthas because the latter were traditionally estate managers for *zamindars* and *taluqdars* and had a reputation for utilizing their control of literacy, the accounts, and the bureaucracies to nefariously acquire title to their patrons' lands; and Muslims and Hindus of course distrusted each other for both political and religious reasons and reflected this distrust and enmity in the factional choices they made.

Thus, in Faizabad-cum-Ayodhya, differential mercantile, agrarian, professional, bureaucratic, and socio-religious interests, honed in the context of the metropolitan social-stratification system, influenced the choices which the members of a limited number of hereditary status groups made, respecting their microparty affiliations. The bulk of the Kayastha party consisted of Kayasthas and Baniyas plus a variable assortment of persons from other, less demographically significant status groups who came and went in response to the way the economic and political winds seemed to be blowing at various times. The bulk of the Khattri party consisted of Khattris and Thakurs plus others whose interest agendas purportedly coincided with the coalition's asserted political objectives. Brahmins and Muslims ebbed and flowed in both coalitions. Muslims did so in accordance with where they believed their communal interests lay at any given time. Brahmins were a consistently significant presence in both microparties, in keeping with their considerable demographic weight, their unique ritual status in the traditional socio-religious order, and their powerful derivative class status in the modern social order.

However, what the study of electoral politics in the municipal and (as they came increasingly into the picture) district boards revealed was that it was not merely the traditional caste and socio-religious stereotypes which determined the composition of microparties, but the relationship of these formations to the existing economic order. It was a subtle intermixture of ascriptive and class traits that was decisive. And the precise nature of this intermixture varied with the social, cultural, and economic characteristics of sub-regions and districts within provinces.

Land control and trade were perhaps the most important variables in determining political allegiances. 'The traditional influence of the commercial and landed groups varied from area to area of [the United Provinces]' 'and so did the impact of economic change' (Robinson 1973: 77). In western UP, between the 1870s and the 1910s, traders and moneylenders prospered in the new political economy and dramatically expanded the scope of their economic power through land purchases at the expense of the traditional agrarian classes. This, in turn, was translated into political power in the municipal and district-board arenas. In eastern UP, the traditional agrarian classes fared better, largely due to the entrenchment there of the taluqdar and zamindar classes. Robinson's data show that in western UP, the so-called moneylending and trading castes, the most prominent of whom were Baniyas, Khattris, Bohras, and Kalwars (with a scattering of Brahmins) had increased their landholdings in most districts from the 1870s onward by between 30 and 233 per cent. In eastern UP , increases of this magnitude were rare except for Lucknow district which, of course, contained the province's capital with its heavier concentrations of traders and moneylenders. Thus, in this portion of the province, the retention of land control by the traditional agrarian elites gave the latter proportionately more political clout in the local bodies. 'In 1907 landlords and zamindars held over thirty-nine per cent of municipal seats, men in the professions, landlord and government service held nearly forty-two per cent, and commercial men no more than seventeen per cent' (Robinson 1973: 85).

These sub-regional differences profoundly affected Muslim performance in the electoral and representational processes. With the common agrarian interests between formidably entrenched Hindu and Muslim landlords in the east, the latter were often able to forge cross-communal coalitions which enhanced their influence, and thus their sense of social security, in local politics. In the west, however, according to Robinson, 'Muslims were not simply in a minority. Their interests tended to clash with those of the Hindus.' Especially, 'where traders were active, dispossessed Muslims found it difficult to get any representation at all' (Robinson 1973: 87).

The drive for separate Muslim constituencies grew as much out of disparities such as these in the grassroots arenas as from rhetorical confrontations between the major leaders of the two communities at mega-political level. However much the national leadership of the Indian National Congress asserted the secular bona fides of their movement, electoral politics in the towns and districts appeared to belie these assertions. Even in eastern UP, let alone in the west, Muslims perceived the new open political system as being disproportionately beneficial to Hindus both because most of the seats went to Hindus in the elections and because the Hindu trading castes blatantly bankrolled candidates (even Congress candidates) who publically asserted their support for such Hindu causes as the effort to have Devnagri adopted either as a co-equal with the Arabic script or even as a replacement in the writing of public documents and records to symbolize the end of Muslim political dominance, the Hindu Sabha, and the Arya Samaj. A passage from the *Allahabad Leader* in 1910 depicted the communal atmosphere which local-level elections were engendering. 'Our Mahommedan friends,' declared the reporter, 'appealing to the religious sentiments of their co-religionists ... succeeded to such a great extent that almost all the Mahommedans went in a body for the Mahommedan candidate.' On the other side of the communal divide, 'Our Kayastha friends followed the footsteps of their Mahommedan brethren and preached Kayastha fraternity.' In his notable study of the local roots of Indian politics between 1880 and 1920, Bayly (1975) showed how different the world looked to Muslims at the grassroots by contrast with the way national-level spokesmen for major political groups were depicting the communal question. 'Organizations in which the *rais* and bankers played an important part such as the People's Association and the Hindu Samaj were also enlisted in support of the Congress and *acted in the early days as its electorate.*' Since the big patrons 'were religious philanthropists', and pointedly voting 'Hindu' in the municipal elections, it was inevitable that 'Congress at the local level was sometimes indistinguishable from the movement for the protection of cattle or for the propagation of Hindi, *even though this may have been contrary to its secular protestations*' (Bayly 1975: 131–2, emphasis added).

It was these grassroots realities that more than anything else appear to have led to the movement for separate Muslim constituencies which were thus first introduced for the provincial assemblies as part of the Morely-Minto reforms of 1909, and in the United Provinces adopted for municipal-board seats in 1916 and for district-board seats in 1922. Henceforth Muslims formed separate blocs in board politics and were rarely found in the ranks of the Hindu-dominated microparties. This was a logical progression for them because, in Robinson's (1973) words, 'they were beginning to be exposed to the force of democratic politics.' Before these changes in constitutional structure, Muslims had been unable to win seats on the provincial councils and because of this they perceived their political situation increasingly in communal terms. Thus, 'uneasy about their position, Muslims began to search for protection through statutory safeguards and communal organization' (Robinson 1973: 94).

In Faizabad, as well as in other districts, this intensification of the communal divide resulted in a pattern of political competition which clearly laid the foundations for the eventual partition of the country as successive constitutional reforms applied the principle of separate franchise to increasingly expanded electoral arenas (Gould 1994).

Communal differentiation was but one by-product of the period from the 1909 Morely-Minto reforms through the Montague-Chelmsford reforms of 1919 to the 1937 elections which followed the Government of India Act of 1935. It was at this time that forms of political behaviour, particularly ethnically structured competition, generated in the limited franchise municipal and district arenas, were by degrees being projected onto a much larger political stage. Electoral politics at the grassroots and nationalist politics emanating from the centre generated by confrontation between Congress, the Muslim League, and the Raj were gradually crystallizing on opposite ends of the social spectrum until finally converging to form the structural basis for India's (and Pakistan's) post-Independence political system. Each of these constitutional milestones came at the conclusion of a political stand-off the solution of which demanded compromise and concessions between nationalists and the colonial government (in 1909, in the aftermath of the failure of the Bengal Partition; in 1919, in the aftermath of the Jalianwala Bagh massacre and the failure of the Rowlatt Acts; in 1935 in the aftermath of the success of Gandhian-style and Muslim League-style mass political mobilization). This situation created progressively more viable legislative bodies and led to an intensification of electoral politics in constituencies increasingly conducive to ethnically based mass mobilization by political parties (namely the Congress, the Muslim League, the Liberal Party, the National Agriculturalists Party of Agra and Oudh, and the Hindu Mahasabha) manifesting effective ideological articulation and clearer agendas for social reform and change.

The first step toward representative government above local-body level was taken with the 1909 Government of India Act. Its importance was not that it mandated real elections for provincial council seats from grassroots constituencies but that non-official nominees and candidates from 'recognized bodies and associations' would occupy a majority of seats. Under this rubric, communal politics was formally introduced into the evolving Indian political system by the adoption of the reservation principle for Muslims.

In the next phase, namely the Government of India Act of 1919, provincial assemblies were profoundly altered. 'Dyarchy' devolved many heretofore centrally administered functions upon the provincial assemblies, increased their size by almost 300 per cent, and, most important from the standpoint of the evolution of grassroots politics, 'the method of indirect election to the Indian Legislative Council which had been prevalent under the Act of 1909 was abolished and, for the first time, direct election was introduced to fill a large majority of the seats in the Assembly' (Pylee 1965: 86). However, seats were still subdivided into 'communal' and 'special' electorates (although more elaborately so) which meant that direct elections to public offices were still limited to seats on local bodies. Despite this fact, and despite Pylee's (1965) conclusion that Dyarchy failed because, in the end, the Act of 1919 failed to achieve 'the principle of responsible government', the foundation was laid for a new round of mobilization and agitation which brought India closer to real representative government and political independence.

The Government of India Act of 1935 was the next, and basically the final, constitutional step toward this end. It came at a point when the Government of India could no longer suppress demands for the establishment of some measure of party-structured self-government. 'British imperial interests', in Pylee's words, 'had to put on a new garb and devise a new constitutional mechanism before the surging tide of Indian nationalism' (1965: 92). The solution included a further enlargement in the number of assembly seats (to a total of 1594 in eleven provinces),[7] major expansion of the franchise (from about 3 to 18 per cent), and the establishment of numerous territorially structured constituencies along with the usual array of special constituencies. This Act also put the Indian political system, perhaps 'the most complex ever known in the history of federalism,' (Pylee 1965: 99) on an irreversible federalizing track that permanently reinforced the trends toward the ethnic structuring of grassroots electorates begun in the municipalities. The most important step in this process was the decision to locate the general constituencies within the compass of districts and use *tahsils* as their building blocks. This guaranteed that political competition would replicate the pattern which developed in the local bodies. Like them, the mosaic of castes and other particularistically structured groups contained within these elemental administrative units were crucial aspects of embedded sub-cultural systems that determined the political strategies pursued by individuals and groups in pursuit of public office.

The elections held in 1937 illustrate how far grassroots politics had progressed under the terms of the 1935 Act. This was especially evident in the so-called general constituencies and in the reserved Muslim constituencies where Congress and its political surrogates fought it out with the Muslim League for voter support. The United Provinces typified the manner in which seats were distributed and electorates were constructed in the new provincial legislatures. There were 17 Urban General (including 4 Scheduled Caste) and 123 Rural General (including 16 Scheduled Caste) constituencies and 13 Muhammadan Urban and 51 Muhammadan Rural constituencies. In addition there were still 24 'specialized' constituencies which assured representation to Europeans, Anglo-Indians, Indian Christians, factory labour, commerce and industry, etc.

The extension of the franchise from a few hundred thousand voters to more than five million immediately brought into play a wide range of social groups whose votes would transform the Congress into a dynamic political machine preoccupied with attracting voters to its standard. The principal source of support in the rural general constituencies, where the largest number of new voters were to be found, was the peasantry. In UP and Bihar, vast numbers of peasants lacked secure titles to the land they cultivated. As tenants they were prey to the whims of landlords who as a class showed little regard for their rights or well-being. Congress had made agrarian reform a major plank in its political platform by the 1930s[8] and ran candidates in the 1937 elections who energetically solicited the votes of the tenantry as well as other small-scale cultivators. Their main agrarian opposition in the United Provinces was the National Agriculturalists Party of Agra and Oudh representing zamindars and talukdars (that is the principal landlord classes). An organization whose creation had been encouraged by the colonial authorities, it hoped to rally its landed clientele against the threat to its class interests being posed by a radicalized Congress whose demographic base under the new franchise provisions now extended to a significant segment of the tenantry (Reeves 1991).

The caste composition of this new electorate signified a scalar increase in the social complexity of grassroots political arenas. Although many of the small cultivators who had been let into the system were Brahmins and Thakurs, the vast majority of those comprising the tenantry were members of what are today called the Backward Castes—Yadavs, Kurmis, Koiris, Muraos, etc. These went in decisive numbers for Congress candidates in the rural general constituencies. For example, in two such constituencies in Faizabad district, Congress won with 77 per cent of the votes in the constituency where Kurmis and Yadavs overwhelmingly outnumbered Brahmins and Thakurs, but narrowly lost to a NAPO candidate in the other where the demographic proportions favoured the elite castes (Reeves et al. 1975; Gould 1994). Differences in the caste composition of legislative constituencies mattered, in other words. Consequently, as in the local bodies, politicians were compelled to factor these differences into their calculations if they were serious about winning elections, ideological protestations about 'casteism' notwithstanding.

The urban and Muslim constituencies generated electorates with different social configurations. But the political utilization of these configurations was the same. In the latter, of course, ethnic mobilization stressed communal identities which fuelled the consolidation of the Muslim League and intensified countervailing socio-religious sub-nationalism among Hindus. In the former, ethnic differentiation between trading castes, Scheduled Castes, and other groups comprising the metropolitan social-stratification system was sharpened. More important than these differences per se, however, was the fact of differentiation itself which bespoke of the manner in which the dialogue of confrontation between nationalism and the Raj was affecting the scope and social complexity of politics at the grassroots.

Post-Independence Darwinian Politics

The achievement of Independence and the adoption of the 1950 Constitution brought about a final convergence of the two strands of Indian political development—namely evolution from the top down and evolution from the bottom up. The founding of the Indian National Congress had been the starting point for creating a political organization dedicated to the eventual establishment of a free and independent Indian state. As the party grew in stature and organizational sophistication, and as other political formations such as the Muslim League, the Hindu Mahasabha, the Congress Socialist Party, and various regional political groups entered the fray over the years, the details of the kind of central-governmental system India would choose for itself gradually emerged from the turmoil of the freedom struggle and inter-party competition. It would be a secular, democratic state whose legislative bodies would be modelled on Great Britain's Westminster system and whose federal structure would be modelled on the American system of government.

The Ripon reforms had been the starting point for creating the grassroots behavioural base upon which the central system would rest. Despite naive assumptions about local bodies being the appropriate way to introduce an untutored Indian population to the rudiments of self-government, the actual result was to create open, pluralistically structured arenas in which ethnic, class, and socio-religious identities were the principal raw materials of political group formation. As subsequent constitutional reforms widened the scope of popular participation in politics and increased the scale of the arenas in which elections and representative government took place, the forms of political behaviour occurring in these arenas replicated, in magnified form those which had originally crystallized in the small-scale municipal arenas.

Because the principal figures who guided India to Independence opted for a political system which stressed accommodative over coercive methods of institution building, the outcome was a balance between centrally, regionally, and locally integrated structures of power. Clearly the decision to pursue this course was profoundly influenced by the subcontinental size and social complexity of India itself and by the democratic liberalism which the Congress leadership in particular had imbibed from their British overlords. But whatever the sources of these perspectives, the post-colonial Indian state, shorn of its Muslim-majority regions, entered its post-colonial phase with a federal structure in which power was dispersed downwards through the system to such a degree that central authority could only be maintained by an elaborate process of bargaining, resource manipulation, and co-optation. The unique mixture of hereditary status groups, socio-religious communities, and social classes found in the provinces and districts were, as noted earlier, taken as a 'given' upon which the central system superimposed itself without attempting to replace or significantly alter it (Barth 1959). These sub-national units, and the sub-units within them in turn, then, became powerful nodes of countervailing power which could impose limits on the capacity of centrally initiated policies to be implemented at grassroots level. The task of central government was, in the words of Sisson and Roy, one of seeking 'the appropriate "balance" between centralization and decentralization' (1990: 19).

As a segmentary state with a democratic constitution, India's central system was from its inception, and continues to be to this day, a loosely integrated structure in which power can be exercised only through, processes of bargaining, resource manipulation, and co-optation. This meant and continues to mean that at grassroots level political groups enjoy a high measure of autonomy—so much so, in fact, that it has prompted some to conclude that politics at this level corresponds to what anthropologists call an 'acephalous system' (see Barth 1959 and Gould 1994). It is this comparative autonomy combined with the profusion of hereditary status groups and socio-religious communities inhabiting the local socio-political environment that has been responsible for the fragility of political coalitions at every level of the political system. It is a major reason why factionalism has been so pervasive in Congress and indeed every political party and why, even at national level, neither the Congress during its heyday nor successor parties at the centre and in the states were (and are today) able to fully carry out their legislative agendas.

The problem for the Congress and its successors was that its legislators were almost invariably 'compromised' in the sense that most had been elected by pluralities consisting of coalitions of supporters spanning the ideological spectrum. In the absence of strong central-party control at local level, few could obey the letter of the party line with impunity. To do so could generate defections from their grassroots support systems that would endanger their chances of remaining in office. Individual legislators, in short, could not afford to blindly obey the party whip. This vulnerability is clearly apparent in the election data. In the Fourth General Elections of 1962, for example, the Congress won 361 (74 per cent) of the Lok Sabha's 488 seats, seemingly an overwhelming majority that should have enabled the party to carry out almost any policy it wished. However, only a small fraction of these incumbents had garnered an absolute majority of the votes in their constituencies. Therefore, their local mandate was limited. In Uttar Pradesh, where Congress won sixty-two of the state's eighty-six seats, only eleven Congressmen obtained absolute majorities in their constituencies. With so many partymen devoid of latitude for political manoeuvre in their home constituencies, the party's central leadership was able to see very few of its most cherished 'socialist' policies effectively implemented. Most of the party's MPs could not afford the luxury of blind obedience. In fact, frustration over the failure of policy implementation by 1963 led to Nehru's famous 'Kamraj plan' which forced several regional party bosses to resign their chief ministerships in 'a calculated effort to save the socialist pattern of society' (Frankel 1978: 229).

Unable to curb or eliminate the ethnically integrated hereditary status groups that pervade the constituencies where elections are decided, Congress, as well as other parties, inevitably based their local-level party building on the competitive manipulation of local structures of power (Gould 1959: Ch. 11). Following the model that began in the municipal boards with Ripon's Resolution on Local Self-Government, coalitions have been built by a 'natural-selection' process. Successful proprietors of local structures of power are selectively co-opted by a faction of the local branch of the party machine and then held in line by providing access to the spoils of public office and opportunities for political mobility through the party organization. Failure to provide expected rewards leads to defections which, if too widespread (whether the context be inter-factional or inter-party competition) lead to loss of a coalition's 'critical mass' which, of course, leads to loss of political power. Mrs Gandhi's unsuccessful attempts (and Rajiv Gandhi's attempts after her) to gain dictatorial control of Congress's political agenda can be said to have arisen from an inability to appreciate the resiliency of boss-controlled power systems at the grassroots. Wherever chief ministers controlling strong indigenous power systems were removed because they seemed to obstruct Mrs Gandhi's or her son's political and policy goals, the party eventually lost control of these state governments. This is because the displaced politicians merely transferred their structures of power to a rival faction or party that, as a consequence, gained the necessary coalitional strength to replace whichever Congress formation had been the basis for Congress(I) dominance.

Conclusion

In conclusion, what has happened to grassroots politics in India since Independence? The scale has increased as more and more layers of political activity have been brought into existence, while the idioms of political interaction have remained consistent. Not only have the number and variety of normal political arenas been increased and increasingly refined, but other types of public arenas, brought into existence in order to provide a wide variety of opportunities for the Indian people to participate in their governance and social and economic development have undergone politicization. Panchayati raj institutions are a noteworthy case in point. So also are the various cooperative institutions that have attempted to improve the public's access to agricultural loans, insurance, basic food supplies, etc. Educational institutions are still another domain where the democratization of control has paved the way for politicization (Rudolph and Rudolph 1972; Gould 1994: Ch. 13). These various governing or legislative bodies that were created to insure public involvement in planning and development have taken on many of the characteristics of formally structured political arenas. Competition for management and control has been phrased in caste, class, and socio-religious terms. Political parties entered these arenas, indeed stimulated their politicization, as it became clear that they could be valuable assets in their machine-building strategies. Panchayati Raj is perhaps the most striking example of this process. *Zilla parishads, taluk* boards, *kshettra samitis*, and *gaon* panchayats throughout India have become vital grassroots venues for party building and the cultivation of 'co-optable' political careers.

The starting point of this narrative was a review of the empirical studies of village-level politics which grew out of the community development and evaluation projects sponsored by the Government of India and various foreign foundations. In retrospect, it is now possible to see that these studies were implicitly documenting the initial stages of the process through which a wide range of public arenas ostensibly designed to stimulate planning and socio-economic development eventually became intertwined with the country's formal, constitutionally mandated political system. Election studies have provided insight into the connections between the country's centralizing national institutions and its acephalous grassroots environments. Decentralized power and politically empowered ethnicity are the principal ingredients which have fuelled competitive politics in these environments. The Darwinian style of 'natural selection' and 'selective co-optation' became, under the terms of a democratic constitution and a federally structured polity, the principal manner in which politically ambitious figures at the grassroots achieved social visibility and made themselves available for recruitment by political parties in search of winning coalitions. To an important extent, the desire of India's nation builders to accommodate diversity and maximize fairness resulted in a political culture in which the power of its local systems severely circumscribes the capacity of any party or parties in power at the centre to successfully carry out to the letter their ideologically conceived programmes. But the trade-off for this programmatic imperfection is a society where political participation is extensive and electorates display a remarkably high level of political sophistication.

ENDNOTES

1. Oscar Lewis was recognized for his contributions to the study of the interplay between peasant communities and an encompassing urban civilization. At this point in his career, Lewis had published a well-recognized restudy of the Mexican community of Tepoztlan, then a few miles north of Mexico City, now a part of its metropolitan system. This study was a critique of an original study of this community conducted by Robert Redfield (1941). Redfield's research had led to his famous 'folk–urban continuum' which held that the impact of 'urban culture' upon peasant communities was essentially disorganizing and disintegrative. Lewis contended that the relationship between folk and urban systems was more complex and subtle than this. On the contrary, averred Lewis, the changes which take place in the village under the impact of urban culture 'do not necessarily imply disorganization'. Instead, 'they involve a new kind of organization or reorganization.' (Lewis 1951: 437). This perspective clearly made Lewis appealing to the Ford Foundation and the Planning Commission at a time when the Government of India was heavily preoccupied with better understanding the complexities of planned social change in rural India.

2. This pamphlet was published in 1954 under the name of Oscar Lewis 'with the assistance of Harvant Singh Dhillon' by The Programme Evaluation Organization of the Planning Commission. Since Lewis had no background in Indian society and culture and knew no Indian languages, the substantive data gathering and analysis were done by Dhillon and a group of young Indian students who participated in the research and are acknowledged in a footnote. They are: R.N. Bansal, Inder Pal Singh Monga, Venu Ramdas, and Rajpal Singh Rathee.

3. These studies were subdivided into urban and rural constituencies. Authors of the urban constituency studies were: Rajni Kothari and Tarun Sheth (Baroda East), V.M. Sirsikar (Poona Constituency), Paul R. Brass (Kanpur city), Wayne Wilcox (Indore city), Roby Chakravorti (Muchipara constituency, central Calcutta), S.N. Roy (Behala constituency, suburban Calcutta), Aloo J. Dastur (North Bombay). The rural studies were by: Baldev Raj Nayar (Sidhwan Bet constituency in Ludhiana district), Rajni Kothari and Ghanshayam Shah (Modasa constituency, Gujarat), Harold Gould (Faizabad city, UP), and Myron Weiner (Ponnur constituency, Andhra Pradesh).

4. Kothari's volume has ten studies following an introduction outlining the basic conceptual issues. These were by Eleanor Zelliot on the Mahars of Maharashtra, Rushikesh Maru on the Kshatriyas of Gujarat, Robert L. Hardgrave on the Nadars of Tamil Nadu, Carolyn Elliot on the Reddis and Kammas of Andhra, Richard Sisson on political factions in Rajasthan, Ramashray Roy on caste and political recruitment in Bihar, André Béteille on caste and political group formations in Tamil Nadu, Anil Bhatt on caste and mobilization in a Gujarat village, and Donald Rosenthal on caste participation in the politics of two cities (Kothari 1972a).

5. Chapters on Uttar Pradesh (Paul R. Brass), Madhya Pradesh (Wayne Wilcox), Maharashtra (Ram Joshi), Jammu and Kashmir (Balraj Puri), West Bengal (Marcus Franda), Rajasthan (Lawrence L. Shrader), Andhra Pradesh (Hugh Grey), and the Punjab (Baldev Raj Nayar).

6. Gladstone's government wished to placate Indian sensibilities at a time when Czarist expansionism in Central Asia was setting off alarm bells in London about the security and fiscal stability of India. Ripon was chosen as Viceroy because of his comparatively enlightened views on how the colony should be run. 'Ripon came to India from an unusually full public life in England: early association with F.D. Maurice and Christian Socialism, an apprenticeship under Sydney Herbert the army reformer, thirty years experience of politics and of the great departments in Whitehall' (Tinker 1967: 43).

7. The breakdown by province: Assam 108, Bihar 152, Bengal 259, Bombay 175, Madras 215, United Provinces 228, Central Provinces 112, North West Frontier Province 50, Orissa 60, Punjab 175, Sind 60. Legislative Councils were additionally created in six provinces: Assam 22, Bihar 30, Bengal 65, Bombay 30, Madras 56, United Provinces 60.

8. Agrarian unrest in many parts of India from the 1920s onwards had generated a number of spontaneous mobilizations by the peasantry. An emerging left wing in the Congress, increasingly imbued with Socialist doctrines, was able to formally organize itself into the Congress Socialist Party (1934) and gradually pressure the party's senior leadership to adopt a measure of class-oriented mobilization. A.R. Desai assembled studies by numerous authors which revealed the subcontinental scope of these uprisings (see Desai 1979). In most cases, the Congress entered this domain of political opportunity by co-opting local movements that had arisen in response to the specific forms of inequity and oppression that were found in the regional environments. The Congress Socialists found a particularly ripe opening for their agitational activities in UP and Bihar. Here, so-called *kisan sabhas* had found wide constituencies among the tenantry. In Avadh, one of the most noteworthy leaders was a rustic revolutionary who called himself Baba Ram Chandra. In Bihar, clearly the most striking manifestation of spontaneously generated peasant leadership was Sahajanand. Apart from their shared charismatic qualities, Ram Chandra and Sahajanand typified what wide disparities could exist in levels of sophistication among such grassroots figures. Baba Ram Chandra achieved a wide following in his local domain but never demonstrated the intellectual articulateness needed to propel himself onto the national political scene. Sahajanand, on the contrary, did possess such talents and produced a formidable body of writings on his views concerning India's agrarian situation. While both of these leaders personally resisted absorption into Congress's version of the kisan sabha movement, much of the tenantry in UP and Bihar were and became a decisive vote bank in the Congress's victories in the 1937 elections.

The definitive scholarship on Sahajanand's writings and contributions to agrarian politics, plus many other aspects of peasant radicalism in Bihar, has been by Professor Walter Hauser of the University of Virginia. See, for example, Hauser (1994; 1993). On Congress's co-optive role in agrarian unrest in UP see Siddiqi (1978); Pandey (1978); Gould (1984).

REFERENCES

Atal, Yogesh. 1972. 'Project CLAPP: Studying Political Behaviour in a Region'. In Satish Saberwal, ed., *Beyond the Village: Sociological Explorations*. Simla: Indian Institute of Advanced Study.

Bailey, F.G. 1958. *Caste and the Economic Frontier: A Village in Highland Orissa*. Delhi: Oxford University Press.

_____. 1963. *Politics and Social Change: Orissa in 1959*. Berkeley: University of California Press.

_____. 1969. *Strategems and Spoils: A Social Anthropology of Politics*. Oxford: Basil Blackwell.

Barth, Frederick. 1959. *Political Leadership among the Swat Pathans*. London: Athelone Press.

_____. 1969. *Ethnic Groups and Their Boundaries*. Boston: Little Brown and Company.

Bayly, C.A. 1975. *The Local Roots of Indian Politics: Allahabad 1880–1920*. Oxford: Clarendon Press.

Béteille, André. 1965. *Caste, Class and Power: Changing Patterns of Stratification in a Tanjore Village*. Berkeley: University of California Press.

_____. 1972. 'Caste and Political Formation in Tamilnad'. In Rajani Kothari, ed., 259–98.

Brass, Paul R. 1965. *Factional Politics in an Indian State: The Congress Party in Uttar Pradesh*. Berkley: University of California Press.

_____. 1974. *Language, Religion and Politics in North India*. New York and Cambridge: Cambridge University Press.

Cohn, Bernard S. 1965. 'The Changing Status of a Depressed Caste'. In Mckim Marriott, ed., *Village India: Studies in the Little Community*. 53–77. Chicago: University of Chicago Press.

Desai, A.R., ed. 1979. *Peasant Struggle in India*. Delhi: Oxford University Press.

Dumont, Louis and David Pocook. 1957–66. *Contributions to Indian Sociology*. I–IX. The Hague: Mouton (annually).

Elliot, M. Carolyn. 1972. 'Caste and Faction among the Dominant Caste: The Reddis and Kammas of Andhra'. In Rajani Kothari, ed.

Fadia, Babulal. 1984. *State Politics in India*. vols 2. New Delhi: Radiant Publishers.

Frankel, Francine. 1978. *India's Political Economy, 1947–97: The General Revolution*. Delhi: Oxford University Press.

Ghurye, G.S. 1957. *Caste and Class in India*. 2nd ed. Bombay: Popular Book Depot.

Gould, Harold A. 1959. 'The Peasant Village: Centrifugal or Centripetal'. *Eastern Anthropologist*. 13:1–16.

_____. 1963. 'The Adaptive Functions of Caste in Contemporary Indian Society'. *Asian Survey*. 3(427–38):156.

_____. 1984. 'Politics of Agrarian Unrest in UP: Who Co-opted Whom 2'. *Economic and Political Weekly*. 19(49), December: 2084–8.

Gould, Harold, A. 1987 and 1988. *The Hindu Caste System*, vol. 1; *The Sacralization of a Social Order*; vol 2: *Caste Adaptatio in Modernizing Indian Society*. Delhi: Chanakya Publications.

———. 1994. *Grass Roots Politics in India: A Century of Political Evolution in Faizabad*. New Delhi: Oxford and IBH.

Hardgrave, Robert L. 1969. *The Nadars of Tamilnadu: The Political Culture of a Community in Change*. New York: Harcourt, Brace and World.

Harold A. Gould, 'Local-level/Grass-roots Political Studies'.

Harrison, Selig S. 1959. *India, The Most Dangerous Decades*. Princeton: Princeton University Press.

Hauser, Walter. 1993. 'Violence, Agrarian Radicalism and Electoral Politics: Reflections on the Indian People's Front'. *The Journal of Peasant Studies*. 21(1), October:85–126.

———. ed. 1994. *Sahajanand on Agricultural Labour and the Rural Poor*. Delhi: Manohar Books.

Kothari, Rajani. 1972. *Politics in India*. Boston: Little Brown and Company.

———. ed. 1972a. *Politics in India*. Beston: Little Brown and Company.

———. 1972b. 'In Rajani Kothari, ed.,

Kothari, Rajani and Tarun Sheth. 1965. 'Extent and Limits of Community Voting: The Case of Baroda East'. In Myron Weiner and Rajani Kothari, eds, *Indian Voting Behaviour: Studies of the 1962 General Elections*, 13–34. Calcutta: Mukhopadhyay.

Lewis, Oscar. 1951. *Life in a Mexican Village: Tepoztlan Restudied*. Urban: University of Illinois Press.

Lewis, Oscar and Harwart Dhillon. 1954. *Group Dynamics in a North Indian Village: A Study of Factions*. Delhi: The Programme Evaluation Organization of the Planning Commission.

Lipset, Beymoni, Martin. 1963. *Political Man*. London.

Marriott, McKim. 1960. *Caste Ranking and Community Structure in Five Regions of India and Pakistan*. Poona: Decan College Monograph Series 23.

———. 1968. 'Multiple Reference in Indian Caste System'. In James Silverbarg, ed., *Social Mobility in the Caste System in India*, 103–14. The Hague: Mouton.

Pandey, Gyanendra. 1978. *The Ascendancy of the Congress in Uttar Pradesh. 1926–34*. Delhi: Oxford University Press.

Patterson, Manoreen. 1954. 'Caste and Political Leadership in Maharashtra'. *Economic and Political Weekly*. 25 September.

Pylee, M.V. 1965. *Constitutional Government in India*. Bombay: Asia Publishing House.

Redfield, Robert. 1941. *Tepotzlan—A Mexican Community*. Chicago: University of Chicago Press.

Reeves, Peter. 1966. 'The Politics of Order: "Anti-Non Cooperation" in the United Provinces, 1921'. *Journal of Asian Studies*. 25(2), February. 261–74.

———. 1991. *Landlords and Governments in Uttar Pradesh: A Study of Their Relations until Zamindari Aboltition*. Delhi: Oxford University Press.

Reeves, P.D., B.D. Graham, and J.M. Goodman, eds. 1975. *Elections in Uttar Pradesh, 1920–5*. Delhi: Manohar Publishers.

Retzlaff, Realph H. 1962. *Village Government in India: A Case Study*. London/New York: Asia Publishing House.

Robinson, Frances. 1973. 'Municipal Government and Muslim Separatism in the United Provinces, 1883 to 1916'. In John Gallagher, Gordon Johns, and Anil Seal, eds, *Locality, Province and Nation: Essays on Indian Politics, 1870–1940*. Cambridge: Cambridge University Press.

_____. 1974. *Separatism among Indian Muslims: The Politics of the United Provinces' Muslims, 1860–1923*. Cambridge: Cambridge University Press.

Rudolph, Lloyd and Sussane. 1967. *The Modernity of Tradition*. Berkeley: University of California Press.

_____. ed. 1972. *Education and Politics in India: Studies in Organization, Society and Policy*. Harvard: Harvard University Press.

Sesson, Richard. 1972. *The Congress Party in Rajasthan: Political Integration and Institution Building in an Indian State*. Berkley and Oxford: University of California Press.

Siddiqi, M.H. 1978. *Agrarian Unrest in North India: The United Provinces, 1918–22*. New Delhi: Vikas Publishing House.

Sisson, Richard and Ramashray Roy. 1990. *Diversity and Dominance in Indian Politics*. New Delhi: Sage Publications.

Srinivas, M.N. 1957. 'Caste in India'. *Journal of Asian Studies*. 4:529–48.

Tinker, High. 1967. *The Foundations of Local Self-Government in India, Pakistan and Burma*. Bombay: Fabion.

Weiner, Myron. 1967. *State Politics in a New Nation: The Indian National Congress*. Chicago: University of Chicago Press.

_____, ed. 1968a. *State Politics in India*. Princeton: Princeton University Press.

_____. 1968b. ' In Myron Weiner, ed., *State Politics in India*. Princeton: Princeton University Press.

Weiner Myron and John Osgood Field, eds. 1974–77. *Electoral Politics in Indian States*, vol. 1: *The Communist Parties of West Bengal*; vol. 2: *The Disadvantaged Sector*; vol. 3: *The Impact of Modernization*; vol. 4: *Party Systems and Cleavages*. Delhi: Manohar Books.

Weiner, Myron and Rajani Kothari, eds. 1965. *Indian Voting Behaviour: Studies of the 1962 General Elections*. Calcutta: Mukhopadhyay.

Social Movements

Martin Fuchs • *Antje Linkenbach*

Systematic and extended research on social movements is a comparatively late development in the social sciences. As the study of social movements has gained in stature, it has altered the understanding of society in academic discourse, highlighting how societies are made or unmade through collective political movement. Simultaneously political events of the 1960s and 1970s, especially the process of decolonization, lent a great deal of legitimacy to social movements. Over time social movements lost the sense of being revolutionary, militant, or anomic events came to be regarded as a regular feature of social life, at least in modern democracies.

The growth of research on social movements has been remarkable in the last three decades in India as in other world regions. Several disciplines have participated in this development. Political science took the longest to accept social movements as a genuine subject, and social anthropology for a long time limited itself to specific types of movements, namely those which were considered anti-modern, or pre-capitalist. Sociology and social history took the lead in research on social movements. It was sociology which first made research on movements a sub-field of its discipline. Whereas the theoretical concern in all the disciplines was directed primarily to specific social or political issues and to particular historical constellations, sociology became the special arena for general conceptual reflections. Recent debates have shown the necessity to reintegrate movement research with general theoretical concerns, while, reciprocally, the focus on social movements has been effective in reformulating the concepts of society and culture. Studies of social movements do not cover a clearly circumscribed phenomenal field.

'Even an implicit, "empirical" agreement about the use of the term is largely missing' (Diani 1992: 2). The term 'social movements' refers to a diverse spectrum of collective social and political phenomena, as heterogeneous as revolutions, religious sects, political organizations or single-issue campaigns, or anti-colonial resistance and resistance against inroads by alleged 'outsiders' (McAdam et al. 1988). Social movements by definition are unstable, transitory phenomena. They do not have a clear beginning nor, in many cases, a clear point of termination, and cannot be easily and precisely separated from the process of social interaction at large. The term 'social movement' is used by many researchers 'in a naively descriptive manner' to refer to a supposedly unified collective subject (Melucci 1989: 29). Two aspects are generally avowed or implied: first, the 'anti-establishment social content' (Touraine 1995: 243), a reference to ideas of autonomy, equity, human dignity or fundamental rights, and, second, the link to social change, especially modernization, as a triggering cause or an objective of social movements. A distinction, broadly accepted in European and American research (but less suited to Indian conditions as we shall see), is that between movements that effect personal change and those which effect political (or institutional) change.

Added to the heterogeneity on the phenomenological level in understanding social movements, is the heterogeneity of narrative strategies, analytical approaches, and theoretical frameworks deployed in movement research, which points to differences in the concepts of action (praxis) and society (sociality), which underlie the analysis. Given the heterogeneity, we start with a provisional definition of social movements used in the chapter. *A social movement takes the forms of collective self-organization for the attainment of social recognition and the assertion of rights or existential interests hitherto denied to a group or category of people. It engages in resistance against the threat of a group's or cateogory of people's rights and basis of existence.*

The main criterion for judging which kinds of inequities or injustices are being addressed may be inferred only from a situational appraisal of the concerned actors in a movement. However, all social movements, in that they are based on an experience of difference from the political society and involve forms of reflexivity, engage actors in the active interpretation of the present and imagination of the future. Even when engaged in struggles for specific causes they draw upon general principles of equity and justice: thus they may be seen to address a 'generalized other' (Mead [1984]). In many cases social movements may come up against the 'limits of compatibility' of a social order (Melucci 1989: 29) and thus get involved in conflict which cannot be contained within the principles of that particular social order.

In organizing this chapter we concentrate on three aspects. Part II gives the main conceptual developments of research on social movements. Part III presents the main topical fields of research on social movements in India—the discussion is exemplary rather than exhaustive. Part IV looks towards the future—indicating the promising perspectives developed in this research.

II
Conceptual Developments

At the risk of some simplification, one may distinguish two basic lines of thought in research on social movements. One line of argument has focused on the behaviour of social actors who joined or organized a movement. The second has centred upon the overall socio-political system, and the conflicts over its future orientation, seeing social movements as 'carriers of political projects', or as 'historical actors' who make attempts to bring about change in the political and social order (Eyerman and Jamison 1991: 26). While the second perspective implies conflict and antagonism as a regular feature of social life, the first assumes collective action to be exceptional or deviant in relation to normatively regulated and institutionalized behaviour (Rule 1989).

Collective Behaviour and Resource Mobilization

The early 'collective behaviour' approaches, centred in the USA, took off from the 'crowd psychology' of authors like Tarde ([1901] 1922), Le Bon (1897), or Freud (1955), and regarded social movements, together with mass panic, craze, hostile outburst, but also riots and revolutionary movements, as *reactions* to 'structural strain' or breakdown of the social order and social disintegration (Smelser 1962). Many authors attributed the increase in social movements in contemporary society to the large-scale, disruptive social change, either inherent in the development of society through modernization and the resultant ideological confrontations, or induced by outside interventions, as in the case of colonial subjection and political repression.

Every movement, smaller or larger, appeared as a singular phenomenon. Social movements were seen as aggregations of individual actions, the participants manifesting identical or similar susceptibilities and behavioural patterns. Coordination of action was seen as secondary only, as not constitutive for the movement. The forms of behaviour exhibited in social movements fell largely outside the scope of conventional, rational forms of action. It was sociologists in the lineage of the Chicago School, like Park and Burgess (1921), Blumer (1939; 1957), and, above all, Turner and Killian (1957) who began to see social movements as interactive endeavour and as phases of social innovation (emergent imageries and norms, invention of new forms of social organization).

It was the double issue of detecting linkages between individual susceptibilities—the transformation of individual decisions into a coordinated collective undertaking—and discovering the particular rationale of social movements, which stood at the beginning of a second phase of research in the 'behaviouristic' line. In this, one may distinguish two kinds of approaches, one starting from socio-psychological assumptions of a frustration–aggression paradigm, the other from the rationalist assumptions of a strategic action model. Those who still clung to the exceptionalist character of social movements concentrated on psychological motivations for participation in social movements, that is on imputed states of apprehension and expectation shared by a group of people, encapsulated in theorems of 'rising expectations', 'relative deprivation', 'downward mobility', or 'status inconsistency' (see Melucci 1989: 32f). This was combined with what Eder (1993: 9n) called stage models which plot the formation and career of a collective actor, and with a set of observational criteria (mobilization, leadership, organization, ideology, strategy, internal dynamics, outcome). These models were often biased towards a top-down perspective, privileging the views of the elite within a movement, assuming these were conceptions also held by other participants. This approach inspired many empirical studies in India, most prominently by M.S.A. Rao, who took up the concept of relative deprivation (Runciman 1966; Aberle 1966; Gurr 1970; see Rao 1979b), and by T.K. Oommen in whose work this concept was enclosed in a discussion of the tension between mobilization and institutionalization (Oommen 1990).

The second group of approaches to social movements, within this genre of theorizing, came to be known under the summary term 'resource mobilization theory'. Developed in the USA as a response to the civil rights, anti-war, women's, and black movements of the 1960s and 1970s, these theories sought to 'rehabilitate' social movements by reincorporating them into the realm of rational action, or rational choice, and organizational politics (Rule 1989). Social movements were analysed as rational undertakings by movement 'entrepreneurs' who accomplish the constitution of a collective project by their mobilizing efforts. Movement 'entrepreneurs', and more or less (prospective) participants too, were seen to calculate costs, risks, and advantages and evaluate the 'political opportunity structure' (Eisinger 1973; and later Tarrow 1983, 1989). The theory of resource mobilization substracted from its model all those aspects of the phenomena analysed which do not conform to this rationalist logic. Thus, for instance, it had no place for emotional dynamics, experiences of *communitas*, consummatory ends of action (Rule 1989), and pre-existing solidarities in its analytical framework. The 'resource-mobilization theory' also remained confined to an individualistic concept of social action. This has become increasingly manifest in the unabating debate on the 'free-rider' issue initiated by Olson in 1965 with respect to common-property resources. Grievances, in this model were not taken as constituting explanatory variables of mobilization but as ubiquitous, constant, and thus rather irrelevant conditions: the role of ideology is consistently downplayed (Snow and Benford 1988; Mayer 1991), while the context of decisions and actions appears as an external structural factor.

In recent years, two kinds of responses have been made to these criticisms within the model of rational strategic action. In his historically oriented research on social movements, Charles Tilly pointed out that though collective action draws upon the existing collective repertoires in a society, this action repertoire is historically grounded and thus changed over a period of time (Tilly et al. 1975; Tilly 1978). This allowed Tilly to accommodate the notion of strategic rational action within a theory of context-specific rationality. On the other hand, some advocates of the resource-mobilization theory have started to look for interpretative linkages between participants in a movement and social organization. While acknowledging the significance of interpretations of grievances by the participants, both 'elite' and 'members', of a movement—as well as the construction of meaning frames (*frame-alignment approach*)—there is still a tendency to reduce the hermeneutic aspects to the strategic task of consensus mobilization and action generation (Snow and Benford 1988). Approaches in the theory of resource mobilization, mainly developed in North America, had little direct impact on Indian studies, whereas with European research a dialogue was instituted in the 1980s (Klandermans et al. 1988; Rucht 1991a; Neidhardt and Rucht 1993). Special mention may be made of Rule (1989) who sets himself the task of including emotional valences and the expressive content with rationalist accounts in an interactionist concept of collective action.

Movements as Historical Actors

The second approach in the research on social movements followed a different trajectory. It took its lead not only from a different concept of society, now seen as characterized by structural conflict, *as a normal feature of its life*, but also showed an inclination to view social movements as macro subjects. Prototypical were the social contradictions and the movements of the working class in the epoch of industrialization and the formation of capitalism. In many cases this led to an identification of social movements with class(es) and thus a perception of social movements as carriers of historical projects. This construction was to be transferred to the peasantries of the non-western ('Third-world') countries in the 1960s and 1970s who came to be considered as revolutionary subjects (Alavi [1965] 1973; Wolf 1971; Dhanagare 1983). However, the historical validity of the identification of movements with classes has been questioned by many scholars (Habermas 1981; Rucht 1991b; Eder 1993) as also the determinism inscribed into the structural notion of class. Many scholars have pointed out that it is not easy to correlate 'objective', structural constraints and contradictions with states of social consciousness and with social conflicts as encountered historically. While this correlation had looked convincing in the case of 'classical' capitalism, in most other cases it is important to keep in mind the contingent character of the precise form that a movement takes.

A resurgence of interest in social movements was stimulated after 1968 by the 'new social movements', such as the students', women's, environmental, human-rights, or peace movements. In this case too, it led to a reconsideration of the concept of social movements. These new approaches were sometimes subsumed under terms such as 'new social movements-approach', or 'identity-oriented paradigm' (Cohen 1985). What was common in these approaches was their acceptance of society as constitutionally conflictual, with an emphasis on macro-social contexts and formative conditions on the one side, and the capacity for critique and reflexivity on the other. The class-theoretical assumptions (and sometimes also the dichotomous conception of a basic social antagonism) were now seen as overlain, qualified, or superseded by other conflicts, at least with respect to what was diagnosed as the new phase of 'late-capitalist', 'postindustrial', or 'programmed' society (Habermas, 1981; Touraine 1978 [1981]). In India too the Hegelian-Marxist idea of *Aufhebung*, of (final) overcoming of social contradictions, began to lose ground, though it continues to find favour in the socio-historical analysis of agrarian movements. In most other cases the focus of social conflicts is seen to have shifted to the sphere of reproduction; emphasis also shifted to the critique of values through which the different kinds of oppression are reproduced. Examples may be found in critiques of patriarchy in feminist movements, of paradigms of development in environmental movements and the critique of education. In Europe, as in India, the writing on new social movements, especially by scholars committed to a particular case, has been prolific. This has been paralleled by a resurgence of interest in older 'culturo-political' conflicts such as issues of collective identity, self-determination or group autonomy, or of social reform movements. It has also been accompanied by a rediscovery of older, historical conflicts in the fields of reproduction and social hermeneutics, like those on concepts of health, or on concepts of religion and the accessibility of religious ritual and salvation (*bhakti*) for all sections of society. This has been connected, more generally, to the rediscovery of distinct 'moral economies' and their clash especially with market economy and rising capitalism both in European and Asian social history (see Thompson 1980; Scott 1976 and 1985; *Subaltern Studies* 1982–99). Despite the related conceptual developments in this field, a split shows up between those who basically, and sometimes even programmatically, want to limit the concept of *social* movement to modern and modernizing society—because only this society is seen to actually work upon itself (Touraine [1978] 1981; Rucht 1994)—and those who derive a perspective applicable to all emancipatory movements and who put the cultural expressions of actors into the foreground. While the first group understands 'tradition' as the reverse of self-proclaimed modernity, the second wants to give a new reading to religious and other ('non-modern') cultural forms of opposition or 'subalternity' (see *Subaltern Studies* 1982–99).

Approaches subsumed under the second trend in social-movement research very often related to the theories of the 'new Left' and post-Marxists. The names of Touraine and Habermas in Europe are especially associated with this. In India it is Gramsci, rediscovered by the Subaltern school, and Foucault in the many post-structuralist critiques who have inspired this research (Arnold 1984). Gandhian concepts have also provided inspiration to many scholars (Chatterjee 1984). The development of research on social movements stimulated and was stimulated by the debate on a theory of agency and praxis on the one hand, and on difference and representation on the other. Though issues pertaining to the individual or collective subjectivity, of autonomy and creativity, were addressed within this research, their interrelation still needs thorough discussion (Fuchs 1999).

The 'culturalist turn' in some parts of the research on social movements has brought anthropological thinking into contact with social-movement research in a new way. It has helped in the discovery of 'everyday resistance' and 'hidden transcripts' in subaltern action (Scott 1985; 1990), notions which then found their way into anthropological research itself. Women's culture, oral tradition, 'folk-religion', ritual practices or everyday life have received new significance and meaning as 'counter' cultures (for example Haynes and Prakash, 1991; Raheja and Gold 1994; Kumar 1994; besides *Subaltern Studies* 1982–99). Before that, anthropological theorizing on social movements, while paralleling the trajectories outlined here, had restricted itself to specific phenomenal clusters and categories of people emphasizing chiliastic, millenaristic or revivalist movements, especially among tribals, and peasant movements. The broadening of scope has helped to bring social anthropology and sociology closer into these fields.

Whatever approach one may take in the study of social movements and collective action, it is not possible to think of these as a distinct sphere of social reality. As a category, some have suggested that social movements are better seen as belonging to a 'meso level', between the micro and the macro (Neidhardt and Rucht 1991; Rucht 1994). In fact, the understanding of social

movements has moved from a marginal to a central position in the analysis of
society, as they are seen to be a central configuration of social life rather than
an aberrant phenomenon (Touraine [1978] 1981). While there may be some
reservations about Touraine's historicist assumptions about the role of social
movements as major actors of change, it is generally accepted that social
movements are ubiquitous quasi-institutional social players situated somewhere
between political parties, associations (*Verbände*), and interest groups (Diani
1992; Rucht 1993). Some would argue that modern societies are better viewed as
engaged in ongoing negotiation, conflict, and construction of relationships with
a central role being assigned to social movements and to collective action
(Kothari 1989; Neidhardt and Rucht 1993).

III

The Indian Context: Four Exemplary Fields

In this section, we discuss four exemplary fields of research on
social movements in India—namely peasant, tribal, dalit, and women's
movements. It is obvious that the distinction between topical fields should not
be reified—considerable overlaps may be found within these fields. Our
discussion on these fields builds upon earlier discussions by Shah (1990) and
Oommen (1990).

Peasant Movements

Systematic interest in peasant movemens can be traced back to the
1960s. It was a period when the 'agrarian question', the unequal distribution
of land, in the 'Third World' became a prominent political issue. This
development had been furthered by revolutionary movements like that which
led into the war in Vietnam, or, in the South Asian context, the uprising in
Naxalbari (northern West Bengal) in 1967 and the ensuing 'Naxalite'
movements and activities in other Indian states, especially Andhra Pradesh
and Bihar. This was accompanied, in India and outside, by renewed interest in
the Russian and the Chinese, or the Mexican revolutions and the significant
role of agrarian issues in them. Peasants came to represent a possible
alternative revolutionary subject (Alavi [1965] 1973; Moore 1967; Wolf 1970).
In the Indian case it seemed particularly difficult to question deep-rooted
notions of the inertia and docility of the Indian peasantry (still upheld even
by Barrington Moore when he tries to contrast India with China).

The interest in the revolutionary role of peasantries connected with
a large-scale reorientation in the social sciences, which had started in the early
1950s. Policies and discourses of 'development' on the one hand, of
decolonization on the other, and the attainment of full citizenship rights by the
population at large in the newly independent states, brought the rural areas,

where the larger part of the population lived, into the limelight. Their disposition for, or their resistance to, modernization was discussed as were the effects of modernization on the rural population. Central issues became the evaluation of the 'green revolution' and the 'terms of trade', and the accompanying tensions, between the rural and the urban, industrializing sectors. The social questions of the agrarian sector was largely discussed in terms of pre-modern (or 'feudal') versus modern (or capitalist) conditions (or modes of production) and their articulation or intersection. The 'discovery' of the peasant translated into sprouting research in the fields of development economics, rural and political sociology, economic anthropology, and social and economic history.

In anthropology, especially, many scholars experienced the political and social changes as a 'loss' of the traditional subject, the small-scale community or tribe, and a compulsion for resetting of intellectual coordinates. While the 'village community' in agrarian states became a kind of *Ersatz*, generic characteristics of, and interlinkages between, the local communities were sought on the civilization and economic plains (Redfield 1965, Wolf 1966, Shanin 1971). Peasants were treated as a comprehensive social category (or even stratum) to whom some economists even ascribed a distinct, common rationality—that of the ideal typical self-employed peasant—transcending differences of social and cultural context. The revival of the thoughts of A.V. Chayanov are characteristic in this context (Chayanov [1925] 1966; cf. Kerblay 1971; see also the assumption of a distinct mode of production of the 'middle peasant' in Alavi [1965] 1973).

The assumption of a shared condition of (all) peasants was to throughout haunt peasant studies and studies of peasant movements all the more. Attempts to determine (contextually) who (all) comes under this social category remained ambiguous. In a broad sense reference is (made) to a way of livelihood, meaning all those who depend on cultivation, while in a more specific sense the occupant of a family farm is taken as prototypical representative of this category (see recently still Ludden 1999: 74), leaving the problem of how to deal with the different scales and mixtures of self-employment and dependence on hired labour. Some authors therefore shift emphasis to dependency and surplus extraction as a defining criterion (Wolf 1970). Usually no attempt is made to start from the categories used by the people concerned (terms like *kisan* originally being more a kind of translation of 'peasant' than a term of self-definition). The problem with the heterogeneity of peasantries translated into two analytical strategies. On one side one finds various attempts (of different sophistication) to distinguish strata or classes amongst the peasantry (and its superiors or dependants), like landlord, rich, middle and poor peasants, and (landless) agricultural labourers (see Patnaik 1987).

Opposing these, authors who recognize the overlapping of rank criteria and (try to) account for the forms of social consciousness, developed positions which foreground the contextually unifying bonds of solidarity of peasant communities, 'incapable of being broken down into constituent parts' (Chatterjee 1982: 34f; cf. Stokes 1978; see also Omvedt 1993: 115 for the contemporary condition). While Hardiman (1992b: 57) refers in general terms to the whole empirical range of bonds of caste, kinship, religion, and locality, Partha Chatterjee combines a theoretical argument on the concept of community with a reference to circumscribed, village-like entities who exhibit an internally non-egalitarian structure (Chatterjee 1982; 1983; 1988).

Differences in the concept of the peasantry reflect in the type of peasant struggles that is being foregrounded. Three main focuses can be distinguished:

1. Movements which address the 'internal' socio-economic, and sometimes also cultural, tensions amongst those who occupy opposite positions in the rural class structure. Special debates concern the role of the 'middle peasant' (the Marxist version of the family farm model) and the question of the development of a 'rich' or capitalist 'peasantry'. The first debate raised the question of the revolutionary potential of the middle peasant. While authors like Alavi ([1965] 1973) and, in a different way, Wolf (1970) emphasize their initial militancy being owed to their relative economic independence, the thesis is rejected for India by D.N. Dhanagare (1983). Critics like Pouchepadass (1980) and Charlesworth (1980) refer to the heterogeneous and changing character of this social category. Conversely Hardiman (1992b) argues against Stokes (1978) who claims the development of a rich peasantry at the end of the nineteenth century which was going to lead the movements of the early twentieth century.

2. Economic and political struggles against 'outside oppression' (Hardiman 1992b: 57) or 'supravillage exploiters' (Omvedt 1993: 104). Centering on the period 1858–1914, Hardiman distinguishes five chief areas of resistance: peasants against European planters; peasants against indigenous landlords; peasants against professional moneylenders (*sahukars*); peasants against the land-tax bureaucracy; and peasants against forest officials (Hardiman 1992b: 11).

3. Peasant (or farmers') movements as part of an intersecting field of social movements. Omvedt (1993), centring on Maharashtra, points out intersections between peasant and tribal, women's as well as ecological movements in contemporary India. On the other hand, cases have been pointed out in which different dimensions of social struggle are intertwined, as the anti-British, anti-Hindu, and anti-landlord struggle in the case of the Moplah movements which took place in Malabar between 1836 and 1921 (Oommen 1990: 93f).

As yet a comprehensive, overall analysis of Indian peasant movements has not been attempted. An early overview of Indian peasant movements was given by Gough (1974), followed by Shah (1990) and Oommen (1990), while Dhanagare (1983) concentrated on the main movements in a particular period (1920–50). Gough as well as Dhanagare tried to classify peasant movements according to their goals, ideology, and methods of organization. They distinguished five/six different types: nativistic or restorative movements, religious or millenarian movements, social banditry, mass insurrection, terrorism, and (only Dhanagare) liberal reformist agitation (see Gough 1974: 1395; Dhanagare 1983: 214), thereby replicating the perspective of the colonial state. A.R. Desai presented a spectrum of studies of different peasant movements in two compilations (1979 and 1986). The literature on peasant movements often includes movements which others specify as tribal movements.

Peasant movements or agrarian struggles have already been reported for pre-colonial days (Habib 1963). The revolt of 1857 is being considered as a landmark from which also the modern history of peasant movements starts. Eric Stokes has analysed the involvement of peasants in this widespread but fragmented revolt (1978 and 1986). The movements in the period between 1858 and 1914 tended to remain localized, disjointed, and confined to particular grievances (Hardiman 1992b). Well-known are the Bengal revolt of 1859–62 against the indigo plantation system and the 'Deccan riots' of 1875 against moneylenders (see Kumar 1992; Catanach 1992; and Charlesworth 1992). Some of these issues continued into the following period, and under the leadership of Mahatma Gandhi became partially linked to the Independence movement. Studies relate prominently to the Bardoli satyagraha (1928, Surat District), a 'non-tax' campaign as part of the nationwide non-cooperative movement (Dhanagare 1983), the Kheda satyagraha 1917–18, a campaign of refusal to pay land revenue (Hardiman 1981), and the Champaran satyagraha 1917–18 directed against indigo plantations (Pouchepadass 1986). The other prominent case was the Moplah rising in Malabar (1921), a movement of a Muslim peasantry against Hindu upper-caste landlords (Dhanagare 1983; Wood 1992; Arnold 1982b). In the 1920s, protest movements against the forest policies of the British government and local rulers arose in certain regions (see Guha 1989). The period between 1920 and 1940 saw the emergence and consolidation of peasant organizations, the *kisan sabhas*, in many parts of India. The first organization to be founded was the Bihar Provincial Kisan Sabha (1929) and in 1936 the All-India Kisan Sabha came into existence. The peasants organized by the Sabhas demanded freedom from economic exploitation for peasants, workers and all other exploited classes (Das 1983; Gupta 1982). The attainment of Independence was marked by two mass insurrections of politicized peasants which have become classical cases: the Tebhaga movement (1946–7) was a struggle of sharecroppers in Bengal for a two-thirds share of the produce (instead of the customary half); (Sen 1972; Sarkar 1986; Dhanagare 1983) which had the support of the Kisan Sabha and the Communist Party of India (CPI); the Telengana revolt (1946–51) against the feudal conditions in the princely state of Hyderabad was launched by the CPI and became the first large movement with communist leadership (Dhanagare 1983; Custers 1987).

Certain issues which had dominated in colonial times lost their significance in independent India, when land reforms, *zamindari* abolition, declining importance of land revenue, and a public-credit system began to alter rural conditions. The period after 1947 was characterized by two major social movements: The Naxalite struggle and the 'new farmers' movements'. The Naxalite movement started from the region of Naxalbari (1967) when—after the consolidation of the United Left Front government in West Bengal—the pro-Peking CPI(M) initiated forcible land occupations. Agitation subsequently spread to other districts (Midnapur 1969–70, Birbhum 1970–1) and to other parts of India. Oommen has worked out several characterizing factors of the revolt, which differentiated it from earlier movements and contributed to the attention it got amongst scholars and public: its anti-national slant, its declared intention to capture state power, violence against 'class enemies', and its emergence out of intense political factionalism in the left (Oommen 1990; see also Mohanty 1977; Roy 1977; Mukherji 1978). The so-called 'new farmer's movements' began in the 1970s (in Punjab and Tamil Nadu). These movements were regionally organized (largely following the principle of linguistic states), were non-party, and involved farmers rather than peasants ('farmers' are said to be market-involved as both commodity producers and purchasers). The basic ideology of the movement was strongly anti-state and anti-urban. The focus of demand were 'price and related issues' (for example price procurement, remunerative prices, prices for agricultural inputs, taxation, non-repayment of loans). Novel methods of agitation were employed: blocking of roads and rails, refusing politicians and bureaucrats entry to villages, and so on. Scholars agree that the farmers' movements are to be distinguished from the older types of peasant movements. Omvedt (1993) and Brass (1995b) especially argue that from the 1980s onwards the farmers' movements have broadened their agenda and ideology and include environment and women's issues. Therefore they can be seen as a part of the worldwide 'new social movements' which embrace post-material values (see Omvedt 1993; Brass 1995a, 1995b).

The debate on the farmers' movements shows the reappearance of a topic which has accompanied the debate on peasant movements in India since their early days: the question of the new affluent farmer/peasant (Dhanagare 1995). But the 'subordinate sections' (Alexander 1989) in the rural encounter have joined in agrarian movements as well. Alexander (1989) shows in a historical overview how in Kerala and Tamil Nadu (low-caste) labourers were mobilized along caste and later class lines and organized in caste associations (agricultural labour unions).

Research on peasant movements had been started on the frequently emphasized assumption that the subjectivity of the peasants had to be rehabilitated and the rationality of their actions acknowledged (Guha 1983a; Ludden [1985] 1989; Hardiman 1992b). Not only colonial, but also historical writings in the nationalist or Marxist vein have been criticized for making peasant movements an adjunct only of some master narrative—the *Raj*, the Nation, or the People (Guha 1983a, 1983b). In their attempts to rectify this, leading members of the early *Subaltern Studies* group themselves became caught in a conceptual dilemma: exploring the insurgent peasants' 'elementary' logic of action, Guha again tended to emphasize the dependency of the rebel consciousness on the model of those whom it opposes. At the same time Guha and other members of the Subaltern group tried to establish the claim for an originary, non-mediated autonomy of the peasants' tradition of resistance (besides Guha 1983a, 1983b, see Chatterjee 1989; for critique O'Hanlon 1988; Fuchs 1999). On the other hand, authors from this group developed hermeneutical strategies of historical analysis which allowed the circumstantial recovery of fragments of peasants' voices and a reconstruction of local modes of interpretive appropriation of nationalist discourses (Amin 1984; 1995). In a different way, others have tried to retrieve the voices of individual movement participants through personal narratives (Stree Shakti Sanghatana 1989; Custers 1987; and following discussion).

Tribal (Adivasi) Movements

Research on tribal movements commenced in the 1940s and 1950s as a topic in social anthropology. The focus was on the study of so-called 'millenarian cults' in Melanesia, Africa, and North and South America (see Worsley [1957] 1968; Linton 1943). The Indian case was marginal in the anthropological discourse. Worsley mentions with amazement the 'absence of millenarism from Hindu India'—the only millenarian cults among two east Indian tribes being a direct result of the Christian missionaries (Worsley [1957] 1968: 232). The first accounts on tribal movements in India were parts of more general studies on the culture and religion of east Indian tribes (see Roy 1912; 1915; 1928). Systematic research on tribal movements started in the 1940s (Datta 1940; of *Man in India* 1945), but most academic work on this topic came in the 1960s and later (see Fuchs [1965] 1992;

Singh [1966] 1983). With the emergence of the critique of elitist historiography and the development of the concept of 'subalternity' in the early, 1980s, tribal movements became the subject of research in the disciplines of sociology and social history. They were integrated into the larger field of peasant studies and interpreted as a particular form of resistance of the subaltern against dominant classes and castes in a dichotomized society (see *Subaltern Studies* 1982–99).

The categories of 'tribe' as well as '*adivasi*' (original inhabitants) have strong evolutionary as well as racial connotations and can lead to misconceptions. The distinct ways of life of many Indian adivasis as well as their geographical location in mountainous and forested areas often encourages certain common stereotypes: tribes are characterized as autochthonous, isolated, without history, economically and culturally primitive (for a critique see Hardiman 1987b; Devalle 1992; Corbridge 1988). In fact, tribal communities often look back on a history of migration and interaction with other (political) communities and the large majority have been settled agriculturists for centuries, with a complex social order and a rich cultural life. Many tribal villages were regularly visited by merchants and moneylenders, and this contact between tribal and non-tribal groups intensified with colonial subjugation, also recognized as the time when the history of tribal movements, as we know them today, began.

Tribal movements are divided in two (Sachchidananda 1990) or three phases (Singh 1985). The first phase (up to 1855/1860) coincided with the rise, expansion, and establishment of the British empire; the rebellions in those days can be classified as 'defensive' (Sachchidananda 1990) or 'resistance' (Singh 1985) movements. In the second phase (from 1857/1860–1920 according to Singh 1985), colonialism was more deeply entrenched in the tribal areas and the movements shared characteristics of both resistance and revitalization (they included the search for reforms). K.S. Singh mentions a third phase (1920–47) which saw the rise of movements of a 'secular and political nature', that is, participation of tribes in the national movement, and the emergence of separatist movements (see Singh 1985:24). Tribal movements in *colonial India* had a certain peculiarity as they basically represented conflicts between adivasis and the so-called 'outsiders', people who did not belong to the tribal communities but operated as exploiters and masters in tribal areas. These outsiders were not necessarily British—they could be Hindus, Muslims, or Parsees 'who established themselves under the protection of the colonial authorities and took advantage of the new judicial system to deprive the adivasis of large tracts of their land'. (Hardiman 1987b: 15). The tribal movements in the nineteenth and the first half of the twentieth century can be regarded as anti-colonial at their core, but the actions of resistance and revolt were primarily directed against the non-British local exploiters.

Tribal movements have predominantly been located in the so called 'tribal belt' in middle India. Comparatively numerous and well documented are the movements of the Santhal Hos, Oraons, and Mundas in Chota Nagpur and the Santhal Parganas (the region constitutes the main part of what has come to be called *Jharkhand*) (see Jay 1961; Singh [1966] 1983; MacDougall 1985; Sachchidananda 1990). Some of these movements have incorporated elements of Christianity (Birsa Munda 1895–1901) and of the Bhakti tradition (Bhagat movements of the Oraons) into their vision (see Jay 1961; Singh [1966] 1983; Fuchs [1965] 1992). Occasional studies concentrate on tribal movements in Gujarat (Hardiman 1987a; 1987b) and in Andhra Pradesh (Arnold 1982a). Some general overviews try to cover the whole of the tribal movements in (British) India (Fuchs [1965] 1992; Singh 1982–83). There was a relative dearth of social movements among tribes in south India, though this could be a reflection of the absence of research on tribes in this area. The movements of the tribes of north-eastern India (Naga, Bodo, Mizo), which are documented in case studies and referred to in the mentioned overviews, occupy a special position as they developed into armed struggles for political autonomy and separate nationhood, which started in pre-independent India but continued after Independence (Bhattacharji 1996; Misra and Misra 1996).

In many ways the research on tribal movements in British India mirrors the history of academic theorizing on social movements in general. Very roughly one may distinguish three main approaches:

Tribal Movements as Reaction to a Clash of Cultures and Relative Deprivation: The Messianistic Movements

This approach is followed by S. Fuchs ([1965] 1992), who draws on Mühlmann (1961) and Lanternari (1963). Two homogeneous but unequal cultures, one 'rather undeveloped and retarded, the other at least technically vastly superior' (Fuchs [1965] 1992: 2), are seen as abruptly confronted. The members of the marginal culture are said to be emotionally and intellectually incapable of dealing with the new situation. Placed 'in a dilemma' they are seen to develop a feeling of relative deprivation and 'confusion', which leads to 'emotional unrest with certain hysterical symptoms' (Fuchs [1965] 1992: 3). People then begin to search for a solution by imagining a future society in which the present state of deprivation will be fully reversed. This reversal may be based on different ideologies and mechanisms: revivalism, nativism, vitalism, syncretism, eschatologism, and millenarism or chiliasm. Ideology and actions depend heavily on the figure of a charismatic leader, a messiah or prophet, who claims to be the recipient of divine revelations as well as to possess magic powers. The leader often succeeds in establishing new hierarchies and solidarities and challenges the dominating culture, generally by violent measures.

Messianistic movements are seen as characteristic for the colonial encounter. They mark an exceptional situation, triggered of by the clash of cultures and economic and political forces. Although the movements often show a 'revolutionary' character, interpretations and actions of leader and subjects are regarded as 'irrational' and the uprisings necessarily are doomed to failure.

Tribal Movements as Expression of Social Disorganization: The Revitalization Movements

The concept of 'revitalization' presented by Anthony Wallace in 1956 aims to replace the more narrow categorizations of movements as 'messianistic', 'nativistic', or 'reformist' by carving out and naming an underlying uniform process. This concept was adopted in his study of east Indian tribal movements by Edward Jay (1961), who gave the originally more psychologically oriented concept a sociological turn. In Jay's approach society or culture is seen as an organism or system which regularly has to undergo periods of cultural distortion and social disorganization to reach a new equilibrium through an adaptive or acculturative process. Under colonial conditions, the revitalization movements of Indian tribals functioned as 'catalysts of acculturation' and means for the creation of a new moral order, in which elements of the opposing culture were integrated.

In the 'revitalization' concept of Jay, movements are not taken as unusual phenomena but as stage-markers in the process of social dynamics. They are an expression of social conflict which itself is seen as 'functional and organizing' (1961:313). The definition of revitalization movements as 'a deliberate, organized, conscious effort by members of a society to construct a more satisfying culture' (Wallace 1956) suggests that the protagonists of tribal movements, leaders and followers, act in rational ways. As strong emphasis is laid upon group solidarity and social cohesion, a leader—even in an outstanding charismatic role—becomes a personification of the collective subject.

Tribal Movements as Resistance of the 'Subaltern'

A central concern of the Subalternist school of history was to give recognition to the peasant (that is subaltern) as a subject of history. This involved a mode of analysis and writing that would bring out his voice emphasizing the 'rebel consciousness'—its sovereignty, consistency, and logic.

In the context of subaltern studies, tribal movements are looked upon as particular case of peasant movements, because the tribal situation is supposed to reflect the fundamental characteristics of subalternity in prototypical manner.

In his analysis of the Gudem-Rampa risings in Andhra Pradesh David Arnold (1982a) points out that subalternity manifested itself in a dual way in the tribal areas: on the one hand, the tribals were opposed to 'outsiders' who threatened their territory and customary ways of life; and, on the other, they were themselves divided into a local elite with wealth, status and political influence, and 'the other peasantry'.

For the Subalternists, tribal as well as peasant movements originate in social oppositions and cultural conflict. But tribal uprisings affect particular strategies of resistance which are somewhat different from those of peasant insurgencies and have their own rationale. Arnold identifies the religious element as constitutive for the imagination of a new society as well as for social cohesion and solidarity—the crime-as-protest element serving as a gesture of defiance. In his studies of the Devi movement in south Gujarat, David Hardiman (1984) mentions social reform (observing new rules of purity such as temperance, vegetarianism, and cleanliness) as another possible strategy of resistance. Hardiman finds the rationale in the way the adivasis relate to the values of the powerful.

Some authors of the Subaltern school draw attention to the significance of the Gandhian national discourse in the context of tribal movements. Certain aspects of the teachings of the Mahatma (purity and temperance, *khadi*, Ram *Rajya*) as well as national politics (civil disobedience) are discovered as central interpretive and strategic elements in the tribal struggles, which have been reinterpreted by the movement itself in accordance with the tribal situation (Hardiman 1984; Arnold 1982a; Sarkar 1985).

Tribal struggles have changed their character in post-Independence India. Adivasis now express their demands in two different ways, which can be called *tribal politics* and *tribal resistance*. On the one hand, tribals have started to organize in political parties, engage in election politics, and follow the parliamentary path to achieve their goals. The best documented case of tribal politics is the struggle for an autonomous state of Jharkhand (Devalle 1992; Das 1992; Corbridge 1988; Singh 1985). Tribal politics often goes along with an 'invention' or reformulation of tribal identity and tradition, which in the case of Jharkhand is being transformed into a regional identity. These processes have often been brought under the rubric of the term ethnicity (Weiner 1978; Sachchidananda 1990). Tribal politics of this kind is largely urban based. The distance between the 'intellectual-organizer' and the 'rural masses' as well as the fragmentation of political organization has been pointed out in the relevant literature. On the other hand, modern forms of tribal resistance, often mediated by political and/or non-governmental organizations, are particularly directed against attacks on the economic and cultural base of tribal existence. These attacks predominantly occur in the form of ecologically destructive, often large-scale projects, which go along with the appropriation of tribal territories and the eviction of the tribal people from their land—the internationally most-debated and best-documented example being the Narmada (Sardar Sarovar dam) case (Baviskar 1995). It should be added that conflicts over natural resources (land, forest, water) undermining or even terminating so-called traditional forms of life are not restricted to tribal groups alone, other sections of the Indian population are involved in 'struggles for survival' as well (Shiva 1991; Agarwal et al. 1982, Agarwal and Narain 1985). Another noteworthy example of a new form of tribal resistance is the strong participation of the Santhals in the Naxalite movement in different districts of West Bengal (Duyker 1987).

It seems difficult to distinguish tribal resistance from other ways of tribal self-articulation. Many such attempts at self-articulation cannot be classified as *movements* in the narrow sense but these aim to bring specific interests and demands of tribal groups into the public sphere. For example, non-governmental organizations (NGOs) or tribal coordinations have evolved in many areas demanding land rights and access to commons as well as to education and to public resources. They have also protested against atrocities on women and demanded equal access to resources in everyday life (see Rao 1996).

Dalit Movements

Social movements of Dalits show a particular character. They cannot be explained satisfactorily by reference to economic exploitation or political oppression, although these dimensions are of great importance. Class-analytic approaches have been tried on Dalit movements, but have not been successful in accounting for the extra-economic oppressive factors (Gokhale 1993). Alternatively the concept of exploitation was sought to be widened to include forms of dominance and violence beyond class, which finally led to the acknowledgement that the symbolic and cultural sphere, whether '"secondary" to the material base or of equal weight', has a 'logic of its own' (see Omvedt 1994 and 1995). What, furthermore, distinguishes the case of Dalits or 'Untouchables' is the fact that they are always a minority. While adivasis are a minority in relation to the total Indian population, but traditionally not in the regions they inhabit, Dalits are dispersed across the country. While insinuating a comprehensive socio-cultural problematique, 'Dalit', or any other equivalent term, does not connote a unified or homogeneous category. 'Dalit', originally meaning 'broken, ground down', has been taken as a summary term for those groups otherwise designated '(ex-)Untouchables', 'Harijans' or, more technically, 'Scheduled Castes' or 'Depressed Classes.' The Dalit Panthers in Maharashtra, who popularized the term in the early 1970s, had advanced 'Dalit' to forge a coalition of all the oppressed, including workers and women, which never materialized. Of all the generic terms 'Dalit' has received the largest approval amongst those concerned, especially in urban contexts. Yet it is not accepted all over by those for whom the term was primarily designed who still make reference to *jati*.

Dalit movements have set themselves wide and fundamental aims. Their inner motive can be conceived best as a 'struggle for recognition' as fellow human beings (Honneth [1992] 1996; Fuchs 1999). On the one hand, it is a struggle for self-confidence and (space for) self-determination, on the other hand, a struggle for an overhaul of the social system. More particularly, but still in general terms, the target can be described as a struggle for the abolishment of stigmatization (inadequately condensed in the notion of 'untouchability') and of all discriminations derived therefrom or connected with it (atrocities and physical violence, sexual harrassment, forced labour, landlessness, public 'disabilities', and exclusion from certain occupations and certain spaces or from religious congregations).

While situationally the opponents of the Untouchables can be more or less specified—often dominant or higher ranking jatis, landowners, or a particular institution—the overall identification of an adversary of the Dalit struggles is possible only in terms which are ill-defined: be it either 'Brahmanism', or 'Hinduism', or 'the dominant castes at large'. Many social movements of the Dalits therefore combine self-reform with appeals to the state as (the) general addressee or organ of society at large. Many Dalit leaders, like Ambedkar, the eminent spokesman of the Dalit struggle, placed hope in such general developments as democratization and industrialization and in the establishment of a state on secular' principles.

Modern Dalit social movements reached their peak in the first half of the twentieth century. They used the space provided by an emerging, restructured public sphere for regional self-organization and trans-regional networking. In some cases Dalit movements fed upon activities of Christian missionaries and social reform movements, initiated by high-caste individuals (like the Arya Samaj and its *shuddhi* campaign). The design to build an autonomous base of (Dalit) organizations collided with the strategy of 'social uplift' pursued by members of higher-ranking castes who took it as the responsibility of the *savarnas* to make good the wrongs the Untouchables had to suffer and to reform the attitude and behaviour of the non-Dalits. Gandhi in particular took that position. He confronted Ambedkar on the issue of separate representation for Dalits, questioning an independent leadership of their own. With a 'fast unto death' he forced Ambedkar in 1932 in Pune to give up the demand for separate constituencies in the future elections (Poona Pact), an event which was to have a long-lasting impact on the Dalit discourse and harden Ambedkar's attitude towards the Congress and towards Hinduism (see Ambedkar [1945] 1946; [1936/1944] 1989; Zelliot 1972; Nagaraj 1993; Rodrigues 1994).

Dalit social movements, or those Dalit efforts classified as social movements, characteristically at first sought to gain or regain autonomy of cultural and religious expression. All those Dalit movements which made a regional impact were associated with the search for a religious alternative: the emancipation from Hinduism, connected sometimes with attacks on Hindu symbols and Hindu exclusivism, the joining of another creed (especially Christianity or Islam), and often the invention or restoration of a 'distinct' faith, which was based on certain Hinduistic ideas or took off from older *sampradayas* such as the Sri Narayana Dharma Paripalana [SNDP], Ad Dharm, or Satnamipanth. While all these religious options had a strong universalist tinge (SNDP: 'One God, one religion, one caste'), only Ambedkar, who opted for a 'non-Hinduistic' religion of Indian background, that is Buddhism, wanted to transcend the particularism of a community religion by propagating a 'civil religion' or moral proviso for the whole of society (Ambedkar [1950] 1970; [1957] 1974). In this there seems to be a resonance also of John Dewey's idea for a 'secular religion' for democratic society (Fuchs 2001). Recently efforts have been made by Christian Dalits for a 'Dalit theology' which could also learn from Ambedkar's ideas (Massey 1994). The strong presence of a religious dimension in Dalit social movements is an expression of a basic religious transformation, shifting emphasis towards ethics, instrumentality, and the collective and 'active appropriation and construction of religious symbols and worlds views' (Aloysius 1998: 1–2).

The provisions for the Scheduled Castes and Scheduled Tribes in the Indian Constitution, including abolition of untouchability, reservation of seats in parliament, and quotas in educational and administrative institutions, are regarded as a major achievement of Dalit struggles. However, these have also deflected the dimension of social reform and bureaucratized the struggle. A strong symbolic value has been imputed by Dalits to the fact that Ambedkar had been in charge of the drafting committee of the Constitution. The post-Independence Dalit movements used the new democratic platform in different ways. On the one hand, pressure groups within political parties became important and pressed for the demands of the Dalits. Earlier attempts to forge independent political parties such as Ambedkar's to form the Independent Labour Party (1936), followed by the Scheduled Castes Federation SCF (1942), and the Republican Party (1957), had little long-term electoral success. These parties had their centres in Maharashtra. In recent years the emergence of the Bahujan Samaj Party which is now a major player in Uttar Pradesh politics has revived the strategy.

The rising number of atrocities against Dalits has been addressed by civil and human rights activists' actions outside party politics, demanding implementation of education and developmental programmes with a special focus on Dalits. But, above all, after 1969, beginning from Maharashtra and spreading to several south Indian regions, Dalits have found a new language and new rhetorical forms for voicing their concerns. Building on Ambedkar's policies and the new identity provided by Ambedkarite Buddhism, the Dalit Panther movement and the Dalit Sahitya (Dalit Literature) movement have begun to give expression to Dalit experiences of oppression and personal as well as collective quests. The large number of Dalit autobiographies, besides poems and short stories are remarkable expressions of this experience and its political articulations (see Pawar 1978; Dangle 1992).

Corresponding to the changes in Dalit politics, the social science literature *on* Dalit social movements reflects differences and changes in attitude. The early literature of the 1950s and 1960s had incorporated these social movements in the programmatic design of social change and of social modernization. Dalit struggles against their stigmatized identities were discussed in relation to the allegedly ubiquitous tendency towards 'Sanskritization' and its contradictory move, 'westernization' (Srinivas 1962; 1966). Similarly their self-organization for claims over political and economic resources was seen as an example of caste politics and of the modern tendency towards founding of caste associations (Rudolph and Rudolph 1967). These approaches, like the class-analytic approach, did not embrace any specific assertion on behalf of Dalits, but simply incorporated their struggles within the wider processes of change.

Research on Dalit movements really came into its own only with the case-study approach which was followed from the late 1960s onwards and focused on particular, more or less jati-centred movements which combined religious manifestation and political assertion. They usually did not concentrate on a single campaign but pursued the movement career of a collective subject whose identity seemed unquestioned. The historical study by Hardgrave (1969) on the social advancement of the Nadars of Tamil Nadu from the beginning of the nineteenth century can be seen as precursor. M.S.A. Rao, besides others, took up the case of the Izhavas, by label 'toddy tappers' like the Nadars, in Kerala (1979); Juergensmeyer ([1982]1988) the case of the Ad Dharm movement in Punjab in the 1920s and 1930s and its later repercussions; Babb (1972); Dube (1992, 1998); and others the example of the Satnamipanth of Chhattisgarh, who started their movement in the first half of the nineteenth century; and Gooptu (1993) discussed the Adi Hindu movement in UP which too developed in the 1920s. The movements covered most extensively related to the Mahars of Maharashtra, especially the period under Ambedkar and the Dalit Sahitya and Dalit Panther activities after the 1960s (see Zelliot 1969, 1992; Gokhale 1990, 1993; Omvedt 1994). In recent years, around and after Ambedkar's 100th birthday in 1991, not only was a multi-volume edition of his writings and speeches published by the Government of Maharasthra, but broader academic circles began to pay attention to his ideas (Gore 1993; Baxi 1995; Viswanathan 1998: Ch. 7). The journalist Arun Shourie made him the object of a heavy attack (1997). Academically, too, the interest in Ambedkarite Buddhism has being growing (see Sangharakshita 1986; Rodrigues 1993; Narain and Ahir 1994; Queen 1994; Sponberg 1996; Beltz 2001). Only recently, the pre-Ambedkarite Buddhist movement amongst Tamilian Dalits under the leadership of Pandit Iyothee Thass (1845–1914) has been rediscovered (Geetha and Rajadurai 1993, Aloysius 1998). A few authors make attempts to re-situate Dalit movement studies in an overall debate on Dalit projects and visions (Mendelsohn and Vieziany 1998; Michael 1999). In his synopses of the literature on Dalits, Robert Deliège (1999) includes on overview of Dalit-movement research.

The case-study approach brought individual subjects and their actions into focus as well as the significance of a religious hermeneutics. But this approach still tends to construct movements as consistent cases. Dispersed and submerged forms of resistance came to the fore only when a new culturalist perspective was introduced which dealt with the hermeneutics of everyday life and reflected on modalities of agency. This led to the discovery of hidden, subdued voices, as in songs of Untouchable women, and a new attention to the hidden rationale of 'mythical' narratives (origin and explanatory myths) and to the strategies of identity construction and their self-reflexion in everyday as well as ritual interaction and communication (Trawick 1988; Vincentnathan 1993; Menon 1993; Clarke 1998). What one has to face is the often contradictory and ambiguous forms these articulations (necessarily) take, pointing to the tensions in Dalit life (Fuchs 1999). Besides, discourse analytical approaches have been brought to bear upon chief Dalit (religious) texts (Rodrigues 1993). Dalit scholars themselves have started to analyse the state of Dalits and the development of Dalit politics and movements (Guru 1993; Jogdand 1991; Ram 1995; Massey 1995; see also Nagaraj 1993; Ilaiah 1996).

The new culturalist approaches to Dalit social movements and Dalit resistance coincides with some new developments in religious studies. Some of the Bhakti- and *sant* movements (like certain Kabirpanthis) are taken to represent a particular low-caste perspective and counter-hegemonic tradition, and Bhakti saints of allegedly 'Untouchable' background, who are partly disapproved of (like Chokhamela) and partly reaffirmed (like Raidas) in modern Dalit discourses, are being rediscovered (Lorenzen 1987, 1996; Gokhale-Turner 1980; Zelliot 1992).

In political and ideological statements of Dalits since the 1920s a strong tendency to ontologize Dalitness can be detected. Claims for a separate ethnic, and even racial, origin of Dalits as a basis of identity formation have been affirmed. This stands in contrast to attempts by Hindu nationalist groups and parties, normally dominated by upper castes, to draw Dalits into their own fold and even to stifle their attempts at self-assertion (Contursi 1989; Guru 1991).

Women's Movement

As distinct from the other fields of social movements, discussed earlier, the women's movement is self-referential and self-reflexive in a particular way. The contemporary agenda of political agitation against patriarchal structures and male oppression goes along with the academic project of women's studies or feminist studies. To a high degree, the Indian women's movement finds its expression in such writing.

In India, women's studies as a new academic genre began in the early 1970s and consolidated during the UN 'Decade of Women' (1975–85). Although the genre itself can, by no means, be seen as homogeneous, two main strands of literature may be distinguished: studies focusing on the *representation* of contemporary and historical *women's struggles*, and *gender studies* which aim to unmask and challenge gender relations as well as the dominant male perspective in social and historical discourse. At the heart of women's studies one can identify the following core objectives:

i. To uncover the dominant modes of *construction and representation of womanhood*, for example in the context of nineteenth-century reform discourse (Southard 1995; Forbes 1996; Chakravarti 1989; Bagchi 1996), the Gandhian nationalist discourse (Kishwar 1985), and the contemporary discourses on community rights (Mani 1989) and on Hindu nationalism (Basu 1993b).

ii. To reflect on processes of *victimization of women and the denial of subjectivity* (Rajan 1993; Das 1995).

iii. To *represent women as endowed with agency*. This intention plays out in a double way: to conceptualize women today and in history as actors and subjects, and to identify women's resisting spaces or counter-discourses (Kumar 1994).

iv. To *see gender as a structuring principle* in economic and social processes and so to combine the critique of class and caste relations with that of patriarchal structures (Sangari and Vaid 1989; Agarwal 1991).

The main emphasis in the following discussion is on the styles of feminist research on women's struggles on which considerable amount of literature has been generated in recent years. Historical reconstructions try to give a general overview of women's struggles (Forbes 1996; Kumar 1993) or focus on a certain period or region (Omvedt 1986 and 1993; Southard 1995). Representations of particular issues and struggles are to be found in (auto)biographical writings which foreground outstanding women. Examples of this genre of writing are O'Hanlon (1994) on Tarabai Shinde; Kosambi (1988), Bapat (1995), and Chakravarti (1996), all on Pandita Ramabai; and Tharu and Lalita (1991) on women writers. The life-history approach has been used to give voice to the 'ordinary' women involved in a certain struggle (the compilation of Stree Shakti Sanghatana 1989). There are also examples of case studies of an important event which place it in a social and historical context. For instance Basu's study on the contrasting modes of activism in Maharashtra and Bengal (1993a); Custers (1987) and Kannabiran and Lalitha (1989) on the Tebhaga/ Telengana uprisings; Kelkar and Gala (1990) on the Bodh Gaya land struggle. Representations of women's struggle as political statements focus especially on the 'new women's movement' which deploy the concept of women's empowerment. Particularly noteworthy in this area are Bhatt (1999) on SEWA; Kelkar (1992); Omvedt (1980); Kishwar and Vanita (1984); Kumar (1993), as well as various contributions to the women's periodicals *Manushi* and *Samya Shakti* on campaigns concerning rape, dowry murder, and equal land rights.

There is general agreement with regard to the *periodization* of the Indian women's movement. Most authors date the emergence of the women's question back to the beginning of the nineteenth century and connect it with the social-reform movements of this period. The first initiative to change women's roles is usually ascribed to men who were members of Hindu revivalist and reformist organizations like the Brahmo and Arya Samajs (for example Rammohun Roy, I.C. Vidyasagar, S. Dayananda). Linking the reform of women's status with the modernization agenda, the reformers opposed practices like child marriage and spoke up for the remarriage of widows and the education of women. Accordingly, the pioneer women educationists of the first generation (Pandita Ramabai Saraswati, Mataji Tapaswini, D.K. Karve) saw as their main responsibility the founding of schools for girls. The nineteenth-century reform movements redefined the concept of the 'perfect wife' and valorized the 'new' educated woman as the true 'companion' and support for reformist Indian men, who were seeking professional advancement. Despite the emphasis on companionship, women were expected to accept the strict division between the public and private spheres and their own restriction to the latter.

Urban upper- and middle class women began to organize in the late nineteenth and early twentieth centuries and started to build up larger networks. Besides a large number of local ones, three major national women's organizations emerged between 1917 and 1927: the Women's Indian Association

(WIA), the National Council of Women in India (NCWI), and the All India Women's Conference (AIWC). These organizations engaged in campaigns against child marriage and for women's suffrage and equality in civil rights. They were successful in opening up new professions for women belonging to the upper social strata: medicine, teaching, and law. Comparatively rare attention was paid to the situation of working women in the industrial, rural, and domestic sectors.

The social and political activities of women became intensified during the nationalist movement, when they supported the politics of *satyagraha* of M.K. Gandhi and took part in the Non-cooperation campaign and the Civil Disobedience movement. While the nationalist involvement meant that the women's movement was 'drawn out of its upperclass enclave' (Kumar 1993: 81), there is a critical debate on the emancipatory potential of this participation (Forbes 1996; Kishwar 1985).

World War II and the early years of independent India saw a weakening of women's organizations and a marginalization of gender issues. As relations between the Congress and the Muslim League became more and more hostile, communal tensions made themselves felt in the women's organizations; by 1944 nearly all Muslim women had left the AIWC (Kumar 1993: 92). Communist women started to work not only with industrial workers but also with peasants and sharecroppers (Tebhaga and first years of Telengana movement) and with adivasis (Warli movement), and so tried to bridge the urban–rural and the upper–lower class divide. Separate communist women's organizations were founded.

Most scholars divide the women's movement in independent India into two main phases: women's struggle up to 1975 and the 'new' women's movement from 1975 onwards (Omvedt 1986, 1993; Kumar 1993). The first years after Independence were marked by the institutionalization of women's organizations and their political integration, a process which did not remain undisputed. Women from different political camps criticized the bureaucratization and the reformist stance of women's organizations and took up other activities: they were involved in grassroots projects and NGO work, others joined activities led by communist parties. In 1974 *Towards Equality*, a landmark report on the status of women in India, was published. It seriously challenged the commitment of the government to gender. The authors of the report came to the conclusion that the status of women in India had not improved but rather declined and that the majority of Indian women 'are still very far from enjoying the rights and opportunities guaranteed to them by the Constitution'. Undoubtedly, the research data and conclusions of *Towards Equality* had stimulated the emergence of the 'new' women's movement.

By the mid-1970s women's groups sprang up all over India. These groups declared themselves as 'autonomous' and 'feminist' and rapidly built close networks amongst each other. The members were from a middle- and upper-class-caste background and often maintained membership in other political, mostly leftist groups. The real 'new' issue of the contemporary women's movement was the focus on violence. This meant 'to break the silence' (Forbes 1996) and to bring to public attention the humiliation, atrocities, and tortures to which women were subjected. This also included an attack on the family and on social institutions which deprived women of control over their own bodies. The new movements included a radical critique of the virtuous woman as in the 'Ram-Sita-paradigm' (Omvedt) and the image of the self-sacrificing women always devoted to husband and family. Women's groups in different cities and regions of India joined in anti-violence campaigns, especially against dowry deaths, rape, and *sati* (see Kumar 1993). Besides the issue of violence, women engaged in grassroots mobilization in order to improve the situation of poor women. Thus women's NGOs engaged in employment-generation schemes, support of industrial and rural workers' strikes, agitation on property rights, health education, trade unions, credit schemes, and environmental issues. They also tried to propagate these views and to engage in political education through production of literature and audio-visual materials.

The increasing communalization of public life and the issue of 'personal law' (in its meaning of different family laws for different religious communities) has become a new challenge for the women's groups. The case of Shah Bano (1985), a Muslim woman, who fought for the right of maintenance after divorce, brought the tension between secular legislation and differentiated community laws, as well as the question of representation and construction of womenhood, on the agenda. It led to large-scale mobilization of women for reform in family laws.

In recent years women activist-scholars have started to draw attention to the fact that a number of women from upper caste, middle class, and urban backgrounds increasingly commit themselves to the Hindutva ideology and actively support the politics of Hindu nationalist organizations like the Rashtriya Swayamsevak Sangh (RSS), Vishwa Hindu Parishad (VHP), and Bhartiya Janata Party (BJP). Participation in this political fold allows these women belonging to a specific conservative mileu to go beyond a purely domestic and feminine identity. In the context of 'feminist studies', a debate on women's role in Hindu militant nationalism has commenced (Basu 1993a, 1993 and 1999; Bacchetta 1993; Sarkar and Butalia 1995). The participants in this debate have generated important material on the symbolic use of women and of the concept of womanhood within religious nationalism. They have traced the strategies and motivations of the women leaders in pro-Hindutva groups, given biographical accounts on militant women of the RSS women's wing, and reflected on the use of violence in the Hindu nationalist discourse. The BJP has made the raped Hindu woman into a symbol of the victimization of the entire Hindu community, thus ironically paying an indirect tribute to the women's movement (Basu 1993b: 29). The concept of women under the new ideology of Hindutva unites the image of suffering and self-sacrificing women with the image of brave and powerful women 'who use violence if necessary to protect their community' (Basu 1993b: 32).

We suggest the following important conclusions which emerge from the literature on the women's movement in India:

i. The history of the women's movement in India cannot be constructed as a straightforward history of increasing emancipation and equality for women, but has to account for the accompanying process of 'recasting' women. Sangari and Vaid claim that 'the history of feminism in India ... is inseparable from a history of anti-feminism' and suggest a differentiation between the 'modernization of patriarchal modes' and the 'democratization of gender relations' (1989: 19).

ii. To locate patriarchy as the primary contradiction in society has its advantage but its shortcomings as well:

> The strength of this position lies in the fact that it foregrounds patriarchal oppression as existing within all historically known modes of production and as a socio-cultural system cutting across class divisions. Its weakness lies in treating women as a 'class' by themselves, leading to a disregard of the fact that women of the exploited classes may indeed have closer group interests with men of their own classes than with women belonging to the dominant classes [Sangari and Vaid 1989: 23].

In other words, to see the women's movement solely as a struggle against patriarchy and male domination tends to neglect the caste-class-based mechanisms of oppression and of solidarity being at work in the rural as well as urban industrial contexts.

iii. A clear distinction has to be made between a women's movement, centring around women-specific demands, and a social movement in which women are involved together with men (Sen 1990). Ignoring this can result in ascribing a basically feminist content to movements which pursue different objectives, as for example in the eco-feminist interpretation of the Chipko movement proposed by Shiva (1988) which ignores the diversity of issues that have been at stake within the local society in which the Chipko movement emerged.

Social movements have become a core feature of social analysis and have begun to play a central role in an interactionist and 'constructivist' social theory. As a result of this, we may observe the following changes in social theory itself:

— New attempts at social theory have started to put emphasis on the self-instituting capacities of society (Sztompka 1991) and the transformative capacities of the actor (Giddens 1984). The 'creative' side (Joas; 1996) and 'pro-active' (Tilly et al. 1975: 249) of action are foregrounded. Social movements are seen as a privileged social form in which the processes of institution and reconstitution of meaning and of social relationships are being manifested.

— Research on social movements demands a concept of interaction which transcends the micro-analytical level and incorporates the aspect of conflict both at micro and macro levels of society. Social movements are interactively constituted, bringing into play different kinds of solidarities which are coordinated. Being, in principle, non-formal and non-institutional structures, social movements are implicated in a process of constant reconstitution. These social movements become nodal points in the social process of negotiation, debate, and struggle between social adversaries, as well as between and across different moral economies, lifestyles, or discourses.

— The interpretive dimension of social movements, and of contestation and resistance in general, has come into greater prominence. The struggle of social movements in a decisive way is to be seen as a struggle about and by means of representations. Social movements are not only acting upon specific problems, but they have to be seen as themselves interpreting, analysing, and communicating. The actors involved in social movements themselves construct concepts of agency and sociality, albeit in a different language from the social sciences. They thematize the mechanisms and modalities of social exchange and interrelationships. They speak about society, they project new relationships, referring to a social imaginary (Castoriadis 1987). Movements, or different participants in a movement, explicitly or implicitly raise claims of validity. Given these claims, we cannot restrict the analysis of social movements to a critique of ideology or an analytics of frame alignment. The vision of society has to be expanded in response to the pressure generated by the analysis offered by the movements themselves.

There is another aspect, which may assume greater importance in future. Social movements not only relate to their respective (direct) adversaries, but as mentioned in the Introduction, they also appeal to a larger public, that is address a 'general other'. As yet this aspect has received little attention in research on social movements. It has been discussed under the rubric of 'civil society' and with respect to certain situations only. Discussions have foregrounded the relationship between society and state. In the Indian context, Rajni Kothari in the 1980s introduced the notion of a 'non-party political process' (Kothari 1989). Recently the debate on civil society (see J.P.S. Uberoi this volume) has concentrated on the role of 'communities' vis-à-vis the state as well as the individual (Chatterjee [1994] 1998; Sangari 1995; Das 1995; Mahajan 1998; Bhargava et al. 1999; Sheth and Mahajan 1999; Alam 1999). Only few social-movements studies as yet concern themselves with the 'traditional' ideas and mechanisms of mediation, public arbitration and redress, and with the obstruction or breakdown of these mechanisms and conceptions, under conditions of colonial rule and modernization (see Guha 1989).

Research on social movements posits the idea of the social subject, individual as well as collective, whose constitution takes shape in an ex-centric relationship with social identities, representations, and cultural discourse. To frame it in differently: movement research implies the 'non-identity of society with itself' (Arnason 1986). The image of society invoked is not that of a principally integrated and centralized structure, but of shifting centres of activity and power. Social movements presume the ability of actors to reflexively distance themselves from their surroundings, a given social environment, from prevalent representations, as well as from particular roles and current positions (what could be termed self-distanciation). For a future analysis of social movements it would be necessary to address the frictions as well as the modes of linkage and modulation between groups, individuals, and representations (Das 1995; Melucci 1989).

REFERENCES

Aberle, David F. 1966. *The Peyote Religion among the Navaho*. New York: Wenner-Gren Foundation.

Agarwal, Anil, Ravi Chopra, and Kalpana Sharmam, eds. 1982. *The State of India's Environment: The First Citizens' Report*. New Delhi: Center for Science and Environment.

Agarwal, Anil and Sunita Narain, eds. 1985. *The State of India's Environment 1984–85 'The Second Citizens' Report*. New Delhi: Center for Science and Environment.

Agarwal, Bina. 1991. *Engendering the Environment Debate: Lessons from the Indian Subcontinent*. East Lansing, Mich.: Center for Advanced Study of International Development.

Alam, Javeed. 1999. *India: Living with Modernity*. Delhi: Oxford University Press.

Alavi, Hamza. [1965] 1973. 'Peasants and Revolution'. In K. Gough, and H.P. Sharma, eds, *Imperialism and Revolution in South Asia*, 291–337. New York: Monthly Review Press.

Alexander, K.C. 1989. 'Caste Mobilization and Class Consciousness: The Emergence of

Agrarian Movements in Kerala and Tamil Nadu'. In F.R. Frankel and M.S.A. Rao, eds, *Dominance and State Power in Modern India: Decline of a Social Order*, vol. 1: 362–413. Delhi: Oxford University Press.

Aloysius, G. 1998. *Religion as Emancipatory Identity: A Buddhist Movement among the Tamils under Colonialism*. New Delhi: New Age International Publishers.

Ambedkar, Bhimrao Ramji. [1945] 1946. *What Congress and Gandhi Have Done to The Untouchables*. Bombay: Thacker.

_____. [1950] 1970. *Buddha and the Future of His Religion*. Jullundur: Bheem Patrika Publications.

_____. [1957] 1974. *The Buddha and His Dhamma*. Bombay: Siddharth Publication.

_____. [1936/1944] 1989. 'Annihilation of Caste—With a reply to Mahatma Gandhi'. In V. Moon, ed., *Dr Babasaheb Ambedkar: Writings and Speeches*, vol. 1:23–96. Bombay: Education Department, Government of Maharashtra.

Amin, Shahid. 1984. 'Gandhi as Mahatma: Gorakhpur District, Eastern UP, 1921–2'. In R. Guha, ed., *Subaltern Studies III: Writings on South Asian History and Society*, 1–61. Delhi: Oxford University Press.

_____. 1995. *Event, Metaphor, Memory: Chauri Chaura 1922–1992*. Delhi: Oxford University Press.

Arnason, Jóhann P. 1986. 'Culture, Historicity and Power. Reflections on Some Themes in the Work of Alain Touraine'. *Theory, Culture & Society*. 3(3):137–52.

_____. 1988. *Praxis and Interpretation. Sozialphibosophiche Studies*. Frankfurt (Main): Suhrkamp.

Arnold, David. 1982a. 'Rebellious Hillmen: The Gudem-Rampa Risings 1839–1924'. In R. Guha, ed., *Subaltern Studies I: Writings on South Asian History and Society*, 88–142. Delhi: Oxford University Press.

_____. 1982b. 'Islam, the Mapillas and the Peasant Revolt in Malabar'. *The Journal of Peasant Studies*. 9(4):258–64.

_____. 1984. 'Gramsci and Peasant Subalternity in India'. *Journal of Peasant Studies*. 11(4):155–77.

Babb, Lawrence A. 1972. 'The Satnamis—Political Involvement of a Religious Movement'. In J.M. Mahar, ed., *The Untouchables in Contemporary India*, 143–51. Tucson: University of Arizona Press.

Bacchetta, Paola. 1993. 'All Our Goddesses Are Armed. Religion, Resistance, and Revenge in the Life of a Militant Hindu Nationalist Woman'. *Bulletin of Concerned Asian Scholars*. 25(4):38–51.

Bagchi, Jasodhara. 1996. 'Ethnicity and the Empowerment of Women: The Colonial Legacy'. In Kumari Jayawardena and Malathi de Alwis, eds, *Embodied Violence: Communalising Women's Sexuality in South Asia*, 113–25. New Delhi: Kali for Women.

Bapat, Ram. 1995. 'Pandita Ramabai: Faith and Reason in the Shadow of the East and West'. In V. Dalmia and H. Stietencron, eds, *Representing Hinduism: The Construction of Religious Traditions and National Identity*, 224–52. New Delhi: Sage Publications.

Basu, Amrita. 1993a. 'Feminism Inverted: The Real Women and Gendered Imagery of Hindu Nationalism'. *Bulletin of Concerned Asian Scholars*. 25(4):25–36.

Basu, Amrita. 1993b. *Two Faces of Protest: Contrasting Modes of Women's Acivism in India.* Delhi: Oxford University Press.

Baviskar, Amita. 1995. *In the Belly of the River: Tribal Conflicts over Development in the Narmada Valley.* Delhi: Oxford University Press.

Baxi, Upendra. 1995. 'Emancipation as Justice: Babasaheb Ambedkar's Legacy and Vision'. In U. Baxi and B. Parekh, eds, *Crisis and Change in Contemporary India,* 122–49. New Delhi: Sage Publications.

Beltz, Johannas. 2001. *Mahar, Bouddhiste et Dalit. Conversion religiouse et émancipation socio politique dams l'Inde des castes.* Bern: Peter Lang.

Bhargava, Rajeev, Amiya Kumar Bagchi, and R. Sudarshan, eds. 1999. *Multiculturalism, Liberalism and Democracy.* New Delhi: Oxford University Press.

Bhatt, Ela R. 1999. 'Towards the Second Freedom'. In Bharati Ray und Aparna Basu, eds, *From Independence towards Freedom: Indian Women since 1947,* 34–55. Delhi: Oxford University Press.

Bhattacharji, Chandana. 1996. *Ethnicity and Autonomy Movement: Case of Bodo-Kacharis of Assam.* New Delhi: Vikas Publishing House.

Blumer, Herbert. 1939. 'Collective Behaviour'. In R.E. Park, ed., *An Outline of the Principles of Sociology,* 221–80. New York: Barnes & Noble.

_____. 1957. 'Collective Behaviour'. In J.B. Gittler, ed., *Review of Sociology: Analysis of a Decade,* 127–58. New York: John Wiley & Sons.

Brass, Tom, ed. 1995a. *New Farmers' Movements in India.* Ilford, Essex: Frank Cass.

Castoriadis, Cornehims. 1987. *The Imaginary Institution of Society.* Cambridge: Polity.

_____. 1995b. 'Introduction. The New Farmers' Movements in India'. In T. Brass, ed., *New Farmers' Movements in India,* 3–26. Ilford, Essex: Frank Cass.

Catanach, I.J. 1992. 'Agrarian disturbance in Nineteenth-century India'. In D. Mandrian, ed., *Persent Resistence in India 1858–19141,* 184–203. Delhi: Oxford University Press.

Chakravarti, Uma. 1989. 'Whatever Happened to the Vedic Dasi? Orientalism, Nationalism and a Script for the Past'. In K. Sangari and S. Vaid, eds, *Recasting Women: Essays in Colonial History,* 27–87. New Delhi: Kali for Women.

_____. 1996. 'The Myth of "Patriots" and "Traitors". Pandita Ramabhai, Brahmanical Patriarchy and Militant Hindu Nationalism'. In K. Jayawardena and M.D. Alwis, eds, *Embodied Violence. Communalising Women's Sexuality in South Asia,* 190–239. New Delhi: Kali for Women.

Charlesworth, Neil. 1980. 'The "Middle Peasant Thesis" and the Roots of Rural Agitation in India, 1914–1947'. *The Journal of Peasant Studies.* 7(3):259–80.

_____. 1992. 'The Myth of the Deccan Riots of 1875'. In D. Hardiman, ed., *Peasant Resistance in India 1858–1914,* 204–26. Delhi: Oxford University Press.

Chatterjee, Partha. 1982. 'Agrarian Relations and Communalism in Bengal, 1926–1935'. In R. Guha, ed., *Subaltern Studies I. Writings on South Asian History and Society,* 9–38. Delhi: Oxford University Press.

_____. 1983. 'More on Modes of Power and the Peasantry'. In R. Guha, ed., *Subaltern Studies II. Writings on South Asian History and Society,* 311–49. Delhi: Oxford University Press.

_____. 1984. 'Gandhi and the Critique of Civil Society'. In R. Guha, ed., *Subaltern*

Studies III. Writings on South Asian History and Society, 153–95. Delhi: Oxford University Press.

———. 1988: 'For an Indian History of Peasant Struggle'. *Social Scientist*. 16(11):3–17.

———. 1989. 'Caste and Subaltern Consciousness'. In R. Guha, ed., *Subaltern Studies VI: Writings on South Asian History and Society*. 169–209. Delhi: Oxford University Press.

———. [1994] 1998. 'Secularism and Tolerance'. In R. Bhargava, ed., *Secularism and Its Critics*, 345–79. Delhi: Oxford University Press.

Chayanov, A.V. [1925] 1966. *The Theory of Peasant Economy*. Eds Daniel Thorner, Basile Kerblay, and R.E.F. Smith. Homawood Ill.: R.D. Irwin.

Clarke, Santhianathan. 1998. *Dalits and Christianity: Subaltern Religion and Liberation Theology in India*. Delhi: Oxford university Press.

Cohen, Jean L. 1985. 'Strategy or Identity: New Theoretical Paradigms and Contemporary Social Movements'. *Social Research*. 52(4):663–716.

Contursi, Janet A. 1989: 'Militant Hindus and Buddhist Dalits: Hegemony and Resistance in an Indian Slum'. *American Ethnologist*. 16(3):441–56.

Corbridge, Stuart. 1988. 'The Ideology of Tribal Economy and Society. Politics in Jharkhand, 1950–80'. *Modern Asian Studies*. 22(1):1–42.

Culshaw, W.J. and W.G. Archer. 1945. 'The Santal Rebellion'. *Man in India*. 25(4):218–39.

Custers, Peter. 1986. 'Women's Role in the Tebhaga Movement'. *Economic and Political Weekly*. 21(43), (25 October):97–104.

———. 1987. *Women in the Tebhaga Uprising: Rural Poor Women and Revolutionary Leadership (1946–47)*. Calcutta: Nava Prokash.

Dale, Stephen F. 1975. 'The Mappila Outbreak. Ideology and Social Conflict in 19th Century Kerala'. *Journal of Asian Studies*. 35(1).

Dangle, Arjun, ed. 1992. *Poisoned Bread. Translations from Modern Marathi Dalit Literature*. Bombay: Orient Longman.

Das, Arvind. 1983. *Agrarian Unrest and Socio-Economic Change in Bihar, 1900–1980*. Delhi: Manohar Publishers.

Das, Veena. 1995. *Critical Events. An Anthropological Perspective on Contemporary India*. Delhi: Oxford University Press.

Das, Victor. 1992. *Castle over the Graves*. New Delhi: Inter-India Publications.

Datta, K.K. 1940. *The Santal Insurrection*. Calcutta: The University of Calcutta.

Deliège, Robert. 1999. *Les intouchables en Inde*. Paris: Editions Imago.

———. 1999. *The Untouchables of India*. Oxford: Berg.

Desai, A.R., ed. 1979. *Peasant Struggles in India*. Delhi: Oxford University Press.

———. 1986. *Agrarian Struggles in India after Independence*. Delhi: Oxford University Press.

Devalle, Susana B.C. 1992. *Discourses of Ethnicity: Culture and Protest in Jharkhand*. New Delhi: Sage Publications.

Dhanagare, D.N. 1983. *Peasant Movements in India 1920–1950*. Delhi: Oxford University Press.

———. 1995. 'The Class Character and Politics of the Farmers' Movement in Maharashtra During the 1980s'. In T. Brass, ed., *New Farmers' Movements in India*, 72–94. Ilford, Essex: Frank Cass.

Diani, Mario. 1992. 'The Concept of Social Movement'. *The Sociological Review*. 40(1):1–25.

Dube, Saurabh. 1992. 'Myths, Symbols and Community: Satnampanth of Chhattisgarh'. In P. Chatterjee and G. Pandey, eds, *Subaltern Studies VII: Writings on South Asian History and Society*, 121–58. Delhi: Oxford University Press.

_____. 1998. *Untouchable Pasts: Religion, Identity, and Power among a Central Indian Community, 1780–1950*. Albany (NY): State University of New York Press.

Duyker, Edward. 1987. *Tribal Guerillas: The Santals of West Bengal and the Naxalite Movement*. Delhi: Oxford University Press.

Eder, Klaus. 1993. *The New Politics of Class: Social Movements and Cultural Dynamics in Advanced Societies*. London: Sage Publications.

Eisinger, P.K. 1973. 'The Conditions of Protest Behaviour in American Cities'. *American Political Science Review*. 67(1):11–28.

Eyerman, Ron and Andrew Jamison. 1991. *Social Movements: A Cognitive Approach*. Cambridge: Polity.

Forbes, Geraldine. 1996. *The New Cambridge History of India. (IV.2), Women in Modern India*. Cambridge: Cambridge University Press.

Freud, Sigmund. 1955. 'Group Psychology and the Analysis of the Ego'. In J. Strachey, et al., eds, *The Standard Edition of the Complete Psychological Works of Sigmund Freud*, 18:65–143. London: Hogarth.

Fuchs, Martin. 1999. *Kampf um Differenz: Repräsentation, Subjektivität und soziale Bewegungen—Das Beispiel Indien*. Frankfurt am Main: Suhrkamp.

_____. 2000. 'A Religion for Civil Society? Ambedkar's Buddhism, the Dalit Issue and the Imagination of Emergent Possibilities'. In V. Dalmia, M. Christof-Füchsle, and A. Malinar, eds, *Charisma and Canon: Essays on the Religious History of the Indian Subcontinent*, 250–73. Delhi: Oxford University Press.

Fuchs, Stephen. [1965] 1992. *Godmen on the Warpath: A Study of Messianic Movements in India*. New Delhi: Munshiram Manoharlal [Orig.: *Rebellious Prophets: A Study of Messianic Movements in Indian Religions*. London: Asia Publishing House].

Geetha, V. and S.V. Rajadurai. 1993. 'Dalits and Non-Brahmin Consciousness in Colonial Tamil Nadu'. *Economic and Political Weekly*. 28(39):2091–98.

Giddens, Anthony. 1984. *The Constitution of Society: Outline of the Theory of Structuration*. Cambridge: Polity.

Gokhale, Jayashree B. 1990. 'The Evolution of a Counter-ideology: Dalit Consciousness in Maharashtra'. In F.R. Frankel, and M.S.A. Rao, eds, *Dominance and State Power in Modern India: Decline of a Social Order*, 212–77. Delhi: Oxford University Press.

_____. 1993. *From Concessions to Confrontation: The Politics of an Indian Untouchable Community*. Bombay: Popular Prakashan.

Gokhale-Turner, Jayashree B. 1980. '*Bhakti* or *Vidroha*: Continuity and Change in Dalit Sahitya'. *Journal of Asian and African Studies*. 15 (1–2):29–42. Special issue 'Tradition and Modernity in Bhakti Movements'. Ed. Jayant Lele.

Gough, Kathleen. 1974. 'Indian Peasant Uprisings'. *Economic and Political Weekly*. 9:(32–4). (Special number):1391–1412.

Gooptu, Nandini. 1993. 'Caste and Labour: Untouchable Social Movements in Urban Uttar Pradesh in the Early Twentieth Century'. In P. Robb, ed., *Dalit Movements and the Meanings of Labour in India*, 277–98. Delhi: Oxford University Press.

Gore, M.S. 1993. *The Social Context of an Ideology: Ambedkar's Political and Social Thought.* New Delhi: Sage Publications.

Guha, Ramachandra. 1989. *The Unquiet Woods: Ecological Change and Peasant Resistance in the Himalaya.* Delhi: Oxford University Press.

Guha, Ranajit. 1983a. *Elementary Aspects of Peasant Insurgency in Colonial India.* Delhi: Oxford University Press.

———. 1983b. 'The Prose of Counter-insurgency'. In R. Guha, ed., *Subaltern Studies II: Writings on South Asian History and Society,* 1–42. Delhi: Oxford University Press.

Gupta, Rakesh. 1982. *Bihar Peasantry and the Kisan Sabha.* Delhi: People's Publishing House.

Gurr, Ted Robert. 1970. *Why Men Rebel.* Princeton: Princeton University Press.

Guru, Gopal. 1991. 'Hinduisation of Ambedkar in Maharashtra'. *Economic and Political Weekly.* 26(7–16 February):339–41.

———. 1993. 'Dalit Movement in Mainstream Sociology'. *Economic and Political Weekly.* 28(14):3 April. 570–73.

Habib, Irfan. 1963. *The Agrarian System of Mughal India (1556–1707).* London: Asia Publishing House.

Habermas, Jürgen. 1981. *Theorie des kommunikativen Handelns,* (Bd. 1) *Handlungsrationalität und gesellschaftliche Rationalisierung.* (BD. 2) *Zur Kritik der funktionalistischen Vernunft.* Frankfurt/Main: Suhrkamp.

Hardgrave, Robert L. 1969. *The Nadars of Tamiland: The Political Culture of a Community in Change.* Bombay: Oxford University Press.

Hardiman, David. 1981. *Peasant Nationalists of Gujarat: Kheda District 1917–1934.* Delhi: Oxford University Press.

———. 1984. 'Adivasi Assertion in South Gujarat: The Devi Movement of 1922–3'. In R. Guha, ed., *Subaltern Studies III. Writings on South Asian History and Society,* 196–230. Delhi: Oxford University Press.

———. 1987a. 'The Bhils and Shahukars of Eastern Gujarat'. In R. Guha, ed., *Subaltern Studies V. Writings on South Asian History and Society,* 1–54. Delhi: Oxford University Press.

———. 1987b. *The Coming of the Devi. Adivasi Assertion in Western India.* Delhi: Oxford University Press.

———. ed. 1992a. *Peasant Resistance in India 1858–1914.* Delhi: Oxford University Press.

———. 1992b. 'Introduction'. In D. Hardiman, ed., *Peasant Resistance in India 1858–1914,* 1–59. Delhi: Oxford University Press.

Haynes, Douglas and Gyan Prakash, eds. 1991. *Contesting Power: Resistance and Everyday Social Relations in South Asia.* Delhi: Oxford University Press.

Honneth, Axel. [1992] 1996. *The Struggle for Recognition: The Moral Grammar for Social Conflicts.* Cambridge: Mass.: MIT Press.

Ilaiah, Kancha. 1996. *Why I Am Not a Hindu: A Sudra Critique of Hindutva Philosophy, Culture and Political Economy.* Calcutta: Samya.

Jay, Edward. 1961. 'Revitalization Movements in Tribal India'. In L.P. Vidyarthi, ed., *Aspects of Religion in Indian Society,* 282–315. Meerut: Kedar Nath Ram Nath.

Joas, Hans. 1996. *The Creativity of Action.* Cambridge: Polity.

Jogdand, Prahlad Gangaram. 1991. *Dalit Movement in Maharashtra.* New Delhi: Kanak.

Juergensmeyer, Mark. [1982] 1988. *Religious Rebels in the Punjab. The Social Vision of*

Untouchables. Delhi: Ajanta [Orig.: *Religion as Social Vision. The Movement against Untouchability in 20th-Century Punjab*. Berkeley: University of California Press].

Kannabiran, Vasantha and Lalitha, K. 1989. 'The Magic Time. Women in the Telengana People's Struggle'. In K. Sangari, and S. Vaid, eds, *Recasting Women: Essays in Colonial History*, 180–203. New Delhi: Kali for Women.

Kelkar, Govind. 1992. *Violence against Women: Perspectives and Strategies in India*. Shimla/New Delhi: Indian Institute of Advanced Study/Manohar.

Kelkar, Govind and Chetna Gala. 1990. 'The Bodhgaya Land Struggle'. In I. Sen, ed., *A Space within the Struggle. Women's Participation in People's Movements*, 82–110. New Delhi: Kali for Women.

Kerblay, Basil. 1971. 'Chayanov and the Theory of Peasantry as a Specific Type of Economy'. In T. Shanin, ed., *Peasants and Peasant Societies: Selected Readings*, 150–60. Harmondsworth: Penguin.

Kishwar, Madhu. 1985. 'Gandhi on Women'. *Economic and Political Weekly*. 20(40 and 41):1691–702; 1753–758.

Kishwar, Madhu and Ruth Vanita, eds. 1984. *In Search of Answers: Indian Women's Voices from Manushi*. Zed: London.

Klandermans, Bert, Hanspeter Kriesi, and Sidney Tarrow, eds. 1988. *From Structure to Action: Comparing Social Movement Research across Cultures*; JAI: Greenwich (Conn.).

Kosambi, Meera. 1988. 'Women, Emancipation and Equality. Pandita Ramabai's Contribution to Women's Cause'. *Economic and Political Weekly*. 23(44):WS–38.

Kothari, Rajni. 1989. *State against Democracy: In Search of Humane Governance*. Delhi: Ajanta.

Kumar, Nita. ed. 1994. *Women as Subjects. South Asian Histories*. Stree: Calcutta.

Kumar, Radha. 1993. *The History of Doing: An Illustrated Account of Movements for Women's Rights and Feminism in India 1800–1900*. New Delhi: Kali for Women.

Kumar, Ravindra. 1992. 'The Deccan Riots of 1875'. In D. Hardiman, ed., *Peasant Resistance in India*. 1858–1914, 153–83. Delhi: Oxford University Press.

Lanternari, V. 1963. *The Religion of the Opposed: A Study of Modern Messianic Cults*. New York: Knoff.

Le Bon, Gustave. 1897. *The Crowd: A Study of the Popular Mind*. London: T.F. Unwin.

Linton, Ralph. 1943. 'Nativistic Movements'. *American Anthropologist*. 45(1):230–40.

Lorenzen, David N. 1987. 'Traditions of Non-caste Hinduism: The Kabir Panth'. *Contributions to Indian Sociology* (n.s.). 21(2):263–83.

———. ed. 1996. *Bhakti Religion in North India: Community Identity and Political Action*. New Delhi: Manohar Publications.

Ludden, David. [1985] 1989. *Peasant History in South India*. Delhi: Oxford University Press.

———. 1999. *An Agrarian History of South Asia*. Cambridge: Cambridge University Press.

MacDougall, John. 1985. *Land or Religion? The Sardar and Kherwar Movements in Bihar, 1858–95*. New Delhi: Manohar Books.

Mahajan, Gurpreet. 1998. *Identities and Rights: Aspects of Liberal Democracy in India*. Delhi: Oxford University Press.

Man in India. 1945. 25 (Special 'Rebellion' number).

Mani, Lata. 1989. 'Contentious Traditions: The Debate on Sati in Colonial India'. In K. Sangari and S. Vaid, eds, *Recasting Women: Essays in Colonial History*, 88–126. New Delhi: Kali for Women, in association with The Book Review Literary Trust.

Massey, James. ed. 1994. *Indigenous People: Dalits. Dalit Issues in Today's Theological Debate*. Delhi: ISPCK.

_____. 1995. *Dalits in India: Religion as a Source of Bondage or Liberation with Special Reference to Christians*. New Delhi: Manohar Books.

Mayer, Margit 1991. 'Social Movement Research and Social Movement Practice: The US Pattern'. In D. Rucht, ed., *Research on Social Movements: The State of the Art in Western Europe and the USA*, 47–120. Frankfurt (Main) and Boulder (Colorado): Campus and Westview Press.

McAdam, Dough, John D. McCarthy, and Mayer N. Zald. 1988. 'Social Movements'. In N.J. Smelser, ed., *Handbook of Sociology*, 695–737. London: Sage Publications.

Mead, George H. 1984. *Mind, Self, and Society: From the Standpoint of a Social Behaviorist*. Ed. C. Morris (Works of George H. Mead, vol. 1). Chicago: University of Chicago Press.

Mendelsohn, Olivar and Marika Vieziany. 1998. *The Untouchables. Subordination, Poverty and the State in Modern India*. Cambridge: Cambridge University Press.

Melucci, Alberto. 1989. *Nomads of the Present: Social Movements and Individual Needs in Contemporary Society*. London: Hutchinson Radius.

Menon, Dilip M. 1993. 'Intimations of Equality: Shrines and Politics in Malabar, 1900–1924'. In P. Robb, ed., *Dalit Movements and the Meanings of Labour in India*, 245–76. Delhi: Oxford University Press.

Michael, S.M., ed. 1999. *Dalits in Modern India. Visions and Values*. New Delhi: Vistaar.

Misra, Tilottama and Udayon Misra. 1996. 'Movements for Autonomy in India's North-east'. In Sathyamurthy, ed., *Region, Religion, Caste, Gender and Culture in Contemporary India*, 107–44. Delhi: Oxford University Press.

Mohanty, Manoranjan. 1977. *Revolutionary Violence: A Study of the Maoist Movement in India*. New Delhi: Sterling.

Moore, Barrington. 1967. *Social Origins of Dictatorship and Democracy*. London: Allen Lane.

Mühlmann, E. 1961. *Chiliasmus and Nativismus: Studien zu einer Psychologie, Soziologie und historischen Kasuistik der Umsturzbewegungen*. Berlin.

Mukherji, Partha N. 1978. 'Naxalbari Movement and the Peasant Revolt in North Bengal'. In M.S.A. Rao, ed., *Social Movements in India*, Delhi: Manohar.

Nagaraj, D.R. 1993. *The Flaming Feet. A Study of the Dalit Movement in India*. Bangalore: South Forum Press & Institute for Cultural Research and Action (ICRA).

Narain, A.K. and D.C. Ahir, eds. 1994. *Dr Ambedkar, Buddhism and Social Change*. Delhi: B.R. Publishing Corp.

Neidhardt, Friedhelm and Dieter Rucht. 1991. 'The Analysis of Social Movements: The State of the Art and Some Perspectives for Further Research'. In D. Rucht, ed., *Research on Social Movements: The State of the Art in Western Europe and the USA*, 421–64. Frankfurt Main & Boulder (Colorado): Campus & Westview Press.

_____. 1993. 'Auf dem Weg in die 'Bewegungsgesellschaft?' Über die Stabilisierbarkeit sozialer Bewegungen'. *Soziale Welt*. 44(1):304–26.

O'Hanlon, Rosalind. 1988. 'Recovering the Subject, Subaltern Studies and Histories of Resistance in Colonial South Asia'. *Modern Asian Studies*. 22(1):189–224.

_____. 1994. *A Comparison between Women and Men: Tarabai Shinde and the Critique of Gender Relations in Colonial India*. Madras: Oxford University Press.

Olson, Mancur. 1965. *The Logic of Collective Action: Public Goods and the Theory of Groups*. Cambridge (Mass): Harvard University Press.

Omvedt, Gail. 1980. *We Will Smash This Prison! Indian Women in Struggle*. London: Zed.

_____. 1986. *Women in Popular Movements: India and Thailand during the Decade of Women*. Geneva: United Nations Research Institute for Social Development (UNRISD).

_____. 1993. *Reinventing Revolution: New Social Movements and the Socialist Tradition in India*. Armonk (New York): M.E. Sharpe.

_____. 1994. *Dalits and the Democratic Revolution: Dr Ambedkar and the Dalit Movement in Colonial India*, New Delhi: Sage Publications.

_____. 1995. *Dalit Visions: The Anti-Caste Movement and the Construction of an Indian Identity*. New Delhi: Orient Longman.

Oommen, T.K. 1990. *Protest and Change: Studies in Social Movements*. New Delhi: Sage Publications.

Patnaik, Utsa. 1987. *Peasant Class Differentiation: A Study in Method with Reference to Haryana*. Delhi: Oxford University Press.

Park, Robert and Burgess, Ernest. 1921. *Introduction to the Science of Sociology*. Chicago: University of Chicago Press.

Pawar, Daya. 1978. *Balute* (in Marathi), Bombay: Granthali [several translations available, English translation under preparation].

Pouchepadass, Jacques. 1980. 'Peasant Classes in Twentieth Century Agrarian Movements in India'. In E. Hobsbawm, W. Kula, A. Mitra, K.N. Raj and I. Sachs, eds, *Peasants in History: Essays in Honour of Daniel Thorner*, 135–55. Calcutta, Delhi: u.a.: Published for Sameeksha Trust by Oxford University Press.

_____. 1986. *Planteurs et Paysans dans l'Inde Coloniale. L'indigo du Bihar et le Mouvement Gandhien du Champaran (1917–1918)*. Paris: Editions L'Harmattan.

Queen, Christopher S. 1994. 'Ambedkar, Modernity and the Hermeneutics of Buddhist Liberation'. In A.K. Narain and D.C. Ahir, eds, *Dr Ambedkar, Buddhism and Social Change*, 99–122. Delhi: B.R. Publishing Corp.

Raheja, Gloria Goodwin and Ann Grodzins Gold. 1994. *Listen to the Heron's Words: Reimagining Gender and Kinship in North India*. Berkeley: University of California Press.

Rajan, Rajeswari Sunder. 1993. 'The Subject of Sati'. In T. Niranjana, P. Sudhir and V. Dhareshwar, eds, *Interrogating Modernity. Culture and Colonialism in India*, 291–318. Calcutta: Seagull Books.

Ram, Nandu. 1995. *Beyond Ambedkar: Essays on Dalits in India*. New Delhi: Har Anand Publishers.

Rao, Janardhan B. 1996. 'Adivasis in India: Characterization of Transition and Development'. In T.V. Sathyamurthy, ed., *Region, Religion, Caste, Gender and Culture in Contemporary India*, 417–43. Delhi: Oxford University Press.

Rao, M.S.A. ed. 1978/1979. *Social Movements in India*. 2 vols. New Delhi: Manohar Books.

Rao, M.S.A. 1979b. *Social Movements and Social Transformation. A Study of Two Backward Classes Movements in India*. Delhi: Macmillan.

Redfield, Robert. 1965. *The Little Community and Peasant Society and Culture*. Chicago: University of Chicago Press.

Rodrigues, Valerian. 1993. 'Making a Tradition Critical: Ambedkar's Reading of Buddhism'. In P. Robb, ed. *Dalit Movements and the Meanings of Labour in India*, 299–338. Delhi: Oxford University Press.

_____. 1994. 'Between Tradition and Modernity: The Gandhi-Ambedkar Debate'. In A.K. Narain and D.C. Ahir, eds, *Dr Ambedkar, Buddhism and Social Change*, 137–61. Delhi: B.R. Publishing Corp.

Roy, Ashish K. 1977. 'Indian Communist Movement and the Peasantry: An Overview'. *China Report*. 13(6).

Roy, S. 1912. *The Mundas and Their Country*. Calcutta: The City Book Society.

_____. 1915. *The Oraon of Chotanagpur*. Calcutta: The Brahmo-Mission Press.

_____. 1928. *Oraon Religion and Customs*. Calcutta: The Industry Press.

Rucht, Dieter, ed. 1991a. *Research on Social Movements. The State of the Art in Western Europe and the USA*. Frankfurt/Main & Boulder (Colorado): Campus & Westview Press.

_____. 1991b. 'Sociological Theory as a Theory of Social Movements'. In D. Rucht, ed., *Research on Social Movements: The State of the Art in Western Europe and the USA*, 355–84. Frankfurt/Main & Boulder (Colorado): Campus & Westview Press.

_____. 1993. 'Parteien, Verbände und Bewegungen als Systeme politischer Interessenvermittlung'. In O. Niedermayen and R. Stöss, eds, *Stand und Perspektiven der Parteienforschung in Deutschland*, 251–75. Opladen: Westdeustscher Verlag.

_____. 1994. *Modernisierung und neue soziale Bewegungen: Deutschland, Frankreich und USA im Vergleich*. Frankfurt/Main, New York: Campus.

Rudolph, Lloyd I. and Susanne Hoeber Rudolph. 1967. *The Modernity of Tradition: Political Development in India*. Chicago: University of Chicago Press.

Rule, James B. 1989. 'Rationality and Non-rationality in Militant Collective Action'. *Sociological Theory*. 7:145–60.

Runciman, W.C. 1966. *Relative Deprivation and Social Justice*. London: Routledge and Kegan Paul.

Sachchidananda. 1990. 'Pattern of Politico-economic Change among Tribals in Middle India'. In F.R. Frankel and M.S.A. Rao, eds, *Dominance and State Power in Modern India: Decline of a Social Order*, 278–317. Delhi: Oxford University Press.

Sangari, Kumkum. 1995. 'Politics of Diversity. Religious Communities and Multiple Patriarchies'. *Economic and Political Weekly*. 30 (51–52):3287–310 & 3381–89.

Sangari, Kumkum and Vaid, Sudesh. eds, 1989. *Recasting Women: Essays in Colonial History*. New Delhi: Kali for Women.

Sangharakshita. 1986. *Ambedkar and Buddhism*. Glasgow: Windhorse.

Sarkar, Krishnakanta. 1986. 'Kakdwip Peasant Insurrection'. In A.R. Desai, ed., *Agrarian Struggles in India after Independence*, 618–659. Delhi: Oxford University Press.

Sarkar, Tanika. 1985. 'Jitu Santal's Movement in Malda, 1924–1932: A Study in Tribal Protest'. In R. Guha, ed., *Subaltern Studies IV. Writings on South Asian History and Society*, 136–64. Delhi: Oxford University Press.

_____. 1991. 'The Woman as Communal Subject. The Rasthrasevika Samiti and the Ramjanambhoomi Movement'. *Economic and Political Weekly*. 26(35):2057.

_____. 1999. 'Women, Community, and Nation: A Historical Trajectory for Hindu Identity Politics'. In P. Jeffery and A. Basu, eds, *Resisting the Sacred and the Secular: Women's Activism and Politicized Religion in South Asia*, 89–104. New Delhi: Kali for Women.

Sarkar, Tanika and Urvashi Butalia, eds. 1995. *Women and the Hindu Right. A Collection of Essays*. New Delhi: Kali for Women:

Scott, James C. 1976. *The Moral Economy of the Peasant: Rebellion and Subsistence in Southeast Asia*. New Haven: Yale University Press.

Scott, James C. 1985. *Weapons of the Weak: Everyday Forms of Peasant Resistance*. New Haven (Comn.): Yale University Press.

———. 1990. *Domination and the Arts of Resistance: Hidden Transcripts*. New Haven (Comn.): Yale University Press.

Sen, Ilina, ed. 1990. *A Space within the Struggle: Women's Participation in People's Movements*. New Delhi: Kali for Women.

Sen, Sunil, 1972. *Agrarian Struggle in Bengal*. New Delhi: People's Publishing House.

Shah, Ghanshyam. 1990. *Social Movements in India: A Review of the Literature*. New Delhi: Sage Publications.

Shanin, Teodor, ed. 1971. *Peasants and Peasant Societies*. Penguin: Harmondsworth (Middlesex).

Sheth, D.L. and Gurpreet Mahajan, eds. 1999. *Minority Identities and the Nation-state*. Delhi: Oxford University Press.

Shiva, Vandana. 1988. *Staying Alive. Women, Ecology and Survival in India*. New Delhi: Kali for women.

———. 1991. *Ecology and the Politics of Survival: Conflicts over Natural Resources in India*. New Delhi/Tokyo: Sage/United Nations University Press.

Shourie, Arun. 1997. *Worshipping False Gods: Ambedkar, and the Facts Which Have Been Erased*. New Delhi: ASA.

Singh, K.S. ed. 1982/1983. *Tribal Movements in India*. 2 vols. New Delhi: Manohar Books.

———. [1966] 1983. *Birsa Munda and His Movement 1874–1901: A Study of a Millenarian Movement in Chotanagpur*. Calcutta: Oxford University Press [Orig.: *The Dust-Storm and the Hanging Mist: A Study of Birsa Munda and His Movement in Chhotanagpur (1874–1901)*. Calcutta: Firma K.L. Mukhopadhyaya].

———. 1985. *Tribal Society in India: An Anthropo-historical Perspective*. New Delhi: Manohar.

Smelser, Neil. 1962. *Theory of Collective Behavior*. New York: Free Press.

Snow, David A. and Robert D. Benford. 1988. 'Ideology, Frame Resonance, and Participant Mobilization'. In B. Klandermans, H. Kriesi, and S. Tarrow, eds, *From Structure to Action: Comparing Social Movement Research across Cultures*, 197–217. Greenwich (Conn.): JAI.

Southard, Barbara. 1995. *The Women's Movement and Colonial Politics in Bengal: The Quest for Political Rights, Education and Social Reform Legislation, 1921–1936*. New Delhi: Manohar.

Sponberg, Alan. 1996. 'TBMSG: A Dhamma Revolution in Contemporary India'. In C.S. Queen, and S.B. King, eds, *Engaged Buddhism: Buddhist Liberation Movements in Asia*, 73–120. Albany: State University of New York Press.

Srinivas, M.N. 1962. *Caste in Modern India and Other Essays*. London: Asia Publishing House.

———. 1966. *Social Change in Modern India*. Berkeley: University of California Press.

Stree Shakti Sanghatana. 1989. *'We Were Making History. ...': Life Stories of Women in the Telengana People's Struggle*. New Delhi: Kali for Women.

Stokes, Eric. 1978. *The Peasant and the Raj: Studies in Agrarian Society and Peasant Rebellion in Colonial India*. Cambridge: Cambridge University Press.

———. 1986. *The Peasant Armed: The Indian Revolt of 1857*. Oxford: Clarendon.

Subaltern Studies. Writings on South Asian History and Society. Vols 1–10. 1982–99. 1–6 Delhi: Oxford University Press.

Sztompka, Piotr. 1991. *Society in Action. The Theory of Social Becoming*. Cambridge: Polity.

Tarde, Gabriel. [1910] 1922. *L'opinion et la foule*. 4th ed. Paris: Alcan.

Tarrow, S. 1983. *Struggling to Reform: Social Movements and Policy Change during Cycles of Protest*. Cornell University.

_____. 1989. *Struggle, Politics, and Reform: Collective Action, Social Movements, and Cycles of Protest*. Cornell University.

Tharu, Susie and K. Lalita, eds. 1993. *Women Writing in India. 600 BC to the Present*. Delhi: Oxford University Press.

Thompson, Edward P. 1980. 'The Moral Economy of the Eglish Crowd in the 18th Century'. *Past and Present*. 50:76–136.

Tilly, Charles. 1978. *From Mobilization to Revolution*. Reading (Mass.): Addison-Wesley.

Tilly, Charles, Louise Tilly, and Richard Tilly. 1975. *The Rebellious Century, 1830–1930*. Cambridge (Mass.): Harvard University Press.

Touraine Alain. 1976. *Was nützt die Soziologie?* Frankfurt (Main): Suhskamp.

_____. [1978] 1981. *The Voice and the Eye: An Analysis of Social Movements*. Cambridge/Paris: Cambridge University Press/Editions de la Maison des Sciences de l'Homme.

_____. 1995. *Critique of Modernity*. Oxford: Blackwell.

Trawick, Margaret. 1988. 'Spirits and Voices in Tamil Songs'. *American Ethnologist*. 15(2):193–215.

Turner, Ralph H. and Lewis M. Killian. 1957. *Collective Behaviour*. Englewood Cliffs (N.J.): Prentice-Hall.

Vincentnathan, Lynn. 1993. 'Untouchable Concepts of Person and Society'. *Contributions to Indian Sociology*. (n.s.). 27(1):53–82.

Viswanathan, Gauri. 1998. *Outside the Fold Conversions Modernity and Belief*. Delhi: Oxford University Press.

Wallace, Anthony, F. 1956. 'Revitalization Movements'. *American Anthropologist*. 58(2):264–81.

Weiner, Myron. 1978. *Sons of the Soil: Migration and Ethnic Conflict in India*. Princeton, N.J.: University Press.

Wolf, Eric R. 1966. *Peasants*. Englewood Cliffs, N.J.: Prentice-Hall.

_____. 1970. *Peasant Wars in the Twentieth Century*. New York: Harper & Row.

Wood, Conrad. 1992. 'Peasant Revolt. An Interpretation of Moplah Violence in the Nineteenth and Twentieth Centuries'. In D. Hardiman, ed., *Peasant Resistance in India 1858–1914*, 126–52. Delhi: Oxford University Press.

Worsely, Peter. [1957] 1968. *The Trumpet Shall Sound: A Study of 'Cargo' Cults in Melanesia*. London: Paladin.

Zelliot, Eleanor Mae. 1969. 'Dr Ambedkar and the Mahar Movement'. University of Pennsylvania, Ph.D. Thesis.

_____. 1972. 'Gandhi and Ambedkar—a Study in Leadership'. In J.M. Mahar, ed., *The Untouchables in Contemporary India*, 69–95. Tucson: University of Arizona Press.

_____. 1992. *From Untouchable to Dalit: Essays on the Ambedkar Movement*. New Delhi: Manohar Books.

Collective Violence

Jonathan Spencer

Collective violence is an expression used to describe certain specific kinds of violence: the violence of the urban crowd (rather than the violence of the state), and the violence of the public arena (rather than the violence of domestic relations). Although the term appears self-evident and satisfactorily value-free, the boundaries between collective violence and the rule of law, between acts of the crowd and acts of warfare, between the aberrant moment of riot and the 'normal' violence of political life, are by no means as clear-cut as is usually implied. In South Asia, 'collective violence' is now often used interchangeably with the more contentious term 'communal violence'. In both Europe and South Asia, the study of collective violence has until recently been dominated by the work of social and economic historians, and it is only relatively recently that it has returned to the empirical agenda of anthropologists and sociologists. In Europe and North America, the urban disturbances of the 1960s provoked a brief flurry of studies on crowd violence, but interest waned until the collapse of the Soviet empire and the break-up of Yugoslavia reminded Europeans of the continued power of the call to community, ethnos, or nation. In South Asia, anthropologists and sociologists have responded to the disturbing rise in collective violence since the late 1970s with a number of important studies emerging in the 1990s.

This chapter will start with a review of the curious position of violence in classic western social theory, as well as the special place it occupies, with its Gandhian alternative, non-violence, in South Asian political theory. It will then briefly review the comparative evidence on violence and non-violence from social and cultural anthropology, before turning to recent empirical and theoretical work from South Asia in the 1980s and 1990s. In keeping with the so-called crisis of representation in the social sciences, since the 1980s the analysis of violence has been preoccupied in part with the political and moral problems of writing about violence.

Violence and Theory

Collective violence could be said to be the evil twin of the Enlightenment march of Reason. The French Revolution can be remembered for both the apparent triumph of the politics of universal reason and the recognition of the radical political potential of the Parisian crowd. For Marx, violence was famously the 'midwife' involved in the birth of any new social order. For Weber (1948), addressing German students in the revolutionary aftermath of the First World War, violence was the 'decisive means' of modern politics, and the fact that the politician's power was in the last analysis based on the command of force presented one of the key ethical dilemmas of modern politics. For Durkheim, somewhat more abstractly, violence was one of those natural human propensities which required the disciplining of the conscience collective if human community was to function. In all these cases, though, violence was in a curious way treated as a given, a necessary part of the theoretical background, rather than an object itself requiring sustained theoretical attention. The writings of leading theorists of violence, such as the syndicalist Georges Sorel (1950), have been ignored for most of the century. If it is true that Hannah Arendt (1969) and Frantz Fanon (1965), probably the two most important mid-century theorists of violence, have returned to intellectual fashion in the 1990s, their specific suggestions on violence and power are still relatively neglected.

Three moments stand out in what Keane (1996) calls this 'long century of violence' in Europe and North America: the experience of the slaughter in the trenches of the First World War; the Nazi project for a Final Solution; and the dropping of atomic bombs on the Japanese cities of Hiroshima and Nagasaki. All involved complex processes of collective agency and enormous suffering, yet, in an odd way, all have been treated as aberrant or atypical, as temporary departures from the smooth road of normal politics in modern societies. The problems they posed for intellectuals were often transposed into the register of morality and aesthetics and not, again until surprisingly recently, into problems of social and political theory. The analogue in India is obviously the experience of Partition, which, as Gyanendra Pandey has recently argued, has become a site of 'collective amnesia', another aberration or departure from the teleological narratives of the Indian nation (Pandey 1992). If it has taken the rather different theoretical efforts of Michel Foucault (1984) and Zygmunt Baumann (1993) to remind western intellectuals of the complicitous relationship between these moments of extreme violence and the institutional forms of political modernity, it has been the mounting tide of so-called communal violence since the early 1980s that has forced South Asian intellectuals to re-examine the relationship between violence and their own local forms of political modernity.

In this century, the great South Asian contribution to the political theory of violence is, of course, the recognition in Gandhian theory and practice of the political potency of collective non-violent action. This is explicitly invoked as an example in Hannah Arendt's radical argument for a distinction between 'power', which is an effect of collective non-violent action, and its obverse, force, which in its reliance on violence betrays an absence of what she sees as real power (Arendt 1969). Yet the very success of Gandhian political practice in the anti-colonial struggle has generated further complicating distortions. Just as India can be stereotypically represented as the land of non-violence, so too is the story of the nationalist movement told as a teleology of non-violence with no intelligible space left for the moments of collective violence which also formed part of it. Recently, though, it has become apparent that historical and sociological investigations in South Asia require the recognition of the coevality and interdependence of both violence and non-violence (Vidal et al. 1993).

Violence and Anthropology

Just as violence has long been taken to be a sign of the primitive, the savage, or the uncivilized, or alternatively, of the deviant, the individual, and the unsocialized, so anthropology has long been concerned to show that violence obeys rules, is part of culture, and even fulfils certain social functions. Classic functionalist accounts of institutions such as the feud stress that these bind people together, through the shared norms and expectations that participants invoke, even as they appear to divide them. But, despite this well-worn interpretative path, violence retains its capacity to unsettle and disturb.

Theoretically, violence lurks behind many important anthropological conceptions of the human and the social. Violence represents 'natural' drives which society must tame and repress if it is to survive: this broad idea can be found in western political philosophy (classically in Hobbes), as well as in Freudian psychoanalysis, Durkheim's notion of humans as 'homo duplex', and Mauss's implicit argument in his essay on 'The Gift' that gifts are society's means of overcoming the inevitability of war. From these perspectives emerges the linked notion of society, or most often the state, as the monopolist of 'legitimate' violence. The place of violence as a sign of the natural and unsocialized is even more marked in socio-biological arguments about human nature and genetics, such as those employed by Napoleon Chagnon (1983) in the complex controversy about Yanomamo violence in lowland South America. Not surprisingly, such emphases have generated a counter-literature in which ethnographic examples are employed to suggest that peaceful sociability is the 'natural' condition (Howell and Willis 1989).

As a comparative discipline, anthropology's most useful contribution has probably been its documentation of the fact that violence is pre-eminently collective rather than individual, social rather than asocial or anti-social, usually culturally structured, and always culturally interpreted. This was already implicit in functionalist interpretations of violence, but in recent years it has been greatly extended as anthropologists have reported the experience and interpretation of violence from the point of view of (among many others) paramilitaries in Northern Ireland, Indian riot victims, and torture survivors in Sri Lanka. Here the anthropology of violence becomes part of a new anthropology of the body in which the body becomes a privileged site for the inscription of signs of power.

What is more difficult is to escape the assumption that questions about violence are inevitably questions about human nature. Simon Harrison (1989), writing about the Avatips of the Sepik river area of New Guinea, argues that the Avatips distinguish between two types of sociality linked to two different concepts of the person. The unmarked type, so to speak, is one in which everyday social relations are lived in an idiom of peaceful equality; the other type of sociality, encountered in the world of men's politics and men's warfare, is marked by assertion, aggression, and potentially uncontrollable violence. This second type is not, however, treated as a natural property of men, but rather as something which has to be created and sutained in ritual action. In order to perform those acts of violence which warfare requires (and warfare itself is politically necessary if Avatip society is not to descend into entropy), Avatip men have to acquire the capacity to be violent.

Harrison's argument is an excellent example of the way in which cultural accounts of other people's ideas about violence, gender, and personhood can serve to undermine powerful western assumptions about human nature. Such cultural accounts do not, though, clarify any of the definitional confusions in the analysis of violence. Even in societies with an explicit concept which we could translate as 'violence', not all acts involving the deliberate inflicting of physical pain, or marking or damage to another's body are defined as 'violent'. Are sacrifice, circumcision, tattooing, fighting, and biomedical procedures ranging from appendectomy to electro-convulsive therapy, all usefully classifiable as acts of 'violence'? How should we classify acts of witchcraft and sorcery, actions which are clearly *intended* to cause bodily harm, even if we doubt their efficacy? What of attempts to break down such literal assessments of violence, like Bourdieu's (1977) use of the term 'symbolic violence' to refer to acts of coercion which are usually unaccompanied by overt physical violence? One way to imagine an anthropology of violence is to see it as a kind of mapping of the different moral and aesthetic evaluations people in different contexts make of their actions on the bodies of others. Instead of constituting a discrete and self-evident object of study, the broad category of 'violence' seems to contain particularly valuable evidence which can help us explore the links between two connected aspects of human life: what Mauss called the 'techniques of the body'; and the inter-subjective world of signs and communications (1950).

Collective Violence in South Asia

When confronted with events like the anti-Tamil riots in Colombo in July 1983, or the killings of Sikhs in Delhi in the wake of Indira Gandhi's assassination the following year, the immediate reaction is usually to ask, how are these things 'still' possible? But in asking this question we are already treating the events as historically 'normal', however bad, wrong, or anachronistic we may think them to be. The view of history implicit in this reaction is brought out in Pandey's reconstruction of colonial interpretations of 'communal violence':

> The violence of the 'native' has other, specifically Oriental, characteristics. It is a helpless, instinctive violence, it takes the form of 'convulsions' and, in India, these are more often than not related to the centuries' old smouldering fire of sectarian strife. That is all there is to the politics of the indigenous community. That is the Indian past [Pandey 1990: 65].

There are, in fact, two components of this view of communal violence. One is the idea that violence happens in 'convulsions' and is 'helpless' and 'instinctive'; the other attaches these convulsions to certain identities—'communities'—and treats this attachment as 'ancient', 'primordial', or (in a peculiarly inappropriate term favoured by political scientists) 'parochial'.

There is, of course, an alternative tradition in the human sciences. This is the idea, which runs in a line from Marx to Fanon and thence to myriad left-wing commentators, that some violence is a necessary accompaniment of social transformation. In the actions of the 'mob' we may, with a little historical digging, recover the structural necessity of class struggle. The best of this work has greatly enriched our understanding of the moral structure of collective action in Europe and America in the eighteenth and nineteenth centuries. It has, however, tended to concentrate on those kinds of violence—grain riots rather than religious riots, machine breaking rather than lynchings—which fit most readily into the template of putative social revolution. The insights of this strand of Marxist social history have been most successfully applied to South Asian examples by the historian Ranajit Guha (1983) and his colleagues involved in the early volumes of *Subaltern Studies*.

Yet what is usually called communal violence seems particularly ill-suited to this explanatory framework, because its distinguishing feature is rarely the powerless attacking the powerful, or the poor taking on the powers that be. Communal violence, especially in the colonial and immediately post-colonial period, most often involves sections of the urban poor attacking each other. Colonial rulers may have seen the resulting 'disorder' as a challenge to their authority, but only the naive would assume that this meant that those involved actually intended to attack their rulers but somehow got sidetracked into attacking each other. More generally, there is a widespread tendency to confuse economic explanations with rational explanations. The sometimes tortuous search for the material 'reality' behind the appearance of religiously, ethnically, or linguistically based violence too often confuses rationality and rationalization, explanation and explaining away, as if the murder of a family is somehow more intellectually and morally acceptable if it can be shown to be connected to the pursuit of land or business, and is morally more problematic if it is connected to religious or cultural symbols. This is not to deny that economic factors play a part in what are characterized as communal riots, even as religious idioms can be detected in what might be thought to be more straightforwardly economic or political actions. What is most discomfiting, though, is the necessary recognition that similar patterns of order and meaning can be found in collective violence of apparently different provenance, that participants in religious riots are as likely to see their actions as being informed by considerations of morality and justice as participants in grain riots or peasant insurgencies.

One great gain of Marxist approaches to collective action and collective violence has been a successful break from the unthinking condemnation and scapegoating which characterize most immediate reactions to crowd violence. The moral intensity of the search for scapegoats has the effect of separating these events off from the processes of 'normal' politics. In 1983, the Sri Lankan government took refuge in a version of events which blamed the anti-Tamil riots on a coterie of left-wing conspirators who were allegedly exploiting the people's sensitivity to the threat of separatism in order to destabilize the regime. Many of the affected Tamils, and not a few left-liberal Sinhala, took comfort in an alternative explanation which heaped all the blame at the door of elements of the ruling United National Party (UNP), who were widely believed to have been prominent in the more overtly 'organized' episodes of the violence. The UNP may well have been involved in the July violence (as sections of the Congress Party were alleged to have been prominent in Delhi the following year), but this in itself 'explains' nothing; it merely indicates that any adequate explanation has to treat the violence of the riots as one moment in a longer political process. This requires us to look more broadly at violence and power in South Asian political systems, especially the 'normal' use of violence by agents of the state, and at the fuzzy borderline between state and civil society, private violence and official violence (Brass 1997).

Morality is, however, important in analysing these events. As was long ago pointed out in two classic studies of European riots (Davis [1973] 1975; Thompson 1971), crowds seem to obey moral imperatives of their own and their violence is often structured in terms of 'legitimate' targets and appropriate punishments. In the case of riots studied by Davis and Thompson these targets and punishments were structured according to values which are widely accepted within the community. In early modern France, Protestants excelled in the destruction of religious objects and religious property, while Catholics were more prone to attack the persons of their religious opponents; Protestants were interested in exhuming the bones of those venerated by Catholics, but Catholics were more concerned with the desecration of Protestant corpses. Ideas of justice were prominent in French religious riots as in English grain riots. But the morality which the crowd sought to impose seems not to have been based on the new heaven of a transformed society. Rather, it invoked a retrospective vision of a world restored to its proper order, where the sinner has been punished and the righteous are left free to go about their business.

Recent violence in South Asia seems also to have been motivated by similar ideas of justice and morality, 'legitimate' targets and appropriate punishments. In Delhi in 1984 these targets were Sikh men and their punishment was not merely death, but death administered in a particular, stylized way: Sikhs caught by the crowds had their skulls cracked and were then burnt. In Colombo, and elsewhere in Sri Lanka in 1983, the appropriate punishment seems to have been the destruction of Tamil property; killing seems to have been mostly reserved for those Tamils (mis)identified as members of the separatist Tigers. Again the killings employed a distinctive repertoire of violence: stabbing and burning were the favoured modes of destruction for those the crowd identified as Tigers. However uncomfortable it may make us feel, we need to confront the possibility that some of these actions may, for those taking part, be interpretable as extensions of 'everyday forms of resistance', even though the source of injustice in this case is defined in religious or ethnic, rather than class, terms.

As Charles Tilly points out, 'at any point in time, the repertoire of collective actions available to a population is surprisingly limited' (Tilly 1978: 151). The evidence suggests that riots are—perhaps not so surprisingly—informed by many of the same values that inform everyday life. This is not to say that Delhi Hindus or Colombo Buddhists go about their daily business wracked with the idea of death and mutilation. But those—generally quite small—sections of the population which actively participate in riots seem to do so in the belief that they are acting morally, imposing a justice which the official organs of the state cannot or will not impose. In doing this, they seem able to invert the most obvious interpretation of their actions: Sinhala rioters seem to have believed they were acting in their own defence when they killed innocent Tamils in 1983, and the few police cases that followed the Delhi riots mention self-defence as the motive for the killings. What the crowd was doing to Sikhs and Tamils was what the crowd believed Sikhs and Tamils were doing, or going to do, to them.

Crowds and Perception

We are, in this context, severely constrained by the shortage of evidence on the ideas and explanations of the rioters, the social composition of the crowds, and the central organizing symbols for their actions. But we do have some evidence concerning what we could call the collective context of collective violence. Violence and disorder have the capacity to create their own characteristic forms of inter-subjectivity. We know this form of inter-subjectivity as it reaches us in the shape of 'rumours'. The crowd usually knows these 'rumours' as 'facts' and acts upon them. In Colombo in 1983 people believed a Tiger attack on the city was imminent. The Tigers, it was said, had travelled from Jaffna, hanging on the undersides of trains, or moving by road wearing military uniforms under the robes of Catholic priests. Tamils who made any display of resistance to the actions of the crowds found themselves identified as 'Tigers' and liable to be murdered. As in earlier riots, there were constant rumours of an attack on the Temple of the Tooth in Kandy. (In 1915 rumours of an army of Muslims making its way up to Kandy from the coast were sufficiently convincing to persuade the colonial authorities to turn out the militia to meet them in several towns.) The rumours inverted what was actually happening. The Tamils were treated as the 'real' aggressors; the response of the crowd was merely self-defence. In some cases the security forces also attacked Tamil civilians, apparently convinced that by doing so they were attacking Tigers.

Similarly in Delhi in 1984, the roles were inverted in the crowd's perception of the situation: the Sikhs who were being attacked were the 'real' aggressors, and recurring rumours supported this view of the situation. What is striking about these rumours to an observer is the tenacity with which people hold them to be true; the collective interpretation, propagated and developed within the crowd, has the power to override the evidence of the witness's own eyes and ears. Again, this evidence from South Asian violence in the 1980s connects to historical reconstructions of the place of rumour in violent disturbance, both in South Asia (Guha 1983) and elsewhere. In the case of communal violence in the 1980s, though, one can no longer simply celebrate rumour as the idiom of the subaltern of marginal.

Confronted with evidence like this, what we seem to need is an adequate theory of the crowd. The theory we need has to be a theory of collective psychology. 'Collective' because this experience of the crowd is the same experience that is at the heart of Durkheim's description of collective effervescence. 'Psychology' because what needs explaining is what it is about these circumstances that predisposes people to accept certain representations as real and true, either in the absence of immediate empirical evidence or, in many cases, in direct contradiction to what they see around them. Nor is it simply a matter of perception; the actions of people in crowds can include inversions of 'normal' behaviour, inversions which range from grown men crying on football terraces to small groups of killers acting out collective fantasies of hell and punishment (which is one way in which we can interpret the killings in Sri Lanka in 1983).

The psychoanalyst Sudhir Kakar has described some of the psychological processes which may underlie the actions of crowds. The ethnic 'other', he suggests, acts as a container for 'one's disavowed aspects' (Kakar 1990: 137). Muslims, for example, become the medium through which Hindus can represent aspects of themselves—particularly in the area of aggression and physical violence—which they cannot openly acknowledge. Crowds—whether gathered for religious purposes or assembled for attack on some other rival group—share the capacity for what he calls 'self-transcendence' and this 'self-transcendence' may then manifest itself either in acts of demonic violence or displays of loving self-sacrifice, depending on the structure of the situation itself. Kakar's conclusion is apparently pessimistic: the possibility of acts of violence and destruction is rooted in our unconscious sense of self and is always liable to erupt in the particular conditions of mass action. It is, therefore, foolish to imagine that we can ever rid ourselves of the threat of ethnic violence; instead, we should concentrate on ways of managing the processes which underlie it.

The main problem with this analysis is Kakar's use of an extremely broad brush. Veena Das stresses that we should not treat all crowds as the same—in particular, we need to investigate the difference between violent and non-violent crowds; non-violent crowds 'who, following Gandhian techniques, are willing to allow their own bodies to be violated, and, conversely, violent crowds who must inflict pain and injury upon surrogate victims in order to be avenged' (1990: 28). We could expand this further. There are the crowds who participate in secular, ludic celebrations of identity—mass sporting events—as well as those who participate in religious festivals; these crowds, as we all know, contain the potential for violence and destruction, but it is nevertheless striking how little this potential is realized. Ritual displays of aggression are more often than not quite sufficient; what Kakar characterizes as 'actual physical violence and destruction' is the exception rather than the rule. When exceptions do occur, they require a more nuanced explanation of their precise causes, although such explanation will have to touch on the psychological processes which Kakar describes.

It is significant that the Sri Lankan anthropologist, Stanley Tambiah, ends his survey of collective violence in South Asia (1996) with a reconsideration of both the turn-of-the-century crowd psychology of Gustave Le Bon, and of Durkheim's ideas about the birth of the sacred in the heightened experience of collective action. But as a consideration of the political context of Le Bon's work should remind us, 'the crowd' itself is a complex representation which serves to personalize, demonize, and homogenize the agents and practices of violence. In fact, local research shows that the spatial distribution of collective violence is anything but homogeneous, as neighbouring areas within the same city suffer quite different levels of violence at the same time. To understand this statistical irregularity, we need specifically to reconstruct the work of political agents and often extremely local, social and political contexts. To the extent that the notion of 'the crowd' glosses over these particularities, it is a hindrance to understanding collective violence (Das 1996).

Violence, the State, and Normal Politics

In the discussion so far, it has been convenient to isolate some kind of collective meta-agent—called 'the crowd'—as our object of concern. In fact, though, we know that rumours and misapprehensions are not confined to participants in collective action, rumours circulate all the time. It is just that they reach a special intensity in particular circumstances. The presence on the street of crowds is not necessarily the causal factor in the dissemination of collective misinterpretations, but is perhaps better viewed as a symptom of some more pervasive cause. The rumours which circulated in Colombo in 1983 and Delhi in 1984 drew on pre-existing stereotypes about Tamils and Sikhs and provided a plausible interpretation of what must otherwise have been a threateningly disorientating time. They can only be interpreted and understood if we treat these 'organizing images', as Das (1990) describes them, as the products of everyday concerns, heightened and distorted by extraordinary circumstances. We need, then, to attempt a more precise delineation of the circumstances which predispose people to accept apparently absurd misrepresentations of what is actually happening. In the past, collective violence was often associated with festivities thought to be periods of ordered licence. Now as often as not they are tied to the events of national political history; the violence following Indira Gandhi's death can be treated as a feature 'of the more general inversion of order which prevails to mark the passing away of a great leader'. Local arguments become transmuted as they are reinterpreted in the terms of national political differences; national political events become the occasion for local disturbances. Sometimes there is a coincidence of both markers of disorder: in Sri Lanka in 1983 (and earlier in 1981) violence broke out in response to news of killings by the Tigers in the north, news which coincided with the time of the Buddhist full-moon holiday.

The evidence reviewed so far throws into question a number of customary responses to collective violence: far from being an irruption of unreasoning pre-social passions, it seems to display not merely a logic, but a logic which is both moral and collective. So the interpretation of the actions of crowds and the symbols and rumours around which they organize can tell us something about how collective violence takes its particular form in South Asia. But it seems unlikely that it can tell us why it occurs at some times rather than others. For that we need to reinsert our category of 'collective disorder' back into the flow of 'normal' political time. Moments of violence are not discontinuous, isolated from the processes of 'normal' politics, and there is much recent evidence from which to question the complacent political distinction between the 'legitimate' violence of the state and the brutality of the crowd. In general, the pattern is the same as we find in Europe: 'repressive forces are themselves the most consistent initiators and performers of collective violence' (Tilly 1978: 177). Again this needs to be interpreted in the context of 'normal' politics in post-colonial South Asia. In Sri Lanka, for example, the police have long been known to be a source of brutality, and from the inception of universal suffrage in 1931 electoral politics has been marked by the selective use of violence and intimidation. But there has, nevertheless, been an escalation in the level of political violence since the 1960s, much as there appears to have been in India. In the months before the 1983 riots in Sri Lanka, groups of government supporters publicly beat up prominent opponents and even tried to intimidate high-court judges. For many observers who were in the country at the time, the riots themselves seemed a logical continuation of the steady growth of 'semi-official' violence over the preceding decade. In Sri Lanka, political use of 'official' and 'semi-official' violence over the decade that followed the UNP's accession to power in 1977 created a situation in which a generation of young people came to believe that the only valid idiom of protest was the same idiom used by the powers that be. The result was the spiral of terror and counter-terror that followed the arrival of the Indian Peace Keeping Force in 1987 and the violent opposition to its arrival led by the Janata Vimukti Peramuna (JVP). There is no sensible way in which we can tell the story of the 1983 riots without referring to the broader use of violence by both the state and its political opponents, both before and after the riots.

The most impressive attempt to construct a full political context for acts of collective violence is Paul Brass's *Theft of an Idol* (1997). This book, based on very rich, long-term field data from UP, analyses the politics of violence in terms of circulating discourses of violence. Why do some acts of violence become politically significant, and other, equally shocking, ones go unnoticed? How is it that some violent clashes become known more widely as 'communal', even when there is little or no 'communal' component at the original moment of conflict? Brass deals with these issues through an uneasy mixture of Foucaultian, and more conventional political scientific, theorizing. Perhaps the most compelling feature of Brass's study, though, is his description of the place of violence in 'normal' political and social relations in rural north India:

> [T]here is no law and order in the countryside. Rather there are sets of forces operating in pursuit of their own interests, which include *dacoits*, police, villagers who belong to distinct castes and communities, and politicians. These forces do not operate on opposite sides of a dichotomous boundary separating the mechanisms of law and order from those of criminals, but are integrated in relationships in which criminal actions bring some or all of them into play with unpredictable results. In this context, a criminal act does not necessarily or even likely lead to a police investigation, a report, the filing of a case, pursuit of the criminals, and their being hauled up before a court. Rather, it provides an occasion for the testing of relationships and alliances or for the forming of new ones. In the ensuing encounters, force and violence are always a possibility [Brass 1997: 75].

Just as a concern with 'the crowd' may occlude our grasp of the local politics of violence, so a concern with the intense moment of collective, or communal, violence can distract our analytic gaze from the high incidence of violence in everyday encounters with the state in much of rural South Asia.

In an important study of Hindu–Muslim violence in Hyderabad in 1990, Sudhir Kakar (1996) has presented some remarkable evidence on the world of the perpetrators of collective violence. In particular, he describes his meetings with two well-known leaders of urban violence—one Hindu, one

Muslim. Although Kakar is concerned with analysing the personality type of the men of violence, his description allows us to glimpse important factors in the socio-political context of contemporary violence. Both men are known to the police for their alleged involvement in acts of violence and intimidation; both have roots in the world of traditional wrestling, and their public personas as men of violence and influence combine old and new concerns about leadership, community, and the cultivation of the male body; and both talk openly about their role in previous Hindu–Muslim disturbances. What is most striking, though, are the telling glimpses of the political milieu in which Kakar's 'warriors' emerge and flourish—a world of dubious property deals and rough politics, in which the roles of police and criminal can be combined or reversed, and in which citizens in pursuit of 'justice' rarely have much confidence in the official procedures of the state and turn instead to local political bosses and their violent enforcers.

In other words, understanding collective violence in South Asia requires an understanding of the political circumstances which make such violence possible. This includes the exploitation of symbols of identity and fears of the other by local and national politicians, as well as the place of violence in the pattern of 'normal' politics and the tolerance of high levels of violence by official agencies. But it also requires a complementary understanding of the symbols, organization, and culture of the crowd, or of the participants, that I pointed to in the earlier discussion.

Language, Narrative, and Reflexivity

Some of the most original and impressive recent analysis of collective violence is contained in the final section of Veena Das's *Mirrors of Violence* (1990) in which Amrit Srinivasan, Valli Kanapathipillai, and Veena Das record and interpret the voices of the survivors of the Colombo and Delhi riots. The strengths of these analyses are the strengths of classic ethnography: clear documentation allied to theoretical sophistication and sensitive interpretation, voices recorded and situated in their social, cultural, and political contexts. But this work differs in one crucial respect from the usual work of the ethnographer—it is explicitly therapeutic. The people whose voices are recorded demanded that their testimony be transcribed and preserved. The title of Das's chapter is taken from one survivor's remark to a visiting academic: 'It is our work to cry and your work to listen.'

Reading the survivors' stories is often harrowing and often moving. Kanapathipillai reproduces the terrifying first-hand account of a middle-aged schoolteacher, locked into a room in her own house with her children while Sinhala men try to break down the door. Das starts her chapter with the impossibly sad case of a woman called Shanti who lost her husband and three sons in the Delhi violence; racked with guilt at her failure to protect her children, Shanti eventually commits suicide; she was the only survivor from her colony to do this. Yet the authors do not merely record the testimony of the witnesses, they also describe the processes by which those affected tried to piece together a world which had been turned upside down and transformed into a scene of terror. There are differences in the reactions of men and women, adults and children, the middle class Tamil whose voices are heard in Kanapathipillai's article. The family emerges as a crucial mediating institution—a source of strength for the Tamils, but also a source of friction for the widowed Sikh women. The experience of violence was also gendered—in Delhi the killers singled out Sikh males and the surviving women found themselves dealing with new, unfamiliar areas of life, lawyers, bureaucrats, and civil rights' activists.

These analyses bring out what has become a major theme of the work of the 1990s—the problems of narrative, representation, and reflexivity involved in writing about violence. In her chapter, Srinivasan talks of the 'epistemic space' of the survivor, a space which mediates between 'life and death, chaos and order, speech and silence' (Srinivasan 1990: 307). In recording the testimony of survivors it seemed best to 'keep lay perceptions and understandings of the collective crisis free of exogenous theory' (Srinivasan 1990: 310). Das also writes about the need to avoid a titillating or voyeuristic style in writing about the experience of survivors. For her, the survivor's record is particularly important because it can show us how suffering 'may be transformed into redemption'; the survivor carries 'the responsibility of creating a reflexive understanding of our situation and our times' (Das 1990: 33–4).

One common experience, of course, is the survivors' demand that their sufferings and injustice are recorded and publicized by the observer. Given the potency of memories of past violence in the motivation of present and future violence, there is an understandable pressure to suppress or play down the testimony of those who have suffered more recently. Moreover, as the discussion of rumour should have made clear, the issue of memory is not at all straightforward. Kakar starts his account of riots (1996) with his memories of the violence of Partition, memories dominated by the horrific eye-witness accounts told by members of his immediate family. Then, disarmingly, he confesses to the reader that he is now unable to sort out what he 'really' saw as a child from the morass of stories, second-hand accounts, rumours, and fantasies that circulated at the time of the violence. He, like other recent writers confesses to being forced to adopt a more personal, less 'objective' tone than might be considered normal or desirable for a social scientist. Valentine Daniel introduces further complexities in his study of the impact of violence on Tamils from the hill country of Sri Lanka (Daniel 1996). He starts his book with the issue of how to write about violence without prurience, to write an 'ethnography' rather than a 'pornography' of violence. Later he describes how during an interview the same woman, describing her father's brutal death at the hands of the security forces, pleaded with him to 'tell the world' exactly what had happened, then later beseeched him not to let anyone know the indignities and shame he had suffered. Daniel uses this moment of powerful ambivalence as the key to meditation on both the necessity and the impossibility of documentation, on the need to challenge the prevailing 'master narrative' of violence, and, perhaps even more radically on the need to realize that even the 'master narrative' was plural and evanescent.

Daniel is not alone in his predicament. Brass (1997) swings between a Foucaultian concern with discourses of violence and a much more conventional urge to establish 'what really happened'. This urge to document, to construct an authoritative version of what happened, is by no means confined to modern social scientists. Colonial officials often conducted enquiries and published reports, seeking to impose narrative coherence on the world of rumour and real or imagined atrocity. The practice has been continued, some of the time at least, by the post-colonial state, although the reports have been read with increased cynicism as the involvement of politicians and police gets quietly swept under the official carpet. Since the early 1980s, there has been a growing trend for groups of academics and activists to visit areas affected by violence in order to compose their own, more independent and trustworthy, reports. In an important article reflecting on his experience as a member of one such team, Gyanendra Pandey acknowledges the impossibility of this task:

> Violence produces the necessity of evidence gathering, of uncovering hidden processes and contradictions that we might normally prefer to ignore, but violence also wipes out 'evidence' and even, to a large extent, the possibility of collecting it in a manner and form that is deemed acceptable by today's social sciences [1992: 35].

In Pandey's expereince volunteers became aware of a sense of rehearsal, or the recitation of 'official versions' of the experience of violence, from the victims they interviewed. There were pressures to create a questionable balance by including stories of violence on 'both sides', although all the evidence suggested that the violence was overwhelmingly directed against one community, and so on.

Pandey reaches two main conclusions. The first is the need to identify and challenge the unspoken assumptions about the nation-state and the teleology of the nation which can be shown to structure much writing about collective violence in post-colonial South Asia. The second is a plea to recognize the necessary limits, the provisionality, of social scientific analyses of collective violence. Both points are explored in telling detail in Shahid Amin's *Event, Metaphor, Memory* (1995). This work focuses on a moment of collective violence—the attack on the north Indian police station of Chauri Chaura by a group of Gandhian volunteers in 1922 in which twenty-three policemen were killed—and combines oral history with archival reconstruction to remarkable effect. Amin demonstrates how the procedures of the colonial legal system produced one, highly tendentious, offical version of the event, even as the shocked reactions of Gandhi and other Congress officials produced another. But Amin discovered that even local memory could not be relied upon to produce a more authoritative account of what had actually happened: sometimes details that were 'remembered' could be shown to be factually 'wrong', at other times the broad shape of memory had been clearly influenced by the later importance of the event as nationalist metaphor.

Given the seriousness of the problem of collective violence in post-colonial South Asia, it would be quite understandable for the reader to express some impatience and dissatisfaction at articles such as mine. Is it not typical of the times, it could be asked, for academics to indulge in fashionably post-modern exercises in deconstruction when what is required is some robust combination of fact and explanation? This criticism would, though, be misplaced. If the important work of the 1980s and 1990s on collective violence has demonstrated one thing, it is the representational potency of violence, or stories about violence, as signs or tokens in the everyday politics of community and exclusion. Tales of who-did-what-to-whom do not merely circulate within communities, to a very great extent they are instrumental in creating those communities. Striking examples of this process can be found in the symbolism of martyrdom among both Sikh and Tamil militants: the suicide bomber who dies in pursuit of a separate state for Sri Lankan Tamils thereby binds the survivors more closely to that ideal with a combination of grief and guilt. Sociologists and anthropologists know far more about all aspects of collective violence than they did in the 1960s or 1970s. Not least, some are now acknowledging that the best critical response to the place of violence in the certainties of communal rhetoric is a careful and sober reminder of our uncertainty, of the necessary limits of our knowledge of complex social and political phenomena.

REFERENCES

Amin, S. 1995. *Event, Metaphor, Memory: Chauri Chaura 1922–1992.* Delhi: Oxford University Press

Arendt, H. 1969. *On Violence.* New York: Harcourt, Brace and World.

Baumann, Zygmunt. 1993. *Modernity and the Holocaust.* Oxford: Polity.

Bourdieu, P. 1977. *Outline of a Theory of Practice.* Cambridge: Cambridge University Press.

Brass, P. 1997. *Theft of an Idol: Text and Context in the Representation of Collective Violence*. Princeton: Princeton University Press.

Chagnon, N. 1983. *Yanomamo: The Fierce People*. New York: Holt Rinehart and Winston.

Daniel, E.V. 1996. *Charred Lullabies: Chapters in an Anthropography of Violence*. Princeton: Princeton University Press

Das, V., ed. 1990. *Mirrors of Violence: Communities, Riots and Survivors in South Asia*. Delhi: Oxford University Press.

———. 1996. 'The Spatialization of Violence: Case Study of a "Communal Riot"'. In K. Basu and S. Subrahmanyam, eds, *Unravelling the Nation: Sectarian Conflict and India's Secular Identity*, 157–203. Delhi: Penguin.

Davis, N.Z. [1973] 1975. 'The Rites of Violence'. In N. Z. Davis, ed., *Society and Culture in Early Modern France*, 152–87. Stanford: Stanford University Press [originally published *Past and Present*. 59].

Fanon, Frantz. 1965. *The Wretched of the Earth*. London: Macgibbon and Kee.

Foucault, M. 1984. 'Space, Knowledge and Power'. In P. Rainbow, ed., *The Focault Reader*, 239–56. London: Penguin.

Guha, R. 1983. *Elementary Aspects of Peasant Insurgency in Colonial North India*. Delhi: Oxford University Press.

Harrison, S. 1989. 'The Symbolic Construction of Aggression and War in a Sepik River Society'. *Man* (n.s.). 24(4):583–99

Howell, S. and R. Willis, eds. 1989. *Societies at Peace: Anthropological Perspectives*. London: Routledge.

Kakar, S. 1990. 'Some Unconscious Aspects of Ethnic Violence in India'. In V. Das, ed., *Mirrors of Violence*, Delhi: Oxford University Press.

———. 1996. *The Colors of Violence: Cultural Identities, Religion, and Conflict*. Chicago: University of Chicago Press.

Keane, J. 1996. *Reflections on Violence*. London: Verso.

Mauss, M. 1950. 'Les Techniques du Corps'. In M. Mauss, ed. *Sociologie et Anthropologie*, 363–86. Paris: Presses Universitaires de France.

Pandey G. 1990. *The Construction of Communalism in Colonial North India*. Delhi: Oxford University Press

———. 1992. 'In Defense of the Fragment: Writing about Hindu-Muslim Riots in India Today'. *Representations*. 37:27–55

Riches, D. ed. 1986. *The Anthropology of Violence*. Oxford: Blackwell.

Sorel, G. 1950. *Reflections on Violence*. Illinois, Glencoe: Free Press.

Srinivasan, A. 1990. 'The Survivor in the Study of Violence'. In V. Das, ed., *Mirrors of Violence*, 305–20. Delhi: Oxford University Press.

Tambiah, S.J. 1996. *Leveling Crowds: Ethnonationalist Conflicts and Collective Violence in South Asia*. Berkeley: University of California Press.

Thompson, E.P. 1971. 'The Moral Economy of the English Crowd in the Eighteenth Century'. *Past and Present*. 50:76–136

Tilly, C. 1978. *From Mobilization to Revolution*. Reading, MA: Addison-Wesley.

Vidal, D., G. Tarabout, and E. Meyer, eds. 1994. *'Violences et Non-Violences en Inde'* (*Purusartha* 16) Paris: EHESS.

Weber, M. 1948. 'Politics as a Vocation'. In H. Gerth and C.W. Mills, eds, *From Max Weber: Essays in Sociology*, 72–128. London: Routledge.

Subject Index

Abhiras, of Mahabharata 227
The Aboriginals 385
aborigines/tribes 377, 1480, 1481
   as backward castes 1481
abortion, of female foetuses 1133
   as form of birth control 1132
   rights 1390
   sex-selective 1079
Abrahamic religion 790
absentee landlords 1226, 1227
Abstract Code 734
abuse (d), child 1136–8
   of elderly person in the family
      1147
   of male child 1138
academic feminism 1165–6
acana, ritual of offering 869
access, to food and clothing, sex-
      differentiated 1079
   to food, education and material
      resources to girls 1139
   to higher education 1046
   to justice 1401
   to land, women's restriction to
      1087
   to Supreme Court and High
      Courts 1400–1
   to women's education 1053
accountability, in democracy 1367
   local 1369, 1370, 1376
   and responsibility, in decision-
      making 1364

Accra, economic activities in 1287
Accreditation Council 1045
'acephalous system' 1516
'achievement motivation' 1322,
      1324
Act of Uniformity 1662 120
Ad dharm movement 1544
Ad Dharm Satnamipanth 1543
Adhagaon 409
Adhavaryu-priest, in Yajurveda 602
Adi-Andhras 1482
Adi-Dravidas 898, 1482
Adi Hindu movement, in Uttar
      Pradesh 1544
Adim Jati Sevak Sangh 394
Adiparasakti 1167
Adithi, organization for
      development of rural
      women, study by 1135
adivasi (s)/tribals 167, 369, 378,
      593n, 1540, 1541, 1548
   categories of 1537
   experience, education and 1026
   identity 590
   as 'indigenous people' 174
   and Narmada Andolan activists,
      against Narmada dam 173,
      174
   school drop-outs among 1019
Adivasi Mahasabha 593n
administration, imperatives of 1,
      1371

   in India during British rule
      106–7
   structure, under Mughal
      empire 1423
'administrative frontier' 1499
*Administrative Report of the
      Civil Justice in Kerala*
      1404n, 1405n
adolescence 1082
adult, franchise 433, 435, 1452,
      1469, 1475
   literacy 1021
   personal relationship, mistrust
      in 1182
   work schedules 1082
Adult Education Programme 1046
adulthood, world of 937
advaita (monism) 782
advertising, in India 564, 659
advocates 1392, 1395
aesthetics, folk and 585–6
   religious practices and ritual
      performances 1191–8
affine(al), links 419
   relatives, marriage and 1115, 1116
Afghan refugees, in Pakistan 283
   Smuggling operations by 273
Afghanistan, Soviet intervention
      in 287
Africa 1288
   research on tribal movements
      in 1536

African Political Systems 129
agamas 782
Agastya, sage 871
age, of consent 1081
    distribution in South India 962
    and gender 965
    at marriage 339, 1140
        of girls/women 339, 1140
        lower 1140
            marital status distribution
                and 197–9
            rise in 1124
    of renunciation 963–5
    in rupture 968
    stratification 968
    theorizing 968
aged/elderly, and abusive
            behaviour by sons and
            daughters-in-law 1148
    discrimination against 1132
    inadequate healthcare and food
            discrimination to 1148
ageism 960
agelessness 967
agglomeration economies 1368
aging, in India 961–3
    laparian version of 956
    normal 959
    person within the home 1146–9
    physiological and pathological
            958
    political economy of 962
aging in difference 968
Aging in India 961
aging and modernization theory
        959
aging is process 968
aging is work 968
aggression, ritual displays of 1573
Aghorī ascetics 806, 808
Agraharams 464
agriculture (al)/agrarian,
            capitalization of 370
    change(s) 1229
        and agricultural labour
            1232–5
        during colonial rule 1219–
            25
        classical theories of 1234–5
        after independence 1225–6
    child employment in
            subsistence 945, 946
    civilization 152, 153

colleges and universities 436
commercialization of 1220–2
conflicts 446
countryside as domain of
        1297–8
crop cultivation, and Vedic
        Hinduism 152
decline in importance of 1288,
        1298
development 1234, 1236
economy 1220, 1289, 1297
elites, political clout of 1510
employment, decline in 1298,
        1299
extensification, in Madhya
        Pradesh 164
and forest-based movements
        403–4
high status in rural India 411–
        12
income 1235
    and food, unequal
            distribution of 1215–16
    tax, absence of 1458
and industry 450
innovation 1206
intensification, impact of
        technology on 162–3
'involution' 140, 162
labour/workforce 160–1, 208,
        209, 411, 1206, 1223,
        1255, 1298
    agrarian change and 1232–5
    cash wages for 1232
    in pre-colonial South India
            1218
    women in 1086
modernization process in 1233
movements 1529
neolithic revolution 141, 142
output, increase in 1229
ownership and labour in 1245
and pastoral transhumance
        158–9
policies 447
    and impact on nomad-
            sedentary relations 238
production 1207, 1220, 1229,
        1385
    mode of 1207, 1231–2
'question' 1214
relations 45, 52, 80, 411, 1214,
        1216, 1227, 1235

in pre-colonial period 1217–
        18
'revolution' 1229
settled, and sedentary villagers
        480
    and subsistence 143, 160–2
and sexual symbolism 167
sociology 1216l
structure 153, 1206, 1217, 1218,
        1226, 1235, 1495
    and their transformation
            1213–36
studies 1214, 1216
technology in 161, 1234, 1235
in Third World 1214, 1216
universities 1045, 1230
*The Agrarian History of Moslem
        India* 104
Agricultural Prices Commission 439
agro-industry 1299
    artisans turning to, in Punjab
            1327
Ag7–lar v. Felton, US 922
Ahimsa (non-injury) 148, 785, 786
Ahirs, pastorals 228, 421
Ahl-i Hadis group 794
Ahmedabad, corporate tradition
            in 468
    textile industries in, and
            conflicts in 543
Ahmadiyah sect 794
AIDS crisis 211, 342, 1081
Ain-I Akbari 327, 328, 1424
    on nomads/hunters 224, 225
'air', as form of leisure 677
Akali Dal 1464, 1467
Akalis 788
Al-Biruni, Muhammad ibn
            Ahmad 327
algebra, development of 1035
Alexander the Great, and the
            Greek army's march into
            India 263
alienation 504, 1223, 1224, 1254
Aligarh Muslim University 1043
All-India Adi Dharm Mission 815
All-India Backward Classes
            Federation 1478
All-India Backward Classes
            League 1478
All-India Congress Committee
            (AICC), annual sessions
            of 1451

All-India Council of Technical Education 1045
All-India Educational Survey, Sixth 981
All-India Judges' Association v. Union of India 1410
All-India Kisan Sabha 446, 1534
All-India Trade Union Congress (AITUC) 1247
All-India Women's Conference (AIWC) 1548
Allahabad High Court, on Indira Gandhi's election 1459
'alliance', approach to kinship studies 1092
    aspect of marriage 1105, 1125
    perspective in family and kinship 1090
'allochronism' 79
allopathy 7–9, 311
alpana decorations 588
Alvārs, poetry of 809
Amar Akbar Anthony 633
Ambedkar, statue of, in Ambedkar Udhyan, Lucknow 625
Ambderkarite Buddhism 1544, 1545
Amending Act of 1781 1038
America see United States of America
American (s), as 'advanced' type, of kinship organization 1066
    family, breakdown of 1065
    transition of 1065–6
    men and women, differences in speaking pattern among 727
American Dilemma 520
American kinship: A cultural account 1075
American modernization theory 67
American sociology 64
amniocentesis tests 1079
    and female foeticides 1133–4
amorphism, semantics and 710
anand 678
Anavil caste 421
ancestor worship 1106
The Ancient City 1106
Andaman Grand Trunk Road 156
Andaman and Nicobar Islands, economies of 157

tribal movement to 389
Anadamanese 225, 247
    as mobile gatherers, fishers and hunters 232
    in state-supervised enclaves 157
Andhra Pradesh 1505
    backwardness in literacy and education 1022
    birth rate in 194
    caste politics in 1502
    nativist agitation in 1468
    People's War Group in 448
    total fertility rate in 194
androgyny 1163
anger, and sexuality 1182
Anglican Christians 789
Anglican diocese, of Calcutta 789
Anglican missionaries 773, 890
Anglicanism, in England 917
Angliscists 1039
Anglo-American nuclear family 1065
Anglo-American writings 709
Anglo-Indians 735
    Representations to 1514
Anglo-Muhammedan law 1120, 1123
Anglophone sociologis5– 40
animal(s), fares 422
    religion and classification of 145
    sacrifice 779, 793
        at Id-ul-Fitr among Muslims 151
        in Vedic times 147
animal husbandry 158, 160, 163
    Vedic Hinduism and 152
animism 585
ankeliya (' horn-game') ritual, in Sri Lanka 1195
Annamalai 714
Anpu (love), Tamil comcept of 1188, 1196
Ansari caste 423, 425
antelop, religious significance of 154
'anthropogeography' 328
Anthropological Linguistics 702
Anthropological Survey of India 57, 373, 374, 401, 404
    people of India project by 379
anthropology, Indian 6, 38, 88, 656, 657, 669, 686, 828, 851, 948, 1062, 1495

child labour and 939–49
enquiry 142
frameworks 862–4
history and 6, 7, 109, 110
of kinship 1061
of old age 938
and sociology 80, 141, 175
study, of markets 1356–7
    on tribes 383
violence and 1566–8
in the West 22
anthopometry 9
anti-Bengali riots, in Assam 298
anti-colonial movement 1207, 1413, 1429, 1430, 1450
'anti-establishment social context' 1525
anti-market rhetoric 1345
anti-migrant movements 278–9
anti-slavery International 944
anti-Western xenophobia 1066
Anveshi, Research Centre in Women's Studies 1128
anxiety 64
    and 'suffering', as core of emotional life in India 1182
    violence and 1128
Ao Naga 894
Apabhramśa (secondary) 734
Apache culture, role of silence in 699, 700, 705
apaurusheya 780
'Apna Utsav' performances 657
apocalyptic old women 965
Apostle of St. Thomas 788
Appellate courts 1390, 1392, 1394, 1397
'Appropriate English' 708
appropriate skills, investments in 1270
appropriate technology, concept of 708
Arab pattern, of patrilineal descent 1120
Arabic education 1038
Arabic-Persian/Muslim tradition, of historiography 100
Arabs, from Baghdad, conquering parts of Punjab and Sind 263
Arahamic religions, monotheism characteristic of 776

aranya (forests) 146
Aranyakas 780
arcane offerings, votive rituals and
    872
architectural forms, religion and
    150, 153
Area Study Programs, in North
    American universities 1
'Areal Linguistics' 698
Argentina 74
Aristotle's theory of poetics 1194
armed guerilla struggle 447
Armanians, migration of, into
    India 264
art, of dying 967
    history 658
Arthashastra 255n, 1380, 1414,
    1416, 1417
    model of 'circle of kings' 1422
    on state 1418
artisans, of Benaras 684
    entrepreneurial ability of, in
        Asia 1335n
        in India 1322
    and merchants, contribution to
        industrialization 1326
    traditional 1321, 1322, 1334n
Arunachal Pradesh, decline in
        tribal population in 389
    Scheduled Tribe population in
        201
Arya Samaj 770, 794–6, 816, 892,
        1007–08, 1511, 1542,
        1547
    educational philosophy of 1008
    movement 794, 795
    and Vedic way of ceremonies 424
Arya Kanya Gurukuls 1007
Aryadesa 251
Aryan civilization 576
Aryans, 779–80
    invasion/migration from Iran
        to India 263, 379
    confrontation with Dravidians
        480
    supremacy, folklore and myth
        of 575
    tribals 381
'Aryanism' 575
Aryavrata 780
a-sa-gotra, patrilineal clan,
        marriages forbidden
        between same 1118

a-sa-pinda, marriage rule and
        1118
ascetic 1160
    lineage/order 818, 820
asceticism, life of 851, 1162
    of Sikh Guru 964
Ashraf groups, marriage rules in
        Shariah 1120
Asian Drama 73
ashrama (s), 680, 781, 803
    as educational institute under
        Vedic learning 1035
    for men 680
Asia 1288
    Buddhism in 783
    collective violence in South
        1387–8
    entrepreneurship in 1319, 1324,
        1331
Asiatic Society of Bengal 103, 373
Asiatic Society of Calcutta 11
Asiatick Researchers 103
Asom Gana Parishad 272, 279, 1467
Assam, Bangladeshi illegal
        migration into 262, 298
    case study of myth from 827
    East Bengali refugees in 271–2
    elections in 1467
    myth of 'mouth-putting' in
        rural 839
    Scheduled Tribes in 201
    total fertility rate in 194
Assamese myth 772, 837
Assamese Vaisnavas, fieldwork
        among 831
assimilation 743
    by tribals 399, 400
Astadhyayi 715
astrology, development of 1035
astronomy, development of 1035
Asur legend, in Munda
        mythology 584
Asur myth 853
Aśvamedha (horse sacrifice) 602
aylum 138
    right of, conflicts and 544
    seekers 283, 292
Atharva Veda 603, 780
Atlas of Tribal India 333
atlases 329, 330
atman-brahman, concept of 832
attached labour, system of 1233,
        1234

attitude studies 696
Aufhebung, Hegelian-Marxist
        idea of 1529
Augustine, and rejection of
        custom 128
auspiciousness, in Hinduism
        863
    inauspiciousness 863
Australoid tribals 381
Austric linguistic category, of
        tribals 381
Austro-Asiatic family/type 1113
    Of kinship organization 1064
auto industry 1268
automated guided vehicle system
        (AGVS) 1266
autonomous linguistics,
        opponents of 724
avant-garde, movements 699
    theatre, West's 601
Avatip, of Sepik River, in New
        Guinea 1567
Awadhi literature 722
Awami League, of East Pakistan
        270–1
'axial arguments' 535–7
Ayodhya, crisis in 497, 535
    In the politics 822–3
Ayurveda (ic) 303, 309, 310, 313
    pathophysiology 311
    texts, on three sexes 1163
    on muscular body 1169

Babri Masjid, destruction of 100,
        657–8
    and violence in Mumbai 663
Babar, 228
    conquest of northern India by
        264
bachelor households 1093n
'Backward'/untouchable castes
        1304, 1383, 1514
    access to opportunities 1474
    in Bihar 1384
    as colonial categories 1478–80
    favouring 1456, 1457
    as legal and political entities
        1474–92
    past and present 1477
    reservation for 1470
    social and political space for
        1475
'Backward classes' 1474, 1478

and central commissions 1488–
90
in the Constitution of India
1484–5
as educational categories 1478–
9
educational concessions to
1481–2
judiciary and 1485–7
as legal and political entities
1474–92
in the State's services 1485, 1486
status, scramble for 1491
and vote-bank politics 1478
Backward Classes Commission,
first see Kaka Kalekar
Commission 1488
Backward Classes Commission,
Second see Mandal
Commission
'backwardness' 1383, 1488
politics of 1485
Bagariya nomadic group, in
Rajasthan 157
Bagdi procession 647
Bahai faith 775
Bahais 770
Bahujan Samaj Party (BSP) 625,
1491, 1543
The Baiga 385
Baiga tribes, myths among 853,
854
Survival and protection of 385
Bakhtin 936
Bairāgīs 808
Bakkarwal nomads, of
Himalayan belt/Jammu
and Kashmir 231, 234,
243–5
migration by 244
sedentiarization of 244
bal 311
bala-pravrajika (renunciation
while still a child) 1104
balance of payment crisis 1991
1438
Baliyan clan 419
balwadis 441
Balwant Rai Mehta Committee
437
Bandhua Mukti Morch v. Union
of India 1391
Bangalore, study of courts in 1394

Bangladesh 74, 271
Behari refugees from, in
Pakistan 270
Bengali refugees from (East
Pakistan), in India 285,
286, 288–9, 291, 293
census courts in 186–7
decentralized development in
1373
decentralized government in
1364
formation of 448, 1441n
illegal migrants from, into
India 202
in Assam 262
Islamization and discourses on
emotion in 1199
Muslim predominance in 779
refugees, resettlement of, in
Andaman Islands 156
Banihara nomads, expulsion from
Jammu and Kashmir 236
Baniya caste 1335n, 1510
local histories of 17
locality and 416
traders 1323
Banjaras 221, 225, 228, 229, 249–
50
Ghormati language of 250
migration by 250
banking facilities 1328, 1423
banking industry, study on
technical changes in 1281
Baptist missionaries 890
Bar association 1398
Barahabhum, principality of 398
Bharatachari mivement 592n
Bardoli, incident 446
Satyagraha 1534
Barelwis group 794
Baroda East assembly constituency,
study of 1501
Baroque 640
barter exchanges, in villages 417
'Basic Education', of Mahatma
Gandhi 746, 936, 1009,
1011, 1025
Bastar, tribal art of 586
Bataidar 1231
battle of Buxar 1426
battle of Palssey 1426
Baul discourse, in Bengal 1194
on goddess Durga 835

bazaars, in cities 465
markets and 1353, 1354
study of, in Bengal 1355
transactions, social and
cultural factors in 1353
behaviour (al), geographers 331
theory of 711
bej, reciting of myth 847
Belgium, State aid to religious
institutions in 929
Benaras Hindu University 1043
Benaras Sanskrit College,
establishment of 1038
Bene Israeli population, in
Bombay 778
Bengal, conquest of 1426
cultural history of 578
Diwani of 1425–6
famines 191, 1221
folk consciousness and
vernacular culture in
575–80
leftist groups, victory in
assembly elections in
1967 447
movement in 569
partition of 1004
peasant categories in rural, and
land ownership 432
revolt of 1859–62, against
indigo plantation system
1534
rural folk culture of 588
Tebhaga struggle in 446
Bengal National College 746
Bengal Permanent Settlement
Regulation Act of 1793
593n
Bengal School 593n
Bengal school painters 587
Bangali academic community
1004
Bengali culture 578
Bengali folklore
Bengali identity 577
Bengali kinship, culture of 1076
Bengali language, H/L standard
styles in 740
Bengali literature 577, 578
Bengali mysticism, ecstatic love in
1194
Bengali renaissance 99
Berar, Ryotwari settlement in 1220

Bhadrakali, goddess, festival 867
    and possession 867
    temple 878
        consecration ritual at 877
bhadralok 964
    colonial culture, and mimicry
        of West 636, 637
bhagal 410
Bhagat movements 40, 1538
Bhagavad (ta) Gita 795, 865, 1419
Bhāgavata, 614
    tradition 809
Bhagavata Purana 608, 613, 614,
    615
    Kannada version of 613
    Kathakali based on stories
        from 615
Bhai Bandh relations 416, 418,
    419
Bhaichara 418
Bhaktamāl narratives 643, 813
bhakti (devotion) 782, 797, 810,
        836, 866, 876, 1529
    concept of 865, 866
    cults, women's involvement in
        1186
    dancing with 874
    donations and sponsorship to
        temple rituals 866–7
    emotional and ecstatic 865
    movements 631, 1194, 1545
    saints 512
    strains, and Vedic revelation 149
    tradition 864, 1538
Bhangi caste 18
    Households of, image-practices
        in 627
Bharatiya Party (BJP) (Jan Sangh)
        262, 270, 657, 658, 1460,
        1461, 1462, 1464, 1472n,
        1549, 1550
    and Hindu unity 496
    and implementation of Mandal
        Report 496
    lamp as symbol of 1018
    opposition to Mandal
        Commission report by
        1489
    and religious minorities 1461
Bharatiya Vidya Bhavan 104
Bharatrashtra 1414
Bharvad nomads, pastoral 228,
    234, 236, 241–2

    magration by 241
    traditions 224
Bhatisuda village, *bhakti* in 631
    Chamars of 644
    Image worship in 627–8, 643
Bhāva (quotidian feelings) 608,
        1180, 1192
Bheruisthans (clan deity shrines)
        630
Bhil (nomads) 225, 245, 253, 382,
        398, 400
    as low castes 250
Bhima Carita, story of Khobā –
        Khubī in 851
Bhoodan movement, of Vinoba
        Bhave 445–6, 451
Bhopa pastorals 227
Bhopal, toxic leak, and disaster in
        168, 175, 315
Bhotiyas, of Nepal 225, 227
Bhumiji tribe 398, 400
    Revolt by 403
bhuts (evil spirit) 841, 842
    belief in 897
Bhutan, Buddhism in 779
    Nepalese from, migration to
        West Bengal 272
    Refugees from, in Nepal 283
Bhuyian landlords 382
Bible 789, 795
    translation into local languages
        773, 894
bi-directional studies 706
Bihar, backwardness in 438
    birth rate in 194, 195
    decline of tribal population in
        389
    famines in 314
    female infanticide in 197
    female population in 197
    fertility rate, total 194
    people's war groups in 448
    tribal revolts in 445
BiharProvincial Kisan Sabha 1534
Bihar State Backwardness Classes
        Federation 1478
Bihari Mata shrine 647
'Bihari Muslims', refugees from
        Bangladesh 285–6
Biharilal, image of Ramdevji 643
Bij parampara 821
bilateral cross cousin marriages
        1109, 1110

bilharziasis 342
bilingualism, degree of 696
Bill of Rights, United States of
        America 922, 923
binary gender 968
Bindusara, State under Mauryan
        dynasty of 1417
Bindu parampara 821
Bineshevar landlords 382
Bint'amn, preferences for, among
        Muslims 1121
biodiversity 169, 254
biological family 1059
biological reproduction 1077–80
biomedical system, research in 10
        State and 140
biomedicine 309–12
biradari 1140
    panchayat, among Muslims in
        Uttar Pradesh 423, 424
Birhor tribe (foragers) 246
    Asur myth among 853–4
Birsa movement 403
Birsa Munda 1538
birth control, forms of 305
    by poor people, in high fertility
        countries 943
    resistance to, by poor 943
birth (rates), and death rates,
        estimates of 188
    and death registration system
        187
    decline in India 193–4, 947
    decline in USA 1065
    fertility and rate of natural
        increase 193–5
    in India 217
Birth, Death and Marriages
        Registration Act of 1886
        187
Black population, and no notion
        of pollution 520–1
Bloom-fieldian tradition 698
Blue Vein Society, in Nashville 520
Board of Education, USA and
        religious education in
        926–7
Bodh Gaya land struggle 1547
Bodo movement 1538
Boby and mind, non-dualism of
        678
Bogardus scale 699
Bohra caste, among Muslims 1510

Bolshevik revolution 572, 574
Bombay (Presidency) 19, 464, 1478
    conversion to Christianity in 889
    Government in 639–40
    Ryotwari Settlement in 1220
Bombay Native Society 1043
Bombay school 6
bondage/bonded labour, abolition of 391, 1310
    agricultural labourers in 1233, 1245, 1293
    rights of 1390–1
'bonded slaves' 1234
Bon Ton Society, Washington 520
Book of Common Prayer and Liturgy 120
Botany, taxomical advances in 165
boundary (ies), -maintenance 422
    concept of, violence and 1129
    sacredness of 471
bourgeoise class, 526
    domestic 1436
    social order 949
    societies 118, 120
bovines, diet and human ecology 345
Boy Scouts movement 577
Brahmā Kumārīs 817
Brahmā Sampradāya, sect of Vaisnavism 809, 810
Brahmacharis 1008
brahmacharya (celibacy), for man 680
Brahmin dialect 720, 722
Brahmins/Brahmans 145, 152, 478, 479, 481, 603, 688, 780, 1415, 1477, 1509, 1514
    anti-Brahmin movements in Maharashtra and Tamil Nadu 13
        see also non-Brahmins
    Aryan origin of 10, 13
    caste system and 1475
    conflicts with Buddhists and Jains 1416, 1418
    on local customs and traditions 148
    and Kshatriya relationship 483
    locality and 416
    orthodoxy among 781, 803

painters 644
position of 13
-priest 603
relations with other Hindus 148–9
status of 482, 516, 518
    temple control by 471
    and tradition 781
    and untouchable community 521
Brahmins, -non, appropriation of Vedic discourses by 148
dialects 721, 722
movements by 10, 518, 1475
Brahmanas (text) 780
Brahmanical Hinduism 582, 889, 1415
Brahmanical ideology 368, 481, 484, 486, 1415, 1416
Brahmanical legal code 220, 480
Brahmanical system of higher education 1035–6
'Brahmanism' 1542
    anti- 807, 1194
    nexus of power between Sanskrit and 16
    and Vedic religion 147
Brahmo Samaj 815, 1014, 1547
    Movement 770
Braj, literature of 722
Brandt Report (1980) 742
Bratachari movement 576
'breaking of teeth' (palkhansna) ritual 853
Brecht's 'epic' theatre 620
bride(s), and bridegroom families, asymmetrical relation between 1119
    burning/murder for dowry 1058, 1143
bride-price/wealth, 1123, 1135
    divorce and return of 423
    payment of 1119, 1121
    see also dowry
Brij Bhumi 421
Brijbasi images 642
Britain 120, 658
    democratic political practices in 1507
    establishment of modern civil society in 120–1
    industrial revolution in 116
    industrialization in 1330

British government/rule/*Raj*, in India 1042, 1413, 1425–9, 1448, 1507
    administration of 1478, 1483
    and Indian joint family 1062
    on 'riots' in cities 368
    agricultural relations during 411
    artisans and handicrafts, deterioration of during 1326, 1335n
    census enumeration and cartography during 106
    confrontation between Congress, Muslim League and 1512
    conversions and economic changes in the hill regions of India 891–2
    disaster and epidemics measure by 428–9
    education policy of 936, 1048
        English education, impact on India 620
        and loyalty to 1039, 1042
    higher 1038–45
    end of 1431
    forest policy of 388
    hatred to stylization of Sanskrit 735
    impact of, on labour market 1245
    industrial entrepreneurship during 1335n
    land settlements during 388, 1206
    marriage laws, inability to reform on 1121–2
    missionary activities during 889
    rebellion against 403
    reinforcement of caste, religion and language 373
    resistance to 106
    and spread of Christianity 789
    village communities during 430–3
    and westernization 70
British capital, role of 1335n
British colonies, in Africa, West Asia and South-East Asia 1426
British Crown 1426, 1428

British Exchequer 1426
British historiography, and
        ethnology, of India 11
British imperialism, and India
        104–8, 1335n
British Indology 91n
British Orientalism, and India
        103–4
British law 1454
British Parliament 1454
British sociology 56
British Town and Country
        Planning Act of 1909 464
British universities, in India 1042–
        3
brokerage, role of, in market
        1210–11, 1353–4
brother-sister bond, sacred 1159
Brown v. Board of Education,
        USA 1390
Buddha, Gautama 148
    and analogy of jati 148
Buddhism 147, 201, 775, 783–5,
        909, 1119, 1331, 1414,
        1416, 1543
    conversion of caste Hindus to
        265, 785
    cultural tradition of 1185
    during Ashoka's time 1416–17
    'eight-fold path' of 783
    monasteries, universities and
        trade under 460
    non-theism of 776
    opposition to animal sacrifice
        by 148
    pilgrimage landscape of 347
    reaction against Brahmanic
        supremacy 1416
    split in 784
        Mahasanghika faction in
        784
        Sthania faction of 784
Buddhist Councils 1416
Buddhist Dhamma 1414, 1419
Buddhist higher education 1036–7
Buddhist monasteries (viharas)
        1036, 1037
Buddhist monks, in Sri Lanka
        1163
Buddhist philosophy, in Bengali
        folklore 578, 579
Buddhist population, in India 777,
        778

Buddhist Sangha, formation of
        1416
Buddhist texts 1440n
budget, government 1361, 1372,
        1373, 1375
Bundelkhand, caste groups in 336
'burden of learning', report of
        981
Bureau of International Affairs,
        US Department of Labor
        948, 950
bureaucracy 444, 1416, 1428, 1433
    and politics 1464
    role of in development 436
burial grounds, building of,
        among Muslims 151

Burma, end of British rule in 285
Burmese Muslims, influx into
        Bangladesh 273
business, corporations, rise of 1325
    communities in Delhi 1347
    networks 1328
    organizations 1333, 1334
bustees 464
byliny, songs in, Russia 572

Cabinet, powers of 1454
Caitanya, mission 811
    movement, in Bengal 810, 811
    sect 809, 812, 813
    tradition 816
Caityavāsīs (temple dwellers) 818
Cakravartin 602
Cākyār actors 616
Calcutta 464
    population of 274
    squatters' movemnt in 297
Calcutta Art Studio 636, 637, 642
Clacutta Madrassah, founding of
        1038
Calcutta University Commission
        (1902), report of 1043
calendar artists 645
'call girls' 1095n
Camār (Chamar) caste 815, 819
Canada, Indian labour in 440
canal irrigation, adverse
        implication of 161
    centralization of India's 1366
    construction of, during British
        rule 428
    in Punjab 231

Canonic law, royal commission to
        review 915
Canarium strictus resin 247
capital, accumulation of 1224,
        1332, 1434
    expenditure, of Central
        government 1439
    formation 666
    and labour 1309
capitalism 111, 142, 1024, 1225, 1232
    and disparities 340
    in Europe 1336n
    liberating role of 510
    rise of 1289
capitalist development 1211, 1320,
        1324, 1330, 1333
    entrepreneurship 1321
    formation 1209
    industrialization 1434
    mode of organization 1236, 1289
    /'rich' peasantry 1533
    production, and exchange 1427
    work roles in 1267
    society, class struggle between
        capitalist and proletariat
        528
    transformation 1290
        Marxist theories of 1320
Caribbean, Indian indentured
        labour to the 265, 440
Casrnegie Corporation 76
carnival 574
'Cartesian perspectivalism' 640
cartography, during British rule
        106
case pending, in Indian courts
        1399–1400, 1403n, 1405n
cash crops, switch from food
        crops to 413, 1221
caste(s) 4, 9, 16, 22, 38, 4, 74, 81,
        373, 41, 477–99, 654, 655,
        687–9, 1327, 1495, 1497
    action 489
    activity, in politics 1491
    'adaptive functions' of 1498
    affiliations 1466
    alliances 417, 433
    anti-, attitudes 865
    associations/organizations 420,
        1383, 1497, 1536, 1544
    and democratic politics 491–
        3
        youth wings in 44

-based political parties 1464
-based reservations, in
     education 991n
     see also reservation
during British/colonial period
     9, 105, 106, 480–1
and citizenship 108
and class relationship 52, 666,
     1207, 1217, 1486
and community 1501, 1509
composition, of legislative
     constituencies 1515
     of new electorate 1514
concept of 17, 69, 368
conflict 49, 518
in contemporary India 487–90
definition of 34
dialects 719–21
discrimination, eradication of
     1455
and dyadic relationship 688
and education 1179
endogamy 276, 477, 487, 490
ethnicity, role of 1498, 1501
ethnography 687, 688
     Dumont's theory of 481–6
and gender-based disparities
     334–5, 339, 795–6
groups 10, 432, 435, 1476
and hierarchy 17, 52, 477, 488,
     515, 516687, 771, 1093n,
     1206, 1235, 1476, 1498
     and Brahmin superiority
          486
     and power in the society
          483
     and regulation of *jati* and
          locality 555
     rigidity in 50
     and rituals 1216
     rules 689
in Hindu scripture 479–80
horizontal alliances of 420–1,
     434
identity 8, 511, 1076, 1348,
     1466, 1508
and inequality 384, 491, 1466
and kinship ties 369, 409, 427,
     452, 964, 1207
-linked occupation 1244
loyalties 18, 511
and marriage, importance of,
     in villages 419

mobilization/mobility 50, 74,
     420–1, 511–14, 524, 555,
     828
among non-Hindus 490–1
and occupation 686, 1170
     and poverty 1486, 1487
     and ritual status 166
order 538
     in pre-colonial India 551
panchayats 417, 422–5
-peasants, tribes and 384–5
and political/electoral power
     10, 18, 49, 53, 435, 491,
     510, 1382, 1466, 1487
politics, 1544
     in Andhr Pradesh 1502
populations, geographical
     literature on 334–7
post-Dumont studies 484–6
Puranas 17, 834
and race 520–2
relations 5, 7, 368
and religion 105, 685
     and India's industrial
          development 1325
and ritual purity-pollution 487,
     488
role of 17, 18, 49, 53, 491
sabhas (associations) 1487
and sects 771, 803, 818–21
and society 395, 506, 1415, 1447
and status 10
     abolition of 1470
     see also caste, hierarchy
system 5, 14, 108, 1093n, 1321,
     14115, 1449
     assault on 556
     breakdown of 478
     colonial model of 687
     and division of labour 478
     nomads and 250–2
     and 'resistance to change'
          1321, 1322
     social and ritual structures
          of 1346
taboos 166
transition of 1497–8
and tribes 66, 383–4, 481, 982,
     984–5
     and gender 332–40
unity of 427, 1064
and warfare for upward
     mobility 512

Caste Disabilities Removal Act
     XXI of 1850 899
Caste, Class and Power 1499
Caste in India 432
Caste in Indian Politics 51
'casteism' 70, 492, 1508, 1515
casual labour 209, 1209, 1234,
     1256, 1307, 1311
     and unskilled workers 1305
'catalysts of acculturation' 1539
Catholic(s), attack on religious
     opponents 1570
     converts 889
     missionaries 890, 898
     participation in Hindu
          ceremonies 896
     population in India 884–5,
          920
Cattle Tresspass Act of 1871 235
catuh-sampradāya 809
celibacy 804, 818
Census of India 105, 106, 185–7,
     190, 428
     on age at marriage 1140
     on caste of citizens 481
     on child work 978, 980
     commissioners 10, 432
     on female labour 1257
     on female sex ratio 1135
     geographic analysis of 329,
          330
     'home' 212n
     on literacy 974, 1019
     on mother tongue 744
     Reports 9, 1482
Census, of 1891 375
     of 1901 376, 383
     of 1911 383, 1482
     of 1921 377, 383
     of 1931 252, 377, 383
     of 1941 191
     of 1951 191, 292
     of 1961 189, 207, 1072
     of 1971 195, 203, 205, 741
     of 1981 186, 197, 204, 205,
          460, 978, 980, 1257
     of 1991 184, 186, 190, 196,
          197, 200, 204, 275, 798n,
          884, 974, 975, 1019, 1135,
          1138, 1140, 1257
Census of India 1991 1393
Central Advisory Board of
     Education 747

Central Provinces, *Mahalwari/ Malguzari* Settlement in 1220
centralization, and decentralization structure 1371, 1516
  under colonial rule 1428
'Centrally Sponsored Scheme of Restructuring and Reorganizing of Teacher Education' 1023
Centre for Development Studies (Trivandrum) 47
Centre for the Study of Developing Societies, Delhi 47
Centre for Science and Environment 170, 172, 1541
Centre for Women's Development Studies, New Delhi 54, 1150n
Chagatay pastoral nomads 255n
Chaitanya 579
Chaitanyalila performances 677
Chakmas, refugees from Bangladesh 270, 283, 286
Challa Yanadi, foragers in Sriharikota 246
Chalukya rulers 1422
Chamar community 521, 1499
  housing problems of 336
  settlements, images/*murtis* in 628
Champaign Council of Religious Education, USA 927
Champaran satyagraha 1534
Chandal caste 521, 1036
Chandramohan V. State of Uttar Pradesh 1405n
Chandramouleshwar V. Patna High Court 1405n
Changpa pastorals, of Himalayan belt 243, 245
'chaos', and semantics 710–11
'Charan', as animal husbandry 228
charkha 1009
Charles Wood Despatch (1854) 1479, 1480
Charter Act of 1813 890, 1001
Charter rights 1425
Charya padas 579

Chaturvarnya 1475
Chau dance 611
Chauri Chaura incident 446, 1579
Chenchu hunters, in Andhra Pradesh 232, 246
Chetna 306
Chho dance, of Purulia 589, 590
Chicago School 1526
child/children, abuse 949, 1136–8
  activity status 980
  -bearing, age-pattern of 199
  as central necessities of life in India 1158
  costs and return on 947
  domestic chores by 945, 946, 978, 980
  exploitation of 937, 947, 948, 1255, 1257
  health 305
    maternal education and 983
  identity 1075
  labour/employment/work 441, 450, 937, 945, 949, 1136, 1258–9, 1293
  age, gender and kinship in 939–40, 946, 047
  in agriculture 945, 946
  and anthropology 939–49
  approaches to 940–4
  bonded 1136
  condemnation of 939–40
  and education 986
  exploitation of, *see* child, exploitation
  in factories/industries 940, 1246
  in Himachal Pradesh 986
  as full-time workers 979
  in informal sector 945, 1303
  and increase in family income 941, 948
  legislation for abolition of 1259
  movement against 979
  obstacles to schooling 937, 979, 980
  paradox of 939–40
  policies 939
  in poor families 942, 979
  and school attendance 982, 997
  and self-respect 949–50
  unpaid 941, 945

  value of 939, 950
  marriage 1052, 1124, 1547, 1548
  morbidity 949, 1079
  mortality 949, 1079, 1361
  nutrition and health 306
  in poverty 940, 945
  rape of 1145
  -rearing, emotion and families 1181, 1182, 1186–91
  rights of 949
  schooling of 1082
  survival 306, 315
Child Marriage Restraint Act (the Sarda Act), of 1929 198
childbirth, sexuality and 1080
childhood 947, 988
  concept of 1082
  disassociation of 939, 948
  ideology 948, 950
  negotiation of 940, 948–50
  sexual trauma 1162
Chile 74
China 936
  decentralized development in 1371, 1375
  education policy in 1020, 1364
  free-market in post-Mao 1292
  and India, literacy rate in 974
  literacy in 936–7, 979, 1021
  population of 184, 191–2212n
Chinese ethnography 45
Chinese immigration, to India 264
Chipko movement 143, 170, 174
  as archetype 170–1
  women's participation in 1550
Chitrashala Press 637
Chittagong Hill Tracts Peoples Solidarity Association 270
Chokhala 423
Chokhamela 1545
Chola period 1420
  society during 1421
  Chola rulers 1422
Cholanickan, foragers of Kerala 246–7
Cholera, spread of 304, 342
Chota Nagpur, Christianity in 582
  protests in, against oppressive social system 582
Christ Ashram 903
Christian (s) (population), in India 770, 773, 777, 778, 884, 1474

caste division among 477, 491, 897–8
Dalits 1543
groups, varieties of 884–94
literacy and education among 202
mission schools 1038
missionaries 884, 892, 893, 897, 899, 1542
  and education 773, 1038, 1039, 1041, 1051, 1479, 1480
  religious bias of 742
  and tribal education and development 394
orthodox 885
societies 120, 910
in south India 894–6, 1419
theology 568
women population among 196, 207
Christian Dalit Liberation Movement 902
Christianity 201, 585, 770, 772–3, 775, 788–90, 885, 1491, 1538
  conversions to 153
    of tribals 382, 398, 582, 584
  in Indian society and culture 884–904
  influence of 773
  and jati and community identity 887
  propagation of 890
  in the United States of America 923–4
chromolithograph images, in India 627, 629, 630, 636, 641–3
'chronotopes', educational thought and 998–9
Chundawat clan 418
Church, autonomy for, and religious liberty 931
  and indigenous modes of worship 903
  national, and the ruler/ monarch 914–16
  protest against extravagance of 913
  and religious discrimination in Europe 928
  role of 803

schools, in USA 922
-sect dichotomy 802
separation of, from politics 910
and the State 120, 121, 908, 916–20, 924, 928–30
and sovereignty of the monarch 917
subordinate to political sovereign 920
tax paid by 915
cinema 659, 661
city (ies) 189, 368, 370, 458–72
  character of 663
  colonial writings on 368
  -industrial complex 1289
Citizen's Reports 174
citizens, civil, political and religious rights, of citizens 911, 927, 931
  system of registration of 272
citizenship 5, 1385
  and religion 773
civic governance, in towns 468–70
civic planning bodies 464
civil and criminal laws, system of 1433
civil disobediance movement, of Mahatma Gandhi 124, 549, 746, 1452
civil judege 1390
Civil Justice Committee Report 1924–25 1403n
'civil society' 114–31, 1552
  concept of 119
  definition of, by opposition 118–20
  of Hegel 118–20
  history of 114
  languages and territory in 131
  and opposition to state 118
  pluralism and 124–7
  politics of 119
civilization 101, 111, 580, 654
  India's 4, 7, 7, 708
  measure of 575
  and nation 13
  and transmission of knowledge 1033
  Western 4
clan 44
  -exogamy 418–19
  organization 418
Clarendon Code, England 917

class 40, 659, 1495
  caste and 52, 489, 1486, 1497, 1499
  differences in Marx 529
  division, in society 469
  identity 1095n
  importance of, in political economy 493, 687
  mobility, in open systems of stratification 514–15
  and occupation 685–7
  relationship 396, 685
  and 'secular' divisions 685
  service, intermediate and working, relations between 525–6
  society, Revolution and, abolition of, in Russia 574
  sociological treatment of 504
  status 1082, 1095n
  and stratification 52, 506, 507
  structure, in USA 511
  struggle 451
  'transformation' 1500
classical anthropology 90n
'classical', definition of 610–11
classical Hinduism, cultural-religious practices of 66
classical theories, of agrarian change 1234–5
closed system, of stratification 508–11, 517–18, 520–2
  hierarchy in 523
  mobility discouraged in 508–10
clothes, and levels of symbolism 681–2
Coalition Against Child Labour (1997) 979
coalitions, non-dominant 1460–2
coal-mining, in eastern India 1207, 1246
coconut sacrifice 873
code-mixing, as a speech process 723–4
code-repertoire 722
'coded substances' 516, 691
Code of Civil Procedure 1397
codification of language 733–7
Cold War 65, 284, 959
  movements, and gerontology and geriatrics 960

collective action 1369, 1526, 1573
  concept of 1528
  social movements and 1530,
    1531
collective identities 15, 16, 19, 53,
    413, 414, 564, 566, 583,
    1059, 1190, 1529
  importance of 53
collective psychology, theory of
    1572
collective violence 35, 1564–79,
    1571, 1573, 1574, 1575,
    1579
  and contests 1387–8
  in South Asia 1568–71, 1576
colleges, in India 1047
  establishment and growth of
    1038–9
  for women 1052
Colombo, violence in 1573, 1576
colonial culture 636
colonial heritage, and
    development 1049–51
colonial historiography 12, 15,
    103
colonial language 718, 733
colonial medicine, on pathology
    of old age 958
colonial struggle, anti- 1566
colonialism 15, 111, 659, 890, 968,
    1005, 1006, 1011, 1024,
    1054, 1325, 1428, 1429,
    1958
  education in post-coloniality
    1003–10
  and hierarchy and alienation
    504
  impact of 16, 45
  opposition to 1450–1
  and tribal movement 1537
colonization 142
  effects of mental-moral forms
    of 84
  modernity and 84
colour hierarchy, racism and, in
    USA 520
combinatorial modes, and culture
    165–7
commerce 663, 668, 1336n, 1353
  and commodification 666
  and consumption 665
  cultures of 665–6
commercial banks, 439

credit to farmers 1228
  nationalization of 128
commercial castes, structure and
    ethos of 666
commercial cities 1342
commercial crops, export of 1221
Commission for Secondary
    Education 746
Commissioner for 1911 Census of
    Bengal 492
Commissioner for Scheduled
    Castes and Scheduled
    Tribes 377, 392
Committee on the Status of
    Women in India 54, 990n
common property resources, local
    management of 417,
    1365–6
  decline of 236–7
  and 'free-rider' issue 1528
Commonwealth Immigrants Act
    267
communal identity 8, 1501, 1508,
    1515
communal riots/violence 7, 11,
    798, 909, 1200, 1564,
    1566, 1568, 1569, 1575
communalism 4, 16, 51, 70, 664,
    689, 909, 1508
communication/communicative,
    696, 706, 707, 729,
    1268
  acts, manipulation of 727–8
  asynchronies 725
  breakdown 726
  and conflicts 537, 548
  cooperation 727
  language and 470, 733, 740
  problems in, male-female
    speech 728
  in rituals 607
  speech act and 718–19
  structure of 716
communism 115
  fall of, in Russia and eastern
    Europe 117
Communist Party of China 448
Communist Party of India (CPI),
    446, 447
  Kisan Sabha and 1535
  split in 1464, 1473n
Communist Party of India
    (Marxist) 1473n, 1535

Communist Party of India
    (Marxist-Leninist) 447
communist(s) (parties) 1460, 1548
  in Kerala 1464, 1467
    Nehru's dismissal of
      government in 1457
  legislators 1453, 1463
  as national party 1463, 1464
  in West Bengal 1464, 1467,
    1506
  and 'People's war' 446
  in Tripura 1464
communitarian division, of urban
    territories 462
communitas, experiences of 1527
community 10, 488
  as applied to village 48
  associations 421, 424
  concept of 1533
  Development Programmes 49,
    73, 76, 390, 435, 437,
    448–9, 1046, 1228–9,
    1496
  identity 569, 573
  life, development and 435
  model of 573
  role of 1552
  towns and 470–1
Community Service Guild of
    Madras, study by 1135
compulsory education 947, 976
  and elimination of child labour
    941
computer, aided design and
    manufacturing (CAD/
    CAM) 1266, 1275
  aided process planning (CAPP)
    1266
  convergence and application of
    1268
  importance of 1260
  integrated manufacturing
    (CIM) technologies 1268
  numerical control (CNC)
    machines 1266
Concepts of Repression 833
Concepts of Person 1076
Conference of Chief Ministers, on
    three-language formula
    747
confidence, and love 64–6
conflicts 5, 284
  caste and 518

catharsis in, realistic and non-
        realistic 546–7
    dimension of 533–5
    genetic and cultural 540–1
    life-cycle of 536–7, 540–5
    modes of 532, 534
    modulating and aggravating
        impulses 542–5
    and order 536–7, 545–50
    over poverty, discrimination
        and urbanization 326
    and social change 548–9
    and strengthening of identities
        and boundaries 548
Confucianism 1331
Congress Party 446, 1381, 1453,
        1461, 1464, 1503–06,
        1512, 1514, 1516, 1522n,
        1548, 1570
    abrogating democratic
        functioning of, by Indira
        Gandhi 1458–9
    alternatives to 1461
    Ambedkar on 1543
    decline of 1381
    dominance at the Centre 1467,
        1503, 1518
    electoral defeat in 1967
        elections 1457
        1977 elections 1437
    electoral success in 1962
        elections 1517
        1971 elections 1437
    factionalism in 1516–17
    government(I) 1489, 1490
    under Indira Gandhi 1381,
        1458
    legacy 1451, 1452
    and liberalization policy 1469
    and Muslim League,
        confrontation between
        1512
    as 'national' party 1463
    in the Nehru period 1467
    opposition to Mandal Report
        1489
    power struggle in 1436
    split in 1452
    tribals' loyalty to 399
Congress Socialist Party 1515,
        1552n
conjugal family/home 1080, 1089
    pattern in the West 1067

violence in 1140–6
conjugal relationship 1080, 1130
conspicuous consumption 424,
        680
Constitution of India 46, 433,
        437, 447, 493, 776, 1387,
        1432, 1433, 1453, 1474,
        1480, 1483, 1503, 1548
    adoption of 1475, 1496, 1515
    amendments, 73rd and 74th
        1369
        for Panchayat Raj
            institutions 437
    Article 1 of 1414
    Article 16 (4) of 1485–8
    Article 15 (4) of 1485, 1488
    Article 21 of, on right to health
        314
    Article 30 of, on right to
        religion 790
    Article 38 and 39 of 1441n
    Article 226 (1) of 1396
    Articles 233–236 of 1398
    on backward classes 1484–5
    on benefits/reservations to
        tribals 386
    compensatory provisions in
        1483–4
    courts' interpretation of 1391
    definition of scheduled tribes
        in 376, 377
    Directive Principles, Article 45
        of 990n
    on distribution of power
        between Centre and the
        states 1433
    framing of 553, 555
    ninth schedule of 1472n
    on officially recognized
        languages 741, 743–4
    uniform civil code under 1123
constitutional structure, of
        democracy 1453–7
Constituent Assembly 378, 1452,
        1455–6, 1472n
construction sector, employment
        in 209
consanguine relatives, marriage
        and 1115, 1116
    Church rules on 901
consumption, ethics of 675
    levels, by human beings 688
    and lifestyle 675–91

and production 564, 565, 666,
        676
    role of 680, 1355
    and social identity 1355–6
continuous hierarchy 514–19, 523,
        524
contraception/contraceptives,
        method of 199, 305, 306
Contributions to Indian Sociology
        42, 52
Convecticle Acts, England 120,
        918
conversation (al), Implicature 703
    strategies 726–8
conversion, to Buddhism 785
    to Christianity 789, 885, 889,
        900
        and education for children
            1038
        in Goa 886, 888
        in north-east India 890
    to Islam in East Bengal and
        Kashmir Vlley 792
    re- 900
cooperative societies 429, 450,
        1495, 1518
    credit societies 1228
    in villages 413
Coorg(s) 421
    social change in 69
    study of religion and society
        among 50, 451–2
core linguistics 710–12, 717
Cornell University Field Research
        Project 1496
Corporation Act of 1661, England
        918, 919
corruption, in credit societies
        1228
    in judiciary 1393, 1394, 1404n
    in local governments 1369
    market, state and 1352
cosmology, and mode of
        livelihood 155–6
cosmography, notions of 609–10
Cote d'Ivoire, decentralization in
        1364
Council for Advancement of
        People's Action and Rural
        Technology (CAPART)
        394
Council for Agricultural Research
        1045

Council for Historical Research 1045

Council for Medical Research 1045

Council for Scientific and Industrial Research 1045

Council for Secondary Education 747

Council for Social Science Research 1045

'counter-cultures' 1530

Cours de Linguistique Generale 714

courtesans, of Lucknow 1164

courts, cases in, and compromise 1394
    delay/pending in 1392–3
    and legal profession 553
    lower *see* lower/subordinate courts
    see also Supreme Court

cow, cultural ecology of sacred 154
    protection, agitation for 637, 638–9
    as sacred symbol 148

craft, and art 587, 1297
    craftsmen in India 1245, 1335n

credit, and insurance markets 1363, 1368
    market, moneylender in 1223
    societies 1228

Crime Against Women Cell, Delhi 1137

Criminal courts, cases in, and delay in 1392, 1396

Criminal Tribes Act, abolition of 235

Criminal Tribes Act Enquiry Committee (1949–50) 235

'critical events', anthropology of 87, 660

critical gerontology 967

cropping pattern 1206, 1221

cross-cousin marriages 1122, 1140
    among Tamil Brahmins 1130
    decline in 1123, 1124
    forbidden among Mundas 1113
    in south India 1106–9, 1112, 1114

Cross Sex Communications Strategies 706

'cross trading' 1272–3

crowd, and perception 1571–4
    psychology 1526, 1573
    theory of 1572
    violent and non-violent 1572–3

'crypto-art historians' 634

crude death rate 193, 217

crude minimum poverty line 1361

Cuba, effective rural education and health services in 1364

cult, beliefs 153
    of Goddess 612

The Cult of the Goddess Pattini 1195

culture (al), 101, 103–4, 111, 123, 1015, 1276
    approach to family and kinship 1077, 1092
    authenticity to 591
    and civilization, India's 658–62
    codes, and conflicts 537, 550–7
    and colonialism 660
    combinational modes and 165–7
    concept of 564, 962
    civil society and 114
    diversity 277, 504, 580
    dynamics 1179
    encounter 551
    forms 591, 659
    geography, social and 326–48
    'heritage' 578
    history of Bengal 578
    identity 569, 580, 657
        Indian diaspora and 267
    image in India 625–48
    landscape studies 344–8
    -linguistic structure of India 709
    performances 599–602
    perspective, of entrepreneurship 1319, 1320–5, 1331, 1332
    and power 15–21
    regions 1495
    representations 141, 565
    scene in India 775
    'schizophernia' 78
    schooling and modernity 998–1027
    sociology 108–9
    and the state 657–8
    study of 44

unity 569, 1381, 1455
    value, in public pan-eating 676

'culturalism', language and 736

curative rituals, myth and 837–43, 846

currency system, during Mughal rule 1423

'custom', and beliefs 583
    concept of 127–9
    'of the country' 127
    habit and 129
    notion of 11
    of people 114, 326

Czarist expansion, in Central Asia 1521n

Dadra and Nagar Haveli, Scheduled Tribes in 201

Dādupanth 814

The Dak and Khanar Vachana 592n

Daker vachana 578

Dalit (s) 478, 625, 644, 776, 1384, 1491
    atrocities on 1544
    -'Bahujan' 18
    Christians 491, 773, 1491
        movements 903
    conversions to Buddhism 19, 771, 785
    killings if, in Mumbai 625
    leadership among 1386
    literature 371
    mohallas 625
    movements 19, 369, 1384, 1386, 1531, 1541–6
    politics 1544, 1545
    struggle against casteism 902
    'theology' 903, 1543

Dalit Panther (s) 1545
    movement 1544

Dlit Sahitya (Dalit Literature) 1544, 1545

dam constructions, by princely states 428

Daman and Diu, conversion to Christianity in 889

Dandakarnya Project 290
    rehabilitation of Bengali refugees in 298

darshan (vision), in temples 626, 627, 632, 781

Darul Uloom 793

Daśarūpa 608
Daśnāmī Naga/Sannyāsīs 806, 808, 819, 822
Daśnāmī order/sect 808, 815, 816
Dāsya bhāva 1180
daughter, education of 983
  preferences 1133
daughter-in-law, dowry and abuse, and neglect of 1171
Dayanand Anglo-Vedic (DAV), colleges 1007, 1008
  Schools 936
death (s) rates, in India 192–3, 217, 409
  due to natural calamities 429
  registration of 187
debt burdens 439, 1225, 1230, 1234
Deccan, farming communities in 222
Deccan cults, pastoral cults and 227
Deccan Education Society 1043
Deccan Relief Act of 1879 1223
'Deccan riots' of 1875 1223, 1534
decentralization 1282, 1366, 1390, 1432, 1518
  concept of 1369
  and the poor 1361–76
decennial census 136, 184
Declaration of Indulgence 919
decolonization movements 12, 22, 84
  in Asia 5
  process of 1524
'deemed' universities 1045
Defence of Children International 944
deficiency disease studies 341
deforestation, British policy and 232
  prevention of 254
'deindustrialization' 1222, 1326
Delhi, population of 274
  riots 1568, 1570, 1571, 1573, 1576–7
  Sultanate, and disappearance of Saiva Siddhanta sect 806–7
democracy 911, 1381, 1382, 1429, 1485, 1498
  constitutional structure of 1381, 1453–7

and economic policy 1468–9
  features of 1462–6
  institutions of 116, 1381, 1382, 1385
  nature of Indian 1447–71
  origins of Indian 1448–53
  and regional interests 1467–8
  and secularism 909
  and social inequality 1469–71
  under Jawaharlal Nehru 1457, 1460
democratic liberalism 1516
democratic politics 1462, 1463, 1468, 1471
  impact of 433–5
  and social conflicts 1470
demography (ic) 88, 1289
  changes 136, 962
  see also population
demon (ic), illness, Sinhalese Buddhists suffering from 1184
  masks 590
  possession 875, 876, 1185
  violence 1572
Deobandi (s) 794
  movement 770
Department of Family Welfare 199
Department of Geography, Varanasi 458
Dependency theory 86, 92n, 1532
Depressed Classes 18, 19, 1475, 1483, 1542
'depression', 450, 1180, 1185
  European and American idea of 1185
  and hostility 1190
deprivation, impact of, on girl child 1132
  tribals and 1538
desa-dharma (customary laws of regions) 1105, 106
'descriptive' art 640
Deshasthe 416
deshya, Shastric classification of 576
desi art 587
design, concept of 1268, 1270
Dispatch of 1854 *see* Charles Wood Dispatch
devadasis 1164
developing countries, child labour in 944

informal sectors in 1290
  language planning and modernizing in 731, 732
  modernization in 729–30
  social transformation in 1289
  structural adjustment programmes in, and poor children 949
  technocratic development projects in 1374
  types of 729–31
  work pattern of children in 939, 940
'developing societies', in anthropology 79–80
  traditional cultures of 1250
development (al) 67, 348
  blocks 1495
  concept of national 68
  economies 66, 1532
    literature and education in 974
  policies, and discourses of 1531
  projects 1385
    and displacement of 393
    state-designated 1362
    for tribal areas 390–2
    in villages 435–8
  schemes, to face natural calamities 429
'Development of Tribal Areas' 392
'Developmental Sociolinguistics' 698
Devi movement, in South Gujarat 1540
Devi (Shakti) worship 782, 783

devolution of power, to local communities 678, 864–7, 1362, 1366, 1370, 1376
devotion, to family and deity 864, 1162
  and divine possession 875
  and piety 866
  and religious activities 1193–4
Dewali festival/syndrome 415
Dhangar pastorals, of Deccan 242
Dhangar pastorals 227
dharma ka bap 417
dharma 675, 777, 783, 1035, 1036, 1104, 1344, 1418, 1429
  Asoka's policy of 1418–19

of householder and king 964
notion of 788
and religion 1471n
Dharmachakra, of emperor
Ashoka 1414
Dharmashastras 484, 780, 1062,
1161, 1162, 1419
on Brahmanical ideal society
480
on marriage 1104–6, 1117–23
on rights and duties of four
varnas 479
Dharma Sutras 780, 1417
dharma-vijaya 1421
dharmayuddha 124
Dhebar Commission *see*
Scheduled Areas and
Scheduled Tribes
Commission
dhundh, ritual of 415
dialect (s), caste and 719–21
'Geography' 698, 702
innovation by upper and lower
classes 721
'dialectology' 698, 702
diaspora/dispersed communities,
659
and concept of language 735
effect of, on South Asian
personhood 1172–4
Indian intellectuals 564
dictionaries, compilation of 773
differences/differentiation,
hierarchy and, in social
stratification 517, 522–3,
526
in Marx and Weber 527–9
and integration, society and
536, 537–40
Digambara tradition 805, 818
'diaglossia' 696, 723
diksa 870
Dimasas 398
Din-el-Ilahi 1424, 1429
directive principles of State policy
438, 444
Director of Public Instruction,
Bombay 1481, 1482
disadvantaged castes/groups, 190,
1475, 1477
educational (deprivation) of
975, 979
literacy rate among 984–5

schools, discrimination in 985
disaster, managing in villages
426–30
disciple succession, principle of
804, 818
discipline, in child rearing 1190
Discovery of India 1451
discrete castes, continuous
hierarchies of 515–18
discrimination 1484, 1542
against girls and women 1139–
40
caste-based 18
reverse, in favour of backward
castes 1456, 1457
disestablishment, and the rhetoric
of separation 920–8
'disinvestment', of public sector
units 1436
'displaced people' 299, 308
Displaced Persons (Compensation
and Rehabilitation) Act
1954 290, 292
dispute resolutions 1395, 1399,
1401
District Cooperative Bank 1506
District Gazetteer 18
district judges 1390
jurisdiction of, appellate 1390
District Level Board 1506
district level courts 1391, 1403n

District Poverty Initiatives
Programmes 441, 490
divine possession 604, 874–6
and speech 606
divine right theory 914
divinity, concept of 776
division of labour 71, 537, 1218,
1243, 1272, 1293
concept of 1267
and economy in villages 411–
13, 482
gendered 139, 983
divorce 1125
frequency of, and remarriage
1085
prohibition among Hindus 117,
118
and right of maintenance 1549
rise of, in United States of
America 1065
stigma to the family 1160

Diwani of Bengal, to East India
Company 1425–6
'doctrine of blood and soil' 570,
573
Dogra tradition, and seasonal
migration 234
dola-dukha, Sinhalese women's
1186
domestic arena, child employment
in 945, 946, 978, 980
'domestic group' 1071, 1085
domestic violence 1058, 1084,
1088, 1127–50, 1165,
1386
'dominant caste' 433
concept of 70
Doon model of education 1016
Doon school, Dehradun 936,
1004, 1011, 1012–17
relevance of, and Indian
modernity 1013
secularism policy in 1016–17
Doon School Weekly 1015
dotage, as mescosm between body
and social order 957
'downward filtration theory'
1040–1
dowry/bride-wealth 901, 1085,
1117, 1123, 1142–3, 1160
communal aspect of 1142
'deaths' 1124, 1142, 1143, 1549
and female infanticide 1134–5
marriage and 424
opposition to 1171
politics of 665
victims of, in Delhi 1143
and violence 1143, 1149
Draft National Policy for
Rehabilitation 280
dramatic performances, and
emotional performances
1192–4
tradition of 655
Draupadi, Terukuttu performance
based on 612
Dravida Munnetra Kazhagham, in
Tamil Nadu 1467, 1468
Dravidian kinship organizations,
in south India 1064
Dravidian languages 719–20, 1106
Dravidian linguistic category, of
tribals 381
Dravidian pattern of marriage,

cross-cousin marriages
1105, 1106–12, 1114
Dravidians, and Aryan
confrontation 480
drinking water, lack of 308
droit common, evolution of, in
France 128
droughts and drought prone areas
429, 450
seasonal migration from 425
dualism/*dvaita,* and discontents
76–80, 782
Indian description of 77
theories, of traditional-modern
1288, 1289
concept of 1294
Dumont's theory of caste 484–6
ethnography of caste and 481–
6
Durga/Kali, complex 857n
cult of 1419
mythical cycle of 835
Durga Puja festival, and sacrifice
415
Dussehra 421
'dyarchy' 1513
dyshoric mood/state, of
spiritlessness 1184–16

earthquakes, deaths due to 429
East Africa, Indian indentured
labour in 265
East Asia, gross domestic product
in 1277
growth in labour force in 1278
East and South-east Asia,
entrepreneurs in 1320
East Bengal *see* Pakistan, East and
Bangladesh
East India Company, English 11,
103, 327, 430, 773, 789,
822, 889–90, 1207, 1393,
1425, 1426
administrators of 450, 451
Charter of 1001, 1038, 1039
and collapse of old handicrafts
1222
Court of Directors of 1040,
1041, 1479
educational policy of 1041
policies of 104
ecofeminism, in India 171, 1165
ecology (cal), degradation 174

and environment 141–76
involution 143, 155, 162–5
issues 717–19
models, towns and 461–2
revolution 142
economy (ic), activities 1323
criminal 1294
participation in 206–8
registered 1291–3
anthropology 1342
backwardness 1320, 1486
bondage, freedom from, in
villages 511
deprivation, and children's
schooling 979–81
of disadvantaged castes 984
development 12, 1308, 1325,
1433, 1434, 1447, 1495
higher education and 1049–
51
in India and Asia 1334
and social change 46
'evolution' 1005
federalism 117
globalization, and rise of
Hindu right 665
growth rate of India's 1321,
1324, 1361
liberalization/reforms 268, 276,
657, 1344, 1438, 1441n,
1469
and cost of welfare
programmes 1066
majoritarian democracy and
1436–9
and religious
majoritarianism 1438
nationalism 658, 1050
organization 1337n, 1343,
1344, 1357
policy, democracy and 1468–9
in villages 1346
sociology 1344
structure, of tribals 395
surplus, investments in
commercial activities
1416
theory 1343
transactions 1333, 1345, 1348
Economic and Political Weekly 42,
52
'economism', protest 523
eco-sociology 175

Edict of Nantes 919
education (al) 74, 936, 1034–5
access to, in Brahmanical
system 1036
achievements, in India 997
administration 1367
aspirations 978–9
backwardness 1482
caste-based reservations/
concessions in 991n,
1383, 1470, 1481
caste, and tribe and
inequalities in 982–4
of daughters 977
and sons 1171
'demand' for 1019
deprivation 975–81, 985, 988
discourse on 999, 1007
disparities in 982–9
elementary 979, 980, 989
and employment 975
of girls/women 1005–6, 1165,
1547
informal and formal 1034
institutions 936, 1518
and literacy, failure of 749
Mahatma Gandhi on 1003,
1009–11, 1024
modern system of 1018, 1429,
1430, 1497
for tribal children 985
among Muslims 793–4
natives and, in the nineteenth
century 999–1003
neglect of, in tribal areas 985
planning 697, 741, 743, 749,
1002
policies, and implementation
of 1018–24
Rabindranath Tagore on 1008
resistance to 990
and social inequality 988
sociolinguistics 702
Western 1450
work and 1168–71
'Education Barons' 1048
Education Commission 253, 747,
1480, 1481
recommendations of 1482
Report 1481
Education and the People of India
999
1857 uprisings, nomadic

pastoralists and 229
elderly/aging population 315,
    1071, 1146–9
  kinship behaviour towards 959,
    1146–9
  medication for 961
  social obsolescence of 960
  status of 959
  violence towards 1146
Election Commission 543
electoral politics 18, 447, 493,
    1382, 1463, 1466, 1469,
    1471, 1498, 1500, 1506,
    1540
  at grass-root level 1512
  in municipal and district
    boards 1507–10
electorate, and mandate 1465
  pluralized 1502
  social and demographic
    characteristics of 1500
  system of separate, for
    minorities 1431
electronic industry 1271
elementary education 979, 988,
    999
elite groups, in India, educational
    and political culture of
    1453
  and discourse in Modern
    Indian languages 736
  lifestyles of 684
  among peasantry 1215
  and Western democratic ideals
    1450
Elwin Committee 392
emancipatory movements 1530
enumeration, classification and
    role of numbers 7–11
Emergency of 1975–77, imposed
    by Indira Gandhi 194,
    1381, 1437, 1459
  and 'compulsory sterilisation'
    194
  intensified family planning
    during 306
  and suspension of political
    rights 1437
emotion(al), abuse of children
    1137
  bonds between parents and
    children 1179, 1181,
    1189

cultural construction of 1179–
    1200
  families, childrearing and
    1186–91
  gender, colonial legacy and
    ideologies of 1198–20
  among lower status groups of
    Hindus and Muslims
    1198
  negative 1196
  and sensations 1181
empirical science of languages 715
employer-employee relations 1245,
    1247, 1248, 1255, 1301
employment 1048, 1277–8
  access to 1302
  of backward castes 1477
  growth in 1277, 1279
  in informal sector 1302, 1309
  labour force and 1286
  gross domestic product and
    1286
  modality 1299–1303
  pattern of 1266, 1297, 1312
  practices 1209
  regulating 1310
  relations 1251, 1253
  reservations for backward
    castes and Scheduled
    Castes 1383
  and unemployment, estimate
    and structure of 188
Employment Assurance scheme
    1022
Employment Guarantee Scheme
    1259
Encyclopedia Britannica 1032
Encyclopedia Mundarica 584
endogamy 17, 411, 899
Engel v. Vitale, USA 922
engineering, education in 1049–50
England, Church of England, the
    official Church 929
  curtailment of Papal
    interference by monarchs
    914
  see also Britain
English Civil Law 1038
English language 726, 742, 1456
  Indianization of 708, 735
  as an instrumental medium
    735
  loan-words, in modern Indian

languages 733
  as medium 1001, 1024, 1040
    by Indian elite 736
  and Sanskrit 727, 734, 736–8
  teaching of 743, 1038, 1041
  Western learning and 1002,
    1003
  writing in 709
Enlightenment 3, 93n, 716, 1008,
    1024
  in Europe 40, 83
  march of Reason 1565
  period, rational-empirical
    phase of 715
  theory 103
enrolment, in school 1019, 1052
enterprises, modern, and unions
    1246–7
entrepreneurship, in India 1211,
    1274, 1319–34
  forms of 1334
environment (al), diseases, areas
    prone to 139
  factors, and constraints on
    health 307–9
  ecology and 141–76
  geography of health hazard
    and 340–4
  movements in India 20–1, 141,
    170, 331, 1529
  pollution 343
    industrial development and
    168
  protection, laws on 169
  and public sphere 169–76
  religious representation and
    143–4, 152–4
  resources 343–4
    degradation of 1365
  studies 32, 54
  voluntary organizations and
    172–3
environmentalization, of the West
    142
epics 618, 659, 834
  oral tradition of 610
  performances based on 601,
    608
  televisual propagation of 657
epidemics, and disease
    management in villages
    426
  and slow growth rates 190, 191

epidemiology 342
epistemology 715
Epperson v. Akansas, USA 926
equality, 124, 570, 690, 903, 1429,
1453
in civil rights 1548
concept of 498
of educational opportunity
1046
educating women for 1051–4
ideals of 1381
and justice, principles of 1525
Western ideas of 1381
of all religions 1430
in the West 53
'equality of all religions', of
Mahatma Gandhi 124,
125
equalitarianism 1485
Eseki, goddess, in Tamil
Hinduism 895
*An Essay on the History of Civil
Society* 118
Establishment Clause, USA 922
Etawah project 436
Ethiopia, developmental projects
in and local self-help
initiatives in 1373
ethnic groups 53
friction/conflict among 284,
298, 537, 727
mobilization of 580, 1515
revolution by, in industrialized
societies 704
segregation of 664
tradition and modernity in the
languages of 732
and violence 1572
ethnic identity 53, 278, 403, 1170
ethnicity 53, 1501, 1509, 1540
and linguistic and discourse
strategies 726
notion of 705
ethnocentrism 89n
ethnology 6, 10, 11
ethnography 23, 33, 35, 45, 655, 965
of communication 703
methodology of 689
and public culture 662
of speaking 599
'of the State' 660
ethnonational identity, and purity
664

'ethnosociology' 968
eugenics, fantasy of 959
Euro-American theatre 620
Eurocentric models 1333, 1336n
Eurocentric paradigms 1330
Europe, Catholic 898
Church and State's view on
custom in the Middle
Ages 128
civil society in 120–2
developments in 1320
higher education in 1049, 1050,
1054
industrial capitalism, rise of
1324
industrial revolution in 141–2
industrialists in 1331
post-Renaissance and
transition to non-secular
absolutist regimes 911–17
refugees from Eastern to
Western 284
religion and politics in 910,
911, 930
social history of 655
social sciences and modernity
in 33
towns in 462
transition from 'feudal to
capitalism' in 1321
urban disturbances/violence in
1564, 1565
European capitalism 1330, 1331
European civilization, and Indian/
Hindu civilization 91n
on tribal people 387
European culture 1038–40, 1042
European education, in India
1039, 1041–2
European Enlightenment 101, 102,
690
European knowledge, and culture
1039–40
European languages,
modernization of 732
European legal and administrative
traditions 554
European modernity 83
European nomadism 229
European scholars 43
European societies 773, 1570
European vocabulary 636
evangelical discourses, on caste 900

Evangelicalism 790
Event, Metaphor, Memory 1579
'evil eye', myth of 840, 853, 1186
evil mouth 840, 841, 853
evil spirit, possession by 875–8
'exchange entitlements', and 1943
Bengal famine 1221
exchange relations 1235, 1344,
1345, 1355
'Exchange Theorists' 700
exit policy 1281
exogamous patrilineal clans
(*gotra*) 1116
exorcism/exorcist 877, 878, 1128,
1179, 1196
expatriate South Asian families
1173
exploitation, 1220, 1224, 1325
of child workers 944, 948,
1246, 1255, 1257, 1259,
1303
concept of 1541
under imperialism 1326, 1433
in informal sector 1302
of labour 1257–9
and oppression of tribals 385
of women workers 1246, 1255,
1257, 1258, 1303
extended/joint families 205, 1160
work and services in 942
Extension Education 1046
externalities, interjurisdictional
1367, 1368
negative 1368
positive 1368
extra-marital relationship 1143

Fabian Socialists 1469
factory, acts, against child
employment under
colonial rule 942
mode of production, and
labour 1245
fairs, at pilgrim centers 422
Faizabad 1509
communal divide in 1512
familism 1062, 1174
family/familial, in India 40, 44,
50, 1062–4, 1069, 1327
as basic unit of production and
consumption 1215
child-rearing and emotion
1186–91

concept of 1062
-controlled firms 1328
and diaspora 1172–4
dilemma 1158–60
discourse on 1058
exploitation and violence on
women within 1129
hierarchy 1150
honour 1084, 1160
and household, and status of
women in 1130
structure, regional variation
in 962
household versus 1068–73
ideology 1059, 1140–1, 1150
and inequalities in society 1131
and kinship studies 1061, 1073,
1092, 1131
life, alternatives to 1162–4
dysfunctional and
pathological aspects of
1091
loyalty 945, 946
and marriage options within
caste system 1160
as mediating institution,
violence and 1577
obligations 1191
patterns 1066, 1068
person beyond the 1158–75
profession 1348
property, sharing of 1063, 1085
'recovering' 1073–88
relations 1084, 1087–8
renunciation of 1172
social functions of 1077–87
socialization and interaction,
theory of 1065
solidarity 1125
in the 'system of families'
1089–90
'values' 1066
violence in 1132
women renouncing
subordination in 1167
work, by children 944
family farm 1532
and peasant's mode of
production 1384
*Family and Kin in Indo-European
Culture* 1063
family planning programme 193,
210, 306, 313

'family of procreation' 1089
famines 429, 450, 1206
in Bengal 191, 1221
and mortality 307
and slow growth rates 190
in southern India 1221
and starvation deaths 1222
of 1866 428
of 1899–1900 212n, 428
farm labourers, patronage and
bondage of 1245, 1256
farmers/peasants 452
affluent 1536
interests in national politics
1458
-labour relationship 1233
-living below subsistence level
1245
movements 1231, 1535
see also peasants
Farmland Improvement
Associations, Korea 1367

fascism 115
fasts (ing), observance of, among
Hindus 867, 1161, 1195
Fateh Sagar 428
father-son relationship 1088, 1182
fecundity, girls 1081
federal structure, in India 1433,
1454–5
based on American model 1515
female/girls, age at marriage of
198
'autonomy' 1078
body, aesthetic evaluation of
1168–9
inferiorization at death of
679–80
notions of perfect 1146
as object of desire and
control 1130
education of 979, 982, 983,
1000
in villages 983
foeticide 196, 197, 1132
as household heads 205–6
infanticide 197, 679, 1051–2,
1081
in Tamil Nadu 137
labour/workforce 207–9, 337,
1257–8
and role of literacy 338

literacy among 997, 1019
a by-product of male
literacy 937, 983
mortality, excess 196, 197
population among Scheduled
Castes and Scheduled
Tribes 200
puberty, and sexuality 1080
reproductive behaviour of 1079
self-employed 338
sexuality 171, 1081
sterlization 199
feminine identity 1082, 1149
feminine socialization 1140, 1145
feminism 658, 1164–8, 1550
feminist expressions, through
cinema and television
shows 1166
feminist ideologies 1164
feminist movements 1054, 1164,
1529
feminist perspectives 337–40
feminist studies 1166, 1546
fertility levels/rate 1077
by age 199–200
and birth rate 193–5
decline in, urbanization and
industrialization and 195,
210–11, 1072
dysfunctional 1078
'explosive' 305
among peasant families 942,
943
Festival of India 1986 657
festivals, in India 684
performance of bizarre rituals
at 873
in villages 415
and votive rituals 873
feudal society 507, 528
'feudalism to capitalism' 1334n
fidelity 20
fiqh traditions 104
Fiji, Indian indentured labour in
265, 440
Indian population in 266–7
filial piety 960, 967
films, as popular medium 564,
656, 661
fine arts tradition 587
'Fire', lesbianism in film 1166
fire sacrifice (*homa*) 873
firewalking ritual 875–6

'first language', concept of 748
fiscal crisis 1435, 1439
fishing, agriculture and 160
    ritual for Lord Murugan, in Sri
        Lanka 865–7
Five Mile Act of 1665, England
    918
Floods 429
A Flowering Tree 836
Fluid zone/fluidity, concept of 748
folk, category of 567–92
    and civilization 567
    community 569–61, 573–5,
        592n
    consciousness, vernacular
        culture in Bengal 575–80
    craft 570
    culture, concept of 568, 569,
        573, 576
    feminism 1167
    forms of literature, in Telugu
        724
    hero 574–5
    Hinduism, 'spiritism' of 776
    identity, and national culture
        568–80
    literature in Bengal 577
    '-popular' 611
    and the primitive societies 579
    race and nation in Nazi
        Germany 570–2
    religion 568, 581–6, 782, 1530
        polytheism of 576
    societies, and modernity 579
    songs, gender-based
        discrimination in 339
        Rajasthani women's 1167
    'spirit', Bengali 576
    tradition 576, 577
    and tribal art 567, 587
    '-urban continuum' 1519n
    wisdom 545
folk art 568, 586–91
    as ritual art 588
    versus popular art 588–91
folklore/folktales 572, 834, 853,
    1161
    and proletarian culture, in
        Soviet Russia 572–5
    role of 574
    scholarship 566, 591
    and women's genres 1088
food, access to 307

consumption 682–3
crops, decline in area under
    1221
    and non-food crops, export
        of 1221
    -gathering as mode of
        livelihood 156
    security 1206–7
Food and Agricultural
    Organization (FAO) 442
foragers/foraging 225, 237, 245–6,
    252
    'forced migrants' 292
Ford Foundation 2, 65, 76, 1230,
    1494–5, 1519n
foreign private capital 1436, 1439
Forest Department, under colonial
    rule 231
Forest Research Institute (FRI)
    1014–15
forest(s), acts 394
    -based, and agrarian
        movements 403–4
    conflicts, between forgers and
        the State 240
    control over 171
    policies, on ban on grazing and
        felling 229, 231, 237
        under British 388, 1534
        and rights of tribals 393
    resources, management of 1371
    revenue from 388
    satyagraha 404
    'tribe' 375, 388
    utilization of 164
formal sector, employment/labour
    in 1293, 1295
formal system, of education, in
    India 1000, 1033–4, 1170
Forum against Oppression of
    Women 306
Foundation for Research in
    Community Health 1134
Fox's Book of Martyrs 121,
    132n
frailty 961
frame alignment approach 1528
France, civil code in 129
    religious persecution and
        intolerance in 918–19
    religious and political rights of
        Huguenots 919
    revolution in 116

separation of religion from
    State 929
supremacy of King in 915
franchise 1508, 1514
fraternity 688, 1453
free and compulsory education
    977, 980
Free exercise clause 922
'free rider' issue, on common
    property resources 1528
freedom 1453
    of belief, expression and
        association 928, 932
    of conscience 922–4
    'natural', reform and 690
    of opinion and expression,
        denial of, during colonial
        rule 1429
    of worship, belief and
        association, in England,
        Sweden and Norway 929
French Cardinals 913
French religious riots 1570
French revolution 2, 3, 117, 129,
    921, 1356, 1565
Friedreich Elbert Stiftung agency,
    Germany 441
Friendship ties 416
frontiers, and nomad territories
    251
fundamental rights 1396, 1433
fundamentalism, in India 33, 770
funeral, Islamic prohibition of
    'loud' wailing at 1199
    post-, ceremonies 424
    rites 415

Gaddis, of Himachal Pradesh 158,
    234, 243–5, 423
    migration pattern of 231, 243
    tradition of Dhaula Dhar 225
Gaduliya Lohars, smiths of
    Rajasthan 226, 239, 248–
    9, 253
    migration by 249
galis, and kuchas 466
Gaṇapati festival, Tilak's co-
    option of 637
Ganapati, worship of, in
    Yaksagana 614
Gandhi, Mahatma/Gandhian,
    concepts 1530
    era 1430

ideology of trust 1208
national discourse 1540
-Nehru friendship 1434–5
-Nehru phase 1413, 1430
and reforms and nationalist
movement 18
and social reconstruction 172
stress on hand-weaving 444
view of self-rule and self-
reform 123, 124
Gandhi Labour Institute 1249
Gandiya Math Institute 811
Ganga river, immersion of ashes
of the dead into 421
Snan at Garh Mukteshwar 422
Ganga-Yamuna region 1422
ganj 1342
gaon/gram 410
panchayats 1518
garibi hatao programme, of
Indira Gandhi 1437, 1458
Gavli pastorals 224
gay kinship, practice of 1058
lovemaking 1163
movement, in USA 1059
gāye halud, emotional songs at
weddings 1199
Gazetter tradition 330
Gender, age and kinship, and
children's work 948
hierarchies based on, and
position of children 948
as basis of disadvantage 1087
bias 338
inequalities in education
977, 981–2, 1054, 1207n
'blindness' 1235
caste and, and discrimination
795–6
colonial legacy and ideologies
of emotion 1198–20
differences/discrimination 678–
83, 1386
division of labour 139, 171
and kinship study in South and
South East Asia 1075
language and 706–7
'Orientalism' 1200
in public areas 466
relations 1130, 1546
and sexuality 1005, 1199
socio-economic position and
power 339–40

-specific conversational
differences 727
and State, refugee studies on
293–5
studies 32, 53–4, 1546
tribes, castes and 332–40
and violence 1129, 1577
and work 337–9
genealogies, of old body 938
General Committee of Public
Instruction 1478
General Election
Elections of 1937, 1514
First (1952) 1496, 1497
Second 1497
Third 1500
Fourth 1517
of 1967 1381
of 1967, Congress Party's
defeat in 1457, 1458
of 1971 1437
of 1977 1437
impact of 1500–2
General Rules (Civil) (1987) 1405n
Gentil's atlas, of Mughal *subas* 327
geography (cal), recent
developments in 329–32
social and cultural 326–48
of social hierarchies, tribes,
castes and gender 332–40
societies 329
geometry, devlopment of 1035
'geriatrics' 957, 959, 960
German Evangelical Mission
Society 891
German Romantics 570
Germany, 575
disestablishment of state and
church 928–9
expansionist policy of 571
race, folk and nation in 570–2
religious persecution and
intolerance in 918
geroanthropology 957, 960
gerontology 938, 957, 960
writing 955
geropsychology 963
geropsychiatric distress 963
Ghana 1287
decentralized government in
1364
Ghasiram, Nathdvara painter 641,
642

Ghatiya Jogi nomads, in
Rajasthan 239
ghatwals 395
Ghaznavid invasion, 327
and migration of Charan
nomads 228
ghunghat (veil), use of, by
women 682
The Gift 1566
'gift of Christianity' 909, 910
gift(s), -giving, a Western culture
1345
marriage and commodification
of 1059
relationship, and market
relationship 1210, 1345,
1349, 1350
and social relation 1345
girl(s), first menstruation of 1169
murder of 1134
as *paraya dhan* 1141
socialization of 1082
unpaid domestic work by 945
victim of discrimination in the
family 1131–2
violence against 1127
see also female
globalization 86, 138, 155, 348,
369, 404, 1050, 1051
combinatorial modes of
subsistence, nation-states
and 168–9
impact of 440–3
Goa, beliefs in *bhut* spirit in 897
conversion to Christianity in
886–8, 893
God of Small Things 1167
Godan 409
Goddess tradition, in Mukkuvar
Christianity 895–6
The Golden Bough 968
Gollas, pastoral, in Mysore 232
Gonds 398, 400
marriage with alternate
generation among 1111
satyagraha 404
Rajas 382
Gorakhanāthīs 807
Gosāis 808
goshalas, shelter for animals 345
Gossner Evangelical Lutheran
Mission 891
gotra, and marriages 1116

gotrantara 1118
governance 936
    and order, Western notion of
        1387
    and research 1247–9
    structures, control rights in
        1376
Government of India Act of 1909,
    importance of 1512
Government of India Act of 1919
    1513
Government of India Act of 1935
    19, 1426, 1433, 1483,
    1512–14
'Graanthika' (H-code) 725
gradational approach,
    stratification and 524–7
Graeco-Italian tradition, and
    spiritual and temporal
    power 115
grain riots, 1568, 1570
Gram swaraj(ya), of Mahatma
    Gandhi 370, 443, 445
Gramadan movement, of Vinoba
    Bhave 445, 451
Grameen Bank, Bangladesh 1363
Grammar (s) 700, 712–14, 714,
    724
    compilation of, by missionaries
        773
    theories of 713–14
    writing 750
grammatical and social
    constructs, of language
    737–8, 751
Grant Medical College, Bombay
    1002
Grants-in-aid Code 1481, 1482
graphization, of language 737
grass-root mobilization, women
    engaged in 1549
grass-root politics 1505, 1507,
    1515, 1518
    research on 1496
Great Revolt of 1857 1425, 1426
Great Tradition, of Hindu society
    66, 71, 729, 730, 733,
    862, 1018
    and languages 730
    and Little Tradition 14
    role of Sanskrit in 13
The Great Transformation 1344
Green Revolution 344, 426, 437,

440, 1208, 1232, 1233,
    1236, 1435, 1532
    and after 1229–32
    areas, children working in 943
    impact of 1207
Grihasthashrama (householder)
    1036, 1162
Grihya Sutras 780
grophization 738
*Group Dynamics in a North
    Indian Village: A Study
    of Factions* 1495
growth rate, size of population
    and 190–2
    see also economy, growth rate
Gudem-Rampa risings, in Andhra
    Pradesh 1540
Guhilot clan 418
guilds (*mahajan*) 1034, 1244, 1321
    socialism 117
guinea worm 342
Gujar caste, pastoral nomads 158,
    231, 418
Gujarat 1505
    birth rate in 194
    crisis over reservation policy in
        495
    entrepreneurs in 1328
    public culture studies of 663
    Scheduled Tribes in 201
    total fertility rate in 194
    tribal movements in 1538
    urbanization of 190
Gupta dynasty 1419
    rulers of 1419
    subcontinental State under
        1414–20
Gupta period, performance of
    Sanskrit in 734
guru, bahin, institution of 417
    bhai, institution of 417
    paramparā 804
    and *shisya* 804, 1009
Gurukul educational movement
    1007–8
Guyana, British, Indian
    immigrants in 266–7
'gypsies' 228
    children 253
'gyroscope' 1182

Habitual Offenders Act 235
Hakims 312

Hakkipikki, of southern India 225
    sedentarization of 246
hajj 790
hali payments 412
Hanafi School 794
Hanbali school 794
Harappan civilization 779
    symbiotic relationship with
        nomads in 222
Harappan culture 779
'Harijans' 18, 478, 776, 1542
    equality for 493
    ideology of 484, 486
Haryana, birth rate in 194, 195
    female infanticide in 197
    pastoralism in 224
    sex-ratio in 196–7
    total fertility rate in 194
hathayoga 807
Hatkar Dhangar group, pastoral
    234
haveli, among Hindus and
    Muslims 153, 463, 467
Havik Brahmin society, women in
    1185
healers/healing 310, 1198
    performances 1179
    rites, in South Asia 1196
health, care, and preference for
    boys 1140
    and diseases 140
        socio-cultural framework of,
            in India 303–15
    facilities 253, 343
    global context of 303–7
    hazards, environment and
        340–4
    inequality, social inequality and
        139
    medicine, study of 54
    services 304, 307, 342
    sickness and suffering, beliefs
        and knowledge about
        309–13
    State and 313–15
'Health for All by the Year 2000'
    313
hearth-group units 1085
heavy industry sector, self-reliance
    in 1435
    in State sector 1434
Hegelian-Marxist idea, of
    Aufhebung 1529

herbal pharmacopcia 310
hereditary, identity 1498
    status groups 1497, 1509, 1516,
        1517
    succession among householders
        821
heretical movements, Buddhism
        and Jainism and 1416
heterogeneity 1094n
hetero-sexuality 20, 1058
hierarchy (cal), 53, 1539
    caste system and 515, 516
    categories of 1499
    in closed system of
        stratification 509
    and difference 503, 506–8, 510,
        517, 522, 523, 526
    ideologies, and division of
        society 152
    male-female 1167
    in Marx and Weber 527–9
    model of 770
    of power 502, 706
    relation 5
    and social change/mobility
        502–29
    status and 52, 518–20, 522
    of wealth 502
High Courts 1389, 1392, 1399
    deterioration of justice in 1400
    Kerala case study 1395–9
    as supervisory/disciplinary
        authority 1398–9
high-fertility countries, and birth
        control by the poor 943
high schools, functions of 1012
high yielding variety (HYV) seeds,
        introduction of 1230
higher education 937–8, 1024,
        1032–54, 1272
    access to 1046
    and economic development
        1049–51
    expansion and upgrading of
        facilities 1045–6
    in pre-colonial India 1035–8
    as a social institution 1033,
        1034
    voluntary bodies for 1043
    for women 1052
    see also women
hijras 1163–4
''Hill and Forest' tribes 377

Hill Pandaram pastorals 240
Himachal Pradesh, educational
        achievement in 1022, 975
    homogeneous character of
        village communities in
        988
    literacy rate in 937, 984, 986,
        989
    social inequalities in 992n, 988
    total fertility rate in 194
    women's economic work in
        1086
Hind Swaraj 132n
Hinayana Buddhism 784
Hindi films, and fantasies 1191–2
    images in 633
    influence of 588
Hindi language, borrowings from
        733
    development of 744
    discontent in south India and
        West Bengal 1456
    and Marathi 720–1
    as official link language 747
    and Urdu language 125–6, 721–
        2
        and Hindustani language
        721–4
Hindu culture, 657
    classical 100
Hindu deity, images of 626, 628,
        632, 636
Hindu doctrine, three paths to
        salvation in 864
Hindu identity 796, 170
    tribal identity and 1385
The Hindu Jajmani System 432
Hindu joint family 1058, 1064
Hindu law 11, 480, 1038, 1063,
        1106
    on marriage 1104
Hindu life-cycle rituals 1080–1
Hindu Mahasabha 1511, 1512,
        1515
Hindu majoritarian vision 1382,
        1461, 1473n
Hindu marriage, hierarchy of
        caste and 1090, 1120
    patterns 1117–20
Hindu Marriage Act 1122–3
Hindu militant nationalism,
        women's role in 1549
Hindu myth 836

Hindu nationalism 132n, 658,
        1380, 1546
    and popular culture 656, 658
    and reformist tradition 1456
    rise of 1460, 1461
Hindu nationalists/groups 1456,
        1461, 1546, 1549
Hindu orthodoxy, in Bengal 578
Hindu 'personal laws' 1058, 1077
Hindu population, differences in
        beliefs and practices
        among 775
    -Muslim relations 5, 11, 1575
    spread of, in India 777
    state-wise distribution of 777–8
Hindu revivalism 665–6, 1489
Hindu Samaj 1511
Hindu/Sanskritic historiographical
        tradition 99–100
Hindu scriptures, caste in 479–89
Hindu and Sikh refugees, from
        Pakistan to India after
        Partition 269–70
Hindu society 13, 20, 379, 1321,
        1477
    assimilation of tribals into 382,
        399, 400
    caste and 1476
    characteristics of 1344
    religious and secular in 879
    symbols and rituals 890, 1017
    towns 463
    tradition 576, 795
    widows, and remarriages,
        legality of 1122, 1123
Hindu Succession Act of 1956
        1086
Hindu Widows' Remarriage Act
        (1856) 1122
Hinduism 108, 201, 581, 593n,
        770, 775–6, 796, 828,
        832–6, 909, 1170, 1321,
        1542, 1543
    Ambedkar's stand on 1543
    classical 66
    devotional 772
    dominant religion 775
    dualism in 862
    folk and tribal religions in 383,
        581
    later 146–50
    notions of karma and
        reincarnation in 830

possession in 874–8
renouncer and individual
mobility 512
supernatural beliefs in 861
Vedism and early 779–83
Hindustan Lever, schooling as
business by 1024–5
Hindustani language 722–3,
1009
Hindi-Urdu- and, borrowings
in 723
Hindutva 123, 649n, 657, 796,
1018, 1170
ideology 1549
women under the new ideology
of 1550
hinterlands, towns and 468–9
Hiroshima, atomic bombing of
1387, 1565
historical sociology 44, 102
historiography, of Indian society
6, 99–111, 659
history 581, 716
and anthropology 6, 7, 109
myth and 828
writing of 100–1, 105
*History and Culture of the Indian
People* 104
History of India 104
The History of Sexuality 958
Ho, movement of 1538
Holi festival 415
holism, in India 4, 52, 53
and hierarchy 483
Holmstrom, Mark 1326
homa (fire sacrifice) 841, 844, 873
homeopathy 313
'homo duplex' 1566
homo economicus 1288
homo-eroticism 1183
Homo Hierarchicus 104, 482, 483,
484, 1183
homo socialis 1289
homogeneity 452, 685
homosexual activities 1163
horse sacrifice (Asvamedha) 602,
603
Hos 403
Satyagraha by 404
Hotar (Rigveda), recitation by 602
Hotoku movements, in Japan 1324
household(s), change, dynamics
of 1070

characteristics of 203–4
as commensal and co-resident
group 1069
composition, formation, and
dispersion 1091
definition of 1093n
family and 1068–72, 1092
head of 1087
ideology 961
inequality in 1138–40
notion of 1062
role of, between individual and
the State 1086
size 187, 1070
work by women 983, 1131
*The household dimension of the
family in India* 1069
'householder' 803, 851, 1160
and ascetic ideals 1163
ideologies of 484, 486
sects 817
householdership 1076, 1162
versus renunciation 1161
'houseless' persons, enumeration
of 186
human geographers 327–9
human resource development
(HRD) 1050, 1254, 1266
human rights, guarantee of 1496
violation of 1385
hunter-gatherers 157, 167, 220
as mode of livelihood 156–8
and subsistence 143
by tribals, and impoverishment
157
husband, purchase of 901
Husain Sagar 428
Hyderabad state, Indian army's
intervention in 1432
revolt by Communist Party of
India (CPI) in 1535
hymns, devotional, in bhakti 866
hypergamous marriages 1120,
1142

iconic mythic 564
identity (ties), -based political
parties 1464
and boundaries, conflicts and
548
and diaspora 340
European 1015
ethnicity and 403

formation 404, 568, 1149, 1546
language and 748–51
nationalism, tradition and 551,
575
-oriented paradigm' 1529
politics 659
ideology 1501, 1528
'idiolect', concept o 697, 701
idol worship 795
illiteracy, among adults 1303,
1361
among children 949, 976, 1018,
1019
illness, and affliction 1179
'idoms' 1186
and psychopathology 1184–6
image (s), empowerment of 631
'fleshly eye' and power of 627
of gods 641
in Indian culture 625–48
power of 627
production, and consumption
of 565
and ideology 644
ritual utility of 641
worship, attack on 816
Images of Aging 967
Immaculate Conception 789
immigrant population 264
Immigration Act of 1965, USA
267
Immunization 306
Immunology 1046
imperial edicts 1424
Imperial Gazetteers 428
imperialism 111, 117
historiography 104 import,
liberalization 1436
substitution strategy 1328
impurity, menstruation and 1124
widows symbol of 680
incest, prohibition of 1089–90
income, from agriculture 1299
fluctuation in 1296
in the informal sector 1298,
1299, 1305
and stratification 507
indebtedness, of farmers/workers
1232–4, 1256
Independence, India's 46, 448
movement 1534
post-, Darwinian politics 1515–
18

Independent Commission on International Humanitarian Issues 292, 293
Independent Labour Party (1936) 1543
indentured labour system, by British planters 265
India/Indian 74, 122–4
  absence of equal liberty in 932
  aging in 961–3
  agrarian context 1216–19
  British imperialism and 104–8
  British Orientalism and 103–4
  changing villages in 436
  China relations 271
  'civilization' 247, 387, 707, 1113
    and ancient Greek civilization 103
    and Western European civilization 91n
  closed system of stratification in 511, 516
  entrepreneurship in, study of 1319–34
  formation of sovereign (1947) 1431
  higher education in pre-colonial 1035–8
  Hindu religio-spritual tradition and culture 80
  judiciary in 1399–1402
  modern contemporary 554–7
  nationalism 45, 575, 1413, 1513
    Mahatma Gandhi's emergence as leader of 1415
  north, marriage among Indo-Aryan families 1114–16
  Partition of in 1947 271
    and refugee flow, and rehabilitation of 287–91
  pre-colonial India 551–3
  riot victims in 1567
  scholars 43
  since Independence 433–40
  social life in, and holism 4
  society, historiography of 99–111
  South 1420
    caste associations in 492
    women's position in 338
  theology, reform of 903

India, Ancient and Modern 626
India Annual Report 1406n
India's Changing Villages 73, 437
Indian Conference of Social Work 377
Indian Council of Social Science Research (ICSSR) 41, 47, 54, 57–8, 331, 1053, 1249
  and Indian Council of Medical Research 303
Indian Diaspora 33, 269
Indian Educational Commission (1882) 1003
Indian Educational Policy of 1904 745
Indian English 708–9
  and native English 709
Indian History Congress 12
Indian Journal of Gender Studies 53
Indian Journal of Labour Economics (IJLE) 1248
Indian Labour Conference 1942 1248
  1957 1280
Indian Labour Journal 1248
Indian Missionary Council 904

Indian nation-state 1413–39
  democratic, secular and developmental 1430–6
Indian National Committee 329, 332, 348
Indian National Congress (INC) 1431, 1451, 1515
  establishment of 1507
  'National Education Movement' of 746
  national leadership of 1511
  organizational structure of 1451
  Pradesh Congress Committee 1451
  reorganization of 1430
  see also Congress Party
'Indian Oedipus' 857n
Indian Peace Keeping Force (IPKF), in Sri Lanka 1575
Indian Penal Code (IPC 1983) 1143
Indian Press Act 1910 639
Indian Psychoanalytical Society 833

'Indian public school' 1013
Indian Society for Labour Economics' 1248
Indian Sociological Society 18, 42, 72, 440
Indian Statistical Institute, Calcutta 188
Indian Trade Union Act 1926 1247
Indian Wildlife (Protection) Act 1972, amendment to 237

Indian Village 73, 436
India's Villages 436
'Indic' religions 775–7, 779–99, 805
indigenous banking, decline of during colonial rule 1428
indigenous educational systems, decline of 999–1002, 1041–2
indigenous groups, in America and Australia 378, 379
indigenous learning v. European learning, controversy over 1039–40
'individualism' 1007, 1008, 1062, 1381, 1449
  values of 1174
  in the West 4, 53
Indo-Anglians 735–6
Indo-Aryan linguistic categories, of tribals 381
Indo-Aryan pattern of marriage 1105, 1114–16
Indo-Bhutanese friendship treaty 1950 286
Indo-European family law 1106
Indo-European hypothesis, on science of language 715
Indo-European towns 463–4
Indo-Nepal Friendship Treaty of 1950 272
Indology 6, 45, 581, 110, 600, 688, 1064
  and sociology 14
  approach to the study of family, society and culture 44, 1085
Indonesia, 1288
  decentralization in, and decline in poverty 1375
Indus Valley civilization 580, 779
  and trading in 224

industries (al), capitalism 1320,
        1330
    in the West 1321, 1324
    development 1321–2, 1326
        and environmental pollution
            168
    enquiry commissions into
        conditions of workers in
        1246, 1248–9
    labour/workers 208–09, 1208,
        1246, 1248, 1250
    socio-economic conditions
        of 1248
    technology and 1266–83
    women and children as 1246
Industrial Courts 543
Industrial Disputes Act 544
Industrial Revolution 116, 121,
        129, 141, 168, 1049, 1220,
        1222
    impact of 1245
industrial robots 1266
industrial societies, stratification
        in 524–7
Industrial and Technical
        Institutions 1046
'industrial zone' 464
industrialists, in India 1327, 1328
    from artisans to 1326–7
industrialization 307, 1050, 1207,
        1246, 1249, 1290, 1528
    colonialism and tardy 12
    concept of 370
    and cultural impediments to
        growth 1250
    in Europe 1321
    factorized 1289
    impact of, on family pattern
        1067–8
    in India and Europe 1330
    native 1334n
    planned process of 1251
    'problems' of 1208
    process of 1066, 1250
    threat to rural livelihood 168
    and uprooting of tribals 388
    urbanization, and fertility
        decline 210–11
inequality (ies) 48, 51–2, 974,
        1375
    forms of, in tribal society 395–
        6
    gender-based 1131

in the household 1138–40
    regional and social 1207
    in rights over land 1218
    social and economic 1370
    stratification and 504
infant mortality rates (IMR) 192–
        3, 212n, 217, 306
    among Muslim population 202
    among Scheduled Castes and
        Scheduled Tribes 201
infanticide, female 1132
    birth order and 1136
    outlaw of 1134
informal sector 1255–7, 1287–
        1313
    bias against women 1258
    child labour in 1259
    concept of 1287, 1293, 1297,
        1303
    definition of 1291
    economy in 1301
    importance of 1209
    size and dynamics of 1295–7
    workers in, problems and
        status of 1261, 1304,
        1307, 1308
information technology (IT) 1208,
        1209, 1267, 1268
    impact of, and labour 1251
    importance of 1260
ing, cult of 900
inheritance rights 1075
    of daughters/women 901, 1086,
        1094n, 1123
    rules of 1058
The Inner World 1183
inquiry commissions, under
        British rule 1246,
        1248–9
inquisitorial witchcraft 957
Inquisition 581, 887, 889
Institution Chretienne 918
Institute of Developmental
        Studies 441
Institute of Economic Growth,
        Delhi 47
Institute of Science, Bangalore
        938, 1043
Institute for the Study of Social
        and Economic Change,
        Bangalore 47
insurgent signs and gestures,
        repertoire of 640

insurgency movements, rise of
        1381
Integrated Rural Development
        Programme (IRDP) 437,
        1234, 1259, 1361
integrated tribal development
        project (ITDP) 391
Intensive Agricultural Areas
        Programme (IAAP) 1230
Intensive Agricultural
        Development Programme
        (IADP) 1230
inter-caste marriages 1120
Interactional Sociolinguistics 703,
        727–8
'interior designers' 467
intermediaries 1301, 1307, 1353
    abolition of 429
    role of 1352–5
intermediary tenures, abolition of
        1227
International Catholic Bureau 944
International Congress of Free
        Trade Unions (ICFTU)
        1308
*International Encyclopadiae of
        the Social Sciences* 131n
International Geographical Union
        Conference 329
International Institute for
        Population Sciences (IIPS)
        198, 984
International Labour
        Organization (ILO) 943,
        947, 1247, 1287, 1291,
        1310
    on child labour 441, 941
    report 941
    study 1280, 1282
International Monetary Fund
        (IMF) 1312, 1437, 1438
International Rice Research
        Institute, Manila 441
International Society for Krishna
        Consciousness (ISCON)
        811
International Women's Decade
        1053
International Year of the Child
        1979 943
International Year of the
        Indigenous People, UN
        378

interracial urban living 705
intra-caste marriages 1120
intra-community marriages 1173
'involuntary migrants' 292–3,
        299
Iraq, war in, and drop in
        remittances 268
irrigation/irrigated, agriculture,
        impact on migrant
        nomads 231
    controlled 1230
    budgets 1366
    groundwater, in agriculture,
        and incidence of salinity
        164
    lack of water for 308
    practices 1206
    in villages 160
*Ishwar Chand Jain v. High Court
    of Punjab and Haryana*
    1398
Islam/Islamic 20, 100, 153, 201,
        770, 775–7, 790–4, 796–7,
        909, 1170, 1331
    arrival in India 791
    conversion to 264
    doctrines 1423
    identity 1170
    in India 581
    law 1424
    learning 1037
    lifestyle 689, 690
    mystic aspects of 150
    orthodoxy 791
    pattern of marriage, and South
        Asian Muslims 1120–1
    religion and encounter with
        150–2
    scripture 581
    sharia, personal laws of 1428
    spread of 792
    as world religion 151
Islamic Law, schools of 794
Israel 74
Italy 1375
itīhas 99
itihāsa-purāṇa tradition 828
Izhavas 1544
izzat (honour), defence of 1395

Jacobite or Orthodox Church 789
Jagannatha, Lord, of Puri, Orissa
        782

Jagannātha temple, Puri 811
jagir(s)/jagirdari system 396, 427,
        1422
    abolition of 1227
jagirdars 395
    in princely states 434
Jai Santoshi Maa 633
Jain community/population, in
        India 777–8, 786, 1321,
        1334n
    against Brahminic supremacy
        1416
    ascetic values among 805, 816
    Banias 1334n
    concern for life 148
    literacy and education among
        202
    women population among 196
Jaina 785
Jainism 147, 201, 775, 783, 785–6,
        776, 805, 1119, 1416,
        1440n, 1414
    Digambara group in 786
    and non-violence 786
    opposition to animal sacrifice 148
    Shvetambara group in 786
Jaintias 398
Jaipur, city based on Vastushastra
        461
jajmani (yajaman) system 147,
        176n, 413, 420, 683, 1244,
        1346–7
    notion of 1218–19
    relations 51, 1233
Jalienawala Bagh massacre 1512
Jama Masjid 470
Jamia Milia 938, 1043
jan sunwayis 1370
Jana, and tribe 374
Janata Party 1469
    coalition government of in
        1977 1437, 1489
Janata Vimuki Peramuna 1575
jangamma, class 820
janjati 369
japā-jarā 842
Jarawas, of Andaman Islands 232
    hunting, gathering and fishing
        by 156–7
    problems faced by 247
Japan 1270, 1565
Japanese management system
        1319

Jats (nomads) 228, 416, 418, 434,
        478
    exogamous status of 418
    occupation of 234
    opposition to education 990n
jati (s) 49, 50, 53, 146–7, 687, 411,
        490, 628, 629, 828, 887,
        1542, 1476
    boundaries, in Kerala 894–5
    and caste 374, 477
    concept of 147
    -dharma 1105
    endogamy 148, 521
    identity in the North 1385
    and Islam 151
    and kinship 469
    and occupation 166
    panchayat-like arrangements
        for regulating 551
    -Rajput conflicts 421
    rural 663
    -varna, dichotomy 1476–7
Jatras 414, 421
Jaunpur District, Uttar Pradesh
        1394
Jawahar Rozgar Yojana (JRY)
        1022, 1259, 1361
Jerome, and rejection of custom
        128
Jesuit missionaries 789
Jesus, Lord, divinity of 789
jewellery, market for 1350
    as symbol of status and wealth
        1350
Jew population, in India 4, 24n,
        777–8
    Iraqi, immigration into India
        264
Jharkhand region 590, 1538
    development and tribal
        population in 390
    electrification and irrigation in
        390
    movement for separate state
        333, 403, 582, 593n, 1385,
        1540
    uprooting of tribals in 388
    urban growth in 389
Jharkhand Morcha 403
Jharkhand Party 279
Jhujhar babji 628
Jhunjhari, cult figure of, in
        Rajasthan 227

Jihad 790
jita payments 412
Jodo Buddhism 1324
joint family system, India's 955,
       1062, 1093n, 1191, 1321
    decline of 961, 963, 965, 1058,
       1062, 1069, 1072
    burden/support on daughter-in-
       law 1130
    concept of 1062
    ideology of 1073, 1076–7
    in modern times 1090
    and security 1083
    strongest in north India 1072
    values 1072
    versus nuclear family 50, 1061–
       92
Jorwe phase, pastoral nomadism
       in 222
The Journal of Arts and Ideas
       659
Juang tribes, myths among 853
Judaism 775, 776
judiciary/judicial system, India's
       1389, 1399–1402, 1433
    and backward classes 1485–7
    and delay 1395
    independent 1433
judicial officers 1398
The Jungle and the Aroma of
       Meats *345*
just-in-time (JIT) principles 1266
justice 1381, 1401, 1453, 1570,
       1571

Kabīrpanth (is) 814, 1545
Kadar nomads, of Cochin 232,
       246
Kashtkari Sangathana, on
       education 1026
kaivalya 1161
Kaka Kalekar Commission, report
       of 1488
kala azar 342
Kalamukha Sannyasins, Brahman
       status for 512
Kālāmukha sect, in Karnataka
       806–7
'Kalashnikav culture' 271
Kalbelia nomadic group, in
       Rajasthan 157
    literacy among 974
Kali, goddess, 643, 646, 831

Kali age 847
'Kali Yug' 639–40
Kallidasa, work in Sanskrit 735
    use of Prakrit by 736
Kalighat Bazar paintings 588
Kalighat Pata 588
Kalighat Temple 857n
Kallar community, in Tamil Nadu
       1135
Kalwar caste 1510
Kamar tribe, myths among 854
'Kamaraj Plan' 1517
Kammas 434
    and Reddys, conflict between
       421
Kanarese/Kannada language 720
Kannada folk tales 836
Kannaujia 416
Kānphaṭa Yogīs 807
kanyadana marriage 1117, 1119,
       1123
Kanyakumari, pilgrim center 421
Kapālika sect 513, 806
karma 22, 784–5, 805, 1082
    doctrine of 1321
    notion of 788, 830
Karmika, women's organization
       1147
Karnataka 1370, 1505
    birth rate in 194
    conversion to Christianity in
       889
    education, female 991n
       in rural 990n
    effective decentralization in
       1364
    reservation for OBCs in 494–5
    sex-ratio in 196
    total fertility rate in 194
    urbanization of 190
Karnataka High Court 1403n
Kashmir, elections in 1467
    incursion of tribesmen from
       Pakistan into 1432
    Islam in 792–3
    secessionist movement in 269
Kashmiri displaced persons 286,
       299
Kashmiri Muslim insurgents, and
       violence 286
Kashmiri Pandits, ideology of 1076
Kashmiri Pantis, understanding of
       child and childhood 1082

Kashmiri Pohol 221
katha exposition 609
Kathaki (dance) 611
    jester in 615
Kathakali, dance theatres in
       Kerala 607, 615–18
kathapravacana 609
Kaviraj, Sudipta 1381
Kavitraya, language of 724
'Kayastha party' 1509
Kayasthas 1509, 1511
Kenya 1287
    Indian labour in 440
    population growth rate in 191
Kerala, birth rate in 194–5
    case study of high courts in
       1390, 1395–9
    Catholic Church's control over
       education in 1457
    Christianity in 788, 885
    civil cases in 1393
    health and social welfare
       programmes in 313–14
    jati boundaries in 894–5
    life expectancy in 193
    literacy rate in 976–7, 986,
       1021, 1393
       'Kerala model' in literacy
       and education 937,
       1021–2
    mobilization of labour in 1536
    mortality level, lowest in 210
    school attendance in 1021
    sex-ratio in 196
    urbanization of 190
    villages in 410
Kerala High Court 1390, 1395–9
    Reports of 1391, 1395, 1403n
*Kesavananda Bharati V. State of
       India* 1390
Kerketta 584, 585
Khalapur village study 410
Khalsa faith 788, 797
Khanar vachana 578
Khanna Study, US-financed 305
Khanp 419
Khari Boli dialect 721–2
Kharwars satyagraha 404
Khasis, of North-East 398, 400
    cohabitation among 901
    matrilineal system among 901
'Khattri party' 1509
Khattris 1509–10

Kheda 446
kheda khunt ki devi, village deity in Rajasthan 415
Kheda satyagraha (1917–18) 1534
Khilafat movement 446
Khoba-Khubi, myth/story of, in Assam 839, 841–5, 847–9, 858n
  Sakam, and ritual in marriage 843–5, 850
  story in *Bhima Carita* 851–2
Khubiram, Nathdvara painter 641–2
Khyampa (nomads), of Almora 227
Killekyatha, peripatetic community 225, 248
kin ties/kinship 11, 38, 44, 49–50, 81, 655, 660, 893, 1105–6, 1115, 1159–60, 1190, 1327, 1380, 1495
  and affinity 1090
  behaviour 958, 1069
  and caste 369, 409, 427, 1207
  and cultural and social structural contexts 1131
  and family 961
  fictive 416–17
  hierarchy 52
  ideology 368, 1074–7
  and marriages 418–20, 482, 1058
  mediating rural-urban interconnections 427
  network 1414
  norms 1061, 1072
  organizations 1064, 1078
  patterns 945, 1091, 1167
  solidarity 416
  study of 656, 1058, 1073
  system 983
  in villages 414–17
kindly ideology 484–5
'kindred of cooperation' 419

King, as head of the State and Church 917, 920
  and the Papacy 886
  religion of, as religion of State 913, 916, 920
kingdoms, in southern India 1380
kingship 16, 1421
  divine 108, 115

religious aspect of 115
  and society 485
Kinsey Report 1081
kīrtan performances 1193
kisan 1532
Kisan Sabhas 447, 1385, 1534
  and Communist Party of India 1535
knowledge, 864, 936, 938
  -building and British administration 107
  and power 139
Koiris 1514
Kol triber, insurrection 403
  myths among 853–4
Koli dilemma 421
Konchi Korava, of Karnataka 253
Konkon, Christians, caste differences in 898
  Dhangar pastorals of 242
Konkanasthe 416
Korea, Republic of 1270
  Irrigation bureaucracy/system in 1366, 1367
Koku noblemen 382
Kotwals 468
Krishna/Kṛṣṇa, Lord, cults 1166, 1194
  description of marriage of 847
  image of Lord 633
  temple 647
Krishna-Tungabhadra Valley, agriculture in 223
Krishnalila performances 677
Krist Puranna 894
Kshatriyas 145, 479, 483, 787, 830, 1415, 1477
  and Brahman relationship 483
  identity 828
  reform movement 823
  values 485
kshatriyzation/rajputization 400
kshettra samitis 1518
Kubrawis 793
kulā burhī 844–5
Kurmis 1514
Kula Burhi dances 845
Kūtiyāṭṭam theatre 611, 616, 619
Kūṭṭu 612, 617
Kuttunad Industrial Relations Committee, Kerala 544
KWDI 1144

L-code 723, 725
'labelling theory', of social deviance 700
labour, absenteeism 1208, 1249
  arisrocracy in the formal sector 1304
  attachment 1304
  conditions 1248, 1251
  contractors 1246, 1307, 1310
  definition of 1243
  demand for 1301
  displacement of 1271
  and employment in informal sector 1255, 1286
  exploitation 1333
  force, growth in 1277
    structure of 136
  legislation/laws 1279, 1281, 1312
  -management relations 1249, 1251, 1255
  market 1234, 1266, 1293–6
    emergence of 1245
    fragmented 1302–03
  movement 1208, 1281
  organization 1243, 1306
  power 1295–6
  in pre-industrial days 1244–5
  productivity 1251
  relations 944, 1245–6, 1248–9, 1256, 1293–4, 1251
  and society 1243–4
  and sociology 1249–50
  system, policy and globalization of 1310–13
  technology and industry 1266–83
  and trade unions 1243–61
Labour Bureau 1248
Labour Institution 1249
Laborian variability model 720
laissez faire 1465
lajya (emotion), in South Asia 1180
Lakshadweep, female households in 206
  Scheduled Tribes in 201
land, acquisition of 13971499–1500
  alienation 388, 391, 1223–4
  commodification of 1222–5
  control over 1236, 1510

disputes 425
grab movement, in Uttar
    Pradesh 447
husbandry 1215
-ownership 411, 1226
    and livestock by nomads 251
redistribution of 448, 1227
reforms 396, 447, 1226–8, 1236,
    1245, 1375, 1435, 1535
    and emergence of new class
      of rich farmers 1463
    legislation on 370, 438
relations 1216, 1225
revenue 413, 439, 451, 468,
    1218, 1221, 1426, 1535
    during British rule 430, 432,
      480
rights 161–2
    of women 1235
tenure, system of 107, 893,
    1058, 1206, 1228
use patterns 329, 409
Land Acquisition Act of 1894 279
Landholders' Association of
    Bengal 1004
landholding (s), castes, political
    power of 493
consolidation of 1227
legislation on 439
pattern of 1206, 1207, 1236
population and labour force in
    small and marginal 205
size of 1226
structure of 189
landless labourers 122, 1245
landlord/landowners, 1225
caste, role of in village 17
big 1235
cum moneylenders 1232
hereditary obligations and
    occupational duties 1219
rich, domination of 1224
-tenant relations 1235
language(s) 123, 326, 373, 1385
accreditation 751
and chaos 711–12
concept of 737
contact 726–7
    and conflict studies 723
controversy 750
and culture 717, 1504
demand for single indigenous
    1455

development 6987, 729, 732–3
-dialect controversy 722–4
and education 749–50
    planning, in developing
      nations 740, 742
    problems of 740, 743, 745
empowerment 697
and gender 706–7
of global discourse 1003
grammatical and social
    construct of 713, 739, 751
horizontal explanation of 712–
    13
and identity 700, 748–51
Indian modernity and analogy
    of 125
loyalty to 696, 709–10
modern 734, 752
modernization and 732–3, 738–
    51, 753
narrative and reflexivity 1576–9
and nation 16, 704
official 729
planning 697, 729, 732, 740–3,
    751
policies, of developing nations
    731–2
'purity' 739, 751
religion 507
role of, in society 125–6, 700,
    729–30
as 'social action' 598
social aspects of 695–753
and social structure 712–14
standardization 718, 722
theory, core elements 726
unifying and dividing functions
    of 718
Language 715
Language Commission 744
Language in a Plural Society 132n
Language Treatment 697
Language of Wider
    Communication (LWC)
    731–2
'Lnguages in Contact' 704
Latin America 1288
law(s)/legislation 11, 88, 1381,
    1386–7, 1485
    and administration, colonial
      tradition of 35, 431
    British interest in native Indian
      104

On child labour 940, 1259
codified 1428
development of 1035
on Hindu marriage, enactment
    by Parliament 1104
need for, to protect workers
    1308–9
on regulating industries 1246
Sanskrit works on 103
Law Commission of India 1392,
    1393
Law Commission of India,
    Fourteenth Report (1956)
    1403n
    Seventy-seventh Report (1978)
    1403n
Lawbook of Yajnavalkya 1419
Laws of Manu 104, 227, 479

leftist groups 452
legal, disputes, delay in settlement
    of 1387
    institutions 1448, 556
    and political entities, backward
      castes/classes as 1474–92
    profession 553
    system 4, 1062–3
    and tradition 433
Legislative Assembly, direct
    elections to 1513
    reservation of seats for
      Scheduled Castes and
      Scheduled Tribes in 1484
Legislative Council, indirect
    elections to 1513
Lemon V. Kurtzman, USA 922
lesbianism 1163
'Lexical innovations' 708, 733, 738
liberal democracies 116, 928
Liberal Party, Britain 1507, 1512
Liberalism, origins of 911
liberalization, economic 1432,
    1436, 1439, 1441n, 1442n,
    1469
    consumerism, childhood and
      adolescence 1082
    and deregulation 1351
liberation 805, 903, 1161, 1168
    European Enlightenment and
      101
Liberation Tigers of Tamil Elam
    (LTTE), in Sri Lanka 286
    female militants in 1167

life, at birth 211
    course, post-modern 965–9
    '-cycle', of development 1071
    rituals 901, 1082–3
    expectancy 191–3, 213n, 217
    in Kerala 10121
    -styles 142, 680, 688, 690–1
    consumption and 675–91
    and constraints on women 681
    identification by cities or
        regions 684–5
Līlakīrtan, divine play of Krsna in
    1193
lineages 564, 558n, 1414
    outside the 815–16
    peasant castes and
        interrelations 416
    sectarian clans and 805–16
Lingāyats 806
    and caste (jatis) 819–20
    movement 806–7, 816
'linguistic', and anthropological
    literature 565
    and 'communicative
        competence' 753
    consciousness 70
    'corruption' 739, 751
    cultures 606, 1456
    diversity in India 125
    empowerment 737, 753
    innovation, and change 721,
        722
    and literary practices in India 15
    policy 1456
    region, caste groups in 1476
    states, formation of 734, 738,
        1472n
    structuralism in 714–16
linguists 695, 697
liquor trade, profits from 1500
literacy 936–7
    and education 974, 1010
        Mahatma Gandhi on 974
    female 338–9, 1257
    gender gap and 975
    patterns of, and their social
        context 973–89
    rates 974, 989n, 1018–20
    situation today 974–6
literature, and art, reinforcement
    of 470
    and literacy, effect of, on ethnic
        groups 1170

    overview of 67–9
lithographs 629
litigants/litigation 1389, 1392,
    1395, 1402
Little Tradition 862
    Great Tradition and 14
    notion of 71
livestock, density 237
    -rearing in India 159
        and ritual/caste taboos 163–4
local, autonomy 1275
    information, access to 1370
    irrigation communities 1375
    -level/grass-roots level politics,
        study of 51, 370, 1382,
        1494–1519
local self-government 1362
    participation in 1496
Lodhi-Rajput caste 421
logic, development of 1035
lok adalats (people's courts) 1393,
    1406n
Lok Sabha, elections to 433
    reservations to, for Scheduled
        Castes and Scheduled
        Tribes 1484
London School of Economics 75
London School of Linguistics 696
London University 1042
'low' Hindu castes 69, 478
    denial of education to 1000
    prevention of entry to temples
        and village wells 479
    and untouchables, and
        principles of caste 485
lower/subordinate courts 1389
    judgements in 1387
    in judicial process 1389–1402
    problems of 1392–5
    proceedings in English in 1391
    reforms in 1401
    significance of 1390–5, 1389–
        1402
    villagers' participation in 1392
loyalties, caste-based 1383
    primordial 7, 11
Lucknow-Cornell project 436

MARG *see* Multiple Action
    Research Group
MHFW 307
Macaulay's minute 1040
The Machine that Changed the

    World 1268
Madhya Pradesh, birth rate in
    194–5
    life expectancy in 193
    mobilization against Narmada
        project in 173
    Scheduled Tribes in 201
    total fertility rate in 194
Madhva monks, child monks in
        Udipi, Karnataka, 1104
Madras 464
Madhubani painting 589
Madiga caste 421
    conversion to Christianity 892
Madinah 790
Madras (Presidency) 70, 464,
    1478–9
    backward classes in 1483
    industrialists, family histories
        of 1068
    Muslims as backward classes in
        1479
    Ryotwari Settlement in 1220
    Survey *1822), on schools 999
Madras Geographical Association
    458
Madras Institute of Development
    Studies 47
Madras Provincial Backward
    Classes League 1478
Madras Schoolbook and
    Vernacular Society 725
Madrassahs (institutions for
    higher education) 1037
The Magic Mountain 830
Mahābhārata 24n, 149, 621, 781,
    851, 1118, 1185, 1414
    Kannada version of 613
    Kathakali based on stories
        from 615
    Shanti Parva in 1380
    Tamil version of 612
Mahakal, Ujjain, pilgrim center 421
Mahalwari/Malguzari Settlement
    411, 1220, 1223
Mahar caste 19
Maharajas 1427
Maharashtra, anti-Brahmin
    movements in 13
    birth rate in 194
    caste and inequality in 335
    peasant movement in 1533
    total fertility rate in 194

Mahars, movement by, in Maharashtra 1544
Mahayana Buddhism 784
Mahdavi Movement 1423
Maheshwari project, halting of 308
Mahila Sakti 306
Majhi tribes 400
majoritarian democracy 1460
and economic liberalization 1436–9
majra 410
maktabs (school), under Mohammedan rule 1037
Malaiman Udayan Christians 898
Malamantaram gatherers/hunters, of Kerala 246
Malapantaram nomads/hunters, of Kerala 232
malaria 342
Malas, conversion into Christianity in Telugu country 892
Malawi Self-Help Water Project, Africa 1371
Malay Archipelgo, spread of Islam in 265
Malaya/Malaysia, Indian immigrants in 266–7
Indian labour in plantations in 265, 440
Malayālam, Kakakali dialogue in 615
Maldives, Islam in 779
male, agricultural workers in 411
body, aesthetic evaluation of 1168–9
child, and security in old age 1078
education, high parental motivation for 980
-female, inequality in 943
literacy rate 1019
oppression 1546
prostitution 1164
sexual anxiety 1182
sterilization, during Indian Emergency 1079
vulnerability 1183
malguzari tenure system, in Punjab and Central Provinces 1206
Maliki School 794

Malimath Committee Report 1405n
Malwa region, Madhya Pradesh, investigation in 50
Mamkootam 1282
Man 1180
Man in India 42
management, 'modern' 1289
new technology and modern 1267–9, 1281–2
Manav Dharma Shastra 687, 780
Mandal Commission 494, 1464, 1473n, 1476
controversy over 494–5
recommendations 1457, 1470, 1491
Report 494, 497, 1382–3, 1477, 1489–90
opposition to 1489, 1491
and reservations 498
'Mandalization'/Mandalized politics 369, 493–7, 498
mandala theory, of the state 1417, 1418, 1422
mandi 1342
mandir and *mandal* politics 665
mangal kavya literature, in Bengal 578, 592n
manic depression 1128
Manipur, Scheduled Tribes in 201
manoratha genre, paintings in 633
mansabdari system 1422
'*mantra*' 804
'for breaking the Mouth' 841, 842
and myth 842–3
Manu Smriti 780
manufacturing automation protocol (MAP) 1266
manufacturing industry/sector 1279
decline in, during colonial rule 1428
job reduction in 1271
workforce in 209
Manushi 1166, 1547
Manusmriti 479, 795
on inter-caste marriages 521
Mapillas, of Kerala 791
mapping 4, 328, 341–2
Mar Thomas Church 789
Marathas 465, 1426
Marathi language 720–1
Nagpuri 720–1

Marvars 478
'mardana' area 467
marg art 587
marga, Shastric classification of 576
marital, alliance 1090
bond 1189
discord 1142
fidelity 1066
rape 1145
relationship, poor and depression 1185
unequal 1141
status, distribution and age at marriage 197–9
markets/marketing, 1333, 1342–57
actors in the 1347–9
in cities 465–6
competition 1372
in China 1373
criticism of 1349
culture 1355
in the West 1357
development of 1206
economy 1343, 1356, 1357
exchanges 1344
dynamics, technology and 1266
'failure' of 1351
'forces' 1441n
-friendly economy 1436
functioning of 1352
importance of 1345–9, 1362
institutions of 1382
for jewelry 1350
mechanism, and information 1363
and monetary transactions 1342, 1345
orientation, agricultural production for 1231
place, culture of 574
principles 1353
process 1373
redefining 1349–52
role of brokerage in 1210–11
and the State 1350–2
and trade 1342
transactions, importance of trust in 1352
in villages 418, 425
marriage(s) 44, 49–50
alliance, role of family 1074

behaviour, changing patterns in
    south India 1109
within caste 488
and childbearing 1158
choices among South Indian
    Dravidians 1108–9, 1112
of close kin forbidden 1116
companionship and 1088
concept of, as gift 1119
cross cousin, in South India
    1106, 1108–9
distinction between North and
    South India 1059
exogamous rules of 1075
and family relationship 1088
of same *gotra* forbidden 1116,
    1118
heterosexuality, reproduction
    and sexual geographies
    and 20
among Hindus 9
intercaste 477
within *jati* 428
of kinship in the Dravidian
    pattern 1112
and kinship in villages 418–20,
    424
'love' 1143, 1146
    and family support structure
        1172, 1191–2
and male physical violence
    1146
migration and, within the caste
    279
and migration by women
    276–7
minimum age at, for girls 339,
    679
mixed, of race and caste 521
among Muslims of South Asia
    1120–1
among parallel cousins,
    forbidden 1106
patterns of 1059, 1104–25
pre-puberty 1419
among relatives, forbidden in
    North India 111–16
and religious traditions 1105
rites, myth in 843–6
rituals 846, 852, 1083
rules of 1059, 1090
sexuality and 1080–1
of text and con-text 846–7

types of 1058
at young age 1078
Marwaris 1325
Marx, Karl, on hierarchy and
    difference 527–9
    theory of inequality 52
Marxism 44, 75, 110, 527, 528
Marxist, analysis of Russian
    countryside 1214
    approach to collective action
        and violence 1569
    approach to peasantry in India
        1206
    on class 524–5
    initiative, for social change 172
    mode of production theories
        1335n
    social history 1569
    sociologists 44
    teleology 1208
    thesis, of images 644
    theories of capitalist
        transformation 1320
    tradition, and civil society 117
Masai ethnology 11
masculility, Indian 1006, 1169
    Europeans and 1200
    modern schooling and 1016
    and procreative ideology 1075
masks, of Chho dance of Purulia
    590
    demonic 590
    Santhal 590
mass-media 74, 88, 668, 734
    and dissemination of standard
        language 740
    feminism 1166
    and public life 667–8
maternal education, and child
    health 981
maternity/maternal, love, notion
    of 1189
    and child welfare 342–3
Matrikundiya, pilgrim center 421
matrilateral cross cousin
    marriages 1109, 1112
matrilineal communities, India's
    1074, 1092
    nature of inheritance in 206
    Nayar joint families 558n
        Marriage rituals among
            1111–12
    women in 1022

Mauritius, Indian indentured
    labour in 265, 440
    Indian population in 266–7
Mauryan State, under Ashoka
    1418
    decline of 1419
    subcontinental state under
        1414–20
Mazdoor Kisan Shakti Sanagthan
    1370
McArthur Foundation 2
McCollum Vs. Board of
    Education, USA 926
Mecca, spiritual center for Islam
    151
medical, anthropology and
    sociology 140, 309
    education 311, 1022
Medical Termination of
    Pregnancy (MTP) 1132
medieval Europe 1032, 1034
meditation, tradition of 834, 1161
    Buddhism and 1036
Mediterrarean immigrants, in
    USA 297
medium of instruction 746, 1001,
    1003, 1040
mega castes 1383
Meghalaya, female household
    heads in 206
    Scheduled Tribes in 201
mehr (bride-price) 1121
Mehrgarh, Quetta, nomads of
    222
Makkah, pilgrims to 790
Melanesia, research on tribal
    movements in 1536
Memoir of a Map of Hindoostan
    327
mental disorders, violence against
    women and 1128
mental impairment, in old age
    958
mental maps 466
merchants, contribution of, to
    industrial development in
    India 1327
merit versus need, and inequality
    1483–4
Mesolithic sites, of Ganga Valley,
    foragers in 222
messianistic movements 1539
Methodist church 789

Methodist missionaries 890
'metropolitan', socio-political
    order and caste 1499
    urban agglomerations 275
Mexican community, of Tepoztlan
    1519n
Mexico, community committees
    in 1364
    population growth rate in 191
microelectronics 1266–7, 1271,
    1277–8
middle class, agitation against
    colonial rule by 1450
    educated 980
        English- 1429, 1430
        tribal 397–8
    elites 65
    growing 1507
    women, purity and tradition of
        682
middlemen, role of 1207
'middle peasant' 1532–33
migration 137–8, 664, 262–81
    and economic change 1347
    chain 278
    by farmers and nomadic
        pastoralism 240
    international 440–1
    inter-state 277–9
    marriage and by women 276,
        277
    nature of 188
    out- 276
    overseas, and family ties 1172–
        3
    permanent 427
    by religious minorities and
        tribes 277
    rural to rural 276–7
    rural to urban 189, 204, 1207,
        1231, 1246, 1256, 1297,
        1298
        and increase in urban
            growth 273–6, 462
    seasonal, from villages 425–6
    and social conflict 281
    theory 281
    transnational 564
    by tribals 1537
migrant(s), as casual labour 1288
    'dependent' families of 1303
    labourers 221
    mobilization of 1299

refugees and 292–3
    resentment against 278
militancy, female 1167
    by peasantry 1533
militant asceticism 771, 821
'millenarian cults' 1536
Millennial Pentecostal movements,
    and Madras Protestants
    903
Mimamsa 1119
    school 781
'mind', as the object of
    educational reform 1006–
    7
mineral resources, exploitation of
    389
minimum wages 1293
    in industries 1248
    for landless labourers 1310
    regulations 1312
    for rural labour 1257
Ministry of Family Planning and
    Welfare 306
Ministry of Rural Development
    1022
Ministry of Labour 1278, 279
Ministry of Health and Family
    Welfare 313
Ministry of Law, Justice and
    Company Affairs 1397,
    1400, 1404n, 1406n
minorities (communities) 1438
    disadvantaged women workers
        from 1258
    freedom and equality to 690
    indigenous and religious, and
        language, education 750
    languages, as 'we' code 707
    and mother tongue in
        education 748
    rights of 288
    role of 772
Memoirs of Violence 1576
missionary (ies), activities and
    education in 19th century
    India 890, 1001
    and conversion to Christianity
        900
    educationists 1483
    in Goa 887
    in Kerala, influence in
        education 1022
    schools 1041

Mitakshara 1106
Mizoram, Scheduled Tribes in 201
Mizos, as tribal community 379,
    398
    separatist movements 1385,
        1468, 1538
mobile population 224, 255n,
    265n
    and sedentarization 253
mobility 221, 370, 1066
    in ancient period 222–4
    forms of 222–4
    limited 1306
    strategies, stratification and
        508–11
    upward 69
mobilization 558n
    of beneficiaries, of local
        infrastructural projects
        1373
    caste 420–1
    concensus 1528
    electoral, of masses 1432
    of lower castes and poor
        peasantry 1463
    of peasants 1207
        and nationalist movement
            1224
    at regional level 1382
    of social groups 1499
    and struggle 541–2
    of voters 1466
    of women 1165
'Model Agreement' 1281
modernity/'modern' 2, 45, 84,
    93n, 660, 661, 659, 752,
    753, 1004, 1005, 1499,
    1507, 1530
    and ageing 961
    and anxiety 85
    and care of the aged 959
    and condemnation of child
        labour 949
    definition of 3
    and disassociation of
        childhood from work 948
    discourse on Indian 1013
    European Enlightenment model
        of 83
    meaning of 93n
    and modernization theory 33
    promissory notes of 21
    schooling culture and 998–1027

situating 1012–18
social life of 668–9
tradition and 3, 14, 45, 68–9,
    75, 77–8, 85–6, 91n,
    93n, 139, 691, 726–7,
    1427
use of the term 82–3
violence of 690
West and 3, 83
The Modernity of Tradition 1498
modernization 45, 63–89, 93n,
    1506, 1525
aging and 963
and break-up of joint families
    955, 1062
demands of 46
and development programmes
    1214
as the ideology of social
    sciences in the West 33
impact of, on family 1092
in Indian politics 75
industrialization and
    mobilization 511
notion of 81–2
resistance to 1532
standardization and, of
    languages 733–5
studies 64, 66–7, 81
theory 21, 32, 65, 84, 90n,
    1320, 1325, 1466
    Marxists on 92n
    modernity and 33
    and old age 958–60
thesis 1064–8
use of the term 83
Modified area development
    approach (MADA) 391
mofussil courts 1398
Moghul rule *see* Mughal
mohalla 462, 1422
    -clusters 464
    identity of 683–4
    and regional politics 687
Mohammadan Anglo-Oriental
    College, Aligarh 794
Mohammedan higher education
    1037–8
Mohammedan law 1038
Mohenjo-Daro, 'great bath' in
    779
moksa 803
Mon-Khmer linguistic affiliation,

of kinship organization
    1064
monarchy, relationship with
    national churches 914
use of religion by 913, 914
monastic life, alternative to family
    life 1163
money/monetary, exchanges 1347
    'famines' 1428
    as symbol of modernity 1210
    system, under colonial rule
        1428
    and trade 1346
    transactions 1210, 1342, 1345
        and market relationship
            1345
        and social relationship 1346
moneylenders 396, 1222–4, 1228,
    1303, 1323
    landlords cum 1232
    traders and, and political
        economy in Uttar
        Pradesh 1510
Mongoloid tribals 381
monogamy 1006
Movement for Zamindari
    Abolition, Uttar Pradesh
    432
Montague-Chelmsford reforms
    (1919) 1512
Moplah(s), migration to India by
    264
    movements in Malabar 1533,
        1534
    rebellion 446
morbidity 201, 341–2, 948, 1140
    female 1138
Morely-Minto reforms (1909)
    1511–12, 1383
Moroccan bazaars 1353
morphology, of cities/towns 461–7
    ecological models 461–2
    Indo-European towns 463
    planning in 464
    urban density 463
morphemes, inflectional 723
mortality 341, 342
    female 1138
    and fertility rates 194–5
    indicators for India 217
    Partition, refugee migration
        and 191
    rate 210

mother(s), abject, figures of 965
    child relationship 304, 1181,
        1186–9
    image 1183
    and son bond 1088, 1183
    oedipal tensions in 1080
    status of 1075
mother goddess, cult of 148
mother-in-law, and daughter-in-
    law, relation between
    1141
mother tongue 741, 744, 750
    education in 747
motherhood, status in Hindu
    society 1075
motifs, 829
    myth and 847, 855, 858n
'Mouth – Breaking Mantra' 842
mud and thatch clusters 464
Mughal empire, in India 264,
    1414, 1420, 1422–5
    Authority, decline of 1425
    cash crops during 1220
    and colonial state 1425
    cultivation rights during 1217–
        18
    education under 1037
    nobility, migration by 234
    patrimonial bureaucracy in
        1380, 1424
Mughal paintings 587, 649n
Muhammedan Rural
    Constituencies 1514–15
Muhammedan Urban
    Constituencies 1514–15
Much laga manuh (mouth-putting
    persons) 840–1
Mukkauvar Christians, fishing
    caste in Goa, and
    conversion to Christianity
    887
    Esaki as goddess of 891
    and Hindus 895–6
    image of Mary and Maataa of
        895
mukti (liberation) 1035
multiculturalism 127, 658
multilingual speech communities
    705, 734
multilingualism 126–7
Multiple Action Research Group
    (MARG) 1132, 1147
Mumbai, population of 274

violence in 663
see also Bambay
Munda(s) (tribe), in Chota
    Nagpur 382, 583–5, 1113
    cosmology 585
    marriage pattern of 1105,
        1111–14
    movement of 1538
    myths of 584, 853–5
Mundaka Upanishad 1414
Mudaliar Commission 1014
Mundari type Kinship
    organization 1064
Municipal government/Boards
    468, 1508
    politics of 1509
munshis 1403n
munsif, jurisdiction of, original
    1390
Muqaddimah 255n
Muraos 1514
Muria Gonds, study on 1350
Murugan, Lord, fishing ritual for
    865–7
    worship of 870–2
Muslim(s), 213n, 632, 770, 1062,
    1474, 1480, 1509
    alienation of 1464
    of Arabian origin 490
    Board politics, separate block
        for 1511
    caste division among 477, 490–
        1
    concept of 'contract' in
        marriage among 1121
    concessions to, in professional
        colleges 1481–2
    constituencies, separate/
        reserved 1383, 1511, 1514
    cults, in Rajasthan 151
    education of 202, 1474
        special treatment in 1481–2
    -Hindu relations 5, 11, 1510–11
        violence in Hyderabad 1575
    images of space of 689
    infant mortlity among 202
    invasion of subcontinent 151
    law, from Shariah, on marriage
        1104
    legalists 1063
    literacy and education among
        202
    lower castes among 490

Meos 490
Migration/refugees, from India
    to Pakistan after
    Partition 269–70,
285, 287–9, 298
    patronage, to literature in
        Bengal 578
    'personal laws' of 1058
    population growth of 137,
        201–2
    reservation principle for 1513
    rituals, in 'syncreticism' 581
    rule of India 104
    separate educational
        institutions for 1000
    state-wise population of 777,
        778
    survey of, in India 331
    women population 196, 1548
        purdah by 208
Muslim League 269, 287, 746,
    1432, 1452–3, 1512,
    1514–15, 1548
    confrontation between
        Congress, the Raj and
        1512
    demand for separate state by
        1431
muttadars 395
mutiny of 1857 *see* Great Revolt
    of 1857
Muttahida Quami Movement
    (MQM), in Pakistan 269
Myanmar 1385, Indian refugees
    from 270
Mysore state 1426
    social change in 69
mysticism, in Rabindranath
    Tagore's educational
    philosophy 1008
myth/mythic 583–5, 772
    in Assam, and link with
        agriculture 837, 842
    and caste 828
    colonial space of 640
    figures 574–5
    and folklore 833
    and group consciousness 835
    and history 828, 835
    in literary context 851–3
    literature 772
    and marriage rites 843–6
    and mythology 847–51

from Palani Murugan temple
    870–2
    and political realms of 564,
        566
    reflections of Indian 832
    signs, among Hindus 626
    text and con-text of 827–55
    use of 827–8
    of the Vedas 827
Myths of Middle India 853
Mythological Deliberations 828,
    832
mythology 827, 829, 830, 834
    classicism and 636
    and myth 836, 847–51

nād parampara 820
Nadar(s) of Tamil Nadu 421, 478,
    1544
    and 'breast-cloth' controversy
        893
    conversion to Christianity by
        892
    relationship with Christian
        Vellas 899
    women, rights of 899
Nāgās 812
    chieftains 382
    conversion into Christianity by
        891
    militants 821
    movement 1385, 1538
    refugees, from Burma, into
        India 283, 287
Nāgā Dādupanthīs 821–2
Nagaland, Scheduled Tribes in
    201
Nagasaki, dropping of atomic
    bombs in 1565
namaz 790
Nalanda, Buddhist education
    center in 1036, 1037
Namdhari movement 788
Nambudiri Brahmins 885
Nanak Pathis 787
Nāndī Purāṇa 843, 846
Nandiwalla/Devwalla, in Andhra
    Pradesh 249
    as middle centers 250
    migration by 249
    Tirumal and Fulamli groups of
        249
Naṅṅyār actresses 616–17

Naṅṅyār Kūttu 617
Napolean era, reinstatement of
        Catholoc Church 921
Narada, myth of 846–7
'Narangwal Experiment' (1967–
        73) 305–6
narcissism 1182, 1183
Narmada Bachao Andolan 174
Narmada anti-dam agitation 143,
        170, 173–6
    eviction of tribals and 1541
Nasik cave inscription 224
Nastika 784
Natal, Indian immigrants in 266
    Indian indentured labour in
        265
natal home 1141
    violence against girls in 1132–
        40
Nāth Yogis (Jogis) 806, 808, 814,
        821–2
    of Saiva sect 907
Nāthdvāra, Rajasthani pilgrim
        town of 640–2, 644, 810
    influence of 643
    pichhavis 650n
    Strinathji at 633
    style of painting 641–2, 644,
        649n
nation(s) 5, 12–15, 40, 119, 569,
        1413, 1495
    civilization and 13
    concept of 131
    as cultural communities 568
    and language, theories of 16
    race and folk, in Nazi
        Germany 570–2
    -state 3, 15, 86, 90n, 117, 120,
        155, 1380, 1413–39, 1506,
        1578
        emergence of 12, 16
        notion of 1440n
        re-imagining 1436–9
        subsistence, and
            globalization 168–9
    teleology of 1578
national boundaries 664
national culture, folk identity and
        568–80
    space and location and 571
national development, social
        consequences of 387–90
    tribal development and 387

national identity 575, 682, 1015
national integration, and
        responsible citizenship
        1046–7
national languages 731–2, 734
national monuments 664national
        pluralism 126
'national space' 664
National Agricultural Bank for
        Rural Development 439
National Agriculturalists Party of
        Agra and Oudh 1512,
        1514
National AIDS Control
        Organisation (NACO)
        211
National Cadet Corporation 1046
National Commission on Labour
        1249
National Commission on Rural
        Labour 1255
National Commission of Self
        Employed Women 1258
National Commission on
        Urbanization 460
National Commission for Women
        1138
National Committee on
        Education of Women,
        report of 1053
National Confederation of
        Labour 1260
National Conference, in Kashmir
        1468
National Coordination
        Committee for Scheduled
        Castes Christians 902
National Council of Education
        1906 746
National Council of Educational
        Research and Training
        (NCERT) 190
National Council of Women in
        India (NCWI) 1548
'National Education Movement'
        746, 1004
National Employment Guarantee
        Programme 437
National Family Health Survey
        (NFHS) 136, 197–9, 201,
        202, 204, 306
National Forest Policy of 1952
        237

National Front government 494,
        1489
National Health Policy 103, 308
National Institute for Rural
        Development 436
'National Institutes' 1046
National Labour Institute 1257
National Muhammadan
        Association 1479
National Museum 634, 648
National Policy on Education
        (1986) 1020, 1053
National Population Policy 195
National Remote Sensing Agency
        237
National Sample Survey (NSS)
        136, 188–9, 206–7,
        212n
    data on household size 204
    on working population 207
National Sample Survey
        Organization (NSSO) 188
National Service Extension
        Programme 76
National Social Service 1046
National Socialism 571
National Socialists, on race and
        culture 580
nationalism 5, 67, 70, 93n, 110,
        247, 568, 575, 579, 661,
        681, 936, 1010, 1013,
        1018, 1200, 1438, 1456,
        1462, 1508
    and democracy 1436
    impact of, on higher education
        1043
    and independence 65
    and Raj, confrontation
        between 1515
    and tradition and identity 575
nationalist artists, on folk art 586
nationalist educational agenda
        1003
nationalist folklorists, of Bengal
        579
nationalist historiography 15, 104
    role of 12
nationalist ideology 80
nationalist movement 11, 13, 66,
        110, 369, 432, 471, 569,
        578, 1380, 1429, 1432,
        1448, 1450, 1455, 1475,
        1504, 1507, 1548

Mahatma Gandhi and 18, 549, 550
and tribals 1537
nationalities 1502
nationalization, of large banks 1436
natural calamities 451
natural differences, and social stratification 505–6
Natural Law and the Political Science 132n
'*Natva vidhaana*' 720
native, English 709
language 732
personality 936, 998
speakers of English, concept of 736–7
States, nomadic groups in 232
natives, and education in the nineteenth century 999–1003
nātya 613
Nātyaśāstra 608
Nautanki theatre, of north India 611
Navaratra festival 415
Navodaya Vidyalayas (NVs) 1016
Naxalbari region, in West Bengal 447, 1531, 1535
events in 448–9
movement 446–7, 541
Naxalite movements, in Andhra Pradesh and Bihar 1473n, 1531, 1535
Naxalites 1473n
Nāyanmars 807
Nayar Service Society 420
Nayars of Kerala, tarawad-to-tarawad relations of ritual marriage 1111–12
Nazakat refinement 459
Nazi architecture 570
Nazi concentration camp, violence and 1387
Negriot tribals 381
Nehru- Liaquat Pact 288
Nehru, Mahatma Gandhi-, leadership/phase 1430, 1434–5
Nehruvian State 1434–6, 1456
Nehruvian strategy, of economic development 1441n
neighbourhood, cities/towns and 462–3

relations 1072
Neo-Buddhists 785
neo-classical approach, criticism of 1343
neo-classic theory 1342, 1349, 1354
neo-grammarian movement 715
neo-liberal flexibilization 1279
Nepal, Hinduism in 779
literacy rate in 991n
local self-help initiatives in development projects 1373
Nepalese, from Bhutan into Nepal 273
refugees, in India 286
Nepali households, dynamics of 1076
Nestorian Church 788–9
New Delhi, building of, by Britishers 465
'new farmers movement' 1535
'new institutional economics' school 1343
New Reproductive Technologies (NRTs), social implications of 1079
'new social movements' 1384, 1529
new technology 1209
in agriculture 1230–1, 1236, 1268
and modern management 1267–9
worker and union response to 1279–83
new women's movement 1548–9
Newars, of Nepal, emotion among 1180
New York Ordinance of 1916, on 'zoning' 464
newspaper industry, study on new technology in 1281
nibanna 783
Nigeria 74
Nijai Bol movement, in Uttar Pradesh 447
Nigiri Game and Fish Preservation Act of 1879 232
NIMHANS, Bangalore 1138
Nirankari movement 788
nirguna bhakti 813–14

niskama karma 1419
nomads (ic), as 'backward' community 235
constraints on movement and interaction with human and natural environments 235–41
as 'criminal tribe' during colonial period 229
as frontier groups 220
hunting by 157
interaction by 227–8
life patterns of 137
mobile clusters of 228
movement patterns of 219–55
and nomadism 252
pastoralism and autonomy 167
and semi-nomadic communities 334
spatial mobility and caste system among 250–2
symbiotic relations with 222
nomadism 250, 254
during colonial period 229–32
in Neolithic and pre-Neolithic period 222
nomads and 252
-sedentism, concept of 220
non-alignment policy 1435
Non-Conformist Christians 789
non-governmental organizations (NGOs) 2, 437, 453, 1541
contribution towards education 1025–6, 1048
gerontological 962
on healthcare 314
natural calamities and 430
organizing workers by 1260
on problems of child labour 947
on social welfare schemes 1083
women's 1548–9, 1165
Non-Resident Indians (NRIs) 440–1
Investments by, in India 268
non-scheduled population 200–1
non-violence 1440n
Mahatma Gandhi and 124, 444
violence and 1564, 1566
normal ageing 958
North America *see* United States of America

Northern Ireland, violence in 1567
Norwegian government 442
Notes on Love in a Tamil Family 1188
nuclear families/households, 204–5
    and child labour 944
    and child rearing in 1078
    cities and 472
    and joint households 50, 1061–92, 1070–1
    in modern societies 1065
Nuer tribe, study of, in Sudan 482
numbers, compilation of 136
    enumeration and role of numbers 7–11
    interpretation of 8
    role of 136
nursing care 441
nutrition (al), 340
    deficiency 341–2
    neglect of 137
    poverty and 342
Nyaya School 781

objectification, analysis of 714
obsessive-compulsive behaviour 1128
oceanic trade 460
occupation (al) 74
    access to modern 1497
    boundaries 1271
    caste-linked 478, 1244
    class and 685–7
    mobility, caste as obstacle to 1322
    in modern sector 478
    multiplicity and casualized labour 1301
    of nomads 252
    skills 1290
    structure 1268–71
'Oedipal'/Oedipus 1188
    complex 832–3
    conflict 1183
    of mother-son relation in India 1080
    myth 833
    theme, universality of 772
Office of the Registrar General 184

Official Language Policy 743
Official languages, modernizing of, in India 732
    Recognized 741
Official Secrets Act of 1923 1370
OECD countries 1277–8
oilseeds, cropping 1236
old age/people, 938, 955–69, 1162
    'abandoning' of 959
    form, sickness in 959
    fraility and *futility* 960
    making 957–62
    medical attention to 957
    medical impairment in 959
    retirement communities of 960
    security, education and 981
    women 958
old madwoman, figures of 965
Old People of Makunti 961
oligarchy 1252, 1507
Omkareshwar, pilgrim center 421
One Hundred Twenty Sixth Report 1988 1393
Onge tribe, 'development' and resettlement of, in Little Andaman 247
    in state-supervised enclaves 157
ontology 1076
open-door economy 1436
open system of stratification 508–11, 517–20
    status in 523
Operation Barga 333
Operation Blackboard (OB) scheme 1020
oppression 1140, 1529
    of women 1129, 1130, 1146
oral cultures 600, 603–7
oral traditions, of narratives 601, 655, 1530
Orangi project, Pakistan, mobilization of local poor in 1373–4
Oraon tribals 403, 891
    movement of 1538
organized crimes/violence, in Mumbai 663
    to realize equality and justice 451
organic theory, of nationality 571
organization (al), of production 1333

changes in 1266, 1274–6, 1279–81
    management, innovative 1290
    and protection 1306–10
    structure 1268, 1272, 1274–6
oriental despotism 115
'Orientalism' 5, 6, 16, 348, 964
    influence of, in art 588
Orientalism 107
orientalists 936, 1039
Orientalist Indology/Indologists 66, 89
    versus Anglicist debates, on education 937
Orissa, birth rate in 194
    fertility rate in 194
    life expectancy in 193
    new economic and political order, and downtrodden castes in 1499
    political process in villages of 434
    politics in 1500
    scheduled castes in 335
    scheduled tribes in 201
    tribal revolts in 445
orthodoxy, and continuation of tradition 836
'Other Backward Castes' (OBC) 18
    reservation for 493–5
'Other Backward Class', rise of 435, 1474
Oxfam, and SOS villages 441
Oxford History of India 104

Padroado 886
Pagan territories 887
Paharis, of hill districts of Uttar Pradesh 685
Pahul (ritual of initiation) 787
Pakistan, census counts in 186
    civil war in 1971 270–1
    creation of (1947) 143
    demand for 792
    modern history of 100
    mohajirs in 269
    Indian Muslim refugees in 298
    India's war with, 1971 1459
    Islam in 779
    split in, and creation of Bangladesh 1441n
    women in 1183, 1190

Pakistan, East, refugees from, in West Bengal 271, 295, 297
    unrest in, and independence of Bangladesh 288
Pallava, period 1420
    society under 1421
pan eating, in Benaras 676, 678
Pandits, role of 11, 13, 14
    traditions 22
Pañcarātra movement 809
panch shila, principles of 386
Panchamas 1482
Panchayati (s) Raj 51, 399, 437, 439, 443–5, 468, 544, 1414, 1496, 1518
    cases in 1393
    study of, in Uttar Pradesh, Maharashtra and Karnataka 1370
Pandavalila performances 677
Pānī kaṭāgā dhowā 842
Papal authority, challenge to 914–15
Papal bulls 887
panigrahana 1117
Pani panchayats 417
Para-language, study of 698
parallel cousins/kin 1113
    marriages forbidden between 1106
paramarthika (extra-referential) 781
Parashara Smriti 1118
Parava fishing caste, in Goa 887, 894, 901
parda, and women 682
Pardhi pastorals 239
parents (al), and children interaction 1173, 1187–8
    and conjugal bonds 1065
    motivation for children's schooling 978–9, 982
    for female education 983
    rights, bourgeois notions of 948–9
pariahs (outcastes), 1482
    rights of 899
Parishads, settlements of learned Brahmins 1036
parkavati rite, in Tamil culture 870
parliamentary democracy/form of government, 1433, 1453

with a Cabinet 1454
parochialization 71
Parsi theatre 588
Parsis 1321, 1325, 1334n
    migration from Persia to Bombay by 264
Parsonian modernization theory 89n
participatory development 449, 450, 1376
'participatory observation' 451
Partition, of India (1947) 151, 792, 1381, 1432, 1453–5, 1512
    experience of 1565
    and population movement 269
    rape/violence of women 1127, 1200
    refugee migration and mortality 191
    refugees in towns /cities 463
    unfamiliar space of 660
    use of religion for 909
    and violence 1084, 1127, 1577
The Passing of Traditional Society 77
'passive revolution' 75
pastoral nomads/pastoralism 158–60, 220, 345
    and claim to Rajput descent and status 251
    and farming 223
    movements/migration of 224–7, 238
    and subsistence 143
    transhumance agriculture 158–9
pastoralists 241–50
Pāśupalā temples 806
Pāśupalas 806
Patels 434
paternalism, and feminism 1166
Pather Panchali 1192
pathology, environment and 312
Patia Kela, snake charmers of Orissa, migration by 248
patriarchal structure /joint family, 1063, 1067
    agitation against 1546
    ideology 1074
    and male domination 1550
patrilateral parallel cousin, marriages between 1121

patrilineal joint family, 1077, 1089
    clans/kinship 419, 1072, 1083
    cross cousin marriages 1109, 1110, 1118
    descent 1075
    solidarity 1189
patrimonial bureaucracy 1380, 1422–5
patron-client relations 17, 51, 1219, 1233, 1235, 1244
patronage 610, 1256, 1352, 1435
    in agricultural labour 1245
    politics, of British India 1475
    of Ramalīlā 609
    to ritual performances 603
    royal, to Kathakali 617, 618
Pattini cult, in Sri Lanka 1195
Pauranikas 782
Pavagadh, images of 643
'pavement shops' 465
peasants/farmers communities 416, 452, 1206, 1214–15, 1298, 1533
    'economy' 1226, 1297
    indebtedness of, to moneylenders 1222–4
    and 'menial' population 1218
    migration by 233, 402, 429, 432
    mobilization, and nationalist movement 1207
    movements 1207, 1384, 1385, 1531–6, 1540
    pauperized 1207
    resistance 1207
    revolt 1218
    'studies' 1216
    'uprisings' 7, 1450–1
        in Telengana 1432
    and urban civilization 1519n
    voting by 1496–7
'peasantry' 1532
    concept of 1214, 1533
    involvement in market 1221
pedagogy, and linguists 702
'pedigreed culture' 519
peepal tree, venerated by Hindus 151–2
peer monitoring 1363
Pentacostal movements 773
People's Association 1511
People of India project 404
Peoples of India 432

People's Union of Democratic
    Rights (PUDR) 1127
'people's war' groups, in Bihar
    and Andhra Pradesh 446,
    448
performances, concept of 598
    in social sciences 598–621
    setting for 599–600
    textual dimension of 600–1
peripatetic communities 220–1,
    225, 226, 248–51
    interaction by 227
    migration by 240
    -sedentary relations 238
    as 'symbiotic' nomads 221
Permanent Settlement, in Bengal
    1206, 1219
Permoli V. New Orleans, US
    Supreme Court on 923
Peru, local community financing
    projects in 1374
Persian Gulf, Indians migrating to
    267–8
Persian language, 723, 735
    as medium of instruction
        1037–8
    use of, in government
        administration 264
'Persian schools' 1000
'personal laws', of Hindus 1058,
    1077
    of Muslims 1058
personality, formation 1182
    traits 1159
personhood, in South Asia 1076,
    1164, 1190
    definition of 1058, 1141
    emotion and 1179
    models of 1059
    women establishing 1165
Peshwas 637
Petty bourgeoise 1305
Phasepardhi nomadic group, in
        Maharashtra 157
philology 10, 1035
Philosophy of right 118
The Philisophy of NEFA 385
Philadelphia Convention 922
Philippines 1287
photography 564, 661
physiography 329
pictorual art, traditional form of
    661

Pierce V. Society of Sisters of the
        Holy Names of Jesus and
        Mary, USA 925
pilgrmage 347, 610, 1161, 1179
    centers 412–2
    as cultural form 662
    to Lord Ayyappan Sabari
        Malai 1196
    social space and 628–9
    for villagers 421
pithāguri 845–6
Pilot Project in Etawah 442
piracankam 612
pirzada women, going into
        esctacy 1198
pisiculture, agriculture and 160
Pitt's India Act, of 1784 1426
plague, in Surat 342
Planning Commission 76, 184,
        392, 1248, 1495, 1519n
Plans, Five Year 388, 1435
    First 193–4
    Fifth 390
    Seventh 1053
    Ninth 1053
plantation workers/labour 440,
        1249
pluralism 114, 123–4, 129, 773,
        1380
    and Christianity 904
    and civil society 124–7, 707
    logic of 126
    notion of 770
    plurality and, of religion 775–
        98
pluriculturalism 742
Pohol, professional Kashmiri
        shepherds 244
policy, and globalization of
        labour system 1310–13
political behaviour 150, 1516
    state-level 1502–6
political development 75, 1495,
        1502
political economy 109–10, 485,
        659, 1074, 1216, 1468
    and Marxism 75
political identities 1059, 1413,
        1487
political marginalization, of the
        masses 988
political mobilization 16, 369,
        402, 663, 1504, 1512

class, caste and 1497, 1499
    role of sects in 771, 821–3
political participation 1504, 1519
    by tribals 399
political parties 279, 1381–2
    identity-based 1382, 1464
    membership of 1505–6
    support base of 1502
political power 512, 625, 1517
    caste forces and 70, 1466
    culture and defence 461
    hierarchy 510
    at regional levels 435
    and stratification 517
political process 1384, 1498
    and social theory 23
political reforms 1508
political science 658, 1496
    and modernization theory 75
    and social movement 1524
political and social equality 1448
political studies, local-level/grass-
        roots 1594–1519
political unity 14, 1420
Political Anthropology 130
Political economy of aging 960
politics, 38, 49, 659, 1383, 1497
    and religion 51, 772, 908–10
    sects in India 821–3
Politics, Law and Ritual in Tribal
        Society 129, 132n
pollution 71, 142, 308, 875,
        1164
    atmospheric and river 165, 304
    backward castes and 1304
    birth and death and 1075
    practice of, among Hindus and
        Christians 899
    purity and, ritual of 482, 483,
        863–4, 874, 1415
    women and 71, 679, 1199
polluting castes 1483
polyandry, 1118
    among Tadas 901
polygamy 900, 1117
    legal ending of 1123
Poona Pact 1543
poor, decentralization and the
        1361–76
    desire for large families 943
    lifestyle of 687
    and the markets 1363
    unorganized 1370

Pope, in medieval Europe 912
and political realm 910
power and prestige of 911–13, 930
spiritual and temporal authority of 912–14
as supreme head of Catholics 885
popular art, folk versus 588–91
popular culture 34, 655–8, 955
nationalization and commodification of 657
popular instructions 1478–80
population, concept of 136
control 304, 1079
density 192, 274
dependent on agriculture 1214, 1233
displaced, forced 279–81
distribution, by religion and domicile 105, 798–9nn
explosion 306
growth, and characteristics of 184–211
and employment 1278
theory of, 942
impact of, on land and water resources 328
policy 305
pressure, on land 1206, 1245, 1246
Population Council 307
Port Blair, establishment of 232
Portuguese, arrival and base in Goa, India 789, 886–7
and conversions to Christianity 773
ecclesiastical dominance of 888
missionaries 887
possessed /possession 607, 864, 867, 872
bhakti and 878–9
case study of 876–8
cults 1162
by deity 875
by evil spirit 875
in Hinduism 874–8
rituals 604–6, 861
during temple festivals 867
of women, by spirits 1128, 1198–9
in Bangladesh 1186
post traumatic stress disorder

(PTSD) syndrome 1128
poultry keeping 345
poverty, in India 12, 308, 686, 1447, 1480, 1486
alleviation programmes 1232, 1361
children in 945
and child labour 940, 944
and disease 305
and living in slums 465
and nutritional deficiency 342
peasants and tribals in 201, 308, 385
and schooling 977
in urban areas 472
power, and civil society 114
culture and 15–21
distribution of, at grass-roots 1500
hierarchy 507
notion of status and 528–9
and patronage 1435
and status 508, 528
structure 1475, 1516
pradesh party organizations 1505
Praja (tenant) party 1499
Prajapati's cosmic body 144–5
Prakrit inscription 734, 736, 752
Telugu in 725–6
Prakrta 735
prāṇ pratiṣṭha 632, 836
prasanga 612, 614–15
Pre-natal Diagnostic Technique Act 1994, (Regulation and Prevention Act 1994) 212n
prejudice, caste and 503, 516, 517–19
Presbyterian missionaries 890, 918
President, as head of the State 1433, 1454, 1462
primary health centers 343
primary education 937, 979, 998, 1020–1, 1023, 1047, 1371, 1482
primary schools 1018–19
Prime Minister's national relief fund, for natural calamities 429
primordial, identities 1500
loyalties 1256, 1414
ties 1250, 1328

versus supernatural 583–6
princely states, integration into India by 1432
inter-marriages among 418
of middle India 426
studies on 1506
print feminism 1166–7
printing press, in Goa by missionaries 894
in Telugu 724
privy purses, abolition of, for former rulers of princely states 1436
procreation, 'ideologies' 1074, 1080
indigenous theories of 1074
and sexuality 1081
production, and consumption 564, 565, 1084–7, 1210–11
forces, under colonial rule 1224–5
importance of, in economic process 1208, 1274, 1355
and market 1356
modes/means of 1290, 1294, 1532
relations 1226, 1415
proletarian culture, and folklore, in Soviet Russia 527, 572–5
property rights 463–4, 1072, 1073, 1085, 1219, 1352, 1365–6
control of, and female infanticide 1134
prostitution 1148, 1164
'protest marches/movements' 471, 522–4
Protestant Christians 789, 884–5, 898, 904
and destruction of religious objects and property 1570
ethic hypothesis 909, 1319–21, 1324
Protestantism 910, 920
persecution against, in France and Germany 918–19
provincial assemblies, altering of 1513
Muslim constituencies for 1511
psychiatric morbidity 963, 1182
psychiatry, science of 998

'psycho-social syndrome', of
 modernity 74
psychoanalytic approaches/studies
 832–4, 1181–3, 1186,
 1187, 1190
psychological anthropology 1186
psychology, science of 963, 998,
 1139, 1572
psychopathology 1182, 1184–6
puberty rituals 1083
public sphere, environment and
 169–76
public culture 564, 654–69
Public Culture 658–9
public distribution system 187,
 212n, 429, 439, 1361
public sector 1247, 1281, 1434–5
public instruction department
 1479, 1482–3
 reports 1481
pūjā 836
Punjab, census of 9
 birth arte in 194
 elections in 1467
 labour migration from, and
  into 276, 440
 life expectancy in 193
 Mahalwari/Malguzari
  settlement in 1220
 pastoralists and pastoralism in
  224
 rehabilitation of refugees from
  West Pakistan in 289–90,
  296
 secessionist movement in 269
 sex-ratio in 196, 197
Punjab Alienation of Land Act of
 1901 1223
Punjabi kinship 1076–7, 1131
Puranas (Puranic) 99, 782, 828
 myths 11
 performances based on 601,
  607, 609
Puranna of St. Peter 894
Purdah, practice of by women
 1083, 1085
purity, and divine contact 875
 and pollution, in caste system
  482–3, 51517, 689, 863,
  864, 874, 1186, 1415
 in Kerala 1138
Pushkar, pilgrim center/festival
 421–2

Pushkarna 416
Puṣṭimṣrg sect 631, 809–10, 812,
 816–17

Qadiyani sect *see* Ahmadiyah
qanun-e-shahi 1424
qasbah 1342
qaum 490
quality, concept/standards of
 1268, 1275, 1281
 of work life 1276–9, 1312,
  1368
Quasi-Permanent Land Allotment
 scheme, in East Punjab
 for refugee
 Rehabilitation 289
'Quantification sociolinguistics'
 697
'quazi-feudal' structures 1220
quda 410
Queen Victoria 1426
Quit India resolution 1451
Quota system, for 'untouchables'
 19
Quran 777, 790, 1423

Rabari pastorals/nomads 224,
 228, 234, 236, 241–2
 material culture 224
 as middle castes 250
race/racism, caste and 7, 520–2
 and culture 580
 folk and nation and, in Nazi
  Germany 570–2
 language, and physical types
  and 9, 11
 people of mixed, origin of 512
 relations, in America 519, 520
  in South Africa 521
 theory, critical 370
Radhasoami movement 815
Raidas 1545
Raikas, nomads of Rajasthan 158,
 167, 232
railways, construction of, during
 British rule 428
 growth of 450
 introduction of 1207, 1220,
  1246
 workers' welfare organizations
  1247
rais, 1427
 conspicuous consumption by 680

rajadharma 1416
rajamandala 1422
Rajasthan 248, 1127, 1370, 1394,
 1506
 birth rate in 194–5
 Congress party in 1506
 female infanticide in 197
 literacy among women in 977
 migration from 241
 nomadic hunters in 223
 Samand lake in 428
 Scheduled tribes in 201
 sex-ratio in 196
Rajasthan Forest Act 1953 255n
Rajasthan Shiksha Karmi Project
 1023
Rājasūya 603
Rajatrangini 327
Rajput miniature paintings 587
Rajputs 157, 416, 418, 478, 484,
 1423, 1509
Rajya Sabha 1454
Ram mandir/temple, at Ayodhya
 638, 644
 and Ramajanmabhumi –Babri
  Masjid dispute at 592n,
  638, 658, 771
Ram Rajya 124
Rāma, cult of 822
Ramakrishna Mission 815
Rāmānandī (Ramavat) sect 809–
 12, 820–3
 advent at Ayodhya 822
 liberation from caste
  restrictions 513
Ramalila dramas, 609–111, 619,
 677
 patronage by Mahārājas of
  Benaras 609, 612
 of Ramnagar 610–12
Rāmānuja 810
Ramāyaṇa 149, 609, 811, 1185
 impact of Doordarshan's
  telecasting of 637
 Kannada version of 613
 Kathakali based on stories
  from 615
 tradition 608
Ramayani-specialists 610, 612
Ramcaritamanas 609, 811
Ramdeora, pilgrim center 421,
 422
Ramdevji, image of 628–9, 643

Rameswaram, pilgrom center 421
Ramkheri village, Madhya
    Pradesh, case study of
    487–9
Rampur village, study on political
    formation 1495
'Rang Roop' 645
Rangbhumi 409
Rankin Committee Report 1405n
rape cases 1077, 1549
    of child 1137–8
    and domestic violence 1127–8
Ras Lila 611
Rasa classical theory of 1192–4,
    concept of 608, 609
Rashtrakuta rulers 1422
Rashtriya Swayamsevak Sangh
    (RSS) 1549
    militant women of 1549
Rasiks 813
    sedentarization of 818
Ravi Varma Lithographic Press
    637, 639, 642
Ravidas, images of 643–4
real estate market 1352
rebirth, concept of 805
reciprocity 114, 1344
'Recognized Educational
    Institutions' 1018
Reddis 434
redistribution 1344, 1347, 1371
reforms/reform movements 681,
    1171, 1386, 1542,
    1547
Reformation 120–1, 129, 732, 911,
    913, 916–17
    on separation of religion from
        politics 930
refugee (s) 283–99
    adaptation and assimilation of
        296–7
    'agency' 297
    definition of 291–3
    ethnic and environmental
        factors 298–9
    migration and 138, 292–3
    and occupational mobility 295
    from Pakistan on Partition of
        India 285, 287–91
    psychological and mental
        aspects of 295–6
    studies on gender and state
        293–5

region (al), autonomy,
    movements/demands for
    1455, 1467
    contrasts, in literacy 984–7
    geography 330
    groups, coalition of 1461, 1462
    identity 576, 1540
    interests, and democracy
        1467–8
    languages, cultures 1455
        modernization of 73, 730,
            731
    lifestyles in rural and urban
        683–5
    patterns of marriage 1105,
        1106
    pluralism 1467
    political parties 1467
    politics, and Indian democracy
        1468
    pressure groups 492
    -specific gender ideologies 338
    tribals classification by 380
regionalist movements, in Punjab,
    Andhra Pradesh, Assam
    and Kashmir 1437
Registration of Births and Deaths
    Act, 1969 187
registration system, of births,
    deaths, marriages and
    divorces 187–8
reincarnation, notion of 830, 1119
relational approach, stratification
    and 524–7
Relative Clause Formation (RCF)
    723
religio 777
religion(s)/religious, 11, 14–16, 38,
    44, 49, 51, 81, 120, 146,
    326, 373, 431, 483, 689–
    90, 775–98, 1211, 1495
    affiliation 1499
    beliefs and, architecture 150
        environment and 143–5
        practices 345, 862
        practices among Coorgs
            50–1
        ritual, social functions of
            1092
    and civil society 117
    communities, affiliations to
        1455
        conflicts between 1464

culture 346, 805
cults, studies on 699
discrimination 923, 931
    Church and 920
    safeguards against, in USA
        924
    state-sponsored 910
education, in schools in USA
    926–7
in everyday life 772, 861–79
environmental interpretation of
    152–4
in Europe in the Middle Ages
    913–14
festivals, crowd participation
    in, and violence 1573–4
fundamentalism 1066
and geographical features 149
heretical movements within
    1416
heterogeneity 201–3
hybridity 150, 153
identities 770–2, 924
images 628
Indian, sects and 802–23
institutions, in USA 925–6, 931
of King, as religion of State
    920
liberty 924–8, 930, 932
    concept of 932
    and the right to worship 910
minorities 1491
and monarchy 913
movements 74
narratives 636
nationalism, mass media and
    667
persecution 918–19, 922
pluralism 794–8, 1471n
    and tolerance, in Gupta
        period 1419
and political rights, denial of
    920
and politics 635, 772, 908–10,
    932
    in Goa 887
    in USA 921–2
practices, aesthetics and ritual
    performances 1179,
    1191–8
reform movements 582, 585
representations, of man and
    nature 141, 143–52

responses 1160–4
  non-religious responses
    1164–72
  riots 1568, 1569
  and secularism 908
  schools 929
  and society 862, 864
    in the West 861
  and State, separation of 921,
    928, 930
  supremacy of, in modern
    nation-state 917–20
  symbols in India 154, 1549,
    1569
  tax 921, 929
  traditions 139, 770
  vows 874
remittances, from the Gulf and
    non-resident Indians 268
  by migrants to villages 275
Renaissance 128, 640, 732, 911,
    913
  critics of *Malleus* 957
  post-, Europe, Protestant
    politics in 910, 917, 920
renewable resources, management
    of 344
renunciation 22, 484, 512, 771,
    804, 816–18, 1104,
    1160–2
  age of 963–5
  alternative to family 1174
  medieval renouncer 964
  and *moksa* 803
  sects and 803–4
reorganization of States, on
    linguistic basis 1456
*Report of the Board of Education
    1840–41* 1002
Report of the Central Advisory
    Board of Education
    (CABE) 1011
*Report on the Administration of
    Justice in the State of UP,
    1976* 1404n
*Report of the Arrears Committee
    1989–90 see* Malimath
    Committee Report
representation, of constituent
    state, principles of 1454
  problems of 1462–6
  for regions 1467
repression, concept of 772

reproduction, family as
    organization of 20, 1073,
    1074, 1078
  and social hermeneutics 1529
Republican Party 1543
research 1, 47, 1045, 1506
  on markets 1349
  sociological 41–3
reservations, for backward castes/
    classes, women and
    tribals, in education and
    jobs 19, 386, 397, 399,
    435, 437, 1457, 1470,
    1484, 1486, 1488–50,
    1543
  for Muslims 1513
  to Parliament 1543
  anti-reservation agitations 1488
reservation policies 368, 497, 498,
    991n, 1051, 1382–4
  during colonial period 1383
  implementation of Mandal
    report 498
  politics of, 493–7, 1383
    in Gujarat 663
Reserve Bank of India 1228
resistance, everyday form of 1570
  against domination 687, 879
  functions of 879
  movements by tribals 1537
  religious form of 878–9
    as non-religious activity 879
  by women 1149
  by workers 1309
retirement communities, of old
    people 959
revenue 107, 1342, 1416
  from agricultural land 1219
  assessment 1220
  under colonial rule 7, 9, 1062,
    1206
  from tribal cultivators 396
  'villages', in rural areas 190,
    1200
'revisionist' movement 1423
'revitalization' movements,
    concept of 1539
'revolution', modern concept of
    445
revolutionary movements 445–8,
    524, 1531
rice cultivation, Japanese method
    of 441

demand for labour for 426
Rig Veda 223, 263, 479, 602, 780,
    794
right(s), of communities 1381
  of cultivation, in pre-colonial
    India 1217–18
  to equality 1470
  to health 314
  of informal workers 1306
  over land 1222
  to property 1062
  to public worship, denial of
    921
Ripon initiative 1507
Ripon Reforms 1508, 1515
Ripon's Resolution on Local Self-
    Government 1517
Rishi order, of Kashmir Valley
    793
ritual(s) offerings/practices, 147,
    149, 413–15, 427, 451,
    565–6, 581, 599–500,
    601–7, 611, 621, 654–5,
    780–1, 836, 864, 1179,
    1207, 1210, 1322, 1497,
    1530
  aesthetics, religious practices
    and performances 1191–8
  cathartic function of 1195
  exorcism, of Sinhalese
    Buddhists 1196
  hierarchy 1415, 1502
  life-cycle 1304
  performances, in oral cultures
    603–7
  rulership, political unity on
    1420
  study of 655
  of weeping 1197
ritualistic-healers 310
Rockefeller Foundation 2, 65,
    1494
Roe V. Wade, USA 1390
Rohingya refugees, Burmese, in
    Bangladesh 283, 287
'Roja', Tamil-Hindi film 1166
Roman lawmakers 553
Roman Catholic Church, in
    Chota Nagpur 583
Roman Catholic Church, in
    Europe 911–12, 930
  breakdown of 913, 916
  and the Pope 913

Roman Catholics 789, 917–18

Romantic movement, of folk art 586

Rome, legal system of ancient 1063

Rowlatt Acts, failure of 1512

Royal Asiatic Society, London 649n

Royal Commission on Agriculture 429

Royal Commission on Labour, in India (1931) 1246, 1249

Royal Geographical Society 328

rozah 790

Rudra Sampradaya, sect of Vaisnavism 809

rule of law 1386, 1429, 1449, 1450, 1564

Rules for the Treatment and Management of Hillman 232

rural (areas), aging population in 1146, 1147

-cum-agrarian identity 1288

'appraisal projects' 449

changes in 453

children, work by 942

class conflicts in 447

development 276, 436, 1229

economy 1299

in pre-British period 1244

female household heads in 205

indebtedness of peasants in colonial period in 1206

labour (households) in 186, 204–5, 1071, 1256

landscape 346, 472

poor, conditions of 449–50, 1365, 1372–3, 1436

population 187, 190, 274–5

psyche 409

schools 981

society 81, 1206, 1215

space 662

systems, legal system for transformation of 430

and urban areas, 'continuum' 452

literary rates in 977

migration 262, 275–7

network 1210

water projects 1374

welfare, NGOs involvement in 441–3

States' action for 453

Rural General constituencies 1514

The Rural Profiles 436

rural sociology 66, 75, 1215

Russian fairy tales 593n

'Russian debate' 1214

Russian history, folklorists on 572

Ryotwari system 411, 1206, 1220, 1223

ryots, as tenants of the state under 1220

sabha, caste association 492

of learned scholars 1036

sacred space and place, theories of 347, 772, 776

sacrifice /sacrificial ritual, 147, 602, 603, 816, 872, 880

animal, by Hindus 145, 147, 152

among Muslims at Id-ul-Fitr 151

coconut 870

of goat 876

symbolism, in votive rituals 870

Vedic, sanctified by Agni 146

victim of 872–3

sadhu sect 812

Saheli 306, 1145

Sahitya Akademi, languages recognized by 741

St Thomas tradition, and Syrian Christians 885–6

Śaiva(s) 688, 808

agamas 806

Dasnāmīs 821

militants 821

and Vaiṣṇavas, division between 805

Siddhanta sect 806–7

Sakta form 1194

sakti (divine power) 863

Sakuntala 958

Salem district, female infanticide in 1135

Sāma Veda 602–3, 610, 780

samaj 488

samhitas 782

sami tree, in ritual and classified texts 148

Samkhya School 781

Sample Registration system(SRS), of births and deaths 136, 188, 192–3, 196, 197

samoradyas 1543

Samskrta (refined) 734

samskaras 1082

samya shakti 1547

Sanakādi (nimbārka) Sampradaya sect, of Vaisnavism 809

sanatana 780

Sangh Parivar 638, 657

Sanghas, assemblies of scholars 784, 1036

Sangharakshita 1545

sannyasin sects 513

sanyasis (renouncers) 250, 781, 808, 964, 1161

Sanskrit (language) 5, 13, 715–16, 734, 779

borrowings from 733, 735

as basic to Brahmin dialect 720

and Brahmanism 16

British hatred to 735

dialects of Tamil Brahmins, and loan words from 721

dramas 608, 617

in educational and cultural system 736

English and 727, 736–8

epics, bardic traditions of 610

translation into Telugu 724

grammar 715

of Gupta period and English 734–5

impact on historical development 715

and Indo-Aryan language 263

loan-words 721

Panani's grammar of 715

power and glory of 734

ruki rule in 719

theoretical treaties 608

West's encounter with 714–15

Works, on law 103

Sanskritic Great Tradition 14

Sanskritic heritage 1064

Sanskritic Hinduism 862

Sanskritization 69–71, 91n, 400, 424, 427, 492, 691, 733, 738, 752, 1093n, 1123, 1135, 1544

caste mobility and 50

concepts of 69
de-Sanskritization 733
and vernacularization 15–21
and Westernization 736
sant panths 814
sant traditions 787, 797, 813–14,
816–17
Sants (poet-saints) 806, 813–15
Santhal (s) 382, 403
converts 885, 891
curio masks of 590
custom of polygny, divorce and
marriage 901
myths among 853, 854
particpation in Naxalite
movement 1541
rebellion of 1857 333, 402–3,
590, 891
ritual hunt by 167
uprising 445
santāner carita gaṭhan 1190
Santiniketan 1010
Santri Muslims, in Indonesia 1324
'*sapinda*', concept in Hindu
kinship 1075, 1105
satpadi 1117
Sarda Act 198
Sardar Sarovar project 173, 308
and displacement of people
280
Sargent Report 101, 1012
Sarva sadharma dharma 781
Sarvodaya 443
sati 665, 1127, 1549
abolition of 1006, 1081
samskaras 1076
satnāmī sect 819, 891, 893
Satnampath 893
of Chhattisgarh 1544
'satva vidhaan' 719
satyagraha 124, 446, 1548
Saur Revolution, in Afghnistan
287
Savanath lion Capital, of emperor
Ashoka 1414
sa-varna 1120, 1542
Save the Children 944
Scheduled Areas and Scheduled
Tribes Commission 392
Scheduled Castes (SCs) 19, 190,
200–1, 207, 332, 478,
776–7, 1464, 1466, 1474,
1480, 1483–5, 1515, 1542

in Andhra Pradesh 1384
discrimination of 335
education for 336
fertility rate among 201
female population among 196,
200
literacy among 339, 975
infant mortality among 201
literacy among 984
poverty among 201, 335
regional disparities among 335
reservation for, in jobs and
education 493–4, 1046,
1457, 1490
school enrolment, decline in
1019
Supreme Court on Mandal
Commission report on
1489–90
as former untouchable castes
1480
Scheduled Castes Federation
(1942) (SCF) 1543
Scheduled Castes Order (1990)
200
Scheduled Tribes (STs) 190, 200–
01, 332, 369, 777, 1474,
1483–5
aborigines as 1480
education of 336
female population among 196,
200
literacy among 339
fertility rate of 210
infant mortality among 201
poverty among 201
reservations for, in jobs and
education 493–4, 1046,
1457, 1490
school enrolment, decline in
1019
worker population ratio of 207
'schismogenesis', concept of 557n
schizophrenia 78, 1128
school/schooling, as antidote to
child labour 946–7
attendance 978, 980–2
during colonial period 1038
costs of 947, 991n
culture and modernity 998–
1027
curriculum, local language and
985

dropouts 937, 980, 982
infrastructure 937, 981
motivation for, by parents 982
negative impact of 947
quality of 937, 981–2, 1016
and space for children 947
system, modern 998
in tribal areas 984
years of 977
and work, by children 947
School-Free Notification (1886)
1481
School of Mining, Dhanbad 1042
Scientific research 54
Scientific Revolution 120–1
'scientific temper' 1005, 1014
Scythians (Sakas), invasion by 263
seclusion (*purdah*), for women
337, 1083
secondary education 998, 1011,
1014
and higher education 1480
sects, and Indian religions 44, 631,
781, 802–23
caste and 771, 803, 818–2
meaning of 802
secular /secularism 12, 40, 51,
932–3, 100, 125, 794, 797,
908–33, 1045, 1163, 1380,
1431–2, 1461
cities of 909, 910
education and 1016–18
legal and politicales over 773
-socialist democracy 1438
transition from absolutism to
920
'secularization' 40,
without separation 928–33
study of 51
'sedentarization' 818
concept of 253
sedentary population 137, 225,
240
and non-sedentary continuum
233–4
segmentation 130–1, 411, 416
segregation, sex 71, 125, 130, 1083
self-denial, in rituals 880
self-employed 1209, 1278, 1287,
1290, 1299–1301, 1311
Self Employed Women's
Association (SEWA)
1306, 1363, 1547

selfhood, and emotions in South
    Asia 1180, 1182
'self-image', shifts in 1183
'self-respect' marriages, in Tamil
    Nadu 424
Selvi, case study of, possessed by
    supernatural beings 876–
    8
'Semantic Differential Technique'
    699
semantics, of confusion 710
Seminar 658
semiotic constraints 711
senility, and dementia 966
Sentinelese, in North Sentinel
    Islands 156–7
Separatist Tigers, in Sri Lanka
    1570
Servants of India Society 1043
sex/sexual, abuse of children 1137
    aggression 1136
    determination/selective tests
        1132–4
sex/sexual, ...
    division of labour 1065, 1085
    harassment 1127, 1304
    morality, in USA 1065
    ratio 137, 190, 196–7, 339,
        1135
    selective abortions 137
    violence 20
    workers 1127
sexuality, domain of 88, 656,
        1058–9, 1080–1
    of girls and early marriage
        1140
    and procreation 1077
    puberty and 1138
Shafii school 794
Shah Bano case 1123, 1549
Shaiva cult 782–3
Shaivism, in Kashmir 793
Shaktawat clan 418
shamanic healers, in Nepal 1196–
    7
shamanic séances 875
shamanism 784
Shantiparva 1417
shariah, Muslim holy law 791,
        793, 1062, 1121–3
    on marriage 1104, 1120
shastric traditions 104
sheep shearing 242

Shiah sect, among Muslims 792,
    793
shifting cultivation 164, 220
Shingaku movement, in Japan
    1324
Shirdhi Sai Baba, murti (image)
    of, at the temple of 633
Shiv Sena 279
    -BJP government in Mumbai
        625
    -Sunni clash 471
Shiva sects 1419
    Kalamukha sect 782
    Kapalika sect 782
    Pashupata sect 782
    see also Shaiva cult
Shivling images 628
Sharmik Mukti Sangathan, on
    education 1026
Shrauta Sutras 780–1
Shree Krishna Janma 641
Shri Ram Centre for Industrial
    Relations 1249
Shrinathji svarup (form) 631, 642
shruti texts 780, 795, 1415
shuddhi campaign, of Arya Samaj
    1542
shudra caste 70, 145, 153, 479,
        1415
    removam of legal
        discrimination against
        1419
'siblings' 1106–08, 1094n, 1113
    bond among 1189
Siddha system 303, 309, 310, 312,
    829
Sign-painting 645–6
Sikhs (population) 202, 770, 777–8,
        821, 1426
    alienation of 1464
    attack on, in Delhi 1148, 1568,
        1570–1, 1577
    caste division among 477, 487–
        8, 491
        Amritdhari Sikhs 788
        Keshdhari Sikhs 788
        Sahajdhari Sikhs 788
    defeat of, by British 788
    identity 771, 787–8
    literacy and education among 202
    migration from Pakistan to
        India after Partition 285,
        287

militancy 660, 1579
    women population among 196
Sikhism 144, 201, 775–8, 814,
        909, 963
    and caste Hinduism 787
    Scheduled Tribes in 201
Sindhur 1117
sindhuradana 1117
Sing Bong, god of Munda Tribes
    584–5
Singapore, Indians' migration to
    115, 267
Sinhala rioters, in Sri Lanka 1517
Sinhalese language 265
Siva, in Bairava form 806
    see also Shaiva cult
Siva temple festival,
        Munnesvaram, in Sri
        Lanka 866
Sivaratri, and observance of fast
        among Hindu Saivas
        1195
Skills, occupational structure and
        1268–76
    mix 1271
    semi-skilled workers 1282
    skilled and unskilled workers
        185
Slavic, social organozation of
    1063
sloka 615
slums, living in, incities 308, 464–
    5
Small Industries Extension
        Training Institute,
        Hyderabad 74, 76
Smartha-Pauranika traditions 782
Smartas 782
Smritichandrika 1118
snakebite healers 309
S.N.D.T. University 938, 1043
social, action concept of 565, 1527
    religion and 689
    activism 1171–2
    change 67–8, 46, 340, 504, 507,
        527, 1069, 1215, 1495,
        1525–6
    conflict and 548–50
    modernization and 64, 82
    study of 46
    'closures' 1474
    conflicts 35, 330–1, 532–57,
        1529, 1539

language and 700
migration and 281
'Contract' of Hobbes 116, 1290
and cultural framework, of
  health and disease in
  India 303–15
and cultural geography 326–48
death of old people 966–7
dialects, caste system and 720
dynamics 505–8, 1298
ecology 136, 138
engineering 90n, 704, 728–49,
  741
equality 494, 1448, 1470
functions of the family 1077–
  87
geographers 331–2, 341
gerontology 962
historical perspectives 1496,
  1507–15
identity 102, 699–70, 1303–6,
  1247–8, 1303–6, 1348,
  1487
inequality 139, 502–3, 1466
  caste and 478
  democracy and 1469–71
justice 449, 1384, 1433, 1490,
  1497
mobility 506–7, 517, 888, 893,
  1244, 1297
  social stratification,
    hierarchy and 502–29
movements 20, 665, 668, 1235,
  1384, 1475, 1524–52
  of Dalits 1541–6
  definition of 1525
  research on 1524, 1526,
    1552
  of tribals 402, 1538
networks 1348, 1352
order 503, 505, 1415, 1475
policies, impact of 1495
-psychological perspectives
  74–5
reconstruction, Gandhian view
  of 172
reforms /movements 835, 1051,
  1081, 1497, 1529, 1540
revolution 527, 1569
'sciences' 1, 2–4, 83
  and discourse on caste
    497–9
security 962, 1312, 1510

rights 1312
Semiotic, language as 696
space 434, 551
  on the cultural practice of
    Indian Muslims 20
  and pilgrims 629
stasis, principles of 505–8
stereotype 718
stratification 370, 502–29,
  1497, 1509
  in USA 514
structure 136, 1324–5, 1447,
  1448, 1462, 1497
  language and 712–14
theory 1210, 1551
  political process and 23
welfare schemes 960, 1083
Social Psychology of Language
  698, 703
socialism 1432, 1434, 1465
Socialist party, as 'national' party
  1463–4
Socialist states 1083
Socialists, in the Hindi area 1467
sociality 564, 1380
  patterns of 370, 1210, 1567
socialization 1081–3, 1149
social anthropology 32, 79, 87,
  669, 1213–14, 1524
  in pre-Independence India
    80–1
  and nationalism 13
  perspectives 69–71
  research in 41
  sociology and 37–59, 568, 1530
social anthropologists 37, 828
Social Change in Modern India 69
Social Class in America 514
Social Mobility in Industrial
  Society 526
society (ies), based on caste and
  community identity 1447
based on religious ideology
  483–4
Christianity in Indian, and
  culture 884–904
'cold' 504
concept of 1528
definition of 4
Dumonts' characterization of
  Indian 4
in histories of the Subcontinent
  101

historiography of India's 34
labour and 1243–4
language and 695–701, 717,
  728–9, 737–8
'modern' and 'backwardness'
  1213
notion of 34, 1566
rigidly-integrated, and conflicts
  539
and State 1552
  without State 129–31
types of 384, 1058
understanding of 88
Society of Jesus 903
sociology (sociological) 6, 32, 57–
  8, 669, 695, 1062, 1495,
  1496
of agriculture 1216
approach to Indian family
  1061, 1069
categories, natural differences
  and 505–6
definition of 37
enquiry 39, 44–5, 47
and Indology 14
influence of, on historiography
  of Indian society 110
labour and 1249–50
'of language' 697–700
  Sociolinguistics and 697,
    701–14
and nationalism 13
and social anthropology 37–59,
  80, 141, 175, 568
research in 41–3, 58
and social history, and social
  movements 1524
study on castes 383
Sociological Bulletin 42
'sociolinguistics', and sociology of
  languages 695–7, 701–14,
  717
socio-centric theory of person,
  emotion and 1059
socio-cultural integration, language
  policies for 730–1
socio-economic inequality/
  development 333, 728–9,
  1375, 1416, 1518
Socio-Economics Status Indexes
  514
'Socio-Historical Linguistics' 697,
  703

soil, conservation 437
    nutrient deficiencies 342
sodomy cases 1138
solidarity, among groups/women
        114, 139, 665, 1527, 1539,
        1551
'somatization' 1182, 1185
    among Indian women 1186
'son-preference' 196, 1078, 1079,
        1133
son-in-law, treatment meted out
        to 415
Sons of the Soil movement, in
        Assam 278
sorcery, and violence 1567
'soul loss' 1179, 1185–6, 1196–7
'soul-calling' rites 1197
South Africa, racism in 505–6,
        521
South America, research on tribal
        movements in 1536
    role religion in political
        movements in 903
South Asia/South Asians, conflicts
        in 545
    diaspora 1172–3
    emigration from 265–9
    experience of consumption and
        lifestyle 675–6
    family bonds in 1174
    gross domestic product in
        1277
    household life-cycle and family
        changes in 1072
    kinship, culture of 1076
    labour force, growth in 1278
    language development in 723,
        724, 732–3
    Louis Dumont's ethnography
        on 688–9
    McKim Marriott on life in 689
    migration into 263–5
        international migration
        within 269–73
    Muslims 791
    political systems, violence and
        power in 1570
    problems of development in 73
    refugees in 283–7
    society in 233
    violence in 1570, 1572
        'collective' 1564, 1568–71,
        1573, 1578–9

vocabulary and power of
        expressions in 732
South Asian area studies 1494–5
    in the United States of
        America 5–23
sovereignty 1420, 1380
    and unity 1433
Soviet Union, collapse of 1564
    folklore and proletarian culture
        in 572–5
    ethnic communities in 592n
    invasion of Afghanistan, and
        refugee flow into
        Pakistan 271
    literature, purge of, and
        'Western' elements 573
    movements in 569
    society, cleavage between
        politically powerful and
        masses 574
soy bean, cropping 1236
S.P. Gupta V. Union of India
        1404n
space 668, 654
    categorization of 145
    and female-male distinctions
        677–8
    forms of 564
    and movement in India 219–21
    politics of 662–4
    and spatiality 668
    of traffic, commerce and
        leisure 663
    and visual culture 636
Spain 1271
spatial ecology, of disease 341,
        342
spatiality, pattern of 137–8
speaking, ethnography of 704–6
    see also speech
Special Marriage Act, of 1872
        1122
    of 1954 1122
speech 710
    acts 598–9, 718, 726, 752
    behaviour, of literate people
        740
    as chaos 751
    communities 699, 701
    constructions 712
    as intermediary agent 710
    standard 740
    and texts 712

varieties 702
    vertical interpretation 712
spinsterhood 1093n
spirit, aversion of evil, by
        worshipping 846
    possession 874, 1162, 1186,
        1190
        Bangladeshi women facing
        1184
'spirit of capitalism', analysis by
        Marx and Weber 1329
'spirit loss', Yolmo communities
        suffering from 1184–6
śrāddha (funeral) rites 871
śṛaṅgāra rasa 1194
Srauta-Sūtras 603
Sri Lanka, disenfranchised Indian
        Tamils from 266–7
    displaces people 299
    disturbances in 1574
    end of British rule in 285
    ethnic conflicts in 286
    India's peace-keeping force in
        286
    Indian labour, in plantations in
        265–7, 440
    police brutality in 1574
    separatist Tigers in 1570
        and assassination of of
        Rajiv Gandhi 273
    torture survivors in 1567
    violence in 1574–5
Sri Lankan Tamils 285, 186
    influx into India 270, 273, 283
Sri Narayana Guru
        Dharamaparipalana
        (SNDP) 1543
    Yogum 420
Sri Visva Vaisnava Raj Sabha 811
Srikrishna Commission, report of
        663
Stalinism 574
'Standard Language' 718, 737,
        740, 751, 773
state 73, 88, 1413, 1566
    centralized 16, 1417
    on child labour 940
    and the Church, in Europe 120,
        121, 908
    and communities, and
        individual 660
    culture and 657–9
    -designated development

projects 1362
and employment 169
formation 398, 1208
Governors 1462
under Mauryan and Gupta
dynasties 1414–20
and health 313–15
and informal sector 1209–10
market and, 1350–2, 1362
and nation 669
pyramidically segmented 1420–
2
regulation, on movements of
people 138
religion, and religion of ruler
914, 921
abolition of, and secularism
policy 921, 923
study of political behaviour at
the level of 1502–6
and tribes 385–98
and welfare responsibilities
1084
State of Assam V. Ranga
Mohammad 1405–6nn
State Census Reports 18
State of West Bengal V. Nripendra
Nath 1406n
State Statistical Bureau 976
Statistics 4, 8, 329
development of science of 106
history of 136
status 504
of the family 1323
and hierarchy 52, 507, 518–20,
522
'inconsistency' 1527
inequality, based on caste 1470
and power, notions of 528–9
size of property and 464
and stratification 506–7
in urban India 489
wealth and power and 1415
of women 1130–1
Statutes of the Realm (1810–28)
915, 917–18
statute of praemunire (1353) 914
steel sector 1282
'stem family' form 1071
'strategic mimicry' 636
stratification 38, 52, 131, 666
closed system of 517
hierarchy and differences in 510

open and closed systems of
508–11, 517
power and 506–7
Stree Shakti Snghatana 1536, 1547
Stri Kriti Samiti 1142
structural, adjustment
programmes 949, 1312,
1439
analysis 130
approach to entrepreneurship
1319–20, 1325–9
consistency, and dynamics 1291
constraints, and contradictions
1529
-functional framework 46, 706,
1089
issues 716–17, 719–25
'structuralism' 701, 714–16
students, in colleges 1047
unions of, and problems 1049
Studies in Agrarian Social
Structure 1216
'sub-sub-caste', phenomenon of,
in South India 419
sub-cultures, in complex societies
698–9
'sub-national' movements 1504
subah 1423
'subaltern Studies' (movement)
80, 100, 101, 110–11, 486,
1224, 1569
Subaltern School 7, 656, 1530,
1539, 1540
'subalternity' 109, 1530
concept of 1537
subsidies, government 1312, 1369
on fertilizer and seeds 1435
subsistence 172, 942
agriculture, child employment
in 944, 945
economy, rural 1289
modes 141–3
combinatorial modes of
154–69
succession, problems of 424–5
Sudra caste 18, 808, 1475, 1477
Suez canal, opening of, and global
market 1220
Sufi (mystics) 791, 792, 797
in Bangladesh 1196
doctrine of tolerance of 552
Order, Chishti 793
Naqshbandi 793

Qadiri 793
Suhrawardi 793
Sufism 792–3, 814
sugarcane cultivation, migrant
labour for 426
suicide rates 8
Sultanism 1424
Sunderban, in West Bengal, tribal
population movement to
389
Sunni sect, among Muslims 792,
793
Supreme Court, in India 1038,
1389, 1398, 1401, 1432
Backward Classes and
reservations, ruling on
1485
deterioration of justice in 1400
use of English in 744, 1391
and High Courts 1403n
increased flow of cases in 1392,
1399
judges, appointment of 1459
on Mandal Commission report
1489–90
Supreme Court of United States
of America 23
Surma Valley, Assam, Scheduled
Castes' movements in 337
surplus extraction 1385, 1532
sutradhara (stage-manager), in
theatrical performances
608
suttee, fight against 1051
Svadhyaya 603
Svaminarayan sect, of Gujarat
810, 819
svarupa 610
svayambhu (self-born) 631
Svetambara Jains 805, 818
female ascetics of 817
swadeshi 124
art 586
ideologies of 666
movement and 576, 588, 746
Swadeshi International
Development Agency 441
swaraj 22, 124–5
Swatantra Party 1460
Sweden, Evangelical Luthen
Church, established
Church in 929
technological change in 1280

Swidish International
Development Agency
442
symbols, conflicts and 534
of excess, women and 1197–98
of identity, and fears 1576
and images, power of 541
and rhetoric 556
Synod of Diamper, Portuguese
ecclesisticial dominance
by 887–8
Syrian Christians, in India 264,
788–9, 885–6,
Holy places of 886
of Kerala 490, 773, 894–5
Patriarch 789
A System of National Education
1006
*Systems of Consanguinity and
Affinity of the Human
Family* 1106

TFR 211
'Taayumaanvar', Tamil television
serial 1166
Tada polyandry 901
tahsils 1513
Taiwan, decentralization in, and
decline in poverty in 1375
taluk development board 1505–6,
1518
taluqdari class 1510, 1514
Tamasa 611
Tamil Brahmins, borrowings of
Sanskrit words by 720–1
Tamil Hinduism, and Eseki as
village goddess in 896
Tamil kinship 1076
Tamil language 721
H/L styles in 740
Tamil literary form 722
Tamil Nadu 864, 1505
anti-Brahmin movement in 13
birth rate in 194–5
conversions to Christianity in
889
female infanticide in 197
fertility rate in 194
during Pallava period 1420
reservations for Other
Backward Castes (OBCs)
in 494–5
urbanization of 190

Tamil Nadu Act, in the Ninth
Schedule 1490
Tamil nationalism 807
Tamil militants 1579
Tamil Tolkappiyam 224
Tamil "tigers", of Sri Lanka 1571,
1574
Tamils (population), anti-Tamil
riots in Sri Lanka 1568–
70
religious experience of, in Sri
Lanka 772
violence and killing of, in Sri
Lanka 1571, 1577
Tantra 576
texts 782
Tantrism, Buddhism and 784
and rituals 782
sects 806
Tantrikas 782
tapra 410
Ta' rich al Hind 327
Tata Institute of Social Sciences
1043
Tavistock Institution 1267
taxation 1292, 1418
Taxila, center of Brahmanical
higher education 1036
teacher/teaching, 43, 937, 981
accountability 937, 981, 991n
and punishments 983
respect for 1035–6
Tebhaga struggle, in Bengal 404,
446, 1535, 1547
technology(cal), change/advances
1050, 1051, 1270, 1277
education in 1049–50
labour and industry 1266–83
new, and industrial revolution
142
and occupational structure and
skills 1269–70
and organization structure
1274–6
'technologically-advanced
metropolis' 1288
Tehri dam project, halting of 308
Tehri Garhwal, UP 541
Tej 311
Tejpal Singh V. State of UP
1406n
Telengana revolt/uprising(1946–51)
445–6, 1432, 1535, 1548

television 661
Telugu *gadya* (oral prose) 724
Telugu language, H/L standard
styles in 740
Telugu literary styles 724
Telugu speech community 699
Telugu verse 724
temples, divine possession in 875
images in 626–7, 631
location of, at *titthas* 150
murtis/statues 631, 634
rituals 600, 866–7
tenancy/tenants, 1223, 1300
ownership rights to 1227
tenkay pali (coconut sacrifice) 873
Terakhaniya Bar Karati 837
'terms of trade' 1532
terror and revival, discourse of
667
Terukkuttu, of Tamil Nadu 612–
15, 619
Test Act of 1673, England 918,
919
text, context of a 667, 834–5
textile industry, and child labour
941
beginning of 1207, 1246
closure of, in Bombay and
Ahmedabad 1311
study on technological change
1282
workers 1304
Textile Lbour Association,
Ahmedabad 1256
Teyyam cult, in Kerala 604–7,
611
possession 607
Thakurs 1499, 1509, 1514
Thanksgiving rights, ritual of, of
deity 867–8
theatre, modern Indian 618–21,
661
theatrical performances 565–6,
598, 601, 460–72
possession 604
Theft of an Idol 1576, 1578
Theology 582
Theravada Buddhism 784–5
Third World countries 65–6, 74,
1229, 1289, 1336n
agriculture in 1214
comparisons across 88–9
metropoles of 1288

modernization, anthropological accounts of 78
population working in informal sector 1287, 1295
Thomas Christians *see* Syrian Christians
thread ceremony, for Hindu Brahmin boys 1117
three-language formula, Nehru on 747
Tibetan influence, in the Himalayas 225
Tibetan refugees, from China, into India 271, 283, 286–7
in Nepal 283
Tibeto-Burman linguistic category, of tribals 381
Ticcadars 396
Tipu Sultan 1424
tirthankars 785
Tiruccentur Murugan temple 871
Tirumal Nandivalla pastorals 239
Tisri Kasam, Hindi film 409
Toleration Act of 1689, England 918
Tonga children, in Zambeszi Valley, schooling and work by 946
'total literacy' 977
campaign 979, 983
Towards Equality, report on status of women 54, 1548
towns/cities 189, 472
classification of 460–1
along river-banks 462
planning 464
township and village enterprises (TVE), in China 1372, 1373, 1375
'Toytism', new model of 1274
trachoma 342
trade-off 1367
trade unions 117, 1208–9, 1268, 1279, 1293, 1306
blue-collar workers of 1254
control of 1252
decline of 1261
emergence of 1246
and informal sector 1307–8
labour in 1243–61

launching of, by Mahatma Gandhi 1247
leadership in 1252
and management 1253
militancy/violence by 1253, 1254
movements 404, 1208
and nationalist movements 1247
new technology and 1276–7, 1279–83
and politics 1247, 1252
studies 1251–5
weakening of 1254
traders 396, 1423
and entrepreneurship 1323
identity of 1348
and moneylenders, in UP 1510
network 1348
ritual seclusion of 1322
'traditions'(al), in India 3, 33, 43, 72, 80–1, 654, 659, 1530
family structure 1167
culture 1471n
great and little 1206
and identities 551
and modernity 14, 45, 68–9, 75, 77–8, 85–6, 91n, 93n, 139, 691, 726, 1289, 1344, 1427
myth and 835
negotiating 894–902
and nationalism 575, 731
of philosophy and history 22
search for 21–3
societies 729
values 45, 71
villages 481, 489
trance 875–6
and performance of rituals 876
training 1273, 1278
transsexuality, in South Asia 1163
tree-felling, resistance to 170
tribals/tribes, acquired characteristics of 381–2
animism, practice of 383
agriculture by 384
backwardness and poverty of 385
base-line study of 451
beliefs 146
'belt', in middle India 1538
and caste dichotomy 383–5

and gender 332–4
conceptualizing 374–85
children and education of 985, 991n
Christianity theologians 582
church 583, 585
classification of 379–80
communities, marginalization of 985
construction of 374–6
culture 579, 589
Dalits 1545
Definition of 376–7
displacement of 395, 449, 1541
folk and 567
identity 582, 1385
importance of land and forests for 387, 412
law 130
literacy among 369, 984–5
middle class and educated 397–8
movements 401–2, 1384–5, 1531, 1536–41
for religious reforms 585
mythology 855, 856n
of north-east India 1385, 1538, 1539
panchayat 582
politics 399, 1540
religion 144, 583
reservation for 386, 397
'revolts' 401
in Bihar and Orissa 445–6
rights of 379, 386
social geography of 332–4
society 130, 376, 384, 1506
without state 130
socio-cultural life of 399–404
state and 385–98
in south India 1385
study of 45, 48
sub-plan (TSP) 391–2
women, gender equality for 337
see also Scheduled Tribes
Tribal Research Institute 373–4
Tribal Welfare Committee of 1951 377
Tribunals 1393
'trickle-down' theory, of economic growth 1229, 1232

tridosham 311
Trinidad and Tobago, Indian
    immigrants in 266–7
Tripartite Delhi Agreement of
    1951, between Nepal and
    India 272
Tripura, tribal population in 201,
    389
tropical medicine 140
trusteeship, Gandhian ideology of
    1255
    theory of 445
tsher glu (songs of pain), among
    Yolms, sung at funerals
    1197
tsungrem, as God 894
tube-wells, in Ganga-
    Brahmaputra delta 308
Tulu, dialect 720
Turkish invaders 263
    Rule in India 264
Twentieth Century Fund 76
'twice-born' caste 69
two-nation theory 1455
Tyagi caste 412, 812, 818

Udgatar (singer), in Samaveda 602
Uganda, expulsion of Indians and
    Pakistanis from 266
Ulama 791–2
Umayyad caliphate 791
umma 791
ummat 102
Unani-Tibb 303, 309–10, 312
underdeveloped countries 1289
underdeveloped societies 74
underprivileged, families,
    education for 978
    speech communities 701
unemployment/unemployed 1254,
    1259, 1277, 1294, 1296
uniform civil code 1123
Uniformity Act of 1662, England
    917
'United Front', phase 446
United Left Front government, in
    West Bengal 1535
United National Party(UNP), in
    Sri Lanka 1569–70
United Nations (UN) 307
    on population estimation 184,
    192
United Nations Children's

Emergency Fund 2441,
    943
UN Conference on Population
    and Development 1994
    306
UN Convention relating to the
    Status of Refugees 1951
    283–4, 291, 299
UN 'Decade of Women' 1546
UN Development Programme
    (UNDP) 441
UNESCO 2, 747
    Conference on higher
    education 1032–3
United Nations High
    Commissioner for
    Refugees (UNHCR) 283,
    284, 287, 299
United Nations International Year
    of the Family 1944 1066
United Nations Sub Commission
    on Prevention of
    Discrimination and
    Protection of Minorities 378
United Provinces, 1514
    Muslim constituencies in 1511
United Provinces of Hindu
    Backward Classes League
    1478
United States of America (USA)
    33, 65, 658, 735
    Catholic migration to 919
    class mobility in 514–15
    Constitution of 923
        First amendment to 923
        Fourteen amendments to 924
        and secular polity 921–2
    disestablishment and
        separation of Church and
        state in 930
    environmental NGOs in, on
        Sardar Sarovar project
        174
    gerontology in 959–61
    green revolution in 1229
    higher education in 1049, 1050,
        1054
    Indians migrating to 267, 440
    kinship system in 1075–6
    movement for 'state rights' in
        1371
    open system of stratification in
        511, 516

religion and politics in 911,
    921, 922
social structures in cities 462
society, nuclear family in 1065
speaking patterns of men and
    women in 728
study programmes, on South
    Asian studies 5–23
urban disturbances/violence in
    1564–5
White population, and
    intolerance towards
    Black population 520
United States Agency for
    International
    Development (USAID)
    76, 211, 306
United States Committee for
    Refugees 283, 287
United States Supreme Court,
    protection of liberty of
    religious
    institutions 925
    on separation of religion from
    politics 922, 925
universal childhood education
    laws 1170
universal elementary education,
    and democracy 975,
    978
universal franchise/suffrage 1309,
    1433, 1453, 1496
'Universal Grammar', notion of
    701
'Universals of Language' 698
universal literacy 210, 988
University of Bombay, department
    of anthropology in 41
University of Calcutta,
    department of
    anthropology in 41
University Departments of
    Sociology and
    Anthropology 373
University Education Commission
    746
University Grants Commission
    (UGC) 54, 1045, 1047, 1053
universities,
    emergence of, in medieaval
    Europe 1034
    in colonial period in India 1042
    in India 1019, 1043, 1047

unorganized workers 1208, 1260
'untouchable castes' 19, 481, 487,
        1415, 1457, 1480, 1541–2
    conversions to Christianity 885,
        891, 898–9, 902, 1491
    emancipation of 1475
    impure status of 482
    opponents of 1542
    political representatives from
        1463
untouchability 478, 628
    abolition of 18, 124, 438, 493,
        1081, 1456, 1475, 1543
    practice of 1457
Upanishads (treatise) 780, 783,
        796, 815
Uraon leaders 382
urban, 'agglomeration' 189,
        1289
    centers 274–5, 438, 452, 470
    culture 1082, 1519n
    demographics 663
    dualism 1290–1
    economy 1288, 1291, 1294,
        1296–7
    General constituencies 1514
    growth 189–90
        migration and 273–6
    history 458–60
    households, nuclear 205
    housing 190
    -industrial culture 1249
    lifestyle 684
    locality, definition of 189
    middle and upper classes in
        south India 71
    morphology 34
    population 187, 189, 203,
        273–4
    and rural sociology 459
    settlement patterns 459–60
    space 662
    tensions 470–1
    violence 1575
*Urban Form and Meaning in
        South Asia* 346
urbanism 459–60, 683
urbanization 74, 274, 276, 326,
        336, 409, 1288, 1290
    concept of 370
    industrialization and fertility
        decline 210–11
    in Nazi Germany 571

and nuclearization 1071
    villages, and level of 189–90
Urdu language, Hindi and 125–6,
        722–3
    and Hindustani language
        721, 723
    Persianization of, and
        Brahminic reaction to
        722
    Perso-Arabic origin of 722
    'purists' on 721
'users' cooperatives 449
usury 1225
Utilitarianism 105
Uttar Pradesh (UP). Assembly
        elections of 1993 in 1491
    Birth rate in 194–5
    caste and occupation in 335
    civil cases in 1393
    Congress governments in 1503,
        1505, 1517
    Courts in 1390
    Fertility rate in 194
    Hindus winning the elections
        1511
    life expectancy in 193
    sex-ratio in 196
Uttar Pradesh Chief Minister's
        Estates Acquisition Act
        of 1953 438
Uttar Pradesh Zamindari
        Abolition Act of 1952
        438

vacanam 613
Vadabalija caste, possession
        rituals among 604–7
vaids 301
Vaisesika school 781
Vaishnava, religious culture 823
    songs 579
    theology 809
Vaishnava(s) /Vaisnavas, 808–13
    Banias 1334n
    cult 782–3
    devotionalism 809, 813–14,
        835, 1193
    Hindus, in Tamil Nadu 1196
    lineages, Caitnayaite tradition
        and Pustimay tradition of
        816
    movement 578, 809
    Nagas 822

and Saivas, division between
        805
    sects in, 'orthodox' sects in 809
        Pancharatra sect in 782
        Sri Sampradaya sect in 809
        Vaikhanasa sect in 782
    tradition 808
Vaishyas 145, 479, 1415, 1477
    Vaishya ethic 1323
Vajrayana 784
Valabhi, Buddhist educational
        center 1036
Vanniyar caste 421
variation studies, languages and
        719–20
varna 105, 144–7, 491, 576, 780,
        1476–7
    and caste 49
    hierarchy 483
    -jati dichotomy 1476–7
    panchayats 417
    system 479, 486, 687, 1475
    theory 485, 1476
varnashrama-dharma 513, 781,
        1416, 1162, 1415
Vastushastra, 'Hindu' towns
        based on 461, 463
Vatican Council 930
    Second 931
Vedas 145–7, 601, 609, 779, 795,
        816
    Learning the 1035
    (Vedic) mantra, and fire at
        weddings 1117
    memorization of, as education
        1035
    myths of 827
    texts, training in 603
    women and Sudras prohibited
        from hearing 603
Vedanta 780, 795
    School 781
Vedantic Hinduism 796, 797
Vedic, beliefs 144–7
    civilization 576
    culture 1007
    heritage 575
    Hinduism, and Brahmanical
        codifer 147, 149
    hymns, ecology and
        environment 143–4
    mythology 856n
    religion and Sanskrit 779

rituals 602–3, 609, 780
sacrifice 145–6, 1117
society, and pastoralism 220, 223, 251
symbols and moulds 146
wedding rituals 1117
Vedism, and early Hinduism 779–93
Vedda nomads, of Sri Lanka 232
vegetarianism 345, 485
Vellals, Christians, in Tamil Nadu 899
vernacular(s), culture and folk consciousness in Bengal 575–80
dialects 745
development of 123
journalism 733
languages, as medium of instruction 1002–3, 1040–1, 1046
literature 16, 1455
maps, of towns 466
movement 17
vernacularization, Sanskritization and 15–21
in South Asia 16
verbal abuse, of women 1129, 1148
vesa 619
'Vidhi', Tamil film 1166
Vidusaka, the jester 608
Vietnam, refugees from, in USA 284
war 1531
Vigyan Shikshan Karyakram, on education 1026
Vijayanagara, a 'Hindu' city 470
kingdom 1421
period 1420
Vikramshila, Buddhist educational center 1036
village(s), in India, and agriculture 1289, 1532
assemblies, meetings of 439
caste system in 434, 479, 481
communities 34, 105, 108, 369, 409–53, 992n, 1063, 1093n, 1414–15, 1244, 1495
during British rule in India 430–3
Mahatma Gandhi on 444

conflicts 48, 448
and customary rights, in land, water and produce 417
deity, temple and 150, 415
development programmes in 435–51
economy 1342, 511
exogamy 417–18
festivals and rituals 414–15
governance 1382
and ideological movements 442–50
-level welfare programmes 441–3
life /lifestyle in 17, 577, 683
markets 425
as moral entity 413–17
morphology of 410–13
organization, for revenue collection 368
panchayats 450
reconstruction 49
and region 417–26
resilience in 427–30
schools, girls studying in 981–2
size distribution of, and urbanization 189–90
social network 1496
society, politics in 17–18
studies 48, 51, 451, 484, 1382, 1494–5
village commons 160, 163
rights of villagers over 161–2
Village Government in India 1496
Village India 1216
Vimmochana 306
vinaya 784
violence, 1387–8
and anthropology 1566–8
culture of 658
definition of 1127–32
discourses of 1578
and disorder 1571
against girls/women 1129–30, 1132–40, 1549
in conjugal home 1140–6
after Indira Gandhi's death 1574
and intimidation 1574, 1576
Marx on 1565
mental health aspect of 1128

and non-violence 1564, 1566
of public arena 1564
social 1567
state and normal politics 1573–6
of urban crowd 1564
and theory 1565–6
Virasaiva gurus 820
Virasaiva movement see Lingayat movement
Visarjan 836
vishishitadvaita 782
Vishnu, Lord, cult/worship of 782, 1419
Vishwa Bharati 938
Vishwa Hindu Parishad (VHP) 638, 649n, 657, 1549
visual culture/visual signs, 627632, 639–40, 660–1, 665
Vithoba (Vitthal) deity, at Pandharpur 813
Void, speech and 710
Vokkaliga, and Lingayat conflicts 421
Volkgeist (folk soul) 570, 580
Voluntary Health Association of India (VHAI) 303, 314, 315
voluntary organizations, 437
and environment 172–3
natural calamities and 430
for tribal development 394
'vote bank' politics 1437, 1478, 1491
votive offerings/rituals 861, 864, 867, 869, 872–3
symbolism of 870–4
vrata (vow) 867–8, 869
'Vyaavaharika' (transactive knowledge) 725, 781
Vyasas 610

Waddar caste 421
wages, 1276, 1282
in agriculture 1245
labour 1300, 1321
self-employment and 1301
Wakf property/land 464
Wallace V. Jefferee, USA 922
Walz V. Tax Commission, USA, Supreme Court on 926
Wardha programme/scheme 1009, 1010

Warli movement 1548
water, collective management 417, 437
    offerings of, as a symbol 677
    rights 160
    sources, exploitation of 162
we/they codes, in post-colonial context 707–10
'weaker sections', of population 451–2
    local governance structure benefiting 1374
    NGOs protecting the rights and interests of 442
weavers, quality of, in India 1322
weaving industry 690
welfare programmes, government's 370, 394, 1066, 1083–4
welfare state 949, 1312, 1434
West Bengal, 1505
    birth rate in 194
    decentralization in rural, 1370, 1372–3
    fertility rate in 194
    refugee population from Bangladesh in, 289–91
Westminister model 1454
West/Western, democracy 1450, 1465
    dominant influence of language of 732
    education, introduction of, in India 1450
    enlightenment and freedom 1450
    forms of ideology 1449
    histories 101
    individualism and equality 53
    influence of, on Bengali cultural heritage 577
        languages 731
    learning, and English language 1002
    and modernity 3
    religion of, and society in 861
        superiority of 861
    scholars, and interest in Indian histories 100
    societies, and freedom 690
    sociological studies of contemporary 43
Westernization 69–70, 93n, 691, 731, 1544

and borrowing of foreign terms
and cultural change 733
and Sanskritization 736
West Asia, and Kerala Christianity 885
wheat cultivation, Mexican method of 440
When a Great Tradition Modernizes 45
Whig historians 911
White-coat labour force 1270
Widmar V. Vincent, USA 925–6
widow(s)/widowhood 963
    abject, in Hindu *tirthas* 965
    disadvantaged position of 1059, 1147
    immolition of 1058
    incidence of 197–8
    oppression /violence 1052, 1148
    re-marriage of 423, 1547
    rights of 956, 965
    social role of 1088
    status of 680, 1148–9
wife/wives, -abuse/beating 1144–5
    and obedience to husband 1145
    position of 945
wildlife, policies 237–8
    preventing depletion of 254
Wisconsin V. Yoder, USA 925
witchcraft 957, 1567
witch-hunt 1127
women ('s), and agency 1546
    agricultural labourers 1235
    and body 679
    and bondage to family 1164
    and child-rearing 679
    colleges 1043, 1046
    cooperatives 1258
    as custodian of tradition 1000
    education in India 1005, 1041, 1051–4
        under Buddhist system 1037
    freedom and equality status to 690
    employment in industries 1246, 1248, 1273
    and household work 983
    impediments to improvement 1083
    in joint families 1064
    land rights of 1235
    lifestyles of, and constraints 681–2

literacy level in Kerala 1021
movements 20, 306, 1085, 1150, 1384, 1531, 1546–52
NGOs in South Asia 1165
organization 1547–8
Partition and, abduction of 293–4
position of 681–2, 1149
power strategies of 681
religious performance by 879
reservation for 437
role and status of 439, 1075, 1165, 1257, 1547
studies on 1053, 1506, 1546
suffrage 1548
violence against 1127
writers, in South Asia 1167
Women's Indian Association (WIA) 1547–8
Wood's Education Dispatch of 1854 1001, 1003, 1041–2, 1052
work/working, arrangements in informal sector 1293, 1296
    children, and clash with childhood ideology 949
        and self-respect 949–50
    conditions 1273
    culture 1274
    and education 1168–71
    and financial support to family 1168
    life, quality of 1276–9
    new technology and 272–3, 1279–83
    organization, in formal sector 1293
worker population ratios (WPRs) 206–7
Working Group on Indigenous People 378
World Assembly on Aging, Vienna 962
World Bank 2, 307, 287, 441, 1312, 1364
    Economic Memorandum on India 1439
    -funded water projects 1365
        to Sardar Sarovar project, revoking 174, 280
    survey on literacy in Nepal 992

World Council of Churches 904
World Development Report 1994
1128, 1364, 1373
World Employment Programme,
of ILO 1287
World Health Assembly 313
World Health Organization
(WHO) 2, 304, 441, 943
'world religion religion' 144, 153,
154
*World revolution and family
patterns* 1066
World War, First 450, 1565
World War, Second 5, 340,
450.746, 960, 1214, 1548
and refugees in Europe 284
worship, offerings during 872–3
space for 607

writ petitions/jurisdiction 1392,
1396–7, 1402
Writing Culture 962

Yadavs, pastoral nomads 158, 421,
823, 1514
Yagnavalkyasmriti, on inter-caste
marriages 521
Yajur Veda 602–3, 780
Yaksagana, of Karnataka 613–16
Yanomamo violence, in South
America 1567
Yatis 818
Year of the Girl Child 1147
Yoga school 781
Yogasutras, *kaivalya* in 1161
Yolma folk songs 1181
Yolma Sherpa, of Nepal 1180

'Yong Bengal', movement in
Calcutta 680, 1471n
Yugoslavia, break-up of 1564

Zakir Hussain Committee Report
(ZHC) 1011
zamindari system 411, 1223
abolition of rights 438, 447, 1535
zamindars 395, 434, 1218–19,
1423, 1425, 1510, 1514
zenana (women's) area 467, 682
zero defect, principle of 1266
Zilla Parishads 1518
Zorach V. Clauson, USA, Supreme
Court on 926
Zoroastrianism 775
Zorastrians (Parsis) population
203, 213n, 777–8

Name Index

Abbasi 423
Abdullah, Farukh 1468
Abercrombie, Nicholas 64
Aberle, David F. 1527
Abhinavagupta 608
Abraham, C.M. 169
Abrahams 607
Abu Ali of Sind 792
Abu Bakr 792
Abu'l-Fazl 224
Acharya, P. 1009, 1026
Acharya, T. 175
Achenbaum, W.Andrew 959
Adam 1040
Adam, William 1000
Adi Nath 807
Advani, L.K. 644
Agarwal, A. 238, 241
Agarwal, Anil 172, 305, 307–8,
    315, 344
Agarwal, Bina 171, 307–8, 338,
    962, 965, 1074–5, 1077–8,
    1083, 1085, 1087, 1091–2,
    1094n, 1546
Agarwal, Kuntal 1133
Agarwala, S.N. 198
Agehananda Bharati, Swami
    1163
Aggarwal, P.C. 1233
Agnes, Flavia 1127, 1144–5, 1150
Agnihotri, Satish Balram 1138
Agrawal, Anuja 1163

Ahir, B.B 334
Ahir, D.C. 1545
Ahuja, K. 238
Ahuja, Mukesh 1148
Ahuja, R. 1144
Ahmad, A. 333–4, 337
Ahmad, Aijaz 101, 659
Ahmad, Aijazuddin 326, 329, 331,
    332, 347, 348
Ahmad, Aziz 791
Ahmad, Imtiaz 20, 490, 581
Ahmad, Mirza Ghulam 794
Ahmad, Qazi 330, 345
Ahmadi, A.M. 1393
Ahmadi, Chief Justice 1404n
Aijaz, R. 336
Aitchism, J. 697
Aiyar, Shankar V. 625
Aiyar, Swarna 288
Ajirotutu 729
Akbar 1414, 1422, 1423–4
Akhilesh, K.B. 1281–2
Akhtar, Rais 340, 341, 342, 343
Akinnaso 729
Al-Biruni 792
Al-Ghazzli 792
Alam, Bjorn 535
Alam, M. 1421, 1423
Alam, Muzaffar 543, 552
Alatis, J.E. 697, 702
Alavi, Hamza 1224, 1225, 1528,
    1531, 1532, 1533

Alexander, of Macedona,
    incursions into India 1417
Alexander, K.C. 1536
Ali, Prophet Muhammad's son-in-
    law 792
Ali, Imran 328
Ali, M. Athar 1423, 1425
Ali, Sabir 465
Alisjahbana, S.T. 704
Allen, Michael 1080, 1199
Alley, R.S. 922, 924
Alonso, Ana Maria 592
Aloysius, G. 1545
Alter, Joseph S. 150, 1169
Alvares, C. 334
Alvares, Claude 72
Amani, K.Z. 348
Ambalal, Amit 633
Ambedkar, B.R. 19, 378, 785,
    1457, 1475, 1542–3, 1545
Amim, A.A. 944, 949
Amin, Shahid 12, 1536, 1578–9
Anand Bhanu, A. 332
Anantaraman M. 342
Anbert, R. 919
Anderson, Benedict 16, 1170
Anderson, Benedict R. 667
Anderson, E.S. 703
Annamalai 713
Anveshi 1129
Ao, Shilu 392
Appadurai, Arjun 7, 9, 23, 65, 85,

90n, 93n, 304, 373, 471, 564, 637, 654, 656, 809, 879, 1024, 1173,1193, 1350, 1355
Appaswamy, Jaya 588
Appel 696
Appel, R. 697
Archard D. 949
Archbishop Warham 915
Archer, Mildred 648n
Archer, W.G. 167
Ardener, Edwin 558n
Arendt Hannah 573, 1565–6
Argyle M. 703
Arie's P. 949
Aries, Philippe 1082
Aristotle 840, 850, 1192
Arnason, Jo'hann 1551–2
Arnberg L. 697
Arnold, David 161, 304, 311, 1530, 1534, 1538, 1540
Aron, Raymond 56
Arora, Sushil 160
Asad, Talal 6, 8, 153
Ashoka, Emperor 1414, 1416–19, 1440n
Askew Ian D. 343
Assayag, Jakie 492
Atal, Yogesh 423, 434, 1495
Athreya V.B. 1135–6
Atkinson, H. 1269
Atmore 251
Attlee, Clement 117
Attwood, Donald W. 549
Aulakh G. 704, 726
Aurobindo, Sri 746
Austin, J.F. 703
Austin, John L 598
Avaradi, S.A. 156
Avineri, Shlomo 431
Ayyar, P.V. Jogadisa 871
Azad, Abul Kalam 796–7
Azad, M.H. 332
A'zami, Altaf Ahmad 312
Aziz, Abdul 1257

Babb Lawrence A. 633, 661, 771, 802, 815–19, 871, 874, 1544
Bacchetta Paola 1549
Bacchhan, Hariwanshrai 1000
Baden-Powel, B.H. 411, 432, 577, 1220
Baetens-Beardsmore, H 696
Bagchi, Amiya Kumar 1232, 1352

Bagchi D. 333, 337–8
Bagchi Jasodhara 1546
Baghel A.S. 333
Bagla, Pallava 304
Bailey 427
Bailey C.J.N. 702
Bailey, E.G. 1223
Bailey, F.G. 376, 385, 410, 424, 426, 434, 452, 1216, 1497, 1499, 1500
Bainbridge, William Sims 802
Baines A. 224, 227
Bainton R.H. 916
Bajpai, Asha 1258
Bakhtin, Mikhail 574–5, 998, 999, 1018
Balagopal, K. 1231
Baland·J.M. 1366
Balandier Georges 129, 132n
Bales, Robert F. 1065, 1066
Ballard, Roger 1173
Baller C.D. 703
Balmain, Colonel 891
Bambawale U. 1133
Banaji, J. 1214, 1224
Banarasidas 469
Bandopadhyay N. 333
Bandopadhya 965
Banerjee, B. 1304
Banerjee, G. 309
Banerjee-Guha, Swapna 343
Banerjee J.N. 633
Banerjee M. 333
Banerjee, N. 337, 943, 945
Banerjee, Sukumar 397
Banerjee, Sumantra 588
Banerjee, Tapas 309
Banerji, Bibhutibhushan 1192, 1193
Banerji Debarar 304, 319, 343
Bani, Upendra 100
Bankimchandra 682
Bannerji, Nirmala 1257
Bansal R.K. 314
Banu, Zainab 278
Banuri, Tariq 72, 76, 85
Bapat, Ram 1547
Barai Dakshal 332, 343
Baral, Lok Raj 284, 286–7
Barani, Zia-ud-din 791
Bardhan Pranab 51, 75, 1232, 1233, 1361, 1366, 1375, 1435
Barkataki, Gangadhar 837

Barnett, Steve 1076, 1092
Barrier N.G. 328
Barrows, Harlan 329
Barsh, Russel 305
Bartelt 705–6
Barthes, Roland 1355
Barthwal, P.D. 814
Bartoni-Ricardo 702
Barua M. 295
Barz Richard 809–10
Basava, (founder of lingayat sect) 807
Basso 699
Basu, A.M. 1139
Basu, Alaka 1072, 1078
Basu, Amrita 1546–7, 1549, 1550
Basu, Durga Das 1398
Basu, K. 1349
Basu, Kaushik 1352, 1357
Basu, Sajal 567
Basu, Salil 308
Basu, T. 1018
Basu, Upendra 1545
Bateson, Gregory 536, 557n
Batliwala, S. 1139
Baudrillard, Jean 1012, 1355
Bauer P.T. 1226
Bauman Richard 148, 598–9, 702
Baumann, Zygmunt 1565
Baviskar, Amrita 173–4, 308–9, 420, 1235, 1541
Bayliss-Smith T.P. 344
Bayly, Christopher A. 101, 102, 107, 109, 461, 471, 481, 552, 902, 1347, 1350, 1511
Bayly, Susan 790, 886–7. 889, 898
Beals, Alan R. 311, 414, 421, 425
Bean, Susan S. 875
Beck 967
Beck, Brenda E.F. 872, 875
Beck, Ulrich 142, 150
Becket, T. 100
Bedell, G.C. 926
Beesley, M. 1271
Beidelman, T.O. 1219
Beittel, M. 945
Bekombo M. 947
Bell, Catherine 599, 1227
Bellafiore, V. 346
Bellah, Robert 1324
Bellotti E.G. 946
Bendix, Reinhard 81, 436, 516, 526

Bendurant Joan 1127
Benford, Robert D. 1528
Bennett, Lynn 1081, 1087–8
Bennett, Tony 657
Bentall, Jim 344
Bentham, Utilitarianism of 103
Bentinck, William 1478
Bequele A. 943
Berger, John 636
Berger, Peter 1227
Berger, Thomas 308
Berna, James 1323
Bernstein, Basil 702
Berry, Brian J.L. 330
Bessant, J. 1269, 1273, 1274, 1276
Béteille, André 1, 18, 32–3, 37, 41,
    47–8, 52–3, 56, 58, 93n, 161,
    174, 374, 376, 379, 383–4,
    410–11, 432, 434, 452, 427,
    433, 435, 483, 488, 498, 507,
    577, 583, 654, 939, 1082,
    1131, 1168, 1214, 1216–17,
    1233, 1236, 1484, 1499, 1502,
Bhabha, Homi 640
Bhadra, M. 338
Bhaduri, A. 1232–3, 1235
Bhaktivedanta Svami Prabhupada,
    A.C, 811
Bhalla G.S. 1230
Bhalla S. 1233
Bhandarkar RG 807, 809–10
Bharat, Shalini 1081, 1084
Bhardwaj, Surinder M. 313, 326,
    327, 347. 1235
Bhargava, Hem Chander 641–2
Bhargava, R. 1432
Bharvad 222–261, 227
Bhasin, Kamala 295, 1127*
Bhasin, Veena 158
Bhat, G.K. 1192
Bhat, P.N. Mari 188, 192, 1072,
    1078–9, 1094n
Bhat, R.L. 279
Bhatacharjee, Chandana 1538
Bhatia, Gautam 468
Bhatia, Gayatri 314
Bhatia, Tej K. 696
Bhatt, Ela R. 1547
Bhatt, M.K. 312–13, 316n
Bhattacharya, Ashutosh 579
Bhattacharya, Kalidas 22
Bhattacharya, N. 225, 254, 1218,
    1223

Bhattacharya, Vidyadhar 461
Bhatty, Kiran 979, 98
Bhave, Vinoba 443–5, 451
Bhowmik P.K. 332
Bhowmick, Sharit K., 397, 404,
    1253*
Bhindranwala, Janail Singh 788
Biardean, Madeleine 100, 145,
    146, 147, 148, 149, 486,
    872
Bickerton D. 704
Bidwai, Praful 1260
Bijlani, H.K. 464
Bird, R.M. 1368
Bird-David, Nurit 156, 167
Bischel, Ulrich 335, 346
Bishop, Mary F. 306
Bisht, N.S. 992n
Biswas, Liny 347
Biswas, Suhas 955
Black, Cyril E. 82, 93n
Black, M. 943, 950
Black, Richard 293
Blackburn, Stuart 601, 610
Blackburn, S.H. 830, 834–5, 855,
    856n, 857n
Bladen, W.A. 343
Blair, Archibald 225
Blanchet, Therese 1184, 1186
Bloch, Jules 734, 736
Bloch, M. 1345
Blom, J.P. 703
Bloomfield, L. 696, 702
Bloomfield, Leonard 714
Blumer, Herbert 1526
Blunt 250
Blyn, G. 1221
Bocke, J.H. 1288–9
Bogard M. 11444
Bohannan, Paul 532, 539
Boltomore, Tom 536
Bompas, C.H. 854
Bonazzoli, 609
Bond, Ruskin 443
Bonnano, A. 1215
Borden, Carla 657
Borker, R.A. 727
Borocz, J. 297
Bose, A.B. 955
Bose, Ajoy 471
Bose, Ashish 307
Bose. Girindrashekhar 772, 833,
    834

Bose, N.K. 7, 13, 44, 384, 401, 458
Bose, Nand Lal 588
Bose, P.K. 396
Bose, Pradip Kumar 1190
Bose, Subhas Chandra 1452
Bose, Sugata 100, 1428
Boserup, Ester 162
Bouhdiba, A. 943
Bourdieu, Pierre 171, 519, 665,
    862, 879, 1109, 1568
Boxer, C.R. 886
Boyd, J. 944, 948, 950
Boyden, J. 943–4, 947–8
Bradford, N.J. 807, 819–20
Bradford, W. 923
Brara, Rita 158–9, 139–40, 141,
    162, 166, 417
Brass, Paul 310, 421, 1504, 1570,
    1575, 1578
Brass, Paul R. 18, 493, 699,1503
Brass, Tom 1234, 1535
Braverman, H. 126, 1266
Brechenridge, Carol A 85, 637,
    656, 659, 1344, 1355
Breman, Jan 49, 51, 654, 663,
    1209, 1210, 1233, 1256,
    1287, 1295, 1299, 1305,
    1309, 1310, 1311, 1357
Brennan, Timothy 569
Briggs, Charles L. 598–9
Briggs, George Weston 807
Bright W. 719, 720
Brijbasi, Shrinathdas 641, 648n
Brijbasi, Shyamsunderlal 641–2,
    648n
Britto, F. 696
Britto, Francis 734
Brockington, J.L. 780, 865
Broehl, W.G. 1329
Bronghton, G.M. 1249
Brook, Peter 621
Brouwer, Jan 148
Brown, Kenneth 459
Brown, Norman 5
Brown, P. 703
Brown, R. 702
Brubaker, Richard L 875
Bruce, S. 916
Brückner, Heidrum 565, 566, 598
Brush, Stephen B. 305
Buchy, Marlene 170
Buddha, Gautama 783–4, 1018
Bullivant, B.M. 696

Burgess Ernest 1526
Burgess, E.W. 462
Burghart, Richard 79, 309, 485,
    486, 513, 804, 811–12, 816,
    819
Burke F. 334, 335
Burns, T. 1276
Burra, N. 947
Burra, Neera 1136, 1259
Butalia, Urvashi 294, 965, 1127,
    1549
Butcher, Melissa 1082
Butler, Judith 879
Butler, Robert N. 959
Bynon 703
Byres, T.J. 1227, 1229

Cadene, P. 1355
Caitanya 810–11, 817
Caldwell, John C. 305, 943,
    946–47
Calhoun, Craig J. 748
Callahan, Daniel 960
Calman, Leslie J 1164
Camden, W. 917
Calvin 129
Campbell A. 1270–1
Campos, R. 945
Canguilhem, Georges 957
Cantlie, Audrey 772, 827
Caplan, Lionel 897, 899, 902, 903
Carr, M. 1258
Carrier, J.G. 1348, 1356–7
Carroll, J.B. 702–3
Carstaivs, G. Morris 1080, 1181–3,
    1187, 1198, 1200, 1127
Carter, Anthony J. 1092
Casimir, Michael 137, 219
Casrithers 1355
Catanach, I.J. 1534
Cater J. 326
Cavell, Stanley 8, 22
Cazden, C.B. 703
Cernea, Michael M. 280
Cesaire, Aime 92n
Cèspedes B.S. 945
Chadha G.K. 1230, 1299, 1327
Chagnon, Napoleon 1567
Chaki-Sivkar, Manjusri 1187
Chakrabarty, Dipesh 6, 94n, 101,
    545
Chakrabarti, P.K. 297
Chakravarti, Anand 974, 1227

Chakravarti, Uma 471, 1546, 1547
Chakravarty, S. 1349
Chakravorty, C. 204–5
Challis J. 942–3, 950
Chambard J.L. 330
Chambers J.K. 702
Chambers Robert 344
Chambers Robert N.C. 308
Champalakshmi, R. 461
Chana, U. 703
Chanana, Karuna 1140
Chand, M. 945
Chandhoke, Neera 119, 132n
Chandra, Baba Ram 1522n
Chandra, Bipen Pal 1349
Chandragupta Maurya 1416,
    1440n
Chandra Gupta II, of Gupta
    empire 1414
Chandragupta, state under
    Mauryan dynasty of 1417
Chandrakanth, M.G. 149
Chang, C. 1372
Changpa 221
Charcot, Jean Martin 956–7
Charlesworth, N. 1533–4
Charlsey, Simon 18, 91n
Chatterjee, Margaret 796
Chatterjee, Meera 303, 1139
Chatterjee, N. 289, 291, 297–8
Chatterjee, Partha 86, 93n, 99,
    1000, 1428, 1432–33, 1552,
    1530, 1533, 1536
Chatterjee, S.P. 328–9
Chatterji, P.C. 909
Chatterji, Roma 151, 566, 589,
    966–7
Chattoo, sangeetha 966–7
Chattopadhyay, B.D. 461
Chattopadhyay, Bankim Chandra
    93n, 1471n
Chattopadhyay, K.P. 43–4
Chaturvedi, Abha 1250
Chaturvedi, M.G. 749
Chaube, S.K. 401
Chaubey, Kailash 342
Chaudhuri, B. 305
Chaudhuri, K.N. 1342
Chaudhuri, S. 305
Chaudhury, D.P. 1136, 1259
Chauhan, Brij Raj 14, 369–70,
    409–10, 412, 414, 420, 423,
    429, 433, 436

Chayanov, A.V. 1214, 1532
Che, J. 1372
Chen. Lincoln C. 305, 1139
Chen, Martha Alter 962, 1147
Chen, R. 1144
Cheng 703–4
Cherian, J. 1258
Cheung, F.M. 1144
Chib, 55, 332
Child J. 1275–6
Childers, C.H 250
Chiplumkar, Vishnu Krishna 637
Chitnis, Suma 937–8, 1032
Chitvalekha R., 342
Choksi, A. 237
Chomsky, N. 701, 710
Chopra, Deepak 967
Chopra, Kanchan R. 344
Chopra, Radhika 1255
Choudhry K. 342
Chowdhry, Prem 1088, 1235
Chowdhury, Brajendra Kishore
    1005
Chowdhury-Sengupta, Indira 835
Chowdhury, Surya Kanta Acharya
    1005
Chud, Nwa-Chil 749
Chunkath, Sheela Rani 1135
Clad, James 1392
Clark, Katerina 573–4
Clauss, Peter J. 310, 604, 1162
Clement VII, anti-pope 913
Clifford, James 23, 87, 960
Clive, Robert 1426
Clothey, Fred W. 871–2
Clyne, M. 704
Coase, R.H. 1351
Cobarrubias, J. 704
Cobbin, Ingram 122, 132n
Coccari, Diane M. 151
Cohen 960, 966
Cohen, Jean L. 1529
Cohen, Lawrence 937–8, 955, 957,
    963–5, 1058, 1164
Cohn, Bernard 6, 10, 66, 90n, 105,
    109, 654, 656, 1394, 1397,
    1427
Cohn, Bernard C. 471
Cohn, Bernard S. 373, 481, 821,
    1217, 1499
Colaco, Miguel 903
Cole, Thomas R. 958, 967
Colebroke, Henry Thomas 103

Collier, Jane Fishburne 1085
Comte 64
Connell, R.W. 999, 1005
Contursi, Janet A. 1546
Cook-Gumperz 727
Coomaraswamy, Ananda K. 587, 589, 1017
Cooper 703
Copley, Antony 900
Corbridge, Stuart 332, 344, 1537, 1540
Cornell 968
Cornia, G. 944, 949
Correa, Charles 465
Cort, Louise Allison 148
Coser 558n
Coser, Lewis 539, 545–9
Cossman, Brenda 1075, 1077, 1150
Coulson 734
Coward, Howard G. 794
Cowgill, Donald Olen 960
Cromwell 121
Crook 1374
Crook, R. 1364, 1370
Culler 697
Cumming, Elaine 959
Cummins, J. 703
Cunningham, A. 327
Cunningham, H. 944, 949
Curtin, Philip 304
Curzon, Lord 745
Custers, Peter 1261, 1535–6

D'Abreo, Desmond 388
D'Costa, Adelyne 899
D'Eaubonne, Francoise 171
D'Souza, A.B. 885, 889
D'Souza, Peter R. 909
D'Souza, V.S. 52
Dadu 814
Dahrendorf 557n
Dak, T.M. 955
Dalai Lama, in India 271, 785
Dale 1534
Dalmia, Vasudha 576
Dandekar, Kumudini 315, 1139, 1146
Dangle, Arjun 1544
Daniel, E. Valentine 303, 309–12, 315, 1076, 1161, 1196, 1577
Daniel, W.W. 1280
Darling, M. 1223

Das 20, 416, 1534
Das, Arvind N. 657
Das, C.R. 1013
Dās, Jagjivan 819*
Das, Kamala 716
Das, S.R. 1013–14
Das, Sujit 314
Das, Veena 1, 17, 55, 72, 79, 87, 145, 168, 294, 311, 315, 545, 568, 581, 592n, 660–1, 667, 816, 828, 961, 966–7, 1000, 1027n, 1075—7, 1082–3, 1087, 1127, 1129, 1131, 1140, 1147, 1158–9, 1166, 1197–8, 1200, 1235, 1546, 1552, 1572–3, 1576–7
Das, Victor· 1540
Das Gupta, Ashin 461
Das Gupta, Monica 303–4, 1139–40, 1073, 1079, 1087
Dasgupta, Atis K. 811, 822
Dasgupta, G. 601, 620–1
Dasgupta Jyotivindra 704
Dasgupta, Probal 707–8, 736, 737–8, 742
Dash N.R. 332
Dastoor 708
Datt, Ruddar 1257, 1260
Datta, K.K. 1536
Datta (Naidu), Ratna 89n
Datta, S.K. 943
Datta-Ray, B. 389, 398, 402–3
Dava, Shikhoh 796–7
Davala, Sarath 1254
Davar, Bhargavi 1128
Dave, A.B. 1137
Davirs, A. 941
Davis 428
Davis, Kingsley 420, 428, 1078
Davis, N.Z. 1570
Davis, Richard H. 633, 658, 806, Dayakrishna 33
Dayal, John 471
Dayanand Saraswati 936, 1007
Dayananda 795
Dāyānanda, Sarasvatī 816, 1547
De, Nitish R. 1251
De, R.K. 332
De Alwis, Malathi 1066
De Camp D. 704
de Certeau, Michel 879
de Coulanges, Fustle 459,1106
De Hondt, P.A. 100

De Mause L. 949
De Soto H. 1311
De Souza Alfred 955, 962
De Tocqueville, Alexis 116, 132n
De Tray D. 945
Deb, Debal 166
Debysingh, M. 345
Deery, S. 1281
Dehon, Rev. Father 853
Deka P. 342
Deliege, Robert 485, 1545
Delphine, Roger 312
Deng 1372
Derne, Steve 1191
Derr, Bruce W. 1070–1
Derrett, J. 11, 1397
Derrida 968
Desai, A. 333
Desai, A.P. 448
Desai, A.R. 45, 74, 378, 401, 1130, 1219, 1224, 1491, 1534
Desai, Anita 709
Desai, Anjana 343
Desai, I.P. 50, 147, 1073, 1120, 1130
Desai, K.G. 955
Desai, Manisha 1165
Desai, Meghnad 212n
Desai, Morarji 1489
Desai, Murli 1084
Desai, Neera 1140
Deshpande, A. 1138
Despande, Satish 33, 35, 63, 76,658, 665
Desjarlais, Robert 1059, 1128, 1179–81, 1184, 1197
Deutsch, Karl 742
Dev, Amar 343
Dev, B.J. 336
Deva, Indra 567
Devalle, Susana 1537, 1540
Devannabhatta 1118
Devgun, S. 345
Devi, 1135
Devi, M. 290
Devi, N.G.S. 332
Dewey, John 329, 1543
Dhagamwar, Vasudha 1160
Dhanagare, D.N. 432, 445–6, 1218, 1223–4, 1229, 1231–2, 1528, 1534, 1535–6
Dharampal 305
Dharampal-Frick, Gita 6, 900

Dhareshwar, Vivek 86–7, 94n
Dharma 212n
Dhavalikar, M.K 222
Dhavan, Rajeev 1400
Dholakia, R.H. 337
Dhussa, R.C. 347
Di, Sciullo, A.M. 697
Diani, Mario 1525, 1531
Dickey, Sara A. 661
Diddee, J.N. 334
Diebold, A.R. 696
Dietrich, Gabriele 175
Dillard, J.L. 704
Diller, K. 696
Dilley, Roy 1357
Dilley Devi, L. 247
Dimock, Edward C. 810–11, 1192
Dirks, Nicholas 5, 6, 105, 108,
    109, 373, 485, 558n, 656
Dittmar, N. 702
Djurfeldt, G. 1219
Dobb, Maurice 1321
Dobbin, Christine 1326
Dong Xing 1144
Doniger, Wendy 154
Donnelley 8
Donzelot, J. 944, 949
Dore, R. 942
Dorian 703
Doshi, Harish 462
Douglas, M. 1355
Douglas, Mary 665
Dove, Michael R. 154
Dreisbach, D.L. 923
Drèze, Jean 305, 936–37, 962, 965,
    974, 975n, 987, 1018, 1020–2,
    1027n, 1087, 1147, 1351–2,
    1364
Drucker, D.P. 1274
Dube, D.P. 347
Dube, Kamala K. 308
Dube, Leela 486, 945, 1074–5,
    1080–3, 1139
Dube, R.S. 342
Dube, S.C. 17, 49, 73, 76, 90n,
    93n, 379, 409–11, 433, 436,
    484, 1229
Dube, Saurabh 891, 1544
Dulean, R. 467
Dumont, Louis 4, 5, 14–15, 22,
    24n, 44, 52–3, 90n, 94n, 104,
    110, 147, 186n, 368, 487,
    512, 515, 551, 654, 688, 770,

803–4, 816, 818–19, 863–64,
    874, 961, 964, 1075, 1090,
    1092, 1105, 1142, 1160,
    1183, 1344, 1416–17
Duncan, James S. 347
Dundas, Paul 785
Dundes, Alan 592n
Dunn 592n
Dupuis, J. 330
Durkheim, Emile 3, 4, 8, 19, 40,
    64, 117, 132n, 144, 776, 863,
    1267, 1565–6, 1572–3
Dutt 107
Dutt 1226
Dutta, A.K. 345, 346, 347
Dutt, Gurusady 576–577, 579,
    592n
Dutt, R.C. 12
Dutt, Srikant 272
Dutta, Ashok K. 342
Dutta, Hiram M. 342
Dutta, B.B. 395
Dutta Barna, Arati 843
Duyker, Edward 1541
Dyer, C. 237
Dyson, Tim 307, 1078, 1072

Easton, David 533
Eaton, Richard M. 102, 109, 153,
    891, 894
Eck, Diana L. 150, 627, 632, 829,
    904
Eder, Klaus 1527–8
Edney, Mathew 328
Edwards, A.D. 702–3
Eels, Kenneth 504, 514
Egnor, Margaret Trawick 310,
    1169
Eisenstalt, Shinuel N. 15, 942,
    1324
Eisinger, P.K. 1527
Elahi, K. Maudood 288–9, 298
Elder, Joseph W. 1323
Eliade, M. 836, 849, 855
Ellen, Roy 155
Elliman, D. 942–3, 950
Elliott, M. Carolyn 1502
Elphinstone, Lord 104, 1040
Elson, D. 943, 946,
Elwin 387, 390, 399
Elwin, Verrrier 68, 72, 91n, 377,
    382, 385, 853–4, 856n
Emerson, C. 22, 999

Engels 368, 528
Ennew, J. 944
Ensminger, Douglas 90n
Entwistle, A.W. 1200
Epstein, T.S. 414, 432, 1070
Erikson E.H. 705, 1082
Erskine, May 1454
Ervin, S. 697
Ervin-Tripp, S 702–4
Escalona, Ana 293
Espinola, B. 948
Estes, Carroll L. 960
Ethrenfels, U.R. 156
Evans, P. 949
Evans-Pritchard E.E 40, 44, 129,
    132n, 436, 482, 544, 558
Evenson, Norma 465, 472
Everett, Jana 1258
Evnst, Kris 635
Evons, D.T. 949
Ewing, Katherine 310, 1183, 1190
Eyerman, Ron 1526
Eyles, J. 326, 332

Fabian, Johannes 79, 568, 626
Fadia, Babulal 1506
Fanon, Frantz 92n, 546, 1565, 1568
Fanselow, Frank S. 490, 1353
Farmer, B.H. 344
Farmer, Victoria 658
Farooqi 342
Farooq, Ghazi Mumtaz 305
Farquhar, J.N. 810, 815
Fasold, R. 702, 704
Fasold, W. 703
Fatima 342
Faust, David 344
Fazl, Abu-al 1424
Fazl, Abul 327, 1423*
Featherstone, Mike 967
Fei, J.C. 1289
Feldhaus, Anne 150
Feldman, Allen 660
Feldman, S. 338
Ferguson, Adam 118
Ferguson, C.A. 696, 702, 704, 725,
    737
Ferishta, Mohammad Kasim 225
Fernandes, Walter 280, 388–9,
    956, 962
Ferris, Elizabeth G. 292
Field, John Osgood 1506
Fina, L. 128

Finkelhor, David 1144
Firishta 100
Firth, J.R. 696
Fischer, David Hackett 960
Fischer-Lichte, Erika 601–2, 607
Fisher, R.J. 157, 250, 335
Fishman, J.A. 696–7, 702, 704, 729–31
FitzGerald, Frances 960
Fleck, J. 1274
Flueckiger, Joyce Burkhalter 591
Flood, Garin 780
Folbre, N. 943, 945, 949–50
Foner 968
Forbes Geraldine 1546, 1548–9
Ford, Allan 719
Forest, D. 726
Forrester, Duncan B. 892–3, 900
Fortes, Meyer 129, 132n, 1071
Foster, Hal 649n
Foucault, Michel 9, 107, 142, 626, 656, 690, 958, 1003, 1013, 1080, 1425, 1428, 1530, 1565
Foucault, Michelle 136 (chk Enrt)
Fox, Richard G. 109, 156, 658, 1323
Fox, Robin 1083
Frake 699
Frank, Jerome 1390
Frankel, F.R. 1229, 1425, 1435
Frankel, Francine 1415
Franklin, B. 949
Frasca, A. 612
Frater 242
Frazer, James George 34, 132n, 959, 968
Freed, Ruth S. 544, 1071
Freed, Stanley A. 544, 1071
Freeman, M.D.A. 949
Freeman, James 863
Freeman, J.M. 335
Freeman, J. Richardson 605, 606, 607
Freitag, Sandria B. 552, 554, 655, 656
Freud, 772, 833–4, 850, 1181, 1183, 1194, 1526, 1566
Fried, M.H. 375
Friedland, W.H. 1215–16
Friedland, William 89n
Friedman, John 344
Fruzzetti, Lina H. 1076, 1083, 1092

Frye, Roland Mushat 585
Frykenberg, Robert E 109, 346
Fuchs, Martin 1384, 1524, 1530, 1536, 1538, 1543, 1545
Fuchs, S. 1538
Fuller, Christopher J. 368, 477, 490, 516, 902, 1347
Furer-Haimendorf, C.Von 400
Fyfe, A. 943–4, 946–50

Gadamer 21
Gadgil, D.R 1222
Gadgil, Madhav 148, 152, 154, 157, 164–5, 170, 173, 307, 308–9, 344
Gadgil, M.V. 1228
Gaiha, R. 1370
Gait, E.A. 383
Gajjala, Radhika 1173
Gal, S. 703
Gala, Chetna 1547
Galanter, Marc/k 19, 498, 1476, 1478*
Galaty, C. 159
Gandhi, Indira 1148, 1381, 1436, 1437–8, 1458–60, 1464, 1467, 1472n, 1489, 1517, 1568 1574
Gandhi, Mahatma 13, 34, 48, 72, 99, 117, 123–4, 132n, 133n, 172, 294, 370, 394, 443–5, 446, 450, 451, 549, 550, 645, 666, 683, 746, 750, 776, 796–7, 855, 936, 1003, 1009, 1010–11, 1024–5, 1052, 1166, 1169, 1171, 1247, 1255, 1381, 1385, 1430, 1450, 1451–2, 1457, 1475, 1534, 1542, 1548, 1579
Gandhi, Nandita 305–6, 1150, 1164–5
Gandhi, Rajiv 268, 273, 657, 1472n, 1489
Gangrade, K.D. 945–6, 956
Gardner 696
Garg, Murlilal 649n
Garratt, G.T. 1426–7
Gartz, Clifford 162, 599
Garvin, Paul 704, 737
Gautam, A. 332
Gatutama Buddha 783, 787
Gazdar 989
Gathia, J.A. 945–6

Geddes, Patrick 43, 458, 461
Geertz, Clifford 140, 144, 1324, 1353
Geetha, V. 1088, 1545
Geiger, Theodor 557n
Gell, Alfred 1350
Gelles, K. 1144
Gelles, Richard 1144
Gellner, Ernest 16, 568–9
Gendzier, Irene 65, 92n
George, Alex 314
George, Sabir 237–8, 1135
Gerow, Edwin 1192, 1194
Ghadially, Rehana 1127
Gharpure, J.R. 1105
Ghatak, Maitreya 1257
Ghose, A.K. 1226
Ghose, Aurobindo 1006–7, 1018
Ghosh, Amitav 659, 1173
Ghosh, Santosh 307, 346
Ghoshal 1418
Ghurye, G.S. 7, 9, 13, 43, 44, 68, 377, 382, 385, 386, 420, 422, 491, 492, 497, 654, 807–10, 821, 1063–4, 1070, 1081, 1105, 1476, 1481, 1491, 1497
Gialombardo 699
Gibbs, M.E. 789
Giddens, Anthony 967, 1329
Giles, H. 703
Gill, C. 1281
Gill, Indermit 277
Gill, M.S 336
Gillespie, Stuart 305
Gillion, K.L. 458, 468
Gilman, A. 702
Ginsberg, Carlo 581
Ginsburg, Faye 648
Girard 968–9
Gladstone 1507
Glissant, Edouard 92n
Gluckman, Max 129, 132n, 557n
Glushkova, Ivina 150
Gobind, Guru 797
Goddard, V.B. 943
Godelier, Maurice 375
Godwin, C.J. 889
Godlewska, A. 328
Goffman, Erving 519
Gokhale, Jayashree 1541, 1545
Gokhale-Turner, Jayashree B. 1545
Gold, Ann Grodzins 486, 655,

820, 879, 1088, 1161, 1167, 1199, 1530

Gold, Daniel 815, 820, 822

Goldberg, G. 923, 925

Goldenweiser, A 162

Goldman, R.P. 832–3

Goldthrope, John 524–7

Gole, Susan 327

Good, Anthony 1080–1, 1083, 1110

Goode, William J. 1066–8, 1077, 1092

Goodenough, W.H. 702

Goodfriend 463

Goodwin-Raheja, Gloria 1167

Goody, Jack 1062, 1071, 1073, 1085, 1142

Gooptu, Nandini 1544

Gopal, S. 336

Gopalan, C. 1139

Gordon, J. 305

Gordon, R.J. 251

Gordon, S.N. 227

Gore, M.S. 1094n, 1130, 1545

Gosal 335

Goswami, Profulladatta 855, 858n

Goud, Laxma 634

Gough, E. Kathlean 52, 410, 485, 1216, 1233, 1092, 1112, 1534

Gould, Harold A 1071, 1382, 1383, 1494, 1498, 1508

Gouldner, A.W. 1218

Gounder 434

Goyal, R. S 276

Graham-Brown, S. 705, 949

Gramsci 34, 99, 110, 114, 119, 1530

Granovetter, M. 1349

Grant, Charles 819, 890, 1001, 1040

Graves, T.D. 702

Gray, John N. 873, 961, 1076, 1085

Green, David 626

Greenough, paul R. 53, 139, 140, 303, 311, 1084, 1221–2

Greogory, M. 703

Grewal. J.S. 787

Grice, H.P. 703

Griffiths, W.G. 854

Grosjean, F. 696

Gross, Robert 804, 808–9, 812

Grove, Richard H. 161, 165, 170, 304

Grover, Neelam 166

Guha 1534

Guha, B.S. 296

Guha, Ramachandra 54, 91n, 101, 148, 152, 161, 164–5, 170–3, 307–9, 344, 388, 541, 548, 1220, 1224–5, 1552, 1572,

Guha, Ranajit 6, 15, 80, 99–100, 110, 402, 581–2, 635, 640, 656, 1536, 1569

Guha, R.C. 1235

Guha, Thakurta, Tapati 587, 593n, 637

Gulati, Leela 268, 1139, 1257, 1304

Gulrajani, M. 945

Gumperz, John J. 437, 703–5, 707, 720, 723, 726–7

Gunasekaran, R. 332

Gunn, S.E. 948

Gupta 1534*

Gupta, A. 339

Gupta, Charu 649n

Gupta, Dipankar 370, 502, 516, 517, 522, 1231

Gupta, Giri Raj 303, 419, 420, 423

Gupta, Narayani 370, 458, 471

Gupta, N.L. 339

Gupta, Roxanne 808

Gupta, S. 342

Gurr, Ted Robert 557n, 1527

Guru Gobind Singh, the tenth guru of Sikhs 787–8, 964

Guru, Gopal 1545–6

Guru Nanak Dev, founder of Sikhism 787–8, 797, 814, 964

Gurumurthy, K.G. 253

Gusfield, Joseph 93n

Gutschow, Niels 466

Haas, Mary R. 702

Habeeb A. 469

Habermas Jurgen 34, 114, 170, 667, 716, 1528–30

Habib, Ifran 101, 307, 468, 1217–18, 1220, 1244, 1342, 1534

Habib, Mohammad 24n

Hacking, Ian 8

Haggard, Henry 957–8

Haksar, Nandita 471

Halder, A.K. 160

Halhed, Nathanied Brassey 103

Hall, R.A. Jr. 704

Hall, Ronald 520

Hallak, J. 947

Halliday, Michael A.K. 696, 704

Halliwell, S. 840, 850

Hamadani, Kubrani Sufi Sayyid Ali 793*

Hamblin, 558

Hamlet 129

Hannington, Captain 891

Hanchett, Suzanne 1083

Hancock, Mary 13–14

Hand, Sean 580

Handy, C.B 1276

Hansen, Kathryn 299, 607, 610–11

Haque, C.E. 293

Hardgrave, Robert L. 893, 1498, 1544

Hardiman, David 403, 878–9, 1346, 1533–4, 1536–8, 1540

Hardy, Friedhelm 148, 593n

Hardy, Peter 100

Haribabu, E. 334

Harley, B. 697, 703

Harper, Edward B. 538, 874, 879, 1346

Harris 697

Harriss, J. 1229–30, 1343

Harris, Marvin 154

Harrison, Mark 304

Harrison, Selig S. 1498

Harrison, Simon 1567

Harriss-White Barbara 1079, 1231, 1347, 1354

Hart, K. 1287, 1292, 1299

Hartman, B. 305

Harvey, Peter 783

Hasan, Mushirul 100, 459, 471

Hasan, Zoya 909, 1066, 1081

Hasley, A.H. 56

Hasnain, Imtiaz 704

Hastings, Warren 104, 1001, 1121

Hatch, E.M. 696

Haugen, Einer 697, 704, 723

Hauser, Walter 1522n

Havell 587, 593n

Hawksworth, R. 1281

Hawley, John Stratton 783

Hawthron, Geoffrey 83

Hayden, R.M. 248

Haynes, Dougles 543, 1530

Hazelhurst, Leighton 1323

Hazra, jayati 342

Heath, S.B. 696, 703
Heestreman, J.C. 110, 147–8, 603
Hegel, G.W.F. 34, 114, 117–20, 131n
Heilborn, Johan 2
Hein, Norvin 1200
Heinsath, Charles, H. 637
Helb, E. 1277
Heller, M. 703
Hembram, P.C. 580
Henderson, D. 703
Henderson, J. 1271
Henry VIII 120, 121, 915
Henry, Edward O. 310
Henry, William E. 959–60
Hepworth 967
Herbolzeimer, E. 1271, 1274, 1280
Herder 570, 580
Herpen, A. 942
Herring, R.J. 1226, 1228
Hershman, Paul 1075
Hertzler 696
Herzfeld, Michael 660
Heston, Alan 154
Hettne, Bjorn 393
Heyman, J.M.C. 1356
Hill, Stephen 64
Hiltebeitel, Alf 146, 148–9, 151, 621
Hilton, James 957–8
Hiriyanna, M. 781, 1192
Hirschon, Renee 1141
Hirway, Indira 1259
Hitchcock, John 410,
Hitchens 1082, 1186
Hitler, Adolf 571
Hobbes, 116, 118, 129, 1566
Hobskawn, E. 1344
Hocart, A.M. 516
Hochschild, Arlie Russell 959, 960*
Hock, Hans 719–20
Hockett 722
Hoebel, E. Adamson 544
Hoff Lee Ann 1144
Hoffman, John 583–4
Holborn, L.W. 291–2
Holla-Bhar, Radha 305
Holmes, Lowell D. 960
Holmstorm, Mark 1256, 1250, 1329
Holquist, Michael 573–4
Honigmann, J.J. 375

Honneth, Axel 1542
Hornby, P. 696, 702
Hosetitz, B.F. 468
Houtart, F. 885, 887, 895
Howard-Jones, N. 304
Howell, S. 1567
Hoyles, M. 949
Hsiao-tung, Fei 45
Hsu, Francis L.K. 1075, 1088
Hudson, D. Dennis 889, 894
Hudson, R.A 696
Hui 967
Hull, T. 942–3
Humphrey, Caroline 148, 1355
Hunter, J. 1343
Hunter, W.W. 1480
Husain, M.F. 634
Hussain, M. 346
Hussain, Sayed 341
Husserl, E. 22
Hutton, J.H. 383, 432
Hyma, A. 312
Hyma, B. 342–3
Hyman, R. 1267
Hymes, D.H. 695–6, 699, 703
Hymes, Dell 591, 599, 704

Ibrahim 790
Ikome, Otto 718
Illaih, Kancha 18, 650n, 1545
Inden, Ronald B. 108–9, 311, 373, 506, 516, 861, 1076, 1088, 1192, 1213, 1420, 1421–2
Inglis, Stephens R. 644
Inkles, Alex 74, 76–7, 79
Irudaya, Rajan 1138
Irvie, Judith 1199
Irving, R.G. 465
Isham, J. 1374
Isherwood, Baron C. 665, 1355
Ishtiaq, M. 332–3
Isidore 128
Ismail, 790
Ivekovie, Rada 22
Ivins, William 649n
Iyer, G. Subramanya 1349
Iyer, K. Gopal 403–4
Iyer, L.A.K. 43, 45
Izhar, Nilofar 312, 341–2

Jackson, Cecile 171
Jackson, Peter 326, 329–30
Jacob, P. 1295, 1298

Jacobson, D.W. 337
Jaffa, Harry V., 116, 131n
Jaganathan, N.V. 1298
Jagjivan, Ram 1463
Jahan, Roushan 1144
Jahangir, Emperor 1425
Jain, D. 943, 945
Jain, Madhu 1125
Jain, Mahaveer 1259
Jain, Meenakshi 495
Jain, P.C. 440
Jain, Ranu 593n
Jain, Ravindra 440
Jakobson, Doranne 1165
Jakobson, Roman 593n
Jalal, Ayesha 100, 1428
Jalal, D.S. 342
James, C.L.R. 92n
James, I 919
Jameson, Frederic 635
Jamison, Andrew 1526
Jamison, Stephanie 603
Jamous, Raymond 146, 490
Jardin, A. 919
Jay, Edward 1538–9
Jay, Martin 626, 640
Jayachandran, S. 342
Jayachandran, Usha 991n
Jayakar, Pupur 648n
Jayaprakash Narayan 49, 443, 444–5, 450–1
Jayaram, N. 532, 557, 1018
Jayawardena, Kumari 1066
Jefferson, Thomas 922–3
Jeffery, P. 1198,
Jeffery, Rogar 303, 314
Jeffrey, Patricia 945
Jeffrey, Robin 558n, 1021–2
Jena, B. 956
Jenks, C. 949
Jernudd, Bjorn H. 704
Jewett, Sarah 348, 344
Jeyapal, P 343
Jhabvala, Rehana 1260
Jhal, H. 336
Jindal, Rajendra 809–10
Jinnah, M.A. 1431, 1452
Joas, Hans 570, 580, 1551
Jodha, N.S. 161, 237, 344
Jodhka, Surinder 371n, 1206–7, 1213, 1217, 1228, 1230, 1234
Jogdand, Prahlad Gangaram 1545

John, Mary 88, 129, 1080–1
Johnston, William 1273
Jomon, M.G. 1255
Jones, T. 326
Jones, Kenneth William 11, 103, 332, 715, 816, 958, 963–4, 1350
Joshi, G.V. 12
Joshi, manohar 625
Joshi, P.C. 432, 438, 1226–7
Joshi, Sanjay 1200
Joshi, Sharad 439
Joshi, Smita 343
Juergensmeyer, Mark 815, 817, 1544
Jugal, B.N. 1304
Jumani, Usha 1258
Juneja, R. 1134
Jung, C.G. 173

Kabīr 123, 813–14, 822
Kachru, Braj 696, 708–9, 720–1, 723, 724
Kadekodi, Gopal K. 344
Kagzi, H.C.J. 744
Kahlons, Raminder Kaur 637
Kakar, Sudhir 309–10, 545, 656, 658, 832, 946, 1081–2, 1088, 1125, 1127–8, 1144, 1182–3, 1187–8, 1194, 1199–1200, 1572–3, 1575–7
Kalia, Ravi 465
Kalidasa 608, 958
Kalpagam, U. 1243
Kaltman, H. 704, 726
Kamat, Vinay R. 309
Kambargi, R. 946–7
Kanappan, A. 1287
Kandinsky, Kclee 587
Kane, P.V. 1062, 1075
Kanhere, Usha 1140, 1254
Kannabiram, Vasantha 1547
Kannan, K.P. 1306
Kapadia, K.M. 7, 43–4, 1064, 1080, 1084, 1105, 1491
Kapadia, Karin 104, 485, 980, 1081
Kapferer, Bruce 600, 1184, 1196
Kaplan, R. 705
Kapur, Anuradha 588, 626, 635–6, 656, 658, 661, 667
Kapur, A.K. 334
Kapur, Geeta 87, 661

Kapur, Promilla 1086
Kapur, R.L. 1182
Kapur, Rajiv 788
Kapur, Ratna 1075, 1077, 1081, 1150
Karan, P.P. 326, 341, 343–4, 347
Karanth, G.K. 246, 1233
Karim, M.E. 1185
Karlekar, Malanika 137, 1058, 1084, 1086, 1127–50, 1130, 1139, 1145, 1160, 1304
Karna, M.N. 395
Karni, V.B. 1252
Karve 414, 418–19, 422
Karve, D.K. 1547
Karve, Irawati Karunakar 7, 44, 962, 1064, 1072, 1078, 1084, 1088, 1105, 1114
Karve, Maharishi 50, 1502
Kasdan, Leonard 1121
Kashyap, S.C. 909
Kasturi, Leela 1130
Kasturi, Malavika 1134
Katariya, G. 339
Katz, Stephen 960–61, 967
Kaushik, Sunanda 1144
Kautilya 1414, 1416–17
Kautsky 1214
Kavapathi Pillai, Valli 1576–77
Kaviraj, Sudipta 75, 99, 1381, 1385, 1431, 1435, 1437, 1447
Kavoori, Purnenda 159, 166, 236
Kaye, J.W. 626
Kayongo, Male D. 946
Keane, John 1565
Kelkar, G. 171
Kelkar, Govind 1130, 1547
Keller, S.R. 289, 296
Kellogg, S.H. 722
Kelly, Donald R. 128–9, 132
Kelly, J.G. 697
Kelman, Herbert 742
Kennedy, Judith T. 346
Kennedy, Robert E. 1325
Kerblay, 1532
Kerblay, Basil 1532
Kerketta, Jonas 582–3
Kern, H. 1267
Keshari, Biseshwar Prasad 593
Kessinger, Tom G. 109, 1070
Kessler, C. 696
Kessler, K. 703

Keylley, Donald R. 128
Khaldun, Ibn 255
Khan, A.Q. 343
Khan, Abdul Gaffar 429
Khan, Chaudhri Zafarullah 1013, 1140
Khan, Joel 1345
Khan, Mumtaz 348
Khanam, M. 1185
Khare, R.S. 305, 310–11, 315, 644, 1077, 1084
Khartar, Gacch 818
Kher, Manik 1250, 1282
Khilnani, Sunil 100, 1435
Khubchandani, L.M. 377, 699, 728–9, 732, 748–50
Khungdim, H 348
Kidder, Robert 1394
Kielman, Arnfried 306
Kierkegaard, Soren 968
Killian, Lewis M. 1526
Kīnā Rām 808
King, A.D. 464–7
Kirbat, Preeti 307
Kirkpatrick, Joanna 309
Kish 699
Kishor, Sunita 1139
Kishwar Madhu 1007, 1142, 1166, 1546–8
Klandermans, Bert 1528
Klein Ira 308
Kleinman, Arthur 315
Kloss, H. 702
Klugman, J. 1373
Knipe, David M. 310
Knudsen, John Chr. 315
Koch, Ebba 465
Kocherry, T 175
Koerner, 697
Kohli, Atul 1438
Kolamma, M. 311
Kolenda 1078, 1094, 1346
Kolenda, Pauline 410, 875, 962, 1069–72
Kolff, Dirk 1342
Kolk, Ans 174
Kondiah, Raju C 644
Kooiman, Dick 810
Kopf, David 90 n, 91n, 1014
Kosambi, D.D. 7, 13, 401, 1418–19
Kosambi, Meera 464, 1547
Koser, Khalid 299
Kothari, Manu L. 312

Kothari, Rajni 51, 75, 421, 434, 1430, 1498, 1500–2, 1531, 1552
Kothari, S. 339, 945, 1235
Kothari, Smita 308
Kowshik, Dinkar 588
Krafft, Thomas 562
Kriesi, Hanspeter 1528
Krishan, G. 348
Krishen, Pradip 656, 659
Krishna, Daya 22
Krishna, P. Murali 342
Krishnamurthi, Anandi 343
Krishnamurthi Bh. 699, 704, 733, 738, 740
Krishnamurti 737
Krishnaraj, Maithreyi 1140
Krober, A.L. 1214
Kropotkin, Pierr 328
Kudaisya, Gyanesh 290
Kuhlman, T. 296
Kuhn, T. 175
Kulkarni, Sanjeev 1134
Kulke, H. 1415, 1422
Kumar 212n
Kumar, A. 332
Kumar, Dharma 1218, 1221 1244, 1256
Kumar, Krishna 1000, 1020, 1023, 1082
Kumar, M.S. 338–9, 342
Kumar, Mina 1163
Kumar, Nita 546, 565, 655–6, 675, 1546
Kumar, R. 1414, 1534
Kumar, Radha 1150, 1164, 1546–9
Kumar, Ravinder 471, 909
Kumar, Sanjay 31, 308, 315
Kumaran, T. Vasantha 343
Kumaraswamy, K. 342
Kumari 1139, 1140
Kumara, V.K. 343
Kundu, Amitabh 330–1
Kung, Bushmen, Study of Speech of 699
Kuntz, Carl 925
Kurien, C.T. 1439
Kurien, John 175
Kurtz, S.N. 857 n
Kurtz, Stanley 1187–8, 1194
Kurz, Otto 635
Kvamisch, Stella 150

Kynch, Jocelyn 1087, 1139

La Fontaine, J.S. 942, 947
Labor, W. 702–4, 720
Lacan, Jacques 1183
Lachaier, P. 1348
Lahiri, D.K. 336
Laidlaw, James 148, 816
Lakoff, R. 699
Lakutisa 806
Lal, Devi 967
Lalita, K. 1547
Lall, John 467
Lamb, 965–6
Lambert, Helen 309
Lambert, John 121–2
Lambert, R.D. 1250–51
Lambert, William 1187
Lambert, W.E. 696, 702
Lanco-Worrall 697
Langford, Jean 309–10
Lanternari, V. 1528
Lardinois, Roland 307, 1067, 1073
Larson, Gerald James 630, 1414
Laslett, Peter 1073
Lavalette, M. 942
Law, J.S. 1144
Lawrence, Denise L 150
Lawton, D. 702
Laxman, R.K. 975
Le Bon, Gustave 1526, 1573
Le Paage, R.B. 703–4
Leach, Edmund R. 549, 1109
Learmonth, A.T.A. 341–2
Leavitt, John 148
Ledbetter, Rosanna 306
Lee-Wright, P. 942, 946
Lefebure, H. 1012
Lehman, Hellmut 570–1
Lehmann, Arno 889
Leibenstein, H. 1329
Leitner, H. 340
Lele, Jayant K. 92n, 719, 726
Lemercinier, G. 885, 887, 895
Lenin, VI 572, 1214
Lerner, Daniel 78–9
Leslie, Charles 310
Leslie, J. 946
Lersinger, Hanna 1173
Levin, Jack 959
Levin, William C. 959
Levinas 580
Levinson, S. 703

Levi-Strauss, Claude 126, 141, 153, 482, 850–1, 957, 1089, 1090, 1092, 1109
Levner, David 77
Levy, Robert 150
Lewis, I.M. 878
Lewis, M. 1343
Lewis, Oscar 419, 879, 1495, 1519n
Lewis, Reina 1200
Lewis, W. Arthur 92n, 1226, 1289
Ley, David 330
Liberman, Anatoly 572
Lievens, 583
Lifton, Ralph 570
Lindberg, S. 1219
Lindholm, Charles 152, 490
Linkenbach, Antje 1384, 1524
Linton 1536
Lipset, Martin 1502
Lipset, S.M. 516, 526
Lipsey 587
Litke, Robert 1129
Livingstone, David N. 328
Llewllyn-Jones, R. 459
Lloyd, G.E.R. 553
Lock, Margaret 315
Locke 116, 118
Lodrick, Deryk O. 345
Logan, Penelope 867
Loh, Jackie 956, 1020–1
Lohr, Oscar 891
Long, Bruce 1195
Lord, Albert B. 600, 605
Lorenzen, David N. 782, 806–7, 814, 1545
Loseke, D.R. 1144
Lotman, Juri 126, 635
Louis XIV, of France 915
Low, Setha M. 150
Luckmann, Thomas 538
Ludden, David E. 109, 658, 1532, 1536
Luke, A. 703
Lutgendorf, Philip 601, 609, 656
Luther, Martin 129, 917
Lyman, Karen A 963
Lynch, Owen 1180

Macaulay 703, 1002
Macaulay, Thomas Babington 1478
MacChendra, (Nath) 807

MacKinder, Halford 328
MacDougall, John 403
MacGaffery, Wyatt 591
MacPherson, S. 742
Madan, T.N. 22, 23, 40, 50, 54,
    68, 72, 74, 76, 80, 90n, 91n,
    150, 309, 484, 486, 654, 770–
    1, 775, 795, 797, 816, 909,
    961, 1075–6, 1085, 1142
Madhava 1118
Madhavan, V.R. 303
Madhuri, S. 1252
Madhurima 783, 1137, 1143–4,
    1146–7
Madhavācārya 809–10
Madison, James 922–3
Madsen, Stig Toft 544, 550, 558n
Magnussen, Lars 2–3
Mahadev, P.D. 343
Mahajan 910, 1152
Mahajan, Amarjit 1137, 1143–4,
    1146–7
Mahajan, Gurpreet 773, 908
Mahalingam, S. 332
Mahapatra, S. 393
Mahar, Michael 410
Maharaj, Man Singh of Jodhpur
    822
Maharaj, R.N. 403–4, 1257
Mahavir, founder of Jainism 1018
Mahavira, Lord Sece Vardhamana
Mahmud of Ghazni, 791
Mahmuda, Islam 312
Mahunnued, Cashin Peristha 100
Maine, Henry 430–1
Maine, Henry Sumner 1063, 1092
Majno, Guido 303
Major, Andren J. 295
Majumdar, D.N. 68, 420, 434, 436
Majumdar, K. 332
Majumdar, Nabendu Dutta 1478
Malamond, Charles 145–6, 176n,
    872, 1162
Malathy, R. 337
Malaviya, Madan Mohan 444,
    1013
Malcolm 104
Malhotra, K.C. 157, 165, 233
Malik, Ashok 625
Malik, Jamal 464
Malini, B. Huma 342
Malinowski 833
Malinowski, B. 702, 828

Mallik, Ross 298
Maltz, D. 727
Mamdani, Mahamood 266, 305,
    942–3
Mamkoottam, K. 1208, 1253,
    1266, 1271, 1274, 1277, 1281
Mandal, B.P. 1488
Mandavdhare, S. 335
Mandelbaum, David G. 74, 90n,
    384, 482, 484, 702, 863,
    1083
Mangeshkar, Lata 967
Mani, Lata 658, 1000, 1546
Manekar, Purnima 637, 1140
Mann, Michael 539
Mann, Thomas 830
Mannheim, Karl 56, 472
Manor, J. 1364, 1370, 1375
Manu 1106, 1161
Manuel, Peter L. 658
Manwaring, T. 1277
Marcoux, R. 943, 945
Marcus, Abraham 472
Marcus, George E. 23, 961
Marglin, Frederique Apffel 309,
    782, 1174
Marks 251
Marn 64, 432, 1565
Marn, Karl 3, 99, 688, 1224, 1329
Marraca, B. 601, 620–1
Marriott 71, 419, 436, 968
Marriott, McKim 17, 44, 70, 72,
    311, 506, 516, 654, 689, 862,
    1076, 1216, 1499
Marshall 699
Marshall, Alfred 1005
Marshall, T.H. 44
Martin, Biddy 1164
Martin, W.G. 945
Martyn, John 1015
Marulasiddaiah 965
Marulasiddaiah, H.M. 961–2
Marx, Karl 118, 368, 426–7, 510,
    1249, 1568
    on villages in India 430–1
Massam, Bryan H. 343
Masselos, Jim 471
Massey, James 1543, 1545
Masson, Jeffrey Moussaeff 1163
Mather, C. 347
Mathew, C.P. 789
Mathew, M. 1282
Mathew, Thomas 314

Mathur, H.S. 342
Mathur, Hari Mohan 441, 449,
Matsuda Motoji 879
Mauss, M. 834, 1349, 1566, 1568
Mauss, Marcel 1175, 1179
Mayawathi 625
Mayer, A.C. 50
Mayer, Adrian 414, 416–17, 419,
    421, 423, 427, 440, 484, 487–
    8, 1085
Mayer, Albert 429, 436
Mayer, Margit 1528
Mayer, P. 1219
Mayer, Peter 1347
Mayo, Katherine 93n
Mayoux, L.C. 338
Mazumdar, Charu 447–8
Mazumdar, D. 1287
Mazumdar, Veena 1133, 1135,
    1138, 1166
McAdam Dough 1525
McAlpin, Michelle Burge 307
McCarthy, John D. 1525
McCarthy, T. 707
McClelland, David C. 74–6, 1322,
    1324, 1326
McCollum, Terry 926–7
McCrory, J.T. 1323
McCully, Patrick 173
McDaniel, June 1161, 1180, 1194,
    1199
McDougall 1538
McEwen, S.A. 945
McNamara, R. 943, 947
McGee, Mary 867
McGee, T.G. 471
McHugh, Ernestine 1190
McIntosh, A. 704
McKenzie, R.D. 462
McLeod, W.H. 787, 802, 819
McNeill, Geraldine 305
Mead, George Herbert 329, 1525
Mead, Margaret 942, 1187
Meeker, Marchia 504, 514
Mehra, Ajay 468
Mehta, A.B. 1250
Mehta, Depa 151, 1166
Mehta, S. 333
Mehta, Tyeb 634
Mehta, V.R. 1417
Meillassoux, C. 945, 968
Meister 465

Melhuus, M. 945
Meluci, Alberto 170, 174, 1525, 1527, 1552
Mencher, Joan P. 160, 485, 1230
Mendelievich, E. 942–3
Menon, Dilip M. 1545
Menon, Ritu 295, 1127, 1200
Mescont, Jim 138
Messer, Elen 307
Metcalf, Thomas 465
Metcalfe, A. 1008
Metcalfe, Charles 431, 1217
Meulenbeld, G. Jan 303, 310
Meyer, E. 1566
Michaelson, K.L. 943
Michaux 129
Michell, Nora 346
Midgley, J. 742
Mies, Maria 171, 338, 945, 1258, 1304
Mignon, Elisabeth 958
Mill, James 45, 103–4, 1217
Mill, John Stuart 1448
Miller, Barbara D. 307, 1078, 1133–4, 1355
Miller, Daniel 587, 591
Miller, S. 702
Milner, J. 122, 132n
Milner, Murray 517
Milroy, J. 702
Milroy, L. 703
Milnault, Gail 467
Millward, N. 1279–80
Mines, Mattison 491
Ming-Kalman W. 941
Minkler, Meredith 960
Minocha, Aneeta 1139
Minois, Georges 956–7
Minto, Lord 1001, 1040
Minturn, Leigh 1082–3, 1088, 1186–7
Minz, Nirmal 582–3, 585
Mirabai 1162
Mishra, Arpita 726
Mishra, G.P. 1259, 1261
Mishra, P.K. 332
Mishra, chief Justice Ranganath 1391, 1401
Mishra, Saraswati 956, 963
Mishra, Subhas
Mishra, U.S. 314
Misra, B.K. 333
Misra, B.P. 398

Misra, H.N. 345
Misra, P.K. 234, 238
Misra, R.P. 342
Misra, Tilottama 1538
Misra, Udayon 1538
Misri, Urvashi 1074–5, 1080, 1082, 1158
Mitchell, George 346
Mitchell-Kernan, C. 703
Mitra, Jyotir 303
Mitra, Subrata 332, 909
Moerat, F. 945
Morice, A. 944, 946
Moffatt, Michael 485, 876, 1077
Mohammad, Noor 326, 341
Mohanti, Chandra Talpade 658, 1164
Mohanty, J.P. 33
Mohanty, J.N. 22
Mohanty, Manoranjan 1535
Mohapatra, P.C. 333
Mondrian 587
Monga, S. 336
Mookerji, Radha Kumud 1004
Moog, Robert 1386, 1389, 1392, 1394, 1398
Moore, Barrington Jr 968, 1218–19, 1222, 1229, 1531
Moore, Erin 1394
Moore, Henrietta 1085
Moore, Melinda A. 150
Moore, Mick 1072, 1078
Moreland 104, 107
Morgan, D.H.J. 1066, 1087
Morgan, Lewis Henry 1064, 1092, 1106
Morice, A. 943
Morinis, R.A. 829
Morris, B. 232, 240
Morris, Morris D. 1250,
Morrison, Charles 1394
Morse, Bradford 308
Morse, M. 1322, 1356
Morson, G.S. 999
Moses, D.G. 904
Moseley, W. Henry 305
Mosse, C.D.E. 888–9, 896, 898, 902
Mosse, David 483
Mother Teresa 967
Mueller, E. 943
Muhlmann, E. 1538
Mujeeb, Muhammad 791

Mukerjee, Ramakrishna 432
Mukerji, A.B. 327
Mukerji, D.P. 43, 6871, 72, 88
Mukerji, R. 22
Mukherjee, Aditi 704
Mukherjee, Ashutosh 577
Mukherjee, Bharati 1173
Mukherjee, H. 1004
Mukherji, Partha N. 297, 447
Mukherjee, R. 1216
Mukherjee, Radhakamal 43
Mukherjee, Ramkrishna 50, 89, 90n
Mukherjee, S. 332
Mukherjee, S.N. 1199
Mukherjee, U.U. 1004
Mukherjee, 1535
Mukhopadhyay, Bhudev 1471n
Mukhtar, A. 1246
Mukul 165, 168
Mulay, Sanjeevanee 342
Mulla, D.F. 1063
Mullick, M.S. I 1185
Munda, Ram Dayal 333, 593n
Muni, S.D. 284, 286–7
Mundle, S. 944, 949
Munro, Lord 1040
Munroe, Thomas 999
Munsi 348
Munson, Fred C. 1252
Murdock, George Peter 1077
Murphey, Robert F. 1121
Murphy, William 591
Murthy 1139
Murthy, M.L.K. 222
Murty, A.B. 344
Muysken, P. 696
Myerhoff, Barbara G. 960
Myers, C.A. 1250
Myers, R. 943, 946–7
Myers, W.E. 948, 950
Myka, Frank 157
Myrdal, Gunnar 65, 73–4, 76, 305, 519–20

Nabhadas 813
Nagar R. 340, 347
Nagaraj, D.R. 1543, 1545
Naicker, E.V. Ramaswamy 1475
Naidu, Ratna 471
Naik, J.P. 1038, 1040
Naik, J.P. S. 999, 1001–2, 1012
Naim, C.M. 1194

Nair, Janaki 88, 1080–1, 1150
Nair, Ravi 283
Nakatani, Tetsuya 138, 283
Namdev 810
Nanda, Gulzarilal 92n
Nanda, Serena 1164
Nandi, R.N. 223
Nandi, S.K. 588
Nandinath, S.C. 807
Nandy, Ashish 21, 34, 72, 85, 99,
    305, 472, 661, 656, 658,
    736, 834, 909, 910, 958,
    1080, 1088, 1127, 1199,
    1200
Nanhaya 724
Naoroji, Dadabhai 12, 1349
Narain, A.K. 1545
Narain, Sunita 307, 344
Narayan, D. 1374
Narayan, J.P. 443–5
Narayan, Kirin 1161
Narayn, R.K. 1161
Narayana Ayyar, K. 311
Narayana Guru 1475
Narayaswami, V. 303
Nardinelli, C. 941
Nascher, Leo Iqnatz 956–9
Nasir 342
Nasrin, Taslima 1167
Natarajan, Nalini 890
Nath, Ayas Dev 822
Nathan, D. 171, 1260
Nayak, D.K. 337
Neale, W. 1217
Needham, R. 829, 849, 855
Negi, D.B. 332
Nehru, J. 386–7, 438, 747,
    1413–14, 1432, 1434,
    1451–2, 1457, 1460,
    1467, 1472, 1517,
Neidhardt, Freidhelm 1528, 1530,
    1531
Neill, Stephen 885, 889
Netting, Robert McC 1073, 1092,
    1131
Neuman, Franz 571
Neustupny, J.V. 729
Newby, H. 1215
Newell, W.H. 234
Newman, R. 903
Nichols, M. 943
Nicholas, Ralph W. 18, 311, 1076,
    1088, 1092

Nichter, Mark 1186
Niehoff, A. 1250
Nieuwenhuys, Olga 937–8, 942,
    944–7
Nietzsche 106
Nilsson, Sten 461
Nimbarka 809
Nimkoff, M.F. 1069
Niranjana, Tejaswini 658, 660
Nityananda 811
Nivedita, Sister 936, 105, 1006
Nobili, Robert 889
Noble, A.G. 345–6
Noble, Margaret
Nongbri, Tiplut 900
Noor, Mohammad 335
Novronha, Evnasto 626
Nuer, of southern Sudan 544
Nugent, J.B. 943
Nuland, Sherwin B. 961
Nuna, S.C. 333–4, 337
Nuruddin, Shaikh 793
Nurullah, S. 999–2, 1012, 1038,
    1040
Nydegger, Corinne 957

Obeyesekere, Gananath 1162,
    1180, 1185–6, 1195
O'Connell, Joseph T. 1200
Oddie 900
Oddie, G.A. 890, 893, 900
O'Flaherty, Wendy Doniger 832,
    849, 1161
O'Hanlon, Rosalind 101, 656,
    1536, 1547
Oinas, Feliz J. 572
Oldenburg, Veena Talwar 459,
    1164
Olivelle, Patrick 803
Olko, B.A. 947
Olshtain, E. 705
Olson, Laura Katz 961
Olson, Mancur 1375, 1528
Omichand 1426
Omissi, D. 1016
Omvedt, Gail 315, 344, 1533,
    1535, 1541, 1545, 1547–8
Oommen, T.K. 119, 433, 437, 445,
    448, 541, 544, 1228, 1527,
    1533–5
Openshaw, Jeanne 835
Oppert, Gustav 873
Oppong, C. 945

Orans, Martin 401, 403
Orenstein, H. 484, 1070
Orland, B. 346
Orr, W.G. 822
Ortner, Sherry B 504
Osella, Caroline 1076, 1169
Osella, Filippo 1076, 1169
Osgood, C 697, 699
Ostas, Z. 948
Ossowski, Stalinslaw 524
Oster, Akos 1076, 1092, 1355
Ostrom, E. 1366
Ozaki, Muneto 1280

Paar, Daya 1544
Pacholi, Sarojini 342
Padmanabhan, M. 1132
Padmsee, Akbar 634
Pakrasi, Kanti, B. 1134
Pal, Pratapaditya 630
Palriwala, Rajni 1074, 1083–4,
    1131
Palsson, Gish(a) 23
Panchbhai, S.C. 403
Pande, Gyanendra 11, 86, 658,
    1013, 1565, 1568, 1578
Pande, J.N. 1398
Pande, K.C. 332
Pandian, M.S.S. 661
Pandit, P.B. 125–7, 132n, 719,
    750
Pandit, R.S. 327
Pandit, S.M. 645
Pandit, S.S. 1007
Pandit, T.N. 156
Pandita, Ramabai 1547
Pandit, Vijay Laxmi 429
Pandya, Vishwajit 157
Panigrahi, Lalita 1134
Panikkar, K.N. 909
Panini 715
Panini, M.N. 88–9, 90n, 495
Panofsky, Erwin 635
Pant, B.R. 342
Pant, Gobind Vallab 432, 1484,
    1488
Pant, S.P. 333
Pantham, T. 1380–1, 1383, 1413,
    1432
Paolosso, M. 946
Papanek, Hanna 1083, 1086–7,
    1138
Papola, T.S. 1278–9, 1296

Parajuli, Pramod 308
Parekh, Bhikhu 100, 1431, 1439
Pareto, Vilfred 143
Parish, Steven M. 146
Park, R.E. 462
Park, Robert 329, 1526
Parkes, Peter 152
Parkin, Robert 1113–14
Parmar, H.S. 333
Parpola, A. 779
Parry, J. 516, 808, 1085, 1345–6
Parry, William J 421
Parsons, Talcott 21, 66, 431, 519, 960, 1065–6, 1088–9
Patanjali 1161
Patel, Kunj 1250
Patel, M.L. 393
Patel, Prasin J 337, 1260
Patel, Sujata 471, 543, 1247
Patel, S.J. 1256
Patel, Sardar Vallabhai 1432
Patel, Tara 304–5, 308
Patel, Tulsi 1079
Pateman, C. 1015
Pathy, J. 377, 396
Pati, Biswamony 1127
Pati, R.N. 956
Patkar, Medha 173–4
Patnaik, M.M. 1142
Patnaik, P. 1436
Patnaik, Utsa 75, 1224, 1226, 1232, 1532
Pattanayak, D.P. 719, 742–3
Patterson, Maureen 1498
Pawar, M.S. 1144
Pawar, R.S. 346
Paxton, Nancy 1200
Payne, Geoffrey 467
Peacock, James L. 621
Pearson, Michael N. 311
Pebley, Anne R. 306
Peet, Richard 344
Peirano, Mariza 23, 35, 89, 94n
Perlin, F. 1425, 1428
Peterson, Indira V. 1159
Pfeffer, Leo 921
Phadke, Anant 20
Phadnans, Nana 649n
Phalke, D.G. 641
Phanishwar, Nath Renu 409
Phillimore, P.R. 225, 243
Phule, Jotirao 1475

Piatigorsky, A. 828, 830, 832, 834–5, 849–50, 855, 856n,
Picasso 587
Pillai, S.M. 1306
Pinch, William R. 812, 821–3, 1163
Pingua, B.P. 333
Pinney, Chris 625
Pinney, Christopher 564, 566, 625–7, 629–30, 636–7, 661
Pitkin, Hanna 8
Platt, H.K. 702
Platt, J.T. 702
Platt, J.P. 1366
Plattner, Stuart 1357
Pluetschan 89
Pocock, D.F. 809–10, 865, 874, 1346
Polanyi 1347
Polanyi, Karl 1343–4
Pollock, Sheldon 14–17, 24n
Poonacha, Veena 1130
Pope, Urban VI 913
Portes, A. 297
Possehl, Gregory L. 779
Postman 949
Potter, Theodore 8
Pouchepadass 1533–4
Prabhakar 903
Prabhu, K. Seeta 276
Prabhu, P.H. 1063, 1080, 1133
Pradhan, M.C. 109, 419
Prakash, Gyan 102, 543, 656, 1530
Pramar, V.S. 153, 467
Prasad, A. 399
Prasad, B. 1416
Prasad, G.J.V. 716
Prasad, K.N. 333, 1233
Prasad, M. 333
Prasad, Madhav 87–8, 661
Prasad, R.R. 334
Prasad, Sheela R 342–3
Prasad, S.N. 333
Pratt, M.L. 1015
Premavati 343
Premchand 409, 682, 965
Premi, M.K. 339
Presler, Franklin A. 656
Preston, James J. 872
Preston, N. 1024
Price, Pamela 656

Prince, N. 172
Pritchett, L. 1374
Prophet, Mohammed 790, 792, 797
Propp, V. 852–3, 858n
Prud homme, R. August 1371
Ptolemy 225
Pugh, Judy 303, 310, 312
Punalekar, S.P. 1304
Punekar, S.D. 1246–7, 1249, 1251–2
Punekar, V.B. 334
Purdy, L. 947, 949
Purkait, B.R. 745
Putnam, R.D. 1366, 1375
Pylee, M.V. 1513

Qian, Y. 1372
Queen, Christopher 1545
Quigley, Declan 486, 516
Quine W.V.O. 715
Qureshi, A. 341

Rabindranath 682
Rabinow, Paul 23
Radcliff, Brown A. R 51, 132n, 452, 1089, 1092
Radhakrishnan, P. 494, 495, 1227, 1383, 1474
Radhakrishnan, S. 776, 1025
Raghav, R. 342
Raghavaiah 394, 401
Raghavan, V. 13
Rāghavānand 811
Raheja, Gloria Goodwin 485–6, 655, 863, 879, 1088, 1199, 1530
Rahman, Fazlur 790
Raina, V. 1023
Rainbow, Paul 2
Raj, K.N. 92n
Raja of Amber 465
Raja, H.R. 644–5
Raja, S.V. 1545
Rajadhyaksha, Ashish 88, 661
Rajadhyaksha, Tanini 1124
Rajadurai, S.V. 1545
Rajagopal, Arvind 626, 658, 651, 665–7
Rajaiah, B. 339
Rajan, Mukund Gobind 172
Rajan, Rajeshwar Sunder 1546
Rajan, S. Irudaya 314
Rajendra, Prasad 429, 1372n

Rajeshwari 343
Raju, K.N.M. 1071–2, 1085, 1094n
Raju, S. 335, 337–9, 1078
Ram, Kalpana 160, 886–7, 895–6
Ram, Nandu 1545
Ram, Suresh 446
Rama, Saraswati 851–2
Ramachandran, J. 333
Ramachandran, R. 458
Ramakrishna 795, 832
Rāmakrishna Paramahamsa 815
Ramamurthi, Iyer T.G. 303, 310
Ramamurthy, P.V. 963
Raman, Vasanthi 1136
Ramanna, A. 1133
Rāmānand 811, 813
Ramanujam, A.K. 472, 558n, 601, 719–20, 782, 809, 812, 822, 828, 833–4, 836, 842, 844, 847, 855, 856n, 857n, 1160
Ramaswamy, E.A. 541, 544, 1078, 1251–4
Ramaswamy, Uma 1250, 1261
Ramaswamy, Vijaya 338, 461
Ramesh, A. 342–3
Ramotra, K.C. 337
Ramprasad, Vanaja 176n
Ranade 1226
Ranade, H.G. 12
Ranade, Justice 1349
Ranade, P.S. 334
Randhawa, T.S. 233
Rangarajan, Mahesh 170
Rangnekar, D.V. 254
Rani, T.J. 339
Ranis, G. 1289
Ranja, K. 343
Ranjan, Haripriya 341, 344, 348
Ranjana, Kumari(1989) 1142–3
Ranjit, Singh, establishment or kingdom of 788
Rao, A. 231
Rao, Aparna 137, 219, 236
Rao, A. Venkoba 1185
Rao, B. Shiva 1484
Rao, H.S.A. 459
Rao, Janardhan 1541
Rao, K.M. 391
Rao, K. Raja 447
Rao, M.S.A. 42, 308, 421, 432, 446, 1527, 1544

Rao, Nitya 1258
Rao, P.V. Narasimha 634, 1472n
Rao, T.A.G. 633
Rao, U. Bhaskar 287–9
Rao, Vijayendra 1144
Rathori, M.S. 238
Ratnagar, S.T. 233
Ratzel 571
Ratzel, Friedrich 328
Ravīdās 813–15
Ravindra, R.P. 1134
Ravitch, Norman 915
Ray, H.M. 334
Ray, H.P. 460
Ray, Niharanjan 374
Ray, Rabindra 94n, 541
Ray, Rajat K. 1326
Ray, S.N. 276
Ray, Satyajit 965
Raychauduri, Tapan 307, 1342
Raza, Rahi Mason 409
Raza, Masoom 469
Raza, Mehdi 333
Raza, Moonis 348
Reagan, Ronald 967
Reclus, Elisee 328
Reddy, G.P. 236, 247
Reddy, P.H. 1138
Reddy, William 1356
Redfield, Robert 13, 17, 66, 70, 85, 90n, 150, 436, 472, 581, 960, 1214, 1216, 1532
Rehman, A. 346
Reindorp, Julian 1252
Rennel, James 327
Renon, Louis 802
Retzlaff, Ralph H. 1496–7
Reynolds, P. 945–6, 969
Rhoads, Ellan C. 960
Rhoads, Lorna A. 309
Richards, J.F. 1424
Richman, Paula 659
Richmond, A.H. 292, 299
Richmond, Farley 611
Rimband, C. 943
Ripon, Governor General 1480
Ripon, Lord 1507–8, 1521n
Risley, H.H. 7, 9, 13, 18, 375, 377, 383, 432, 480
Risseuw, Carla 1074, 1084
Rivers, W.H.R. 1092
Rizvi, Saiyid Athar Abbas 793
Roberts, John M. 544

Robertson, A.F. 1071, 1073, 1082
Robinson, Francis 20, 1507, 1510, 1512
Robinson, J.A. 226
Robinson, Rowena 773, 884, 887–8
Robinson, W.P. 702
Roche, P.A. 470
Rocher, L. 843
Rockefeller, Foundation 76
Rodgers, G. 943, 1304
Rodney, Walter 92n
Rodrigues, Valerian 1543, 1545
Roe, Thomas 327
Rohner, Ronald 1187
Roland, Alan 1158, 1182, 1186
Romaine, Suzanne 696, 703
Romm, Jeff 149
Rontledge, Paul 341, 344, 348
Rosaldo, Michelle 1085
Rose, Jacqueline 649n
Rosen, H. 703
Rosen, George 76, 90n
Rosencranz, A. 169
Ross, Aileen D. 962, 1087
Ross, R. 459
Rastogi, Yogendra 645–6
Rostow 959
Rostow, W.W. 92n
Rothermund, D. 1415
Roy, Arundhati 1167
Roy, Ashis K. 1535
Roy, Beth 151
Roy, B.K. 330, 333, 374, 379, 382, 399, 400, 401
Roy, Jasmine 588
Roy, Mamata 1281
Roy, Ramashray 1516
Roy, Ram Mohan 579, 815, 1006, 1547
Roy, S. 285, 1536
Roy, S.C. 45, 853–4
Rubin, J. 704
Ruchela, S.P. 253
Rucht, Dieter 1528, 1530–1
Rudolph, Lloyd I. 63, 75, 83, 492, 1498, 1544
Rudolph, Susanne Hoeber 63, 75, 83, 492, 1498, 1544
Rudra, A. 1233–4
Rusel, Malcolm 151
Rule, James B. 1526–8
Runciman, W.C. 1527

Rush, H. 1276
Rushdie, Salman 709, 1173
Russel, Kathy 520
Rutten, Mario 1211, 1231, 1319
Ryerson, Charles A. 807

Saberwal, Satish 89, 90n, 532, 539,
    550, 553, 557n, 558n, 1326
Saberwal, V.K. 231
Sachchidananda 436, 1537–8, 1540
Sachse, W.L. 915, 917–18, 923
Sadnal, M.K. 1142
Sadri, S. 1254, 1260
Sah, R.K. 1373
Saha, P. 335
Sahajanand 810, 1522n
Sahajiyās, Tantrik 811
Sahay, Keshari N. 891, 899
Sahlins 1355
Sahlins, M.D. 375
Sahoo, U.C. 944, 1304
Said, Edward W. 6, 103, 107, 348,
    656
Sainath, P. 305
Salazar, M.C. 946
Saldanha 1025, 1026
Saldanha, D. 1018–20
Salzman, P.C. 236–7, 238, 241
Samaddar, Ranabir 1281
Samanta, P.K. 333
Samuel, Hazal 1127
Samuel, M.J. 343
Sandhya 1148
Sangari, Kumkum 1546, 1550,
    1552
Sānkaracārya 808
Sankara 782
Sankoff, G. 702, 704
Sankrtyayon, Rahul 13
Sanyal, B. 1299
Sapir, Edward 702, 716
Saradamoni, S. 1081
Saran, A.K. 21–2, 44, 71–2, 90n,
    91n, 94n, 654
Saran, K.M. 1244
Saran, M. 1364
Saratchandra 681–2
Sardar, Mata 648n
Sargent, John 1011–12, 1014
Sarkar 1535
Sarkar, Benoy 44, 68, 149, 576–7
Sarkar, Jayanta 238
Sarkar, R.M. 334

Sarkar, Sumit 101, 658
Sarkar, S.C. 1008, 1010
Sarkar, Sir Jadunath 808
Sarkar, Tanika 1088, 1127, 1540,
    1549
Satyanarayana, A. 433, 1221
Sau, S. 333
Sauer, Carl 328
Saumarez-Smith, Richard 99
Saussure 751
Saussure, Ferdinand De 697, 701,
    714
Savarkar, V.D. 123–4, 132n
Saville, Troike Muriels 703
Savur, M.G. 1251
Savyasaaachi 164
Sax, Williams S 609
Saxena, Jyotirmaya 410
Saxena, N.C. 344
Saxena, Rajni 347
Scarcella, R. 706
Schaller, Joseph 815
Schechner, Richard 598, 601, 610,
    655
Schegloff, E.A. 703
Scheper, Huges N. 945
Schermerhorn, R.A. 700
Schieffelin, Edward L. 621
Schildkrout, E. 943
Schleicher, Fritz 639
Schlemmer, B. 943–4
Schluchter, Wolfgang 15
Schneider, David M. 1074–6,
    1092
Schneiderman 960
Schneiderman, Lawrence 979
Scömbucher, Elizabeth 565–6, 598,
    605, 607
Schomer, Karine 813
Schrivers, J. 943
Schumann, M. 1267, 1271
Schumpeter, J.A. 1329
Schur, Edmin 700
Schwartzberg 348
Schwartzberg, Joseph E. 326–8,
    341
Schwarz, Henry 99
Schwarzweller, H.K. 1215
Scott, David 6
Scott, J. 1219
Scott, J.C. 879, 1309, 1529–30
Scott, Reginald 957
Scarse, T.J. 1016

Seal, Anil 637
Seal, Brajendranath 68
Searle, John 703
Sekhar, P. Satya 304
Sen, Amartya 305, 945, 1087,
    1139, 1221, 1351–2, 1535
Sen, D.C. 577–8, 592n
Sen, Geeti 305, 307
Sen, Ilina 1550
Sen, Sukumar 578–9, 592n
Sen, Sunil 395–6
Senapathy, Manju 983
Sengupta, N. 377, 388–90
Sengupta, S. 945, 1139, 1551
Sengupta, Sankar 577
Sengupta, Smita 347
Senker, J. 1276
Senker, P. 1271, 1276
Seth, Jagath 1426
Sethi, Harsh 344
Sethuraman, S.V. 1287
Seymour, Susan 1187
Shah, A.M. 42, 50, 147, 213n,
    416, 423, 581, 654, 955,
    961, 1061, 1063–4,
    1069–71, 1093n, 1120,
    1130–1, 1534
Shah, Ganshyam 305, 396, 398,
    403
Shah, Gita 315
Shah, Mihir 80
Shah, Nandita 305–6, 1150,
    1164–5
Shah, Tushaar 344
Shah, Emperor 465
Shanin 1215
Shanin, Teodor 1213, 1532
Shankardas, Mala 1146
Sharar, Abdul 459
Sharma, Anju 308
Sharma, B.C. 333
Sharma, B.G. 640, 643–4
Sharma, B.K. 1259
Sharma, Baldev R. 1250–1
Sharma, G.K. 1246–7, 1249
Sharma, Indra 644
Sharma, Jagdish 647
Sharma, K.D. 334
Sharma, K.N. 440
Sharma, L.N. 640, 646–7
Sharma, Manoj 314
Sharma, Miriam 1394
Sharma, M.L. 956

Sharma, N.L. 644, 646–8
Sharma, Narayana Narottam 641, 642
Sharma, Pandit Shiv 303, 310
Sharma, R.C. 330
Sharma, S.L. 440
Sharma, Ursula 1072, 1083–4, 1142
Sharp, H. 746
Shastri, Lal Bahadur 645
Shaw, Annapurna 331
Sheath 1208
Sheath, Narayan 1207
Sheifer 1369
Sheth, Narayan 1243
Sheth, N.R. 1250, 1252, 1254, 1261
Sheth, Tarun 1501
Sherlock, Stephen 1253
Sherzer, J. 702
Shils, Edward 44, 94n, 116, 132n
Shinde, S.D. 342
Shinde, Tarabai 1547
Shiva, Vandana 171, 176n, 305, 308, 334, 338, 344, 945, 1165, 1541, 1550
Shivaji 637
Shobha, V. 1258
Shourie, Arun 1545
Shrinathdas 642
Shrunathji, at Nathdwara 633
Shrivastava, Rashmi 309
Shukla, Laxmi 342
Shulman, Davis 871–2
Shuy, R.W. 702–3
Shweder, Richard A. 1180–1, 1185
Shyam, Sunder L 333
Sibbons, M. 307
Siddiqui, Javed 305
Siddiqui, Mohammed Khalid 312
Siddique, N.A. 341, 347
Sil, A.K. 333
Sillima, Jael 316n
Silverman, S. 1214
Simmel, George 64, 532, 545–6, 548, 557n, 1210
Simmons, F.J. 327, 345
Simson, William 626
Singer, J. David 534–5
Singer, M. 1018
Singer, Milton 13, 70, 85, 90n, 91n, 150, 598–9, 654, 667,
865–6, 1068–9, 1080, 1163, 1324
Singer, Yogendra 45
Singh, A.K. 204–5
Singh, Alok K. 308
Singh, Amar Kumar 91n
Singh, B. 336
Singh, Baij Nath 436
Singh, C. 225, 227, 231, 252
Singh, Chandra Pal 343
Singh, Darshan 815
Singh, Fateh 428
Singh, H. 332
Singh, J. 348
Singh, Jaipal 378
Singh, J.P. 332
Singh, Katan 344
Singh, K.N. 335
Singh, Justice K.N. 1398
Singh, K.S. 374, 380, 395–6, 399, 402–3, 1078, 1091, 1537–8, 1540
Singh, Mani Shekhar 589
Singh, Manjit 1255, 1261
Singh, Mehr 347
Singh, Prem 715
Singh, R. 736
Singh, R.D. 332
Singh, R.K. 277
Singh, R.L. 329, 347, 466
Singh, R.P. 327, 332, 347
Singh, R.P.B. 326, 329, 334, 335, 347
Singh, R.Y. 333
Singh, Raj 428
Singh, Raja Jai 461
Singh, Rajendra 446, 700–1, 719
Singh, Ram 645
Singh, Ravindra 342
Singh, S. 346, 1017
Singh, Shiv Dayal 815
Singh, Talveen 909
Singh, Udaya Narayan 565, 695, 699, 701, 713, 748
Singh, V.P. 494, 1382, 1489, 1491
Singh, Yogendra 72–3, 76, 91n, 742–3
Sinha 398, 956
Sinha, A. 346
Sinha, Amita 346
Sinha, B.K. 281
Sinha, B.N. 333
Sinha, D.K. 340
Sinha Jwala Nand Prasad 955
Sinha, S. 333, 339–40, 343, 383, 384, 395, 401
Sinha, S.K. 946
Sinha, Sachidanand 346–8
Sinha, Surajit 305, 398, 581, 583
Sinha, Richard 1506, 1516
Sita, K. 276
Sitaramayya, Pattabhi 1452
Sjoberg, Gideon 462
Sivard, R.L. 69
Skeltm, Robert 631, 649n
Skinner, Quenten 913
Smailes, Arthur E. 164
Smelser, Neil 1526
Smith, Adam 688, 1348
Smith, Anthony 571
Smith, A.G.R. 915, 917
Smith, B.K. 145–7, 149, 154
Smith, David 74, 77, 79
Smith, Donal Eugene 797, 909, 1122, 1432
Smith, G. 703, 1300
Smith, H. Daniel 630, 650n
Smith, N. 328
Smith, Richard S. 7, 9–10, 34, 105, 107, 328
Smith, Susan J. 329–30
Smith, Vincent 104
Smith, William Robertson 959
Snow, David A. 1528
Som, T.K. 333
Sombart, Werner 1355
Soodan, Kripal Singh 956, 961
Sopher, David E. 345, 347
Sorel, Georges 1565
Sorge, A. 1267
Sorokin, Pitrin 502
Soundakaff, Stephen 572
Southall, A. 945
Southard Barbara 1546–7
Southeimer, Gunther D. 149, 220, 227, 581, 593n
Spadek, Howard 346
Spate, O.H.K. 345
Spencer, Jonathan 1387–8, 1564
Spivak, Gayatri Chakravorty 658, 1166
Sponberg, Alan 1545
Spring 923
Sreenivasan, N. 1254

Sridhar, S.N. 704
Srinath, Shoba 1138
Srinivas, M.N. 17–18, 42, 48–50,
    63, 69–70, 74, 76–7, 80,
    88–9, 90n, 92n, 93n, 149,
    264, 401, 410, 414, 419–22,
    431, 433, 435–37, 451–2,
    478, 492, 496–7, 581,
    654, 667, 691, 818, 862,
    863, 1069, 1078, 1088,
    1093n, 1123, 1163, 1164,
    1187, 1231, 1235, 1474,
    1476, 1484, 1498, 1544,
    5051
Srinivas, S.V. 661
Srinivasan, A. 1576–7
Srinivasan, Doris M. 346
Srinivasan, Viji 1135
Srivastava, K. 1261
Srivaisnavas 812
Srivastava, H.C. 333
Srivastava, Jaya 1148
Srivastava, P. 168
Srivastava, S. 1016
Srivastava, Sanjay 936, 998
Srivastava, Saroj 342
Srivastava, Vinay Kumar 148, 167
Srivatsan, T. 659, 661
St. Clair 703
Stadium, B. 941
Staley, E. 1322
Stalin 572, 573
Stalker, G.M. 1276
Standing, G. 943, 1304
Stark, R. 699
Stark, Rodney 802
Stawp, Dudley 329
Stien 109, 1422, 1425
Stien, B. 1420–1
Stien, Burton 108
Stien, M.A. 327
Stephens 894
Stephen, James Fitzjmes 1410n
Stiglitz, J.E. 1373
Stocking, George W. 568
Stoddard, Robert 326
Stokes, E. 231, 432, 1220,
    1533–4
Stoler, Ann Laura 958
Strathern, M. 157, 175, 1141
Strauss, M.A. 1144
Streeck, W. 1267
Streefkark, Hein 1327–9

Strevens, P. 704
Subdara, Ravindran T.K. 306
Subramanyam, Chandra 343
Subramanyam, K.N. 1246–7,
    1249
Subramanyam. S.V. 303, 312, 987
Subramanyam, Sanjay 34, 108,
    461, 1342, 1346, 1357, 1421,
    1423
Sudarshan, R. 1429
Sullivan, Bruce M. 1180
Sultana, D. 288. 289
Sundar, Pushpa 470
Sunder, Rajan, Rajeshwari 1127
Suresh, Ram 445
Sutherland 699
Sutherland, N.M. 919
Svalastoga, Kaare 539
Swaminathan, M.S. 445, 586–7
Swann 611
Swartz, Mare J 541
Sweester, Anne Thompson 312
Symes, C. 1024

Tagg, John 630
 Tagore, Rabindranath 48, 124,
    588, 593n, 1008, 1010, 1018
Talgeri, Pramod 717
Tamaskar, B.G. 327
Tambhiah, S.J. 621, 1075, 1085,
    1142, 1573
Tanaka 875
Tanaka, M. 772, 861, 864
Tannen 705
Tapaswini 1547
Tapper, Bruce Elliot 171
Tarabout 1566
Tarde, Gabriel 1526
Tarlo, E. 663, 1348, 1355–6
Tarrow, S. 1527–8
Taussig, Michael 660, 868
Tayfar, Abu Yazid of Iran 792
Taylor, Carl C. 306
Taylor, R.W. 582
Telang, K.T. 1349
Telkamp, G.J. 459
Tewari, A.K. 347
Thackeray, Bal 625
Thakkar, Bapa 377, 394
Thakur, B. 326, 328–9
Thakur, Bhativinode 811
Thakurta, Guha Tapati 661
Thangamani, K. 343

Thankappan, T.R. 175
Thapan, Meenakshi 656, 1130,
    1146
Thapar, N. 348
Thapar, Romila 34, 100, 110,
    223, 459, 513, 803,
    1416–19
Tharamangalam, J. 491, 885, 899
Tharu, Susie 1547
Thass, Pandit Iyothee 1545
Thewlis, Malford Wilcox 957
Thomas, Frederic C. 308
Thomas, M.M. 582, 789
Thompson, Edward 1426–7
Thompson, E.P. 1529, 1570
Thorburn, S.S. 1223
Thoren, 22
Thorner, Alice 471, 1232
Thorner, D. 75, 1225–8, 1235,
    1250, 1256
Thukral, Enakshi G. 308, 315,
Thurston, Edger 1482
Tiemann, G. 228, 251
Tikait, Mahinder 471
Tilak, Bal Gangadhar 637
Tilak, Shrinivas 956–7, 963,
Tilly, C. 44, 1528, 1571, 1574
Tilly, Louise 1528
Tilly, Richard 1528
Tilson, David 961
Timberg, Thomas A. 1325
Timmers, Jaap 591
Timur 255n
Tinker, Hugh 265
Tipps, Dean 81, 90n
Tiwari, D.D. 342
Tiwari, S.C. 334
Tom, T. 1304
Tonnies 64
Tooke, Horne 715
Touraine, Alain 170, 172, 1525,
    1529–31, 1551–2
Traube, Elizabeth G. 591
Trautmann 1107–8, 1110,
    1111–12
Trautman, 10
Trautman, Thomas 91n, 1059
Trautmann, Thomas E. 103
Trautmann, Thomas R. 148, 576,
    1075, 1078, 1090, 1104, 1119
Trawick, M. 1169, 1194
Trawick, Margaret 1058,
    1076,1077, 1158–9, 1162,

1163, 1167, 1188–90, 1545
Treu, T. 1281
Trevelyan, Charles 999
Tripathi, B.D. 808–9
Tripathi, Dwijjendra 1321
Tripathi, R.S. 334, 336
Trivedi, Harshad 1112
Troeltsch, Ernst 802
Troisi, Joseph 891, 901
Trudgill, Peter 698, 702, 722
Tsing 969
Tucker, Richard P. 243, 161
Tudesq, A.J. 919
Tulsidas 609
Tulsidas, *Ramayana* of 610, 810
Tulsi, Shahib, of Hatras 815
Turner 967–8
Turner, Bryan S. 64, 1011
Turner, Ralph H. 1526
Turner, Terrence 648
Turner, Victor 598–9
Tyagi, Nutan 346
Tyler, Stephen 627, 1180

Uberoi, J.P. Singh 22, 34, 54, 72, 89, 114, 127, 132n, 656, 661, 817–18, 963–4, 1075, 1088, 1092
Uberoi, Patricia 20, 88, 630, 1058, 1061, 1075, 1077, 1080, 1083–4, 1129, 1142,
Uberoi, U. 1081
Ulrich, Helen. 1185
Uma, Shankari 866, 873
Upadhyay, C.B. 1231
Upadhyay, G. 303

Vaid, N.K. 392
Vaid, Sudesh 1546, 1550
Vaidnathan, A. 154
Valdman, A. 704
Valentine, T. 703, 706,
Vallabhācārya 631, 810, 817
Van den Bogaert Michael 582
Van der, Dennen 557n, 558n
Van der, Dennen, Johan M.G. 541, 548
Van der, Veer P. 667, 803, 805, 808, 811–13, 818–23, 1000, 1344
Van Gennep, A. 942
Vanagisako, Syhia Jemko 1085

Vanaik, Achin 100
Vandeville, Charoltte 813–14, 1197
Vamitha, Ruth 1547
Van, Emden, Arthur 584
Van, Exem A. 548, 585
Van Parijis, Philippe 550
Varadande, M.L. 621
Vardhamana Mahavira, Lord 785, 787, 805
Varickayil, R. 1249
Varma, Raja, Ram, founding father of visual culture 634–6
Varma, Ravi 640
Vartak, V.D. 154
Vasari, A.R. 167
Vasudevan, Ravi S. 661, 667
Vatuk, Sylvia 490, 962, 965–6, 1070–2, 1083, 1115, 1142, 1189
Veblen, Thorstein 1355
Veen, J.H. Van der 1328
Veer, Peter, Van der 658–9
Venkatachalan, C.S. 1255
Venkatachalan, R. 1135
Venkoba, Rao A.K. 963
Venniyoor, E.M.J. 637
Verghese, J. 1142
Verhasselt, Yola 340, 342
Verlet, M. 944
Verma, R.C. 391
Verma, R.S.P. 333
Vieziiamy, Marika 306
Vidal, Denis 1210–11, 1346, 1355, 1566
Vidal de la Blache, Paul 328
Vidusaka 608
Vidhyarthi 382, 397, 399–400
Vidhyarthi, L.P. 333, 373, 380, 395
Vijaygopalan, S. 946
Vidyasagar, Ishwarchand 1006, 1547
Vincentnathan, Lynn 1545
Visania, L. 136–7, 184, 195, 200, 203, 211, 274, 307, 1079
Visania, P. 136–7, 184, 190, 192, 194, 200, 208–9, 211, 274, 307, 1257, 1295, 1298
Vishny 1369
Vishwakarma, J.P. 336
Visnuswami 809

Visvanathan, Shiv 54, 72, 305, 308, 312, 656
Visvanathan, Susan 789, 885–6, 888, 895
Viwanath, Kalpana 307
Viswanath, G. 1020
Vittachi, A. 949
Vitthalnath 810
Vivekanand, Swami 795, 815, 1005, 1018, 1471n,
Vlassoff, C. 943
Vyas, Anju 315, 1127, 1129
Vyas, V.S. 1244

Wade, Robert 160, 1366
Wadhwa, S. 1138
Wadia 1247
Wadley, Susan 661, 861, 863, 1070–1, 1073, 1091, 1165, 1197
Wales, James 649n
Walji, P. 946
Walker, Barbara G. 958
Walker, L.E. 1144
Wall, Richard 1073
Wallace, Anthony 1539
Wallace, Anthony F. 1539
Wallerstein, I. 943, 945
Walvin, J. 941
Walz, Frederick 926
Wang, W.S.Y. 703, 1371
Wanmali, S. 34
Warner, Lloyd 504, 514–15, 526
Warner, M. 1270–1
Waren, D. Michael 305, 309
Warthin, Aldred Scott 959
Waseem, Mohammed 298
Washbrook, David 101
Washington, George 923
Watson, O.M. 702
Wattenberg, Ben J 307
Watts, Michael 344
Weaver, Mary Ann 1167
Weber, Max 3, 4, 40, 58, 64, 68, 117, 144, 152, 444, 461, 470, 489, 527, 547, 1211, 1223, 1249, 1319–22, 1324, 1329, 1331–3, 1565
Webster, J.C.B. 892, 899
Weiner, Myron 74, 138, 262, 269, 287, 298, 389, 395, 421, 434, 435, 447, 941, 947, 1505–6, 1540, 1550

Weigast, B.R. 1372
Weinreich, U. 704, 709, 723,
Weissbach, L.S. 941
Wiser, 413
Wernick 967
Wersch, H. Van 1253
Wescoat, Jim L. 326, 346–8
Westphal, H. 224
Westphal-Hellbusch, S. 224, 241
Weyer, Johann 957
White, B. 942–3, 946–7, 949
White, R. 1004
Whiting, B.B. 942
Whiting, Beatrice 1187
Whiting, John 1187
Whorf, B.L. 702
Wilce, James M. 1179, 1197–8
Wild, R.A. 52
Wile, James 1059, 1179
Wilk, Richard R. 1092
Williams, Eric 92n
Williams, Raymond B. 82, 93n,
    810, 819,
Williams, S. 942
Williamson, J.A. 915
Williamson, Oliver E. 1351
Willis, R. 1567
Willman, O. 1280
Wilson, Kalpana 1260

Wilson, Midge 520
Wilson, R. 704
Winter, David G. 74–6, 1322
Winter, S.G. 1351
Wiser, Charlotte Viall 961
Wiser, W.H. 147, 412–13, 432,
    961, 1218, 1346
Wittengstein, Ludwig 1186
Wittrock, Bjorn 2–3, 15, 21
Wolf, E. 1215,
Wolf, Eric R. 1528, 1531–3
Wolfe, Patrick 581
Wolfenstein, M. 942
Wolfram, W.A. 702
Wolschke, Bulman J. 346
Womack, jame 1268
Wood, 1534
Woodburn, J. 156
Woodward, J. 126
Woodward, Kathleen 967–8,
Worsely, Peter 1536
Worster, Donald 142
Wright, C. 916
Wright, Erick Olin 524–7
Wuff, Donna 835
Wuers, J. 945
Wulff, Donna. 1193–4
Wulff, Donna Marie 783
Wyan, J.B. 305

Xaxa, Viginius 369, 373, 397

Yadava, K.N.S. 315
Yalman, Nur 1075, 1081
Yalney, B.S. 1226
Yang, A.A. 229
Yapa, L. 344
Yesudian, Patrick 342
Yocum, Glenn E. 866
Yue, Chi 262

Zaidi, S. Akbar 269
Zald, Mayer N. 1525
Zarrilli, Phillip 613, 615–16, 618,
    1611
Zarama, M.I.V. 945
Zbavitel, Dusan 1197
Zdizer, V. 949
Zelizer, V. 942
Zelizer, Vianana 1345
Zelliot 1545
Zelliot, Eleanor Mae 1543,
    1545
Ziegenbalg 889
Zimmerman, Francis 154, 310,
    345, 1169
Zolberg, A.R. 284, 287
Zwingli 122